DRAMA
CRITICISM

Guide to Gale Literary Criticism Series

For criticism on	Consult these Gale series
Authors now living or who died after December 31, 1999	**CONTEMPORARY LITERARY CRITICISM (CLC)**
Authors who died between 1900 and 1999	**TWENTIETH-CENTURY LITERARY CRITICISM (TCLC)**
Authors who died between 1800 and 1899	**NINETEENTH-CENTURY LITERATURE CRITICISM (NCLC)**
Authors who died between 1400 and 1799	**LITERATURE CRITICISM FROM 1400 TO 1800 (LC)** **SHAKESPEAREAN CRITICISM (SC)**
Authors who died before 1400	**CLASSICAL AND MEDIEVAL LITERATURE CRITICISM (CMLC)**
Authors of books for children and young adults	**CHILDREN'S LITERATURE REVIEW (CLR)**
Dramatists	**DRAMA CRITICISM (DC)**
Poets	**POETRY CRITICISM (PC)**
Short story writers	**SHORT STORY CRITICISM (SSC)**
Black writers of the past two hundred years	**BLACK LITERATURE CRITICISM (BLC)** **BLACK LITERATURE CRITICISM SUPPLEMENT (BLCS)**
Hispanic writers of the late nineteenth and twentieth centuries	**HISPANIC LITERATURE CRITICISM (HLC)** **HISPANIC LITERATURE CRITICISM SUPPLEMENT (HLCS)**
Native North American writers and orators of the eighteenth, nineteenth, and twentieth centuries	**NATIVE NORTH AMERICAN LITERATURE (NNAL)**
Major authors from the Renaissance to the present	**WORLD LITERATURE CRITICISM, 1500 TO THE PRESENT (WLC)** **WORLD LITERATURE CRITICISM SUPPLEMENT (WLCS)**

ISSN 1056-4349

DRAMA
CRITICISM

Criticism of the Most Significant and Widely Studied
Dramatic Works from all the World's Literatures

VOLUME 14

Justin Karr, Editor

GALE GROUP

Detroit
New York
San Francisco
London
Boston
Woodbridge, CT

STAFF

Lynn M. Spampinato, Janet Witalec, *Managing Editors, Literature Product*
Kathy D. Darrow, *Product Liaison*
Justin Karr, *Editor*
Mark W. Scott, *Publisher, Literature Product*

Jeffrey W. Hunter, *Senior Editor*
Mary Ruby, *Technical Training Specialist*
Deborah J. Morad, Kathleen Lopez Nolan, *Managing Editors*
Susan M. Trosky, *Director, Literature Content*

Maria L. Franklin, *Permissions Manager*
Ryan Thomason, *Permissions Assistant*

Victoria B. Cariappa, *Research Manager*
Tracie A. Richardson, *Project Coordinator*
Sarah Genik, Ron Morelli, Tamara C. Nott, *Research Associates*
Nicodemus Ford, *Research Assistant*

Dorothy Maki, *Manufacturing Manager*
Stacy L. Melson, *Buyer*

Mary Beth Trimper, *Manager, Composition and Electronic Prepress*
Gary Leach, *Composition Specialist*

Michael Logusz, *Graphic Artist*
Randy Bassett, *Imaging Supervisor*
Robert Duncan, Dan Newell, *Imaging Specialists*
Pamela A. Reed, *Imaging Coordinator*
Kelly A. Quin, *Editor, Image and Multimedia Content*

Library of Congress Catalog Card Number 92-648805
ISBN 0-7876-3142-6
ISSN 1056-4349
Printed in the United States of America

10 9 8 7 6 5 4 3 2 1

Contents

Preface

*D*rama Criticism (*DC*) is principally intended for beginning students of literature and theater as well as the average playgoer. The series is therefore designed to introduce readers to the most frequently studied playwrights of all time periods and nationalities and to present discerning commentary on dramatic works of enduring interest. Furthermore, *DC* seeks to acquaint the reader with the uses and functions of criticism itself. Selected from a diverse body of commentary, the essays in *DC* offer insights into the authors and their works but do not require that the reader possess a wide background in literary studies. Where appropriate, reviews of important productions of the plays discussed are also included to give students a heightened awareness of drama as a dynamic art form, one that many claim is fully realized only in performance.

DC was created in response to suggestions by the staffs of high school, college, and public libraries. These librarians observed a need for a series that assembles critical commentary on the world's most renowned dramatists in the same manner as Gale's *Short Story Criticism* (*SSC*) and *Poetry Criticism* (*PC*), which present material on writers of short fiction and poetry. Although playwrights are covered in such Gale literary criticism series as *Contemporary Literary Criticism* (*CLC*), *Twentieth-Century Literary Criticism* (*TCLC*), *Nineteenth-Century Literature Criticism* (*NCLC*), *Literature Criticism from 1400 to 1800* (*LC*), and *Classical and Medieval Literature Criticism* (*CMLC*), *DC* directs more concentrated attention on individual dramatists than is possible in the broader, survey-oriented entries in these Gale series. Commentary on the works of William Shakespeare may be found in *Shakespearean Criticism* (*SC*).

Scope of the Series

By collecting and organizing commentary on dramatists, *DC* assists students in their efforts to gain insight into literature, achieve better understanding of the texts, and formulate ideas for papers and assignments. A variety of interpretations and assessments is offered, allowing students to pursue their own interests and promoting awareness that literature is dynamic and responsive to many different opinions.

Approximately five to ten authors are included in each volume, and each entry presents a historical survey of the critical response to that playwright's work. The length of an entry is intended to reflect the amount of critical attention the author has received from critics writing in English and from foreign critics in translation. Every attempt has been made to identify and include the most significant essays on each author's work. In order to provide these important critical pieces, the editors sometimes reprint essays that have appeared elsewhere in Gale's literary criticism series. Such duplication, however, never exceeds twenty percent of a *DC* volume.

Organization of the Book

A *DC* entry consists of the following elements:

- The **Author Heading** consists of the playwright's most commonly used name, followed by birth and death dates. If an author consistently wrote under a pseudonym, the pseudonym is listed in the author heading and the real name given in parentheses on the first line of the introduction. Also located at the beginning of the introduction are any name variations under which the dramatist wrote, including transliterated forms of the names of authors whose languages use nonroman alphabets.

- The **Introduction** contains background information that introduces the reader to the author and the critical debates surrounding his or her work.

- A **Portrait of the Author** is included when available.

- The list of **Principal Works** is divided into two sections. The first section contains the author's dramatic pieces and is organized chronologically by date of first performance. If this has not been conclusively determined, the composition or publication date is used. The second section provides information on the author's major works in other genres.

- Essays offering **overviews and general studies of the dramatist's entire literary career** give the student broad perspectives on the writer's artistic development, themes, and concerns that recur in several of his or her works, the author's place in literary history, and other wide-ranging topics.

- **Criticism** of individual plays offers the reader in-depth discussions of a select number of the author's most important works. In some cases, the criticism is divided into two sections, each arranged chronologically. When a significant performance of a play can be identified (typically, the premier of a twentieth-century work), the first section of criticism will feature **production reviews** of this staging. Most entries include sections devoted to **critical commentary** that assesses the literary merit of the selected plays. When necessary, essays are carefully excerpted to focus on the work under consideration; often, however, essays and reviews are reprinted in their entirety. Footnotes are reprinted at the end of each essay or excerpt. In the case of excerpted criticism, only those footnotes that pertain to the excerpted texts are included.

- Critical essays are prefaced by brief **Annotations** explicating each piece.

- A complete **Bibliographic Citation,** designed to help the interested reader locate the original essay or book, precedes each piece of criticism.

- An annotated bibliography of **Further Reading** appears at the end of each entry and suggests resources for additional study. In some cases, significant essays for which the editors could not obtain reprint rights are included here. Boxed material following the further reading list provides references to other biographical and critical sources on the author in series published by Gale.

Cumulative Indexes

A **Cumulative Author Index** lists all of the authors that appear in a wide variety of reference sources published by the Gale Group, including *DC*. A complete list of these sources is found facing the first page of the Author Index. The index also includes birth and death dates and cross references between pseudonyms and actual names.

A **Cumulative Nationality Index** lists all authors featured in *DC* by nationality, followed by the number of the *DC* volume in which their entry appears.

A **Cumulative Title Index** lists in alphabetical order the individual plays discussed in the criticism contained in *DC*. Each title is followed by the author's last name and corresponding volume and page numbers where commentary on the work is located. English-language translations of original foreign-language titles are cross-referenced to the foreign titles so that all references to discussion of a work are combined in one listing.

Citing *Drama Criticism*

When writing papers, students who quote directly from any volume in *Drama Criticism* may use the following general formats to footnote reprinted criticism. The first example pertains to material drawn from periodicals, the second to materials reprinted from books.

Susan Sontag, "Going to the Theater, Etc.," *Partisan Review* XXXI, no. 3 (Summer 1964), 389-94; excerpted and reprinted in *Drama Criticism*, vol. 1, ed. Lawrence J. Trudeau (Detroit: Gale Research, 1991), 17-20.

Eugene M. Waith, *The Herculean Hero in Marlowe, Chapman, Shakespeare and Dryden* (Chatto & Windus, 1962); excerpted and reprinted in *Drama Criticism*, vol. 1, ed. Lawrence J. Trudeau (Detroit: Gale Research, 1991), 237-47.

Suggestions are Welcome

Readers who wish to suggest new features, topics, or authors to appear in future volumes, or who have other suggestions or comments are cordially invited to call, write, or fax the Managing Editor:

Managing Editor, Literary Criticism Series
The Gale Group
27500 Drake Road
Farmington Hills, MI 48331-3535
1-800-347-4253 (GALE)
Fax: 248-699-8054

Acknowledgments

The editors wish to thank the copyright holders of the excerpted criticism included in this volume and the permissions managers of many book and magazine publishing companies for assisting us in securing reproduction rights. We are also grateful to the staffs of the Detroit Public Library, the Library of Congress, the University of Detroit Mercy Library, Wayne State University Purdy/Kresge Library Complex, and the University of Michigan Libraries for making their resources available to us. Following is a list of the copyright holders who have granted us permission to reproduce material in this volume of *DC*. Every effort has been made to trace copyright, but if omissions have been made, please let us know.

COPYRIGHTED EXCERPTS IN *DC*, VOLUME 14, WERE REPRODUCED FROM THE FOLLOWING PERIODICALS:

America, v. 163, December 8, 1990. Reproduced by permission.—*American Literature,* v. 42, March, 1970. Reproduced by permission.—*Booklist,* v. 79, July, 1983. Copyright © 1983 by the American Library Association. Reproduced by permission.—*Books Abroad,* v. 49, Summer, 1975. Copyright 1975 by the University of Oklahoma Press. Reproduced by permission of the publisher.—*Colloquia Germanica,* v. 19, 1986 for "Grillparzer's 'Konig Ottokars Gluck und Ende' and Shakespeare's 'Richard II'" by Roger A. Nicholls. Reproduced by permission of the author.—*Comparative Drama,* v. 21, Summer, 1987. © 1987, by the Editors of *Comparative Drama*. Reproduced by permission.—*Educational Theater Journal,* v. 20, December, 1968. © 1968, University and College Theatre Association of the American Theatre Association. Reproduced by permission of The Johns Hopkins University Press.—*English Studies,* v. 75, May, 1994. © 1994, Swets & Zeitlinger. Reproduced by permission.—*Film Comment,* v. 25, May-June, 1989 for "Beth's Beauties" by Karen Jaehne. Copyright © 1989 by Film Comment Publishing Corporation. Reproduced by permission of the author.—*Forum for Modern Language Studies,* v. 12, April, 1976 for "An Off-Stage Decision: An Examination of an Incident in Grillparzer's 'Ein Bruderzwist in Habsburg'" by Bruce Thompson. Reproduced by permission of the publisher and author.—*The French Review,* v. 41, February, 1968. Copyright © 1968 by the American Association of Teachers of French. Reproduced by permission.—*The Germanic Review,* v. 39, 1964 for "Grillparzer's Ottokar" by Walter Silz. Reproduced by permission.—*Jahrbuch fur Internationale,* v. 16, 1984. Reproduced by permission.—*Michigan Germanic Studies,* v. 1, Fall, 1975. Reproduced by permission.—*Modern Austrian Literature,* v. 11, 1978; v. 17, December, 1984; v. 18, December, 1985; v. 21, 1988. © copyright International Arthur Schnitzler Association 1978, 1984, 1985, 1988. All reproduced by permission.—*Modern Drama,* v. 15, March, 1973; v. 23, January, 1981; v. 30, March, 1987; v. 35, March, 1992; v. 36, March, 1993, v. 38, Fall, 1995. Copyright © 1973, 1981, 1987, 1992, 1993, 1995 University of Toronto, Graduate Centre for Study of Drama. All reproduced by permission.—*Modern Language Notes,* v. 111, April, 1996. © 1996 by The Johns Hopkins University Press. Reproduced by permission.—*Modern Language Quarterly,* v. 25, March, 1964; v. 43, March, 1982. Both reproduced by permission.—*Modern Language Review,* v. 66, April, 1971 for "'Weh dem, der lugt:' Grillparzer and the Avoidance of Tragedy" by Ruth Kluger. © Modern Humanities Research Association 1971. Reproduced by permission of the publisher and the author.—*Modernism/Modernity,* v. 3, May, 1996. Reproduced by permission.—*Mosaic,* v. 30, March, 1997; v. 31, December, 1998. © Mosaic 1997, 1998. Acknowledgment of previous publication is herewith made.—*The National Observer,* v. 10, November 20, 1971. © 1971 Dow Jones & Company, Inc. Reprinted by permission The Wall Street Journal. All rights reserved worldwide.—*New York,* v. 23, November 12, 1990; v. 31, October 26, 1998. Copyright © 1990, 1998 PRIMEDIA Magazine Corporation. All rights reserved. Both reproduced with the permission of *New York* Magazine.—*The New Yorker,* v. 66, November 12, 1990. © 1990 by the author. All rights reserved. Reproduced by permission.—*October,* v. 64, Spring, 1993. © 1993 October Magazine, Ltd. and Massachusetts Institute of Technology. Reproduced by permission of The MIT Press, Cambridge, MA.—*The Paris Review,* v. 34, Winter, 1992. © 1992 The Paris Review, Inc. Reproduced by permission.—*Performing Arts Journal,* v. 3, Spring-Summer, 1978; v. 6, 1981. © 1978, 1981 The Johns Hopkins University Press. Both reproduced by permission.—*Players Magazine,* v. 51, October, 1975 for "A Rhetoric of American Popular Drama: The Comedies of Neil Simon" by Helen McMahon. Reproduced by permission of the author.—*Romance Notes,* v. 33, Winter, 1992. Reproduced by permission.—*Studies in American Drama, 1945- Present,* v. 6, 1991. Reproduced by permission.—*Theater,* v. 15, Winter, 1983. Copyright © 1983 by Duke University Press, Durham, NC. Reproduced by permission.—*Variety,* v. 335, May 10, 1989; v. 351, August 9, 1993. Both reproduced by permission.—*World Literature Today,* v. 51, Summer, 1977; v. 54, Summer, 1980; v. 55, Winter, 1981; v. 58, Summer, 1984; v. 60, Winter, 1986; v. 62, Summer, 1988. Copyright 1977, 1980, 1981, 1984, 1986, 1988 by the University of Oklahoma Press. All reproduced by permission of the publisher.—*Yale French Studies,* n. 31, 1964 for "Artaud: A New Type of Magic" by Bettina Knapp; n. 39, 1967 for "Antonin Artaud: Metaphysical Revolutionary" by Naomi Greene. Copyright © Yale French Studies 1964, 1967. Both reproduced by permission.

Antonin Artaud
1896-1948

(Full name Antoine-Marie-Joseph Artaud; also wrote under the pseudonym Le Révélé) French essayist, dramatist, poet, novelist, screenwriter, and actor.

INTRODUCTION

Poet and theorist of revolutionary theater, avant-garde novelist and surrealist screenwriter, actor, drug addict, and madman, Antonin Artaud is famous for the influence he exerted through his writings and performances—especially after death—on the way writers, directors, actors, and communal theater companies conceive of theater, its production, and its function. Progenitor of a form of theater whose aim is to unsettle and radically transform its audience and its culture, such as happenings, theater of the absurd, or experimental theater, Artaud called for an end to a drama of rationality, masterpieces, and psychological exploration. Artaud advocated a "theatre of cruelty"—a probing, goading, and provocative theater drawing on Symbolist sensory derangement, psychoanalytic theory, and the Balinese theater. Such a theater, according to Artaud, should employ expressive breathing, animal sounds, uninhibited gestures, huge masks, puppets, and an architecture that destroys the barrier between actors and audience in order to turn spectators into participants, and bring them to a level of visceral experience Artaud deemed more profound than any experience accessible through passive understanding or absorption of language, plot, or coherently structured action. Artaud's aim was to unblock repression and to purge violence, hypocrisy, and the malaise he saw as endemic to society.

BIOGRAPHICAL INFORMATION

Born in Marseilles—his father a wealthy shipbuilder, his mother of Greek heritage—Artaud suffered a lifetime of ill-health, physically and mentally debilitated by a severe case of meningitis contracted when he was five. During his early teen years, while a student at a Marist Catholic school, he started a literary magazine in which he published his own poetry. Suffering from depression and sharp head pains, at the age of nineteen Artaud sought treatment at a local sanatorium. Drafted into the army the following year, he was given a medical discharge after only a few months. Artaud then spent two years in a Swiss hospital, where his literary inclinations were encouraged as part of his therapy. At twenty-two, upon release from a clinic in Switzerland, Artaud went to Paris where he remained under the care of Dr. Edouard Toulouse who was

both editor of the literary magazine *Demain* and a psychiatrist. Toulouse published Artaud's poetry and employed him as an editorial assistant. In 1923, Jacques Riviére, editor of the *Nouvelle revue française* rejected several poems Artaud submitted to the magazine as incomprehensible, but published a series of letters by Artaud defending his work, advancing his theories about poetry, and discussing his mental distress. Around this time Artaud began taking laudanum—a solution of opium in alcohol—for his pains, and continued to use opium, heroin, and other drugs until his death. It was also at this time that Artaud allied himself with the surrealists, and began working in the theater and the cinema. He was featured in Carl Dreyer's *Passion of Joan of Arc* (1928) as Jean Massieu with Maria Falconetti, and wrote the screenplay for the surrealist film, *La Coquille et le Clergyman* (1927). Artaud broke with the surrealists when Andre Breton, the leader of the movement, joined the communist party. Communism seemed to Artaud to be more of the same debilitating European rationality he wanted to destroy. In 1926, Artaud formed the Theâtre Alfred Jarry with Roger Vitrac and Robert Aron. Soon after the failure of his adaptation of *Les Cenci* (1935), Artaud traveled to live with the Tarahumaras in Mexico, where he took peyote and studied their ceremonies. He then traveled to Ireland, where he suffered a mental collapse, and returned to France in a straight jacket to be hospitalized and subjected against his will to several rounds of electroshock treatments for the next nine years. Nevertheless, Artaud continued to write. Upon his release, he made a triumphant return to Paris and the limelight, receiving the Prix Sainte-Beuve for *Van Gogh, le suicide de la societe* (1947), lecturing to audiences that included Andre Gide, Albert Camus and Andre Breton, and writing a play for radio commissioned by the French government radio station. This work was recorded but never broadcast because of obscenity and anti-Americanism. In 1948, Artaud died of sphincteral cancer.

MAJOR WORKS

Les Cenci, Artaud's play about a man who rapes his own daughter and is then murdered by men the girl hires to eliminate him, typifies Artaud's theater of cruelty. *Les Cenci* was produced in Paris in 1935 but was closed after seventeen dismal performances. Another illustration of Artaud's work is *Le jet de sang* or *The Fountain of Blood* (1925), a farce about the creation of the world and its destruction by humans, especially women. Like many of Artaud's other plays, scenarios, and prose, *Les Cenci* and *The Fountain of Blood* were designed to challenge conventional, civilized values and bring out the natural, barbaric instincts Artaud felt lurked beneath the refined, human facade. Of *The Fountain of Blood,* Albert Bermel wrote in *Artaud's Theater of Cruelty*: "All in all, *The Fountain of Blood* is a tragic, repulsive, impassioned farce, a marvelous wellspring for speculation, and a unique contribution to the history of the drama." More than for any particular work, Artaud is remembered more for his tormented life, for having turned himself inside out in the attempt to discover a way to transform theater and society, and for the concepts he developed for effectuating transformation. *Le Théâtre de la cruauté* (1933) and *Le Théâtre et son double* (1938; *The Theater and Its Double*)—Artaud's most famous works—along with the novel *Héliogabale* (1934; *Heliogabalus*) and his blasphemous play *Le jet de sang,* rather than having an independent artistic existence, stand as manifestos and vehicles for approaching, if not achieving, the transformations Artaud proclaimed. According to author Susan Sontag: "Not until the great outburst of writing in the period between 1945 and 1948 . . . did Artaud, by then indifferent to the idea of poetry as a closed lyric statement, find a long-breathed voice that was adequate to the range of his imaginative needs—a voice that was free of established forms and open-ended, like the poetry of [Ezra] Pound."

CRITICAL RECEPTION

In *Antonin Artaud: Man of Vision,* Bettina Knapp offered an explanation of Artaud's popularity long after his death: "In his time, he was a man alienated from his society, divided within himself, a victim of inner and outer forces beyond his control. . . . The tidal force of his imagination

and the urgency of his therapeutic quest were disregarded and cast aside as the ravings of a madman. . . . Modern man can respond to Artaud now because they share so many psychological similarities and affinities." Artaud's individual works, throughout his lifetime, were often received badly. However, the body of his work—seen as a call for the creation of a new theater—and his life—seen as the forge upon which his theories were fashioned—gained in the latter part of the twentieth century a numinous force, and a celebrated following.

PRINCIPAL WORKS

Plays

Le jet de sang [*The Blood Jet, The Fountain of Blood,* and *The Spurt of Blood*] 1925
L'Ombilic des limbes [*The Umbilicus of Limbo*] (poetry, essays, and dramatic dialogues) 1925
La Coquille et le Clergyman [*The Seashell and the Clergyman*] (screenplay) 1927
Les Cenci 1935
Pour en finir avec le jugement de dieu (radio play) 1947

Other Major Works

Tric-trac du ciek (poetry) 1923
Le Pese-nerfs [published with *Fragments d'un journal d'enfer,* 1927; translated as *The Nerve Meter* and *Fragments of a Diary of Hell*] (poetry) 1925
Correspondance avev Jacques Riviére [*Artaud-Riviere Correspondence*] (letters) 1927
L'Art et la mort [*Art and Death*] (essays) 1929
Le Theatre Alfred Jarry et l'hostilite du publique [with Roger Vitrac] (essays) 1930
Le Théâtre de la cruauté (manifesto) 1933
Héliogabale; ou, l'anarchiste couronné [*Heliogabalus* or *The Anarchist Crowned*] (novel) 1934
Les Nouvelles révélations de l'être [*The New Revelations of Being*] (essays) 1937
Le Théâtre et son double [*The Theater and Its Double*] (essays) 1938
D'Un Voyage au pays de Tarahumaras [*Concerning a Journey to the Land of the Tarahumaras*] (essays and letters) 1945
Artaud le momo (poetry) 1947
Ce-git, precede de la culture indienne [*Indian Culture* or *Here Lies*] (poetry) 1947
"Tutuguri, the Rite of the Black Sun" (poetry) 1947
"Une note sur le peyot" (essay) 1947
Van Gogh, le suicidé de la société [*Van Gogh: The Man Suicided by Society*] (essays) 1947
Supplement aux Lettres de Rodez, suivi de Coleridge, le traitre (letters and essays) 1949

Les Tarahumaras [*The Peyote Dance*] (letters and essays) 1955

Oeuvres Complêtes [revised edition, 1970] 20 vols. (collection) 1956-1984

Artaud Anthology (collection) 1965

Collected Works [translated by Victor Corti, Calder and Boyars] 4 vols. (collection) 1968-1975

Love Is a Tree That Always Is High: An Artaud Anthology (collection) 1972

Antonin Artaud: Selected Writings (collection) 1976

The Peyote Dance (essays) 1976

Nouvelles escrits de Rodez (letters and essays) 1977

Artaud on Theatre (collection) 1991

OVERVIEWS AND GENERAL STUDIES

Wallace Fowlie (essay date October-December 1959)

"The New French Theatre: Artaud, Beckett, Genet, Ionesco," in *The Sewanee Review,* Vol. LXVII, No. 4, October-December, 1959, pp. 643-57.

[*In the following essay, Fowlie outlines Artaud's theory of theatrical ritual and dramatic cruelty, and analyzes his influence on Samuel Beckett, Jean Genet, and Eugene Ionesco.*]

Jacques Copeau's Vieux Colombier was the most famous and most fecund of the little theatres of the 20th century. All subsequent little theatres have continued the example of Le Vieux Colombier in opposing what Copeau called the double pest of the theatre: industrialization and *cabotinage*. The meaning of the first word is obvious. But the second word, which is purely French, is more difficult to define. It has to do with the art of the actor which in its lowest manifestation can equal a degrading kind of parody. The *cabotin* is vulgar and vain; he can even be ferocious. The weariness of rehearsals and backstage intrigues, gossip and desultoriness are able to sterilize the energies and moral character of an actor. *Le cabotinage* is a sickness which infects a good deal of the theatre—and the world outside the theatre: it is, fundamentally, the sickness of insincerity and falseness. The person suffering from *cabotinage* ceases to be authentic as a human being. He never recognizes the malady in himself. In his training, an actor risks the complete mechanization of his personality and the loss of much of his intelligence and spirituality. Copeau often spoke of the need for the actor of reaching a total simplicity: the opposite of *cabotinage*. This simplicity in the actor would give to the work of art, to the play, its maximum human quality, its power of pathos and poetry.

The little theatre movement was, for Copeau, precisely the means of reaching this simplicity. It was the teaching not so much of a new technique but of ways of feeling and living and reacting. Copeau wanted his actors to be human beings. That is why he welcomed non-professionals in his company. (For the same reason certain movie directors today, notably the Italians, use non-professional actors.) Copeau revindicated the place of the amateur in the theatre, the unaffected unpretentious actor who has not been subjected to the hardening experience of professionalism. He deplored the tendency to overtrain the professional actor, to separate him from the normal contacts of daily life, and to make him into a virtuoso, a star.

The little theatre is a corporation based upon a spirit of abnegation, of discipline and enthusiasm. It protects the dramatic masterpieces of the past and offers a place of refuge to the masterpieces of the future. It will not allow the over-elaborate pretentious *mise-en-scène* which, starting in Germany and spreading to other countries, has become today another form of *cabotinage*. The little theatre movement has always emphasized an almost rudimentary form of production because it is the richest in possibilities and because it is that kind which prevailed in ancient Greece and Elizabethan England. Such a theatre will allow a new dramatic poet, when he arises, to impose his own mode of interpretation, his own dramatic form.

The emergence of the new experimental theatre in Paris is the consequence of the decline and death of *le théâtre bourgeois*. These plays bear almost no relationship to our world; when they are performed (and they still are performed much more often than the experimental plays), they seem apart from the tempo and the problems of the present. They can still appear as skillfully written plays and often serve as vehicles for stars: *La Dame aux Camélias,* for example, of Dumas *fils*. Two major wars within less than thirty years have changed many aspects of the social structure in France, and especially of the bourgeoisie. The majority of the Paris theatres continue to give plays from a repertory that has not evolved with the times. Those newer plays which reflect more faithfully the psychic and social problems of our day are still looked upon as experimental and are usually confined to the little theatres. Since the Liberation, fourteen years ago, several new and youthful companies, dedicated to the production of the new plays, have occupied the little theatres intermittently and usually for short runs.

The new playwrights are first those attracted to a poetic kind of play, lyric in tone but not written in verse: Ghelderode (a Belgian), Supervielle, Audiberti, Pichette and Shehadé; and a second group, more philosophical in intention: Adamov, Ionesco, Genet and Beckett. It may well be that the three most important new playwrights in France are Adamov (of Russian origin), Ionesco (of Rumanian origin) and the Irishman Samuel Beckett. What all these writers have in common is a scorn for the traditional form of play writing, for the well-made play which has flourished in France for almost one hundred years. In the work of these writers a new kind of play has finally come into prominence, twenty or thirty years after the same revolution was realized in poetry and painting. This is normal in the history of the theatre: its revolutions occur twenty or thirty years late.

For these new plays a new kind of production has been evolved. Poverty was the material condition of the younger theatrical companies: they had no money, no stage equipment and almost no stage. Jean Dasté has had a great influence in this domain. His famous sets for *Les Frères Karamazov* and *Le Cercle de Craie* of Brecht were reduced to bare essentials, but were as powerful and suggestive as the spectacular settings of the early 20th century. Jean Vilar has continued the use of this kind of set in his productions at the Théâtre National Populaire. To this theatre has come a new kind of public, from the large working class. Vilar first took his productions to them, to the populous outskirts of Paris, the *banlieue,* and to the provinces.

THE THEORIST: ANTONIN ARTAUD

Artaud's name is associated with a fundamental revolt against insincerity. His most cherished dream was to found a new kind of theatre in France which would be, not an artistic spectacle, but a communion between spectators and actors. As in primitive societies it would be a theatre of magic, a mass participation in which the entire culture would find its vitality and its truest expression. In January 1947, a year before his death, Artaud gave a lecture in Copeau's old theatre, Le Vieux Colombier. Among those present, and mingled with a youthful fervent audience, were such writers as Gide, Breton, Michaux, Camus. Artaud symbolized for all the generations in his audience an exceptional fidelity to a very great belief, a life devoted to a cause.

Artaud's greatest activity in the theatre fell between 1930 and 1935. They were productive years for the Paris theatres in general. Jouvet produced three new plays of Giraudoux: *Electre, La Guerre de Troie n'aura pas lieu* and *Ondine.* Dullin was responsible for a fine production of *Richard III.* Pitoeff put on three plays of Tchekov: *The Sea Gull, Three Sisters* and *Uncle Vanya.* But even such repertories as these were unsatisfactory for Artaud. He wanted to go much farther in dramatic experimentation. He wanted for the theatre the same kind of frenzy and moving violence which he found in the paintings of Van Gogh. He claimed that a new kind of civilization was needed, one that would consummate a break with the sensitivity and the logical mentality of the 19th century. Thunderingly he denounced his age for having failed to understand the principal message of Arthur Rimbaud.

Artaud summarized the classical tradition of the French theatre, which he found still dominant, as that art which states a problem at the beginning of a play and solves it by the end, which presents a character as the beginning and then proceeds to analyze the character during the remainder of the play. Artaud asks, "Who says that the theatre was created to elucidate a character and to solve a conflict?" He sees the beginnings of a new kind of theatre, characterized by freedom, by the surreal and by mystery, in Mallarmé, in Maeterlinck and in Alfred Jarry, and finds an instance of it in Apollinaire's *Les Mamelles de Tirésias.*

Artaud divides humanity into the primitive or prelogical group and the civilized or logical group. The roots of the real theatre are to be found in the first group. At the Colonial Exposition of 1931, where he saw the Indonesian or Balinese theatre, he was struck by the tremendous difference between those plays and our traditional Western play. He felt that the Balinese dramatic art must be comparable to the Orphic mysteries which interested Mallarmé. A dramatic presentation should be an act of initiation during which the spectator will be awed and even terrified—and to such a degree that he will lose control of his reason. During that experience of terror or frenzy, instigated by the dramatic action, the spectator will be in a position to understand a new set of truths, superhuman in quality.

The method Artaud proposes by which this will be brought about is to associate the theatre with danger and cruelty. "This will bring the demons to the surface," he says. Words spoken on the stage will then have the power they possess in dreams. Language will become an incantation. Here again Artaud draws upon the poetic theory of Mallarmé and Rimbaud. Action will remain the center of the play, but its purpose is to reveal the presence of extraordinary forces in man. The *metteur-en-scène* becomes a kind of magician, a holy man, in a sense, because he calls to life themes which are not purely human. The principal tenet of Artaud's essay, *Le Théâtre et son Double,* is that reform in the modern theatre must begin with the production itself, with the *mise-en-scène.* Artaud looks upon it as something far more than a mere spectacle. It is a power able to move the spectator closer to the absolute. The theatre is not a direct copy of reality, it is another kind of dangerous reality where the principles of life are always just disappearing from beyond our vision, like dolphins who, as soon as they show their heads above the surface of the water, plunge down into the depths. This reality is beyond man, with his habits and character; it is "bloodthirsty and inhuman" (*sanguinaire et inhumain*). Artaud has acknowledged that in this conception of the theatre, he is calling uupon an elementary magical idea used by modern psychoanalysis wherein the patient is cured by making him take an exterior attitude of the very state which he should recover or discover. A play which contains the repressed forces of man will liberate him from them. By plastic graphic means, the stage production will appeal to the spectators, will even bewitch them and induce them into a kind of trance. Artaud would like to see stage gesticulations elevated to the rank of exorcisms. In keeping with the principal theories of surrealism, Artaud would claim that art is a real experience which goes far beyond human understanding and attempts to reach a metaphysical truth. The artist is always a man inspired who reveals a new aspect of the world.

THE PLAYWRIGHTS: BECKETT, GENET, IONESCO

From Mr. Beckett's first play, a phrase has passed into the French language, *j'attends Godot,* which means that what is going on now will continue to go on for an unidentifiable length of time. But if the phrase has reached an exceptional degree of popular consumption, the play itself still remains enigmatical. The public is held by it—Beckett is a skillful dramatist—but the after-effect is one of worry and wonderment.

The two tramps of Beckett, in their total dispossession and in their antics with hats and tight shoes, are reminiscent of Chaplin and the American burlesque comedy team. Pozzo and Lucky, the master and slave, are half vaudeville characters and half marionettes. The purely comic aspect of the play involves traditional routines which come from the entire history of farce, from the Romans and the Italians, and the red-nosed clown of the modern circus. The utter simplicity of the play, in the histrionic sense, places it in the classical tradition of French play writing. Its close adherence to the three unities is a clue to its dramaturgy. The unity of place is a muddy plateau with one tree, a kind of gallows which invites the tramps to consider hanging themselves. The unity of time is two days, but this might be any sequence of days in anyone's life. The act of waiting is never over, and yet it mysteriously starts up again each day. The action, in the same way, describes a circle. Each day is the return to the beginning. Nothing is completed because nothing can be completed. The despair in the play, which is never defined as such but which pervades all the lack of action and which gives the play its metaphysical color, is the fact that the two tramps cannot not wait for Godot, and the corollary fact that he cannot come.

Many ingenious theories have been advanced to provide satisfactory interpretations for the characters of Beckett's play. Religious or mythical interpretations prevail. The two tramps Estragon (Gogo) and Vladimir (Didi) may be Everyman and his conscience. Estragon is the one who has trouble with his boots. He is less confident than his companion and at one moment is ready to hang himself. Vladimir is more hopeful, more even in temperament. One thinks of the mediaeval debate between the body and the soul, between the intellect and the nonrational in man. Certain of their speeches about Christ might substantiate the theory that they are the two crucified thieves. Pozzo would seem to be the evil master, the exploiter. But perhaps he is Godot, or an evil incarnation of Godot. The most obvious interpretation of Godot is that of God. As the name Pierrot comes from Pierre, so Godot may come from God. (One thinks also of the combination of God and Charlot, the name used by the French for Charlie Chaplin. . . .) Mr. Beckett himself has repudiated all theories of a symbolic nature. But this does not necessarily mean that it is useless to search for such clues. The fundamental imagery of the play is Christian. Even the tree recalls the Tree of Knowledge and the Cross. The life of the tramps at many points in the text seems synonymous with the fallen state of man. Their strange relationship is a kind of marriage. The action of the play is a series of actions which are aborted and which give a despairing uniformity to the time of the action.

The new play, *Fin de Partie,* was finished in 1956 and produced in 1957. The title is a term used in chess to designate the third and final part of the game. (This technical meaning is not recognized by most of the French.) It was perhaps chosen for its indeterminateness, for its capacity to designate the end of many things, the end of life itself. The approach to "the end" is indeed one of the principal themes of all of Beckett's writings.

Two of the characters, Nagg and Nell, placed in ashcans, raise their covers from time to time and speak. But most of the dialogue is carried on between their son Hamm, who is a paralytic and blind and who is confined to a wheelchair, and his male attendant Clov. Throughout the action of *Fin de Partie,* Clov is constantly expressing a desire to leave. When Beckett was asked to summarize his new play, he stated that whereas in his first play, everyone expects the arrival of Godot, in the second play, they will be expecting the departure of Clov.

Whereas *Godot* was concerned with the theme of waiting, *Fin de Partie* is on the subject of leaving, on the necessity of reaching the door. We have the impression of watching the end of something, the end possibly of the human race. All movement has slowed down. Hamm is paralyzed and confined to his chair. Clov walks with difficulty. Nagg and Nell are legless and occupy little space in their ashcans. The setting vaguely resembles a womb and the ashcans are wombs within the womb. The two windows look out onto the sea and the earth, both without trace of mankind. The fundamental tragedy or hopelessness of the situation is offset by a fairly steady tone of burlesque and farce. The metaphysical conclusion of the play—and this is the same for Godot—belongs to each individual spectator who will interpret it in accord with his own sensibility and his own philosophy.

Concerning his play, *Les Bonnes (The Maids),* Jean Genet has said that it is a "tragedy of the confidants." In a classical tragedy, the confidant listens to the hero discuss his loves and his exploits. The subject of M. Genet's play is the unfolding of the confidant's thought after he has left the stage. There are two confidants here, two maids who devotedly serve their mistress, and who gratefully receive Madame's cast-off dresses. Their life has been so reduced by this service, by the silence imposed upon them, that the only way they feel they can exist independently and truthfully is by committing a crime. But the planned murder of their mistress turns against them.

The sense of horror which this play creates seems almost more intense and more menacing than the horror generated in countless scenes of Genet's books. When performed on the stage, with living actors, such a story as *Les Bonnes* reveals a violence that is almost unbearable. This is an example of the theatre of cruelty Artaud speaks of. It is not the revelation of scandal which hastily written dramatic criticism has often called it. It is the revelation of a moral distress, able to turn human beings into sufferers whom we often live close to without recognizing. These sufferers often speak in words of sumptuous beauty because Jean Genet is a very great writer.

The action of Genet's second play, *Haute Surveillance* (*Death Watch*) transpires in a prison cell where a very precise and powerful hierarchy exists among three young men. Yeux-Verts (also called Paolo les Dents Fleuries) is the murderer of a girl. He expects in two months time to be guillotined: "D'un côté de la machine j'aurai ma tête, et mon corps de l'autre côté." He dilates at such length on this situation of horror that it becomes something monstrous and fabulous. He loses himself in admiration over the magnitude of his own condemnation and fate. He is the *maudit* but without the romantic halo of rebel and apostle. He is the exalted criminal. By his prestige he dominates a second prisoner, who in his turn dominates a third prisoner, a mere thief. This is the hierarchy of the cell where seductiveness (essentially of a sexual nature) comes from the power of evil.

The heroes of *Haute Surveillance* walk back and forth in their close cell and provide thereby a picture of their obsessions from which they cannot escape. It is a self-contained world of damnation. Genet does not move outside of the world of the damned; he gives to it the inverted vocation of evil. His subject matter is that which is condemned by society and to it he gives, as an authentic playwright in *Les Bonnes* and *Haute Surveillance,* an infernal order, a presentation of evil conceived of in terms of a criminal hierarchy. Yeux-Verts, the protagonist of *Haute Surveillance,* has his own prestige and magnificence. He is the beneficiary of a perverted kind of grace and power.

In Sartre's critical work, *Saint Genet comédien et martyr,* he has meticulously pointed out the strong relationship between the two plays. In writing for the stage, Genet was unquestionably drawn by the artifice of the theatre, by its pretense and lie. In the text of *Les Bonnes,* he gives the formal direction that the two maids be played by adolescent boys in order to enhance even more drastically the ludicrousness of their appearance and the strangeness of their strategy. In the uniform structure of the two plays the important male figure is absent: the husband of the house in *Les Bonnes,* and the negro criminal Boule-de-Neige who obsesses the minds of all three prisoners in *Haute Surveillance.* There are three visible actors in each play. One of these actors, Madame in *Les Bonnes,* and Yeux-Verts in *Haute Surveillance,* serves as a kind of intermediary between the absent actor, whose power and authority have been somewhat transmitted to him, and the couple: the two maids in *Les Bonnes* and the other two prisoners Maurice and Lefranc in *Haute Surveillance.* In each play the couple is a weird pair of beings, who are simultaneously drawn to one another and hate one another, and who dream of committing a murder. One play ends with a suicide and the other with a murder.

Most men are able to play some kind of role in society. By feeling thus integrated with a social group, they justify their existence. Jean Genet is concerned in his two plays, as well as in all of his books, with the type of man who is alienated from society, who has been given a role outside of society and accepts it. Sartre can easily find in the writings of Genet examples of a gratuitous and absurd existence. The maids and the criminals in the two plays, in the acceptance of their alienation, have only one recourse. They have to play at being normal, at being integrated characters. So the maids play at being their mistress and the criminals form a hierarchical society in their cell. But the characters of Genet know what they are doing. They know they are counterfeiting society. They know that the actions which they invent will justify their existence. So in reality they are always playing their own alienated selves. We are therefore always watching simultaneously two actions in the plays of Genet: the invented actions of the characters playing at being something they are not, and the fatal drama of alienation.

In a new edition of *The Maids* (*Les Bonnes et l'Atelier d'Alberto Giacometti,* L'Arbalète, 1958), Genet has published an important letter on his play and on the theatre in general. On the whole, he feels repulsed by the clichés and formulas of the Western theatre. In the tradition of our theatrical performances, the actor identifies himself with a character in the play, and this, for Genet, is basically exhibitionism. He claims that our Western plays are masquerades and not ceremonies: what transpires on the stage is always childish. Genet wrote *Les Bonnes* through vanity, he says, because he was asked to by a famous actor, but he was bored during the writing, depressed by his knowledge that it would be performed in accord with the conventions of the modern theatre where everything is visible on the stage, where the actions of men, and not of the gods, are depicted.

In a recent interview Eugène Ionesco pointed out the futility of wishing for a healthy, comfortable and comprehensive theatre. To achieve this kind of theatre would be equivalent to killing it. To be in a state of crisis is characteristic not only of the theatre, but of humanity itself. Ionesco reminds us once again that man is a sick animal, the only animal in the universe which is dissatisfied with its condition. But this is why man has a history. The function of art, literature and the theatre is to express the permanent crisis of man. M. Ionesco does not believe, for example, that an economic crisis really affects the theatre, since it lives by and through much more serious crises. There is no minority theatre, he claims, which cannot become a majority theatre. It was once said that Anouilh's plays were accessible only to a bourgeois public. This has been disproved. He has had success in the popular theatres where also the experimentalists Audiberti, Beckett, Ghelderode and Ionesco have been warmly received.

As is usually the case for a new playwright, the critics are divided over Ionesco in praise and blame. His admirers find in his writings the abstractions of a philosophy of language, and his detractors grant him no talent, no importance. At the performance of an Ionesco play, there is considerable laughter in the audience. The source of this laughter is as old as the theatre itself. It is man laughing at his own vacuity, his own emptiness, his own intimate triviality. This kind of laughter has been excessively exploited by the surrealists and by those close to surrealism, by Jarry in *Ubu-Roi*, by Cocteau in *Les Mariés de la Tour Eiffel*, by Desnos and Queneau and Michaux. It is language and miming which plunge the reader into the very heart of his own foibles and imbecilities.

The text of *La Cantatrice Chauve (The Bald Soprano)* is an example of the burlesque inventiveness of Ionesco, of the verbal fantasies he can create, but the laughter the text generates is not very pure. It covers up a rather serious worry of man, a *malaise*. It is a text made up of commonplaces very skillfully reconstructed, or placed just a bit out of context. We laugh because of the persistent disparity which lies between the words as they are said and the behavior of the characters speaking the words. The spectacle which transpires on the stage (and which in no wise resembles a plot or a story) is very close to the spectacle going on in us or around us almost all the time.

La Cantatrice Chauve, which Ionesco calls an "anti-play," was first performed in May 1950. The roof over the stage leaked that night and the rain fell directly on the actors. This added to the confusion of a puzzling text and an absurd title, a bald soprano who never appeared. A few of the spectators enjoyed themselves, but most were furious with the conviction they were being made fun of. The theme of *La Cantatrice Chauve,* which occurs often enough in the other plays of Ionesco to be called his principal theme, is that of the aging couple, the husband and wife who have made a failure of living together, or at least suffer from some feeling of guilt. There are many Freudian aspects to his writing, but centrally this feeling of guilt which provides pathos as well as monotony. As the dialogue continues its clowning and the non-sensical answers are given back and forth, a pathos slowly emerges and the tragedy of the married couple is faintly sketched. It is not the young couple, in love with one another but quarrelling and misunderstanding one another, such as Molière, Marivaux and Goldoni gave us.

At this first play, when no bald soprano appeared, the public was first irritated and then resigned to the trick. So when the second play, *La Leçon (The Lesson)* was announced, the public knew there would be no lesson. They did not know that Ionesco was going to be unpredictable from one play to another. The play turned out to be an authentic private lesson given by a teacher to a rather stupid pupil, and this lesson lasts the full length of the play. The teacher is nervous and tense, and grows more irritable as he continues to teach his young pupil who is preparing the full doctorate (*le doctorat total*). At the end, the teacher kills his pupil.

Already *La Leçon* has become a kind of classic of the new French theatre throughout the world. It has been performed in England, America, Germany, Turkey, Japan. The first two plays are more simple than the subsequent ones, but they contain the essence of Ionesco's dramaturgy. They are filled with a ludicrous babbling and chattering. The speech of man seems unable to adapt itself to the sentiments and the truths which the language is attempting to express. The dialogue of Ionesco often resembles the monotonous whining of an animal unable to articulate the cause of its suffering, unable to make its suffering understood. The ritual of commonplaces can become so cruel that the laughter of the spectator is uncomfortable.

Ionesco published in *La Nouvelle Revue Française* of February 1958 an important article in which he describes his early dislike for the theatre. He attended the theatre rarely because everything about it disturbed him: the acting of the players, the arbitrariness of the so-called dramatic situation, the artificiallity and the trickiness of the productions. He found no magic in the theatre, but on the contrary an intricate system of tricks and deceptions and patterns. These he calls *les ficelles*. The living presence of men and women on the stage, playing parts foreign to their nature, was an unpleasant spectacle for him. He could not accept the art of the actor, as defined by Diderot and refined on by Jouvet and by Brecht, the art of the actor who is in full possession of the character he is playing. Ionesco remained attached to some of the great dramatic texts of the past: Aeschylus, Sophocles and Shakespeare; but this was a literary attachment. The comedies of Molière bored him, and he found the greatness of Shakespeare's plays seriously diminished when they were performed. Ionesco was the opposite of what might be called an amateur of the theatre. His judgments on playwrights are briefly stated in this article, and they are negative. Corneille is tiresome, Marivaux frothy, Musset thin, Hugo laughable, Giraudoux already unplayable, Cocteau artificial, Pirandello outmoded. Only Racine escapes total condemnation when Ionesco claims that he is played today not because of his psychological understanding but because of his poetry. By comparison with music and painting, the art of play writing has accumulated very few masterpieces which have lasted: twenty or thirty, at the most. As a tentative theory to explain this paltry number of enduring successes, Ionesco wonders whether the playwright's habit of writing for his own time, of trying to remain close to his immediate audience, does not account for the dismally small number of dramatic masterpieces.

In M. Ionesco's early experimentations with play-writing and with the productions of the plays, he discovered that the essence of the theatre for him was in the exaggeration of its effects. Rather than trying to conceal the various artificialities and conventions of a performance (*les ficelles*), he believed that they should be made more visible. Playwright and director should go as far as possible in grotesqueness and caricature. Ionesco recalls theories of Antonin Artaud when he advocates a theatre of violence where the psychological study of characters will be replaced by metaphysical themes. He does not recognize any clearly marked distinction between the comic and the tragic. He deliberately calls his plays "comic dramas" or "tragic farces." In *Les Chaises* he purposely disguised the tragic element by means of a comic treatment. The comic and tragic are not fused, for Ionesco; they coexist. Each stands as a criticism for the other.

No pre-determined plan, no pre-arranged set of ideas guides M. Ionesco in the writing of his plays. Artistic creation appears to him essentially spontaneous. Yet this creation of a possibly new theatre is associated in his mind with the coexistence of contradictory principles: tragedy and farce; the poetic and the prosaic; fantasy and realism; the familiar and the unusual. His texts would seem to indicate a belief that the playwright remains more separated from his characters than the novelist, and that he is therefore a more accurate observer of their lives. In his greater detachment, he can perhaps be a more authentic witness.

Bettina Knapp (essay date 1964)

"Artaud: A New Type of Magic," in *Yale French Studies,* No. 31, 1964, pp. 87-98.

[*In the following essay, Knapp interprets several works of Artaud, arguing that they represent his medium for expressing and transforming the sick and sordid aspects of the human psyche.*]

As actor, director, poet, scenario writer or art critic, in whatever field of endeavor Antonin Artaud[1] chose to express himself, he sought to penetrate deep within man's unconscious into what became known as "the world of sur-reality." He wanted to extract from it and materialize those painful and frightening thoughts and clusters of sensations which man wants to conceal from himself or hesitates to confront. Dreams, hallucinations, magic and alchemy were the instruments Artaud used to effect such revelation.

It was as a theoretician of the theatre that Artaud made his singular contribution, influencing a whole generation of writers. Artaud advocated a "theatre of cruelty," where archetypes would war with each other on stage, where man would unmask himself and stand confronted with his naked ugliness. Artaud would utilize both abstract and plastic elements, that is, gesture and symbol, to give a broader base and a richer significance to the dialogue. In this way "another language" would be subsumed under the "spoken language" and would restore to it "its old magic, its essential spellbinding power" (*The Theatre and Its Double,* p. 110-11).

Artaud lived out his visions in his writings which in themselves were inspired by a series of painful experiences, the more so because he sought in them to unite the dualities within himself which reflected the dualities inherent in the knowable world: between the material and spiritual; language and all it conceals; body and soul. In

his periods of lucidity he became a visionary, creating works of beauty, and a prophet; during those months and years spent in institutions, he dwelt in a world he was unable to control. At the same time he was ironically carrying to the extremes the dualism he spent his life trying to fuse. Even death (which came to him on 4th March 1948) he considered only a separation and not a break.

When Artaud first arrived in Paris in 1920 at the age of twenty-four, he was passionately in love with art in all forms (the theatre, cinema, poetry, painting) and threw himself into every medium with the violence of his highly pitched temperament. In due time he entered a circle of artists sympathetic with his aims: Max Jacob, Elie Lascaux, Joan Miró, all of them dissatisfied with the logic of their times and bent upon casting down hermetically sealed doors to explore the vaster world of the unconscious. In 1924, when Artaud met the Surrealists André Breton, Louis Aragon, Robert Desnos and Roger Vitrac, it seemed to him as if two worlds, the observable and the unconscious, had been blended into one by the visionary energy and outlook of these men and their principles which answered a deep-seated need in Artaud. Their techniques appealed to him: automatic writing, strange word associations, the notation of dreams during waking and sleeping hours, the dislocation of fixed or grammatical rules in both prose and poetry, the sinking and losing of themselves in the fathomless reservoirs of life, and the interest they took in the Orient. Artaud became an active member of the Surrealist group and one of the principal contributors to its periodical, *La Révolution Surréaliste.* Indeed, the third number of this magazine was edited entirely by Artaud. But in 1926, when the Surrealists rallied around and supported the aims of the Communist party, Artaud refused to follow them into what he considered to be a superficial, rational, external world. It did not essentially matter to him whether political power resided in the hands of the bourgeoisie or the proletariat: his interests cut deeper through these crusts. A year later, in 1927, when the Surrealists published a pamphlet *Au Grand Jour* (signed by Aragon, Breton, Eluard, Péret and Unik), in which they made public their exclusion of Artaud from the group, he countered with *La Grande Nuit ou le Bluff Surréaliste,* deriding this particular group as a "grotesque sham," a "masquerade." The final break came after he had contributed to the 1928 issue of *La Révolution Surréaliste.*

Artaud's personal drama during his Surrealist youth represents the painful struggle of an isolated individual trying to unify conflicting aspects of a chaotic personality, and so attempting to make living possible and meaningful. It was hard. "I am suffering from a horrible sickness of the mind," he wrote to Jacques Rivière in 1924; "thoughts seem to disintegrate on all levels: words, sentences, interior directives, simple mental reactions banish" (See *La Nouvelle Revue Française,* September 1925). Whenever Artaud thought he had seized upon just the right word to express the rich compass of sensations he was experiencing and attempted to put these down on paper, and so organize all these fresh clusters of impressions and emotional encounters, a "wicked" and overmastering will robbed him of the key expressions, slacked off his mental tensions, attacked "the soul like vitriol," and left him "gasping at the very doors of life." To fight what he called "mental erosion," while attempting to exteriorize and materialize his immediate visions, was Artaud's problem. The pain, the revulsion, the brutal onslaught of his feelings both toward himself and others, did not arise from some ostensible daily or occasional distasteful experience, some common everyday setback, but rather from sources within himself, the agony he suffered from a rootless, self-torturing activity in flesh and soul. He was unlike his friend Breton and the other Surrealists in that they were not *physically* stricken. Artaud sought relief from his excruciating headaches in opium, marijuana, and peyotl.

Artaud's very sickness, however, served as a curious link between himself and the other Surrealists. For Breton and his group, the delving into the unconscious was fascinating, sometimes a joyous or frightening game; for Artaud, it was this and a great deal more, for he believed it was a dire *necessity* to establish his well-being and balance (such as it was) by burrowing into the interior and bringing forth what he found. It was through the unconscious mind and the relevations his dreams presented to him that he hoped to find "himself," his "identity." In his poetry, plays, movie scenarios and art criticisms, Artaud wanted to jar his audiences into this same receptive attitude and awareness of a surreality in which, somewhere, "wholeness of self" could be miraculously achieved and retained. His aim, as he wrote in *L'Ombilic des Limbes,* was to "equilibrate what is falling, to unite what is separated, to resurrect what has been destroyed" within himself as well as within any sympathetic audience.

In the following surrealistic poem Artaud tried to achieve his aims and effects by creating subtle and bizarre word associations, lugubrious and repetitious sonorities, a sort of undercurrent of noise and movement. His thoughts and images, activated by his emotions, are rapid and compressed, frequently terrifying, like "blades of knives or flashes of lightning in a choked up sky" (*Oeuvres complètes,* I, p. 107). For him poetry is a descent into the darkness and shadows of a submerged soul, like the "tearing of a membrane" or the "lifting of a veil." (*ibid.*)

> Avec moi dieu-le-chien, et sa langue
> qui comme un trait perce la croute
> de la double calotte en voûte
> de la terre qui le démange.
>
> Et voici le triangle d'eau
> qui marche d'un pas de punaise,
> mais qui sous la punaise en braise
> se retourne en coup de couteau.
>
> Sous les seins de la terre hideuse
> dieu-la-chienne s'est retirée,
> des seins de terre et d'eau gelée
> qui pourissent sa langue creuse.
>
> Et voici la vierge-au-marteau,

> pour broyer les caves de terre
> dont le crane du chien stellaire
> sent monter l'horrible niveau.
>
> (With me God-the-dog, and his tongue
> like a dart pierces the crust
> of the double-vaulted dome
> of the earth which itches him.
>
> (And here the triangle of water
> is walking at a bug's pace,
> but under the bug turned to glowing ember
> turns upon it like a knife thrust.
>
> (Under the breasts of the hideous earth
> god-the-bitch has withdrawn,
> breasts of earth and iced water
> which rot its hollow tongue.
>
> (And here the virgin-with-hammer
> comes to crush the earth's caves
> in which the stellar dog's cranium
> feels the horrible leveling rise.)

God-the-dog refers to the dog-headed Egyptian God Anubis, the divine embalmer and the guardian of the tombs of men and kings. For Artaud, who steeped himself in Oriental mysteries, God-the-dog is that divine power which protects the dead who are not dead but simulate deadness. They are like thoughts lying dormant until they are awakened and reveal themselves actually for what they are. When Artaud, speaking as an Occidental, associates the divine with the canine, the ambivalence here revealed has an almost saturnine quality about it. God in the poem may also represent pure thought, the divine spark. The dog then comes to mean something different: the materialization of thought in the word, its corporeality which expresses only a tiny particle of the thought the poet wishes to present, as a dog can only bark out more or less unintelligible sounds. Artaud, the poet, is therefore part God and part dog. The God-dog's "tongue" symbolizes the passage of "thought" from one sphere to another, it "pierces the crust" of man's outer flea-ridden flesh; or it is the word put down on paper. The "calotte" refers to a skull cap worn by both priests and rabbis; it also denotes man's cranium box as well as a "vaulted dome." So the "double calotte" serves to protect, according to Artaud, or stifle thought as the church or cathedral protects or stifles God's revelations, as the family stifles or protects the child. The "calotte" is vault-shaped, like the cathedral and cranium box, and reverberations and echoes of every sort issue from it, which the poet will try to duplicate. As the "tongue pierces the crust," or as thought tries to escape from the confines of the cathedral or cranium box, from the earth's surface, the poet similarly tries to escape his hurt, his itchiness and longings. The breakthrough, then, from the unconscious to the conscious mind, from the spiritual to the material, from the confining and containing objects which are female symbols, to their opposite—that is an agonizing process. And the "tongue," a male symbol, will be instrumental in attempting this liberation.

The second verse gains in momentum and violence. The "triangle" may symbolize the trinity or the spiritual. It may also represent the family: mind, soul and flesh constantly vying with each other. The "water," transparent and unseizable, in a constant state of flux, represents "thought" which is similarly fleeting. The "triangle of water" walks like a bug or bed-bug that reproduces prolifically; it is ugly and sordid, representing instincts which flow forth like a scourge, sucking and draining the blood, strength and vitality, leaving its victim limp and exhausted. It turns into a glowing ember, consuming all in its path, yet capable of producing singular beauty. And like a knife, another male symbol, the "triangle of water" jabs and penetrates the skin, lacerates the protective tissues and inflicts pain as it tries to destroy the vault which had prevented "thought" or "spirituality" from gaining free access to the exterior or conscious world—the land of the living.

"Under the breasts of the hideous earth" which symbolizes the mother and women in general, "God-the-bitch," as opposed to "God-the-dog," has "withdrawn." When the spiritual, the thought-image, or the immaterial tries to transmute itself into material form, basely, like a female, through the written word, thought vanishes, freezes, and the "triangle of water" of the second verse has turned into "ice" in the third. "The earth's breasts," the materially productive or the written word, "rots," leaving the once-piercing tongue or pure thought "hollow," unproductive and empty.

The fourth verse, still more bitter and vindictive, describes the pain the poet endures as he tries to find the right word to express his thought. "The Virgin-with-hammer," an image which completes the trinity of "God-the-dog" and "God-the-bitch," "pounds" away, crushing the "earth's caves" or pulverizing and smashing the female principle, the material or the protective caves in the cranium box where unborn thoughts lie dormant and distant as in the "stellar dog's cranium." From the heights to the depths, from the dog-star to the caves, the poet feels himself powerless, succumbing to the onslaught of mediocrity, "the horrible leveling," aware of his failure to unite opposing forces: spiritual and physical, life and death, male and female, thought (immaterial) and the written word (material), God and church. Artaud, the poet, half-God and half-animal, will remain isolated and gasping on a peak amidst this wreckage and debris.

In the domain of the theatre Artaud also wished to portray man's reality.[2] The spectator, Artaud proclaimed, will be shaken and shattered both mentally and physically when his own personal anguishes and preoccupations are revealed to him on stage. People will go to the theatre in much the same way as they go to a dentist or surgeon, aware they will not succumb from the visit but rather will cure what ails them. Each theatrical performance, even when repeated, will be distinct, unique and unpredictable, as is every action in daily life. Artaud did not want to continue traditional theatre which gives the illusion of

what does not exist, but wanted to bring to light all that is obscure, buried deep and baffling within man. The theatre must be a solid material projection of our internal drama. Deeply influenced by Oriental dancers, Artaud wrote that sets and actors must be considered as the visible signs of an "invisible or secret language." Each gesture must be emblematic of some "fatality of life and the mysterious encounters in dreams." The somber layers of vitality and the magnetic fascination of dreams must eventually triumph on stage because the theatre is associated with magic and its mysterious powers. Accessories, décors, fanfares, parades, fireworks, bombs, strange lights, echoes, reflections, apparitions, mannequins, dismembered parts, strange sonorities, loudspeakers, shreds of eroticism will be used to break down the spectator's reserves and produce in him the equivalent of a vertigo, induced by the onslaught of even more wide-ranging, startling and pressing thoughts and sensations.

Artaud put his "surrealistic" theatrical conceptions to test in his drama *Le Jet de Sang.* As the curtain rises, a pair of lovers repeat: "I love you and all is beautiful." The young man, a moment later, explains: "Ah! the world is so well-balanced." The following void and silence are broken by a howling wind, a tornado, stars smashing into each other, a series of dismembered bodies, three scorpions and a frog falling from the sky. The man and girl dash out. A knight in medieval armor now appears, his big-breasted nurse in his wake. The knight demands his parcels, which his nurse withdraws from her pockets and throws at him; she then exits. The knight unwraps the parcels and eats the gruyère cheese contained within; he too leaves. A priest, a procuress and several others, among them the young man who has lost his girl friend, arrive on the scene. The priest tells the young man that he only likes to listen to "dirty little stories" told at confession. All present are terrified by a clap of thunder and a huge hand descends and seizes the procuress by the hair. "Leave me alone, God," she says, biting his wrist. Blood runs from the wrist. Darkness ensues and the subsequent light makes visible the corpses of the protagonists. All are dead except the young man and the procuress, who fall into each other's arms. The nurse returns carrying in the girl the young man loves, now also dead. The nurse's breasts have vanished. The knight follows his nurse, shakes her, demands his cheese. The nurse raises her skirts; out drops the gruyère. "Don't hurt mother," the young man shouts, behaving like a marionette and talking like a ventriloquist. A multitude of scorpions wriggle forth from under the nurse's skirts. The young man runs off with the procuress. The young girl, risen from the dead, announces: "The Virgin! Ah! That's whom they were looking for."

The young man and girl represent "idealistic" or, one may say, superficial love. This relationship is blotted out and we observe another side of the young man's character manifesting itself as the knight in shining armor—the bold, brave, romantic hero. Artaud is knifing both these myths: the idealization as well as the romanticising of love. Behind the pretensions of the hero-knight, we observe a weak, greedy, brutal individual who craves only to snatch the gruyère from his nurse-mother. He consumes the cheese, made of cow's milk which symbolizes the nourishing and health-giving aspects of women. The knight hungrily biting into the cheese symbolizes his aggressions, his passions for destruction: his blind use of his mother for nourishment; his use of the girl to satisfy a need for idealization, and of the procuress for sexual fulfilment. The young man, who mocks the priest and the priest's own sordid mouthpiece, indicates a hatred and contempt for organized religion with its superficial and gruesome exploitation of a profoundly mystical experience; the struggle between the physical and spiritual in mankind. When God seizes the procuress and she bites in turn, aggression reaches its peak and turns into supreme blasphemy. Man will be punished for his transgressions; scorpions, cadavers and such proliferate on the scene. God the father, cruel and murderous, has wreaked his vengeance. The young man is frightened and guilt-ridden when he observes the knight, his other self, taking it out on his mother-nurse, and so in response to this, he talks like a ventriloquist, thereby confirming this duality. When scorpions run wild under the nurse's skirts, the destructive side of this young man-knight again is uppermost. Scorpions sting and their venom is dangerous, indicating the potential for danger of all such mother-children and man-women relationships; when the child or the man regresses into such a primitive state, it is psychologically fatal. The girl, who after her resurrection says "The Virgin! Ah! That's whom they were looking for," speaks of the opposite extreme, man's need and desire for idealization of women, of purity and perfection. But these are simply myths to embroider the interior realities, which are sordid.

In the field of the cinema,[3] Artaud felt the objective should also be to search out and reveal the darkest truths in man, stated in images which "do not take on [any extraneous] meaning from the situation which develops around them, but rather from an interior and powerful necessity which brings them to light" (*Oeuvres complètes,* I, p. 23). Pure cinema would then be a restoration of certain instinctual sensations and vibrations which reveal experiences or imagined states, presented in patterns and rhythms intrinsic to this new art form.

La Coquille et le Clergyman[4] is a series of illogical and disparate images and sequences, which do not follow any unified story form. The first scene shows an alchemist's workshop. A figure garbed in black like a clergyman, is performing an alchemist's experiment, pouring liquids from one vial into another (using an oyster shell for this purpose). He then smashes the emptied vial. The door opens; a much decorated officer, wearing an enormous sword, enters. He stands, shadow-like, behind the Clergyman. Suddenly he grabs the oyster shell and smashes it with his sword. The room trembles. The officer exits; the Clergyman follows, walking on all fours. Change of scene: a street. A carriage passes with the officer and a beautiful woman beside him. Now the pair are in a confessional. The Clergyman, pursuing them, lunges at the officer who

turns out to be a priest; he vanishes into space. The Clergyman throws himself upon the woman and is about to lacerate her breasts, which become transformed into shells. A succession of scenes. A dark road along which the Clergyman and woman are running; a shadow, which the Clergyman strangles; an immense glass bowl into which he puts the shadow's head; a ship on deck of which the officer lies enchained; the Clergyman running under high vaults and stalactites; a ship passing back and forth; lights penetrating a ship's cabin; women cleaning the cabin and smashing the glass bowl in which a head appears and disappears; a governess in black holding a Bible; a priest running into a house; a young couple prepared to be married who are none other than the Clergyman and beautiful woman. The Clergyman, now headless, descends a stairway which seems to be coming from heaven. He unwraps a package he is carrying and pulls out the glass bowl which he smashes; then from within it he withdraws his head. He rests it on an oyster shell. He puts the oyster shell to his lips, the head melts and is transformed into a type of blackish liquid which he imbibes.

The medieval alchemist—whom the Clergyman represents—spun out his life trying to transmute, and finally unite, opposing substances. The secrets of chemical transformation, the alteration of substance, have parallels in psychic processes, "the unconscious phenomenon of nature." Artaud is bent on discovering the secret of transforming substance, the activating "spirit" in every individual which, when penetrated and used to a purpose, may make him whole again.

The Clergyman-alchemist in his workshop is searching for something definite. The fluid which he pours from one vial to another represents the life force, the primal energy he is constantly trying to mold into diverse forms. The officer, the Clergyman's shadow, is the darker side of his psyche. The sword he drags is symbolic of the aggressive brutality of the male. The oyster shell, a natural container, represents the feminine, protective forces. The glass bowl and the vials stand for the textures enclosing the soul or mind, imprisoned in some seemingly transparent glass. The successive smashings and cleansings of the bowl imply dissatisfaction with the casings or enclosing quality of the vessels. Yet, without some kind of casings, can man exist? The Clergyman who follows the officer on all fours is reverting to his child-like or animal-like state where hideous nightmares have a severe impact on the not yet solidly formed psyche. The same is true of the young couple who accept parental and religious domination without quibble. The beautiful woman, whose breasts the Clergyman attacks inside the confessional, discloses ambivalent attitudes toward the sexual opponent; attraction, rejection, love, hate. The clergyman vivifies the religiously oriented attitude toward life; the soldier, the opposite attitude of a world governed by power and brutality, or matter contending against spirit. There is mutual attraction and antagonisms, excesses on both sides. The overly spiritual attitude may consequently be as destructive as the overly physical. The church, parents, the woman

in black holding a Bible, all represent in one way or
another a safe and protective institution which man needs
and yet will seek to destroy. The priest, in conflict with the
Clergyman, symbolically declares the inadequacy of man-
made dogmas. The ship which carries the dreamer over
seas toward the depths of his unconscious is instrumental
in helping him get his bearings toward safe harbor. The
dark roads on which the Clergyman and woman are running are those which lead nowhere in particualr, symbol-
izing therefore both a search for and a succession of
fluctuating psychological attitudes. The headless Clergyman descending the ladder, the living communication
between God and man, indicates man's inclination toward
inflation; but what is inflation from one standpoint, is
inadequacy from another. His head, severed from his body,
reveals the split between the rational or spiritual and the
physical, between the brighter side of him which is in no
way related to the body or human condition, and the dark
side, his instinctual self. The black fluid which he absorbs
will turn into its opposite: indicating that spirituality when
pushed to extremes becomes as black and as hurtful as
brute unchannelled instincts.

Artaud's fragmentary, bizarre and somewhat chaotic
scenario is a confession of his own gnawing loneliness
and passionate desire to stabilize the conflicting forces
within him. It is a dossier on one of the most candid figures
of his time.

Artaud, meteor-like, arrived on the Surrealist scene during
its heyday. He sought in it a certain eternity, the "sur-real,"
the outward reflection of man's replete inner reality. Today,
Artaud's influence as a theatrical innovator, has made
itself felt. The whole roster of playwrights such as Ionesco, Beckett, Adamov, Genet, Vauthier, and others are
Artaud's literary heirs in one way or another. They, too,
wish to smash the recalcitrant glass casings, to discredit
the logical, the rational in order to reach down into the
primitive stuff in us all, to see man in his fundamentals, in
his baseness as well as his falseness and absurdity, which
is the first step toward a rebuilding process—toward making him whole again. The world as we once used to know
it has vanished. A new theatrical convention has been
established, as Adamov wrote, which makes "a stage play
. . . the point of intersection between the visible and the
invisible worlds. . . ."

Prophetically enough, in a letter Artaud wrote to Louis
Jouvet (27th August, 1931), he stated: "It [the theatre] will
follow the path I prescribe. This will come to pass with or
without me." And though Artaud broke with the Surrealists in 1928 and declared the movement dead the day Breton and his group opted for Communism, he announced
himself unequivocally to be the true continuator of Surrealism which was "never anything else" for him *"but a
new type of magic"* (*Oeuvres complètes*, I, p. 287).

Notes

1. Antonin Artaud was born on 4th September 1896.
His father came from the south of France and his

mother, born in Smyrna, was of Greek origin. A
good student, steeped in the works of Baudelaire
and Poe, Artaud began writing poetry at the age of
fourteen. Four years later, when he finished his
preliminary studies, he began suffering from
melancholia and was sent to a private rest home in
Switzerland for a period of two years. This was the
first of a series of rest homes and institutions which
Artaud was to frequent during the course of his
lifetime. In 1920, his parents sent him to Paris to
further his artistic inclinations. In 1929, he acted in
Lugné-Poe's Théâtre de l'Oeuvre; a year later,
Charles Dullin took him on as a pupil at the Théâtre
de l'Atelier; in 1923, he was engaged by Georges
Pitoëff to play at the Comédie des Champs-Elysées.

2. The Théâtre Alfred Jarry which Artaud founded in
1927 gave *Ventre brulé ou la Mère folle* by Artaud,
Les Mystères de l'Amour by Roger Vitrac, *Gigogne*
by Robert Aron. In 1928 it presented *Le Partage de
Midi* by Claudel, the revolutionary film *La Mère de
Gorky,* and *Le Songe de Strindberg*; in 1929, *Victor
ou les Enfants au pouvoir* by Vitrac.

3. Artaud's best known roles were Marat in *Napoléon*
(1926), and the monk Massieu in *La Passion de
Jeanne d'Arc* (1928).

4. *La Coquille et le Clergyman* was directed by
Germaine Dulac and shown for the first time on 9th
February 1928. Artaud had hoped to play the part of
the Clergyman as well as direct the film, but Mme
Dulac made it impossible for him to do so. Artaud
and his friends, the Surrealists, present at the first
showing, accused Mme Dulac of betrayal. During
the showing a voice spoke from the audience: "Who
made that film?" Another voice: "Germaine Dulac."
First voice: "Who is Madame Dulac?" Second
voice: "A cow." Armand Tallier, the director of the
theatre, turned up the houselights whereupon Artaud
and his friends launched into a series of invectives.
They were forced out of the theatre, but not without
putting up a fight which resulted in the mirrors in
the entrance hall of the theatre being smashed. It
was believed that the other voice heard was Robert
Desnos'.

George E. Wellwarth (essay date 1964)

"Antonin Artaud: The Prophet of the Avant-Garde
Theater," in *The Theater of Protest and Paradox: Develop-
ments in the Avant-Garde Drama,* New York University
Press, 1964, pp. 14-27.

[*In the following essay, Wellwarth compares Artaud's
dramatic theories to the work of Alfred Jarry.*]

[This essay appeared in a slightly different form in *Drama
Survey,* Vol. 2, Winter, 1963, pp. 276–87.]

One of the more curious and paradoxical aspects of modern
theatrical history is that trends in the drama have been

started not by the playwrights but by the critics. The dramatist presents the thesis, but it is the critical commentator who presents the counterthesis that is necessary before the final synthesis of a new theatrical movement can be produced. The drama of the past (the ancient Greek plays, the Roman comedy, the medieval mysteries and moralities, the Elizabethan heroic play, the eighteenth century sentimental drama, the nineteenth century melodrama and well-made jigsaw puzzle play) was "written down" to its particular audience: it was designed to be immediately comprehensible to its spectators. If it was not, it suffered the relegation to the closet shelf. In modern times, however, the drama has become more intellectual and sophisticated; and although the goal still is, as it always has been, to communicate directly to the audience, it has become something mysterious and puzzling. The simplicity of the drama of the past was such that dramatic movements were not discovered until they were dead; today the complexity of the drama is such that dramatic movements must be discovered by the critic before they can come to life.

The contemporary avant-garde theater—the theater of Ionesco, Beckett, Adamov, and Genet—is for most people a theater of mystification. Many go to see the plays of these authors because it is currently the fashionable thing to do. Crowds of people sit in darkened theaters and stare incredulously at lighted stages where plays are performed. Much of the confusion caused by these apparently willfully obscure playwrights might be cleared up by a study of the source of the ideas that animate them. All of the plays of the current avant-garde experimental drama have a common source in the theories of Antonin Artaud (1896-1948).

The dramatic theories of Artaud, as outlined in his chief critical work, *Le Théâtre et son Double,* represent the counterthesis to the thesis of Alfred Jarry's seminal work, *Ubu roi.* Together they lead to the synthesis of the twentieth century avant-garde drama. Before Artaud had formulated his theories, the very real significance of Jarry's drama had passed unnoticed; and indeed it is only very recently that Jarry has come to be recognized as something more than an infantile prankster. The situation is in many ways analogous to the start given the modern problem-play movement by Shaw's criticism of Ibsen, who had previously been shunted aside—by the British public at any rate—as a tasteless trouble-maker. The spectacular riot that took place at the opening of *Ubu roi* in 1896 instantly established Jarry as France's leading enfant terrible. The play itself, however, was brushed aside as a piece of wantonly mischievous nonsense. Only a very few critics had the perceptiveness to observe the significance behind Jarry's nebulous overlay of apparent nonsense. One of them was William Butler Yeats, who attended the first performance. Rather wistfully, Yeats recognized that what he had seen was an important and irrevocable step forward in the development of comedy. Speaking of himself and the writers of his school, he said, "After us, the Savage God." Yeats' characterization of Jar-

ry's comedy, and the movement it would breed, as the comedy of "the Savage God" was one of those instinctive insights that mark the great critic. "The Comedy of the Savage God" might almost be a catch phrase to describe the whole avant-garde movement. It is doubtful whether Jarry himself realized the full extent of what he was starting. His play, like the plays of the avant-gardists who came after him, is a play of pure rebellion, a comedy of the Savage God remorselessly trampling over everything that exists. The avant-grade drama is the comedy of nihilism and despair.

It took a critic of Antonin Artaud's temperament to perceive the far-reaching implications of Jarry's play. He saw Ubu as a powerful destructive force that had eliminated forever the convention-bound "drama as entertainment" or "drama with a purpose," which had dominated the stage for so long. After Ubu, drama had to return to its primal origins as an atavistic folk rite.

As Artaud saw it, what was wrong with drama, as well as with all the other arts, was culture. By "culture" Artaud meant the overlay of artificialities that civilization had imposed upon human nature. The *essence* of human nature, its basic and intrinsic quality, had become obscured by the unreal formal masks—the socially acceptable behavior patterns arbitrarily imposed on us by custom and tradition. Since art is reality, the artist's task was to strip away the layers of artificiality and expose the core of reality that had been hidden for so long. To Artaud this core was pure emotion; and the emotion was latent, instinctual savagery. He perceived that men are, as they always have been, basically barbaric, that the thick protective wall of urbane, civilized behavior they have acquired through centuries of hiding from psychological self-realization is easily crumbled by a forceful appeal to irrational emotion.

Culture, then, must be swept away. Only the instinctive human desires (anger, hate, longing, the physical desires, etc.) are worthy of consideration by the artist. Everything must be elemental—culture and all it implies, including form in art, is out of harmony with instinctive human emotion. We can see from this the real significance of Jarry's Ubu figure. No longer a mere tasteless prank, he becomes, through Artaud's scheme, the prototype of the elemental figure unencumbered by inhibition or respect for the veneer of law and order. The mere existence of a figure like Ubu, whose heedless freedom makes "civilized behavior" look ridiculous, is a protest in itself. And once something has been made to look ridiculous, it can never carry the same authority again.

The apparent perverseness and obscurity of the avant-garde drama is a direct outcome of the Ubu figure and the subsequent Artaud theories. It is an inevitable result of the confusion created in the human mind by its acquired fear of instinct and its ingrained habit of analyzing action. The spectator is confused because he shies away from overt displays of his own instinctual self and because he tries to analyze, i.e., understand, instead of responding and participating emotionally. The vitality of this new drama, despite the puzzlement of the audiences, indicates that the old intensity of instinct is still there, though it has hitherto been stifled.

The function of the drama, according to Artaud, is two-fold: it must, by being consistently uninhibited, protest against the artificial hierarchy of values imposed by culture, and it must, by a "drama of cruelty," demonstrate the true reality of the human soul and the relentless conditions under which it lives.

The manner in which this violent attack on the everyday is to be accomplished involves a fantastic, larger-than-life callousness that enables the characters to disregard the amenities of social behavior, and a rejection of speech as a means of communication. Speech, according to Artaud, is nontheatrical; therefore, strictly speaking, it has no place in the theater. The paradox forming the basis of Artaud's system of theatrical practice is that instead of clarifying the meaning of drama, instead of using the various elements of the theater (scenery, lighting, costumes, stage movement, etc.) to make the plays easier to understand, it is necessary to make the plays less easy to understand in order to make them the more accessible to instinctive human emotion. What Artaud meant by this was that ever since the theater had descended (as he saw it) from ritual to art form, all the essentially theatrical elements—those elements that distinguish the theater from other forms of expression—had been subordinated to speech. Everything that has ever been done in the theater since ancient Greece has been predicated on the assumption that the function of the theater is communication through speech. But speech—communication of rational thoughts—is the very thing that does not and cannot distinguish the theater from anything else—which makes it, in short, merely a branch of literature. If rational communication through speech is really the ultimate goal of the theater, then, according to Artaud, there is no point at all in going to the enormous trouble and expense of producing a play: it is obviously enough simply to read it. One can obtain information from the written word just as easily as from the spoken. Theater, Artaud decreed, must be theatrical, and speech is not theatrical, but literary. Therefore we must concentrate exclusively on those elements of the theater peculiar to it alone.

Through the ages the true nature of the theater had become obscured. The demands of society shaped theater into something national, even local, reflecting the current mores and points of view of particular segments of humanity rather than universal human feeling. In this way the rational, imitative theater came into being; and problem plays (dealing with some specific aspect of some specific society) or irresponsible comedies designed for superficial entertainment became the vehicles of theatrical expression. Artaud's theater was therefore a return to the original purity of drama.

Artaud did consciously what Jarry had done instinctively when he wrote *Ubu roi*: he went back to the most primi-

tive forms of the theater. To Artaud, theater was something that had been perfect in its beginnings and had been degenerating ever since as a result of contamination by civilized convention. Artaud felt that the theater had originally been the medium through which men expressed their unconscious feelings—the mysterious, nonrational essence of their beings. Inevitably, the first step in Artaud's program was the destruction of the present-day theater. He rebelled against everything that the contemporary theater represented: against society, against convention, against modern dramaturgy, even against the physical structure of the theater itself. Artaud had no wish to compromise or modify: he did not have the temperament to slither deviously to his objective. Revolt, overthrow, and complete, merciless destruction were the steps he recommended. The new theater had to be created as it had been created in the first place—from its original motivating forces.

Artaud rebelled not only against current methods of production, but against the current matter of production as well. He wanted drama to return to its elemental beginnings—yes; but Artaud was not merely an intellectual purist or a passionate dramatic archaeologist with a fetish for restoring originals. His reason for going back to the original form of drama was his conviction that the drama was an expression of the human condition. Unlike the ceremonies of religious worship, in which man abased himself before a superior power with the object of propitiating it, the ritual of the drama was man's assertion of his dignity and independence and was therefore a defiance and *protest* against the superior power. In religious observances man is nothing; in the self-expression of drama he is everything. Both are forms of worship, for both recognize the existence of a superior power. To love and to bow down to that superior power is no more an acknowledgement of its power and superiority than to hate and defy it. And the latter course is the nobler course because it is the truer: man has a right to his own feelings and his own dignity as a being. Reasoning thus, Artaud arrived at his concept of a theater pervaded by a sense of cosmic powers and by an attitude on the part of actors and audiences that simultaneously implied awe and defiance. Like Jarry and like all the other avant-garde writers who came after him, Artaud looked at mankind in much the same way that Pascal did, although the latter drew radically different conclusions from his view: "*Condition de l'homme: inconstance, ennui, inquiétude.*" The condition of man was such because of the unrelenting malignancy of the incomprehensible cosmic powers that govern him. Hence the theater, which reflects the condition of man, must be a "theater of cruelty."

Cruelty in the theater does not mean, as Artaud was careful to emphasize, mere sadism: it is the impersonal, mindless—and therefore implacable—cruelty to which all men are subject. The universe with its violent natural forces was cruel in Artaud's eyes, and this cruelty, he felt, was the one single most important fact of which man must be aware. This cruelty is seen to some extent as viciousness between human beings. But such scenes must be presented in a manner calculated to purge the spectator of the corresponding emotions in him rather than to arouse in him the desire to imitate. At the same time, the spectator must be made aware of the violence dormant within himself and the omnipotence of the forces outside himself: each theatrical performance must shatter the foundations of the spectator's existence. It must show the spectator his own helplessness in the presence of the awesome and ineluctable forces that control the world. The theater must entangle the emotions, for the majority of the people use their senses rather than their intellect. It must be *ecstatic.* It must crush and hypnotize the onlooker's sense. It must have the same effect on the audience as the dances of the whirling dervishes and the ritual incantations and ceremonies of black magic. Like these ceremonies, the theater must combine submission and mystic union with protest and defiance.

The natural consequence of all this is that theater must be spontaneous. Since theater for Artaud is essentially a primitive ritual, it draws the spectators into the vortex of emotion generated by the actors. Unlike the separated and dispassionate onlookers in the modern theater, the audience should always be like extras who are part of the performance.

If, then, theater is to be spontaneous, it must use only works inspired by the emotion of the moment. In his essay "No More Masterpieces," Artaud explains that all the so-called masterpieces of dramatic literature must either be eliminated or brought up to date. The scholar's slavish cringing before and the layman's passive acceptance of the classics have no place in the new theater. Artaud maintains that there is no reason whatever to suppose that a work can be equally valid at all times. Even if its theme is still as valid as it was in the time the work was written, its structure must be altered to bring it into close harmony with the feelings of a contemporary audience. Artaud attacked the faithful rendition of masterpieces as "bourgeois conformism"—that clapboard superstructure of civilized behavior so antipathetic to his atavistic spirit. "Bourgeois conformism" makes us confuse sublime ideas with the forms they have taken in time. What must be said must be said in a way that is immediately accessible to the masses: "It is idiotic to reproach the masses for having no sense of the sublime when the sublime is confused with one or another of its formal manifestations, which are, moreover, always defunct manifestations."[1] Thus, for example, the themes of Sophocles's *Oedipus Rex* are as sublime as ever, but the form in which Sophocles embodied them, i.e., the dramatic form peculiar to the needs of the ancient Greek theater, is not. Sophocles's stately language, for one thing, is inappropriate for the "rude and epileptic rhythm" of our time. *Oedipus Rex* does have all the elements that Artaud requires in a play. The relentless cruelty of the implacable forces that control man, the violence of human nature, the defiance of common mores in the incest theme—all are there. But they mean nothing if presented in the archaic form and language of the ancient Greek drama:

. . . a public that shudders at train wrecks, that is familiar with earthquakes, plagues, revolutions, wars; that is sensitive to the disordered anguish of love, can be affected by all these grand notions and asks only to become aware of them, but on condition that it is addressed in its own language, and that its knowledge of these things does not come to it through adulterated trappings and speech that belong to extinct eras which will never live again.[2]

This statement crystallizes Artaud's aesthetic theory. Form, as such, has no meaning for him. All that matters is the theme of the play and the technique by which it can be presented most effectively. Plays must be changed in form and language in order to make them clear to the public. The only objection that might be made against this is that form is self-evidently an integral part of a work of art. Change the form of *Oedipus Rex* and you no longer have *Oedipus Rex.* What you have is a different play on the same theme, like the modern reinterpretations of the classical drama by Sartre, Giraudoux, and Anouilh. Artaud's answer to this would be that if modernizing a play means destroying it, then it must be destroyed. In short, Artaud sees drama as a set of important themes floating around amorphously, ready to be shaped into whatever form the all-powerful *metteur en scène* (a combination of producer, director, and author in Artaud's system) wishes to give them.

Artaud was above all a practical—and practicing—theater man. His theories may sound vague, but he described very specifically how he wanted them carried out in actual practice. Artaud maintained that a production should concentrate only on those aspects of the drama that are purely *theatrical,* i.e., that require the medium of the stage to be intelligible. Music, dance, plastic art, pantomime, vocal mimicry, lighting, and scenery fall into this category. When properly combined, they form what Artaud called the "poetry of space." Thus the "poetry of speech," which has always been the theater's chief medium of expression, is eliminated. This is not to say that Artaud intended to transform the theater into a vehicle for pure mime. Speech might still be used in the theater, but not for the communication of ideas and not in such a way as to make it an end in itself. Words can be used on the stage as sound per se—as intonations. As such, their purpose would no longer be to communicate thought, but to bring about an emotional effect. For example, a hoarse, rasping, aspirated roar might indicate a feeling of terror. Artaud's idea of the function of words is rather similar to that of Ionesco's Professor in *The Lesson*: "words charged with significance will fall, weighted down by their meaning, and in the end they always collapse, fall . . . on deaf ears." Like the Professor, Artaud would like to have only "purely irrational assemblages of sounds, denuded of all sense" floating allusively around at high altitudes, where they can charge the atmosphere with a pervading emotion, far above the "deaf ears" of the mind. Insofar as there is to be anything at all even remotely approaching the communication we are accustomed to in the ordinary theater, Artaud would like to convey to the onlookers a generalized impression of a state of mind rather than the communication of facts. Clearly this can only be managed by means of symbols—which on the stage would have to take the form of a formalized sign language. In this "unperverted pantomime" (a term Artaud uses to distinguish it from the type of pantomime ordinarily seen in the theater, which merely substitutes gestures for words as a means of communicating specific ideas) the gestures represent "ideas, attitudes of mind, aspects of nature" instead of words and sentences. As an example Artaud cites the oriental device of representing Night by a tree on which a bird that has already closed one eye is beginning to close the other. This evocation of images or states of mind rather than specific thoughts may be termed a macrocosmic approach to theatrical art rather than the microcosmic one now in use. Like all visionaries, Artaud always saw the large view, the ecstatic, all-embracing concept; thinkers and analyzers, on the other hand, always work through specific instances. In a sense, Artaud was going back to the intellectual method of the Scholastics, rejecting the reform of the inductively minded Renaissance thinkers.

In the drama of Artaud, the *metteur en scène* is responsible both for the text and for the manner of its presentation. The text as written has no authority whatsoever, and the *metteur en scène* is perfectly free to alter it at will. It is his business to transform the text into a set of "animated hieroglyphs" that will involve everyone's emotions. Artaud suggested that this can best be done by a technique of interpenetration of action and audience. That is to say, the old partition between action and audience, which was achieved by the artificial dividing line of the proscenium arch or the barrier of the front-row seats, must be eliminated. The stage will continue to exist, but a great part of the action will be carried on *in* the audience and all around it. Instead of the auditorium being lined-up in front of the stage, as in the theater of conventional design, or around the stage, as in the arena theater, *the stage will surround the audience.* In this way, the audience, seated on swivel chairs, will be encompassed by the action and will feel itself to be part of it instead of hovering over it like students at a surgical demonstration. The theatrical devices that will involve the audience will consist of music, lights, color, masks, and rhythmic physical movement. In addition, Artaud planned to insert novel devices that would serve as hieroglyphs indicating the supernatural forces surrounding man. These would include apparitions, effigies yards high dressed in costumes based on old ritual models, stereophonic sound, and "new and surprising objects."[3] Thus every play would be rewritten by the Supreme Godhead of the New Theater, the Director-Author or *metteur en scène,* in order to fit into the new hieroglyphic language of the stage. The stage will surround the audience, and the auditorium will resound to the eerie wails, the unearthly moans, and the nerve-rending screams of Artaud's apparitions. Often, instead of rearranging already existing plays, the *metteur en scène* will piece together a "drama" on some appropriately awe-inspiring theme as he goes along. A quote from Artaud's tentative repertoire for his new theater makes this clearer:

We shall stage, without regard for text:

1] An adaptation of a work from the time of Shakespeare, a work entirely consistent with our present troubled state of mind, whether one of the apocryphal plays of Shakespeare, such as *Arden of Feversham,* or an entirely different play from the same period.

2] A play of extreme poetic freedom by Léon-Paul Fargue.

3] An extract from the *Zohar:* "The Story of Rabbi Simeon," which has the ever-present violence and force of a conflagration.

4] The story of Bluebeard reconstructed according to the historical records and with a new idea of eroticism and cruelty.

5] The Fall of Jerusalem, according to the Bible and history; with the blood-red color that trickles from it and the people's feeling of abandon and panic visible even in the light; and on the other hand the metaphysical disputes of the prophets, the frightful intellectual agitation they create and the repercussions of which physically affect the King, the Temple, the People, and Events themselves.

6] A Tale by the Marquis de Sade, in which the eroticism will be transposed, allegorically mounted and figured, to create a violent exteriorization of cruelty, and a dissimulation of the remainder.

7] One or more romantic melodramas in which the improbability will become an active and concrete element of poetry.

8] Büchner's *Wozzeck,* in a spirit of reaction against our principles and as an example of what can be drawn from a formal text in terms of the stage.

9] Works from the Elizabethan theater stripped of their text and retaining only the accoutrements of period, situations, characters, and action.[4]

This list of tentative productions was never realized in fact. Artaud's only opportunity to put his theories into practice with absolute freedom came between 1927 and 1929, when he and Roger Vitrac ran their own theater, significantly named the Théâtre Alfred Jarry. Here he produced **Les Cenci,** which he adapted from the Shelley and Stendhal versions, several of Vitrac's plays, Strindberg's *Dream Play,* the third act of Claudel's *Partage du Midi* (acted as a farce), and several other things. But Artaud is not important as a mere transformer of other men's work. He was the catalytic agent for an entirely new drama that used the complex resources of the modern theater to express the age-old cry of fear and protest, the most elemental human impulse from the most primitive man to the present. Taking the sudden outburst of primitive elemental force that Jarry's *Ubu roi* projected into the theater as his starting point, Artaud continued to define a drama denuded of all the excess and essentially nondramatic elements which had accumulated around the art of the theater through the ages. Artaud's drama may be compared to the bare trunk of a tree stripped of all the shrubbery that usually obscures its reality; but the only tree that would have satisfied Artaud would have been Yggdrasil, the sacred, magical, awe-inspiring ash which penetrates to the center of the earth and to the core of life itself. From this tree sprang the modern avant-garde drama—the plays of Beckett, Ionesco, and Adamov (who in 1947 called Artaud the greatest living poet), of Genet, Audiberti, and Jean Tardieu, and of the other avant-garde playwrights. All their plays are concerned with man's subjection to a malignant fate, all of them discard sociology and psychology as media for building characters, and all of them move in a purely theatric, dreamlike atmosphere. This dreamlike atmosphere (which becomes overt in plays like Adamov's *Professor Taranne,* Ionesco's *Victims of Duty,* and Beckett's *Embers*) is not accidental, but is rather the key to the whole technique. Artaud felt that men see themselves clearly only in dreams; and that it was through dreams that men could reach back to the primeval past when drama was born as the ritual observance of the myths whose creation is coeval with the beginning of human thought itself. Artaud's theory of the dream is allied to the Jungian theory, in which dreams bind men together through their demonstration of an inherited collective unconscious. Artaud opposed Freud's theory of dreams because it showed the effects of individually different psychoneurotic repressions—and so is closely allied to the modern drama of individual character analysis.

The use of the dream technique is basic to Artaud's drama. It enabled him to use speech in a purely theatrical and nonliterary manner; and it enabled him to justify his use of visual communication through hieroglyphic symbols, which is the method by which dream communication takes place. It was through the use of the dream technique, too, that Artaud could present the apparitions, effigies, and other "shocks and surprises" which could bring the audience into the desired mystic union with one another, with the action, and with the cruel, primeval, juggernautlike forces governing the world.

Notes

1. Antonin Artaud, *The Theatre and Its Double,* translated by Mary C. Richards. Copyright © 1958 by the Grove Press, Inc. (New York: Grove Press, Inc., 1958), p. 74.

2. *Ibid.,* p. 75.

3. For example, the Ubu figure, the "terrible cry" and "menace" in *Waiting for Godot,* the "awful presence" outside the room in *Endgame,* the growing body in Ionesco's *Amédée,* the loud speaker in Adamov's *La grande et la petite Manoeuvre,* Jarry's disembraining machine, the mausoleum in Genet's *The Balcony.*

4. Artaud, *op. cit.,* pp. 99-100.

Naomi Greene (essay date 1967)

"Antonin Artaud: Metaphysical Revolutionary," in *Yale French Studies,* No. 39, 1967, pp. 188-97.

[*In the following essay, Greene traces Artaud's concept of language, his distinction between political and cultural revolution, and the changes in his thought regarding whether body or spirit has primacy.*]

Albert Camus has written that there are fundamentally two types of revolution: one—characterized as revolt—is metaphysical; the other, political. A metaphysical revolutionary rebels against the limitations placed upon him by the very nature of human existence, against the laws governing life and death. Unlike a political revolutionary, involved with the problems of society, he concerns himself with only the most universal and unchanging aspects of human life. His quest is absolute, for he demands not a new or better society, but a radical change in life itself—a transformation of the human condition. In this sense, Sade, Nietzsche, Dostoyevsky, Blake, Rimbaud, and Lautréamont were all metaphysical, or spiritual, revolutionaries. The most desperate, and the most pathetic, metaphysical rebel of recent years was a poet named Antonin Artaud.

Artaud first found himself forced to define the nature of revolution in the 1920s. At that time a member of the Surrealist group, he was shocked when many of his fellow members welcomed Marxist doctrines. Although his own ideas concerning the form a spiritual, or metaphysical, revolution should assume were not yet formulated, he completely rejected the notion that a purely political upheaval could serve any purpose. For this reason, his scorn for the Surrealists who turned to Marxism was unqualified:

> They believe that they can laugh at me when I write about a metamorphosis of the inner state of the soul, as if I had the same vile notion of the soul that they do, and, as if from any absolute viewpoint, it could be of the slightest interest to change the social structure of the world, or to transfer power from the bourgeoisie to the proletariat.[1]

Political differences served to deepen an existing temperamental cleavage between Artaud and other poets of the group. Unable to share the enthusiasm of an André Breton for life and love, Artaud was emotionally alienated from them; he could not conceive of anything less than an absolute change in life itself that would be capable of solving man's problems.

Artaud was first attracted to the Surrealists because he thought that they shared his desire to penetrate and understand hidden realities in man and the universe. Believing that man's essential character was still to be discovered, Artaud rejected any philosophy presuming to already understand human nature. Years later, he wrote that "The revolt for knowledge, that the Surrealist revolution had striven for, had nothing to do with a revolution that claimed to know man, and that made him a prisoner within the framework of his most bestial needs."[2]

At the time, Artaud was perhaps the only one among the Surrealists to grasp the essential contradiction between the avowed aims of the group and those of Marxism. In *L'Homme révolté*, Camus has clearly shown that the Surrealists' attempt to reconcile Marxist doctrines with their own philosophy was doomed to failure because they were as dedicated to the irrational and the *merveilleux* as the Marxists were to rationality and fact. Artaud's perception of this fundamental contradiction is not surprising, for throughout his life he was horrified by the world of pure fact and matter. Indeed, he constantly sought spiritual and metaphysical realities in which the duality he saw between matter and mind, body and soul, fact and idea, could be reconciled. His desire to find a principle transcending the duality is at the base of his fascination for various mystical doctrines and esoteric religions. Increasingly disillusioned with the dualistic way of thinking that he found in Europe, in 1936 he undertook a trip to Mexico in the hope of finding a people whose metaphysical outlook had not yet been distorted. His writings in and about Mexico delve further into the nature of revolution and the necessity for a spiritual transformation of man. He became convinced that until man understood the reality of his role in the cosmos, until he perceived the nature of his metaphysical position, no spiritual revolution would be possible. Although, ideally, man should be directed by a metaphysical philosophy, in Europe men were being repeatedly misled by a series of political parties, each one erecting a philosophical system to justify materialistic aims.

Distinguishing between culture and civilization, Artaud maintained that a culture reflects man's metaphysical outlook, while a civilization is the body of arbitrary forms that social institutions assume. Every true revolution must stem from a cultural or spiritual transformation—a transformation which necessitates a return to the past, to the "great epochs" of history. Artaud loved to envisage a chaotic mythical past of humanity, when the world was being formed and man was still in touch with universal life-forces and gods that were immanent in nature. During these great epochs, natural phenomena embodied metaphysical principles, thereby bridging the dichotomy between idea and fact, between mind and matter. The Nietzschean idea that man can merge, in a Dionysian frenzy, with the oneness of being, or nature, is reflected in Artaud's dream of a mystical union of man and the cosmos in which the individual, as such, is annihilated and becomes one with universal forces. By alienating himself from nature, European man had lost sight of his metaphysical position and no longer functioned in harmony with cosmic forces.

A cultural revolution must be led not by politicians or statesmen but by artists. They alone are able to penetrate and understand the essential harmony that exists between man and nature; only they can awaken man to the true character of his cosmic role. Although different forms of art may coexist in a culture, if artists are in contact with primitive forces, all art forms should reveal man's metaphysical condition. The tragedy is that European artists, lost in the seeming duality of matter and spirit, have lost the capacity to capture and reflect primordial forces. Art in Europe both reflects and helps perpetuate the decadent state of Western culture.

Once Artaud introduced this rather romantic conception of the role of art, he raised another vital issue, touching on the nature of language. If the artist is to lead man to a new, metaphysical understanding of himself, he must do so through his particular artistic medium. Artaud, as a poet, had to deal with language, which he felt had to be utterly transformed. He believed that any writer who used language traditionally could not reveal metaphysical truths to man, for ordinary language obscured the spiritual realities of the universe. Europe's cultural decadence was closely related to a linguistic degeneration, in which language had become completely separated from the actual being of things. Words, losing all true meaning, had become mere signs for the objects themselves; as such, they could only distort reality. The duality between mind and matter in Western culture was reflected in the separation of the word and its object.

Seeking a form of language which would not be distinct from its object, Artaud eventually formulated the idea of a physical language in which all ideas and emotions are evoked by physical entities, obviating the necessity for words. Since physical objects suggest, rather than state, ideas and emotions, the possible interpretations of such a language are unlimited. Ideas and sentiments are normally circumscribed by the words expressing them, especially since words, meant for general use and communication, can never exactly correspond to the inner state of each individual. Lacking the words to describe our fundamental states of being, we never become fully aware of our deepest reality. "Therefore I maintain that theoretically words cannot express everything and that because of their predetermined nature, fixed once and for all, they hinder and paralyze thought instead of permitting and aiding its development."[3] Artaud's ideas concerning the relation between a cultural or spiritual transformation of man and a linguistic revolution are clear: in order to achieve a spiritual revolution we must first understand the true nature of our being—an understanding that must be preceded by a radical change in our language.

Best able at first to envisage a physical language in theatrical terms, Artaud was preoccupied with the stage during the early 1930s. The theater had only to emphasize its nonverbal aspects—sounds, lighting, costumes, decor—to achieve a perfect physical language. This theatrical language could make man aware of primordial forces existing beneath his acquired cultural characteristics. One of the most important of these characteristics, if not the most important, since it shapes the way man thinks, is traditional verbal language. With its new language, the theater could finally show man in his preverbal, prelogical state: "In this theater every creation comes from the stage and finds its translation and even its origins in a secret psychical impulse which is the Word before words."[4] Transcending man's social and psychological problems, which form an integral part of his cultural environment, the theater should evoke man's prototypal drives and the universal forces under whose sway he exists. The few concrete suggestions Artaud gives to illustrate how the theater could actually accomplish these ambitious aims were inspired largely by a Balinese theatrical troupe he had seen in Paris. He thought that many of the theatrical techniques employed by the Balinese actors served a metaphysical purpose; their gestures, for example, reflected cosmic motions. The Balinese theater illustrated the relationships that exist between animate and inanimate entities, between man and nature, concerning itself not with the individual self but with a kind of universal life: "The theater must be the equal of life, not of individual life, not of the individual aspect of life in which CHARACTERS triumph, but of a sort of liberated life which sweeps away human individuality, in which man becomes a mere reflection."[5]

Since Artaud's only play, **Les Cenci,** was totally unable to attain the lyrical heights of his theoretical writings, it is not surprising that his experimental group, "Le Théâtre de la Cruauté," failed miserably in 1935. Artaud then turned to Mexico in the hope of finding the key to a new language. When, in 1936, he visited the Tarahumara tribe in the mountains of Northern Mexico, he felt that at last he had found this key. Deeply impressed by the physiognomy of the terrain, he saw in the natural configurations, in the rocks and mountains, different "signs." Nature herself had become language and suggested a myriad of ideas and emotions. Here was the primeval, physical language he had so ardently sought: "The country of the Tarahumari is full of signs, forms, and natural effigies which seem to have been born, not by accident, but as if the gods, that can be sensed everywhere here, had wanted to indicate their powers by these strange signatures."[6] For the Tarahumari, idea and being, mind and matter, language and objects, were one and the same. The Indians understood that the basic principles of life are incarnated in material elements and that essential life-forces have a concrete existence. Their language, both natural and physical, was universal since, unlike conventional languages, it revealed fundamental and ultimate realities of existence. Consequently, Artaud's attempt to utterly transform and revolutionize traditional language, to create a new language capable of expressing man's inner reality, ended in a return to the past, a return to the nonverbal language of animistic primitive societies.

Shortly after his return from Mexico toward the end of 1936, Artaud left France for Ireland. There, his already tenuous grip on reality slipped and for the next nine years he was committed to various asylums. Released in 1946, he enjoyed his new-found freedom very briefly, for two years later he was dead. In the course of these last years his ideas concerning spiritual and linguistic revolution underwent a radical change, a change that could have resulted from the mental and physical sufferings he endured or from the terrible realization that his great metaphysical quest had been in vain. In any case, during his grim confinement, he began to focus all of his atten-

tion on the human body. The duality between mind and matter that had so long consumed him ceased to exist, as he proclaimed that matter was the source of all, that man was nothing but a body. Violently repudiating all the great metaphysical systems that had formerly fascinated him, he derided with great venom spiritual concepts concerning the soul, God, and metaphysics. The cosmos, with its eternal life-forces, held no more interest for him, as he now impatiently urged not a spiritual revolution but a transformation of the body.

Although proclaiming the absolute superiority of the human body, he could not overcome his lifelong horror of it nor could he manage to divest himself of his former desire to find a spiritual reality beyond the material world. He could resolve this impossible ambiguity only by demanding that the body itself be transformed and purified: he thereby transposed his need for spirituality to the very plane of matter itself. Curiously enough, his affirmation that the body was the sole reality led him to a total refusal of its present state. True reality was attainable only in a pure body; man had first to rid himself of his organs, sexual drives, and bestial instincts. Paradoxically, corporeal transformation was linked to spiritual concepts of immortality, such as resurrection and metempsychosis. Having lost his former belief in an immortal soul and in eternal universal forces, Artaud found himself forced to seek immortality through matter and the body. If man could rid himself of all that is physical, all that is subject to decomposition and decay, he would not die. Man's body decays and dies because it has not purged itself of its animal instincts. True freedom, which is ultimately freedom from death, depends upon man's complete liberation from all that is corporeal:

> When you will have given him a body without organs
> then you will have delivered him from all his automatic
> responses and given him back his true liberty.[7]

No political revolution will be possible until man is transformed physically:

> And no political or moral revolution will be pos-
> sible as long as man is magnetically held down,
>   by his simplest and most elementary organic and
> nervous reactions,
>   by the sordid influence
>   of all the suspicious centers of Initiates,
>   who, cozy in the foot-warmers of their psyches
>   laugh at revolutions as well as wars,
>   sure that the anatomical order at the base of
> existence and the duration of present society
>   will no longer be changeable.[8]

Artaud's ideas concerning revolution did not evolve without a concurrent change in his theories involving language. And, for the first time, his poetry really illustrated his theories. No longer eager to find a language uniting being and thought, he sought one that stemmed from man's physical being. He ceased to reject verbal language and demanded instead that it liberate itself from the control of the intellect and, in so doing, that it precede any logical, rational formulation of ideas and emotions. Language was not meant to communicate ideas, which reflect the superficial level of man's being, but rather to express man's physical presence. In his later poems, he repeatedly asserts that he has reached a realm prior to thought:

> I, the poet, I hear voices which no longer
> come from the world of ideas.
> For, here where I am, there is no more to
> be thought.[9]

He even maintained that this language was for the illiterate, referring to men who, like himself, rejected rational, discursive language:

> But let the swollen words of my life swell up them completely alone to live in the abc of writing. It is for the illiterates that I write.[10]

Artaud's cult of spontaneous writing has seen its logical development not only in his own poems, but in the work of writers such as Genet, Henry Miller, and Céline.

Artaud believed that true poetry, unlike discursive language, does not appeal to the intellect, but evokes emotional and physical responses. For him, emotions were largely physical in origin: certain sounds, for example, create various sentiments and feelings. Language could call forth man's most elemental reactions only if the word were used for its sound rather than its rational meaning. Throughout his later writings, Artaud never ceased to stress the importance of the sound of words in poetry.

> All poetic lines have been written primarily to be heard, to be concretized by voices speaking them aloud, and, it is not only that they are clarified by their music and that they can then speak by simple modulations of sounds, sound by sound, but it is that only once removed from the written or printed page, does an authentic line make sense.[11]

In the last few years before his death, Artaud wrote the major poems of his life, such as *Ci-Gît, précédé de la Culture Indienne* and *Artaud le Momo*—poems that are still virtually unknown in France and the United States. They are "sound poems" whose words often convey no meaning until they are spoken or heard aloud. In the short poem "Histoire du Popocatepel," "double vé cé" and "ésse vé pé" make no sense until they are sounded out to give us WC and SVP. Sounds may not even suggest actual words, but may merely awaken ideas or emotions. Deprecating life in the poem "Il fallait d'abord avoir envie de vivre," Artaud wrote,

> larme de larve
> larve de larme
> de cette langhate,

thereby intermingling real words with created ones to produce a series of sounds evoking something that is slimy and obscene. Like Joyce, he was fascinated by puns and

delighted in those that were, at the same time, erudite and pornographic. A frequent pun concerns the words "Ka" and "Ka Ka." "Kâ," in the ancient Egyptian religion, was the noncorporeal double of the body, conserved in the mummy, while "caca" of course is excrement. Incantatory passages, which reflect his preoccupation with pure sounds as well as his belief in the absolute efficacy and magical value of words, appear very often. Incantation is used in the most precise sense of that word—to exorcise something or someone. In one poem, Artaud uses a number of words containing an anagram of his own name, thereby attempting self-exorcism:

> Talachtis talachti tsapoula
> koiman koima nara
> ara trafund arakulda

The rhythm in this passage, as in all the incantatory sequences, is quite definite and of great importance. These few examples may give some idea of the different ways Artaud experimented with the sounds of words.

It is clear that Artaud's conception of the role language should play in effecting a transformation of man changed radically during the last few years of his life. Before his death, he had completely rejected his former conviction that language could reveal metaphysical truths or influence man's spiritual nature; instead, he asserted that it was directly related to man's physical being, stripped of any nonmaterial quality. Having lost all hope that man could unite with universal forces, he desperately longed for an immortality to be found through a transformation of the human body. Although so many of his earlier ideas underwent a violent reversal, one belief remained constant throughout his life: man's very being had to be altered before any political or social upheaval could be effective. True revolution had to be, first and foremost, metaphysical.

Notes

1. "Ils croient pouvoir se permettre de me railler quand je parle d'une métamorphose des conditions intérieures de l'âme, comme si j'entendais l'âme sous de sens infect sous lequel euxmêmes l'entendent et comme si du point de vue de l'absolu il pouvait être du moindre intérêt de voir changer l'armature sociale du monde ou de voir passer le pouvoir des mains de la bourgeoisie dans celles du prolétariat" ("A la Grande Nuit ou le Bluff Surréliste," *OC* [Gallimard, 1956], *1*, 284-85).

2. "Cette révolte pour la connaissance, que la révolution surréaliste voulait être, n'avait rien à voir avec une révolution qui prétend déjà connaître l'homme, et le fait prisonnier dans le cadre de ses plus grossières nécessités" ("Surréalisme et Révolution," *Les Tarahumaras* [Arbalète, 1963], p. 177).

3. "Car je pose en principe que les mots ne veulent pas tout dire et que par nature et à cause de leur

caractère déterminé, fixé une fois pour toutes, ils arrêtent et paralysent la pensée au lieu d'en permettre, et d'en favoriser le développement" ("Le Théâtre et son double," *OC* [Gallimard, 1964], *4*, 132).

4. "Dans ce théâtre toute création vient de la scène, trouve sa traduction et ses origines mêmes dans une impulsion psychique secrète qui est la Parole d'avant les mots" (ibid., p. 72).

5. "Le théâtre doit s'égaler à la vie, non pas à la vie individuelle, à cet aspect de la vie où triomphent le CARACTERES, mais à une sorte de vie libérée, qui balaye l'individualité humaine et où l'homme n'est plus qu'un reflet" (ibid., p. 139).

6. "Le pays des Tarahumaras est plein de signes, de formes, d'effigies naturelles qui ne semblent point nés du hasard, comme si les dieux, qu'on sent partout ici, avaient voulu signifier leurs pouvoirs dans ces étranges signatures" ("La Montagne des Signes," *Les Tarahumaras,* p. 43).

7. "Lorsque vous lui aurez fait un corps sans organes alors vous l'aurez délivré de tous ses automatismes et rendu à sa véritable liberté"

Pour en finir avec le jugement de dieu (Editions K, 1948), p. 40.

8. "Et il n'y aura pas de révolution politique ou morale possible tant que l'homme demeurera magnétiquement tenu, dans ses réactions organiques et nerveuses les plus élémentaires et les plus simples, par la sordide influence de tous les centres douteux d'initiés, qui, bien au chaud dans les chaufferettes de leur psychisme se rient aussi bein des révolutions que des guerres, sûrs que l' ordre anatomique sur lequel est basée aussi bien l'existence que la durée de la société actuelle ne saurait plus être changé."

"Le Théâtre et la Science," *Théâtre Populaire,* No. 5 (janvier-février 1954), p. 7.

9. "Moi poète j'entends des voix qui ne sont plus du monde des idées.

Car là où je suis il n'y a plus à penser."

"Préambule," *OC, 1,* 11.

10. "Mais que les mots enflés de ma vie s'enflent ensuite tout seuls de vivre dans le b a ba de l'écrit. C'est pour les analphabètes que j'écris" (ibid.).

11. "Tous les vers ont été écrits pour être entendus d'abord, concrétisés par le haut plein des voix, et ce n'est même pas que leur musique les éclaire et qu'ils puissent alors parler par les modulations simples du son, et son par son, car ce n'est que hors de la page imprimée ou écrite qu'un vers authentique peut prendre sens" ("Sur les Chimères," *Tel Quel,* No. 22 [été 1965], p. 5).

Mary Ann Caws (essay date February 1968)

"Artaud's Myth of Motion," in *The French Review,* Vol. 41, No. 4, February, 1968, pp. 532-38.

[*In the following essay, Caws describes the illness which paralyzed Artaud's thought and movement in the context of his belief in a theater of myth created through the expressive language not of words but of mental and physical mnovement.*]

> *J'estime avoir assez emmerdé les hommes par le comple-rendu de mon contingentement spirituel, de mon atroce disette psychique, et je pense qu'ils sont en droit d'attendre de moi autre chose que des cris d'impuissance et que le dénombrement de mes impossibilités, ou que je me taise. Mais le problème est justement que je vis.*

> Artaud, "*Nouvelle Lettre sur moi-même*"[1]

Antonin Artaud, like the surrealists Breton and Péret, was strongly attracted to Mexican folklore, in which they all saw a manifestation of the peculiarly unitary quality of the Mexican mind. The firm denial of any split between logic and irrationality, between reason and poetry, or between the objective and the subjective is natural to the Mexican people, according to Benjamin Péret in his *Anthologie des mythes, légendes et contes populaires d'Amérique.* He describes this attitude as being in open conflict with the practical necessities of modern life and with our ordinary vocabulary, and as an excellent example of the surviving "état mental générateur des mythes."[2]

Artaud's admiration for Mexican mythology is, as he explains in *Le Théâtre et les dieux,* based on its recognition of movement as the essential character of human thought in its contacts with the world. This mythology of motion he calls an "open" mythology; the Mexican landscape and traditional Mexican art are full of "formes ouvertes," he says, and the Mexican gods have "des lignes ouvertes, ils indiquent tout ce qui est sorti, mais ils donnent en même temps le moyen de rentrer dans quelque chose."[3] Here man can learn a pattern of thinking which will enable him to come out of himself, to move beyond his psychologically fixed or closed situation. In a rhythm that Artaud sees as geometrically active, human thought moves from the dead point or abstract emptiness at the center of things out toward the concrete world of color and events. To follow this rhythm suggested by the Mexican landscape and traditions is to lead "une vie occulte . . . à la surface de la vie," to participate at once in death and in life through a difficult metaphysical discipline that leads the way to "culture":

> *La culture est un mouvement de l'esprit qui va du vide vers les formes, et des formes rentre dans le vide, dans le vide comme dans la mort. Etre cultivé, c'est brûler des formes, brûler des formes pour gagner la vie. C'est apprendre à se tenir droit dans le mouvement incessant des formes qu'on détruit successivement.*

> *Les anciens Mexicains ne connaissaient pas d'autre attitude que ce va-et-vient de la mort à la vie.*

> *Cette terrible station intérieure, ce mouvement de respiration, c'est cela qui est la culture, qui bouge à la fois dans la nature et dans l'esprit.*

> (*T,* 203)

Artaud's own conception of the theatre is closely related to this interpretation of Mexican mythology. He discusses at some length how the fear of the empty center acts as a motor for the outward motion toward the world of fullness and forms, how the theatrical burning of exterior forms releases the energy for the motion back to the center. *Gesture,* or the double of thought in the realm of matter, he explains as the concrete realization of the dynamics of leaving and returning in a continuous staging. While the act of writing by its lack of movement can stifle the "vaste respiration" of the spirit in a silent crystallization, Artaud claims that his theatre corresponds exactly to "l'image d'un bruit," absorbing and reflecting within itself all the noise and movement of life. Like the "civilisation spasmodique" of Mexico and in direct opposition to the vain estheticism of a lifeless "art fermé," an art that bears reference only to its own gratuitous surface of forms, language and appearance and does not push beyond the sign to the reality signified, Artaud's theatre of thought is a theatre of mobility, depending on an open and necessary rhythm:

> L'essentiel: voir les correspondances, apprendre les lois, trouver à tout instant la loi,
>
> replacer le geste inutile et gratuit dans son ambiance utile, celle qui le relie à des lois principes, le met en conformité avec tout,
>
> ce minimum de connaissance qui permet de se diriger, et cette connaissance exemplaire qui vient d'images liées à l'énergie inséparable de l'exercice de toute loi (IV, 312).

The final goal of Artaud's theatre is, like that of the games of antiquity, "cette connaissance qui, par l'action, dompte le destin." What must be known is the totality of nature, "la nature que l'homme rythme de sa pensée," and in man, "la conscience complète, mise au rythme des évènements" (*T,* 194). This complete and active interpenetration makes up the reality which must be represented in the theatrical gesture as it is the exterior manifestation of thought. To the "marche" of thought Artaud applies a series of highly active descriptions—it is cruelty, intensity, action, presence of life, conflict of adverse forces; it is vigorous, energetic and bloody. And conversely, his descriptions of gesture appear indeed at first sight more appropriate to thought than to action—it is bare, pure, essential, precious, rare, precise, intellectual, and of a quintessence and a necessity that are absolute. These unexpected switches of vocabulary are an important indication of the intermingling of categories Artaud insists on, in accordance with his ideal mobility of thought in all its openness of line. Both of these traits, as we have seen, are characteristics he perceives in Mexican thought, and the fact that he perceives them is for us more significant than whether or not they are in fact characteristic of that thought.

Artaud's theatre is also a *théâtre par la poésie*: he defines poetry as a special sort of knowledge, that of the internal and dynamic workings of thought itself or again, as the translation *into action* of the most extreme ideas (III, 241). While the alchemical or poetic theatre attempts to construct

an "édifice du mouvement" in the objective world where motion is easily grasped, it must at the same time "intérioriser" the actor's playing, in strict accordance with the interior and necessary movement of thought (III, 120, 277). This theatre replaces the "classic" theatre of individual psychological motivation where feeling is studied as an inert and lifeless object "on pourrait dire photographique . . ." (III, 216). A good example of "closed" art, psychological theatre is totally anti-heroic and devoid of action, says Artaud; the reality it presents is desolate and flat, suggestive of no value beyond itself. Artaud shares the Pirandellian conception of man as a scattered and many-sided being in a room of mirrors and demands a theatre of movements sufficiently diverse in their meaning and their presentation to convey human complexity (III, 216). For this reason, it is not surprising that his objections to the staging of certain plays (such as Passeur's *Les Tricheurs* and Bruckner's *Mal de la jeunesse*) are based on their immobile quality. Artaud insists above all on the enlarging function of the theatre, which must open out beyond the narrow limits we often set for it. This is his basis for refusing the purely verbal theatre of the West: "Or, il faut bien admettre même au point de vue de l'Occident que la parole s'est ossifiée, que les mots, que tous les mots sont gelés, sont engoncés dans leur signification, dans une terminologie schématique et restreinte" (IV, 141).

One can easily see, therefore, why Artaud should have been so enthusiastic about the silent cinema. In the 1920's he had found its mobile structure far more promising than that of the theatre because it more skillfully created an atmosphere of mystery, revealing the secret transformations of the "moi interne" and blurring the usual clarity that paralyzes the life of the spirit. In the ideal film human psychology would be devoured by the dynamics of *action,* and the film in general should have been the perfect successor to the outmoded theatre. But in the 1930's Artaud became disillusioned with the cinema; in his view, the addition of sound disrupts the flow of images in their implications and extension. In a scathing article of 1933 entitled "La Vieillesse précoce du cinéma," he claims that films supply us with an instant diet, fragmentary and facile, their order relating only to certain exterior habits of vision and memory, their formal technique limited to the representation of an accidental and incomplete world, "fini et sec."[4] If the world we are shown is not the unitary and open one Artaud takes as his beginning point, it is the fault of the medium. Since the filmmaker's choice is not spontaneous but is, Artaud thinks, generally made before the moment of presentation, the gesture is given to us as already perfected and the world seems closed to the mobilizing influence of the human mind. "Le monde du cinéma est un monde clos, sans relations avec l'existence" (III, 98). Frozen, or glued, into immobility, lacking in any possibility of change or becoming, the structure of the cinema has no relationship to the active structure of thought or to the laws of reality, which Artaud always sees as closely related to thought. Since it cannot surround real things or enter the movement of life, "Le monde cinématographique est un monde mort, illusoire et tronçonné" (III, 97). Cut off from action and expansion, it can go no farther than a kind of excitation of the nerves. Because it is empty of depth, of density, of distance and of "fréquence intérieure . . . ce n'est pas du cinéma qu'il faut attendre qu'il nous restitue les Mythes de l'homme et de la vie d'aujourd'hui" (II, 99). After this disappointment, Artaud is forced to confine all his hope for the restoration of the Myths to his idea of the theatre.

But the unitary basis Artaud always insists on threatens even his conception of the mythic theatre. "Car de plus en plus la vie, ce que nous appelons la vie, deviendra inséparable de l'esprit" (III, 81): he clings to the principle of a mobile continuity between spirit and life, language and reality, mind and the works of the mind, and between the stages of personality that individual works manifest. In *L'Ombilic des limbes* he attacks the separations usually made between these elements for provoking a "rétrécissement" of the person, saying of his own writing: "Ce livre je le mets en suspension dans la vie, je veux qu'il soit mordu par les choses extérieures et d'abord par tous les sobresauts en cisaille, toutes les cillations de mon moi à venir" (I, 49). His parallel refusal to distinguish between temporary states—"les minutes de moi-même"—is genuine and must be taken into account in any discussion of his work. If Artaud sees his individual anguish as inseparable from his poetic and theoretical productions, they should not be, though they often are, considered in isolation from his personality. Such an attitude he might have characterized as a "critique fermée," partial and discontinuous and therefore of necessity superficial and immobile.

Artaud's sickness, which he refers to as "Le poison de l'être. Une véritable paralysie" (I, 40), is graver and more difficult than a purely metaphysical or psychological limitation would be. When he calls this a physical and almost exterior anguish and thus distinguishes it from the anguish characteristic of the other writers of his time,[5] he is calling attention to the totality of his own sickness and to its permanence; the only possible escapes from it, he says, are in total madness or in the grave. A metaphysical paralysis or temporary absence of the mind could be overcome by action in the objective exterior world, whereas this all-penetrating paralysis has no solution on either the exterior or the interior level. It is, of course, an ironically fitting illness for a man who depends so heavily on the unity of levels. The sickness affects his being in all its representations: that he should be so conscious of it is doubly pathetic in view of his repeated insistence on motion, energy, purity, continuity and presence:

Je n'ai pas de vie, je n'ai pas de vie! Mon effervescence interne est morte. . . . Comprenez-moi. Ce n'est même pas une question de qualité d'images, de quantité de pensées. C'est une question de VIVACITÉ *fulgurante, de vérité, de réalité. Il n'y a plus de vie. . . . Je sens mon noyau mort. . . . Je n'arrive pas à penser. Comprenez-vous ce creux, cet intense et durable néant. Cette végétation. Comme affreusement je végète. Je ne puis ni avancer ni reculer. Je suis fixé, localisé autour*

d'un point toujours le même. . . . C'est que ma pensée ne se développe plus ni dans l'espace, ni dans le temps. Je ne suis rien. Je n'ai pas de moi-même. . . . Je ne suis pas là. Je ne suis plus là, à jamais (I, 298-300).

It may be argued that in Artaud it is hard to determine the exact proportion of pose, to separate voluntary dramatics from genuine feeling. But the recurrence of particular terms and patterns of feeling must at least be seen as significant of his preoccupations.

Since one of the primary determinations of *l'être* as Artaud defines it is expansion and mobility of thought, he believes any reduction of this mobility to be a reduction in essence. In one letter of 1929 he complains of being *arrêté* in a physical sense, and in another, of "un véritable envoûtement de désordre, d'impuissance, d'incohérence" he is fated to undergo (III, 148, 178).[6] In a later letter to Paulhan describing his interior battle where his mind rarely wins, the adjectives he applies to his sickness suggest an immobility in both the physical and mental realms: "enlisé," "ligoté" (III, 272). And in letters to Dr. Allendy about his "vide intellectuel" and his intense *ennui,* Artaud finds that his thought has neither extension nor continuity, that his stuttering speech is paralleled by the contraction of his thinking which "hardens" and then stops altogether. Certain as he is of the necessary union of outward form and inward reality, he sees these things as linked to the same problem of immobility which he hoped to overcome through his theatre. In this perspective what might otherwise seem trivial takes on an entirely different appearance. We have no choice but to accept Artaud's intentions as to the interpenetration of mind and work and to listen to his own warning: "L'exercice vrai de l'esprit creuse la vie comme une maladie" (IV, 286).

This does not simply mean that the Theatre can be compared to the Plague. If life is essentially the "marche de la pensée," then the sickness attacking thought threatens life at its root and with it, the notion of the theatre Artaud so intimately connects with life and above all, with thought. The structure of the metaphysical or theatrical connection between the abstract center of emptiness and the world full of forms cannot be sustained when the possibility of the individual to act is sapped or when the movement of the mind comes to a stop. If thought lacks the energy to "brûler les formes" it will not push beyond the formal surface, and the thrust of theatre may become as ineffectual and its representation as incomplete as that of the cinema. "L'édifice du mouvement" cannot be built on an immobile structure or an inactive imagination: "Créer des Mythes voilà le véritable objet du théâtre . . ." (IV, 139). If the signs and the gesture lose their expansion or if the pure mobility is paralyzed, then the mythic theatre becomes in its turn a closed art and an outworn myth. Artaud's conception of the theatre, if it is connected as closely to his thought as he intended, is endangered by his own sickness—a destiny he was unable to dominate even through knowledge. His lament in *Les Tarahumaras* should not be forgotten: "Car le danger des mythes, si hauts soient-ils et si tenaces, c'est qu'ils s'éteignent" (*T,* 163).

Notes

1. *OEuvres complètes* (Paris, 1961), I, 273. References to this work will be made by volume number in the text.

2. Benjamin Péret, *Anthologie des mythes, légendes et contes d'Amérique* (Paris, 1960), p. 33.

3. *Les Tarahumaras* (Décines, 1963), p. 207. Referred to in the text as *T.*

4. The chief distinction he makes between his own film *La Coquille et le clergyman* and other surrealist films is that while the latter are *gratuitous* in their action, his scenario is based on a *necessary* flow of images.

5. In a letter of 1924 Artaud explains to Jacques Rivière that the leaps and sudden stops in his poetry are the result of his mental inability to concentrate on any object, a weakness he calls typical of the age and of other poets such as Reverdy, Breton and Tzara. But he goes on to say that for them the weakness touches only the area of thought, whereas for him it is physical and constant: "Cette inapplication à l'objet qui caractérise toute la littérature, est chez moi une inapplication à la vie. Je puis dire, moi, vraiment, que je ne suis pas au monde, et ce n'est pas une simple attitude d'esprit" (I, 39).

6. Artaud, totally conscious of the dangers of pose discussed above, calls these feelings a phony romanticism and struggles against them with an effort that cannot be interpreted as insincere.

Charles Gattnig Jr. (essay date December 1968)

"Artaud and the Participatory Drama of the Now Generation," in *Educational Theater Journal*, Vol. 20, No. 29, December, 1968, pp. 485-91.

[*In the following essay, Gattnig shows Artaud's influence on the de-emphasis of text and the convention of a passive audience in the theater of the late 1960s.*]

Some recent visitors to New York's theatres have been surprised and shocked by the kind of involvement required of them in the productions they merely came to view. The audience (which seems to dress less and less formally) is bedazzled by electric equipment: amplifiers scream; strobe lights flash; technicolor slides are projected on the walls and on the audience. The actors perform the play by moving through, over, and around the spectators. There are frequent, and often successful, attempts made by the performers to communicate with the spectators in a personal and non-illusory manner. Language seems less important than visual action and non-linguistic sounds. The total effect seems to be designed to stir the audience to active participation. There seems to be little or no interest in telling a story. Instead, short but highly charged instants of intense energy are transmitted in every direction. Slowly, one becomes aware that what has happened is that the traditional barrier between the cast and the audience has been dropped. We are with the nobles once again, sitting on Garrick's stage and waiting to be kicked off again.

The avant-garde theatre represents a trend which is not primarily concerned with a change in stage form although that will also come soon.[1] Rather, this new theatre is attempting a change in the definition of the term "drama." Simply stated, this new drama is theatre in which both the creation and the performance of the play is a total sensory experience for everyone in the area of the activity.

Sometime between 1963 and 1965 the so-called Theatre of the Absurd faded away and was replaced by Happenings and today's avant-garde theatre. However, it should be noted that while absurdist drama celebrated chaos, as Mordecai Gorelik has so often stressed,[2] its dramaturgy was masterfully constructed along classical lines; that is, its language was often poetic; its ambience tragic; its form compressed, severe, and disciplined. Most importantly, it was a literary drama which remained safely beshind the proscenium arch and politely allowed the audience to storm out in protest, or go to sleep, or watch from a distance—an aesthetic distance. It did not attempt to reach its audience physically but cerebrally. While the plot seemed obfuscated, words remained more important than spectacle.

As Marshall McLuhan has pointed out, we seem to be returning to a tribal-village society in which each member of the tribe (or planet) is afforded heightened multi-sensory involvement.[3] This audience desire for greater participation is evident in other areas. In many baseball stadiums now, the spectators are warned that the penalty for running onto the field is arrest. (It seems too many fans cannot overcome the desire to join the players.) When promoters attempted to initiate soccer as a national sport in this country a few years ago, they were astounded by the fact that in several early games spectators in large groups swarmed onto the playing field when they objected to a decision. Our museums and art galleries are filled with notes which instruct the visitor not to touch the art, and an amazing number of guards see to it that this rule of aesthetic distance is strictly enforced.

The spectator, especially today's youth, has gotten the message; he wants to be where the action is. By touching a painting, he is getting closer to its nature; in a sense, he is touching the painter as well as the action of painting. For the first time in recorded history, a public school system has instructed the masses in art. Now, these masses want to perform. In a democratic society, participation is not a privilege but a right—even an obligation. That this concept is being explored has been clearly demonstrated by the movements of Afro-Americans, youth in general, and the poor across this country.

1

In a Hippy production of *Beggar's Opera,* presented in a church loft in downtown New York City, we sat on folding chairs which had been placed all around the room in a seemingly haphazard fashion. We were bombarded by amplified noise while strobe lights flashed and technicolor slides were projected on our faces and on the walls. A series of vaudeville-type songs and skits barely told the story of the hardships of a Hippy singer and addict named MacHeath. The program indicated that this *Beggar's Opera* was written by Tom Sankey who also played the leading role. At the outset, a young man with a microphone introduced himself as the "master of ceremonies," and he proceeded to walk around the room asking various spectators questions. For example: "Do you like Hippies?" "What do you think about the war in Vietnam?" "Have you ever heard of *Beggar's Opera?*" "John Gay?" "You've heard of him?" "Good." (My wife grabbed my arm and frantically demanded that I answer for her if she should be asked a question. I laughed at her, but found myself getting nervous about making a fool of myself in such a situation. "Fortunately," our m.c. did not reach us.) While this was happening, and later during the intermission, three girls, who seemed to be between eleven and thirteen years of age, frugged in the center area. In parting, the m.c. told us that he would return and invited us to join the singing and dancing. During the intermission, some audience members danced in the center of the room while others chatted amiably with the actors.

In Joseph Papp's *Hamlet,* various characters walked through the aisles amongst the audience, sometimes sitting in empty chairs or on the step of an aisle. Hamlet offered the spectators balloons and peanuts while he himself munched on, discarding the shells as he ambled around. During Polonius' speech of advice to Laertes, the actor playing the old man turned to the audience and soundlessly mouthed the famous words ". . . Neither a borrower nor a lender be," while gesturing to the audience to fill in the words for him.

In O'Horgan's production of *Tom Paine,* actors invite the audience to join in an informal discussion of politics and current events. Schechner's *Dionysus in '69* offers the spectator the opportunity to participate in a series of sexual games. In *Hair,* actors walk through the audience passing out flowers, leaflets, and abuse. One actor, dressed as a policeman, came out into the house at intermission and announced that we were all under arrest for observing a display of nudity onstage. (It is interesting to note that a large number of spectators never noticed that at one point near the end of the first act, at least six boys and girls stood onstage stark naked for approximately four minutes. Attention was focused on a singer who sat on a table under which various lights were flashing.) In *The Concept,* amateur performers, a group of ex-addicts, move through the audience imploring us to embrace them and asking, "Will you love me?"

2

To understand the avant-garde theatre, especially in its relation to the audience, one should first study the theories of Antonin Artaud for therein lie the seminal influence of our new theatre.

Artaud called for a theatre of participatory action:

> We need above all a theatre that wakes us up: nerves and heart. . . . In the anguished, catastrophic period we live in, we feel an urgent need for a theatre which events do not exceed, whose resonance is deep within us, dominating the instability of the times.[4]

Conceiving a Theatre of Cruelty, Artaud outlined its function in relation to its audience:

> The Theatre of Cruelty proposes to resort to a mass spectacle; to seek in the agitation of tremendous masses, convulsed and hurled against each other, a little of that poetry of festivals and crowds when, all too rarely nowadays, the people pour out into the streets.
>
> The theatre must give us everything that is in crime, love, war, or madness, if it wants to recover its necessity.
>
> In a word, we believe that there are living forces in what is called poetry and that the image of a crime presented in the requisite theatrical conditions is something infinitely more terrible for the spirit than that same crime when actually committed.[5]

And in the Second Manifesto for a Theatre of Cruelty, Artaud begins by claiming:

> Admittedly or not, conscious or unconscious, the poetic state, a transcendent experience of life, is what the public is fundamentally seeking through love, crime, drugs, war, or insurrection.[6]

In a new, non-Aristotelian *Poetics* (*The Theatre and Its Double*), Artaud attacked the classical literary tradition of the French theatre. Denigrating the playwright's function, Artaud called for a visual theatre. "Dialogue—a thing written and spoken—does not belong specifically to the stage, it belongs to books."[7] Whereas Aristotle had addressed himself primarily to the playwright and his *audience,* Artaud's *Poetics* was intended for the director and his *spectators.* Artaud subordinated plot, character, and diction to *mise en scène* or spectacle.

> And thus we rejoin the ancient popular drama, sensed and experienced directly by the mind without deformations of language and the barrier of speech.
>
> We intend to base the theatre upon spectacle [*mise en scène*] before everything else. . . .[8]

For Artaud, the superior poet is more concerned with the language of gesture than the language of words. He delineates the *mise en scène* as the heart of theatre and extends a new definition for the word "stage":

> It has not been definitely proved that the language of words is the best possible language. And it seems that on *the stage, which is above all a space to fill and a place where something happens,* the language of words may have to give way before a language of "signs."[9] (my emphasis)

Having identified the *mise en scène* as a more important element of theatre than plot, Artaud then set about dissipating the playwright:

> The old duality between author and director will be dissolved, replaced by a sort of unique Creator upon whom will devolve the double responsibility of the spectacle and plot.[10]

According to Artaud, the director or master of the spectacle ("master of ceremonies") would not use a written play, or, rather, a text would be used as a point of departure. He says, "Thus we shall renounce the theatrical superstition of the text and the dictatorship of the writer."[11]

Of all of Artaud's concepts, the subordinate position of the playwright to the director during the production is the least original contribution he makes. For, we may say that almost all the most important directors of this century have adapted the text to suit their plans, Stanislavsky being no exception. The transcripts of Meyerhold's rehearsals of *The Inspector General* clearly show that he made numerous changes in Gogol's play. Meyerhold, by the way, always listed himself on the programs of his productions as the "Producer of the Spectacle (*Mise en Scène*)." Certainly, Sophocles, Shakespeare, Molière, and Brecht altered their scripts during rehearsals.

However, when Papp's *Hamlet* opened, many of the critics who attacked him did so on the grounds that Papp had no right to adapt the play and make cuts the way he did. (How often does one see an uncut version of *Hamlet*?) The Board of Education in New York City threatened to bar the touring of the show to various city high schools, because some parents and teachers complained that this was not the way Shakespeare intended his play to be produced, and not the way to introduce the Bard to youngsters.[12] Incidentally, the youngsters seemed to enjoy this production (unlike the Gielgud-Burton *Hamlet* during which many people nodded off to sleep by 10:30).

This discussion is relevant because a theatre in which the director is master allows for the possibilities of audience participation. On the other hand, when the playwright is a literary author in control of the theatre, the auditorium becomes literally a listening room and the audience becomes an absorbent sponge which sops up words and then departs.

Artaud was also interested in doing away with the scene designer. "There will not be a set. This function will be sufficiently undertaken by hieroglyphic characters, ritual costumes, mannikins ten feet high. . . ."[13]

In the Broadway production of *Hair,* all tormentors, teasers, and portals were removed. Audience members could see all the lighting instruments, the wings, and the stage-hands. Some actors could be seen lounging offstage while waiting for their entrance cue. They wore the beads and feathers and the long hair of the American Indian. During a scene in which the Supremes were caricatured, three girls appeared on a huge rolling platform. We soon saw that they were wrapped up in one enormous sequin dress. Observing such a sight would help one to realize what Artaud may have meant by "hieroglyphic characters" and "ritual costumes" and "mannikins ten feet high." Also, in the musical adaptation of Shakespeare's *Twelfth Night, Your Own Thing,* it was evident that the scenic artist had been replaced by the psychedelic, electronic artist. The entire stage was painted white and the scenery was projected on the walls.

What did Artaud say specifically about the relationship between the theatre and the spectator? According to Artaud, the Theatre of Cruelty would be

> a theatre that induces trance . . . [14]
>
> . . . furnishing the spectator with the truthful precipitates of dreams, in which his taste for crime, his erotic obsessions, his savagery, his chimeras, his utopian sense of life and matter, even his cannibalism, pours out, on a level not counterfeit and illusory, but interior.[15]

While admitting man's perversity and the existence of evil in the world, Artaud believed that man's nature was basically heroic. The Theatre of Cruelty would ennoble society by purging it of its irrational appetites.

> The action of theatre, like that of plague, is beneficial, for, impelling men to see themselves as they are, it causes the mask to fall, reveals the lie, the slackness, baseness, and hypocrisy of our world; . . . and in revealing to collectivities of men their dark power, their hidden force, it invites them to take, in the face of destiny, a superior and heroic attitude they would never have assumed without it.[16]

However, Artaud warns the audience member:

> The spectator who comes to our theatre knows that he is taking part in a true action involving not only his mind but his very senses and flesh. Thenceforth he will go to the theatre as he goes to the surgeon or dentist; in the same frame of mind, knowing that he will not die, but that it is serious, and that he will not leave intact. He must be thoroughly convinced that we can make him cry.[17]

In the end, there is Artaud's description of a new kind of theatre. This is probably the most valuable contribution in his entire construct. He speaks arrogantly:

> We abolish the stage and the auditorium and replace them by a single site, without partition or barrier of

any kind, which will become the theatre of action. A direct communication will be re-established between the spectator and the spectacle . . . from the fact that *the spectator, placed in the middle of the action,* is engulfed and physically affected by it. . . .

Thus, abandoning the architecture of present-day theatres, we shall take some hangar or barn. . . . [18] (my emphasis)

[*Dionysus in '69* is being presented in a garage; other avant-garde productions take place in church basements and old lofts that resemble barns.]

The hall will be enclosed by four walls, without any kind of ornament, and the public will be seated in the middle of the room, on the ground floor, on mobile chairs which will allow them to follow the spectacle which will take place all around them. . . . *The scenes will be played in front of whitewashed wall-backgrounds designed to absorb the light.* . . . Galleries overhead will permit the *actors . . . to be deployed on all levels and in all perspectives of height and depth.* . . . [19] (my emphasis)

Near the conclusion of his latter-day *Poetics,* Artaud explains what he thinks is the key to capturing audience attention; at the same time he makes a startling reference to multi-sensory mixed media which prefigures McLuhan's discussions of "cool" media:

Intensities of color, lights, or sounds, which utilize vibration, tremors, repetition . . . or a general diffusion of light, can obtain their full effect only by the use of 'dissonances.'

But instead of limiting these dissonances to the orbit of a single sense, *we shall cause them to overlap from one sense to the other,* from a color to a noise, a word to a light, a fluttering gesture to a flat tonality of sound, etc. [20] (my emphasis)

He continues:

The spectacle . . . by elimination of the stage . . . will physically envelop the spectator and immerse him in a constant bath of lights, images, movements, and noises.
. . .

And just as there will be no unoccupied point in space, there will be neither respite nor vacancy in the spectator's mind or sensibility. That is, *between life and the theatre there will be no distinct division, but instead a continuity.* Anyone who has watched a scene of any movies being filmed will understand exactly what we mean. [21] (my emphasis)

"In theatre, poetry and science must henceforth be identical." [22] Thus, Artaud's theories, enunciated in the thirties, seem finally to be coming to fruition. The Off Off-Broadway theatre is becoming a scientific world in which electronic equipment is substituted for what Beckett calls "the barnacles of Shakespeare's language." The words become lost in the vibrations, but the beat goes on. This new-old drama is visual and tactile rather than linguistic.

Brustein's claim that this theatre overindulges itself in sexual matters and obscenity because, as he says, "sex is the great equalizer," is valid. [23] This trend toward the democratization of art, which Brustein deplores, celebrates sex through song and dance—the stock-in-trade of vaudeville—because these activities bring people together. (It was Gorelik who pointed out years ago that since the fifties there has been a trend toward vaudeville in the avant-garde theatre.) This new theatre of "mixed means," as Richard Kostelanetz labels it, [24] is anti-literary because young people consider language to be the "great separator." It is no secret that the traditional language of the Broadway theatre has been and continues to be anti-black, anti-high school dropout *and* graduate, anti-poor, and anti-commonfolk. One must have a college degree in liberal arts (science will not suffice) to comprehend the linguistic tomfoolery of an Albee or a Pinter.

The avant-garde theatre has made us aware of a fundamental question of theatre; that is, what is the true relationship between the performers and the audience? Is the stage essentially a vehicle for the playwright, that is, a place for the dramatist to present his art? If so, it is merely a museum which is actually nothing more than a graveyard for art.

In conclusion, viewing theatre from the audience's point of view, we find that there seem to be three stages or kinds of art:

(1) "Tribal," i.e., spectators, performers, and authors are indistinguishable; everyone is an artist united by communal, multi-sensory participation. Architecturally, this theatre is all stage.

(2) "Aristocratic," i.e., the artist (represented by a Rembrandt or a Shakespeare—an elevated, special personage of "genius") is totally responsible for the work; a coterie audience may only look or listen—from a distance.

(3) "Impressionistic," i.e., the artist (represented by the "madman" figure of a van Gogh) initiates the artifact but forces the spectator to participate by completing the scene. Painting and sculpture seem to have come full cycle and are returning to a "tribal" stage. [25]

Since Aristotle, the Western world has perpetuated an "aristocratic" theatre (Middle Ages excepted) whose ruler is the playwright and whose tradition is literary. The avant-garde theatre seems to be approaching the "impressionistic" stage, and its progenitor is Antonin Artaud, that "madman" who spent one-third of his life in asylums.

Notes

1. In this context, there is no difference between the "arena" stage and the proscenium arch stage from the audience point of view; in both structures the focus is linear, and there is a clear, architectural separation between performer and spectator. For what appear to be some differing opinions see Roger

Pierce, "'Intimacy' in the Theatre," *ETJ*, XX (May, 1968), 147-151.

2. For one example see "The Absurd Absurdists," *New York Times,* August 8, 1965, Sec. 2, pp. 1, 3.

3. Marshall McLuhan and Quentin Fiore. *The Medium Is the Massage* (New York: Bantam Books, 1967), p. 63.

4. Antonin Artaud, *The Theatre and Its Double,* trans. Mary Caroline Richards (New York: Grove Press, 1958), p. 84.

5. Artaud, p. 85.

6. Artaud, p. 122.

7. Artaud, p. 37.

8. Artaud, p. 124.

9. Artaud, p. 107.

10. Artaud, p. 94.

11. Artaud, p 124.

12. Richard Severo, "Papp Gives 'Hamlet' to Catch Conscience of School Board," New York *Times,* January 31, 1968, p. 43.

13. Artaud, p. 97.

14. Artaud, p. 83.

15. Artaud, p. 92.

16. Artaud, pp. 31-32.

17. "States of Mind: 1921-1945," trans. Ruby Cohn, *TDR,* VIII (Winter, 1963), 45.

18. Artaud, *The Theatre and Its Double,* p. 96.

19. Artaud, pp 96-97.

20. Artaud, p. 125.

21. Artaud, pp. 125-126.

22. Artaud, p. 140.

23. Robert Brustein, "The Democratization of Art," *New Republic,* August 10, 1968, p. 19.

24. *The Theatre of Mixed Means* (New York: Dial Press, 1968).

25. For example, I think it was Dali who years ago pontificated, "One thing I ask of sculpture is that it should not move." Today, that is the one thing one cannot ask of sculpture. A multitude of so-called "kinetic" artists (beginning with Alexander Calder) have set art in motion. The patron takes the artifact home, and it is he who turns it on, who sets it in motion, and thus participates in its creation and performance.

Maurice M. Labelle (essay date March 1973)

"Artaud's Use of Language, Sound, and Tone," in *Modern Drama,* Vol. 15, No. 4, March, 1973, pp. 383-90.

[*In the following essay, Labelle discusses Artaud's use of sound, tone, pitch, and volume in his attempt to undermine conventional language and traditional theater.*]

"Oh, for a language to write drama in," Eugene O'Neill wrote in 1929. "I'm so strait-jacketed by writing in terms of talk! But where to find that language?"[1] His cry of frustration reiterated the feelings of one of his French contemporaries, Antonin Artaud (1896-1948). Although O'Neill failed to answer his question, Artaud, in his plays and poems, undertook a long series of experiments in language, sound, and tone in an attempt to develop new means of communication.

The Spurt of Blood (***Le Jet de sang***) (1925), a play which was the highpoint of his early period (1924-1931), demonstrates the subservient role Artaud assigned to language. The work is a montage of short, highly visual episodes. Briefly, the work opens with a love scene between a young couple, which is interrupted by a cosmic convulsion in which parts of human anatomy, temples, and insects fall from the sky. After the storm, the man and girl leave, and then a Knight and Nurse enter. Following their sexually suggestive actions and discussion, the Young Man returns. His conversation with a Priest is terminated when God reaches down and grabs a Whore, who has appeared on the scene. Resisting His action, she bites His wrist; at once blood spurts across the stage. God, wounded, retreats in a fury of lightning. The action then quickly moves to a highly imagistic and erotic scene which concludes the play.

Experimenting with sound in ***The Spurt of Blood,*** Artaud manipulates rhythm and voice qualities, such as tone and volume, to expose the natures of the characters. In the opening scene, the Young Girl, initially hesitant to become truly sexual, has a strong tremolo in her voice (*OC,* I, 74).[2] Counterpointed to her limited affection is the male, who states his love in a deep and resonant tone, a technique Artaud used earlier in *Paul the Bird-Like* (*Paul les oiseaux*) (c. 1924) to show the carnal nature of one of the characters, Brunelleschi. As the girl in ***The Spurt of Blood*** loses her fear, her voice quality becomes lower than the man's; however, her love remains inadequate because she selfishly continues to view the male's affection as being centered around her. Because of this egotism, she fails to surrender her primitive concept of reality. Forcing her to do so, the Young Man expresses his love in highly sensuous terms (*OC,* I, 75). He communicates the elevated nature of his sexuality by his voice; the tone changes from being deep and resonant to "exalted and piercing" (*OC,* I, 75). The Young Girl succumbs, relinquishes her egotism, and acknowledges, in equally shrill tones, her love for him (*OC,* I, 75).

This experiment in the manipulation of language in ***The Spurt of Blood*** is unsuccessful because it disrupts the effect of the presentation. At least a titter from the audience would be expected when a girl's voice is lower than a man's and his voice, in turn, becomes shrill. The value of this technique is lost unless the spectator is aware of its significance, which would probably require an understanding of *Paul the Bird-Like.* Artaud himself must have recognized the inadequacies of this method of using language because he did not utilize it again. Although his demonstration was foolish—it would not be the last experiment to misfire for him—he showed that the human animal can communicate by other means than language. Moreover, these methods can be non-rational and non-didactic.

Artaud also used words in the accustomed manner to highlight sexuality. The Knight and the Nurse in *The Spurt of Blood* exemplify the mysterious love, like that of Brunelleschi in *Paul the Bird-Like,* which enables man to free himself from mundane reality and to experience "an indescribable vibration" which unifies him with the cosmos (*OC,* IV, 62). When the two characters are first seen shortly after the cosmic convulsion, the Nurse is holding her swollen breasts (*OC,* I, 76). The Knight directs the audience's notice to them when he orders her to leave her breasts alone (*OC,* I, 76). Through words, the observer is attracted sexually to the action and prepared to accept the extraordinarily visual scene at the end of the play when the spectator's interest in the Nurse's bosom is transferred to her sex organ. After she enters without her inflated breasts, she raises her dress. Suddenly, scorpions come out from under her dress, swarm over the Knight's sex organ, which swells and "becomes glassy and shiny like a sun" (*OC,* I, 81). The audience is so transfixed by this time that snickers would be most unexpected.

Artaud manipulates the spectator's religious sensibility with an astute use of words. In the stage directions for *The Spurt of Blood,* the Priest is to speak as if he were in the confessional booth. It is in this context that he asks the Young Man to which part of the girl's body he refers most often, to which the youth replies "To God" (*OC,* I, 78). Bettina Knapp concludes that the Priest hopes for "some kind of a lewd answer."[3] This assessment is justified; however, the reply also links God with the heavily sexual nature of the play. Before the audience can analyze the relationship between God and sex, Artaud interposes the illogical action of suddenly having the Priest begin speaking in a Swiss accent. This transformation startles the spectator and thereby weakens, but does not disrupt, his identification with the preceding confessional episode. This manipulation prepares the observer emotionally to accept the shock of seeing God in the next scene.

Language, then, has an integral and significant role in Artaud's creations during the early period of his life. These works reflect, however, his dissatisfaction with words, his recognition of their limits, and his willingness to utilize them in novel fashions. His most important and successful experiment, *The Spurt of Blood,* showed how he minimizes dialogue and subordinates words to images. In some instances, which the same work exemplifies, the experiments were ridiculous; in other places the trials were rich in promise. Before Artaud brought the latter techniques to fruition, he had to recover from following a wrong path when he devoted himself to films.

In 1922, Artaud began to experiment with the cinema as a medium for bringing about "a complete reversal of values . . . and of logic" (*OC,* III, 73), both of which were fundamental to gaining his goals. Significantly, this was the era of silent films, and Artaud used his resources well in *The Scallop and the Clergyman* (*La Coquille et le Clergyman*), which was published in November, 1927, to achieve a modicum of success. In this film, an *étude* in the use of images, Artaud bombarded the spectator's visual sense in order to excite the memory and subconscious (*OC,* III, 96). Try as he might, sound film could not be ignored; it was a veritable invasion from the United States.

Recognizing that the era of silent films was over, Artaud decided to demonstrate proper sound techniques in *The Butcher's Revolt* (*La Révolte du Boucher*), which he wrote shortly after he finished *The Scallop and the Clergyman* (*OC,* III, 164). The principal function of the scenario's five lines of speech is to blend images together (*OC,* III, 47); the success of this technique, however, is questionable. In the first scene, a Woman enters a café and after being accosted by a gigolo, announces her preference for a madman who has been watching her. The insane man, responding to the gigolo's ensuing threats, hits him in the face and warns him: "Be careful—your head will be on the butcher's block" (*OC,* III, 48). Shortly afterward, the noise of a butcher's wagon is heard in the street. While the connection between the words and the sound is recognizable, the relationship is not sufficiently obvious to be understood by the audience. Artaud integrated language and image more effectively in *The Spurt of Blood* when he used words to attract the audience's attention to the Nurse's enormous breasts.

Although Artaud continued to act in films for many years, his interest in the cinema as a medium for his creativity waned shortly after he wrote *The Butcher's Revolt.* Simultaneously, his attention returned to the theater. In November, 1926, Artaud announced that he and two of his friends, Roger Vitrac and Robert Aron, had founded the Theatre Alfred Jarry. Again Artaud transformed his attitudes toward language. His selections for the theater, such as Vitrac's *The Mysteries of Love* (*Les Mystères de l'amour*), and *Victor or Child at the Helm* (*Victor ou les enfants au pouvoir*); the third act of Paul Claudel's *Break of Noon* (*Partage de midi*); and *A Dream Play* by August Strindberg demonstrate that Artaud was willing to allow words to be used in art. However, his scenario for Strindberg's *The Ghost Sonata,* which Artaud wrote at this time, shows that he was not truly content with language and that he was still attempting to manipulate it in new ways. For instance, a mysterious force operates in the play which enables the enigmatic Hummel to meet the Student, who then encounters the Colonel and his daughter exactly as Hummel has predicted. All other actions stem from this assignation. Accentuating the element of mystery which surrounds Hummel, Artaud has the beggars speak in rhythm when Hummel enters for the first time. The noise, Artaud writes, should duplicate the sound made by "a large tongue striking the front of the mouth" (*OC,* II, 118).

Artaud entered his richest period shortly after seeing a production of the Balinese dance-drama in 1931. In several letters he wrote within a month of seeing the Balinese, he disparaged words because, he maintained, they paralyze thought instead of favoring its development (*OC,* IV, 129). Music, he contended, could be an important substitute for language if it were properly used. He had theorized in *Backgammon with the Sky (Tric trac du ciel)* (1923) that music can overpower reason and liberate the subconscious so that the individual could experience the cosmic source of life. Failing to refine this embryonic idea, Artaud did not return to the subject of music until the performance of the Balinese theater rekindled his interest in it. Modifying his earlier contention considerably, he integrated his concept of music with his new views of language: music should have the form of incantation (*OC,* IV, 56) because the "rhythmic repetition of syllables and vocal modulation . . . stimulate numerous images to be formed in the mind, resulting in a more or less hallucinatory condition" (*OC,* IV, 145). The validity of Artaud's concept had been demonstrated by Edgar Allan Poe in "The Raven" and "The Bells." Artaud had found a touchstone, and he demonstrates his find in *The Cenci (Les Cenci)* (1935).

This play, which he borrowed and adapted from versions by Shelley and Stendhal, is based on a story of Francesco Cenci (1549-1598), a Roman nobleman. Following the death of his first wife, by whom he had seven children, he married Lucretia Petroni. Seized with sadistic and homicidal desires, the Count planned to murder his sons and rape his daughter, Beatrice. His schemes miscarried, and in retaliation, Beatrice and her step-mother hired assassins to kill him. They succeeded: nails were driven through one of his eyes and his throat. The guilt of Lucretia and Beatrice was revealed, and, after Pope Clement VII refused to pardon them, they and Giacomo, Beatrice's brother, were beheaded on September 11, 1599. All of Artaud's hopes for the triumph of his efforts and concepts depended on the success of this play. Representing the peak of his creative and intellectual abilities, this work remains his best theatrical creation.

Artaud exemplifies his concept of incantation when Cenci walks into an ambush which Beatrice has planned (II, ii). Just as the Count's deathknell is about to sound, the spectator hears mysterious voices chanting Cenci's name. Warned, he escapes. A bizarre rapport is established between the action and the spectator when the Count addresses the mysterious voices, which the other characters do not hear (*OC,* IV, 245). This use of sound is designed to numb the spectator's desire to reason and to place him in a state of nonrationality so he cannot question why Cenci escapes the assassins. One "knows" that it is not the Count's destiny to die at that time.

Artaud, in *The Spurt of Blood,* directs the audience's attention and stimulates the spectator's sexual nature; repeating this technique in *The Cenci,* he utilizes language to appeal to the observer's intellect. The Count, for example, had long desired the death of his sons. During the Banquet

Scene he receives word that two of them are dead—one of whom, Cenci gleefully tells his guests, was crushed to death when the dome of a church fell on him (*OC,* IV, 204). Enraptured, Cenci raises a glass of wine in celebration and challenges his guests to prove that God has not favored him by destroying his sons. The audience must judge the rectitude of the Count's statement, and ultimately agree that Cenci is correct. This conclusion strengthens the atmosphere of evil which permeates the work. Artaud, then, effectively employs logic and language to gain his ends.

Words, however, have their limits, which Artaud demonstrated in a dialogue between Beatrice and Lucretia. The former says "!!!!!!!!!!!" and the latter replies "!!!!!!!!!!!" (*OC,* IV, 241). At such a moment, the actors must use their own sensitivity and acquaintance with life and cosmos to express what words cannot. For the original performances, Artaud had two such professionals: himself as the Count, and Mme Iya Abdy, whom he selected for the role of Beatrice (*OC,* V, 302).

The production of *The Cenci* was shortlived; poor reception forced its closure after seventeen days. The play was more than a financial catastrophe: "The poet, from that moment, was completely discouraged and he abandoned all activity in the theater," according to Mme Marie-Ange Malausséna.[4] His period of creativity was over. Artaud left France, travelled to Mexico, returned to France and Belgium briefly, and then departed for his disastrous trip to Ireland. There he suffered a mental breakdown. When his ship docked at Le Havre in 1937, he was committed to a mental hospital. After he had been transferred from one asylum to another, and undergone electro-shock therapy, Artaud's mental health began to improve. In 1943, he began to write again, and in 1946 he was released. Once again he returned to the realm of aesthetics which he had abandoned eleven years before.

Artaud continued to search for a language which would liberate instead of enchain, stimulate rather than suppress. In "Shit on the Spirit" ("Chiote à l'esprit") (March, 1947), he gave an example of this new medium of art. The proper effect of his experiment, he instructed, is gained only when the words are spoken rapidly:[5]

> lo kundum
> a papa
> da mama
> la mamama
> a papa
> dama
>
> lokin
> a kata
> repara
> o leptura
> o ema
> lema
>
> o ersti
> o popo
> erstura

o erstura
o popo
dima[6]

In a letter to Henri Parisot (September 22, 1945), Artaud gave another illustration of the "new" language:

ratara ratara ratara
atara tatara rana

otara otara katar
otara ratara kana

ortura ortura konara
kokona kokona koma

kurbura kurbura kurbura
kurbata kurbata kenya

pesti anti pestantum putara
pest anti pestantum putra.[7]

Eric Sellin, who has researched this phase of Artaud's attempt to develop a new language, notes that some of the sound units resemble real words: papa, mama, kenya, and anti. Others, he contends, stem from Artaud's experiences: *koma* is "related to the shock treatments Artaud received which induced comas; *pesti* and *pestantum* bring to mind Artaud's frequent references to the plague . . . *kurbata* may relate to "courbé," "courbature," and especially "courbette," which Artaud used in describing the dramatic ritual of the peyote dance.[8] Sellin believes, and correctly so, that the expressions are "essentially meaningless utterances, objectified word-sounds."[9]

Fascinating as the experiment in language which Artaud gave in "Shit on the Spirit" may be, it is highly questionable whether it is suitable for stage presentation or, as it stands, useful for any art form. Basically, it would be extremely difficult to sustain the "objectivied word-sounds" for the length necessary to tranquillize the spectator's desire to use his reason and then excite his nature.

Artaud's subsequent experiments with language show that he struggled to refine his attitudes about the function of words and tried to make his views artistically functional. In *Here Lies* (*Ci-Gît*) (1947), Artaud took a step forward when he carefully prepared the reader's mind to accept the "word-sounds." His solution recalls his successful experiments in using language, first of all, to prepare the spectator to receive the impact of the principal emotional barrage. In *Here Lies,* he uses recognizable expressions to introduce the meaningless terms. One section begins with the statement that "All true language/ is incomprehensible;"[10] then the sounds are equated with the noise false teeth make. By punning on the word "claque," he gives the sound a sexual connotation. At this point, the words do not have a comprehensible syntax. The organization of this part of *Here Lies* allows the individual to formulate his own connotations of the unintelligible "words." The technique is reminiscent of "surrealist dialogue," such as

"What is your name?" "Forty-five houses." According to André Breton, the "patient" is forced to seize upon the last words and find some trace of them in his own mind.[11]

In late 1947, Artaud made a recording for the *Radio-diffusion francaise*; unfortunately, the performance was never aired. Artaud did not include a demonstration of the "new" language during the presentation; however, he depended heavily upon sound effects, shouts, yelps, and "xylophonics." In "Tutuguri, the Rite of the Black Sun" ("Tutuguri, le rite du soleil noir"), the voice levels, volumes and qualities, either by error or by design, assume an importance all their own and have little relevance to the meaning of the words. The impact upon the listener is striking to say the least. Yells, screams, and "xylophonics," while effective in moderation, can be so irritating that they cause revulsion, resentment, and rejection, rather than the desired mystical awareness of life. Nevertheless, the techniques are intriguing. However, Artaud's ability to develop and refine these tools was hindered by the increasingly severe pain caused by cancer. Under great strain, he completed "Tutuguri," a poem (February 16, 1948); sixteen days later he was dead.

Artaud's theories of language, sound, and tone frequently ended in confusion, ridicule, and failure. Nevertheless, his experiments in non-verbal techniques, despite their inadequacies, have made him a seminal figure in the modern theater.

Notes

1. Cited in Arthur and Barbara Gelb, *O'Neill,* New York, 1962, p. 399.

2. Antonin Artaud, *Oeuvres complètes,* I, Paris, 1956, p. 74. Hereafter cited in the text and abbreviated as *OC.*

3. Bettina Knapp, *Antonin Artaud, Man of Vision,* New York, 1969, p. 33.

4. Marie-Ange Malausséna, "Antonin Artaud," *La Revue théâtrale,* 8, no. 23, 1953, p. 51.

5. Antonin Artaud, *Lettres de Rodez,* Paris, 1948, pp. 17-18.

6. Antonin Artaud, "Chiote à l'esprit," *Tel Quel,* 2, été, 1960, p. 4.

7. *Lettres de Rodez,* pp. 17-18.

8. Eric Sellin, *The Dramatic Concepts of Antonin Artaud,* Chicago, 1968, p. 143, n. 38.

9. *Ibid.,* p. 89.

10. Antonin Artaud, *Ci-Gît,* Paris, 1947. No pagination given.

11. André Breton, *Manifestes du surrealisme,* Paris, 1966, p. 48.

Gilles Deleuze (essay date 1979)

"The Schizophrenic and Language: Surface and Depth in Lewis Carroll and Antonin Artaud," in *Textual Strategies:*

Perspectives in Post-Structuralist Criticism, edited by Josue V. Harari, Cornell University Press, 1979, pp. 277-95.

[*In the following essay, Deleuze explores the differences between the languages constructed by Artaud, Lewis Carroll, and schizophrenics.*]

The presence of esoteric words and portmanteau words has been pointed out in the rhyming chants of little girls, in poetry, and in the language of madness. Such an amalgamation is troubling, however. A great poet can write in a direct relation to the child that he was and the children that he loves; a madman can produce a great body of poetry in direct relation to the poet that he was and has not ceased to be. This in no way justifies the grotesque trinity of child, poet, and madman. We must be attentive to the displacements which reveal a profound difference beneath superficial resemblances. We must note the different functions and depths of *non-sense* and the heterogeneity of portmanteau words, which do not authorize grouping together those who invent them or even those who employ them. A little girl can sing "pimpanicaille" (in French, a mixture of "pimpant" + "nique" + "canaille"), a poet write "frumious" (furious + fuming) or "slithy" (lithe + slimy), and a schizophrenic say "perspendicacious" (perpendicular + perspicacious)[1]: we have no reason to believe that the problem is the same because of superficially analogous results. There can be no serious association of the little elephant Babar's song with Artaud's breath-screams, "Ratara ratara ratara Atara tatara rara Otara otara katara. . . ."[2] Let us add that the logicians' error when speaking of non-sense, is to give disembodied examples which they construct laboriously for the needs of their demonstration, as if they had never heard a little girl sing, a great poet recite, or a schizophrenic speak. Such is the poverty of these "logical" examples (except in the case of Russell, who was inspired by Lewis Carroll). Here, again, the inadequacies of the logicians do not authorize us to construct a new trinity in opposition to theirs, however. The problem is a clinical one: that of the displacement from one mode of organization to another, or of the formation of a progressive and creative disorganization. The problem is also one of criticism, that is, of determining differential levels at which change occurs in the form of non-sense, in the nature of portmanteau words, in the dimension of language as a whole.

We would like to consider two great poetic texts containing such traps of resemblance: Antonin Artaud confronts Lewis Carroll first in an extraordinary transcription—a counterequivalence—of Carroll's "Jabberwocky" and then in one of his letters written from the insane asylum in Rodez. Reading the opening stanza of "Jabberwocky" as it was rendered into French by Artaud, one has the impression that the first two lines still correspond to Carroll's criteria, and conform to the rules of other French translations of Carroll.[3] Beginning with the last word of the second line, however, a displacement, and even a central, creative breakdown, occurs, one which transports us to another world and to a completely different language. In

fright we recognize this language without difficulty: it is the language of schizophrenia. Caught up in grammatical syncopes and overburdened with gutturals, even the portmanteau words seem to have another function. At the same time, we see the distance separating Carroll's language, which is emitted at the surface, from Artaud's language, which is hewn from the depths of bodies—a distance which reflects the difference between their problems. We then understand the full significance of Artaud's declarations in one of the letters from Rodez:

> I did not do a translation of "Jabberwocky." I tried to translate a fragment of it, but it bored me. I never liked the poem, which always seemed to me to smack of affected infantilism. . . . *I do not like surface poems or languages* which smell of happy leisure moments and intellectual triumphs. . . . One can invent one's language and make pure language speak with an a-grammatical meaning, but this meaning must be valid in itself, it must come from anguish. . . . "Jabberwocky" is the work of a profiteer who wanted—while filled with a well-served meal—to fill up intellectually on others' suffering. . . . When one digs into the shit of the individual being and his language, the poem must necessarily smell bad; "Jabberwocky" is a poem that its author has taken special pains to keep outside the uterine being of suffering into which all great poets have dipped, and from which, delivering themselves into the world, they smell bad. In "Jabberwocky" there are passages of fecality, but it is the fecality of an English snob who curls the obscene in himself like ringlets around a hot curling iron. . . . It is the work of a man who ate well, and you can smell it in his writing.

> [IX, 184-186]

In short, Artaud considers Lewis Carroll a pervert, a minor pervert, who limits himself to the creation of a surface language and does not sense the true problem of language in its depth—the schizophrenic problem of suffering, of death, and of life. Carroll's games seem puerile to him, his nourishment too worldly, even his fecality hypocritical and too well-bred.

Let us briefly consider *Alice.* A strange evolution takes place throughout all of Alice's adventures. One can sum it up as the conquest or discovery of surfaces. At the beginning of *Alice in Wonderland,* the search for the secret of things and events goes on in the depths of the earth: in deeply dug wells and rabbit holes, as well as in the mixtures of bodies which penetrate each other and coexist. As one advances in the narrative, however, the sinking and burrowing movements give way to lateral, sliding movements: from left to right and right to left. The animals of the depths become secondary, and are replaced by playing card characters, characters without thickness. One might say that the former depth has spread itself out, has become breadth. Here lies the secret of the stammerer [Carroll]—it no longer consists in sinking into the depths, but in sliding along in such a way that depth is reduced to nothing but the reverse side of the surface. If there is nothing to see behind the curtain, it is because everything visible (or rather, all possible knowledge) is found along the surface of the curtain. It suffices to follow the curtain far enough and closely enough—which is to say superficially enough—in order to turn it inside out so that right becomes left, and vice versa. Consequently, there are no adventures of Alice; there is but *one* adventure: her rising to the surface, her disavowal of the false depths, and her discovery that everything happens at the borderline. For this reason, Carroll abandoned the first title that he had in mind, *Alice's Adventures Underground.*

This is even more true of *Alice's* sequel, *Through the Looking Glass.* Events, in their radical difference from things, are no longer sought in the depths, but at the surface: a mirror that reflects them, a chess-board that "flattens" them to a two-dimensional plane. By running along the surface, along the edge, one passes to the other side; from bodies to incorporeal events. The continuity of front and back replaces all levels of depth. In *Sylvia and Bruno,* Carroll's major novel, one witnesses the completion of this evolution: a stretching machine elongates even songs; the barometer neither rises nor falls, but moves sideways, giving horizontal weather; Bruno learns his lessons backward and forward, up and down, but never in depth; and Fortunatus' purse, presented as a Moebius strip, is made of handkerchiefs sewn together "in the wrong way," so that its external surface is in continuity with its internal surface, and inside and outside become one.

This discovery that the strangest things are on the surface or, as Valéry would say, that "the skin is deepmost" [*le plus profond, c'est la peau*], would be unimportant if it did not carry with it an entire organization of language: Carrollian language. It is clear that, throughout his literary work, Carroll speaks of a very particular type of thing, of *events* (of growing, shrinking, eating, cutting, and so on), and he interprets the nature of these events in a strange manner whose equivalent one finds only in the logic of the Stoics.

[The privileged position of the Stoics comes from the fact that they were the initiators of a paradoxical theory of meaning which imposed a new division between beings and things on the one hand, and concepts on the other.[4] The Stoics distinguished between two states of *being*: (1) real beings, that is, *bodies* with their depth, their physical qualities, their interrelationships, their *actions* and *passions*; (2) the *effects* that take place on the surface of beings. Effects are not states of things, but *incorporeal events*; they are not physical qualities, but logical attributes. Emile Bréhier, for instance, explains incorporeal events in these terms: "When a scalpel slices into the flesh, the first agent produces, not a new property in the second body, but a new attribute, that of having been cut. The *attribute* does not designate a real *quality* . . . , on the contrary, it is always expressed by a verb, which means that it is not a being, but a *manner of being.*"[5]

It is in this sense that we must understand the events of which Carroll speaks. "To grow," "to shrink," "to cut," or

"to be cut" are not states of things, but incorporeal events that occur on the surface of things. Carroll's entire work consists precisely in marking this difference between events on the one hand, and corporeal beings, things, and states of things on the other.

The first great duality of Stoic origin is therefore the opposition between causes and effects, between corporeal things and incorporeal events. But to the extent that the event-effect does not exist outside the *proposition* that expresses it, the duality body/event is carried over into the duality things/propositions, that is, bodies/language. From this comes the alternative which recurs throughout Carroll's work: to eat or to speak. In *Sylvia and Bruno,* the choice is between "bits of things," and "bits of Shakespeare." Eating is the operational model for bodies, for their actions and passions, and for their modes of coexistence with(in) each other. Speaking, on the other hand, is the movement of the surface; it is the operational model for incorporeal events.

The second duality, body/language or eating/speaking, is not sufficient for an understanding of Carroll. We know that although meaning does not exist outside of the proposition that expresses it, it is nevertheless an attribute of things (bodies) or states of things (physical qualities) and not of the proposition. Things and propositions are positioned not so much in a radical duality as on the two sides of the borderline constituted by meaning.[6] This borderline neither mixes nor unites them. It is rather the articulation of their difference: body versus language, things versus propositions. This duality is reflected on both sides, in each of the two terms. On the side of things, there are, on the one hand, physical qualities and real relationships; on the other hand are logical attributes indicating incorporeal events. And, on the side of propositions, there are, on the one hand, nouns and adjectives which *designate* the state of things, and on the other, verbs which *express* events or logical attributes.

The duality in the proposition is thus between two levels of the proposition itself: between *designation* and *expression,* that is the designation of things (bodies and consumable objects) and the expression of meaning. We have here something similar to the two sides of a mirror except that what is on one side does not resemble what is on the other. To pass to the other side of the mirror is to move from a relationship of designation to one of expression, to enter a region in which language no longer has any relationship to bodies or designated objects (which are always consumable) but only to meanings (which are always expressible).]

This abstractly presented schema of the logic of the Stoics comes to life in Carroll's work. As he said in an article entitled "The Dynamics of a Parti-cle," "*plain superficiality* is the character of a speech." Throughout Carroll's work, the reader will encounter: (1) exits from tunnels in order to discover surfaces and the incorporeal events that are spread out on these surfaces; (2) the essential affinity of events with language; (3) the constant organization of the two surface series into the dualities eating/speaking, consumption/proposition, and designation/expression; and (4) the manner in which these series are organized around a paradoxical element, which is expressed sometimes by a hollow word, sometimes by an esoteric word, and sometimes by a portmanteau word whose function is to fuse and ramify these heterogeneous series.[7] In this way "snark" ramifies an alimentary series ("snark" is of animalish origin, and belongs therefore to the class of consumable objects) and a linguistic series ("snark" is an incorporeal meaning); "Jabberwocky" subsumes an animal and a conversation at the same time; and finally, there is the admirable gardener's song in *Sylvia and Bruno,* in which each couplet brings into play two different types of terms that elicit two distinct perceptions: "He thought he saw . . . He looked again, and found it was. . . ." The couplets develop two heterogeneous series: one of animals, of beings, or of consumable objects described according to physical and sensory (sonorous) qualities; the other, of symbolic objects and characters, defined by logical attributes which are bearers of meaning.[8]

The organization of language described above must be called poetic, because it reflects that which makes language possible. One will not be surprised to discover that events make language possible, even though the event does not exist outside of the proposition that expresses it, since as an "expressed" it does not mix with its expression. It does not exist prior to it and has no existence by itself, but possesses an "insistence" which is peculiar to it. "To make language possible" has a very particular meaning. It signifies to "distinguish" language, to prevent sounds from becoming confused with the sonorous qualities of things, with the noisiness of bodies, with their actions and passions, and with their so-called "oral-anal" determinations. What makes language possible is that which separates sounds from bodies, organizes them into propositions, and thus makes them available to assume an expressive function. Without this surface that distinguishes itself from the depths of bodies, without this line that separates things from propositions, sounds would become inseparable from bodies, becoming simple physical qualities contiguous with them, and propositions would be impossible. This is why *the organization of language is not separable from the poetic discovery of surface,* or from Alice's adventure. The greatness of language consists in speaking only at the surface of things, and thereby in capturing the pure event and the combinations of events that take place on the surface. It becomes a question of reascending to the surface, of discovering surface entities and their games of meaning and of non-sense, of expressing these games in portmanteau words, and of resisting the vertigo of the bodies' depths and their alimentary, poisonous mixtures.

Let us consider another text, far removed from the genius of Artaud and the surface games of Carroll, one whose beauty and density lie in the clinical realm.[9] This text concerns a schizophrenic language student who experiences an eating/speaking duality, and who transposes it into propositions, or rather, into two sorts of language: his mother tongue (English), which is essentially *alimentary* and excremental, and foreign languages, which are essentially *expressive* and which he strives to acquire. In order to hinder the progress of his study of foreign languages, his mother threatens him in two equivalent ways: either she waves before him tempting but indigestible foods packaged in cans, or else she jumps out at him suddenly and abruptly speaks English to him before he has time to plug his ears.

He fends off this double threat with a set of ever more perfected procedures. He eats like a glutton, stuffs himself with food, and stomps on the cans, all the while repeating several foreign words. At a deeper level, he establishes a resonance between the alimentary and the expressive series, and a conversion from one to the other, by translating English words into foreign words according to their phonetic elements (consonants being the most important). For example, *tree* is converted by use of the *R* that reappears in the French vocable (*arbre*), and then by use of the *T* which reappears in the Hebrew term. Finally, since the Russians say *devero* (tree), one can equally transform *tree* into *tere, T* then becoming *D.* This already complex procedure gives way to a more generalized one when the idea occurs to the schizophrenic student to employ certain associations: *early,* whose consonants (*R* and *L*) raise particularly delicate problems, is transformed into French expressions dealing with time like "*suR Le champ,*" "*de bonne heuRe,*" "*matinaLement,*" "*dévoRer L'espace,*" or even into an esoteric and fictive word of German consonance, "*uRLich.*"

Here, again, what is it that gives us the impression that this language is both very close to, and yet totally different from, Carroll's? Are we talking of a different organization of language, or something worse and more dangerous? One is reminded of Artaud's vehement denunciation of Carroll: "I do not like surface poems or languages. . . ." Consequently, how could Carroll appear to Artaud as anything but a well-mannered little girl, sheltered from all the problems of the depths?

The discovery that *there is no more surface* is familiar to and experienced by any schizophrenic. The great problem, the first evidence of schizophrenia, is that the surface is punctured. Bodies no longer have a surface. The schizophrenic body appears as a kind of body-sieve. Freud emphasized this schizophrenic aptitude for perceiving the surface and the skin as if each were pierced by an infinite number of little holes.[10] As a result, the entire body is nothing but depth; it snatches and carries off all things in this gaping depth, which represents a fundamental involution. Everything is body and corporeal. Everything is a mixture of bodies and, within the body, telescoping, nesting in and penetrating each other. It is all a question of physics, as Artaud says: "We have in the back filled vertebra, which are pierced by the nail of pain, and which through walking and the effort of lifting, become cans by being encased upon each other."[11] A tree, a column, a flower, a cane pushes through the body; other bodies always penetrate into our body and coexist with its parts. As there is no surface, interior and exterior, container and content no longer have precise limits; they plunge into universal depth. From this comes the schizophrenic way of living contradictions: either in the deep cleavage that traverses the body, or in the fragmented parts of the body which are nested in each other and whirl around. Body-sieve, fragmented body, and dissociated body form the first three dimensions of the schizophrenic body—they give evidence of the general breakdown of surfaces.

In this breakdown of the surface, all words lose their meaning. They may retain a certain power of designation, but one which is experienced as empty; a certain power of manifestation, but experienced as indifferent; a certain signification, but experienced as "false." But words, in any case, lose their meaning, their power to set down or express incorporeal effects (events) distinct from the body's actions and passions. All words become physical and affect the body immediately. The process is of the following type: a word, often of an alimentary nature, appears in capital letters printed as in a collage that fixes it and divests it of its meaning. Yet as the pinned word loses its meaning, it bursts into fragments, decomposes into syllables, letters, and above all into consonants which act directly on the body, penetrating it and bruising it. We have seen this in the case of the schizophrenic language student: the mother tongue is emptied of its meaning at the same time that its *phonetic elements* gain an uncommon power to inflict pain. Words cease to express attributes of the state of things. Their fragments mix with unbearable sonorous qualities and break into parts of the body where they form a mixture, a new state of things, as if they themselves were noisy, poisonous foods and encased excrements. The organs of the body become defined and determined as a function of the decomposed elements which affect and attack them.[12] In this process of passion, a pure *language-affect* is substituted for the *language-effect*: "All Writing is Pig-Shit," says Artaud (I, 120); that is, all fixed, written words are decomposed into noisy, alimentary, and excremental fragments.

In this way an awesome primary order, namely, language-affect, replaces the organization of language. It is within this primary order that the schizophrenic fights and strives to affirm the rights of another sort of word over the passion-word. It is henceforth less a matter for the schizophrenic of recuperating meaning than of destroying words, of warding off affects, or of transforming the body's painful passion into a triumphant action. All this takes place in the depths beneath the punctured surface. The language student offers an example of the means by which the painful splinters of words in the mother tongue are converted into actions through foreign languages. Just as, earlier, the power of wounding was in the phonetic elements affecting the encased or dislocated parts of the body, so victory now can be obtained only by establishing breath-words, screamwords in which all values are exclusively tonic and nonwritten. To these values cor-

responds a superior body, a new dimension of the schizophrenic body. The body has become a superior organism without parts, one that functions entirely by insufflation, inhaling, evaporation, and transmission of fluids.[13]

This determination of the active process, in opposition to the process of passion, doubtless seems insufficient at first. Indeed, fluids seem no less maleficent than fragments. But they seem so only because of the action/passion ambivalence. It is here that the contradiction experienced in schizophrenia finds its true point of application: passion and action are the inseparable poles of an ambivalence only because the two languages that they form belong inseparably to the body, to the depths of bodies. One is therefore never sure that the ideal fluids of a partless organism do not carry with them parasitic worms, fragments of organs and solid foods, and remnants of excrements; one can even be certain that maleficent powers use fluids and insufflations in order to make fragments of passion pass into the body. The fluid is necessarily corrupted, but not by itself—only by the other pole, from which it is inseparable. Nevertheless, the fact remains that it represents the active pole, or the state of perfect mixture, in opposition to the encasing and bruising of imperfect mixtures, which constitute the passive pole. In schizophrenia there is a way of living the distinction between two corporeal mixtures, the partial mixture, which corrupts, and the total and liquid mixture, which leaves the body intact. In the insufflated fluid or liquid element there is the unwritten secret of an active mixture that is like the liquefying "principle of the Sea," in opposition to the passive mixtures of the encased parts. It is in this sense that Artaud transforms the Humpty Dumpty poem about the sea and the fishes into a poem about the problem of obedience and command.[14]

This second language, this process of action, is defined in practice by an overload of consonants, gutturals, and aspirates, as well as interior apostrophes and accents, breaths and scansions, and a modulation which replaces all the syllabic and even literal values. It is a matter of making an action out of a word by rendering it indecomposable, impossible to disintegrate: language without articulation. Here, however, the bond is a palatalized, an-organic principle, a block or mass of sea. In the case of the Russian word *devero* (tree), the language student rejoices over the existence of a plural—*derev'ya*—in which the interior apostrophe ("yod," the linguists' soft sign) seems to assure him of a fusion of the consonants. Instead of separating them and making them pronounceable, one could say that the vowel reduced to the "yod" makes the consonants indissociable by liquefying them, that it leaves them unreadable, and even unpronounceable, but it turns them into vocal outbursts in a continuous breath. The outbursts are welded together in the breath, like the consonants in the sign which liquefies them, like the fish in the mass of the sea, like the bones in the blood of the organless body, or like a sign of fire, a wave "that hesitates between gas and water," as Artaud said.[15] These outbursts become sputterings in the breath.

When Antonin Artaud says in his "Jabberwocky": "Up to the point where rourghe is to rouarghe to rangmbde and rangmbde to rouarghambde," it is precisely a question of articulating, insufflating, or palatalizing a word, causing it to blaze out so that it becomes the action of a partless body, rather than the passion of a fragmented organism. It is a question of turning the word into a consolidated, inde-composable mass of consonants by using soft signs. In this language one can always find equivalents for portmanteau words. For "rourghe" and "rouarghe," Artaud himself indicates *ruée* (onslaught), *roue* (wheel), *route* (route), *règle* (rule), *route à régler* (a route to be regulated). (One can add le Rouergue, the region of Rodez in which Artaud happened to be.) In the same way, when he says "Uk'hatis" (with the interior apostrophe), he indicates *ukhase* (ukase), *hâte* (haste), and *abruti* (idiot), and adds "a nocturnal jolt beneath Hecate which means the moon pigs thrown off the straight path" (IX, 167).

However, at the very moment in which the word appears to be a portmanteau word, its structure and the commentary adjoined to it persuade us of something entirely different: Artaud's "Ghoré Uk'hatis" are not equivalent to the "pigs who have lost their way," to Carroll's "mome raths," or to Parisot's "verchons fourgus." They do not function on the same level. Far from assuring a ramification of series according to meaning, they bring about a chain of associations between tonic and consonantal elements, in a region of infra-meaning, according to a fluid and burning principle that absorbs or actually resorbs the meaning as it is produced: Uk'hatis (or the strayed moon pigs), is K'H (*cahot*—jolt), 'KT (*nocturne*—nocturnal), H'KT (*Hécate*—Hecate).

The duality of schizophrenic words has not received adequate attention. It consists of *passion-words which explode in wounding phonetic values,* and *action-words which weld together inarticulated tonic values.* These two types of words develop in relation to the state of the body, which is either fragmented or organless. They also refer to two types of theater—the theater of terror and passion, and the theater of cruelty, which is essentially active—as well as to two types of non-sense, passive and active: the non-sense of words emptied of meaning, which decompose into phonetic elements, and the non-sense of tonic elements which form indecomposable words that are no less empty. In both these cases everything happens below meaning, far from the surface. It is here a matter of under-meaning [*sous-sens*], of un-meaning [*insens*], of *Untersinn,* which must be distinguished from the non-sense at the surface. In both of its aspects, language is, to quote Höld-erlin, "a sign empty of meaning." It is still a sign, but one that merges with an action or passion of the body. This is why it is insufficient to say that schizophrenic language is defined by an incessant and mad sliding of the signifying series onto the signified series. In fact, no series remains at all; both have disappeared. They now exist only in appear-ance. "Speaking" has collapsed onto "eating," and into all the imitations of a "chewing mouth," of a primitive oral depth. Non-sense has ceased to give meaning at the

surface; it absorbs, it engulfs all meaning from both sides, that of the signifier and that of the signified. Artaud says that Being, which is nonsense, has teeth.

In the surface organization which we described earlier as secondary, physical bodies and sonorous words were at the same time separated and articulated by an incorporeal borderline—that of meaning, which represents the pure "expressed" of words, on the one side, and logical at-tributes of bodies on the other. It follows then, that although meaning results from the body's actions and pas-sions, it is a result that is different in nature (is neither ac-tion nor passion), and that protects sonorous language against being confused with the physical body. In the primary order of schizophrenia, on the contrary, there is no duality except that between the actions and passions of the body; language is both of these at the same time and is entirely resorbed into the body's gaping depths. There is no longer anything to prevent propositions from collapsing onto bodies and mixing their sonorous elements with the olfactive, gustative, digestive, and excremental affects of bodies. Not only is there no longer any meaning, but there is no longer any grammar or syntax, nor even any articulated syllabic, literal, or phonetic elements. Antonin Artaud can entitle his essay "An Antigrammatical Endeavor against Lewis Carroll."[16] Carroll needs a very strict gram-mar, one responsible for preserving the inflexion and articulation of words as separated from the flexion and articulation of bodies, if only by mirrors that reflect these words and "send" a meaning back to them. For this reason we can oppose Artaud and Carroll, point by point—the primary order in opposition to the secondary organization. Surface series of the "eating/speaking" type really have nothing in common with those poles of the depths that ap-parently resemble them. The two configurations of non-sense which, at the surface, distribute meaning between different series have nothing to do with the two descents of non-sense (*Untersinn*) that pull, engulf, and resorb meaning. The two forms of stuttering—clonic and tonic—have only the most superficial analogy with the two schizophrenic languages. The break at the surface has nothing in common with the deep cleavage (*Spaltung*). Even portmanteau words have entirely heterogeneous func-tions.

One can find a schizoid "position" in the child before he rises to or conquers the surface. In addition, one can always find schizoid fragments at the surface itself, since its role is precisely that of organizing and displaying ele-ments that have come from the depths. Still, it is no less erroneous and condemnable to confuse the conquest of the surface in the child, the breakdown of the surface in the schizophrenic, and the mastery of surfaces by a "minor pervert." Lewis Carroll's work can always be turned into a kind of schizophrenic tale. Some English psychoanalysts have rashly done so, pointing out the telescopings and en-casings of Alice's body, her manifest alimentary (and latent excremental) obsessions, the fragments that designate morsels of food as well as "choice morsels," the collages and labels of alimentary words that are quick to decompose, the losses of identity, the fishes in the sea, and so on. One may also ask what sort of madness is represented clinically by the Mad Hatter, the March Hare, and the Dormouse. In the opposition between Alice and Humpty Dumpty,[17] one can always recognize the two ambivalent poles: fragmented organs/organless body, body-sieve/ superior body. Artaud himself had no other reason at first for confronting the Humpty Dumpty text. But it is at this moment that Artaud's warning rings out: "I did not do a translation. . . . I never liked the poem. . . . I do not like surface poems or languages."

Bad psychoanalysis has two ways of deceiving itself: it can believe that it has discovered identical subject matters, which necessarily can be found everywhere, or it can believe that is has found analogous forms which create false differences. In doing either, psychoanalysis fails on both grounds: those of clinical psychiatry and literary criticism. Structuralism is right in reminding us that form and content matter only within the original and irreducible structures in which they are organized. Psychoanalysis should have geometric dimensions rather than merely consisting of personal anecdotes. It is first of all the organization and the orientation of these geometric dimensions, rather than reproductive materials or reproduced forms, that constitute both life and sexuality. Psychoanalysis should not be content with designating cases, analyzing personal histories, or diagnosing complexes. As a psychoanalysis of meaning, it should be geographic before being anecdotal: it should distinguish between different regions. Artaud is neither Carroll nor Alice, Carroll is not Artaud, Carroll is not even Alice. Artaud plunges the child into an extremely violent alternative between corporeal passion and action that conforms to the two languages of depth. Either the child must not be born, which is to say, must not leave the chambers of his future spinal column, upon which his parents fornicate (which amounts to an inverse suicide)—or else he must become a fluid, "superior," flaming body, without organs or parents (like those whom Artaud called his "daughters" yet-to-be-born).

Carroll, on the contrary, awaits the child in accordance with his language of incorporeal meaning. He awaits her at the moment at which the child leaves the depths of the maternal body without yet having discovered the depths of her own body, that brief moment of surface when the little girl breaks the surface of the water, like Alice in the pool of her own tears. Carroll and Artaud are worlds apart. We may believe that the surface has its monsters (the Snark and the Jabberwock), its terrors and its cruelties which, though not from the depths, nevertheless have claws and can snatch laterally, or even pull us back into the depths whose dangers we thought we had averted. Carroll and Artaud are nonetheless different; at no point do their worlds coincide. Only the commentator can move from one dimension to the other, and that is his great weakness, the sign that he himself inhabits neither. We would not give one page of Antonin Artaud for all of Carroll; Artaud is the only person to have experienced absolute depth in literature, to have discovered a "vital" body and its

prodigious language (through suffering, as he says). He explored the infra-meaning, which today is still unknown. Carroll, on the other hand, remains the master or the surveyor of surfaces we thought we knew so well that we never explored them. Yet it is on these surfaces that the entire logic of meaning is held.

Notes

1. "Perspendicacious" is a portmanteau word used by a schizophrenic to designate spirits that are suspended above the subject's head (*perpendicular*) and that are very *perspicacious.* Mentioned in Georges Dumas, *Le Surnaturel et les dieux d'après les maladies mentales* (Paris: Presses Universitaires de France, 1946), p. 303.

2. Antonin Artaud, *Oeuvres complètes* (Paris: Gallimard, 1970), IX, 188. Henceforth, references will be to the volume and page of this edition. All translations are the editor's. Breath-screams are used in Artaud's theater of cruelty as a means of preventing spectators from relating to the "intellectual" content of language. (The scream is a specific system of breathing derived from the Kabbala, and is designed to free the feminine or repressed side of the self.)—Ed.

3. The original text of "Jabberwocky" which Humpty Dumpty explicates is found in *Through the Looking Glass* (Lewis Carroll, *Complete Works,* Modern Library ed., p. 215. Henceforth, all references will be to this edition) and goes as follows:

   'Twas brillig, and the slithy toves
   Did gyre and gymble in the wabe
   All mimsy were the borogoves,
   And the mome raths outgrabe.

   Artaud's version (taken from "L'Arve et l'aume, tentative anti-grammaticale contre Lewis Carroll," IX, 156-174) is as follows:

   Il était roparant, et les vliqueux tarands
   Allaient en gibroyant et en brimbulkdriquant

   Jusque là où la rourghe est à rouarghe à rangmbde et rangmbde à rouarghambde:

   Tous les falomitards étaient les chats-huants
   Et les Ghoré Uk'hatis dans le grabugeument.

   Whereas Henri Parisot's translation (cf. *Lewis Carroll,* Seghers ed.) reads:

   Il était grilheure; les slictueux toves
   Gyraient sur l'alloinde et vriblaient;
   Tout flivoreux allaient les borogoves;
   Les verchons fourgus bourniflaient.
   —Ed.

4. Editor's note: My long interpolation here about the Stoics attempts to define: (1) the parameters within which Deleuze's essay was written; (2) the concepts Deleuze develops and uses further on in his study. In order to facilitate the reader's task, brief definitions of the key Stoic concepts at work in

Deleuze's text follow: *Action* and *Passion*: in the interaction among bodies, *actions* are the active principles by which bodies act, and passions are the *passive* principles by which bodies are acted upon. This establishes the duality agent-body versus patient-body. *Proposition*: that which allows the expression of *events* (or *effects*) in language. *Designation* and *expression*: two dimensions of the proposition. The first, *designation* (consisting of nouns and adjectives), is what links the proposition to physical things (bodies or consumable objects) which are exterior to it. The second, *expression* (consisting of verbs), links the proposition to incorporeal events and logical attributes; it *expresses* them and thus represents the conceptual link between the proposition and meaning.

5. *La Théorie des incorporels dans l'ancien stoïcisme* (Paris: Vrin, 1928), p. 11.

6. On the one hand, meaning doesn't exist outside of the proposition that expresses it. But, on the other hand, it is not to be equated with the proposition; it has its own completely distinct "objectivity." The *expressed* does not resemble the *expression* at all. Meaning is not an attribute of the proposition; it is the attribute of a thing or of the state of a thing. It deals, on the one hand, with things, and, on the other, with propositions. But is is no more to be equated with the proposition that expresses it than with either the state of things or the physical quality that the proposition designates. Meaning is exactly on the borderline between propositions and things.—Ed.

7. An esoteric word can be defined as the point of convergence of two different series of propositions. A first type of esoteric word is limited to a contraction of the syllabic elements of a proposition ("y'reince" for "your royal highness"). Another type is concerned with affirming, within the esoteric word, the conjunction and the coexistence of two series of heterogeneous propositions. (Snark = shark + snake). Finally, there exists a third type of esoteric word—the portmanteau word—which is the contraction of several words and thus englobes several meanings. The essential characteristic of the portmanteau word is that is is based on a strict *disjunctive synthesis*. Its function always consists of ramifying the series in which it is placed (frumious = fuming + furious *or* furious + fuming).—Ed.

8. The song of the gardener, in *Sylvia and Bruno,* is made up of nine verses, eight of which are in the first volume, the ninth appearing in *Sylvia and Bruno Concluded,* chapter 20. We quote here two of the verses.—Ed.

> He thought he saw an Albatross
>   That fluttered round the lamp;
> He looked again, and found it was
>   A Penny-Postage-Stamp.

[p. 347]

> He thought he saw an Argument
>   That proved he was the Pope:
> He looked again, and found it was
>   A Bar of Mottled Soap.

[p. 701]

9. Louis Wolfson, *Le Schizo et les langues* (Paris: Gallimard, 1971). On this subject see the introduction written by Deleuze to Wolfson's book and the articles by Alain Rey ("Le Schizolexe" in *Critique,* Nos. 279-80 [1970]) and Jeffrey Mehlman ("Portnoy in Paris" in *Diacritics,* 2 [Winter 1972]).—Ed.

10. "The Unconscious," in *Metapsychology* (1915). Citing the cases of two patients, one of whom perceives his skin, and the other his sock, as systems of small holes in continual risk of expansion, Freud shows that this symptom is peculiar to schizophrenia, and could belong neither to a hysteric nor to an obsessional neurotic.

11. In *La Tour de feu,* April 1961.

12. On the subject of organ-letters, see Artaud, "Le Rite de Peyotl," in *Les Tarahumaras* (IX, 32-38)—Ed.

13. Cf. Artaud's superior, or "organless" body made only of bone and blood: "No mouth No tongue No teeth No larynx No esophagus No stomach No belly No anus I will reconstruct the man that I am" (*84,* November 1947, p. 102).

14. Compare Carroll's and Artaud's versions of the same poem—Ed.

> But he was very stiff and proud:
> He said, 'You needn't shout so loud!'
> And he was very proud and stiff:
> He said, 'I'd go and wake them, if—'
> I took a corkscrew from the shelf:
> I went to wake them up myself.
> And when I found the door was locked,
> I pulled and pushed and kicked and knocked.
> And when I found the door was shut,
> I tried to turn the handle, but—

[Carroll, p. 220]

> He who is not does not know
> The obedient one does not suffer.
> It is for him who is to know
> Why total obedience
> Is that which has never suffered
> When the being is what disintegrates
> Like the mass of the sea.
>   . . . . .
> God only is that which obeys not,
> All other beings do not yet exist,
> And they suffer.
>   . . . . .
> The being is he who imagines himself to be
> To be enough to dispense with himself
> From learning what the sea wants . . .
> But every little fish knows it.

[Artaud, IX, 171-172; Editor's translation]

15. "One feels as if one is inside a gaseous wave which emits an incessant crackling from all sides. Things are released, as from what was your spleen, your liver, your heart, or your lungs; they escape untiringly, and burst in this atmosphere which hesitates between gas and water, but which seems to call things to itself and to command them to regroup.

   "What escaped from my spleen or my liver was in the shape of letters from a very ancient and mysterious alphabet chewed by an enormous mouth" (IX, 32-33).—Ed.

16. "And I will add that I have always despised Lewis Carroll (see my letters from Rodez concerning the 'Jabberwocky'): for me this was an antigrammatical endeavor not *following* Carroll, but *against* him" (IX, 273-274).—Ed.

17. Cf. *Through the Looking Glass,* in which Humpty Dumpty introduces himself as an egg, or a body without organs, and reproaches Alice for the organic differentiation of her face, which he judges to be too ordinary.

Jane Goodall (essay date Summer 1987)

"Artaud's Revision of Shelley's *The Cenci*: The Text and its Double," in *Comparative Drama,* Vol. 21, No. 2, Summer, 1987, pp. 115-26.

[*In the following essay, comparing Artaud's version of* The Cenci *to Shelley's, Goodall pays particular attention to showing how Artaud reframes a narrative dependent on language into a play of forces realized by the language of movement and gesture.*]

   The plague takes images that are dormant, a latent disorder, and suddenly extends them into the most extreme gestures; the theater also takes gestures and pushes them as far as they will go: like the plague it reforges the chain between what is and what is not, between the virtuality of the possible and what already exists in materialized nature.

   (Antonin Artaud's *The Theater and its Double,* p. 27)

This image represents the theater as a bridge from the virtual to the actual, a convergence of physical and metaphysical operations. Artaud's metaphors betray an obsessional concern with this physical/metaphysical interface, a concern which drives him in quest of an "alchemical theater," capable of resolving "every conflict produced by the antagonism of matter and mind." His own endeavors to bring about such a resolution through practical work in the theater present a special problem where critical assessment is concerned. At one extreme, critics like Jacques Derrida and Susan Sontag, whose interest in Artaud is exclusively conceptual, are intrigued by the paradoxical phenomenon of "an art without works." Sontag gives a disparaging summary of his Theater of Cruelty

enterprise and his production of *The Cenci* in particular, asserting that his incompetence as a practitioner is "a constituent part of the authority of his ideas"; and she summarizes his achievement as "a singular presence, a poetics, an aesthetics of thought, a theology of culture and a phenomenology of suffering."[1] Derrida, having acknowledged that an art without works defies exegesis and leaves the critic without resource, contemplates the aporia of a "metaphysics of flesh" which can produce works only as a form of excretion:

   Like excrement, like the turd, which is, as is well known, a metaphor for the penis, the work *should* stand upright. But the work, as excrement, is but matter without life, without force or form. It always falls and collapses as soon as it is outside me.[2]

Such an approach to the relationship between work and creator as one of somatic contiguity excludes the possibility of bridging the gulf between physical and metaphysical awareness through the expression of creative impulse in palpable form. But Artaud envisages "*matter as revelation,*" "culture-in-action" (as he declares in his Preface), which is not a material product but a *materialization.*[3] In describing the manifestations of creative impulse, Artaud chooses metaphors of eruption, explosion and ejaculation, of transformation, dissolution and apotheosis. The artist is represented as a medium, the center of a psychic force-field. His relationship to the tangible effects of this force-field—described in metaphors of earthquake, whirlwind, lightning, tidal wave—is never metonymic. Alchemy works outside the terms of physical cause and effect.

If a concentration on Artaud's metaphysics has tended to lead to the dismissal of his theatrical enterprises as aberration, the reverse has also been the case. Christopher Innes finds Artaud's theoretical writings "positively Delphic in their poetic obscurity" and suggests that this has been "largely responsible for the way his stage work has been ignored or disparaged."[4] Innes' decision to regard *The Cenci* as a work in its own right rather than an attempt to realize the principles of the alchemical theater leaves him unembarrassed by the ontological paradox which Derrida and Sontag find in Artaud's very attempt to give tangible form to his ideas.

Innes makes a revealing study of the dramaturgical qualities of the script, which he sees as a framework for mathematically calculated sound and movement patterns, a performance text as distinct from a dramatic text. His preference for a critical vocabulary borrowed from technical subjects (geometry and kinetics especially) is symptomatic of his reaction against what he sees as a misleading emphasis on the abstruse and the abstract in preceding studies of Artaud's work. Certainly he is effective in countering the dismissive appraisals of *The Cenci* given by Sontag and Martin Esslin, and in answering Grotowski's charge that "Artaud left no concrete technique behind him, indicated no method."[5]

As an exegesis, though, Innes' offering is fragmentary and evasive. He complains of a lack of inherent logic in the thematic development of the text and concludes that "coherence of vision is obviously not as important to Artaud as the intensity, passion and extremity of the action." In as far as he acknowledges a governing idea behind the proliferation of carefully articulated stage effects, it is as vague as this:

> By applying geometric shapes to a vision of anarchy and primitive excess, which should make the perspectives on life that they represent seem artificial and arbitrary, Artaud could hope to make his audience uncertain of their familiar assumptions about the physical universe.[6]

In spite of his careful attention to the details of its craftsmanship, Innes conveys no sense of *The Cenci* as a composition.

In "Metaphysics and the Mise en Scène," Artaud analyzes a painting, Lucas van den Leyden's *The Daughters of Lot.* In his description of the work, he correlates a painstaking observance of detail with a highly charged response to the "thunderous visual harmony" of the whole, in its revelatory fusion of physical and metaphysical awareness. The painting, he claims, is what the theater should be "if it knew how to speak the language that belongs to it."[7] Artaud's description is an impassioned tribute to the work as an organic creation and as such is difficult to reconcile with Derrida's image of the work-as-turd, "without life, without force, without form." Moreover, vitality, forcefulness, and form are seen to be inextricably related in the painting which Artaud cites as his exemplary "text."

A reading of *The Cenci* which set out to acknowledge both the details of its craftsmanship and the metaphysical dynamics of its overall composition, then, might go some way towards reconciling the incompatible positions of Innes on the one hand and Sontag and Derrida on the other. We need to investigate the script as at least an attempt to discover and transcribe the "language" that belongs to the alchemical theater. At the same time, however, it is necessary to take account of Artaud's maverick attitude to the use of sign systems of any kind.

Raymond Rouleau describes Artaud rolling round the stage at the start of a rehearsal, practicing extreme vocal and physical distortions.[8] But perhaps this ritual of semantic and kinesic dissociation is something more than a tantrum. Artaud's analogy between the theater and the plague draws upon Saint Augustine's idea that both are a dangerous scourge—the one to the body of the state as the other is to the body of the individual. Artaud develops from it an image of the psyche as "occupied" by culturally determined programs of thought and expression which must be overthrown so that "ripe powers previously held in servitude and unavailable to reality, burst forth in the guise of incredible images which give freedom of the city and of existence to acts that are by nature hostile to the life of societies."[9] This involves an insurrection against the thought-traps set by established sign systems. The systems themselves must still be put to use, but in a coalescence that enables the constraints of any one of them to be transcended.

Artaud repeatedly asserts his conviction that certain conjunctions of signs are explosive to the culturally determined syntax which delivers most forms of human expression still-born. The alchemical theater works through "commanding interpenetrations" ("les correspondences les plus imperieuses")[10], a phenomenon more prosaically described by the semioticians' term "transcodification." A study of the relationship between Artaud's *The Cenci* and Shelley's is a particularly effective means of highlighting this technique of correspondence or transcodification. In spite of Artaud's insistence that his own play is not an adaptation, it is in the true sense a *dramatization*: he has scored Shelley's work for performance by translating its central ideas from verbal exposition into a multiple coded arrangement involving complex interplay between different modes of expression.

To Artaud, one of the most repellent characteristics of the logocentric theater is its preoccupation with psychological exegesis, and he cites Shakespeare as a prime culprit in this. Shelley's play draws heavily on the literary subcodes of Shakespearian drama: rhetorics of guilt, pathos and strategy; patterns of metaphor; involved motivational analysis. Artaud dismantles the elaborate framework of Shelley's characterizations by substituting force for motive. The problematic relationship between will and action is the subject of most of the verbalized thought processes which are the primary substance of Shelley's text.

For Artaud's Cenci, will and action are fused, not set in relation to each other. He describes himself as a force of nature, unable to resist the charge of energy that compels him. The theoretical implications of this are trenchantly stated in *The Theater and its Double*:

> If our life lacks brimstone, i.e., a constant magic, it is because we choose to observe our acts and lose ourselves in considerations of their imagined form instead of being impelled by their force.[11]

Dramaturgically, Artaud's approach entails a radical and pervasive re-shaping of his source material. He shifts the emphasis from diegetic to mimetic forms of representation: details of the subject are cut back as the focus is concentrated almost exclusively on what the audience is to witness. Cenci's demonic power is conveyed not so much through what he says and aims to do as through the disruptive impact of his *presence,* so that reaction to him on the part of other characters is conveyed primarily in gestic and kinesic terms.

The predominance of action over reflection accelerates the development of events so that the whole dramatic structure seems to be wrenched by the impetus of Cenci's course. The monologues with which Shelley habitually concludes his scenes all are cut in favor of sudden, jarring transitions. These uninterrupted transitions from one scene to another are counterpointed by moments of stasis and quandary during the course of the most frenetic scenes so that a spasmodic effect is created. The even rhythms of Shelley's blank verse give place to a volatile surface texture. Extreme fluctuations in pace, pitch, and tone heighten sensory awareness and intensify the isolated moment, the here and now of performance.

Artaud's instinct for what was theatrically practicable was determined largely by his experience with Charles Dullin's company. He joined Dullin late in 1921 and spent 18 months with him on an intensive training program (ten to twelve hours a day) which included mime, voice production, gymnastics, and concentration exercises designed to sharpen sensory perception. Artaud's use of bells as acoustic framing for the banquet scene and of amplified footsteps as a *leitmotif* is specific evidence of Dullin's strong influence on his dramatic imagination. These particular sounds were the focus for an exercise designed by Dullin to attune the actors to "la voix du monde," and would therefore have acquired significance to Artaud as catalysts for inducing heightened awareness of the objective world. Mime exercises involving identification with or struggle against elemental forces also were standard. Dullin records giving this exercise to Artaud:

> You must cross a mountain stream. You fight against the current. You have overestimated your strength, the stream carries you away. You fight desperately, you are out of your depths.[12]

Very similar mime sequences are prescribed in the banquet scene and in the storm scene, where the first murder attempt takes place.

The availability of Roger Blin's promptbook notations for the banquet scene makes this a useful starting point for an investigation of Artaud's dramaturgical techniques. The kinetic paradigms established here can, in particular, be studied with some precision. The stage directions in the published text indicate that he envisaged the opening scenario as suggestive of extreme atmospheric turbulence, with wind-blown drapes, waves of suddenly amplified sound, and crowded figures engaged in "furious orgy." A chorus of church bells was to accent the "spinning rhythm" of the scenario, which overall was to be like a wild exaggeration of Veronese's *Marriage Feast at Cana*.

This massive tableau is held in the Louvre, so Artaud would have been familiar with the original. Its densely arranged groupings of figures and objects, forming numerous, disparate fields of concentration, conveys a general impression of conspiratorial tension. It is a stage manager's nightmare, and small wonder that the photographs of the scene in performance bear so little resemblence to it, though its semiotic influence is clear in the underlying semantics of Artaud's own stage picture. Veronese's composition highlights the ironic discrepancy between two planes of awareness; amidst the turmoil of diversely preoccupied figures an alchemical miracle is taking place. (More sinister models for the association of the banquet and the revelatory gesture are to be found in *Thyestes* and *The Revenger's Tragedy,* both of which were listed by Artaud as potential Theater of Cruelty texts.)

Blin's notations for this opening sequence give evidence of major alterations to the stage directions as printed in the text. Instead of having Cenci on stage and central to the stage picture at the outset, Artaud prescribes his entry some minutes after the start of the scene, which is very low key. The blocking plans indicate slow eddies of individual movement as the guests trace aimless paths across the stage with stilted, pantomimic gestures. Dummies accompany the human automatons in a "slow and sluggish promenade."[13] This allows the mounting turbulence of the scene to be unambiguously associated with Cenci's presence. On his appearance, the free use of the center stage immediately ceases and the figures are confined to fixed positions around the periphery.

Where Shelley's Cenci maintains a semblance of formal courtesy for some minutes, soothing his guests with announcements about the "pious cause" of the feast,[14] Artaud's Cenci sets up an immediate antagonism with the announcement that "the Cenci myth has come to an end," that he is "ready to give teeth to the legend." Camillo senses a *frisson* of psychic electricity. He rises from his seat, but sits again. This is the first of a series of comically futile gestures of protest. During Cenci's ensuing report of the murder of his sons, Beatrice rises and sits again three times, Lucretia twice, Camillo a second time and Colonna once. It is as though some external pressure fixes them in their places until, compelled *en masse* to active rebellion, the guests "fling themselves towards the centre and are scattered in all directions." The stage has become a cyclonic force-field, and they are hurled from its vortex. As they attempt to converge on him they are caught in a series of whirlwind formations and are seen battling against the currents as though against an onslaught of ghostly antagonists.[15]

There is no physical disorder in Shelley's version of the banquet, which culminates in a verbal confrontation between Cenci and Beatrice. Shelley's Beatrice is the eloquent protagonist in a fierce moral conflict, her uncompromising resistence to corruption being the primary source of pathos and dramatic tension. Artaud, determined to strip the situation of its moral connotations and their attendant rhetoric, presents the relationship between Cenci and Beatrice as a matter of elemental dynamics. Her defiance of him takes the form of an attempt to generate a rival force-field; she traces an orbit of her own, temporarily holding possession of the central arena as she issues threats on behalf of her remaining brothers. After the rest of the company have left, she and Cenci come face to face, and the frenetic pitch and tempo of the scene drop to a mesmeric calm, punctuated by a low, sonorous echo of bells and the sustained note of a viola. Cenci is the eye of the cyclone, and as she enters his personal space she shares its quiescence. Blin's diagram for this section shows them tracing slow paths around each other as, in trance-like state, she responds to his veiled overture:

> Your father is thirsty, Beatrice.
> Will you not give your father something to drink?[16]

The coalescence of verbal and visual symbolism here creates a theme statement fraught with discordant reverberations. Earlier, Cenci has designated the wine goblet as a sacriligious icon containing the blood of his sons. The savage god who turns wine into blood now sets about another kind of alchemy, another revelation.

In Shelley's version, incest is the deed without a name, a "formless horror," the unsignifiable phenomenon which dislocates all normal thought processes. After the rape, Shelley's Beatrice rushes onto the stage in a state of wild spatial and cognitive disorientation. The ground sinks beneath her, the walls spin round her, her flesh seems to be dissolving into a formless mass. Her thoughts "rise, shadow after shadow, darkening each other."[17] In spite of this condition, she manages during the course of the scene to speak some one hundred and seventy lines of flawless blank verse which, moreover, exhibit prodigious metalingual sophistication. In one extraordinary metaphor after another, she describes the experience of not being able to describe her experience. After this crisis, almost exactly at the mid-point of the play, Beatrice proceeds to wind her way unerringly from the heart of darkness, with language as her guiding thread. Rhetoric enables her to justify the crime of her father's murder and prevent the rift between will and conscience which threatens to divide her against herself. Rhetoric enables her to distinguish between the violation of the body and the violation of the soul and to rebuild a holistic consciousness "as firm as the world's center."

It is from this scene that Artaud seems to have taken his cue for the deconstruction of Shelley's dramatic world, for Shelley solves the problem of how to designate the "formless horror" by using graphic plague imagery:

> There creeps
> A clinging, black, contaminating mist
> About me . . . 'tis substantial, heavy, thick,
> I cannot pluck it from me, for it glues
> My fingers and my limbs to one another,
> And eats my sinews, and dissolves
> My flesh to a pollution, poisoning
> The subtle, pure and inmost spirit of life.[18]

To Artaud, the plague is an alchemical agent: it brings about a revelatory metamorphosis. It is this that he hopes to re-activate, through the dissolution of Shelley's dramatic language and by resorting to forms of expression that are not shackled to a whole epistemological framework.

At the end of Artaud's banquet scene Cenci allows Beatrice to make her escape, secure in the knowledge that she cannot break free of the sphere of his influence, for she cannot escape a force that is at work within herself. Drawing on Freudian insights, Artaud treats incest as a generalized syndrome rather than an individually deliberated act. As its victim, Beatrice has no difficulty when the time comes in articulating what has happened to her (her bald pronouncement "My father has raped me" reads like a purposed gesture of contempt for Shelley's lyrical

circumlocutions) but she cannot acknowledge such instincts in herself or in other family relationships. Cenci identifies with the plague that has taken possession of him, harnessing the full power of his conscious volition to the impulses it generates; Beatrice, Lucretia, and his sons are like those plague victims described in *The Theater and its Double* who proudly examine their unblemished bodies in the mirror, unaware of their advanced state of internal dissolution. The irony of this situation lends itself to varied means of dramatic representation.

Cenci's symbolic overture to Beatrice is facetiously juxtaposed with the opening of a scene featuring a vast bed in the center, on which Lucretia sits cradling Bernardo, a satirical *pieta*. It is against the languid intimacy of this tableau that Beatrice hurls herself onto the stage, as though flung from a vortex. The precipitateness of her entry and the urgency of her speech are intermittently disrupted, as she listens for the sound of Cenci's footsteps. The concentration of the audience is thus shifted from the visual to the auditory, the proximal to the distal, from an immediate to an anticipated source of disturbance. The footsteps, straightforwardly metonymic on one level, also have metaphysical significance as the radiating signal of an active presence, of a motivated "other" which threatens to burst in with consuming malevolence. (Shelley, too, has Beatrice allude to Cenci's approaching footsteps, but without Artaud's distorted sonic coding, this is no more than a common indexical sign.) Cenci's entry is accompanied by sonic peaks—a crescendo of amplified footsteps, an outcry from Beatrice, an outcry from Cenci himself—and, again, there is the suggestion that his presence generates a force-field. Beatrice clings to the walls of the room for stability; Lucretia and Bernardo gravitate towards her, into a huddle.

Shelley's references to Lucretia as the "shield" and the "nurse" of the family take on suggestive connotations when transferred to mimetic forms of representation. Artaud's blocking patterns undermine the moralistic protestations in the dialogue, changing the scene into a deeply ambiguous charade which highlights the dynamics of sexual rivalry within the family. Cenci moves in on Beatrice, but Lucretia steps between them; Bernardo clings to Lucretia as she stands face to face with Cenci. Lucretia signals for Bernardo to leave and he transfers his fixation to Beatrice. As sister and brother escape, hand in hand, Cenci resists the impulse to detain them, signalling the confidence of his dominant position by stretching out comfortably on the bed. Lucretia moves close to comfort him, creating an ironic echo of the opening tableau.

Artaud's ambiguous treatment of Cenci's family consciously destroys the pathos of the dramatic situation as Shelley presents it and consciously runs the risk of serious clashes in the emotional coloring of his own work. In his letter to André Gide about the recently completed manuscript, he warned:

> In this play, nothing is treated with respect. I want to
> make everyone understand that I attack the social

superstition of the family without asking that one take up arms against any particular individual.[19]

Critics of Artaud's production recorded the disconcerting mixture of ridicule and awe with which the performance was received. In dismantling the psychological framework of Shelley's play, Artaud is wrenching the generic norms of cohesion which determine the expectations of an audience at a tragedy, and the effects of this are most acutely evident in the handling of the crisis scenes, such as that which follows the rape.

This moment is designed as a close parallel to the first family scene. Beatrice's entry again takes the form of a wild trajectory. The opening dialogue reads like crude melodrama, and its gestic accompaniment is equally unconvincing. When Artaud's Beatrice attempts pathos through overcoding of Christian iconography, the effect is parodic:

> My only crime was being born. I am free to choose how to die, but I did not choose to be born. That was the fateful blow. (She clasps Lucretia's legs, like Mary Magdalen at the foot of the cross).

Artaud shows that people behave like pantomime figures when they attempt to combat or deny the elemental forces that govern them, and instead "lose themselves in consideration of their imagined form." A few moments later, the emotional reality of Beatrice's experience is starkly conveyed as she begins to recount a dream. This presentation of the schism between conscious and unconscious awareness is a Freudian recasting of Shelley's theme of the divided self. Artaud's framing of the speech against the over-presented artificial pathos of the preceding sequence accentuates its candor:

> When I was little I had the same dream every night. I was naked, alone in a vast bedroom with a wild animal such as only exists in dreams. I could hear it breathing. I could escape but I had to hide my glaring nudity. At that moment a door opened. I felt hungry and thirsty. Suddenly, I found I was not alone.

This ingenuously delivered allegory belies the rhetoric of Beatrice's conscious behaviour. Thirst, as we remember from the banquet scene, is a metaphor for lust. Finding herself couched with a wild beast, Beatrice, is thirsty. She runs away, but can only escape by waking up, closing off the eloquent world of the unconscious.

The full meaning of Lucretia's response—"Your dream simply confirms what I already know. One cannot escape one's destiny"—only becomes evident as the action evolves towards its final stages. Where Shelley's Beatrice escapes from the "plague" and its attendant revelation by means of the life-line of axiological rhetoric, Artaud's Beatrice comes to experience the metaphysical cruelty of a world that works inexorably to unite the self with the monstrous other. The whirlwind gives place to the grinding wheels of destiny in the form of the machinery of state justice, "as noisy as a factory in full production." Beat-

rice's attempts to escape the alien force have brought her, physically and metaphysically, full circle. Death, she fears, will only reunite her with her father and teach her that, ultimately, she is "not unlike him."

In his scenario for *The Conquest of Mexico,* Artaud envisaged the characters being "carried along like straws" by the "lines of force" which shape the drama.[20] In literary drama, character is sculpted in language, in the rhetoric of self-representation. Artaud, like Wittgenstein, is "engaged in a struggle with language," that "immense network of wrong turnings."[21] By transcribing Shelley's rhetorically formulated tragedy to forms of representation that break the mould of rhetoric, he reveals the shadowy double at its heart.

Notes

1. Susan Sontag, "Approaching Artaud," in *Under The Sign of Saturn* (London: Writers and Readers Publishing Co-operative Society, 1983), p. 17.

2. Jacques Derrida, *Writing and Difference,* trans. Alan Bass (London: Routledge and Kegan Paul, 1978), p. 183.

3. Antonin Artaud, *The Theater and Its Double,* trans. Mary Caroline Richards (New York: Grove Press, 1958), p. 59.

4. Christopher Innes, *Holy Theater: Ritual and the Avant-Garde* (Cambridge: Cambridge Univ. Press, 1981), p. 60.

5. Jerzy Grotowski, *Towards a Poor Theatre,* ed. Eugenio Barba (London: Methuen, 1975), p. 86.

6. Innes, p. 70.

7. Artaud, *The Theater and Its Double,* p. 37.

8. Raymond Rouleau, Letter on Artaud's *Dream Play* production, cited Innes, p. 64.

9. Artaud, *The Theater and Its Double,* p. 28.

10. Ibid, p. 55.

11. Ibid, p. 8.

12. Charles Dullin, *Souvenirs et notes de travail d'un acteur* (Paris: 1946), p. 110.

13. *The Drama Review,* 16 (June, 1972). Material on Antonin Artaud's *Les Cenci,* p. 100.

14. Percy Bysshe Shelley, *The Cenci,* in *Poetical Works,* ed. Thomas Hutchinson (New York: Oxford Univ. Press, 1967), p. 284.

15. *The Drama Review,* p. 121.

16. Antonin Artaud, *The Cenci* in *Collected Works,* Vol. IV, trans. Victor Corti (London: Calder & Boyars, 1974), p. 130. All quotations from Artaud's *The Cenci* are from this edition.

17. Shelley, *The Cenci,* p. 300.

18. Ibid, p. 297.

19. *The Drama Review,* p. 92.

20. Artaud, *Collected Works,* Vol. IV, p. 99.

21. Ludwig Wittgenstein, *Culture and Value,* trans. Peter Winch (Oxford: Basil Blackwell, 1980), pp. 11, 18.

Lawrence R. Schehr (essay date Winter 1992)

"Artaud's Revolution: Nowhere to Turn," in *Romance Notes,* Vol. 33, No. 2, Winter, 1992, pp. 109-17.

[*In the following essay, Schehr argues that Artaud did not consider the transfer of social, economic, and political power from one class to another revolutionary if there was not also a continual subversion of the self, and of the language and grammar which enable its expression.*]

We owe Jacques Derrida and Julia Kristeva debts of gratitude for having made Artaud the focus of contemporary literary inquiry. As early as 1967 in "La Parole soufflée," Derrida reflects on a corpus that extends from Artaud's early work on the theater to the letters written at Rodez; of interest to him is the import of the pre-semiotic at work in Artaud's writing, a concept that informs his view of the theater. In 1972 at Cerisy, Philippe Sollers organized a session on Artaud in which both he and Julia Kristeva engaged the question of revolution in Artaud's writing. Despite subsequent differences between Tel Quel and deconstruction, the three writers agree in their assessment of the concept of revolution in Artaud's writing. For Derrida (283-84), the revolutionary affirmation relates to the depth of the unreadable in which the distinctions among the various organs of the theater, such as play, writer, and audience, would not be possible. What is not revolutionary is also clear. As Derrida notes (284n), Artaud, in *Manifeste pour un théâtre avorté,* rejects the Surrealists' revolution as one in which it is a question merely of the transmission of power (2:25). In "L'Etat Artaud," Sollers reflects on the center in Artaud's revolution; this center is the absolute antithesis of the calm at the eye of the storm: "Ce n'est pas *autour* de ce centre qu'il faut être, baiser, se branler, gigoter, mouiller, ça l'arrangerait plutôt, la machine, mais au coeur du centre, dans le *re* du produit centré . . ." (24). And Kristeva follows through with her conception of the pre-semiotic center as *chora* as she talks about the rotation of the *chora* ("Le Sujet en procès," in Sollers 74-89). This pre-semiotic center, which Kristeva, Sollers, and Derrida all see as the heart of the Artaudian revolution, becomes for Sollers and Kristeva, though not explicitly for Derrida, the link to a revolutionary practice.

To articulate Artaud's revolution means recognizing this confrontation between sign and *chora* and exploring the changes in the sign of "revolution" predicated on this confrontational difference. Of course, it is not toward the Surrealists' Marx that we must look, for even despite their rejection of the Stalinism of the thirties, the Surrealists remain bound to Euro-Marxism. Kristeva's and Sollers' models return Artaud to a Marxist revolutionary practice

to make him the clarion of Mao and the permanent revolution. As Kristeva points out, for Artaud, the Communist revolution (in the USSR) is merely "a simple transmission of power from the bourgeoisie to the proletariat" (107). To leave Artaud there makes him (especially from what has become a post-Marxist perspective in the West) merely the other path, the alternative to Stalinism. Considering both the failure of the Cultural Revolution and the shift of Sollers and Kristeva away from their Maoist position, it seems unfair to Artaud to leave him as the herald of a failure.

Artaud's revolution is described in the *Messages révolutionnaires* (8:157), where he says that there are three forces: "la force répulsive et dilatante, la force compressive et astringente, la force rotatoire." These form a revolution that rejects the power exchanges of European thought—"l'esprit d'analyse où l'Europe s'est égarée." This is a far cry from the Surrealist revolution that seeks a liberation through a Marxist revolution coupled with a liberation of the unconscious. For Artaud, Surrealism dwells in the mythology and ossified ideology of the West. For Artaud the problem is that even through that liberation of the unconscious, there is no internal revolution, no upsetting, change, rotation, redefinition, or explosion in the categories that are—and determine—the divisions of the mind into conscious and unconscious.

For Artaud, the revolution is not defined as the negation of another revolution—Surrealism—and even less as the predecessor of anything other than Artaud himself. Even his revolutionary messages announce nothing more than their own revolution, his own revolution. Nevertheless, despite this return onto himself, we should not hurtle into the "garde-fou" of Artaud criticism that reads Artaud teleologically. As Derrida maintains and as Jacques Garelli summarizes, though the medical facts cannot be ignored, we cannot interpret "every aspect of the work in accordance with this point of departure," that is to say, Artaud's madness and/or incarceration (21). In this modest text then, I would like to propose a path that includes both the singularity of the subject and the question of the *effet de sujet* in its historical context. At the same time, I would like to attempt a reading that is not teleological even by implication: this is not an Artaud that is pre-psychotic or pre-Maoist, but rather an Artaud in the process of engendering and becoming his own revolution. Hence, I am proposing a reading of the word "revolution" in a changing historic and subjective context in Artaud's work.

"Revolution" is a singular word, found both *sous rature* and as a *point de capiton.* No one could doubt the importance of this word situated at a conjunction between the self-effectuating change in the subject and the change effectuated by the subject in a historical context. Especially for the later Artaud, "revolution" becomes a word that cannot be said, a word that disappears by and large from his vocabulary; that disappearance enables a whole host of other words, other texts that are truly revolutionary. For ultimately, by its act of complacent self-nomination, even the word "revolution" becomes a betrayal of the revolution *de lettres / de l'être.*

Certainly in the twenties and early thirties, the revolution starts out as a very present, real event defined in terms of its historical context. The text is seen both as a vanguard of this change and as a means of effectuating a change in the world. Thus a revolutionary discourse has a polemical and pragmatic side intended to affect the outside world. This aesthetic of revolution is present in the early critical works such as *Le Théâtre et son double,* where the construct of the revolution is given in the figures of cruelty, the rhetoric of disaster, and the specularity of the *spectacle* (4:7-137). Along with the performative aspect of this work, there is both an illocutionary force and a perlocutionary force attached to the program. The work is a manifesto for change and a promise that change will occur through an effectuation of the discourse of the revolutionary theater of cruelty. Artaud's endeavor is thus double: the manifesto describes what the theater accomplishes; the manifesto takes the place of a theater that may only be accomplishable in the virtual reality of the cinema. And as a manifesto, it is not far from miming the Surrealist manifestos of the previous decade in rhetoric, style, and desired effect: Artaud's double repeats Surrealism, copies the theater, and sets up the critical subject as the *sosie,* caught, yet effective in a discourse that is the conjunction of a textual revolution with a praxis and with a historical context of societal change.

As a sometime member of the Surrealist group, Artaud is committed to their ideal of social and political revolution. The political position of the Surrealists is anything but stable, but at least on the surface, there is a united front that still includes Artaud. In fact, he pointedly joins the words "Surrealism" and "revolution" together as the byword of his vision of the project: "Nous sommes bien décidés à faire une Révolution. Nous avons accolé le mot de *surréalisme* au mot de *révolution* uniquement pour montrer le caractère désintéressé, détachée, et même tout à fait désespéré, de cette révolution" (1bis:29). Despite the seeming solidarity with the position of the Surrealists, the situation is already complicated within Artaud's version of the figure of revolution: for the Surrealists themselves, the revolution is anything but "désespéré." This linguistic evidence shows that the eventual rift between Artaud and the other Surrealists cannot merely be chalked up to a political difference and/or to a mimetic rivalry. The despair of the situation shows that Artaud's revolution is on a different register. For him, the political occurs first and foremost at the level of the subject. For Aragon and Breton, there was a legitimate political reason for the break with Artaud, as they make a materialist critique of his self-centered spiritual revolution. According to them, the only matter Artaud recognized was "the matter of his mind" (qtd. in 1[bis]:241). Breton and Aragon fail to realize that, for Artaud, for there to be a true revolution at the level of the material means that the very perception of the material must undergo a spiritual revolution. Without such a movement, matter is still prey to the structures in which a detheatricalized society has blithely forced it.

For Artaud, it is wrong to "plot like children" and to reduce revolution to a political reordering and a uniquely poetic reordering of the world; by poetic he refers specifically to the literary production of the Surrealists (1[bis]:118). For Breton *et al.,* the distance between this proposed materialist or political revolution and the poetic revolution is bridged by the belief in Surrealism, in the power of these revolutions, and especially, in the link the Surrealists proposed between these two events. For Artaud however, the link is not necessarily there; an article of faith for Aragon and Breton is a false structure for Artaud. For him, revolution should be used as a means of reordering the world, but more importantly, the soul and the mind. It is a point that he continues to make as late as the *Messages révolutionnaires*: ". . . il n'y a pas de révolution sans révolution dans la culture, c'est-à-dire sans une révolution de la conscience moderne face à l'homme, à la nature et à la vie" (8:240). Thus the transformational poetry of surrealism that transcribes the aberrance already in the world is not nearly as radical a revolt for Artaud as the one he is proposing that includes a revision of consciousness itself, without which the structures would remain fundamentally unchanged. He foresees an overthrow of everything *including* the already present dissonances, aberrances, or elements of the unconscious in the world. There is a dissonant element in Artaud's conception of the revolution that does not jive with the engaged political position of the Surrealists. Despite the freeing of the unconscious implied in processes like automatic writing, their position does not go as far as his in the grammatical and linguistic upheavals that he feels necessary to a revolutionary position: "cette révolution vise . . . à une confusion absolue et renouelée des langues" (1bis:45).

So for Artaud, revolution is not defined by a class struggle, by solidarity, or by the linguistic equivalent of this solidarity that is the ability to say the word "nous." Artaud defines revolution as a dislocation of language and the mind, and *a fortiori* of the linguistic system that provides support for discourse. Much later he will define it implicitly as the Tower of Babel, a linguistic system in a permanent state of confusion. In Mexico, he says: "Quant à la France, on peut dire qu'elle se trouve virtuellement en état de révolution. Nous sommes comme à la veille d'une nouvelle *Confusion des Langues*" (8:231). What is named is what has been agreed on: it is the name given by "nous" to things that serve as the base for the Surrealists and the target for Artaud: "Tout ce qui a un nom . . . passe dans les girations de ce feu où se rebroussent les vagues de la chair même" (1bis:58). Thus naming, consensus, and agreement, signs of a materialist political revolution whose discourse is one of revolutionary solidarity, are at the antipodes of the proper revolution. The proper Artaudian revolution is the act of gyration, an inward turn of mind that is endlessly turning, endlessly confusing, and endlessly revolutionary. As he will eventually write in his translation of Lewis Carroll's *Jabberwocky*: "Gilroyer, c'est tourner rond sur rond sur soi-même, en mettant tout le temps sa tête à la place de sa queue et sa queue à la place de sa tête . . ." (9:141). For the revolution to work, it must be "antigrammaticale" (9:133).

We should thus understand Artaud literally when he says that "Tout le fond, toutes les exaspérations de notre querelle roulent autour du mot Révolution" (1bis:59n). For the Surrealists, the revolution is fundamentally materialist, and therefore anchored; for Artaud, this rolling around repeats the endless, unpinnable gyration of the revolution itself. The problem is literally linguistic: how can someone who cannot define his pronouns participate in a revolution defined as a political movement of solidarity? And conversely, what good can a revolution be to someone who already defines himself in an alienated fashion, alienated from the world and from himself, and for whom revolution is a hope of *zu sich selbst kommen,* a linguistic act whose perlocutionary force should be to bring him back to himself? Without this gyration, this gyre that is a return, the revolution is meaningless for Artaud: "Mais que me fait à moi toute la Révolution du monde si je sais demeurer éternellement douloureux et misérable au sein de mon propre charnier . . . il n'y a de bonne révolution que celle qui me profite, à moi, et à des gens comme moi" (1bis:60).

The three constitutive elements of Artaud's revolution are now in place. First of all, on the negative side, is the act of repression of the word in Artaud's vocabulary. Because the word has become the by-word of the Surrealists who define it relative to an adhesion to the French Communist Party, the word disappears. The disappearance is the site of an irritation: the disappearance of the word is not a simple erasure but a combination of a repression and alienation. The split from the Surrealists has a profound effect on Artaud that could be characterized as an alienation not only from them, but also from the concept of a joint venture with anyone, a permanent difference from the word "nous." And yet with this repression comes the beginning of an explosive variant of revolution defined solipsistically, a pattern that will emerge in the texts of the thirties. Artaud's eventual concept of revolution is not defined merely as the organic result of his own difference from Surrealism but rather as the dynamic combination of this difference with an internalized repression and alienation.

Though Artaud's most valid critique of the Surrealists is that they are incapable of "se représenter une Révolution qui n'évoluerait pas dans les cadres désespérants de la matière" (1bis:62), the result of the rift is that he is no longer capable of representing revolution to himself in any way. If the inability to establish a valid hierarchy of personal pronouns for himself has always been there, the remarking of this inability by the Surrealists and the internalization of this remark by Artaud is the double irritation that will push him much further along his solitary road. Artaud cannot say "we," as later he will not be able to say "*tu,*" either to another or to himself, but the worst of it is that everyone knows it. As long as his internalized gyre is unremarked, it is not dangerous. Now however, the gyre of revolution occurs entirely within his mind.

The repression of irritation of this word in a cryptonymy begins to work on the very nature of linguistic representa-

tion for Artaud. Of course when he is in Rodez this will be patently and pathologically clear: "Je ne suis pas masculin affirmatif mais neutre expulsif" (15:195), but the basis of this linguistic dislocation is present very early on. If thematically, *Héliogabale* is a call to replace the materialistic revolution of the Surrealists with an anarchistic explosion that respects no laws or dichotomies, not even those that divide mind from matter, Artaud cannot maintain any preconceived linguistic or hierarchic notion. Artaud takes the Surrealists' literary production and turns it on its head: for Artaud, poetry is always fundamentally a contradiction; to use poetry is to bring into play a state of permanent revolution, against, for example, the vulgar materialist revolution of the French Communist Party that adheres to the Soviet model.

A textual revolution has already occurred in *Héliogabale* based on the inversion of all values and of base and summit. No longer a figure meant principally to convince others, Artaud's figure of revolution occurs in the persona of the revolutionary figure, Héliogabale himself, who is a literal and figurative inversion of Artaud's discourse of revolution. The revolutionary is the one who performs the revolution on himself, thus unseating and over-turning himself in the process. In accomplishing his act, the revolutionary destroys the point at which the revolution started. This is not simply a dialectical reversal but an act of upheaval continually refigured in the rest of the works. As Carol Jacobs notes: "This endless layering of symbolical strata creates the semblance of a certain meaning, but one that then violently denies its own apparent logic" (56).

This permanent state of war is even more radical than one might think at first. For as Artaud states in *Les Nouvelles Révélations de l'Etre,* the world will accomplish the revolution against us that we could not accomplish, for "la Révolution aussi se souvient qu'elle est femme" (7:160). Revolution thus is anything but a political machine. Recused from a political position, Artaud turns revolution into a cosmogony that does not know the limitation of a linguistic or textual system. Instead of politics, revolution becomes the woman who simultaneously seduces and betrays by bringing out fantasies of a multiply inverted sexuality. Within Artaud, at the point of gyrating revolution, is the internalized figure of the woman: mother and genetrix of Artaud himself, the figure of the woman as revolution replaces and redefines the position at which revolution had earlier been repressed. If he is not fully feminized, if he is only neuter expulsive instead of feminine negative, as long as he is no longer masculine affirmative, that will be enough for now.

Within himself at the point of internalized gyration, in Mexico where the "eternal betrayal of white men" seems far away, Artaud can simultaneously re-enunciate the revolution and his own past. He can finally bring his relation to the Surrealists back up to the surface to retell the event. Revolution is no longer repressed, nor does it take the alternative form of the anarchistic rebellion he proposed in *Héliogabale.* Rather, revolution is told from the position of the betrayed woman, the feminine whose gap or difference from the materialistic defines the core of being. Now revolution is the sign of Artaud's renewed view of Surrealism that can be enunciated because he is far from the pernicious white men who betrayed the true revolution by making it a materialist event. Even if Surrealism maintains its Marxism against the perverse forms of Stalinism, any Marxism is a perversion for Artaud: "la révolution inventée par Marx est une caricature de la vie" (8:151). In part it is a caricature because it is a synecdoche; it is a part substituted for the whole: "La révolution de Marx a posé d'une façon technique le problème de la révolution sociale. Nous pensons, nous, que la révolution sociale n'est qu'un aspect séparé de la révolution totale . . ." (8:236). Artaud cannot accept a figure of revolution based on contiguity; the revolution must be based on a total dislocation. If Marx's revolution is a caricature, the means by which it is sustained is blasphemously unsupportable: "le Surréalisme était lui aussi devenu un parti" (8:147). As understood by the Surrealists, the Marxist revolution erects a "we" into a block, a monolithic basis for the material world. Yet this "*nous*" is a false god because the pronoun excludes what is within. This partisan revolution cannot penetrate the mind of man to which it is blind; it cannot penetrate the mind of Artaud, feminine figure in his own text, which it has excluded. And Artaud has built his being on that exclusion, a being linguistically defined by the feminine neuter at its core: "Entre le réel et moi, il y a moi, et ma déformation personnelle des fantômes de la réalité" (8:148).

The alternative to the monolith is the separation that is equally problematic to Artaud; the revolution must fight "le dédale de la science séparée" (8:154). For this fragmented maze is "une invraisemblable poussière de cultures" (8:210) from which no new unity *can* be drawn but from which a new unity *must* be drawn: "Tirer une nouvelle unité de cette poussière de cultures est une nécessité" (8:210). There lies the problem for Artaud who seeks the impossible and whose solution is the introduction of the completely other as the new source of the same. *Quid* this rebirth or renaissance?

The generative function of the alterity will lead to a text like *Les Tarahumaras,* where the figure of revolution has itself almost dissolved into a semiotics of re-turn to the signs of the earth, with its "mountain of signs" (9:35) and an incomprehensible, divine cosmology. If the project is clear, the impossibility of fulfilling it is also clear, though never avowed. It is the realization of the impossibility of the project that must be—but cannot be—founded on a new order, both real and linguistic, that is fundamental in Artaud's alienation. The "they"—initially the Mexicans and more specifically the Tarahumaras themselves—was supposed to produce a rebirth in the "we." This "they" transformed into "we" is the will to abolishing the distance of representation announced in *Le Théâtre et son double.* For Artaud, the revolution is also the common fusion, infusion, and confusion that go beyond the individual. Despite the positive announcement, no rebirth is possible.

The "they" that was to liberate finally forms the basis of the paranoid alienation whose endless graphomania we witness in the notebooks. In those works, and neither the centripetal force of the world nor the centrifugal force of the inner mind ever again affect the dominant force: the rotational force of a verbal gyre that spins around an empty, pronoun-less center.

Works Cited

Artaud, Antonin. *Oeuvres complètes.* 24 vols. Paris: Gallimard, 1961-88.

Derrida, Jacques. *L'Ecriture et la différence.* Paris: Seuil, 1967.

Garelli, Jacques. "Ontology and Madness: The Question of Clinical and 'Eidetic' Reduction." *SubStance* 39 (1983): 21-25.

Jacobs, Carol. *The Dissimulating Harmony: The Image of Interpretation in Nietzsche, Rilke, Artaud, and Benjamin.* Baltimore: Johns Hopkins, 1978.

Sollers, Philippe, ed. *Artaud.* Paris: U.G.E. [10/18], 1973.

Kathy Foley (essay date March 1992)

"Trading Art(s): Artaud, Spies, and Current Indonesian/ American Artistic Exchange and Collaboration," in *Modern Drama,* Vol. 35, No. 1, March, 1992, pp. 10-19.

[*In the following excerpt, Foley analyzes the influence of Balinese theater on Artaud's ideas about the form, function, and possibilites of his own theater.*]

In 1990-91 as part of the Festival of Indonesia, a government to government exchange of the arts, a wealth of Indonesian performance toured American cities. Over the same eighteen-month period there were an equivalent number of collaborative productions mounted by Indonesian directors, writers, choreographers, and U.S. groups (Keith Terry and I Wayan Dibia's *Body Tjak* in San Francisco and Arifin C. Noer's *Ozone* with students from the University of California at Santa Cruz), which followed the earlier collaboration between Putu Wijaya and Phillip Zarrilli in the mid-eighties. In some cases cultural roles were reversed, as at the San Francisco and Los Angeles museums where Larry Reed performed Balinese Wayang Parwa (shadow theatre) under the auspices of the Festival, while Indonesian artists were showing their avant-garde batik paintings in the foyer. P.T. Barnum's museum of curiosities. The Americans are the primitives, and the Indonesians are the moderns![1]

The questions inherent in the on-going process of artistic interaction between Indonesia and the U.S. are obvious. Are cross-culture drama, dance, and music the ultimate in cultural tourism: Club Med experiences of "the real thing" without any substantive connection to the internal stuff that codes a performance? Of is it the very reality of the arts to allow us to test the boundaries of self and other where the experience stretches us toward realizing the other is only a possibility of the self that for cultural reasons is suppressed?

There can be no definitive answers. The process of Indonesian-American cross-fertilization, while linked to older cross-cultural encounters, has only exploded in the last two decades as Americans and Indonesians have become for perhaps the first time well-trained in each other's arts and without the clear barriers of colonial relationships to impede their explorations. It will take more time to see the long term results of this work. My aim here will be to begin to chart some of the earlier history and see how models of the past may structure such Festival exchanges.

1930 Intersections

In looking for ancestors for the fusion work of today, the work of the French actor/director Antonin Artaud and the Russian-born German painter/musician Walter Spies demand acknowledgement. In addition to drawing attention to Balinese performance, they set up a number of the presuppositions that have largely prevailed in the West until the present. Among these suppositions I include (1) the sense in Balinese (and Indonesian) theatre that the arts of music, dance, and theatre fuse; (2) the belief that this is a theatre where the sacred is nigh; and (3) the idea that this is a theatre where text is minimized. Artaud propagated these ideas via writing that responded to a performance seen in Europe. Spies shared some of these ideas in his writing, but also importantly communicated his values through commissioning the prototype of what has become a significant performance genre of the Balinese.

Artaud on The Exposition Coloniale

Colonial exhibits like the one Artaud attended in July 1931[2] had from the prior century whet the appetites of European and American artists for non-Western work. Claude Debussy, hearing gamelan at the 1889 Paris World Exhibition, had introduced the sounds of gongchimes into some of his works, but the impact of the 1931 performance was on theatrical circles. Artists like Artaud, who had become disillusioned with "fourth wall" illusionism that swept over the European theatre in the first quarter of the century in the wake of Stanislavski, Chekhov, and Ibsen, saw in the masks and movement of Asian culture presented at such exhibitions, tools to shatter realistic modes. What African art was for Picasso, what Chinese theatre was for Brecht, Balinese dance was for Artaud—a way to get beyond the perceived constraints of realism.

Artaud had already primed himself, by reading material on various types of Asian performance and by seeing the Cambodian court troupe that had appeared at Marseilles in 1922; and his response to the 1931 performance inflames

to this day. "The spectacle of Balinese theater, which draws upon dance, song, pantomime—and little of the theater as we understand it in the Occident—restores the theater, by means of ceremonies of indubitable age and well-tried efficacity, to its original destiny which it presents as a combination of all these elements fused together in a perspective of hallucination and fear."[3] An aspect of Balinese performance that he prized was the synethesia of the arts. Artaud correctly sensed that the connective tissue between music, movement, and vocalization was essential to the impact of this theatre. Drums accent movements, modal scales define vocal placement, etc.

More importantly, Artaud found in this theatre the figure of the double which, for Artaud, represented life in both its creative and destructive essence. In a letter he wrote to Jean Paulhan (25 January 1936) he explained the concept in the following terms, "By this double I mean the great magical agent of which the theatre, through its forms, is only a figuration waiting to become the transfiguration."[4] While the letter was written five years later when the idea of the double was more fully formulated, it is apparent in the essay written for the October 1931 *Nouvelle Revue Française* that Artaud considers the double of central importance. He uses the term in reference to the effect of costuming, the linking of the noble characters with a more comic companion, and as an image of theatre at its moment of apotheosis. "The hieratic quality of the costumes gives each actor a double body and a double set of limbs—and the dancer bundled into his costume seems to be nothing more than his own effigy."[5] The clothing that Artaud saw would have included the wrapping of the torso and chest of refined characters in a mode that approximates swaddling with long, thin colored bands with gold overlays. This wrapping flattens and supports the upper body below the arms, allowing elbows and shoulders to maintain the high diagonals needed for the dance, and is combined with a cloth of gold skirt that sheathes the hips and thighs. For stronger characters he would have seen the dangling ribbons and cape of cloth of gold fabric over white pants and shirt characteristic of the military Baris dancer. When the refined dancer grasps the trailing yards of the cloth of gold skirt and extends its width to his side, or when the strong male Baris twirls to send his ribbons flying—the costume magnifies the dancer's movement, seeming to expand his implications toward the superhuman.

What then was the particular representation of this double that evoked Artaud's use of the term? The Barong play that ended the performance was an episode from *Arjuna's Meditation* which shows how the great hero of the *Mahabharata*, Arjuna, sits in meditation. Unmoved by the seduction of heavenly nymph, Arjuna only rises to stop an ogre named Mamangmurka (murka = passion) who has transformed into a Barong (a mythical beast). In this confrontation of Arjuna and the dragon (Barong) which represents the meditator subduing his passions, Artaud saw the double: "And behind the Warrior, bristling from the formidable cosmic tempest, is the Double who struts about, given up to the childishness of his schoolboy gibes, and who, roused by the repercussion of the turmoil, moves unaware in the midst of spells of which he has understood nothing."[6]

The "double" of the quotation above is almost certainly Artaud's interpretation of the typical clown-follower of the hero who would have appeared in this dance drama. This clown character is, by comparison with the epic character he serves, more realistic and less the "animated hieroglyph" (Artaud, p. 54) which Artaud felt in the other characters.[7]

While just a joker, the clown is paradoxically also semi-sacral. In the Wayang Parwa puppet theatre the main clown, Twalen, is considered a high god of the universe. In folk performances around the Indonesian archipelago the clown player often doubles as shaman for the troupe, as in Ludruk in East Java. In trance performances like Sintren in Java the clown player often protects the trancer and may interpret the garbled messages of the spirit world that emerge from the séance. While no one form or explanation can sum up the multitudinous aspects of clown archetype, the idea of "double" is a reasonable try. The clown, in Balinese performance, linguistically translates the Kawi experience of the hero back into mundanely understandable Balinese terms. He becomes the double that can talk the local language and clarify what the hero's epic experience might mean in current practice. Due to this translation function the hero and the play cannot exist without him. It would be as if English language plays were in Latin with the clown roughly interpolating the text in the vernacular. The heroes and their opponents eventually die and the story continues with their descendants—but the same clown lives on, appearing in every story. The clown is the traditional mediator through whom each story comes into the Balinese audience's purview.

Artaud's double is probably the central concept of his theatre. The ideas of the plague, of alchemy, and of cruelty, can be argued to be permutations of it. The double is the dark and dazzling entity that dances behind the rational surface of human existence. Artaud feels it is the central mission of theatre to allow this energy to appear and clarify itself via performance. He warns us that if this energy is suppressed it is apt to burst through in less savory manifestations. For Artaud the double is the most important discovery in the Balinese performance, for it is a pathway to the sacred.

However, field research would have forced Artaud to revise some of his initial impressions about Balinese performance. He feels, for example, that the theatre was lacking in improvisational possibilities. He implies that music dictates and circumscribes movement. He assumes that the prime creator of the performance he saw was a director who was successful in purging this theatre of words. In each instance he misses the mark *vis-à-vis* Balinese performance. Improvisation within the strict constraints of the form is central, and music follows the dancer rather than the opposite, as Artaud supposes.

Perhaps Artaud was most mistaken in his feeling that the constraints of language were finally broken in this theatre. Those who know Balinese performance will understand that the *dalang,* the puppeteer of Wayang Parwa who uses figure, dance and music in conjunction with language and story is the central performer of this society. In this puppeteer's repertoire language is indubitably the most powerful of his tools: in various charms used for opening and making the transition into certain scenes, language reaches an apotheosis, becoming a mantra. Exorcism is linked with the performer's command of sacred texts and Kawi language. Significant trance forms also reach their climax in language, since what the spirit says needs an interpreter. For the average audience member it may be that the movement, sound, and image allow for the emotional trigger. But if you ask anyone what it really means they will refer you to the puppeteer or priest, who by command of archaic language and ability to interpret that into modern language, is the empowered performer. Structurally speaking the puppeteer or priest is in some ways analogous and complementary to the clown. All are translators of the alternative reality [the story (for the dalang), the spirit (for the priest), or the hero (for the clown)] to the here and now. Language is needed to make the connection with that powerful world possible and then understandable. Communication comes in the performer's command of Kawi language, and translation comes in his command of the vernacular.

Artaud's impressions—"age-old rites," "*Gestures made to last,*" "An exorcism," "A state prior to language," "Intoxication which restores to us the very elements of ecstasy . . . Bestiality and every trace of animality are reduced to their spare gestures: mutinous noises of the splitting earth, the sap of trees, animal yawns"[8]—could today be critiqued in hindsight for their orientalist tone. In the post-Colonial milieu, Artaud would no doubt have been more politically correct in his choice of words, making sure he would not confine images of intoxication, ecstasy, and animality only to the Balinese, and recognizing the historicity and cultural specificity of the performance he saw.

But if Artaud did not follow through on the particulars, he was right on intuitions. The Balinese theatre conceptualized itself somewhat differently from European art theatre—the energy and focus of the Balinese theatre is in assessing and accessing archetypical emotional experience. Artaud was interested in playing with the primal and, in his search for the sacred, stumbled upon the Balinese model. For him it was unencumbered by its history. Nor did he seek the particular Balinese messages of religion and culture that were in the language. The theatre became for him, instead, a weapon against European realism and all its pomps and works. Music, movement, puppet, mask became ways to exorcise realism. Artaud saw a way of working—visual, sound and movement orientated—and a concept of theatre as the reality, and the world as a dim representation thereof. Despite, or perhaps because of its orientalist aspects, his essay remains a significant statement of how the Westerner is apt to conceptualize theatre of this area. Fusion of the arts and a sense of awe will be recognized, but a minimization of text is likely to prevail.

Notes

1. Performances by Westerners of traditional theatre as well as fusion pieces such as those of Julie Taymer (*Way of Snow, Tirai*) and John Emigh (*Little Red Riding Shawl*) are increasingly frequent in Indonesia (see Stephen Snow, "Intercultural Performances: The Balinese-American Model," *Asian Theatre Journal* 3, 2 [Fall, 1986], 204-232). Director Ron Jenkins, mime Leonard Pitt, and performance artist Sha Sha Higby have been affected by Indonesian work. Tours by American groups are frequent, Sekar Jaya, a San Francisco based Balinese gamelan that Terry has been associated with is preparing for its second Balinese tour in 1992. The University of Hawaii gamelan has taken performances to Indonesia on occasion, and the UCSC gamelan did a 1988 tour under the auspices of the government of West Java.

2. The program as reported in Leonard Pronko, *Theatre East and West* (Berkeley, 1967), p. 24, included Gong, Gong dance, Kebyar, Janger, Lasem, Legong, Baris, Rakshasa, and Barong. Gong and Lasem were musical. While it is difficult to establish the nature of the "Gong dance," the other pieces have recognizable names. Kebyar was a fast and dynamic sitting dance by a young male, Djanger is a popular group dance of young males and females which involves group formations and singing between episodes of solo or small group theatre performance, Legong is a court dance done by prepubescent girls, Baris is a warrior dance, Rakshasa is an ogre dance and Barong is a dance-drama in which a protective animal, analogous to the Chinese/Buddhist lion, appears in a drama of some sort. While the Balinese performers found Paris cold and alienating the economic success of the venture was apparent in the relative wealth of this gamelan on their return to Bali (Colin McPhee, *A House in Bali* [New York 1944], p. 161).

3. Antonin Artaud, trans. M.C. Richards, *The Theater and its Double* (New York, 1958), p. 53.

4. Julia Costich, *Antonin Artaud* (Boston, 1978), pp. 45, 118.

5. Artaud, p. 58.

6. Artaud, p. 67.

7. In "Artaud and the Balinese Theatre," *Modern Drama*, 28 (1985), 397-412, Patricia Clancy identifies the clown as Artaud's double but finds the use of the term strange.

8. Artaud, pp. 58, 59, 60, 62, 65-66.

Thomas Akstens (essay date 1994)

"Representation and De-realization: Artaud, Genet, and Sartre," in *Antonin Artaud and the Modern Theater*, edited by Gene A. Plunka, Fairleigh Dickinson University Press, 1994, pp. 170-82.

[*In the following essay, Akstens argues that there is a similar attempt in the work of Artaud and Jean Genet to "de-realize" accepted images and definitions of reality.*]

This paper concerns two writers who have been highly mythologized: Antonin Artaud and Jean Genet. There is an *idea* of Artaud; there is an *idea* of Genet. It is profoundly ironic that Artaud, who complained bitterly of "a rupture between things and words, between things and the ideas and signs that are their representation,"[1] has himself often been treated as an abstraction of his "theories" and his supposed persona in a manner that seems quite divorced from any actual text.[2] This may be a fate common to the writers of manifestos—the same might be said of Ezra Pound. Be that as it may, there is surely an idea of Artaud: the revolutionary conceptualist of the Theatre of Cruelty, the victim of the asylum, the brooding profile in the familiar Man Ray photograph. This abstraction of Artaud, even while it stands "ruptured" away from his text, has acquired a textuality of its own. Like it or not, the idea of Artaud informs our reading of his text; the idea of Artaud has itself become a text.[3] Likewise, there is the matter of "Sartre's Genet"—Genet the sanctified scatologist, the convict, the homosexual—an idea of Genet that has recently been subjected to critical scrutiny.[4] I will leave the task of systematic demythologizing to abler hands. My attention in this paper will be on the question of theatrical representation; Sartre's treatment of representation in Artaud and Genet will serve to focus my discussion. My purpose will be to offer a fresh appraisal of the affinities between Artaud and Genet that I believe become evident when we actually consider the function of representation in their texts—most particularly in *The Theater and Its Double* and *The Maids*.

I will begin with the observation that, in addition to the all-too-familiar Sartre's Genet, there is also a Sartre's Artaud. This Artaud—the "fellow-traveler of the Surrealists"[5]—appears in Sartre's lecture, "Myth and Reality in Theater," as a virtual antithesis to Genet. Sartre grounds his discussion of twentieth-century theater in the ostensibly polar opposition between Artaud's demand for evanescent theater and Genet's obsessive use of ceremony and ritual as a basis for his own dramaturgy.[6] Sartre delivered this lecture in 1966; he did not invent his Artaud in the same way as he might be said to have invented his Genet. It is interesting to note that, five years earlier, Jacques Guicharnaud had reaffirmed André Frank's assertion that "Artaud is 'an influence more than a presence, a presence more than a work.'"[7] Indeed, when we read "Myth and Reality," we are struck with a sense of familiarity with the absolutist Artaud who is portrayed—and ultimately remythologized—in the course of Sartre's lecture.

Sartre found in the idea of Artaud a convenient construct that suited the dialectical method of his analysis. He sees the synthesis of his dialectic in "the emergence of what we may call *critical theater* around 1950," a theater whose practitioners "are trying to convert the very inadequacies of theater into instruments for communication" (*MRT*, 137). The inadequacies Sartre discusses are primarily ontological. What is important for our immediate consideration is that Sartre's focus is squarely on the problem of theatrical representation: "This is the meaning of theater: its essential value is the representation of something which does not exist" (*MRT*, 143). The contradictions inherent in this problem appeal to Sartre, as does the idea that there is a new theater in emergence that "recongnize[s] the totally illusory character of dramatic representation . . . [and] exploit[s] it as such—as a denial of reality . . . and not as an imitation of it" (*MRT*, 149-50). "Myth and Reality in Theater" raises what we have come to identify more recently as fundamental issues of the metaphysics and semiotics of the theater and the textuality of plays.

What I wish to point out, because I believe that it is ultimately important to the question of representation in Artaud and Genet, is the method by which Sartre uses Artaud's thesis to discredit itself. Sartre identifies Artaud's thesis in the statement, "I regard theater as an act" (*MRT*, 141), and he extends it to what he assures his listeners is a logical extreme, through and beyond the contemporaneous phenomenon of *le happening*. In doing so, he presents his listeners with a reading of *The Theater and Its Double* that at least plays at consistency with Artaud's already mythologized theories. It is a reading that invites commentary—a commentary that has been implicitly provided by Derrida's provocative consideration of Artaud and "the closure of representation."[8] But when Sartre hyperextends Artaud's thesis, he arrives not at the zero point of representation, but at an essentially distinct *telos*: "the crisis of the image." The image (for which we may read "sign") survives the crisis, Sartre tells us, because it is axiomatic that "the real serves the unreal" (*MRT*, 149). In this way, Sartre's analysis is an elaborate pun on the most loaded word in the sentence he identifies as Artaud's statement of thesis. Every "act" is fundamentally an "*act*." The pun itself is a metaphor of the dialectic that is at the heart of the crisis. A "real action" is at one polarity; "something nonreal . . . the representation of the imaginary" occupies the other (*MRT*, 141).

The ostensible differences between the scheme for ***The Conquest of Mexico*** and *The Maids* or *The Balcony* would seem to match the dialectics of Sartre's analysis and would appear to serve his dichotomy between Artaud's demand for evanescent action and Genet's fascination with the practice of ritual. As Sartre himself tells us, it all appears to fit "very neatly" (*MRT*, 140). But it is interesting to note that, in Sartre's analysis, Genet is both the antithesis to Artaud and a practitioner of the "critical theater" that is the synthesis of the dialectic. Sartre's Genet is here rather like Lionel Abel's; at least the premises are the same: "We cannot have it both ways: a gain for consciousness means a loss for the reality of its objects."[9]

In actuality, Sartre's entire discussion in "Myth and Reality" is heavily dependent on a notion of theatrical experi-

ence as the net sensory effect of the specta*cle* upon the specta*tor*. His dialectic is based on the apparent contrast between the theatrical "result" that he envisions for an event like ***The Conquest of Mexico*** and a performance of a Genet play. In the cases of ***The Conquest of Mexico*** and *The Maids,* at least, Sartre's argument would have to be sustained by his own hypothesized actualizations of a theatrical text[10]—both plays remained unrealized to a degree that would require (or allow) Sartre to hypothesize. ***The Conquest of Mexico*** existed only as a literary text (in effect, as a massive stage direction), and Louis Jouvet's refusal to stage *The Maids* with a male cast radically affected the theatrical text of 17 April 1947 and of any subsequent performance. In fact, the theatrical "result" upon which Sartre bases his dialectic may be seen as substantially a product of his own hypotheses.

The dichotomy that Sartre postulated between Artaud and Genet has been influential; I have attempted to show how it was constructed and its function in his treatment of the problem of representation in postwar theater. But others, like Guicharnaud, have seen affinities between Artaud's "theories" and Genet's theatrical practice.[11] Robert Brustein, in a book published two years before "Myth and Reality," advanced an Artaudian reading of Genet—a reading that was the subject of a curt dismissal in one of the more important recent studies of Genet's semiotics.[12] Granted that Brustein's methodology now seems dated and that his consideration of the affinities between Artaud and Genet ultimately becomes muddled when he brings Pirandello into the discussion, it is still true that he emphasizes something important that other readers have seemed to discount. Artaud, the "theorist," is also a superb fabulist.

Reading "The Theater and the Plague," Brustein makes an interesting assertion: "Artaud, in fact, uses this analogy [of the abscess] in the same way he would use the theater—as an image-producing agency instead of as a literal fact."[13] The notion that the writer who railed against the "rupture between things and the ideas and signs that are their representation" would traffic in analogies and employ the theater as a medium to produce images may seem paradoxical. But we must remember that a few pages later Artaud elucidates what he means when he tells us that the theater has a "double": "Every real effigy has a shadow which is its double. . . . The theater, which is in *no thing,* but makes use of everything—gestures, sounds, words, screams, light, darkness—rediscovers itself at precisely the point where the mind requires a language to express its manifestations" (*TD,* 12). These shadows have power, and Brustein was correct to call our attention to the metaphoric power of Artaud's text.[14] What Artaud's text tells us is that theater is forced into existence by the demand of the mind for *manifestation,* for images of the compelling shadows. What the text also tells us is that Artaud does not despise representation. What he despises are "*false* shadows" (*TD,* 12, emphasis mine), culturally contrived significations and arbitrary *mis*-representations.

Artaud concludes his preface to *The Theater and Its Double* with another metaphor:

> And if there is still one hellish, truly accursed thing in our time, it is our artistic dallying with forms, instead of being like victims burnt at the stake, signaling through the flames.
>
> (*TD*, 13)

Artaud writes with passion, but he is not an absolutist when it comes to the question of representation. He employs metaphoric representation in his own texts, and it seems that he does so specifically at those moments in his writing when the shadow of the theater he desires enforces its demand for manifestation most urgently. Even in his scenario for ***The Conquest of Mexico,*** Artaud repeatedly resorts to metaphor to convey his vision of the spectacle: "Everything trembles and groans, like a shop window in a hurricane" (*TD*, 128-29). And the spectacle itself is a vortex of "images" (*TD*, 128) and "signs" in which action is transformed into "a genuine physical language" (*TD*, 124). In Artaud's projection of ***The Conquest of Mexico,*** the *mise-en-scène* effectively becomes the text, but the physical poetry of movement, sound, and light is endowed with representational value as an immediate manifestation of "the reality of imagination and dreams" and of "primitive Myths" (*TD*, 123). Moreover, the chaotic spectacle of the *mise-en-scène* has an explicit metaphoric correspondence to what Artaud saw as the "moral disorder" of colonialism, both historically and in his own time (*TD*, 127).

It is ironic that Sartre, who gave us an absolutist reading of Artaud in "Myth and Reality," also provided us with a key to the methodology we require to consider the actual affinity between the function of representation in Artaud's writings and Genet's theater. We discover the key in Sartre's earlier essay on *The Maids.*

The framework of this methodology is to be found in one of Sartre's most formidable verbal constructs: "theatrical procedure."[15] With his invention of this phrase, Sartre turns our attention to the process of what happens in the theater; he places us in the immediacy of the event itself. This is a completely different approach to the textuality of the theater than the one we see in "Myth and Reality," where theater is considered as a "result," or product—as the net sensory effect of the event upon the audience. Sartre's phrase also implies that there is at least a potential for the institutionalization of the process through which any theatrical text is actualized; a "procedure" may become conventionalized. This framework directs our attention to the metaphysics of the theatrical text in the process of *becoming* and, in the context of Sartre's discussion, calls our attention to representation as one of the vehicles that establish the reflexive correspondence between the writer and the audience that allows the text to *become.*

Sartre concludes his paragraph with this gloss on Genet's "algebra of the imagination": "Anything can be a woman: a flower, an animal, an inkwell" (*M*, 10). I am reminded of Borges's admonition, "If literature were nothing but verbal algebra, anyone could produce any book simply by practic-

ing variations."[16] We have a glimpse of both writers at the moment of their confrontation with the inexhaustibility of representation. Sartre tells us that for Genet, who "wishes from the very start to *strike at the root of the apparent*" (*M*, 8), a man can be a woman, or a tin knife can be a penis—that "as the distance increases between itself and what it signifies, the symbolic nature of the sign is heightened" (*M*, 11). And it is at this point that Sartre discloses the key itself: his notion of "de-realization."

It is necessary to emphasize that Sartre's exposition of de-realization here is enclosed within the framework established by his phrase "theatrical procedure." De-realization is not an effect or a device of theatrical rhetoric. De-realization is an integral element of the process of Genet's theater, and it involves everyone who is engaged in the process—Genet, the audience, and even actors themselves, as "the shock boomerangs" (*M*, 11). Sartre postulates de-realization as a state of cognitive anarchy, deliberately provoked in the audience and on the stage by the strategies of the playwright—in this specific instance by crossgendered representation. It is as if Genet has found the perfect way to celebrate "the falsehood of the stage" (*M*, 8). In the crossgendered performance of *The Maids* that Sartre envisions, and which both he and Odette Aslan contend that Genet wanted,[17] the dissociative action of de-realization is simultaneously the dominant mode of representation and the process by which the theatrical text is actualized.

When Genet wrote in 1954 of the "failure" of the 1947 production of *The Maids,* he appeared to refer to his capitulation to Jouvet on the issue of the gender of the actors. The basis for his complaint is that "the Western actor does not seek to become a sign charged with signs," and he contends that he was frustrated in his effort to "do away with characters . . . to the advantage of signs as remote as possible from what they are meant to signify. . . ." As Sartre suggested, the remoteness of the sign is the source of its energy, of what Genet refers to here as its "displacement." Genet tells us that his characters were to "be only the metaphors of what they were supposed to represent," and he is openly contemptuous of the "air of masquerade" in Western theater.[18]

The representation of character in *The Maids* is not a masquerade. It is the "displacement" of the familiar patterns of cognitive association that attend character representation and, in this way, is the essence of the de-realization. In a lucid discussion of crossgendered representation in Lyly, Jonson, and Shakespeare, Phyllis Rackin has called attention to the "subversive power of theatrical representation," suggesting that theatrical cross-dressing is inherently dissociative.[19] Rackin, and before her the controversial Jan Kott, contested the notion that Elizabethan boy actors were so skilled as female impersonators and that the convention itself was so entrenched, that the audience unflinchingly accepted the representative illusion. In her consideration of *As You Like It*, Rackin contends that an illusory masquerade was not the point, that Rosalind's carefully contrived layering of gender identities had subversive political implications.[20] Kott, who saw affinities between Shakespeare's comedies and "Genet's brutal poetry,"[21] was greeted with suspicion in the 1960s when he suggested that Shakespeare deliberately played upon his audience's conscious awareness that Rosalind was, first of all, a young man. But Rackin's analysis at least implicitly vindicates the idea. Both discussions appear to acknowledge that these Elizabethan representations of women by boys might *now* be considered to have functioned as Sartrean de-realizations only to the extent that the audience was overtly aware of the "mis"-representation and the "sustained contradiction"[22] of the male body in female clothing and only to the extent that the audience was also made aware of its own resultant social, political, or gender anxiety.

Sartre makes a great deal of the passage in *Our Lady of the Flowers* where the narrative voice declares that the audience of his crossgendered play would be continuously reminded by placards that the actresses on the stage were adolescent boys.[23] The audience's anxiety—and Sartre suggests, the anxiety of the players themselves—would be intensified by the arrogance of this gesture, which calls attention to the very gratuitousness (I am deliberately using Artaud's terminology)[24] of the crossgendered representation. In a crossgendered performance of *The Maids*, the male gender of the actors is irrelevant in every sense to the internal structural integrity of the dramatic action.[25] Any possibility of dramatic irony is deliberately precluded. The portrayals are manifestly baseless and false and, for Genet, both theatrically and erotically charged *because* of the falseness and uselessness of the image. It is the tension between the masculine body and its feminine apparel that empowers the image as a "sign charged with signs" and a source of anxiety for the audience. As Genet notes on the first page of *The Thief's Journal,* "My excitement is the oscillation from one to the other"[26]—from the male physicality of his fellow convicts to their uniforms, which suggest flowers to him. Similarly, Our Lady is "naked under the silk" of his dress; "he doesn't give a damn that they see he has a hard-on."[27]

This degree of overt "displacement," which seeks to display arrogantly its own erotic and dissociative potential, may seem quite far removed from either Rackin's or Kott's reading of *As You Like It.* I believe that this is the case because Genet takes us beyond subversion to the point of anarchy. If, as Rackin contends, "the actor [and particularly the transvestic actor] . . . trangresses the social and ontological categories that keep the world an orderly place,"[28] then Genet's phallic Claire allows his audience no hope of refuge in either familiar patterns of psychological association or a secure social hierarchy:

> Hand me the towel! Hand me the clothespins! Peel the onions! Scrape the carrots! Scrub the tiles! It's over. Over. Ah! I almost forgot! Turn off the tap! It's over. [*Exalted*] I'll run the world!
>
> (*M,* 62)

Genet's Claire and Solange bear no relation to any archetype of the androgyne as an embodiment of prelapsarian perfection; they are Saturnalian figures of misrule—sometimes rampant, but always at least implicitly threatening.[29]

With this in mind, it may be productive to make note of the contrast between Claire and Song Liling, whose very presence on the stage in David Henry Hwang's 1988 play, *M. Butterfly,* is essential to that play's deconstruction of Western culture as "a world of surfaces."[30] Unlike *The Maids, M. Butterfly* employs dramatic irony as a fundamental structural device; the audience's knowledge of Song Liling's male gender is ultimately turned against itself. Dramatic irony, more than Sartrean de-realization, becomes Hwang's vehicle of deconstruction—because, in any conventional technical sense, dramatic irony necessarily involves the collective complicity of the audience. The audience's voyeuristic fascination with the spectacle of a man who is a woman becoming a man at the end of Act 2 stands as an incrimination of its own decadent and exploitative cultural values. Genet, on the other hand, can allow no possibility of dramatic irony concerning the gender of his actors because he cannot admit the possibility of complicity with his audience. The de-realization that is evident in *The Maids* is a provocation and a gesture of defiance.

Sartre also makes the point in his essay on *The Maids* that "Genet prefers imaginary murder to real murder" (*M,* 24). As Genet himself put it in a 1976 interview, "There are literary categories and categories of experience. The idea of murder can be very beautiful. An actual murder is something else."[31] It is well known that in his own explanation of the Theatre of Cruelty, Artaud warned that "the word 'cruelty' must be taken in a broad sense," that it was not to be considered literally as the "gratuitous pursuit of physical suffering" (*TD,* 101-2). The "cruelty" of Artaud's manifesto is, in actuality, a representation itself: "From the point of view of the mind, cruelty *signifies* rigor, implacable intention and decision, irreversible and absolute determination" (*TD,* 101; emphasis mine). What is equally remarkable in terms of our consideration of representation is Artaud's suggestion in "The Theater and Cruelty" that "the image of a crime presented in the requisite theatrical conditions is something infinitely more terrible for the spirit than that same crime when actually committed" (*TD,* 85).

It is interesting enough that these texts appear to be coincident. Even more interesting is the fact that *idea* of Artaud to which I referred at the beginning of this paper does not prepare us to consider the extent to which Artaud actually employed representation and acknowledged its power. I have already suggested that I believe that Artaud resorted to metaphoric representation when he had to make the shadow of his theater evident. The clearest example of this, of course, is in his fable of the plague.

Artaud's fable begins with the sentence, "Once the plague is established in a city, the regular forms collapse," and concludes with the "surge of erotic fever" and necrophilia he recounts on the following page (*TD,* 23-24). As with any fable, the narrative illustrates a point that is essentially a moral lesson. Artaud concludes his fable with the suggestion that "perhaps we can determine the value of this gratuitousness . . ." (*TD,* 24), and he appears to find his moral several pages later: ". . . the action of theater, like that of plague, is beneficial, for, impelling men to see themselves as they are, it causes the mask to fall, reveals the lie . . ." (*TD,* 31). The moral of the fable—that the theater destroys the pervasive "hypocrisy" of a "slippery world" (*TD,* 31-32)—emerges from the metaphoric correspondence between the theater and the plague that is inherent within the fable itself. The rhetorical structure of Artaud's narrative of the plague is decidedly analogical.

The plague tears away the mask of false representation and reveals not simply the truth of chaos, but the truth of an image: the theater is *like* the plague. And within the narrative itself, the plague engenders the theater. The chaos of the mob—which has been provoked by disease and madness—in turn provokes a text into being. The dissociative actions of arson, sodomy, and murder change the mob into its own audience (as well as *act*ors) and cause its own anarchy (which is ostensibly evanescent) to become institutionalized in the form of the theater. Indeed, Artaud calls at the end of his essay for the establishment of a new theater. The theater that has been engendered by the anarchy of the plague and created in an explosion of false images is apparently capable of endurance.

As in the case of a crossgendered performance of *The Maids,* the dissociative action that is given metaphoric form in Artaud's fable of the plague has the potential to become conventionalized as "theatrical procedure"—as a process by which a theatrical text is brought into being. There is an affinity in function between Artaud's "warrior hero [who] sets fire to the city he once risked his life to save" (*TD,* 24) and the young man who is Claire, who is Solange, who is Claire, who is Madame, who is himself.[32] Both are de-realized, and both are agents of de-realization. In both cases, de-realization destroys false images, liberates "extreme gestures" (*TD,* 27), and reveals the truth of the actor.

The effect of de-realization in a crossgendered performance of *The Maids,* according to Sartre, is that "the pantomime of a young male who pretends to be a woman *seems to* [the audience] *to be the truth*" (*M,* 30). Sartre characterized de-realization as a state of cognitive anarchy in which "the volatile unity of the being of non-being and the non-being of being is achieved in semi-darkness, this perfect and perverse instant . . . the moment of evil" (*M,* 30). Likewise, the theater that is born of chaos in Artaud's fable "reforges the chain between what is and what is not." It is a theater in which "before our eyes is fought a battle of symbols," a theater that exists "only from the moment when the impossible really begins . . ." (*TD,* 27-28).

There are challenging similarities between the sensory and psychological "virtual revolt" (*TD,* 28) that Artaud envi-

sions at the core of his theater, which is "born out of a kind of organized anarchy" (*TD,* 51), and the process of de-realization that Sartre contends is basic to a fully actualized text of *The Maids.* De-realization in *The Maids* originates with a deliberately "displaced" representation— and with our anxious sense not only of the jarring incongruity of the representation, but also of the truth of that incongruity. As Artaud's plague infects the city and disorders it with crime and madness, the theater is liberated to reveal the truth of its own "delirium" (*TD,* 27). Both theaters discover their textuality through a process that subverts conventional patterns of associational and representational correspondence. And while I do not suggest that my reading begins to exhaust the possibilities of such a highly charged text, it seems apparent to me that "The Theater and the Plague" gives metaphoric expression to a state of cognitive anarchy in the theater that is very like Sartre's notion of de-realization. What I am quite sure of is that the conundrum of a young *man* ". . . wearing a slip . . . standing with her back to the dressing table" (*M,* 35) and "the dandy [who] decks himself out in his finest clothes and promenades before the charnel houses" (*TD,* 24) are both true images of what Artaud showed us to be "the anarchistic principle of all genuine poetry" (*TD,* 125).

Notes

1. Antonin Artaud, *The Theater and Its Double,* trans. Mary Caroline Richards (New York: Grove Press, 1958), 7. Subsequent citations are made in the text, using the abbreviation *TD.*

2. Jacques Derrida was correct to point out that "[Artaud's] texts are more *solicitations* than sums of precepts"; see note 8. Jane Goodall's reading of "the association of revelation with abomination in Artaudian theater" represents a departure from the treatment of Artaud's texts purely as documents of "theory." See "The Plague and Its Powers in Artaudian Theatre," *Modern Drama* 33, no. 4 (1990): 529—42.

3. In this respect, Julia F. Costich's *Antonin Artaud* (Boston: Twayne, 1978) is typical of a number of quasi-biographical treatments of Artaud: ". . . [Artaud's] life has the qualities of a text" (107).

4. Una Chaudhuri comments negatively on the pervasive influence of "Sartre's Genet" in her *No Man's Stage: A Semiotic Study of Jean Genet's Major Plays* (Ann Arbor, Mich.: UMI Research Press, 1986), 2-7.

5. Jean-Paul Sartre, "Myth and Reality in Theater," in *Sartre on Theater,* ed. Michel Contat and Michel Rybalka, trans. Frank Jellinek (New York: Pantheon Books, 1976), 143. Subsequent citations are made in the text, using the abbreviation *MRT.*

6. Gene A. Plunka has argued that Artaud's theater was also highly ritualistic. See *Peter Shaffer: Roles, Rites, and Rituals in the Theater* (Rutherford, N.J.: Fairleigh Dickinson University Press; London and Toronto: Associated University Presses, 1988),

42-46. See also Susan Sontag, "Approaching Artaud," in *Under the Sign of Saturn* (New York and London: Doubleday, 1991), 54.

7. Jacques Guicharnaud, with June Beckelman, *Modern French Theater: From Giraudoux to Beckett* (New Haven: Yale University Press, 1961), 224.

8. Jacques Derrida, "The Theater of Cruelty and the Closure of Representation," in *Writing and Difference,* trans. Alan Bass (Chicago: University of Chicago Press, 1978), 232-50.

9. Lionel Abel, *Metatheater: A New View of Dramatic Form* (New York: Hill and Wang, 1963), 78.

10. My use of the terminology "theatrical text" and "literary text" to clarify the textuality of performance is adapted from Marco De Marinis's article, "Dramaturgy of the Spectator," *TDR* 31 (1987): 100–112.

11. The reference is to Guicharnaud's discussion of Genet: "Following the theories of Antonin Artaud . . ." (169). But the question of the direct influence of Artaud on Genet remains problematical. See Robert Brustein, *The Theatre of Revolt: An Approach to the Modern Drama* (Boston: Little, Brown and Co., 1964), particularly his note, 378. See also Laura Oswald, *Jean Genet and the Semiotics of Performance* (Bloomington and Indianapolis: Indiana University Press, 1989), xiv-xv and 131, and Ronald Hayman, *Artaud and After* (Oxford: Oxford University Press, 1977), 153.

12. Chaudhuri, *Semiotic Study,* 4.

13. Brustein, *Theatre of Revolt,* 370.

14. Goodall's reading of *The Theater and Its Double* also acknowledges the metaphoric vitality of Artaud's texts: "Artaud's writings on theater abound with metaphors of awakening" (540).

15. Jean Genet, *The Maids and Deathwatch,* introd. Jean-Paul Sartre, trans. Bernard Frechtman (New York: Grove Press, 1962), 10. Subsequent citations are made in the text, using the abbreviation *M.*

16. Jorge Luis Borges, *Other Inquisitions: 1937-1952,* trans. Ruth L. C. Simms (Austin: University of Texas Press, 1965), 164.

17. See Aslan's "Genet, His Actors and Directors," in *Genet: A Collection of Critical Essays,* ed. Peter Brooks and Joseph Halpern (Englewood Cliffs, N.J.: Prentice-Hall, 1979), 146-55.

18. Jean Genet, "A Note on Theatre," *TDR* 7, no. 3 (1963): 37–38.

19. Phyllis Rackin, "Androgyny, Mimesis, and the Marriage of the Boy Heroine on the English Renaissance Stage," *PMLA* 102 (1987): 35.

20. Camille Paglia's reading of the play is apparently self-contradictory on this point: "The use of virtuoso boy actors in all female roles conditioned Elizabethan playgoers to a suspension of sexual disbelief. The textual ambiguities of the transvestite comedies would be heightened by the presence of boys in the lead roles"; see *Sexual Personae: Art and Decadence from Nefertiti to Emily Dickinson* (1990; reprint, New York: Vintage Books, 1991), 204-5. Rosalind's gender status has attracted the attention of many of the recent practitioners of cultural theory. For two of these perspectives, see Marjorie Garber, *Vested Interests: Cross-dressing and Cultural Anxiety* (New York and London: Routledge, 1992), 36-40 and 71–77, and Stephen Greenblatt, *Shakespearean Negotiations: The Circulation of Social Energy in Renaissance England* (Berkeley and Los Angeles: University of California Press, 1988), 66-93.

21. Jan Kott, *Shakespeare Our Contemporary* (1964; reprint, New York: W. W. Norton & Co., 1974), 229.

22. The phrase is Sartre's (*M,* 9).

23. See Jean Genet, *Our Lady of the Flowers,* trans. Bernard Frechtman (New York: Grove Press, 1963), 221.

24. Artaud, *TD,* 24-25.

25. By contrast, Diouf's gender crossing in *The Blacks* is subject to the internal logic of the action.

26. Jean Genet, *The Thief's Journal,* trans. Bernard Frechtman (New York: Grove Press, 1964), 9.

27. Genet, *Our Lady of the Flowers,* 219.

28. Rackin, "Boy Heroine," 35.

29. Both Rackin and Kott give some treatment to the complex sociocultural implications of crossdressing, which are sometimes liturgical or shamanistic, sometimes subversive. See also Paglia, 44-47 and 89-92. My reading of Genet's phallic Claire is clearly at odds with Garber's Lacanian generalization that "the theatrical transvestite literalizes the anxiety of phallic loss" (356). In the case of this representation, the phallus itself, "displaced" beneath the dress, is a source of anxiety for the audience.

30. David Henry Hwang, *M. Butterfly* (New York: Plume, 1989), 100. Robert Skloot discusses the cultural and gender politics of the play in "Breaking the Butterfly: The Politics of David Henry Hwang," *Modern Drama* 33 (1990): 59–66.

31. "I Allow Myself to Revolt: Jean Genet Interviewed by Hubert Fichte," in Brooks and Halpern, eds., 183.

32. Goodall refers to the miser, the sodomite, and the parricide in Artaud's fable as "denatured" (534), a term that invites comparison with Genet's "displaced" and Sartre's "de-realized."

Leonard R. Koos (essay date 1994)

"Comic Cruelty: Artaud and Jarry," in *Antonin Artaud and the Modern Theater,* edited by Gene A. Plunka, Fairleigh Dickinson University Press, 1994, pp. 37-50.

[In the following essay, Koos argues that Alfred Jarry strongly influenced Artaud's concept of comedy and of its importance to the theater of cruelty.]

> Our speaking on the theme of comedy will appear almost a libertine proceeding to one, while the other will think that the speaking of it seriously brings us into violent conflict with the subject.
>
> —George Meredith, *An Essay on Comedy*

> By providing us with the lovely illusion of human greatness, the tragic brings us consolation. The comic is crueler: it brutally reveals the meaninglessness of everything.
>
> —Milan Kundera, *The Art of the Novel*

In a characteristically outrageous moment in the classic Marx Brothers' film *Monkey Business* (1931), Groucho, being chased by the ship's captain, enters a cabin, interrupts an argument between a gangster and his wife by announcing that he is the tailor, and proceeds to disappear into the walk-in closet. In the subsequent scene, first with the gangster's wife then with the gangster himself, Groucho alternately plays, in the space of a few minutes, the part of a lawyer, a guitar player, a cheating husband, a tango dancer, an outraged husband, a hero, a housewife, a teacher, and a child. His evasionary tactics prove so successful that, rather than getting shot for having been found in a compromising position with the gangster's wife, he is offered a job as the gangster's bodyguard. It is certainly this sort of scene, replete with its anarchical articulation of character and dialogue, that attracted the attention of the French avant-garde theorist and playwright Antonin Artaud. So impressed was Artaud by the Marx Brothers' film, *Monkey Business,* and its predecessor, *Animal Crackers* (1930), that he included in an appendix to his seminal collection of essays, *Le Théâtre et son double,* a short note on the American comedians.[1] This note offers itself as a useful point of departure for examining the role that comedy plays in the subsequent Artaudian conceptions of theater.

Artaud's enthusiastic commentary on the Marx Brothers contextualizes their work in the landscape of the European avant-garde with the residual identification of their films as authentically surrealist (this assertation, however, would seem to be tinged with political overtones as Artaud began to stray from André Breton and the surrealist group by late 1926).[2] In turn, this surrealist essense exemplifies a poetic state that Artaud, in a redefinitional operation that recalls his previous reworkings of the conventional images of the plague, alchemy and cruelty, associates with the particular brand of comedy found in the Marx Brothers' films:

> La qualité poétique d'un film comme *Animal Crackers* pourrait répondre à la définition de l'humour, si ce mot n'avez pas depuis longtemps perdu son sens de libération intégrale, de déchirement de toute réalité dans l'esprit.

> (The poetic quality of a film like *Animal Crackers* would fit the definition of humor if this word had not

long since lost its sense of essential liberation, of destruction of all reality of the mind.)[3]

The affinities between this brand of supposedly original and primitive humor and Artaud's prescriptions elsewhere for theatrical form are striking. Comedy, then, is a deadly serious business. As Artaud refines his definition of this type of humor, in which one recognizes the existing traditions of the farce and the grotesque, its generic precision becomes thwarted by the emergent disjunctive hybrid that monstrously fuses comedy with elements of tragedy:

> . . . il faudrait ajouter à l'humour la notion d'un quelque chose d'inquiétant et de tragique, d'une fatalité (ni heureuse ni malheureuse, mais difficile à formuler) qui se glisserait derrière lui comme la révélation d'une maladie atroce sur le profil d'une absolue beauté.
>
> (*TE*, 214)

> (. . . you would have to add to humor the notion of something disquieting and tragic, a fatality [not happy nor unhappy, but difficult to formulate] which would hover over it like the cast of an appalling malady upon an exquisitely beautiful profile.)
>
> (*TA*, 142-43)

Reminiscent of the aesthetic paroxysm Artaud saw in the plague, the Marx Brothers' humor exhibits a primordial potential for disrupting the ordering systems of conventional albeit arbitrary relations in society and language. These relationships, which the prefatory essay of *Le Théâtre et son double* has already characterized as shadowless because they have radically separated systems of thought from existence, are unmasked and discarded by the intrusive humoristic weapon. Humor bubbles up from the shadows and destroys any possible relevance of the systems of thought that cerebrally construct notions of reality. This kind of humor, quintessentially poetic, comprises a sort of vital energy that "tend toujours à une espèce d'anarchie bouillante, à une désintégration intégrale du réel par la poésie" (*TE*, 216) ("leads toward a kind of boiling anarchy, an essential disintegration of the real by poetry" [*TA,* 144]).[4]

The casual reader of the essays of *Le Théâtre et son double* might be tempted to dismiss the remarks Artaud makes in discussing the humor of the Marx Brothers as at best tangential and perhaps even antithetical to such conceptions so seemingly far removed from the realm of the comic as, for example, the plague or cruelty. In the major essays of the collection, neither in the occasional references to existing plays nor in the proposed programs for the Theatre of Cruelty are comedies of any sort mentioned. And yet Artaud's conception of humor articulated explicitly in his commentary on the Marx Brothers anticipates a number of ideas that he would develop in his work for the Theatre of Cruelty.

The concept of cruelty that dominates Artaud's two manifestos for the theater he had planned to establish as early as 1932 and realized with a single production of his own play, *Les Cenci,* in 1935 has often confounded readers. In a later essay included in the volume, "Le Théâtre et la Cruauté," Artaud comes closest to providing a definition of this concept: "Tout ce qui agit est une cruauté" (*TE,* 132) ("Everything that acts is a cruelty" [*TA,* 85]). When applied to the theater, reviving the etymological origin of the "drama" as action, the fundamental dynamism of cruelty becomes preeminently exploited in order to renew theatrical form and imbue the theatrical experience with regenerative qualities. The distillation of action in theatrical cruelty, then, for Artaud, must embrace the virtual violence and destruction in all action in effecting this regeneration. This violence, with its attendant implications of catastrophe and chaos, provides the contextual frame within which Artaud considers the option of humor in the first manifesto for the Theatre of Cruelty.

A key terminological cluster in the two manifestos centers around the idea of dissonance—linguistic, spatial, visual, acoustic, and so on—which, in its inherent mobility, appropriately translates cruelty into the theatrical medium. Dissociation, deformation, disruption, debauchery, and destruction all exhibit a particular degree of dissonance and therefore can be reasonably included in the total spectacle of theatrical cruelty. Humor, in the first manifesto, is appreciated by Artaud precisely for its dissonant and destructive nature, for its dual suggestion of creation and chaos:

> Et l'humour avec son anarchie, la poésie avec son symbolisme et ses images, donnent comme une première notion des moyens de canaliser la tentation de ces idées.
>
> (*TE,* 139)

> (And humor with its anarchy, poetry with its symbolism and its images, furnish a basic notion of ways to channel the temptation of these ideas).
>
> (*TA,* 90)

Humor, again like poetry in the note on the Marx Brothers, then, has the power to cast metaphysical shadows onto the spectator who, having witnessed the "destruction anarchique, productrice d'une prodigieuse volée de formes" (*TE,* 142) ("anarchistic destruction generating a prodigious flight of forms" [*TA,* 92]), will undergo a purge that will strip away the psychological and social shell that society has imposed. This purge will result in "remettre en cause organiquement l'homme, ses idées sur la réalité et sa place poétique dans la réalité" (*TE,* 142) ("organically reinvolving man, his ideas about reality, and his poetic place in reality" [*TA,* 92]). This purge, as Eric Sellin has noted,[5] irrevocably diverges from Aristotle's conception of catharsis in classical tragedy precisely on this point of method of its realization. Humor, in fact, throughout the first manifesto, remains perhaps the most effective of instruments for establishing theatrical cruelty due to its dangerously subversive virtuality: ". . . L'HUMOUR-DESTRUCTION, par le rire, peut servir à lui concilier les habitudes de la raison" (*TE,* 140) (". . . HUMOR AS DESTRUCTION can serve to reconcile the corrosive nature of laughter to the habits of reason" [*TA,* 91][6]). In

this way, perhaps more effectively than any other method in the arsenal of the Theatre of Cruelty, humor as an everyday phenomenon that surreptitiously couples itself with the structures of reason and rationality incarnates the sought-after subversion of the systems of language and society to which Artaud's theater ultimately aspires, an aspiration whose result would reside in a transcendent realm of purity and eternal forces.[7]

The genesis of Artaud's ideas on comedy made in the various essays of *Le Théâtre et son double* can be directly traced to his theatrical activity and experiments of the decade previous to the publication of that seminal volume.[8] Of the plays Artaud authored, the comic genres play an ongoing role in the experimental scenarios of this period. The early play, *Le Jet de sang* (*The Fountain of Blood,* 1923), consistent with the dadaist and surrealist penchant for black humor,[9] contains a parody of Shakespeare's *Romeo and Juliet,* as well as a number of allusions to Guillaume Apollinaire's 1917 absurdist, protosurrealist farce, *Les Mamelles de Tirésias* (*The Breasts of Tiresias*).[10] In the scenario for *La Pierre philosophale* (*The Philosopher's Stone,* 1931), Artaud combined elements of the commedia dell'arte with those of the grotesque. Harlequin, having been caught in a compromising position with the Doctor's wife, is clinically dismembered by him in his laboratory, only to reassemble himself magically in the night and return to the wife. Both of these examples illustrate Artaud's interest in radicalizing comic form which, while decontextualizing existing traditions, attempts to distill its essence of anarchy and destruction and whose closest contemporary model would be that of the absurdist farce.

The culmination of Artaud's theatrical endeavors in the 1920s came in his association with the founding and subsequent productions of the short-lived Théâtre Alfred Jarry. Founded in late 1926 with Robert Aron and Roger Vitrac, the Théâtre Alfred Jarry provided Artaud with a practical as well as theatrical forum for the development of his dramatic aesthetic. Not surprisingly, the comic plays a significant role in the theater's conjectural orientation, as well as in its eventual productions. Once again, a particular brand of comedy is evoked, as the Théâtre Alfred Jarry's brochure for the 1926-27 season notes: "Comique ou tragique, notre jeu ne sera l'un de ces jeux dont à un moment donné on rit jaune"[11] ("Comic or tragic, our play will be one in which at any moment one will offer a sickly smile"). As with the later Theatre of Cruelty, the Théâtre Alfred Jarry attempted to position itself in the avant-garde landscape, explicitly breaking with existing conventions and seeking to reevaluate the role of theater through the theatrical experience: "Le Théâtre Alfred Jarry a été créé pour se servir du théâtre et non pour le servir" (*O,* 29) ("The Théâtre Alfred Jarry was created in order to use theater and not serve it"). Its first season's program proposed a number of selections from Jarry and Vitrac (in reality, the first program of the Théâtre Alfred Jarry, which took place on 1 and 2 June 1927, consisted of Roger Vitrac's *Les Mystères de l'amour,* a now lost musical sketch by Artaud entitled *Ventre brûlé, ou la mère folle* [*Burned Belly or the Mad Mother*], and a play by Robert Aron under the pseudonym Max Rebour: *Gigogne*). On 19 January 1928, the second presentation of the Théâtre Alfred Jarry included, along with the Paris premiere of V. I. Pudovkin's film, *Mother,* a version of the third act of Paul Claudel's *Partage de midi*. Announced on the program as an "acte inédit d'un écrivain 'notaire' joué sans l'autorisation de l'auteur"[12] ("unpublished act of a noted writer played without the author's permission"), the third act of Claudel's play, in theatrical terms somewhat traditional and decidedly not avant-garde, was played as an absurdist farce, punctuated with disruptive shouts and cries, which ultimately provoked its audience.[13] Following the next two productions of the Théâtre Alfred Jarry, the first of Strindberg's *Dream Play* on 2 and 9 June 1928 and the second of Vitrac's *Victor ou les enfants au pouvoir* on 24 and 29 December 1928 and again on 5 January 1929, a statement was produced by the theater company in 1930 that sought to respond not only to the hostility on the part of critics and audiences alike, but also to clarify the position and goals of the financially floundering Théâtre Alfred Jarry. In this pamphlet, the reader finds perhaps the most explicit remarks from Artaud and his collaborators on the subject of humor:

> L'humour sera la seule lanterne verte ou rouge qui éclairera les drames et signalera au spectateur si la voie est libéré ou fermée, s'il est convenable de crier ou de se taire, de rire tout haut ou tout bas. Le Théâtre Alfred Jarry compte devenir le théâtre de tous les rires.
>
> (*O*, 44)

> (Humor will be the only green or red light that will illuminate the dramas and signal to the audience if the path is open or closed, if it is proper to shout or keep quiet, to laugh out loud or to oneself. The Théâtre Alfred Jarry counts on becoming the theater of all laughter.)

Humor and the barometer of its resulting laughter, then, is propounded here for its ability to activate its audience, not unlike certain elements of Brecht's epic theater, and to link fundamentally the performative and receptive poles of the theatrical experience. As an instrument for realizing "l'actualité entendue dans tous les sens" (*O*, 44) ("the actuality understood in all of its meanings"), humor becomes the pathway to "'le rire absolu,' le rire qui va de l'immobilité baveuse à la grande secousse des larmes" (*O*, 44) ("the absolute laughter, the laughter that goes from the dribbling immobility to the great shock of tears"). This radicalized view, which already evinces a particular turn towards a ritualized theater, goes so far as to state that all the efforts of the Théâtre Alfred Jarry "vise très exactement à préciser expérimentalement cette notion de l'humour" (*O*, 44) ("very exactly aims at specifying experimentally this notion of humor"). Logic or any other criteria exterior to the dynamics of the theatrical experience, this portion of the pamphlet concludes, are doomed to misapprehend the nature of the plays produced by the Théâtre Alfred Jarry.

In another passage in the 1930 pamphlet for the Théâtre Alfred Jarry, its authors mention several influences that mark an avowed heritage for the theater company. Among the allusions that include Elizabethan theater, Chekhov, Strindberg, Feydeau, and Roussel, none stands more prominently than the playwright whose name had been chosen to inaugurate the theater: "Quant à l'esprit qui le dirige, il participe à l'enseignement humoristique inégalé d'*Ubu roi* . . ." (*O*, 45-46) ("Regarding the spirit that guides it, it participates in the humoristic teachings of *Ubu Roi*"). Although Artaud never actually produced a work of Jarry's for the stage,[14] the shadow cast by the fin de siècle playwright's absurdist masterpiece, *Ubu roi,* informs on a number of Artaud's fragments of a theory of comedy.

In the careers of both Antonin Artaud and Alfred Jarry, the significance of the Théâtre de l'Oeuvre provides another link between them. When Artaud arrived in Paris in 1920, he shortly thereafter met Aurélien Lugné-Poë, the Théâtre de l'Oeuvre's director since 1893, who gave him his first acting job on the Parisian stage, a bit part in Henri de Régnier's *Les Scruples de Sganarelle*. In 1921, he met Firmin Gémier, the first actor to play Ubu, who referred him to Charles Dullin whose Théâtre de l'Atelier provided Artaud with a solid basis for his early theatrical experience. The Théâtre de l'Oeuvre, as well, served as the site of perhaps one of the two most important theatrical events of the nineteenth century (the other being the premiere of Victor Hugo's *Hernani* in 1830), the first production of Alfred Jarry's harbinger of modernist theater on 10 December 1896, *Ubu roi*.[15]

"Merdre,"[16] that word first publicly uttered in 1896, heralds Père Ubu's relation to language, perhaps one of the few organizing principles of *Ubu roi*. Ubu's first and most significant gesture is linguistic. At first glance, Jarry's play might seem entirely inconsistent with Artaud's later devaluation of articulated language as an appropriate medium for the Theatre of Cruelty. And yet, Jarry's version of language in *Ubu roi* decisively diverges from conventional notions of linguistic articulation as to allow this comparison to be pursued. The entire play—its language, its characters, its themes—belongs to well-established traditions of popular comedy that include guignol, farce, vaudeville, and satire. In these popular traditions, the verbal elasticity of Ubu language is not foreign. The first articulated word of the play, the invective "merdre!," unveils the method to the madness of Ubu's particular speech patterns: deformation. While appropriating the material of language—recognizable in its referential context both as thing and invective—Ubu forges a new word that carries the mark of the ubuesque beast. Ubu's continual neologizing results in stretching the referential chain to the pont of crisis. This would seem to fulfill Artaud's desire, in the first manifesto for the Theatre of Cruelty, to employ a language that realizes "ces possibilités d'expansion hors des mots, de développement dans l'espace, d'action dissociatrice et vibratoire sur la sensibilité" (*TE*, 138) ("its possibilities for extension beyond words, for development in space, for dissociative and vibratory action upon the sensibility" [*TA*, 89]). Moreover, as "merdre" travels through the text, as a word whose privileged status derives from Ubu's liberating gesture, it becomes a protean utterance that attests to Ubu's linguistic contamination of the world. "Merdre" becomes potentially appended to any noun in any situation (another of these protean utterances in *Ubu roi*, "de par ma chandelle verte" ["by my green candle"], actually an allusion to a poetic text by Jarry, attests to the absurdity effect created by this semantic anarchy). The system to signification, invaded by the referential excess of "merdre," begins to break down transforming the text into a series of semantic gestures. These utterances take on the tone of incantations, a form of linguistic representation proposed by Artaud in order to "retrouver la notion d'une sorte de langage unique à mi-chemin entre le geste et la pensée" (*TE*, 137-38) ("to recover the notion of a kind of language half-way between gesture and thought" [*TA*, 89]). In another example, the menu of the first act banquet, Ubu-speak continues its assault on language. Mère Ubu enumerates the menu:

> Soupe polonaise, côtes des rastron, veau, poulet, pâté de chien, croupions de dinde, charlotte russe . . . [. . .] Bombe, salade, fruits, dessert, bouilli, topi-nambours, choux-fleaurs à la merdre.
>
> (Polish broth, spare ribes of Polish bison, veal, chicken and hound pie, parson's noses from the royal Polish turkeys, charlotte russe . . . [. . .] Ice-pudding, salad, fruit, cheese, boiled beef, Jerusalem fartichokes, cauli-flower à la pschitt.)[17]

Although certain dishes may not be familiar as existing signifying structures, they are not ultimately problematic in their signifying, just unfamiliar and exotic (as well as perhaps distasteful). It remains the celebrated "côtes des rastron," which Ubu uses later in the act as a projectile weapon to clear the room, that challenges notions of reference and signification. "Côtes," of course, is recognizable and, in fact, encourages a signifying structure of meat, but "rastron," unlike the other pure neologisms of *Ubu roi* ("gidouille," "bouzine," and "boudouille"), which through usage refer back to the ubuesque belly, remains a pure neologism whose reference and meaning can never be determined. Nevertheless, inscribed in a series of signifying edibles, we assign a categorical meaning to "rastron," but its specific referential structure remains opaque and ultimately empty.[18] In a final example from the last act, Mère and Père Ubu engage in a duel of insults with Bougrelas that ends in the following way: "Tiens, capon, cochon, félon, histron, fripon, souillon, polochon!" (*TU*, 125) ("Take that, pork-snout, layabout, whore's tout, pox-riddled sprout, idle lout, boy scout, Polish Kraut" [*U*, 70][19]). Evidently, the organization of the Ubus' insults, again recalling Artaud's proposition of an incantatory language for the Theatre of Cruelty, rests on sound, but in enumerating the words that facilitate an acoustic assonance, a sematic dissonance emerges. The series that originates in the realm of traditional and comprehensible signification and figured reference progressively abandons meaning and meaninglessly reassigns a figurative value regardless of the precedent of previous usage. Although, as

with the "rastron," the basic categorical frame maintains the incomprehensible figure as insult, the referential and associative chain between Bougrelas, the motivation and original reference of the insult, and "polochon," a bed bolster, which sounds suspiciously like "polisson," a scamp or depraved person, cannot be reconstructed beyond sound. The production of meaning in Jarry becomes a function of the depotentiality of a contagious deformation and the increasing imprecision that it invites such that layers of linguistic excrement pile up, distancing the reader or the spectator further from the possibility of meaning. The biological basis for Père Ubu's deformation of language, his Rabelaisian-like belly from which issues his excremental speech as well as his anarchical laughter, incarnates to a great extent Artaud's prescription for "la création d'un véritable langage physique à base de signes et non plus de mots" (*TE*, 192) ("the creation of a genuine physical language with signs, not words, as its root" [*TA*, 124]). Language in *Ubu roi*, submitted to a dangerous game of referential disruption that leads it to the brink of nonsense, is stripped of its signifying function and reduced to a dynamic, performative essence.

The linguistic acrobatics of *Ubu roi*, suggestively called by Michel Arrivé "l'existence d'une véritable hantise du signe" ("the existence of a veritable obsession of the sign"),[20] problematizes conventional signifying processes in language and characteristically expands the limits of absurdist farce as it enters the realm of Artaudian "HUMOR AS DESTRUCTION." The drama of language that Jarry's play enacts distills the comic to an essential state that, in a truly cruel manner, initiates the dissociate movements that will illustrate the complete relativity of all value in the human plane. Embodying this fundamental, extra-human chaos in the theater was a primary goal of the ritualized Theatre of Cruelty, a modern ritual that would allow the theatrical experience, like the Great Mysteries of antiquity, to access the essential drama through "le second temps de la Création, celui de la difficulté et du Double, celui de la matière et de l'épaississement de l'idée" (*TE*, 77) ("the second phase of Creation, that of difficulty and of the Double, that of matter and the materialization of the idea" [*TA*, 51]).[21] Through the "humoristic teachings" of Jarry, Artaud was able to appreciate the absurdist farce's propensity for destroying reality and envision the possibilities for the savage god of comedy in the post-representational spectacle of theatrical cruelty.

Notes

1. Artaud's short essay on the Marx Brothers was first published as a film review of *Monkey Business* in *La Nouvelle Revue Française* (no. 220, January 1932, 156-58). It was not reedited when it appeared in *Le Théâtre et son double* (Paris: Gallimard, 1938).

2. Artaud's ouster from the surrealist group, along with that of Philippe Soupault at the same time, would prefigure the subsequent "excommunication" of Vitrac, Leiris, Queneau, Ribemont-Dessaignes, and others in the next five years. Breton, in his 1930

Second manifeste du surréalisme, would claim that Artaud and the others had betrayed the cause of surrealism by having become concerned about art for its own sake. This criticism, whether justified or not, conformed to the general rhetorical strategy of the second manifesto wherein Breton unsuccessfully attempted to promote the sociopolitical dimensions of the surrealist aesthetic. The motivation for this attack, however, would seem to have originated in an article that Artaud published in the 10 September 1929 issue of the review *L'Intransigéant* in which the author reacted negatively to the 1929 reediting of the first *Manifeste du surréalisme* (1924). Breton, in the new edition, had conveniently deleted the names of those writers and artists who, by 1929, had been excluded from the surrealist group. Artaud's reaction, in turn, was part of an ongoing feud with Breton who, the previous year, had severely criticized both the motivations and the methods of Artaud's 1928 production of Strindberg's *Dream Play* at the Théâtre Alfred Jarry.

3. Antonin Artaud, *Le Théâtre et son double* (Paris: Gallimard, 1964), 214; idem., *The Theater and Its Double,* trans. Mary Caroline Richards (New York: Grove Press, 1958), 142. Artaud is subsequently cited as *TE,* Richards as *TA.*

4. The chronology of the publication of Artaud's note on the Marx Brothers and the subsequent manifestos for the Theatre of Cruelty is illuminating because they were all produced during the same period. The first manifesto was published in *La Nouvelle Revue Française* (no. 229, October 1932, 603-14). Artaud would slightly edit this version before publishing it in *Le Théâtre et son double.* The second manifesto was published as a pamphlet by Editions Denoël et Steele in 1933. Also included in the sixteen-page pamphlet was an account of the repertoire and critical reception of the earlier Théâtre Alfred Jarry (1926-30).

5. Eric Sellin, *The Dramatic Concepts of Antonin Artaud* (Chicago: University of Chicago Press, 1968), 101-2.

6. In the translation of Artaud's original, the phrase "corrosive nature" does not appear, although it conforms to the general tone of Artaud's remarks in this passage.

7. This idea, which appears in the first manifesto, was reiterated in one of the 1936 Mexican conferences included in the *Messages révolutionnaires* in which Artaud, when speaking of the theater of Jean-Louis Barrault, contends that "C'est un théâtre qui sait pleurer, mais qui a une conscience énorme du rire, et qui sait qu'il y a dans le rire une idée pure, une idée bienfaisante et pure des forces éternelles de la vie." (In *Oeuvres complètes,* vol. 8 [Paris: Gallimard, 1961], 227.) ("It is a theater that knows how to cry, but has an enormous conscience for laughter, and that knows that there is in laughter a

pure idea, a beneficial and pure idea of the eternal forces of life") [my translation.]

8. The earliest remark on comedy by Artaud can be found in a 1923 letter to Génica Athanasiou wherein Artaud, being disappointed by the Fratellini brothers, muses, "Je pense à des farces qu'on pourrait créer sur les marges du sinistre, quelque chose de fou où, le ton de la voix même aurait un sens, avec des oppositions de burlesque et d'humanité réelle, d'humanité de tous les jours." (cited in Alain Virmaux, *Antonin Artaud et le théâtre* [Paris: Seghers, 1970], 120) ("I think about farces that one could create on the margins of calamity, something crazy where, the very tone of the voice would have a meaning, with oppositions of burlesque and real humanity, everyday humanity")[my translation]. For a detailed account of Artaud's work on theater and film in the 1920s, see Jean-Louis Brau, *Antonin Artaud* (Paris: Éditions de la Table Ronde, 1971), 25-113.

9. The widespread use of humor by the dadaists and the surrealists raises the question of the centrality of that genre in those aesthetics. From dada works like Marcel Duchamp's scatological defacement of a reproduction of the Mona Lisa entitled "L.H.O.O.Q." (1919), to the homophonic word play of Robert Desnos's *Rrose Sélavy* (1922-3) and *L'Aumonyme* (1923), Michel Leiris's *Glossaire; j'y serre mes gloses* (1925), and Louis Aragon's *Le Mouvement perpetuel* (1925) to the surrealist films of René Clair, Germaine Dulac, and Luis Buñuel, to André Breton's later *Anthologie de l'humour noire* (1940), humor would seem to be an important pathway (particularly in its black, absurdist, and grotesque manifestations) to the domain of the surreal. While Breton does not specifically evoke humor as a means for attaining surreality in the first manifesto (despite the fact that a number of its passages are satirically humorous), he certainly does allow for the possibility of its inclusion with other states, like love, dreams, hallucinations, and madness, that are able to circumvent reality and liberate "real" thoughts, that is to say, the unconscious mind. Of course, in this respect, one thinks of Freud's treatise, *Jokes and Their Relation of the Unconscious,* which would provide a psychoanalytic validation of this contention. While the surrealists were acquainted with certain works of Freud, it is doubtful that this text was among those with which they were familiar. For a discussion of the influences of psychoanalysis on surrealism, see Anna Balakian, *Surrealism: The Road to the Absolute* (Chicago: University of Chicago Press, 1986), 125-34, and S. Dresden, "Psychoanalysis and Surrealism," in *Freud and the Humanities,* ed. Peregrine Horden (New York: St. Martin's Press, 1985), 110-29.

10. Apollinaire's delirious version of the depopulation question seems all the more remarkable as a

precursing text for surrealism as it was written in 1903, long before the author's explicit turn to modernist aesthetics. When it was finally produced for the stage in 1917 (at the Théâtre Maubel on 24 June), it included a preface by Apollinaire that coined the term "surreality," which Breton and his group would appropriate and propose as surrealism in the 1920s.

11. Antonin Artaud, *Oeuvres complètes,* vol. 2 (Paris: Gallimard, 1961), 18. All subsequent documents on the Théâtre Alfred Jarry are cited as O and are followed by my translations. For an English language version of certain of the documents of the Théâtre Alfred Jarry, see Antonin Artaud, "States of Mind: 1921-45," trans. Ruby Cohn, *Tulane Drama Review* 8, no. 2 (Winter 1963), 30-73.

12. Cited in Gérard Durozoi, *Artaud; l'alienation et la folie* (Paris: Larousse, 1972), 131; my translation.

13. The scandal that was provoked by the production of the third act of Claudel's play is an interesting story that illustrates certain of the interworkings of the avant-grade in the 1920s. Most of the audience in attendance were present to view Pudovkin's film, which had previously been banned in France. Others in the audience included André Gide, Breton, and some of the surrealist group. After the third act of the play had been presented, Artaud greeted the booing, shouting crowd with the announcement of the piece's author (adding Claudel's then current title of French Ambassador to the United States). Although Breton took the side of Artaud in the resulting uproar, a number of the other surrealists disapproved of his use of such a traditional author. One wonders if this evening was not the beginning of the eventual rift between Artaud and the surrealists that materialized later that year after the Strindberg production.

14. The program for the 1926-27 season proposed a *mise-en-scène* of two fragments of a little-known work by Alfred Jarry, *L'Amour en suites* (dialogue eight entitled "La peur chez l'Amour" and the last part entitled "Au paradis ou le Vieux de la montagne"). In a circular printed in 1929 by S. G. I. E., Artaud contends that the next year the Théâtre Alfred Jarry was planning to produce *Ubu roi* "adapté aux circonstances présentes et joué sans stylisation" (O, 35) ("adapted to present circumstances and played without stylization"). Due to the increasing financial problems of the theater, however, this production was never pursued.

15. For an account of the first production and premiere of *Ubu roi,* see Martin Esslin, *The Theater of the Absurd* (New York: Doubleday, 1961), 254-58, and Maurice Marc LaBelle, *Alfred Jarry: Nihilism and the Theater of the Absurd* (New York: New York University Press, 1980), 81-100.

16. Throughout this discussion, the reader must remain aware of the difficulty of translation of the language

of Jarry's play. "Merdre," for example, has been translated by Cyril Connoly and Simon Watson Taylor in Alfred Jarry, *The Ubu Plays* (New York: Grove Weidenfeld, 1968) as "pschitt." While this is an original solution for the translation of the neologism, it neutralizes to a certain extent the scatological force of the original in which the sole deforming letter comes at the end of the neologism. For the purposes of this discussion, this neologism has been kept in the original.

17. Alfred Jarry, *Ubu Roi,* in *Tout Ubu,* ed. Maurice Saillet (Paris: Livre de Poche, 1985), 39, and idem., in *The Ubu Plays,* trans. Cyril Connoly and Simon Watson Taylor (New York: Grove Weidenfeld, 1968), 24. Jarry is subsequently cited as TU, Connolly as U. Once again, a certain amount of liberty has been taken with the translation here. "Côtes de rastron" has been rendered as "spare ribs of Polish bison" which, as with the previous example of "merdre," tends to neutralize the neological force of the original French. As the discussion will demonstrate, the permanent opacity of the pure neologism is an important element in the strategy of its use. By rendering it with words that do exist, one realizes that any potential ambiguity or incomprehensibility (knowing whether or not the European species of bison or wisent, *Bison bonasus,* is native to, or can be commonly found in, Poland) has been shifted from the signifier to the referent.

18. While neologisms are not a staple technique of farce (most often, one finds in traditional farce a reliance on the polysemantic characteristics of language that can lead to miscommunication), they ultimately can fit into the linguistic idiosyncrasies of that genre. Consider Linda Klieger Stillman's remarks on farce in her excellent article, "The Absent Structure of Farce: ça Biche" (*Romanic Review* 76, no. 4 [November 1985]: 405-14): "In La Biche's farce [*Le Plus heureux des trois*], and in farce generically, signifying structures must be invented to name what the established code does not express. Frequent unsettling of conventional links between signifier and signified contributes to ambivalence and ambiguity initially perceived as non-sense. In order to accommodate a communications system overburdened by a criss-crossing of tracks, by unpredicatable switch throwing and by probable derailment, expected semantic rules are suspended" (406-7).

19. The translation here has made an attempt to reproduce in English the acoustic assonance of the words and completely replaced the corresponding French words. The literal translation of the French is "Take that, coward, pig, traitor, actor, rogue, scullion, bed bolster."

20. Michel Arrivé, *Les Langages de Jarry; Essai de sémiotique littéraire* (Paris: Publications de l'Université de Paris, 1972), 97. For more on the semiotic reading of *Ubu Roi,* see Linda Kliger

Stillman, "The Morphophonetic Universe of Ubu," *French Review* 50, no. 4 (March 1977): 586–95.

21. The same issue of the ritualization of modern theater through comedy is addressed by Friedrich Dürrenmatt in an essay entitled "Problems of the Theater," trans. Gerhard Nellhaus, in *Theater in the 20th Century,* ed. R. W. Corrigan (New York: Grove Press, 1963), 49–76. In this essay, the author contends that tragedy, as a genre, is no longer possible because it necessitates a "true" community in order to function effectively. However, Dürrenmatt writes, "But the tragic is still possible even if pure tragedy is not. We can achieve the tragic out of comedy. We can bring it forth at a frightening moment, as an abyss that suddenly opens up . . ." (70).

Louis Sass (essay date May 1996)

"'The Catastrophes of Heaven': Modernism, Primitivism, and the Madness of Antonin Artaud," in *Modernism / Modernity,* Vol. 3, No. 2, May, 1996, pp. 73-91.

[*In the following essay, Sass presents a case history of Artaud as artist, primitivist, and madman, arguing that neither Artaud's art nor his madness led him out of the "malaise of modern existence," characterized by the conflict between consciousness and instinctual being, but deeper into it.*]

To heal the catastrophes of heaven, Voyage to the land of speaking blood.[1]

I.

These words, with their suggestion of a hoped-for remedy for world catastrophe, are those of the poet and playwright Antonin Artaud (1896-1948), the exemplary madman of the modernist avant-garde. They were written in 1935, shortly before Artaud embarked on his own quest for the primitive, a journey to visit the Tarahumara Indians of Mexico. Artaud was, by then, thoroughly disgusted with modern civilization and profoundly disillusioned about the possibility of redemption through art. He believed that "reason, a European faculty, exalted beyond measure by the European mentality, is always an image of death"; that reason had "created the contemporary despair and the material anarchy of the world by separating the elements of the world which a real culture would bring together" (*SW,* 358-59). In Mexico, in the land of the Tarahumara, Artaud expected to find a true culture, a land of speaking blood where consciousness and language, instead of causing a rupture in being, would be the medium of a deep unity between self and world, spirit and body, intellect and emotion. "Because I kept seeing around me men lying . . . I felt the need . . . to go away to a place where I could at least freely advance with my heart," he wrote (*PD,* 71). "I came to Mexico to make contact with the red earth" (*SW,* 537). Stopping off in Mexico City, Artaud was dismayed to find that the city dwellers there had no interest in the Indian cultures surrounding them. He took this as a bad omen. "Nevertheless," he wrote in a letter home, "*the Indians exist. . . .* and soon I am going to reach the Indians . . . and there I hope to be understood" (*SW,* 365).

There is no figure who better illuminates the complex relationships among three closely related *topoi* of our age: modernism, madness, and the primitive or tribal mind. A profound influence on modernist art, perhaps the decisive influence on avant-garde theater, Artaud clearly had a critical attitude toward many of the central trends of modern culture and thought. He also spent nine of his last eleven years in asylums. There he displayed many classical signs and symptoms of paranoid, catatonic, and deteriorated forms of schizophrenia—an illness that many psychoanalysts and psychiatrists, as well as many anti-psychiatrists and members of the artistic avant-garde, have seen as involving a regression to the earliest, most unreflective and instinct-ridden stages of human life.

In Artaud's embarking for the land of the Tarahumara, we have the spectacle of a schizophrenic artist, a person of immense influence on twentieth-century culture, setting out on his own quest for the primitive.[2] Ironically enough, he too yearns for the very mode of life—primal and undivided, imbued with passion, immediacy, and a sense of mystical participation—that, according to traditional theoretical accounts, underlies his own psychological condition.[3] It seems, then, that the schizophrenic, at least *this* schizophrenic, can be as susceptible as anyone else to the myth and the lure of the primitive; and it is worth asking why this should be the case. Does Artaud sense a fundamental affinity between his own mode of being and that of the Tarahumara of his imagination, living in immediate connection with their emotions and in symbiosis with the surrounding world? Or could it be just the reverse: namely, that for Artaud the Tarahumara seemed to offer the haven of an existence quite antithetical to his own?

In both worlds where he has been a figure of importance, anti-psychiatry and the artistic avant-garde, Artaud has been primarily understood in the first way. Since the 1960s he has served as the paradigmatic instance of the madman as wildman or primitive, a person who is supposed to incarnate the irrationalist and primitivist esthetic of which he is perhaps the most influential modern exponent.[4] He is the emblematic figure for those who adopt Dionysian notions of madness, of modernism (and postmodernism), and of modernism as a kind of madness; and he is thought to embody a postromantic or romantic-modernist esthetic in which insanity has become the privileged "metaphor for passion," the logical consequence of all strong emotion.[5] Perhaps the classic modern expression of this conception is Nietzsche's vision, in *The Birth of Tragedy,* of an ecstatic surrender of self-control that obliterates all doubt and hesitation to make way for the raptures of unrestrained instinct and primordial unity. Such a conception of madness has often served as a kind of objective correlative. It has been used to exemplify the supposedly Dionysiac nature of the forms of boundary dissolution, self-fragmentation, and social withdrawal that are common in the twentieth century avant-garde—a condition in which the coherent self is said, for instance, to be "dismembered by the very fertility of its resources" in a "triumph of desiring fantasy," dissolved in "exuberant fusion with those scenes which offer themselves, literally, as the theater of our desires."[6] Thus for Sylvère Lotringer, Leo Bersani, and Martin Esslin, Artaud's literary works display the "uncontrollable, polymorphous movement," "heterogeneous multiplicity," or "pornographic tyrannies intrinsic to all desire." They illustrate the triumph of "concrete experience" and "the unrestrained ecstasies of Dionysus" over abstract thought and the "Apollonian principle." Artaud's texts demonstrate that "emotion released from all restraint of logic . . . can result in a glorious rhetoric of unbridled passion."[7]

The major works of anti-psychiatry—R. D. Laing's *The Politics of Experience,* Foucault's *Madness and Civilization,* and Deleuze and Guattari's *Anti-Oedipus: Capitalism and Schizophrenia*—were all profoundly inspired by their authors' reading of Artaud. In all of them similar images prevail. Foucault speaks, for instance, of madness as a "sovereign enterprise of unreason," a "wild state" of an "inaccessible primitive purity." Laing describes insanity as a release from constraint and a return to "primal man" that offers the hope of healing "our own appalling state of alienation called normality"; while Deleuze and Guattari celebrate the schizophrenic as the "true hero of desire," who is "closest to the beating heart of reality" and the "vital biology of the body."[8]

This Dionysian or primitivist image is largely based on the middle years of Artaud's career, the time of his most famous work, *The Theater and its Double* (written 1931-36), and a period that culminated in his trip to Mexico in 1936. During this, his second period of literary production, consciousness was conceived altogether negatively, and Artaud threw himself into activities designed to eclipse it. We will need to pay closer attention to the lesser-known but, in many respects, more fundamental first period of Artaud's writing, the decade of the 1920s and early thirties during which he offers the most direct descriptions of the anguish that was to plague him throughout his life, motivating yet at the same time undermining his later attempts to escape into immediacy and absorption. As we shall see, it is this first, in a sense Apollonian or Socratic phase, that forms the indispensable ground for understanding not only Artaud's middle or Dionysian period, but also the strangest, final decade of his life.[9]

The present paper is not a work of intellectual or cultural history, but a case study of a single individual—an individual who, however, is the most prominent figure to stand at the crossroads of psychiatry and the arts in our century. Investigating Artaud's life and work reveals a great irony of twentieth-century thought: that the madness so often imagined to be antithetical to, even perhaps to of-

fer refuge from, the malaise of modern existence, may in fact be a particularly excruciating case of this very same condition—bearing, in heightened form, all its familiar stigmata of distance, deadness, and self-division.

II.

Artaud's major preoccupations in his first period, the 1920s and early thirties, could hardly be less Dionysian in character. His most persistent theme in this period is, as he terms it in ***The Umbilicus of Limbo*** (1925), "a *congealing* of the marrow, an absence of mental fire, a failure of the circulation of life" (*SW,* 72). In *Fragments of a Diary from Hell* (written 1925), he describes himself as "definitively apart from life . . . stigmatized by a living death" (*SW,* 92), and elsewhere he writes, "I am made of blood, obviously I am made of blood. But I cannot see myself right now. I do not think of myself as being alive" (*PWW,* 82). In a typical passage from this period lasting eight to ten years, Artaud compares himself to an emptiness or absence and to a robot that is nevertheless aware of some inner rift: "God . . . has kept me alive in a void of negations and stubborn self-disavowals. . . . He has reduced me to being a walking robot, but a robot who can feel the rupture of his unconscious" (*PWW,* 81).[10]

In such texts as *The Nerve Meter* (1925), Artaud speaks repeatedly of the "disembodiment of reality" and of "a kind of constant leakage of the normal level of reality" (*SW,* 82)—a leakage that originates in the realm of thought but quickly contaminates even his own most fundamental sense of bodily existence. "I feel the ground slipping out from under my thoughts. . . . More than the mind which stays intact . . . it is the nervous trajectory of thought which this erosion affects and subverts. This absence and this standstill are especially felt in the limbs and blood" (*PWW,* 68; also *SW,* 94). Even bodily sensations seem unreal to him, like fugitive images from a dream he cannot quite recall: "*description of a physical state*: . . . Probably localized in the skin, but felt as the radical elimination of a limb, and presenting to the brain only images of limbs that are threadlike and woolly, images of limbs that are far away and not where they should be. A sort of internal fracturing of the whole nervous system" (*SW,* 65).

Artaud complains of a "lack of normal vitality" which, he says, "prevents me from keeping track of my ideas . . . and from reviewing at will my opinions and decisions" (*PWW,* 83). One eerie passage describes a "great cold, an excruciating abstinence, the limbo of a nightmare of bones and muscle, with the sensation of the gastric functions snapping like a flag in the phosphorescence of the storm. Larval images that are pushed about as if with a finger and bear no relation to any substance" (*SW,* 94). Artaud speaks of a "shifting vertigo," a state of "oblique bewilderment" (*SW,* 65) in which he cannot represent any sort of stable world, either in his consciousness or in words. Body, mind, and external reality: all seem distant, uncoordinated, unreal. He lives instead with a chronic ontological nausea, always on the brink of some vaguely sensed and ineffable, yet horrifying devastation. Some years later Artaud would refer to "this private intellectual vacuum" as the main theme of his writing and the "dominant characteristic of my condition" (*SW,* 290). Artaud's psychological difficulties had begun in his youth, and he spent considerable time in sanatoria between 1915 and 1920. A lifelong struggle with drug addiction, with periodic attempts at detoxification, began when laudanum was prescribed for him by a doctor at a sanatorium in Neuchâtel.

In his writing of the 1920s, Artaud clearly sees his thinking as the main locus and source of his problems, which he describes as "a frightful illness of the mind" (*PWW,* 60). "I suffer because the Mind is not in life and life is not the Mind; I suffer from the Mind as organ, the Mind as interpreter, the Mind as intimidator of things to force them to enter the Mind," he writes in **The Umbilicus of Limbo** (*SW,* 59). For the most part, however, he does not attempt to escape or suppress thinking. Indeed, at this stage he tends to see thinking as indispensible to human existence and, potentially at least, the richest source of the sentiment of being, the feeling of reality and vitality that constitutes life itself. "That which is true in life always gives the feeling of intelligence," he writes (*SW,* 189), equating "absolute thought" with "life" (*PWW,* 71), and defying anyone "to imagine that absolutely unthinkable being, a mind that could really exist without thinking" (*SW,* 193). Thinking, for Artaud, is not to be identified with the spontaneous or semiconscious activities of object-directed awareness; not, for instance, with a "pure consciousness" that "forbids itself all self-expression" (*SW,* 193), but only with some form of reflexive self-recognition or self-awareness. "Thinking means something more to me than not being completely dead," he writes.

> It means being in touch with oneself at every moment. It means not creasing for a single moment to feel oneself in one's inmost being, in the unformulated mass of one's life, in the substance of one's reality; it means not feeling in oneself an enormous hole, a crucial absence; it means always feeling one's thought equal to one's thought, however inadequate the form one is able to give it.
>
> [*SW,* 70]

A "living mind," he explains, is one that is "still conscious, lucid, capable of observing and measuring its own life, capable, if necessary and at certain moments, of weighing and judging its own thought" (*SW,* 192).

Given this identification of thought with self-consciousness, this conceptualization of thinking as a self-sustaining mode of self-awareness, it is understandable that Artaud often attempted to overcome the sense of non-being through compulsive attempts to contemplate, control, or describe his own thinking. It was not enough, it seems, for him to open his eyes and see; or, for that matter, to close his eyes and think. To gain a feeling of ontological grounding, experience had somehow to be registered, held fast, and seen twice. Not only did Artaud need to see, he

had to watch his own seeing; and not only think, but contemplate his thoughts, constantly testing their responsiveness to his will. Thus he explains that what constitutes thought is not its external reference, accuracy, or transparency, but some reflexive inner sense of its thereness and its myness: "for by *having thought* I do not mean seeing correctly or even *thinking* correctly; having thought to me means *sustaining* one's thought, being able to manifest it to oneself" (*SW,* 69).

Artaud's writings of this period reflect intense self-preoccupation of two kinds: on the one hand, anguished attempts to trace the fitful and ultimately ineffable contents of his inner life; and, on the other, equally anguished attempts to state the problem of ineffability itself—to express precisely how it feels to be unable to express oneself, and to explain how this inability undermined his literary endeavours and provided him with his central theme. In such explicitly introspective works as his correspondance with the editor Jacques Rivière (1923-24) and the *Fragments of a Diary from Hell* (1925), Artaud speaks of "persist[ing] in this pursuit, in this need to pin down once and for all the state of my suffocation": "I am definitively apart from life," he writes. "My torment is as subtle and refined as it is bitter. It is necessary for me to make insane efforts of the imagination, multiplied tenfold by the grip of this strangling asphyxia, in order to succeed in *thinking* my disease" (*SW,* 92).

To capture precisely his own unique inner sensations, to pin down or state his condition, to think his disease—to Artaud such acts of effortful and controlled self-awareness seemed to offer the best chance of shoring up his eroding self and world and of mastering the linguistic forms that always seemed to dissolve on approach.[11] But inherent in this yearning is a vicious paradox: the very self-consciousness by which Artaud tried to shore things up appears, in fact, to have further exacerbated (and perhaps all along contributed to) the fragmentation and collapse that afflicted his thinking and language as well as his general sense of existence. "Yes, my thought knows itself," writes Artaud in **The Umbilicus of Limbo** (1925), "and it now despairs of reaching itself. It knows itself, by which I mean that it suspects itself; and in any case it no longer feels itself" (*SW,* 69). Artaud describes his mind as "present at the profound decline and non-manifestation of its own powers"; his experience takes the form of an "inner dialogue between consciousness and mind, that kind of soliloquy to which everything is reduced and by which everything is ultimately measured in the inner domain, which sees its words burst, its phrases abort, its stability scattered, curiously undermined, full of flight, full of a horrible suspended absence" (*SW,* 192-93).

Artaud's most explicit descriptions of this sort of mental self-subversion can be found in his letters to the doctor George Soulie de Morant. In 1932, when the Apollonian phase was nearly over and he had already begun his essays on the theater of cruelty, Artaud looks back over his past in an attempt "to illuminate once and for all . . . the dominant characteristic" of the "horribly cruel" and nearly ineffable condition that continues to plague him (*SW,* 290). The lack of "continuity" or "persistence" in his thinking might, he writes,

> in some sense be regarded as analogous to the stammering which possesses my outward elocution almost every time I want to speak. It is as if each time my thought tries to manifest itself it contracts, and it is this contraction that shuts off my thought from within, makes it rigid as in a spasm; the thought, the expression stops because the flow is too violent, because the brain wants to say too many things which it thinks of all at once, ten thoughts instead of one rush toward the exit . . .
>
> [*SW,* 293]

On reading this passage, it is natural to assume that Artaud's thought-blocking or stammering is a consequence of his consciousness being overly full, an assumption that is also consistent with two of the most common characterizations of schizophrenic cognition: the cognitivist notion that such individuals are overwhelmed by internal and external stimuli due to their lack of an attentional gating mechanism or filter capable of blocking out the irrelevant; and the psychoanalytic notion of schizophrenic consciousness as dominated by wildly proliferating primary-process modes of thought. A bit later in the same letter, however, Artaud rejects the idea that his consciousness is a plenitude. As he explains, there is a more profound sense in which his mind is too empty:

> [B]ut if one really analyzes a state of this kind it is not by being too full that consciousness errs at these moments but by being too empty, for this prolific and above all unstable and shifting juxtaposition is an illusion. Originally there was no juxtaposition, for it seems that in every state of consciousness there is always a dominant theme, and if the mind has not *automatically* decided on a dominant theme it is through weakness and because at that moment nothing dominated, nothing presented itself with enough force or continuity in the field of consciousness to be recorded. The truth is, therefore, that rather than an overflow or an excess there was a deficiency; in the absence of some precise thought that was able to develop, there was slackening, confusion, fragility.
>
> [*SW,* 293]

Artaud also denies that the confusion besetting his thinking is the product of a dominance of instinctual over rational processes. What is impaired, he says, is "not merely the thought but the personality, the life" (*SW,* 294). In the absence of vital impulse, there emerges no charged purpose or idea around which the mind can spontaneously organize itself. "Things have no more odor, no more sex," he writes in **The Umbilicus of Limbo**; "their logical order is also sometimes broken precisely because of their lack of emotional aroma" (*SW,* 65). "My thought can no longer go where my emotions and the images that arise within me drive it. I feel castrated even in my slightest impulses" (*SW,* 92).

It turns out, then, that Artaud's consciousness is not in fact filled with mental contents—not, at least, with mental content of the usual kind. The violent "flow" of which he speaks is composed neither of instinctual urges nor of stimuli nor even of normal images or thoughts, but of something more like meta-levels—perspectives on himself and his own thinking. "[T]en thoughts instead of one rush toward the exit," he says in the letter to George Soulie de Morant, then goes on to explain what these thoughts actually involve:

> [T]he brain sees the whole thought at once with all its circumstances, and it also sees all the points of view it could take and all the forms with which it could invest them, a vast juxtaposition of concepts, each of which seems more necessary and also more dubious than the others, which all the complexities of syntax would never suffice to express and expound.
>
> [*SW,* 293]

What plagues Artaud is actually a form of maniacal, reflexive self-awareness. Instead of simply grasping its own content and nothing more, his mind tends to be occupied with levels of awareness that would normally be known only by some other person who observes his subjectivity from without. Indeed, he can become so preoccupied with states of mind as such that there is hardly any interest, or any room, left over for more standard kinds of mental contents. One consequence is a destabilization and undermining of foundations; Artaud describes himself as "losing contact with all those first assumptions which are at the foundation of thought." It is "this catastrophe at a higher level," he explains, that is "the destructive element which demineralizes the mind and deprives it of its first assumptions," thereby making "the ground under my thought crumble" (*SW,* 290, 94):

> It so happens that this slackening, this confusion, this fragility express themselves in an infinite number of ways and correspond to an infinite number of new impressions and sensations, the most characteristic of which is a kind of disappearance or disintegration or collapse of first assumptions which even causes me to wonder why, for example, red (the color) is considered red and affects me as red, why a judgment affects me as a judgment and not as a pain, why I feel a pain, and why this particular pain, which I feel without understanding it . . . for after all there is no reason why what is simply a perverse and perverted way of being and feeling should be the cause of a state that makes me miserable. No doubt that idiotic and crude reaction of people who, when confronted by someone else's pain, say, Don't think about it, is right, but they are metaphysically right and do not know it.
>
> [*SW,* 293-94]

III.

The Dionysian project central to Artaud's second period of writing cannot be understood apart from the forms of experience that precede, underlie, and in the end undermine it. This is not to say that such texts as *The Theater and its*

Double, Artaud's most exciting work and his most significant contribution to esthetics, can be dismissed as of no intrinsic interest. Still, it hardly requires a deep committment to a hermeneutics of suspicion to recognize that Artaud's advocacy of a theater of cruelty is something other than the "uncontrollable, polymorphous movement of desire" imagined by certain champions of his work.[12] Artaud's own words virtually demand that we see his ecstatic project as (at least in part) what one might call a Dionysian defense (and a rather unsuccessful one) against what is essentially an Apollonian or Socratic condition.

Anaïs Nin recounts a time when Artaud, leaving a cafe in an open taxi, stood up, stretched out his arms toward the crowded street, and said, "The revolution will come soon. All this will be destroyed. The world must be destroyed. It is corrupt and full of ugliness. It is full of mummies, I tell you. Roman decadence. Death. I wanted a theater that would be like a shock treatment, galvanize, shock people into feeling."[13] In the preface to *The Theater and its Double,* he writes of "the unprecedented number of crimes whose perverse gratuitousness is explained only by our powerlessness to take complete possession of life" (*TID,* 9). And in his essay on the Balinese theater, he praises the frenzied dance in which "one suddenly senses the headlong fall of the mind," and manages "to cover over the void with fear" (*SW,* 225).

True theater, Artaud believed, had to be a massive assault putting "direct pressure on the senses" (*TID,* 125), an arousal of instincts so extreme as to obliterate normal consciousness. Through a Satanic "total exorcism" of intellect and superego, such a theater would overwhelm all scruples and hesitations, all concern with rational purpose, and any tendency to dote upon the future or any other absent world. Distantiated estheticism—that "hellish, truly accursed thing in our time . . . our artistic dallying with forms"—should disappear, to be replaced by a total theater that rivets the attention and eclipses all sense of distance, a theater in which both actors and spectators become "like victims burnt at the stake, signaling through the flames" (*TID,* 13). In this period Artaud no longer yearns for a private language, a language adequate to the unique intricacies of his inner life, as he had in the 1920s. He calls instead for a nondiscursive and alogical, an affective and respiratory language: "a different language of nature . . . whose sources will be tapped at a point still deeper, more remote from thought" (*TID,* 110), and which will restore to speech "its old magic, its essential spellbinding power" (*TID,* 111). No longer does he seek to know and control his mind, for he now recognizes that "all true freedom is dark, and infallibly identified with sexual freedom" (*TID,* 30).

Artaud's views on the theater of cruelty are well known, and I do not wish to dwell upon them here. In many respects they are an attempt to foster the kind of pure Dionysiac experience described in Nietzsche's *Birth of Tragedy* (a book Artaud is likely to have read). Consciousness—now understood not as the true source of being but

as the inclination to nihilate the world and feeling, to hold things off at a distance—is Artaud's ever-present enemy during this period; its obliteration is the central purpose of his new esthetic demands. Artaud's attempts to instantiate such a theater were, in any case, rather unsuccessful, both with audiences and as a curative medium for Artaud himself. Artaud knew, however, of another way to pursue his end. This was to return to what, in Nietzsche's view, is the true origin of theater and the theatrical impulse: the orgiastic rituals of primitive cultures, rituals where there is no audience but only participants, where nothing is symbolized or represented because everything is present, including even the deities and demons who will seem quite literally brought down to earth.

Artaud had long dreamed of cultures more primitive or more innocent: of the ancient Syrians, the Europeans of the Middle Ages, and contemporary tribal peoples, all of whom he imagined as pursuing the mystic project of glimpsing "the great All." "Ever since the genesis of the elements," he wrote, the ancient religions "neither separated the sky from man, nor man from the entire creation" (*PWW,* 136). Artaud yearned for an "organic culture" in which to drown his increasing estrangement: "a culture based on the mind in relationship to the organs, and the mind bathing in all the organs, and responding to each of them at the same time."[14] After the devastating failure of his play, **Les Cenci,** Artaud decided to leave Paris and travel to a land where such a culture would really exist. He would go to the Mexico of the Tarahumara, that "Primeval Race" of "pure red Indians" who exist "in a feeling of spontaneous solidarity" in touch with the "natural Unconscious"; people whose "magic culture . . . spring[s] forth from the power of the Indian soil," who are "physically strong like Nature" because they are "made of the same substance as nature" (*PD,* 3-11; *PWW,* 142).

Like the Surrealists and many others of his generation, Artaud considered tribal man to be free of what Breton termed "the hegemony of consciousness," and therefore as able "to concentrate on the conquest of revelatory emotions."[15] It is hardly surprising that Artaud, an admirer of Breton and sometime member of the Surrealist group, should have imbibed the evolutionist notions popular in his own cultural milieu. More interesting, and more revealing of Artaud's own preoccupations, is the shifting or contradictory quality of his attitudes. The Tarahumara and other pagans and primitives of Artaud's imagination are not, in fact, conceived in simple antithesis to his own alienation and hyperreflexivity: though largely defined in opposition to European consciousness as well as to his own inner state, Artaud does not always imagine them as devoid of alienation so much as, in effect, engaged in effortful struggle against it. "What distinguished the pagans from us," he writes in one passage, "is that at the origin of all their beliefs there is *a terrific effort not to think as men,* in order to stay in contact with the entire creation, that is, with the divinity" (*PWW,* 140; emphasis added). At times, in fact, Artaud describes the Tarahumara as living as if they were already dead, as obsessed with philosophy and ideas, and as despising the life of their bodies.[16] Like Artaud himself, the Indians he imagines seem not to be spontaneous primitives so much as willful ones, or better, primitiv*ists* who have glimpsed the trajectory of human consciousness and now recoil defensively from its demands. They exist, says Artaud, "in defiance of this age" (*PD,* 7).

Artaud spent a number of months in Mexico City before he managed to obtain financial support for a visit to the Tarahumara Indians, who lived in the Sierra Madre mountains of northern Mexico. The trip began ominously. Artaud was exhausted and in great physical pain. Among other problems, he was withdrawing from drugs; wanting to rid himself of his European addictions, he had thrown away the last of his heroin before entering the mountainous region. He traveled on horseback into the back country, immersed in a quasi-delusional mood in which everything in the landscape had a doubled look—as if "represent[ing] an experience I had had before" (*PD,* 84)—or seemed to be filled with an ineffable portentousness: "The land of the Tarahumara is full of signs, forms, and natural effigies which in no way seem the result of chance" (*SW,* 379).[17]

When he finally arrived among the Indians, Artaud was unable at first to get them to perform their peyote rituals, and had to wait some weeks in what felt like "heavy captivity." As so often before, Artaud's body felt to him now like a "cataclysm" or a "dislocated assemblage, [a] piece of damaged geology." For twenty-eight days, he felt that "this ill-assembled heap of organs which I was and which I had the impression of witnessing [was] like a vast landscape of ice on the point of breaking up" (*SW,* 382-83). Not surprisingly, Artaud was moved to doubt the worth of his pilgrimage and his primitivism:

> For to have come this far, to find myself at last on the threshold of an encounter and of this place from which I expected so many revelations, and to feel so lost, so abandoned, so deposed. . . . And all this, for what? For a dance, for a rite of lost Indians who no longer even know who they are or where they come from and who, when you question them, answer with tales whose connection and secret they have lost. . . . And what was it then, what false presentiment, what illusory and artificial intuition caused me to expect some sort of liberation for my body and also and above all a force, an illumination throughout the reaches of my inner landscape, which I felt at that precise minute to be beyond any kind of dimensions? . . . Why this terrible sensation of loss, of a void to be filled, of an event that miscarries?
>
> [*SW,* 384]

But then, at last, the Indians did perform their ritual. As Artaud watched, the priest-sorcerers began pounding the ground and tracing magical numbers and symbols in the dirt. The dancers whirled, lacerating space with their "coyote calls" and tinkling strange bells, while the priests uttered incantations and sprinkled water on the initiates, striking their heads with magical sticks (*PD,* 31). Artaud,

who had taken peyote, felt at moments that he was inside the ultimate theater of cruelty. The Indians lay him on the ground "so that the ritual would descend upon me, so that fire, litany, screams, dance and the night itself like a living human vault might wheel as a living being over me."[18] "To this I knew that my physical destiny was irrevocably bound. I was ready for any burning, and I awaited the first fruits of the fire in view of a conflagration that would soon be universal" (*PD,* 57-58).

The experience was clearly ecstatic, but its impact, unfortunately, was short-lived (*PD,* 82). Before long, Artaud's sense of cosmic transformation seems to have turned negative, his sense of mystical union undermined by an encroaching and all too familiar sense of ontological insecurity and catastrophe. In *The New Revelations of Being,* a pamphlet written shortly after his return to Europe, Artaud predicts a cosmic holocaust, a destruction of civilization or ruination brought on by Fire, Water, Earth, and by "a Star which will occupy the entire surface of the air, in which the Spirit of Man had been immersed."[19]

In other passages in *The New Revelations of Being,* Artaud comes close to admitting the essentially reactive or defensive nature of his Dionysian project, this attempt to cover the void with fear that now seemed to him to have been doomed from the start:

> For a long time I have felt the Void, but I have refused to throw myself into the Void. . . .
>
> When I believed that I was denying this world, I know now that I was denying the Void. . . .
>
> What I have suffered from until now is having denied the Void.
>
> The void which was already within me.
>
> [*SW,* 413]

Now he prefers to accept rather than to fight separation and nonbeing, as if the only possible act of affirmation was the paradoxical one of affirming nonbeing itself:

> I know that someone wanted to enlighten me by means of the Void and that I refused to let myself be enlightened. . . .
>
> I struggled to exist, to try to accept the forms (all the forms) with which the delirious illusion of being in the world has clothed reality.
>
> I no longer want to be one of the deluded.
>
> Dead to the world, to what composes the world for everyone else, fallen at last, fallen, risen in this void which I was denying, I have a body which suffers the world and disgorges reality. . . .
>
> It is a real Desperate Person who speaks to you and who has not known the happiness of being in the world until now that he has left this world, now that he is absolutely separated from it.
>
> The others who have died are not separated. They still turn around their dead bodies.

I am not dead, but I am separated.

[SW, 413-14]

The New Revelations of Being was the last work Artaud completed before breaking down into frank psychosis. Shortly after finishing it, he embarked on a final desperate journey to Ireland, where he believed he was meant to await the impending holocaust. The trip went badly; there were reports of violent or threatening behavior; and on arriving back in France, Artaud was in a straitjacket. It was the beginning of nine years of confinement in mental hospitals.

IV.

After his arrival at Le Havre in September 1937, Artaud was placed in a series of mental hospitals. Following the acutely disturbed phase of his trip to Ireland, he now lapsed into a state more characteristic of chronic schizophrenia. For a year and a half he was nearly catatonic, refusing to respond to visitors or write to his friends. On being declared incurable, he was transferred, in February 1939, to a hospital on the outskirts of Paris. There he began to write letters and receive visitors, who were appalled to see what had happened to their friend. After four years, Artaud was again transferred, this time to an asylum in Rodez in southern France where he remained until 1946, when intercession by friends and admirers willing to guarantee his financial support made possible his release and return to Paris.

From the time of the ill-fated trip to Ireland, Artaud was frequently preoccupied with grandiose and violent fantasies that had a more overtly psychotic quality than did the eccentricities of his earlier years. At Rodez, for example, he would frequently circle his room uttering wild cries and, at meals, would sometimes engage in such strange rituals as belching in rhythmic patterns or getting down on his hands and knees to draw magic circles. At times he felt his body was occupied by a succession of different souls, whose conversation he was able to overhear; and he declared that all "things and *beings* inevitably obey the commandment of my breath" (*PWW*, 188).

In these last ten years of his life, Artaud continued to be plagued by feelings of ontological insecurity and nonbeing. In letters written in Rodez, for instance, he complains of horrible splittings of the personality that make him "absolutely incapable of working, thinking, *and feeling that I was alive*" (*SW*, 438). Though he blamed these feelings on the electroshock treatments he received, they can, in fact, be difficult to distinguish from those he had described so often before, as in his early texts, *The Umbilicus of Limbo* (1925) and *The Nerve Meter* (1925). Artaud's continuing sense of ontological insecurity, at the limit a fear of world catastrophe, is apparent in his descriptions of van Gogh, an important alter-ego figure of this period. Artaud speaks of van Gogh as a man who "understood the phenomenal nature of the problem," the fact that in him "every real landscape is as if latent in the

crucible where it is going to be reborn" (*SW*, 505). The sense of cosmic or godlike responsibility thereby implied was accompanied by feelings of all-encompassing threat: van Gogh's paintings, says Artaud, are like atomic bombs or bursts of fire (*SW*, 483); "the apocalypse, a consummated apocalypse, is brooding right now in the paintings of old martyred van Gogh," the artist who "has caught the moment when the pupil is about to pour itself out in the void" (*SW*, 497, 510). And, writes Artaud in 1947, "I am also like poor van Gogh. I no longer think but each day I come nearer to the explosions I am producing."[20]

At first glance, Artaud's third phase may well appear to perpetuate and exaggerate his second phase, with its revulsion for consciousness and its valorization of the body. In "Chiote à l'Esprit" (Shit to the Mind), a poem written about a year before his death, he declares:

the mind is pretentious and phony.
        A kind of larval smoke which only lives upon
what it has drawn out from the body
struggling to make a gesture and not an idea or fact.
        For really, what are these ideas, facts, values
and qualities?
        Lifeless terms which only become real when
the body has sweated them out.

[*PWW*, 166]

Now more than ever, Artaud believes in the redemptive power of bodily being, and yearns for an existence in which "there is no inside, no mind, no outside or consciousness, nothing but the body just as you see it—a body whose existence doesn't cease even when the eye looking at it turns away. And this body is a fact: me" (*PWW*, 168).[21]

Unlike in the Dionysian phase, however, Artaud no longer looks to instinct and desire, or to pleasure and pain, as offering refuge from the deadening, distantiating tendencies of the mind. The following passage is an implicit critique of the theater-of-cruelty aesthetic, for it suggests that even the most intense physical sensations are now vulnerable to consciousness's derealizing power: "When my hand burns, / there is the fact that my hand burns which, considered as a fact, is already in trouble, / having the feeling that my hand is burning means entering another domain. / If I have the idea that my hand burns, I am no longer in my hand but in a state of supervision" (*PWW*, 167).[22] Even basic biological facts have lost their incontrovertible, anchoring power; and are now liable to feel like absurd phenomena, arbitrary products of human will that might just as well not have existed, or have existed in some very different form: "There where it smells of shit / it smells of being. / Man could very well have avoided shitting, / and kept his anal pocket closed, / but he chose to shit / like he could've chosen to live / instead of consenting to live dead" (*WRS*, 291).

But it is not merely that instinct and sensuality are *vulnerable* to the depredations of consciousness; the Dionysian realm now takes on certain of the ontological characteristics previously associated with the realm of mind. Lust and all the other imperatives of the flesh had previously been experienced as plenitude, sources of a heightened sentiment of being. Now, like the mind, they are felt to constitute an essential lack, aptly expressed through the motif of the hole or the void. In "Le Visage Humain," an essay published the year before his death, it is the organs of sense perception, the bodily sites of intentional, world-directed consciousness, that appear as grotesque voids: "But this means that the human face as it is is still searching with two eyes, a nose, a mouth and four openings of the burial vault of approaching death" (*WRS*, 277). In another work from the same period, *Artaud le Momo*, desire is represented in similar terms: thus Artaud describes the human body as: "This tongue between four gums, / this meat between two knees, / this piece of hole / for madmen" (*SW*, 524). A passage from his radio play of 1947, "To Have Done with the Judgment of God," describes human life as an "electric battery"

> whose abilities and emphases
> have been oriented toward sexual life
> while it is made
> precisely for absorbing
> by its voltaic displacements
> all the errant availabilities
> of the infinity of the void,
> of the increasingly incommensurable
> holes of void
> of a never fulfilled organic possibility.
>
> [*WRS*, 312]

In contrast with his earlier polarizing of the sensual and the cerebral, Artaud now sees the mental self as a parasite that corrupts an otherwise self-sufficient and innocent body, transforming it into an organ of desire:

> The anchored mind
> screwed into me
> by the psycho-lubricious
> thrust
> of heaven
> is the one that thinks
> every temptation
> every desire
> every inhibition.
>
> [*SW*, 523]

In his later years, Artaud was obsessed with thoughts of parasitic beings bent on destroying him by sucking life from him, by robbing him of his masculinity, as well as by appealing to corporeal desires. The essence of these "psycholascivious parasites" is the same as what, for Artaud, now characterizes both consciousness and desire: namely, pure nothingness, a condition they create and by which they are also created. Thus the parasites are "born without cessation, / from each other, / from the holes of the air, / from the roaming vacuities of space" (*PWW*, 181).[23]

Since Artaud now believes that both "feelings and the mind have poisoned life" (*PWW*, 167), he wants to cut off

every sort of connection with the external world, to be "chaste and pure, / virgin, intact, untouchable" (*PWW*, 192):

> there is no learning, no knowledge,
> life has been lost from the day that one single
> thing was known.
>
> I am not of your world
>
> mine is on the other side of everything that is, knows
> and is aware of itself, desires and
> makes itself.
>
> [*PWW*, 165]

The body he now wishes to become is a purified body, a "body without organs." The psycholascivious parasites are dependent creatures who corrupt by inducing the dependencies of desire. To evade their corrupting influence it is necessary that all holes be covered over and all organs extirpated—those of consciousness as well as of instinct, eyes and ears as well as genitals, anus, and mouth. At the end of ***"To Have Done with the Judgment of God,"*** Artaud dreams of an operation on an "autopsy table" in which all the organs of the human body are removed:

> When you will have made [Man] a body without organs,
> then you will have delivered him from all his automatic reactions
> and restored him to his true freedom.
>
> [*SW*, 571]

In his attempt to remove everything that might evoke any hint of ontological dependency, or of the absence and non-being this now implies, Artaud was forced to deny virtually every conceivable form of sapient or sensate human existence: "I hate and denounce as a coward all sensations and all being. / I hate and denounce the so-called sensations of being. / I am by nature clean and pure" (*PWW*, 192). What Artaud desires in this final year of his life is a paradoxical and impossible state: to *be* the kind of being that has no sensation of being, and, at the same time, to experience this condition. He wants to return to a time before mind existed, a time when, "as for consciousness, no one had ever thought of it" (*SW*, 505). Thus he wants to create a theater very different from that of *The Theater and its Double*, a theater in which man would be a "sculptural object" rather than a "swollen creature"; and he insists that Man could, indeed should, have made up his mind "to lose being, that is, to die alive" (*SW*, 559).[24]

The state of grace that Artaud now imagines is antithetical to that of the psycholascivious parasites: devoid as it is not only of all need for ingestion, excretion, or desire, but also of any consciousness of the ambient world. Now his great wish is to become "an old tree with grooves / which didn't eat / didn't drink / didn't breathe" (*PWW*, 182); and he dreams of an idyllic golden age, a time

> when man was a tree without organs or function, but possessed of will, [this time] will return. For the great

lie has been to make man an organism, / ingestion, / assimilation, / incubation, / excretion, / thus creating a whole order of hidden functions which are outside / the realm of the *deliberative* will; / the will that determines itself at each instant; for it was this, that human tree that walks, / a will that determines itself at each instant, / without functions that were hidden, underlying, governed *by the unconscious.*

[*SW,* 515][25]

The pure will of this "tree without organs or functions" is not that of "digestive humanity" (*SW,* 519). It is an uncontaminated, self-determining, utterly independent will, a will that is conscious through and through, and free of any determination by underlying motives. It is the will of a creature supreme in its indifference and harboring no desire other than the wish to constitute itself beyond any risk of neediness or nonbeing.

Artaud's body without organs is obviously not a Dionysian body. It is also different from the synthesis inherent in a romantic or Hegelian unification of body with soul, mind with universe, self with other, or a Nietzschean union of the Apollonian and Dionysian principles. To reconcile the psychical with the physical in the form of the organic would, for Artaud, be tantamount to creating a psycholascivious parasite, the loathsome creature who combines the dependencies inherent in both knowing mind and yearning body. Artaud's "body without organs," his "tree without organs or function," implies a strange coming-together of spirit and substance—a denaturing of both mind and body in which each element is purified to a point of self-negation that is also a point of convergence between the two. As we have seen, the body without organs is a body without desire and sentience, almost a mere substance. In one sense, then, it might be seen as the final stage in an anti-Hegelian progression whereby Artaud passes from self-consciousness back through the imperatives of passion and pain, and on toward states of vegetal or even inorganic matter. In another way, however, it can seem a return to the condition of his first, highly cerebral phase. Artaud's body without organs is, after all, a pure and worldless will—self-determining, self-identical, and self-aware. If it is a body, it is a curiously Apollonian one. If it is a synthesis, it is one founded on negation rather than reconciliation: all the elements are there, but denied rather than affirmed. The body without organs of this supposed champion of unbridled passion is not, then, a bodymind but a not-body / not-mind, apotheosis of pure negation.

Notes

1. Antonin Artaud, in Susan Sontag, ed., *Antonin Artaud: Selected Writings,* trans. Helen Weaver (New York: Farrar, Straus, and Giroux, 1976), 353; hereafter abbreviated *SW.* References to other works by Artaud will be given from the following editions: Naomi Greene, ed., *Antonin Artaud: Poet Without Words* (New York: Simon and Schuster, 1970), hereafter abbreviated *PWW*; Antonin Artaud, *The Peyote Dance,* trans. Helen Weaver (New York: Farrar, Straus, and Giroux, 1976), hereafter abbreviated *PD*; Antonin Artaud, *The Theater and its Double,* trans. Mary Caroline Richards (New York: Grove Press, 1958), hereafter abbreviated *TID*; and Antonin Artaud, *Watchfiends and Rack Screams; Works from the Final Period,* edited and translated by Clayton Eshleman with Bernard Bador (Boston: Exact Change, 1995), hereafter abbreviated *WRS.*

2. In order to escape "the habits of modern thinking," Artaud seeks what he calls "a regression into time" (*SW,* 162).

3. On the prominence of primitivist and Dionysian images of schizophrenia, see Louis Sass, *Madness and Modernism: Insanity in the Light of Modern Art, Literature, and Thought* (Cambridge: Harvard University Press, 1992), 1-23.

4. Martin Esslin, for example, refers to Artaud as "always the complete incarnation of his own thought"; see his *Antonin Artaud* (Harmondsworth: Penguin Books, 1977), 123.

5. Susan Sontag, *Against Interpretation* (New York: Dell, 1969), 170.

6. Leo Bersani, *A Future for Astyanax: Character and Desire in Literature* (New York: Columbia University, 1984), 272. Such a conception seems, incidentally, to betray the hidden romanticism inherent in some postmodern discourses that would like to present themselves as, above all, *anti*romantic.

7. Sylvère Lotringer, "Libido Unbound: The Politics of 'Schizophrenia,'" *Semiotexte* 2, no. 3 (1977): 8-10. See Esslin, *Antonin Artaud,* 122-27, and Bersani, *Future for Astyanax,* 272. For these authors, as for André Breton in his first manifesto of Surrealism, madness becomes "the emblem of creative insurrection against rationalist repression linked to social power" (J. H. Matthews, *Surrealism, Insanity, and Poetry* [Syracuse: Syracuse University Press, 1982], 4-5).

8. R. D. Laing, *The Politics of Experience* (New York: Ballantine Books, 1967), 126, 167. Michel Foucault, *Madness and Civilization,* trans. Richard Howard (New York: Vintage Books, 1988), 278. Also, Foucault quoted in Jacques Derrida, *Writing and Difference,* trans. Alan Bass (Chicago: University of Chicago Press, 1978), 37. Gilles Deleuze and Félix Guattari, *Anti-Oedipus: Capitalism and Schizophrenia,* trans. R. Hurley, M. Seem, and H. Lane (New York: Viking, 1971), 87-88. Deleuze and Guattari reject the notion of the schizophrenic as "the autistic rag—separated from the real and cut off from life" (19-20). When such a state occurs, they claim, it is not the result of the schizophrenic process itself but rather of its interruption, whether through incarceration or through the deadening effect of a society that recoils from those who

threaten it. The figure of Artaud lies behind their image of schizophrenia as a state hyper-imbued with passion and the life force.

9. It goes without saying that I adopt the terms Apollonian and Dionysian from Nietzsche's *Birth of Tragedy.* My purpose here is to capture the dominant and distinctive features of each of these three phases, and thereby to bring out the main lines of Artaud's psychological and esthetic development. I recognize that, in doing so, I exaggerate somewhat the unity of Artaud's concerns in each period: there is more heterogeneity within, and more overlap between, these periods than is reflected in my presentation. I am indebted to various works on Artaud's life and work, including Martin Esslin, *Antonin Artaud*; Ronald Hayman, *Artaud and After* (Oxford: Oxford University Press, 1977); Bettina Knapp, *Antonin Artaud: Man of Vision* (New York: David Lewis, 1969); and, especially, Naomi Greene, *Antonin Artaud.*

10. André Breton, more clear-sighted than many of Artaud's devotees, once described Artaud as having led him to a place that was "abstract, a gallery of ice . . . a place of lacunae and ellipses where personally I could no longer communicate with the innumerable things I like" (quoted in Greene, *PWW,* 23). Artaud himself once wrote that what made him different from the Surrealists was the fact that he despised life as much as they loved it (*PWW,* 23).

11. Artaud could be said to yearn for a "private language," in Wittgenstein's sense of the phrase. See Louis Sass, "Antonin Artaud, Modernism, and the Yearning for a Private Language," in Kjell S. Johannessen and Tore Nordenstam, eds., *Culture and Value: Philosophy and the Cultural Sciences,* vol. 3 (Kirchberg am Wechsel, Austria: Austrian Ludwig Wittgenstein Society, 1995), 255-60.

12. Lotringer, "Libido Unbound," 8.

13. Anaïs Nin quoted in Esslin, *Artaud,* 37.

14. Artaud quoted in Knapp, *Antonin Artaud,* 135.

15. Breton quoted in Greene, *PWW,* 128.

16. See *PD,* 3, 9, 10. Later, when the trip was over, Artaud would recall a conversation with the Tarahumara priest who gave him peyote. The priest had described his own world in terms reminiscent of decadent, alienated Europe. "The world in the beginning was completely real," Artaud reports him as saying. "It resounded in the human heart and with the human heart. Now the heart is no longer in it, nor is the soul because God has withdrawn from it" (*PD,* 34).

17. Even the number of times Artaud perceived certain forms in shadows and rock formations seemed significant: "I saw repeated eight times the same rock which projected two shadows on the ground. . . . And everything I saw seemed to correspond to a number" (*SW,* 380-81). He looked about him with

the kind of scrutiny that forces the object to yield up some special yet elusive meaning: "I noticed in the mountain that it is useful to have *the obsession of counting.* There was not a shadow that I did not count, when I felt it creep around something; and it was often by adding up shadows that I found my way back to strange centers." For discussion of this sort of predelusional mood, see Sass, *Madness and Modernism,* "The Truth-Taking Stare," 43-74; and Sass, *The Paradoxes of Delusion: Wittgenstein, Schreber, and the Schizophrenic Mind* (Ithaca: Cornell University Press, 1994), 97-113.

18. See Knapp, *Antonin Artaud,* 151, and *SW,* 391.

19. Artaud quoted in Esslin, *Artaud,* 48.

20. Artaud quoted in Hayman, *Artaud and After,* 18. For more on the experience of world catastrophe in schizophrenia, see Sass, *Madness and Modernism,* "World Catastrophe," 300-323.

21. "The self is not the body, it is the body that is the self," wrote Artaud in 1946-47 (*WRS,* 251). In a letter from 1948, Artaud speaks of

> a nauseating flocculation of the infectious life of being
> which the PURE BODY
> repulses
> but which
> the PURE SPIRIT
> accepts
> and which the Mass
> through its rites brings about. . . .
> But this is what popular consciousness will never understand,
> that a macerated and trampled body . . .
> will be superior to a spirit handed over to all the phantasms of the interior life
> which is merely the leaven
> and the seed
> for all the stinking phantasmagorical bestializa-tions.
>
> [*WRS,* 330]

22. This sense of derealization was a persistent fear even during Artaud's Dionysian phase. In the preface to *The Theater and its Double,* he writes, "If our life lacks brimstone, i.e., a constant magic, it is because we choose to observe our acts and lose ourselves in considerations of their imagined form instead of being impelled by their force" (*TID,* 8). Artaud's comments on his play *Les Cenci* make a related point: "There will be between the Theater of Cruelty and *The Cenci* the difference which exists between the roaring of a waterfall or the unleashing of a natural storm, and all that remains of their violence once it has been recorded in an image" (quoted in Stephen Barber, *Antonin Artaud: Blows and Bombs* [London: Faber and Faber, 1993], 70).

23. In "To Have Done with the Judgment of God," Artaud speaks of "the void which advances with all

its forms / of which the most perfect representation / is the march of an incalculable group of crab lice." To the question, "And what exactly is consciousness?" he answers, "It is nothingness. . . . It seems that consciousness / is in us / linked / to sexual desire / and hunger" (*WRS,* 294, 297-98).

24. Artaud's attitude toward language in his final period partakes of this same paradoxicality: at times he advocated a language that seems totally devoid of meaning, incomprehensible to everyone, the self included. It appears that Artaud had arrived at a point where, at moments, only utter eschewal of meaning, complete opacity of language, could ward off the nihilating potentiality of human awareness and proclaim a bedrock of existence independent of consciousness's nihilating power. In the following poem he shifts from the theme of ontological suffering toward the undeniable reality of sound, of pure word-objects utterly devoid of sense: ". . . therefore no more suffering. / no more illness / dysentery / suffocation . . . / ka loughin / re te ka la gouda / ka lagouda / e te ka loughin" (*PWW,* 213). Just as the body had to be rid of consciousness and desire, of anything that points or yearns beyond itself, so language had to be rid of any tendency for the signifier to refer to a distant or separate realm: "All true language is incomprehensible,/ like the clack / of chattering teeth; / or the clack (whorehouse) / of the toothy femur (bloody)" (*PWW,* 169).

25. In a passage from *Supports et Supplications* (dictated 1946-47), Artaud speaks of a "stone [that] has an aura which is being, and it is in the aura of being, the integral aura of being, the tide of inexhaustible will" (*WRS,* 252).

Z. Bart Thornton (essay date March 1997)

"Linguistic Disenchantment and Architectural Solace in DeLillo and Artaud," in *Mosaic,* Vol. 30, No. 1, March, 1997, pp. 97-112.

[*In the following essay, Thornton argues that in their work both Artaud and the novelist Don DeLillo transform language into an architecture of sounds.*]

Contemporary literary criticism and modern philosophy are rife with architectural metaphors: just as literary critics speak of *surfaces* and *structures, foundations, frames,* and *fissures,* so philosophers from Kant to Heidegger to Derrida have invoked structural concepts in their theorizing. Without the architectural figure, as Mark Wigley has claimed, much of Heidegger's work would be groundless: "It is not that [Heidegger] simply theorizes architecture as such, but that theorizing is itself understood in architectural terms" (7). It is only recently, however, that critics have begun to focus specifically on the matrices between architectural theory and literary fiction. An example of this

concentrated attention is Jennifer Bloomer's *Architecture and the Text,* in which she argues that Joyce's *Finnegans Wake* and Piranesi's etchings both "approach the literary in their ambiguity and invitation to a kind of narrative interpretation. . . . Both texts are presented as white pages upon which black marks have been made" (6). Similarly, literary critics like Fredric Jameson and Linda Hutcheon have been seeking new ways to textualize architectural space, while architectural practitioners like Bernard Tschumi and Peter Eisenman have been proclaiming that "there is no longer any essential difference between architecture and text" (Graafland 96).

Indeed, Eisenman's houses—which aim to complicate the relationship between inhabitants and structures—mirror the textual constructions of contemporary novelists, whose truncated plots and enigmatic characters are the literary equivalents of Eisenman's slanted walls and half-missing staircases. In particular, Eisenman's architectural theory seems to correspond with the linguistic philosophy that informs the work of Don DeLillo. In essays and interviews Eisenman has argued that in order to remain vibrant, architecture must continually reinvent itself by "dislocat-[ing] [the idea of] dwelling" (54). In order to rethink what it means to "dwell," we must first dissociate architecture from the comfortable complacency of functionalism; while a building has to stand up and function, Eisenman contends that it does not have to *look* like it stands up and functions (52). In his novels DeLillo similarly dislocates the idea of dwelling by depicting characters who are alternately welcomed and repelled by the buildings they inhabit and by the texts themselves.

My purpose in this essay, however, is not directly to correlate Eisenman and DeLillo; rather my objective is to show how DeLillo invokes architectural concepts and metaphors to address and combat the linguistic detachment experienced by his characters. Thus, in contrast to critics like Leonard Wilcox and Scott Bukatman who have hailed DeLillo as a paradigmatic postmodernist, in tune with the Baudrillardian vision of a hyperreal America, I will argue that DeLillo's cynicism about language and communication is undercut by his architectural esthetics and accordingly that his "postmodernism" is rooted in a modernism very similar to that of the surrealist theatrical auteur Antonin Artaud. What links them, as I see it, is their mutual concern with the quest for an idiom that conjoins inner speech, social utterance, and physical space, and the optimism that ultimately comes from finding such a "space." Although my purpose is in no way to suggest any direct connection between Artaud and DeLillo—I am quite aware of the dangers of collapsing theater and fiction and different historical periods—I will begin by outlining the linguistic and architectural components of Artaud's project and then go on to show how these components can be used to illumine DeLillo's theory and practice.

Skeptical about the value of conventional language and inclined to treat the body as an architectonic presence, Artaud urged his actors to develop a rhetoric of visuality in an effort to say the unsayable. In *The Theater and Its Double* (1938) Artaud proposed a new theater—the *theater of cruelty*—that would surmount "the boredom, stupidity, and inertia of it all" (83). Refusing to surrender to a seemingly all-encompassing *malaise* (one which resembles that which postmodernists myopically see as endemic and restricted to their own age), Artaud suggests that we need "something to get us out of our *marasmus*," or cultural quagmire (*Theater* 83): namely, a submersion in a world of affective athleticism, reconfigured space, and dynamic intonations. In Artaud's theater, which privileges emotive enunciation and renders verbal meaning superfluous, an abstract language supersedes "the expressive potential of the language of words" (Schulte-Sasse xxxi).

Although some of Artaud's ideas are drawn directly from the linguist Ferdinand de Saussure—like Saussure, Artaud sees "at the root of [contemporary] confusion a rupture between things and words" (*Theater* 7)—it is important to note that Artaud ultimately rejects the Saussurean idea that "the subject's use of language manifests . . . an utter absence of authenticity" (Nehring 138). Instead, throughout his *Selected Writings*, in searching for an *authentic* language, Artaud finds himself working through the Bakhtinian division between an official, *authoritative* discourse and an individual, *internally persuasive* discourse. There is a complicated relationship between these types of discourses, which are anything but mutually exclusive: "Meanings," according to Patrick Brantlinger, "are dialectically or dialogically produced, at once conflictual and communal, individual and social" (71). Rather than focus, as did Saussure, on the ineluctability of linguistic practices, Bakhtin concentrates on the dynamics of individual utterances. Like Bakhtin, Artaud insists that "the concrete and particular" should be seen as "*the* object of thought"; like Bakhtin, Artaud valorizes "positive and affirmative forms of expression that . . . vigorously renew our capacity to perceive [a] particular experience" (Schulte-Sasse xxxii). In his *Selected Writings* Artaud dramatizes precisely what happens at the intersection between bodies, buildings, and utterances.

In notes for an unproduced screenplay, which he worked on sporadically from 1925 to 1926, Artaud describes a character who faces a bizarre malady: "He has become incapable of reading his [own] thoughts . . . no matter what thought occurs to him, he can no longer give it external form, that is, translate it into appropriate gestures and words" (*Writings* 115). Brilliant but unable to verbalize (or "act out") his ideas, the protagonist of this screenplay faces a quintessentially Artaudian predicament. Throughout the letters included in *Selected Writings* Artaud laments his inability to translate his imagistic thoughts into meaningfully coherent prose. He tells Jacques Rivière, the publisher of *La Nouvelle Revue Française*, "My thought abandons me at every level . . . as soon as I *can grasp a form*, however imperfect, I pin it down, for fear of losing the whole thought" (*Writings* 31). To prevent mental images from escaping, they must be pursued, grasped, and wrestled with; for Artaud, thinking is an inescapably physi-

cal endeavor, wherein it is the body that provides the entryway into a keener awareness of the self.

Artaud imagined the theater as the "place where the body would be reborn in thought and thought would be reborn in the body" (Sontag xxxvi). In Artaud's enterprise such categories—body, thought, theater, text—become all but indistinguishable. Onstage, however, the body remains a troublesome entity: what does it do? where does it go? how does it communicate its own material presence? Herbert Blau articulates the paradoxes inherent in the body when he calls it "that clinical object with a fantasy life: house of pleasure or prison house; interpellated subject or subject of entropic decay" (111). Significantly, Blau refers to the body as a "house," an architectural presence in an architectural space. A similar emphasis on architecture and on the architectonics of the body can be seen throughout Artaud's writing. The body is a house that, in Eisenman's terms, functions and stands differently.

Although a number of critics have noted the architectural aspects of Artaud's work, the tendency unfortunately has been to focus on the more pessimistic instances. In her introduction to his works, for example, Susan Sontag notes that he often describes his failures in architectural terms: he speaks of "the chronic *erosion* of his ideas, the way his thought *crumbles*"; he describes his mind as "*fissured, deteriorating, petrifying*" (xx; emphases mine). In a comment to Abel Gance, who in 1927 was commissioned to direct a cinematic version of Poe's "The Fall of the House of Usher," Artaud said, "My life *is* the life of Usher and of his sinister hovel" (*Writings* 168). What is frequently overlooked, therefore, is the positive inflection which architecture assumes in the writings of Artaud, who also sees built space as a refuge from the problematics of the body. In an early poem called "Love" (1923), Artaud writes,

> She who lies in my bed
> And shares the air of my room
> Can throw dice on the table
> The very ceiling of my mind.

>   (*Writings* 6)

Here architecture becomes the bonding agent between disparate bodies: "She" establishes an intimate relation with the narrator's private domestic space, and "she" participates alongside the narrator in the magical transformation of the decor (table becomes ceiling, ceiling becomes mind). Elsewhere, Artaud further emphasizes this connection between thoughts, spaces, and buildings. In *Fragments of a Diary from Hell* (1925), he writes, "I am on the moon as others are on their balconies. I participate in planetary gravitation in the fissures of my mind" (*Writings* 96). Here architecture is posited as that which can be transcended (Artaud goes to the moon while others can go only to their balconies); later in the *Diary* buildings are subsumed by what Artaud calls "the ether of a new space." As he reveals in *The Nerve Meter* (1925), Artaud yearns for an internal architecture: a space that, if located within the body, does not exclude the presence of real things.

For every passage in *Selected Writings* in which Artaud depicts himself as a Roderick Usher, a victim of eroded foundations, there is another in which he displays a more sentimental view of architectural pleasures. In a letter to Génica Athanasiou, "the most important woman in Artaud's life" (Sontag 599), Artaud shows how integral architecture is to his imaginative life when he imagines seeing Athanasiou's face hovering peacefully above the thatched roof of a house overlooking the sea (*Writings* 19). For Artaud, architecture is that which allows for (and even produces) contemplation; architecture alone can reweave the tangled fibers of the body and the mind.

In the theater, too, Artaud expresses his epiphanies in architectural terms. In the bodies of Balinese actors "everything that might correspond to immediate psychological necessities . . . corresponds as well to *a sort of spiritual architecture* created out of gesture and mime but also out of the evocative power of a system" (*Theater* 55; emphasis mine). The system whose "evocative power" informs the bodies of the Balinese actors is architecture, and the spectators of their performance cannot but respond in architectural terms: "Here we are suddenly in deep metaphysical anguish, and the rigid aspect of the body in trance, stiffened by the tide of cosmic forces which besiege it, is admirably expressed by that frenetic dance of rigidity and angles, in which one suddenly begins to feel the mind begin to plummet downwards" (*Theater* 65). In the course of this "frenetic dance of rigidity and angles," the Balinese actor becomes architectural; the actor's body becomes a constructed space which replaces (but also resembles) the building which houses the performance.

Artaud's recourse to architecture in *The Theater and Its Double* has a remarkable affinity with DeLillo's handling of linguistic issues in his *End Zone* (1973), a novel which chronicles a year in the life of a West Texas football team. Gary Harkness, the narrator and a star running-back at Logos College, struggles to understand his role on a team marked by ambiguity, in a world shaped by indeterminacy. Isolated in what he calls a "remote and unfed place . . . set apart from all styles of civilization" (5), Gary divides his time among tyrannical coaches, ranting ROTC professors, and alienated teammates, all of whom speak in cryptic codes. Like Artaud's actors, DeLillo's football players counter lassitude with physicality as they create hieroglyphic languages through their poetic rhythms and disembodied sounds.

Even if the characters in the novel cannot escape the domain of language, they frequently attempt to devalue communication, which nonetheless impacts them more than they care to admit. Early in the novel, Gary espouses a utilitarian theory of language: "What men say," he tells his roommate Anatole Bloomberg, "is relevant only to the point at which language moves masses of people or a few momentous objects into significant juxtaposition" (45). Throughout the novel Gary, an aficionado of nuclear-war narratives, yearns to have intimate knowledge of a cataclysm, and it is not surprising that his definition of

linguistic relevance hinges on such words as *momentous* and *significant*. If the content of words is largely irrelevant, except on momentous and significant occasions, the process of vocalizing is, for Gary (as for Artaud and Bakhtin), indispensable. When Gary and Anatole converse rather superficially about everything from their place in history to their professional football prospects, Gary distances himself from the dialogue long enough to make the following observation:

> Our words seemed to rise toward the ceiling. . . . Our words floated in the dimness, in the room's mild moonlight, weightless phrases polished by the cool confident knowledge of centuries. I was eager for subjects to envelop, timeless questions demanding men of antic dimension, riddles as yet unsolved, large bloody meat-hunks we might rip apart with mastiff teeth.
>
> (48)

It is a telling moment: even as weightless words rise toward the ceiling, escaping from everything (speakers, meanings, contexts), Gary hungers to address those "timeless questions" that could be answered only by words that retain some of their substantiality. The passage's optimism is playfully undercut by the final personification ("large bloody meat-hunks"), which suggests that the world's riddles will not be solved but annihilated. Beginning in a spirit of ethereality and ending with an evocation of animalistic brutality, the quotation seems almost cautionary in its suggestion of the insidious power of imagery to usurp the place left behind by the departure of words.

Those characters in DeLillo's novels who place an uncomplicated faith in the power of verbal language often come across as reactionary and bullying; theirs is the most seemingly insurmountable form of *authoritative discourse*. Midway through *End Zone*, Gary receives a letter from his father concerning Gary's trip home at Christmas. The letter opens with a chipper proclamation ("Flying is easy if you keep alert and know what you're doing") and ends with a pessimistic reminder ("And be sure to carry some identification in case of a crash" [162]). In the space between these extremes, the father attempts to lead his son through a virtual airport ("All right, you're at the counter now"), one which houses every contingency. After reading the letter Gary knows that he must: a) hand his ticket to the person whose duty it is to collect it; b) carry his boarding pass on the inside left pocket of his jacket—since, as his father helpfully points out, he is right-handed; and c) go at once to the gate in order to avoid the "headaches" resulting from a missed plane. In a novel animated by different sorts of chaos—the chaos of football, the chaos of language, the chaos of composition—the father's certitude is anachronistic. Gary's attitude is much more indicative of the text's attitude toward traditional strategies of verbal communication; he tells his friend and military advisor Major Staley that words "don't explain," "don't clarify," "don't express" (85).

Gary's refusal to grant *any* abilities to words is, of course, problematic. What he seems to be affirming is that, to use

Artaud's phrase, "the language of words may have to give way to a language of signs" (*Theater* 107). As I have suggested, this language of signs—which in a novel is unavoidably filtered through words—comes into being when characters express themselves through bodily rhythms, visual images, and architectural allusions. Words become signs, perhaps, when they cease to be primarily communicative tools. In "Discourse in the Novel," Bakhtin speaks of the generic novel as being comprised of "heteroglot, multi-voiced, multi-styled [and] multilanguaged elements" (265). Bakhtin's assertion is validated by the idiosyncratic register of discourses we see in *End Zone*. A tackle named Raymond Toon speaks in a bizarre blend of economic terms and sportscasting metaphors; other players must continually ask him what he is *trying* to say (23-24). Major Staley's language is notable not only for its graphic detail but also for its syntactical uniformity and its reliance on copulative verbs: "There *are* problems with microcephalic offspring. . . . There *is* formation of abnormal lens tissue in offspring. . . . There *is* general reduction of body size of male offspring" (87; emphases mine). Like Gary's father, Major Staley seeks comfort in predictability and assertiveness; but, unlike Gary's father, Major Staley is attuned to the rhythms of confusion. He is aware that in the case of a nuclear war his self-assured syntax will provide little defense. Gary's other mentor, Professor Zapalac, is a paranoid "exobiologist" who is convinced that science fiction has finally "caught up with the Old Testament" (160) and who offers his dazed students space-age prophesies: "We'll all end as astroplankton" (159). These characters are united in their refusal to adjust their discourse to the needs and demands of their listeners.

Yet the more that language is abstracted and removed from the realm of conversation, the more it becomes a physical extension of the individual psyche and of the body. The psyche does not always speak in complete sentences. Bakhtin, Artaud, and DeLillo share an emphasis on the value of *concrete* intonations. For Bakhtin *intonation* is a vital and concrete feature of the communicative matrix. Intonation, according to Bakhtin and Volosinov, "lies on the border of the verbal and the nonverbal, the said and the unsaid" (399). The word *concrete* appears frequently in *The Theater and Its Double,* in which Artaud claims that his thoughts "find their ideal expression [only] in the *concrete* language of the stage" and that what is most needed on stage is a "solidified, materialized language"; he speaks of the "*concrete* value of intonations" (38) and of the ability of *concrete* gesticulations "to shatter as well as to manifest something" (46); "I shall return a little later," he says at one point, "to this poetry which can be fully effective only if *concrete*" (39; all emphases mine). This drive toward *the concrete* is also an affirmation of built space, for it is only within the walls of architecture that spatial security is a recognizable possibility. Artaud declares that "[t]o change the role of speech in theater is to make use of it in a concrete and spatial sense, combining it with everything in the theater that is spatial and significant in the concrete domain—to manipulate it like a solid object, one which overturns and disturbs things,

in the air first of all, then in an infinitely mysterious and secret domain" (72). By the terms he chooses—*spatial, significant in the concrete domain, a solid object*—Artaud emphasizes the architectonic foundation of his theater.

At the outset of *End Zone* Gary refers to "the phenomenon of anti-applause [in which] words [are] broken into brute sound, a consequent silence of metallic texture" (3). It is a phenomenon which haunts him—or which he willingly follows—throughout the narrative. In the novel, internalized forms of language are associated with football players. Before a big game, "a few people made their private sounds, fierce alien noises having nothing to do with speech or communication of any kind" (105). These "fierce alien noises" seem straight out of *The Theater and Its Double*; loudly poetic, they are clearly in opposition to what Artaud terms language's "basely utilitarian" function (46).

The character in *End Zone* who best exemplifies the Artaudian spirit is Billy Mast, a reserve defensive back who has become meaningfully attached to words whose definitions he does not know. For a course he is taking in "the untellable," he memorizes Rilke's *Ninth Duino Elegy* in German, a language he does not understand (64). After a hard game, he recites this poem about architecture, language, and the unsayable. It is no coincidence that the words (house, bridge, gate, window) in which Billy seeks solace have an architectural resonance. In these abstracted German words Billy finds habitation and what architectural theorists call *Geborgenheit* (spatial security).

Like Billy, Gary has a history of transforming the verbal into the visual. From ages fourteen to seventeen, Gary stares at the placard—"WHEN THE GOING GETS TOUGH, THE TOUGH GET GOING"—that his father had placed in Gary's bedroom. Although the sentiment has little appeal, Gary finds a beauty that emanates from the words themselves. Gary gazes at the sign until "All meaning faded" and "The words became pictures" (17). This picturesque alphabet offers Gary what the German language offers Billy Mast: a way out of the "marasmus" of the everyday. As Gary watches the transformation of words into pictures, he offers us a sense of the density of abstracted language. The placard, which cannot be reduced to any one platitudinous sentiment, becomes a storehouse of all the images that its viewer finds in it.

Throughout the novel Gary attempts to replay his adolescent abstraction of language into visuality. After listening to Major Staley's harrowing account of the possibilities of nuclear apocalypse, Gary takes a long walk through the desert. Anguished by Major Staley's narrative, Gary desperately attempts to think of other things. The abstract world he creates, however, is post-apocalyptic: "What we must know must be learned from blanked-out pages" (89). This image of "blanked-out pages" is replicated in Gary's frequent close readings of the walls that surround him. In blanked-out pages and on austere walls Gary is able to "perceive varieties of silence, small corners, rectangular planes of stillness" (191). In the walls of Logos College, Gary finds the solidity that elsewhere seems so elusive. Yet in *End Zone,* as in *The Theater and Its Double,* there is a tension between a desire for containment and a fear of enclosure.

In a discussion of walls in "Complexity and Contradiction in Architecture," Robert Venturi claims that "[a]rchitecture occurs at the meeting of interior and exterior forces of space. . . . Architecture as well as the wall between the inside and the outside becomes the spatial record of this resolution and its drama" (88-89). Both *The Theater and Its Double* and *End Zone* are animated by the tensions between walls and those whom they protect and enclose; in both works architecture successfully staves off attempts to undermine its structures. Consider first the way that Artaud speaks of placing spectators at the center of a "revolving spectacle" (86), whereby they become "engulfed and physically affected" by the performers and by the production (96). His desire to dissolve the "wall" between the audience and the spectacle is related to his "protest against the idea of culture as distinct from life" (10). Yet although frequently he articulates the magnificent possibility of living in "a culture without space or time" (10), he is adamant about maintaining control over the demarcated architecture of his own stage. "The domain of the theater," he stresses, "is not psychological but plastic and physical" (71); consequently, the stage setting must be in precise accord with the metaphysics of the *theater of cruelty.*

Interestingly, these metaphysics have less to do with the dissolution of barriers than with the re-placement of walls. Although Artaud wants to "abolish the stage and the auditorium," he insists that the hall in which his spectacles are enacted "be enclosed by four walls" and that the scenes be "played in front of whitewashed wall-backgrounds" (96-97). Here we see the architectural paradox at the heart of the Artaudian project. As much as Artaud wants to abolish the border between the spectators and the spectacle, in the end he reproduces the four-walled environment of the prototypical theater. What he challenges is the idea of the theatrical *fourth wall,* the invisible line that announces to spectators that they are watching "theater."

In a sense, Artaud is carrying on the project of the late-19th-century naturalist Émile Zola, who envisioned the theatrical innovator as one who "smash[es] the imposed patterns [and] remark[es] the stage until it is continuous with the auditorium" (351). Like Zola, Artaud emphasizes the role of the walls in the creation of the production. Far from being claustrophobic enclosures, the walls—which "act" in every scene—provide actors with the freedom of mobility that they need to chase each other around the periphery of the theatrical space. For Artaudian actors, wordlessness is an objective, but *placelessness* is a nightmare.

In *End Zone,* as in Artaud's theater, the wall acts as the point of psychological and physical change. At this intersection of "interior and exterior forces of space,"

characters also find themselves attempting to reconcile interior and exterior forms of language. Walls provide a backdrop for the characters' discursive practices (recall Gary's description of words escaping their users and rising toward the ceiling), and they also serve as the concrete embodiments of the characters' worldviews.

In the course of the novel Gary changes his mind about the nature of the relationship between language and walls. Since he initially sees walls as extensions of syntax, parts of familiar phrases ("He'll go to the wall for you"; "I'm up against a wall"), it is not surprising that he dismisses them so readily. Failing to see the Bakhtinian *inner-life* of such expressions, which are transformed by their users in certain meaningful ways, Gary initially equates walls with what he sees as a corrupt system of linguistic representation. About a tenacious player named Bobby he says: "He was famous for saying he would *go through a brick wall* for Coach Creed. Young athletes were always saying that sort of thing about their coaches. . . . Men followed such words to their death because other men before them had done the same, and perhaps it was easier to die than admit that words had lost their meaning" (53-54; emphasis mine). If Gary is flippant about Bobby's devotion to Coach Creed—"Young athletes were *always* saying that sort of thing"—he is also careful to place Bobby's "eager violence" within a larger context, Bobby ritualistically repeats what Gary sees as a platitude in order to reinvigorate through continual repetition the idea that keeps him focused. What does it mean, after all, to be willing to "go through a brick wall"? For Gary, to go through a wall is to reanimate the dialectic between *inside* and *outside*. To go through a wall is to experience the ultimate in the transcendence of architecture. Gary may be skeptical of Bobby's *gung ho* promises, but he is also envious of Bobby's cultivation of a spatial-demolition-man *persona.*

As this passage shows, Gary correlates walls to verbal clichés. He does so even more directly elsewhere in the first half of the novel. Gary notes that the "trite saying is never more comforting" than when the speaker and listener are in the presence of death, which is "the best soil for cliché" (69). At wakes, for instance, "flowers are set around the room; we stand *very close to walls,* uttering the lush benalities" (69; emphasis mine). Here Gary displays his gradually increasing awareness of the potency of spoken language, even (especially?) language that seems clichéd. As he visualizes the layers of sentiment that must be peeled away to reveal the essence of the utterance, Gary finds an *internally persuasive discourse* at the heart of the *authoritative* cliché. Even if the menace of clichés is "hidden within the darker crimes of thought and language," this menace becomes, at times of tragedy, forgivable, when "lush banalities" fill the (social and linguistic) spaces between what is said and what is unsayable. Offering our "trite sayings" we are standing "very close to walls" because walls, like verbal clichés, provide support. They are a distraction and a comfort, but they are also as multivalenced, as potentially salutary, as the densely-layered sentiments that fill the room.

During the time that he is beginning to see a new complexity in utterances and physical spaces, Gary befriends a tailback named Taft Robinson, an African-American transfer student from Columbia who zealously guards his silence. While Gary and Anatole fill the silence of their shared room with words that do not mean much, Taft sits alone and stares at his walls, at his things. Proud of the "play of shapes" of the objects in his room, and speaking of the pleasures of "creat[ing] degrees of silence," Taft gives Gary a tutorial in the mechanics of interior space. "When I change something slightly," Taft says, "everything changes" (239). Like a *De Stijl* artist, Taft has created a room of a few precise horizontal and vertical shapes; the result is a space (like that of the cliché) that is abstract and minimal but intensely connected to the physical presence of its creator, so connected that when something changes, everything changes, for the room and for Taft. The room allows Taft, in Eisenman's terms, to stand differently.

Because of Taft's influence, Gary alters his view of walls as merely components of unsatisfying linguistic utterances; because of Taft he works assiduously to "read" the nuances of blankness on Taft's walls:

> The walls were bare [observes Gary] except for an inch of transparent tape curling into itself, thumb-smudged, just one corner sticking now, a small light imprint on the wall indicating (to anyone who was interested) exactly how the tape had first been applied, at what angle to the ceiling, at what approximate angle to the intersection of that wall with each adjacent wall, at what angle to all other fixed lines in the room. The complete and absolute barrenness of the walls (tapeless) made the tape seem historic.
>
> (189-90)

Intent on safeguarding his personal identity from his teammates, Taft—who often appears around campus in dark, aviator-style sunglasses—has nevertheless left a trace of himself for others to find. This inch of transparent tape jumpstarts Gary's imagination as he attempts to understand Taft through its presence. Gary wonders what sort of poster it was that the tape pressed to the wall; he realizes, though, that the tape may be a deliberate mystery designed to throw off those who would pin down Taft's identity. "In his austerity," Gary thinks, "[Taft] blended with the shadowless room" (191). Gary, who mentally transformed his father's placard into a non-representational form, longs for an specific image that he can synecdochally connect to Taft. He knows, however, that the absence of a knowable image conveys *exactly* the image that Taft has cultivated. And Gary soon finds himself, like Taft, able to surrender himself to the contemplative abstraction of the walls themselves.

Because he finds meaningful conversation with his father difficult, Gary turns his father's platitude into a picture, which explodes into a vibrant blend of official and internal discourses. Because he cannot talk easily with Taft, for whom silence is sacred, Gary adopts a spatial vocabulary with which to express the sculptural power in the surfaces of Taft's walls. He realizes that architecture can offer "new ways to hold ourselves, to move and to be" (Kolb 46). Like his roommate Anatole, who faces tragedy by lining himself up "parallel to the horizon and [trying to] walk in a perfectly straight line" (188), Gary locates in geometry what is more difficult to find (but by no means lost) in language: beauty, precision, and truth.

Both Artaud and DeLillo envision ideal spectators for their theatrical, athletic, and literary performances. For Artaud, these spectators sit at the center of the action, which swirls around them as they become increasingly immersed. According to Artaud, the more violent the performance, the more *cathartic* the experience is for spectators. Artaud wants to provoke in their minds "a bloodstream of images, a bleeding spurt of images" (*Theater* 82), and he does not seem at all concerned that members of his audience will be tempted to re-enact these aggressive fantasias in the world beyond the theater. In fact, he defies "any spectator to whom such scenes have transferred their blood, who will have felt in himself the transit of a superior action . . . to give himself up, once outside the theater, to ideas of war, riot, and blatant murder" (*Theater* 82). Dramatized mayhem, then, serves a quietistic function. Artaud's ideal spectators are able to lose themselves completely in moments of theatrical brutality but immediately regain their composure upon leaving the architecture of the theater. Just as DeLillo counts on the ordered lines of the football field to contain the madness of the game, so Artaud trusts that his edifice will absorb all of the negative energies that are released during a production. Despite his desire to demolish the walls of traditional theatrical architecture, Artaud is compelled once again to buttress the original structure, to solidify the barrier between "art" and "lived culture."

There is, however, a difference between the ways that Artaud and DeLillo handle the issue of the spectator. Whereas Artaud's spectators sit in the center of a newly refigured space, DeLillo's spectators are forced onto the periphery. In the novel's second section—a thirty-page football *ekphrasis* (or verbal description of the visual action)—DeLillo first delineates and then abuses an "exemplary spectator." Because this spectator is uninterested in intellectual analysis of the game, DeLillo provides pages and pages of unadorned commentary ("I went ahead for five"). He offers, then, a sadistic extension of the spectator's desire for the facts. Because this spectator feels that the sport provides the illusion that order is possible, DeLillo provides him (the masculine pronoun is DeLillo's) with thirty pages of authorless text, the only order of which is projected by the reader, who seeks connections between the game's abstracted terminology—"blue turk right, zero snag delay" (113)—and earlier, more compelling textual images. Because the spectator has "a lust for details"— "impressions, colors, statistics, patterns, mysteries, numbers, idioms, symbols" (112)—DeLillo keeps the language as uninformative and as flat as he can. Because the spectator is so obsessed with football that he must struggle "not to panic at the final game's final gun," De-

Lillo treats him to a game that even Fox TV sportscaster John Madden would find forgettable. In creating a flawed space—one which is the antithesis of everything the exemplary spectator/reader wants from a text—DeLillo builds one wall between himself and the reader, and another between the numbing second part of his novel and the more vigorous sections that bookend it.

Paradoxically, the concentration in the middle section on a public event, a football game, provides the book's most private language. We do not understand much of the lingo, which seems to owe less to the conventional terms of football than to the secret languages of science fiction: "Monsoon sweep, string-in left, ready right. Cradle-out, drill-9 shiver, ends chuff" (116). This manipulation of words that exist as performative commands—telling Gary where to line up, where to feint, and where to move—is what Artaud calls "metaphysics-in-action" (*Theater* 44). It is a language that is expressive because it is so inextricably connected to what it prompts the players to do with their bodies. In this section the players engage a "whole complex of gestures, signs, postures, and sonorities" (Artaud, *Theater* 44), and if we readers feel alienated by the action, perhaps it is because our own interpretive abilities have flown and fled in the face of the more idiosyncratic registers of football. In this section, DeLillo relies on what Bakhtin calls *stylized language,* which "joins the stylized world with the world of contemporary consciousness, projects the stylized language into new scenarios, testing it in situations that would have been impossible for it on its own" (363).

I began this necessarily verbal and thus abstract essay by enlisting the theories of practicing architects; and by way of conclusion I would like, therefore, to return to a concrete example of the affinities between architecture and literary fiction. Specifically, I would like to refer to the *Gehry House,* the Santa Monica residence that architect Frank Gehry designed—actually redesigned—for himself, and suggest some parallels between this revolutionary piece of architecture and DeLillo's *End Zone.* In the light of the way that Gehry worked on the house for a number of years, continually modifying the extant structure, his project could be called *dialogical.* Indeed, in the following account by Aaron Betsky it is difficult not to hear echoes of DeLillo's cultivation of the deliberately disjunctive in *End Zone:*

> Gehry first removed the protective skin from this building, exposing its descriptive anatomy. . . . Interior walls of a pre-existing house, to which he added a U-shaped addition, were stripped, revealing wood studs and the electrical conduits snaking through them. [F]unctional boxes gave way to a flowing space defined by an asphalt floor, a corner was replaced by a distorted glass insert, and a tumbling cube . . . crashed into the kitchen area. This house confounds any traditional sense of composition, *façade,* scale, or plan; yet, it is made of original materials, which provide an internal scale and which unearth the original craft of the house.
>
> (48)

At the same time that the *Gehry House* thus violates the usual architectural expectations of beauty, symmetry, and unity, its transgression of such dictates gives it an unexpected potency. In this successful disavowal of the rules, the *Gehry House* "reads" very much like a DeLillo text (or an Artaud production).

According to Betsky, "Gehry shows that the act of building can capture the unknowable" (53). This desire to "capture the unknowable," to speak the unspeakable, is at the heart of the efforts of DeLillo. The *Gehry House,* like DeLillo's characters and Artaud's actors, is simultaneously transparent and opaque: just when we think we know it, and them, we find a new gap between structure and *façade.* The beauty of the house, like that of any DeLillo text, arises unexpectedly and departs abruptly: Gehry's house and DeLillo's novels both offer flowing spaces and asphalt floors. Even with its mysteries fully exhibited, its stripped walls showing, the *Gehry House* offers its visitors a terrific challenge, one that is analogous to the challenge held out by much contemporary literature and theory. Engaged in the house's dance of rigidities and angles, vowing to *become* the walls that once confined us, we realize what Artaud's actors and DeLillo's characters were trying to tell us all along: architecture plays a pivotal role in the construction of language and meaning.

Works Cited

Artaud, Antonin. *Selected Writings of Antonin Artaud.* Ed. Susan Sontag. Trans. Helen Weaver. Berkeley: U of California P, 1988.

———. *The Theater and Its Double.* New York: Grove, 1959.

Bakhtin, Mikhail. "Discourse in the Novel." *The Dialogic Imagination.* Ed. Michael Holquist. Trans. Caryl Emerson and Michael Holquist. Austin: U of Texas P, 1981. 259-422.

———, and V. N. Volosinov. "Discourse in Life and Discourse in Art (Concerning Sociological Poetics)." *Contemporary Literary Criticism.* Ed. Robert Con Davis and Ronald Schleifer. New York: Longman, 1989. 391-410.

Betsky, Aaron. *Violated Perfection: Architecture and the Fragmentation of the Modern.* New York: Rizzoli, 1990.

Blau, Herbert. *To All Appearances: Ideology and Performance.* New York: Routledge, 1992.

Bloomer, Jennifer. *Architecture and the Text: The (S)crypts of Joyce and Piranesi.* New Haven: Yale UP, 1993.

Brantlinger, Patrick. *Crusoe's Footsteps: Cultural Studies in Britain and America.* New York: Routledge, 1990.

Bukatman, Scott. *Terminal Identity: The Virtual Subject in Postmodern Science Fiction.* Durham: Duke UP, 1993.

DeLillo, Don. *Americana.* 1971. New York: Penguin, 1989.

————. *End Zone.* 1973. New York: Penguin, 1986.

Eisenman, Peter. *Re: Working Eisenman.* London: Academy, 1993.

Graafland, Arie. *Peter Eisenman: Recent Projects.* Nijmegen, Neth.: SUN P, 1992.

Hutcheon, Linda. *A Poetics of Postmodernism: History, Theory, Fiction.* London: Routledge, 1988.

Jameson, Fredric. *Postmodernism, or, The Cultural Logic of Late Capitalism.* Durham: Duke UP, 1991.

Kolb, David. *Postmodern Sophistications: Philosophy, Architecture, and Tradition.* Chicago: U of Chicago P, 1990.

Nehring, Neil. *Flowers in the Dustbin: Culture, Anarchy, and Postwar England.* Ann Arbor: U of Michigan P, 1993.

Saussure, Ferdinand de. *Course in General Linguistics.* Ed. Charles Bally and Albert Sechehaye. Trans. Wade Baskin. New York: McGraw-Hill, 1966.

Schulte-Sasse, Jochen. "Foreword: Theory of Modernism versus Theory of the Avant-Garde." *Theory of the Avant-Garde.* By Peter Burger. Minneapolis: U of Minnesota P, 1984. vii-xlvii.

Sontag, Susan. "Introduction." *Selected Writings of Antonin Artaud.* xvii-lix.

Tschumi, Bernard. *Architecture and Disjunction.* Cambridge: MIT P, 1994.

Venturi, Robert. *Complexity and Contradiction in Architecture.* New York: Museum of Modern Art, 1966.

Wigley, Mark. *The Architecture of Deconstruction: Derrida's Haunt.* Cambridge: MIT P, 1985.

Wilcox, Leonard. "Baudrillard, DeLillo's *White Noise,* and the End of Heroic Narrative." *Contemporary Literature* 32.3 (1991): 346-65.

Zola, Émile. "Naturalism in the Theater." Trans. Albert Bermel. *Theory of the Modern Stage.* Ed. Eric Bentley. New York: Penguin, 1968. 351-72.

David Sterritt (essay date December 1998)

"Kerouac, Artaud, and the Baroque Period of the Three Stooges," in *Mosaic,* Vol. 31, No. 4, December, 1998, pp. 83-98.

[*In the following essay, Sterritt argues that the writings of Jack Kerouac, the comedy of the Three Stooges, Kerouac's riffs on the Stooges, Artaud's writings about the theater of cruelty, and his wish for a body without organs are all related attempts to transcend the constraints of everyday life by the spirit of carnival.*]

American life in the 1950s era was famously marked by conservative discourses of consumerism, consensus, conformity, and cold war. Less frequently noted is the fact that these ideologies were challenged by a variety of interrogative, hostile, or downright negational counterparts—or "contravisions," to borrow a term from Stan Brakhage, perhaps the most radical avant-garde filmmaker to emerge during the period (143). Such oppositional currents ranged from the socially skeptical writings of Paul Goodman and David Riesman to far-reaching artistic explorations like those of Miles Davis and Thelonious Monk in music, Jackson Pollock and the New York School in painting, Judith Malina and Julian Beck in theater, and Kenneth Anger and Gregory J. Markopoulos in film, among others in sundry fields.

Central to this activity was the literature of the Beat Generation. Allen Ginsberg's jazzlike poetry, William S. Burroughs's cut-up texts, and Jack Kerouac's outpourings of spontaneous prose were at once expressions of assertively "individualistic" personalities, explorations of fecund yet officially disregarded aesthetic possibilities, and deliberately chosen sociolinguistic responses to the homogenized tone of "authoritative" literature sanctioned by the academy and/or the bestseller list.

To be sure, the Beats were not organized guerrillas recruiting partisans for group assaults on square ideology. Their rebellion took place on the dispersed terrain of scattered individual consciousness, not so much confronting the centers of organized power as ignoring or evading them. Yet this insurrection was no less carefully conceived or passionately pursued for being carried out through a combination of personal adventurism, aesthetic experimentalism, and intellectual eccentricity. It chipped away at dehumanizing norms by interrogating, demystifying, and ridiculing them, anchoring its own key values in the very oddness and unconventionality that rendered the Beats suspect in the eyes of the American mainstream.

Focusing specifically on works by Kerouac (1922-69), in many ways the group's most complex and representative member, this essay will use Mikhail Bakhtin's theory of carnivalism to explore the Beat critique of postwar society, emphasizing such key Beat strategies as ambivalent rhetorical tropes and transgressive grotesque-body imagery. Within this context, I will then argue that Kerouac's jazzlike riffs on such seemingly whimsical subjects as a movie actress's photo, an old folk song, and the Hollywood slapstick fantasy exemplified by the Three Stooges share revealing characteristics with the similarly radical assault on 20th-century sociocultural norms launched earlier by Antonin Artaud (1896-1948), the French cultural theorist who called for a "theater of cruelty" that would represent the modern human condition with unprecedented fullness and ferocity. My goal in juxtaposing these figures is to trace an underrecognized thread of socially subversive expression woven through the dense fabric of Western culture in what many think of as the monologized and homogenized years after World War II.

Kerouac thought of his work as "spontaneous bop prosody," and used his writing to rediscover in words, memories, and ideas an array of hidden or overlooked contextual meanings buried in the layers of his own consciousness and in the cultural forces surrounding him. This is especially clear in such early works as *Doctor Sax: Faust Part Three* (1959) and *Visions of Cody* (written in the early 1950s but not published until 1972, illustrating the uneasy relationship between Kerouac's unconventional style and the book business). Two of Kerouac's most complex achievements, these novels are characterized by an allusiveness, polysemia, and slippage of conventional rationality that exemplify the opposition of Beat writing to the unity and authority of most mainstream expression in the 1950s period. Viewing them from a Bakhtinian perspective, one can describe them as being rooted in the carnivalesque tradition that has mounted a centuries-long challenge to social hierarchy, constructing visions of "life drawn out of its *usual* rut" and of "'life turned inside out,' 'the reverse side of the world' ('*monde à l'envers*')" (*Problems* 122-26).

Carnival, as Bakhtin noted, has special importance in times of strong normative pressure. Pointing to the medieval period as such an era, Bakhtin notes that a typical person of that time lived two parallel lives. One was the "official" life, "subjugated to a strict hierarchical order, full of terror, dogmatism, reverence, and piety." Opposed to this was the life of carnival and the public square, "free and unrestricted, full of ambivalent laughter, blasphemy, the profanation of everything sacred . . . familiar contact with everyone and everything" (*Problems* 129-30).

Bakhtin's analysis may be applied *mutatis mutandum* to the period after World War II, when American culture attempted to nourish only the first of these two "lives," supporting this effort with claims of political and social-scientific rationality while discouraging tendencies toward pararational or "free and unrestricted" existence. Dominant discourses did not eradicate the carnivalistic sensibility, of course, but they did manage to divide the two kinds of "lives" among two highly asymmetrical groups. Proper middle-class citizens lived out something like the "official" life of the medieval subject—trudging through a round of socially sanctified activities, filling strictly designated niches in home and workplace, undergoing the terrors of cold-war paranoia while internalizing the dogmas of a culture obsessed with normality and averageness. It was left for the Beats and other self-styled rebels to live—or try to live—a more carnivalesque existence. One of their strategies was to nurture what Bakhtin calls the "image of the contradictory, perpetually becoming and unfinished being" within individual consciousness (*Rabelais* 118). *Doctor Sax* and *Visions of Cody* provide strong evidence of how much the young Kerouac belongs in this tradition—how free of restriction, how charged with laughing ambivalence, how blasphemous and profane, how fruitfully familiar and radically vulgar he wanted his daily life, and the daily lives of everyone with whom he came into contact, to be.

To make this argument, of course, is not to posit rigid or impermeable distinctions between a straitjacketed bourgeoisie, on one hand, and an anything-goes bohemia, on the other, glaring at each other across some unbreachable boundary running from the reverentially hushed churches of the former to the wild-and-woolly coffeehouses of the latter. Respectable citizens of the Eisenhower age seized numerous opportunities for carnivalesque laughter and glancing contact with the subversive and profane. Looking just at commercially marketed culture, examples of this phenomenon range from Frank Tashlin's ribald movies (e.g., *Will Success Spoil Rock Hunter?*) and Ernie Kovacs's surreal TV shows (e.g., the Brechtian blackout jokes in his weekly network series) to the drug-related inflections of Jack Gelber's plays (e.g., *The Connection*) and the burgeoning bebop scene. Conversely, many a Beat rebel experienced moments of uncertainty, submissiveness, dogmatism, and even out-and-out traditionalism. Tracing the term "Beat" to the joys of "beatitude," Kerouac himself scorned sensationalistic phrases like "Beat mutiny" and "Beat insurrection," which were repeated ad nauseam in media accounts. "Being a Catholic," he told conservative journalist William F. Buckley Jr. in a 1968 appearance on Buckley's television program *Firing Line,* "I believe in order, tenderness, and piety." In sum, while middle-class conformity and Beat contentiousness reflected radically different perspectives on the human condition, they were less sharply divided than ideologies on either side were eager to acknowledge.

Kerouac's ability to scamper nimbly along this cultural continuum, embracing insights that less flexible minds would call contradictory, is echoed by what Regina Weinreich calls an "oscillating linguistic design" in his most important novels (120). This design asserts itself in rhetorical tensions such as dream/reality, comedy/tragedy, racing up/down, raging action/gentle sweetness, and, more sweepingly, Lost Bliss/Bliss Achieved, a tension that arches through entire novels and groups of novels (122). Kerouac's predilection for mutually contesting tropes plunges his work into the "ambivalence" that Bakhtin finds at the heart of carnivalism. Such ambivalence is related to parody and also to practices of literary doubling; this is especially so when doubling goes beyond the neat binarism of opposed essences and expresses the boisterous multiplicity of dialogic dissemination, bringing together such polar distinctions as those described by Bakhtin as "birth and death (the image of pregnant death)" and "blessing and curse (benedictory carnival curses which call simultaneously for death and rebirth)." Highly characteristic of carnival thinking, Bakhtin notes, are "paired images, chosen for their contrast (high/low, fat/thin, etc.) or for their similarity (doubles/twins)" (*Problems* 126).

Kerouac's work is filled with doubles, in both its rhetorical oscillations and its narrative moments. Most immediately, one thinks of the many masks and disguises he wears as the thinly veiled protagonist of his various autobiographical novels. One also thinks of the resonant word and image conjunctions that he uses to carnivalize "proper" novelistic discourse. One may say of his creative linkages what Bakhtin said of comparable inventions in François Rabelais's prose: that they aim "at destroying the established hierarchy of values, at bringing down the high and raising up the low, at destroying every nook and cranny of the habitual picture of the world" ("Forms" 177).

Kerouac frequently accomplishes his carnivalization through an emphasis on physicality that has (at least by 1950s standards) a decidedly Rabelaisan ring. Like his 16th-century predecessor as described by Bakhtin, he often seeks an expansively comic tonality that "not only destroys traditional connections and abolishes idealized strata [but] also brings out the crude, unmediated connections between things that people otherwise wish to keep separate, in pharisaical error." By doing this he wishes, again like the Rabelais that Bakhtin describes, "to uncover a new meaning, a new place for human corporeality in the real spatial-temporal world," thus allowing the world itself to enter "a contact with human beings that is no longer symbolic but material" (*Rabelais* 170).

Kerouac's materialization is itself a deeply ambivalent enterprise, however, since yet another pairing in his life and work—an affinity with both Christian and Buddhist philosophy—leads him to complex religious inclinations that oscillate among affirmations of the flesh, of the spirit, and of flesh *and* spirit as commingled in the Roman Catholic theology (with its doctrines of incarnation and transubstantiation) that always played a part in his thinking. In his writing and in his life, he never lost an ultimately mystical fascination with what John Tytell describes as "the bared power of the actual and the ordinary, the natural and the commonplace—like the road that became his primal metaphor" (141).

The actual and the ordinary often mean the bodily for Kerouac, who peppered his 1958 article on "Essentials of Spontaneous Prose" with a noteworthy number of somatic references. In punctuation, he likens the "vigorous space dash" to "jazz musician drawing breath between outblown phrases"; in composition, he recommends not "pause to think of proper word" but rather "the infantile pileup of scatological buildup words till satisfaction is gained"; in rhythm, he recommends working "excitedly, swiftly, with writing-or-typing-cramps, in accordance (as from center to periphery) with laws of orgasm, Reich's 'beclouding of consciousness.' *Come* from within, out—to relaxed and said" (57-58).

Kerouac draws on the oral, anal, and genital levels of activity not merely to offer a string of suggestive metaphors, but to invoke verbal creation as an act of physical exchange and interpenetration with the world outside the self. In this way he aligns himself with the carnivalesque tradition of discourse about the "grotesque body" and the "material bodily lower stratum," which Bakhtin studied and celebrated in *Rabelais and His World*. The grotesque image is, for Bakhtin, that which "reflects a phenomenon in transformation, an as yet unfinished metamorphosis, of death and birth, growth and becoming" (24). His favored example is a group of figurines (in the Kerch terracotta collection) representing senile, pregnant, laughing hags who embody "a pregnant death, a death that gives birth" (25). The grotesque body "is not a closed, completed unit; it is unfinished, outgrows itself, transgresses its own limits"; its imagery emphasizes "those parts of the body that are open to the outside world," most notably "the apertures or the convexities, or . . . various ramifications and offshoots: the open mouth, the genital organs, the breasts, the phallus, the potbelly, the nose" (26).

Kerouac would surely have approved this enumeration. Mouths, genitals, and breasts recur with generous regularity in his prose adventures, as do other body parts. It is not mere coincidence, for example, that the Hollywood figure with whom he most repeatedly conflates his father's image is W. C. Fields, known throughout his film career for the proud potbelly and glowing nose that accompanied his drawling, insinuating voice. Kerouac was also familiar with intimations of life, pregnancy, and death as aspects of a single grotesque (and sometimes terrifying) cycle—as is clear from his description of the Hindu goddess Kali in his important 1968 novel *Vanity of Duluoz: An Adventurous Education, 1935-46*:

> Mother Kali of ancient India and its wisdom aeons with all her arms bejeweled, legs and belly too, gyrating insanely to eat back thru the only part of her that's not jeweled, her yoni, or yin, everything she's given birth to. Ha ha ha ha she's laughing as she dances on the dead she gave birth to. Mother Nature giving you birth and eating you back.
>
> (273)

Kerouac generally leans toward orality as the privileged site of interaction between self and world. He refers often to food, eating, and drinking, as well as talking, conversing, and singing; at times, as in the highly carnivalesque *Doctor Sax*, orality and anality are implicitly linked. Genitality enters his work through (among other things) frequent references to the promiscuous sexual relations that were a hectic part of his life as a young adult; there is also a good deal of childhood sexuality in *Doctor Sax*, which has youthful experiences with masturbation and homosexuality among its many concerns. Its oral/anal interests are even stronger. In this novel—a free-associative, often phantasmatic romance based on a calamitous flood and other incidents from Kerouac's early years in the Massachusetts industrial town where he grew up—there are a variety of grotesque (and often media-inspired) characterizations: the title character, based partly on Fields and partly on "The Shadow" of radio and magazine fame, prized by Kerouac for his orally extravagant "Mwee hee hee ha ha" laugh; Wizard Faustus, a "Master of Earthly Evil" with a "moveable jaw-bird beak" and front teeth that are "missing" (50) yet paradoxically in need of cleaning by the Wizard's own "sensual tongue" (51); and Count Condu, who is a vampire and therefore belongs to the most orally insatiable (and insatiably oral) category of horror-movie monsters. Food also plays a strong part in the book, as does the color brown. This trajectory begins to gather momentum in an early passage where the narrator, young Jackie Duluoz, remembers what he calls his Great Bathrobe Vision, which came to him while

> sitting in my mother's arms in a brown aura of gloom sent up by her bathrobe—it has cords hanging, like the cords in movies, bellrope for Catherine Empress, but brown, hanging around the bathrobe belt—the bathrobe of the family, I saw it for 15 or 20 years—that people were sick in . . . the brown of the color of life, the color of the brain, the gray brown brain, and the first color I noticed after the rainy grays of my first views of the world in the spectrum from the crib so dumb. . . . I am the pudding, winter is the gray mist. A shudder of joy ran through me—when I read of Proust's teacup—all those saucers in a crumb—all of History by thumb—all of a city in a tasty crumb—I got all my boyhood in vanilla winter waves around the kitchen stove. It's exactly like cold milk on hot bread pudding, the meeting of hot and cold is a hollow hole between memories of childhood.
>
> (18-19)

Here mother and child form an interconnected union of contradictions and complements (old/young, female/male, outside/inside, etc.) that is not closed and completed, but intertwines within itself as well as interconnecting with the world of things, of people, of movies. Its associations in the protagonist's mind with early-childhood brownness—of life/organicism, brains/thought, food/nourishment—anticipate later immersions in the brownnesses of death, decay, and rebirth. A high point of the novel comes when Doctor Sax counsels Jackie not to fear dying because "all and every moment is yearning to stay grown to you even as the pee-rade passes it—you'll take up your place in the hierarchal racks of vegetabalized heaven with a garland of carrots in your hair . . . in your death you'll know the *death* part of your life. And re-gain all that green, and browns" (204).

Oblivion and fecundity mingle with carnivalesque flamboyance in such passages. Although Kerouac's investment in the physical often serves a symbolic function, it always maintains an emphatically concrete quality rooted in his own sense of bodily reality. He shares with Bakhtin a hearty respect for the lower body, and a conviction that—as Bakhtin puts it, paraphrasing Rabelais's priestess of the Holy Bottle—the "riches hidden in this underground . . . are superior to all that is in heaven, on the surface of the earth, or in the seas and rivers. True wealth and abundance are not on the highest or medium level [of the metaphorical body] but only in the lower stratum" (368-69), whence the head of intellect is at its farthest remove, and excretion and copulation reign supreme.

Kerouac's affinity with the dialogically grotesque, carnivalistic, and material erupts more robustly still in *Visions*

of Cody, again narrated by Duluoz, now old enough to be called Jack rather than Jackie. This novel is a structurally intricate account of the freewheeling life, picaresque adventures, and passionate human relationships of Beat Generation ego ideal Neal Cassady, as seen through the eyes and filtered through the sensibility of Kerouac, his closely attached friend and admirer. The tone of the narrative is established with a boldly cinematic description (mimicking a lengthy tracking shot) of Hector's Cafeteria in New York, featuring a rich cascade of food-related imagery, and strongly evoking the carnival tradition of feasts, banquets, and cornucopia, here found in the commodified form given to it by modern consumer society.

As the novel proceeds, even passing references may find biology, mythology, scatology, and theology jangling against one another—as when Duluoz riffs out an acknowledgment that "all my life I've dreamed on breasts (and of course thighs, but now we're talking of breasts, hold your Venus, we're talking about Mars, and your water, we're talking about milk)—the dirty magazines of boyhood become the religious publications of manhood. . . ." The reference here is to a photograph described as "a pix of Ruth Maytime (the famous Hollywood actress)," with which Jack Duluoz becomes infatuated precisely because it is a simulacrum, and therefore a suitable site for the projection of fantasies and lusts generated by his own corporeality. "I can hardly think or control myself—I even know this [gazing at the photo] is infinitely more delicious than touching Ruth's breast itself (though I'd do anything for the chance)," he declares (76). Later he adds that the photo's lack of color further enhances its sexual "reality" since he "was brought up in the balconies of B-movie theaters" (77).

The filmic allusions in such passages as this and the Great Bathrobe Vision of *Doctor Sax*—with its evocation of Marlene Dietrich in *The Scarlet Empress,* conjured up by the sash of a mother's cloak—are deliberate and revealing, pointing to movies as an ideal (and idealized) site for grotesque-body imagery. This reflects Kerouac's commitment to the conversion of thought (i.e., writerly imagination) into the physicality of prose modeled less upon traditional literary conceits than upon musical, painterly, and cinematic precedents. The bodily image in cinema has rich potential for grotesquerie, since it lacks such real-world properties as solidity, three-dimensionality, and perceptibility by tactile and olfactory means. Kerouac recognizes this with particular acuteness in *Visions of Cody* when he describes the spectacle of Joan Crawford performing an on-location movie scene (which he inadvertently encountered in San Francisco one evening) and spins from it the simulacrum-upon-simulacrum of his "Joan Rawshanks in the Fog" improvisation, wherein he blows manic riffs that echo and parody cinematic procedure.

It is also in *Visions of Cody* that one finds what is possibly the most explosive combination of cinematic and grotesque-body aesthetics in all of Kerouac's work: his masterful aria on the Three Stooges, whose surreal antics become all the more phantasmatic when—in a clever extension of the appearance/reality ambivalence found in the passage on the Ruth Maytime photo—he considers the comedy trio not as illusory shadows on a screen, but as corporeal beings in the realm of the actual.

"Supposing the Three Stooges were real?" he asks with disarming directness. Then he envisions them springing to life at Cody's side, and almost instantly his prose takes on the crude, exhilarating physicality of their crude, exhilarating identities:

> Moe the leader, mopish, mowbry, mope-mouthed, mealy, mad, hanking, making the others quake; whacking Curly on the iron pate, backhanding Larry (who wonders); picking up a sledgehammer, honk, and ramming it down nozzle first on the flatpan of Curly's skull, boing, and all big dumb convict Curly does is muckle and yukkle and squeal, pressing his lips, shaking his old butt like jelly, knotting his Jello fists, eyeing Moe, who looks back and at him with that lowered and surly "Well what are you gonna do about it?" under thunderstorm eyebrows like the eyebrows of Beethoven.
> . . .
>
> (304)

As in the Three Stooges' own work—and work by some other film artists, such as the surrealist Luis Buñuel and the body-intensive Jerry Lewis—outrageous escalation is one of Kerouac's basic strategies here: "it gets worse and worse, it started on an innocent thumbing, which led to backhand, then the pastries, then the nose yanks, blap, bloop, going, going, gong . . ." (304). The setting also undergoes expressive changes, from "the street right there in front of the Station" to "a sticky dream set in syrup universe" and then "an underground hell of their own invention." Yet the reality of these Stooges is insisted upon:

> like Cody and me [they] were going to work, only they forget about that, and tragically mistaken and interallied, begin pasting and cuffing each other at the employment office desk as clerks stare; supposing in real gray day and not the gray day of movies and all those afternoons we spent looking at them . . . you saw them coming down Seventh Street looking for jobs—as ushers, insurance salesmen. . . .

And finally, looking at the notion of Stooge-Reality from yet another perspective, Kerouac acknowledges them as performers but takes *this* actuality as an ironic counterpoint to their on-screen personae:

> they are photographed in Hollywood by serious crews . . . until . . . they've been at it for so many years in a thousand climactic efforts superclimbing and worked out every refinement of bopping one another so much that now, in the end, if it isn't already over, in the baroque period of the Three Stooges they are finally bopping mechanically and sometimes so hard it's impossible to bear (wince), but by now they've learned not only how to master the style of the blows but the

symbol and acceptance of them also, as though inured in their souls and of course long ago in their bodies.
. . .

(305)

From these spectacles of Stoogeish grotesquerie, Cody derives a deep and comforting insight, realizing that "all the goofs he felt in him were justified in the outside world and he had nothing to reproach himself for, bonk, boing, crash, skittely boom, pow, slam, bang, boom, wham, blam, crack, frap, kerplunk, clatter, clap, blap, fap, slapmap, splat, crunch, crowsh, bong, splat, splat, *BONG!*" Cody's consolation is not a result of mere amusement at the Stooges' antics, or of mere diversion from the cares and conflicts that torment him. It derives rather from the Stooges' embodiment and exemplification—for Cody and for Kerouac himself—of two of the most potent transcendental possibilities to be found in Kerouac's universe.

One of these potentials is the ability of art to summon and sustain the most profound passions with which the human spirit is capable of communing; the Stooges do not simply caper and cavort, but in the untrammeled madness of their improvisations they provide "scenes for wild vibrating hysterias as great as the hysterias of hipsters at Jazz at the Philharmonics." The other is the ability of the (finite) human spirit to penetrate the realm of the (divine) transhuman spirit through the most appalling throes of materiality. "Larry, goofhaired, mopple-lipped, lisped, muxed and completely flunk—trips over a pail of whitewash and falls face first on a seven-inch nail that remains imbedded in his eyebone," Duluoz reports with matter-of-fact respect for this extreme instance of earthly suffering. And then, astonishingly, he continues:

> the eyebone's connected to the shadowbone, shadowbone's connected to the luck bone, luck bone's connected to the, foul bone, foul bone's connected to the, high bone, high bone's connected to the, air bone, air bone's connected to the, sky bone, sky bone's connected to the, angel bone, angel bone's connected to the, God bone, *God bone's connected to the bone bone.*
> . . .
>
> (304)

As wildly carnivalesque figures whose relationship to "real" character types is tenuous at best, and whose "real" existence for Kerouac transpired wholly on movie screens—he saw Joan Crawford behind the scenes, but never this crazy trio—the Three Stooges are perfect grotesqueries, capable of executing any irrationality, surviving any torment, sustaining any transfiguration that may come their way. Kerouac's trajectory for Larry's ultimate adventure begins with a Rabelaisian linkage of incongruities—eye to bone, bone to shadow—and then proceeds to an inversion of the conventionally proper (foul connects to high) and a transcendence of the materially possible (bone connects to God). Most audacious in this itemization of Larry's spiritual anatomy is its circularity, foreshadowing the cyclical configuration of Kerouac's novelistic *oeuvre* while culminating its own escalating etherreality (air-to-sky-to-angel-to-God) with a return to earthly, obdurate bone. The latter figure is doubly affirmed (*bone bone*) in its ineluctable corporeality, yet wholly transformed by its contextualization in a catalog of sublimely grotesque body parts.

Observing that the sound of one's own voice is heard largely through bone conduction, media theorist Douglas Kahn notes that the phonographically reproduced voice "returns to its parent through air conduction, that is, without the bones. The phonographed selfsame voice is deboned." Kahn concludes that such deboning constitutes "a machine-critique of Western metaphysics" since it "uproots an experiential centerpiece for sustaining notions of the presence of the voice—hearing oneself speak—and moves the selfsame voice from its sacrosanct location into the contaminating realms of writing, society, and afterlife" (93-94).

This point about phonography cannot be transferred directly to discourse about cinema, as Kahn recognizes (93, 103), because visual reflections (in mirrors, etc.) have always been comparatively accessible and familiar (sonic echoes are a weak competitor for them) and because the anatomical apparatus for vision is configured quite differently from that employed in hearing oneself speak. It remains true, however, that Kerouac's unremitting fascination with *precisely* the realms of writing, society, and afterlife led him to divine—on the "real" movie screens of B-movie theaters, and on the phantasmatic "movie screens" of his own propulsively visual imagination—a sublimated Stooge whose haplessly punctured eyebone opens on a vision that simultaneously accepts and transcends the human condition in all its ambiguous *écriture,* carnivalistic sociality, and yearning for redemption in a beyond at which even the inspired irrationality of a Stooge and Kerouac combined can only dimly hint.

Points of intersection among hysteria, corporeality, and phonography were familiar terrain for Antonin Artaud, who was famously prone to glossolalia, a nonreferential speech form—often associated with the mentally ill, the spiritually possessed, and the very young—that transforms language into a string of impenetrable signifiers, repudiating all meaning and valorizing the unadulterated voice. An instance is found in a 1945 letter he wrote to Henri Parisot, an editor and friend of the Surrealist group, from the asylum at Rodez where Artaud was confined for many years: "ortura ortura konara/kokona kokona koma/kurbura kurbura kurbura/kurbata kurbata keyna/pesti anti pestantum putara/pest anti pestantum putra" (*Selected Writings* 451). Kerouac was also fascinated with vocal sound (and its graphological transcription) as a material substance stripped of conventional signification. Examples appear at the end of his novel *Big Sur* in the appended poem "Sea," which takes its inspiration from noises of the ocean, as in this excerpt:

> Ami go—da—che pop
> Go—Come—Cark

> Care—Kee ter da vo
> Kataketa pow! Kek kek kek!

(231-32)

Like these syllables, the catalogs of onomatopoetic Stooge-abuse in *Visions of Cody* have the musicated ring of Artaud's raving glossolalia. Of particular note is the frequency of /k/ sounds in nonsemic utterances by Artaud and Kerouac alike. Looking at Artaud's late work through Roland Barthes's idea of the "grain of the voice" and Artaud's own fascination with conflating the mouth and the anus, Allen S. Weiss calls attention to Artaud's ingenuity in forging a linkage between these anatomical parts by deploying glottal sounds as a "symbolic—and physiognomic—reflection of defecation," since closure of the glottis in speech constitutes a material echo of sphincter activity in anal functioning (288-89).

Kerouac's evocation of dematerialized/rematerialized bones also carries the reader into an Artaudian domain, recalling the French author's ruminations on the convulsively reconfigured body in such a work as his 1947 radio play, *To Have Done With the Judgment of God*:

> In order to exist you need only let yourself go until you are,
>> but in order to live
>> you must be somebody,
>> in order to be somebody,
>> you must have a BONE,
>> not be afraid of showing the
>>> bone,
>> and of losing the meat on the way.

(316)

The nonplace that Artaud mentally inhabited in his later mad years appeared to him as the realm of Bardo, a liminal territory identified by ancient Tibetan theology as the home of the soul during the forty-nine days between bodily death and rebirth. Artaud describes Bardo in "Insanity and Black Magic," the final text in his 1947 book *Artaud le Mômo*—the latter word means simpleton or fool—as "the pang of death into which the self falls with a splash" (*Selected Writings* 530). For his electroshocked psyche, this represents a natural destination for the "body without organs" that he prescribes as a corrective for humanity's ills in the valedictory portion of *To Have Done With the Judgment of God*:

> Man is sick because he is badly
>> constructed.
> We must decide to strip him in order to
>> scratch
> out this animalcule which makes him itch
>> to death,
>
>> god,
>> and with god
>> his organs.
> For tie me down if you want to,
>> but there is nothing more useless than an
>> organ.

When you have given him a body without
  organs,
     then you will have delivered him from
       all his automatisms
        and restored him to his
         true liberty.

Then you will teach him again to dance inside
  out
     as in the delirium of our accordion
      dance halls
      and that inside out will be his true
       side out.

                         (328-29)

Artaud associated this deconstructed *corps à l'envers* with the invisible spaces of the radiophonic airwaves. Yet the paramorphic freedom and grandiose grotesquerie of the body without organs might also be situated in the hyperrealist realm of cinematic simulacra. In an essay entitled "The Premature Old Age of the Cinema," the skeptical Artaud asserted that in film he found only a limited "poetry of contingency, the poetry of what might be" (*Selected Writings* 314). Still, he experimented with film during his artistic career, and he perceived its capacity for deorganicizing the stuff of life when he observed in his essay "On *The Seashell and the Clergyman*," about a film made by Germaine Dulac from a screenplay he had written, that it "exalts matter and reveals it to us in its profound spirituality" while constructing a "pure play of appearances" and a "so to speak transubstantiation of elements" (*Selected Writings* 151-52). He adds that a cinema "studded with dreams" and "the physical sensation of pure life" finds its ultimate expression in "the most excessive form of humor. A certain excitement of objects, forms, and expressions can only be translated into the convulsions and surprises of a reality that seems to destroy itself with an irony in which you can hear a scream from the extremities of the mind" (*Selected Writings* 152).

Despite his conclusion in the "Cinema" essay that film "remains a fragmentary and . . . stratified and frozen . . . conquest of reality" (*Selected Writings* 314), and despite his eventual abandonment of even radio as an expressive medium, Artaud appears to have suspected that from the radiating surfaces of film might conceivably spring the supremely superficial body of which he dreamed. In the formulation of audiophonist Gregory Whitehead, this would be a body "rolling on some stunning ground"—like Captain Ahab, whose "whole beaten brain seems as beheaded"—and quoting Artaud le Mômo's late chant:

The
world,
but it's no longer me.
And what do you care,
says Bardo,
it's me.

                         (261)

The existential limbo between me and not-me, and the performative limbo between not-me and not-not-me

(Schechner 111-13), are territories of liminality that the Beat writers found haunted with dark beauties and daunting possibilities. Gilles Deleuze and Félix Guattari recognize this when they list Kerouac and Ginsberg among Anglo-American authors who "know how to leave, to scramble the codes, to cause flows to circulate, to traverse the desert of the body without organs" yet simultaneously "never cease failing" to complete a transgressive project dogged by the demons of its age. "Never has delirium oscillated more between its two poles," these philosophers conclude, lamenting the closures of "neurotic impasse . . . exotic territorialities . . . or worse still, an old fascist dream" (132-33).

Kerouac's longing for order, tenderness, and piety bears out his centrality to an American literature whose destiny is, Deleuze and Guattari suggest, "crossing limits and frontiers, causing deterritorialized flows of desire to circulate, but also always making these flows transport fascisizing, moralizing, Puritan, and familialist territorialities" (277-78). To acknowledge Kerouac's turbulent "oscillations of the unconscious," however, is not to slight the ecstatic revolutionism that erupted from the best, most paradoxical intuitions of his Bardobound spirit. Artaud reached that sublimely metaphysicized realm before him, and—grotesquely and incredibly—so did the Three Stooges, at least the way Kerouac tells it. Jackie Duluoz was perceptive when he called the Proustian meeting of hot and cold a hollow hole between memories of childhood; but it takes the older, wiser Jack Duluoz to decode those differentials of molecular motion into dialogic poles of existence and oblivion, potentiality and void, life in death and death in life; and to apprise cold-war America of the liberating news that History's carnivalesque contravisions may travel a nail-poked route to revelation through organless film-bodies like Larry the Stooge.

Works Cited

Artaud, Antonin. *Antonin Artaud: Selected Writings*. Ed. Susan Sontag. Trans. Helen Weaver. Berkeley: U of California P, 1988.

———. *To Have Done With the Judgment of God*. Trans. Clayton Eshleman. Kahn and Whitehead 309-29.

Bakhtin, Mikhail M. "Forms of Time and of the Chronotope in the Novel: Notes toward a Historical Poetics." *The Dialogic Imagination: Four Essays*. Trans. Caryl Emerson and Michael Holquist. Austin: U of Texas P, 1981. 84-258.

———. *Problems of Dostoevsky's Poetics*. Trans. Caryl Emerson. Minneapolis: U of Minnesota P, 1984.

———. *Rabelais and His World*. Trans. Hélène Iswolsky. Bloomington: Indiana UP, 1984.

Brakhage, Stan. *Film at Wit's End: Eight Avant-Garde Filmmakers*. Kingston: McPherson, 1989.

Deleuze, Gilles, and Félix Guattari. *Anti-Oedipus: Capitalism and Schizophrenia*. Trans. Robert Hurley,

Mark Seem, and Helen R. Lane. Minneapolis: U of Minnesota P, 1983.

Kahn, Douglas. "Death in Light of the Phonograph: Raymond Roussel's *Locus Solus.*" Kahn and Whitehead 69-103.

————, and Gregory Whitehead, eds. *Wireless Imagination: Sound, Radio, and the Avant-Garde.* Cambridge: MIT P, 1992.

Kerouac, Jack. *Big Sur.* New York: Penguin, 1981.

————. *Doctor Sax: Faust Part Three.* New York: Grove Weidenfeld, 1987.

————. "Essentials of Spontaneous Prose." 1958. *The Portable Beat Reader.* Ed. Ann Charters. New York: Viking, 1992. 57-58.

————. *Vanity of Duluoz: An Adventurous Education, 1935-46.* New York: Coward-McCann, 1968.

————. *Visions of Cody.* New York: Penguin, 1993.

Schechner, Richard. *Between Theater and Anthropology.* Philadelphia: U of Pennsylvania P, 1985.

Tytell, John. *Naked Angels: The Lives & Literature of the Beat Generation.* New York: McGrawHill, 1976.

Weinreich, Regina. *The Spontaneous Poetics of Jack Kerouac: A Study of the Fiction.* New York: Paragon, 1990.

Weiss, Allen S. "Radio, Death, and the Devil: Artaud's *Pour en finir avec le jugement de dieu.*" Kahn and Whitehead 269-307.

Whitehead, Gregory. "Out of the Dark: Notes on the Nobodies of Radio Art." Kahn and Whitehead 253-63.

FURTHER READING

Criticism

Arnold, Paul. "The Artaud Experiment." *Tulane Drama Review* 8, No. 2 (Winter 1963): 15-29.

> Although supporting Artaud's vision, argues that the liberation from destruction and evil through engaging in "a time of evil," which Artaud espoused, failed in theatrical practice.

Brown, Erella. "Cruelty and Affirmation in the Postmodern Theater: Antonin Artaud and Hanoch Levin."*Modern Drama* 35 (1992): 585-606.

> Considers the devaluation of the verbal in postmodern drama within the context of Artaud's elevation of gesture over language.

Brustein, Robert. "Antonin Artaud and Jean Genet: The Theatre of Cruelty." In *The Theatre of Revolt: An Approach to the Modern Drama,* pp. 363-411. Boston: Little, Brown and Company, 1962, 435p.

> Considers playwright Jean Genet as Artaud's heir.

Caws, Mary Ann. "Inappropriations: A Problematics of Response." In *Understanding French Poetry: Essays for a New Millenium,* edited by Stamos Metzidakis, pp. 237-48. New York: Garland Publishing, 1994, 271p.

> Using Artaud as well as other poets analyzes the varieties and values of several possible types of reader responses.

Croyden, Margaret. "Artaud's Plague." In *Lunatics, Lovers, and Poets: The Contemporary Experimental Theater,* pp. 55-77. New York: McGraw-Hill Book Company, 1974, 320p.

> Analyzes Artaud as one of the antecedents to experimental theater companies like The Living Theatre and The Open Theatre.

Docherty, Brian. "Artaud and Genet's *The Maids*: Like Father, Like Son?" In *Twentieth Century European Drama,* edited by Brian Docherty, pp. 146-161. New York: St. Martin's Press, 1994, 228p.

> Questions the "received wisdom" that Artaud was a significant influence on Genet.

Koch, Stephen. "On Artaud." In *The American Literary Anthology 1: The First Annual Collection of the Best from the Literary Magazines,* pp.91-107. New York: Farrar, Straus & Giroux, 1968, 495p.

> An explication of Artaud himself as a text whose core is the tension between an inexpressible inner violence and the elusive attempt to express it.

Mauriac, Claude. "Antonin Artaud." In *The New Literature,* pp. 35-49, translated by Samuel I. Stone. New York: George Braziller, Inc., 1959, 251p.

> A study of Artaud's work grounded in the study of the man himself.

Sontag, Susan.. "Approaching Artaud." In *Under the Sign of Satum,* pp. 13-72. New York: Farar, Straus & Giroux, 1980, 204p.

> Analyzes Artaud as an author whose works can inspire or repel, but which cannot be culturally assimilated.

Tonelli, Franco. "From Cruelty to Theater: Antonin Artaud and the Marquis de Sade." *Comparative Drama* 3, No. 2 (Summer 1969): 79-86.

> A study of the difference between the dramas and the stories of de Sade illuminated by Artaud's use of de Sade's stories rather than his plays for the presentation of cruelty.

Weingarten, Romain, translated by Ruby Cohn. "Re-read Artaud." *Tulane Drama Review* 8, No. 2 (1963): 74-84.

A meditation, using *The Theater and Its Double* as the text on theater, action, and ritual.

Additional coverage of Artaud's life and career is contained in the following sources published by the Gale Group: *Contemporary Authors,* **Vols. 104, 149;** *DISCovering Authors: Modules, Dramatists;* *DIS-Covering Authors 3.0;* *Major 20th-Century Writers,* **Vol. 1; and** *Twentieth-Century Literary Criticism* **Vols. 3, 36.**

Thomas Bernhard
1931-1989

Dutch-born Austrian dramatist, novelist, autobiographer, short story writer, poet, critic, and scriptwriter.

INTRODUCTION

Considered one of the most original German-language prose stylists to emerge after World War II, Thomas Bernhard earned a reputation as an intellectual *enfant terrible* for his emphasis on philosophical pessimism and his vituperative attacks upon values, institutions, and cultural and political figures of modern Austria. Compared to Franz Kafka, Peter Handke, and Samuel Beckett for his vision of isolation and despair, Bernhard often explores such subjects as physical and mental illness, death, cruelty, and decay. While his works often comment upon what he termed his "love-hate" attitude toward Austria, he chose to reside in that country throughout his life, and many critics have noted a contradiction between his preoccupation with hopelessness and failure and his prodigious literary output.

BIOGRAPHICAL INFORMATION

Raised in Austria and southeastern Bavaria during the Depression, Bernhard witnessed both the rise of Nazism and the aftereffects of World War II. He was largely cared for by his maternal grandparents, especially his grandfather, Johannes Freumbichler, a respected but impoverished novelist who introduced him to a pessimistic view of existence influenced by his reading of such authors as Michel Montaigne, Arthur Schopenhauer, Blaise Pascal, and Friedrich Nietzsche. Bernhard was sent to a boarding school for disturbed youths in Salzburg, where he was able to discern no difference between the school's Nazi supervision and the Catholic administration, which replaced it following World War II. At eighteen years of age, Bernhard developed a form of lung disease that was considered terminal, and in 1949 he came close to death. He also contracted tuberculosis while recovering in a sanatorium, an experience that resulted in a permanent hatred and distrust of the medical establishment.

In 1951 Bernhard decided to study music and acting in Vienna. He attended the Mozarteum in Salzburg a year later and in 1956 graduated with his thesis on Antonin Artaud and Bertolt Brecht. His initial literary work drew scant critical attention. In 1963 his first major work of fiction, *Frost,* was published and attracted some critical comment. At that time, his work as a dramatist was sparking controversy. Despite his expressed disdain for Austria, he

continued to live there. His final drama, *Heldenplatz,* debuted in 1988 and inspired acrimonious public debate. The play examined Austrian anti-Semitism and the country's complicity in Nazi atrocities during World War II. Bernhard died of heart failure and lung problems on February 12, 1989, in Gmunden, Austria.

MAJOR WORKS

Employing a musical yet tumultuous style in which atonality and dissonance serve to reflect the emotional states of his characters, Bernhard often focused on withdrawn, compulsive men obsessed with utopian ideals of artistic perfection who are offered no hope of religious, aesthetic, or political transcendence. Composed in unrhymed free verse, Bernhard's plays are usually surreal in atmosphere and eschew plot development and characterization in favor of compelling icons and situations that become gradually intensified and elaborated. Bernhard's first drama, *Ein Fest für Boris* (1968), reflects the influence of absurdism and the Theater of Cruelty in its blackly humorous story of a birthday party attended by a group of legless characters in wheelchairs. After presenting the hostess's husband, Boris, with long underwear and boots, the guests discuss their various maladies as Boris pounds a drum. No one notices that he has died until the drama's end. In *Die Macht der Gewohnheit* (1974; *The Force of Habit*), an elderly ringmaster with a wooden leg commands a caravan of musically-illiterate circus performers to rehearse Schubert's *Trout Quintet.* At the play's conclusion, he listens jealously to a perfect rendition of the piece on the radio. *Helenplatz* prompted heated controversy by claiming many contemporary Austrians harbor anti-Semitic sentiments. This work focuses on a Jewish professor who leaves Germany in 1938 after the rise of Nazism and commits suicide upon his return to the country in the present day.

CRITICAL RECEPTION

Bernhard's controversial plays have garnered much critical attention through the years. Many commentators have debated his place in Austrian literature as well as the playwright's attitude toward Austrian history and culture. Several reviewers have compared his work to that of Franz Kafka, Peter Handke, and Samuel Beckett. Stylistically, his dense and compulsively repetitive prose, dominated by monologues, was considered disaffecting and strange. Yet others assert that this style is effective in depicting the fragmentation of modern existence. Although some critics have faulted Bernhard's plots and characterizations as two-dimensional or undeveloped, critic Martin Esslin commented: "Bernhard's theatre is essentially a *mannerist* theatre. If his characters are puppets, all the greater the skill with which they perform their intricate dance; if his subject-matter is venom and derision, all the more admirable the perfection of the language in which the venom is spat out, the intricacy of the patterns it creates." Although notorious for the contempt he visited upon those who offered him literary prizes, Bernhard received many major awards, including the Bremen Prize, the Georg Büchner Prize, and the Austrian Prize for Literature.

PRINCIPAL WORKS

Plays

Ein Fest für Boris [*A Party for Boris* or *A Feast for Boris*] 1968

Der Ignorant und der Wahnsinnige [*The Ignoramus and the Madman*] 1972

Die Jagdgesellschaft [*The Hunting Party*] 1974

Die Macht der Gewohnheit [*The Force of Habit*] 1974

Der Präsident [*The President*] 1975

Die Berühmten [*The Famous Ones, The Stars, Notabilities,* and *The Big Names*] 1976

Minetti: ein Portrait des Künstlers als alter Mann [*Minetti: Portrait of the Artist as an Old Man*] 1977

Immanuel Kant 1978

Vor dem Ruhestand [*Eve of Retirement* or *Before Retirement*] 1979

Der Weltverbesserer [*The World Reformer*] 1979

Am Ziel [*At One's Goal* or *The Goal Attained*] 1981

Über allen Gipfeln ist Ruh: Ein deutscher Dichtertag um 1989 [*Rest Beyond the Peaks*] 1981

Der Schein trügt [*Appearances Are Deceiving*] 1983

Ritter, Dene, Voss 1984

Der Theatermacher [*Histrionics*] 1984

Einfach kompliziert [*Simply Complicated*] 1986

Elisabeth II 1987

Heldenplatz 1988

Other Major Works

Auf der Erde und in der Hölle (poetry) 1957

In hora mortis (poetry) 1958

Unter dem Eisen des Mondes (poetry) 1958

Die Rosen der Einöde (ballet sketch) 1959

Frost (novel) 1963

Amras (novel) 1964

Prosa (prose) 1967

Ungenach (prose) 1968

An der Baumgrenze (short stories) 1969

Ereignisse (prose) 1969

Verstörung [*Gargoyles*] (novel) 1969

Watten: Ein Nachlass (prose) 1969

Das Kalkwerk [*The Lime Works*] (novel) 1970

Midland in Stilfs (short stories) 1971

Korrektur [*Correction*] (novel) 1975

Die Ursache: eine Andeutung [*An Indication of the Cause*] (memoir) 1975

Der Keller: eine Entziehung [*The Cellar: An Escape*] (memoir) 1976

Der Wetterfleck (short stories) 1976

Der Atem: eine Entscheidung [*Breath: A Decision*] (memoir) 1978

Der Stimmenimitator [*The Voice Imitator*] (short stories) 1978

Ave Virgil (poetry) 1981

Die Kälte: eine Isolation [*In the Cold*] (memoir) 1981

Beton [*Concrete*] (novel) 1982

Ein Kind [*A Child*] (memoir) 1982

Wittgensteins Neffe: eine Freundschaft [*Wittgenstein's Nephew: A Friendship*] (memoir) 1982

Der Untergeher [*The Loser*] (novel) 1983

Holzfällen: eine Erregung [*Woodcutters*] (novel) 1984

Alte Meister [*Old Masters*] (novel) 1985

Auslöschung: Ein Zerfall [*Extinction*] (novel) 1986

In der Höhe: Rettungsversuch, Unsinn [*On the Mountain: Rescue Attempt, Nonsense*] (memoir) 1989

OVERVIEWS AND GENERAL STUDIES

Alfred Barthofer (essay date 1978)

SOURCE: "The Plays of Thomas Bernhard—A Report," in *Modern Austrian Literature*, Vol. 11, No. 1, 1978, pp. 21–48.

[*In the following essay, Barthofer explores possible influences on Bernhard's dramatic style and provides an overview of his early plays, contending that they do not "fit easily into commonly accepted categories of literary classification."*]

Thomas Bernhard is at the moment not only one of the most prolific and versatile but also one of the most successful young writers in the field of German drama. His plays have been performed in Berlin, Hamburg, Munich, Frankfurt, Essen, Zürich, Basel, at the Salzburg Festivals, and even in as conservative a place as the Burgtheater in Vienna. He won the Büchner-Prize, the Austrian *Staatspreis*, the Wildgans-Prize, the *Literaturpreis der Freien und Hansestadt Bremen,* and most of his plays have been shown on television in Germany, Austria and Switzerland. All in all Thomas Bernhard is widely acknowledged as one of the leading contemporary playwrights in German.

After having written almost exclusively poetry and narrative prose for many years, Bernhard shifted his creative interest to the dramatic genre. He has written seven plays so far: *Ein Fest für Boris* (1968), *Der Ignorant und der Wahnsinnige* (1972), *Die Jagdgesellschaft* (1974), *Die Macht der Gewohnheit* (1974), *Der Präsident* (1975), *Die Berühmten* (1976) and *Minetti* (1976).

Bernhard's present preoccupation with drama is not purely accidental but the artistic fruition of a long-standing interest in the theater: he worked as a theater critic for the Austrian weekly *Die Furche,* he studied Brecht and Artaud in his final year at the Musikakademie in Vienna, he wrote short dramatic sketches along with poetry at the outset of his career, and he dealt with the theatricality of human existence in his narrative prose:

> Komödie. Die Welt ist tatsächlich, wie schon so oft gesagt, eine Probebühne, auf der ununterbrochen geprobt wird. Es ist, wo wir hinschauen, ein ununterbrochenes Redenlernen und Gehenlernen und Denkenlernen und Auswendiglernen, Betrügenlernen, Sterbenlernen und Totseinlernen, das unsere Zeit in Anspruch nimmt. Die Menschen nichts als Schauspieler, die uns etwas vormachen, das uns bekannt ist.[1]

In spite of the temporary preoccupation with Brecht no major formative influence is discernible. Bernhard's plays lack Brecht's social concern and the belief in the alterability of the world. They resemble at best Brecht's early pessimistic visions of anarchy and despair. Everything centers around death as the all-determining absolute:

> Wenn wir einen Menschen anschauen
> gleich was für einen Menschen
> sehen wir einen Sterbenden
> ein Sterbender ist es
> . . . . .
> Wir sind zur Bewegungslosigkeit verurteilt
> Verstehen Sie
> wir sind tot
> alles ist tot
> alles in uns ist tot
> alles ist tot.[2]

The frequency of the death vision in his plays leads many critics to view Bernhard's works within the context of the Theater of the Absurd. Reinhard Baumgart thus talks about "Collagen aus lauter Genet-, Beckett-, Bunuel-Motiven,[3] Rolf Michaelis links Bernhard with Ionesco,[4] Franz Schonauer and Humbert Fink stress a strong affinity to Beckett,[5] and Michel Demet even claims that Bernhard is going beyond Beckett:

> Les oeuvres théâtrales de S. Beckett pourraient toutes s'appeler "fin de partie." Ce dont il s'agit chez Thomas Bernhard devrait s'appeler "après la fin de la partie," puisqu'en effet tout est joué désormais, y compris le théâtre.[6]

Siegfried Melchinger points to the influence of Büchner,[7] Céline, Lorka, Artaud, Kleist and Nestroy are also considered to have had some influence on Bernhard's dramatic style, but most attempts to place Bernhard within familiar systems of literary classifications are superficial. The similarities to Antonin Artaud's conception of the

theater as outlined by Elke Kummer and Ernst Wendt[8] for example are too vague and general to constitute a basis broad enough for valid comparison. With the exception of perhaps *Ein Fest für Boris* Thomas Bernhard's plays do not have that unique quality of language which Artaud postulates in his *First Manifesto,* nor do they explore the thematic and formal possibilities of the Theater of Cruelty as outlined in the *Second Manifesto* and put partly into practice by such German dramatists as Peter Weiss and Heiner Müller. Bernhard's plays lack the ritualistic projection of terror, violence and dissonance. The unbearable inhuman reality Artaud speaks of and its artistic transformation into powerful and overwhelming dramatic ritual can be found only in Bernhard's first play in which the blasphemous Last Supper echoes of the birthday-party conjure up an atmosphere of hypnotic horror and madness. The grotesque birthday presents and the bizarre conversation heighten the grisly atmosphere of macabre farce and semi-religious frenzy.

Although Bernhard's theatrical world is full of horror, menace and cruelty, none of the other plays shows such a strong affinity to the Theater of Cruelty as *Ein Fest für Boris.* The monologic structure of most of these plays is based on the sterile verbosity of the protagonists; this structure in turn destroys the ritualistic conception of reality postulated by Artaud as the only basis of drama. The legless cripples, the wheelchairs, the empty and restricting interior, the mysterious bond between the main characters, the verbal inhibition silencing the majority of characters, and numerous minor details of Bernhard's first play echo in more than a distant way the gloomy picture of man in Samuel Beckett's *Endgame.* All of Bernhard's plays have something in common with Beckett's plays: namely, a pessimistic outlook. Both playwrights present a frightening vision of a decisive endphase in the development of human behaviour, institutions and beliefs. But Thomas Bernhard's plays are not ambiguous in their final resolution. With the exception of *Die Macht der Gewohnheit* they all end in a climactic vindication of death, anarchy and universal stasis. The presentation of an advanced stage of physical, intellectual and emotional disintegration constitutes, in fact, the central concern of Bernhard's plays. The lack of comic elements and mythical and literary allusions, elements which give depth to Beckett's elliptic plots, reduces human existence as presented by Bernhard to unbearable monotony and barrenness.

In his first play, *Ein Fest für Boris,* Thomas Bernhard anticipates already the major themes and formal characteristics of his later plays. Man is seen as being trapped in an empty meaningless world which is threatened by disintegration from within and by physical destruction from without. Attempts to break out of this situation are defined as pointless and illusory. There is no divine plan at work in man's immediate universe, and productive value systems, even in their most rudimentary form, are almost nonexistent or simply figments of deranged minds. Enriching human relationships no longer exist because man cannot extend beyond himself. He lives in suffocating artificiality, hopelessly cut off from nature's regenerative resources. The inarticulateness of the majority of characters and the unbearable monologo-mania of the principal characters reflect accurately the irrevocable breakdown of meaningful communication.

Thomas Bernhard's plays mirror one central concern: sickness decay and death. And yet, in spite of this almost pathological obsession with the dark and unpleasant aspects of the human condition, a very serious attempt is made to interpret the maddening chaos of this world and to determine whether the aggressive force which continuously threaten man's existence are a biological necessity or manifestations of corrupt value-systems. The very fact that his plays (and novels) offer hardly any hope for optimism should not distract from this major concern of his artistic endeavour.

In the first play, ***Ein Fest für Boris,*** which is structured around the birthday-party of cripples, Bernhard demonstrates that the world of goodness ("Haus der Guten") as defined by modern secularized society is just as sick and absurd as the world of the *Krüppelasyl.* The vaguely altruistic gestures of the "good woman" are revealed as selfish, irrelevant, and even destructive. This revelation is worked out in the confrontation, or rather attempted synthesis, of the value-system of the "good woman" and the world of suffering (*Asylwelt*). The latter may very well assume grotesque and macabre dimensions, but it is indicative of man's destruction by inhuman systems set up by society to serve society. In spite of the multiple breaking of reality (e.g. the cripples' dream world) the desire of the cripples for a new *Asylordnung* is neither extravagant nor exotic:

DER ÄLTESTE KRÜPPEL:

> Es gehört schon lange eine neue
> Asylordnung

ALLE

> Eine neue Asylordnung

> (99)[9]

They specify that the *Asylwelt* should include "allmonatliche gründliche Inspektionen" (99), "besseres Essen," "frische Bettwäsche," "neue Rollstühle," "mehr Schwestern," "weniger faule Ärzte," "bessere Medikamente," "einen neuen Chirurgen" (100), and "mehr Abwechslung" (101). Their wishes could be found in any socially minded party platform. And in view of the *KZ*-like conditions prevailing in the cripple-asylum they are undoubtedly modest proposals for urgently needed improvements. Reviewers frequently ignore these issues altogether. They fail to recognize that the bleak world conjured up in Thomas Bernhard's plays is to a large extent man-made, an idea which also plays a major role in Dürrenmatt's dramatic model of the human condition.

The cripples are highly realistic and down to earth when they define their basic needs: in an almost Brechtian fashion they deny the relevance of art to human suffering:

> Wir brauchen besseres Essen
> längere Betten
> Verbesserungen unseres Allgemeinzustandes
> keine Künstler
> keine gescheiten Menschen liebe Frau.

> (102)

They realize that the *Asyldirektor* and his dehumanized collaborators are at best indifferent to their suffering. One is instantly reminded of Kafka when the oldest cripple says: "Es stimmt meine Dame / Wir dürfen uns beschweren / aber es nützt nichts" (97). Torture, neglect, repression and sadism are the most striking features of the asylum:

> Er tut jedem weh
> er schneidet jedem ins Gesicht
> ins Ohr
> in den Hinterkopf
> in den Hals
> ins Kinn.

> (97–98)

It is highly ironic that this system has been devised by a minority whose task it is to alleviate the suffering of the cripples. Neither collective lamentations, nor the shallow rhetorical outbursts of the "good woman" will and can change the plight of the people concerned:

> Eine Schande
> Eine Schande für die Anstalt
> eine Schande für das Asyl
> eine Schande für den Anstaltsdirektor
> eine Schande für den Staat
> Das ist doch absurd.

> (80)

Being aware of the unalterability of their condition, the cripples withdraw into a bizarre dream-and-fantasy world in which no ultimate development towards optimism is possible. This is brought out particularly strongly by the powerful alienation-, withdrawal- and death-imagery which dominates their utterances.

The marked emphasis on intellectualism (cf. the numerous head references) and the continuous association of the head area with darkness point at disproportionate cerebration as a chaos-generating force:

> Große sehr große Köpfe
> in der Finsternis
> Ihr müßt euch vorstellen
> sehr große Köpfe
> in der Finsternis
> aufeinmal waren die größten Köpfe da.

> (65)

This view brings Thomas Bernhard very much in line with two other Austrian writers who were most ardent adherents of this idea: Alfred Kubin and Fritz von Herzmanovsky-Orlando. Some critics interpret Bernhard's concept of nature in a completely negative way. Chaos and darkness are seen as integral aspects of nature and not as phenomena associated with man's intellect: "Because the 'normal' state of nature is 'Finsternis' and 'Chaos,' it is natural that man too should move toward that state. Natural too therefore that disease, madness and crime are end products of nature whereas health, sanity and temperate living are unnatural."[10] Their interpretative models which are based on this assumption should be re-examined and modified in the light of the plays. It is worth mentioning in this context that the stronghold of destruction and annihilation is clearly the man-dominated sphere and not nature. With the exception of *Die Jagdgesellschaft* nature receives little attention in Bernhard's plays.[11]

Moreover, physical mutilation is not presented as an unavoidable natural phenomenon. It is associated with war and modern technology: "Im Krieg im Krieg / Aber die andern haben ihre Beine / nach dem Krieg verloren wie ich / nach dem Krieg" (87). (Cf. also the semi-cryptic references to Ireland, 104). Although the accident of the "good woman" is surrounded by a shroud of mystery, everything points to modern technology as the real cause of the disaster (24–25). There are also clear indications that poor judgment and mistakes, and not uncontrollable cosmic forces, have contributed their share to the cripples' present predicament: "die Fehler die wir gemacht haben / die Unvorsichtigkeiten die dazu geführt haben / daß wir keine Beine mehr haben liebe Dame" (104). This does, of course, not remove the overall pessimism of the play, but it places some of the responsibility for human suffering on man himself. The cripples in Thomas Bernhard's play are certainly not like Gödicke in Hermann Broch's novel *Die Schlafwandler*. Gödicke succeeds in re-establishing his viciously mutilated *Ich* at least in his wish-dream fantasies. The cripples are worse off. They are exposed to immense suffering (83), but they do not even have the strength to reject life in its present humiliating form: "Wir denken darüber nach / wir besprechen es / aber wir tun es nicht" (89). Their existence turns into an obsessive preoccupation with death.

The inhuman conditions prevailing in the asylum are due to the viciousness of those running it and the unconcern of those not directly involved. The all-pervasive disintegration process illustrated in the play (physical mutilation and mental derangement being its most conspicuous aspects, but by no means the only ones) is to a large extent man-inflicted. The depressing fact that wholeness and happiness turn out to be a madman's dream does not necessarily invalidate these notions, but it reflects the advanced stage of perversion in commonly accepted standards. This perversion is also brought out in the description of man in animal terms. The religious area is associated with apes: "Erinnern Sie sich an den Affen / an den Affen / mit dem ich gesprochen habe / diese plötzliche Unterhaltung mit dem Affen / Der Affe hat mich erkannt / der einzige der mich sofort erkannt hat der Affe / der Kaplan / der Affe ist unser Kaplan" (46–47). The doctors in the asylum are continuously referred to as pigs (e.g. 98, 100). Johanna

who has to wear a pighead at the costume ball and in the house of the "good woman" is not part of this image field. With her the pighead represents a negatively qualified fertility area. Her attempts to take it off (44–45) in order to break away from the "good woman" and to establish her identity in a more natural environment are indicative of her repressed natural instincts (46). Johanna's unique position is supported by the fact that she is the only one with legs among a party of fifteen leg-amputated cripples. Her role of a "Beinlose" during Boris's birthday celebration is only temporary and not real: "Sie spielen ja heute nur / daß Sie keine Beine mehr haben" (69). And yet, Johanna is a rather ambiguous character. The numerous references to her intellectual faculties are in sharp contrast to her inarticulateness and her complete failure to extricate herself from the sterile influence of the "good woman." Her mute obedience to her opponent can be explained only in terms of a strong sexual bondage. One is, indeed, reminded of Werner Faßbinder's lesbians, whose initial affection has turned into fathomless hatred but who cannot live without each other.

The "good woman" is just as important in the play as Boris and his crippled friends in the asylum. In spite of her name, her close links with the Church, her preoccupation with charity (90), and her inflated caritative gesture towards Boris (50) the "good woman" (and all she stands for) does not offer any prospects for hope and optimism. The crown and the royal attire at the costume ball are just as much out of place as her claims to goodness. With her some of the most basic positive areas of life have become grossly perverted and farcically meaningless. Her social charities and her superficial benevolence have no permanent palliative impact on the suffering of the cripples. The birthday party which she arranges for Boris is a grotesquely ludicrous charity luncheon with strong Last Supper connotations. Shortlived escapism is actually all she has to offer. She echoes not only the words of Karl Kraus[12] but also those of Christ at the Last Supper: "eßt eßt trinkt trinkt / trinkt alle eßt alle / essen Sie doch Johanna essen Sie / trinken Sie" (70). In so doing she reduces Christ's ultimate gesture of love to grotesque irrelevance.[13] While most of the birthday-presents (90–91) are indicative of the cripples' regression into childhood, the "Offiziersstiefel" (92) of the "good woman" lay bare the true but repressed layers of her personality. Everything in her is in a state of hopeless confusion. Her desire to have a strong husband is mixed up with warped Christian principles. Her desire to have children gives way to perverted possessiveness (51). Her self-inflicted isolation is in sharp contrast to her intense longing for sympathy. Her orders to cut down all the trees of the park (54) reflect her destructive unnaturalness. Her immobility, which she herself defines as the "Todeskrankheit der Natur" (33) highlights a fatal stasis. Wealth and luxury offer little help. Anxiety has become a permanent condition. (28) The house of the "good woman" turns out to be a diabolic trap of death and despair and not a genuine alternative to the absurdities of the asylum for cripples.

Thomas Bernhard's second play, ***Der Ignorant und der Wahnsinnige*** (1972), was written specially for the *Salzburger Festspiele* and performed at the Salzburger Landestheater only once.[14] At first sight it has very little in common with ***Ein Fest für Boris***. The depressing shadow world of the cripples is left behind in favour of unsurpassable artistic perfection (79) and rare scientific achievement: "Der Doktor / ist eine Kapazität / in ganz Europa / schätzt man ihn / seine Bücher / und seine Schriften / sind in sämtliche / Sprachen übersetzt" (96). These two areas are set up as unique and autonomous realms of heightened human experience. The question of the ultimate contribution of artistic experience and scientific knowledge to the enrichment of man's life is scrutinized and becomes a major issue of the play. The answer is finally in the negative: artistic perfection and scholarly pursuit fail to have a positive and lasting impact on man's existence. They lead, as the play convincingly demonstrates, to soulless mechanization (cf. *Koloraturmaschine* (7, 80) and to death (99) on the one hand, and to man-alienated, inhuman specialization on the other:

> wie die Medizin ja überhaupt nichts
> mit dem Menschen zu tun hat
> verstehen Sie
> diesen Irrtum geehrter Herr
> weil die Medizin überhaupt nichts mit dem Menschen
> zu tun haben kann.
>
>   (36–37)

The Doctor's sciento-mania, as reflected in the numerous lengthy passages dealing with anatomical subtleties, exhausts itself in mechanical descriptiveness and does not go beyond man's phenomenological reality. It is hardly more than a morbid preoccupation with death and the worst form of self-congratulatory academic scholarship divorced from social responsibility and human concern:

> Das Gewebe ist das Interessante geehrter Herr
> nicht das darunter
> oder dahinter
> oder wie immer.
>
>   (37)

The play has no action. Its most conspicuous structural feature is to be found in the endless monologues of the Doctor and the *Königin der Nacht*. The father of this world-famous coloratura soprano is impatiently waiting for his daughter to sing her part for the two-hundred-and-twenty-second time (42). With him in the dressing room is the Doctor, an eminent scholar and close friend of the soprano. Since she arrives at the very last moment the two have plenty of time to talk about anatomy, music, and life in general. Finally the *Königin der Nacht* arrives and is made ready for another brilliant performance. Afterwards the three meet in a most exclusive restaurant. The celebration, however, opens up an abyss of unhappiness and futility in the life of the soprano and ends in complete darkness with her death. (Part Two) Success does not alter the fact that life is a torture. The father of the soprano lives in the shadow of the twin peaks of artistic and scientific

achievement without higher aspirations. He is "ein völlig heruntergekommener Mensch" (49) and lives more for his "Schnaps" than for anything else. His inarticulateness shows striking parallels to ***Boris*** and to the majority of characters in Thomas Bernhard's later plays. All he actually does is to interrupt the Doctor's never ending flow of words and to repeat mechanically fragments of it.

The problem area associated with the father highlights irreparably damaged family relationships and common patterns of escapism. The family is no longer a wholesome unit. Paternal possessiveness and suspicion distort affection and make life unbearable: "Zwischen Ihnen Herr / und Ihrer Tochter / ist nichts als Mißtrauen / Ursache aller möglichen Krankheiten" (38). The inability of the older generation to face reality, which is brought out in the numerous references to blindness, forces them back into a completely inappropriate childhood world (38) or makes them seek refuge in meaningless activities without being aware of it: "man flüchtet / in eine unsinnige Tätigkeit / und sei es / daß man von einem bestimmten Zeitpunkt an / nur mehr noch trinkt / oder auf und ab geht / oder die ganze Zeit / nur mehr noch mit Kartenaufschlagen verbringt / mit Handlesen / der eigenen Hände / geehrter Herr / oder mit Briefschreiben / oder mit wahnsinniger Lektüre / daß man jedesmal / wenn man aufwacht / wieder ein Medikament einnimmt / um wieder einzuschlafen / und so jahrelang / Jahrzehntelang geehrter Herr" (40–41). Whereas the other people are unaware of the monotonous emptiness and superficiality of life, the artist and the scientist are only temporarily fooled. They recognize man's futile attempt to hide behind a smoke-screen of existential irrelevancies:

> Hätten wir nicht die Fähigkeit uns abzulenken
> geehrter Herr
> müßten wir zugeben
> daß wir überhaupt nicht mehr existierten
> die Existenz ist wohlgemerkt immer
> Ablenkung von der Existenz
> dadurch existieren wir
> daß wir uns von unserem Existieren ablenken.
>
>   (22–23)

The scientist makes this insight an essential part of his "Lebens-philosophie." The artist becomes its victim.[15] The endeavours of the artist and the scientist are also designed to distract from the real issues of life. For that reason they must fail to fill human existence with true meaning and satisfaction. The scientist contributes very little to the understanding of the universe: "Aber was erklären / wenn doch überhaupt nichts / erklärt werden kann" (74). The work of the artist is identified with artificiality and is defined as a life-alienating activity which transforms people into "Maschinen" (7, 53, 80), "künstliche Geschöpfe" (17) and into lifeless puppets: "Wie Sie wissen Frau Vargo / handelt es sich / um ein Puppentheater / nicht Menschen agieren hier / Puppen / Hier bewegt sich alles / unnatürlich / was das natürlichste / von der Welt ist." (55) The *Scheinwelt* of the theater is therefore totally unsuitable for man's self-realisation:

Das Theater
insbesondere die Oper
ist nichts
für einen natürlichen Menschen.

(97)

The same is said about highly specialized scientists. The Doctor is probably the best example to illustrate this point. True self-realisation can be attained only in the conscious confrontation with suffering:

das Leben ist eine Tortur
wer das nicht begreift
und die Platitüde
nicht wieder gut
und zur Tatsache die schmerzt macht
hat nichts begriffen
andererseits kommen wir
gerade in den Angstzuständen
zu uns selbst.

(18)

A marked step towards total pessimism occurs in Thomas Bernhard's third play *Die Jagdgesellschaft*. As in previous works, man is again defined as sick and unable to understand the world around him (cf. theme of blindness): "Dadurch sind wir krank / dadurch haben wir / jeder von uns / eine Todeskrankheit" (70–71).[16] Physically he is an invalid (104). The artistic-intellectual side of man as represented by the *Schriftsteller* turns out to be completely death-oriented and without positive potentials. The artist's obsessive preoccupation with sickness and death reduces the cognitive force behind his experience of reality to purely negative unproductive observations. This becomes particularly obvious in the middle and final sections of the play. The new aspect introduced in *Die Jagdgesellschaft* is, however, the extension of decay and death to nature in form of a sudden and mysterious infestation of a huge forest area in which the play is set with a most destructive species of *Borkenkäfer*:

Tatsache ist
daß der Borkenkäfer
alles hier
alles mit dem Jagdhaus Zusammenhängende
zerstört
zerfrißt
alles.

(44)

In this atmosphere of doom and imminent death the irrevocable breakdown of human relationships moves also in its final phase. The *Jagdgesellschaft,* which comprises a general, his wife, two ministers, a prince, a princess and a writer, gathers in one of the "schönsten Jagdhäuser / in einer gänzlich von der Außenwelt abgeschnittenen Gegend" (104). The continuous references to snow (49), coldness (39) and darkness (39) create an atmosphere of hopelessness. The unregenerative quality of nature around the *Jagdhaus* is final. Nature even becomes the destructive agent of circumstance as the death of the young woman in

Warsaw (10) illustrates. Similarly, the Christian festival no longer offers hope. It has become a superficial *Theaterstück* (90) with angels in white dresses (88). The religious area is just as much in danger as the General's forest and the party in the hunting lodge. There is no divine force at work in the plays of Thomas Bernhard. The *Schriftsteller* identifies with the philosophy he has found in one of Lermontow's novels:

und da ich es mir zur Regel gemacht habe
nichts bedingungslos zu verwerfen
und mich auf nichts blind zu verlassen
so warf ich die Metaphysik über Bord
und richtete den Blick wieder auf den Boden zu
meinen Füßen.

(107)

But all he discovers is a dead pig. The writer's attitude towards metaphysics is a fairly common one in Bernhard's theatrical world. In this chaotic world of ours in which only material values and private obsessions matter everything is transitory. All human activities are demasked as futile attempts to ignore this basic truth:

Die Leute kaufen sich an
sichern sich ab
eine Wissenschaft
eine Partei
eine Kunst ist es
alle suchen aufeinmal Zuflucht
plötzlich werden sie katholisch
oder werden wieder katholisch
um nicht verrückt zu werden.

(108–109)

Self-deception and fear reduce man's life to a "schäbigen Unteraltungsmechanismus" (102), to something completely artificial and frequently purely mechanical. Cardplaying (55–76), hunting and talking for the sake of talking are the most striking examples. The substitutive quality of these activities is obvious. The numerous allusions to sex during the cardplay highlight not only the players' incapability of establishing an appropriate relationship but also the irreversible breakdown of the General's marriage. Although the General attributes rejuvenating qualities to hunting (30), its real purpose is *Ablenkung* (82). His suicide finally results from the Writer's aggressive frankness (104–105) and the General's inability to face reality. The General embodies aristocratic decadence and a deep-seated guilt feeling connected with his role in World War II: "Jedesmal wenn er in den Wald geht / und er findet ein erfrorenes Wild / denkt er an die erfrorenen Soldaten" (109). The numerous allusions to war thus link man again unambiguously with death and destruction. The desperate attempts to save the forest by destroying it stress man's predicament.

In Bernhard's fourth play *Die Macht der Gewohnheit* (1974) man's life is identified with the circus. The essential aspect of the metaphor, however, is not the glamor and splendor of the opening night but the almost unbearable drudgery of everyday life and work. To escape the stultifying boredom of the circus and the repulsive smell of the arena, *Caribaldi,* the ringmaster and key figure of the comedy, decides to play Franz Schubert's *Trout Quintett.* His incessant endeavours connected with this idea reduce the actual circus reality to insignificance. For more than twenty years *Caribaldi* has been pursuing this idea with incredible ruthlessness and brutality:

> Die Probe findet statt
> und wenn ich sie alle mit Fußtritten
> an ihre Instrumente treten muß.
>
> (83)

The play, which is just one of these daily rehearsal-rituals illustrates that he has achieved nothing so far:

> In diesen zweiundzwanzig Jahren
> ist es nicht ein einziges Mal gelungen
> das Forellenquintett
> fehlerfrei
> geschweige denn als Kunstwerk
> zu Ende zu bringen.
>
> (22)

The very fact that the Ringmaster and his subordinates never get beyond the tuning cacophony and a sporadic *Zupfen, Streichen* and *Kolophonieren* indicates the impossibility of breaking through the oppressive confines of human imperfection and suffering:

> Mit schmerzverzerrtem Gesicht
> kann man nicht Schubert spielen
> schon gar nicht das Forellenquintett.
>
> (23)

Man is trapped in the suffocating narrowness of his job. He is homeless (cf. *Wohnwagen*) and compelled by brute force to an empty, meaningless existence. Life has become a nightmare in Caribaldi's empty caravan. Yet, nothing can be done about it:

> Wir wollen das Leben nicht
> aber es muß gelebt werden.
>
> (43)

Everybody is sick in some way, above all, the Ringmaster whose art-motivated brutality keeps everything going. He is invalid, old and embodies Thomas Bernhard's ever recurring idea of *Herrschaft des Kranken und Häßlichen*:

> Der Kranke und der Verkrüppelte
> beherrschen die Welt
> alles wird von den Kranken
> und Verkrüppelten beherrscht.
>
> (34)

With a whip the Ringmaster reduces the people around him to unreflective puppets and animals: "Wir sind nichts / als Tiere / . . . / Tiere / nichts als Tiere" (69). In spite of his noble aspirations Caribaldi's personality is indicative

of man's easy regression into his animal past. It is therefore not surprising that the Lion Tamer, who is continuously linked with violence, though a "durch und durch bürgerliche Existenz" (40), should be his "fleischlicher Neffe" (30). The Lion Tamer illustrates a very important truth: repression does not make free, it only creates further dependence:

> Die Tiere gehorchen mir
> umgekehrt
> gehorche ich den Tieren.
>
> (60)

The only character with the potential of self-realisation is the Juggler. He is never identified with the aggressive animals of the circus and he lacks the inarticulateness of the others. His intellectual faculties are not idle—he even reflects on the detrimental impact the German language has on him: "Die deutsche Sprache / verdummt mit der Zeit / die deutsche Sprache / drückt auf den Kopf" (24). He also expresses a deep desire for freedom (54). Nevertheless, he is not strong enough to extricate himself from his humiliating (27) doglike condition (70). The dream of an eternal spring at the Riviera (23) and of a life together with his sister (54)[17] are the only alleviations.

The most vulnerable character of the play is Caribaldi's grandchild. Her work on the tightrope is associated with the beautiful (78) and even divine (75). However, the numerous death qualifications and the fact that the tightrope work is defined in terms of unreflective mechanical functionalism destroys its inherent elevating potential. The grandchild, like all the other characters, becomes a lifeless puppet. Dirt, illness, domestic trivialities, coldness and suffering are the most important forces in her world. Happiness and harmony as hinted at in the cryptic references to Casals are uniquely rare phenomena of a distant and foreign world. Childhood becomes a traumatic experience, and life is drudgery. The hope of rejuvenation and renewal normally associated with the child is irrevocably destroyed, and this situation constitutes perhaps the most depressing aspect of this play.

Thomas Bernhard's fifth play *Der Präsident* (1975) purports to deal with political issues. The central character is an omnipotent dictator-president whose assassination finally exposes his country to anarchy. This play consists of two disjointed monologues characterized by such key lexical items as anarchy, terrorism, revolution, hatred, fear and death:

> Haben Sie denn nicht Angst vor den Terroristen
> Daß Ihnen ein Anarchist auflauert
> Sie glauben Sie machen ein Buch auf um zu lesen
> und werden in Stücke gerissen
> haben Sie nicht Angst davor
> Alle haben Angst
> alle
> alle
> in diesem Staat herrscht nurmehr noch die Angst.
>
> (47)

The dictator-president's lying-in-state at the end of the play highlights the temporary end of mass-executions (46) and the victory of a new generation headed by the president's son and intellectual malcontents: "Das Proletariat ist es nicht / Frau Frölich / die Intellektuellen sind es" (74). But their attempt to overthrow the repressive system in power and to improve the chaotic conditions prevailing in the world amounts to nothing:

> Die Welt ist ein Sauhaufen
> mein Kind
> ein Sauhaufen
> nichts als ein Sauhaufen
> Schweinerei
> nichts als Schweinerei.
>
> (139)

The revolution is a kind of *Spiel* (138) which ensures the replacement of figureheads and functionaries but not a genuine renewal of the human socio-political unit. For at the end of the play the scene seems to be set for even more effective and brutal repression. The basic political philosophy underlying Bernhard's play is thus similar to that of Max Frisch's *Graf Öderland* or Büchner's *Dantons Tod*. Moreover, the many allusions to the president's unprecedented rise from "ganz unten" (117) where he knew the "Bratengeruch der Wohlhabenden nur aus den Fenstern" (139) and to his present social indifference and vicious brutality as well as his contempt for the lower classes as the "Abschaum der Menschheit" (138) emphasize the corrupting influence of power and wealth. The very accusation tabled against the ordinary people epitomizes the president's own direction of development:

> Wenn es dem Volk zu gut geht
> wird es größenwahnsinnig
> und die Verrückten
> zünden den Staat an
> Das Volk wird größenwahnsinnig
> und verliert den Verstand
> Dann kann man es nicht mehr eindämmen meine
> Herren.
>
> (158–159)

Thomas Bernhard's *Der Präsident* is not a political play in the strict sense of the word. Unlike some of the political plays that have appeared in Germany in recent years it demasks the idea of the alterability of the world as a fatal illusion. The extremely pessimistic interpretation of the human condition presented in it and the implications arising from it are just another artistic manifestation of Bernhard's gloomy pessimism:

> Die Welt ist ein Unrat
> sonst nichts
> Und durch diesen Unrat gehen wie durch eine große
> Bewußtlosigkeit
> gehen und gehen und gehen mein Kind.
>
> (121)

The obsessive vigour with which the successful Austrian playwright gives artistic expression to the universality of

death and man's tragi-comical inability to come to terms with it, separates him distinctly from the mainstream of contemporary German drama. Man is no longer seen within the narrow confines of his social environment as is the case in the works of most dramatists writing "im Bannkreis Brechts."[18] At this point, something ought to be said about Bernhard's dramatic strategy in general, because it might help to appreciate the unique structure of his plays morefully. Bernhard dislikes above all well developed stories and plots.

> Ich bin ein Geschichtenzerstörer, ich bin der typische Geschichtenzerstörer. In meiner Arbeit, wenn sich irgendwo Anzeichen einer Geschichte bilden, oder wenn ich nur in der Ferne irgendwo hinter einem Prosahügel die Andeutung einer Geschichte auftauchen sehe, schieße ich sie ab.[19]

This dislike is clearly reflected in all his works. Moreover, he claims to write primarily for actors and *not* for an audience:

> Es hat mich als ehemaliger und wahrscheinlich lebenslänglicher sogenannter Schauspielschüler immer nur interessiert, *für* Schauspieler zu schreiben *gegen* das Publikum, wie ich ja immer alles gegen das Publikum getan habe, alles gegen meine *Leser* oder meine Zuschauer, um mich retten, mich bis zu dem äußersten höchsten Grade meiner Fähigkeiten disziplinieren zu können.[20]

His arrogant remarks concerning the *Geistfeindlichkeit* of audiences have angered many people: "Das Publikum ist der Feind des Geistes, deshalb habe ich für das Publikum nichts übrig, es haßt den Geist und es haßt die Kunst und es will nur das Dümmste zur Unterhaltung, alles andere ist nichts als Lüge, mir aber ist das Dümmste zur Unterhaltung immer verhaßt gewesen, also muß mir das Publikum verhaßt sein, es ist und muß Feind bleiben . . ."[21]

Bernhard's more recent play *Die Berühmten* (1976) needs somewhat less attention. It does not differ markedly from previous plays as far as dramatic technique is concerned. However, the texture of ideas is thinner than in most of the other plays. Some of the issues discussed have been dealt with in a similar context elsewhere. The play is basically a long-winded send-up of the commercialization of art:

> Die Kunst insgesamt ist heute
> nichts anderes
> als eine gigantische Gesellschaftsausbeutung
> und hat mit Kunst so wenig zu tun
> wie Musiknoten mit den Banknoten
> die großen Opernhäuser wie die großen Theater
> sind heute nur große Bankhäuser
> auf welchen die sogenannten großen Künstler
> tagtäglich
> gigantische Vermögen anhäufen.
>
> (17)

In a loose sequence of five scenes the myth of the greatness of artists is ridiculed and destroyed. The essence of present-day art turns out to be money:

Der Künstler ist der ideale Künstler
wenn er auch ein guter Geschäftsmann ist
denn sonst geht er ja alle Augenblicke
unweigerlich in die Falle
Die Opernhäuser sind Fallen.

(112–113)

Art is defined as a mass-product (13). Bernhard seems to attack what Horkheimer and Adorno call *Kulturindustrie*. Salzburg, where the play is set, is one of its centers. The very fact that there are hardly any references to Salzburg throughout the play indicates, however, that Bernhard is not primarily interested in a specifically local facet of a widespread cultural phenomenon. The issues raised in the play must therefore not be seen in the narrow context of Salzburg but as pertaining to art and artists in general.[22] Seven world-famous artists (musicians, actors, singers and a publisher) gather in the summer residence of an equally famous basso to eat, drink and to celebrate their host's splendid achievement as Ochs in Richard Strauss's opera *Der Rosenkavalier*: "Aber es war ihre Idee / Sie alle heute einzuladen / zur Feier meines zweihundertsten Ochsen / zweihundertmal der Ochs" (36). In the ensuing table-conversation which forms the structural skeleton of the play the eight celebrated artists reveal themselves as comically lifeless puppets. Their conversation consists of nostalgic reminiscences of a grotesquely trivial nature and cultural chit-chat. The content of their talk and the language they use bring out their true nature. The initially harmless dinner party turns suddenly into a frightening nightmare when the eight artists turn spontaneously against the puppets representing their idols and destroy them:

schlägt auf den Kopf der Lotte Lehmann
Regisseur zieht blitzartig ein Messer und stößt es
Max Reinhardt in den Rücken
Tenor würgt und erwürgt Richard Tauber,
gleichzeitig erschlägt der Kapellmeister mit einem
einzigen Faustschlag Toscanini
Verleger zieht eine Pistole und schießt Samuel
Fischer in das Genick
Pianistin springt auf und bekommt einen Schrei-
krampf und stürzt sich auf die immer noch gleich-
mäßig spielende Elly Ney und packt ihren Kopf
von hinten und schlägt ihn mit beiden Händen
mehrere Male auf den Bösendorferflügel. . . .

(69–70)

In the final scene the artists wear animal masks and produce deafening animal noises. The *Offenbarung der Künstler* is thus complete.

The key character of Thomas Bernhard's most recent play *Minetti: Ein Porträt des Künstlers als alter Mann* (1976) is the brilliant German actor Bernhard Minetti whose interpretation of *Caribaldi* made headlines in Germany and Austria. The play was originally planned to be performed in Stuttgart on New Year's Eve 1975 with Bernhard Minetti in the title role. However, Bernhard did not finish the play in time and the plan had to be dropped.

In a short letter to Henning Rischbieter the author indicates why he wrote the play especially for Bernhard Minetti:

Diesen großen, wahrscheinlich größten spielenden und also lebenden und seinen Beruf und also seinen und also unseren bühnendramatischen Wahnsinn verhexenden Schauspieler muß ich noch ausnützen bevor er nicht mehr ausgenützt werden kann, diesen durch and durch elementaren *Geistestheaterkopf*. Wir haben in einem Jahrhundert nicht viele solche uns *tatsächlich* auf die Nerven gehenden Künstler![23]

The very fact that a living actor is given the task to act out his own life as an actor highlights Thomas Bernhard's basic belief in the theatricality of life:

Das Leben ist eine Posse
die der Intelligente Existenz nennt.[24]

The play, which is set in a shabby old hotel in Ostend on a stormy New Year's Eve, is above all a play about waiting. The hotel personnel is waiting for new guests to arrive, a lonely middle-aged woman is waiting for the time to pass (45), a young girl is waiting for her lover (52), and an old actor is waiting for the theater-director who has offered him a job:

Ich erwarte den Schauspieldirektor von
Flensburg
Zur Zweihundertjahrfeier des Theaters in
Flensburg
spiele ich den Lear
Shakespeare
Ich habe dreißig Jahre nicht mehr gespielt
ich bin dreißig Jahre nicht mehr aufgetreten.

(46)

During the thirty years of humiliating isolation in Dinkelsbühl he devoted all his time to the study of classical literature (which he hates) and Shakespeare's *Lear*:

In der Dachkammer meiner Schwester
in Dinkelsbühl
spielte ich an jedem Dreizehnten des Monats
vor dem Spiegel den Lear
immer pünktlich um acht am Abend
in Ensors Maske mein Kind
um nicht aus der Übung zu kommen.

(53)

Now he is anxiously waiting for the theater-director to arrive, but he is continuously disappointed:

Ich glaube
der Schauspieldirektor ist es
aber ein Liliputaner kommt herein
oder ein Verkrüppelter
Jedesmal wenn die Tür aufgeht glaube ich
es ist der Schauspieldirektor
zum Mädchen
Ich habe das Beweismittel verloren
das Telegramm
in welchem mich der Schauspieldirektor auffordert
nach Ostende zu kommen.

(53)

The theater-director, of course, never arrives. Finally, the old actor opens his huge trunk and puts on his much cherished Lear-mask, sits down on a bench and perishes in the snow storm.

The allusions to Shakespeare, Beckett, and Joyce are obvious. And yet, Thomas Bernhard's new play is by no means a superficial imitation of these writers. It is uniquely Bernhard. As a matter of fact, it is one of the most moving plays he has written so far. The bitter experience of a life in isolation shines gently through the protagonist's monologues, and in the scene with the young girl the monologue turns unobtrusively into a dialogue reflecting genuine concern and interest for others. This is something new in Bernhard's plays.

Thomas Bernhard's overriding concern with death as the central issue of life and the final absurdity of man's existence makes his world akin to that of Ionesco, Beckett, Genet and other representatives of the Theater of the Absurd. However, just as Thomas Bernhard's preoccupation with Artaud and the Théâtre de la Cruauté had no direct and tangible impact on his dramatic writing, neither did his study of Beckett and Brecht impoverish his own creative stance. Like Williams, Miller, Albee and Inge, Thomas Bernhard is intensely concerned with man's inability to relate productively to others without accepting their rigid rationalistic framework of psychology. The flat monotonous repetitiveness in his characters' monologues echoes Harold Pinter, and his perceptive observations in regard to the communicative depreciation of language show a strong affinity to one of Peter Handke's major artistic concerns. It is perhaps in this area as well as in his interpretation of the futility of man's existence and in the imprisoning irrelevancy of inflated human endeavours where his real achievements are to be found.

Thomas Bernhard is not a typical representative of the thinking of his generation, nor do his plays fit easily into commonly accepted categories of literary classification. They are unique in their own way and whether they will eventually become landmarks of modern German drama is a question which only the future will be able to answer.

Notes

1. Thomas Bernhard, *Verstörung,* Frankfurt/M. 1967 (Insel Verlag), p. 164f.

2. Thomas Bernhard, *Die Jagdgesellschaft,* Frankfurt/M. 1974 (Bibliothek Suhrkamp 376), p. 67.

3. Reinhard Baumgart, "Der Pomp des Elends." In *Süddeutsche Zeitung,* 20.2.1973, p. 13.

4. Rolf Michaelis, "Elegie für 15 Rollstühle." In *Frankfurter Allgemeine Zeitung,* 1.7.1970, p. 32.

5. Franz Schonauer, "Die Welt kann ruhig Gesundheit vortäuschen." In *Kölner Stadt-Anzeiger,* 29.7.1967, p. 9. Humbert Fink, "Beckett in Tirol?" In *Allgemeines deutsches Sonntagsblatt,* Hamburg, 20.9.1964, p. 12. See also: Franz J. Görtz, "Hier

spukt natürlich Beckett." In *Text und Kritik, Thomas Bernhard,* Nr. 43 (Juli 1974), pp. 36–44.

6. Michel Demet, "Le Théâtre de Thomas Bernhard, Nostalgie de la Nature et Triomphe de l'Artifice." In *Etudes Germaniques,* vol. 31 (Janvier-Mars 1976), p. 66.

7. Siegfried Melchinger, "Das Material ist die Wahrheit der Welt." In: *Theater heute,* Heft 6 (Juni 1974), p. 8.

8. Elke Kummer und Ernst Wendt, "Die Schauspieler in den Schauspielern der Schauspieler." In *Theater heute,* Heft 12 (Dezember 1969), pp. 37–38.

9. Thomas Bernhard, *Ein Fest für Boris,* Frankfurt/M. 1968 (edition suhrkamp 440). All references to the other plays are to the following Suhrkamp editions: Thomas Bernhard, *Der Ignorant und der Wahnsinnige,* Frankfurt/M. 1972. (Bibliothek Suhrkamp 317). Thomas Bernhard, *Die Macht der Gewohnheit,* Frankfurt/M. 1974. (Bibliothek Suhrkamp 415). Thomas Bernhard, *Der Präsident,* Zürich 1975 (Bibliothek Suhrkamp 440). Thomas Bernhard, *Die Berühmten,* Frankfurt/M. 1976 (Bibliothek Suhrkamp 495).

10. D.A. Craig, "The Novels of Thomas Bernhard." In *German Life and Letters,* XXV (1971–72), p. 346.

11. In Thomas Bernhard's poetry "nature" plays an immensely important but highly ambiguous role. See Alfred Barthofer, "Berge schwarzer Qual. Zur Lyrik Thomas Bernhards." In: *Acta Germanica,* Bd. 9 (1976), pp. 187–211.

12. Karl Kraus, *Die letzten Tage der Menschheit,* Teil I, Akt I, Szene 23.

13. Rolf Michaelis, "Elegie für 15 Rollstühle." In: *Frankfurter Allgemeine Zeitung,* 1.7.1970, p. 32.

14. Heinz Beckmann, "Das Notlicht ist dunkel genug." In: *Rheinischer Merkur,* 11. August 1972, p. 16. (The ORF (Austrian Television) showed the play even twice: 8.11.1972 and on 30.11.1974).

15. See the soprano's experience in the Teatre Fenice (p. 28) and the Falstaff theme.

16. See also p. 42, p. 44, p. 69, p. 101, p. 104.

17. This problem is raised frequently in Thomas Bernhard's works. It forms the nucleus of the early short story *An der Baumgrenze* and of his latest novel *Korrektur,* Frankfurt/M. 1975 (Suhrkamp).

18. Walter Hinck, Das moderne Drama in Deutschland, Göttingen 1973, p. 152 and p. 206.

19. Thomas Bernhard, *Drei Tage.* In: Thomas Bernhard, *Der Italiener,* Salzburg 1971, p. 152.

20. Thomas Bernhard, "Bernhard Minetti." In: *Theater 1975.* Sonderheft der Zeitschrift *Theater heute,* p. 38.

21. *Ibid.*

22. Thomas Bernhard attacks Salzburg for similar reasons (and others) in his two semi-biographical books *Die Ursache,* Salzburg 1975 and *Der Keller,* Salzburg 1976. In the former he writes: "Im Sommer wird unter dem Namen Salzburger Festspiele in dieser Stadt Universalität geheuchelt und das Mittel der sogenannten Weltkunst ist nur ein Mittel, über diesen Ungeist als Perversität wegzutäuschen, wie alles in den Sommern hier nur ein Wegtäuschen und ein Wegheucheln und ein Wegmusizieren und Wegspielen ist, die sogenannte Hohe Kunst wird in diesen Sommern von dieser Stadt und ihren Einwohnern für nichts anderes als ihre gemeinen Geschäftszwecke mißbraucht, die Festspiele werden aufgezogen, um den Morast dieser Stadt zuzudecken. Aber auch das muß Andeutung bleiben, hier ist nicht der Platz und jetzt nicht die Zeit für eine diese ganze damalige und heutige Stadt betreffende Analyse, Gedankenklarheit und gleichzeitig Gnade dem, der eine solche Analyse jemals macht" (112).

23. Thomas Bernhard, "Bernhard Minetti." In: *Theater 1975.* Sonderheft der Zeitschrift *Theater heute,* p. 38.

24. Thomas Bernhard, "Minetti. Ein Porträt des Künstler als alter Mann." In: *Theater heute,* Jg. 17/10 (Oktober 1976) p. 51. This play is presently not available in book form. The complete text of the play can be found in the above journal pp. 45–55.

Martin Esslin (essay date Spring-Summer 1978)

SOURCE: "Contemporary Austrian Playwrights," in *Performing Arts Journal,* Vol. 3, Nos. i–ii, Spring-Summer, 1978, pp. 93–8.

[*In the following essay, Esslin places Bernhard within the context of contemporary Austrian dramatists and compares his plays to those of Irish writer Samuel Beckett.*]

Austrian writers use the German language and there is thus not little confusion about whether a world-renowned playwright and novelist like Peter Handke is German or Austrian. Yet the distinction is not without importance, and is becoming increasingly so. Present-day Austria is the remnant of the nucleus of what was, until 1918, one of Europe's great Empires, rivaling Germany and Russia in extent and population. Between 1918 and 1938 Austria was, it is true, independent, but unwillingly so: the German-speaking part of the rump of the Austro-Hungarian Empire wanted to join Germany, and it was only through the compulsion of the victorious powers after World War I that the little country remained independent. Then, in 1938, Hitler achieved the unification of Austria and Germany. It looked as though the end of Austria as a country had arrived. But, so tactlessly and cruelly did the Germans behave, so openly did they treat the Austrians as inferior, and, as the war broke out, so evident did it become that being one with Germany was far from comfortable (and Austrians are proverbially addicted to comfort) that, for the first time, a genuine desire to be free of the German connection developed. After World War II there thus arose a genuine Austrian national feeling, a genuine Austrian national identity. No longer did educated Austrians try to speak as clear and dialect-free a German as possible; suddenly it was socially acceptable, even desirable, to have a recognizably different language. And that could not remain without influence on literature.

Moreover, after the holocaust of World War II, German literature had to deal with the overwhelming topic of German national consciousness, the question of guilt and its expiation. The Austrians, because they had felt occupied and oppressed by the Germans and saw themselves as victims rather than instigators of the war, felt no such compulsion to devote themselves to bitter heartsearchings about the sources of the relapse into barbarism which preoccupied their German colleagues. So not only the language but the subject matter of post-World War II Austrian literature became different.

Austrian writers and intellectuals began busily to rediscover the roots of their different national tradition and identity: the Baroque theatre, the Viennese folk theatre of the early nineteenth century, Schnitzler, Hofmannsthal and the great satirist Karl Kraus were re-defined as the forebears and creators of a specifically Austrian attitude to drama. These newly consecrated classics were eagerly cultivated by the many theatres of Vienna and the other Austrian cities—Linz, Graz, Innsbruck, Salzburg and Klagenfurt. What is it that differentiates these dramatists from the German tradition?

Whereas in Germany the main trend in the literature of the eighteenth century had been the endeavor to create a "respectable" German literature, which could rival the achievements of the other great nations of Europe—England's Shakespeare, Spain's Calderon and Lope de Vega, Italy's Dante, France's Racine and Molière—so that the cruelly divided German nation could make a valid claim to political unity and national identity, Austria, the center of a powerful Empire and secure in its power as a major country, was free from this somewhat hysterical effort. Hence, while in Germany the folk theatre was being frantically cleaned-up and academics established classical standards of "high" literature as against the vulgar entertainments of the people, in Austria this division into a serious and a trivial stream in the theatre never took root. The greatest achievements of Austrian theatre were works in the "vulgar" tradition: the fantastical fairy tale plays of Raimund, the broad but brilliantly witty farces of Nestroy, the entire tradition of Viennese operetta which culminated in works like Johann Strauss's *Die Fledermaus* and ultimately helped to inspire the American musical. Much of this dramatic literature was, being folk theatre, in broad Austrian dialect.

And this is where the younger generation of Austrian playwrights took their inspiration after World War II. Even writers who do not use dialect, like Peter Handke and Thomas Bernhard, are deeply preoccupied with the problem of language and are in open revolt against the prevailing German tradition of serious, thoughtful, and didactic theatre which characterizes the works of the German giants from Schiller and Goethe to Brecht and Peter Weiss. There is always a light, almost cabaret-like touch in the work of these Austrians and even their gloomiest pronouncements are somehow uttered tongue-in-cheek. In Austria, the old saying goes, the situation is always desperate but never hopeless. The country's deepest melancholia (and the popular image of a jolly, *gemütlich* Austria is a fake, perpetrated for the benefit of tourism) is ultimately reducible to a mood of gallow's humor, black comedy, laughter among ruins and decay.

Of the three playwrights who have become pre-eminent in the last decade (and are now, undoubtedly, among the most successful in the whole German-speaking area), the oldest is Thomas Bernhard. Born in 1931, he is also, at least on the face of it, the gloomiest. Bernhard, a most accomplished novelist and brilliant stylist, writes his plays in a very characteristic free verse; there are many parallels in his work to that of Samuel Beckett, although he claims that he developed his style long before he had read any of Beckett's work. And it may well be that there is a deeper affinity between the two writers, as Bernhard, like Beckett, is in his novels and stories deeply preoccupied with mental breakdown, schizophrenic states of mind, and feelings of alienation from the world of men. Bernhard's plays lack plot; they are, essentially, explorations of mood and conceived as series of images, poetic metaphors that are brought to concrete existence on the stage. His first great success, *Ein Fest für Boris* (*A Party for Boris,* 1970), for example, shows a rich lady, only referred to as *Die Güte* (*The Good Soul*), who has lost both legs in an accident. To make her feel less disadvantaged she is surrounding herself exclusively with other legless people, has married a cripple and is giving a party for him, so that the stage is full of legless cripples careering around in wheelchairs. The action of the play, which revolves around "the good soul's" relationship with the only character with legs in the play, her secretary, pales before the gruesome humor of that image. Similarly, in *Der Ignorant und der Wahnsinnige* (*The Ignoramus and the Madman,* 1972), we are in the dressing room of a great coloratura soprano in her decline, who is appearing as the Queen of the Night in Mozart's *Magic Flute* that evening, and is only referred to as the Queen of the Night. Her voice teacher is talking learnedly about the mechanism by which the human voice can be made beautiful and artistic, while the singer's doctor discourses at great and gruesome length about the way a corpse is dissected and illustrates his words on a big chart. We are thus shown the tension between the human body as the vessel from which the most sublime spirituality, Mozart's music, can emerge but which at the same time is a veritable cesspit of decay and corruption. Bernhard's only play which he has actually labeled a comedy, *Die Macht der Gewohnheit* (*The Force of Habit,* 1974), deals with a similar tension in the human condition. Here a

circus director, Caribaldi, has been trying to make his staff (the lion tamer, the tightrope walker, the juggler, and the clown) perform the *Trout Quintet* by Schubert. For years they have been rehearsing under his guidance and yet they have not mastered anything beyond the first notes, but Caribaldi relentlessly forces them to go on with it. The whole play presents us with just one such rehearsal, a hopeless quest for artistic perfection. And when, as usual, the rehearsal breaks up in angry recrimination and Caribaldi despairingly sinks back in his armchair, he turns on the radio from which emerges the perfect harmonies of a superb performance of the *Trout Quintet.* Here again what is at issue is the gap between the vulgar world of everyday life (the circus) and the high spiritual sphere which, we know, exists somewhere out in the empyrean, but which seems beyond our reach. In the first performance of *The Force of Habit* the part of Caribaldi was played by the great old German actor, Bernhard Minetti. Bernhard's latest play is called *Minetti* (1976) and shows an old actor who has come to a town where he believes he has been invited to play the part of Lear. But, Godot-like, the director with whom he thinks he has a date never appears and the play ends with the old man sitting in the street in a snowstorm, still waiting to play Lear, while having himself *become* Lear. . . .

. . . Austria has always been a major power among the nations of Europe as far as the theatre and playwrights have been concerned—from Raimund and Nestroy to Grillparzer, Schnitzler, Hofmannsthal and a host of other great names. The present generation is even more clearly and characteristically Austrian, both in the special flavor of their language and their very individually slanted subject matter. . . .

Hans Wolfschütz (essay date 1980)

SOURCE: "Thomas Bernhard: The Mask of Death," in *Modern Austrian Writing: Literature and Society After 1945,* edited by Alan Best and Hans Wolfschütz, Oswald Wolff Ltd., 1980, pp. 214–35.

[*In the following essay, Wolfschütz traces Bernhard's literary career and investigates the thematic and formal consistency found in his poetry, novels, and plays.*]

Thomas Bernhard's early prose collection *Ereignisse* (*Events,* written in 1957) takes the form of a sequence of anecdotally-fashioned episodes each presenting a variation on that most central of concepts in modernist writing, the intrusion of 'Schrecken' of terror and horror, into everyday reality. In such a moment of shock the victim inevitably looks at his own existence and his relationship with the world about him in a new light, as, for example, does the painter in one of Bernhard's episodes; at work on his scaffolding high above the people in the street, he is suddenly struck by the ridiculous nature of his elevated position:

> Ein entsetzlich lächerlicher Mensch! Jetzt ist ihm, als stürze er in diese Überlegung hinein, tief hinein und hi-

nunter, in Sekundenschnelle, und man hört Aufschreie, und als der junge Mann unten aufgeplatzt ist, stürzen die Leute auseinander. Sie sehen den umgestülpten Kübel auf ihn fallen und gleich ist der Anstreicher mit gelber Fassadenfarbe übergossen. Jetzt heben die Passanten die Köpfe. Aber der Anstreicher ist natürlich nicht mehr oben.[1]

All Bernhard's characters are marked by such an 'event', whether this takes the form of some personal misfortune or shock, or has been experienced as part of a general or historical 'catastrophe'. But whereas in his early prose Bernhard is still primarily concerned with the actual moment when a sense of normality gives way to a sense of alienation, in most of his more typical work of the 1960s and 1970s the emphasis is switched to the effects of this new awareness, to the presentation of a mind and consciousness that have been wholly deranged by the experience. The connection with external reality has disappeared. Bernhard's typical character is, to use the image of the 'Anstreicher', suspended between the scaffolding and his death in the abyss of his own inner world. He is a 'survivor' whose monomanic visions of decay and dissolution are the last hold to which he clings before his final fall.

The episode of the 'Anstreicher' also illustrates the second basic pre-condition for Bernhard's writing—the experience of the inward collapse of illusionistic art and art-forms. Bernhard's dislike for such painters of façades, who from their bird's-eye-view paint a harmonizing gloss over the world, that is his hatred of 'high art', is evident in most of his work. The grotesque image of the yellow wash running over the dead painter's body expresses an awareness of the death of such art and its artistic means, an awareness which forms the basis of the author's own iconoclastic approach to literary conventions.

Bernhard's uncompromising vision of man caught in the web of a solipsistic universe together with the far-reaching formal consequences of his defection from a belief in art as an organizing structure account for the fascination (and frustration) of his readers and critics. Critics may describe his work as akin to torture but this has not prevented them from writing extensively about it. Bernhard must rank as Austria's most widely-discussed and controversial writer, arousing such dissenting views as angry denunciations of his obsessive obscurantism or the high praise of George Steiner, who regards him as 'the most original and concentrated novelist writing in German'.[2] His status in the Austrian literary scene may be described as 'that of being at the same time a kind of "modern classic" and required reading, and, at least in the eyes of some, an *enfant terrible,* a poseur or even a charlatan'.[3]

It was not until the early 1960s that critics started to take an interest in Bernhard's writing. By then he had already published three volumes of poetry written under the haunting shadow of a serious illness which had very nearly proved fatal. These poems, for the most part an expression of his religious and mystical search for meaning, speak of a world full of suffering, brutality and coldness, but they are too close to personal experience to escape the charge of sentimental melancholia and self-indulgence. Even in the volume *In hora mortis* (1958) written several years after his brush with death, Bernhard shows but a fleeting glimpse of the rebellious self-assertion that was to become such a characteristic feature of his later writing. In these poems the lyrical 'I' is attempting to overcome his fear of death through religious faith, but without success, for he receives no answer from his God. The cycle ends in a cry of mental anguish that is clearly expressionistic in both idiom and pathos:

> tot ist längst
> mein Rot
> mein Grün
> mein Stachel
> zerschnitten
> ach zerschnitten
> ach zerschnitten
> ach
> ach
> ach
> mein Ach.[4]

In his early prose work, on the other hand, Bernhard shows a much greater control over his personal pain. *Ereignisse* illustrates his new-found capacity to invest an individual dilemma with universal significance and to create a new norm, that of a life lived in the aftermath of the experience of 'Schrecken'. This is particularly evident in the progression from the opening to the closing episode. *Ereignisse* begins with the hasty flight of two lovers into a tower where, in each others arms, they attempt to blot out the memory of an unspecified horrific experience. Their flight is echoed in the final episode, but this time it is a mass flight, the flight of a crowd seeking sanctuary from air-raids in tunnels bored into the mountains. Bernhard's conclusion is grotesquely macabre:

> Als nun aber der Krieg zu Ende ist, geschieht etwas, das niemand begreifen kann: sie schütten die Stollen nicht zu, sondern gehen, wie es ihnen zur Gewohnheit geworden ist, hinein. Sie werden, solange sie leben, die Stollen aufsuchen.[5]

The escape gained by the two lovers promised a momentary release, now, at the close of the collection, there is nothing but permanent incarceration in a mind frozen by fear. Those who return to the tunnels have become automatons controlled by a force whose power-source has long been extinguished.[6] Having survived their experience of war and death, life for them is but an empty ritual.

Even the narrator in *Ereignisse,* whose traditional function would involve drawing the various strands together in a meaningful pattern, is seen at the end of the sequence to be as much a 'survivor' as those whose fate he has described, and must be accounted part of the world he depicts. Thus there are no standards which might help the reader to assess the distortions portrayed. The narrator cannot interpret the world or put it into perspective but he is able to present it in a detached manner with occasional moments of grotesque and ironic lightening. This dual aspect to the narrator prefigures one of the most striking features of Bernhard's later narratives—the objective and dispassionate presentation of extremely subjective experience.[7]

Both of Bernhard's early novels *Frost* (1963) and *Verstörung* (Disturbance, 1967) follow this pattern and begin realistically enough before probing deep into the minds of their protagonists. The narrator in *Frost,* a young medical student, is given the task of observing and reporting on a painter, Strauch, who is allegedly mad and who has retreated to a mountain village. He begins his study with a fascinated and yet critical attitude but gradually loses the scientific detachment of the mere observer. By the end of the novel he can only express himself in the language and idiom of his 'case history':

> Er schiebt ganz einfach seine Hinfälligkeit in Form von Sätzen in mich hinein, wie photographische Bilder in einen Lichtbilderapparat, der dann diese Schrecken an den immer vorhandenen gegenüberliegenden Wänden meiner (und seiner) selbst zeigt.[8]

In *Verstörung* the narrator accompanies his father, a doctor, as he makes his house-calls. Their journey proceeds via stages of physical and psychological mutilation until it ends at Hochgobernitz, the seat of the mad Prince Saurau. In much the same manner as the young medical student in *Frost,* the doctor's son also suffers a process of depersonalization: he falls prey to the fascinating charm of the darker world represented by Saurau and finds himself reduced to a silent transmitter of his gigantic monologue (which covers about two thirds of the novel).

Both novels reflect Bernhard's penchant for adapting traditional elements of narrative fiction for his own idiosyncratic presentation of a monomanic world. The journey which the doctor's son undertakes for 'educational purposes' and which, as so often with Bernhard, takes him upwards, clearly echoes the structure of the *Bildungsroman*. The outcome of this educative journey is, however, not self-awareness and self-recognition but self-loss. The narrators of both novels are taken over by the characters they encounter, characters whose deranged talking it becomes their function to record and transmit.

Such a reduction of the narrator to a mere transmitter shatters the basis of traditional realism—the dialectical relationship of inner and outer reality. In most of Bernhard's subsequent narratives the narrators cease to exist as identifiable characters with recognizable features, but even so the reader remains aware of their narrative presence. It is a shadow existence, often suggested by nothing more substantial than extensive and sustained passages in the subjunctive mood, or by means of the reported speech in which they record the monologues of the central characters.

Within the hermetic world of these monologues there is nothing that exists in its own right. Topography, events

and all the minor characters are merely the outward manifestation of a single psyche; thus the nightmarish village in *Frost* with its cripples, drunkards, lunatics and criminals is merely the outer shell of the disturbed workings of the painter Strauch's mind, and the house-calls in the first part of *Verstörung* are merely the first, basic, often animal-like steps towards the rarified philosophical derangements of Prince Saurau.

In much the same manner Bernhard's work as a whole presents a sequence of variations on a set of identical situations, characters and settings. There is no individuality to these settings and they are well-nigh interchangable, whether they are isolated hamlets, menacing valleys, impenetrable forests, or castles and estates which in earlier times were centres of economic power but are now no more than dilapidated anachronisms. Bernhard's central characters are shadowy figures too, for the most part psychological cripples on the threshold of madness with no hope of escape into the sanctuary of former times nor any prospect of a meaningful future; having withdrawn to the extreme solitude of some bleak mountain retreat they lead a life of total introspection and philosophical contemplation devoting themselves to such topics as the irrelevance of the state, the senselessness of historical development, the hostility of nature, disease, madness and above all, death.

Thematic and formal consistency is the hallmark of all Bernhard's work. He deliberately turns his back on such contemporary preoccupations as the relevance of literature in the political and social context, or the search for new artistic forms and methods, and concentrates on the one recurrent image of the world—an organism inescapably caught in its own vacuity. His writing thus acquires an uncanny immediacy as each new work provokes a moment of recognition when the reader detects the familiar set pieces, quotations and ideas rearranged in a new and unfamiliar context. Any 'development' there has been in Bernhard's work after the appearance of *Frost* must be seen in terms of increasing emphasis on a limited spectrum of stock-situations. In Bernhard's plays this has led to a measure of self-parody which can be seen in the shift from **Die Macht der Gewohnheit** (**The Force of Habit,** 1974), still largely a parable, to the sheer self-caricature and self-denunication of **Die Berühmten** (**Notabilities,** 1976) or **Immanuel Kant** (1978). The shrinking world of Bernhard's narrative fiction reaches its ultimate stage in his novels *Kalkwerk* (The Limestone Works, 1970) and *Korrektur* (Correction, 1975).

Not surprisingly such an insistent pattern of repetition and variation has led many critics to charge Bernhard with increasing sterility and a consequent failure to provoke and irritate his public. His most recent narrative *Der Stimmenimitator* (The Mimic, 1978), a collection of some hundred short episodes, does, however, suggest a welcome change of direction. As Ulrich Greiner notes:

> Im *Stimmenimitator* hat Bernhard kein neues Thema, wohl aber eine neue Methode gefunden. Während er

früher aus dem absolut Ungewöhnlichen die Lust des Schreckens saugte, holt er sie hier aus dem scheinbar Gewöhnlichen.[9]

In its preoccupation with the absurdities of everyday life but also in its anecdotal form and its combination of the deadly serious with elements of comedy *Der Stimmenimitator* is very reminiscent of Bernhard's first narrative work, the collection *Ereignisse*. This may well indicate that the author, by going back to his own beginnings, is searching for a way out of the solipsistic world which his literary explorations of the last twenty years have increasingly sealed off from any recognizable reality. But as Uwe Schweikert writes, 'Bernhards Werk ist ein "work in progress". Über ein solches läßt Endgültiges sich nicht ausmachen'.[10]

Bernhard's emergence from the relatively minor role of 'literary talent' in the 1950s to his pre-eminence in the Austrian literary revival of the late 1960s and 1970s coincided with the spread of a new political and cultural radicalism amongst the young in the western world. It must be said that his writing has little in common with the politically inspired student revolts of the late sixties and yet both his work and his life-style are in harmony with the spirit of revolt in their anarchic rejection of preconceived ideas, their aggressive defiance of authority in any form and the delight they take in shocking 'respectable' society. Conventions and established patterns of meaning are seen as fetters from which the individual consciousness is to be liberated.

Bernhard's own rebellious streak is primarily rooted in the agony of his own existence. For him 'Vergangenheitsbewältigung', the attempt to come to terms with the past, is not a political problem but a personal one. In an essay on his childhood he describes his writing as a search for the origins of his personal disaster,[11] as an attempt to ward off the mists of despair which threaten to engulf him. Thus the act of writing becomes an expression of self-assertion; its function is therapeutic but not in a psychotherapeutic sense. While a psychoanalyst believes that the establishment of a chain of cause and effect, of action and reaction will assist understanding and enlightenment and thus help overcome the trauma of personal experience, Bernhard takes the opposite road and seeks freedom in a form of self-exorcism. It is in this sense that in a television interview, *Drei Tage* (Three Days, 1971), he described himself as a surgeon desperately performing a series of operations on himself to rid his body of the cancerous growths which keep on forming.[12]

The overwhelming negativity of Bernhard's world is the product of the writer's chosen form of therapy. Rather than search for a meaningful pattern to his personal suffering, Bernhard, through writing, intensifies his agony and raises it to an absolute and universal condition in which all traces of personal experience are lost. This attempt to transcend authentic, personal experience implies entry 'in die *andere, in die zweite, in die endgültige* Finsternis', the eternal darkness that comes when hope and illusion have

had their day.[13] There is only one vantage point for such an absolute panorama: the finality of death. 'Wenn man an den Tod denkt', Bernhard suggests, everything about human life seems ridiculous.[14] Viewed from the perspective of death, he argues, everything becomes relative and is reduced to little more than the stage properties for some drawing-room comedy; from this perspective—and it is the perspective that informs all Bernhard's work—life itself, society, the state, historical development and even such personally-based experience as fear and disorientation lose their specific significance and become interchangeable elements in a uniform panoply of darkness.

It is death which enables Bernhard to escape the limitations of an objective, balanced view of the world and grants him the freedom to experiment within the framework of a world that is artificial and wholly aesthetic in its origins.

Bernhard's autobiographical novels illustrate this paradoxical attempt to assuage existential suffering by a process of intensification; it is an attempt inextricably linked to a central concept of Bernhard's writing: resistance. In the purely existentialist sense this implies a revolt against the norms of a world in which, as for example *Der Keller* (The Cellar, 1976) shows, the writer has experienced nothing but pain. *Der Keller* constantly harks back to Bernhard's decision to abandon the grammar school education envisaged for him and to take up an apprenticeship in a poky grocer's shop in the worst part of Salzburg. Only by summoning up the strength to reject an existence which Bernhard felt was being imposed on him from outside, was he able to find the conditions in which he could survive. His chosen path away from the 'normality' of a conventional career to life at the periphery of society amongst its flotsam and jetsam is an outward manifestation of the road from illusion to an all-embracing preoccupation with the 'ultimate darkness' referred to in *Drei Tage*:

> hier war alles zu finden, was die Stadt zu verschweigen oder zu vertuschen versuchte, alles, was der normale Mensch flieht, wenn er in der Lage ist, es zu fliehen, hier war der Schmutzfleck Salzburgs . . . ein einziger Schmutzfleck aus Armut und also ein Schmutzfleck zusammengesetzt aus Hunger, Verbrechen und Dreck.[15]

The road to this world beyond hope, to the extremities of society is, at the same time, a road to the inner mind, a descent into the abyss of Bernhard's own personal existence. As such it is given symbolic expression in the total isolation of his private world which he secures in *Die Ursache* (The Cause, 1975) in a narrow, stinking shoe-cupboard of the boarding-school where the young pupil sought refuge from the humiliations he suffered at the hands of his teachers and fellow pupils:

> In die Schuhkammer ist nichts hineingedrungen, als ob sie hermetisch für mich und meine Phantasien und Träume und Selbstmordgedanken abgeschlossen wäre.[16]

In this 'fürchterlichsten Raum im ganzen Internat'[17], a further example of Bernhard's methodical pursuit of obscurity in all its forms, the young boy is able to allow his despair and thoughts of suicide full rein, while at the same time resolving and dispelling them through the 'creativity' of his violin which he is practising in this room. His playing is both unconventional and contrary to all instruction, but, in intensifying his morbid tendencies it also serves to counter them by consciously directing his mind from thoughts of suicide to the creative possibilities afforded by the violin. Thus the shoe-cupboard is not merely a place of extreme isolation and morbidity but one of resistance through creative activity; in this Bernhard depicts the second aspect of the motif of resistance—the resolution of existential difficulties by their transformation into an aesthetic world.

Bernhard's shoe-cupboard is a compelling image of that creative activity which depends on an almost autistic detachment from the outside world, and whose goal is the eradication of the original stimulus to such activity, namely suffering. Pure, self-sufficient aesthetic experience offers a significant prospect of release from the pain and suffering of life. In a literary context this would imply the ideal of *poésie pure,* the *absolute Prosa* which Bernhard finds in the work of Ezra Pound and above all in Valéry's *Monsieur Teste*.[18] It would be a literature in which language ceased to be a 'window on reality' and would stand or fall by its immanent possibilities. In the idiom of *Die Ursache* this would be the creative range and possibilities of the violin.

Bernhard's work testifies to this continual struggle to achieve an ideal literature constructed according to musical and mathematical principles. It is an enterprise whose roots lie in the misery of existence and which, while never fully losing contact with the existential realm, is decided on an aesthetic plane. Since language, as opposed to musical sound, is not merely an autonomous sign, but always carries a signifying element in its transmission, Bernhard must seek to destroy all those linguistic elements which threaten to communicate by reflection and image, or, in other words, he must seek to 'musicalize' his language. To this end he uses a consciously contrived and very distinctive style of writing whose most prominent features are density and exaggeration, repetition and variation. His prose is characterized by geometrically-constructed sentence-complexes, some of which may run on for more than a page in a manner reminiscent of the formal and laborious style of official or legal documents. It is his exaggerated precision in these mammoth constructions—the abundance of conjunctions such as 'because' or 'although'—which enables Bernhard to undermine the development of logical arguments. As he himself writes:

> In meiner Arbeit, wenn sich irgendwo Anzeichen einer Geschichte bilden, oder wenn ich nur in der Ferne irgendwo hinter einem Prosahügel die Andeutung einer Geschichte auftauchen sehe, schieße ich sie ab. Es ist auch mit den Sätzen so, ich hätte fast die Lust, ganze Sätze, die sich *möglicherweise* bilden könnten, schon im vornhinein abzutöten.[19]

In his plays he achieves the same purpose of preventing the development of a logical sequence by using rhythmi-cally accentuated blocks of paratactical sentences. A number of his public speeches have a similar effect, in that the meaning is not so much conveyed by the sentences as a whole, but by the use of selected words with clear negative overtones.

Bernhard's writing thus suggests a state of constant tension. On the one hand, by making use of language at all, he inevitably conveys meaning while with the other he retracts it, and such reflections of the world as he does create are promptly shattered. The emphasis is firmly on structure and the rhythmical patterns of language rather than on content; there is little place for the referential element in language in the systematic abstraction to which Bernhard's absolutism leads. His predilection for superlatives, his recurrent use of such adverbs as 'all', 'nothing', 'every', 'always' etc. are similar means to the ultimate goal of aesthetic redemption through pure formal experimentation. It is an ideal which, given the dual nature of language as sign and signifier, can never be wholly attained.

The consequent ambivalence in Bernhard's presentation of material from the world at large and his concealment of that reference behind a veil of methodical abstraction is particularly evident in his use of material with specifically Austrian overtones. Nearly all the settings of his works, although in themselves devoid of any clearly identifiable features, are given names of actual villages and communities in Austria. In addition, Bernhard is constantly deriding Austria, not only in his public speeches and autobiographical accounts, but in his creative writing as well. A third point of reference to Austria can be traced in Bernhard's inclusion in his work of examples of the gradual decline and dispersal of the massive estates which had been held by individual families down the ages. While granting economic freedom to their owners in former times, these estates are regarded by Bernhard's central characters as an unbearable burden of which they desperately attempt to rid themselves.

These heirs of the feudal aristocracy are depicted as inhabiting residences situated high above the realm their families used to control. Thus Festung Hochgobernitz, the world of Prince Saurau, is a typical example of these centres of former economic and cultural import. Land and property bestowed power, and the landowners themselves embodied a tradition of universal values. Like the Zoiss family in the narrative *Ungenach* (the name of an actual Austrian village; 1968), they 'made' history. Their decline is seen as the direct result of a loss of purpose, of a growing impotence and of the aggressive advances made by representatives of the 'masses' from their lowland dwellings into the feudal heights. Such an incursion is documented in the novel *Korrektur* in which the thoughts of the central figure, Roithamer, continually return to the destructive influence of his mother, who, having fought her way up from the cultural wasteland of life as a butcher's daughter to become the mistress of the Altensam estate, presides over its destruction with devastating effect.[20]

Bernhard is not, however, writing specifically Austrian versions of such family chronicles as *Buddenbrooks* or *The Forsyte Saga*. His novels have, as it were, already 'taken place' and what is presented to the reader is the product of the memory and imagination of his central characters, a pageant acted out on a stage which they themselves will never tread. Their thinking is conditioned by concepts which are inextricably linked to their own heritage, but, as they are all-too aware, their whole existence has become an anachronism and can no longer be defined in terms of belonging to a particular social environment. Prince Saurau in *Verstörung* provides a characteristic illustration of this dilemma:

> Ich fühlte unter meinen eigenen Leuten, daβ ich für sie längst unsichtbar geworden bin, und fühlte das immer mehr. Auf einmal war ich für sie überhaupt nicht mehr vorhanden, nicht mehr *da*.[21]

The parallel to the 'Anstreicher' in *Ereignisse* who was suddenly 'no longer up there' any more is evident, but the anecdotal reference to a purely existential problem is now presented within a historical framework. Saurau measures his own existence, as might be expected of the head of a feudal hierarchy, in terms of his property, that is of 'his own people'. 'The Prince' was indeed to have been the original title of the novel, but Saurau is a mere shadow of the preeminence outlined by Machiavelli in his treatise. His sense of disorientation within any meaningful external reality, his feeling that in social terms he is as good as dead, leaves him with one recourse, and that is to defy social yardsticks completely and establish his own inner standards and codes. It is a solution shared by most of Bernhard's characters, not least the doctor in *Watten* (1969; 'Watten' is an Austrian card-game), whose social alienation leads him to seek a different reality within himself:

> Ich muβ in der Isolierung *sein* . . . Ich gehöre nicht in die Masse, höre ich die Masse, ich gehöre in mich selbst, höre ich mich. Da die Masse mich ausscheidet, habe ich keine andere Wahl, als mich nach einem Tod in mir selbst umzuschauen . . . [22]

Like Saurau, the doctor also has an aristocratic background; however, rather than shut himself off within the walls of his inherited castle, he seeks refuge in the isolation of a forest-hut. For both characters death represents a surrogate for a social pattern that has been lost—a clear echo of Bernhard's own paradoxical step from personal alienation to what he called 'the ultimate darkness'.

The elevation of death to such absolute pitch is no mere exercise in excessive morbidity but an attempt to establish a new, abstract universality totally devoid of all reference to historical reality. It is an attempt that demands the shedding of physical and psychological limits to the experiencing mind. Thus Bernhard's central characters seek the deliberate destruction of their heritage in both the literal sense (by running-down such property as they have inherited) and the figurative (by thinking through and re-thinking their own past to the point at which it no longer

has any meaning). The heir-cum-philosopher Roithamer in *Korrektur* not only allows Altensam to go to rack and ruin, but writes a treatise on the estate and everything related to it as part of his attempt to extinguish within himself all traces of the past:

> Er hatte sich den Kopf frei gemacht von Altensam und von Österreich . . . er hatte praktisch alles, was er gewesen war, aufgegeben, um alles zu erreichen, was er nicht gewesen war und schließlich geworden ist durch die übermenschliche Überanstrengung.[23]

Roithamer's almost Nietzschean 'self-correction', his attempt to achieve 'what he had not been', is at the same time matched by his equally Nietzschean attempt at absolute creativity: he plans and directs the construction of the 'Kegel', an extraordinary cone-shaped building in the middle of an impenetrable forest. This building, intended as a home for his beloved sister, represents a kind of 'counter-Altensam' and as such is the external manifestation of the new zenith of pure thought for which Roithamer is striving. As Sorg notes, the 'Kegel' is:

> konzentriertester Ausdruck einer radikalen Untergangssehnsucht, die noch einmal, vor dem Erlöschen, das Vollkommene will und plant und gegen alle und alles durchsetzt.[24]

Inevitably, Roithamer's attempt to invoke extremes of analytical thought as an instrument to achieve the destruction and annihilation of those concepts that condition his mind can only lead to self-annihilation. His final suicide leaves the 'Kegel' as a defiant symbol of unfulfilled utopia abandoned in the forest where it will be reclaimed by nature.

Most of Bernhard's characters dream of such a wholly different reality to what they perceive as a dying world. There every thought and deed is guided by the ideal of an a-directional, a-practical existence, by mystical visions permeated with concepts from a fairy-tale utopia, as described by the painter Strauch in *Frost*:

> Es gibt hier auch ganz eigensinnige Täler und in diesen Tälern Herrenhäuser und Schlösser. Man geht in diese Herrenhäuser und in diese Schlösser hinein und man sieht gleich: die Welt, aus der man ist, hat hier nichts mehr zu suchen. Das müssen Sie sich alles ganz unwirklich vorstellen, *so wie die tiefste Wirklichkeit*, wissen Sie. Türen gehen auf, hinter denen Menschen in kostbaren Kleidern sitzen, Thronsesselmenschen . . . Einfachheit wölbt sich wie ein klarer Himmel über das, was man denkt. Nichts Phantastisches, obwohl alles der Phantasie entsprungen. Wohlhabenheit, die einfach, Menschenwärme, die ohne die Spur eines Verbrechens ist . . . Geist und Charakter sind schön in der Menschennatur vereint. Logik ist in Musik gesetzt. Das Alter plötzlich wieder zur Schönheit fähig, die Jugend wohl wie ein Vorgebirge. Die Wahrheit liegt auf dem Grund wie das Unerforschliche'.[25]

Such an utopian vision, cast as it is against the background of an aristocratic social structure, with its emphasis on the synthesis of mind and body, thought and deed, imagination and reality and man and nature in the simplicity and geometric clarity of a new order, is clearly indebted to the specifically Austrian tradition which sought to escape from historical reality into an abstract order.[26]

Even so, Bernhard cannot be seen as a latter-day exponent of that literary trend which Claudio Magris so tellingly designated 'the Hapsburg myth'. There is no one explanation of Bernhard's idiosyncratic approach. The socio-historical perspective, his realization that a social class and indeed a whole historical era has come to an end, would, in a political sense, undoubtedly label him as a conservative defector into the ranks of anarchy. Yet this is but one of so many different perspectives ranging from the purely existential to the metaphysical and philosophical. Bernhard's literary explorations defy all categorization; he hints at solutions while at the same time throwing a veil of mystery around their implications—'Die Antwort muß ausbleiben'.[27] His style, his linguistic abstractions and the circular structure of his works leads to a broad spectrum of interpretations which are at the same time congruent yet disparate.

This is well shown in the play *Die Macht der Gewohnheit.* This comedy turns on the vain, artistic ambitions of an ageing ringmaster in a small family circus. For the past twenty-two years he has been unsuccessfully attempting to bring his small troupe of artistes to the point at which they can achieve a perfect performance of Schubert's quintet 'The Trout'—an activity clearly echoing Roithamer's projected perfect home, the 'Kegel'. Despite the ringmaster's awareness that he can never achieve such an ideal of universal beauty he refuses to give up. On this level the play appears to be little more than a straightforward parable in the absurd manner employing the familiar absurdist circus metaphor and an equally familiar bleak message conveyed to the audience by the ringmaster himself:

> Wir wollen das Leben nicht / aber es muß gelebt werden . . .
> Wir hassen das Forellenquintett / aber es muß gespielt werden[28]

Die Macht der Gewohnheit is so overloaded with such 'universal truths' that the validity of individual statements is immediately cast into doubt. While clearly an absurdist parable at base, the play could equally well be seen as a political parable or as a parody of the very Salzburg Festival for which it was written. It is to music, however, that the reader should look for the most telling parallel, to the musical structure of Schubert's quintet with its central theme woven around with a sequence of variations. From this point of view *Die Macht der Gewohnheit* ceases to be piece of literature 'about' something; with its rhythmically reiterated set of phrases and actions it comes closest to Bernhard's ideal of musicalized writing and its theme, if indeed it can be said to have one, is the death of meaning.

Bernhard's obsession with death suggests a close affinity to that Austrian modernism which turns aside from reality in favour of introspection and the cultivated pursuit of melancholy, ascribing to death a mythical quality as the ultimate source of truth. It is, however, open to question whether Bernhard's apocalyptic visions suggest that the 'purgatory' at present experienced will in fact necessarily lead to 'paradise'. In the speech he gave when receiving the Austrian State Prize, Bernhard insisted that all thinking was 'second-hand', and in this he must have included thinking and speaking about death. Thus he sees speaking as a form of speaking in inverted commas, a form of role-playing within a carefully-set theatre, and he includes both his own work and his own public image in this definition. By choosing to live in the solitude of an out-of-the-way farm he not merely reflects the isolation of his characters, but his infrequent public appearances to receive prizes or to give interviews show him obsessed with death and apparently unable to talk about anything else. It is as if he were constantly quoting from his own work.

Bernhard's fine sense of the theatrical is well-shown in the speech he prepared for his receipt of the Wildgans Prize in 1968. He was not allowed to deliver this speech lest this too might provoke yet another of the many scandals surrounding his public appearances. What he had written was a fairly lengthy speech, yet another variation on the theme of death, the end of which seems to parody 'memento mori':

> . . . und mit dem Hinweis darauf, daß nämlich alles mit dem Tode zu tun hat, daß alles der Tod ist, das ganze Leben ist ja nichts anderes als der Tod, werde ich Ihnen einen guten, möglicherweise einen merkwürdigen Abend wünschen und aus diesem Saal hinausgehen, fortgehen aus Wien, aus Österreich eine Zeit fortgehen an das Vergnügen und an die Arbeit und ich . . . erinnere Sie noch einmal nachdrücklich an den Tod, daran, daß alles mit dem Tode zu tun hat, vergessen Sie den Tod nicht . . . vergessen Sie ihn nicht, vergessen Sie ihn nicht. . . . [29]

The evening which Bernhard, cast in his role of voice crying in the wilderness, would have given his culturally-polished audience, would have been memorable indeed. Those listening would have found themselves presented with what was tantamount to a play, but one whose conclusion was still unclear, so that they would not have known whether they were being given answers to the problems of life (or the realization that there are no answers) or made to witness a brilliant piece of clowning.

There is a similar deliberate 'staginess' in much of Bernhard's work, a staginess with strong morbid overtones. The dark overtones of his story *Ja* (Yes, 1978) conceal the mystery of the affirmative title, so untypical of Bernhard's style, until the very last sentence. At the end of the story the narrator is recalling a series of conversations he had had with a woman, who, he has just learned, has committed suicide. This news reminds him that he had asked her during a discussion about suicide whether she had ever considered the possibility that she might take her own life:

> Darauf hatte sie nur gelacht und *Ja* gesagt.[30]

In this, the last sentence of the story, Bernhard uses the grotesque element in this paean of self-destruction as a counter to the gloomy seriousness and philosophical profundity of what has gone before. As in the grotesque climax to the episode of the 'Anstreicher' in *Ereignisse,* the author fuses comic and tragic elements into a new and original union.

Ultimately, the reader realizes that Bernhard's preoccupation with death is a pose in which he plays the part of the poet of death, transcending mundane social and political considerations to draw hidden treasures of truths from the shadows for all to experience. His relationship to the literary tradition, his life and work, are first and last a game played at the edge of the abyss, a game which not only reflects the loss of any objective value-system, but also the demise of that modernist view which sees the artist as the interpreter and sooth-sayer of a disjointed and fragmented world. There is no better phrase to describe his attitude than the romantic 'höheren Witz' to which he refers in *Der Keller.*[31]

Bernhard's sceptical attitude to the possibilities of artistic integrity and meaningful interpretation is the paradoxical conclusion to that Austrian tradition whose roots lie in the linguistic and philosophical dilemmas of the turn of the century. Hugo von Hofmannsthal, despite the despair of the Chandos Letter, still believed in a new form of poetic language and in the possibility of salvation through art; for Bernhard this avenue is no longer open. Language does not bring contact with the world but, on the contrary, reemphasizes the isolation of the individual:

> Ich spreche die Sprache, die nur ich allein verstehe, sonst niemand, wie jeder nur seine eigene Sprache versteht.[32]

Here too, as in so many other Austrian writers, we find an echo of Wittgenstein's solipsistical 'The limits of my language signify the limits of my world'.

Even so Bernhard is not the value-free observer of the world that Wittgenstein would have his new philosopher be, nor is he the mere recorder of phenomena as Robbe-Grillet sees the new writer in the technological era. Bernhard maintains the humanistic tradition of searching for meaning, he remains an interpreter of the world, but always keenly aware that the artist can create nothing but lies and deceit. The ringmaster in **Die Macht der Gewohnheit** grandly proclaims his belief that anyone who trusts art is a fool, and yet he pursues his obsessive quest for perfection through art in much the same way as Bernhard continues to write. It is another character in the comedy—the juggler—who may well provide the clue to Bernhard's artistic goal:

> Das Leben besteht darin / Fragen zu vernichten[33]

It is not just that Bernhard refuses to provide answers, leaving the search for meaning in some absurd vaccum, but rather that he makes the validity of the very act of questioning the focal point of his work. However, whereas some other younger writers have abandoned altogether the search for a justification of life and reality, Bernhard, while doubting the existence of any justification, is nonetheless peculiarly susceptible to this basic human aspiration to attach meanings to all phenomena and experiences. Like Beckett, his work

> retains a link with traditional western rational humanism by virtue of its felt sense of the pathos of this tradition's demise. Such literature may be said to affirm an objective order of values, not by permitting the assumption that such an objective order actually exists, but by assuming that the loss of such an order is deprivation.[34]

In its manic obsession with death, Bernhard's 'anti-literature' may be said not to deal with death itself, but rather with the death of meaning and truths, including the absurdist meaning of the meaninglessness of the world. There is here more than an echo of Nietzsche's dictum that all truths are illusions, only mankind has forgotten this fact. Bernhard's writing is closely involved with his own country and its own traditions; it is a fluctuating love-hate relationship that is perhaps inevitable in one steeped as he is in the Austrian tradition which, on the one hand lays claim to culture as the ultimate repository of human values and truths, and on the other, breeds scepticism and radical self-doubt in its creative offspring.

An author such as Bernhard, who questions the validity of his own role as writer, can find himself in a paradoxical cul de sac. In attempting in his own very peculiar way to take the mystique out of art he cannot but see himself caught in the cultural process he derides. This vicious circle is neatly illustrated in the three plays written for the Salzburg Festival, perhaps *the* shrine of the Austrian cultural myth. It is surprising enough, perhaps, that Bernhard should write these plays, but, despite parting company with the festival on the bitterest of terms, he then had them published in a single volume under the collective title of *Salzburger Stücke*!

Notes

1. 'A horribly ridiculous person! Now it seems to him as if he were plunging into this awareness, deep into it and down, at tremendous speed, and cries are heard and when the young man lies crumpled on the ground all the people run apart. They see the turned-up paint pot fall on him and all at once the painter is covered in yellow. Now the passers-by look up, but, naturally, the painter is no longer up there'. Thomas Bernhard, 'Ereignisse', in: Thomas Bernhard, *An der Baumgrenze,* Munich, 1969 (=sonderreihe dtv 99), pp. 41–91. This quotation pp. 57f.

2. George Steiner, 'Conic sections', in: *The Times Literary Supplement,* 13.2.1976.

3. A.P. Dierick, 'Thomas Bernhard's Austria: Neurosis, Symbol or Expedient?', in: *Modern Austrian Literature,* 12 (1979), No. 1, 73–93. This quotation p. 73.

4. 'Long since dead / my red / my green / my sting / broken / oh broken / oh broken / oh / oh / oh / my oh'.

Thomas Bernhard, *In hora mortis,* Salzburg, 1958, p. 30.

5. 'Now that the war is over, something inexplicable happens and no-one knows why. Instead of closing up the tunnels, they keep going back into them. It has become a habit. Every day, at the same time they go back into them. As long as they live they will keep on returning to the tunnels'.

Bernhard, 'Ereignisse', in: *An der Baumgrenze,* p. 91.

6. In *Die Ursache* (The Cause, 1975) Bernhard reveals the documentary basis for these tunnels. He describes them as air-raid shelters used by the citizens of Salzburg during the Second World War, and shows that these places of refuge are themselves filled with the presence of fear and death and devoid of all hope of safety.

7. cf. Uwe Schweikert, '"Im Grunde ist alles, was gesagt wird, zitiert"', in: Heinz Ludwig Arnold (ed), *Thomas Bernhard,* Munich, 1974 (= Text und Kritik 43), pp. 1–8.

8. 'He slips his vulnerability into me in sentences like slides into a projector, which casts these terrors onto the ever present walls of my (and his) self'.

Thomas Bernhard, *Frost,* Munich/Zurich, 1965, (= Knaurs Taschenbuch 80), p. 257.

9. 'The *Stimmenimitator* does not represent a new theme for Bernhard but rather a new method. In his earlier work he was drawn by the horrific elements in existence which were wholly out of the ordinary, but now he depicts them in a context which has all the appearance of everyday reality'. Ulrich Greiner, 'Thomas Bernhards gewöhnlicher Schrecken', in: *Frankfurter Allgemeine Zeitung,* 21.11.1978.

10. 'Bernhard's work is "work in progress". There is nothing definite that could be said about it'.

Uwe Schweikert, op. cit., p. 8.

11. cf. Thomas Bernhard, 'Unsterblichkeit ist unmöglich. Landschaft der Kindheit', in: *Neues Forum,* 15 (1968), 95–97.

12. cf. Thomas Bernhard, 'Drei Tage', in: Thomas Bernhard, *Der Italiener,* Munich, 1973, (= sonderreihe dtv 122), pp. 78–92. This reference p. 80.

13. Bernhard, 'Drei Tage', in: *Der Italiener,* p. 89.

14. 'If we think of death . . .' Thomas Bernhard, 'Rede', (On receipt of the Austrian State Prize for Literature, 1968) in: Anneliese Botond (ed), *Über Thomas Bernhard,* Frankfurt/M., 1970 (= edition suhrkamp 401), p. 7.

15. 'Here was everything which the city would rather forget or gloss over, everything from which the normal individual would flee if he had the opportunity, here was the garbage-can of Salzburg . . . one huge garbage-can of poverty, of hunger, crime and filth'.

Thomas Bernhard, *Der Keller, Eine Entziehung,* Salzburg, 1976, p. 34.

16. 'Nothing could penetrate the shoe-cupboard, it was seemingly hermetically sealed so that I could indulge in my fantasies and dreams and think of suicide'.

Thomas Bernhard, *Die Ursache, Eine Andeutung,* Salzburg, 1975, p. 78.

17. 'the most terrible room in the whole boarding-school', Bernhard, *Die Ursache,* p. 15.

18. cf. Bernhard, 'Drei Tage', in: *Der Italiener,* p. 87.

19. 'Whenever I see a story about to take shape, or catch a glimpse of a story lurking somewhere in the distance behind a mountain of words, I reach for my revolver. It's the same with sentences—I get this strong desire to take sentences which might just take shape and wring their necks before they have a chance to breathe'.

Bernhard, 'Drei Tage', in: *Der Italiener,* pp. 83f.

20. Here and elsewhere (as, for example, in *Ungenach*) Bernhard links the decline of a former ruling-class to the intrusion of women into the sphere of male domination and patriarchal rule.

21. 'Even amongst my own people I felt I had long since become invisible as far as they were concerned. I simply did not exist any more. I just wasn't *there*'.

Thomas Bernhard, *Verstörung,* Frankfurt/M., 1967, p. 134.

22. 'I must exist in my isolation. I don't belong to the masses when I hear the masses, I belong to myself when I hear myself. Since the masses have closed their ranks against me, I have no option but to seek out a death within myself'.

Thomas Bernhard, *Watten, Ein Nachlaß,* Frankfurt/M, 1969 (= edition suhrkamp 353), p. 23.

23. 'He had rid his mind of Altensam and Austria (. . .), he had as good as given up everything which he had been, in order to achieve what he had not been, and this he finally achieved through his superhuman effort'.

Thomas Bernhard, *Korrektur,* Frankfurt/M., 1975, p. 39.

24. 'a highly concentrated symbol for a radical death-wish which, before the final collapse, seeks to achieve perfection and lays its plans and carries them through against all opposition'.

Bernhard Sorg, *Thomas Bernhard,* Munich, 1977 (= Autorenbücher 7), p. 181.

25. 'There are quite wilful valleys here too, and these valleys have castles and manors. If you go into these manor-houses and into these castles you can see at once that the world you have come from is another world completely. But you have to imagine things in a quite unreal way, *as if it were absolute reality.* Doors open and reveal people sitting there in precious clothes, fit for a throne . . . Everything you think is beautifully simple, like a cloudless sky. Nothing strikes you as being fantastic but it is all fantasy. There is a simple well-being and a genuine human kindness without a touch of wrong-doing . . . Mind and character have been harmoniously united in human nature and logic has become music. Old age can regain its youthful beauty and youth seems no more than a foothill. And truth lies around like some unfathomable puzzle'.

   Bernhard, *Frost*, p. 193f.

26. cf. Herbert Gamper, *Thomas Bernhard*, Munich, 1977 (= dtv 6870), pp. 43ff.

   Hans Höller, *Kritik einer literarischen Form. Versuch über Thomas Bernhard*, Stuttgart, 1979, (= Stuttgarter Arbeiten zur Germanistik 50).

27. 'There cannot be any answer'.

   Bernhard, *Der Keller*, p. 157.

28. 'We do not want life / but we have to live it. We hate 'The Trout' / but we have got to play it.

   Thomas Bernhard, *Die Macht der Gewohnheit*, Frankfurt/M., 1974 (= Bibliothek Suhrkamp 415), p. 43.

29. '. . . and with the reminder that everything has to do with death, everything is death, the whole of life after all is nothing but death, let me wish you a good, perhaps even remarkable and strange evening. I leave this hall, leave Vienna, leave Austria, to pursue my pleasure, pursue my work for a time, and let me say again . . . let me again remind you quite expressly of death, of the fact that everything has to do with death; don't forget death, don't forget death . . . don't forget death . . .'

   Thomas Bernhard, 'Der Wahrheit und dem Tod auf der Spur. Zwei Reden', in: *Neues Forum*, 15(1968), No. 173, p. 349.

30. 'Thereupon she had laughed and answered 'Yes''

   Thomas Bernhard, *Ja,* Frankfurt/M., 1978 (= Bibliothek Suhrkamp 600), p. 148.

31. 'I speak a language which I alone understand, and everyone else speaks their own private language as well'.

   Bernhard, *Der Keller*, p. 156.

32. Bernhard, *Der Keller*, p. 156.

33. 'Life is a question of destroying questions'.

   Bernhard, *Die Macht der Gewohnheit*, pp. 144f.

34. Gerald Graff, 'The Myth of the Postmodernist Breakthrough', in: Malcolm Bradbury (ed.), *The Novel Today,* Glasgow, 1977, pp. 215–249. This quotation p. 226.

Martin Esslin (essay date January 1981)

SOURCE: "A Drama of Disease and Derision: The Plays of Thomas Bernhard," in *Modern Drama,* Vol. 23, No. 4, January, 1981, pp. 367–84.

[*In the following essay, Esslin summarizes the plots of Bernhard's major plays, noting his use of repetitious dialogue and "almost total absence of surprise, suspense or development."*]

> The diseased and the crippled
> rule the world
> everything is ruled by the diseased
> and by the crippled
> It is a comedy
> an evil humiliation

Thomas Bernhard, **Die Macht der Gewohnheit,** Scene I[1]

> We stand towards each other in a relationship of disease
> the whole world consists of such sickness
> all of it undiagnosed

Thomas Bernhard, **Ein Fest fuer Boris,** First Prologue[2]

> On the theatre, dear Sir, even the impossible
> becomes entertainment and the monstrous
> becomes an object of study as being
> improbable, and all by allusion.

Thomas Bernhard, *Watten*[3]

> "Everybody merely talks to himself" said
> the Prince, "we are in an age of monologues
> The art of the monologue is, moreover,
> a much higher art than the art of
> conversation" he said "but monologues
> are just as meaningless as conversations,"
> said the Prince, "albeit much less meaningless."

Thomas Bernhard, *Verstoerung*[4]

In the German-speaking world, and in the whole of continental Europe, Thomas Bernhard, born in Holland of Austrian parents in 1931 (on the 10 February, the date also of Brecht's birth), is generally accepted as one of the leading literary figures of his time, the author of a remarkable series of short stories, seven major novels and ten successful plays; yet in the English-speaking sphere, he is still practically unknown. One of his plays, **Die Macht der Gewohnheit** (**The Force of Habit**), has been translated, was briefly performed at the National Theatre in London in 1976, and proved a resounding failure. But apart from that, his name has hardly been mentioned.

And, admittedly, Bernhard is a strange and bewildering writer. His deep pessimism, the blackness of his humour, his predilection for a basically monologic form, both in the novel and the short story, and in the theatre, point to a kinship with Beckett; yet there are very profound differences between them as well. Bernhard is a wholly original writer whose roots might perhaps be sought in Kleist and Stifter (as the sources of the remarkable purity and directness of his style in his prose and the free verse of his dramatic works) as well as in the German expressionist theatre, Wedekind and Strindberg, rather than in any contemporary models.

By all accounts, Bernhard's childhood and youth were extremely unhappy: he seems to have been an illegitimate child, brought up by his maternal grandparents in Austria (Vienna and Salzburg) and Bavaria. From the age of fourteen, he began training as a musician, studying singing, the violin and musical theory, but his studies were interrupted by lengthy stays at various sanatoria for lung ailments. Hence perhaps his obsessive preoccupation with disease in all its forms, physical as well as mental. Although he graduated from the Salzburg Mozarteum and the Academy for Music and the Performing Arts in Vienna, Bernhard did not take up a musical career, but travelled widely, worked as the court-room reporter for a socialist newspaper and began to publish poetry in 1957; he wrote the libretto for a ballet-oratorio; and he had a number of short dramatic sketches performed at a rural festival in 1960.

His novel *Frost,* a brilliantly written study of a man's mental disintegration, appeared in 1963 and immediately propelled him into fame. A second novel, *Verstoerung (Disorientation),* followed in 1967. His breakthrough in the theatre came in 1970, when the Hamburg Schauspielhaus scored a great success with his play ***Ein Fest fuer Boris (A Feast for Boris),*** which, apparently, he had written as early as 1967. His output, both of plays and narrative prose since then, has been abundant.

As his work is practically unknown in the English-speaking world, it may be useful to precede a discussion of his dramatic work with brief summaries of the outlines of his ten full-length plays:

> ***Ein Fest fuer Boris*** (1967; first performed 1970). An extremely rich lady, referred to only as "Die Gute" (the Good Lady), has lost both her legs in an accident in which her husband was killed. She has used her wealth to finance an asylum for legless cripples, and has married the most repulsive and miserable among them, Boris. In the first scene, labelled "First Prologue," we see the Good Lady tormenting her servant/companion Johanna with her capriciousness while trying on hats and gloves before attending a charity costume ball. The "Second Prologue" takes place after the ball, with the Good Lady in the costume of a queen, Johanna with the mask of a pig's head. The third scene, "The Feast," is Boris's birthday party, attended by thirteen legless paraplegic cripples, including Boris, the Good Lady, and Johanna, who is now also in a wheelchair, having had to assume at least the appearance of a legless cripple so as not to offend the sensibilities of the oth-

ers. The cripples talk about their dreams, mainly concerned with imagining that they still have legs and that therefore their beds are too short; Boris is given his presents, which include two enormous officer's boots and long underpants; but at the end of the party, Boris is found to have died. When left alone with the corpse, the Good Lady bursts out in uncontrollable laughter.

> ***Der Ignorant und der Wahnsinnige (The Ignoramus and the Madman*;** 1972). The first act takes place in the dressing room of a famous coloratura soprano, referred to as the Queen of the Night, before and during a performance of *The Magic Flute* in which she sings that part. Her father, a drunkard in the last stages of alcoholism, and her doctor, a world-famous expert in the dissection of corpses, are anxiously waiting for the prima donna's arrival; the doctor speaks of her as a mere mechanism, a beautiful voice. Throughout the play he lectures the father, in the greatest medical detail, on the procedure for cutting up a dead body from head to toe, with specially detailed accounts of the dissection of the brain and the genitals. The great singer arrives, is dressed, expresses her disgust with the theatre and leaves for the stage, whence we hear her performance through the loudspeaker. The second scene takes place in one of Vienna's best-known restaurants, The Three Hussars, after the performance. The singer, now coughing incessantly, cancels a number of engagements.

> ***Die Jagdgesellschaft (The Hunting-Party*;** 1973/74). In a hunting-lodge in the depth of winter, a writer and the general's wife play incessantly at *vingt-et-un.* In the first scene—"Before the Hunt"—they are waiting for the arrival of the general and two of his fellow cabinet ministers for a hunt. We learn that the general, who has lost an arm at Stalingrad, is not only going blind but also suffering from an incurable disease from which he is bound to die soon. The immense forests around the hunting-lodge which are his main delight have been attacked by a parasite and are due to be cut down; moreover, it is certain that the two cabinet ministers are coming down to inform the general that he has been dismissed from the government. "During the Hunt" (second scene), the exposition of these dire circumstances is continued. In the third scene, "After the Hunt," the general expresses his suspicion of the writer, and writers in general; the writer reads a passage from Lermontov's novel *A Hero of his Time,* after which the general leaves the room and shoots himself.

> ***Die Macht der Gewohnheit (The Force of Habit*;** 1974). The scene is the interior of a circus-wagon belonging to Caribaldi, the ring-master of the Caribaldi Circus. For more than twenty years, Caribaldi has been trying to add a performance of Schubert's *Trout Quintet* to the repertoire of his establishment. Each evening since then he has been rehearsing this piece of music with performers of his circus. He is expecting the juggler, the girl tightrope dancer (who is his granddaughter), the lion-tamer (his nephew), and the clown for this night's rehearsal. But exactly like each rehearsal in the last twenty years, this one also is a disaster and never progresses beyond the first bar. The lion-tamer has been bitten by one of the animals and has a bandaged hand which makes it impossible for

him to play the piano; the clown disrupts everything by constantly losing his hat—part of his comic routine during performances—thus inducing the girl tightrope dancer to giggle; and the juggler is threatening to leave the circus for a better engagement. The rehearsal breaks up in disorder. Caribaldi, left alone, turns on the radio from which a perfect rendering of *The Trout Quintet* floods his wagon.

Der Praesident (*The President*; 1975). The President of an unnamed country has just escaped an attempt on his life during which an aide-de-camp and his close friend, a colonel, has been killed. It is possible that the anarchist who fired the shot might have been the president's own son, who has disappeared and joined the anarchists. The president's wife is lamenting, at great length, the loss of her favourite dog, which she was carrying in her arms when the shots were fired. The poor animal was so frightened that it instantly died of a heart attack. In the second scene, the president and his wife are getting ready for the state funeral of the murdered colonel. In scenes three and four, the president is on holiday in Estoril (Portugal) with his mistress, a vulgar actress to whom he gives vast sums of money which she loses at the gaming-table. In the brief fifth scene, we see the president, who has at last been murdered by the anarchists, lying in state while his wife and the government file past his coffin in deep mourning.

Die Beruehmten (*The Famous Ones/The Stars?*; 1976). At his palatial home in Salzburg, a famous singer, a bass, has assembled eight of his prominent and famous friends to celebrate his two hundredth performance of the role of Ochs von Lerchenau in *Der Rosenkavalier*. In the first scene ("First Prologue"), these are seated around a table next to wax figures of their professional ideals: the host himself next to an effigy of Richard Mayr (the great Ochs of the nineteen thirties); the tenor next to one of Richard Tauber; the soprano with Lotte Lehmann; the actor with Alexander Moissi; the actress with Helene Thimig; the director with Max Reinhardt; the conductor with Toscanini; the lady pianist with Elly Ney; and the publisher with Samuel Fischer (the founder of the S. Fischer Verlag, publisher of Hauptmann and Thomas Mann). After exchanging bitchy gossip, the characteristic small talk of prominent and successful people in the arts, the guests fall upon the wax effigies and smash them. In the second scene (labelled "first scene"), the stars are seen sitting under paintings of their ideal figures. The same kind of malicious conversation continues. In the third (second) scene, the same stars, somewhat drunk, have animal heads and are served by valets in rats' heads: the bass has become an ox; the conductor, a cock; the publisher, a fox; the actress, a cow; the lady pianist, a goat; the soprano, a cat; the actor, a dog; the director, a pig (the tenor's animality is not specified in the printed text). In the last scene, all language has disappeared; we merely hear a cacophony of animal sounds proceeding both from the animal-headed characters and from loudspeakers on all sides of the theatre.

Minetti (1976). The hero of this play bears the name of the great German actor Bernhard Minetti, who played Caribaldi in *The Force of Habit*. This Minetti,

however, is an old actor who has an appointment in a hotel in Ostend (shades of Ensor!) to meet a producer who has promised to cast him as King Lear. Godot-like, this producer never arrives. In the end, the old actor is thrown out of the hotel lobby (he has no money to take a room). The play ends with the old actor sitting in the open during a blizzard being slowly covered with snow. He has become Lear in reality.

Immanuel Kant (1978). On an ocean liner, Immanuel Kant, his wife, his parrot Friedrich (whom he regards as his most precious possession because it can repeat everything he has ever said), and his servant are on the way to New York, where Kant has, he believes, been invited to receive an honorary degree from Columbia University. Kant, greatly admired by a millionairess and other passengers, spouts nonsensical profundities. On arrival in New York, he is met by a delegation of white-coated male nurses from the University who are obviously going to study him as a prime example of madness.

Der Weltverbesserer (*The World Reformer*; 1979). A sixty-eight year old cranky philosopher who has published a treatise about the improvement of the world torments his common-law wife (whom he refuses to marry) while waiting for, and being dressed to receive, a delegation from Frankfurt University who are going to bring him his diploma for an honorary degree. When the delegation of vice-chancellor, burgomaster, etc., arrives, the world reformer treats them with disdain and throws them out of the house after having unceremoniously taken the diploma.

Vor dem Ruhestand (*Before Retirement*; 1979). Hoeller, chief justice and member of the state legislature somewhere in West Germany, lives with his two sisters: Vera, with whom he has an incestuous relationship; and the crippled Clara (paralysed in an American air raid just before the end of the war). Hoeller is an ex-Nazi who was deputy commandant of an extermination camp. Today is the 7 October, Himmler's birthday, which he always celebrates with a party for which the guests arrive in their old S.S. uniforms. But this year these old Nazis have got cold feet and excused themselves. So the party has to take place among the family alone. Clara, the crippled sister, sympathizes with the political left and hates her brother. As he gets more and more drunk, Hoeller threatens her with his gun. In the excitement, he has a stroke and collapses. Vera undresses the dying man and puts him back into his everyday clothes before she phones for the doctor—who is a Jew.

Bernhard's theatre, as even these brief summaries show, is devoid of plot in the conventional sense. It is, essentially, a theatre of images, static situations that are merely gradually elaborated and intensified: the grotesquerie and despair of the legless cripples in *A Feast for Boris* become ever more grotesque and desperate; the bloated, conceited VIPs in *The Stars* become more and more nasty and beastly; the accumulation of gloom and disaster in *The Hunting-Party* is more and more intensely stressed until the general shoots himself; Kant becomes more and more nonsensical; the world reformer grows more and more hypochondriacally self-possessed; the doctor's descriptions of anatomy and dissections become more and more disgusting in **The Ignoramus and the Madman,** while the alcoholic father turns more and more drunk, and the fragility of the great soprano's voice is more and more made manifest; the vanity of Minetti's hope ever to play Lear is clear from the beginning and becomes ever clearer; and the picture of the unhappy household of an ex-Nazi war criminal now holding one of the highest positions in West Germany (inspired by actual events that were in the news shortly before the play was written) is simply more and more graphically elaborated; the impossibility of the rehearsal of *The Trout Quintet* ever proceeding beyond the first note is inherent in the opening scene of **The Force of Habit**; the image in **The President** is a double one: in the first part, it is dominated by the president's silly and sentimental wife; in the second, by the president himself, but here too there can be no doubt from the outset that the president is doomed and *will* be shot.

In each of these plays, then, there is an almost total absence of surprise, suspense or development. The opening scene, the opening image tells us all. And yet audiences are held by them. Why?

Above all, perhaps, because the images themselves are visually compelling: a stage populated by paraplegics in wheelchairs, a wagon filled with costumed circus performers trying to rehearse chamber music, ridiculously vain VIPs sitting next to the wax images of their authentically great predecessors—these are images interesting enough to be contemplated at length, even if the dialogue is endlessly repetitious. Indeed, repetition is the main verbal device employed by Bernhard to achieve an almost hypnotic effect. To illustrate this, one has to quote at some length. Here is a passage from **The World Reformer** in which he and his woman discuss the suit he is to put on for the ceremony:

> THE WORLD REFORMER (*calls to her off-stage*)
> The suit I wore in Treves
>
> *The Woman enters with a black-striped suit*
>
> THE WORLD REFORMER The one I wore in Treves
> THE WOMAN You wore this one in Treves
> THE WORLD REFORMER I wore this one in Treves
> I did not wear this one in Treves
> not in Treves
> not this one
> not this one in Treves
> THE WOMAN Of course you wore this one in Treves
> THE WORLD REFORMER In Treves
> worn in Treves
> perhaps you are right
> perhaps I wore it in Treves
> are you sure
> THE WOMAN Sure
> you wore it in Treves
> THE WORLD REFORMER In Treves
> where we missed the train
> THE WOMAN You wore it
> THE WORLD REFORMER That I don't remember
> that I wore it in Treves
> do you think

> it fits me
> THE WOMAN It certainly fits you
> THE WORLD REFORMER Are you certain
> THE WOMAN It certainly fits you
>
> *She holds up the suit*
>
> THE WORLD REFORMER *pokes the suit with his ear trumpet*
> I cannot remember
> that I wore this suit in Treves
> No good memory
> of Treves
> THE WOMAN You were upset
> THE WORLD REFORMER People did not deserve my lecture
> One does not go to Treves without regretting it
> one goes to Treves and makes oneself ridiculous
> Do I not have another suit
> for this occasion
>
> *pokes the suit again with his ear trumpet*
>
> THE WOMAN Why don't you want to wear the suit
> put it on
> What do you care
> that you wore it in Treves
> What do you care
> such a fine suit
> merely because you wore it in Treves
> it seems not good enough
> THE WORLD REFORMER In Treves intelligence
> is not at home
> THE WOMAN Such a nice suit
> THE WORLD REFORMER If the tailors were not so insolent
> The tailors are insolent
> and infamous
> I know the infamousness of tailors
> THE WOMAN Are you going to wear the suit
> or not
> THE WORLD REFORMER In Treves I wore it
> you are right
> this is my Treves suit
> But what do I care
> that I wore it in Treves
> where they ridiculed me
>
> THE WOMAN *holding the suit up*
> It is eight years
> since we were in Treves[5]

And so on for a considerable time, with the hypnotically repeated name Treves only gradually receding. All of Bernhard's plays are written in this characteristic form of unrhymed free verse without punctuation signs. Only the occasional appearance of a capital letter at the beginning of a line indicates a new sentence.

It will perhaps become clear from this example that Bernhard—trained musician that he is—adopts a musical principle of construction. He uses words in endlessly varied repetition as musical structural elements: a phrase—"I wore it in Treves"—is stated, inverted, varied, repeated and then repeated again in its inverted form. Then a new structural element is brought in—the ridicule that followed the lecture at Treves—and combined with the first one, the new combination inverted and varied, till another fresh element is introduced and added to the previously used elements—the insolence of tailors, in this instance—and after a while the earlier *motif* becomes sparser and is finally dropped—but only to reappear suddenly and unexpectedly at a later stage. In most of his plays, moreover, Bernhard uses certain phrases as constantly recurring *leitmotifs*: in **The Force of Habit,** for example, the sentence "tomorrow in Augsburg" (referring to the circus's next stop on its tour) occurs on almost every page. Simple as it is, it carries a multitude of associations and overtones in a number of different contexts: it is used as an indication of the transitoriness of the present situation and a hope of better things to come ("tomorrow things will go better"); it also functions in the opposite sense, in connection with phrases expressing contempt for Augsburg as a filthy second-rate provincial city ("another hopeless place tomorrow"); it is used as a threat when, for example, Caribaldi tells his granddaughter that tomorrow in Augsburg he will buy her the textbooks she will have to learn by heart; and the phrase—the last one spoken in the play—functions as the final expression of hopelessness and defeat when Caribaldi utters it as he sinks, discomfited, into his armchair. And for those in the know, it carries an additional malicious overtone: for Augsburg is Brecht's home town and thus exemplifies an epic theatre of plot and meaning, everything that Bernhard's theatre emphatically tries *not* to be.

The use of repetition as a musical, structural element differentiates Bernhard's utilisation of this device from that of other contemporary dramatists—notably Pinter—who are mainly concerned to show that real speech in real situations *is* largely repetitious. In Bernhard's case, there is no pretence to naturalism. His dramatic language—he uses quite different devices in his narrative prose—is strictly rhythmical. Each line of verse contains one rhythmical element; at the end of each line there must be a pause for breath. There is no *enjambement*. Every new sentence indicated by the use of a capital letter must start at the beginning of a line.

But, without ever pretending to naturalism, Bernhard also uses his rhythmic structural pattern to indicate the disintegration of human speech and communication. Language frequently literally *crumbles* in the mouths of his characters, dissolves into crumbs of half-expressed meaning.

Take the opening of the second scene of **The Hunting-Party**: when the curtain rises, the writer and the general's wife are seen playing cards, drinking brandy and laughing:

> GENERAL'S WIFE *throwing her cards on the table; to the end of the scene she notes down winnings and losses on a piece of paper*
>
>> I have won
>> I have won
>
> *she takes the cards, shuffles them and deals*
>
> WRITER This loud laughter
>> your loud laughter
>
> *looks into the cards and takes two more*
>
>> There is great interest
>> in fatal diseases
>> really

> *throws the cards on the table*
>
>> I have won
>> in theatrical events
>
> *The general's wife shuffles, deals. The writer drinks*
>> When we are observers
>> and not part of what is happening
>
> *looks into the cards, takes three more*
>> The stupidity
>> and the senselessness
>> the means by which people
>> who are not made for it at all
>
> GENERAL'S WIFE *hitting the table with both hands*
>> I have won
>> I have won
>> I have won
>
> *she drinks*
> WRITER We need not take part
>> partake yes
>> but not *take* part
>> If we put our powers of observation
>
> *throws his cards on the table*
>> You have won
>> shuffle
>> shuffle
>
> *the general's wife shuffles quickly*
>> A large sum
>> a large sum
>> really a large sum
>
> *takes some cards*
>> Possibly
>> possibly
>
> GENERAL'S WIFE *takes unusually many cards*
>> What is possibly
> WRITER Possibly
>> it is not a fatal disease after all
>> *he laughs*[6]

Several strands of thought run here, half expressed, parallel to the action of card-playing. A kind of syncopated rhythm is created by excessive repetition combined with large holes—omissions of half sentences—in the dialogue. The suggestion here is that the general's wife and the writer are discussing her husband's fatal disease in a completely casual and offhanded manner while laughing and playing cards, and that the movement of the card-game is so much more important to them that each minor climax of the game is enough to divert them from the discussion of what is a matter of life and death for the lady's husband. At the same time, the interrupted, staccato rhythm produced establishes the character of this, the second movement of the musical structure. It becomes clear that this scene is the *scherzo* of the symphonic structure of the play, of which Bernhard himself says in a note at the end: "The play is written in three movements, the last movement is the 'slow movement'."[7]

The stylisation of halting, panting and half-completed speech into poetic patterns has only one striking parallel in classical German literature—in the work of Kleist. It is not without significance that in **The Hunting-Party** the writer (who is shown as writing a play about a hunting-party and thus clearly represents Bernhard himself) refers to Kleist when he tells the general's wife that the general seeks to draw him into conversations about his writing:

> About literature he wants to talk
> for example about Heinrich von Kleist
> but I
> do not like talking about it.[8]

Nor is it without significance that Heinrich von Kleist committed suicide. Suicide is one of Bernhard's main themes, both in his narrative prose and in his plays.

Even though in the passage of dialogue just quoted both characters appear to be speaking to each other, nevertheless the basic structure remains essentially monologic. As the writer's half sentences are never finished, their meaning remains known only to himself. And indeed such passages of relatively equal interaction of two characters are rare in Bernhard's dramatic *œuvre*. The essential pattern is that of a dominant speaker holding forth to a second character who either is completely speechless or only occasionally answers a question or makes a monosyllabic remark. *A Feast for Boris* is basically a monologue of the Good Lady in the two opening scenes with Johanna, and then a succession of monologues (the cripples' dreams and life stories) during the feast itself. In *Immanuel Kant,* it is the pseudo-philosopher who holds forth almost without interruption, except for a brief interlude when the millionairess relates her life story. The world reformer in the play of that title and Caribaldi in *The Force of Habit* dominate throughout the entire action. In *The President,* the president's wife is the principal monologist in the first two scenes, the president himself in the subsequent two, whereas the fifth, that of the lying-in-state, is practically silent. In *The Stars,* the bass singer dominates. In *Before Retirement,* the three characters are given about equal weight, yet each of them is addicted to non-communicatory, monologic utterance. *Minetti* is virtually one long monologue, although other characters appear simply as listeners to his logorrhoea. In *The Ignoramus and the Madman,* the doctor dominates with his long and detailed anatomical disquisitions. It is only in *The Hunting-Party* that a certain amount of actual interchange takes place among the three principal characters, the writer, the general and the general's wife, but here too basically each of them merely states his or her position rather than allowing any genuine give-and-take of communication to happen.

Throughout all these plays, form and thematic content are strictly one: there is no genuine dialogue in Bernhard because his chief characters are entirely enclosed in separate inner worlds. There are no love scenes or love interests in any of Bernhard's works—narrative or dramatic—because monologue does not allow genuine interaction between human beings. Any interaction that takes place is thus purely mechanical, as that between puppets. Bernhard's earliest dramatic efforts were written for marionettes. He regards and deliberately designs his characters as basically no different from puppets—simply

because he is convinced that people in real life are, with very few exceptions, barely conscious, let alone able to act otherwise than as merely propelled by mechanical instincts and reflexes; that, in fact, living human beings, in the mass, are no better than marionettes. In the epigraph to *The Hunting-Party,* Bernhard quotes Kleist's famous treatise on the puppet theatre: "I inquired after the mechanism of these figures and how it was possible to govern their individual parts and points without having myriads of threads on one's fingers, in the manner required by the rhythm of their movements or their dance." Clearly his own solution for producing this kind of movement or rhythm of his puppets is to create a pattern of rhythmical, intersecting monologues uttered by puppet-like characters.

In the real world, the chief triggers for the mechanism that actuates man, the marionette, and makes him twitch and jump are madness and disease. Both in his narrative prose and in his plays, Bernhard never stops stressing that point. Life itself is a disease only curable by death. Cripples and madmen merely exhibit, more plainly and therefore perhaps more frankly, what all men suffer from beneath the surface. And even "genius is a disease,"[9] as the doctor asserts in *The Ignoramus and the Madman.*

In Bernhard's short stories, novellas and novels, this point of view is relentlessly expounded in deep seriousness. Yet his dramatic work is different: the themes are the same, but the atmosphere is ambivalent. The artificiality of the prosody, the clarity of the musical structure combined with the compression and exaggeration caused by the absence of the subtler half-tones of the *internal* monologue of the novels or their long passages of reported speech, produces a strangely disturbing effect. Is this theatre stark tragedy? Or crude horror-mongering melodrama? Or is it intended to be comic, almost farcical?

Here, I believe, lies one of the sources of the peculiar fascination of Bernhard's theatre. In West Germany, where he has had his most spectacular triumphs, most of his plays, notably *A Feast for Boris, The Force of Habit* and *The Hunting-Party,* have been received with solemn seriousness, although *The Force of Habit,* for one, is actually subtitled "comedy" by the author himself. The West German theatre public, following the West German critics, tends to look for deep significance and profound philosophical and social meaning. One might say that this public veritably wallows in self-laceration, gloom and tragedy. I should venture to suggest that as an Austrian—and the Austrian tradition of theatre is one of pure entertainment, light-hearted amusement—Bernhard is tempted to make fun of this tendency of the German theatre-going public. As the mad Prince says in the novel *Die Verstoerung* (*Disorientation*): "These are people who are carrying their pain onto the street and thereby turn the world into a comedy, which, naturally, is laughable. In this comedy they all suffer from ulcers of a mental or spiritual nature and actually *enjoy* their fatal diseases."[10] The writer in *The Hunting-Party* is writing a play exactly like *The Hunting-Party*:

Imagine a comedy
in which a general plays the leading part
and this general has a fatal illness
in Stalingrad they tore off his left arm
And one day he goes into the forest
and injures his leg on a motorised saw
and at the same time it is found
that he suffers from glaucoma
And on top of that two ministers dear lady
who force the general to resign from the government
I imagine a hunt
a hunting-party
in one of our finest hunting-lodges
in an area totally cut off from the outside world[11]

And shortly afterwards the writer adds:

Everything is different
perhaps a philosophy
the general might say
If a one-armed general appears in my play
it is a different one
And perhaps dear lady it will be said
I myself was in my theatre
But it is a different person[12]

In the same play, the general himself feels uneasy about the writer's enterprise:

The writer in his madness
writes a comedy
more of an operetta
and the actors are taken in
by this comedy
operetta
And then the world the world of educated people
believes
that this is something philosophical
The writer attacks philosophy
or a whole lot of different philosophies
and simply puts his own head upon the actors
and if it is a tragedy
he asserts
it is a comedy
and if it is a comedy
he asserts
it's tragedy
when it's nothing but operetta[13]

Bernhard's theatre thus does not merely seem to me to be basically comic in intention, but arguably the chief comic effect produced by it is that of the audience solemnly taking it as tragedy. The person who is really amused by it, the one who has the best laugh, is the playwright himself. These plays are, at least in one important regard (they are, of course, so complex and multilayered that they also display many other intriguing aspects), aggressions against the solemn, educated audience—the "Bildungsbourgeoisie"—as it only exists in West Germany today. As the unnamed hero of the story *Watten* puts it: "We live in a cabarettistic world, in which the high art of imagining life as well as the even higher art of Life and Existence itself are being derided. When I wake up I connect with my name a cabarettistic existence. Every day I commit suicide in a cabarettistic manner. Philosophy cabarettistic. Religion cabarettistic. A war, a huge heap of corpses, dear Sir, a whole mendacious continent, today they are but a joke."[14]

Despair thus turns into derision, and that derision crystallizes in Bernhard's theatre, which can be seen as a savage aggression against the public itself. Bernhard's work is full of remarks displaying a burning hatred not only of the masses of humanity in general, but of the theatre audience in particular. "For society, and I mean the whole of society, but in particular the stratum of society that comes to the theatre, is a nauseating rabble,"[15] says the mad Prince in *Disorientation*. The great cmloratura soprano in **The Ignoramus and the Madman** agrees:

and secretly we hate the public
is it not so
our tormentors[16]

while the doctor concludes:

The Theatre
and in particular the opera
is nothing
for a natural human being
If we compound the imbecility
which reigns in this art form
dear Sir
with the vulgarity
of the spectators
we get near madness[17]

And Caribaldi in **The Force of Habit**:

I merely smell
this evil odour
the spectators exude
It is ridiculous
to make this remark again and again
but the smell of the spectators
is repulsive[18]

And in a short story which predates his first full-length play, significantly enough entitled "Is it a comedy? Is it a tragedy?", the narrator expresses these sentiments in an even more telling prose:

. . . I despise the theatre, I hate the actors, the theatre is one big perfidious outrage, an outrageous perfidy. . . . You know the theatre is a piggishness, I said to myself, and you will write a study about the theatre that you already carry in your head, this theatre study that once and for all slaps the theatre in its face! What the theatre *is,* what the actors *are,* the playwrights, the theatre directors, etc. . . . .[19]

And yet, a few years later, Bernhard began to write a long series of plays for the theatre. Is he, in piling horror upon horror, repetition upon repetition, venting his outrage upon the spectators, cocking a snook at their readiness to read deep philosophical profundities into what are often quite clearly parodies of famous plays (think of the numerous parallels between **The Hunting-Party** and *The Cherry*

Orchard, Minetti and *King Lear*) or accumulations of grotesque images of that audience's own humourlessness?

The clearest indication of this derisive aggression against the audience is furnished by ***Immanuel Kant.*** Here the audience is presented with Immanuel Kant crossing the Atlantic on a luxury liner accompanied by his wife. Everyone knows that Kant died before the age of luxury liners and that he never married. Yet a modern, earnest theatre audience, in the age of the Theatre of the Absurd, is prepared for everything. After all, we have seen Hamlet in modern dress, the Trojan women of Euripides as Vietnamese war victims. There might, after all, be a profound meaning in putting the greatest of all German philosophers into our own time. Kant is famous for never having left his native Koenigsberg. But here perhaps there is a deep truth in his own pronouncement:

> Kant
> on the high seas
> Kant never
> got out of Koenigsberg
> they say
> Where Kant is there is Koenigsberg[20]

So will the great Kant not utter great truths even in this anachronistic allegorical modern theatrical situation? He does make pronouncements like:

> Everything that is
> is
> everything that is not
> is not
> The world is the flip side
> of the world
> Truth is the flip side
> of the truth[21]

or, when talking of the poisonous nature of fish:

> The problem
> at all times was
> that of the holes
> in the nets
> A cousin of mine
> introduced sea fish
> to the Alps
> He was the inventor of the refrigerated truck
> His monument stands in Innsbruck
> *suddenly*
> But it has not yet been unveiled[22]

Here the author clearly is testing the audience's capacity to remain solemnly interested in what is a deliberate flood of derisive nonsense unleashed upon them. Will they remain in eager expectancy to receive a final allegorically encoded message? Is the author polemizing against Kantian philosophy? In the last scene, abruptly Bernhard shows that the man on whose lips the audience has been hanging because he called himself Kant is a harmless madman. As the writer puts it in ***The Hunting-Party***:

> Suddenly a turn of speech dear lady
> that's philosophical
> but the whole philosophy is nonsense[23]

And, indeed, the chief characters of *all* of Bernhard's plays are plainly mad: the Good Lady; Caribaldi; the mad doctor and the ignoramus; the president; the bloated, animal-headed VIPs with their bitchy show business talk; Minetti; Kant; the cantankerous world reformer; Hoeller, the complacent ex-Nazi judge. The writer of ***The Hunting-Party*** is the solitary exception, but he is writing a play in which improbable horrors are accumulated for an audience who will take them for tragedy while they are in fact parody, farce.

Bernhard's theatre, if this analysis is correct, can thus be seen as a gigantic practical joke against the "consumers of culture," the solemn, pretentious German theatre audience. Bernhard is—or presents himself in his public persona—as a confirmed misanthrope whose hatred of mankind, of course, includes self-hatred.

> I have never loved my life
> I have always hated it
> hated everything
> to do with it
> And to the utmost exploited
> that self-hatred[24]

says the world reformer. Bernhard's main impulse appears as a destructive one. He presents himself in public as an arch destroyer. In an interview which predated his emergence as a major playwright he said, talking about his work as a writer of fiction: "I am . . . not a teller of tales, I basically hate stories. I am a destroyer of stories, I am the typical destroyer of stories."[25] There is doubtless a similarly destructive motivation behind his activity as a playwright.

But if we are faced here with a gigantic act of provocation ("I will bite my thumb at them, which is disgrace to them if they bear it," as Sampson puts it in *Romeo and Juliet*), an enormous rude gesture at the audience—and the critics who indulge in solemn exegesis of that rude gesture—what is its value?

Seen from the angle from which it is here contemplated, Bernhard's theatrical *œuvre* can be valued as an exuberant comic creation, a grotesque Dance of Death, an exuberant release of destructive impulses, of Swiftian *saeva indignatio,* an impassioned Philippic against all the pretentiousness and folly of his civilization. What makes this outburst of misanthropy and self-hatred remarkable and puts it into proximity to such similar outpourings of misanthropy as Goya's or Daumier's grotesques or the visions of Hieronymus Bosch is not their misanthropy or the hatred they exude but the artistry with which these impulses are hammered into shape. Bernhard's theatre is essentially a *mannerist* theatre. If his characters are puppets, all the greater the skill with which they perform their intricate dance; if his subject-matter is venom and derision, all the more admirable the perfection of the language in which the venom is spat out, the intricacy of the patterns it creates.

If Caribaldi in ***The Force of Habit*** miserably fails in extracting the divine music of Schubert from his grotesque, debased circus performers, Bernhard, in patterning that very play—and others like it—as an intricate musical structure, actually succeeds triumphantly in converting madness and hatred into a kind of chamber music.

Notes

1. Bernhard, *Die Macht der Gewohnheit* (Frankfurt, 1974), p. 34.

2. Bernhard, *Ein Fest fuer Boris* (Frankfurt, 1968), p. 22.

3. Bernhard, *Watten. Ein Nachlass* (Frankfurt, 1969), p. 40.

4. Bernhard, *Verstoerung* (Frankfurt, 1972), p. 138.

5. Bernhard, *Der Weltverbesserer* (Frankfurt, 1979), pp. 46–49. All translations in this article are mine, in spite of what the world reformer has to say on the subject:

> A translator cannot be helped
> the translator must go his way alone
> They have totally distorted my treatise
> totally distorted
> The translators distort the originals
> The translated work only reaches the market as a distortion
> It is the dilettantism
> and the filth of the translator
> that makes a translation so repulsive
> Translated works are always disgusting
> But they have brought me a lot of money
>
> (Ibid., p. 28)

6. Bernhard, *Die Jagdgesellschaft* (Frankfurt, 1974), pp. 55–56.

7. Ibid., p. 112.

8. Ibid., p. 103.

9. Bernhard, *Der Ignorant und der Wahnsinnige* (Frankfurt, 1972), p. 52.

10. Bernhard, *Verstoerung,* p. 136.

11. Bernhard, *Die Jagdgesellschaft,* p. 104.

12. Ibid., p. 105.

13. Ibid., pp. 51–52.

14. Bernhard, *Watten,* p. 70.

15. Bernhard, *Verstoerung,* p. 108.

16. Bernhard, *Der Ignorant und der Wahnsinnige,* p. 43.

17. Ibid., pp. 57–58.

18. Bernhard, *Die Macht der Gewohnheit,* p. 87.

19. Thomas Bernhard, "Ist es eine Komoedie? Ist es eine Tragoedie?", in Thomas Bernhard, *Prosa* (Frankfurt, 1967), p. 38.

20. Thomas Bernhard, *Immanuel Kant* (Frankfurt, 1978), p. 26.

21. Ibid., p. 46.

22. Ibid., pp. 61–62.

23. Bernhard, *Die Jagdgesellschaft,* p. 76.

24. Bernhard, *Der Weltverbesserer,* p. 80.

25. Quoted in U. Schweikert, "Im Grunde ist alles, was gesagt wird, zitiert," in *Text + Kritik,* 43 (July 1974), 2.

Gita Honegger (essay date Winter 1983)

SOURCE: "Wittgenstein's Children: The Writings of Thomas Bernhard," in *Theater,* Vol. 15, No. 1, Winter, 1983, pp. 52–62.

[*In the following essay, Honegger discusses the influence of philosopher Ludwig Wittgenstein on Bernhard's work and philosophy.*]

> *I with the German language*
> *this cloud around me*
> *that I keep as a house*
> *drive through all languages*
>
> (Ingeborg Bachmann)

> *The stupidity of entrusting oneself*
> *to the German language, my dear Doctor—*
> *absurd! And not only the German language,*
> *I think, but still the German language above*
> *all. The stupidity resulting from German,*
> *I think. . . . . . ."*
>
> (from Thomas Bernhard's "Gargoyles")

When I left Austria twenty years ago I thought that I could also escape my native language with all its historical resonances and traps as well as the stock temperament and mentality locked forever in its syntax and rhythm. It took over ten years before I ventured out of my voluntary exile in the English language. Some long forgotten words, along with astonishing new word combinations had managed to penetrate the harness of my Americanized persona that was to protect me from the eerie silence of a Viennese postwar childhood, from a language which, in my mind, had lost forever all integrity, usefulness and promise. Words like *faulen* (rot), *Unzucht* (fornication), *Ungeist* (unreason, "un-spirit", the German *Geist,* like the French *esprit,* implies both), *Wilderer* (poacher), *Blutvergiftung* (bloodpoisoning): faint, dark echoes from distant childhood nightmares on the edge of consciousness, long since rendered harmless through trivialization and abuse, suddenly emerged with the full force of their archaic authenticity as they named a world that deserved them.

There were other, rarely used or new words, combinations of several nouns or transformations of verbs into nouns. It is impossible to translate them into English which doesn't permit such flexibility, words like *Selbstverletzungsstrategie* (a "strategy to hurt oneself," condensed into one noun), *Geistesmuell* (mental garbage), *Geistesgegenteil* (the opposite of mind/spirit, "counter-mind," "counter-spirit," "counter-reason," all three meanings resonate in the German *Geist*), *Verstandeserschuetterung* (literally: "concussion of the mind" which could be simplifed as: mental trauma, shock, but the German term is intentionally artificial to differentiate it from *Gehirnerschuetterrung*, concussion, from "concussion of the mind," i.c. the biological from the intellectual function of the brain), etc. . . . name fragments, extracted from the signs of a dead world, grafted onto each other, disquieting artifacts, words with physical impact and the effect of viruses; words strung together in long, breathless sentences, each sentence moving across several pages, stretching the German syntax to its utmost limits, balancing along the edge of madness, suspended between life and death with the controlled intensity and unrelenting concentration of a superb tightrope act. I had discovered Thomas Bernhard. I began to rediscover my native language, a language after the catastrophe, created by a writer, who, like Walter Benjamin's Angel of History is blown into the future while looking back on history, not as a series of single, specific events, but one single castastrophe.

Following the long-winded sentence structures of Bernhard's earlier stories and novels (*Frost, Amras, Verstoerung,*[1] *Das Kalkwerk,*[2] *Midland in Stilfs, Ungenach, Watten, Gehen* and more) becomes an archeological dig in a horrifying landscape of decay and death for fragmented traces of the human mind, minds literally broken, captured at their breaking point in states of extreme tension, when the names of people, objects, landscapes become physically threatening, contagious, where the sign has more power than the signified and there is no more dividing line between outer and inner realities. The writing itself is located in what Foucault calls the "frontier situation" shared by the madman and the poet, the one "alienated in analogy," the other searching beneath the named differences for the language of resemblance, "where their words unceasingly renew the power of their strangeness and the strength of their contestation."[3]

It is dangerous territory, to be sure, and Bernhard is constantly testing, challenging its most extreme consequences, fully if defiantly aware that they may finally catch up with him, the writer/poet as well. Most of his prose pieces introduce two or more "languages" through an elaborate system of quoting. There is the author quoting a narrator as he quotes the actual central figure, usually a dead person, driven to death by an overriding obsession (illness in this context is an obsession too) which led to madness and frequently suicide. The thought process culminating in total collapse is revealed in letters, journals, notes and personal conversations until the narrator's voice merges with the quoted voice to the point where he becomes the impersonator of a dead man's mind. The process in these novels and stories is profoundly theatrical: the narrator, by elaborately quoting another, no longer functions as the conventional story teller, but rather as performer, "impersonator." Appropriately enough, one collection of Bernhard's short satirical tales is entitled *Der Stimmenimitator* (literally: "The Imitator of Voices," whose

English equivalent is an impersonator. Incidentally, the *Stimmenimitator* of one of the stories can imitate many different voices, but not his own). The author himself is, of course, the supreme performer—of all the voices introduced by him, which is to say, ultimately, of himself. Only by an extreme act of artistic consciousness—the consciousness of the performer who is able to distance himself from what he impersonates, most importantly from himself—can he save himself from succumbing to the madness of his voices.

All of Bernhard's writing takes the form of monomaniacal soliloquies, bravura performances of the mind which is both tragic hero and sole spectator in this drama of life that is a tragedy for the subject, and becomes a grotesque comedy for his "other," who is watching himself perform the futile struggle against his limitations, his better knowledge. *Is it a Tragedy? Is it a Comedy?* is the title of one of Bernhard's stories. It is the key to his philosophy and aesthetics. If the question sounds banal, Bernhard would be the last one to deny it. On the contrary, its banality is quite to the point in his vision (and personal experience) of life, where the tragic hero becomes a clown (as such as much a cliché as any other theatrical convention), when observed in action, in performance.

The place of action is always Austria. More specifically, it is the landscape between Salzburg, where Bernhard grew up and Gmunden, where he has been living for the past twenty years. Over-shadowed by looming mountains, darkened by damp forests, peopled by stuporous, brutal peasants and pompous, equally stupid representatives of the educated, so-called "civilized" classes (notably doctors, his favorite targets), Bernhard's Austria is invariably outlined in clusters of outraged superlatives racing each other from deepest despair to the heights of deadly derision, from biblical to satirical wrath. In his theater of the mind, it is not a naturalistic landscape, but a set, a "foreign body," its persistent exaggerations linked to the other world like malignant tumors from a virus which has infiltrated the brain from outside.

No one, least of all the writer himself, is safe from contagion. We are all part of the disease, be it specifically cultural or basically human, a tragic predicament, no doubt, but ultimately a comic spectacle as our efforts to protect ourselves from it are the surest symptoms of our contamination. There is no way out. Teutonic prediliction for *Weltschmerz*, pathos and the commonplace? Yes, of course, except that in Bernhard's world these aspects are already part of a performance and, in the process, subject to exaggeration which invariably leads to ridicule. Moreover, with his characteristic obsessive insistency Bernhard in his most recent work does not shy away from the ultimate consequence: self-parody. For Bernhard, the writer who has won the most prestigious literary awards as the twentieth century visionary of doom, successor to Kafka in the pantheon of Middle-European literary geniuses and subject of an ever increasing body of secondary literature, this may seem an outrageous act of self-destruction. But it is totally consistent with his radical theatrical philosophy, a particularly Austrian sensibility which links him to such desperately funny satirists as Johann Nestroy and Karl Kraus and the self-deflating, deadly serious irony of Ludwig Wittgenstein, who begins his *Tractatus logico-philosophicus* with a quote from Nestroy and ends it with the complete negation of everything he said before.

> "The question is not 'How do I write about Wittgenstein?' but rather: "Is it possible for me to be Wittgenstein for just *one* moment without destroying either him (W) or me (B)?"[4]
>
> (Thomas Bernhard)

Ludwig Wittgenstein has haunted the imagination and challenged the craft of Austria's post-war generation of writers from Ingeborg Bachmann to Peter Handke. But while Handke attempted to apply Wittgenstein's logical positivism directly to his writing, Bachmann and Bernhard share a much deeper affinity to the source of Wittgenstein's philosophy, to Wittgenstein as "metaphysical subject" who cannot be described because he is situated at the frontier between the speakable and the unspeakable. It is Wittgenstein, the mystic, as Bachmann pointed out[5], who truly opened up new, dangerous territory, precisely that vast field of silence, closed to the philosopher's discourse, which the poet must dare to transgress. It is here that Bernhard must meet Wittgenstein in full knowledge of the philosopher's rigorous critique of language and its possible consequence for the writer, namely self-annihilation. Wittgenstein's genius, his full impact on our century, as Bernhard (and Bachmann before him) understands so well, lies in the consciously sustained dialectic of his failure: if the positivist thinker failed the mystic, it is the latter's unthinkable silence that finally eclipses the philosopher's most brilliant achievement.

Approaching Wittgenstein ("Is it possible for me to be Wittgenstein. . . . ?") in Bernhard's dramaturgy of the mind is a performance act: he must enter a particular state of mind (the stage) and lock into the mechanism of its thought processes (the rhythmical foundation of theater: music/text) with its built-in self-destructive power which may not spare the intruder (performer: the red shoes dancing their dancer to death): he may be exposed as a phony (impersonator/impostor) or completely lose all sense of personal self in his attempted identification with another— Wittgenstein as "metaphysical subject" (the "soul" of the stage character behind a "voice") which at best is never more concrete than the "focal vanishing point behind the mirror of his language".[6]

Bernhard's novel *Correction*[7]—generally acknowledged as a seminal masterpiece of twentieth century literature—is a triumph totally in tune with the legacy of Wittgenstein's spirit, precisely because it is *not* about Wittgenstein, although it is quite possibly the most accurate approximation of the philosopher's uncompromising temperament and intellectual/spiritual integrity. Bernhard's language originates in the same cultural/geographical space as

Wittgenstein's. But in response to that space, which is to say, in response to itself, it transforms all regional, biographical and temperamental similarities between Wittgenstein, Roithamer, the book's central figure and Bernhard himself. They become correspondences which designate the cultural as mental space which contains both the origin and destruction of thought in its struggle to achieve perfection and verification through matter. The house in the shape of a perfect cone that Roithamer, the Austrian born Cambridge scientist, builds for his beloved sister in the middle of the forest which is their native landscape, is to be the perfect expression of his sister's nature, that is, of his, Roithamer's complete understanding of his sister, hence the perfect expression of both himself and his sister. It is the mystic's age-old attempt to reconcile all differences: between spirit/matter, inside/outside: the cone as shelter and monument, male/female: as a sign of total penetration (perfect understanding) as well as enclosure (home/womb) incestuous/self-love, self/other, through the triumph of the spirit that has completely penetrated the other and given birth to itself in a perfect expression of their joint nature. This is impossible since all matter (including man's biological self) is part of nature, hence subject to decay and death. Perfection in accordance with nature can therefore only be achieved through illness (both physical and mental, since the mind is part of nature as well) in death. All that is left in the end is the empty space: "The end is not process. Clearing." The clearing is the site both of the cone (in the forest) and its origin and destruction (in the mind). Only that space is left intact. It marks the survival of Bernhard, the writer/poet as author of this particular book. But the victory is only temporary, as Bernhard would be quick to point out not with self-pity, but with that profound sense of irony which so often is mistaken for nihilistic black humor. It is the awareness that death is only deferred through the act of writing in the space which also contains his (B's) destruction.

> Am I right in saying
> that what you write
> has to do with philosophy
> even though you call it comedy
> Or am I right in saying
> that what you write is comedy
> while you insist
> that it is philosophy[8]

"*Ist ja alles ein Theater* is a popular Austrian expression which implies much more than its English translation: "Everything's just theater." It stands for an entire *Lebenseinstellung,* an attitude toward life, which accepts the fun and futility, the illusion as well as the vanity and perversity of all our efforts in view of the fact that the final curtain will come down for good. The traditional Austrian *gestus* accompanying this statement is a shrug which takes the edge off any pathos that might arise from all too reverential associations with Shakespeare's famous "*All the world's a stage . . .*"

In this spirit the theater has provided Bernhard with a theoretical basis for his philosophy and aesthetics and with a perspective on himself as writer, survivor, clown: tireless performer and spectator of himself. Therefore it should come as no surprise that besides a substantial body of prose literature, Bernhard has also written about 15 plays.[9] What might be more surprising is his repeatedly expressed disgust with theater, which goes beyond his more obvious attacks on the present state of the theater and is frequently aimed at himself. But such an attitude is also totally consistent with his unrelenting self-investigation in the context of his philosophy. Theater as an idea, as a philosophical challenge, is quite different from theater as a practiced artform or, as he calls it, an "entertainment mechanism." A theatrical performance, in its original attraction, must hold the same promise for Bernhard as the cone did for Roithamer: Thought turned into matter, the temptation of the perfect expression (embodiment) of self in another. Only that theater, by its very nature, quickly exposes the illusory nature of all such attempts and in its temporality makes a mockery of all claims to permanence. If thought seeks its expression in a medium that already renders reality as an illusion, it is one step further removed from its aim and doomed to failure from the start. In this sense theater becomes the perfect sign for failure. No wonder Bernhard jumps on it with masochistic self-disgust (and joy) as the most useful (and delightful and despicable) model for his philosophy, which, performed on stage, must naturally imply the mockery of itself. Gloucester's jump from the cliffs of Dover is, as Jan Kott pointed out[10], a blind man's pantomime set up by his son on an empty stage. Even death, in performance, becomes a grotesque spectacle, a clown act, once we have severed all connections to the metaphysical realm (the Gods), and the rest is Wittgenstein's irrevocable silence.

The most equivocal, deceitful aspect of theatrical convention is language: an actor who pretends to be another speaking spontaneously, actually quotes a text that pretends to quote that most elusive original, called "character." Bernhard's theatrical language never attempts to create the illusion of spontaneity. On the contrary, a language based on quotes is his most essential means of characterization which points to the deadly traps of culture and tradition. His characters are always quoting, whether they speak a literary, "theatrical" language, or express themselves in commonplaces, phrases and slogans, all of which are part of their cultural history. Moreover, the language they are locked into also carries the traditional mode of delivery so that very often it is the language which incites the emotion rather than the other way around, as is common in naturalistic, "psychological" drama. His built-in critique of the use of language makes its most effective, chilling point in the play *Eve of Retirement,* which shows how fascist rhetoric has succeeded in perverting so-called "traditional values" passed on through generations in popular idioms and sayings and stubbornly persists today in the most "innocent" use of language. Bernhard's theater demonstrates the process of mortification of a society which is solely animated and eventually destroyed by a historical mechanism which has long been cut off from its source and is

kept in motion on the strings of language which activate their desperate speakers like pitiful marionettes.

Bernhard doesn't exclude himself from the process. While in his earlier plays the prevailing mood is an ominous, if often grotesque sense of tragic despair over this human predicament, his later plays reveal more and more how the fatal mechanism eventually takes hold of the writer himself. He is locked into it by his own language, trapped as it were, in his own texts. Several of his recent plays[11] contain ironic reflections of the legend he himself has become. But self-parody, self-quotes are more than in-jokes or symptoms of a writer who has run dry or simply exploits his proven technique. Even if they are that too, they are necessarily part of a writer who is honest enough (or shameless enough as he may put it) not to claim that he can place himself outside his culture.

His last play, *Appearances Are Deceiving*[12] shows how the mechanism of language, like the lives of its speakers, is slowly coming to a halt, burning itself out "like cigarettes left burning in an ashtray" as Bernhard himself described it recently. It is much quieter, gentler, more openly compassionate and vulnerable than anything he had written before. For the first time the ironies are touching rather than cruel as they point to the writer who is playing out the familiar strategies of his own language (his life) until there is, like for Beckett's R[13] "nothing left to tell".

> If I hadn't actually lived through everything that led up to my present existence, I would have probably invented it and come up with the same results.[14]

In the second part of *Don Quixote,* notes Michel Foucault[15], Cervantes' text turns back upon itself and becomes the object of its own narrative. Don Quixote meets people who have read the first part and recognize him. He has become the book and what he is (represents) must correspond with the way he is read. Don Quixote's truth, according to Foucault, is not in the relation of the words to the world, but in the complex relationship of verbal signs between themselves. The "disappointed" fiction (*la fiction déçue*) of the great epic romances has brought out the representative power of language.

Similarly, Bernhard's earlier work keeps reappearing in his later work. As much as he himself has become text through his earlier books, he makes himself the object of his later work which, aside from five autobiographical books about his youth[16], contains more and more of what we can now recognize as "biographical" elements. But those, too, have emerged exclusively from his earlier texts. It seems relatively easy to track him down through his many repetitions, thematic obsessions, stylistic patterns and essentially the same mind driving itself again and again into the same excruciating tension. But with his reclusive life-style and personality which covers itself in his rare public appearances through skillful "auto-performances" (clownish exaggerations of his "literary" image, layered masks of impenetrability), he makes sure that his biography is never anything but *fiction déçue,* text interacting with text from which he, Bernhard, like Don Quixote, emerges as yet another—still the same—book.

The fact that in this country only three of his novels have been published rather sporadically[17] and disappeared with hardly any notice[18] is a serious loss which drastically limits any full appreciation of his literary achievement, and, more importantly, any insight into the drama of his writing: the interaction between the texts, between writing and writer constantly threatening to annihilate, or, at the very least, outwit each other.

"I kept watching the desk until I saw myself sitting at my desk, from the back, so to speak, I saw how I bent over, according to my illness, in order to write" writes Rudolf, the central character of *Beton* (Concrete) who is unable to find the first sentence for his study on Mendelssohn-Bartholdy after ten years of intense research and preparation.[19] He continues to watch, create himself like a stage-character in his frantically comic struggle to write which may well kill him even before his life-threatening illness: "I saw that my posture was pathological, but then again, I am not a healthy man, I actually am sick, through and through, I told myself. The way you sit there, I told myself, you have already written a few pages about Mendelssohn-Bartholdy, maybe ten or twelve pages already, this is how I sit at my desk when I have already written ten or twelve pages, I said to myself." This is the *writer* as we know him from previous texts, writing about a writer writing about himself in the process of writing which he is unable to do but actually does, since *a text is* being written. The book which is "about" not writing contradicts, annihilates its premise by its very existence. What it does confirm, once again, is the survival of Bernhard, the *writer,* in and of the text.

Don Quixote himself, says Foucault, has become a sign, in his personal appearance and through the book. Bernhard, too, has become a sign, through his personal life-long struggle with illness which he keeps challenging and fighting through his writing which in turn has assumed the function of another life-long illness as a necessary, if equally deadly, survival mechanism. He himself has become the sign of the survivor, of the *writer as survivor.*

In his latest book, *Wittgensteins Neffe* (Wittgenstein's Nephew)[20], an incurable madman and an incurable writer secretly meet on top of the hill that separates the mental ward from the lung cancer pavillion, their respective places of confinement. The writer is Bernhard. The other is his friend Paul Wittgenstein, nephew of Ludwig, like his uncle black sheep of the powerful clan, potential genius turned public madman, the *Herr Baron* as he was called, a tragically flamboyant figure in Vienna's literary cafes and nightclubs where he used to recite from memory long passages from a philosophical mammoth work he never wrote; who, like his uncle, gave away his family fortune until it ran out and, at the age of 60, was sent by the Wittgensteins to work as a clerk in an insurance company. He died in 1979 in a mental institution in Upper Austria, a pathetically abandoned, broken old man. At the time of their peculiar meeting in 1967 Bernhard had just undergone one of his many lung operations he was not expected to survive, while Paul had suffered another one of his many mental breakdowns.

"The only difference between Paul and me" writes Bernhard, "is that Paul let himself be *completely* consumed by his madness while I never let myself be *completely* consumed by my equally intense madness. . . . Paul had only his madness and he existed through his madness, I had, in addition to my madness, my lung disease and I have taken advantage of both: my madness and my lung disease; one day, from one moment to the next, I have made both the *source of my existence* for the rest of my life. Just as Paul has lived the lunatic for decades I have lived for decades the man with the lung disease and just as Paul has *played* the lunatic for decades, I have *played* for decades the man with the lung disease and as he used the lunatic for his purposes, I used the man with the lung disease for mine."

And if Paul's uncle compared philosophical questions to a disease which called for treatment rather than solutions, he too needed and exploited this disease as his life-long illness in order to survive. The philosopher's undaunted approaches toward a philosophy to end all philosophies is as suicidal as his nephew's obsessive performance acts of madness and Bernhard's textual auto-performances, which may eventually, like Roithamer's corrections, eclipse themselves in the process.

The paradox of incurability casts the madman, the philosopher and the poet in a mad ritual of manic productivity toward self-destruction. Yet they keep fighting for their lives *like madmen, as* madmen, shamans, enacting the catastrophe to defuse it for one last moment. Genius or insanity? Our standard definitions might hinge on no more than more or less accidental priorities of vanity:

"The one, Ludwig, might have been more philosophical, while the other, Paul, was crazier, but it might also be possible that we only believe the philosophical one that he indeed is a philosopher, because he put his philosophy on paper rather than his madness, while we consider the other, Paul, a lunatic, because he suppressed his philosophy and didn't publish it, but exhibited his madness instead." To which the quintessential Austrian genius, the *Ueberlebenskuenstler* (survival artist) would reply with Nestroy's sense for irony and double entendre: "*Geh, mach doch net so ein Theater!*" (Come on, stop putting on such a show!)

Notes

1. Published by Knopf as *Gargoyles.*

2. Knopf; *In the Lime Works.*

3. Michel Foucault *The Order of Things.*

4. Thomas Bernhard, 1971, in a letter to Austrian writer Hilde Spiel.

5. Ingeborg Bachmann: *Sagbares und Unsagbares— Die Philosophie Ludwig Wittgensteins.*

6. David Pears *Ludwig Wittgenstein*; (*Penguin Modern Masters.*)

7. Published by Knopf in 1976; published by Ventura on an imprint of Random House.

8. From Bernhard's play *The Hunting Party,* published in *Performing Arts Journal, #13.*

9. They are performed by the best repertory companies all over Europe. In the U.S. only his *Eve of Retirement* has been staged by Liviu Ciulei at the Guthrie Theater in Minneapolis. It has been published together with *The President* by Performing Arts Journal Publications.

10. Jan Kott: *King Lear and Endgame* in *Shakespeare Our Contemporary.*

11. Most obviously his last two plays, *Am Ziel* (Arrived) and *Ueber allen Gipfeln ist Ruh* (a mocking reference to the Goethe poem, to the all-time *master* of German language).

12. Published in this issue and first staged at the Schauspielhaus Bochum by Claus Peymann who directed almost all premiere productions of Bernhard's plays.

13. The "reader" in *Ohio Impromptu.*

14. From Bernhard's autobiographical book *Die Kaelte* (The Cold).

15. In *The Order of Things.*

16. *Die Ursache* (The Cause), *Der Keller* (The Cellar), *Der Atem* (Breath), *Die Kaelte* (The Cold), *Ein Kind* (A Child).

17. *Gargoyles, In the Lime Works* and *Correction.*

18. Betty Falkenberg and Richard Gilman were the only critics who wrote very perceptive reviews of *Correction,* in the *Partisan Review* and *The Nation,* respectively..

19. Published by Suhrkamp in 1982 and presently in the process of being translated in England.

20. Suhrkamp, 1982.

Gerald A. Fetz (essay date December 1984)

SOURCE: "The Works of Thomas Bernhard: 'Austrian Literature?'" in *Modern Austrian Literature,* Vol. 17, Nos. 3–4, December, 1984, pp. 171–92.

[*In the following essay, Fetz discusses the defining characteristics of Austrian literature and how Bernhard's work fits within that category.*]

I: INTRODUCTION

The question posed in the title of this essay appears, at least on the most literal level, to be rather simple if not downright simplistic. Certainly the works of Thomas Bernhard form a part, even a very significant part of Austrian literature. Bernhard's ancestors far into the past were Austrians and he still resides in Austria today. The doubts sometimes expressed about the legitimacy of claiming "Austrian writer" status for such authors as Rilke, Celan, or Canetti, who grew up in parts of the Habsburg Empire long lost to Austria and who spent most of their adult, creative lives away fom Austria, are not applicable to Bernhard: with the exception of short stays abroad he has continued to reside in Austria since his earliest years in the First Republic, through the "Ständestaat" and "Anschluß" in the Third Reich, to the present day in Austria's Second Republic.[1] And at one point in a taped conversation, in which Bernhard relates the significance of the various locations where he spent time as a child—Henndorf, Salzburg, Vienna—, he even asserts: "Ich bin nur Österreicher!"[2] Examples of Bernhard's writings can be found in virtually every anthology of contemporary Austrian literature since the mid-1950s, and he is discussed extensively in every study of post-1945 Austrian literature which has appeared during the past two decades. But does such factual information, or even Bernhard's assertion about himself, really answer the question, and is the question really as simple as it initially appears?

If we move very far beyond the question as one which requires or is satisfied by a yes-or-no answer, it becomes much more complex. We are suddenly confronted by the necessity of defining, describing, and trying to explain both the works of Thomas Bernhard, a formidable and controversial task in itself, and just what is meant by the term "Austrian Literature," an even more controversial undertaking. The numerous attempts in both directions are characterized by contradictions, over-simplifications, rebuttals, emotional responses, and even skepticism about the usefulness and possibility of the attempts altogether.

The secondary literature contains direct warnings about the dangers inherent in any confrontation with these two subjects as well as clear warnings that one should not expect to reach definitive answers or understanding of either Thomas Bernhard or the *nature* of "Austrian Literature." About Thomas Bernhard, for example, one can read: "Weder zu Bernhard noch seinen Figuren kann man mit vernünftigen oder plausiblen Argumenten kommen."[3] In another commentary Bernhard is described as being ". . . ein Autor, der ganze Scharen Berufskritiker auf den Holzweg führt und vielleicht selber nicht einmal weiß, was er da Verheerendes anrichtet. Anzuraten ist, dem Mann vorerst einmal kein Wort aufs Wort zu glauben."[4] And even Bernhard himself issues an unambiguous warning when he says: "Ich spreche die Sprache, die nur ich allein verstehe, sonst niemand, wie jeder nur seine eigene Sprache versteht, und die glauben, sie verstünden, sind Dummköpfe oder Scharlatane."[5] About the attempts to define "Austrian Literature" one can read comments which are merely skeptical: "So unverzichtbar das Österreichische für die deutsche Literatur der Moderne ist, so schwer läßt es sich—über die Namen der Schriftsteller hinaus—

definieren."⁶ Others deny the possibility completely, claiming: ". . . daβ jede literarische Arbeit, die deutsch geschrieben ist, zur deutschen Literatur gehört und dieser Umstand für die meisten österreichichen Autoren recht glücklich ist; diese verhungerten, wenn es nicht so wäre."⁷

Difficult and controversial questions such as these, for which simple answers are foolish and result in untenable generalizations and over-simplifications, underscore the nature of literary criticism and commentary as art rather than science. Art, merely because it refuses to provide definitive or absolute answers, cannot be dismissed as useless, for the insights which it offers to those who look carefully are often far more profound than simple answers can hope to be. Literary criticism, like the art with which it concerns itself, can make few claims to definitive answers; yet it too is far from being useless, for, if founded in careful and extensive reading and reflection, it can also provide insights both varied and profound. The following attempt to confront the not-so-simple question posed in the title above, a question which will not be satisfied with a simple yes-or-no answer, will be undertaken with these assertions in mind.

The fact that these questions and subjects, Thomas Bernhard and "Austrian Literature," are significant and worthy of further reflection is substantiated by the extensive, thoughtful attention they continue to receive, here in the pages of *Modern Austrian Literature* and elsewhere. Consequently, and in spite of the qualifications and warnings offered above, it should not be surprising that still one more critic would choose to approach them. Before doing so, however, the initial question of the title should perhaps be rephrased, in light of those qualifications and warnings to read: To what extent should the works of Thomas Bernhard be regarded as "Austrian Literature?" That is the question we will address in the remainder of this essay.

II: "Austrian Literature"—Can one describe it?

The controversy over whether one can legitimately speak of "Austrian Literature" separate from "German Literature" and if so, what the differentiating characteristics between the two actually are, extends at least as far back as the 18th century and Alois Blumauer's *Beobachtungen über Österreichs Aufklärung und Literatur.*⁸ Since then an almost indeterminable number of attempts have been made to answer those questions, a very high percentage of these since 1945. A majority of these attempts, as one would expect, have been undertaken by Austrians, although Germans and other non-Austrians have frequently confronted these questions as well. The first question, whether there is a distinct "Austrian Literature," has been asked most often in a form similar to the following: "Gibt es eine eigenständige österreichische Literatur? Oder gibt es nur eine deutsche Literatur in Österreich, bzw, eine österreichische Literatur als Teil der gesamtdeutschen?"⁹ Critics who affirm the uniqueness or separateness of an "Austrian Literature" must then face the problem of defining or

describing that uniqueness. The diversity of the attempts and conclusions is both impressive and astounding, but truly convincing, thoroughgoing definitions or descriptions have proven rather elusive. As one commentator has suggested: ". . . das Problem, was österreichische Dichtung eigentlich sei, gehört zu den Fragen, deren Antwort jeder zu wissen meint, die aber keiner definieren kann."¹⁰

The efforts to define "Austrian Literature" have been made with a variety of purposes in mind, not all of which have been primarily literary in nature. Most, of course, were made with the intention of drawing a clear line between "Austrian" and "German Literature," the major difficulty of which lies in the fact that they share not only a common language but more than a few cultural and literary traditions as well. Not infrequently the most ambitious attempts to differentiate between the two have been undertaken by critics who were trying to underline Austria's uniqueness and independence from Germany in general, especially politically. Conversely, the attempts to minimize or even deny any uniqueness for "Austrian Literature" have frequently been proposed by critics who were seeking to minimize the differences between Austria and Germany as political entities.¹¹ The variety and nature of answers to the question cannot be understood independently of the ideological and political considerations which have often informed them. The radical change in Hofmannsthal's response to this question where-by he stresses in 1917 the separateness of "Austrian Literature," only to deny it in 1931, can be understood only in this context and as a clear reflection of the extra-literary and political factors which influence such answers.¹²

The attempts to describe and define "Austrian Literature" have increased steadily since the early years of the Second Republic. Well-known to those familiar with the secondary literature are among others the analyses of Helmut Olles (1957), Joseph Strelka (1966), Herbert Seidler (1970), Robert Mühlher (1970), and Viktor Suchy (1975), the essays by Otto Basil, Herbert Eisenreich, and Ivar Ivask in the collection *Das groβe Erbe* (1962), as well as the numerous short, but representative answers to the question—"Gibt es eine österreichische Literatur?"—in the 1965 issues of *Wort in der Zeit,* edited by Gerhard Fritsch.¹³ Many of the earlier descriptions in the postwar period were written with Nadler's *Literaturgeschichte der deutschen Stämme und Landschaften* in mind and as clear refutations of his denial of the uniqueness of "Austrian Literature," a denial which had been accepted as fact, for obvious reasons, by official and semi-official Nazi culture. His monumental work had served as a convenient, "scientific" justification for the "Anschluβ" of "Austrian Literature" as well.

In that context and in the zeal of wanting to (re-)establish the independence and spell out the uniqueness of "Austrian Literature," the case was frequently over-simplified and over-stated. What often emerged was a rather static image of "Austrian Literature," an image in which individual works and writers were forced to fit a universal, timeless outline, an image in which the similarities, real and imagined, were emphasized at the expense of significant differences. Some excellent surveys of the evolution of the concept "Austrian Literature" have appeared recently (Mádl, Schmidt-Dengler, Roger Bauer, Dagmar Lorenz),[14] thus there is no need to repeat that intriguing history here. For our purposes let it suffice to generalize somewhat and merely indicate the major characteristics which the post-1945 critics have most often claimed to find in "Austrian Literature." Very frequently mentioned—and these became the oft-repeated clichés and commonplaces about "Austrian Literature"—were its continuing indebtedness to the Baroque tradition, its conservative and anti-realistic nature, its musicality, its melancholy mood, its emphasis on language and theater as central themes, the passivity of its protagonists and lack of action in its plots, and, last but not least, its fascination with decay and death.[15] In addition to the continuous significance of the Baroque, certain other literary movements or eras—Biedermeier, Jugendstil-Impressionism, Surrealism, and more recently both linguistic experimentation (Concrete Poetry) and a "New Subjectivity"—have been portrayed as genuinely "Austrian" movements or eras, whereas others—Enlightenment, Storm and Stress, Romanticism, Realism, Naturalism, Expressionism, and politically or socially engaged literature—have been regarded as primarily "German" phenomena.[16]

Such generalized assertions are, of course, not completely false. The problem with them and others like them, however, is that they tend to be very vague, they too often lay exclusive claim to these characteristics for "Austrian Literature," they deny the significance, even presence, of others which might contradict or fail to fit the pattern, and they are based on rather superficial readings of the literary works themselves. All too frequently it appears that "Austrian Literature" has been read with one eye closed. It is precisely such definitions at which the editors of the special "Literatur in Österreich" issue of *Tintenfisch* (1979) aimed their criticism when they exclaimed: "Die herrschende Meinung gibt vor, die Wahrheit über die österreichische Literatur zu verbreiten, während in Wahrheit die österreichische Literatur ein paar Wahrheiten über die herrschende Meinung bereithält."[17] This with-one-eye-closed approach to "Austrian Literature" is certainly the overriding weakness of Claudio Magris' often-cited study, *Der habsburgische Mythos in der österreichischen Literatur* (1966),[18] a weakness blindly adopted by Ulrich Greiner in his disappointing book, *Der Tod des Nachsommers* (1979).[19] Since Walter Weiss had so convincingly elucidated the short-comings of Magris' approach, it is surprising that Greiner tried to revive and apply Magris' major thesis to contemporary "Austrian Literature." This basic thesis contends that "Austrian Literature" is conservative, passive, unengaged politically, oriented toward the past, and obsessed with that (Habsburg) past and its myths. It is claimed that no significant tradition of realistic, liberal-progressive, social or politically critical literature exists in Austria, that it is, in fact, "un-Austrian."[20] Even if one chooses to overlook such aspects in the works of Lenau,

Nestroy, Kraus, Horváth, Musil, or Handke (as many have done), or simply brand their works in which these aspects are absolutely undeniable as anomalies and thus exceptions to the rule (as many have done), then the recent scholarship by critics such as Weiss, Mádl, Bodi, and Jarka, which has illuminated a significant tradition of realistic and engaged literature in Austria, has made such a thesis totally untenable.[21]

In spite of the extensiveness of the secondary literature on "Austrian Literature" as a concept, then, new and significant insights continue to emerge. The number of recent scholarly symposia and sessions at professional meetings devoted to the topic,[22] as well as the scores of longer newspaper and journal articles on the subject in the last decade alone is very impressive. This special issue of *Modern Austrian Literature* is itself based in part on three special sessions at the annual MLA meeting in 1979.[23]

Unlike Greiner's work most of these more recent discussions of the concept "Austrian Literature" have been much more modest in their goal, less intent on claiming exclusive "Austrianness" for certain literary themes or traits, less interested in finding timeless threads which would neatly tie all of "Austrian Literature" together from beginning to end. In these recent discussions one also finds a real hesitancy to pursue the idea of an "Austrian National Literature" very far.[24] Such a concept has been rendered problematical not only by its abuse during the Nazi period, but also by the fact that in the present German-speaking world one not only has to differentiate between "German" and "Austrian Literature" but also between and among "Austrian," "West German," "East German," and "Swiss-German" as well. And these most recent discussions, although they do not deny that there are certain elements, concerns, and traditions which tie writers in each of these political-social realms together, willingly admit and affirm the significance of literary and intellectual influences, traditions, and impulses which cross not only the borders between these countries, but also the borders of the rest of the Western world. With regard to "Austrian Literature" there have been very few recent attempts to build universal, timeless, and exclusive constructs or paradigms.[25] In addition to the efforts mentioned earlier to uncover and elucidate the realistic and social-politically critical aspects of the Austrian literary tradition the most informative and useful studies recently have cautiously probed the affinities and similarities among Austrian writers or between them and individual but not exclusive Austrian literary traditions.[26] No attempt will be made here to deal with the wide range of these discussions, but in order to provide a context for viewing Bernhard's works as "Austrian Literatur" in a meaningful and legitimate way, I will draw insights from two of the most compelling of these recent discussions.

In general the attitudes about our central questions which prevail in the best of these discussions, particularly in those which focus on contemporary "Austrian Literature," are reflected in the opening lines of Walter Weiss' introduction to *Zwischenbilanz,* an anthology of modern Austrian writing:

"Österreichische Beiträge," das ist nicht im Sinne einer Abgrenzungshysterie oder eines literarischen Imperialismus aufzufassen. "Österreichisch" meint hier nichts unhistorisch Absolutes und Feststehendes, sondern bezeichnet zunächst nur eine Minimalgemeinsamkeit der in dieser Anthologie vertretenen Autoren: Sie sind im heutigen oder ehemaligen Österreich, zumindest aber in dessen Ausstrahlungsbereich; geboren und aufgewachsen. Sie bleiben später, auch aus der Distanz, in verschiedenen Formen und Intensitätsgraden darauf bezogen. Es geht um ihre besonderen Beiträge zur Gegenwartsliteratur und nicht etwa vorrangig und abgehoben davon um ihren Beitrag zum Österreichischen als solchen.[27]

For our purposes in this portion of the essay one final complementary example of these more circumspect recent approaches to "Austrian Literature" deserves mention. Wendelin Schmidt-Dengler argues in his essay, "Nationalliteraturen I: Österreich-Pathos der Immobilität,'" that the elaborate attempts to construct timeless outlines of "Austrian Literature" have clearly overstated the affinities and continuity and understated or neglected both the significant differences among Austrian writers as well as affinities which exist between those Austrian and non-Austrian writers. Near the end of his essay one reads: "Ist nun die Literatur, die aus Österreich kommt, doch eine deutsche und keine österreichische? Sie ist auf jeden Fall keine bundes-deutsche. Von einer österreichischen Nationalliteratur zu sprechen, ist heute nicht sinnvoll . . ."[28] Thus, in spite of his disclaimer about the usefulness of speaking about an "Austrian National Literature," he also finds it inappropriate to portray such Austrian writers as Handke, Bachmann, and Bernhard as West German writers. These writers were all included, for example, in the Kindler volume on contemporary West German literature as well as in the volume on Austria.[29]

In spite of their reservations about the possibility of describing a timeless unified Austrian literary tradition, which they claim simply does not exist, critics such as Mádl, Weiss, and Schmidt-Dengler all contend that there are certain themes, concerns, even character types that recur in almost endless variation in the works of many Austrian writers, Bernhard included. One cannot help but be struck, for instance, by the frequent focus on language itself as a major theme: linguistic consciousness, language criticism, language skepticism, linguistic experimentation.[30] The frequent emphasis placed on theater and music as theme, metaphor, and symbol is also readily discernible. Noticeable, too, is the fact that numerous protagonists in the works of Austrian writers appear to be direct descendants of Jakob, the quintessential un-Faustian hero, in Grillparzer's *Der arme Spielmann*: from Hofmannsthal's Hans Karl Bühl (*Der Schwierige*) and Canetti's Peter Kien (*Die Blendung*) to Bernhard's Strauch (*Frost*) or Konrad (*Das Kalkwerk*). As the traditional descriptions of "Austrian Literature" have asserted, there does in fact appear to be a widespread fascination with decay and death, and not only in the Baroque and Fin-de-siècle periods. Yet, in direct contradiction to those same descriptions, there also emerges a long line of examples of aggressive social

and political criticism, often directed at Austria's government, society, institutions, and people—a line stretching from Lenau to Soyfer, from Kraus and Horváth to Innerhofer and Bernhard.

The fact that important affinities exist among Austrian writers, especially among contemporaries, is hardly surprising. They share a common, if ever-changing, political, social, and cultural environment as well as a common history, traditions, and myths, all of which influence significantly both the way in which they view the world and their works, none of which are created in a vacuum: Vienna is neither Berlin nor Zürich; the Habsburgs were considerably different from the Hohenzollerns; the Catholic heritage differs from the Lutheran; Wittgenstein's philosophy distinguishes itself from that of Hegel or Kant; a *Vielvölkerstaat* is not comparable to an essentially monolingual empire; and the Second Austrian Republic is neither the Federal Republic nor the German Democratic Republic. These differences, simplified here to illustrate a point, cannot help but be reflected to some degree in the literature which emerges from the different socio-political realms. If that were not the case, the many recently published social histories of literature would hardly be valid.[31] To keep things in perspective, however, and to avoid the dangers of thinking in too exclusive terms, we should perhaps remind ourselves that Austria and Germany have shared and continue to share more than a common language, that Kleist, too, was skeptical of language, Goethe interested in theater as metaphor, E.T.A. Hoffmann in music, that Tucholsky's social-political criticism has much in common with that of Soyfer, that F.X. Kroetz's portrayal of rural life corresponds clearly to Innerhofer's, and that Thomas Mann also was fascinated with decay and death.

Schmidt-Dengler concludes his essay with the following comments:

> Es hat aber seine guten Gründe, die aus Österreich kommende Literatur *auch*, beileibe nicht ausschließlich in ihrem konkreten historischen (österreichischen) Kontext zu begreifen, nicht um einen verschämten, dafür aber umso hartnäckigeren neuen österreichischen Chauvinismus zu nähren, sondern um Schwächen und Stärken dieser Literatur besser zu würdigen oder kritisieren zu können.[32]

With the comments of Weiss and Schmidt-Dengler clearly in mind, and in the context of our discussion of the difficulties and dangers in trying to describe "Austrian Literature" as a unified concept, let us turn our attention to Thomas Bernhard and his relationship to that literature.

III: THOMAS BERNHARD AND "AUSTRIAN LITERATURE"

My intention is not to catalogue and discuss the multitude of ways in which the works of Thomas Bernhard are tied to, derive from, negate, or extend a variety of Austrian literary traditions.[33] That has been attempted elsewhere. Instead, by focusing on his works in the context of two recent representative descriptions of specific emphases in

"Austrian Literature"—essays by Walter Weiss and Karin Kathrein[34]—, I hope to offer examples of the extent to which his works can be read as "Austrian Literature," and then, in conclusion, I intend to outline very briefly the limitations of approaching Bernhard as an "Austrian writer" and offer some thoughts on the extent to which his works should be read as German-language literature of Europe or even the entire Western world.

Bernhard's works abound in contradictions and paradoxes, providing, like the Bible and other terribly ambiguous works, material and "proof" for opposing and contradictory interpretations and conclusions. Some critics, for instance, have stated that they can read him only in the context of Austria and "Austrian Literature." Jean Améry, after reading *Die Ursache,* claimed for example: "Ich kann dieses Werk *nur* (emphasis added) im Kontext 'Österreich' lesen, erfahren und als Erfahrenes wiedergeben, kann in ihm *nur* (emphasis added) das Pathogramm des 'morbus austriacus' sehen, dem Trakl, der engere Landsmann Thomas Bernhards, so gut, bzw. so schlimm erlag wie Kafka, wie Joseph Roth, wie Ernst Weiss und Otto Weininger . . ."[35] Others, however, have minimized, even denied, the importance of Austria, its landscapes, its cities and villages, its people, institutions, and traditions for Bernhard's works, insisting that these elements are superficial, serving essentially as accidental or coincidental chiffres for the universal condition of (at least Western) man. One can read in an article by Heinz Ehrig comparing Bernhard with Beckett, for instance, that regardless of the concrete Austrian details, in Bernhard it is always ". . . eine aussage über den zustand der *welt,* für den die österreichische 'umgebung' *nur* (emphasis added) ein zufälliger stellvertreter sein kann."[36] Yet, Bernhard's works simply cannot be categorized convincingly in such either/or fashion.

Of the two essays mentioned above, let us focus our attention initially on Walter Weiss' "Thematisierung der 'Ordnung' in der österreichischen Literatur" from 1975. The fact that his goals are in keeping with our description of the more circumspect, recent approaches to the question of "Austrian Literature" is obvious when he portrays his essay as an attempt ". . . konkrete *Teil*zusammenhänge (emphasis added), 'literarische Reihen' herauszuarbeiten, die spezifisch, aber auch über die Grenzen der 'österreichischen Literatur' hinaus anschlußfähig sein können."[37] It is clear then that Weiss makes no claim either to exclusivity for, or to a universal applicability of, the theme of "order" to all of "Austrian Literature."

Rather than offering an a priori definition of "order," Weiss discusses numerous works of literature in terms of their various approaches to "order," starting with contemporary works and proceeding backward chronologically. He divides these various approaches into four major categories: 1) the acceptance of or belief in "die zeitlos-lebendige Universalordnung." This includes faith in God's order as well as the order of the Habsburg Empire, which for many were very closely related; 2) the attempt to renew this

universal order once its validity and viability have been called into question; 3) a so-called "Zurückweichen und ästhetische Verklärung der Ordnung" which takes place as the decline or disintegration of this order becomes impossible to overlook; and 4) the "problematisierte Ordnung" or "Ordnung als Negativum."[38]

One does not need to contemplate these categories very long before several Austrian writers come to mind for each. Not surprisingly, Weiss discovers among contemporary Austrian writers the most radical statements and examples of his fourth and last category: the "problematisierte Ordnung" or "Ordnung als Negativum." He claims, for instance: "Nicht um elegische Beschwörung von Ordnungstraditionen und Ordnungsbildern gegenüber einer chaotischen Gegenwart, nicht um aktuelle Drohungen für die Ordnung geht es . . . , sondern um aktuelle Bedrohungen durch die Ordnung, durch die Mächte der Ordnung für die bzw. den Menschen."[39] Upon reflection this assertion certainly applies to works by Kolleritsch, G.F. Jonke, Rosei, Bachmann, Innerhofer, Handke, and many others. It is particularly true for the works of Bernhard. The number of Bernhard protagonists for whom the external order—society in general, its institutions, officials, rules, and expectations—is virtual anathema and from which they either withdraw in a futile effort to maintain even minimal control over their lives or are pushed away because they are non-conformists is considerable. Consider such figures as Strauch (*Frost*), Walter and his narrator brother (*Amras*), the Prince (*Verstörung*), Konrad (*Kalkwerk*), Minetti (*Minetti*), Koller (*Die Billigesser*), etc. For many, the remnants of the old (Habsburg, aristocratic) order are burdens which weigh heavily on their lives. One of Roithamer's primary intentions in building the elaborate "Kegel im Walde" (in *Korrektur*) is to use up his inheritance; i.e., to destroy all that remains of the old order.[40]

The characters in Bernhard's works—Konrad, Caribaldi (*Die Macht der Gewohnheit*), or Koller, for example—are, however, also frequently obsessed with creating and maintaining order in their daily routines, many of which tend to be rather idiosyncratic. These routines (or attempts at routines) quickly emerge as desperate efforts to keep the chaos of their lives and minds, and of life in general, at bay. Ironically, having withdrawn from the externally imposed order, they desperately try to establish their own. Yet their orderly routines are constantly disrupted by others, by distractions both real and imagined, and by their own inability to accept any real order in their chaotic lives: neither Konrad nor Koller can actually get his "study" written down, and Caribaldi's rehearsals of the "Forellenquintett" with the members of his circus troupe never get past the first few notes. The overwhelming artificiality of the order they try to bring to their lives and thoughts is frighteningly apparent. This is also the case with Roithamer, who single-mindedly tries to impose order onto his and his sister's lives by constructing his incredible "Kegel," even though, or paradoxically and precisely because, he knows it can only result in both the liquidation of the old order and in the ultimate realization of the chaos in life: death. All of these protagonists sense, if they do not actually perceive fully, that they are not confronting and falling victim to a universal order per se, as did the tragic heroes of the past, but rather to the omnipresent *lie* of an order which no longer exists, and perhaps never did exist. The central paradox of their lives—Konrad's, Caribaldi's, Koller's, Roithamer's—lies in the fact that they must invent an artificial order so that they might continue to exist, even though they are painfully aware of the artificiality of their attempts and know that their inventions will be ultimately futile.

The artificial and therefore false order, expressed most often in repetitive speech and actions, appears in Bernhard's works to be simultaneously necessary for survival then and the justifiable target of attack and destruction *because it is a lie.* In Schnitzler's novel *Der Weg ins Freie* one can read: "Wir versuchen wohl, Ordnung in uns zu schaffen, so gut es geht, aber diese Ordnung ist doch nur etwas Künstliches. Das Natürliche . . . ist das Chaos."[41] Any artificial order in Bernhard's works is Weiss' "Ordnung als Negativum" and must therefore be destroyed. And wherever signs of harmony or order do appear in Bernhard, they are destroyed. One frequently senses a moral impulse behind Bernhard's insistence on such destruction: "Es darf nichts Ganzes geben, man muß es zerhauen . . ."[42] He also exclaims at another point: "Harmonie ist immer und überall Irrtum,"[43] and at still another: "Die Vollkommenheit ist für nichts möglich . . ."[44] And finally in the interview "Drei Tage" he claims: "In meiner Arbeit, wenn sich irgendwo Anzeichen einer Geschichte bilden, oder wenn ich nur in der Ferne irgendwo hinter einem Prosahügel die Andeutung einer Geschichte auftauchen sehe, schieße ich sie ab. Es ist auch mit den Sätzen so, ich hätte fast die Lust, ganze Sätze, die sich *möglicherweise* bilden könnten, schon im vorhinein abzutöten. Andererseits . . ."[45]

Andererseits. And here is another paradox, for Bernhard's attitude toward order is not so unambiguously negative as it first appears. It is therefore necessary to view it not just as "Ordnung als Negativum" but as "problematisierte Ordnung" as well. On both a metaphysical and historical level one sometimes senses and even reads about a feeling of loss in Bernhard, if not of an actual universal order—God or the Habsburg Empire or both—then at least of the possibility to believe in such an order, whether it in fact ever existed or not.[46] Despair over the loss of faith in God has been noted in the commentaries on Bernhard's early poetry,[47] and a sense of loss arising from the necessity of denying a worldly order—such as that represented by the Habsburg Empire—has also been commented upon in the secondary literature.[48] But in spite of the loss there is no attempt on Bernhard's part either to renew it (Weiss' category 2) or to aestheticize it in a transfigured form (Weiss' category 3). Bernhard understands clearly and asserts boldly: "Wir finden nicht mehr zurück / nicht mehr."[49]

There is at least one more possibility for viewing the attempts of Bernhard's protagonists to establish order in their lives, even though it is an artificial order, as something positive. Especially in Bernhard's more recent prose works, *Das Kalkwerk, Korrektur, Ja,* and *Die Billigesser,* the main characters spend less time talking incessantly about the utter chaos which surrounds them (as do Strauch in *Frost* and the Prince in *Verstörung*) and actually try to establish some kind of order in their lives while simultaneously trying to expose and destroy the artificial order of society at large. They distinguish themselves in their attempts from the majority of people whom Bernhard consistently criticizes for their dullness and unconscious acceptance of society's and life's artificiality and lies without recognizing them as such—"Die Gute" in **Ein Fest für Boris,** the general's wife in **Die Jagdgesellschaft,** or the musicians and artists in **Die Berühmten**—in that they are aware of the lie and artificial nature of their efforts and harbor no illusions about the fact that these efforts are doomed to failure.[50] As outsiders who have withdrawn from the ordinary artificial routines of life, most of Bernhard's protagonists achieve a certain moral stature in their isolation, their (albeit confused and confusing) intellectual reflection, and in their idiosyncratic refusal to participate in the ordinary lies of society at large. The more recent protagonists in Bernhard's prose works—Konrad, Roithamer, Koller—achieve additional moral stature in their willingness to fail.

From our discussion of the role and problematics of "order" in Bernhard's works at least one way in which Bernhard's works reflect a major emphasis of "Austrian Literature," as Weiss has convincingly argued it, is evident. Weiss' elucidation of this emphasis, or "literarische Reihe," clearly serves a useful purpose by underlining some of the affinities and common concerns among Austrian, particularly contemporary Austrian, writers. And although the theme of order is hardly unique to "Austrian Literature," one can recognize in these writers' approaches to the theme certain features which are peculiarly Austrian: the frequent use of castles and large estates as symbols of a past order which is now lifeless; the hints and direct allusions to the Habsburg Empire as that which represents a worldly, even spiritual order which is lost forever; or the frequent portrayal of theater, role-playing, and clichéd language as the most pervasive, artificial means of creating the illusion of order. Yet Weiss makes no claims that only Austrian writers are concerned with the theme of order. Certainly Thomas Mann, Bertolt Brecht, Friedrich Dürrenmatt, Franz Xaver Kroetz and many other non-Austrian writers are equally concerned in their diverse ways with order and chaos, with the destruction of the traditional visions of order and with the possibilities of creating new ones.

The second and final inquiry into one central theme or motif in modern "Austrian Literature" to consider here in our discussion of Bernhard is an article by Karin Kathrein that appeared in the Viennese newspaper *Die Presse* in April 1975: "Die Umwelt als Mordschauplatz. Von den Dichtern gezeichnet und von den Mitbürgern nicht wiedererkannt: das Menschenbild der 2. Republik."[51] Kathrein is even less interested in proposing a theoretical framework for reading the literary works of Austria than was Weiss. She is also more exclusively concerned with contemporary literature, even though she does mention briefly some possibilities for relating the contemporary writers whom she discusses—Handke, Turrini, Frischmuth, Bachmann, Innerhofer, Bauer, and Bernhard—to several early twentieth century writers. Her analysis is based clearly on extensive reading of these and other contemporary Austrian writers, during which she was struck by the similarities which led to the observations presented here. She claims, for instance: "Überblickt man nun die dichterischen Spiegelungen des Menschen der Zweiten Republik, so sind die Gemeinsamkeiten bestürzend massiert."

The basic elements which Kathrein observes in the literary portrayals of the Second Republic and its society, whether in its rural or urban forms, are described as follows: "Da haben sich Bilder eingefressen von Brutalität und Gemeinheit, von Vulgarität und Verrohung, einem 'Sauschlachten' der Individualität, von Terror, Verstörung, Wahnsinn." These words, as anyone who reads Bernhard will immediately recognize, are the backbone of his vocabulary in describing the society in which his characters exist. When Kathrein recalls Hofmannsthal's "Komödie unserer Seele," she notes that the "böse Dinge" remain, but the "hübsche Formel" is nowhere in sight. The mask which at least superficially covered and distracted from the terror which lay beneath has been torn away. This literature ". . . ist alles Aufschrei, Demaskierung, schonungslose Entlarvung. Provokant, rücksichtslos, roh. Da wird eine ungeheuerliche Welt so gezeigt, wie sie ist. Hinter den kunstvoll errichteten Fassaden. Wenn sich ein Mensch mit Erlaubnis des Dichters noch verstecken darf, so hinter der Brutalität und dem Wahnsinn." Clearly the *Maskenball* is over, there are no more *schöne Leichen,* and the abyss over which literary characters of the turn-of-the-century still danced has been unambiguously exposed.

The typical picture of Austria with its quaint mountain villages, its robust farmers, its culture, and high life style, this is not. It corresponds neither to the image of Austria held by tourists and marketed by the tourist industry not to that held by most Austrians, as the subtitle of Kathrein's article suggests. Yet that seems to be precisely the reason for the aggressiveness and explicitness of these literary portrayals: they all seem intent on destroying the myths and exposing the artificiality and lies through which the unrealistic, fairytale-like image of Austria is maintained. "In ihrer Bedingsungslosigkeit entlarven sie Oberflächlichkeit, Heuchelei, Gefühlsträgheit einer Gesellschaft, die Illusionen verkauft und die wahren Werte durch ein Kostüm, zugeschnitten auf ein sinnentleertes Spiel, getauscht hat." They obviously want their readers to see a different reality than the one which they ordinarily buy and sell. We need only to consider some of the most significant Austrian literary works in recent years—Handke's *Wunschloses Unglück,* Turrini's *Kindsmord,* Bachmann's *Malina,* Frischmuth's *Haschen nach Wind,* Innerhofer's ironically titled *Schöne Tage,* Bauer's *Change,* or virtually any of Bernhard's works, as Kathrein has done, and add others

which quickly come to mind: Jonke's *Geometrischer Heimatroman,* Wolfgruber's *Herrenjahre,* or Jelinek's *Die Liebhaberinnen,* to see just how frequently this portrait of a brutalized Austria has been painted.

Although Bernhard is therefore not unique in the fact that he paints such pictures, he is certainly the most consistent painter of such anti-idyllic portrayals of Austria. If the secondary literature on Bernhard agrees on any one point, it is that his works, plays and prose alike, concern themselves for whatever reasons with this dark side of life. His characters manipulate and abuse others ("Die Gute" in **Ein Fest für Boris** or Rudolf in **Vor dem Ruhestand**); they live isolated and lonely lives (Strauch in *Frost* or the Prince in *Verstörung*); they border on and frequently succumb to insanity (Karrer in *Gehen* or Konrad in *Das Kalkwerk*); they are sick, crippled, or deformed (Boris in **Ein Fest für Boris** or Koller in *Die Billigesser*); and they often kill themselves (Roithamer in *Korrektur* and virtually everyone in *Amras*). Everywhere one looks in Bernhard's works one is confronted with incurable disease, crime and brutality, physical and psychological abuse, insanity and decadence, despair and death.

The focus on these negative, horrifying, and often unspoken aspects of life (and death) is noticeably prevalent in the works of contemporary Austrian writers, as Kathrein observes, and, although one can find works of literature in the other German-speaking countries which share a similar focus—Sperr's *Jagdszenen aus Niederbayern,* Kroetz's *Stallerhof,* Walser's *Überlebensgroß Herr Krott,* E.Y. Meyers *In Trubschachen,* or Frisch's *Triptychon,* for example—certainly the fact that this is such a predominant focus is unique to contemporary "Austrian Literature."

In numerous analyses and commentaries on Bernhard and his many works he has frequently been compared with, and claims have been made about his affinities with, a vast array of Austrian writers and thinkers. Without going into any detail here and without discussing the merits of each citation, let us merely indicate those most frequently mentioned: Raimund and Nestroy, Grillparzer and Stifter, Trakl and Hofmannsthal, Kafka and Canetti, Celan and Handke, Bachmann and Fritsch.[52] He is also frequently mentioned, as was pointed out above, in the context of the "Austrian" school of "Sprachskepsis und -kritik": Nestroy, Hofmannsthal, Kraus, Mauthner, Wittgenstein, Horváth, and Handke.[53] And still other studies have portrayed Bernhard's indebtedness and relationship to a wide variety of literary traditions claimed to be "Austrian."[54] Often mentioned in the secondary literature are also the various remarks Bernhard has made about his Austrian roots, familial and intellectual, and his strong but ambivalent ties to Austria in "Politische Morgenandacht," the interview "Drei Tage," the several acceptance speeches for literary prizes, letters and essays in newspapers, and in his five autobiographical volumes.[55]

It is clearly illustrated then, by the two essays of Weiss and Kathrein, that Bernhard not only shares much in common with other Austrian writers but that he is even assigned, implicitly or explicitly, the status of a representative contemporary Austrian writer. Other approaches we could have taken to his works would have underlined other aspects of the *Austrianness* of his works. Yet, as the numerous and increasing number of translations of his works into English, French, Italian, and other languages, as well as the extensive reception of his work throughout the Western world demonstrate, neither Bernhard nor his works are the least bit provincial in their *Austrianness*. Any attempt to brand him an exclusively "Austrian" writer of exclusively "Austrian Literature" fails to account for the breadth and universal applicability of his literary concerns and themes, the wealth of his literary and intellectual relationships and affinities, and the acknowledged significance of his works for the non-Austrian audience.

IV: CONCLUSION

In the second section of this essay I pointed out several of the most serious difficulties and weaknesses of many traditional attempts to answer the question—"Gibt es eine österreichische Literatur?"—and to define and describe that literature in a way which would distinguish it clearly from "German Literature." In the last section, however, we have seen through our discussion of the two essays by Weiss and Kathrein how less ambitious approaches to the question of "Austrian Literature," approaches which are satisfied with indicating single thematic affinities among numerous Austrian writers, can be exceedingly helpful in showing us some of the common concerns which link those writers and their works to each other and to Austria while allowing that they have other concerns and affinities which link them to non-Austrian writers and their works or make them unique in their own right. Using those two essays as the context for a discussion of Bernhard's works, I then tried to demonstrate how those works can and must be read, and not only on a superficial level as some critics have claimed, as "Austrian Literature," regardless of how one chooses to describe it. Yet, as was suggested above, Bernhard is not provincial Austrian, nor are his works, and there are definite limits to the usefulness of interpreting him as an Austrian writer.

The literary and intellectual traditions with which Bernhard connects and which he extends are not only Austrian. His sense of indebtedness to such writers and thinkers as Pascal, Montaigne, or Novalis is evident not only from the mottos introducing many of his works, but also from his own statements in interviews and from the content of the works as well. Particularly apparent in many of his works is the heritage of Romanticism: the musicality of the prose, the almost endless variations on a theme, the fragmentary quality of the texts, the insoluble paradoxes, the fascination with sickness and death, and the search for light in darkness. The influence of Kierkegaard, Kleist, and Novalis are all present here. And we should remind ourselves that Romanticism has often been described as a singularly un-Austrian literary movement.[56] Much, of course, has been written about the impact of Wittgenstein's philosophy on Bernhard but, as recent studies have convincingly argued, the influence of both Schopenhauer and Heidegger in Bernhard's works is equally strong.[57] It was asserted earlier that many of Bernhard's protagonists are modern descendants of Jakob in Grillparzer's *Der arme Spielmann*; an equally valid claim can be made that these same protagonists are the direct descendants of Büchner's Lenz. There can also be little doubt that Bernhard is indebted to both the literature and philosophy of existentialism (here one senses again the imprint of Kierkegaard, Novalis, Kleist, and Heidegger) and the theater of the absurd. In fact, although his works must be read on other levels as well, Bernhard can legitimately be regarded as one of the most important writers of existentialistic and absurdist literature in the German language. In this regard the comparisons which have been drawn between Bernhard and Beckett have been very informative for the differences and similarities which they illuminate.[58] Yet additional comparisons between Bernhard and writers such as Ionesco, Artaud, Sartre, Pinter, and Bond would undoubtedly add helpful perspective and perceptions to our understanding of Bernhard as a European writer.

To the extent that it makes sense to speak of "East German Literature" as being distinguishable in any meaningful way from "West German Literature"—and the vast secondary literature on the distinctions shows clearly that numerous critics think it makes very good sense—it also makes sense to speak of "Austrian Literature," at least in the contemporary setting, as distinguishable in some meaningful ways from the other three German-language literatures. In all cases, however, one must recognize that such designations underline the differences, but say nothing about the substantial similarities among these various German-language literatures. These literatures, regardless of their country of origin, share much in the way of literary, cultural, and intellectual heritage which cannot help but inform the works of writers in all of those countries, and the mutual influences from the literary works of one German-language country to another and back again on several levels cannot help but be more extensive and more profound than those which emanate from further abroad.

Like Kafka, with whom he has often been compared, Bernhard is a difficult and complex writer whose contradictory and paradoxical works lend themselves to and even require being approached from a number of levels and angles. His works are ambiguous in the best and richest sense of the word. No one approach can lay claim to exclusive validity or truth. Not only to the extent that his works grow out of the Austrian context but also to the extent that they reflect concerns and criticism of Austria and Austrians can and should we view Bernhard as an author of "Austrian Literature." But to the extent that his concerns and criticisms, themes and metaphors speak to Europeans and Americans from many different countries we should be able to look past that regional designation, valid and useful on several accounts to be sure, and regard Thomas Bernhard as a German-language writer from Austria who writes books that are significant contributions to Western Literature.

Notes

1. Some confusion did exist in the earliest commentaries on Bernhard about the circumstances of his birth, which took place in Heerlen, Holland. His unmarried mother, the daughter of the writer Johannes Freumbichler, had fled to Holland to give birth to her illegitimate child in a cloister there. She returned with her son Thomas to Austria ca. one year later. Cf. Thomas Gamper, *Thomas Bernhard* (München: dtv., 1977), 215–218.

2. Tape DST 90 (1977), *Dokumentationsstelle für neuere österreichische Literatur,* Vienna.

3. Wendelin Schmidt-Dengler, "Thomas Bernhard," in *Deutsche Literatur der Gegenwart,* ed. Dietrich Weber (Stuttgart: Kröner, 1977), 70.

4. Eckehard Henscheid, "Der Krypto-Komiker," in *pardon,* 7 (1973), 23.

5. Thomas Bernhard, *Der Keller* (Salzburg: Residenz, 1976), 156.

6. Matthias Schreiber, "Die Heimat der Phantasie," in *Kölner Stadtanzeiger,* 3. September 1977.

7. Egon Schwarz, "Das Gemeinsame," in *Wort in der Zeit,* 5 (1965), 2.

8. See Roger Bauer, "Österreichischë Literatur: Der Bedeutungswandel eines Begriffes," in *Literatur aus Österreich-Österreichische Literatur. Ein Bonner Symposion,* ed. K. Polheim (Bonn: Bouvier, 1981), 23ff. for discussion of the earliest comments on the question of the uniqueness of Austrian Literature.

9. Karl Werner, "Kultureller Separatismus. 'Eine österreichische Literatur?'" in *Deutsche National-Zeitung,* 28. January 1977.

10. Eugen Thurnher, "Der österreichische Staatsgedanke und die österreichische Dichtung," in *Sprachkunst* VI, 2 (1975), 169.

11. See, for example, Josef Nadler, *Literaturgeschichte der deutschen Stämme und Landschaften,* 3 Vols. (Regensburg: 1912–18) and its later revisions.

12. Although Hofmannsthal expressed himself on several occasions about this issue, the two essays to which I refer here are "Österreich im Spiegel seiner Dichtung" (1917) and "Österreichische Geistesform und österreichische Dichtung" (1931). A further pro-Austrian Literature essay, of course, is his "Die österreichische Idee" (1917).

13. Helmut Olles, "Gibt es eine österreichische Literatur?" in *Wort und Wahrheit,* 12 (1957), 115–34; Joseph Strelka, "Von Wesen und Eigenart der österreichischen Literatur," in J.S. *Brücke zu vielen Ufern* (Vienna: Europa Verlag, 1966), 9–16; Herbert Seidler, "Die österreichische Literatur als Problem der Forschung," in *Österreich in Geschichte und Literatur,* 14 (1970), 354–68; Robert Mühlher, "Das 'Historische' als Baustein der österreichischen Moderne," in *Geschichte in der österreichischen Literatur,* ed. Inst. für Österreichkunde (Vienna: Hirt, 1970), 93–109; Viktor Suchy, "Kontinuität und Traditionsbruch in der österreichischen Dichtung der Gegenwart," in *Dauer im Wandel,* ed. W. Strolz (Vienna: Herder, 1975), 45–61; Otto Basil, et al., *Das große Erbe* (Graz, Vienna: Stiasny, 1962); *Wort in der Zeit,* 1 and 5 (1965).

14. See, for example: Antal Mádl, "Entwicklung der österreichischen Literatur," in *helikon.* Sondernummer, ed. Ilona T. Erdély (1979), 17–42; W. Schmidt-Dengler, "Europäische Nationalliteraturen I: Österreich-'Pathos der Immobilität,'" in *Frankfurter Hefte* 34, 10 (Oktober 1979), 54–62; Roger Bauer, "Österreichische Literatur . . ." (see note 8 above); Dagmar Lorenz, "Ein Definitionsproblem: Österreichische Literatur," in *Modern Austrian Lit.,* 12, 2 (1979), 1–22.

15. See Basil et al., *Das große Erbe*; Eugen Thurnher, "Der österreichische Staatsgedanke . . ."

16. Thurnher, p. 176.

17. *Tintenfisch,* 16 (1979), 8.

18. Claudio Magris, *Der habsburgische Mythos in der österreichischen Literatur* (Salzburg: Otto Müller Verlag, 1966).

19. Ulrich Greiner, *Der Tod des Nachsommers* (München: Hanser, 1979).

20. Cf. Greiner, p. 51.

21. In addition to the work by Mádl cited above in note 14, see A. Mádl, *Politische Dichtung in Österreich 1830–1848* (Budapest: 1969); Walter Weiss, "Österreichisches in der österreichischen Literatur seit 1945," in *Literatur aus Österreich- Österreichische Literatur. Ein Bonner Symposion,* pp. 73–92; Leslie Bodi, *Tauwetter in Wien. Zur Prosa der österreichischen Aufklärung 1781–1795* (Frankfurt: 1977); Horst Jarka, ed. *Jura Soyfer. Das Gesamtwerk.* (Vienna: Europa Verlag, 1980), etc.

22. Symposia on this topic have been held for example in Bonn (1980), at Monash University in Australia (1980), at Amherst (1978), and a special session on the topic was included in the VI. Internationaler Germanisten-Kongress in Basel (1980).

23. These sessions, in which twelve papers were presented, took place at the annual MLA Meeting in San Francisco, December 1979.

24. Cf. Schmidt-Dengler, "Europäische Nationalliteraturen . . ."

25. Exceptions are Greiner's book and an essay by Claudio Magris, "Der unauffindbare Sinn," (Klagenfurt: Carinthia, 1978), in which he broadens his view of Austrian Literature but still makes too many claims to exclusivity.

26. In addition to the works already cited by Mádl, Bauer, Weiss, and Schmidt-Dengler, worth men-

tioning here are Karin Kathrein, "Die Umwelt als Mordschauplatz," *Die Presse,* 26/27, April 1975, and Alan Best, "The Austrian Tradition. Continuity and Change," in Best and Wolfschütz, eds., *Modern Austrian Writing* (London: Oswald Wolff, 1980), 23–43.

27. Walter Weiss, "Ein Essay," in *Zwischenbilanz,* Weiss and Schmid, eds. (Salzburg: Residenz, 1976), 11.

28. Schmidt-Dengler, "Europäische Nationalliteraturen . . .," p. 61.

29. Hilde Spiel, ed., *Die zeitgenössische Literatur Österreichs* (Zürich, München: Kindler, 1976); Dieter Lattmann, ed., *Die Literatur der Bundesrepublik Deutschland* (Zürich, München: Kindler, 1973).

30. Cf. Gerald A. Fetz, "Thomas Bernhard und die österreichische Tradition," in *Österreichische Gegenwart. Die moderne Literatur und ihr Verhältnis zur Tradition,* ed. W. Paulsen (Bern, München: Francke, 1980), 200ff.

31. An excellent recent example in which the advantages of such an approach is made clear is *Die Sozialgeschichte der deutschen Literatur von 1918 bis zur Gegenwart,* ed. Jan Berg et al. (Frankfurt a.M.: Fischer, 1981).

32. Schmidt-Dengler, "Europäische Nationalliteraturen..," p. 62.

33. For such a discussion see my essay, "Thomas Bernhard und die österreichische Tradition."

34. Walter Weiss, "Thematisierung der 'Ordnung' in der österreichischen Literatur," *Dauer im Wandel,* W. Strolz, ed. (Vienna: Herder, 1975), 19–44; Karin Kathrein, "Die Umwelt als Mordschauplatz." (See note 26).

35. Jean Améry, "Morbus Austriacus." Bemerkungen zu Thomas Bernhards 'Die Ursache' und 'Korrektur,'" in *Merkur,* 1 (30. Januar 1976), 92.

36. Heinz Ehrig, "Probleme des Absurden. Vergleichende Bemerkungen zu Thomas Bernhard und Samuel Beckett," in *Wirkendes Wort,* 29, 1 (1979), 47.

37. Weiss, "Ordnung," p. 19.

38. Ibid., p. 28ff.

39. Ibid., p. 25.

40. Cf. Fetz, p. 191.

41. Schnitzler, *Der Weg ins Freie* (Berlin: S. Fischer, 1928), 453.

42. Bernhard, "Drei Tage," in *Der Italiener* (München: dtv, 1973), 87.

43. Bernhard, in Andreas Müller, "Harmonie ist Irrtum," *Abendzeitung* (München), 25. November 1978.

44. Bernhard, *Der Atem* (Salzburg: Residenz, 1978), 87.

45. Bernhard, "Drei Tage," pp. 83–4.

46. Cf. Fetz, p. 203; Weiss, "Ordnung," p. 27: "Eine vorangegangene, positive Ordnung der Dinge taucht auf als meist verborgener Maßstab für Bernhard's Gegenwartskritik."

47. Cf. Heinz Beckmann, "Die Welt des Thomas Bernhard," in *Zeitwende,* 44 (1973), 271ff.; Alfred Barthofer, "Berge schwarzer Qual," *Acta Germanica,* 9 (1976), 187ff.

48. Cf. Fetz, p. 203.

49. Bernhard, "Der Berg," in *Literatur und Kritik,* 46 (1970), 340.

50. Cf. Erika Tunner, "Scheitern mit Vorbedacht," in *Bernhard: Annäherungen,* ed. Manfred Jurgensen (Bern, München: Francke, 1981), 231–242, and Jürgen H. Petersen, "Beschreibung einer sinnentleerten Welt," in *Bernhard: Annäherungen,* pp. 143–176.

51. Kathrein, see note 26.

52. See, for example, Schmidt-Dengler, "Thomas Bernhard," (note 3), p. 59ff. and Fetz, p. 194ff.

53. For an extended discussion of this aspect of Bernhard's works see Albrecht Weber, "Wittgenstein's Gestalt und Theorie und ihre Wirkung im Werk Thomas Bernhards," in *Österreich in Gesch, u. Lit.,* 25, 2 (1981), 86ff.

54. Cf. Fetz; Josef Donnenberg, "Thomas Bernhard und Österreich," in *Österreich in Gesch, u. Lit.,* 14 (1970), 237–51.

55. Bernhard: "Politische Morgenandacht," in *Wort in der Zeit,* 1 (1966), 11–13; "In Österreich hat sich nichts geändert," in *Theater heute,* Sonderheft (1969), 144; "Büchner Preisrede," in *Büchner-Preis-Reden* (Stuttgart: Reclam, 1972), 215–16; "Der Wahrheit und dem Tod auf der Spur. Zwei Reden," (for Wildgans Pr8ze and Austrian State Prize), in *Neues Forum,* XV, 173 (Mai 1968), 347–349; and the autobiographical works, *Die Ursache* (1975), *Der Keller* (1976), *Der Atem* (1978), *Die Kälte* (1981), and *Ein Kind* (1982), all in Salzburg: Residenz Verlag.

56. Cf. Eugen Thurnher, p. 176.

57. See, for instance, David Roberts, "Korrektur der Korrektur? Zu Thomas Bernhards Lebenskunstwerk 'Korrektur,'" in *Bernhard: Annäherungen* (see note 50).

58. See, for instance, Heinz Ehrig, "Probleme des Absurden . . .," (see note 36).

Martin Esslin (essay date 1985)

SOURCE: "Beckett and Bernhard: A Comparison," in *Modern Austrian Literature,* Vol. 18, No. 2, 1985, pp. 67–78.

[In the following essay, Esslin presents several parallels between the lives and works of Samuel Beckett and Thomas Bernhard.]

It occasionally happens that I am asked to name some of the more important continental playwrights. And occasionally, if I mention among them the name of Thomas Bernhard and am asked what kind of writer he is, I am tempted to sum it all up by saying: "A kind of Austrian Beckett." Like all such attempts at a snap judgment, this is, of course, highly superficial. But there is also a grain of truth in it. That is why it may be worthwhile to go into the matter at a little greater depth and attempt something like a comparison.

Certainly the parallel has been noticed more than once. In 1972 the German magazine *Der Spiegel* summed it up in a telling, if somewhat cheap jibe, by calling Bernhard—varying a famous Austrian play's title—an "Alpenbeckett und Menschenfeind."

Bernhard is twenty-five years younger than Beckett, but like Beckett he has written an impressive volume of poetry, narrative prose, and drama. Like Beckett he first emerged as a poet, then as a prose writer and only relatively late in his career as a playwright, and like Beckett he is better known, at least outside the German-speaking world as a dramatist than as a prose-writer (although, like Beckett, he takes his prose works more seriously than his drama in spite of having since 1970 had thirteen major plays produced, almost one a year).

But these are superficial parallels. There are some much more significant ones. First, however, I want to stress that I am not concerned with the question of direct influence. Whether such a direct influence by Beckett on Bernhard exists or not is a moot point, but one that is not only impossible to verify as Bernhard's oeuvre is wholly personal in form and content, so that any direct influence would have to have been exerted at second remove, but also I think not a very important one. There certainly cannot be any question of conscious imitation, not even in Bernhard's earliest phase. In fact, according to the few people who have seen it, an early work by Bernhard, **Mrs. Nightflowers Monolog,** which has remained unpublished, shows some striking similarities with Beckett's play *Happy Days.* But the manuscript by Bernhard dates from 1958[1] (when he was twenty-six), while *Happy Days* was not performed or published till 1961—a clear indication here that the similarities were due to deeper affinities of temperament and attitude rather than direct imitation or influence.

Bernhard's world, like much of Beckett's, whether in his poetry, prose or drama, is an essentially *monologic* universe, a universe of characters caught up in the prison house of their own consciousness, compulsive solipsistic talkers, experiencing their own selves, or rather, the hopeless quest for their true identities, as an endless stream of language erupting from their brains in the form of stories,

stories made up of voices. In Beckett's narrative prose usually one voice follows another, as the narrator, in quest of his own self assumes one fictional persona after another. Bernhard's technique is different: his usually unnamed narrator carries a whole plethora of voices with him, voices he quotes as the highly unreliable and contradictory sources of his story. Take the opening passage of his second major novel *Das Kalkwerk* (1971). The book starts in midnarration, even midsentence, with three dots followed by a clause in lower case:

> . . . wie Konrad vor fünfeinhalb Jahren das Kalkwerk gekauft hat, sei das erste die Anschaffung eines Klaviers gewesen, das er in seinem im ersten Stock liegenden Zimmer habe aufstellen lassen, heißt es im Laska, nicht aus Vorliebe für die Kunst, so Wieser, der Verwalter der mußnerschen Liegenschaft, sondern zur Beruhigung seiner durch jahrzehntelange Geistesarbeit überanstrengten Nerven, so Fro, der Verwalter der trattnerschen Liegenschaft, mit Kunst, die er Konrad hasse, habe sein Klavierspiel nicht das Geringste zu tun gehabt, er improvisierte, so Fro, und habe, so Wieser, an jedem Tag eine sehr frühe und eine sehr späte Stunde bei geöffneten Fenstern und bei eingeschaltetem Metronom auf dem Instrument dilettiert . . .[2]

Over 270 pages the story is thus built up out of the reported speech of various sources, both actual people and the consensus of public opinion in a number of bars and cafes—"heißt es im Laska"—with the effect that this novel, and many of Bernhard's other stories and novels, becomes a veritable Babel of voices, uttering unverifiable and contradictory versions of the same event and the opinions of various people. The manic, compulsive power of this type of logorrheic utterance has a hypnotic effect, analogous to that of the long and equally logorrheic monologues of Beckett's trilogy or his *Texts for Nothing.*

Beckett has, more than once, dealt with this compulsion to talk. In Beckett's radio play *Embers* (and his radio plays are in many ways the most revealing, as radio itself is a direct concretization of such voices) the leading character, Henry, hears a continuous roar, rather like the noise of the tide flowing over shingle, in his head. To drown this out he must keep talking incessantly. As his wife tells him:

> You should see a doctor about your talking, it's worse, what must it be like for Addie [their daughter]? Do you know what she said to me once, when she was quite small, she said Mummy why does Daddy keep on talking all the time? She heard you in the lavatory. I didn't know what to answer.

To which Henry replies: "I told you to tell her I was praying. Roaring prayers at God and his saints." Ada continues: "It's very bad for the child. It's silly to say it keeps you from hearing it and even if it does you shouldn't be hearing it, there must be something wrong with your brain."[3]

In another of his important radio plays, *Cascando,* Beckett represents the human consciousness as divided into two voices, an "opener" who is in partial control and opens a

stream of continuous sound, consisting equally of a logorrhea of words and a strand of music. The "opener" says:

> What do I open? They say he opens nothing, he has
> nothing to open, it's in his head. . . . They say that is
> not his life, he does not live on that. They don't see
> me, they don't see what my life is, they don't see what
> I live on, and they say, That is not his life, he does not
> live on that. (Pause) I have lived on it . . . pretty long.
> Long enough.[4]

And in one of his early poems Beckett speaks of "the sky
/ of my skull shell of sky and earth."[5]

Similarly, one of Bernhard's manic talkers, the Prince Saurau in his novel *Verstörung* says: "Wie du weißt, sage ich
immer zu mir, ist immer alles und alles immer in deinem
Kopf. Alles ist immer in den Köpfen. Nur in allen Köpfen.
Außerhalb der Köpfe ist nichts."[6] It would be tedious to
quote many more of the passages that show that Bernhard,
like Beckett, considers every individual's world to be
confined to the inside of his skull, to exist solely within
his brain.

If the world can never be more accurately perceived than
as the projection of a single individual's consciousness,
there can obviously be no certainty, no solid framework to
our understanding of the world. Nevertheless in Bernhard's
stories the principal character is frequently a scientist who
is trying to unravel some of the secrets of the real world,
nature. In a number of his stories, moreover, we find a pair
of brothers, or a brother and a sister in the center, usually
living in a lonely farmhouse, castle or tower, one of whom
is an artist, often a musician or musicologist, while the
other is concerned with the real world, nature or business.
(This is quite analogous to the pairs of interdependent
characters in Beckett, Hamm and Clov, Pozzo and Lucky,
Vladimir and Estragon, who represent Beckett's conviction
that one of the basic dilemmas of human existence is that
expressed by the Latin adage "nec tecum nec sine te," that
is, the fact that a human being cannot live alone but is
also being driven mad by living with someone else. In
Bernhard's work the endeavor by the more creative partner
of these tragically interdependent pairs might presuppose
the existence of a solid outside reality. In fact it again and
again turns out to be no more than a conscious stratagem
by which the character concerned is trying to invent a
reason to go on living, a task to be fulfilled, while at the
same time he knows full well that all such projects are
bound to be illusory, illusions we merely create to infuse
some sense into a senseless universe. Konrad, the scientist
and protagonist of *Das Kalkwerk* (who murders his partner,
a crippled wife) is, for example, reported as saying:

> Jede Erklärung führe zu einem vollkommen falschen
> Ergebnis, daran kranke alles, daß alles erklärt werde
> und in jedem Fall immer falsch erklärt werde und die
> Ergebnisse aller Erklärungen immer falsche Ergebnisse
> seien.[7]

Adding later that

Andererseits, soll Konrad . . . gesagt haben, wäre alles
ganz sinn- und zwecklos, man denke etwas und das sei
zwecklos, man tue etwas und das sei zwecklos, man
unterlasse etwas, und das sei immer zwecklos, sinnlos
sei was man denke, wie zwecklos sei, worin man
handle.[8]

(Compare this with the first words of *Waiting for Godot*:
"Nothing to be done"!)

This solipsistic view of the universe, which Bernhard
shares with Beckett, logically leads to the conclusion that
the fact of death which will extinguish the world within
the skull guarantees the ultimate futility of all human
endeavors. As the narrator of the story *Amras* puts it:

> das Bewußtsein, daß du nichts bist als Fragmente, daß
> kurze und längere und längste Zeiten nichts als Frag-
> mente sind . . . daß die Dauer von Städten und
> Ländern nichts als Fragmente sind . . . und die Erde
> Fragment . . . daß die *ganze Entwicklung* Fragment ist
> . . . daß die Vollkommenheit nicht ist . . . daß die
> Fragmente entstanden sind und entstehen . . . kein
> Weg, nur Ankünfte . . . daß das Ende ohne Bewußtsein
> ist . . . und daß nichts ohne dich und daß folglich
> nichts ist. . . .[9]

What, then, of the artist and his endeavor? Beckett has
answered that question in a famous passage in the first of
his three dialogues on modern painters in which he
describes the situation of the modern artist as having to
face "The expression that there is nothing to express, nothing with which to express, no power to express, no desire
to express, together with the obligation to express."[10] The
"obligation to express"—here we approach the root of the
compulsion to talk in a meaningless universe, even if the
impossibility of success in expressing anything is only too
apparent. In the third of his *Three Dialogues*, the one
devoted to his friend Bram van Velde, Beckett speaks of
the need for an artist to admit

> that to be an artist is to fail, as no other dare fail, that
> failure is his world and to shrink from it desertion, art
> and craft, good housekeeping, living . . . all that is
> required now . . . is to make of this submission, this
> admission, this fidelity to failure, a new occasion, a
> new term of relation, and of the act, which unable to
> act, obliged to act, he makes, an expressive act, even if
> only of itself, of its impossibility, of its obligation.[11]

In exactly the same way Bernhard's musicologist who
lives in a hate-love symbiosis with a highly practical sister
and is vainly attempting to write an essay on the composer
Felix Mendelssohn Bartholdy in the novel *Beton* says of it,
"daß sie meine gelungenste, oder besser noch, die am
wenigsten mißlungene [Arbeit] ist."[12] Thus Bernhard and
Beckett share the same paradox at the basis of one of the
main themes of their work, the dilemma of the artist in a
society without an accepted and acceptable philosophy, a
solid structure of its universe. Both Beckett's and
Bernhard's protagonists tend to be artists, philosophers,
scientists engaged in such futile and paradoxical pursuits.

Their narrative prose is essentially monologic as the pairs of characters also obviously tend to represent parts of the same personality, in other words, voices buzzing within the same head. Both Beckett's and Bernhard's worlds could be described as essentially schizoid universes and as such illustrate the attempts by psychologists like Deleuze and Guettari to replace Freudian psychoanalysis by an antio-edipal psychology, and to create a schizo-analysis instead, which would, by basing itself on the concept of alienation, combine Marx and Freud. Many of the features of Bernhard's and Beckett's oeuvre fit the diagnosis of a schizoid state of mind to perfection: the voices in the head; the logorrhea; the withdrawal from the world, in remote castles and towers; the compulsive need to enumerate and to permutate, the preoccupation with counting and abstruse mathematical speculation; to name but the most obvious.

Which, of course, is not to say that Beckett or Bernhard are schizophrenics, merely that they tend to look at the world from the vantage point of an extreme state of consciousness that approximates schizoid mentality, which is precisely what enables them to arrive at insights that may be inaccessible to people enmeshed in the routine perceptions of everyday life. In that sense, all artists who experience life more intensely are exploring extreme states of consciousness and awareness beyond the normal.

So much for a broad comparison of the two writers' subject matter; perhaps, we might briefly turn to look at some of the formal aspects of their art, always remembering that, of course, form is content and content form, in this case more than in most others. For the alienation of the characters in the work of both Beckett and Bernhard is closely reflected in their use of language. It is in both their cases based on an intensive *Sprachskepsis,* a scepticism about language as an adequate instrument of expression for concepts or the existential reality of the individual. As the mad prince is quoted as saying in Bernhard's *Ver-störung*: "Die Wörter, mit welchen wir sprechen, exis-tieren eigentlich garnicht mehr, sagte der Saurau. Das ganze Wortinstrumentarium, das wir gebrauchen, existiert garnicht mehr. Aber es ist auch nicht möglich, ganz zu verstummen."[13] Beckett's attitude to language becomes particularly clear from an early letter of his which has only recently been published in the collection of Beckett's rare theoretical pronouncement *Disjecta*. This letter dated July 1937, when Beckett was thirty-one, was incidentally written in German and shows how brilliantly Beckett

> Es wird mir tatsächlich immer schwieriger, ja sinnloser, ein offizielles Englisch zu schreiben. Und immer mehr wie ein Schleier kommt mir meine Sprache vor, den man zerreißen muß, um an die dahinterliegenden Dinge (oder das dahinterliegende Nichts) zu kommen. Grammatik und Stil: mir scheinen sie ebenso hinfällig geworden zu sein wie ein Biedermeier Badeanzug oder die Unerschütterlichkeit eines Gentlemans. Eine Larve. Hoffentlich kommt die Zeit . . . wo die Sprache da am besten gebraucht wird, wo sie am tüchtigsten mißbraucht wird. . . . Ein Loch nach dem anderen in

ihr zu bohren, bis das Dahinterkauernde, sei es etwas oder nichts, durchzusickern anfängt. Ich kann mir für den heutigen Schriftsteller kein höheres Ziel vorstellen. . . .[14]

Both in Beckett's and Bernhard's practice, thus, we are in the situation described by Wittgenstein when he spoke, in his *Tractatus,* of his words as a ladder which has to be discarded after one has climbed up on it—to the point, that is, where language can be transcended after it has carried the writer to its utmost limit. In Beckett's early novel *Watt* some critics have actually detected allusions to that very ladder of Wittgenstein's. Bernhard has never made a secret of his debt to Wittgenstein, quite apart from his friendship with Wittgenstein's mad nephew Paul, which forms the subject of his most recent autobiographical volume, *Wittgensteins Neffe.*

Another philosopher to whom both Bernhard and Beckett are deeply indebted is Schopenhauer, not only as regards Schopenhauer's pessimism, but also with respect to his aesthetics. For Schopenhauer the visual arts represent the world of *Vorstellung,* the mimetic representation of its appearance, while music alone directly depicts the flow, the incessant pressure of the compulsion "to be," the ultimate reality, which Schopenhauer calls the "will." It is I think in trying to express this dichotomy that both writers turned to the theater after they had already produced some of their major works of poetry and prose. For the theater (or indeed drama in film and television as well) not only enables the writer to escape the tyranny of mere words, he can in performance reach an approximation to musical rather than conceptual structures, quite apart from the fact that performance also allows him to use music directly as an element in a complex contrapuntal dialectic of visuals, language, and sound.

At first sight there may appear to be a contradiction in writers of solipsistic proseworks containing the manic monologues of characters imprisoned within their own consciousness turning towards what seems to be the most objective of all artforms, the mimesis of three-dimensional human beings interacting, the theater. Yet both in Beckett's and in Bernhard's case this seeming paradox easily resolves itself: their dramatic works are as monologic as their narrative prose; they are highly individual visions in which the characters frequently are no more than concretizations of the voices that resound in the heads of the manic speakers of their monologues. And these visions are, ultimately, all metaphors, complex metaphors, or clusters of metaphors for the human condition itself.

Thus both Beckett's and Bernhard's dramatic oeuvre concentrates on such *images,* complex structures of visuals, melodic patterns of language rather than conceptual argument, coalescing in scenic metaphors. Bernhard's first play to get a major production ***Ein Fest für Boris*** (1970), for example, deals with a rich lady who lost both her legs in a car accident. As she cannot bear to be surrounded by people with superior mobility, she now moves exclusively among legless cripples, having made herself the patroness of a hostel for legless cripples. The image of a stage populated by thirteen wheel-chairs madly careering about is a very powerful metaphor of human frailty. It can be compared to Beckett's image of Winnie, the heroine of *Happy Days* sinking into a mound of earth in the first scene up to her waist and in the second up to her neck. In Bernhard's play *Die Prominenten* a group of eminent artists and writers is assembled, each of them accompanied by a waxwork portrait of his ideal predecessor as tenor, writer, critic, etc. Or in *Die Macht der Gewohnheit* we find a more complex image: the inside of a circus wagon, where a mad circus director is forcing his clown, his bareback rider, his lion tamer, and his juggler to join him in the vain attempt for the hundredth time to rehearse Schubert's *Trout Quintet*, a grotesquely sardonic image of the vanity of great art, which says more in a single moment, than reams of theoretical statements.

In his later plays Beckett has become ever more concise and his images ever more compressed; Bernhard's images also have become more restrained, but also more subtle. In Bernhard's more recent plays the image tends to concentrate on a central monologic character whose speeches have lost almost all conceptual content and have become musical structures. In these later plays, *Der Weltverbesserer, Immanuel Kant,* and *Der Schein Trügt,* Bernhard constructs a kind of sonata form by using a limited number of statements which are repeated, varied, combined, and recombined as though they were musical motifs. Analagously Beckett's latest dramatic works, like the stage play *Rockaby* or the television plays *Ghost Trio* or *Quadrat I & II* have become almost entirely visual; and when using verbal elements, the language functions mainly as a vehicle for pace and rhythm. Beckett's favorite actress Billy Whitelaw once asked me to decipher Beckett's handwriting on a postcard he had written her after she had complained that she could not understand the meaning of his play *Footfalls,* in which she was to play the leading part. Beckett's reply ran: "Dear Billy, don't worry about the meaning. What matters is the rhythm and the pace. The words are merely what pharmacists call 'the excipient'" [from memory].

It is surely also significant that both Beckett and Bernhard like writing for television and film—media even more independent of the spoken word than the theater. Bernhard is a fully trained musician; Beckett a devoted music lover, who is most meticulous in his musical references. It may be no coincidence that both writers' favorite composer is Schubert, who plays his part in *Die Macht der Gewohnheit* and in Beckett's *Nacht und Träume* as well as in *All that Fall,* where the strains of Schubert's *Der Tod und das Mädchen* are heard from one of the houses that Maddy Rooney passes.

Both Bernhard's and Beckett's dramatic oeuvre, however dark its subject matter, is essentially comic, black comedy, tragicomedy, but ultimately comedy. Beckett has stressed more than once that he regards himself as essentially a comic writer. In his famous list of the types of laugh in *Watt* he speaks of the highest form of laughter as the "mirthless laugh" which laughs at human unhappiness.

Bernhard's attitude is, it seems to me, wholly analogous, if even more extreme. In his play *Die Jagdgesellschaft* a playwright is among the principal characters assembled in a savage parody of Chekhov's *Cherry Orchard,* in which the protagonist, a general who has been wounded in the war, not only loses his political office as a member of the government, but also has his beloved wood cut down, must learn of his wife's adultery, and hear that he is incurably ill—an accumulation of misfortunes which is positively hilarious (no wonder he shoots himself at the end). This general is aware of the tragicomic quality of human existence and the ambiguity of the theory of genres. He tells the playwright, who he knows is turning his life into a play, the play that the audience is now seeing:

> Der Schriftsteller in seinem Wahnsinn
> schreibt eine Komödie
> mehr eine Operette
> und die Schauspieler fallen
> auf diese Komödie
> Operette
> herein
> Und dann glaubt die gebildete Welt
> Es handelt sich um etwas Philosophisches
> Der Schriftsteller attackiert die Philosophie
> oder eine ganze Menge von Philosophen
> und setzt den Schauspielern ganz einfach seinen Kopf
> auf
> Und handelt es sich um eine Tragödie
> behauptet er
> eine Komödie sei es
> und ist es eine Komödie
> behauptet er
> eine Tragödie
> wo es doch nichts als Operette ist[15]

Both Beckett and Bernhard look at the world and at themselves in a mood of savage black humor, gallows humor in the true sense of the word, aware as they are of the inevitability of death and the eternal elusiveness of human identity which turns each consciousness into a split self—an observer who is constantly observing himself as his own object of observation. This leads Beckett again and again not only to the monologues of endlessly shifting selves or the image of old Krapp not understanding his former self while listening to tapes he recorded decades ago, but also to repeated self-parody. Bernhard's whole dramatic oeuvre is deeply imbued with a similar self-parodistic element, witness the figures of playwrights appearing in a number of his plays. He sums it all up in a significant passage of the novel *Beton:*

> . . . ich bin mein Beobachter, ich beobachte mich tatsächlich seit Jahren, wenn nicht Jahrzehnten ununterbrochen selbst, ich lebe nurmehr in der Selbstbeobachtung und in der Selbstbetrachtung und naturgemäß dadurch in der Selbstverdammung und Selbstverleugnung und Selbstverspottung zu welcher ich letztenends immer Zuflucht nehmen muß um mich zu retten. . . .[16]

While I have established a number of parallels and similarities between Beckett and Bernhard, there are of course also some very big differences between them. Beckett is an Irishman in exile; Bernhard an Austrian who lives in a kind of internal exile in Austria. Bernhard's writing is far more specific in referring to real locations, real geographical and political circumstances, than Beckett's much more abstract approach allows him. Both of them are nonreligious, but obviously marked by coming from deeply Roman Catholic societies. But, whereas Beckett's attitude is deeply quietistic, Bernhard is a violently aggressive personality, whose pugnacity frequently fills the headlines, when, for example, he insults the members of the government who are awarding him a literature prize or withdraws from the Academy of Poets in West Germany, because they have given the ex-President of the Republic, whom he regards as a philistine idiot, an honorary membership. Bernhard also does not hesitate to involve himself in the politics of the day; one of his later plays, **Vor dem Ruhestand,** is a savage attack on the ex-Nazis who have reached high positions in West Germany. But his special wrath is reserved for his native Austria, a country he pursues with the savagery of a rejected and deeply disappointed lover. His most violent love-hate is directed against his home town of Salzburg, the very beauty of which he feels is sullied by the petty bourgeois philistinism and stupidity of its inhabitants. In Bernhard's case the schizoid perspective of his work certainly shades towards the paranoiac.

It is in this light that his dramatic oeuvre also assumes the aspect of a gigantic assault on the bourgeois audience. Bernhard's prose and plays are full of expressions of deep contempt for his audience; his dramatic oeuvre is, among other things, a monumental example of what another important Austrian playwright of our time has called "Publikumsbeschimpfung." Bernhard's is the *saeva indignatio* of a great satirist of truly Swiftian proportions. It makes his position in society truly paradoxical; a celebrated and highly rewarded writer who rejects the very society which heaps these honors on him, and yet by accepting the honors, however grudgingly, negates his own negation of that society. In that respect Samuel Beckett, who refuses to give interviews, to appear on television, and did not even accept the Nobel Prize in person acts far more consistently.

I personally regard Beckett as one of the most important writers of this or any other time. The fact that Bernhard can be compared to him as the creator of an impressive body of work, exhibiting not only an analogous fascination but also affinities arising from a deep similarity in temperament and attitude, highly symptomatic of the position of the individual in an alienated and ideologically vacuous society, shows, I think, that he too is a writer of considerable stature and significance for our time, far beyond the confines of his country and language. Thomas Bernhard deserves to be recognized in the English-speaking world as a major creative presence.

Notes

1. According to Manfred Mixner, "Vom Leben zum Tode" in *Bernhard: Annäherungen,* ed. Manfred Jurgenssen (Bern: Francke, 1981), p. 90.

2. Thomas Bernhard, *Das Kalkwerk* (Frankfurt: Suhrkamp, 1971), p. 7.

3. Beckett, *Embers,* in *Krapp's Last Tape and Other Dramatic Pieces* (New York: Grove Press, 1978), pp. 111–12.

4. Beckett, *Cascando and Other Short Dramatic Pieces* (New York: Grove Press, 1977), p. 13.

5. Beckett, *Poems in English* (New York: Grove Press 1961), p. 21.

6. Bernhard, *Verstörung* (Frankfurt: Suhrkamp, 1976), p. 139.

7. Bernhard, *Das Kalkwerk,* p. 82.

8. *Ibid.,* p. 165.

9. Bernhard, *Amras* (Frankfurt: Suhrkamp, 1976), p. 78.

10. Beckett, *Disjecta,* ed. Ruby Cohn (London: Calder, 1983), p. 139.

11. *Ibid.,* p. 145.

12. Bernhard, *Beton* (Frankfurt: Suhrkamp, 1982), p. 50.

13. Bernhard, *Verstörung,* p. 146.

14. Beckett, *Disjecta,* p. 52.

15. Bernhard, *Die Jagdgesellschaft,* in *Die Stücke 1969–1981* (Frankfurt: Suhrkamp, 1983), p. 206.

16. Bernhard, *Beton,* p. 142.

Gudrun Brokoph-Mauch (essay date 1987)

SOURCE: "Thomas Bernhard," in *Major Figures of Contemporary Austrian Literature,* edited by Donald G. Daviau, Peter Lang, 1987, pp. 89–115.

[*In the following essay, Brokoph-Mauch explores the defining characteristics of Bernhard's poetry, novels, and plays.*]

Thomas Bernhard, the grandson of the Austrian writer Johann Freumbichler, was born 10 February 1931 out of wedlock as the son of a peasant. He grew up in Southern Bavaria and lived there until he entered a boarding school in Salzburg in 1943. In 1946 he exchanged school for a two-year apprenticeship in a grocery store in a poverty-stricken district of Salzburg. There he contracted a lung disease that sent him to several hospitals and lung sanatoriums for the following three years. During that time his grandfather and his mother died (1949 and 1950), severing both his most rewarding and his most difficult relationship up to this point in his life. At the sanatorium Grafenberg he started to write his first prose out of a lack of anything else to do. After his recovery, however, he did not immediately launch into a writing career but pursued his longstanding interest in music. Thus he enrolled at the music academy in Vienna in 1951 and a year later at the Mozarteum in Salzburg, from where he graduated in 1956 with a thesis on Artaud and Brecht. With no family to support him Bernhard worked in Vienna as a laborer as well as an attendant for a seventy-year-old insane woman and in Salzburg as a courtroom reporter and free-lance writer. In 1965 he purchased a farm in Ohlsdorf, Austria, where he has been living ever since.

Bernhard's literary career began with some poems written at the age of sixteen and the publication of a short prose piece, "Vor eines Dichters Grab" (At a Poet's Grave) in the *Salzburger Volksblatt* in 1950. In 1959 he wrote a ballet sketch, *Die Rosen der Einöde* (The Roses of Solitude), and a year later created several short plays that were performed in Maria Saal in Kärnten. His fame as a prose writer was established with his first novel *Frost* (1963) and as a playwright with **Ein Fest für Boris** (1970, **A Party for Boris**).

Twenty-one years ago Thomas Bernhard published his first novel, *Frost,* which brought him as much criticism as praise, both tinged with pathos.[1] He was misunderstood as a dilettante linguist and psychologist;[2] further it was said that the narcissistic quality of his naggings served merely as "confirmation literature" for a circle of elite readers who gloried in their intellectual and social isolation.[3] Still "the unbelievably controlled dynamics" of his language[4] and his unerring search for truth[5] were soon recognized, for they captivated and moved readers. Also for a long time critics could not agree whether his novels were new or anachronistic. But with the publication of *Kalkwerk* (1970, *Lime Works*) scholars concluded: "Here was a writer who, regardless of whether he was modern or not, could write."[6]

Thomas Bernhard is not only a master of prose; he also belongs to the German avant-garde in drama. Yet as a young man he wrote sentimental religious lyrics. Their biblical references, ecstatic mysticism, and intense yearning for salvation surprise us today. Indeed, the very titles convey the melancholy and spirituality of these early poems: "November Sacrifice," "Putrefaction," "Sadness," "Black Hills," "Death and Thymian," "Death." Death and mourning provide the dominant vocabulary:

> Behind the trees there is another world,
> a grass that does not taste of mourning, a black sun,
> a moon of the dead,
> a nightingale, which does not stop lamenting
> about bread and wine
> and milk in large jugs
> in the night of the prisoners
>
> (*EH,* 27).

The images of death and mourning originate in uncertainty about the existence of God, a doubt that wounds the faith of the young poet:

> I die before the sun and
> before the wind and before the children who fight
> about the dog I die
> on a morning which will not become a poem
> only sad and green and endless
> in this morning . . .
>
> (*EH,* 62).

In other poems Bernhard speaks of the "uncertainty of the dim Gods" (*EH,* 69), and he sees God "as a drowning God with open mouth above the world" (*EH,* 70).

Bernhard's "Nine Psalms" bear witness to his swaying between loss of faith and confession of faith, his despair and his hope, his yearning for death and his longing for life:

> You, however, are the unending rain of sadness,
> the unending rain of forsakenness,
> the rain of the stars.
> The rain of the weak
> which makes my eyes powerless
>
> (*EH,* 73).

Contrasting with this litany of resignation are passages in which his will to resurrect God in his writing creates Him with his own words:

> I will fill my hands with earth
> and speak my words,
> the words which will become stone on my tongue
> to rebuild God,
> the great God,
> the one and only God . . .
>
> (*EH,* 74).

When death replaces religion,[7] the author turns from poetry to prose, the form in which he would make his fame. Yet, as he says, "The most terrible thing for me is to write prose. . . . And from that moment on, when I became aware of that, I swore that I would write prose" (*DT,* 154). When Bernhard says he writes prose against his nature, he also characterizes the most prominent gesture of his works: repulsion from and destruction of the aesthetic forms, philosophical assumptions, and social practices of the consciousness that ignore the finality of death and despair. For this "disappointed metaphysicist"[8] is now fixed on one goal: namely, to demonstrate in an unmistakable and "relentless" way that everything is ridiculous in the face of death.[9] From his first volume of prose, the short narratives *Ereignisse* (1963–1969, Incidents), up to his last prose work, *Beton* (1982, Concrete), he is on the track of death and truth;[10] and he searches with a decisiveness that does not shrink from linguistic excess when he attempts to prove that life is "an amnesis of death" and every quest for knowledge actually "a method of death,"[11] which is therefore evil and void.

In 1968 Bernhard remarked, "Death is my theme because life is my theme,"[12] a statement that applies unmistakably to the tales in *Ereignisse.* The themes of guilt, fear, disgust, sickness, crime, insanity, and death anticipate themes in the later writings. But the horror of the earlier works is dimmed somewhat by the dream-logic that perhaps protects the reader through its apparent fictionality, as in "Der Kassierer" (The Cashier) in the volume *Ereignisse*. Notice the pattern of escalation, catastrophe, and anticlimax (the revelation that it is all a dream):

> The cashier in an iron work marries a woman eight or nine years older than he. Shortly after the wedding the quarrels begin. There is an enormous hostility with which both fall asleep and wake up. Finally the woman becomes very ill, which may have something to do with her childlessness, with her hands, at home she writes everything on calendar pages: "I want to go away," for example, or "It is beautiful outside." She hates it when people pity her. Finally she feels pain in her legs and becomes completely stiff. She has to be pushed in a wheelchair. She waits at the window. When her husband comes home, he has to push her around outside. Always the same stretch. Further and further. She threatens with clenched fists. She is more and more hungry for new houses, new trees, new people. She looks out of her winter cape through the trees of the alley. One evening, pushing her in front of him close to the edge of the road, he turns the wheelchair over and tosses it into the abyss. She cannot scream. The metal chair bursts into splinters. This event he dreams. But he will do something like that with her, he thinks.[13]

The actual event, the "Ereignis," is retracted at the very moment it happens by the statement that it is a dream. Thus the impulse to murder is satisfied momentarily, and indeed the mounting tension finds an explosive release in the description of the murder; but the statement, "This event he dreams," deflates the effect. Of course, the positioning of this sentence allows for both the fulfillment of the reader's secret identification with the husband's pent-up feelings of hate, the wish that his wife were dead, while at the moment of its satisfaction the necessary defense mechanism or "emergency break" takes hold. However, the last sentence does allude to the possible actualization of the dream and maintains a certain tension to the very end.

Bernhard's later works forsake this method of dream "framing."[14] Although the *Ereignisse* already contain the material for the fables of the later works, their objective and epigrammatic style sets them apart as a distinct literary form.

The novel *Frost* (1963) is the first prose work that structurally leads to a new form. It is "literature of the most harsh, hostile, and hurting kind."[15] The content may at best be sketched, for the largest part of the book consists of reflective monologues that can hardly be narrated here. A young medical student travels to Weng, a small mountain village in the Austrian Alps, in order to observe the painter Strauch, who seems to be insane. He is assigned to this task by his superior, who is also Strauch's brother. The nameless narrator's observations about the painter and the surroundings are written in the form of diary notes and let-

ters. These diary entries mirror on the one hand the progressive mental decay of the painter and on the other the progressive loss of identity of the narrator as he drowns in the painter's flow of egomaniacal suicidal speech. The letters of the medical student to Strauch's brother demonstrate in style and language this gradual mental rape of the young man by the elder.

The condition of the mind and the condition of the world mirror each other. The village Weng is painted in the colors of disgust; it is a vestibule of Hell, a place dominated by death. The inhabitants are sick and feebleminded alcoholics. They have lice and gonorrhea and suffer from what Bernhard simply calls the "land plague" (*F,* 172). Excesses of drunkenness, arson, injury, murder, and accidental death (often caused by the brain-dissolving frost of a hostile nature) are a constant threat to everyday existence, which is meaningless anyway. Over the entire landscape hovers a suffocating odor of slaughterhouses and corpses, the ubiquitous "world stench," and through it all the dogs bark and howl. Relentlessly Bernhard dismantles here the postcard idyll of the Austrian tourist business and hits at a vulnerable but until now protected spot in his fellow Austrians. The "stupidity in shirt sleeves" that he portrays (*F,* 172) negates the picture of the wholesome simple country people of Adalbert Stifter and Peter Rosegger. Thus this "wasteland" is not confined to one region. No, it represents the world's condition as Bernhard sees it. It is equally one-sided to categorize Bernhard as a "Heimatdichter" (provincial writer)[16] as it is to call him a social and cultural critic. Donnenberg has demonstrated convincingly that Bernhard does not fit nicely into either category in spite of his polemical tendencies.[17]

The figure of the painter recalls Büchner's Lenz and the medical student Hans Castorp just as the entire snow and mountain landscape refers to the mythic associations of Thomas Mann's *Der Zauberberg* (*Magic Mountain*).[18] Like Hans Castorp the narrator faces disease and death as "punishment" (*F,* 346); and this confrontation incites his consciousness and his destructive self-reflection. When he abruptly ends his stay at Weng after twenty-six days, leaving the painter to his suicidal end, he who was originally described as lacking in sensitivity and imagination is deeply scarred. He has to pay for his "expeditions into the jungles of solitude" (*F,* 20) and his spying on another man's suffering with the loss of his own spiritual security.

The novel *Frost* lays the philosophical, material, and stylistic basis for Bernhard's following work to such a degree that the author has been said to be writing with "maniacal tenacity" on a single novel.[19] Although the horror does lose its pictorial explicitness, it increases its effect through abstraction. Repetition takes the place of variation. The action narrows more and more and merely serves to launch the endless monologues behind which looms a gaping emptiness. The theme of disease is intensified in *Amras* (1965) and in *Verstörung* (1967, *Gargoyles*), but in the later novels it remains more in the background. While in *Frost* the specific cause of the painter's physical illness remains unclear, it is already a "literary symptom"[20] of an equally undefinable mental illness and further of the condition of the world. In *Amras* the "mental confusion" has a clear and fitting "objective correlative"[21] in epilepsy, while in *Verstörung* the author goes as far as to establish a distinct hierarchy of the various diseases, beginning with physical sepsis and ending with highly spiritual insanity. Each disease correlates with the social rank and intellectual capacity of the individual and is located in a landscape divided into high, middle, and low regions.

The Prince, whose monologue fills up the last third of the novel, lives on top of a mountain and suffers from the highest degree of sensitivity and mental confusion. Its cause lies in the act of thinking which, as for the painter Strauch in *Frost,* is "an amoral blank space, thinking without a real function" (*F,* 339). "Diseases lead man on the shortest path to himself" (*V,* 228), says Bernhard in *Verstörung,* but the goal is always insanity or death. In *Korrektur* (1975, *Correction*) this theme is expressly connected with the narrator's search for identity. But in the last analysis all diseases are for Bernhard a symptom of the one "sickness unto death," which like suicide has its seed in the womb.

The knowledge that the highly sensitive and intellectual gain in their condition of confusion and permanent mental excitement is of a special kind: "A great vision is constructed out of a very small observation" (*F,* 296). Here the visionary often loses himself in the solipsistic swirls of thought and reflection. The protagonist or narrator in other words is confined within his own cerebral mechanism, a universe in his own head. His is not cognition of the world because there is nothing out there to be understood. Furthermore, the borders between inside and outside are nebulous, shifting, and not clearly definable, corresponding to the narrative perspective that switches back and forth between personal and projected thoughts. The mental condition of other persons cannot be judged objectively. Consequently, the reader does not gain any insight into personal or universal relationships; instead, he is confronted only with the "brain on printed paper" (*F,* 343), with a novel as interior monologue. Nevertheless, the reader will come to accept that these terrifying fantasies of insanity mirror the unbearable condition of the world as it is experienced by other splintered and solipsistic souls.

The novel *Kalkwerk* (*Lime Works*), published in 1970, is also indebted to *Frost,* but its form is developed and its content streamlined in such a sophisticated way that it sets a standard of literary craftsmanship and philosophical insight against which other works will be judged.[22] New for Bernhard is the perspective of a narrator who stands completely apart from the event refracted through two other reporters. The result is an extreme indirectness—an "event twice removed"—combined with precision of language and effect alternately bringing the reader into close contact with the object of narration through speech and distancing him through the presence of the intermediary narrator: "We are simultaneously inside and outside":[23]

". . . Konrad and his crippled wife have lived in the lime works for several years, I think, Höller thinks, Konrad supposedly said to Fro" (*K,* 122). This technique of narrative framing demonstrates how complicated it is to arrive at the authenticity of any statement; it also represents the isolation of the inhabitant of the lime works from nature, society, and tradition. The tension of "bipolarity"[24] between experiencing and narrating narrator, which was already veiled in *Frost,* is completely absent here in order to bring into the foreground the "fictionality of the narrative form."[25]

Again the plot is reduced to a minimum. After years of traveling around in the world Konrad has bought the longed-for lime works into which he and his crippled wife withdraw from the world. There he wants to write a scientific study on hearing that he carries in his head completely finished. After five and a half years of mutual torment and constant irritation preventing the composition of the study Konrad murders his wife. The whole novel is a single cry of anguish about the inability to actualize one's thoughts. The language absorbs the frustrations and aggressions that build up in Konrad and transmits them to the reader in the endless, circular sentences, which become sheer torture in their constant repetitions. In this way the reader is forced to participate directly in Konrad's verbal torture of his wife and the mental and emotional exhaustion of both, for neither has any means of escape.

Already in his earlier novels the place sought out as a protective refuge changed gradually into a hostile and death-inducing prison: Weng in *Frost,* Hochgobernsitz in *Verstörung,* the tower in *Amras* (1965), the shack in *Watten* (1969). However, nowhere did Bernhard succeed so completely and so convincingly in the evocation of this phenomenon as in *Kalkwerk.* Konrad's goal of writing down his research proves fatal for him, his wife, and his work: "Our goal was the lime works, our goal was death through the lime works" (*K,* 225).

The comical grotesque, which is present more allusively in *Frost* and more substantially in *Watten,* is realized fully in *Kalkwerk.* It responds to the abyss that opens once ideology and religion are rejected; it points to the ever-present danger of violence and downfall and as a style achieves the opposite of comic relief: anxiety.

The lament about the difficulty of transforming knowledge into language that *Frost* voices is central to the narrative of the *Kalkwerk.* Thus, paradoxically, the description of the impossibility of language to say what it means becomes itself a successful and complete work of literary art.[26] But despite this triumph it is clear that the author has reached the last stage of the separation of the writer from his audience that had begun in Romanticism; for Bernhard no longer concerns himself with the loneliness, suppression, and desires of the artist for understanding and social acceptance but instead attacks his readers hatefully and finally turns away from them indifferently.[27] The meaning of writing for Bernhard as well as his fictional creations no longer lies in a dialogue with the world but only in the actualization of their own personality. We are witness to an amazing event: literature succeeds here by including its own destruction.[28]

The latest novel, *Korrektur,* continues the premises of *Frost* while adding something that enlarges the basic thesis: "Research, realization, completion, destruction, eradication. In every case and in every matter in this sequence . . ." (*Ko,* 358). Nowhere else can one find realization and completion in Bernhard's works. Up to this novel science and research have always directly led to destruction and eradication. This is precisely the main theme of *Kalkwerk.* But in *Korrektur* the author for the first time has constructed "an architectural piece of art" and only then does he "correct," i.e., destroy it. The novel concerns a type of protagonist who has become typical for Bernhard ever since *Amras, Ungenach, Verstörung,* and *Watten*: namely, a man from a wealthy family, a gentleman scholar who refuses to maintain the family estate. He invests his huge inheritance in a cone-shaped house for his beloved sister who dies a mysterious death shortly after its completion.[29] He himself commits suicide after he has tried in vain to write down the planning and construction of the cone.

The work moves back and forth between the two poles already alluded to above: on the one hand, affirmation of existence through the building of the cone that opposes the hostile world into which man is thrown ("geworfen")[30] with its own realm, "so that we can say after a while, *we live in our world not in the existing world,* namely, a world which does not concern us and which wants to destroy and eradicate us" (*Ko,* 237). On the other hand there is the knowledge of inevitable failure, a knowledge that leads to suicide, as expressed in *Frost.* 'Life is a trial which one loses regardless of what one does" (*F,* 233).

Bernhard's basic premise that the goal of all science is death has not changed. But the question of whether Pascal's totalizing belief that "death makes everything infamous" (*F,* 315) applies here, or whether the author strikes a more conciliatory note this time must be asked at least. For even if there is no meaningful way to live in Bernhard's works, are there not degrees of meaninglessness? Death has perhaps two faces. The reader has known the one face since the beginning and immediately recognized it in the title: suicide as a correction of life. For the first time though Bernhard allows for a second kind of death, namely, death at a moment of intense happiness and fulfillment through the experience of dwelling ("wohnen") in the perfect place. However, since the symbolic form of this living space suggests the tomb (the relationship to the pyramid[31] and to the pole in the tombs of the Etruscans[32] is evident), it is difficult to say how far the relationship of happiness and death, of perfect building and mausoleum can be taken seriously; must it instead be understood as a bitter irony? Roithamer constructs the cone after the philosophy of space of the twentieth century,[33] which tries to overcome existentialism by actualizing Heidegger's theory of the unity of building, dwell-

ing, and thinking. Yet the death of Roithamer's sister parodies the philosophy of the protective place that assumes naively that the existential situation of modern man can be overcome architecturally.[34]

Just as futile is Roithamer's attempt to create his own center in a world without metaphysical principles. After all his focus reveals itself as a place of death. This essential absence of a true philosophical center is mirrored in language and in style. The rotating, circular motion of the sentences seems to suck up bits and pieces of information and swirl them along. Indeed, all sentences and groups of sentences in the first third of the novel, for example, start with "Höller's attic room" and return to it eventually. Höller's attic room as center of these syntactical spirals functions as a grotesque attempt to make up for the "middle," the focus, of missing meaning. The result of rhetorical strain is, of course, that nothingness becomes not covered up but painfully evident. Maier understands the intentions and effects of this style, which is already present in the earlier works, as an expression of a "dissatisfaction with the world plan (world center)."[35] Bernhard's language lacks an anchor, it has nothing to tell. As Spinner observes, one cannot "dwell" ("wohnen") in it any longer.[36]

The construction of the cone reveals very clearly a dialectic that is basic to Bernhard's work: the opposition to tradition coupled with a love for the past. As Gamper says, the aggression against tradition—in this case the family residence Altensam—functions, in reality, as a "utopia projected backwards,"[37] it originates in the frustrated understanding that, although the past is truly valuable, it cannot be experienced truthfully in the present.[38] In *Korrektur* Roithamer tries to escape this destructive dilemma by creating a new place for the idealized past that his sister embodies. The irony of this attempted rescue of tradition lies in the symbolic representation of the cone as tomb, as we have seen.

In *Korrektur* and especially in *Kalkwerk* the reader must not forget that everything said is quoted (G, 22).[39] This means that the closeness between narrator and story, typical in the diary and epistolary novel, is defamiliarized through the reflection of quotation. Once more then Bernhard constructs the scaffold of a traditional fiction only to tear it down before the reader's eyes. Moreover, the first person narrator no longer intends to tell a story but only wants to take "notes" and to "inspect and order" the "scraps of paper" of the other narrator. Bernhard acknowledges this process in his autobiographical television sketch *Drei Tage* (1971, Three Days), in which he admits that he is a "destroyer of stories" (*DT,* 151).

Just as Bernhard's novel appeared to dissolve itself, leaving the reader to wonder what would happen next, the author took a sudden turn in his prose. He turned to autobiography and hence to telling a story. The five prose works. *Die Ursache* (1975, The Cause), *Der Keller* (1976, The Cellar), *Der Atem* (1978, The Breath), *Die Kälte*

(1981, The Cold), and *Das Kind* (1982, The Child), form a novel in series about the life of the man Thomas Bernhard. These five works divide the most important phases of Bernhard's youth into five chronological stages. The author wants the reader to interpret the experiences in these five works as the "cause" of his special way of living, thinking, and writing.

With this series Bernhard joins in a movement in contemporary Austrian literature which, apparently tired of the concreteness, objectivity, and emotional coldness of the 1960s and early 1970s, views the autobiographical novel as a chance to return to subjectivity as a medium for discovering and researching one's own personality. Bernhard even goes a step further than his colleagues; he writes a real autobiography not an autobiographical novel. He says "I" without the least bit of disguise. So far it seems safe to say that this autobiographical quintet shows Bernhard again experimenting with a new form of expression, an attempt very much like his discovery of the theater in 1970 and of film in 1973.

After the aggressive, radical declaration of cognitive and metaphysical bankruptcy in *Korrektur,* Bernhard paused understandably for a time of self-reflection. He seemed to wish for a way out of the dead-end road along which he had traveled further and further in each new novel. In an early poem, "Biography of Pain" ("Biographie des Schmerzes"), Bernhard wrote tellingly: "The place I slept in yesterday is closed today. In front of the entrance the chairs are stacked one upon the other, and none whom I ask about me has seen me."[40]

Nevertheless, in his autobiography he opens the dwelling place of his youth; he sets up the chairs in a very distinct pattern. His research into the "cause of my misfortune"[41] concentrates mainly on the geography of Salzburg, the home of his parents, and the state of his youth, the "deadly soil," the "deadly region" (*Ur,* 69), and only secondarily does it focus on catastrophic occurrences there: his adolescent stay in the boarding school during and after the bombing of Salzburg in *Die Ursache,* his apprenticeship in a grocery store in the slums of the city in *Der Keller,* his struggle with death in the Municipal Hospital in *Der Atem,* his experience of isolation at the sanatorium Grafenberg in *Die Kälte.* These "constellations of severe misfortune," to use a phrase of Ingeborg Bachmann, end temporarily in Grafenberg (*At,* 237), and the reader is left waiting for the continuation of this autobiography.

Of course no autobiography is written spontaneously; some intention determines the selection, composition, and interpretation of the historical material. For this reason Bernhard limits his research of the "Ursachen" (causes) to the occurrences in his life that can lend authenticity to his depictions of sickness, insanity, and death in fiction. The causality imposed on the relationships and events of life changes the chronicle into a work of art. The will to poetic creation the urge to place detail into a totality, is as strong here as the will to truth in his fiction. As André Maurois

observed, memory itself is an artist, making a work of art out of everyone's life.[42]

This aesthetic arrangement of historical material makes the locations and events translucent; that is, facts become metaphors. For example, attendance in the *Gymnasium* (equivalent to high school and two years of college) is interpreted as the adult world's betrayal of the child. The school, under its brutal directors, is an inferno; it exemplifies all oppressive political and religious ideology, contemporary and historical. The director's blow to the head of a pupil, the slap of a face, do damage to the souls of the boys as much as the bombs to the city; for they all symbolize the destructive fury in human nature. Driven to a type of narcosis for refuge, a talented pupil daily plays his violin in the narrow, evil-smelling shoe closet. His playing stimulates and accompanies his meditations about suicide, thoughts that are the result of this oppressive education. Bernhard's frequent condemnations of the Salzburg Festival as a paradigm of cultural decadence and the desire for intoxication, escape, and adolescent masturbation come to mind here.[43]

In the second part of the autobiography the cellar also becomes a metaphor. Obviously it contrasts with the hypocritical façade of bourgeois life. But the metaphor of the cellar refers to yet another realm of interpretation lying in the Pascal quotation at the beginning of *Der Atem*: "Since mankind was incapable of overcoming death, poverty, and ignorance, it decided not to think of them in order to be happy." However, Bernhard does not allow his reader any diversion from the unresolved problems of existence. He turns off the electric light in our modern cellars, to use a metaphor of Bachelard,[44] and leads us mercilessly down the cellar steps with a flickering candle in his hand, not just in this autobiography but in all of his works beginning with his first novel. Only by directly confronting sickness, vice, squalor, and death, the madness and horror beneath reason, can he conceive of a new beginning, if indeed it is at all possible. The stay in the "Scherzhauserfeldsiedlung" is a necessary stage during which the apprentice passes from adolescence to adulthood, ending the escapism of his meditations on suicide and making contact with his inner nature before starting a new life: "I had my life again. Suddenly I had it completely in my hand" (*Ke,* 16), Bernhard's autobiography is truly a biography of pain because this search for his lost ego does not lead him back to society but rather to a lung disease, the well-known "literary symptom" for "the sickness unto death" in his works. The search leads him away from social intercourse and brings him closer to the edge of human existence.

Again in *Der Atem* the factual yields symbolic meaning. The death chamber, which only Bernhard survives in this work, is the last scene in the theater farce of life. Everyone leaves the stage in a different manner, but the significance of these various ways of dying is not clear. In any case death does not pause; it knows no social distinctions here, in contrast to *Der Italiener* (1971) in which different social classes die differently. In *Der Atem* everyone is thrown into the same tin coffin after the corpse has spent two hours under a sheet with a number on his big toe.

In the foreground is the accusation against the conditions of Bernhard's youth: the political dilemma of the war period, the social chaos of the postwar era, the callousness of those who think themselves charitable in the hospitals. The immediate family is introduced: the daily life of three generations in the most inadequate living space—parents, grandparents, brothers, sisters, and one uncle, all of whom have been led into this tiny apartment at the end of the war to experience fright and horror: "My home was hell" (*Ke,* 94). The author, though, expressly denies the reader more details of these horrible conditions. Just exactly how unbearable his life with his mother, stepfather, half brothers, and sisters must have been we can only guess. He does not even elaborate the difficult relationship with his mother, a bond tainted with suspicion and mutual dislike. Its elucidation would help us understand why his female characters are always either passed over or portrayed unsympathetically; and perhaps it would clue us as to why there are no normal erotic relationships in his works.

This gap of information is finally closed in his last autobiographical volume, *Das Kind* (1982, The Child), which reads like an afterthought: instead of continuing the series in chronological sequence, *Das Kind* prefaces it with the hitherto undisclosed early childhood of the author. The book opens with the first bicycle ride of the eight-year-old and closes with the application of the adolescent to the Salzburg boarding school, which serves as a bridge to *Die Ursache*. It is the most intimate volume of the quintet describing in detail his illegitimate birth, his difficult life with his mother, his warm and loving friendship with his grandfather, and his misery and torment as an unsuccessful pupil in grammar school. Because his mother was ill prepared to raise such a precocious child, she turned to frequent corporal punishment in her helplessness and to yelling at him and cursing him. As much as he feared the leather strap on his skin, nothing would wound him as deeply as her "diabolical words": "You are the cause of my unhappiness. The devil shall take you. You have destroyed my life. It's all your fault! You are my death! You are nothing! I am ashamed of you . . . ! (*Ki,* 38). His close resemblance to his father, the man who had deserted her at a young age, was a constant reminder for her of her greatest disappointment. Therefore her instinctive love for her child was obstructed by her hatred of his father and her beatings, harsh words, and lamentations were not so much directed toward the child but toward the father. His mother's life was further complicated by her constant struggle against poverty and entrapment in her father's (the author's beloved grandfather) provocative, anachronistic, revolutionary mental escapades while she longed for normality and harmony.

All the while the child loved his mother but through the unfortunate circumstances of his birth and the economic and emotional pressures on his family was denied the comfort of motherly love and affection. His salvation was his grandfather who would always be his ally in difficult situations and essentially rescued him from the destructive forces around him. "We understood each other. A few steps with him, and I was rescued" (*Ki,* 79). He is his mentor who teaches him how to think, to ask questions, and to find answers. As a writer and as an eccentric he becomes influential for Bernhard's profession.

Bernhard's noticeable preoccupation with death in his works seems to go back to his childhood visits to the graveyard in Seekirchen (one of the several places of residence of the restless family). "The dead were already then my dearest friends, I approached them without reservations. For hours I would sit on the edge of a grave pondering being and its opposite" (*Ki,* 70–71). By offering valuable insight into a disturbing childhood this last autobiographical volume solicits deeper understanding for the author's predisposition toward isolation, insanity, self-destruction, and death in his writings.

Like his novels the autobiographic quintet is filled with voluminous reflections and lengthy commentaries that keep the reader in a constant tension between fascination and irritation. Their compulsive exaggerations rob the historical events of their authenticity. The result is a primarily apologetic tone that stands in the way of a true search for the self. Still it cannot be denied that these commentaries draw the reader into their magic circle; they largely make up the tension and emotional appeal of these works, not so much through content as style, particularly in the circular sentences, which absorb more material here than in the novels. This artificial style, imbued with a power of persuasion, intensifies the subjectivity of Bernhard's confrontation with life and overpowers the readers through its combination of absolute terms and syntactical breathlessness, forcing him into the author's perspective at least as long as he is reading. This narrative strategy satisfies a compulsion to justify oneself, typical in autobiography, and at the same time it addresses the aesthetic and emotional needs of the reader.

Compared with his novels and short stories, Bernhard's autobiography appears conservative in form. The chronological-causal order of the phases of his life in the four volumes releases the reader from the usual labor of piecing a life story together like a puzzle from shreds of quotations and reports of other narrators. Rather, a linear story is told here by an author who has consistently called himself a "destroyer of stories" (*DT,* 151).

The tracing of his artistic development is very sketchy in this autobiography, probably because Bernhard decided late to become a writer. However, as compensation the five volumes serve up much of the intellectual and factual matter of his works, making them more accessible but without changing them into autobiographical writings. For the historical events and emotional turmoils have been filtered through a process of abstraction and reconfiguration in the individual works. As a result they are not easily recognizable. The confusion, terror, and deadly experiences of the author's youth have been rendered in the novels as general confusion, fright, and death in the form of an apocalyptic vision, which has dissolved the historical moment with its claim of absolute truth.

Bernhard's prose does not consist exclusively of novels and autobiography; it also includes shorter forms: the short stories in the volumes *An der Baumgrenze* (1969, At the Timber Line) and *Midland in Stilfs* (1969–1970, Midland at Stilfs) and the short novels *Amras* (1965), *Ungenach* (1968), *Watten* (1969), and *Ja* (1978, Yes). In the collection *Der Stimmenimitator* (1978, The Voice Imitator) he returns to the "short short story" of his first work, *Ereignisse*. Although very similar in content—insanity, suicide, murder, fatal accidents, mysterious deaths, macabre occurrences, and contradictions of a great variety these works are very dissimilar in style and meaning. While the *Ereignisse* are characterized by sentences consisting of short main clauses in the present tense. which produce rapidly mounting tension and direct emotional impact, the stories in *Der Stimmenimitator* display long periods abounding in relative and dependent clauses as well as the indirect speech of the novels. This syntax requires great mental concentration from the reader and consequently does not yield the intense identification with the narrated event as happens in *Ereignisse*. Rather, one is led to a detached, intellectual observation of the story's development and direction and often of its paradoxical or ironical turn at the end.

The structure of the stories is often that of the anecdote—short narration of a single event that aims from the very first sentence at the goal, at the "Pointe" at the end—while the character of the story is taken from a news item in a local paper. Thus the title "Voice Imitator" refers not only to one of the stories in the volume about an artist who imitates the voices of celebrities, while he cannot imitate his own voice, but also to the peculiar ability of the author to invoke the voices of the newspapers in their columns about catastrophes. Bernhard is very successful in his attempt to bring out the ludicrous, the illogical, and the contradictory in journalistic style, which typically uses naive language, introduces immaterial detail, and misplaces the focus of the report. The piece "Too Much" illustrates this technique well: "A family father, who had been praised and liked for decades because of his so-called *extraordinary family sense,* and who on a Saturday afternoon—to be sure while the weather was extremely humid—murdered four of his six children, defended himself in front of the judge with the argument that the children had suddenly been *too much* for him" (*St,* 49).

In contrast to the man in *Der Stimmenimitator* Bernhard not only succeeds in imitating other voices but also seems to have little difficulty in imitating his own voice. The degree to which *Der Stimmenimitator* seems to be a summary of the characters, events, localities, and topics of his previous writings is striking, and the "voice" in this volume rings a familiar tune in the reader's ear with its occasional note of self-irony.

The discussion of the short novel *Beton* (1982, *Concrete*) will conclude our consideration of Bernhard's prose writings. It harks back to the *Kalkwerk* (*Lime Works*) of ten years earlier. Again we have a protagonist who is possessed by the single wish to write down a work of great importance to him, this time a thesis on Mendelssohn, and again is incapable of doing so because of his neurotic sensitivity toward the smallest inner and outer distractions. Although he never does write his Mendelssohn abstract in the course of this book, and it is doubtful that he ever will, his preoccupation with this and similar projects in the past serves as a justification for his life style, which is as expensive as it is absurd: "I attacked Schönberg in order to justify myself, Reger, Joachim and even Bach, only to justify myself, as I now attack Mendelssohn for the same reason" (*B,* 70), he admits, only to come to the conclusion that neither he nor anyone else needs justification, because no one asked to be born.

The theme of the writer whose creativity is stifled because of an excessive degree of perfectionism is combined also in this work with the theme of extreme isolation. Robert lives alone in his country house in Peiskam communicating on a regular basis only with his housekeeper and on an irregular basis with his sister, who imposes upon him at her own will and convenience. And again; as we have seen in previous works, the main character is incapable of freeing himself from the intrusion of another human being on his mind to the degree that the preoccupation turns into obsession. Thus the novel opens with Robert's attempt to resume his normal, carefully orchestrated routine of living through yet another unproductive day after one of those spontaneous visits by his sister, only to find his thoughts totally dominated by her personality, her thoughts and opinions, and her way of life. The contrast between brother and sister that emerges gradually in the usual gyrations of language, the protestations and accusations against each and everyone, could not be starker: she is the picture of health and vitality with a sheer insatiable appetite for life's mundane gifts and adventures, a charming and skillful manipulator of people, a successful businesswoman, in short the guest of honor at the banquet of life, while he—a chronically ailing neurasthenic, hypersensitive man who depends on heavy medication for his mere survival, shunning human contact and the pursuit of ordinary tasks and pleasures—merely nibbles at the crumbs that fall off the table. While the sister is a familiar figure in Bernhard's works, she does not normally appear as such an independent and vital personality, but is usually crippled, tied to a wheelchair or otherwise totally subservient to her brother and dependent on him. Here the roles are almost reversed, for although not dependent upon her financially or physically he is preoccupied with her with that envious fascination of the unsuccessful toward the successful, whereas she on the other hand prods and nudges her little brother toward a more fruitful life.

In the end, unable to free himself from her spell over him, he journeys to Palma, Mallorca, where he recalls the sad fate of a woman he had met there two years ago and who had since committed suicide. Her grave, a slab of concrete, gives this novel its title. Anna Härtl's fate with its progressive stages of misfortune only accidentally forms a contrast to the success story of Rudolf's sister. It is of no consequence to the narrator, who merely uses her story to fill his own empty life and the empty pages that should be filled with the story of Mendelssohn and is an inadequate substitute for the project in his mind. And—as is typical for Bernhard—death has won the day again and has succeeded in making everything else seem insignificant and irrelevant.

If one disregards here the very early theater and ballet sketches,[45] then *Ein Fest für Boris* is Bernhard's first play. He has since written a great number of others, which repeat the themes, images, and motifs of this one as well as of his novels and short stories. Not surprisingly, the main characteristics of Bernhard's dramas are closely related to those of his prose writings: endlessly long monologues, scarcity of action, the joining of two partners in conversation, one of whom talks almost without interruption while the other—inferior in appearance but intellectually often superior—is silent.

Thus the relationship between the "Good Woman," the main character in *Ein Fest für Boris,* and Johanna, her nurse, servant, and companion, is characterized by mutual dependence and mutual hatred, by the overt tyranny of the one and the subversive rebellion of the other; and this relationship is typical of most others in Bernhard's plays. Also typical is the main character's obsession with one problem throughout the play—a familiar occurrence in the novels, too. In this case the "Good Woman," rich, capricious, and tyrannical, is obsessed with only one event in her life: the car accident in which her husband was killed and she lost both of her legs. The mutual dependence of two persons who torment one another and the obsession with one unresolved problem are also found in *Der Präsident* (1975, *The President*) and *Der Weltverbesserer* (1979, *The World Reformer*). Both complexes are metaphors for the torturous coexistence of human beings and the absorption of each individual in his own condition.

The play *Ein Fest für Boris* centers on a birthday banquet for Boris, a cripple and glutton. He celebrates among his former friends from the asylum where he lived before the "Good Woman" rescued and married him. The "Good Woman" plays the sympathetic benefactor: she listens to the cripple's scurrilous and frightening dreams and fantasies, the complaints about the poor treatment of the inmates. Soon their tales turn into war cries and the feast into a rebellious chaos during which Boris collapses quietly and dies. The play ends with the "Good Woman's" "terrible laughter" (*B,* 107).

Comedy or tragedy? They are interchangeable for Bernhard simply because death lies in ambush at the end of almost every play, robbing tragedy of its dignity and comedy of its final serenity. As he says:

> We continuously develop
> a tragedy

> or a comedy
> when we develop the tragedy
> we really develop only a comedy
> and vice versa

(*M,* 18).

Also in the later plays Death concludes the masquerade that is life, as in *Die Jagdgesellschaft* (1974, *The Hunting Party*). In the play *Minetti* (1976) Bernhard combines death with art. An eccentric and possibly mad actor claims to have been asked by a director to perform *Lear* after thirty years retirement. Yet he commits suicide in the ongoing war between artist and audience.

Art is the central theme in several plays. In *Minetti* the artist struggles with his "intellectual object" against the "intellectual garbage" (*M,* 26) in society. He wants to suppress the common stupidity under the "intellectual cap" (*M,* 26), but he is not strong enough. In the end he is destroyed by his public. The other plays—*Der Ignorant und der Wahnsinnige* (1972, *The Ignorant and the Mad*), the comedy *Die Macht der Gewohnheit* (1974, *The Force of Habit*), and the satire *Die Berühmten* (1976, *The Famous*) deal with the ineffectiveness of today's art and its inability to influence society. Bernhard sees several reasons for this. In *Minetti* the trouble is the public's desire for the perfection and harmony of classical literature, in which one can be protected from assuming responsibility for a perplexing and disturbing reality: Minetti refuses to be part of this "shamelessness" (*M,* 48). He declines every offer and resists all pressure to perform classical roles with the exception of *Lear,* a role which is his fate and which drives him to insanity. As a result he is chased from the theater and lives in depravity. *Die Berühmten,* on the other hand, provides a contrast to Minetti's protest, for it is the protagonists' ambition to imitate and possibly surpass those "classical" stars of the theater, opera, and concert hall whom society has placed on a pedestal. The public rewards these efforts with money and the comforts of an opulent lifestyle. Bernhard calls this ambition to be the public's favorite at any cost "the insolence of the artist."

Of a different nature is Bernhard's criticism of art and the artist in *Der Ignorant und der Wahnsinnige.* Here he attacks the reduction of art to mechanical virtuosity, which in its inexhaustible exertion to reach the perfection of form has forgotten human content and descended to the level of empty mechanism. Such striving for artificial perfection also transforms the performing artist, in this case a soprano, into a machine, a "Koleraturmaschine."

While the performing artist's obsession for perfection in *Der Ignorant und der Wahnsinnige* is treated in a morbidly serious way, it is caricatured in the play *Die Macht der Gewohnheit.* The circus director Caribaldi has been practicing the "Forellenquintet" daily for twenty-two years. His single goal in life is to be able to perform the quintet once with absolute perfection. But he never succeeds because he is dependent both on circumstances—the instruments that break down—and on the cooperation and ability of the other performers, who periodically sabotage his efforts. Then too his own failing health undermines his performance. Bernhard borrows the characters and situations from the *commedia dell' arte*; these comical elements are successfully combined with a fundamental skepticism.[46] Caribaldi's wish to make "perfect music" does not originate from the true joy of playing an instrument well but rather from a sincere revulsion against it: "But we must play!" he exclaims (*Gew,* 42), just as we must live life, which is equally unloved. The performance of art appears as a discipline, a therapy, even a diversion from life.

The idea that the talent and the genius are essentially a kind of disease or deformation of human nature runs like a red thread through this play: "The extraordinary is always crippled. That which happens in it a deformation" (*Ber,* 35). This idea of course is not new but a variation of the well-known equation of genius and illness by writers since German Romanticism: but this definition of the creative mind as a sick deviation from the healthy norm is just another way for Bernhard to express his disappointment with art and culture.

Bernhard's cultural pessimism does not end with art and the performing artists but includes also philosophy and the philosophers. In his comedy ***Immanuel Kant*** (1979), for instance, the philosopher is portrayed as a lunatic traveling on a luxury liner from Königsberg to the United States in order to undergo an eye operation and to receive an honorary degree from Columbia University. In reality he is taken into custody by employees of an insane asylum as soon as the ship lands.

Two themes supply the targets for Bernhard's mockery in the play: first, Kant's eye problem, which prevents him from seeing the "thing itself"—in this case the artificial kneecap of the millionairess—an attack on the basic premise of Kant's philosophy; second, his constant companion, the parrot, who repeats Kant's own thoughts and themes on command. Obviously the parrot plays the role of the epigones who accepted and repeated Kant's philosophy thoughtlessly, without constructive skepticism. Bernhard also finds humor and satire in the fact that Kant's presence in the twentieth century is accepted as perfectly natural by his fellow voyagers. That he is not questioned by anyone shows that a madman appears perfectly normal among lunatics.

Among Bernhard's political plays, ***Die Jagdgesellschaft, Der Präsident,*** and ***Vor dem Ruhestand*** (1979, *Eve of Retirement*), the latter is the most significant. It offers a provocative challenge to the remaining secret obsession of postwar Germany with the ideology of National Socialism, its longing for the glorious past and its belief in the return of the Golden Age, the utopian millennium. Every year for the past forty years Rudolf and Vera Höller celebrate Himmler's birthday as a ritual that transcends a past historical moment to the higher order of eternal cosmic forces. Accidental occurrences and incidents that repeat themselves annually on that day give Himmler's birthday

as well as the entire National Socialist ideology a "supernatural legitimation."[47] Robert and Vera have created a symbolic universe with their Nazism, which they must protect and defend against Germany's postwar reality, denigrated as "heretical," "decadent," and "destroyed," as well as against their crippled sister Clara, a Socialist and subversive rebel to their belief. They subdue her spoken and unspoken revolt with repeated threats of institutionalization and annihilation, diminishing her by calling her perverse and crazy, and incorporating her into their universe by assigning her a role in it. She has to play the KZ-victim during their ritualistic birthday celebration. By bestowing ontological status on social roles through the process of reification,[48] all individual responsibility for past and present inhuman acts can be abandoned as inherent in the "office" held: "I only did my duty . . . I am not to be blamed for anything" (*R* 62). Their toast to "the idea, to this one idea" (*R,* 99) unites them all with Nazi sympathizers in Germany and gives this private celebration a collective dimension.

"Reduction," "scarcity," "artificiality" (*IW,* 65)—these three terms characterize Bernhard's plays. One can hardly find rounded individuals. The persons are named only according to their professions and their roles in the drama; personal names are rare. Plots are reduced to a few compulsive gestures, such as the repetitious trying on of hat and gloves by the "Good Woman" or the singing and arm raising exercises of the diva. The language, which often consists only of a few provocations, half sentences, and exclamations, has lost its power to communicate: "Language is a mathematical instrument of ideas / The poet / Rhetorician and philosopher / play and compose grammatically" (*Ber,* 48).

The artificiality inherent in the stage is carried to such an extreme that the term "head theater" ("Kopftheater") has become commonplace among the critics. Bernhard's characters are not real people but figures out of the mind of the writer who manipulates them like puppets on a string:

> As you know
> it is a
> puppet show
> not people act here
> puppets
> everything moves
> unnaturally here
>
> (*IW,* 47)

The structural principle is musical; it corresponds with the serial form of composition of the "Second Viennese School," which like Bernhard's writing is characterized by reduction, scarcity, and artificiality.[49] The musical structure follows either the classical sonata form in three movements, as in the *Jagdgesellschaft,* or rests upon the disharmony of two contrary semantic and linguistic elements, as in *Der Ignorant und der Wahnsinnige.* Besides music the other sources of inspiration for Bernhard's peculiar style are the natural sciences and mathematics: "art is a mathematical art" (**Gew,** 153). But still death alone delivers the only truly "exact work" (**Jagd,** 68).

Ever since the publication of his first novel Thomas Bernhard has written with an undiminished and indeed astonishing productivity. His works give the impression that he is trying anxiously to create order in a chaotic world. His carefully constructed sentences, mammoth in length, proceed breathlessly yet seem in their very length and complexity to forestall conclusion out of fear that the end might bring on the chaos just beyond language and thought. His novels are without plots, and his dramas are without action. However, both are rich in emotions, mostly hostile and aggressive. Both undertake to dismantle traditional forms; they are "anti-novels" and "anti-plays" with a peculiar power to fascinate. Bernhard's endless complaints about the corruption of the Austrian character, culture, and politics, his despair over the human condition, his interest in the deformities of mind and body, and his love affair with death have been called by the distinguished critic Jean Améry the pathology of the "morbus austriacus," a widespread disease of the Austrian writers' soul.[50] Trakl, Kafka, Roth, Weiss, Weininger, and Hofmannsthal were all similarly infected. But they found ways either to sublimate their morbidity or convert it into something greater than itself. In Thomas Bernhard this disease breaks out furiously; it is released, perhaps disciplined, only in the acrobatics of language and syntax. Two sentences, both in the same essay by Bernhard, establish the limits and possibilities of his work: "Death makes everything, unbearable," and "Death makes everything possible."[51]

Notes

1. Anneliese Botond, "Schlußbemerkung," *Über Thomas Bernhard,* edited by A.B. Botond (Frankfurt: Suhrkamp, 1970), p. 139.

2. Marcel Reich-Ranicki, "Konfessionen eines Besessenen," Ibid., pp. 94–99.

3. Jens Tismar, "Thomas Bernhards Erzählerfiguren," Ibid., pp. 76–77.

4. Hartmut Zelinski, "Thomas Bernhards Amras und Novalis," Ibid., p. 31.

5. Karl Heinz Bohrer, "Es gibt keinen Schlußstrich," Ibid., pp. 114–115.

6. A. Botond, "Schlußbemerkung," Ibid., p. 139.

7. Peter Lämmle, "Stimmt die 'partielle Wahrheit' noch? Notizen eines abtrünnigen Thomas Bernhard Lesers," *Text und Kritik,* 43, (July 1974), 48.

8. Ibid., p. 49.

9. Thomas Bernhard, "Rede," *Über Thomas Bernhard,* p. 71.

10. Title of a speech by Thomas Bernhard, *Neues Forum,* pp. 173, 347–349.

11. Ibid., p. 347.

12. Ibid., p. 349.

13. Walter Schönau, "Thomas Bernhards 'Ereignisse' oder die Wiederkehr des Verdrängten," *Wissen aus Erfahrungen, Festschrift für Hermann Meyer* (Tübingen: Niemeyer, 1976), p. 831.

14. Ibid.

15. Urs Jenny, "Österreichische Agonie," *Über Thomas Bernhard,* p. 108.

16. Marcel Reich-Ranicki, "Konfessionen eines Besessenen," p. 95.

17. Josef Donnenberg, "Zeitkritik bei Thomas Bernhard," *Zeit- und Gesellschaftskritik in der österreichischen Literatur des 19. und 20. Jahrhunderts,* edited by the Institut für Österreichkunde (Wien: Hirt, 1973), p. 138.

18. Erwin Koller, "Beobachtungen eines Zauberberg-Lesers zu Thomas Bernhards Roman 'Frost,'" *Amsterdamer Beiträge zur neueren Germanistik,* 2, (1973), 122.

19. Wolfgang Maier, "Die Abstraktion vor ihrem Hintergrund gesehen," *Über Thomas Bernhard,* p. 22.

20. Koller, p. 120.

21. Ibid.

22. Bernhard Sorg, *Thomas Bernhard* (Frankfurt: Suhrkamp, 1977), p. 154.

23. Günter Blöcker, "Rede auf den Preisträger," *Deutsche Akademie für Sprache und Dichtung* (Jahrbuch, 1970), p. 81.

24. Franz Stanzel, *Typische Formen des Romans* (Göttingen: Vandenhoeck, 1969), p. 33.

25. Sorg, p. 148.

26. Ibid.

27. Ibid., pp. 150–151.

28. Ibid, p. 154.

29. George Steiner and Jean Améry have proved that this course of life corresponds to Wittgenstein's biography, and they have interpreted *Korrektur* accordingly as a "Schlüsselroman." See George Steiner, "Thomas Bernhard: Korrektur," *Times Literary Supplement* (London, 13 February 1976), p. 158 and Jean Améry, "Morbus Austriacus, Bemerkungen zu Thomas Bernhards 'Die Ursache' and 'Korrektur,'" *Merkur* Nr. 332 (January 1976), 91–94.

30. Bernhard uses Heidegger's terms here intentionally when he calls Roithamer's mother "die Frau mit dem guten Wurf" (the woman with the good throw), *Korrektur,* p. 246.

31. Sorg, p. 180.

32. O.W. Vacano, "Die Etrusker in der Welt der Antike," *Rowohlts deutsche Enzyklopädie,* Vol. 54 (1957), 85; quoted from Otto Bollnow, *Mensch und Raum* (Stuttgart: Kohlhammer, 1963), p. 61.

33. See Otto Bollnow, *Mensch und Raum*; Gaston Bachelard, *Die Poetik des Raumes,* translated by Kurt Leonhard (München: Hanser, 1960); Martin Heidegger, "Bauen, Wohnen, Denken," M. H. *Vorträge und Aufsätze* (Pfullingen: Neske, 1954).

34. "Das ewige Schweigen dieser unendlichen Räume macht mich schaudern." Pascal ("The eternal silence of these infinite spaces makes me shudder").

35. Wolfgang Maier, "Die Abstraktion vor ihrem Hintergrund gesehen," A. Botond, *Über Thomas Bernhard,* p. 18.

36. Kaspar H. Spinner, "Prosaanalysen, Aus Thomas Bernhards 'Watten,'" *Literatur und Kritik,* 90 (1974), 613.

37. Herbert Gamper, "'Eine durchinstrumentierte Partitur Wahnsinn,'" A. Botond, *Über Thomas Bernhard,* p. 131.

38. Ibid.

39. See Uwe Schweikert, "Im Grunde ist alles, was gesagt wird, zitiert," *Text und Kritik,* 43 (July 1974), 1–8.

40. Thomas Bernhard, *Auf der Erde und in der Hölle, Gedichte* (Salzburg: Otto Müller, 1957), p. 60.

41. Thomas Bernhard, "Unsterblichkeit ist unmöglich," *Neues Forum,* Vol. 15, (1968), 96.

42. Quoted from James Olney, *Metaphors of Self, The Meaning of Autobiography* (Princeton: Princeton University Press, 1972), p. 263.

43. Anton Krättle, "Eine Algebra des Untergangs. Über Thomas Bernhard, 'Die Ursache' und 'Korrektur,'" *Schweizer Monatshefte,* 55 (1975/1976), 822.

44. Gaston Bachelard, *The Poetics of Space,* translated by Maria Jolas (New York: Orion Press, 1964), p. 19.

45. Herbert Gamper, *Thomas Bernhard* (München: Deutscher Taschenbuchverlag, 1977), pp. 179–181.

46. F. N. Mennemeier. "Nachhall des absurden Dramas," in *Modernes Deutsches Drama* 2 (München, 1975), p. 318.

47. Joseph Federico, "Millenarianism, Legitimation, and the National Socialist Universe in Thomas Bernhard's 'Vor dem Ruhestand,'" *Germanic Review,* Vol. 59, No. 4 (1984), 145.

48. Ibid., p. 143.

49. Herbert Gamper, p. 85.

50. Jean Améry, "Morbus Austriacus," in *Merkur,* 332 (January 1976), 92.

51. Thomas Bernhard, "Unsterblichkeit ist unmöglich," in *Neues Forum,* Vol. 15 (1968), 94.

Nicholas Eisner (essay date March 1987)

SOURCE: "*Theatertheater/Theaterspiele*: The Plays of Thomas Bernhard," in *Modern Drama,* Vol. 30, No. 1, March, 1987, pp. 104–14.

[*In the following essay, Eisner contests Bernhard's reputation as a nihilist.*]

Because of the concentration on illness, madness and death in his work as a whole, Thomas Bernhard and his work have until recently often been classified—and dismissed—as nihilistic, without further thought being given to the matter. As can be seen from a reading of any of Bernhard's texts, whether prose or drama, nihilistic is a suitable, but nevertheless incomplete, classification of this product. It is incomplete because the ease with which the nihilism is perceived leads one to suspect that it is perhaps a façade covering something else and that Bernhard might well be a poseur, "a literary figure excelling in brilliant but destructive artistry using nihilism as an expedient" rather than a "true nihilist who bases his beliefs on valid data about the world surrounding him," as A. P. Dierick has suggested.[1] And, from a similar perspective, Martin Esslin has observed that, as far as Bernhard's plays are concerned, although the themes are the same as those of his prose works, there is an atmosphere of ambivalence about them. This, combined with certain changes in style resulting from the move from prose to drama, produces what Esslin calls "a strangely disturbing effect"[2] and leads one to question the grimness and nihilism which otherwise dominate. This is especially so when one considers the complexities and ironies of Bernhard's work, which are more fully developed and thus more easily perceived in his plays than in his prose works. However, it seems to me that although Esslin pinpoints an essential element of Bernhard's plays he does little more than observe that the audience willingly subjects itself to a stream of ridicule from Bernhard. This would make Bernhard simply an aggressive and cynical writer. In performance, however, his plays have a sly, humorous air about them which belies this conclusion. Such observations raise questions regarding the contrast between the nihilism and the irony in these plays. And upon examination of this contrast we encounter an interesting and, to my knowledge, as yet overlooked feature of Bernhard's plays. It seems to me that the ambivalence and disturbing effect of these plays is not only carefully engineered to place the audience in an unusual situation, but that Bernhard has also developed a form of theatre which is in keeping with trends in (post-modern) writing in recent years which I shall examine more closely later.

The main point to note about the nihilism of Bernhard's plays—as of his prose—is that it is derived essentially from a highly repetitive style of language, which does not allow the development of plot, character and genuine dialogue. In addition to this linguistic device are the dramatic ones of portraying grotesque situations and of using visibly oppressive settings. The continued concentration on these elements and the fact that Bernhard has consistently used the same style for all of his published work has led Esslin to suggest that Bernhard is indulging in a form of mannerism. He defines mannerism as the predominance of technique over content, in which "how" becomes more important than "what."[3] This predominance of form or technique over content definitely seems to be the case with Bernhard. As far as drama is concerned, this means that it is no longer simply a literary genre, but in its very form is a physical presentation of an idea ("eine dargestellte Idee")—or in other words, the form is the idea.[4] Consequently, Bernhard's figures are merely "verkörperte Funktionen," (personified functions) used to illustrate the concept which generates them. What they are and what they say is entirely subordinated to a concept which extends beyond each individual play and which governs Bernhard's dramatic production as a whole. As such they are instruments in a performance and exposition of an idea or technique—a metaphor which is given concrete form in the figures and instruments of the play *Die Macht der Gewohnheit* (*The Force of Habit*).[5] Once it is accepted that the structure is more important than the content we can see that the nihilism of Bernhard's work—at least on the level of the expression of a personal philosophy of "Weltanschauung"—is hard to take seriously.

This is especially so when one considers the ironies surrounding his work, particularly his plays. These ironies, which seem as intentional as the static form of the monologues which dominate the plays, soften the harsh impressions of grimness and gloom which Bernhard goes to such lengths to create, so much so, in fact, that one begins to question both the purpose behind the plays and their artistic seriousness. As Hans Wolfschütz says, one ultimately realizes that:

> Bernhard's preoccupation with death is a pose in which he plays the part of the poet of death, transcending mundane social and political considerations to draw hidden treasures of truths from the shadows for all to experience. His relationship to the literary tradition, his life and work, are first and last a game played at the edge of the abyss, a game which not only reflects the loss of any objective value-system, but also the demise of that modernist view which sees the artist as the interpreter and sooth-sayer of a disjointed and fragmented world.[6]

This analysis would seem to place Bernhard firmly into the movement loosely described as post-modernism, one of whose features is the break with the traditional conventions of literary form. More specifically, considering its mannerism, Bernhard's work seems to fit into the category known as metafiction—or, more appropriately for the plays, "metadrama"—in which the conventions of narrative form are made the narrative's focal subject. In a metadrama this refocalisation is the result of the text self-consciously and systematically declaring its status as a (dramatic) artifact. In other words, it makes clear that it is a *performance* of a prepared text by a group of actors who have either rehearsed or performed this text previously. Such a performance draws attention not only to the involvement of many people beyond the actors on the stage, but also to the very nature of drama and the cultural phenomenon of theatre-going itself. In order to draw attention to its artificiality the metadramatic text replaces "the logic of the everyday world . . . [with] forms of contradic-

tion and discontinuity, [and] radical shifts of context."[7] Rather than relying on randomness or excess for this effect, metadrama depends upon a carefully constructed "tension of opposition."[8] The means of creating this tension of opposition include such techniques as irony, parody, self-reflexiveness, the "nesting" of narrative layers within each other (known as *mise en abyme*), and even the open or vaguely disguised discussion of what is being presented/performed. The use of such techniques naturally results in the lack of any final certainty in these texts. But this is actually the playwright's intention—he *wants* to make his audience aware of the doubtfulness of a sense of certainty in relation to this text and, by extension, to any literary text, so that it examines the relationship between the text and reality. As such, the status of Literature as a "sacred system" is challenged, as is the position of the Artist as an "inspirational alchemist."[9] Once these attitudes have been discarded it might seem that literature has nowhere to go and that subsequent texts will be dull, theoretical ones capable only of proclaiming their inability to comment on either literature or the world. This, however, is not the case. Rather than destroying itself, metadrama opens up the possibilities of exploring and revealing its own inherent structures and systems. Thus it not only leads to a greater awareness of what can actually be done with and in a text, but because of the uncertainty inherent in the text it also allows for the possibility of playing with an audience, of making the text a game.

As can be seen in this brief outline of metadrama there are many similarities between it and certain features of Bernhard's plays which I have already mentioned. For instance, the presence of irony in these "nihilistic" plays is contradictory and results in a sense of uncertainty—a tension of opposition; the mannerism involved in the creation of this nihilism is clearly self-conscious and appears to be structured according to a set literary programme,[10] and as a result of the combination of these two features we begin to see the "game" Bernhard is playing in which he seems to be toying with, or teasing, his audience. And as further evidence of the metadramatic and game-like nature of Bernhard's plays we can see that they embody another feature common in metafiction—self-reflexiveness. This is most obvious in the passages depicting or discussing the artist's own creative experience, but is also involved in the use of general and self-referential parody. In this last respect we can see the title figures of the plays *Immanuel Kant* (1978) and *Der Weltverbesserer* (*The World Reformer,* 1979) as (ironic) references to Bernhard himself. In the play *Immanuel Kant* the title character is not the Kant of historical fame but a madman who is celebrated as a great philosopher. And in *Der Weltverbesserer* the title figure is celebrated for his treatise on the improvement of the world, but as he himself tells us he seems to have been badly misunderstood because his plans call for the destruction of the world before it can be improved. As can be seen, there appears to be a strong element of self-irony on Bernhard's part in these two plays. Both figures are misunderstood in a similar way to which he has been generally misunderstood, but in reverse: Whereas the Kant of the play is mad, Bernhard is not, and although the "Weltverbesserer" calls for the destruction of the world, Bernhard does not. However, these are similar to accusations which have been levelled at Bernhard himself. What better way to mock his accusers than to write more plays generated by their accusations, and thus further increase his literary fame? In similar vein the title of the play *Der Schein trügt* (*Appearances are Deceptive,* 1983) can also be seen as evidence of his sense of having been misinterpreted, although it begins to appear that he wanted this to happen in the first place as it seems to be a vital part of the whole concept. Further irony is to be found in the titles of the plays *Vor dem Ruhestand* (*Eve of Retirement,* 1979), *Am Ziel* (*At One's Goal,* 1981) and *Über allen Gipfeln ist Ruh* (*Rest Beyond the Peaks,* 1981). The irony here lies in the optimism hinted at in these titles. Such optimism contrasts strongly with the nihilism which is often observed in Bernhard's work and which is to be found primarily in the continual struggle against fear and despair. Therefore, these titles would seem to be highly ironic because it simply is not possible to achieve any respite from the torments of life in his world—and none is shown in these plays.[11]

However, the most striking irony has to do with the theme of communication and seems to encompass his work as a whole. Bernhard's "nihilism" is a concept which is well worked out, and it rests largely on the problems of language as our main means of communication. As I mentioned above, Bernhard's figures are constantly struggling against fear and despair. One of the main reasons for this is that they are unable to discuss this with those around them and thus relieve their pain because language disguises the truth. Therefore, the figures must continue suffering in isolation as they are unable to communicate. According to Bernhard this is a universal phenomenon and all he is doing in his work is to portray this reality.[12] However, although Bernhard constantly denies the possibility of communication in his work as well as in interviews and speeches, he not only publishes "in steter Folge"[13] (in constant succession) but is also commercially successful both as an author and a playwright. This would seem to indicate that he is communicating to at least some of his readers and audience on some level or other, otherwise he would have been rejected long ago. In fact, this potential for understanding his work is actually built-in by Bernhard, despite his claims to the contrary.

One of the features of his work which is clearly meant to be understood is, of course, the irony itself. For example, in the play *Die Macht der Gewohnheit* (*The Force of Habit,* 1974) we have the recurrent phrase "Morgen in Augsburg" (Augsburg tomorrow). Esslin points out that this phrase carries four separate overtones within the play itself, and one which goes beyond this particular play. Within the play the phrase is used in the following ways: as an indication of the transitoriness of the present situation and of hope for the future; contempt for Augsburg as a filthy second-rate provincial city; a threat to the ringmaster Caribaldi's grand-daughter; and as the final line

in the play an admission of hopelessness and defeat. But beyond the confines of the play itself we have a further meaning, one which refers to Bernhard's basic dramatic concept. For, as Esslin notes, Augsburg is Brecht's home town and thus "exemplifies an epic theatre of plot and meaning, everything that Bernhard's theatre emphatically tries *not* to be."[14] None of these first four overtones can be felt unless we understand the rest of the play, and the fifth requires an understanding of drama history and dramatic theory. However, while this fifth overtone is less obvious, all five must be understood if they are to be effective. In fact, if the play is to be effective at all, then at least the first four must be understood—a requirement that would appear to be expected by Bernhard. As such he is contradicting himself (consciously, it seems). While he claims on the one hand that communication is not possible, on the other he implants these ironic overtones in his plays which need to be understood for these plays to be successful.

A further example of irony and the possibility of understanding it is to be found in the play *Der Präsident* (*The President,* 1975). In this play the dictatorial President of the title drinks a toast to Metternich,[15] in apparent reference to the Austrian arch-reactionary. However, to a German-speaking audience there is a further (ironical) meaning, for Metternich is also a brand of champagne—presumably the kind the President is drinking as he makes the toast. Again, although this second meaning will only be understood by those in the know, it *can* be understood and is clearly meant to be.

By way of contrast, a phrase which can be understood by everyone and not just by those in the know is the final line of *Immanuel Kant*—"Sie haben mich erkannt" (They have recognised me / They have seen through me).[16] In this play the title character is not the Kant of historical fame but a madman who is celebrated as a great philosopher and who is on his way to America to have his eyes operated on. Yet when he arrives in New York, instead of being met by doctors who are to operate on his eyes as expected, he is met by doctors from a mental hospital who take him away to their asylum. Kant's final line, therefore, is not only loaded with irony and ambiguity, but also refers back to the play itself and makes clear the true nature of Kant's "philosophy" and of the play as a whole. For this Kant is unquestionably a madman but is revered as a great philosopher because he makes such profound statements as:

> Alles was ist
> ist
> alles was nicht ist
> ist nicht
> Die Welt ist die Kehrseite
> der Welt
> Die Wahrheit ist die Kehrseite
> der Wahrheit
>
> (Everything that is
> is

everything that is not
is not
The world is the flip side
of the world
Truth is the flip side
of the truth)[17]

The play is full of such statements, which Esslin calls a "deliberate flood of derisive nonsense," and which he feels are there to test the audience's capacity to remain solemnly interested in the play.[18] Consequently, the final line can be seen as a jibe at the audience for having sat out this performance, but a jibe which depends on their having (or not having!) understood the rest of the play. The other figures in the play accept Kant as a great philosopher because of his "profound" statements. Clearly they are fools and are mockingly treated by their creator, Bernhard. By analogy, if the audience accepts Kant's supposed philosophical greatness on the strength of what they hear and see during the performance, then Bernhard is mocking them too. However—and this is the point Esslin makes—if the audience understands that Kant is mad, but waits until the end for confirmation of this, then Bernhard is also mocking them for having sat through the rest of the performance. It is this toying with the audience that finally undermines Bernhard's nihilism and makes one question the seriousness with which his plays are received and which leads us to a further re-assessment of Bernhard's play complex.

In this respect Esslin feels that the public is being confronted with a mass of horror which it believes is a reflection of itself and, because it is inclined to take such things seriously, ignores the possibility of irony and is blissfully unaware of the joke being played on it.[19] From this perspective it seems that Bernhard goes to great lengths to create a performance of such stunning grimness that, as Herbert Gamper says, the members of the audience will be left at the end "wie erschlagen" (as if thunderstruck), and "reglos in ihren Sesseln" (motionless in their seats), while he sits watching them, laughing at their failure to see the deception being played on them.[20] Consequently, because of this radical alteration in the focus of these plays, they are not simply plays in the usual sense, but what Gamper calls "Theatertheater"[21] in which the whole process of a dramatic performance—including the audience's reaction—is made the actual subject of the play, and in which the conventions and artificiality of such a performance are laid bare for examination.

This, of course, is highly metadramatic. But to support this observation we have to be able to find examples not only of elements of a "game" resulting from Bernhard's playfulness, but also of such a "laying bare" of the conventions and artificiality of a theatrical performance. For this we can turn to the figure of the playwright in *Die Jagdgesellschaft (The Hunting-Party,* 1974), who, as we shall see, is engaged in the same activity as Bernhard when he creates him and the play itself. Within the play it is the function of the playwright figure to reveal to the General the realities of the latter's existence. Working in tandem with

this is an awareness on the part of the General that the playwright is turning his life into a play—which is, of course, the one the audience is now seeing.[22] Thus the playwright is doing exactly what Bernhard claims to be doing in his plays—revealing to his audience that life is made up of illness, madness and death. Consequently it comes as no surprise when we are told that the playwright is in the process of writing a play about a similar hunting-party—one that will presumably be entitled *Die Jagdgesellschaft.* As Esslin says, there can be no doubt that this playwright clearly represents Bernhard himself.[23] Further confirmation of this self-representation is to be found in the fact that the play this figure is writing is one in which "improbable horrors are accumulated for an audience who will take them for tragedy while they are in fact parody, farce."[24] Again, it comes as no surprise that this is exactly what *Die Jagdgesellschaft* is. The "improbable horrors" which accumulate in this play all concern the General— his sight is failing, he loses his political office as a member of the Government, has his beloved wood cut down because it is diseased, learns of his wife's adultery, and hears that he is incurably ill. But, although it appears to be a tragedy, this play is actually a savage parody—of Chekhov's *The Cherry Orchard.*[25] This combination of internal self-reflexivity and external parody puts into question, if not completely destroys, the ostensibly tragic nature of this play. It is also an extremely metadramatic combination.

A similar mix of "traditional" dramatic elements combines in *Die Macht der Gewohnheit* to produce a somewhat different effect to that of *Die Jagdgesellschaft.* The basic situation of this play is obviously ridiculous—a group of circus artists attempting a perfect rendition of Schubert's *Forellenquintett (Trout Quintet)* in a circus caravan—and the possibilities of the situation are played out to the full. Therefore we have the ever-hopeful, but desperately resigned phrase "Morgen in Augsburg" recurring throughout, plus the slapstick of the clown's hat falling off and the forcing of the lion-tamer to play the piano with bandaged hands after having being mauled by his animals. As has been noted by some critics, the presence of so many humorous elements weakens the horror of the play,[26] but such criticism ignores the fact that it purposely carries the mood of the play into the realm of the absurd. However, to class Bernhard's plays as absurd is to miss what seems to me to be both their purpose and their most interesting feature. Like so many of Bernhard's plays *Die Macht der Gewohnheit* focusses on artists and one aspect of the artistic process—in this case performance. What is so remarkable about this particular play is that it is about one type of artist, the circus performer, attempting perfection in another artistic field, music, but which in turn is being performed in the theatre by yet another type of artist, an actor. It is this telescoping of the layers of performance, this sense of *mise en abyme* (also present in *Die Jagdgesellschaft*), which is important here and which adds to the metadramatic nature of Bernhard's play complex.[27]

A final example of this metadramatic use of *mise en abyme,* combined with strong elements of intertextuality and internal self-reflexivity is the play *Minetti* (1977) which was written to be performed by Bernhard Minetti, the actor who has become closely associated with Bernhard's leading roles. In this play the character Minetti is a retired actor who wants to return to the stage as the lead in *King Lear* and who, like Shakespeare's Lear, eventually dies, deserted and alone. However, just like *Die Jagdgesellschaft* this play contains—we can go so far as to say consists of—many deeper parodic self-referential elements to accompany these "surface" and intertextual ones. For instance, we have a play about a retired actor, who like Bernhard's Kant is not supposed to be identified with the real person of that name, but in the case of Minetti is intended to be played by that real person. More than this, though, the character Minetti has been duped into attending a non-existent meeting at which he was to discuss his return to the stage, but of course he is on stage all the time. These conceptual twists occur on so many levels in this play that one has to step back and take note of them before dealing with the (secondary) content of the text itself. Such complex and confusing structuring naturally leads to a sense of uncertainty about the validity of any nihilistic comments made in the text.

Although they do not all contain such clear-cut examples, many of Bernhard's plays do seem to be made up of several internal layers plus some external ones. Therefore, the particular text in question is like a Chinese box which not only has many ever smaller ones inside it, but is itself also contained within many ever larger ones. Our smaller boxes are the internal references of the text (such as the playwright writing the play in which he is presently appearing, in *Die Jagdgesellschaft*) and the larger ones are the intertextual references (such as to *The Cherry Orchard* or *King Lear*) and, extending beyond that, the whole concept of drama, literature and, especially in the case of Bernhard, to the theatrical nature of life itself.[28] Therefore, in this structure of Chinese boxes the members of the audience are no longer passive observers of a performance of a dramatic text, but have been drawn into a never-ending cycle of active participation. It is only when we distance ourselves from Bernhard's texts that we can see the whole process: Bernhard plays out the "game" so consistently and successfully that we must do this to see the whole process from start to finish—from the commencement of writing, through the actors' rehearsals, to the actual performance—which includes the procedure of people buying tickets and going to the theatre, etc.—and beyond, to the critical response to this performance. All of this becomes the subject of Bernhard's plays, not just what is printed in the text. Consequently, the audience is just as much the subject of each performance as the text itself. This means that it will have difficulty in interpreting the play it is attending because it is too close to this deceptive core to have a broad enough critical perspective to assess the whole. Because of this the audience tends to come to the conclusion that Bernhard is (deadly) serious and to say that his nihilistic plays are a metaphor for man's tragic condition. However, if we step back and look more deeply into the ironies and structural layers of these plays, we can

see that this reaction has been carefully engineered by Bernhard: It is the result of what Esslin calls the serious-minded "consumers of culture"[29] having been unwittingly drawn into the centre of the "game," from which position they can only superficially interpret his theatrical work. As such, Bernhard cannot be classed as a nihilist. Prankster would be more apt, for he has perfected a form of drama in which the audience is no longer a passive observer, but is the active subject and victim of a gigantic hoax.[30]

Notes

1. A. P. Dierick, "Thomas Bernhard's Austria: Symbol, Neurosis or Expedient?" in *Modern Austrian Literature,* 12 (1979), 74.

2. Martin Esslin, "A Drama of Disease and Derision: The Plays of Thomas Bernhard," in *Modern Drama,* 23 (1981), 378.

3. Martin Esslin, "Ein neuer Manierismus? Randbemerkungen zu einigen Werken von Gert F. Jonke und Thomas Bernhard," in *Modern Austrian Literature,* 13 (1980), 111.

4. See Manfred Jurgensen, *Thomas Bernhard. Der Kegel im Wald oder die Geometrie der Verneinung* (Bern, 1981), p. 37.

5. See Herbert Gamper, *Thomas Bernhard* (Munich, 1977), p. 82.

6. Hans Wolfschütz, "Thomas Bernhard: The Mask of Death," in *Modern Austrian Writing. Literature and Society after 1945,* eds. Alan Best and Hans Wolfschütz (London, 1980), p. 230.

7. Patricia Waugh, *Metafiction. The Theory and Practice of Self-Conscious Fiction* (London and New York, 1984), pp. 136–137.

8. Ibid.

9. Ibid. See the above quotation from Wolfschütz for a remarkably similar comment in relation to Bernhard's writing.

10. See Dierick, p. 73.

11. See Thomas Bernhard, "Nie und mit nichts fertig werden," in *Deutsche Akademie für Sprache und Dichtung. Jahrbuch* (1970), pp. 83–84. The irony of Bernhard's titles is evident in the prose-work too. For instance, the unusually positive title of the novel *Ja* is left unexplained until the last few lines when it is revealed that this was the answer given by a now dead woman, whose recent suicide is the inspiration for the content of the book, to the question as to whether she would ever contemplate taking her own life. See Wolfschütz, p. 229.

12. Bernhard's poetological standpoint is formulated most clearly in three speeches given in the late 60s. These are recorded in the following places: *Neues Forum,* 15 (1968), pp. 347–349 (two together); and *Deutsche Akademie für Sprache und Dichtung. Jahrbuch* (1970), pp. 83–84 (see note 11 above).

13. See Wendelin Schmidt-Dengler, "Thomas Bernhard" in *Deutsche Literatur der Gegenwart in Einzeldarstellungen Bd.2* ed. Dietrich Weber (Stuttgart, 1977), p. 74.

14. Esslin, "A Drama of Disease," p. 374. If this is the case then this fifth overtone would seem to be a key to Bernhard's whole dramatic concept.

15. Thomas Bernhard, *Der Präsident* (Frankfurt am Main, 1974), p. 125.

16. The German is intentionally ambiguous here. Although both of these meanings are implied in the German there is no suitable equivalent for this one phrase in English.

17. *Immanuel Kant* (Frankfurt am Main, 1978), p. 46. Translation by Esslin, "A Drama of Disease," 381.

18. Esslin, "A Drama of Disease," 382.

19. Esslin, "Ein neuer Manierismus," 125.

20. Gamper, p. 151; Esslin, "A Drama of Disease," 378–379, and "Bernhard and Beckett: A Comparison," in *Modern Austrian Literature,* 18 (1985), 77.

21. Gamper, p. 151.

22. See Esslin, "Beckett and Bernhard," 75.

23. Esslin, "A Drama of Disease," 376.

24. Ibid., 382.

25. See Esslin, "Beckett and Bernhard," 75.

26. See, for example, Gamper, p. 160, and Franz Norbert Mennemeier, "Nachhall des Absurden Dramas," in *Modernes deutsches Drama. Kritiken und Charakteristiken. Bd.2: 1933 bis zur Gegenwart* (Munich, 1975), pp. 319–320.

27. The play *Über allen Gipfeln ist Ruh* may be considered a "crossover" in this respect. Rather than focussing on theatrical production or performance like *Die Jagdgesellschaft, Der Ignorant und der Wahnsinnige* (*The Ignoramus and the Madman,* 1972), or *Die Macht der Gewohnheit,* this play concerns the efforts of an egomaniacal prose-writer (Bernhard?) who has just completed a tetralogy. This figure spends the play talking about the difficulties of writing this tetralogy—which seems to be about just that, the difficulties of writing a tetralogy. As such it is very much like *Die Jagdgesellschaft* in its sense of *mise en abyme.*

28. On the theatricality of life in Bernhard's world see Thomas Bernhard, "Nie und mit nichts fertig werden," Esslin, "Beckett and Bernhard," 74, and Gita Honegger, "Acoustic Masks: Strategies of Language in the Theater of Canetti, Bernhard, and Handke," in *Modern Austrian Literature,* 18 (1985), 63.

29. Esslin, "A Drama of Disease," 382.

30. A version of this paper was presented to the CAUTG section of the Learned Societies Conference in Winnipeg on 3 June 1986, under the title "Manipulating the Audience—Thomas Bernhard and the Art of Metadrama."

Rüdiger Görner (essay date 1988)

SOURCE: "The Excitement of Boredom—Thomas Bernhard," in *A Radical Stage: Theatre in Germany in the 1970s and 1980s,* edited by W.G. Sebald, St. Martin's Press, 1988, pp. 161–73.

[*In the following essay, Görner asserts that "the question of what sustains the individual, given the overwhelming sense of pointlessness, is one of the main concerns in Thomas Bernhard's dramatic works."*]

'Sometimes boredom was unobtrusive and sometimes nauseating and when I could no longer stand it', Sartre wrote in his autobiographical essay *Les Mots,* 'I would succumb to the deadliest temptation. Orpheus lost Eurydice through impatience; I often lost myself through impatience.'[1] There can be no doubt that ennui has become one of the most debilitating and chronic afflictions of our age. Moreover, the diagnosis is now almost as commonplace as is the syndrome. All needs seem to be satiated, all unknown terrain has been explored, all taboos have been broken. The disillusionment is complete. Only inveterate humanists like the psychoanalyst Bruno Bettelheim will still speak out publicly against the *ennui général* and maintain that human life is not pointless.[2] Such claims, however, have become curiously dated. By the same token, the recognition that ennui is one of the most pervasive phenomena of post-industrialist society is no longer merely the prerogative of the cynic. Sartre's statement is not just meant as a verdict, it marks the moralist's position and holds out the hope that ennui might become productive if it were to lead to self-analysis, that it is not necessarily a depraved form of self-love as another Frenchman, André Glucksmann, suggested.[3] The question of what sustains the individual, given the overwhelming sense of pointlessness, is one of the main concerns in Thomas Bernhard's dramatic works. This is not a mere coincidence but an integral part of Bernhard's artistic message. His play **Am Ziel** focuses on a dramatist who feels quite unable to create a truly dramatic situation—in the classical sense of the word. If there is any tension, it is only in the accounts of how the characters try to extract themselves from the tedium of their lives. Not surprisingly, Bernhard's young dramatist makes his debut with a piece entitled 'Save yourself if you can'.

Bernhard's own first play, **Ein Fest für Boris,** set the tone for a whole sequence of dramatic sketches, all of them characterised by a feeling of futility so irredeemable that it borders on the grotesque. The protagonist in **Ein Fest für Boris** is the embodiment of this mood. She is disabled but her handicap seems only to have increased her resoluteness and her thirst for power. Despite her indefatigable will, this monstrous female, like most of Bernhard's dramatis personae, is subject to fits of excessive boredom: 'Everything', she says, 'is just a daily grind, day after day, a repeating of repetitions.'[4]

In his *Ethics* Aristotle argued that living to a set pattern was one of the preconditions for a virtuous life. Nothing could be further removed from Bernhard's position. For the latter-day characters in Bernhard's plays, reduced and exhausted as they are, the habitual is sheer hell. Their lives are made up of a series of 'blue Mondays', days of repentance one might say, for blue used to be the colour of repentance in medieval times. But what is it that they repent? Nothing less, it seems, than their own presence, reprehensible to themselves, in this world of unrelieved boredom. They know that the curse which prescribes the endless repetition of the same can only be broken if they turn around to take a last look at Eurydice, at the burning Gomorrah or, as Sartre would have put it, at their own madness.[5]

In Bernhard's scenarios we encounter people weighed down by depression. Their virtual immobility has nothing to do with a calm or composed state of mind, rather it is marked by acute inhibition and extreme fretfulness. Most of his characters suffer from mental and/or physical defects. They are hypochondriacs, dissatisfied and eccentric individuals, failures who have lost all sense of direction. Their only true possessions are their anxieties and their madness and perhaps their hatred of those equally as pathetic as they are themselves, with whom they share their lives.

Nietzsche's counterpoint to his own vitalistic aspirations, the idea of 'eternal recurrence of the same', is unfolded into a complete pathology of autistic behaviour in Bernhard's plays. One of Bernhard's characters, Moritz Meister, summarises this connection as follows: 'Nietzsche Stieglitz and back again you understand . . .'.[6] And back again—from one artificial world into another equally artificial one. In *Ein Fest für Boris* the possibilities of coming to terms with such limitations are reduced to a single idea, a veritable *idée fixe*. The crippled and ostracised characters who make up the cast of this play 'constantly wonder what kind of / suicide / would be the most bearable one'.[7] Whatever reaches these people from the outside is immediately transformed into a litany of repetitions. Thus, in *Ein Fest für Boris,* 'The Song of the Wagtail' is meant to bring hope to the crippled outcasts, but they receive only its somewhat sombre refrain which becomes the signature tune of their meaningless lives. 'In the dark, in the dark / it has ceased to fly.'[8] In this world steeped in *taedium vitae* the word 'change' is unknown. Everything is dominated by an irreconcilable hatred, a hatred which absorbs all energies. Whether Thomas Bernhard shares his characters' by now almost proverbial hatred is a moot point. It is clear, however, that he seems to try and free himself from his pent-up resentments through incessant writing and it remains to be seen whether his literary excesses will prove more therapeutic than his characters' monomaniacal pursuits.

In Camus's *Etat de Siège* Diego exclaims at one point 'I prefer hatred to your smile. I despise you'[9]—a statement which could be adopted to describe Bernhard's fraught relationship with his native Austria. Apart from his preoccupation with the monstrosity that is human life, it is primarily Austria and the Austrian past which compel Bernhard to write; his relationship with his native country is clearly determined by a double bind. The emotional pressure generated by this constellation is, however, balanced by an extra-ordinary degree of formal control. Bernhard's cascades of words are by no means the result of random verbal proliferation. The method of composition is that of 'a musician in words', to use Busoni's characterisation of Rilke. The dramaturgic principle behind Bernhard's scenes—in both senses of the word—is a kind of serialism in words which, almost by definition, tends towards an eternal monologue. Bernhard likes to structure these monologues by inserting the phrases 'on the one hand . . . on the other hand . . .'. Unlike Kierkegaard's famous existentialist challenge *Either . . . Or,* the pseudo-alternatives thus introduced do not oblige the characters to make up their minds, but provide a mechanism which allows them to encircle their pet hatreds again and again.

It goes without saying that Bernhard rejects the amorphous Austrian myth which is propagated, with differing degrees of intensity, by writers such as Schnitzler, Hofmannsthal, Stefan Zweig and Joseph Roth. Bernhard's resentment centres on what he sees as an unreflected, opportunistic glorification of a defunct past which gave rise to one of the most despicable collective aberrations of this century. Compared with Bernhard's relentless onslaughts, Hofmannsthal's critique of language looks positively tame and timid and even Schnitzler's discoveries in the field of social psychology seem no more than an innocuous divertissement.

There is no indication in Bernhard's work that he is interested in a sophisticated critique of language of the kind developed by other contemporary playwrights such as Botho Strauss or Peter Handke. The destructive diatribes into which Bernhard's characters almost habitually launch themselves assault the audience and in this they are reminiscent of the earliest position adopted by Handke in his play *Publikumsbeschimpfung*. These recurrent verbal assaults are rehearsals for a rebellion that can never really be unleashed because its champions are emotionally attached to the objects of their hatred.

Nor are Bernhard's plays based on plots in the accepted sense of the term. When the curtain rises we are presented with a situation which became petrified and irredeemable a long time ago. It is clear from the outset that nothing will give any more. The characters, perfectionists of despair, will keep on going through their motions. They no longer even entertain the hope that they might be liberated by a sudden turn of events or at least a *coup de théâtre*. Bernhard provides scarcely any stage directions. The settings are bare: last resorts, much like the minimal environments of zoos in which animals eke out the remainder of their lives.

Despite these singularly unattractive facets of Bernhard's dramatic works, they have acquired an absolutely devoted following. In their complete faithfulness Bernhard enthusiasts almost resemble the congregation at Bayreuth. Yet there is a difference. Wagner's music has frequently been described as an addictive drug. Bernhard's tirades, however, could be said to be infused with poison. Amazingly, though, the audience gobbles up the unwholesome meal, knowing that it is virtually indigestible. At the end, when paralysis has set in all round, Bernhard himself occasionally appears upon the stage where, having subjected the audience to his venom throughout the evening, he takes a deep bow in front of those whom he so unremittingly despises. Hatred has become an ornament, part of a complex game of double standards which culminates, appropriately, in a gesture of utter malice, a sort of silent monologue on the theme of contempt.

But let us return to what the plays actually do articulate. No matter who is holding forth in Bernhard's plays, the speeches invariably revolve round certain grandiloquent terms which seem to act as stabilisers in a linguistic realm threatened by centrifugal forces. 'Life', 'fear', 'death', 'art', 'science', 'the state', 'the world', 'nature', 'everything' and 'nothing'—these wholesale concepts are invoked in Bernhard's rhetorical effusions but are never differentiated or tested against any concrete reality. As hypostatised notions they are the cornerstones in monologues employed as a means to power by those who are both ignorant and impotent. This is what Bernhard's plays demonstrate in a unique way. Monologue stands for arrogance or presumption and, ultimately, for tyranny.

Hardly any writer since Thomas Mann has dedicated himself so exclusively to the subject of art as has Thomas Bernhard. What is the place of art or its message in this agonising pandemonium which we call life? Can it provide a measure of diversion or relief in this tiresome gamut of repetitions? These are questions which Bernhard and his characters ask obsessively and to which—quite naturally, as Bernhard would say—there can be no answer. On the one hand, Bernhard presents art as the object of repetitive exercises which wear everything down. An instance of this is the farce *Die Macht der Gewohnheit* in which a number of oddly assorted musicians try—in vain—to produce a passable rendering of Schubert's *Forellenquintett*. On the other hand repetition is seen as the object of art, for example when one of the characters in *Die Berühmten* mocks the eternal recurrence of the same by imitating the voices of animals.

Inscribed in Bernhard's plays is, therefore, not only a pathology of the eternal recurrence of the same but also a pathology of the arts which is revealed through a visit backstage. In *Der Ignorant und der Wahnsinnige,* one of the central figures is the 'Queen of the Night', a world famous soprano who has sacrificed her personal life and become one with the role she has sung so many times. Through constant practice she has completely mastered her art, at the price of her own humanity—she has turned into an art machine. Her outlook is jaded. 'We know all operas / all plays / we have read everything / we know all the most beautiful places / and secretly we hate the audience.'[10] It is the selfsame feeling of ennui at the endless recurrence of both natural and artificial phenomena that not only inspires Bernhard's writing but has, in fact, become its substance. The repetitive pattern so completely dominates Bernhard's style that there is no appreciable difference between his prose and his dramatic language. And whatever the theme, it is subjected to the same stylistic treatment. Bernhard's readers know after the first few words that they are reading Bernhard. It almost seems as though, out of a deep-seated fear of anonymity, Bernhard feels compelled to assert his identity by cultivating his extremely mannered and unmistakable style.

Although Bernhard does put the patience of his audience to the test by presenting it with his unending variations on the theme of pointlessness, this does not mean that he is incapable of inventing profoundly moving scenes. His short piece *Minetti* comes to mind, a play at the centre of which there is a clapped-out actor in his late seventies who is reduced to day-dreaming about the great roles of the dramatic repertoire. He still entertains the hope that the artistic director of the Flensburg Theatre, not exactly the focal point of West Germany's cultural life, will engage him to play King Lear. But it is obvious that nothing will come of such dreams. Minetti is finished. Only the ability to survive on the absolute minimum fulfilment of his wishes keeps him going. That and a substantial dose of hatred which he vents by denouncing his own origins: 'The place where one is born is one's murderer.'[11]

Claus Peymann once remarked that in each of Bernhard's plays the bourgeoisie is made to perform a *danse macabre.* At the same time Peymann referred to the almost 'classical' aspects in Bernhard's works for the stage. The terminal decline of the bourgeoisie and the desire for self-sacrifice which the classical line of development suggests, complement and permeate each other in bizarre arabesques. Peymann argues that the more complex and idiosyncratic Bernhard's plays are, the more they demand a realistic and literal production, a meticulously straight transposition of 'the text'.[12] Peymann, however, ignored his own prescriptions when he produced *Die Jagdgesellschaft.* Where Bernhard wanted to see trees in the hunting lodge, Peymann put them outside and, in consequence, distorted the meaning of the play at that particular point. Bernhard knew what he was alluding to. After all, there is only one scene in the history of European drama where trees form part of an interior setting representing the unity of inside and outside world: the hunting lodge in *Die Jagdgesellschaft* is intended as a reference to Hunding's abode in *Die Walküre.* Bernhard, who is given to quoting his own chapter and verse, repeating, almost compulsively apodictic statements from earlier works, also likes to quote the great names and works of the past. Quotations of this sort reveal the artistic heritage as a sham. Travesty remains the only possible answer. Yet the comic elements which arise from the destruction of exalted precedents provide no more of an answer than did the aborted tragedies. Bernhard's point and counterpoint never lead to any kind of resolution. The contradictions are patently irreconcilable.

A central paradigm of this is perhaps that of health and sickness. In Bernhard's plays, those who are able-bodied and enjoy seemingly everlasting health, generally display fascist or crypto-fascist traits. On the other hand, moral and intellectual superiority is predicated upon physical handicaps. 'My paralysis is possibly / the cause of my 'genius', speculates' the eponymous hero in *Der Weltverbesserer*,[13] and in *Vor dem Ruhestand* Rudolf tells his sister who is paralysed but intellectually far superior to him: 'Only your crippled state / gave you the chance to survive.'[14] Misfortune in Bernhard's plays is compounded because 'healthiness' is a state no less chronic and incurable than most severe forms of paralysis.

Pathological deformations wherever one turns. It is this state of affairs that informs Bernhard's highly charged, extremist diction of which Ingeborg Bachmann said: 'Bernhard's words are full of pathos, if we still know what this term originally meant, full of sorrow and suffering.'[15] True, there is a great deal of authentic pathos in Bernhard's language but also much eccentric ranting. His characters quite literally talk everything to pieces. The objective correlative of these exercises in dissolution is the debris of culture. Herr von Wegener, the ultra-conservative journalist in *Über allen Gipfeln ist Ruh,* serves up the following hotch-potch: 'This reminds me of Kierkegaard / Enten Eller / Either Or / even this giant up there in the North / what we have in him is our Liszt as philosopher / as aesthetic and ethical thinker living in desperation / I am convinced it was your husband's attachment to Kierkegaard / that made him into the extraordinary man / he is today / And at one point in the Germania novel he actually speaks / of My inner Copenhagen.'[16]

Bernhard's characters continue to function as language machines even though they have long since died an inner death. Their words, generated by the resounding emptiness inside them, are as redundant as their atrophied lives. For the audience the point of fascination lies in the question as to how long these wretched creatures will be able to endure themselves, let alone others. In *Der Präsident* the president's wife seems to have reached the end of her tether. Outraged by her husband's favourite pastime, she exclaims: 'He is reading Metternich / nothing but Metternich / Metternich / Metternich.'[17] Clearly, it is repetitiveness that renders everything absurd and that is the cause of the stalemate the characters have reached. Bernhard's plays are, essentially, about stalemates. There is no room for manoeuvre. The pattern is broken only occasionally when the characters discover something 'new' that will preoccupy them for a while, distract them from their pedantic rituals. In *Der Präsident* the temporary relief is provided by a game called 'being afraid of anarchists'. At last there is something to talk about. Paranoia as a new lease of life. Not that this leads anywhere. The excitement subsides, doleful silence sets in.

There is also a different kind of silence in Bernhard's plays, the silence of those who at one point in their lives appear to have encountered something like 'meaning', who got to know themselves and others (a horrifying experience, according to Nietzsche). Clara's silences, in *Vor dem Ruhestand,* are a means of revenge. By simply not saying anything, Clara makes the rules of a game which implies incestuous feelings between Rudolf and Vera, her brother and sister. The emotions escalate because of Clara's persistent silence and eventually lead to Rudolf's death. Vera's reaction: 'You are to be blamed / you and your silence / you and your endless silence.'[18]

Whether Clara really is guilty remains an unresolved point. She is guilty in one sense because through her relentless silence she literally extinguished her brother; and in another because she failed to inform the authorities that Rudolf was a committed fascist. The two forms of guilt cancel and compound each other, a prototypical Bernhard paradox. This is as close as Bernhard ever gets to making concrete allegations. The crimes of his protagonists are anonymous. Of course those who were (and are) fascists are despicable. But those who resisted passively and claim some kind of moral superiority are not any less despicable for all that. They are all in the same family. Philosophically, the vigour of Bernhard's pessimism owes much to Schopenhauer; in terms of dramaturgic dispositions it is influenced by the recognition that the most debilitating influence on our lives is the family bond, as the play *Ritter, Dene, Voss* with its echoes of Chekhov demonstrates. In Bernhard, the dream of love between brothers and sisters, which bourgeois culture both relegated and secretly entertained, has finally come to an end. We are all united now—not by our love but by the pathetic beastliness which Bernhard identifies as being the hallmark of the human condition in our age.

When boredom regularly turns into hatred and hatred into boredom the main purpose of the exercise seems to be an exposition of the *élan négatif.* Paradoxically, the idea of negativity in Bernhard's plays is often introduced by characters who say 'yes' to everything. Yet they only appear to represent what has been termed by Marcuse 'affirmative culture'; in fact they only say 'yes' because they have lost all interest in a critical investigation of the conditions of their lives.

Those who take a critical stance do so compulsively and to the point of self-caricature. Bernhard's *Weltverbesserer* represents this particular type of character deformation. We are given to understand that he has elaborated a complex scheme for wide-ranging and general improvements but we do not learn anything about its actual content. The constant references to 'factual logic' and the manifest desire to undermine the conventional suggests that the *Traktat zur Verbesserung der Welt* is a cross between the *Tractatus-logico-philosophicus* and the *Steppenwolf.*

Many of Bernhard's characters dream of a self-liberating revolt, of subversion and anarchy; but they are too weak to translate their dreams into practice. The 'mother' in Bernhard's scenic eschatology *Am Ziel* is an example of this. She tries to break free from her personal prison by talking ceaselessly; she talks until she comes to feel a certain strength that might enable her to change her life. Even so she needs additional support from someone else. The prop in her case happens to be a young writer who describes himself as an anarchist. But he too is capable only of *talking* about anarchism and ultimately the curious pair's options are limited to the destruction of their own mirror images.

Nietzsche once characterised the theatrical world of his time by saying that it reflected both the utter boredom that governed society and its frantic search for distraction.[19] Bernhard's stage characters do not even know the difference between ennui and *divertissement* any more. Pain and pleasure have merged, forming an erratic bloc that serves as pedestal for negativity. Despite this pronounced tendency towards petrification Bernhard's plays undeniably generate an element of excitement, chiefly because the author contrives to construct a kind of *machina ex deo,* that is to say he creates a sense of mechanical repetition which might, or so the spectator is made to believe, eventually wear itself out and be replaced by something yet to come. However, this messianic 'something' never materialises. Prophecy, for Bernhard, has lost its enigma and turned into the enunciation of platitudes like 'Death completes / life'.[20]

Bernhard's at once elliptic and rambling style poses special problems for his interpreters. Vast generalisations of deliberate imprecision obscure rather than reveal meaning. The characters' monologues have, for the most part, a cyclic structure, but the circles never become hermeneutic. Nor does it help to take the temporal and spatial structures in Bernhard's plays as points of reference since both space and time are of minor importance in his stage works.[21] Bernhard shows people who might be anywhere, at any time, going through their motions; there is no sense of teleology, no indication of where we are at. All calendars have been suspended, the roads are no longer passable. Condemned to remaining at home with nothing to relate to but their own company Bernhard's characters lose all sense of proportion, of nearness and distance. It is indicative of this state that outsize conjectures and myopic observations are virtually interchangeable. Reasoning under these circumstances becomes a kind of dunces' game, a form of banishing the fear of darkness and any attempt to create order is reduced to the counting of steps and similar rituals of regularity and security.

It is for these reasons that interpreters of the roles Bernhard has written often find it difficult to provide more than approximations of uncertainties. They inherit the disorientation of the characters and in order to find their way about they have to look for hints other than those given by the traditional meaning of words. They have to sense the various degrees of imbalance between how much is said and what is said. Moreover the varying rhythms have to

be considered as well as the ever-changing relationships between the mass of spoken words and the sudden silences that break into the 'dialogue'. A passage from *Die Jagdgesellschaft* illustrates this point.

> WRITER. [*pouring a glass of sherry for himself, another one for the Generalin and returning to the window*]
> Two hours of Lermontov
> and then another two hours of Lermontov
> GENERALIN. Or two hours of Majakowski
> and then another two hours of Majakowski
> WRITER. Or Pushkin
> All of a sudden I remembered that aphorism
> It is stillness puts things right
> But I did not come back
> Nothing but that phrase It is
> Stillness puts things right
> *after a pause*[22]

Both Writer and Generalin follow, to begin with, the same rhythmical pattern indicating the identity of their mood and view. When this pattern breaks up (after 'Or Pushkin') there appears to be a sort of prospect of change, but it remains unrealised since the aphoristic fragment which comes to the Writer's mind itself produces a different pattern, both in terms of rhythm and of thought. The sudden silence which then sets in renounces the idea expressed in the wistful phrase though this scarcely makes an appreciable difference in the oblique exchanges between the two characters.

An endless comedy of words, reminiscent perhaps of Arthur Schnitzler and his verbal relativism as expressed in his *Komödie der Worte.* The lines of tradition connecting Austrian playwrights are fairly pronounced and it is therefore not surprising that in Schnitzler's *Stunde des Erkennens* we come across the following passage:

> ORMIN. We do not wish to take the words
> too seriously, do we.
> KLARA. Take them as seriously or
> literally as you like.[23]

This extract would be an apposite motto for most of Bernhard's plays, except that Bernhard, in contrast to Schnitzler, has stripped his particular brand of verbal relativism of any residual human feeling and hope. Schnitzler had always reserved for himself the right to sketch into his dialogues faint glimmers of hope, even in plays like *Der einsame Weg* where he introduces people who are very tired of life and surrounded by a deep sense of melancholy.

Despite (or because of) his relativistic use of language, Bernhard frequently employs the vocabulary of ontology but, as would be expected, with parodistic inflections. The linguistic relics of Existentialism are presented as alien, erratic verbal blocs that will not fit into any rhythmic scheme. We hear of 'the becoming of the being' and of 'the being of the becoming' and realise what it is that attracts Bernhard to these resoundingly vacuous concepts.

They allow him to demonstrate how the language of (Heidegger's) existentialism, which serves as a paradigm for all corrupted language, spins out of control, generates more and more words and almost buries the questions of life which gave rise to philosophical investigation in the first place. Much of Bernhard's indefatigable hatred stems from his awareness that he has to work with a totally spoiled language; at the same time there is, as with any other writer, the sheer love of expressing himself. This love-hate relationship with language results in a form of rhetorical invective which, in contrast to Dürrenmatt or Ionesco, avoids all metaphors. Metaphors throughout Bernhard's plays are replaced by obdurate repetition, a device which refers the audience to the one and only truth of the 'eternal recurrence of the same'. The objective correlative of this is the experience of boredom documented in literature since the early nineteenth century. Büchner's *Lenz* believes boredom to be the cause of all human actions, emotions and thoughts: 'Most of us pray out of boredom, others fall in love out of boredom, some are virtuous and some are evil—only I am nothing, nothing—I do not even feel like doing away with myself; it really is too boring!'[24] Any of Bernhard's stage characters could have said that too. Each of them is his own organ-grinder whose mind is gnawed by his repetitive tune. All fantasies and dreams have been abandoned; the great myths are defunct. Bernhard does not try to revive them. If he alludes to them at all—as for instance in **Die Jagdgesellschaft** where he evokes memories of the myth of nature—the attempt reminds one of a coroner's inquest. The indictment inherent in this is that the very nature of life has changed, that life no longer lives but has become a simulation of something we have long since lost and gambled away.

Notes

1. Jean-Paul Sartre, *Words,* trans. Irene Clephane, Harmondsworth 1986, p. 152.

2. In *The Listener,* 24 April 1987. See also Viktor E. Frankl, *Der Mensch vor der Frage nach dem Sinn,* Munich 1980, pp. 180–86.

3. *Frankfurter Allgemeine Zeitung,* 27 March 1987.

4. 'Alles ist jeden Tag tagtäglich / eine Wiederholung von Wiederholungen', Bernhard, *Die Stücke 1969–1981,* Frankfurt 1983 (henceforward *DS*), p. 12.

5. *Words,* p. 152.

6. 'Nietzsche Stieglitz und wieder zurück verstehen Sie . . . !, *DS,* p. 281.

7. 'Wir denken fortwährend darüber nach auf welche Weise / der Selbstmord / für uns am erträglichsten ist', *DS,* p. 67.

8. 'Im Finstern im Finstern / sie fliegt schon lang nicht mehr', *DS,* p. 68.

9. Paris 1948, p. 29.

10. 'Wir kennen alle Opern / alle Schauspiele / wir haben alles gelesen / und wir kennen die schönsten

Gegenden auf der Welt / und insgeheim hassen wir das Publikum', *DS,* p. 116.

11. 'Der Geburtsort ist der Mörder des Menschen', *DS,* p. 581.

12. Claus Peymann, 'Mündliches Statement zum Thema: Thomas Bernhard auf der Bühne'. In *Literarisches Kolloquium Linz 1984: Thomas Bernhard,* ed. A. Pittertschatscher and J. Laichinger, Linz 1985, p. 191.

13. 'Möglicherweise ist meine Lähmung / die Urheberin meines Genies', *DS,* p. 912.

14. 'nur mit deiner Verkrüppelung / hattest du eine Überlebenschance', *DS,* p. 739.

15. Ingeborg Bachmann, *Thomas Bernhard.* In *Werke,* vol. IV ed. C. Koschel, I. Weidenbaum and C. Münster, Munich and Zürich 1978, p. 364. ('Sie sind voll Pathos, wenn man noch weiß, was dieses Wort wirklich bedeutet, sie sind voll Leiden, und die Erträglichkeit und Unerträglichkeit hängen damit aufs Engste zusammen.')

16. 'Dazu fällt mir Kierkegaard ein / Enten Eller / Entweder Oder / selbst ein derartig im Norden Ringender / hier haben wir Liszt als Philosophen / Asthetiker und Ethiker und Verzweiflungsmenschen / Ich glaube die Kierkegaardbeziehung Ihres Mannes / hat ihn zu dem Außerordentlichen gemacht / der er heute ist / An irgendeiner Stelle im Germaniaroman steht ja auch / Mein Kopenhagen des Geistes,' *DS,* p. 868.

17. *DS,* p. 383.

18. 'Du bist schuld / mit deinem Schweigen / du mit deinem ewigen Schweigen', *DS,* p. 792.

19. *Werke,* vol I, Munich, Vienna, Berlin 1978, p. 410.

20. 'Der Tod komplettiert / das Leben', *DS,* p. 377.

21. This is in contrast to his prose. In *Beton* and in *Wittgenstein's Neffe,* for instance, space is of great importance.

22. SCHRIFTSTELLER. [*schenkt sich ein Glas Sherry ein, auch der Generalin, und er geht wieder zum Fenster zurück*] Zwei Stunden Lermontow / und dann wieder zwei Stunden Lermontow

   GENERALIN. Oder zwei Stunden Majakowski / und dann wieder zwei Stunden Majakowski

   SCHRIFTSTELLER. Oder Puschkin / Auf einmal fiel mir der Aphorismus ein / Die Ruhe macht es wider gut / Aber ich kam nicht wider / nur immer Die Ruhe macht es wieder gut / *nach einer Pause*', *DS,* p. 177.

23. *Das dramatische Werk,* vol VII, Frankfurt 1979, p. 21.

   ORMIN. Wir wollen die Wörte nicht gar zu schwer und wichtig nehmen.

   KLARA. Nehmen Sie aut so wichtig und / wörtlich als Sie wollen.

24. *Lenz,* trans. Michael Hamburger, Chicago 1972, p. 56.

Stephen D. Dowden (essay date 1991)

SOURCE: "Bernhard as Playwright," in *Understanding Thomas Bernhard,* University of South Carolina Press, 1991, pp. 71–84.

[*In the following essay, Dowden asserts that for Bernhard's plays to be fully understood and appreciated, they should be considered in light of how they were performed as well as the conditions surrounding their performance.*]

The last Thomas Bernhard drama to premiere was *Elisabeth II.* The play was published in 1987 and appeared on the stage two years later, at the Schiller-Theater in Berlin in November 1989, nine months after Bernhard's death. The play was vintage Bernhard—hard-bitten, uncompromising, and musical—but Claus Peymann, Bernhard's usual director, did not stage the production; the usual Bernhard stars (Bernhard Minetti, Bruno Ganz, Edith Heerdegen, Paula Wessely) did not participate; and the master himself was dead. The play was a failure with the public and the critics. Somehow the fire had gone out.

The reasons seem clear enough. Bernhard's dramas are not intended to be masterpieces. They are immediate and direct, sensational and spontaneous, tied to time, place, and even to particular actors. The plays are brief spectacles that pierce the heart of a transient mood and then die. When read, Bernhard's works for the stage seem thin and ephemeral in comparison with his prose fiction. They lack the concentrated intellectual energy that he lavished on his novels. Though it does not ring true at all, Bernhard spoke of the theater dismissively, even disparagingly: "The curtain goes up, there's a dungheap on the stage, more and more flies show up, the curtain goes down." In addition, he claimed that his prose works did not produce much income ("press runs of only a few thousand copies, as is the case with unknown beginners"). He referred to his plays, with the attendant nuance of triviality, as moneymakers. And Bernhard did not have a great deal of respect for the theater or for theater people (with certain exceptions; e.g., the actor Bernhard Minetti)—or at least that was his claim.[1] Nevertheless, he wrote eighteen full-length plays and a number of brief dramas between 1967 and 1989, and he had two more unfinished plays on his desk when he died. His works for the stage were highly successful in German theaters during the 1970s and 1980s. For them to be understood properly, two basic features must be considered. The plays should be seen in the light of performance, first of all, but also in the context of their then contemporary setting.

Bernhard's musical verbal style—always stripped of punctuation and printed on the page with the appearance of verse—is a difficult medium that calls for a special dec-

lamatory performance. Only the finest actors, those trained in classical theater, can make Bernhard's theater work. "In my opinion drama is primarily a matter of language," says Bernhard; "of course there is also the theater of somersaults, where people flipflop around, constantly running in and out of doors, deciding fates every few minutes. . . . My dramas are different. You have to listen. My drama evolves slowly, out of the language itself, and by that I do not mean my personal experience but my idea of dramatic literature."[2] Minetti is the master of Bernhardian language. But in the hands of lesser actors, even actors who work well in the conventional stage idiom, Bernhard's plays seem bloodless and dull. *Einfach kompliziert* (*Simply Complicated,* 1986), to name only one of many possible examples, was a monologue written with Minetti in mind. And in fact Minetti's performance of the piece was mesmerizing. Still, the fascination does not carry over into reading. The play becomes flat, even boring, because the music has evaporated and because Minetti's strong stage presence is missing.

Die Jagdgesellschaft (1974; translated as *The Hunting Party,* 1980) is another example of the relative fragility of Bernhard's theater writing. It was the first of Bernhard's plays to be performed at Vienna's venerable Burgtheater. The play had been written, according to Bernhard, with Bruno Ganz and Paula Wessely in mind. Unfortunately, the Burgtheater ensemble objected to outsiders performing lead roles in the play. Because he was bound by contract, Bernhard reluctantly (to say the least) let the Burgtheater cast the play. In Bernhard's opinion, and in the critics' opinions, the play was a flop, though by all accounts the Burgtheater is one of the finest theaters in the German-speaking world.

Bernhard considered himself an actor's dramatist. As he said on more than one occasion, he wrote plays intending to offer his actors the opportunity to unfold their talents. In fact, he often wrote for specific actors, and above all for Bernhard Minetti. *Minetti: Porträt des Künstlers als alter Mann* (*Minetti: Portrait of the Artist as an Old Man,* 1976) is unabashedly a vehicle for the talent of Bernhard's favorite actor. *Ritter, Dene, Voss* (1984; translated as *Ritter, Dene, Voss,* 1990) was written and named for actors in Claus Peymann's troupe: Gert Voss, Kirsten Dene, Ilse Ritter. Works so closely tied to specific actors and troupes easily droop and fade when performed by other actors in places not attuned to the intellectual fashion of following Bernhard, the celebrity playwright, and Peymann, the celebrity director.

But there is yet another element of performance that must be considered: that of Bernhard himself. I suggested that one reason for the failure of *Elisabeth II* in Berlin was its author's death. In a wider sense than acting on the stage, Bernhard contributed to the "performance" of his works. Even before the 1970 premiere of his first play, *Ein Fest für Boris* (translated as *A Party for Boris,* 1990), he had a reputation for cantankerous behavior and a scorched-earth tactics in satirical writing. His public was eager to see what powerful figure he would insult next, what enraged outcry he would elicit, who would try to sue him, and how he would respond. To put it baldly, Bernhard's plays were also media events.[3] In 1972, for example, *Der Ignorant und der Wahnsinnige* (The Ignoramus and the Madman) premiered at the Salzburg Festival. Bernhard insisted that for symbolic effect the house lights should go out at the end of the play, fire exit signs included. The fire marshal refused; the festival authorities refused; Bernhard insisted; and the whole incident became histrionically inflated with articles, heated exchanges, and telegrams.

Die Berühmten (*The Big Names*) caused a similar flap in 1975. The Salzburg Festival commissioned Bernhard to write a play for its 1976 season. But when festival officials learned that Bernhard was writing a play that lampooned the big names associated with the Salzburg Festival, they reneged. The usual spate of public and private letters, angry accusations and newspaper editorials ensued. Observers thought that Bernhard's association with the Salzburg Festival had surely come to an end. Astonishingly, he was again invited to write for the festival in 1981 (*Am Ziel* [*The Goal Attained*]) and in 1984. In *Der Theatermacher* (1984; *Histrionics,* 1990) Bernhard satirized himself and the fire exit episode of 1972.

But theater and art as such also come under attack. According to Bruscon, the protagonist of *Histrionics,* human beings are liars and hypocrites, "and nowhere else in this humanity / is the falseness greater and more fascinating / than in the theater." Bruscon, who is an actor, "says that theater is an absurdity":

> but if we are honest
> we can't put on a show
> nor can we if we are honest
> write a stage play
> or act in a stage play
> if we are honest
> we can't do anything anymore
> except kill ourselves
> but since we don't kill ourselves
> because we don't want to kill ourselves
> at least not up to now and not so far
> so since we have not up to now and not so far killed
> ourselves
> we keep giving the theater another try[.]

Now, Bruscon's attitude is not exactly in the spirit of the Salzburg Festival tradition. It is ironic that Bernhard was ever invited to write plays for the festival at all. Given the undisguised aesthetic nihilism of Bernhard's writing, the Salzburg Festival seems an unlikely setting for his attack on the premises of the Western theatrical tradition.

The festival was established in 1920 by dramatist Hugo von Hofmannsthal, composer Richard Strauss, and stage director Max Reinhardt as a symbol of Austrian national identity and spiritual unity. The gradual disintegration and final collapse of the Habsburg empire after World War I created a vacuum in the Austrian sense of national identity.

Robbed of a continuous political history, intellectuals sought to renew for Austria its historical legitimation and self-definition by way of the artistic tradition. Hofmannsthal, Strauss, and Reinhardt specifically were attempting to reconnect a war-battered Austria with itself through art.[4] Cultural unity was to compensate for military defeat and political dissolution.

Music and theater lent themselves well to the task of refashioning Austrian identity because cultural ideals seemed fixed beyond the contingencies of history: the Catholic tradition of Austrian baroque that Hofmannsthal worked to renew in his dramas and libretti; the music of Mozart and Beethoven, and the new compositions of Strauss; the stagecraft of Vienna's brilliant director Max Reinhardt employed to renew the classics. In the high-flown rhetoric of Richard Strauss, the festival was to be "a symbol filled with the light of truth and the reflected glory of our culture. All Europe shall know that our future lies in art. . . . In times during which the possessions of the spirit are rarer than material goods and during which egoism, envy, hate and mistrust appear to rule, he who supports our proposition will have done something good and helped to reestablish brotherly love and human kindness."[5] It is instructive to compare Strauss's post-World War I pathos with Bernhard's post-World War II bathos:

> The spirit of Salzburg therefore is throughout the year the *perverted* spirit ["*Ungeist*"] of Catholicism and National Socialism, and the rest is a lie. In the summertime under the name of the Salzburg Festival, the city hypocritically affects a pose of universality, and the medium of so-called international art is only a means of disguising the perversity of its perverted spirit, just like all the summers here are fakery, hypocrisy, attempts at setting to music and playing away [the perversity] of a city and its residents who during the summers misuse so-called Great Art for vulgar ends of commerce, the Festivals are put on in order to cover up the mire of the city.

His words here could serve as a gloss on the plays he wrote for the Salzburg Festival.[6] Of them the most characteristic is probably his comedy entitled *Die Macht der Gewohnheit* (1974; *The Force of Habit,* 1976). It, too, satirizes the Salzburg Festival, but with more finesse than *Die Berühmten*. Bernhard repackages the festival as a small and shabby family circus. As always the idea of family echoes the idea of nation. At its center is Caribaldi (originally played by Minetti), the paterfamilias and circus director, who for twenty-two years has been trying to extract a perfect performance of Schubert's *Trout Quintet* from his inept circus performers. They, the performers, have neither talent nor interest. Even Caribaldi's hopes have faded, yet the ill-tempered tyrant continues to enforce a regimen of daily rehearsals on the unwilling quintet. Caribaldi speaks here to his juggler:

> The truth is
> I do not love the cello
> It tortures me
> but it has to be played

my granddaughter does not love the viola
but it has to be played
the clown does not love the bass violin
but it has to be played
the lion tamer does not love the piano
but it has to be played
And you do not love the violin
We do not want life
but it has to be lived
We hate the Trout Quintet
but it has to be played[.]

In this play, which was composed especially for the festival, Bernhard is speaking primarily to the Salzburg Festival audience, to its participants, and to the festival authorities. What has kept the music alive all these years in Salzburg, he asserts, is only the force of habit. The grand festival is at bottom a small-time family circus undone by ineptitude and chaos. Thus *The Force of Habit* embodies one of Bernhard's two basic themes in drama: the failure of art to redeem the individual, the nation, the family, or anything else. Art, like life, is a burden borne unwillingly.

The other fundamental theme is historical. Bernhard confronts the problem of the Nazi past with great directness, especially in *Vor dem Ruhestand* (1979; *Eve of Retirement,* 1982) and *Heldenplatz* (1988). Both plays were directed by Claus Peymann, and they excited a great deal of controversy. Bernhard favored the ensemble of the avant-garde director, who staged nearly all the Bernhard premieres. Along with other self-willed directors of the period (e.g., George Tabori, Peter Stein, Peter Zadek), Peymann bucked the prevailing taste of West German theater in the 1970s for conservative productions of the classics on the one hand, and for politically committed Brechtian theater on the other. His productions emphasized directorial imagination and interpretation. Bernhard's plays, with minimal stage directions and a tendency toward the outrageous and offensive, suited his talents well.

Bernhard wrote *Eve of Retirement* for Peymann in 1979, at a time when West Germany was in the grip of a conservative wave of reaction to terrorist acts by the Red Army Faction and the Baader-Meinhof gang. Peymann, who at that time was the artistic director of the Staatstheater in Stuttgart (capital of Baden-Württemberg), had long been criticized by the conservative politicians of the Christian Democratic Union. His theater, like most German theaters, was heavily subsidized by the state, and its leading politicians wondered if its money was being well spent by the avant-garde director. Not the least of his critics was the Minister President of Baden-Württemberg, the outspoken law-and-order conservative Hans Karl Filbinger.

Apart from their general dislike of his theater, a particular incident irritated the state authorities. In 1977 Peymann was approached by the mother of convicted terrorist Gudrun Ennslin. She asked the theater director to solicit contributions on behalf of her daughter who, while imprisoned in a maximum security facility near Stuttgart, needed some expensive dental work. Peymann posted a notice on the Staatstheater bulletin board, which soon caused an uproar in the papers and in conservative political circles. Some branded Peymann a sympathizer with the terrorist cause, while others (notably Stuttgart mayor Rommel) supported his right to solicit funds for anyone he wanted as long as it was legal. Minister President Filbinger and his allies eventually forced Peymann to resign as artistic director of the Württembergisches Staatstheater.

But Peymann's main detractors soon found themselves in an awkward position. In July of 1978 it was discovered that Minister President Filbinger, whose name was being passed around the Christian Democratic Union as a potential presidential candidate for the whole of West Germany, had long concealed his sordid activities as a naval judge during and after the Second World War. At issue were the numerous death sentences he handed down as a zealous agent of Nazi justice, including capital sentences for trivial offenses. In a pattern that the Austrian presidential candidate Kurt Waldheim would repeat in the 1980s, Filbinger at first lied stubbornly about ever having given out death sentences at all. When the truth became incontrovertible, Filbinger—incredibly—tried to trivialize their importance. After vigorous persuasion by his embarrassed colleagues in the Christian Democratic Union, Filbinger finally resigned his post and retired from politics.

The Filbinger affair unfolded and was completed before Peymann's resignation as artistic director in Stuttgart took effect. As his swan song he had planned to stage Rolf Hochhuth's docudrama *Die Juristen* (The Lawyers), which was based on the Filbinger affair. But when Hochhuth failed to meet the deadline, Peymann staged Bernhard's *Eve of Retirement* instead (June 1979). While Bernhard's drama is not directly based on the Filbinger case, it is best understood as a response to the controversy that affair aroused and the public issues that it raised.

The play's subtitle, "A Comedy of the German Soul," gives a good indication of what Bernhard was attempting, even if his "comedy" is not funny. As always Bernhard is interested in plumbing the inner realm of outward events, which means in *Eve of Retirement* an unblinking exploration of German repression of the past. Filbinger represented for Bernhard, and many others, a larger German failure to reckon adequately with the meaning of National Socialism. Particularly galling, obviously, was the rise of the Nazi hanging judge to a place of wealth, prestige, and public trust in a democratic country that had putatively settled with its past. Filbinger served as a symbol for the pernicious continuity between past and present in Germany, and at a time when state policy on terrorism had brought to a seeming impasse the conflict between the government (represented in the authoritarian person of Filbinger himself) and individual rights. Bernhard responded with a glimpse into the family life of a Filbinger-like German chief justice on the eve of his retirement from the bench.

The domestic scenes of his family life stand for the private, taboo, repressed past of a whole nation, the "German soul" of Bernhard's subtitle. On the seventh of every October, Justice Rudolf Höller and his two sisters, Vera and Clara, have for decades secretly celebrated the birthday of SS chief Heinrich Himmler. Höller had served as a concentration camp commandant under Himmler during the war, and remembers those days with warm nostalgia. Champagne, a fine meal set to strains of Mozart and Beethoven, and a ramble through the family photo album begin an evening that is peppered with Höller's demented tirades against Jewry, Americans, and democracy.

Once the Höllers have finished wallowing in memories of National Socialism, the chief justice and his sister Vera top off the evening by retiring to bed for their annual session of incestuous lovemaking. The other sister, Clara, belongs to the ranks of Bernhard's oppressed and powerless female characters. She does not share the obscene pleasures of her brother and sister. Clara sympathizes with democracy and socialism, but she cannot defend herself against Rudolf and Vera. Clara is an invalid, bound to a wheelchair as a result of an American bombing mission during the war. The voice of liberal reason in "the Höller family" is unable to assert its rights.

Eve of Retirement succeeds as satire because it ruthlessly probes the open wounds of German consciousness and historical identity. Not only do its characters speak the unspeakable, but they do so in a blood-chilling matter-of-fact way that lends to the play its eerie, even frightening nimbus of authenticity. "Who would have thought it Vera," says Rudolf as he cheerfully ponders his life since the war:

> Times change so much
> First ten years of hiding in a miserable cellar
> hidden by you and Clara
> then all of a sudden this change for the better
> I don't have a bad conscience
> Now and again things look dark that is still true today
> but I don't have a bad conscience
> I should be the last one to have a bad conscience
> I only did my duty
> and I spared no effort
> I went to work and got more done
> than anyone could have demanded
> I spared no effort
> I find nothing to fault myself for[.]

Höller's clean conscience, which is Bernhard's satirical image of German national consciousness, is harrowing. Still, Bernhard does not become a political playwright with *Eve of Retirement.* He offers no positive vision of critical reason, which he embodies in the sad and permanently disabled Clara.

The vitriolic rage that Bernhard pours into his play is not that of a liberal intellectual committed to a politics based on the application of critical reason. Instead, Bernhard's views are those of a *moral anarchist.* Intellectual liberals—especially those associated with the influential Hamburg weekly journal of opinion *Die Zeit*—followed

Bernhard closely and sympathetically for the most part, and Bernhard frequently published in their pages. They shared his critically incisive views on Germany's past (and Austria's), and they encouraged the discussion that his irreverent books and plays generated. But in spite of the intellectual company he kept, Bernhard himself remained a moral anarchist: "anarchical" in the sense that his views represent a moral revolt against the natural tendency to forgive and forget with the passage of time. "I always take up the subject of those dreadful times," writes Bernhard of the Nazi era, "but people just shake their heads. In me these terrible experiences are just as present as if they had been only yesterday." Bernhard refuses to accept the passage of time and its process of forgetting (and healing) because it is ethically unacceptable. His revolt has nothing to do with a systematic platform of ideas and values that could be translated into a political agenda. Bernhard's ethical standards stem from an internal moral absolute that is personal and hopelessly pessimistic, one that knows no compromise, no forgiveness, and no political praxis outside of literature.

Nevertheless, certain of Bernhard's works have a political, social, and historical dimension with implications for political life, as the editors of *Die Zeit* plainly understood. Apart from *Eve of Retirement* the most important of them is his final published drama, *Heldenplatz,* written for the Burgtheater, which in 1987 had come under the leadership of Claus Peymann. Bernhard wrote the play for a double occasion. The year 1988 marked not only the hundredth anniversary of Vienna's Burgtheater; it was also the fiftieth anniversary of Hitler's triumphant arrival in Vienna. On 15 March 1938 Hitler spoke before throngs of Austrians jubilant over their country's annexation to the prosperous Third Reich. Vienna's Heldenplatz, which is only a short walk down the Ringstrasse from the Burgtheater, was the scene of Hitler's speech.

In *Heldenplatz* Bernhard grinds salt in the open wound of Austrian anti-Semitism. "The situation is much worse now than fifty years ago" is a refrain that recurs throughout the drama with awful insistence. The play concentrates on a group of Austrian Jews—in an apartment near the Heldenplatz and the Volksgarten, within sight of the Burgtheater—who have gathered in March of 1988 for the funeral of Professor Josef Schuster. Five decades earlier the Nazis had driven the philosopher Schuster into English exile because he was a Jew, but after the war, now a famous Oxford professor, he was coaxed back to his native Vienna. Ultimately, however, he found Austria intolerable, and committed suicide shortly before he had planned to return permanently with his wife to England.

His wife is the key to Bernhard's less-than-subtle theme. Frau Schuster suffers acutely from the inability to forget. In Vienna she still hears the raving masses of 1938 from the nearby Heldenplatz. In this context Bernhard's personal view about the Third Reich bears repeating once more. "In me," he says, the terrible experiences of the Nazi era "are just as present as if they had been only yesterday." Frau

Schuster embodies his rejection of time. Even electrotherapy at Steinhof, the local mental institution, has not obliterated her vivid memories of persecution and dehumanization. From Bernhard's perspective her madness is a form of moral sanity.

Basically, the death and funeral that serve as the drama's focal point represent the end of Austria. Schuster is not so much an Austrian *Jew* as an *Austrian* Jew. The persecution of Austrians by Austrians signals the inward collapse of whatever spirit once made the concept of Austria cohere—an empire of multiple nationalities and races—into a cohesive whole. The Austrian in Schuster makes life elsewhere an impossibility, and Austria itself makes life in his homeland an impossibility. The conflict is strongly reminiscent of the impasse experienced by the essayist Jean Améry, which he writes about in his penetrating memoir *At the Mind's Limits* (1966). Bernhard may or may not have had the Austrian émigré philosopher in mind when he invented Schuster. Even if he did not, the parallels are too revealing to pass over without discussion.

Améry is an anagram of Maier, the name he was born with in Vienna in 1912. Hans Maier's father was an Austrian patriot, a Jewish soldier who died fighting for Emperor Franz Joseph in World War I. His mother was a German Austrian. Hans Maier never thought much about his Jewishness until the Nuremberg Laws of 1935 cut through the middle of his identity. His Jewish blood suddenly transformed him into an alien in his own homeland, whether he liked it or not. With the incorporation of Austria into Nazi Germany, Maier fled to Belgium, where he became a member of the underground resistance. He was captured in 1943, tortured by the Gestapo, and eventually interned in a series of concentration camps, including Auschwitz. But Maier survived, and then tried to shape a new identity for himself in Belgium as Jean Améry—philosopher, journalist, photographer.

During the 1970s Améry became a well-known figure in German and Austrian intellectual life. Without surrendering to the sentimentalities of the holocaust industry that was beginning to flourish, he expressed his resentments and hatred of what the Germans and Austrians had done to him with precise insight. It is not without relevance that Améry wrote approvingly of Bernhard's memoir *The Cause* and his novel *Correction.*[7] But what seems most important is the attitude of permanent resentment that the two writers share. Like Bernhard, Améry refuses to let bygones be bygones. Neither writer believes that true progress has been made in the postwar era. Despite the best efforts of right-thinking Germans and others, writes Améry with sober pessimism, "Hitler's Reich will, for the time being, continue to be regarded as an operational accident of history." He continues:

> Finally, however, it will be purely and simply history, no better and no worse than dramatic historical epochs just happen to be, bloodstained perhaps, but after all also a Reich that had its everyday family life. . . . The former general staff officer Prince Ferdinand von der

Leyen writes, ". . . from one of our detachments came even more horrible news. SS units had broken into the houses there and from the upper floors they had thrown children, who were still unable to walk, through the windows onto the pavement." But such murder of millions as this, carried out by a highly civilized people, with organizational dependability and almost scientific precision, will be lumped with the bloody expulsion of the Armenians by the Turks or with the shameful acts of the colonial French: as regrettable, but in no way unique. Everything will be submerged in a "Century of Barbarism." *We,* the victims, will appear as the truly incorrigible, irreconcilable ones, as the antihistorical reactionaries in the exact sense of the word, and in the end it will seem like a technical mishap that some of us survived.[8]

Bernhard's most horrific inventions pale by comparison with Prince von der Leyen's report. But comparison also suggests a possible spiritual source for Bernhard's teratology of the German soul. Like Jean Améry, Bernhard seems incorrigible in his animus against Austria, irreconcilable to history and therefore "antihistorical" in his refusal to let the passage of time do its work of healing. *Heldenplatz,* however rude and mean-spirited it may seem, forces a moral confrontation between past and present—and all the more so in Vienna during the amnesiac presidency of Kurt Waldheim.

There is one other significant link between Améry and Bernhard. It is the resemblance between Améry and Josef Schuster (and Franz-Josef Murau of *Auslöschung*). Améry never really freed himself of his Austrian identity. He changed his name and his country, but he continued to write in his native language, the language of the oppressors; like it or not, his cultural and intellectual background remained Austrian-German, even though he was morally unable to identity with the nation that had driven him into exile, murdered his kind, and robbed the survivors of the right to feel at home in their own past, in their own language, and in their own culture. In 1978 Améry returned to Austria, and in fact to Bernhard's hometown of Salzburg, evidently for the express purpose of hanging himself. He did not explain his reasons for taking his own life, yet it is difficult not to connect his suicide with the resentments, losses, and hatred that he expresses in *At the Mind's Limits.*

Schuster's leap from his apartment window in *Heldenplatz* (and Frau Schuster's sudden death at the end of the play) can be interpreted from the perspective of Améry's suicide. Schuster was not at home in England so he came back to his native Austria, but he discovered that it could no longer be his home. The past, symbolized as a home with a view of the notorious Heldenplatz, was too much for both husband and wife. One actively takes his own life, and the other simply collapses under the strain of life among the people who had once tried to destroy her, her family, and her entire race.

Understandably, Austrian Jews, a tiny minority in present-day Austria, did not greet Bernhard's play with enthusiasm.

Some objected to the apparently self-righteous Thomas Bernhard, a non-Jew, arrogating to himself the right to speak out against Austria in their interest. To make matters worse, Kurt Waldheim's sordid campaign for the presidency of Austria and his subsequent election in 1986 left a residue of anti-Jewish sentiment among some Austrians. The last thing an Austrian Jew needed was a wildly accusatory drama by Thomas Bernhard stirring up anti-semitic feelings. Of course it would be a mistake to suppose that Bernhard intended to speak on behalf of the Jewish community. No doubt he identified to a certain extent with Austrian Jewry; their fate belongs to his basic idea of the way Austria deals with its children. But the more compelling reason for his portrayal of Jews in contemporary Austria must have been his anarchic morality. Always intransigent in his ethics, always eager to make himself known at any cost, Bernhard was willing to offend anyone—and everyone—in the interest of a bitter moral truth.

Bernhard's theater was total theater, especially in Austria. It transcended the stage and spilled over into the streets. Hardly a soul, it seemed, was left uninvolved in the histrionic controversy around **Heldenplatz.** As one of the characters in the play puts it:

> What remains to this poor disenfranchised people
> is nothing but the theater
> Austria itself is nothing but a stage
> on which everything is ruined squandered and wasted.

Trouble began early, when it was announced that Bernhard was working in secret on an offering for the Burgtheater jubilee. Objections were raised at the choice of Bernhard to write for the occasion at all, but also against Claus Peymann, a West German, dominating Austria's most historically important theater. Originally the play was scheduled for an October 1988 debut. But when excerpts appeared in the press, a public scandal erupted. Some of the Burgtheater ensemble refused to participate in Bernhard's drama, which resulted in the premiere being postponed until November.

The public furor around the production was astonishing.[9] Politicians fulminated against Bernhard's anti-Austrian play and against the "waste" of public funds on his works. Kurt Waldheim denounced the play as "a vulgar insult to the Austrian people." There were demonstrations in the streets against Bernhard and his play. His supporters, too, staged demonstrations of their own against the opponents and in support of the play. Heated exchanges occurred in newspapers, coffee houses, and living rooms all over Austria. Poison pen letters and even death threats were sent to both Bernhard and Peymann. But the play went on.

Heldenplatz was the last Bernhard play to appear on the Austrian stage. In February of 1989 Bernhard died of Boek's disease (sarcoidosis) but not without fomenting a posthumous scandal. When his will became public, it was learned that Bernhard had made a strange entailment: none of his books is to be published in Austria and none of his

plays is to be staged there for the duration of his copyright, seventy years. As the news of his will spread in Austria, there was an immediate run on his works in bookstores.

Notes

1. Kurt Hofmann, ed., *Aus Gesprächen mit Thomas Bernhard* (Vienna: Löcker, 1988) 78–79.

2. Quoted in Jens Dittmar, ed., *Thomas Bernhard Werkgeschichte,* 2d rev. ed. (Frankfurt am Main: Suhrkamp, 1990) 231.

3. Because they were difficult to read and had a smaller following, his novels did not lend themselves to the same media excitement as his plays. The notable exception was *Cutting Timber,* which generated the kind of circus that was common for the plays.

4. Michael P. Steinberg has written an illuminating history of the festival: *The Meaning of the Salzburg Festival: Austria as Theater and Ideology 1890–1938* (Ithaca: Cornell University Press, 1990).

5. Walter Pankofsky, *Richard Strauss: Partitur eines Lebens* (Munich: Piper, 1965) 235.

6. *Der Ignorant und der Wahnsinnige,* Salzburg Festival, 29 July 1972; *Die Macht der Gewohnheit,* Salzburg Festival, 27 July 1974; *Die Berühmten,* Vienna, Theater an der Wien, 8 June 1976; *Am Ziel,* a co-production of the Salzburg Festival (18 Aug. 1981) and the Bochum Schauspielhaus (22 Oct. 1981); *Der Theatermacher,* a co-production of the Salzburg Festival (17 Aug. 1985) and the Bochum Schauspielhaus (21 Sept. 1985); *Ritter, Dene, Voss,* a co-production of the Salzburg Festival (18 Aug. 1986) and the Burgtheater in Vienna (4 Sept. 1986).

7. Jean Améry, "Morbus Austriacus," *Merkur* 30 (1976): 91–96.

8. Jean Améry, *At the Mind's Limits: Contemplations by a Survivor on Auschwitz and Its Realities,* trans. Sidney Rosenfeld and Stella P. Rosenfeld (New York: Schocken, 1990) 79–80.

9. Jens Dittmar offers a representative selection of the responses in his indispensable *Thomas Bernhard Werkgeschichte* 330–37.

William E. Gruber (essay date 1994)

SOURCE: "Mental Life in Thomas Bernhard's Comic Types," in *Missing Persons: Character and Characterization in Modern Drama,* The University of Georgia Press, 1994, pp. 108–54.

[*In the following essay, Gruber provides a psychological analysis of Bernhard's characters and surveys his literary techniques.*]

> Answer M D's and Mrs. Dingley's letter, Pdfr, d'ye hear? No, says Pdfr, I won't yet, I'm busy: you're a saucy rogue. Who talks?
>
> *Journal to Stella*

What time is it No don't tell me what time it is. . . .

It is good that you are there and that you are listening
to me We are a conspiracy.

Ein Fest für Boris

Of character in the works of Thomas Bernhard one might
say what Claude Rawson said once of character in Swift's
satires, that discussing it led only to "deserts of circularity."[1] Certainly the figures in Bernhard's plays are as
stupidly and savagely hostile as any of Swift's cannibals,
clergy, or politicians, and, like Swift's characters, they
profess with heartfelt conviction the most appalling
opinions. Sadists, megalomaniacs, pedophiles, Nazis-in-
exile—no mask, no manner of hatred, no gross violation
of culture or common decency is too outré for Bernhard to
dramatize; as a matter of fact, his characters' irrational
viciousness seems to be the main source of their popular
appeal. No human nor any human institution escapes
Bernhard's scorn; his plays, like Swift's works, are wildly
implausible satires of folly and madness.

Nothing in Bernhard's work or life, so far as I am aware,
links his art directly to Swift's; in fact, Bernhard's explicit
denials that his art means anything or has any practical
consequences differ radically from Swift's express interest
in righting social wrongs. But there is much room for
instructive comparisons between the two writers, whether
in their running and bitterly polemical feuds with their
respective countries and compatriots or in their wholesale
misanthropy or, finally, in their preference for literature
that is both funny and mad. And there are legitimate correspondences of literary form: for example, the apparent
instability of Swift's "I" has long been a question central
to Swift studies, and in analogous fashion the plays of
Bernhard highlight problems with character similar to
those that I have been pursuing in this study. Chief among
these is the question of the speaker's responsibility for apparently personal or self-expressive statements. Who talks?
Is it the speaker or the discourse? That is to say, are
characters' words supposed to express the original thoughts
of discrete individuals or are they more on the nature of
borrowings (quotations, echoes, repetitions, imitations)
whose use defines character ironically, as it were, from
without?

Bernhard's stance toward his own work is instructive here.
Even though Bernhard's personal investments in his
characters' utterances are everywhere apparent—many
plays, for example, include characters whose diatribes
against Austria and Austrians resemble Bernhard's own—
more often than not those authorial commitments are
impossible to specify very precisely. In an early novel, for
example (*Der Italiener*), we encounter a narrator who
says, "In my work, if I see the signs of a story developing
anywhere, or if somewhere in the distance between the
mountains of prose I spot even the hint of a story beginning to appear, I shoot it. It is the same with sentences: I
have the urge to take entire sentences and annihilate them
before they can *possibly* take shape."[2] Which is (as Bern-

hard surely knew) almost precisely what Nazis liked to
say of "culture": "When I hear the word 'culture,' I reach
for my Browning."[3] A character speaking an author speaking a Nazi propagandist: how does one come to terms with
such intimidating abysses of personation? How does one
distinguish the voice of the author from those of his
represented personae?

Most of the problems one encounters reading Bernhard's
plays have to do in some way with interpreting the stance
of the speaker toward his or her words, problems therefore
in some sense with character, for the actors in Bernhard's
plays (unlike Beckett's actors) are not discouraged from
inventing psychological subtexts for their various speeches.
On the one hand, Bernhard has insisted repeatedly that he
writes nonnaturalistic theater; on the other hand, as we
have seen in the work of Beckett, to abandon naturalistic
or novelistic portraiture as a means of *representing*
character under no circumstances means abandoning
character. Even in Beckett's most expressly formal works,
where actors cannot imitate specific personalities, character
indelibly stains the work. *Quad,* for example, has apparently been stripped of agency, and yet agency clearly
remains as the central problem. To reiterate for the sake of
emphasis, ruling out psychological modes of portraiture
does not automatically erase an audience's sense of
individual psychology, let alone their sense of character;
as Gordon Craig long ago discovered, simply to place a
living actor on stage is to create a powerful illusion of
character. "We need to confront the fact," says Charles Lyons, "that the image of character in space and time
constitutes an irreducible aesthetic unit."[4]

Because his plays demand what Stephen Dowden calls "a
special declamatory performance," Bernhard has frequently
been described as a philosophical playwright.[5] His plays
often have been compared to music or to geometry, but
hardly ever to nature. In America especially it has become
customary to see Bernhard's characters as puppets or
abstractions or, more recently, as "pithed" souls for whom
language is the sole source of being. Gitta Honegger
(among others) finds in Bernhard compelling evidence for
lost subjectivity:

> The idea of language as a mechanism that sets us in
> motion and keeps us alive, that provides the cues and
> patterns for our actions, the notion of the loss of the
> subject, although accepted in theoretical discourse is
> very hard to introduce to the American theater with its
> deeply engrained belief in psychological motivation as
> the basis for a character throughline which must be
> unbroken and free of contradictions.[6]

It has been clear from the beginning of this study that the
study of character in drama cannot be separated from
modern discourse such as Honegger alludes to about the
nature of the self and personal identity. Much modern
criticism of literature has documented the dwindling
emphasis (if not the vanishing) of the individual, the
authentic subject, the coherent character. In the case of
Bernhard, for example, Dowden writes that "the weight of

the self always turns out to be inconsequential."[7] I would argue, in contrast, that Bernhard's plays are a good deal more hospitable to character than is normally supposed. This is a proposition that will have to be tested over the course of the chapter; in the main, I will follow two related lines of thought. I want to discuss Bernhard's characters in ways that describe as fully as possible their mental landscapes, and I want also to see what remains to be said of character when the usual stage criteria for identifying ethos, namely, the illusions of autonomy and authenticity, have been discarded.

Until recently nearly every person to write on Bernhard's dramas has stressed a direct relationship between his austere style and his flat characters. For most readers, Bernhard's extreme formalism all but eliminates individual personalities and egos. Thus Martin Esslin:

> [There] is no genuine dialogue in Bernhard because his chief characters are entirely enclosed in separate inner worlds. There are no love scenes or love interests in any of Bernhard's works—narrative or dramatic— because monologue does not allow genuine interaction between human beings. Any interaction that takes place is thus purely mechanical, as that between puppets. Bernhard's earliest dramatic efforts were written for marionettes. He regards and deliberately designs his characters as basically no different from puppets— simply because he is convinced that people in real life are, with very few exceptions, barely conscious, let alone able to act otherwise than as merely propelled by mechanical instincts and reflexes; that, in fact, living human beings, in the mass, are no better than marionettes."[8]

Or Nicholas Eisner:

> The main point to note about the nihilism of Bernhard's plays—as of his prose—is that it is derived essentially from a highly repetitive style of language, which does not allow the development of plot, character, and genuine dialogue. . . . Bernhard's figures are merely "verkörperte Funktionen," (personified functions) used to illustrate the concept which generates them.[9]

Or Denis Calandra, who writes that Bernhard and his "chief exponent," Claus Peymann, "share a concern with the purely linguistic features of their dramas, to the neglect of conventional plot and rounded character."[10] Even Stephen Dowden, who cites individuality as one of Bernhard's principal themes, rules out any concern on Bernhard's part with his characters' affective psychologies: "[P]sychology is beside the point in Bernhard's hyperconscious world because what he aims to capture in his fiction—for the imagination alone can capture it—is the spirit of the conscious intellect as it vies with death for supremacy."[11] Bernhard's figures, says Dowden, are not psychological but allegorical. Not only do they "lack psychological depth," but "[t]hey exist more as personified ideas than as plausibly imagined people."[12] "Bernhard operates," he continues, "under the assumption that we cannot fathom the true interior of a human being. . . . The self is

unique and so cannot be described in conventional language. It is a hidden process, ephemeral and unfathomable as a whole."[13] Such assumptions about "flat" and "round" characters, in particular the notion that subjectivity belongs to the latter but not to the former, are hypotheses about character that I want to question by examining some of Bernhard's plays.

A TRAGEDY OF HUMORS

Bernhard seems to have needed no apprenticeship in playwriting; his first play (*A Party for Boris, Ein Fest für Boris,* 1968) provides the model for nearly all that follow. In this and other works, characters seem to lack internal structuring; rather than existing as discrete individuals, they seem bound together into relational units in which emotional intimacy is assumed but rarely dramatized. To an audience these relationships give the appearance of being mechanical or possibly theatrical because the people involved so clearly do and say things they have said and done before. In such an atmosphere even the most intensely personal statements can sound like humorous caricatures of selfhood; "A person," says the protagonist in *A Party for Boris* (named, ironically, Der Gute, "the good one"), "is a person who is in hate with another person."

Bons mots like these are typical of Bernhard's mad satires; one can hear the burst of laughter as the sentence is spoken. At the same time the remark is not only a farcical inversion; there is a real sense in which The Good Woman here exposes the truth of her own situation. The relationship she has with Johanna, her servant, consists of verbal abuse—it is an almost ritualistic tirade—directed by the employer at her employee. Both women hate each other, and yet both in some fundamental way also seemingly need each other. Why otherwise continue this painful relationship? One feels, in other words, that circumstances have conspired to draw together with diabolically humorous symmetry two people who cannot stand one another.

The President's Wife and Mrs. Frolick (*The President*), Vera and Clara (*Eve of Retirement*), or Bruscon and The Innkeeper (*Histrionics*) provide variations on this infernal comedy of odd couples. The relationship is invariably politicized, normally by class or status, creating a situation in which one member is empowered to speak and another expected more or less submissively to listen. Typically the scene takes the form of a rambling disquisition on the current sorry state of the world, Austria in particular; also typically the speaker maliciously degrades the listener, criticizing him or her for lacking education, sense, taste, imagination, social background, even for choosing the wrong village to be born in. Against these charges the listener is compelled because of his or her station to keep silent.

Yet silence on Bernhard's stage functions as powerfully as speech, and in many cases the longer the monologist talks, the more his or her words become ironically self-expressive—expressing, by indirection, the psychic reality they intended to avoid in the first place. Against the background of the listener's continuing silence, the speaker's words become a desperate attempt to fill a bottomless existential void. It is a dramaturgy of surprising power. Bernhard's characters have little new to say to each other; on the contrary, we get the clear impression that what is being said and done has been said and done many times before. Yet the repetitiousness is not banal or uniformly comedic; indeed, at times it can be unexpectedly moving to watch Bernhard's eccentric pairs circle repeatedly round one another, locked forever in a mutually destructive and mutually supportive pas de deux. Ultimately, rather than seeing individual characters progress toward intellectual or emotional insight, we become aware of their profoundly empty spiritual state—in Kundera's marvelous phrase, of their "unbearable lightness of being."

The inner landscape of such terrible lunacy has never been more acutely explored than on Bernhard's stage. Bernhard depicts character, in part, by means of a play of mutual echoes and deep-seated if mysterious psychological collusions. The significant psychological unit for Bernhard is less an individual than a dyad. Here is a small portion of The Good Woman's harangue to Johanna; throughout much of the scene, while talking, she has been aimlessly trying on hats and gloves:

> *tries on a green glove*
> But if you travel to England
> and do not understand the English language
> or to Russia and understand no Russian
> It is good
> that I put a stop to it
> put a stop to it
> *wholly soft*
> put a stop to it
> *admiring the green glove*
> It wasn't as if I had been surprised by the accident.
> it wasn't so.
> *takes the green glove off again*
> To be dead
> to plunge down a light shaft
> to be dead like my husband
> In truth I have not dreamed about him for weeks
> not for years
> When you clean your shoes
> do you not then think about me[.][14]

How can it possibly be said that the speaker of such discourse lacks psychological depth? The mention of dreams alone, quite apart from any psychological portraiture an actor may wish to give to the part, produces clear evidence of this character's narrative extensiveness. One senses not only that The Good Woman *has* a mind, one also imagines her mind following its own inner pathways. Various cues or signs, for example the sudden recurrence of dreams about the dead husband, allow us to imagine several different possibilities. Certainly The Good Woman's words have none of the self-conscious analysis typical of earlier forms of stage realism. Taken at a different level, however, the speech makes perfect sense as an

instance in which verbal repetition signifies the mind's—*a mind's*—unwillingness or inability to let go of a particular subject.

Or consider the moment briefly from an actor's point of view: why does The Good Woman not dream of her dead husband? It is a provocative remark, to say the least brutally frank. How is it to be spoken? With regret? relief? Or perhaps she is lying and if so, to whom? It should be evident that no one of these possible representations, whether denial or regret or some other mental strategy, by itself accounts for the inner workings of her mind. But it should be evident also that Bernhard's actor, in sharp contrast to Beckett's, cannot in such circumstances rely on sculptural portraiture or stylized speech. The moment insists that the actor construe behavior (speech) in firm relation to *some* mental strategy and so allows for a model of mind to be staged.

That Bernhard intends any single specific psychological profile to be staged in this or most other instances is unlikely; the psychological depth here apparent is more illusory than clinically certifiable. But the illusion of depth is present nevertheless, and crucial; it identifies the deepest motive power of the play, the instinctive conjunction of one person to another. To be joined is, for better or worse in Bernhard's world, the primary condition of character.

Over the course of the play Bernhard provides considerable evidence that The Good Woman's acts are symptomatic of a buried mental life. First, like many of Bernhard's protagonists, her psyche has been scarred by the intrusion of terror into everyday life.[15] Next, The Good Woman mentions the dead man only three times, each time briefly. Upon scrutiny, none of the references is random. As in the above instance, her narrative accounts of the dead husband are triggered involuntarily by an accidental association—a double-edged phrase, the color black, the circumstances of remembering her first year with Johanna. We know too that part of Johanna's obligation to her employer is never to speak of the husband—though if we believe The Good Woman, she has a morbid obsession about the subject. Both women are therefore bound together in part by means of the single obscure trauma; barely manifest, the accident is nevertheless crucially important. One might say that it becomes a subtext that secretly directs their daily lives:

> You always wanted to hear something in connection
> with the accident
> in connection with that evening
> whenever you asked me something
> whenever you ask me about my nightdress
> about my necklace
> whenever you ask me if I want to go out or downstairs
> you only ask
> how the accident was[.]
>
> (P. 25)

Bernhard's play interweaves trauma, memory, and speech: yet of the key event, the accident, we know relatively little except that it occurs before the play begins in so-called diegetic space, that is, within a narrated or "virtual" past. To plunge down a light shaft! It is an outrageous way to die. Among the multitude of shocks literary flesh is heir to, it is one of the more novel. Apart from Stephen Dowling Bots, whose death by falling down a well was immortalized hilariously by Mark Twain, I cannot think of a similar literary misfortune. It is not that such things do not happen naturally in real life, but rather that this is assuredly not a "natural" way for characters in imaginative literature to die. Stabbings, poisonings, shootings, illnesses, suicides of one sort of another—these are the kinds of dyings one expects on stage. But characters in literature do not fall down light shafts, and the lack of conventional literary support makes almost impossible interpretive demands. Are we to laugh? are we to sympathize? (It is worth mentioning in passing that students almost always misread this passage. They assume that the accident involves motor vehicles, and that "to plunge down a light shaft" represents a near-death experience. Presumably their awareness of literary convention is insufficiently broad to help them guess that convention itself is here being exposed.)

Our response to the event is made even more difficult by the attitude of The Good Woman. She is not melancholy, but neither is she bitter or reflective. Indeed, she seems suspiciously unaffected by it at all. She seems deficient in the marks—the affects, the insights—by which we customarily recognize individual literary mentality.

But if we look more carefully at the implicit relation between trauma and its remembered recurrence, we may discover that many of The Good Woman's acts point to a bizarre individuation. She writes letters but never mails them, tries on costumes with no intention ever of buying one; legless herself, she sends her servant on daily excursions to purchase stockings and shoes, dreams of travel and "walking the pavement" (p. 37), and marries (there is some evidence she views it as an act of expiation) a legless cripple from a nearby asylum. This bundle of acts does not define a "self," perhaps, but if we cannot derive from them a clinically coherent psychology we cannot also imagine them without simultaneously imagining behind them a center of human energy or will.

It would be incorrect to say that Bernhard is interested primarily in detailing the inner life of The Good Woman; in a way, her obsessive behavior forestalls full insight into her unconscious. In a very real sense, she has within her that which "passes show." In another sense, however, it is precisely such an unconsciousness, and how the landscape of that unconsciousness haunts the play and its action, that determines character in this play. Consider, for example, how we are introduced to the new husband, Boris, of the play's title:

> A cripple I said
> a cripple who like me
> has no legs any more

> in the house
> marry
> Boris[.]

(P. 25)

Bernhard plays upon what he knows will be viewers' predilections to seek psychologically plausible motives for characters' words and acts. Only the slightest hint is necessary to establish for modern audiences the illusion of a hidden psychological agenda. We intuit this directly by way of numerous hints or allusions. At times, for instance, it seems almost as if Boris, the new husband, is indistinguishable rhetorically from the anonymous first husband. Having got used to hearing The Good Woman refer to the dead man as "my husband," it comes as a mild shock to discover in the following passage that the referent has shifted:

> is my husband sleeping
> I said, is my husband sleeping
> is Boris sleeping[.]

(P. 48)

To the degree that we allow for such overlapping, one might suspect that The Good Woman has chosen a husband who mimes in life the condition of her first husband, dead ten years. A number of physical congruencies suggest several levels on which the two men symbolically might be linked. Boris is crippled, immobile, and sleeps incessantly. Much, too, is made of the fact that he sleeps in her first husband's bed; The Good Woman says that

> Boris has a long bed
> in which he can stretch out
> that is the least he can ask of me
> that I give him a bed in which he can stretch out
> *to* BORIS
> right
> you can stretch out in your bed
> BORIS *nods*
> Tell your friends
> that you can stretch out
> when you like
> Only he never stretches himself out
> Never
> I know that he never stretches out
> but if he wants to stretch out
> he can stretch out
> He has the bed of my first husband
> He was one ninety
> *to* BORIS
> Say that you can stretch out in your bed
> when you like
> BORIS *nods*[.]

(Pp. 81–82)

Moreover, the action takes place on Boris's birthday, an anniversary that is specially significant to The Good Woman. "How I look forward to this party," says The Good Woman; "the whole year I look forward to the party on Boris's birthday" (p. 94). Boris receives a great variety of presents from his friends at the asylum, including a drum, a rattle, a hat, telescope, a stuffed raven, a bottle of mead, and—from The Good Woman—officer's boots and long underwear. Of course these latter presents are superbly useless.

The relationship with Boris, is short, despite its contradictory nature and in contrast to that with the first husband, is amply documented, richly suggestive, emotionally turbulent. That it is satire adds complexity to the representation but hardly renders it psychologically empty. At one point The Good Woman reminds Johanna of how she chose her husband:

> What is the point
> of talking to him
> when he has no understanding
> when he has that foul smell
> But I have him
> I have sought him out myself
> *to* JOHANNA
> We went to the asylum and sought him out ourselves
> And I married him
> him
> him
> Say that we sought him out ourselves
> you forced me
> He feels nothing
> he is nothing and he feels nothing
> He knows nothing[.]

(P. 50)

The apparent contradictions themselves are significant. By assuming and then denying responsibility for choosing Boris, The Good Woman can in effect act independently to produce events while yet maintaining an illusion of her own passivity. In a sense, The Good Woman marries Boris to kill the memory of her husband and so gain power over it. By electing a stand-in or double for the dead husband she can both have the husband (that is, cause him to return) and at the same time will him to die by dominating his replacement. Only by selecting a hopeless cripple could she exercise so completely her desire for revenge; like the little boy Freud describes in *Beyond the Pleasure Principle*, The Good Woman plays with Boris as if he were an inanimate object. Acting on whim, she orders his hair parted and forbids him to finish an apple he has been eating:

> THE GOOD WOMAN
> Why has he no part
> I told you to give him a part
> Why has he no part
> BORIS
> I don't want a part
> THE GOOD WOMAN *to* BORIS
> I want you to have a part
> *to* JOHANNA
> Give him a part in the middle
> BORIS
> I don't want a part
> THE GOOD WOMAN
> a part in the middle
> BORIS *makes a point of taking an apple from his*

> *pocket and biting into it*
> THE GOOD WOMAN *shocked*
> He has an apple an apple
> JOHANNA *takes the apple away and hides it*
> THE GOOD WOMAN
> Make certain
> that he gets no apples
> I can't stand to hear it when he bites into an apple
> *to* BORIS
> Does your food taste good Boris
> BORIS *nods*[.]

(Pp. 59–60)

It is probably a mistake to try to make too clinical a descriptive frame for The Good Woman's acts. As a matter of fact, the drama achieves much of its force by satirizing concepts such as emotional unity and voluntary agency. But in calling attention to Bernhard's characters' "mental life" I mean to suggest the survival of something like the psychology of character within a dramaturgy apparently inhospitable to it. In what follows I want to try specifically to reestablish psychology and psychic experience as relevant components of Bernhard's dramatis personae.

LAYERED CHARACTERS

At the time of his death Bernhard had become one of Europe's most controversial and widely admired playwrights, yet his works remain largely unknown to English-speaking audiences, especially Americans. Few of his plays have been translated, and productions are almost nonexistent, even though in academic journals his works receive considerable attention. Much of his commercial unpopularity seems a case of mistaken genres. Bernhard is an expressly comic writer, but the laughter that sounds throughout his plays is derisory, cruel, grisly. That does not make the plays any less funny—comedy is not often fair—but it disturbs audiences who think that the comic spirit is civilized and genial. Exposure to bourgeois comedy (and overexposure to Shakespeare's festive comedy) predisposes English and American audiences to interpret satire as misanthropy or outright nihilism. In addition, topical satire such as the following harangue, spoken by the protagonist, Bruscon, in *Histrionics* (*Der Theatermacher,* 1985), proves extremely difficult to transfer outside Austria:

> A thoroughly stupid country
> populated
> by people who are thoroughly stupid
> It doesn't matter who we talk to
> it turns out
> that it's a fool
> it doesn't matter who we listen to
> it turns out that
> it's an illiterate
> they're socialists
> they claim
> and are only national socialists
> they're Catholic
> they claim
> and are only national socialists

they say they're human
and are only idiots
looking round
Austria
Osterreich
L'Autriche
It seems to me
as if we're touring
in a cesspool
in the pus-filled boil of Europe
beckoning to the LANDLORD
whispering in his ear
Why does everything stink round here
What a horrible return
my dear sir
in a normal tone again
At every street corner
there's something to turn your stomach
Where there was once a wood
now there's gravel pit
where there was once a meadow
there's a cement works
where there was once a human being
there's a nazi
And always on top of everything else
this electrically charged atmosphere of the Lower Alps
in which a sensitive person
is in constant fear
of an apoplectic fit
This tour is proof positive
This country
is not worth the paper
its travel brochures are printed on[.][16]

The self-characterization in this tirade has as much to do with Bernhard as with Bruscon, nominally the speaker. Indeed, part of learning to appreciate Bernhard seems to involve learning to read speeches and personae such as these in terms of the "family relations" between them and characters and speeches in other plays, as well as between them and Bernhard himself. (As is sometimes said of literary villains, such are the characters we love to hate. At the premiere of **Der Theatermacher,** it is said that "the audience broke into gleeful laughter as the protagonist went into the anticipated tirade about the present-day Nazification of Austria."[17])

Doubtless "character" in the conventional sense is inadequate to describe Bruscon. For one thing, he cannot stably be described as round or flat, individual or type. Like most of Bernhard's protagonists, Bruscon is in some ways a figure out of humors comedy. But his humor is subtly modern. He is a megalomaniac—he says so himself—and in fact he displays the requisite symptoms of megalomania, clinically described as a delusional disorder marked by infantile feelings of personal grandeur and omnipotence. Despite their repetitiousness, his speeches clearly depict a mind fixed upon some goal and proceeding logically toward that goal by means of numerous contradictions and conflicting emotions. As was true of the speeches of The Good Woman, Bruscon's monologues constitute an open invitation to actors to invent for themselves plausible narrative subtexts for representing character.[18]

But Bernhard freely compromises even predictably humorous moments of character representation. Consider the play's ending, a comedic explosion of cries and confusion caused by the offstage burning of the local parsonage:

> BRUSCON *staring at the ceiling through which it has already begun to rain while loud cries are heard in the hall*
>
> The parsonage is on fire
> the parsonage is on fire
> on fire
> the parsonage is on fire
>
> *the whole audience rushes out*
>
> BRUSCON *and* SARAH *peer through the curtain until the hall is empty*
>
> BRUSCON *after a pause*
>
> The hall is empty
> an empty hall
> perfectly empty
>
> *rain drips on them all*
>
> SARAH *embracing her father, kissing him on the forehead, very tenderly*
>
> My dear father
>
> *brings him an armchair into which he collapses*
>
> BRUSCON *after a pause in which the thunder and rain have reached the highest pitch of ferocity*
>
> I might have known that it would come to this[.][19]

The way one responds to this scene will doubtless depend on the way the actor plays Sarah's overall relationship with her father, but surely Bernhard's rare affective specification, "very tenderly," indicates the moment is one of exquisite personal sorrow. As he paints this scene, however, Bernhard cannot help but mock his own efforts. The catastrophe seems to echo an older theatrical moment, specifically the burning of the orphanage and the grim pietà of Ibsen's *Ghosts.*[20] It is a little like the realizations so popular on the Victorian stage, those climactic moments when the stage picture suddenly composed itself according to a familiar work of pictorial art. As for its effect on the apparent representation of heartfelt emotion, Bernhard implies that even grief might reveal nothing more of character than any other artificially constructed response.

If the foregoing comparison with Ibsen can suggest some of the power of Bernhard's modes of figuration, it can suggest as well one of the misconceptions involving his work, namely, its seeming derivativeness. As Amity Shlaes writes in a review of Bernhard and contemporary German literature, "The problem with all these plays is that they feel derivative. Bernhard studied Artaud and Beckett, and his plays are often "German" reworkings of postwar existentialist theater. . . . [F]or those not born on the Danube or Rhine, Bernhard too often remains too much the German student of the great originals. Why see **Force of Habit** when one can see *Endgame?*"[21]

Parallels with the works of Samuel Beckett are indeed numerous. Bernhard's characters, like Beckett's, must cope with an uncooperative and imperfect world. Trains are always late, hats always fall off, and appointments are never kept. Bernhard shares also with Beckett an apparent fascination with wounds, disease, or physical impairment, for the majority of both men's plays feature characters who are crippled or partly immobilized. And Bernhard, like Beckett, values aesthetic technique often at the expense of subject matter. Beckett more than once asserted the primacy of form over content, and Bernhard's notorious criticisms of art and artists paradoxically confer on aesthetics a kind of legitimacy. (Of theater, he once wrote: "The curtain goes up, and a pile of shit is lying there, and more and more flies come in, and then the curtain falls again."[22]) Nobody could protest so much and mean it. The list of comparisons with Beckett is so long, in fact, that it is easy to see in Bernhard an Alpine Beckett.[23]

But there are difficulties with this view. One of the most striking involves the different use each playwright makes of stage objects. For Beckett, a prop—and there are not many in his works for theater—often involves several levels of significance. It can be a symbol, an extension of the human figure, an opportunity for stage business, even an aesthetic luxury. One thinks of the tree in *Godot,* of Winnie's umbrella or Krapp's tape recorder, of the dazzling sequins on W's black dress in *Rockaby.* In contrast, the props in Bernhard's works are shallow, and they seem somehow drained of the heightened semiotic capacity we expect of stage objects. Yet paradoxically they are at the same time more aggressive. One example: during the first act of **The President,** The First Lady talks to her dead dog's empty basket. The basket is a natural object, and her grief for her pet seems real. Yet Bernhard's unrelenting scrutiny of the object—some twenty times during the course of the scene The First Lady stares at the basket or refers to it directly—makes it hard to say whether the object is being parodied or honored. In such a context the basket is reduced phenomenologically to a neutral "basket-ness": like a word endlessly repeated, it becomes sheer presence, drained of any referential capacity whatsoever.

Another crucial difference concerns the respective attitudes Beckett and Bernhard take toward another aspect of the dramatic script, stage directions. Beckett's stage directions are perhaps the most explicit in theater history; most of his later plays and especially the plays he wrote for television are created with an extraordinary sense of their detailed pictorial realization. But Bernhard's texts include almost no information about production mechanics—lighting, blocking, pacing, and so on. It is not as if Bernhard were uninterested in figural aspects of character; his texts contain numerous objective instructions to actors to perform specific acts—actors are told to look in the mirror or to stare at a dog basket, to puff on a cigar or to shoot a pistol—but they rarely give information regarding individual affects. (The notation "very tenderly" in *Histrionics* is a remarkable exception.) His plays are a reaction not only against what commonly passes for character

determinants in playtexts—the elaborate narrative specification of states of consciousness or affect such as is widespread in much modernist drama, for example, in Ibsen or Kaiser or O'Neill—but also against the modernist fondness for figural abstraction.

It is all the more surprising, then, that in performance Bernhard's plays are not formal abstractions but remarkably naturalistic; Bernhard Minetti (who is Bernhard's favorite actor) has said that Bernhard's monologues are especially challenging for actors who must themselves determine the numerous movements of characters' minds. Actors must choose "which spoken words are merely private reflection, which are less controlled emotional outbursts, and finally, which are uttered for the sole purpose of evoking responses from others on stage."[24] This variation creates the impression of a ceaseless self-awareness; in contrast to Beckett's actors, who are normally enjoined to speak neutrally and with "no color," Bernhard's actors are free (even encouraged) to color their representations with "character."

Perhaps the best example of inappropriately drawn parallels between Bernhard and Beckett concerns the formal doubling or patterning so typical of their stages. It is here, of course, that Beckett's theater seems definitionally antinarrative; nearly all of the late works replace plot (mythos) with verbal or visual design. In Bernhard's drama also repetition forms an important aesthetic element. In all of the plays, for example, banal catch-phrases are distributed among several characters and repeated insistently (and often unconsciously). Such repetitions give rise to the peculiar impression that certain thoughts are "in the air," part of a Zeitgeist, possibly, or at the least an identifying structural feature, like a rhyme in poetry or a song's refrain. In **Force of Habit,** for example, the phrase "tomorrow Augsburg" (*Morgen Augsburg*) and its variants ("tomorrow in Augsburg," "tomorrow we will be in Augsburg") occurs (so it seems) on every other page. Spoken repeatedly by four of the five characters, it surely carries, as Martin Esslin writes, "a multitude of associations and overtones in a number of different contexts."[25] Esslin calls such visible recurrence a structural element analogous to music more than to drama.

This being the case, however, it is ironic that one might equally plausibly call such echolalia a sign of genuine subjectivity. The formal (almost ritual) display of mirrorings and echoes in Beckett seems at times to approach an autonomous aesthetic system, independent of the individual. Because of the naturalistic subtext from which they originate, however, Bernhard's figures' repetitions suggest a palpable attempt to show the eerie theatricality on which human character ultimately rests. When words spread so infectiously from one individual to others, the separate characters from which they normally issue become alarmingly similar; a new identity is created, what one might call the mimetic subject.

The mimetic existence binds one character to another in various ways in various plays; at its most innocent it takes the form of a congenial assent of one person to another, as when The Niece repeats "in Nuremberg" in response to her grandfather's promise to tour "in Nuremberg" in the fall. We all perform such repetitions dozens of times daily, and here mimesis simply indicates an empathic attentiveness to what the other person is saying. In other circumstances, however, such automatic repetition of another's words seems to break down the apparent integrity of character. When, in **The President,** The First Lady defers repeatedly in her opinions to her friend The Chaplain ("the chaplain says . . .") and The Chaplain, in turn, obtains *his* opinions on manners and morals from the great European authors (Goethe, Voltaire, Proust, among others), individuality in the conventional sense of self against world becomes gravely threatened.

Does this mean that character has been forfeited in favor of formal or philosophical objectives? Not at all. Suppose character is not something essential, unchanging, or intrinsic, but a state of existence more like that imagined by social psychologists or like the social or dialogic self described by Mikhail Bakhtin or the dramatistic self Kenneth Burke invents to account for our verbal exchanges with others.[26] Selfhood is not to be understood exclusively as the expression of an original or private voice; rather it is something one acquires naturally by way of affiliation with others. Character, then, is acquired almost as a form of contagion, and subjectivity spreads as a system of ethics and values from person to person and from generation to generation. It is a curiously Platonic insight: one "catches" character by way of mimesis, by falling, that is, into imitative modes of being. Originality and individuality, of course, have significantly less value in this world, for everybody, it turns out, is a clone of everyone else.

A world peopled by characters cut from the same pattern is by definition humorous, yet in Bernhard's hands the follies of typically humorous characters are transmuted into an appalling bizarreness. It is one thing to parrot a chaplain who parrots Voltaire; it is quite another, however, to push psychological collectivity to its logical and (inevitably) political limits. One example: In **Eve of Retirement (Vor dem Ruhestand,** 1979) two contemporary Nazis, a sister and brother, secretly celebrate Himmler's birthday. The celebration is an annual ritual and involves, among other things, wearing clothes from the Nazi era and committing incest. At one point during the party the pair turn to a photo album and begin to reminisce about their life during the National Socialist regime. It is a scene of unparalleled sardonicism: idyllic country views and family snapshots from their childhood are nestled alongside photographs of corpses and concentration camps. At one point Vera, the sister, turns to her brother, Rudolph, and says, after a nostalgic pause, "Oh Rudolf that we have to hide / and look at this so secretly."[27]

Theater history has never known such a brother and sister, and yet Bernhard seems not to have considered his characters fantastic or even extraordinary. (Indeed the play was written during a time when the problem of ex-Nazis establishing themselves in high government positions was real.) But the most striking feature of the play is its comic underlayment. Despite its credible horror the foregoing scene is uncomfortably risible. Vera and Rudolph seem less individuals than one-dimensional caricatures, mindless generic Germans of the sort one sees in propagandistic cartoons from the Second World War or in more recent films such as Zero Mostel's and Gene Wilder's *The Producers.* And the play's conclusion is downright farcical. Rudolph, impossibly drunk, waves his pistol wildly about the room, then collapses of a heart attack. As he lies groaning, Vera tries desperately to revive him with kisses and at the same time starts to remove his SS uniform. Meanwhile Beethoven's Fifth Symphony plays loudly in the background. The play ends with the summoning of a physician, apparently (and of course ironically) Jewish: as the curtain falls we hear Vera speaking on the phone, "Doctor Fromm, please."

The behavior of these characters is as mechanically predictable as that of any of the protagonists of Jonson or Molière. But to call Vera and Rudolph humorous parodies of past or present Nazis seems dangerously inept. Nothing in the play proves that unrepentant and vicious anti-Semitism is any less a reality now than in 1940. Also wide of the mark, however, is the description of **Eve of Retirement** as "a humorless mix of Strindberg and Beckett . . . as repulsive as Fassbinder's, though more upscale."[28] The objections of Robert Skloot (who wrote the preceding comment) to Bernhard's Holocaust drama cannot be waived arbitrarily. He regards the lack of a humane voice in the play as a damning ethical mistake on Bernhard's part, and I have taught the play unsuccessfully often enough to half-believe him. Told to read **Eve of Retirement** as comedy, students are aghast; told to read it as politics, they miss the humor and so (in my opinion) miss the point. In this humors comedy, buffoons have the power to play out exaggerated, violent fantasies. Of the characters who endow **Eve of Retirement** with the horrors of the National Socialist era, Bernhard has written that such people "are in me, just as they are in everyone else."[29] If his plays are any guide, these remarks must be interpreted as more than a metaphoric expression of innate human depravity. Bernhard suggests here for drama a heterogeneous model for selfhood, one whose component parts are by no means complete and exclusive. Other people are part of us as we, in turn, are part of them. It is a model for character that is multiple, relativistic, open, and, as Bernhard dramatizes it, psychologically plausible.

The issue of character arises also in a work like **Der Präsident (The President,** 1975). Like **Histrionics, The President** presents characters who seem at first almost featureless. No assembly of traits can describe them, and indeed there seems little to describe: they lack determinate pasts, consistent opinions, coherent affects. The play begins just after a group of anarchists have bungled an attempt to assassinate the president of an unspecified European country. Instead of shooting The President, the assassins kill a nearby colonel and The First Lady's beloved pet dog, who apparently dies of fright. The play ends several days later with the anarchists' second, and successful, strike. In the meantime, with crushing finality, The President waits for death.

The President can be read as a *pièce à thèse,* a cheerless lecture on mortality and the relative irrelevance of literary form. Since all plots end in death, Bernhard seems to be saying, why pretend that one is different from any other? By conventional standards the play seems monochromatic: its plot is emphatically static, and its characters are powerless to act in their own interests. The President's situation is of dramatic interest only as an exemplar of "the blight man was born for." Like the child in Hopkins's poem, The President is psychically oriented toward death, even though he cannot bear to acknowledge it. Thus he spends his remaining time in a frantic effort to deny what he knows to be true.

Even though the play dramatizes a moral as succinct as that of any medieval allegory, it cannot be said that Bernhard creates characters mainly to illustrate philosophical principles or to conform to abstract formal patterns. (One might for a start point to its mordant political realism. No one aware of the ghastly ironies of contemporary international events can think Bernhard dwells entirely in fancy.) Next, the play draws odd emotive power from its haunting images of individuals. Even though their words do not directly express the inwardness that in conventional drama passes for psychological realism, one responds empathically to the bleakness of their situation and the extremity of their suffering. These people are mutilated so far beyond recognition that, like the grisaille figures in Picasso's *Guernica,* their pathos is convincingly real.

It is the latter dimension of Bernhard's characters that has thus far gone unrecognized. If they do not fit familiar norms for the depiction of mentality, neither do they conform to our notions for "flat" characters in literature. Consider the following speech in which the representation of character seems largely subordinated to formal matters; The President speaks to his lover, an actress:

> And what does the director plan for you
> a leading role or a supporting role
> You can renounce the lead role my child
> you play it with me
> you play your supporting roles in the theater
> *kisses her on the cheek*
> with me you play the lead role
> *suddenly pathetic, raises the glass*
> You are the greatest actress
> that I know
> and so you play the lead role with me
> you play the greatest role that any actress
> in any of our theaters has played
> Duse
> You Duse
> Duse
> *throws his glass in her face*
> You Duse
> *The actress raises her glass even higher and throws it*

> *in his face*
> My Duse
> my Duse you[.]
> *Curtain*[30]

Like so much of Bernhard's theater, the scene defies easy classification or explanation. It takes place in a "flat" or neutral space, and on the page seems largely empty of subjective interiority. On the one hand, it is a satiric portrait of a comic type (again, a megalomaniac); on the other hand, even though the scene takes place on the edge of slapstick—the head of state is revealed to be nothing but a drunken lecher—the speech cannot be played for laughs. The President's monologue differs qualitatively from a speech by, say, Volpone or Harpagon, mainly because its mode of expression and its peculiar mechanisms suggest a state of mind that is paralytic rather than intent upon action. Its attraction for an audience is therefore more mesmeric than comedic. The speech manifests fear, a sinister hysteria that means nothing in itself because it is only an unreasonable deferral or displacement of emotion. The "I" expressed by the monologue is again infantile, and, incidentally, pathologically accurate. At the same time the repetitive, patterned style adds a pathetic counterpoint to the childish outbursts:

> You can renounce the lead role my child
> you play it with me . . .
> with me you play the lead role . . .
> and so you play the lead role with me[.]

From the point of view of an actor the speech is as complex psychologically as any of Ibsen's characters' revelatory declamations. The President represents his needs symbolically; his words suggest, for example, the protective devices that schizoid individuals use to avoid the dangers of emotional involvement. Early in the scene he speaks of his wife's infidelity with a bizarre objectivity:

> she lies in her bed
> she thinks about her butcher
> about the butcher on the one hand
> about the chaplain on the other
> in the night they both run through her head
> and they won't reconcile themselves in her head
> but neither can she go mad
> in this stage
> And if she is ever with me
> she is still with the butcher
> or with the chaplain
> This explains her increasing nervousness
> This also causes her to torture
> the servants[.]

(P. 130)

The speech first of all structures individual identity as a schizophrenic attempt to reconcile disparate (or other) components of the self: The President's wife's nervousness and cruelty can both be attributed to her awareness of the sway competing authorities hold over her. And The President's monologue carries out his own unapprehended willing. The President claims to be indifferent to his wife's behavior, but the peculiar references to her in his monologue suggest otherwise. There seems to be a causal relationship between his rambling, bitter narrative and an unexpressed wish to deny that his wife means anything to him. His ramblings make perfect sense, for example, if they are understood as coming from the mind of a man who dreads meaningful emotional connections. In one instance during The President's monologue, for example, he begins to link himself with his wife in a sympathetic, caring way; his language, however, almost immediately becomes abusive and repetitious:

> a hair's difference my child
> and I would not now be in Estoril
> The assassination is the reason
> that I am here
> You have suffered a shock
> said my wife
> go to Estoril
> she said
> And she said it only
> so that I would go away
> so that she could go to the mountains herself
> with her butcher
> or she might go with the chaplain to the mountains
> With the butcher
> or with the chaplain
> it is all the same to me with whom she goes to the
> mountains
> the main thing is that I am with you in Estoril my
> child
> *drinks*
> two thousand police all to look after
> my person
> And you my child
> my little actress
> with the diplomatic passport
> and with the official protection of the president
> the day after tomorrow we'll travel to Sintra
> on official business
> and enjoy ourselves
> like that waiter in Sintra last year
> didn't I read him a lecture
> a lecture
> first in French
> which he didn't understand
> then in English
> which he didn't understand either
> finally in Portuguese
> In the night we never sleep together
> my wife and I
> not for twenty years
> when she lies in her bed
> she thinks about her butcher
> about the butcher on the one hand
> about the chaplain on the other[.]

(Pp. 128–30)

The foregoing speech hints at a psychic reality that determines the course of the fragmented, repetitive, hostile verbal surface. The memory of Sintra, for instance, although introduced apparently at random, masks a subtle attempt on the part of The President to recover through memory a situation in which he could dominate events

and persons absolutely. His pleasure in remembering the incident at table seems therefore the product of a blunted psychic need. By repeating the story he reconstitutes the power he held over a waiter who knew neither French nor English and could not respond therefore to verbal abuse. Of course this part of The President's speech can be interpreted conventionally—evidence, perhaps, of a sadistic streak that can never be understood—but given his imperiled situation his words suggest an instinctive psychological strategy. This portion of his monologue is clearly motivated and, from one perspective, perfectly coherent. In context—a nostalgic recollection that contrasts markedly with the bitter commentary on his wife's sexual infidelity—the story of the waiter at Sintra seems to be a delaying tactic, an attempt to kill the memory of his wife.

Bernhard here opens a void beneath The President's humor, thereby giving the effect of genuine interiority. When The President strikes his various poses or discards one personality in favor of another, he defines character as a problem in itself. Indeed, much of the melancholy power of this scene derives from our sense of a character struggling to win a stable sense of self. The President is not talking gibberish; his speech is a performance, a complex tangle of contradictions, assertions, and denials the sum of which testifies to a severely damaged and tormented psyche struggling to articulate itself. His consciousness, to the extent that it can be inferred from his discourse, attracts psychological interpretation. The repetitions, the sudden outbursts, the bitterness, the nostalgic lapses—these are not merely formal elements of a "musical" drama, they are distinctive marks of character. In **The President,** Bernhard dramatizes character effects appropriate for our own age—"the age of the schizoid," as it has been called.[31] For example, the apparent digressions contained in his speech can be interpreted as attacks on "linking," the purpose of which is to deny meaningful relationships.[32] Significantly, the apparent digression via the waiter at Sintra ironically leads The President back to his subject:

> In the night we never sleep together
> my wife and I
> not for twenty years[.]

Digressive topics in The President's speech almost always mark the return of the repressed. The more we observe the peculiar repetitions of The President's monologue, the clearer it becomes that they are closely tied to his obsession with his wife's infidelity. He may not understand fully what moves him to speak, and, indeed, at times his words take on a life weirdly remote from their speaker. To the extent that he is in the grip of his repetition compulsion, he is constituted exclusively by it. But if his own interiority is not always available for The President himself to explain consciously, his repetitions are for us the signs of a pathetic subjectivity. The mental journey the President takes during the course of his monologue has about it the same sinister quality of the Italian walk Freud describes in his essay on "The Uncanny" in which time after time he arrived at the same red-light district from which he was trying to escape. Freud likens his experience of apparently unintended repetition to the helplessness one sometimes feels in dreams, and a similar anxiety pervades The President's speech as, like Freud, he returns by devious paths to the very place he intends to leave. The recognizable landmark in The President's speech is his obsession with the butcher and the chaplain. It is the sign of a repetition compulsion that appears so often and so clearly out of context that it marks his real concern.

The President's speech is as unintentionally revealing of character, therefore, as any of Browning's dramatic monologues, and it is possible to read it for similar kinds of insights into the speaker's mental life. There is a single crucial exception, however. Browning's characters' monologues are invariably gratuitous; their utterances, as Robert Langbaum once observed, remain largely unmotivated.[33] Hence the peculiar formal expressiveness of the dramatic monologue: lacking exterior motive for speech, characters' speech then approaches the condition of lyric poetry. The poem becomes (in Langbaum's description) "the occasion for a total outpouring of soul, the expression of the speaker's whole life until that moment."[34] Bernhard's characters too feel compelled to burst into speech, but for entirely different reasons. The President cannot help but produce himself by speaking, but in another sense (a sense that distinguishes his monologue from, say, that of Browning's Bishop), he loses his command over words to such an extent that he is possessed by them.

The President, therefore, is in some sense an effect or product of discourse. But to say this does not foreclose discussion of The President as a character. Human presence dominates this scene, though it is no longer centralized as it was, say, in Renaissance or nineteenth-century realist drama. Certainly it would be wrong to invest The President with the kind of autonomous expressive power one finds in Shakespeare's or Ibsen's protagonists. But this may well be for Bernhard the crucial issue, to define figures for the self in terms of a revolutionary and expressly negative dramatic language. Characters on stage are not ipso facto deprived of mentality—Forster's illusion of "roundness"—because they lack existence apart from the discourse that animates them. In the foregoing speech, for example, the mental life of The President is individuated, coherent, and to a great extent knowable. Bernhard's figuration of character is archaeological; like Freud's model of Rome as a psychical entity, The President is a site for cumulative layerings or doublings.

To read The President's speech in this way permits the speaker a measure of psychological credibility or wholeness without at the same time reducing him to conventional grammars for character. The President's repetitions are consistent with an internalized struggle, for his monologue reproduces the familiar double structure of a compulsion. Like anyone driven by compulsion, he both controls it and is controlled by it. On the one hand, this makes him a puppet whose repetitions are entirely out of his hands; on the other hand, however, there are moments when, during his infantile outbursts, one senses a self struggling through

repetition to assert control. For The President, in other words, repetitive language dramatizes a complex psychological duality involving surrender and control.

Seen in this way, character is a critical issue for Bernhard, and his stage functions as a forum for contemporary definitions of identity that stress the self's multiplicity. Beneath their torrent of posturings, accusations, repetitions, evasions, and silences, Bernhard's characters struggle to articulate their tortured experience. To substantiate this claim fully will require the rest of the chapter, and perhaps the best way to begin will be to discuss in greater detail the kinds of mimetic involvement with others—repeating, imitating, mirroring, echoing, quoting—that distinguish Bernhard's characters.

REPETITION, SELF-FASHIONING, AND THE FORCE OF HABIT

One of the most remarkable features of all Bernhard's dramas is the extent to which they are infused with linguistic repetitions: all characters repeat the same stories, situations, catchphrases, and allusions. In *The President,* for example, the phrase "ambition, hate, nothing else" is spoken eleven times. Such repetitions at first seem common literary devices. Like the refrain of a ballad or the phrase from Vinteuil's sonata in *Swann's Way,* their significance depends on their being repeated so often as to become a motif or signpost rather than an expression that distinguishes one individual from another. As this bitter phrase echoes throughout Bernhard's play, its significance becomes increasingly ironic until it finally indicates little about its speaker. Like the women's "talking of Michelangelo" in Eliot's poem, the repetition eventually highlights the discrepancy between an original and its subsequent abuse through thoughtless duplication. By the time we hear for the eleventh time, "ambition, hate, nothing else," it has become a prefabricated linguistic response, in effect a kind of comic malapropism. Bernhard coldly mocks the characters whose failures he exposes. Entrapment within language depicts character, but negatively; as in conventional humors comedy, it signifies the absence of thought, the loss of individuality.

Repetition of this kind can also serve formal ends. It can become a unifying structural element as in music, adding intensity or significance, synthesizing or centering the work. Of a similarly repeated phrase in *Die Macht der Gewohnheit* (*Force of Habit*), for example, Martin Esslin remarks that "the sentence 'tomorrow in Augsburg' (referring to the circus's next stop on its tour) occurs on almost every page. Simple as it is, it carries a multitude of associations and overtones in a number of different contexts."[35] Esslin classifies repetitions of this sort as autonomous, technical features of the work of art, unlike the repetitive conversations of other contemporary dramatists (notably Harold Pinter) "who are mainly concerned to show that real speech in real situations *is* largely repetitious." Esslin writes that, "In Bernhard's case, there is no pretence to naturalism. His dramatic language . . . is strictly rhythmical."[36]

Bernhard is a trained musician, and he often borrows from music structural elements for his plays. But the musical or rhythmical analogy, while accurate, does not fully account for the wide-ranging effects of Bernhard's imitative patterns. As we saw in the foregoing analysis of a portion of The President's monologue, repetitions tend in spite of their definitional formalism to cluster around character and to stamp language with individual desire. Whatever their logic as formal elements of a composition, in other words, the repetitions tell an enigmatic story. The President's repetitious language can be read narratively as the symptom of a drive mechanism that holds constant sway over his life and through which he tries to articulate himself. One can track, for example, traces of The President by means of the texts he articulates. Or one can (using late Freudian theory) describe a psychic economy that governs The President's various defensive strategies. When The President returns again and again to "the butcher or the chaplain" he deals with highly negative feelings. He can be said to discover repetition (as Freud theorized in discussing the now-famous *fort/da* game in *Beyond the Pleasure Principle*) as a tactic that transforms passive suffering into a game of control. His compulsion to repeat combines infantile pleasure with a perverse, sterile, and cruel mode of mimesis.

The President cannot see into his repetition, of course, but his monologue clearly tells his story—the story of one who cannot see. Obsessed with his wife's sexuality, he complains incessantly about her lovers, her dead dog, her charities and intellectual pursuits, and even her manner of chewing. And the scene culminates in a pathetic moment of insight and denial:

> The wife of the president of the Republic
> is a whore
> a whore
> *after a pause*
> A whore who now only
> stares into an empty dog basket
> stares into it you understand
> stares
> stares into it
> into the empty dog basket
> *both empty their glasses*
> It is a play my child
> in which alternately
> the most impossible people and arrangements occur
> and possibly
> it is already the revolution[.]

(Pp. 137–38)

The world is a drama staged by actors who inevitably betray the roles they find themselves obliged to play. Bernhard identifies the self's inherent theatricality and pursues that concept to its macabre extreme. His experimental dramaturgy represents inner experience by linking it with external caricatures—a definition of the ego in terms of a set of mechanistic and mimetic responses. Character can be identified as a primary subject of Bernhard's concern, in other words, even though his characters rarely use words

or acts to explain what they are doing and why. Consider evidence from another play, the introductory scene of *Force of Habit*:

> *A piano left*
> *Four music stands in front*
> *Chest, table with radio, armchair, mirror, pictures*
> *The "Trout Quintet" on the floor*
>
> CARIBALDI *looking for something under the chest*
>
> JUGGLER *enters*
> What are you doing there
> The Quintet is lying on the floor
> Mr Caribaldi
> Tomorrow Augsburg
> right
>
> CARIBALDI
> Tomorrow Augsburg
>
> JUGGLER
> The lovely Quintet
> *lifts the Quintet up*
> By the way I have
> received the letter from France
> *puts the Quintet on one of the music stands*
> Imagine
> a guaranteed sum
> Experience proves however
> that an offer
> should not
> be accepted immediately
> That is what experience proves
> *straightens the Quintet on the music stand*
> In Bordeaux above all
> the white wine
> What are you looking for then
> Mr Caribaldi
> *takes the cello leaning against the music stands*
> *wipes it with his right sleeve and leans it back*
> *against the music stands*
> Covered with dust
> everything covered with dust
> Because we play in such a dusty place
> It's windy here
> and dusty
>
> CARIBALDI
> Tomorrow Augsburg
>
> JUGGLER
> Tomorrow Augsburg
> Why are we playing here
> I ask myself
> Why should I ask
> That is your business
> Mr Caribaldi
>
> CARIBALDI
> Tomorrow Augsburg
>
> JUGGLER
> Tomorrow Augsburg
> naturally

The cello
let stand open
for only a few moments
blows dust from the cello
Carelessness
Mr Caribaldi
takes the cello
The Maggini
right
No
the Salo
the so called
Ferrara cello
leans the cello against the music stands again and
takes a step back, contemplating it
an instrumental
expenditure
But naturally it should
not only
be played
in concrete arenas
North of the Alps
the Salo
south of the Alps
the Maggini
or
afternoons before five o'clock
the Maggini
and after five o'clock in the afternoon
the Ferrara cello
the Salo
blows dust off the cello
A dying occupation
suddenly to CARIBALDI
What are you looking for then[.][37]

The scene (like so much of Bernhard's theater) at first glance seems barren of motive and strictly formal, as if we are being told nothing essential about The Juggler and Caribaldi. But in fact the text generates a character-centered aesthetic. The Juggler's incessant speech seems almost surreal in contrast to Caribaldi's relative wordlessness. Why does Caribaldi not respond when The Juggler asks what he is doing on the floor? Why does The Juggler not repeat his question but instead change the subject, not once but twice? Why does he perform a sequence of highly specific acts during his speech—straightening sheets of paper, perfunctory dusting? Why does he devote so much attention to the two cellos? And what motivates him to visit Caribaldi in the first place?

Such practical questions cannot be brushed aside as irrelevant speculations; they are the salient grounds of the dramatic encounter. Actors performing the scene need to know the answers to such questions, and audiences or readers too may profitably institute similar inquiries. It is not true, in other words, that everything we need to know to read this play is contained within it. The need to read The Juggler's monologue for its implicit narrativity is proved first by Caribaldi's relative silence and next by the sequence of linguistic repetitions. Despite its stylization the scene remains rooted in personal neuroses and family relationships. Motives that we would call psychological

give this encounter (and most of *Force of Habit*) its extraordinary blending of abstraction and verisimilitude.

The Juggler several times begins to speak by repeating Caribaldi's phrase, "Tomorrow Augsburg"; this suggests, by extension, that his speech is both mimetic and inauthentic, that it is conditioned by response to exterior authority. By establishing echolalia as a point of reference, Bernhard mocks the convention that words are the distinct property of the person who speaks them. The Juggler's speeches and actions are usually triggered by an interpenetration of his discourse by Caribaldi's, or—more important—by his perception of Caribaldi's mood or needs. As the scene develops, The Juggler's individuality is gradually revealed to be a function of Caribaldi's. (And vice versa: as I show later, Caribaldi cannot act in character, as he is here in character, unless there is someone present whom he can dominate; his behavior, too, is the product of emotional need.)

Under these circumstances, it is impossible to displace character as a legitimate object of inquiry. Awareness of individual psychologies or distinct movements of mind beyond (or beneath) language is certainly central to our experience of the play. Those inner realities are necessarily experienced imperfectly, fleetingly. Likewise their relation to language is problematic; no character's rhetoric is conventionally self-dramatizing or self-expressive. Still, the scene seems to depend on our awareness of language as somehow expressive of character. It is character's shadow, or its sign, and it presupposes the existence of a subject in much the same way that symptoms of a disease presuppose the existence of a host. When, for example, Caribaldi and The Juggler repeatedly speak the phrase, "Tomorrow Augsburg," their words are rhetorical and expressly ethical. At the very least the scene presents individuals who receive language and respond to it with a waxlike impressionability. Even from the very first moments of the play, when The Juggler says "Tomorrow Augsburg" in hope of setting his own rhetoric in accord with that of his employer, one senses the formal linguistic ties that convey to us the play of mimetic correspondences on which character depends for its production.

The continuity of language from speaker to speaker indicates how easily and naturally men and women fall into familiar, repetitive configurations. *Force of Habit* shows a reality that has lately become a sociological commonplace, that human relationships at any level are weirdly choreographed. The play contains sequences of mechanistic actions that are both predictable and comedic, and, as is true of many of Bernhard's plays, its structure resembles conventional humors comedy. The story develops as follows: Caribaldi, a ringmaster of a small troupe of traveling circus performers, is also an amateur cellist. Each day for more than twenty years he and the other four members of his circus have tried to play Schubert's "Trout Quintet." Yet not once have they been able to complete the piece without error; always someone makes a mistake. Bernhard's thesis is ingenious if not exactly novel: perfection, as everyone knows, belongs to another world. (One might note in passing that earlier generations might simply have praised Bernhard for being "true to life"; it is hard to imagine anyone who could not supply his or her own examples of the kind of aspirations and frustrations that Bernhard's formalist art represents.)

In any case, Caribaldi's desire to perform the quintet successfully eventually becomes an obsession, and, when the play begins, he tries to assemble his musicians for yet another rehearsal. Among the players, in addition to Caribaldi and The Juggler, are a Clown, a Lion Tamer (Caribaldi's nephew), and a tightrope dancer (Caribaldi's Granddaughter). Almost as soon as the performance begins, things go wrong. Caribaldi loses the resin for his bow, and The Juggler whines constantly that his artistic talents are unappreciated. The Clown keeps losing his hat, and each time the hat falls he loses his place in the score; and each time the hat falls the dancer giggles and loses *her* place too. Worst of all is The Lion Tamer. He is drunk, and his left arm is bandaged like a club because one of his big cats recently bit it. All he can do with his wounded hand is to pound the piano. Predictably, this rehearsal, like every other rehearsal for the past two decades, never proceeds beyond the first few notes. Screaming in frustration and fury, Caribaldi finally banishes his sorry collection of "art destroyers." Alone on stage, near despair, he putters about the wagon, slowly restoring to order a mess of instruments, music stands, and scattered sheets of music. He turns on the radio, and suddenly the stage is filled with the "Trout Quintet": five measures of music, then silence. These last seconds of the play are moving almost beyond belief: Schubert's music never seems so incomparably beautiful.

Caribaldi is a perfectionist in a fallen world. Driven by his humor, he is surrounded by other humorous types. He and the rest of the characters in *Force of Habit* are puppets, and each of them is basically an archetypal clown whose contours are easily recognizable from several comic traditions—*commedia,* medieval farce, Renaissance humors comedy, Plautine theater. But these formal referents establish the frame for an elaborate subtext. The introductory scene between Caribaldi and The Juggler, for example, is a comic routine involving the relationship between a worker and his boss. The Juggler enters the stage intending to ask Caribaldi to raise his salary, and he brings with him for bargaining power a letter containing a contract offer from a carnival in Bordeaux. In outline the scene has the features of a cartoon, and, in fact, one could easily supply an appropriate caption: The Employee Asks for a Raise.

The key to the encounter, however, is that it is not an original confrontation between The Juggler and Caribaldi but an imitation or duplication of a scene that has been played out numerous times before. Created first and foremost as a fall guy, The Juggler is likeable but dimwitted. He knows when he enters that "the letter from France" is a fiction, and, what is more remarkable, he knows that

all his past attempts to fool his employer with contract offers from France have failed. Caribaldi says as much toward the end of the scene when he accuses The Juggler of trying to dupe him with an old trick. So Caribaldi too knows that the letter from France is an illusion. This foreknowledge is not literally part of the text, but it constitutes nevertheless a vital element of the working relationship established between the two men; competent actors would surely have to consider it as part of their representation. Because spectators understand this relationship implicitly, its repetitive quality is the essence of the joke; it is funny because we discern it has all happened before. The Juggler must know, therefore, that Caribaldi will recognize his strategy. How then does he request a raise? Incredibly, like an animal that has been taught only a single trick, he produces the fictitious contract offer from France. This is force of habit with a vengeance.

One can see clearly underlying the scene Bernhard's humors approach to theater. Dramatic action results not from antagonism between two discrete individuals but from the programmatic harmony of interdependent subjects who carry out a prefigured behavioral pattern. J. Henri Fabré once described the "abysmal stupidity" of a group of moth caterpillars who took seven days to discover that their food supply had been shifted nine inches. In the meantime the insects circled wearyingly round and round the empty track that had once contained their supply of nourishment. Like Fabré's caterpillars, Bernhard's Juggler clings to familiar behavior because he lacks the rudimentary sense of opportunism that would enable him to abandon or alter it. He enters Caribaldi's room, one imagines, after having rehearsed a scenario such as the following: greet Caribaldi, confirm tomorrow's booking, introduce the letter into the conversation, and so on. But habit betrays him. He is surprised to discover Caribaldi on the floor—bosses do not normally crawl on their bellies—and that novelty renders his prearranged script useless. Before he can begin to play his part, The Juggler must first acknowledge Caribaldi's location, and he never recovers from that reversal of expectations. He pins his hopes on a direct encounter with his employer, but how can he ask for a raise when his boss is lying on the floor? Withdrawing immediately to a defensive position—"What are you doing there?"—he cannot at the same time break free of habit. So he clings desperately to a repetitive text that subjects him to increasing confusion and humiliation. In the artificial way he introduces the subject of his raise we see his lack of imagination: "By the way [*übrigens*] I have received the letter from France." But Caribaldi's silence compels The Juggler to abandon the subject, and the lame repetition ("That is what experience proves") signifies that the question of the raise is dead. Only at the end of the long first scene is the matter reintroduced, this time by Caribaldi as a way of cruelly humiliating The Juggler:

> And your letter from the manager of Sarrasani
> is one of hundreds of forged letters
> that in the whole ten or twelve years
> you have been with me

you have held under my nose
Show me the offer
Show me the offer
*plucks the strings briefly a few times and holds the
bow steady, as if to
play.* THE JUGGLER *takes one, then another step
back*[.]

(P. 54)

Bernhard's text suggests that humans cannot achieve
spontaneous behavior or original thought. But this is not to
say that he displaces or down-grades character as an element of the dramatic text. The director of an American
production of **Force of Habit** told me that Caribaldi as a
character is more difficult to perform than Shakespeare's
Lear, mainly because he requires an actor to display a
range of subjecthood that stretches mimesis to its limits.
Not only must the actor speak with his body and by way
of Bernhard's text, he must over the course of rehearsals
become skilled enough with the cello to be able to "speak"
as well through the instrument.

To permit actors so great a range of expressive power
surely militates against the nihilism that is often attributed
to Bernhard's artifice and abstract patternings. In fact, one
may well describe art such as this as "postmodernist
humanism." If, for example, The Juggler's unthinking
repetitions make him into a humorous type, they also
constitute part of his unique "character-armor"[38]—a
personality borne of suffering, pathetically manifest as a
mechanism of displacement, deferral, and denial.

Let me sketch this more elaborately: in repeating the fiction of his "contract offer from France," The Juggler stands
no chance of fooling Caribaldi, but that repetition—even
though it does not win what he requests—enables him to
avoid facing his own extinction. It is as if he repeats the
very strategy he knows will fail precisely because he can
predict its failure. The abundance of references to France
suggests that The Juggler to some extent believes in his
own fiction, and that *he,* not Caribaldi, is the person for
whom the story is told. As The Juggler develops his
rambling monologue, he returns again and again, obliquely
or directly, to the subject of France. "France" thus appears
at the center of his particular narrative fantasy of self-
definition. In truth, hardly anything The Juggler says or
does lacks a French connection; images of France weave
in and out of his speech as though his life there were a living presence to him:

In Bordeaux above all
the white wine

(P. 10)

They are expecting me
in Bordeaux
a five year contract
Mr Caribaldi
My plate number by the way
is decidedly a French number

(P. 13)

and the possibility
to work together with my sister
CARIBALDI *lets the resin fall*
THE JUGGLER *picks it up*
Above all else
in France
Mr Caribaldi
the greatest impossibility
a blessing

(Pp. 23–24)

extra clothing allowance
and the French fresh air[.]

(P. 24)

Interspersed among The Juggler's repetitious conversation
with Caribaldi are repetitions of a particular sort—
memories, anecdotes, confessions that seem to indicate
that in an indirect (and perhaps unconscious or automatic)
way The Juggler is once again telling his own story. As
with The President's speech to The Actress, character here
develops as a weird and yet deeply moving narrative of
loss. The Juggler cannot speak directly for himself, but his
repetitious and disintegrating discourse conveys eloquently
his interior solitude and his emotional distress. The speech
is a broken-down autobiography: The Juggler recollects a
memory from his childhood when he played the violin,
storing extra pieces of resin in "emerald green boxes." He
describes his mother with pride: "French was the mother
tongue / of my mother" (p. 15); "That exceptional woman
/ my mother / by the way in Nantes / left the Church" (p.
15). He alludes briefly to his father—"As you know / my
father was from Gelsenkirchen / an unlucky man" (p.
26)—and to his sister, from whom he has long been
separated. He often mentions cellist Pablo Casals, who apparently has inspired him since childhood. And he repeatedly speaks of himself as an "artist," even though he makes
his living juggling plates and training poodles. In his
opinion such juggling is "art" and he himself is "admittedly a genius" (p. 34). Even when he performs in the
most humiliating conditions, playing out his act as the tent
is pulled down, The Juggler imagines that "the concentration of the audience / is centered on me" (p. 26).

That this last sequence of self-references exposes his
unthinking folly cannot completely subvert our sense that
there is a "being" under this text. Knowing so much about
his background, we have difficulty dismissing The Juggler
as a comic effect of discourse. He is as vain as any
Restoration fop. But is this simply a satiric exposure of
folly? In my view the repetitions that run throughout The
Juggler's monologue—while they are not, properly speaking, a coherent narrative—reveal an impulse toward a narrativity that could, ideally, organize the disorder of his life.
Repetition in this respect is not a sign of the Juggler's lack
of ideal sociability but the symptom of a subject desperately struggling to consolidate itself. The problem is that
The Juggler cannot find a way to act that does not lead
him to repeat himself, and so repetition both affirms and
denies his authenticity. If he attempts to create a life apart
from habit, he cannot act except according to a pattern

that guarantees his failure. If, on the other hand, The Juggler attempts to use the principle of repetition to sustain or to define himself, he is similarly humiliated to discover that exact repetition is impossible. Even his habits of dress betray him. The Juggler prides himself on maintaining an impeccable appearance. He always carries a handkerchief and a shoecloth, but toward the end of scene 2 he is discovered to have placed these items in the wrong pockets:

> [CARIBALDI] A polished, gleaming mirror
> you love that
> your shoes glistening
> THE JUGGLER *and* CARIBALDI *and the* GRAND-
> DAUGHTER *look*
> *at* THE JUGGLER'*s highly polished shoes*
> You have
> as I know
> a shoecloth always
> in your pants pocket
> in your right pants pocket
> in the right a shoe cloth
> in the left a handkerchief
> shoe cloth
> handkerchief
> shoe cloth
> handkerchief
> *ordering* THE JUGGLER
> Yes show
> show
> *orders* THE JUGGLER *with motions of the cello bow*
> *to turn his*
> *pockets inside out*
> Turn
> your pants pockets out
> Turn them out
> THE JUGGLER *turns his pants pockets inside out,*
> *but the shoe cloth*
> *comes into view out of the left and out of the right the*
> *handkerchief,*
> *not the other way round*
> You see
> you have the handkerchief
> not in the left pants pocket
> but in the right
> in the left you have the shoe cloth
> Even you err
> Mr. Juggler
> Put it all back again[.]

> (Pp. 93–94)

Of course this is the theme of **Force of Habit,** that the world leaves little room for perfection or original creativity. But my point is that Bernhard's Juggler, despite his manifest humor, ought not to be seen as an experiment in dramatic formalism but as an attempt to characterize the deserts of selfhood.

Caribaldi too is a "flat" character, and in some ways his mechanistic behavior is a metaphor for broad social or aesthetic matters. It is possible, for example, to see Bernhard's protagonist at the center of a treatise on power and subjection, perfection and human fallibility, art and the artist, and discipline and freedom. But the ringmaster,

like The Juggler, possesses a haunting inner landscape. In his interactions with others he is often brutal and insensitive, as, for example, when he compels his granddaughter to perform an exhausting series of calisthenics:

> CARIBALDI *keeping time with the cello bow*
> Onetwo
> onetwo
> onetwo
> onetwo
> onetwo
> onetwo
> onetwo
> onetwo
> onetwo
> onetwo
> onetwo
> onetwo
> onetwo
> onetwo
> onetwo
> onetwo
> Now stop
> GRANDDAUGHTER *stops, exhausted;* CARIBALDI
> *orders*:
> Peel the apples
> Polish the shoes
> Boil the milk
> Brush the clothes
> And get to rehearsal on time
> do you understand
> You can go[.]

> (Pp. 50–51)

Caribaldi's behavior is not particularly funny, although clearly the scene resurrects older forms of comic theater— the master-slave relationship of New Comedy is one parallel, *commedia* violence another. But there is an important distinction between Caribaldi's compulsive behavior and that of his theatrical antecedents. The blur of commands— onetwoonetwoonetwo—is sadistic but also compulsive, almost as if it were an incantation or a conjuring ritual. The outburst—it is not really speech—cannot easily be played without conferring on Caribaldi a distinct interiority that drives him to act as he does. Like The Juggler in the first scene, Caribaldi here is "not his own." The effect is to remind us of the extent to which the self can be corroded by orders of mimesis, namely, drive mechanisms or transferences. We know, for example, that Caribaldi imagines resemblances between his granddaughter and his own daughter, her mother. Repeatedly he refers to the young dancer as "my child," and it seems as if he uses that patronizing idiom more than idiomatically. On one occasion at least he seems unconsciously to be superimposing the image of the mother on the girl, as in dream:

> Tomorrow Augsburg
> do you sleep well
> in the night
> I don't sleep
> I don't dream
> Show your legs

GRANDDAUGHTER *shows her legs*
Your capital
Your mother
had the most beautiful legs
You must practice
in the strictest way
Practice
Wake up
Get up
Practice
Practice
Practice[.]

(Pp. 74–75)

The Granddaughter seems to provoke two kinds of responses from Caribaldi, both of which involve repetition as the basis for the production of character. First of all, his language creates a humorous monomaniac. But Caribaldi's brutal treatment of the girl often manifests itself as part of a network of habitual associations. In the foregoing scene, for example, it is the memory of the mother's beauty that provokes him to demand incessant practice on the part of The Granddaughter. Breaking off from his memory, he becomes a machine suddenly animated by hidden springs. His sudden reversion to habit (one order of repetition) is motivated, in other words, by another kind of repetition, the likeness of daughter to granddaughter. Caribaldi cannot deal consistently (or lovingly) with his granddaughter because he is unable to separate her from her mother. But that woman died some years ago, the result of a grisly accident on the high wire. Built into Bernhard's drama once again is the pathos of family tragedy, and even though the behavior demonstrated here is essentially humorous, its source is once again a *particular* mental life. Forces that are clearly psychological operate to produce an image of the subject that seems devoid of the marks of individual character precisely because it is compulsively characteristic.

In *Force of Habit* Bernhard poses some challenging questions about the interior structure of subjecthood. Working within the familiar conventions of humors characters, Bernhard isolates psychological realities on which mechanistic (hence characterless, in the sense of lacking individuating control) behavior can be founded. Some of the examples are innovative and ultimately mysterious, as in the case of The Juggler; others are almost textbook case histories. For example, a likely explanation for Caribaldi's tendency to confuse his daughter and granddaughter is given earlier in the scene by The Lion Tamer. He tells The Clown about the way Caribaldi's daughter died:

His daughter
you should have seen her
a beauty
she was completely mangled
Before that her father
made her practice
the drill How does one bow
fourteen times
just as he makes
his granddaughter

perform the same drill
fourteen times
She made a mistake
do you understand
The collarbone
driven into the temple
indicates this
THE CLOWN *imitates him*
Into the temple

JUGGLER
A third class funeral
the father so loved the daughter
she was buried in such haste[39]
that a year later
not a single person knew
where
he looked for her in vain
in the cemetery
Since then he never returns
to Osnabrück
Osnabrück no more

CLOWN
No more Osnabrück

LION TAMER
Like a dog
his own daughter
the dirt just thrown over her
do you understand[.]

(Pp. 62–63)

The Lion Tamer despises Caribaldi because he fails to show expected remorse. He cannot understand why the father seems so little affected by the daughter's death, and so he condemns Caribaldi as an unfeeling brute. But could Caribaldi's apparent indifference and his hostility toward his grand-daughter indicate paradoxically an unmanageable excess of grief? There is some reason to think so. For example, there is considerable overlap between Bernhard's character's behavior and the descriptions of pathological mourning to be found in psychoanalytic literature. I am not trying to prove that psychoanalysis uncovers the secret of Bernhard's art. But it is striking to see how closely the behavior described in actual clinical studies corresponds with Bernhard's bizarre stage fictions, and while that correspondence is probably neither Bernhard's ambition nor his greatest success, it is surely not irrelevant. This does not make *Force of Habit* a work of naturalistic psychology, but it does suggest how "painting the hero's mind" might be an important part of Bernhard's drama.

To see more clearly how Bernhard's drama might illustrate how individuality or society unfold themselves in literary forms, we might turn for a moment toward recent psychoanalytic literature. In that literature, as on Bernhard's stage, we can see a concern with a variety of affective disorders of the self that defy those represented by classic neuroses or conventional dramaturgies. For example, Julien Bigras, in an essay entitled "French Psychoanalysis," tells of a former patient, a young girl "who had been sent to me on the advice of her schoolteacher because she had shown absolutely no reaction after her mother had been killed in a car accident." Bigras writes that

> [t]he girl had also been involved in the crash but has suffered only a very slight brain concussion.
>
> Her teacher could not understand why the girl's conduct at school had not changed in any way whatsoever; she behaved as though absolutely nothing unusual had occurred. I too was at a loss to understand the phenomenon. I therefore accepted her as a patient. I had already dealt with several cases of traumatic neuroses and thus knew that spontaneous sketches, dreams, and fantasies of the patient should reveal violent scenes linked to the accident in which her mother had been killed. This was not the case; the girl would say, "I don't have dreams. No, I'm not afraid. Everything is fine, I assure you."
>
> There was nothing left but to hope that, as a last resort, the spontaneous sketches done by the girl would clear up the mystery. But here also I drew a blank: a cozy little house, a road, a tree; in short, the ingredients of the typical child's drawing. True, a little star or two were in the first drawing, but who would have paid any attention to them? And since it was around Christmas, who would see anything unusual in stars at the tips of the branches of a Christmas tree? Yet in subsequent drawings the stars reappeared again and again scattered among blue flowers or atop a mountain and even at times next to a dazzling yellow sun. Six months went by and still I saw nothing significant in this fact.
>
> Then one day I had a kind of illumination. "Tell me," I said, "when the accident happened I'll bet you saw stars."
>
> She had indeed seen stars at the moment of impact. She immediately burst into tears and told me that she saw stars every night. She was afraid to fall asleep and see them appear again. In addition, from that day forward, she became sad both in my presence and at school. Only at that point was she able to comprehend that before it was neither possible nor permissible for her to mourn her mother's death.
>
> As I listened to "On Death-Work" [a lecture which prompted Bigras to remember his experience with this patient] it was my turn to become aware of something: the subtle and cunning ways in which the death drive works. Suddenly this notion became tangible and vital. It was the "work of death" which, without my young patient or myself being aware of it, had held constant and silent sway over the life of a child and continued to exert its influence upon the cure process she was going through with me. Surely it is striking to see how awesomely the death drive worked its way into the very cure, even concealing itself beneath the things children are so fond of, like wonderful scenes depicting nature or Christmas.[40]

Caribaldi's repetitious behavior, like that of the little girl who added stars to all her drawings, accords with the existence of an unseen drive or instinct. From this perspective, it looks less like "humorous" cruelty or artistic formalism and more like the frenzied activity often associated with actual narcissistic personality disorders. Certainly

Caribaldi's behavior with respect to his daughter is more complex and more pathetic than The Lion Tamer imagines. The acts immediately following her death—the swift burial, the period of denial, and then the desperate search for the grave and the subsequent taboo that he attaches to Osnabrück—are consonant with the compulsive actions one finds in case studies of pathological mourning or in accounts of so-called narcissistic disorders or schizoid fractures of the self. The central experience in the lives of such people, writes Ernest Wolf, is "the experience of unbearable emptiness that comes with loneliness . . . a loneliness that almost immediately elicits some relieving action to restitute the crumbling self." This activity commonly is frenzied, according to Wolf; it is "often tinged with the excitements of sexuality or of aggression, is used to create a sense of aliveness, to banish the dreaded nothingness that comes with the loss of self."[41]

Bernhard's work extends character, then, in two directions simultaneously. In the texts I have chosen to discuss, individuality tends to be represented as dependent both on interior as well as on exterior repetitions. In the latter case Bernhard's characters are almost neoclassical—the image not of an individual but a species or type. They show us what people habitually do (or are), and as characters they can be imaged theatrically as masks or humors. The force of habit requires that we behave like automata. At the same time, however, Bernhard's characters own a discrete core of individuality, and this in turn makes it hard to efface Romantic (or individualist) impressions of subjectivity from the text. Caribaldi's humorous mask does not rule out his possessing a hidden self. On the contrary, his mask is clearly the sign of his inner distress. His behavior is like the tip of an iceberg—a misleading distortion, a clinical symptom with limited reference to the actual malaise. There is more than enough material in the text to prove that Caribaldi attempts to control the mother, whom he cannot reach, by controlling her daughter. His desire to turn his granddaughter into a marionette indicates that he has a control instinct and is using her as a child might use a toy. The comic humor in this case represents the individual's response to pain. Caribaldi invents a game whose express purpose is to effect the illusion of control. Thus Caribaldi's humor is not imposed on him from without, nor does it indicate a complete lack of subjectivity. Insofar as it results in predictable or characteristic behavior, it is an aggressive mode of self-production. The passive and annihilating situation imposed on him by death can be transformed into an aggressive reaction. Not only can Caribaldi control the trauma of losing the mother by dominating the granddaughter, he can even enact on the missing mother a kind of revenge: onetwoonetwoonetwo, daughter away, daughter dead.

To be sure, Caribaldi's humorous behavior in this scene is a defensive strategy only. Of the trigger mechanism we know almost nothing except that it is an event that is neither possible nor permissible for him to accept. From The Lion Tamer's point of view, Caribaldi is inhuman, a megalomaniac. From another perspective, one can see that his life is a profoundly moving horror. His aberrant behavior hints at disordering forces that exist at the foundation of character and yet conceal themselves beneath the masks of egoism, motion, and tyranny—ironically, those very forms of behavior that most suggest the power of individual will.

"The most remarkable peculiarity of melancholia," writes Freud, "and one most in need of explanation, is the tendency it displays to turn into mania accompanied by a completely opposite symptomology."[42] Caribaldi is a textbook melancholic; common sense tells us that his humor imitates something real. Caribaldi's megalomania, his insane quest for perfection, his absurdly repetitive schedule, all are instinctive strategies that have no other aim than their own ceaseless accomplishment. The aim of such repetition (as Freud postulated) is not to obtain pleasure but to ward off death. Ironically, only the force of habit sustains the illusion of life. The perception is both fearful and funny: funny, like the coyote in the children's cartoon, who falls only when he looks down and his legs stop churning; fearful, as when Caribaldi responds to The Clown's monotonous bowing of his instrument by saying that

> if he stops
> he's dead
> with his bow
> in death
> laid out[.]

(P. 103)

The final irony is that all the characters in *Force of Habit* owe their identities to habit itself. On Bernhard's stage, however, habit does not constitute a mask that must be dropped if the wearer is to recover his or her "self." Against textual or centerless grammars for character Bernhard sets distinct signs of innerness, and the resulting gaps or inconsistencies give his characters their unsettling reality. Caribaldi, like the majority of Bernhard's characters, exists because of a grammar of identity sufficiently sophisticated to redefine literary flatness with both psychology and sociology. Likewise, Bernhard's experimental stylistics and conscious deformation of genre create a new topography on stage for self-experience and self-definition. He writes humors comedy as if authorized in turn by Plato and Freud—a theater in which character is a function of mimesis and where images of the self and its representations create a remarkably chilling hilarity.

Notes

1. Claude Rawson, "Order and Cruelty," in *Essays in Criticism* 20 (1970): 24–56. Stephen Dowden, in *Understanding Thomas Bernhard* (Columbia, S.C.: University of South Carolina Press, 1991), reads Bernhard's work as "similar in nature" to that of Swift and other great satirists. Dowden's book in my opinion is the best work by far to appear on Bernhard in English, and while I disagree in many cases with his readings of individual works, I acknowledge his influence in this and the following several paragraphs.

2. Thomas Bernhard, *Der Italiener* (Salzburg: Residenz, 1971), p. 83; my translation.

3. Attributed often to Hermann Göring, but originally said by Hanns Johst, *Schlageter* (1933), cited in *Bartlett's Familiar Quotations,* 16th ed. (Boston: Little, Brown, 1992), p. 679.

4. Lyons, "Character and Theatrical Space," p. 30.

5. Dowden, *Understanding Thomas Bernhard,* p. 72.

6. Gitta Honegger, "Acoustic Masks: Strategies of Language in the Theater of Canetti, Bernhard, and Handke," *Modern Austrian Literature* 18 (1985): 64.

7. Dowden, *Understanding Thomas Bernhard,* p. 5.

8. Martin Esslin, "A Drama of Disease and Derision: The Plays of Thomas Bernhard," *Modern Drama* 23 (1981): 377.

9. Nicholas Eisner, *"Theatertheater/Theaterspiele*: The Plays of Thomas Bernhard," *Modern Drama* 30 (1987): 105.

10. Denis Calandra, *New German Dramatists: A Study of Peter Handke, Franz Xaver Kroetz, Rainer Werner Fassbinder, Heiner Müller, Thomas Brasch, Thomas Bernhard and Botho Strauss* (New York: Grove Press, 1983), p. 27.

11. Dowden, *Understanding Thomas Bernhard,* p. 7.

12. Ibid, p. 24.

13. Ibid., p. 32.

14. Thomas Bernhard, *Ein Fest für Boris* (Frankfurt: Suhrkamp, 1968), p. 34; translations of Bernhard's works unless otherwise noted are mine.

15. See Hans Wolfschütz, "Thomas Bernhard: The Mask of Death," in *Modern Austrian Writing: Literature and Society after 1945,* ed. Alan Best and Hans Wolfschütz (Totowa, N.J.: Barnes and Noble, 1980), pp. 214–35. Wolfschütz writes that "all Bernhard's characters are marked by such an 'event,' whether this takes the form of some personal misfortune or shock, or has been experienced as part of a general or historical 'catastrophe'" (p. 214).

16. Thomas Bernhard, *Histrionics,* trans. Peter Jansen and Kenneth Northcott (Chicago: The University of Chicago Press, 1990), pp. 218–19.

17. Nicholas J. Meyerhofer, "The Laughing Sisyphus: Reflections on Bernhard as (Self-) Dramatist in Light of His *Der Theatermacher,*" *Modern Austrian Literature* 21 (1988): 108.

18. Calandra, *New German Dramatists,* p. 144.

19. Bernhard, *Histrionics,* p. 282.

20. In Ibsen's play, of course, the child is comforted by the parent. But Sarah's role in *Histrionics* is to minister to Bruscon's emotional needs, in effect a kind of mothering.

21. Amity Shlaes, "Thomas Bernhard and the German Literary Scene," *The New Criterion* 5 (January 1987): 30.

22. Quoted in Kurt Hofmann, *Aus Gesprächen mit Thomas Bernhard* (Vienna: Löcker, 1988), p. 79.

23. Martin Esslin says Bernhard is "a kind of Austrian Beckett," in "Beckett and Bernhard: A Comparison," *Modern Austrian Literature* 18 (1985): 67. Esslin also discounts any direct influence of one writer on the other.

24. Cited in Calandra, *New German Dramatists*, p. 145.

25. Esslin, "Drama of Disease and Derision," p. 374.

26. Bakhtin's "dialogic" (or "heteroglossic") self and Burke's "dramatistic" readings of behavior are well known; it should not be necessary to develop an extended comparison between their respective theories and Bernhard's models for character. Such an extended comparison would prove little, though of course the points of comparison are many. See M.M. Bakhtin, *The Dialogic Imagination: Four Essays,* ed. Michael Holquist, trans. Caryl Emerson and Michael Holquist (Austin: University of Texas Press, 1981), and Kenneth Burke, *Language as Symbolic Action: Essays on Life, Literature, and Method* (Berkeley: University of California Press, 1966).

27. Thomas Bernhard, *Eve of Retirement,* trans. Gitta Honegger (New York: Performing Arts Journal Publications, 1982), p. 204.

28. Robert Skloot, *The Darkness We Carry: The Drama of the Holocaust* (Madison: University of Wisconsin Press, 1988), p. 110.

29. Thomas Bernhard, *Der Spiegel,* 23 June 1980, quoted in Calandra, *New German Dramatists,* p. 149.

30. Text is *Der Präsident* (Frankfurt: Suhrkamp, n.d.), p. 140. My translation.

31. Bennett Simon, *Tragic Drama and the Family,* p. 237.

32. See W.R. Bion, "Attacks on Linking," *International Journal of Psycho-Analysis* 40 (1959): 308–15.

33. Robert Langbaum, *The Poetry of Experience: The Dramatic Monologue in Modern Literary Tradition* (New York: Norton, 1963), p. 182.

34. Ibid., p. 183.

35. Esslin, "Drama of Disease and Derision," p. 374.

36. Ibid.

37. Thomas Bernhard, *Force of Habit* (*Die Macht der Gewohnheit,* Frankfurt: Suhrkamp, 1974), pp. 9–12. All references to *Force of Habit* are to this text; translations are mine.

38. "Character-armor" is Wilhelm Reich's term for describing repeated defensive acts. For an application of the concept to stage characters, see Edward Burns, *Character: Acting and Being on the Pre-Modern Stage* (London: Macmillan, 1990), p. 228.

39. *Verscharren,* "to cover with earth secretly or hurriedly," implies shame.

40. Julien Bigras, "French Psychoanalysis," in *Psychoanalysis, Creativity, and Literature: A French-American Inquiry,* ed. Alan Roland (New York: Columbia University Press, 1978), pp. 15–16.

41. Ernest S. Wolf, "The Disconnected Self," in Roland, *Psychoanalysis, Creativity, and Literature,* pp. 104–6.

42. Freud, "Mourning and Melancholia" (1917), in *General Psychological Theory,* ed. Philip Rieff (New York: Macmillan, 1963), p. 173.

Bianca Theisen (essay date April 1996)

SOURCE: "Comitragedies: Thomas Bernhard's Marionette Theater," in *Modern Language Notes,* Vol. 111, No. 3, April, 1996, pp. 533–59.

[*In the following essay, Theisen examines Bernhard's treatment of genre in his work—particularly comedy and tragedy—and asserts that the playwright "experiments with the delimitations of genre, which he dissolves and draws anew as observations of observations."*]

Almost everything comic depends on the appearance of self-annihilation.

—Friedrich Schlegel

Unsatisfied with what comedy writers have to offer, four actors band together to write their own comedy. Although each actor is supposed to write a role for himself, "each one naturally only [writes] about himself." The actors could not have titled the comedy "they produced after weeks of painstaking study anything but *The Author.*" "But even with this *Author,* it is reported, they had no success."[1] Thomas Bernhard could not have titled this anecdote in *Stimmenimitator* anything but *Komödie.* A different title could not have both captured the self-referentiality of the situation and comically broken it. What the actors perform is evidently not comic, but their own *comedy* becomes in a sense their *own* comedy. Insofar as the actors, portraying only themselves, no longer differentiate between role and self or between actor and author, their play *The Author* fails to distinguish itself from the dull productions of the standard comedy writers. The actors have no more success with themselves as authors than with the other authors.

Bernhard's *Komödie* interrupts the self-reference of this "author" by differentiating, almost imperceptibly, between various levels. It is in these terms that the anecdote provides the framework in which I would like to discuss Bernhard's treatment of genre delimitations, above all of comedy, but also indirectly of tragedy. I also want to call attention to an intertextual invocation of Kleist which is relevant for this re-drawing of genre borders. If in his first novel *Frost,* Bernhard already brings together the two dramatic species in a single word, "Komödientragödien,"[2] this does not amount to an affirmation of the simple exchangeability or admixture of comedy and tragedy[3] (although the literature on Bernhard has repeatedly claimed as much, thereby posing questions of genre aesthetics as existential questions which are concealed by their translation into a theatrical metaphorics).[4] Bernhard experiments with the delimitations of genre, which he dissolves and draws anew as observations of observations. This experimentation with genre borders whose installation is dependent on an observer is also implicitly intertextual, if one invokes Mikhail Bakhtin's concept of ambivalence as the coincidence and differentiation of levels by which one word is embedded *in* another but at the same time remains a word *about* the other word. With this formulation, Bakhtin intended to provide an alternative to Tarski's distinction between object-language and meta-language.[5] Rather than speaking of one word being embedded in another, one could speak—using the conceptual models developed by Heinz von Foerster and Niklas Luhmann—about different levels of observation or about the unity of the distinction between self-reference and hetero-reference. The texts I shall be examining relate the recursivity of all observation to a new delimitation of comedy and are connected intertextually with Kleist, particularly to the latter's essay "Über das Marionettentheater," a text which also confounds us with the paradoxes of distinction-driven observation. With the literary processes of intertextuality and genre differentiation, Bernhard also displaces the problem of reference. His texts do not refer to the world as a world of pre-given history or representable objects, but construct a world intertextually out of other texts, a world which only develops from recursive observations.[6] In short, a world as a case (*Fall*) of distinction.

I

In the title of his short story, "Is it a comedy? Is it a tragedy?", which first appeared in 1967, three years before his first drama, Bernhard already seems to give the distinction between these two dramatic forms conceptual priority, evidently deciding at the end of the story in favor of comedy. The first-person narrator, who visits the theater precisely because he hates it, abandons his visit and sits in the park in front of the theater where he watches the other theater-goers enter. A man in women's clothes addresses him, repeating the question posed in the title without expecting an answer from the narrator: "What will be performed, a comedy, or a tragedy?" The man claims that studying the narrator ought to be a way of getting information "about everything that takes place in the theater and everything that takes place outside the theater, about everything in the world."[7] Through the observation of the other—the transvestite sees that the first-person narrator sees that he is wearing women's clothes—he primarily provides information about himself: he is wearing the

clothes of a woman he had thrown into the Donau Canal twenty-two years earlier, and every evening he repeats the play's opening scenario which is concerned with this "incident" (E 85). In the final sentence of the story, he concludes that what is performed in the theater is "*really* a comedy" (E 89).

The transvestite concludes that a comedy is being performed *in* the theater on the basis of the situation *outside* the theater.[8] The travesty of genre corresponds to the transvestism of the murderer of women dressed as a woman. If the transvestite claims that he can infer from the observation of his interlocutor what takes place in the theater, outside the theater, and in the world on account of the fact that everything in the world is always connected to everything else, then the observation of the other is revealed to be a self-observation unfolding in the relation between theater and world. In the observation of the other, the transvestite appears to observe what he himself does not see: the paradoxical simultaneity of his transvestism, the unity of the distinction between man and woman, aggressor and victim, the paradoxical situation of a murderer of women dressed as a woman. Observing the first-person narrator's observations thus makes possible the transvestite's self-observation as a second-order phenomenon from which transvestism can be seen as transvestism. On the other hand, if the transvestite mistakes himself for a woman, he also takes the place of the narrator (in whose person he believes he is able to read both what will be performed in the theater and what takes place in the world). The world, the man repeats twice, is a juridical world; it is a "penitentiary" (E 86, 89), an institution which regulates exclusion through inclusion, while what is performed in the theater, is "really a comedy" (as the man in women's clothes establishes outside the theater, and that is, in the world).

Bernhard intensifies the topos of the world theater into the paradox of a unity of inclusion and exclusion. *Outside* the theater, but *in* the world, which as penitentiary again includes the excluded, one knows what is performed *in* the theater through the observation of observers. Bernhard's paradox cannot simply be explained with Friedrich Dürrenmatt's insight that comedy is suspiciously paradoxical. Dürrenmatt argues that if comedy is to become the world theater, only the plot has to be comic. Not only are the characters often not comic, but they can even be tragic. The comic plot, argues Dürrenmatt, must be understood in terms of paradox. A plot is paradoxical "when it has been thought through to the end."[9] In Bernhard's case, the point is not only that the comic plot becomes paradoxical, but also that in this narrative he presents the form of the drama as a paradox, evidenced in the distinction between comedy and tragedy on the one hand, and the delimitation of theater from world on the other. Recursively, the world theater includes the whole in the part, the world in the theater, and vice versa, the part in the whole, the theater in the world. All the world is a stage, and the stage planks signify the world. In order to think the topos of the world theater in its paradox "through to the end," one must ask from what point in the world one could see that all the world is a stage. The actors must simultaneously become their own audience, a constraint which is normally presented as the problem of the play within a play. The play within a play renders visible each demarcation *within* the play that makes the play into a play in that it differentiates it from something, for instance, from the world. Otherwise, this demarcation or distinction remains invisible. The play within a play can thus be understood as the re-entry of form into form.[10] Bernhard does not fall back on this representation of the play within a play, but mobilizes its logic of recursive inclusion in order to make it simultaneously visible "from the outside" through exclusion. The actors do not become their own audience, rather the audience becomes the audience of the audience. The first-person narrator observes the visitors to the theater at the precise moment that they enter the theater and thereby cross the boundary between world and theater, turning from players (*Spielern*) in the world into the audience in the theater which observes actors (*Spieler*) in the theater. Outside the theater, the transvestite observes the observer of these observers.

Instead of the border between world and theater being represented *in* the theater through the play within a play, the border is here represented *outside* the theater as the world in the world. The fact that penal institutions in the world are no joy and that the entire world is a penal institution has to be juxtaposed with the observation that in the theater comedy is being performed and is, like the observation of the theater, an observation of the world, an observation that, in the world, is only possible as an observation of observers. As observers, "we distinguish ourselves," as Francisco Varela has formulated it, "precisely by distinguishing what we apparently are not, the world."[11] The world is therefore neither this nor that; it is not a world of things; it *is* neither theater nor penal institution. Rather, the world is, as Niklas Luhmann says, nothing but the "blind spot of its self-observation,"[12] and as such, with Bernhard, "really a comedy." In the case of Bernhard's story, one could reformulate this and say that the world is everything that is the incident (*die Welt is alles, was der (Zwischen) fall ist*). After all, the observation of observers as self-observation is always connected to the repeated "incident." Bernhard is evidently reading Wittgenstein with Kleist. For Wittgenstein, the world is everything that is the case (*Fall*), and that means that it is not an inventory of pre-given things, but the totality of facts into which it disintegrates.[13] That which is the case (*Fall*) can now only be interpreted with Kleist as the Fall (*Fall*) into distinction and observation. In his "Über das Marionettentheater," Kleist thus interprets the theologeme of the Fall into sin. He presents not only his familiar thesis about the grace of the mechanistic, but, in suggesting that we eat from the tree of knowledge a second time and thereby repeat the fall, he also argues for the application of the fall to the fall, or, in other words, for the re-entry of the form of distinction-making into the distinction (be it between good and evil or between graceful and graceless). Through a second fall, we might be able to cross the border

which made the world into the post-lapsarian world. This border, as that which makes the world into the world, is the fall. As in Bernhard's story the incident (*Zwischenfall*), the fall (*Fall*) in Kleist's "Marionette Theater" is everything that is the case (*Fall*).

II

Reformulating the genre-definitions of comedy in terms of distinction theory, one could say that comedy observes tragedy with regards to its form. It is a second-order observation of tragedy. If Bernhard already speaks in *Frost* of "comitragedies," he is not aiming, as the transposition of comedy and tragedy already indicates, for the sublation of both into the synthetic category of tragicomedy.[14] Bernhard increasingly has genre concepts oscillate, for instance, in *Watten*: "Man kann in Verzweiflung, sage ich, gleich, wo man ist, gleich, wo man sich aufhalten muß in dieser Welt, von einem Augenblick auf den anderen aus der Tragödie (in der man ist) in das Lustspiel eintreten (in dem man ist), umgekehrt jederzeit aus dem Lustspiel (in dem man ist) in die Tragödie (in der man ist)." And one day, one is "alles auf einmal" and "dadurch in einem Augenblick alles."[15] Constantly switching out of tragedy into comedy and out of comedy into tragedy presupposes a crossing of borders, a crossing which takes time ("from one moment to the next"), but which is synchronized in the coincidence of tragedy and comedy ("everything in a moment"). With such a coincidence, Bernhard neither aims for the sublation of comedy and tragedy in a synthesis, nor for the collision of the two into one another in a sort of toppling-phenomenon which, as Christian Klug has argued, would guarantee the partial identity of comedy and tragedy.[16] One can only speak of such a toppling if, instead of identity, one means an alteration of the viewpoint which treats border displacements in terms of a relation between figure and ground.[17] Even the eighteenth-century category of the *rührenden* or *weinerlichen Lustspiel*—defined by Lessing not as a mediating category between the tragic and the comic, but as a subgenre of comedy—does not help with Bernhard's comitragedies.[18] The apparent lack of distinction in Bernhard's bringing-together of comedy and tragedy, which nevertheless directly calls attention to their distinction (the composite "comitragedy" makes this distinction-in-coincidence visible), cannot be adequately grasped with concepts of mediation or subcategories drawn from genre theory. It requires another definition of form alltogether. The suggestion to define comedy as a second-order observation of tragedy may in this regard prove helpful.

In the ancient tragedy, the polis presents itself to itself. The world of the polis is not simply reflected in tragedy. In the tragic conflict, tragedy represents the demarcation of the borders which made the polis into a polis in the first place. Tragedy plays a mythical past off against the present of the polis. The hero and the chorus confront one another as the protagonists of this conflictual distinction. Heroic legend and mythic tradition are brought to the stage in the person of the hero, whereas the chorus speaks as the representative of the polis. This distinction between past and present, myth and polis, hero and chorus, is taken up again in the duality of language, but is thereby inverted: the older, lyric form of the chorus is opposed to the contemporary prose of the hero. Vernant has described this crossing of myth and polis in the language of tragedy as an ambiguous logic by which the hero, as the representative of a past world, becomes, through his language, the contemporary of the audience (which actually sees itself represented in the chorus).[19] This means that the dialogical character of language once again takes up the contradiction in an inverted form in that it re-introduces the form of tragedy (namely the conflict of past and present) into its form and presents it as the simultaneity of the unsimultaneous.[20] If one conceives of this unity as self-differentiating, then one can reformulate the Aristotelian demand for the "unity of time" in tragedy, a demand which, despite the uni-linear interpretations it has been given in normative poetics, can perhaps assume a new value. The two sides, past/present, are presented both simultaneously and sequentially, as an earlier/later distinction. This paradox of tragedy, which takes its starkest form in its temporal relations, can be described in terms of the simultaneity of the unsimultaneous implicit in Niklas Luhmann's concept of form.[21] In any case, what is at issue here is the crossing of a border whose two sides are given simultaneously, although the crossing of a border from one side to the other takes time.

Sophocles' tragedies turn on the axis of such liminal zones, which Lacan has characterized with reference to *Antigone* as the border zone between two deaths. Lacan anchors them in the splitting of the signifier, which introduces (e.g., with the pleonastic "not" of Oedipus' last words, μηφυναι—in Lacan's translation: "better not to be") a split between the levels of utterance and assertion, a split which erases one's actual being.[22] Whether "linguistically," in the pleonasm of the negating particle, or "logically," in the tautology in which for Antigone the brother is who he is and only he who can be who he is (he is he, a tautology whose law Antigone takes to the limit of the law), tragedy deals with the paradox of demarcation. One could also say: tragedy reintroduces the form (of demarcation or distinction) into the form, and thus lets the audience see to what the hero remains blind—his own limits.

The object of comedy is not this or that comic phenomenon, this or that comic type, nor is it the semantics of oppositional pairs such as order and the breaking of norm. The object of comedy, rather, is the paradox of form in tragedy. Whereas tragedy digs in to paradox, introduces a demarcation which delimits itself internally, and endures the conflict between mythos and polis, comedy presents the conflict in all its facets in comic distance, observing it as the blindness of pure self-reference and unfolding the paradox of tragedy in that it introduces an external, or better, an eccentric, standpoint. It is the function of ancient comedy's parabasis, in which the chorus turns to the audience and disrupts the theatrical illusion, to break open the pure self-reference of the polis in tragedy from such an ec-centric standpoint. Parabasis evades the deathly tautology of the tragic border zone in that it displaces that border, inserting it between the play and the audience in such a way that it is momentarily suspended. According to Lacan, comedy makes us laugh because it presents life as something merely fleeting, something which slips away, something which constantly tears apart its demarcations and barriers, which Lacan regards as constituted through the instance of the signifier.[23] In Lacan's logic of the signifier, the relation between tragedy and comedy can also be described as a displacement of demarcations. The border zone between two deaths is observed from a comic distance as a life in flight. After all, the comic is, for Friedrich Schlegel, the *appearance* of self-annihilation. If in the blindness of the tragic hero the audience sees that it cannot see what it does not see, then it could be argued that comedy puts the audience on stage in order that it can see itself seeing in the auditorium in precisely this non-seeing.[24] Through parabasis, self-reference can be unfolded as hetero-reference. In comedy, the "form" of tragedy (its pure self-reference in the paradox of the internally self-delimiting limitation, which for Luhmann, like every form observed as paradox, symbolizes world, itself also a case of pure self-reference[25]) becomes the "content," and therefore comic.[26]

Looked at in this way, the relation between tragedy and comedy could be regarded as a genre-poetological version of Wittgenstein's problem that every language is based on demarcations, or on a structure about which one can say nothing *in* this language, so that another language is needed in order to be able to express something *about* the structure of the first language, and still another language in order to be able to speak about the structure of the second. If comedy can say something about the structure of tragedy, if it is a second-order observation, with what "language" can one then say something about the structure of comedy? For modern literature, the answer may be: narrativization.[27] The narrative must thus provide a third level of observation from which the observation of second-order observations can be observed. It is thus not by chance that Bernhard deals with the difference between first and second orders of observation ("Is it a tragedy? Is it a comedy?") in a short-story. With its genre of genres, the romantic novel, Romanticism already sought a third-order level of observation, which was supposed to transcend genre borders in the poetry of poetry and the unity of literature and criticism. The parabasis, the external, eccentric viewpoint erected by the ancient Attic comedy between audience and stage, reality and fiction, in order to be able to observe the demarcation as a demarcation, is thereby carried over into the epic. "Parabasis and chorus necessary for each novel (as exponential)" (Parekbase und Chor jedem Roman nothwendig (als Potenz), writes Friedrich Schlegel.[28] Parabasis offers no meta-position from which something would be said through genre borders *about* the play. Meta-positions disappear in the recursivity of the languages of genre and the levels of observation. Parabasis makes possible the leap from one genre border to another, from one observation level to another, which each time unfolds the pure self-reference of a form *as* form. In the genre theory of early German Romanticism, parabasis is therefore promoted, as Werner Hamacher has argued, to the "form of the generation of genre."[29]

Following the historicization of genres in the eighteenth century and their differentiation from one another in terms of temporality, the genre theorists of the Age of Goethe experiment with a differentiation between levels of observation and dynamize genre borders within the field of Idealism's conceptualization of reflection. When Bernhard's German poet Moritz Meister says, "Das Tragische habe ich so herausgearbeitet / daß es die Lust am Denken nicht verdirbt / die Komödie entstehen lassen aus der Tragödie,"[30] he thereby invokes the genre definition of comedy that was formulated by, for instance, Schiller and Hegel. For Schiller, comedy (a genre inclined towards the subjective, towards understanding and "intellectual freedom") emerges from tragedy (which for its part has the objective as object). As a reflexive genre, in which, "nothing takes place through the object and everything takes place through the poet," comedy would, in the end, "make all tragedies superfluous and impossible." Schiller defines this genre difference with reference to his distinction between the sensible and the intelligible. If tragedy arouses passions, comedy turns to understanding and demands the freedom to stand reflective and sovereign above all things rather than passionately mourning for them. In contradistinction to the tragic poet, who treats his object practically, the comic poet always approaches his object theoretically in order to achieve this reflexive effect. Comedy thus emerges from tragedy and overcomes it because (as Schiller only implies) it can reflect on the contradiction in which tragedy remains trapped. Comedy aims to be "free from passion, always clear, always calm, in order to be able to look in and around itself."[31] To put this another way, when it looks in and around itself, thereby differentiating between self- and hetero-reference, comedy moves on a level of second-order observation, without thereby becoming implicated in "passion." Comedy observes how tragedy observes.

Such attempts to bring genre borders into the context of observations organized around distinction remain stuck, however, in a synthesis-based philosophy of the subject. This is also true of Hegel's aesthetics. For Hegel, the unity of the distinction between tragedy and comedy is at first not the drama, but the mediating "middle-genre" between the two, the satyr play or tragicomedy.[32] As for the drama itself, it spans these types of the dramatic and is itself in turn differentiated from both the objectivity of the epic and the subjectivity of the lyric. In the drama's law of unity, a concentration or a "coherence," as much objective as subjective, is opposed to both the shaky coherence of epic episodes in their "objective independence" and the subjective individuation of lyric self-expression. This law of unity is objective with reference to the dramatic conflict, which pits individuals against one another, and subjective in the appearance of this conflict as the passion of each

particular character, a transposition or representation on the level of the subjective which reduplicates the conflict.[33] For Hegel, the drama is defined by this contradiction or collision, but he insists that this contradiction must sublate itself as contradiction in the dramatic resolution.[34] From this sublation of the contradiction in the dramatic resolution, Hegel deduces the distinction between tragedy and comedy. With the resolution of the contradiction—the triumph of the objective in tragedy, of the subjective in comedy—Hegel reintroduces in his distinction of these two dramatic types the distinction between objective and subjective canceled and synthesized in the drama, in order to then bring the distinction in the tragicomedy to a synthesis once again. Whereas in tragedy the individuals destroy themselves in the one-sidedness of their passions, and thus each subjective particularity erases itself in the triumph of an objectivity (which Hegel names eternal justice or moral force), in comedy, by contrast, the objective resolves itself into a self-confirming subjectivity. Unlike tragedy, in which individuals are destroyed by the resolution of the contradiction, comedy brings forth individuals who are raised above their own contradiction in their self-confirming subjectivity. For Hegel, it is precisely this sovereignty in the face of contradiction which makes comedy stand out and distinguishes it from the ludicrous.[35] Unlike the ludicrous, comedy is not produced through the representation of flaws, deficits, vices, or other deviations from the norm; and, according to Hegel, comedy should not simply present a topsy-turvy world and its collapse. Because it could be said that the contradiction appears in it twice, comedy must represent the mastery of this inverted world riddled with false contradictions through a subject who for his part is in contradiction with the world, but is at the same time elevated above the contradiction. In the middle-genre of tragicomedy, the tragic and comic are not opposites which pass over into one another. In this dramatic genre, which for Hegel is specifically modern, they are instead drawn into a balance in which the subjective wrests itself from the purely comic reversals, fortifies itself with earnestness, and thus ameliorates the tragic conflict. In Hegel's historicizing dialecticization of genres, tragedy thus appears as something past which is replaced by comedy in order finally to be synthesized with it in the tragicomedy as the most modern version of the self-implication of dramatic form. Tragedy and comedy are sublated in tragicomedy. This historicization of tragedy and comedy reappears again, extended across the historical process as such, in Marx's dictum that the last phase of a world-historical formation is its comedy.[36]

The genre theories of Schiller and Hegel can be summarized as saying that comedy raises itself above tragedy's objective tendency and the contradiction it suffers insofar as it reflects on them. Comedy becomes the genre of the subject, which remains free even with respect to its own contradiction. One can follow Jean Paul when he defines the comic as an "observed contradiction" and conceptualizes it as the "free play" of understanding through which the subject, in that it sees both self and other in a "picture-light" (Vexier-Lichte) cast from itself and into itself, achieves a new freedom of self-determination.[37] Because these genre theories understand comedy in terms of such contradictions, they define it not in terms of a semantics of norm and deviation, or of an order disturbed and restored, but in terms of its form. These theories attempt to unfold the formal determination of the contradictions treated in comedy as a subject-object relation, and to mediate between them. If the object becomes independent and even occupies the status of a subject in the comic reversal, if, in turn, the subject is mechanized and pushed into the status of an object, this crossing of subject-object positions has no telos out of which a generic definition of comedy could be deduced in terms of an independent object or an objectified, mechanized subject. According to Idealism's genre theory, comedy can always only deal with the subject: even as a mechanized subject who has become object, this subject can now observe itself differently *as* subject, re-drawing its own borders and relating to them freely.

Although the idealistic definitions of comedy do not present a theory of contrasts according to which the comic would be defined in terms of semanticized oppositions, as the other of order or reason, they nevertheless pacify contradictions with conceptions of mediation such as the tragicomedy, or with a dialectic unfolded in the subject-object relation. In order to be able to see how the treatment of contradictions and paradoxes becomes the *form* of comedy, it is necessary to distance oneself both from theories of contrast and from efforts at dialectical mediation. Joachim Ritter attempts this in his essay "On Laughter" where he defines the comic as the double movement of exclusion and the re-inclusion of the excluded. Comedy arises not from the contrast between what is excluding and what is excluded, but through their parallelization. In the process, Ritter envisions an overlapping of the two realms through which the "the excluded realm is itself made visible in and to the realm which excludes it." Whereas for Ritter, comedy aims to produce "the identity of the excluded and the excluding,"[38] we could, instead of talking about identity, speak of a unity of the distinction between excluded and excluding in comedy, and thus describe the form of the contradiction, which is exhibited in the re-entry of the excluded into the excluding as a paradox of demarcation. We would thereby describe comedy as a second-order observation of the paradox of demarcation in tragedy. Thomas Bernhard radicalizes the dependency of genre differentiations on such an observer: "Für die Außenwelt ist eine Komödie / was in Wirklichkeit / eine Tragödie ist,"[39] he writes in *Der Ignorant und der Wahnsinnige,* a play which takes the reflection on the blindness of each individual distinction-driven observation so far that it not only displays it in the play, but draws the spectator himself into this blindness at the end of the play in a darkness so total that Bernhard did not even allow the emergency lights to be left on in the theater.

III

"The Marionette Theater is the genuinely comic theater" (Das Marionettentheater ist das eigentlich komische Theater), Novalis once noted.[40] When Bernhard prefaces his play *Die Jagdgesellschaft* with a citation from Kleist's "Über das Marionettentheater," he is not necessarily invoking the comic character of the mechanical that has been described by Bergson. Kleist's question is evidently no longer a question for Bernhard, for when he cites Kleist, he strikes out the question mark: "Ich erkundigte mich nach dem Mechanismus dieser Figuren, und wie es möglich wäre, die einzelnen Glieder derselben und ihre Punkte, ohne Myriaden von Fäden an den Fingern zu haben, so zu regieren, als es der Rhythmus der Bewegungen oder der Tanz erfordere."[41] The narrator in Kleist's essay calls into question the dancer's hypothesis that the marionettes are more graceful than human dancers. He doubts the self-volition of the marionettes and tries to attribute their grace to the puppet-master who is a kind of unmoved mover. Kleist's dancer refutes this objection, claiming that the puppeteer must place himself in the marionette's center of gravity and is therefore drawn into the movement of the dance. Kleist thereby eliminates any quasi-external standpoint which, itself motionless, could control the movement, and in the course of the argument, he also eliminates any privileged observer's point of observation, itself unobserved, from which the movement could be observed. Such metapositions disappear into an identification of marionette and god which is presented as a paradox.

For Kleist, as for Bernhard, the marionette is therefore more than an "anthropological metaphor" for "people determined by external forces," a metaphor which, as Oliver Jahraus has argued, is linked in the *Jagdgesellschaft* to the problem of freedom and determination, and which is also referred to in passing via the references to Lermontov's novel *A Hero of our Time.*[42] The general who appears in Bernhard's play, and who is deathly ill and convinced that he is going to be ousted by his ministers, at the end suddenly shoots himself. In the terms suggested by Jahraus' reading, he could be seen as externally determined, guided by his wife, who keeps the seriousness of his condition from him, and by the writer, who presents the general and his wife as characters in his comedies. Although he is set off from the others in the catalogue of the dramatic personae, the writer is far from a puppeteer who, strings in hand, is directing everyone like puppets. Bernhard does not only cite the question of freedom and determination thematically, a question which for Lermontov is posed in a Russian roulette bet about the existence of providence, but he above all invokes the structural tendency of Lermontov's novel to perspectivize and engage its hero Petshorin, who is also one of the narrators, in self-observation.[43] Lermontov is thus linked to Kleist through their common concern with the problem of observation and self-observation.

The marionette topos, which prefaces the play through the Kleist citation, points to a relation between rest and movement, which traditionally had made possible the representation of time in terms of movement, but which in Kleist already leads to the problem of simultanization and therefore to an indication of time which is dependent on an observer. At the beginning of Bernhard's play, the author can no longer quite remember an aphorism that suddenly dawns upon him while he is reading Lermontov and Pushkin:

> Der Aphorismus dachte ich fortwährend Der Aphorismus
> Die Ruhe macht es wieder gut
> und die Fortsetzung
> Nein die Ruhe macht nichts wieder gut
> Sondern sondern sondern
> verstehen Sie die ganze Zeit[44]

"Die ganze Zeit" refers, of course, to the time when the writer continuously thought about an aphorism he cannot continue so that the temporal duration arises from a comic insistence on the interruption. The writer lingers at precisely the point of articulation in the aphorism, at the adverbial connection "sondern." At this point, *sondern* becomes ambiguous through its mechanical repetition: as an adverbial connection, it marks the place of breaking-off, and can therefore be understood in the sense of "dividing" or "differentiating." "Die ganze Zeit," as the general's wife should know, is thus, as it were, separated ("gesondert"). *Sondern* thus parallels and distinguishes between three observation-dependent schemas of time: for the writer, the time of wondering how the aphorism will continue; for the general's wife, the time of understanding; and "die ganze Zeit" as the time around which the play revolves, namely, the time since the Second World War.[45] The completed aphorism which the writer finally remembers reads:

> Die Ruhe macht es wieder gut
> Nein die Ruhe macht gar nichts wieder gut
> sondern
> Die günstigere Bewegung
> sondern
> die günstigere Bewegung
>
> (*J,* p. 179)

Here, too, the point of scission is highlighted by the isolation of *sondern* in the text and its repetition, a scission which distinguishes between rest and movement by binding them adverbially. The isolation of the point of scission as the unity of binding and distinction, or connection and break, contains *in nuce* the dynamic which the play unfolds through the device of a play within a play.

The self-implication of the writer's observations in what he observes is above all presented with reference to various temporal levels within the structure of the play within a play. In the first instance, the card game between the writer and the general's wife is obviously a play within a play. As the time "during the hunt," it links the time "before the hunt" with the time "after the hunt," and thus the first with the third "movement" (as Bernhard, using a

musical concept, re-named the acts) of the play. The play within a play flip-flops levels of time: in the first movement, the general mentions one of the writer's comedies which has already been performed; in the third movement, the writer announces a play that would represent the hunting party itself. Speaking of the comedy which has already been performed, the general criticizes the observer-dependency of the changing genre differentiation: "Handelt es sich um eine Tragödie / behauptet er / eine Komödie sei es / und ist es eine Komödie / behauptet er / eine Tragödie," even though everything was "nichts als eine Widerspruch" (*J,* p. 206). At the same time, the general warns that the writer will put everything he observes on the stage (i.e., their hunting party, too), but that what he is observing in the process will be anything but reality (*J,* p. 207). The comedy projected for the future once again contains all the elements which characterize the play as a whole:

> Eine Komödie stellen Sie sich vor
> in welcher ein General eine Hauptrolle spielt
> und dieser General hat eine Todeskrankheit
> in Stalingrad haben sie ihm den linken Arm abgerissen
> Und eines Tages geht er in den Wald
> und verletzt sich mit der Motorsäge am Bein
> und zur gleichen Zeit wird festgestellt
> daß er den Grauen Star hat
> Dazu zwei Minister gnädige Frau
> die den General zum Rücktritt zwingen
> eine Jagd stelle ich mir vor
> eine Jagdgesellschaft
> in einem unserer schönsten Jagdhäuser [. . .]
> Und möglicherweise gnädige Frau
> gestatte ich mir den Borkenkäfer auftreten zu lassen
> *zu den Ministern*
> Das Beschriebene meine Herren
> ist etwas Anderes
> wie ja schon das Beobachtete etwas Anderes ist
> Alles ist anders
> *zur Generalin*
> möglicherweise eine Philosophie
> würde der General sagen
> Kommt ein einarmiger General vor in meinem Stück
> ist es ein Anderer
> Und möglicherweise gnädige Frau wird gesagt
> ich selbst sei in meinem Theater
> Aber es ist ein Anderer
>
> (*J,* pp. 244–45)

As a play within a play, the planned comedy dramatizes the recursivity of the observation of observations in which the writer is himself implicated as an observer. He does not simply depict reality, but observes the observations of the general and his wife, as he does his own, thereby construing the world of the hunting party as one that can only be deciphered recursively: what is described, the planned comedy about a hunting party, is thus different from what is observed, the hunting party[46]—and it is naturally also something different from Bernhard's play *Die Jagdgesellschaft.* The planned comedy about the hunting party is a second-order observation of the play *Die Jagdgesellschaft* implicit in the play itself. The play ends in the suicide of the general, and thus seems to flirt with tragedy. In that the play, *Die Jagdgesellschaft* differentiates itself from itself and observes itself through the doubly inserted structure of the play within a play, it installs the temporal schema of the present and temporalizes the paradox of simultaneity which would characterize a tragic structure, and which is also being played on in the piece. Contrary to the laws of nature, the bark-beetle appears everywhere at once (*J*, p. 193), and the death of the general is simultaneous with the writer's remarks about the general's own premonitions of death that are conditioned by his Stalingrad experience (*J*, p. 249). The past comedy which has already been performed and the planned comedy of the future are linked to one another by the play that takes place in the present, similar to the linking of *sondern* and the card game in the Second Act. The recursive structure of the play within a play is thereby delimited so that the play, as the play *Die Jagdgesellschaft*, no longer encompasses the play within the play, but rather becomes the play's play within a play. The general's remark, "Der Vorhang geht auf / Da sitzen wir / und sind eine Komödie" (*J*, p. 238), highlights the insertion of temporal levels of past and future into the present of the play at hand.[47] On the one hand, this remark refers to the fact that the writer had already staged, and would stage again in the future, what he observes in the hunting lodge. On the other hand, the remark, formulated in an ambiguous present tense, can also refer to the situation of the actors in the play *Die Jagdgesellschaft* who are at that point sitting there acting out a comedy.[48] It thus turns to the audience as a parabasis, disrupting the dramatic illusion and commenting on the play. The parabasis, we had argued, displaces the demarcations of the structure of tragedy: in *Die Jagdgesellschaft*, one could also describe the parabasis in Lacanian terms as the border zone between two deaths, namely, the general's experience of death at Stalingrad and his suicide at the end of the play. Following Lacan, this border zone can be seen in comedy through distancing observations such as those of the parabasis as a life in flight. Bernhard's comic writer continually thematizes this fleeting life as a general death and decay, or with the reference to the deathly preoccupations of the play and of the hunt (*J*, p. 241). Beyond this, however, the comitragedy itself ends in the appearance of self-annihilation" which Friedrich Schlegel perceived as constitutive of the comic. At the end, when the wood begins to fall beneath the saws of the lumber jacks, *Die Jagdgesellschaft* could be said to obliterate what makes it into a hunting party in the first place, that is, the play ultimately erases both itself and its iterability. It was probably for good reason that Bernhard insisted that the trees should be right in the room for the production of *Die Jagdgesellschaft*.[49] When the outside is represented in the inside, the borders are thereby re-drawn. The fall (*Fall*) of the woods is what makes the hunting party into a hunting party, and is thus in the end everything that is the case (*Fall*). This fall, one could say, is the Eigen-value of the hunting party in *The Hunting Party*.

IV

If Thomas Bernhard were to re-write a work of world literature as Borges' Pierre Menard does *Don Quixote*, the play would be Kleist's *Der Zerbrochene Krug* and the novel Lermontov's *A Hero of our Time*.[50] Indeed, he appears to have tried to do just that through a crossing of genres in *Die Jagdgesellschaft* and his novel *Alte Meister. Eine Komödie*. The references to Kleist's comedy, which towards the end of the novel is characterized as "the greatest German comedy,"[51] are just as subtle because they are just as formalized as the references in Borges' story to Cervantes' *Don Quixote*. Totally out of character with his more than thirty-year-old habit of going to the art museum every other day, the music critic Reger has made an appointment there with Atzbacher for the next day, in order to invite him, as we learn only at the end, to a performance of Kleist's *Der Zerbrochene Krug* in the Burgtheater. Bernhard's "comedy" is organized around its relation to the "old masters" of painting, music, philosophy, and literature, around the problem of imitation, and around the relation between forgery and original. Because—as is maintained of Tintoretto's "White-bearded Man," which appears as two originals—each original is already in itself a forgery (*AM*, p. 118), a comedy like Kleist's *Zerbrochener Krug*, which for its part is already a forgery, can once again be forged as a novel.

Borges had already conceptualized this transpositional paradox. On the one hand, Pierre Menard rejects merely being identified with the author: he writes the *Quixote* not as Miguel de Cervantes, but as Pierre Menard, therefore omitting the prologue to the second part (in which Cervantes steps out of the editorial role that he had maintained in the first and gets agitated about a competitor's continuation of his novel that has appeared in the meantime). To have included this prologue would have meant introducing another literary figure, namely Cervantes himself, and it would have meant presenting the *Quixote* as the work of this figure. On the other hand, Menard rejects the simple transposition of past into present whereby Don Quixote would, for instance, appear on Wall Street. Such a simple transposition positions the epochs as different *or* as the same, thus proceeding from a disjunction without being able to grasp the paradox of a conjunction *and* disjunction of the levels of time.[52] In order to outdo both these methods, Menard's project to re-write the *Quixote* must both demonstrate the unity of the distinction between author and reader, and solve the problem of the simultaneity of the non-simultaneous. The new *Quixote* is ultimately characterized as a palimpsest which makes the old text visible in the new. The new text, which should make the old one visible, is, however, itself invisible. Menard realizes his project through erasure: as is first remarked in passing in a footnote towards the end of the story, Menard always burned his manuscripts, which were written in his barely legible handwriting anyway. All that remains of the project is the so-called "visible work" of Menard listed at the beginning of the story, an alphabetical list of his publications. With this list, Borges' story copies, if in a very formal way, the prologue to *Don Quixote,* which itself solved the impossibility of writing a prologue through copying and parody.[53]

In Bernhard's imitation of Kleist's comedy, the genre problem of writing a comedy of comedy which already imitates a tragedy corresponds to Borges' paradoxical task of copying a text which is already presented as the copy of an injunction to copy. As is well known, Kleist tried to re-write *Oedipus Rex* with *Der Zerbrochene Krug* as Pierre Menard did with *Don Quixote.* At first glance, it may appear as though Kleist were merely transposing the old into the new, for example, when Oedipus re-appears in Husum as the corrupt village judge Adam in order to judge himself through an analytical process of searching for the truth. This process of self-judgment can certainly be found in Bernhard's novel, for with his rigorous complaints against the old masters, contemporary art, and the Austrian state, the critic Reger is also always complaining about himself and his subversive critical talent. But to put the relation of Bernhard to Kleist and Kleist to the Oedipus story in terms of self-judgment is still too superficial. The strategy of merely transposing the past into the present—so, for instance, from Oedipus to the village court in Husum and from Adam to the art museum in Vienna—was of course rejected by Borges because it could only tackle the simultaneity of the non-simultaneous through a logic of disjunction. Taking up the Oedipus tragedy anew, it is precisely this paradox that Kleist addresses. In Sophocles' tragedy, the simultaneity of the non-simultaneous—which we had defined with Vernant as the paradox of the form of tragedy played out on temporal levels—could be said to be resolved hypogrammatically in the riddle of the sphinx and Oedipus' solution of it. Indeed, the riddle of the sphinx—"What being is *dipous, tripous,* and *tetrapous?*"—short-circuits the distinction between life's stages, a distinction which *Oi-dipous,* spelling out his own name, reintroduces when he solves the riddle through a narrative sequence of life's stages. Admittedly only in order then himself to become the question of the riddle in turn: both the husband of his mother and the brother of his children, he further blurs the temporal distinctions between generations.[54] Oedipus de-paradoxifies the riddle only himself to become the paradox of the riddle.

In Kleist's *Zerbrochene Krug,* this paradox of a simultaneity of the non-simultaneous is broken comically by the coincidence of the levels of representation in which Marthe lets the historical event represented on the jug and the history of the jug itself become contemporaneous with the present fact that the jug is broken. Kleist's comedy transposes the tragic paradox of the simultaneity of the non-simultaneous onto the biblical story of the Fall, and with the Fall, it introduces a distinction between timelessness and the fall into time, thereby temporalizing the tragic paradox through a different temporal schema. Bernhard's attempt to re-write Kleist's comic transposition of the Oedipus tragedy into the story of the Fall in his novel *Alte Meister* correspondingly de-paradoxifies its own paradoxi-

cal plan through temporal schemata. In the first sentence, Bernhard already takes up the temporal determinations of Kleist's comedy in which the time of the deed at which Adam was supposed to have been in Eve's room and broken the jug is calculated, through contradictory reports, to have been between 10:30 and 12:00. In Bernhard, this narrative time is doubled in that more than thirty years out of Reger's life are comprised, almost indistinguishably, into the time between 10:30 and just after 12:00. Reger and Atzbacher have made a date for 11:30 in the art museum. Atzbacher appears right after 10:30 in order to be able to observe Reger undisturbed in his regular seat in the Bordone Room in front of Tintoretto's "White-bearded Man." They meet at 11:30 and leave the museum after 12:00. Only then does Reger suggest to Atzbacher that he go with him to *Der Zerbrochene Krug,* a suggestion which for the first time throws light on the interruption of Reger's more than thirty-year-old habit of going to the museum every other day.

Only one other event besides this suggestion to see Kleist's comedy in the Burg Theater had also interrupted his regular museum visit: the fall of Reger's wife in front of the art museum as a result of which she died. Reger blames the death of his wife on the city of Vienna because it had not cleared the paths in front of the museum in wintertime, on the state, because the state museum had not called an ambulance quickly enough, and finally on the church, because the surgeons in the Hospital of the Merciful Brethren had bungled the operation. In any case, the question of guilt so constructed falls back on Reger himself in a way that is implied only by the encapsulation of temporal levels. He had met his wife in the museum and then, against her wishes (as was the case with all his habits), had sworn her to the custom of going with him to the museum every day. The fall—here the event around which Reger's observations and the observations of him by Atzbacher appear to circle—could thus also be seen, as is already the case in Kleist's parody of the unity of insight and blindness in tragic self-analysis, as the blind spot of self-observation. "The city of Vienna and the Austrian state and the Catholic Church are responsible for the death of my wife, Reger said at the Ambassador, I now reflected while sitting next to him on the Bordone Room settee."[55] (Die Stadt Wien und der österreichische Staat und die katholische Kirche sind am Tod meiner Frau schuld, sagte Reger im Ambassador, dachte ich neben ihm auf der Bordone-Saal-Sitzbank sitzend, denke ich *AM* p. 248). Various temporal levels are short-circuited and rendered simultaneous: when Reger tells Atzbacher for the ump-teenth time in the art museum just after 12:00 how he had met his wife in the museum over thirty years ago, Atzbacher thinks about the day in the Hotel Ambassador when he saw Reger for the first time after the death of his wife and reports what Reger had told him back then about her fall. Whereas imperfect tense and indirect speech render different levels of the past simultaneous, thereby bringing together two widely diverse events, namely Reger's first encounter with his wife and the fall which caused her death, the present tense, "denke ich," introduces a level of the present which presumably refers to the moment at which Atzbacher writes all this down. Opposed to this barely conspicuous level of the present at the beginning and end of the text is a second level of the present, the introduction of a second narrator in addition to Atzbacher through the simple remark "writes Atzbacher" ("schreibt Atzbacher"). Whereas the narrative time of the levels of the past makes the non-simultaneous simultaneous, the narrative time of the levels of the present introduces a temporal succession: the moment when Atzbacher thinks and writes precedes the second moment at which the second narrator, who only pops up on the margins of the text, confirms that Atzbacher "writes." It could be said that this second narrator poses as the reader and the editor, for Atzbacher, as we learn from Reger (i.e., mediated by Atzbacher himself), has for decades been writing one particular work but has never published anything (*AM,* p. 175). If another narrator, a reader and editor, did not appear on its margins (again, as in Borges' story), then the existing text, *Alte Meister,* could not in fact be available; it would, like Pierre Menard's new version of the *Quixote,* erase itself. With this narrator, a third-order observer is introduced, who for his part observes what Atzbacher, as a second-order observer, observes about Reger. Atzbacher could have observed Reger as a first-order observer of his dealings with the paradox and his attempt to resolve it: his interpretation of his wife's fall and the way he assigns guilt. When at the same time Atzbacher attempts to characterize this paradox and its solution on a second level of observation (by rendering simultaneous events which are not simultaneous), he himself lands in paradox, namely, the paradox of paradox and de-paradoxification[56] (which the narrator on the third level of observation then unfolds in that he temporalizes and sequentializes Atzbacher's observations).

One could formulate such a procession of paradoxes and their resolution through various levels of observation, transposing them into genre distinctions so that the paradox of tragedy is unfolded by comedy as a second-order observation, and the pure self-reference of tragedy is broken comically by a newly inserted observer's standpoint. Comedy, however, when it is rendered simultaneous, can lead anew into paradoxes, which can then be resolved and sequentialized through narrativization. Narrativization dissolves the generic borders of drama in that it makes them, as observations, in turn dependent on observers. For Reger, the generic borders of comedy and tragedy become differentiated from one another through a principle of negative self-reference. As a rule, Reger's statements negate what they say and say what they negate.[57] After we have heard over 300 pages of his opinions and observations about art, he concludes: "The things we think and the things we say, believing that we are competent and yet we are not, *that is the comedy,* and when we ask *how is it all to continue? that is the tragedy,* my dear Atzbacher."[58] (Was denken wir und was reden wir nicht alles und glauben, wir sind kompetent und sind es doch nicht, *das ist die Komödie,* und wenn wir fragen, wie soll es weitergehn? *ist es die Tragödie,* mein lieber Atzbacher. *AM,* p.

308). While in the first instance the proposition summarizes what to this point was presented as Reger's critical competence, it then revokes this alleged competence and, implicitly, itself as a competent proposition, which would be able to differentiate convincingly between the competent and the incompetent. "This is comedy," says the proposition about this proposition. Comedy is not simply characterized by incompetence and a laughable self-deception about what would constitute real competence, rather, it surpasses this traditional conception of comedy through the principle of self-reference. If one then asks how this could be taken further, asking, for instance, if the proposition about the proposition "this is comedy" will be revoked the way that the first proposition about competence was, then that would be tragedy. Indeed, one ends up in tragedy because one is now inescapably caught in self-reference. In order to avoid this, i.e., in order not to end up in tragedy, the proposition, taken as a whole, should not be taken seriously in its self-referentiality.[59] Of course, this does not mean that this proposition, embedded in a story, would opt unambiguously for comedy. Self-referentially, the proposition as a whole revokes itself through its distinction between comedy and tragedy. Its Eigen-value, as the interruption of this self-reference, appears, in a similar fashion as the end of the ***Jagdgesellschaft,*** to lie in self-erasure. With regard to the observation of genre delimitations, one could say of Bernhard what Wittgenstein said about his propositions: "My propositions are elucidatory in this way: he who understands me finally recognizes them as senseless when he has climbed out through them, on them, over them. (He must, so to speak, throw away the ladder after he has climbed up on it.) He must surmount these propositions; then he sees the world rightly."[60]

Notes

1. Thomas Bernhard, *Der Stimmenimitator,* Frankfurt a.M. 1991, p. 59.

2. Thomas Bernhard, *Frost,* Frankfurt a.M. 1972, p. 189.

3. Herbert Gamper, (*Thomas Bernhard,* Munich 1977, p. 160) speaks of "interchangeable concepts"; Wolfram Buddecke and Helmut Fuhrmann ("Thomas Bernhard," in *Das deutschsprachige Drama seit 1945,* Munich 1981, pp. 215–22, here p. 220) see Bernhard's tragicomedy as a "mixture of tragedy and comedy which emphasizes the ambiguous, particularly the grotesque, character of performed events;" Alfred Barthofer ("Vorliebe für die Komödie: Todesangst. Anmerkungen zum Komödienbegriff bei Thomas Bernhard," in *Viertelsjahresschrift* 31 (1982): pp. 77–100, here p. 86) argues for the thematic sublation of conventional categories of genre poetics" into "a petrified craze for masks" through a theatricalization of history and tradition.

4. Christian Klug, *Thomas Bernhards Theaterstücke,* Stuttgart 1991, p. 96. Helmut Rath and Wend Kässens also argue in existentialist terms that

comedy for Bernhard can only be understood against the backdrop of death, transitoriness, and sickness ("Eine Komödie, die eine Tragödie ist. Thomas Bernhard und sein Werk. Radioessay," *NDR 3,* 14.11.1989). Stephen D. Dowden speaks of a "comic insight into basic human plight" (*Understanding Thomas Bernhard,* Columbia 1991).

5. Mikhail Bakhtin, *Die Ästhetik des Wortes,* ed. R. Grübel, Frankfurt a.M. 1979. For the concept of intertextuality derived from Bakhtin, see Julia Kristeva: "Wort, Dialog und Roman bei Bachtin," in *Literaturwissenschaft und Linguistik,* ed. J. Ihwe, Frankfurt a.M. 1972, vol. 3, pp. 345–75.

6. Niklas Luhmann describes this displacement of reference as specific to modern art, which he characterizes as world-art in contrast to the older object-art ("Weltkunst," in *Unbeobachtbare Welt,* eds. F.D. Bunsen, N. Luhmann, and D. Baecker, Bielefeld 1990, pp. 7–45).

7. Thomas Bernhard, "Ist es eine Komödie? Ist es eine Tragödie?" in *Erzählungen,* Frankfurt a.M. 1979, p. 87, hereafter cited as E and page number.

8. Friedhelm Roth suggests that "the reality of the theater and the theatricality of reality pass over into one another" and that Bernhard thus aims for the topos of a world theater ("'Das Gewesene ist es das Fortwährende Gewesene'—Thomas Bernhard: Der Theatermacher," in *Deutsches Drama der 80er Jahre,* ed. R. Weber, Frankfurt a.M. 1992, pp. 15–34, here p. 17).

9. Friedrich Dürrenmatt, "Die Wiedertäufer. Eine Komödie in zwei Teilen. Urfassung," in *Werkausgabe in 30 Bänden,* ed. in conjunction with the author, Zürich 1986, vol. 10, p. 133.

10. David Roberts, "Die Paradoxie der Form in der Literatur," in *Probleme der Form,* ed. D. Baecker, Frankfurt a.M. 1993, pp. 22–44.

11. Francisco J. Varela, "A Calculus for Self-Reference," in *International Journal for General Systems,* 1975, 2: pp. 5–24, here p. 22.

12. Niklas Luhmann, "Weltkunst," p. 15.

13. Ludwig Wittgenstein, *Tractatus logico-philosophicus,* London 1988, p. 31.

14. As for instance Karl S. Guthke has defined it as a specifically modern genre (*Geschichte und Poetik der deutschen Tragikomödie,* Göttingen 1961, p. 22).

15. Thomas Bernhard, *Watten,* Frankfurt a.M. 1978, p. 87.

16. Klug, *Thomas Bernhards Theaterstücke,* p. 103 sees "the partial identity of the tragic and comic as a toppling-phenomenon."

17. Wolfgang Iser has described this as specific to the comic ("Das Komische: ein Kipp-Phänomen," in *Das Komische,* ed. W. Preisendanz und R. Warning, *Poetik und Hermeneutik VII,* Munich 1976, pp. 398–402.

18. Gotthold Ephraim Lessing, "Abhandlungen von dem weinerlichen oder rührenden Lustspiele," in *Werke,* ed. H.G. Göpfert, Munich 1970, vol. 4, pp. 12–58.

19. Jean-Pierre Vernant, "Tensions and Ambiguities in Greek Tragedy," *Myth and Tragedy in Ancient Greece,* New York 1988, pp. 29–48.

20. The Romantics also formulated the genre distinction between tragedy and comedy in terms of their respective representations of temporal difference. Novalis writes: "Alle Darstellung der Vergangenheit ist ein Trauerspiel im eigentlichen Sinn—Alle Darstellung des Kommenden—des Zukünftigen—ein Lustspiel." (Friedrich von Hardenberg, *Werke Tagebücher und Briefe,* ed. H.J. Mähl, Munich 1978, vol. II, p. 326 #58).

21. Niklas Luhmann, *Die Wissenschaft der Gesellschaft,* Frankfurt a.M. 1992, p. 80.

22. Jacques Lacan, *The Ethics of Psychoanalysis,* Seminar VII, New York 1992, p. 306.

23. For Lacan, comedy is organized around a hidden signifier, a reference to comedy's descent from the cult of the phallus. See *The Ethics of Psychoanalysis,* p. 314.

24. Adam Müller, for example, also suggests this in his definition of comedy as that which should ironize even the "holiest," namely, the self-representation of the polis in tragedy: "Die Zeit wird schon noch kommen, wo der Vorhang nicht blos deshalb aufgehen wird, damit ihr den Schauspieler sehen könnt, sondern auch, damit der Schauspieler euch sieht." Friedrich Schlegel had already defined irony as a "permanent parabasis." See "Ironie, Lustspiel, Aristophanes: Aus Adam Müllers Vorlesungen über dramatische Poesie und Kunst," in *Phöbus,* ed. H.v. Kleist and A. Müller, April/Mai 1808. 4. and 5. Stück, pp. 56–67, photomechanical reprint, Darmstadt 1961, pp. 238–39, here p. 237.

25. Niklas Luhmann, "Die Paradoxie der Form," in *Kalkül der Form,* ed. D. Baecker, Frankfurt a.M. 1993, pp. 197–212, here p. 201.

26. Plessner established that the comic offers a border experience almost in the sense of a double bind: one experiences the limit of the comic "not only subjectively, as one's inability to be done with the matter, but also at the same time as the structure of the matter it prohibits." See Helmut Plessner, "Lachen und Weinen—Eine Untersuchung nach den Grenzen menschlichen Verhaltens," in *Philosophische Anthropologie,* ed. G. Dux, Frankfurt a.M. 1970, pp. 11–172, here p. 100.

27. Peter Szondi has argued for the dissolution of the drama in the direction of narrativization in his description of the modern drama, which is oriented around Hegel's dialecticization of genres. See Peter Szondi, *Theorie des modernen Dramas,* Frankfurt a.M. 1963.

28. Friedrich Schlegel, *Literary Notebooks,* ed. H. Eichner, Frankfurt a.M. 1980, p. 172, # 1682.

29. Werner Hamacher, "Der Satz der Gattung: Friedrich Schlegels poetologische Unisetzung von Fichtes unbedingtem Grundsatz," *MLN* 95 (1980), pp. 1155–80, here p. 1174.

30. Thomas Bernhard, "Über allen Gipfeln ist Ruh," in *Stücke 3,* Frankfurt a.M. 1988, p. 250.

31. Friedrich Schiller, "Über naive und sentimentalische Dichtung," in *Werke in drei Bänden,* ed. H. Göpfert, vol. II, Munich 1966, p. 564. For Schiller, this goal of the comedy is also "einerlei mit dem Höchsten, wornach der Mensch zu ringen hat," and in turn reduplicates the basic tasks of the logic of reflection as a genre demarcation.

32. Georg Wilhelm Friedrich Hegel, *Vorlesungen über die Ästhetik,* in *Werke,* ed. E. Moldenhauer and K.M. Michel, Frankfurt a.M. 1986, vol. 15, p. 351.

33. Ibid., p. 482.

34. Ibid., p. 524.

35. Ibid., pp. 527–28.

36. Karl Marx, *Einleitung zur Kritik der Hegelschen Rechtsphilosophie,* in *Frühe Schriften,* ed. H.-J. Lieber und P. Furth, Darmstadt 1989, vol. I, pp. 488–505, here p. 493.

37. Jean Paul, *Vorschule der Ästhetik,* in *Sämtliche Werke,* Historisch-Kritische Ausgabe, ed. Preußische Akademie der Wissenschaften, section I, vol. 11, Weimar 1935, p. 108.

38. Joachim Ritter, "Über das Lachen," in *Blätter für deutsche Philosophie* 14 (1940/41), pp. 1–21, here p. 9 and p. 12.

39. Thomas Bernhard, *Der Ignorant und der Wahnsinnige,* in *Stücke 1,* Frankfurt a.M. 1988, p. 113.

40. Friedrich von Hardenberg, *Werke,* vol. II, p. 773, # 159.

41. Heinrich von Kleist, "Über das Marionettentheater" in *Sämtliche Werke und Briefe,* ed. H. Sembdner, Munich 1985, pp. 338–45, here p. 339.

42. Oliver Jahraus, *Das 'monomanische' Werk. Eine strukturale Werkanalyse des Oeuvres von Thomas Bernhard,* Frankfurt a.M. 1992, p. 240.

43. See Mikhail Lermontov, *Ein Held unserer Zeit,* in *Ausgewählte Werke,* ed. Roland Opitz, Frankfurt a.M. 1989, vol. II, pp. 253–428. Lermontov's narrator distinguishes between, for instance, his remarks and his observations (which are then fleshed out by Petshorin's self-observations), and stresses that his readers should by no means "trust in them blindly," p. 304.

44. Thomas Bernhard, *Die Jagdgesellschaft,* in *Stücke 1,* Frankfurt a.M. 1988, p. 177, hereafter cited as J and page number.

45. Herbert Gamper, "Einerseits Wissenschaft, Kunststücke anderseits. Zum Theater Thomas Bernhards," *Test und Kritik* 43 (1974), pp. 9–21. Gamper points out that Bernhard's texts often deal with a shock in the past (e.g., the General and Stalingrad, or the experience with the Poles in *Der Italiener*). The historical event in the foreground of all these shocks is the Second World War (to which all the recurring figures refer, for instance, two decades or 22 years: in *Die Jagdgesellschaft,* there are 22 hunters, in *Der Ignorant und der Wahnsinnige* the princess' aria is sung 222 times). While Gamper sees history divided by World War II into a before and after (which he describes as *histoire* and *post-histoire*), one could read the figures of 22 not as a historical index, but simply as an intertextual reference to Kleist, in whose texts the numbers 11 and 22 are insistent.

46. Manfred Jurgensen has described a simple change in perspective which can also see something as "different," namely "not only in accordance with socially codified guidelines" (*Thomas Bernhard, Der Kegel im Wald oder die Geometrie der Verneinung,* Bern 1981, p. 25). But the recursivity of observation sketched out here goes beyond this as well because it conceives of art not, as does Jurgensen, as the total other, "something opposed to society," but as an observation of society within society, which specializes in the observation of that which a society—understood in terms of observers—cannot observe.

47. On this unfolding of temporal schemas in observation governed by distinction, see Niklas Luhmann, *Die Wissenschaft der Gesellschaft,* p. 103ff.

48. Christian Klug (*Thomas Bernhards Theaterstücke,* p. 290) works through the temporal encapsulation of the play within a play, reading this remark of the General's, however, as a hypotyposis which makes it possible to skip over the difference of the play within a play of play. Through the "rhetorische Doppeldeutigkeit des Präsens," it can be seen "zugleich als ein ad spectatores gesprochener Kommentar über die gegenwärtige Bühnenexistenz."

49. In his production of the play, Peymann did not follow this instruction and only put the trees close enough to the window that "man praktisch die Schatten im Raum sah, wie es eben in einer realistischen Jagdhütte unter Umständen bei einem bestimmten Sonnenstand sein kann." In the text itself, however, the fact that the woods bring about an utter darkness is stressed, making Peymann's realistic shadows seem somewhat questionable. See Claus Peymann, "Thomas Bernhard auf der Bühne" in *Thomas Bernhard, Portraits,* ed. S. Dressinger, Weitra 1992, pp. 213–17.

50. Conversation with Rita Cirio, "Austriacus Infelix," *L'Espresso,* July 11, 1982, trans. Sabine Gruber, in *Von einer Katastrophe in die andere. 13 Gespräche mit Thomas Bernhard,* ed. S. Dreissinger, Weitra 1992, pp. 95–103.

51. Thomas Bernhard, *Alte Meister. Eine Komödie,* Frankfurt a.M. 1988, p. 310; hereafter cited as *AM* and page number.

52. Jorge Luis Borges, "Pierre Menard, Author of the Quixote," in *Labyrinths,* ed. D.A. Yates and J.E. Irby, New York 1964.

53. Faced with a blank piece of paper, the "editor," Cervantes, works in his prologue on the impossibility of writing a prologue. In the custom of the time, the prologue should authorize the work by citing the great authors in alphabetical order and being able to guarantee its great erudition through notations and references. The problem of being unable to write resolves itself when a friend advises him simply to copy the alphabetical list of prominent authorities out of another book and to fall back on truisms for the notations and references. The impossibility of writing is thus remedied in that this friendly instruction to copy is now simply copied into the prologue. See Miguel de Cervantes Saavedra, *Der sinnreiche Junker Don Quixote von der Mancha,* Munich 1993, pp. 7–13.

54. Jean Paul Vernant, "Ambiguity and Reversal: On the Enigmatic Structure of Oedipus Rex," *Myth and Tragedy,* pp. 113–40, here p. 124.

55. Thomas Bernhard, *Old Masters,* trans. E. Osers, Chicago 1992, p. 124.

56. See Niklas Luhmann, *Die Wissenschaft der Gesellschaft,* p. 98.

57. In contrast, Herwig Walitsch (*Thomas Bernhard und das Komische, Versuch über den Komikbegriff Thomas Bernhards anhand der Texte Alte Meister und Die Macht der Gewohnheit,* Erlangen 1992, pp. 36, 54, and 108) sees paradoxes like Reger's proposition, "Die Kunst ist das Höchste und das Wider wärtigste gleichzeitig" (*AM* 79), or the sublation of statements about competence, comedy and tragedy (*AM* 308) as the "aesthetic correlate" to Bernhard's "dialectical world view" which connects to Hegel's dialectic of the tragic.

58. Thomas Bernhard, *Old Masters,* p. 154.

59. Thomas Anz argues that anyone who takes Bernhard seriously misunderstands him, for he is a "theatrical comedian" who was able to make comedy out of tragedy. ("Thomas Bernhard, Der irrwitzige Komödiant des Grauens," *SFB,* October 22, 1983.

60. Ludwig Wittgenstein, *Tractatus Logico-Philosophicus,* London 1988, p. 189.

DER IGNORANT UND DER WAHNSINNIGE

CRITICAL COMMENTARY

Robert F. Gross, Jr. (essay date January 1981)

SOURCE: "'The Greatest Uncertainty': The Perils of Performance in Thomas Bernhard's *Der Ignorant und der Wahnsinnige,*" in *Modern Drama,* Vol. 23, No. 4, January, 1981, pp. 385–92.

[*In the following essay, Gross discusses Bernhard's treatment of death in* Der Ignorant und der Wahnsinnige.]

Thomas Bernhard's recognition of the omnipresence of death has provided the background for all of his dramatic works to appear thus far. For Bernhard, death is not a single, unique event that occurs at the conclusion of each life, but a current of negation that runs throughout the whole of human existence, manifesting itself in sickness, exhaustion and decay. The Writer in *Die Jagdgesellschaft* presents the Bernhardian vision of death in its most unadorned form:

> Wir sind allein
> oder nicht allein
> wir hören Musik
> oder wir hören nicht Musik
> Jeder Gegenstand gnädige Frau
> ist der Tod[1]
> (We are alone
> or not alone
> we hear music
> or we do not hear music
> Every circumstance dear lady
> is death).

This is not simply another occurrence of the *memento mori* trope; death is not personified as a character who hovers around unsuspecting mortals, waiting to carry them off at any moment. For Bernhard, all persons carry their mortality within them every moment of their lives. This belief in the imminence of death within the living places Bernhard closer to Martin Heidegger and his analysis of death in *Sein und Zeit* than to the conventional view of death in the Western tradition.[2]

In *Sein und Zeit,* Heidegger explains that death does not stand in opposition to *Dasein,* but exists as a fundamental ontological moment of it.[3] *Dasein* exists in incompleteness; so long as human beings exist, they are constantly changing and are subject to further becoming. Only death can complete Being-in-the-world; *Dasein,* by virtue of its finitude, is oriented toward death as the utmost possibility of its being. The fundamental orientation of *Dasein* leads to the experience of anxiety. For both Bernhard and Heidegger, the experience of anxiety is a special locus in which *Dasein's* Being-unto-death is revealed. But Bernhard's characters never learn to confront the fact of their mortality with the "gerüstete Freude"[4] ("fortified joy") that Heidegger finds in the authentic orientation toward death. Instead, they exist in a perpetual flight from death that verges on the hysterical.

Bernhard's dramatic presentation of the flight from death is first emphasized in his second play, *Der Ignorant und der Wahnsinnige* (*The Ignoramus and the Madman*). The death of the title character in his first play, *Ein Fest für Boris* (*A Party for Boris*), virtually fails to make any impression on its audience whatsoever, since it has been so numbed and desensitized by a series of far more ingenious grotesqueries in the course of the play. In retrospect, it is clear that the cruel rituals of *Ein Fest für Boris* are a response to the omnipresence of death in its manifestation as physical mutilation, but the theme is not presented with the precision and subtlety that distinguishes *Der Ignorant und der Wahnsinnige.*

The play's title describes the two forms the flight from death can take: willed ignorance or madness. The Father, an alcoholic approaching total blindness, has chosen ignorance. Although his blindness is not yet total, he has given up the use of his sight, relies on sound for all of his information, and walks with a blind man's cane. His chosen blindness becomes associated with the ignorance and vulgarity of the operatic world:

> Wenn wir den Schwachsinn
> der in dieser Kunstgattung herrscht
> geehrter Herr
> mit der Gemeinheit
> der Zuschauer verrechnen
> kommen wir in den Wahnsinn[5]
> (If we consider the feeble-mindedness
> that reigns in this art form
> dear sir
> along with the vulgarity
> of the audience
> we go insane).

The Father, who is the most faithful and attentive auditor of his daughter, a world-renowned coloratura soprano, is an image of the theatrical spectator, sitting safely in the dark while the performers attempt dangerous acts under the intense lighting of the stage:

> In solcher Intensität
> existieren nicht viele
> Das Licht
> ist ein Unglück . . .
> Wie auf offener Bühne
> geehrter Herr
> wodurch alles die grösste
> Unsicherheit ist (p. 98)
> (Not many exist
> in such intensity
> The light
> is a misfortune . . .
> As on the open stage
> dear sir
> where the greatest uncertainty
> is found throughout it).

The Father, like the public, prefers not to recognize how difficult and destructive the artist's life is.

The world of the operatic stage exemplifies the second form the flight from death can take, insanity. Fleeing from the decay and deterioration that proclaim the omnipotence and omnipresence of death, people look for a structure that appears impervious to death. They accept the rigorous and inhuman demands of the structure, laboring under the illusion that it will free them from the constant threat of annihilation. There are two madpersons in *Der Ignorant und der Wahnsinnige,* the Doctor and the Queen of the Night. The Doctor is the madman referred to in the title. He passes his time backstage at the opera house by explaining to the Father how to dissect a cadaver. He presents the process in detail as a rigorous and inflexible sequence of precise actions. It even demands special virtues from its practitioner:

> die Aufmerksamkeit
> wie die Entschiedenheit
> wie die Rücksichtslosigkeit
> diese drei fortwährend unerlässlich (p. II)
> (Attentiveness
> as well as determination
> as well as ruthlessness
> these three continually indispensable).

The ritualized action of dissection attempts to defy death in its impersonal and inviolable structure, but cannot help to flee from the awareness of death. If anything, it heightens one's awareness of death by confronting one with a naked image of it. It is in the impossibility of a successful flight from death through structure that madness lies.

In Bernhard's world, the artist is no more removed from death than the anatomist. The Father's daughter, known only as the Queen of the Night (after the role she sings in Mozart's *Die Zauberflöte*), is the second character involved in insane flight from death. Subjecting herself to the rigorous discipline of operatic singing, she has tried to escape mortality by transforming herself into a "Koloraturmaschine" (p. 7; "coloratura-machine"). Since the world of artifice superficially appears to be opposed to the world of nature and death, she has striven to become completely artificial, like the golden bird in Yeats's "Sailing to Byzantium," but Bernhard refuses to let his artists escape into any artifice of eternity. The Queen of the Night instructs her dresser, Mrs. Vargo, to cover her entire face with white make-up for her performance that evening:

> Tragen Sie Weiss auf
> viel Weiss
> das Gesicht
> muss ein vollkommen künstliches Gesicht sein
> mein Körper
> ein künstlicher
> alles künstlich (p. 55)
> (Lay the white on
> lots of white
> the face
> must be a completely artificial face
> my body
> an artificial one
> everything artificial).

This white make-up will cover her natural visage, giving her the appearance of an artificial being. Similarly, all of her hair will be hidden beneath her crown (p. 50). Her success as a coloratura-machine resides in her ability to submit herself completely to the impersonal stricture of her art. For Bernhard, the performing arts are not forms of expression, but forms of depersonalization. Musicians are allowed no more self-expression or eccentricity in the performance of their tasks than anatomists.

The pursuit of an operatic career has not only failed to provide the Queen with a means of self-expression; it has also crippled her. Just as her father has lost his eyesight and become little more than a highly sensitive ear for his daughter, the Queen is dwindling away into the disembodied voice that has made her famous. The Doctor observes that her continual state of anxiety is bad for her singing, not considering the mental strain caused by such continual tension (p. 54). The first act ends with her vanishing as a physical presence, as we see the Father and the Doctor listening to her singing the Queen of the Night's first-act recitative and aria over the intercom in the dressing room. In the second act, the Queen's repeated coughs, signalling the breakdown of the coloratura-machine, are more significant than anything else she says or does in the act. By a strange synecdochical operation, the voice becomes the entire character.

This grotesque reduction of a person to a musical instrument might have given the Queen some consolation if it had succeeded in alleviating her anxiety in the face of death, but art has granted her neither safety nor ignorance. Like the Doctor's dissection, the performing arts only heighten one's awareness of death. The Queen dreams that the fire curtain will fall during a performance and kill her (p. 66). She is repeatedly made aware of the fragility of the vocal mechanism on which her art depends (pp. 54, 74). Each night before she goes onstage, the sleeve of her costume tears and must be repaired at the last moment, leaving barely enough time for her to reach the stage in time for her first entrance. She always worries that her costume will tear while she is onstage:

> das ist entsetzlich
> plötzlich
> zerreisst das Kostüm unter dem Arm
> und das Publikum
> bricht in Gelächter aus (p. 56)
> (That is awful
> suddenly
> the costume tears under the arm
> and the public
> breaks out in laughter).

Any accident is capable of destroying the illusion created by a work of art, which, by its very nature, seeks to control all of its elements completely. The rip in the costume spells the death of the illusion, the triumph of chance over order. The tear is a farcical reduction of the abyss, a void that reveals the ultimate impotence and ridiculousness of art. Thus, the work of art is continually threatened by its own disintegration. Death appears in the opera house in every chance event that threatens to upset its precarious aesthetic order. The Queen's madness is founded on her

realization that art is always vulnerable to chance occurrences, whether in the form of a torn costume or a falling fire curtain:

> Die Künstler existieren
> glaube ich
> in ständiger Angst
> vor dem augenblicklichen Verlust (pp. 73–74)
> (The artists exist
> I believe
> in constant dread
> of sudden destruction).

The Doctor compares the life of an opera singer to that of a tightrope walker (pp. 52–53). Like a tightrope walker, the Queen performs an action that is not expressive, but rigorously self-effacing. Despite that self-effacement, however, she is put in mortal danger by her art, which demands that she tread an exceedingly narrow path bounded by the possibility of disaster on either side. She is afforded no opportunity for relaxation, that is, ignorance, since she is aware that her performance could be destroyed at any instant, either by her own carelessness or by forces outside of her control.

The first act of **Der Ignorant und der Wahnsinnige** places in the foreground the anxiety that underlies every artistic performance and the constant threats posed to the artist. The characters are concerned that the Queen might not be ready to go onstage in time for her aria. This tension is heightened by the sound of the opera being performed as it is transmitted into the dressing room by the intercom system. Since the conflicts among the characters fail to influence the action in the scene to any appreciable extent, the dramatic tension is almost entirely the result of this race against the clock. At the end of the act, as we hear the Queen singing, we are relieved to see that order has once again triumphed, however narrowly, over the forces of death and chaos.

Bernhard suggests that those darker forces will inevitably intervene and triumph, since no one can defeat them for once and for all. The Father must continually drink more liquor to keep himself intoxicated, the Doctor must continue with his recitation of his multi-volumed treatise on anatomy, and the Queen of the Night must relive her anxiety at every performance. In the second act, the Queen capitulates to the forces of death. This act is more difficult to perform than the first, since it lacks the energy generated by the impending performance of *Die Zauberflöte* and the problems encountered in preparing for it. Instead, we see a gradual deterioration of the artistic realm induced by anxiety and exhaustion. Whereas the first act ends with the organization of sound in the form of the Mozartian aria, the second act ends with the triumph of chaos in coughing and the sound of objects falling off a table. We see the triumph of exhaustion, as the Queen begins to cough and cancels all of her professional engagements. Her final speech, which is also the final speech in the play, reads, "Erschöpfung / nichts als Erschöpfung" (p. 99; "Exhaustion / nothing but exhaustion"). This speech not only refers to the major, entropic force in the play and indicates its omnipotence, but also implies that life itself is nothing but exhaustion.

In ***Der Ignorant und der Wahnsinnige,*** the flight from death leads the characters into patterns of obsessive repetition that eventually succeed in exhausting their resistance to death and decay. The verbal repetitions that are a salient feature of Bernhard's dramatic style are formulae uttered with compulsive energy in an effort to keep mortality at bay. Both the mad and the ignorant are locked into patterns of repetition. In the face of death, the great annihilator of all individuality, the division between the mad and ignorant breaks down. The anonymous subject of the Doctor's autopsy is a *memento mori,* an invisible corpse that represents the future of all the characters. From the point of view of death, alcohol, the crutch of the ignorant, can be seen as "ein Kunstmittel" (p. 41; "an artistic device"); dissection, opera, alcoholism, cards, correspondence can all be reduced to the same end. As a result, there is little conflict in the play between the various types of characters; the major source of tension is the struggle of each individual with his own mortality.

Because this internal struggle is Bernhard's primary source of dramatic conflict, he tends to neglect the more familiar tensions latent in his material. Although he establishes the animosity between the Queen and her father, they do not communicate directly with each other, but speak to the Doctor, who acts as a neutral figure between them. This mediation prevents the conflict from developing into a major source of tension. Bernhard also refrains from showing us the conflicts that the Queen undergoes with the other members of the opera company. He is not interested in a satire of backstage life; rather, he uses the perils of artistic performance as an image of the tension that exists between mortals and the structures they create to escape their own mortality.

This interest in the agonies of the performing artist places in the foreground the difficulties of performing ***Der Ignorant und der Wahnsinnige.*** In hearing the Doctor and the Queen rail against the stupidity of audiences, the spectator at Bernhard's play may well be led to ask if the dramatist's vision of the artist is not an evasion of the truth. The speeches on the agonies of the performer highlight the difficulties of performing Bernhard's play: sustaining the Doctor's lengthy anatomical monologues, supporting the repetition of phrases that threaten to lose any possible theatrical impact with one more repetition, and overcoming the paucity of traditional dramatic conflict. Bernhard makes his actors submit to a rigorous structure that requires great skill and virtuosity. His mode of virtuosity, however, is not that of the nineteenth-century actor, based on flamboyance and self-expression. He elicits, or, more accurately, he demands virtuoso performances from his actors, presenting them with difficulties rather than easy vehicles.[6] As a result, histrionic virtuosity, achieved through material that might be considered static and untheatrical by some, becomes a testimony to the brilliance of

its performers as well as an image of the impossible demands that intellectual and aesthetic structures make on our limited and death-ridden beings. Art becomes a form of voluntary servitude to an unrewarding master, an impossible task that exhausts the artist without recompense. It becomes, in short, a metaphor for the cruelty of existence.

Notes

1. Thomas Bernhard, *Die Jagdgesellschaft* (Frankfurt am Main, 1974), p. 69. All translations from Bernhard's works are my own, and are included in parentheses after the German quotation.

2. For a detailed and lucid analysis of Heidegger's treatment of death, see James M. Demske, *Being, Man, and Death* (Lexington, KY, 1970), especially pp. 5–73.

3. See Martin Heidegger, *Sein und Zeit,* Band 2 of *Gesamtausgabe* (Frankfurt am Main, 1977), sections 46–53, pp. 314–354.

4. Heidegger, p. 410.

5. Thomas Bernhard, *Der Ignorant und der Wahnsinnige* (Frankfurt am Main, 1972), pp. 97–98. Page references for citations from this edition will appear parenthetically in my text.

6. Bernhard has written certain plays with particular actors in mind. *Minetti* was especially written for Bernhard Minetti. *Die Jagdgesellschaft* was written for Bruno Ganz, who had created the role of the Doctor in *Der Ignorant und der Wahnsinnige.*

DIE MACHT DER GEWOHNHEIT

CRITICAL COMMENTARY

Michael Bachem (review date Summer 1975)

SOURCE: A review of *Die Macht der Gewohnheit,* in *Books Abroad,* Vol. 49, No. 3, Summer, 1975, pp. 537–38.

[*In the following review, Bachem provides a mixed assessment of* Force of Habit.]

In his earlier play ***Die Jagdgesellschaft*** Thomas Bernhard had already commented that we never know what is a comedy and what a tragedy. Certainly this is true of ***Die Macht der Gewohnheit*** (***Force of Habit***), which is superficially designated as a comedy. But what could be comical about a three-act play featuring an aging circus director, a vain juggler, an obscene lion tamer, a silly clown whose only routine seems to be to let his cap slip off his head and catch it again, and the director's equally silly granddaughter. The comedy is merely external, due to the presence of stock comic characters in a stock comic setting.

The action is at best ludicrous: for years the director Caribaldi has been obsessed with the idea of practicing Schubert's "Trout" Quintet. As the title suggests, rehearsals, if one may call them that, are eternally carried on, but the group never plays together. One hears a sequence of long and deep notes from one of Caribaldi's celli—he has three—and an occasional pizzicato from a violin. Caribaldi has forced four of his employees to take up instruments which they hate to play; in fact he himself hates his instrument, but some time ago a doctor recommended cello-playing as a therapeutic routine. The lion tamer is forever eating huge radishes which he stores inside the piano. Little wonder that the instrument stinks. Once the lion tamer even had an axe poised to demolish the piano. The juggler is forever waving a spurious job offer from a competing circus, threatening to quit Caribaldi's outfit. But no one has the courage to quit or at least not to play.

Gradually the real intent of Bernhard's "comedy" clarifies itself. The megalomaniac Caribaldi, who suffers from constant backaches and hobbles around on a wooden leg, only mouths his slogans "precision, consistency, concentration." They are artificial values for him. He intensely desires them, but they are not an organic part of his being, not even *in nuce*; they are willed, but the distance is too great. His continued non-success is thus assured. The juggler provides us with one of the insights (?) of the play: "The sick and the crippled reign over the world: Everything is ruled by the sick and the crippled. It's a comedy, an evil humiliation." Only the words for great ideas or emotions remain. No one can personify them, no one can "fill them out." The words are like empty shells, library categories, respected but benignly neglected. In this vein the word "Casals" is uttered again and again by Caribaldi, but it carries no meaning; it is simply and only a word. What is real is brutality, stupidity (represented by the lion tamer), ridiculousness (the granddaughter and the clown) and vanity and delusion (the juggler and Caribaldi himself). In short: "Everything disgusting / Everything that happens / happens disgustingly / Life existence / disgusting . . ." Or: "We don't want life / but it must be lived."

As reading material, the play could easily be dismissed. But the language of Thomas Bernhard possesses considerable force, and a successful staging of this play would produce a very unsettling theatrical experience.

DIE BERÜHMTEN

CRITICAL COMMENTARY

Ernestine Schlant (review date Summer 1977)

SOURCE: A review of *Die Berühmten,* Vol. 51, No. 3, Summer, 1977, p. 436.

[*In the following essay, Schlant offers a negative review of* Die Berühmten.]

Die Berühmten is one of Thomas Bernhard's four recent plays to deal with the performing arts and artists. The other plays are *Der Ignorant und der Wahnsinnige* (1972), *Die Macht der Gewohnheit* (1974; see *BA* 49:3, pp. 537–38) and *Minetti* (1976). In *Die Berühmten* the high life of international opera performers is mercilessly ridiculed. There is no action to speak of in the two *Vorspiele* and the three scenes of the play. On three different occasions the "famous ones" assemble for dinner or afternoon collation in a castle near Salzburg (and near the Salzburger *Festspiele*), bought and renovated with "half a season's salary" by a basso. In this "natural" environment the "famous ones" are off duty and off guard. They eat, drink and talk. Throughout the play the characters remain nameless, identified only by their artistic skills (basso, soprano, tenor, conductor, et cetera) and the hero images they have picked for themselves and which, in the course of an evening, they destroy.

Language is the exclusive tool for revealing who these "famous ones" are. Thomas Bernhard reflects in the inanity of their conversations the shallowness of their characters and their aspirations. They believe, above all, in the impressiveness of dropping names and in the myth of fame, and they conceive of their art as so much business. Bernhard's criticism veers toward caricature when, in the final scenes, the performers have assumed their "true" nature and speak with their "true" voices. The soprano wears a cat's mask, the female pianist that of a goat, the actress that of a cow, the basso that of an ox, the conductor that of a rooster, et cetera. The play ends with the senseless intermingling and chaotic yelling of these animal voices, outdone by the rooster's three *kikerikis.*

The play can be seen as a social satire of the rich and the dumb. But the exclusive concentration on the performing artists raises questions which Thomas Bernhard leaves unattended. In addition to being rich, dumb and famous, these characters *are* presented as successful artists. Does Bernhard want to question the validity of their artistic skills? And, by implication, of the performances, notably during the *Festspiele,* in which they feature so prominently? Does he want to say there is an unbridgeable gap between the artist as private person and as performer? Is he attempting to demythologize the artist but leave the art intact? Bernard juxtaposes two areas of potential criticism which do not mesh. As satire of the nouveaux riches of the late 1960s, his choice of characters is too narrow and the social and economic background too sketchily drawn. As caricature of a certain kind of performer, his generalizations are too vast. Since no criteria indicate which artists are exempt from these ridicules, the indictments spill over and include all artists of the recent era of economic prosperity. If such a radical attack is indeed Bernhard's intention, then opera performers are an unrepresentative group of spokesmen. And the further question remains: when the artist is debunked, what happens to the art?

DER WELTVERBESSERER

CRITICAL COMMENTARY

Stella P. Rosenfeld (review date Summer 1980)

SOURCE: A review of *Der Weltverbesserer,* in *World Literature Today,* Vol. 54, No. 3, Summer, 1980, pp. 424–25.

[*In the following negative review of* Der Weltverbesserer, *Rosenfeld finds the play "tedious and boring."*]

When the curtain rises on Thomas Bernhard's play, which bears as its motto Voltaire's "Ich bin krank. Ich leide von Kopf bis zu den Füssen," it is five o'clock in the morning. The "Weltverbesserer," a real or perhaps only imaginary invalid, seemingly confined to his sickroom by disease but possibly by self-imposed isolation from the outside world, is preparing to receive representatives from the town and university, who bear him an honorary degree. For the "Weltverbesserer" is the author of a treatise on improving the world, which has received wide acclaim and has been translated into many languages, although it is understood by no one and in truth proposes nothing less than the radical abolition of everything.

Dedicated to the actor Minetti (to whom, in 1976, Bernhard had devoted his *Minetti: Ein Porträt des Künstlers als alter Mann*) and intended to be played by him, *Der Weltverbesserer* is a monumental monologue, delivered by the central figure almost without interruption. When the curtain falls after the *Nachspiel,* it is noon of the same day, and while much has been spoken, little has happened. The invalid has donned a wig and removed it from his totally bald head several times and has soaked his apparently sick feet (both activities intended, no doubt, to establish a clear link between the play and its motto): he has eaten, gotten dressed, and throughout has persistently bullied his housekeeper-companion of twenty years, whose almost total silence and consummate patience in the face of her master's vitriolic outbursts are strangely comforting. The honorable guests have come and gone, and the "Weltverbesserer," in a rare benevolent mood, has performed a good deed for the day by releasing a trapped mouse.

Although the play suggests parallels between its central figure and Voltaire, the "Weltverbesserer" is not Voltaire but rather Thomas Bernhard in disguise. The eccentric, egocentric, cantankerous benefactor of the world is the author's mouthpiece. Through him Bernhard attempts to express his anger and horror at the banality, absurdity and hopelessness of existence, at life as a sickness unto death. But while the reader familiar with Bernhard's work and world view may sense the author's design and respect the honesty of his effort, the play falls short of its apparent intentions. The frequent juxtaposition of the serious and the trivial and the obsessively repetitious concern with the banal, indeed the preponderance of the ludicrous, rob the message of its graveness and detract from the unity of purpose, from the obviously intended condemnation of the human condition. In the final analysis, Bernhard's *Der Weltverbesserer* is more a rambling compilation of life's inanities than a vision of its deadliness.

Whether the play can be more effective on the stage is a question that cannot be answered here. For the exceptional actor it may well be a bravura piece. In print, however, it often becomes tedious and boring, and one cannot help but feel that one has encountered all this before—while reading Thomas Bernhard.

VOR DEM RUHESTAND

PRODUCTION REVIEW

Gitta Honegger (essay date 1981)

SOURCE: "How German Is It? Thomas Bernhard at the Guthrie," in *Performing Arts Journal,* Vol. 6, No. 1, 1981, pp. 7–25.

[*In the following essay, Honegger chronicles the 1981 Minneapolis production of* Eve of Retirement.]

. . . I'm returning from the edge of forgetfulness.

Walter Abish

The day I arrived in Minneapolis, Guthrie Managing Director Don Schoenbaum gave an Open House Party. It was a beautiful midsummer afternoon. A live band evoked what I assumed a beautiful-people affair in the heyday of Glenn Miller must have looked like as Guthrie dignitaries, including many familiar New York theatre faces, mingled with the local corporate aristocracy, headed by Mr. and Mrs. Pillsbury, on the back lawn of a stately, well, not mansion, but in any case, impressive, home. Meeting all those New York actors, among them some friends, gave me the feeling that I had just arrived from the mainland, on a visit to a very prosperous colony. There was a spirit of exuberance and triumph—after all, Liviu Ciulei, the new artistic director, and his team had just conquered not only this city but the whole country, with two nationally acclaimed productions: Ciulei's own *Tempest* and Richard Foreman's *Don Juan,* followed by Alan Schneider's much less breathtaking, but extremely popular production of *Our Town.* But there was also a sense of isolation as I, the newcomer, was eagerly questioned for news from the city, from civilization.

* * *

Donald Madden doesn't fly. He took the train all the way from New York to Chicago and from there to Minneapolis. He arrived a day later. I was asked to welcome him at his hotel. Don will play Chief Justice Hoeller, a former concentration camp commander in Thomas Bernhard's *Eve of Retirement,* which I translated and Liviu will direct. Train service isn't what it used to be, Donald said, and he began to talk about the days of a bygone era of lovely dining cars, sophisticated personnel and exquisitely cultured service. Somehow I have visions of magnolias. The hotel is an old actors' hotel. Touring companies and vaudevillians stopped there and you could almost smell the spilled champagne in the faded carpeting, and sense old theatrical ghosts lurking behind the peeling plaster. It would make the perfect setting for another Bernhard play—*Minetti,* where an old actor, Minetti, is waiting for the artistic director of a small provincial theatre to talk to him about playing Lear at that theatre's 200th anniversary.

I had never met Don before. The first thing he showed me was a case filled with Nazi medals and orders, which he had tracked down in New York in preparation for his part. I was scared to touch those things. It must be my Austrian childhood. After all, we were made to believe in the power of the relics of saints. These then were the relics of the devil and I was sure they would ignite any minute or bring some other fatal curse upon us. In any case, it was a peculiar feeling to be confronted—for the first time—with tangible remnants of a time nobody spoke of when, and where, I grew up.

* * *

Minneapolis is an Austrian childhood dream come true. This isolated outpost of civilization in the middle of the prairie (the prairie!!!—how many wonderful associations are triggered off by that word alone!) in the state with the Sioux name "Land of the Sky-Tinted Waters" and resonating with all the picturesque lakes and rivers leads me back to Karl May and his fifty odd volumes of adventure novels about the "Wild West," which, although the author himself had never been there, became the American Dream for many a generation of German-language children.

How do I get there representing one of the most serious, intense, contemporary German-language writers and, what's even more amazing, what does Bernhard with his very European vision of a decaying, dying world have to do with Minneapolis, the town of the Jolly Green Giant, Betty Crocker, Land o'Lakes, Wheaties and Mary Tyler Moore and its wholesome Nordic population whose genuine good will and friendliness is unsettling even to the cynic?

* * *

The Guthrie is enormous, with its 1500 seats and thrust stage. The raked seats on one side drop down from the ceiling to the stage like a dangerous ski slope.

"I am scared to death," Liviu had said to me during auditions in New York. "Not about the play. I know it well. I am scared of that theatre. I don't even know if the play

should be done here at all. I finally decided to do it, because it is very important to do this play now, to introduce Bernhard now."

Liviu, as I was to find out again and again, is most commanding when he expresses himself in such simple terms. There is no way to contradict him, no more need for any doubt. He has arrived there after much questioning and he has gone to the bottom of the toughest questions. When he finally comes up with an answer, it usually is the right one. As simple as that.

The Guthrie used to have a second, smaller theatre. But in his first season, Liviu wanted to concentrate on the main stage.

* * *

Eve of Retirement is a three-character play, featuring Rudolf Hoeller and his two sisters Vera and Clara, who are preparing to celebrate Himmler's birthday, as they have been doing every year since the end of the war. For this occasion, Rudolf puts on his full SS uniform, he might ask Vera to shave Clara's head and dress her up as a camp inmate. Clara is paraplegic due to a war-time injury from an American bombing attack. She is also a leftist who despises her brother and sister for their political views and for their sleeping together on Himmler's birthday "after the second bottle of champagne." The highlight of the celebration and what has to be one of the most brilliant dramaturgical coups in contemporary theatre occurs during the last act, when Vera and Rudolf leaf through the family photo-album, reliving their childhood and Nazi past.

How will this play on a thrust stage in a 1500-seat house, following such heart-warming pieces of Americana as *Our Town* and *Fox Fire,* the latter starring Hume Cronyn and Jessica Tandy as the old Appalachian couple who finally yield to "progress," that is, the commercialization of their property? Furthermore, *Eve of Retirement* is scheduled to open back to back with *Eli,* Nelly Sachs' poetic evocation of a small Polish village after the Holocaust.

A daring combination, proving what Arthur Ballet, former dramaturg and now dramaturgical consultant calls the Guthrie's "political commitment" to a theatre that provokes thought and further investigation of the function and limit of Art. I think of Schiller's definition of Theatre as Moral Institution, which I haven't read since my high school days.

* * *

In the above sense, Ciulei's *Tempest* can stand as his own, and the Guthrie's, signature piece.

As he says in a program note "Prospero is for me a metaphor for the power of art" and he questions "How great an influence can an artist-scientist-philosopher have on the human conscience? On the human condition? Can he trigger changes in people's minds? . . . When does art inevitably become powerless? . . . Can art help to return to Man his own majesty?"

Working with Liviu one knows that these are not empty phrases but the driving energy behind the intensity and integrity of his work, and possibly behind his survival as an artist, a Rumanian artist confronting, participating in, and in many ways probably victim of his country's many historical transformations.

I am moved to tears by the beauty of his *Tempest.* Not just by the visual beauty—by now everybody has heard about the moat of blood filled with the artifacts of Western civilization that surrounds Prospero's lab. There is a beauty of the creative spirit, a dignity, an absolutely pure intelligence illuminating every directorial choice, every move and counter-move of human strife, ambition, love. What makes it so moving is the tension resulting from the director's obvious commitment to beauty, so romantic in its insistence and at the same time so sad in the face of constant betrayal and decay.

Ferdinand and Miranda are so luminous in their love, they almost seem surrounded by a halo—but only almost—the moment Ciulei tempts us with the most beautifully sensuous image of their innocence, he has Miranda dip her fingers in the moat and that moat is filled with blood.

If I was moved by the beauty of this production I was also awed by its perfection. And this is what kept me ultimately at a distance from Shakespeare. Lucid, transparent as this *Tempest* was, it was also very clearly someone else's forceful, even authoritarian, approach to the play. There was no raw spot that permitted me to move in with my own feelings and imagination. I was moved by the director's experience of the play, not by Shakespeare.

Ironically, I felt closer in retrospect, more loving, toward Lee Breuer's Central Park failure. Its flaws forced me to make my own connections to Shakespeare, to Breuer's world in relation to Shakespeare. I felt included in Breuer's attempt to construct a framework of references from the immediate culture, or rather the odds and ends, bits and pieces of pop-culture surrounding us. Ciulei's cultural points of reference were relics floating in blood, Breuer's were as alive as the immediate environment of Central Park, where he located the play. I felt very protective about the production, because I was part of that environment. Its failure included all of us participating in the event.

* * *

The office I shared with dramaturg Michael Lupu was cluttered with literature about the holocaust. Every now and then someone would drop in with a new book, more pictures, more articles about the camps, about Nazi VIP's. The *Eli* cast watched reels and reels of films, documentaries, Hitler propaganda movies, for hours, many mornings. Don Madden continued to track down Nazi memorabilia,

in uniform shops, from people he involved in conversations who happened to have some relative who collected the stuff and was willing to sell it for a healthy profit.

Everyone was very serious. We felt very good feeling bad, amazed, enraged and horror-struck. There was something perverted about it. I was reminded of Bernhard's repeated attacks on the theatre as the ultimate diversion from confronting the truth about our existence. The ultimate irony: by recreating the horror of human nature we keep distracting ourselves from the horror of human nature— the old magic power of the theatre, of the shaman: preventing evil by enacting it.

* * *

I buy myself a book about Minnesota and find out who Messrs. Hennepin, Nicolet and Marquette of the respective avenues are. I escape into the prairie and the American myth. It still is amazingly seductive.

* * *

A young Austrian professor of German literature at the University of Minnesota who lives on the campus of St. Olaf's College—North Country's answer to Ivy League— where his American wife also teaches German literature, talks of his frustration with a student body that doesn't understand the concept of a disintegrating, decaying world, let alone a sarcastic, cynical interpretation of human nature as it runs through German-language literature. Their world is still intact, their view optimistic. Apple Pie. Sunday School. Minnesota Mining.

* * *

I met a woman from Hibing, Minnesota, who has a high school yearbook with a picture of her and Robert Zimmerman/Bob Dylan.

* * *

Alan Schneider's production of *Our Town* is as drippy as Vermont Maple Syrup. It's very popular with local audiences. Liviu defends it as a play about order. Schneider's nostalgic vision does not suggest any cracks in the shingled facades, therefore the graveyard scene is hopelessly melodramatic.

* * *

I bought myself a 1970 Oldsmobile, once gold, now covered with rust, big as an airplane with all the pushbutton-convenience past of the American luxury car. For 195. Yes. With the windows down and the stereo blasting country music, I drive over the super-highways like through a Wim Wenders movie, I think of Sam Shepard, hear Dolly Parton, and feel very assimilated.

* * *

Eve of Retirement Liviu explains, is about potentially good people. It is essentially good that Vera cares for and protects her brother. Only she goes much too far and ends up doing the worst. The play is about the reversal of values. One critic would compare Vera to Lady Macbeth.

Don insists on playing his part with an accent. He is very good at it. He has acquired it hanging around Yorkville bars as part of his homework. Liviu is concerned it might distance the character too much. The audience could brush him off as yet another demented Kraut (my wording, never Liviu's!) instead of making a connection between Fascism and their own backyards.

Initially, I was very excited about Don's accent. It seemed that the rhythm brought him to the source of that typically German mixture of pathetic sentimentalism and bloodless rhetoric, resulting from the continuous fear and repression of genuine passion and feelings. These people's repertoire of truisms, clichés, quotes and lofty phrases, passed on to them through centuries, predetermined even their emotional responses. The choice of certain words and standard phrases catapult them into their outbursts, rather than the other way around where genuine emotions lead to spontaneous expressions of feelings.

* * *

Molière's or, rather Foreman's *Don Juan*. I am very annoyed the first time I see it. I came unprepared. I didn't reread the play, I am not an expert on Molière, I didn't get it. I know Foreman's work which is puzzling enough when it deals strictly with his own world let alone with a classic. However, the production, on first viewing, made one thing convincingly clear—the interaction of images of a decomposing French society with visual quotes from popular American culture such as the Star War-inspired statue of the commander, which suggests a very American interpretation without negating the French context (I began to understand even better where Breuer failed—his imagery was totally autonomous and finally cut itself off completely from the original text).

* * *

The Guthrie programs are so voluminous and erudite, it's impossible to get through them at the performance they are meant for. In fact, they are so forbiddingly scholarly and detailed that they scare you off altogether. At home I start to read through Foreman's program notes in search of an access to his production.

He writes about *Don Juan*:

> Although he quite properly isolates and speaks out against the stupidities and false pieties of the society in which he finds himself embroiled, he still is, inevitably so, a product of that society; *moreover, the self-defining language of that society is unavoidably coursing through his own discourse* (my italics). He is therefore often 'falling out of his positions,' as it were. Then,

through an effort of reason, he tries to force himself back in his 'chosen' intellectual position. So it is with most of the characters: they start to speak, define themselves and then the drift of their inherited language invariably takes them to places in which they didn't quite expect to end.

This gives me new clues, not to Molière, but to the language of Bernhard's characters: how their fossilized speech patterns and truisms enshrine their Nazi attitudes and make it nearly impossible to leave them behind, how Rudolf in particular lacks this "effort of reason" Foreman speaks about.

* * *

Liviu's motto for his production is Goya's etching "When reason sleeps, monsters are born."

The mad prince in Bernhard's brilliant novel *Gargoyles* (Knopf, 1970) speaks of cultures making "exorbitant demands on us. The oldest cultures the greatest demands. But what destroys us is our own religions though we assert it is nature doing it. What's needed . . . is for us to destroy the image of the world, no matter what it is like. We must always destroy all images." "Reason," he says, "is dictatorial. There is no such thing as republican reason."

Bernhard has a more cynical attitude toward reason, it seems, than either Ciulei or Foreman. Perhaps this proves Foreman's premise that he can't escape the language of his culture; coursing through the author's discourse it shapes the lucid madness of the prince's logic.

* * *

Liviu stresses again that what makes this play so important not only as a political but as a human statement is Bernhard's own attitude. He doesn't put himself on the artist's pedestal, from where he looks down on and judges his fellow-Germans, he includes himself in the culture he attacks. Foreman's thoughts helped to articulate the position of the rebel, the critic of society and his own conditioning by that society.

The luxury of working in an environment where the work of one artist leads to the understanding of another, where everyone's work feeds into one's own in some way!

* * *

Something dangerous is happening to Donald Madden: instead of playing the character's sentimentality, he plays the character sentimentally. He doesn't expose the cliché, he gets trapped in the cliché. He loses the sharp humor that lies in that distance and tends to get pathetic.

Richard Foreman talks about "the ways in which man is being forced to circulate within the codes and forms and social options which are available to him in a given society. He is victimized by his own (inherited) discourse, trapped by his own language, tortured by his own impossible effort to escape 'what his language would have him say.'"

The humor lies in exposing man in this impossible situation. This holds true for Molière as well as for Bernhard, whose characters become laughable, because they don't know their predicament. They are monstrous, to be sure—so is Molière's society, who in their ignorance rejoice over the death of Don Juan, who did know. Vera too, as Liviu points out, knows: she knows it is madness to defend and support her family's values, but in order for her to survive, she must immediately take back those insights. This painful, knowing contradiction gives her a tragic dimension. Liviu speaks of her as the victim (the victim of her language). He speaks of "the guilt of not accepting the guilt."

* * *

I am often asked what led me to translate Thomas Bernhard. Being Austrian like him, this has much to do with sharing the same language (in Foreman's definition) and, therefore, with my own ambivalent reaction to my cultural heritage, including my various attempts to come to terms with it.

My fascination with English started early. In second grade. It was the door to another, a bigger world. And when, at the age of twenty, I decided to live in this country I tried to literally exile myself in another language, to escape a suffocating burden which I felt but didn't understand at that time.

When I first read Thomas Bernhard in German it was after I had avoided speaking German for years. I thought I could reconstruct myself in the English language. Bernhard showed me how to confront and break through the cliché, the lie. He had created his very own, truthful language from the shattered fragments we inherited. I relearned my own language through Bernhard. At the same time he sharpened my perception for the traps and possibilities of language *per se*.

Following Foreman's tracks further I read Foucault's *Madness and Civilization* for clues to Bernhard's constant preoccupation with madness (*Eve of Retirement,* in its exposure of the Nazi mentality, is yet another variation of his persistent obsession with the madness of human existence). In the process I finally discover Derrida and read in his critique of Foucault:

> All our European languages, the language of everything that has participated from near or far in the adventure of Western reason—all this is the immense delegation of the project defined by Foucault under the rubric of the capture or objectification of madness. Nothing within this language and no one among those who speak it can escape the historical guilt.

Within the context of my present involvement with the Guthrie this statement resonates with many meanings. It could stand as a manifesto for the Guthrie's political commitment in the specific sense of presenting the "German plays" (as *Eli* and *Eve of Retirement* have become known by now); it becomes even more significant when one considers the Eastern European experience brought into the Guthrie by Liviu himself, his Rumanian dramaturg and Czech actor Jan Triska. And finally, in our interpretation of *Eve of Retirement* it establishes the cultural link between clinical, political and existential madness.

* * *

Betty Miller plays Vera Hoeller. My fourteen-year-old daughter is watching a rehearsal. She doesn't speak any German, she has been brought up in this country. Suddenly she whispers in my ear: "Betty sounds just like Grandma." My mother doesn't speak any English. Obviously my daughter was referring to the tone of voice, rhythms in speech and movement. Betty didn't approach the part through a German accent, she had discovered the universal language beneath a very specific character.

Suddenly I felt very good about my translation.

* * *

The production will have reached its goal when the audiences first identify with certain character traits and, as soon as they laugh with recognition, suddenly realize that they had just identified with monsters.

* * *

After the first run-through for people whose opinion Liviu values, he is disturbed by the comment that Clara, the paraplegic sister, comes across as a radical, a communist.

His dramaturg comes running up to me and tells me that all references to her being a socialist must be changed to "liberal."

I am enraged. I feel we have already made enough concessions to the audiences. In press releases and program notes, Rudolf and Vera never just "sleep together," instead, they "maintain an incestuous relationship."

In the second act Bernhard has Rudolf slowly transform—with Vera's help—from the uptight perfect German citizen in his business suit into a rather unappetizing, flabby slob as he first slips down his suspenders, then unbuttons his shirt, and finally, in order to pull off his shirt, opens his pants while Vera takes off his shoes and socks and proceeds to massage first his feet, then his back. A lengthy procedure, obviously full of unappealing sexual innuendos. Betty and Don are far too good looking to make this scene anything but tasteful. More importantly, Liviu limited their physical contact to two very brief, discreet images. Aside from Liviu's personal aesthetics which strongly embrace the tasteful, it seems, he insists that it wouldn't do any good to turn the audiences off by emphasizing the ugly sexuality, because this would only close them off to the political impact of the play.

The possibility of offending the Guthrie's rather large handicapped audiences was another problem.

In one very dramatic confrontation between Rudolf and Clara, Rudolf yells at his sister:

> But you won't make it
> People like you
> who squat in their wheelchairs for decades
> fall over suddenly and drop dead
> I've never heard of anyone getting very old

Liviu was afraid that such a brutal statement may not only offend but actually hurt the handicapped in the audience. Donald argued that the remark is no more brutal than his attitude toward Jews. Liviu agreed but maintained that as a direct reference to a physical deformity it could be personally offensive to an audience member, while Rudolf's relationship to the Jews was shown in a critical, larger context. The main thing, he pointed out once again, was to avoid making the characters so repulsive that the audiences would refuse to deal with them.

I had asked Liviu once if he would direct the play differently in Germany.

Yes, he said, he would make the characters harder, less emotional.

There was no need to make the characters recognizable in Germany. Clearly they are natives. Here they first had to become humanly accessible to prepare for the larger impact of their monstrosity.

The line was finally adjusted to:

> But you won't make it
> one day you'll topple over
> suddenly
> In your wheelchair and be dead

* * *

But I can't accept the modification of Clara's political views. I had been suspicious right from the start, when Liviu defined Clara as the voice of reason (ironically she is the one who doesn't talk). She is not on the left, he keeps insisting, she represents the middle, which ultra-rightists like Vera and Rudolf consider leftist. We need her, he repeats again and again, to represent the audience, she must provide the audience with an access to the play. If the audience is confronted with a conflict between Communists and Nazis it can again exclude itself.

I try to point out that there are clear indications that she is reading Marxist literature (not to speak of references to Rosa Luxembourg, which had been cut earlier, since local audiences might not know who she was and miss the

humor of that particular moment). Yes, surely, Liviu agreed, she is a Marxist, but in the European, philosophical sense. Americans, however, would immediately associate Marxism with Stalinism and again miss the main point that Fascism is possible everywhere.

He finally convinces me by pointing out that Bernhard never calls her a Communist. He always refers to her as a Socialist, which after all is the ruling party in Germany, the middle, while Americans always think of Socialism in terms of Communism.

I am not sure I totally agree with his concept but I feel that it is the right approach under the given circumstances.

"We must always keep our main target in mind," Liviu says, after things had calmed down again.

The main target is to get American audiences to recognize something about themselves. Clara becomes a liberal in the city of Humphrey, Gene McCarthy and Mondale.

* * *

Liviu has an uncanny sense for the essence of a play. In order to get to it he keeps peeling off layers and layers of secondary strains of actions and themes as he cuts through all the trimmings which either add up to or obscure the total picture. Once he has located the center he reconstructs the verbal excesses in visual images, which he supports, as necessary, with words.

"Create the space around the line," he repeats again and again.

And again and again I am surprised by what he extracts from those spaces—they are haunted with images from the repertoire of Western theatre: at one point, a family grouping evokes a moment of Chekhov, at another, when he has Vera and Rudolf pacing up and down the room, arm in arm, I immediately think of Mephistopheles' and Martha's famous Easter stroll in Goethe's *Faust*. Once Liviu points out the lyrical quality of certain lines and I think of Gretchen at the spinning wheel.

In his *Tempest* he consciously used relics and visual quotes from Western civilization. Watching him work on ***Eve of Retirement*** I feel that images from our theatrical and cultural history are constantly present somewhere in the back of his mind to suddenly materialize spontaneously, often unintentionally revealing in the briefest moments the rich tradition both play and director are heir to.

* * *

"Am I crazy that I like this play so much," Liviu asks once during rehearsal, with this typical puckish grin of his.

I love him so much!

* * *

Don Juan revisited: Foreman hasn't led me to a better understanding of Molière, but Molière has given me a better understanding of Richard Foreman.

* * *

A young actor, whose work I know and respect very much, has been at the Guthrie since his graduation from Juilliard two years ago. The parts I see him play are small and don't really show his talent, his strength. Yes, he says, he prefers the atmosphere here, the steady work, of course, the exposure to first rate directors as opposed to the hustle in New York. He is able to focus all his energy on his work and development as an actor. He never read as much, he said; he is much more centered now. He even bought himself skates last year. "In winter," he tells me, "you can actually hear the ice freeze on the lake."

* * *

It's getting close to the opening of *Eve* and *Eli*. Holocaust mania is sweeping the theatre. A symposium "Fascism and the Holocaust—The Artist's Response" is scheduled for the Sunday afternoon following the openings. There will also be readings from an appropriate selection of poems, prose pieces and plays. We are all very well-meaning, very committed, very earnest as we trade information, run to the libraries and talk to actual survivors of concentration camps.

Perhaps I have lived too long with Bernhard's vision, but I can't help detecting a certain lustful immersion in the subject matter. There is something dangerously gratifying in our research of history's most unbelievable horrors.

* * *

I want to see a musical comedy!

* * *

One day as I walk down the dressing room area, Don Madden stands there in full SS uniform. The effect of confronting the real thing, swastika arm-band and all, is chilling enough. But huddled around him are members of the *Eli* cast, in their torn traditional Jewish costumes. The immediate presence of a Nazi next to his Jewish victims was spine-curdling. It was as if all the taboos of my childhood, the haunted silence of those years growing up in post-war Vienna, came suddenly to life. At the same time the scene had a grotesque, operetta-like quality. These were costumes, after all, no different than any other theatrical costumes. (The idea that the Holocaust could be reconstructed out of a prop-box seemed hysterical.) That moment I felt very close to Bernhard's dark, horror-struck sense of humor.

* * *

A woman survivor of Auschwitz brought in a concentration camp jacket which would be used to copy the jacket

for our show. The other side to our genuine awe is voyeuristic excitement. The fascination with horror.

* * *

Minneapolis is a city without a clearly identifiable face. There are no century-old facades indicating a past somehow similar to mine, no old homes with the marks of generations of families and, therefore, identifiable pains and joys on them. Before those forbidding red brick buildings there was wilderness. Once I imagined that this was romantic, but after living here for a while I begin to feel the insecurity of living without a foundation, without a past to provide the comfort of continuity or at least an answer to my rage. Perhaps a perfect counterpoint to Bernhard's present, which seems at the tail end of history, "a horrifying history growing increasingly sinister as it recedes back to its origins, into a ghastly stench of generations . . . into a labyrinth of dead horror stories . . . from which from time to time I actually keep hearing cries of horror . . . coming out of the labyrinth of my family," says the prince in *Gargoyles*.

* * *

Holocaust madness: The motives are pure, the commitment is genuine, the effects increasingly bizarre. Survivors of various camps are talked about, pointed out, visited, ushered in and out of the theatre. Everyone knows at least one Holocaust story. I see myself at a cocktail party, the kind where men with martini glasses in their hands used to drop their Ivy League credentials: Yale '52, Harvard '48, Princeton '49. Only now it reads Buchenwald '42, Mauthausen '43, Auschwitz '44. A sick *New Yorker* cartoon. I am horrified. I feel awful. How could I come up with and admit to a perverse joke like that? I had to quickly share the image with others, just to test how sick they thought I was. But we all laughed. Working on those two plays had affected everybody. We wanted to laugh, we needed to laugh to keep our own sanity, exposed as we were to the ultimate limits of human madness.

* * *

The set for *Eve* is magnificent. Along the back wall (the only wall on the thrust stage) there is a stark gray facade with awesomely oversized windows suggesting the architecture of Martin Sperr. Vera, according to the script, opens the curtains at the beginning of the play. Liviu surrounds the entire thrust stage with floor-to-ceiling drapes, creating an atmosphere that is "shrouded in gloom" as Vera calls Clara. It also is a brilliant approximation of the effect of a proscenium stage, for which this play has been written.

* * *

The play I see on opening night is a play about paralysis. The theme is strongly stated with the opening image of Clara entering alone, in her wheeelchair, criss-crossing the stage. It is concluded with the paradigmatic Bernhardian image of Rudolf on the floor, propped up against the table; after his attack, still in his SS uniform: a lifeless puppet.

In the first act, Vera says to her sister:

> How fortunate that you can't walk
> You'd be in jail by now
> with your crazy ideas
>   . . . . .
> That wheelchair saves you
> from imprisonment

This premise is true for all of them: if they weren't crippled, they wouldn't survive. Clara's physical paralysis prevents her from becoming a political activist. Rudolf is protected by his stubborn blindness from an honest confrontation with the past, his guilt. Vera's human potential is paralyzed by her perverted sense of loyalty toward her family. But without it she may not be able to bear the admission of guilt.

All three are ultimately paralyzed by a culture, a "language system" (thank you, Richard Foreman) that passes on the guilt as well as the antibodies to combat that guilt, therefore continuing it *ad infinitum*. The prince in *Gargoyles* tells of holding a long speech about the "antibody in nature." He speaks to drown out the noises in his head, in which he hears "the belated cries of horror of those who died before me."

"None of us can get away," says Vera in one of her vulnerable moments.

In that sense, Bernhard suggests that we are all potential Fascists and he doesn't hesitate to cast himself, at least his namesake, in an outrageous four-page satire, *The German Lunch Table* which was the starting point for *Eve of Retirement.*

And if Liviu created his signature piece with *The Tempest* I offer mine, a staged presentation of the piece (reprinted below) for the symposium "Fascism and Holocaust: The Artists' Response" as a P.S. to his production of my translation of *Eve of Retirement.*

Addendum

Sunday afternoon after the symposium there is a party at Jan Triska's house for his daughter's twelfth birthday. Jan and his beautiful wife Carla are actors from Czechoslovakia. She has given up her career to help Jan and his family establish themselves in a foreign country, in another language.

It's a Guthrie family affair. My farewell party.

The children show my daughter the family photo album with pictures of their glamorous parents holding their glamorous babies in a Beverly Hills-type glamorous home. But that was in Prague, not too long ago. Jan, as I was

told by a German critic who knew him then, was the Gerard Phillipe of Eastern Europe. The house they live in now is one of those tidy ranches in some loop of a highway network outside the city, which looks like all ranches in loops of highway systems surrounding cities everywhere in America.

The kitchen smells like my grandmother's. Both my grandparents were Czech. But the Viennese of my parents' generation didn't emphasize their Slavic background. There is another Czech couple, architects who have lived here for twenty years. I find them beautiful. I feel reassured. Somehow I feel rooted in their beauty. I am very moved. Maybe it's the smell of the paprika-soaked sauerkraut in the kitchen or the realization that I have to come to the prairie to confront my cultural past, maybe it's just because I am leaving for New York the next morning and I haven't even packed. I don't want to. I drink a lot of wine and a lot of cognac. I get stuck with a man whom I had noticed at many Guthrie affairs. He's hard to overlook with his all-American-of-the-good-old-days good looks, including a white-haired crew cut, plaid pants, a rather loud voice and brash sense of humor. He is one of the founders of the Guthrie. I am surprised to find out that he is an expert on *fin-de-siecle* Vienna and particularly well read in the philosophical school from Carnap to Wittgenstein.

I drink more cognac.

Sitting on the plane the next day I try to piece together my scattered memories of the preceding night. I remember Jan standing in the middle of the street saying good night to his guests. I remember myself hugging him and sobbing, actually sobbing on his shoulder for a long time, in the middle of the street! I rarely sob. Then I lost my way in those damned highway loops. I remember ending up in front of a forbiddingly huge spoon-shaped sign saying "Betty Crocker." On my last night in Minneapolis I get stuck in the parking lot of Betty Crocker headquarters! I just sit there and laugh.

Somehow I found my way home. I remember leaving again for Liviu's house around midnight to say good bye to him and his wife.

I remember sitting there with him and Helga and Richard Nelson, the new dramaturg. I drink some more cognac.

On my flight back to New York I realize with great concern that I can't remember a thing I said in this last hour with Liviu. I can't remember having ever been drunk like that, and with Liviu and Helga of all people, who are always so lucid, so articulate in their conversation. Hard as I try I can't remember a word I said to Liviu whom I wanted to tell somehow how rich an experience my stay in Minneapolis was, how much I admire his commitment, his great understanding of art, his human knowledge, his absolute integrity, all the things we never say, yet the things which keep us going.

Much later, on the plane still, I slowly remember, although I am still not quite sure if it wasn't a dream that I tried to call Bernhard at 1:00 a.m. in the coffee house of the small Austrian village where he usually has his breakfast. Since he has no phone on his isolated farm it's the only way to catch him. But over there it's only 7:00 a.m. and the place isn't open yet. The woman who picks up the phone knows Bernhard and now, suddenly, I remember very clearly shouting into the phone, in German: "This is America calling. America! This is America calling. Tell him it went really well! Please don't forget to tell him, it went really well!"

CRITICAL COMMENTARY

Robert Acker (review date Winter 1981)

SOURCE: A review of *Vor dem Ruhestand,* in *World Literature Today,* Vol. 55, No. 1, Winter, 1981, p. 92.

[*In the following negative assessment of* Vor dem Ruhestand, *Acker contends the play reinforces several of Bernhard's recurring themes and stylistic techniques.*]

At first glance it might appear that Thomas Bernhard has written a drama [*Vor dem Ruhestand*] that is vastly different from his previous contributions to this genre, for the play is a direct allusion to recent political events centering around the former Minister President of Baden-Württemberg. It is set in the concrete milieu of contemporary Germany and seems to take a committed stance against aberrations in the West German political system. Yet a sublayer of ideas emerges which remains consistent with the pattern Bernhard has established in his other nine plays.

Each year on the 7th of October Rudolf Höller, a chief judge, dresses up in his old SS officer's uniform in order to celebrate with his sisters Clara and Vera the birthday of his former Nazi commander Heinrich Himmler. This year is slightly different from others, for Höller is near retirement and fearful of the loneliness that will soon be his lot. In reviewing the sorrows and glories of his past life and their possible present consequences, he becomes quite drunk at the birthday party and excites himself to such fervor over the Nazi ideas he still advocates that he suffers a sudden heart attack. The play documents the conversations between the characters from late afternoon, when the sisters are making final preparations for the party, until Höller's collapse in the late evening.

Beyond the harsh indictment of current political practices and the shocking claim that there is a pervasive Nazism inherent in the "German soul," the play contains many elements the Bernhard reader has encountered before. The plot is negligible, and the long, often repetitive monologues of the characters seem to represent sides of

Bernhard's own personality: Vera, the eloquent linguistic virtuoso; Clara, the silent and brooding intellectual; Höller, the pensioner anxious about his future and unable to escape his past. The little skit that the three attempt to perform every year during the birthday party is also illustrative of a recurrent Bernhard theme: the dulling, mechanical existence of man who is unwilling to pierce beyond the surface of reality, content instead to dwell in a world of make-believe.

DER SCHEIN TRÜGT

CRITICAL COMMENTARY

Marjorie L. Hoover (review date Summer 1984)

SOURCE: A review of *Der Schein trügt,* in *World Literature Today,* Vol. 58, No. 3, Summer, 1984, pp. 408–09.

[*In the following review, Hoover offers a laudatory review of* Der Schein trügt *and compares Bernhard with the dramatists Samuel Beckett and Harold Pinter.*]

With the play *Der Schein trügt* (*Appearances Are Deceptive*) Thomas Bernhard transcends earlier critical perceptions of his work (see *WLT* 55:4, pp. 603–607). His initial literary success, crowned by several prizes in the 1960s, rested on novels of gloom and morbidity stemming from his homeland, Austria. His first play too, *Ein Fest für Boris* (*A Party for Boris*; 1970), however comic, projected a grotesquely limited picture: a birthday celebration among about a dozen persons, all in wheelchairs and without legs. The party ends with the title character's fatal collapse. Though *Der Schein trügt* is hardly more hopeful, it gives a broader view of, alas, likewise all too human characters.

The play's eight scenes, divided asymmetrically into two acts, show in the six scenes of act 1 the ugly, uncomfortable room of Karl on a Tuesday, when he can always expect the visit of his younger brother Robert. The two scenes of act 2 then represent about the same lapse of an hour's time in Robert's comfortable room on the Thursday thereafter, the day of Karl's regular visit to him. Karl's stream-of-consciousness monologue in the first three scenes betrays his disgust with himself as he advances in age. Crawling in long winter underwear, he searches for the nail file he dropped while cutting his toenails. Now awkward and half-blind, he was once a juggler who kept twenty-one plates simultaneously flying through the air. He is wracked by envy of Robert, who, despite a lisp and a lack of sensitivity, achieved success as an actor, especially in the role of Goethe's Tasso. Karl remained the craftsman, as opposed to Robert the artist.

The woman's clothes in disorder in Karl's room belonged to the recently deceased Mathilde, who, though Karl's mistress, has bequeathed her weekend cottage to Robert. In five scenes of dialogue the two brothers, the only characters, betray through their opaque-transparent random reminiscences their love-hate relationship, their limited talents yet pretense to culture, and the drab pettiness of their narrow urban existence. In *Krapp's Last Tape* Beckett effectively exposed the habitus of age almost without words. Bernhard adroitly orchestrates his free-verse recollections into a revelatory picture of two lives devoted to art—if, indeed, one may pay the vaudevillian and the half-failed actor the compliment of calling them artists. For, like Chekhov and Pinter, who both have written comedies about art in language which tells most in what it does not say, Bernhard too satirizes the art of the stage in this brief drama without dramatic action. His long perspective on the two whole lives, so shrewdly observed, here opens out on the broader scope of human self-awareness, or lack of it. With *Der Schein trügt* Bernhard shows himself more the dramatist of dark and decaying Austrian forests. If appearances do not deceive, he may herewith be considered world-class like Beckett and Pinter.

RITTER, DENE, VOSS

CRITICAL COMMENTARY

F. P. Haberl (review date Winter 1986)

SOURCE: A review of *Ritter, Dene, Voss,* in *World Literature Today,* Vol. 60, No. 1, Winter, 1986, p. 105.

[*In the following essay, Haberl offers a negative review of* Ritter, Dene, Voss.]

The book jacket informs the reader that the three characters mentioned in the title of Bernhard's play *Ritter, Dene, Voss* are derived from the names of the actresses Ilse Ritter and Kirsten Dene and of the actor Gert Voss. This is confirmed in a brief note by the author at the end of the play in which he also mentions that, while writing the work, he concentrated his thoughts on Ludwig Wittgenstein. Thus the protagonists of the play emerge as Ludwig Worringer and his two sisters. Ludwig is meant to be a portrait of the Austrian philosopher Wittgenstein (1889–1951).

The action, such as it is, takes place in a dining room in a villa in the fashionable Viennese district of Döbling. Ludwig has just come home (at Dene's insistence) from the insane asylum Steinhof. During the first act the two sisters make preparations for an elaborate lunch and converse, mostly about themselves and Ludwig. During this exposition their fatuousness, the emptiness of their lives, and certain incestuous tendencies vis-à-vis Ludwig become ap-

parent. During the interminable lunch (act 2) Ludwig dominates the scene, alternating between madness and lucidity, discoursing on the futility of his life and that of his sisters, who are actresses of sorts, but only because their rich father had bought them 51 percent of the shares in a Viennese theatre. The sole flash of insight occurs when Ludwig states that life is only a fatal disease, but that the process of dying can be slowed down by thinking; man's only raison d'être is thought. The single moment of dramatic intensity occurs when Ludwig, repeatedly urged to eat by Dene, spits out a piece of pastry and yanks the tablecloth off the table, smashing all the dishes. The third act continues in a similar vein, replete with ennui and incestuous innuendo. Finally, the "action" mercifully peters out, as the three siblings drink their coffee. If it is still the function of literature to illuminate the human condition or the function of drama to achieve a measure of audience identification with the characters onstage, then Bernhard's latest play must be judged an abysmal failure.

DER THEATERMACHER

CRITICAL COMMENTARY

Nicholas J. Meyerhofer (essay date 1988)

SOURCE: "The Laughing Sisyphus: Reflections on Bernhard as (Self-) Dramatist in Light of His *Der Theatermacher*," in *Modern Austrian Literature,* Vol. 21, Nos. 3–4, 1988, pp. 107–15.

[*In the following essay, Meyerhofer analyzes the autobiographical elements of Bernhard's work, particularly his play* Der Theatermacher.]

> Die Idee ist gewesen, der Existenz auf die Spur zu kommen, der eigenen wie den andern. Wir erkennen uns in jedem Menschen, gleich, wie er ist, und sind zu jedem dieser Menschen verurteilt, solange wir existieren. Wir sind alle diese Existenzen und Existierenden zusammen und sind auf der Suche nach uns und finden uns doch nicht, so inständig wir uns darum bemühen. Wir haben von Aufrichtigkeit und von Klarheit geträumt, aber es ist beim Träumen geblieben. Wir haben oft aufgegeben und wieder angefangen, und wir werden noch oft aufgeben und wieder anfangen.[1]

Readers familiar with contemporary German literature already know that Thomas Bernhard is one of the most prodigious writers of the twentieth century. Since 1957, when he published his first book, a slender volume of poems entitled *Auf der Erde und in der Hölle,* he has maintained his literary output at a truly prolific pace. Two more collections of lyric poetry appeared in 1957 and 1958, but not until Bernhard turned to prose did the German-speaking public begin to take a serious interest in him. With the publication of *Frost* (1963) and his short prose of the mid-1960s critics recognized in Bernhard an original voice and an extraordinary, if uncompromisingly bleak, literary vision. This critical fascination with Bernhard's prose works continued for nearly a decade with reviewers as notable as George Steiner and Marcel Reich-Ranicki praising the young Austrian author as "the most original, concentrated novelist writing in German" (Steiner) and as a contemporary relative of Novalis, Kleist, Kafka, and Musil (Reich-Ranicki).

By the mid-1970s, however, critics had begun to fault Bernhard's prose for a lack of new insight. The writer had, it was felt, become totally predictable in his obsessive repetition of formulaic themes given expression in the same stock manner. This prose typically consisted of monomaniacal soliloquies which were in effect archeological digs in the mental landscape of some obsessive central figure who was being driven to madness and/or suicide. Lacerating relationships, paralysis of creative will, physical deformity, and even nature itself propel these protagonists into self-destructive isolation, where they knowingly and defiantly blur the dividing line between inner and outer realities, and where they gradually succumb. The distended but controlled clause repetitions in Bernhard's prose mimed in an almost musical manner the psychic circularity and hypertrophy which was thematized, the processes of a mind no longer in control of its own momentum. This pattern applied to his novels of these years (*Verstörung,* 1967; *Das Kalkwerk,* 1970; *Korrektur,* 1975) as well as to his shorter fiction; perhaps in some measure the accusations of poverty of inspiration in his fiction caused Bernhard to turn to drama so often in the 1970s. Moreover, drama offered Bernhard greater creative possibilities than prose, since performance and staging go beyond conceptual structures in wedding visuals, sound, and gesture to language.

Ein Fest für Boris was Bernhard's first play, and it premiered in 1970, the same year in which he was awarded the Georg-Büchner Prize. Those German critics who had already labeled Bernhard as an inveterate "Untergangshofer" and as a "todessüchtiger Selbstmordkandidat" were not long impressed with the transition, however, since it became immediately clear that the writer was not about to give up his characteristic negativity. *Ein Fest für Boris* featured a cast of fourteen legless and mentally debilitated cripples, all abused by a tyrannical and sadistic woman known simply and cynically as "die Gute." The thirteen full-length dramas which Bernhard has written since this initial "Dreiakter" have in general followed suit: They are dominated by egomaniacal monologists whose logorrhea typically gives expression to litanies of hate. Favorite targets in these diatribes are Austria, women, and artistic dilettantes. So familiar and predictable are the Bernhardian "Hasskataloge" in his plays that they no longer elicit surprise or anger because of their brutality but rather evoke the opposite response. When Bernhard's play *Der Theatermacher*[2] was premiered at the Salzburger Festspiele in 1985, the audience broke into gleeful laughter as the protagonists went into the anticipated tirade about the present-day Nazification of Austria.

Like all of Bernhard's plays this recent "Bühnenstück" is nearly devoid of action and can be easily summarized. The protagonist and "Theatermacher" of the title, Herr Bruscon, is an itinerant "Staatsschauspieler" who with his wife and two children as the hopelessly weak supporting cast is currently "on tour" in provincial Austrian villages. What the rural public is treated to is a play of Bruscon's own creation entitled "Das Rad der Geschichte." The piece is seen by Bruscon to be "eine Schöpfungskomödie, eine Menschheitskomödie, ein Jahrhundertwerk," not merely because he has been at work on it for nine years, but also because he is convinced of its universality and greatness. One soon gets the distinct impression, however, that "Das Rad der Geschichte" is in fact a hopeless historical smorgasbord. Nero, Hitler, Metternich, Napoleon, and Madame Curie (among many others) appear in the course of the play's events, but Bruscon is resolute in his conviction that the work is incontrovertibly a masterpiece, just as he is certain that he himself is "der größte aller Schauspieler, die es jemals gegeben hat." He makes constant references both to his own greatness ("Shakespeare, Voltaire und ich") and to the fact that he is an unrecognized genius who is doomed to be unsuccessful—through no fault of his own—in terms of both staging (he sees his family members as "Antitalente" inimical to dramatic success) and appreciation. Bruscon is forced to cast his dramatic pearls before the swine in the village of Utzbach ("Utzbach wie Butzbach"), and this in the most literal sense of the phrase. While attempting to rehearse with wife and children in the dilapidated hall of the village inn "Zum Schwarzen Hirschen" ("nicht einmal zum Wasserlassen / habe ich diese Art von Gasthäusern betreten"), the troupe is constantly interrupted by the energetic grunting of the pigs next door. Pigs seem to be in fact a rather frequent problem for the Bruscon players:

> In Mattighofen wurden die Schweine
> wegen eines Todesfalls wie uns gesagt worden war
> um halbneun gefüttert
> und zergrunzten alles
> das Schweinegrunzen ruinierte das ganze Stück
> Wir hatten es zuerst abbrechen wollen
> aber dann hatten wir uns entschlossen
> es weiter zu spielen
> Auf dem Höhepunkt ist es uns durch das Schweinegrunzen
> vernichtet worden

(47)

Finally, both man and nature conspire to keep Bruscon from realizing his Utzbach production of "Das Rad der Geschichte." His daughter Sarah is to play Madame Curie, but she is an intractable nose-picker of small intellectual stature for whom adequate theatrical performance is an impossibility. His son Ferruccio is to play all significant historical figures who had a "crippled" right arm (Hitler, Nero, Caesar, Churchill), since he himself has a broken right hand. He possesses, however, no appreciation for historical greatness, and Bruscon constantly refers to him as a "stumpfsinniger Dummkopf," adding at one point: "jetzt ist der Dummkopf / auch noch ein Krüppel."

Bruscon's wife has the smallest of roles, since he sees women and theater as incompatible ("was die Frauen betrifft / Jahrzehntelang müssen sie trainiert werden / um das Einfachste zu begreifen / Und wie schwer ist es erst / wenn es sich um die eigene Frau handelt . . . mit Frauen Theater zu machen / ist eine Katastrophe"), and she appears only sporadically to accept meekly an insult from her husband. Of her and her incessant coughing Bruscon punningly states: "Der einzige Reiz an dir / ist der Hustenreiz." *Der Theatermacher* concludes with the outbreak of a storm so violent that it panics the villagers who have assembled in the inn. Bruscon looks on helplessly as his would-be audience flees in terror and as the rain drips down on him from the leaky roof above.

Der Theatermacher displays in its lack of any real dramatic action strong similarities to Bernhard's prose, since both Bernhard's prose and his plays are rooted in his person, albeit in different ways and with different results. Bernhard has stated that writing is for him both a search for the origins of his personal disaster and an attempt—an ultimately Sisyphean attempt—to maintain equilibrium in the face of despair. Writing is thus for Bernhard a form of therapy, but therapy conducted in a never-ending session, since there is no ultimate healing. In one of his relatively rare interviews he once compared himself to a surgeon who desperately performs a series of operations on himself to rid his body of cancerous growths which reappear as fast as they are removed. The metaphor of disease and the hopelessness of the situation are reminiscent of Kafka. Bernhard's prose protagonists are typically arrogant and reclusive individuals who are overwhelmed by the demands and ultimate futility of a life of the mind, and they live in a state of heightened awareness of the inevitability of death. As Bernhard once told his audience in a scandalous "acceptance speech" for a prestigious literary award, everything in life, most especially literary awards, is ridiculous in the face of death's ineluctability: "Es ist nichts zu loben, nichts zu verdammen, nichts anzuklagen, aber es ist vieles lächerlich, wenn man an den Tod denkt."[3]

In Bernhard's earlier plays the prevailing mood was likewise frequently ominous, and they can be characterized as dominated by an often grotesque sense of tragic despair in the face of the human condition. This situation has changed noticeably in his more recent dramatic pieces, however, since the latter have become progressively more autobiographical, more self-referential in nature. As a result they do not shed their negativity, but their bleakness is mollified by ironic self-reflections and by a humor that is integral to the works. Sisyphus is still rolling his stone up the hill, but now he is doing so with a broad grin on his face. A brief examination of some of these self-reflective elements in *Der Theatermacher* may be seen as illustrative of this recent pattern and can at the same time shed further light on Bernhard's philosophy of the theater.

"Ein gewisses Talent für das Theater / schon als Kind / geborener Theatermensch wissen Sie / Theatermacher / Fall-

ensteller schon sehr früh" (28). These words stand as the motto to Bernhard's play, and the protagonist uses them to characterize himself near the beginning of *Der Theatermacher,* a title which in itself is a self-parodying pun.[4] One need not look far in Bernhard's other dramatic works to discover similar statements in the words of the frequent playwright-protagonists, and the same autobiographical remarks are made directly in many of the author's prose pieces. In *Der Keller,* volume two of Bernhard's five-volume autobiography, the author says of himself something very reminiscent of the words of Bruscon: "Das Theater, das ich mit vier und mit fünf und mit sechs Jahren für mein ganzes Leben eröffnet habe, ist schon eine in die Hunderttausende von Figuren vernarrte Bühne. Jede dieser Figuren bin ich, alle diese Requisiten bin ich, der Direktor bin ich."[5] Or again in a passage from the novel *Beton:* ". . . ich bin mein Beobachter, ich beobachte mich tatsächlich seit Jahren, wenn nicht seit Jahrzehnten ununter-brochen selbst, ich lebe nurmehr in der Selbstbeobachtung und in der Selbst-betrachtung und naturgemäß dadurch in der Selbstverdammung und Selbstverleugnung und Selbstverspottung . . . , zu welcher ich letztenendes immer Zuflucht nehmen muß, um mich zu retten. . . ."[6] In this sense the theater has provided Bernhard with a theoretical basis for his philosophy and aesthetics and with a perspective on himself as a writer, as survivor, as tireless performer and spectator of himself. It is small wonder therefore that theater is for Bernhard less centered on action than on language itself and on the idea of theater. "Wie alle große dramatische Literatur / existiert meine Komödie / aus dem Wort," says Bruscon, echoing the words of Bernhard in a newspaper interview of 1981:

> Na, meiner Meinung nach ist Dramatik doch etwas, was in erster Linie mit Sprache zu tun hat. Es gibt natürlich auch ein Theater der Purzelbäume, wo die Leute sich überschlagen, ununterbrochen Türen auf- und zugehen, alle Augenblicke Schicksale sich vollenden und das dann vielleicht alle fünf Minuten fad ist. Bei meinen Stücken ist das anders: man muß hinhören. Aus der Sprache, langsam entwickelt sich mein Drama.[7]

Language is the true chief protagonist of any Bernhard play, but not theatrical language or its attendant conventions. Bernhard knows that the most equivocal and deceitful aspect of theatrical convention involves language, namely, an actor pretending to be another speaking spontaneously but actually quoting a text. Bernhard's theatrical language never attempts to create the illusion of spontaneity; on the contrary, it is a language based on quotes and repetition. In this repetition in fact the author finds, much like Camus's hero Sisyphus, a purpose in life: ". . . gegen die Sinnlosigkeit auf-stehen und anfangen, arbeiten . . . und am nächsten Morgen wieder das gleiche, mit der größten Genauigkeit, mit der größten Eindringlichkeit" is how Bernhard describes it in volume four of his autobiography,[8] and Bruscon characterizes the process as existing "immer aus dem Widerstand / aus dem Anstrengungsmechanismus."

At the same time, however, Bernhard and his protagonists entertain no false illusions about the search for truth in language or about the potential success of their artistic efforts. Bernhard's theater, by its very disavowal of theater as practiced art form, quickly exposes the illusory nature of all such attempts and in its temporality makes a mockery of all claims to permanence. Similarly, Bernhard considers language an imperfect medium for communication, for the imparting of truth: "Die Wahrheit, denke ich, kennt nur der Betroffene, will er sie mitteilen, wird er automatisch zum Lügner."[9] What Bernhard's plays represent is thought seeking expression in a medium that inherently renders reality falsely, i.e. is doomed to failure from the outset. In this sense theater is for Bernhard the perfect sign for failure, and he seizes upon it with masochistic self-disgust and joy as the most useful and despicable model for his philosophy, which if performed on stage must naturally deride itself. Bruscon states directly: "In gewisser Weise ist alles Kompromiß / auch wenn wir die allerhöchste Perfektion im Auge haben," just as he admits: "Wenn wir ehrlich sind / ist das Theater an sich eine Absurdität" (36). Perhaps out of deference to the absurdity of the very notion of "theater" Bernhard is not above parodying one of the theater's great moments by placing the words "Leberknödelsuppe / oder Frittatensuppe / das war immer die Frage" in the mouth of Bruscon and makes the psycho-history of this rather ridiculous but art-obsessed petty tyrant that of himself: "Ausbruch von Zuhause / Ohrfeigen Hiebe / Kopfstücke väterlicherseits / In gewisser Weise Infamie / Selbstinfamie / Von ganz unten herauf gearbeitet" (28).

The quotations just cited are also representative of two facets or sides of Bernhard's humor in recent plays, namely of parody and of a thinly veiled autobiographical allusion which serves as both self-parody and as an "in-joke" for those familiar with the author. Somewhat more problematic and controversial, however, is the question of whether it should be considered funny when Bernhard's more traditional or older targets of abuse, alluded to earlier in this essay, are flayed by the tongue of a Bruscon. Is it humorous, for instance, when he fulminates

> Österreich
> grotesk
> minderbemittelt
> ist das richtige Wort
> unzurechnungsfähig
> ist der richtige Ausdruck
> Mozart Schubert
> widerwärtige Präpotenz
> Glauben Sie mir
> an diesem Volk ist nicht das geringste
> mehr liebenswürdig
> Wo wir hinkommen
> Mißgunst
> hiederträchtige Gesinnung
> Fremdenfeindlichkeit
> Kunsthaß

(39f.).

Or when he fires the following misogynistic salvos:

> Mit Frauen Theater zu machen
> ist eine Katastrophe
> Wenn wir einen weiblichen Darsteller beschäftigen
> beschäftigen wir sozusagen einen Theaterhemmschuh
> und es sind immer die weiblichen Darsteller
> die das Theater umbringen
> wenn wir das auch niemals offen aussprechen
> weil wir dazu zu galant sind
> eine weibliche Tragödin
> ist ja schon immer eine Absurdität gewesen

(36)

Does Bernhard really mean what is said here? Without wishing to equivocate too obviously the answer would seem to be "yes and no." On the one hand it is difficult to take such exaggerated and/or neurotic attacks seriously, but on the other hand they appear too often in his works to be coincidence, to be without autobiographical foundation. This too is typical, however, since so much of these recent plays is an "einerseits/andererseits." On the one hand Bruscon is a new variant and tragi-heroic allegory of the eternally misunderstood lonely artist who is vainly in quest of perfection, and on the other hand he is a shrill parody of precisely such an artist. On the one hand *Der Theatermacher* is a comedy with obvious light moments, and on the other hand it is a tragedy which revolves around the creation of "absolute Finsternis" as a prerequisite for verisimilitude: ". . . in meiner Komödie / die in Wahrheit / eine Tragödie ist / . . . hat es am Ende / vollkommen finster zu sein" (15).

"Ist es eine Tragödie? Ist es eine Komödie?" is the banal title of one of Bernhard's rather early short stories which remains a programmatic key to his philosophy and aesthetics. Bernhard's prose typically reveals the world as reflected in the schizoid prism of one individual's consciousness, an individual who is engaged in a hopeless quest for self-identity via artistic or creative realization. If this is utter solipsism, it is also according to Bernhard the only accurate manner in which to observe and detail "reality." Bernhard's recent plays are tragicomedies whose monologic protagonists ground their lives in senseless repetition and who are by Bernhard's own admission self-parodistic projections. One can argue as to whether a work such as *Der Theatermacher* is predominantly comedy or tragedy, but it is certainly an example of dramatist as performer and spectator of himself, and it is a performance which will most certainly be repeated again and again in Bernhard's future works. Odd as it may seem, Bernhard sees in this self-dramaturgy and self-preoccupation a kind of bond to all humankind since, as the motto to this essay indicates, a clearer conception of self is for him the key to a better understanding of human "existence" in general, and since, in the words of Bruscon "Opfer unserer Leidenschaft / sind wir alle / gleich was wir tun / wir sind die Opfer unserer Leidenschaft."

Notes

1. Cited in Reinhard Tschapke, *Hölle und zurück. Das Initiationsthema in den Jugenderinnerungen Thomas Bernhards* (Zürich: Georg Olms Verlag, 1984), p. vi.

2. Thomas Bernhard, *Der Theatermacher* (Frankfurt a.M.: Suhrkamp, 1984). Future paginal references to this work will be given in parentheses.

3. Spoken on 4 March 1968 at a banquet honoring Bernhard with the "Österreichischer Staatspreis für Literatur." The Austrian education minister Dr. Piffl-Percevic responded by calling Bernhard a "Hund" and by storming out of the banquet hall, while the president of the "Kunstsenat" shook his fist and called the ungrateful author a "Schwein." Cited in Jens Dittmar, *Thomas Bernhard: Werkgeschichte* (Frankfurt a.M., Suhrkamp, 1981), p. 98f.

4. I am referring of course to the colloquial "Mach' doch kein Theater!", which is always used in a denigrating manner.

5. Thomas Bernhard, *Der Keller* (Frankfurt a.M.: Suhrkamp, 1976), p. 121.

6. Thomas Bernhard, *Beton* (Frankfurt a.M.: Suhrkamp, 1982), p. 142.

7. See the "Salzburger Nachrichten" of 30 January 1981, p. 3.

8. Thomas Bernhard, *Die Kälte* (Frankfurt a.M.: Suhrkamp, 1981), p. 33.

9. Thomas Bernhard, *Der Keller,* p. 43.

ELISABETH II

CRITICAL COMMENTARY

Donald G. Daviau (review date Summer 1988)

SOURCE: A review of *Elisabeth II,* in *World Literature Today,* Vol. 62, No. 3, Summer, 1988, pp. 452–53.

[*In the following mixed assessment of* Elisabeth II, *Daviau maintains that "Bernhard offers a very small slice of life here, and though the trip through the work is pleasant enough, one is left wondering whether the journey has been worthwhile."*]

Thomas Bernhard has convincingly proved to everyone's satisfaction that he is a virtuoso of linguistic technique. No author in Austria today uses language more effectively to express character. His protagonists give the impression that they are talking in everyday terms, arguing, complaining, criticizing, and nagging, but the result is a total exposure of the inner being of the individual. We have experienced this technique in drama after drama in rapid succession, and the latest play, **Elisabeth II,** which bears the designation "Keine Komödie," fits into the same pattern.

The play is neither a comedy nor a tragedy but a character study, essentially in the form of a monologue with a few other *Stichwortbringer* to give it the marginal semblance of a dialogue. On the basis of the contents it could just as well have been written in narrative form using the stream-of-consciousness technique. The result would be the same: an unfolding of the personality of Herr von Ehrenstein, a wealthy industrialist, who is eighty-two years old and manifesting all the crotchety behavior of a rich boor in ill health, confined to a wheelchair, and facing death. Through his conversations, primarily with his servant Richard and his secretary Fräulein Zallinger, we learn more about him than we really care to know, because as a human being he is not significant in any way. Since he has no redeeming value in himself, Bernhard must be offering him to us as a representative of a certain class or type and in this way making a comment on Austria. Thus we learn of Ehrenstein's selfish, cruel, and domineering nature, his misogyny, his hostility against the provinces, particularly against Alt Aussee because of the Nazi presence there, his dependency on his servant Richard and his willingness to go to any lengths to keep him, his domination over his secretary (whom he has trained as a concert pianist), and his dislike of his opportunistic nephew.

Bernhard has learned the lesson well that most conversation consists of repetitiousness and that people usually talk in circles, even contradicting themselves. He has built his technique on this principle, and very successfully. This style may become monotonous after a while, but it maintains sufficient interest to keep one reading or listening. One keeps thinking that by the end of the work the unilinear progression of the conversation will suddenly open new vistas and suggest some deeper meaning, hidden insight, or universal truth. Unfortunately, such is not the case here. The guests invited by the nephew to view the arrival of Queen Elizabeth II in Vienna from Ehrenstein's apartment overload the balcony when they all rush out to see the queen and fall to their deaths. Only Ehrenstein, who is annoyed by the guests and refuses to take part in the viewing, is spared, along with his servant Richard. This ironic touch makes an effective theatrical ending but contains no other discernible significance.

Nothing is changed by the events of the play, and there is no character development. Bernhard offers a very small slice of life here, and though the trip through the work is pleasant enough, one is left wondering whether the journey has been worthwhile.

HELDENPLATZ

CRITICAL COMMENTARY

Christine Kiebuzinska (essay date Fall 1995)

SOURCE: "The Scandal Maker: Thomas Bernhard and the Reception of *Heldenplatz,* in *Modern Drama,* Vol. 38, No. 3, Fall, 1995, pp. 378–88.

[*In the following essay, Kiebuzinska enumerates the many reasons for the controversy surrounding Bernhard's* Heldenplatz.]

The violent discussions in reaction to Thomas Bernhard's *Heldenplatz* (Heroes' Square)[1] in the Austrian press even before its opening on 14 October 1988 (as the play selected to celebrate the one-hundredth-year anniversary of the Burgtheater) were influenced by a number of factors. The Burgtheater represents a tradition rooted in the Austro-Hungarian Empire, and the repertoire of the Burgtheater historically reflected that tradition. Consequently, the appointment, not too long before the commemorative celebrations, of the tradition-breaking German theater director Claus Peymann to what is considered the most prestigious and influential post in the performing arts in Austria set off heated discussions in the press about the nature and responsibility of the Burgtheater to foster Austrian culture. Peymann, who before assuming the post at the Burgtheater had been the artistic director in Stuttgart and Bochum, has a reputation of provoking the public, and as a result, criticism against Peymann focused not only on the fact that he was a "foreigner" but also on his open sympathies for the left. At the same time, Bernhard was already viewed in his native country with distaste, reflected in such invectives associated with his name as "*Alpen-Beckett,*" "*Menschenfeind*" or misanthrope, and "*Untersghofer*" or doom promoter, for even before the *Heldenplatz* scandal he had achieved notoriety in 1984 when he was charged with slandering his country's honor and insulting its citizens in his biographical novel *Holzfällen* (*Woodcutters,* 1987).[2]

One must also remember that Heldenplatz was the scene of the Austrians' tumultuous welcome of Hitler in 1938, and consequently, Bernhard's intentional foregrounding of the fiftieth anniversary of the Heldenplatz events was immediately seen as a provocation. In the play, taking his cue from the upheavals generated by the election of Kurt Waldheim in 1986, Bernhard not only dismisses the postwar image of Austria as victim of Nazi Germany, but maintains that Austria's retreat into nostalgia for its imperial past, implied in the celebrations of the Burgtheater's one-hundred-year history, represents yet another problem of Austria's inability of *Vergangenheitsbewältigung,* or attempts to come to terms with the horrors of the past, with its not-so-latent anti-Semitic and pro-fascist sentiments. Thus one could say that the *Heldenplatz* scandal was staged even before Peymann's decision to commission Bernhard to write a new play for the Burgtheater's commemorative celebrations.[3] It was then hardly surprising that because of the antagonism to his tenure, Peymann encountered problems during rehearsals of *Heldenplatz* when six of the Burgtheater's resident actors walked out of their parts under the pretext of moral indignation over having to act in a play so strongly execrating their country. As a result, the première of *Heldenplatz* had to be shifted to the later date of the 4th of November, 1988; however, despite this delay, Peymann continued to bill *Heldenplatz* as the official play for the Burgtheater's centennial celebration.

In addition, the problems that beset the production of *Heldenplatz* were fueled by the highly ructious Austrian scandal sheets. Initially, the outcry focused on the choice of the depressing Bernhard, frequently referred to as the *Übertreibungskünstler,* the exaggeration-artist, as the playwright to open such a significant celebration. Letters poured in demanding a "traditional" Austrian play such as Grillparzer's *König Ottokars Glück und Ende* with its famous "*Lob Österreichs,*" or ode to Austria: "it is a good land . . . look all around you."[4] The discussion of the Burgtheater's repertoire, however, soon escalated to outcries and shrieks of protest as passages from the unpublished script appeared in the *Neue Kronen Zeitung* and the *Wochenpresse.* Since it had been agreed that Suhrkamp, the press publishing Bernhard's work, was not to release *Heldenplatz* until the morning of the première, these illegally published excerpts were quoted out of context, and without any reference to plot or characters.

The focus of the indignation concerned passages from the play that circumscribed Austria as "a stage on which everything had rotted, been annihilated, and had become totally demoralized," by the "disgusting six and a half million supernumeraries of mentally deformed and raving mad Austrians" (89). The excerpts also foregrounded the quotation that "present day Austria has more National Socialists than in 1938" and that to survive in Austria "you have to be either Catholic or National Socialist," since no other point of view is to be tolerated (63–64). The president of Austria is named "a crafty liar," and the Bundeskanzler as "nothing but a tricky dealer in the sell-out of his country" (102). Not to exclude any institution, the university faculty was described as reflecting "the unbelievable primitivism, and catastrophic ignorance" of the "provincial idiots, ninety per cent of whom are Nazis from Tyrol, Salzburg, and Graz" (66). The tirade ends with the dark words that "in this most execrable of countries, the only choice is between black or red swine," and their unbearable stench "spreads out from the Hofburg, the Opera, the Parliament, and football stadium over the entire damned and degenerate land" (164).

Many actors who felt empowered to defend Austria against Bernhard's insults immediately leapt upon the stage. And even though on vacation in Majorca, the retired Chancellor Bruno Kreisky was the first to telephone his indignation that this insult to Austria "should not be allowed to take place." "I find it incomprehensible," he protested, while indirectly insulting his successor Franz Vranitzky, "that no one in power has taken a position until now. Look, Thomas Bernhard can write what he wants. But one shouldn't take this with noble disdain. Rudeness must be met with rudeness."[5] Kreisky had been a target of Bernhard's vitriolic remarks previously when in a series of articles and letters to the press Bernhard had denounced the mediocrity of Kreisky's regime as *Wurstelprater,* a comedy for marionettes;[6] consequently, this was Kreisky's opportunity to have his turn at stirring up opposition against Bernhard.

However, since Bernhard had not left any Austrian politician unscathed in his critiques, virtually every politician, as each one tried to outdo the other in the defense of Austria's "honor," took this opportunity to fuel the climate of anger and hate even further. Nor was anyone to be outdone in demands for purging the "Peymann/Bernhard duo" out of Austria. As was to be expected, within a day, President Kurt Waldheim responded. "I speak out when harm threatens the country," he objected, calling *Heldenplatz* "an outrage against the Austrian people." Feeling that some justification was necessary, he added "that it shouldn't be taken for granted that only we are the *Bösen Buben* and that it's better elsewhere. Look only at some of our neighbors." As a defender of Austrian honor, he could not keep silent in voicing his opinion that the Burgtheater was most certainly not the place for staging such insults.[7] Egged on by the official voice of their President, letters poured in to the Viennese scandal sheets demanding the resignation of Peymann and the institutionalization of Bernhard. The outcry was so vehement that one observer characterized the protests as *Peymannschlacht.*

At this point, not to be outdone by Waldheim, party leader Alois Mock and Jorg Haider provoked further outbursts in their demand that such insults to Austria should not be financed by the taxes "of the hard-working Austrian folk." However, the outcries demanding that the Burgtheater's repertoire must reflect the taxpayers' taste also called attention to the questions censorship in a republic committed to "freedom of expression" in art. At this juncture, the minister of Education and Culture, Professor Hilde Hawlicek, decided to play a role despite the fact that she seemed undecided as to what her lines were. While she protested that freedom of expression in art must be defended, she felt that "had she been Bernhard she would not have written such a play," nor "had she been Peymann would she have chosen it for the opening of the Burgtheater's anniversary celebrations." This evasive defense of "freedom of expression" provided ammunition to Haider, who, strained to the utmost by the audacity of the Bernhard/ Peymann "nest-soilers," cried out, citing Karl Kraus "out, out of Vienna with these rotten scoundrels." When reminded in one editorial that Kraus' words had instead to do with the casting out of scandal-mongering journalists, Haider ironically referred to Hawlicek's defense of "artistic freedom of expression" as justification for the appropriation of Kraus' stinging commentary against Peymann and Bernhard.[8]

In response to the questions raised by Hawlicek's attempts to define artistic freedom, once again letters deluged the press, each trying to outdo the other in terms of erudition, liberalism, or aesthetic sensibility. Indeed, everyone automatically voiced that they were for freedom of expression in art, since "after all this was fundamental to the liberties established by the Austrian constitution"; however, they insisted that there "should be limits" as to what should be considered as art. The "buts" and "howevers" continued using such evasions that of course *Heldenplatz* should be presented, but not in a theater supported by the taxes of its citizens. Others relying on the quasi-intellectual authority of their titles as *Herr Doktor* or *Herr Professor* insisted that according to their informed opinions *Heldenplatz* did not answer to any of the criteria established by Aristotle or Horace. The press, in turn, incited the public to express their "freedom of expression" by boycotting the play.[9]

Nor did the diatribes restrict themselves exclusively to the press, since letters and threats against Bernhard and Peymann also poured into the Burgtheater. Both Peymann and Bernhard were subjected to personal insults as well. On his way to rehearsal, Peymann was attacked by an old-lady-dervish with an umbrella, and Bernhard was threatened with a walking stick by a defender of morality who shouted as he chased him, "one ought to eliminate you." A woman on crutches was about to attack him, Bernhard recounts, but decided that in lifting her crutches she might lose her balance and had to resort to shrill abuse instead. In response to the raging theatrics in the press and by the performers in the political arena, Bernhard decided to make an entrance on the stage of the public theater as well, and in an "exclusive interview" in *Basta* insisted that as a result of the public histrionics, he had enough material to make the dialogue in his play even stronger and sharper. He agreed with the interviewer that his play was "horrible" but called attention to the fact that the theatrics being played out in the public theater were even more horrible. However, he noted "the one belongs to the sphere of art, the other to life."[10]

An examination of the plot of *Heldenplatz* reveals to what extent Austria had become the stage, and all Austrians central characters in Bernhard's exploration of the obsessive nature of discourse on both sides of the stage of the Burgtheater. The plot concerns the central character, Professor Josef Schuster, who has thrown himself out of the window of his Heldenplatz apartment on the day before his return to Oxford. Since his suicide occurs on the fiftieth anniversary of the events on Heldenplatz in 1938, one could say that the professor's death is a consequence of exaggerated hypercriticism and pedantry. Despite his absence on stage, the professor continues to be a presence, as the first act presents the housekeeper, Frau Zittel, and Herda, the maid, preparing dinner for the bereaved family. Through endless quotations of the professor's opinions by Frau Zittel, we find out that the professor was an egotist, a shoe fetishist, and a tyrant regarding the ironing and folding of his shirts to the degree that despite numerous demonstrations of the correct folding of his shirts by the professor, Frau Zittel, out of sheer terror, couldn't master the precise order of the folds. The freeing of Frau Zittel and Herda from the professor's obsessive exactingness emerges subtly as Frau Zittel and Herda open windows to let the spring air in, and since the professor loathed flowers, for the first time set flowers on the table. Most significantly, Frau Zittel dares serve soup with caraway seeds, yet another ingredient that the professor found repugnant. Despite these signs of freedom, Frau Zittel continues to iron the professor's shirts and Herda to shine his shoes fastidiously throughout the first act.

We also discover that the history of the Schuster family represents the history of the Austrian Jews in general. Professor Josef Schuster and his brother, Professor Robert Schuster, emigrated in 1938 to Oxford and Cambridge respectively, barely making it out of Austria alive after Hitler's triumphant rally at the Heldenplatz. Following the war, upon the invitation by the Austrian government to resume their university posts, both brothers return to the Vienna of the 1950s only to discover that from their perspective, anti-Semitism and the Nazi mentality have remained virtually unchanged. Ultimately, Professor Josef's wife, Hedwig, despite many prolonged stays at Steinhof, the Viennese mental institution, has become so hyper-sensitive to the anti-Semitic climate that she begins to hear shouts of *Sieg Heil* from their Heldenplatz apartment. Though Professor Josef, according to Frau Zittel, makes his wife endure these horrors, in the end he gives in to her pressure to return to Oxford. As his brother, Professor Robert, recounts, Josef commits suicide realizing that the return to Oxford is nothing but an *Alptraum,* since alternative locations, even Oxford, have no chance as long as the modern psyche continues to be dominated by its darker historical obsessions. Following the funeral his brother explains the terrible event as the consequence of his brother's inability to deal with "living in a nation of six and a half million retards" (89) ruled by a "caricature of a Nazi" (147).

The second scene takes place in the Volksgarten next to the Heldenplatz with the Burgtheater visible in the foggy, cold March afternoon. The deceased professor's two daughters and his brother are returning from the cemetery. One of the daughters mentions that Robert should protest the fact that a road is to be built through the beautiful grounds and orchards of his retreat in Neuhaus. He insists that he has no intention of protesting since "all protests subvert themselves in the end"; he only wants peace, no more protests, against anything whatsoever (86). And yet, in recounting his interpretation of his brother's suicide, he assumes Josef's discourse of immense anger and negation to such a degree that it becomes impossible to distinguish between quotation and Robert's individual speech. Josef's monomaniacal vision of decay and dissolution represents the last hold to which he clings before the final fall, and it is evident from Robert's "quoted" tirades that his situation is just as desperate: according to him, even the music at the Musikverein has become "*national-sozialistisch,*" and one has shut out "the cries of the six and a half million abandoned, passive idiots who scream at the top of their lungs for a director, a director who when he comes will ultimately throw them into the abyss, from reaching one's ears" (89).

The third scene shows the family, including the widow and a few family friends, gathering amidst the trunks with labels "to Oxford" for the last meal in the apartment at Heldenplatz. The widow, Frau Professor Hedwig Schuster, obsessed by the cries in her head, falls into silence as the others debate the benefit of moving to Oxford versus staying in Vienna. The sounds of *Sieg Heil* become audible to

the spectators as well and become louder and louder until they are virtually unbearable as Frau Schuster falls dead with her head in the plate, and the shouts from the Heldenplatz link the past and present in a continuous shrill scream.

When, prior to the opening, the Burgtheater released a plot-synopsis which revealed that the insults to Austrian honor came out of the mouth of a Jewish professor, several reactions occurred. The immediate response on the extremist side was to blame Bernhard for using the "untouchable" figure of a Jew as a mouthpiece. Other questioned the need to characterize the Jewish professor so negatively both in his inclination for authoritarianism and the bitterness of his emotions. Some voiced the anxiety that "Bernhard by ascribing such disparaging language to a Jew may give the impression to bred-in-the-bone anti-Semites that this is the manner in which Jews think of us. This, in turn, will certainly feed outbreaks of hatred."[11] In fact, anti-Semitic diatribes appeared almost immediately in response, and in an editorial appearing in *Der Standard,* Bernhard's strategy is effectively illustrated as the writer falls into the trap of reinforcing Bernhard's obsessive discourse in ***Heldenplatz***:

> Bernhard uses a synthetic figure to present his insults. This figure, in order to suitably represent the anniversaries of the year, is a Jew. A Jew, analytical and intelligent (naturally, all Jews), occupies himself as a returning emigrant with the Austrian soul. His analysis (in contrast to an intelligent one) is a stupid one. The conclusion—a hysterical, stupefied, undifferentiated, neurotic scream.[12]

One genteel writer insisted that of course she had nothing against a Jewish theme in the repertory of the Burgtheater and suggested instead that "a more pleasant play" such as *Fiddler on the Roof* should perhaps be presented.[13] Yet others protested the debasement of the Austrian, highly cultured Jewish professor by making him appear to "howl like a German Alsatian hound." Others saw the play as nothing but a general provocation by the Jews themselves and concluded that ***Heldenplatz*** and the about-to-open film by Scorsese, *The Last Temptation of Christ,* were all part of the same plot to undermine Austrian-Christian values.[14] Ironically, some Austrians used as examples of their tolerance and lack of anti-Semitism such formulations as "the worst is that Hitler had killed all the best Jews and only the worst have returned."[15] When the press reached the "Nazi-hunter" Simon Wiesenthal for comments, his reply fed the anti-Bernhard/Peymann tirades even more, since according to Wiesenthal "every generalization, every accusation playing up collective guilt, contradicts Jewish ethics and is to be abandoned for fear of throwing together the bad with the good."[16]

A few more perceptive critics from the German press, among them Benjamin Heinrichs, observed that one can only exaggerate that which actually exists. Bernhard's bold and also diabolical construction refuses to show the Austrian Jews in a role which would force tears to the eyes of even the most hard-boiled anti-Semites. Nor does he show them as decent, cultivated victims of barbarism but instead characterizes them as Austrians, as that which they themselves despise but continue to be to the end of their days. Through this alienation effect of presenting the professor's narrow-mindedness, his authoritarianism, and his biases against the middle class, peasants, and the proletariat, Bernhard denies the public the "good Jew" as an object of identification. Nor does he cater to the pseudo-liberalism and supposed open-mindedness of the more humanistically inclined sector of the public by allowing them to wallow in benign philo-Semitism.[17]

As the première approached, *Der Standard* called for a storming of the Burgtheater, and reminded its readers that, owing to public outcry and the storming of the stage in Frankfurt at the première of Fassbinder's *Die Stadt, der Müll, und der Tod,* the play had to be withdrawn.[18] The article ends with the remarks that "it is wonderful that in a democracy everything is possible." And on the day of the première, the front page of the *Neue Kronen Zeitung* presented an incendiary photograph of the Burgtheater in flames with the caption "nothing is too hot for us."[19] This provocation was picked up by the foreign press, and the *Frankfurter Allgemeine* noted that this incitement appeared on the anniversary of the Austrian *Kristallnacht* when rampaging crowds burned down Jewish synagogues.[20]

The press, having fired up its readership since the early days of October, awaited a massive demonstration and turned out in full force many hours before the beginning of the première on the 4th of November. And since counter-demonstrations by the defenders of Bernhard and Peymann, particularly from the Austrian Federation of Writers, were also announced, a clash between the two camps was anticipated. However, despite all their attempts at escalation and agitation, the mass demonstration proved to be a disappointment as small groups of skinheads, Christian defenders of morality, and so on milled before the entrance with placards with such expressive displays as "*Pfui,*" "*Nestbeschmutzer,*" "*Raus mit Peymann,*" etc. The only theatrical event worth playing up was the dumping of a wagonload of horse manure in front of the Burgtheater. Thus, a line in Bernhard's text that "this small town is a huge manure pile" (164) once more showed the liminal border between the theater on the stage and the theater playing itself out at the entrance to the playhouse.

Inside the theater, the reactionary contingent attempted to undermine the performance with loud booing; whistling; stamping; shouts of "boring," "banal," "stupid"; outcries of "God preserve Austria"; and the unfurling of a huge banner, "Away with Peymann," from the third balcony. "Blasphemy," cried out one protestor, and since the play, as a commentator observed, didn't attack God as such, but the Nazis, the outcry reaffirmed the text that Austria was "nothing but a nest for Nazis" (35). Despite the outcries, or indeed perhaps because of them, the ovation, as Peymann and Bernhard appeared on the stage at the conclusion of the performance, continued for forty-five minutes

with tumultuous applause which ultimately suppressed the equally loud booing by the outraged contingent. Following the première, the press, perhaps somewhat chagrined at the failure of the boycott, used the strategy of no longer attacking Bernhard and Peymann for insulting Austria's honor but rather of discrediting the play and production as "boring," "cynical," and "stupid."

These examples of the responses generated by Bernhard's discourse in *Heldenplatz* illustrate the particular dynamics and potential for conflict evoked by his excessive language. The arguments for or against Bernhard frequently have little to do with what he actually said, for as he himself has observed, reality is almost entirely circumscribed by discourse, not as individual creation, but as part of the general field of discourse itself. Consequently, the reception of *Heldenplatz* does not represent a unique reaction to the play but continues the discourse set into motion by the conflation of all of Bernhard's texts, as the obsessive monologue, the single droning voice, is endlessly reformulated, corrected, and filtered through a hundred different registers. What emerges is language spinning on itself in a perpetually arrested inconclusiveness. There is no respite from despair in Bernhard's plays, and *Heldenplatz* like *Eve of Retirement, The President,* and *Histrionics,* shows characters as roles that are reified and detached from human intentionality and expressivity to be transformed into an inevitable destiny for their bearers. Racism is shown to be institutionalized, reified, and accepted as inevitable, and anti-Semitism not as the result of socio-historical development, but, as quite simply, the natural state of affairs.

The merging of the stage and reality from the months of diatribes in the press and in the arena of politics appeared in Bernhard's *Heldenplatz* as a refraction of the degenerate language used so automatically in the press, and which by virtue of its ready-made, dead clichés denied all the actors, those on stage and off, any possibility of individualism and expression. What also emerged was the realization that the actors on stage and off, as well as the spectators as actors, had carefully studied their entrances onto the stage. Theater thus became not only a metaphor for human experience but also denied possibility of representation as the actors both on stage and off merged in the continuous utterances. Bernhard's theater became an arena for obsessiveness and obscenity to be played out as "THE PERFORMERS INSIDE THE PERFORMERS," and "PERFORMERS INSIDE THE PERFORMERS OF THE PERFORMERS" foregrounded the artificiality and excesses of this extended theatrical space.[21] And in the case of *Heldenplatz,* the theatrical space had been extended to include all of Austria as tirades similar to those "quoted" in the play pervaded the land. One German critic observed that Bernhard's technique depended on reversal:

> That there are more Nazis in Vienna now than in 1938 is not true; nor is it true that the universities are filled with idiots. That Vienna is in a total stupefied state of abjection is also not true. Bernhard has the effect of an old Austrian mortar. He doesn't strike the target, but the effect of demoralization is enormous. Everything that isn't true, is true.[22]

Austria as theatrical space was to be the last stage on which Bernhard was to play out the role of provocateur, for Bernhard, already deathly ill during the histrionics surrounding *Heldenplatz,* died three months after the opening on the 15th of February, 1989. His will states that he "explicitly" stresses that he wants nothing to do with the Austrian state and "rejects every attempt by the state to associate itself with his person and his work for all time." To ensure that his last will would be followed, he forbids the performance of any of his works in Austria for the full copywright term of seventy years, with the exception of the five plays already in the Burgtheater's repertory, including *Heldenplatz,* which too must be withdrawn once the terms of the contract expire.[23] Having withdrawn into the silence beyond the grave, Bernhard leaves the theater an opportunity to work out the anguish of his hatred and his love for Austria, since as he writes in an early novel *Der Keller,* "We want to say the truth, but we don't say the truth. We describe something approaching the truth, but that which is described is something different from the truth."

Notes

1. Thomas Bernhard, *Heldenplatz* (Frankfurt, 1988). Subsequent references to the play are to this edition and will appear parenthetically in the text. All translations from the German are mine.

2. Eva Schindlecker, "Thomas Bernhard: *Holzfällen. Eine Erregung,*" in *Statt Bernhard,* ed. Wendelin Schmidt-Dengler and Martin Huber (Vienna, 1984), 13–58.

3. The best source for background discussions of the reception of *Heldenplatz* is a 297-page volume published by the Burgtheater consisting of clippings from the local and foreign press, letters to the editor, and letters to the Burgtheater. See *Heldenplatz: Eine Dokumentation* (Vienna, 1989).

4. See letter to Peymann, 10 October 1988. The letter quotes Grillparzer's "Lob Österreichs!" speech in full with carefully underlined lines directed towards Peymann or Peymann/Bernard. The lines describing the Austrian soul as "open and gay" with "a clear look" and "a steadfast disposition" were directed towards Peymann, while the lines, "God preserve the youthful spirit / and repair what others have corrupted" were specifically called to Bernhard's attention. See *Heldenplatz: Eine Dokumentation,* 28–29.

5. Dieter Kindermann, "Kreisky zu Skandalstück: 'Das darf man sich nicht gefallen lassen,'" *Neue Kronen Zeitung,* 10 October 1988, reprinted in *Heldenplatz: Eine Dokumentation,* 24.

6. Thomas Bernhard quoted by Josef Donnenberg, "Thomas Bernhards Zeitkritik und Österreich," in *Literarisches Kolloquium 1984 Linz: Thomas Bernhard* (Linz, 1984), 52.

7. Kotanko Kittner, "Waldheim: In der Burg kein Platz für *Heldenplatz,*" *Kurier,* 11 October 1988, in *Heldenplatz: Eine Dokumentation,* 35.

8. Fritz Dittlbacher, "Wirbel um Bernhards *Heldenplatz.* Hawlicek: 'Kunst muss provozieren,'" *AZ Tagblatt,* 11 October 1988; Dieter Kindermann, "Hinaus aus Wien mit dem Schuft," *Neue Kronen Zeitung,* 12 October 1988; Kotanko Kittner, "VP-Mock will Bernhards *Heldenplatz* privatisieren," *Kurier,* 12 October 1988. These columns have been collected in *Heldenplatz: Eine Dokumentation,* 38–46.

9. The discourse generated in the press fills endless pages of *Heldenplatz: Eine Dokumentation;* most typical is the column "Staberl" appearing in the *Neue Kronen Zeitung,* 26 October 1988 under the title "Provokation tolerieren!" inciting the readership not to swallow the "insults to Austria" as "expressions of artistic creativity."

10. Conny Bischofberger and Heinz Sichrovsky, interview with Bernhard, "Bernhard bricht sein Schweigen," *Basta,* 26 October 1988, in *Heldenplatz: Eine Dokumentation,* 158–59.

11. See a letter to the "Staberl" column in *Neue Kronen Zeitung,* 18 October 1988, in *Heldenplatz: Eine Dokumentation,* 104.

12. See Peter Sichrovsky, "Stürmt den Heldenplatz," *Der Standard,* 4 November 1988, in *Heldenplatz: Eine Dokumentation,* 187.

13. See letter to Peymann reprinted in *Heldenplatz: Eine Dokumentation,* 101.

14. See letters to the "Staberl" column in the *Neue Kronen Zeitung,* 18 October 1988, reprinted in *Heldenplatz: Eine Dokumentation,* 104; also Peter Sichrovsky, "Stürmt den Heldenplatz," *Der Standard,* 4 November 1988, in *Heldenplatz: Eine Dokumentation,* 187.

15. See C. Bernd Sucher, "Notwendige Wahrheit, gefährliche Provokation," *Süddeutsche Zeitung,* 7 November 1988, in *Heldenplatz: Eine Dokumentation,* 235.

16. See Dieter Kindermann, "Kreisky zu Skandalstück: 'Das darf man sich nicht gefallen lassen,'" *Neue Kronen Zeitung,* 10 October 1988, in *Heldenplatz: Eine Dokumentation,* 24.

17. Benjamin Heinrichs, "Heldenplatz," *Die Zeit,* 21 October 1988, *Heldenplatz: Eine Dokumentation,* 134.

18. The writer conveniently forgot that the "storming" of Fassbinder's play in Frankfurt had to do with the audience's outrage against the play's anti-Semitic content.

19. See photograph and heading in the *Neue Kronen Zeitung,* 4 November 1988, in *Heldenplatz: Eine Dokumentation,* 182.

20. Andreas Razumovsky, "Das Virtuosentum der Wutanfälle," *Frankfurter Allgemeine,* 7 November 1988, in *Heldenplatz: Eine Dokumentation,* 230–31.

21. See Thomas Bernhard, "Is It a Comedy? Is It a Tragedy?" *The President & Eve of Retirement,* trans. Gitta Honegger (New York, 1982), 211.

22. Günther Nenning, "Peymanns Wiener Welttheater," *Die Zeit,* 4 November 1988, in *Heldenplatz: Eine Dokumentation,* 192.

23. See Peter von Becker, "Thomas Bernhard (1931–1989)," *Theater heute,* 8 (1989), 1.

FURTHER READING

Criticism

Dowden, Stephen D. *Understanding Thomas Bernhard.* Columbia: University of South Carolina Press, 1991, 99 p.

Critical study of Bernhard's plays, novels, short fiction, and memoirs.

Honegger, Gitta. "Acoustic Masks: Strategies of Language in the Theater of Canetti, Bernhard, and Handke." *Modern Austrian Literature* 18, No. 2 (1985): 57–66.

Discusses the works of Elias Canetti, Peter Handke, and Thomas Bernard and analyzes the role of language in their plays.

Modern Austrian Literature 21 (1988).

Special issue devoted entirely to Bernhard.

Franz Grillparzer
1791-1872

Austrian dramatist, novella writer, poet, and critic.

INTRODUCTION

Franz Grillparzer wrote in an age of transition, between the classical Romanticism of Johann Wolfgang von Goethe and Friedrich Schiller and the realism of the middle and late nineteenth century. Drawing from one period and sensing the approach of the other, Grillparzer successfully employed the poetic form and Romantic tone of the first to depict the subtle psychological states characteristic of the second. Grillparzer's work also reflects the influences of Shakespeare, the Spanish dramatists Pedro Calderón and Lope de Vega, and the popular theater of his home city, Vienna. His rich and varied oeuvre—little appreciated in his own time—is today widely studied and respected.

BIOGRAPHICAL INFORMATION

Grillparzer was born in Vienna on January 15, 1791. His father was a court lawyer, and the family was esteemed and wealthy. The personalities of Grillparzer's moody, indulgent mother and cold father reflect the opposition between poetic idealism and reality that dominates his work. Grillparzer shared his mother's love of music, and the cadence and structure of his dramas reflect his melodic sense. The Grillparzers were involved in the rich musical culture of Vienna, and Grillparzer shared a lifelong friendship with Ludwig von Beethoven. After studying law at the University of Vienna, Grillparzer briefly acted as a tutor and worked at the court library. Eventually, he became an administrator at the Imperial Archives. In 1817 his first play, *Die Ahnfrau* (*The Ancestress*), was produced in Vienna. The censorship imposed under the rule of Prince Metternich, which intervened especially in the productions of historical tragedies such as *König Ottokar's Glück und Ende* (1825; *King Ottocar: His Rise and Fall*), hindered Grillparzer's success. In 1838, broken by Vienna's resounding rejection of his one comedy, *Weh dem, der lügt!* (1838; *Thou Shall Not Lie*), Grillparzer retreated from the theater, neither publishing nor producing another drama, although he continued to write for thirty years.

MAJOR WORKS

Grillparzer's first produced play, *Die Ahnfrau,* was dismissed by critics as a *Schicksalstragödie* or "fate-tragedy," despite its obvious poetic promise and dramatic power. In his second play, *Sappho* (1818), Grillparzer

employed the literary effects that characterize his work from that point on: the classical blank verse form, serious subject matter derived mainly from classical or historical themes, and an emphasis on psychological motivation. His trilogy, *Das goldene Vlieβ* (1821; *The Golden Fleece*)— *Der Gastfreund* (*The Guest-Friend*), *Die Argonauten* (*The Argonauts*), and *Medea*—utilizes Greek mythology as subject matter. A few of his works, like *König Ottokar's Glück und Ende* and *Ein treuer Diener seines Herrn* (1828; *A Faithful Servant of His Master*), focus on the history of Vienna and its monarchy.

CRITICAL RECEPTION

During his lifetime, many critics deemed Grillparzer a "fate-tragedian." This charge of sensationalism devastated Grillparzer, who always adhered to the highest artistic ideals, and he struggled during the rest of his career to shake off the label with which he was branded. Although many of his plays were commercially and critically successful, the recognition he craved did not come until after his death. Commentators agree that Grillparzer drew from the theatrical traditions of classical Romanticism, Spanish baroque, Shakespeare, and popular theater. That in synthesizing these influences he presaged the realism of the next dramatic age is testimony to the genius that has earned Grillparzer his position as the most distinguished Austrian dramatist.

PRINCIPAL WORKS

Plays

Die Ahnfrau [*The Ancestress*] 1817

*Blanka von Kastilien 1817

Sappho 1818

†Das goldene Vließ: Dramatisches Gedicht in drei Abtheilungen [*The Golden Fleece*] 1821

König Ottokars Glück und Ende [*King Ottocar: His Rise and Fall*] 1825

Ein treuer Diener seines Herrn [*A Faithful Servant of His Master*] 1828

Des Meeres und der Liebe Wellen [*Hero and Leander*] 1831

Der Traum ein Leben [*A Dream Is Life*] 1834

Weh dem, der lügt! [*Thou Shalt Not Lie*] 1838

Ein Bruderzwist in Habsburg [*Family Strife in Habsburg*] 1872

Die Jüdin von Toledo [*The Jewess of Toledo*] 1872

Libussa 1874

Other Major Works

Tristia ex ponto (poetry) 1835

Der arme Spielmann [*The Poor Fiddler*] (novella) 1848

Sämlichte Werke 42 vols. (drama, novella, poetry, and criticism) 1909-48

*This is the date of composition.

†Trilogy comprised of the plays *Der Gastfreund* [*The Guest-Friend*], *Die Argonauten* [*The Argonauts*], and *Medea*.

OVERVIEWS AND GENERAL STUDIES

F. W. Kaufmann (essay date June 1936)

SOURCE: "Grillparzer's Relation to Classical Idealism," in *MLN*, Vol. 51, June, 1936, pp. 359-63.

[*In the following essay, Kaufmann examines the major influences on Grillparzer's work, in particular the effect of classical idealism.*]

Literary criticism rather early recognized the fact that Grillparzer followed Schiller's model in his earliest dramatic attempts and plans, as in *Lucretia Creinwell, Seelengrösze, Robert von der Normandie,* and that from about 1809 on, besides that of Shakespeare and the Romanticists, he yielded more to the influence of Goethe, as *e. g.,* in his *Faustplan, Irenens Wiederkehr* and the dramatic sketch *Spartakus.* As to Grillparzer's mature works, Goethe's influence is especially seen in the characters of Sappho and Hero and in the Greek setting of *Sappho, Das goldene Vlies,* and *Des Meeres und der Liebe Wellen;* a Goethean desire for classical simplicity and harmony is attributed to the recurring inspiration from *Iphigenie.*

This more or less exterior influence, however, is not the subject at hand. Our question is rather: what was Grillparzer's inner response to classical idealism, and what influence had this response as such on the composition of his dramas?

Blanka von Kastilien most closely follows the example of Schiller's *Don Karlos.* The classic-idealistic antithesis of despotism and political freedom, of moral heteronomy and autonomy is still noticeable in the theme of Grillparzer's drama. Especially the impudent passion of Maria de Padilla, the cold rationalism of Rodrigo de Padilla's intrigue and the brutality of King Pedro reflect the dependence on the classical model. The antipole, however, is no longer moral antonomy in the classic-idealistic meaning of the word. Fedriko's conception of duty toward the king is not based on an insight into the moral value of allegiance, but on tradition; it is heteronomous and amoral, if not immoral, according to classical standards; and his relation to Blanka is, in spite of all Schillerean influence, just as much determined by a conventional respect for the empty form of a marriage which hardly ever existed in fact. The logic of this situation requires a non-Schillerean solution; but only death is allowed to join those who naturally belong together. This uncertainty with respect to moral decisions, proves that Grillparzer tries to break away from classical idealism, that he begins to doubt absolute moral postulates and their realization; that, on the other hand, he is still dependent on those postulates, that he does not dare yet to substitute for them a solution which would do better justice to the life situation of his drama.

This doubt grows to skepticism in Grillparzer's *Die Ahnfrau,* a play which suggests not only the often made comparison with Schiller's *Braut von Messina,* but also with Goethe's *Iphigenie.* Schiller submits his characters to fate, in order to show how the moral freedom of man is able to maintain itself against the strongest pressure of necessity; and Goethe's Orestes is lifted through the sisterly love of Iphigenie to the idealism of humanity. The difference in Grillparzer's treatment is not sufficiently explained by a reference to the fate-dramas of the late

Romanticists. It is at least as important to state that the idealistic moral postulate manifests itself in his drama. The Ahnfrau herself impersonates the conflict between idealistic and vitalistic will, a conflict which is clearly expressed in Günther's words:

> Haszt sie die vergangne Sünde,
> Liebt sie die vergangne Glut.

It is significant for Grillparzer's own dilemma that Jaromir is longing for a life of innocence and goodness and that he hopes to find the realization of this ideal through his love for Berta. This ideal intention, however, has, contrary to all idealistic belief in a moral world order, a depravating effect; it is responsible for Jaromir's fatal love for his sister. He is completely blinded by his passion after he has discovered that Berta is his sister, and thus the irresistibility of his desire is an extreme expression of Grillparzer's doubt in the possibility of idealistic conduct; it reveals the sensualistic basis of idealistic striving; it evidences a disillusion comparable only to that expressed in Grabbe's *Herzog Theodor von Gothland* or in Büchner's *Danton's Tod*. Besides that, Grillparzer develops—again in clear, although hardly conscious contrast with Goethe's *Iphigenie*—the idea of rootedness in an organic environment and its opposite, eradication. This existential rootedness has an almost deterministic effect on moral conduct. Goethe's Iphigenie, too, suffers from the separation from her native land, but this suffering develops her character to greater purity and constancy. Grillparzer's Jaromir, however, becomes a robber in the separation from his home-environment. The fact that Jaromir was robbed as a child does not detract from the validity of this interpretation, since the idea of existential rootedness is applied in subsequent dramas in more and more conscious reaction against classical idealism in the characterization of Medea, Jason, Kunigunde (in *König Ottokars Glück und Ende*) and of Otto von Meran (in *Ein treuer Diener seines Herrn*).

The idealistic starting point is also apparent in *Sappho*. Grillparzer's ideas, to be sure, do not differ quite as radically from Goethe's as from Schiller's ideas, because Goethe and Grillparzer represent a more organic conception of life than Schiller. Thus, Goethe's Torquato Tasso doubts, like Sappho, the value of art in comparison to that of life; but Tasso's antipode, the statesman Antonio, in turn envies the poet, and the result is but a tragic resignation to the inescapable one-sidedness of every great talent. Sappho's fate, however, cannot be interpreted as a tragic and heroic resignation to her ideal calling, but only as a disillusioned estrangement from idealism. Sappho is disappointed in life, because she realizes the isolation from concrete existence imposed on her by ideal pursuits. In the last analysis, her tragedy can only be understood as an expression of Grillparzer's development away from idealism, as reluctant yielding to his growing conviction that man cannot rise from his concrete existential basis into a free, independent realm of ideality. It is the tragedy of the idealist who believes that he is able to free himself from the elementary

basis of his existence and who finds it impossible to readjust himself to the demands of reality.

At this point the most essential axioms of classical idealism are abandoned. In *Das goldene Vlies* moral freedom becomes almost illusive, if one interprets freedom in the classical sense as freedom to choose moral goods and freedom to restrict one's will by the recognition of moral principles. Medea and Jason are doomed to moral decline by the fact that they leave the sphere allotted to them by birth and symbiosis, and that is also the tragic fate of Kunigunde in *König Ottokars Glück und Ende* and of Otto von Meran in *Ein treuer Diener seines Herrn.*

Whereas in his first dramas Grillparzer struggles with idealistic beliefs and although they are defeated, assigns them a prominent active part in the motivation of the play, in his later dramas, especially from *Das goldene Vlies* on, the positive moral will is almost completely reduced to the self-limitation in an appropriate environment and to a definite stage in life, and the negative side is represented by the transgression or absence of these limitations. Classical idealism conceived moral goodness as an active decision and badness as a passive yielding to heteronomous influences. Grillparzer arrives at the opposite view that moral goodness is mainly inactive rootedness in an environment, and that evil arises from the transgression of limitations in the concrete existential situation of man. Accordingly, reason gradually loses its highest dignity as supreme judge on moral issues; it becomes mainly an instrument of the will to live, and as such it exerts the dubious function of enabling man to transcend his organic sphere of existence and to strive for aims regardless of existential limitations, thereby menacing the originally organic structure of his environment and preparing ruin for himself and for the environment.

The transition from classical idealism to Grillparzer is a transition from an individualistic conception of man to an existential conception, *i. e.,* man's existence is conceived as essentially symbiotic, as being together with others, as being in active and reactive communication with others. The implications of this change and their influence on the problematic structure of Grillparzer's later dramas transcend the scope of this paper which is only concerned with Grillparzer's breaking away from the classical inheritance.

This development is similar to that of Schopenhauer who inverted the classical relation of idea and will in favor of the unreflected, instinctive rootedness of man in his existential environment. Like Schopenhauer, Grillparzer arrives in and through his work at the tragic conclusion that reason severs man from his existential basis and drives him into an isolation in which he faces physical and moral catastrophe.

The relation to classical idealism as outlined in this paper should eliminate all doubt about Grillparzer's place in the literary history of the nineteenth century. Like Grabbe, he inherited the classical belief in the existence of an ideal order and developed through a stage of disillusion to a more realistic conception of the world; but, belonging to an older generation than Grabbe, he was more inbued with idealistic views and as an Austrian more deeply rooted in an organic environment, so that his adjustment to the realistic trend of the nineteenth century was never as complete as Grabbe's. In the development of the nineteenth century he always regretted the progress of disintegration of an organic structure.—In this respect for the organic structure of life Grillparzer remained in spiritual affinity with Goethe.

T. C. Dunham (essay date October 1938)

SOURCE: "The Monologue as Monodrama in Grillparzer's Hellenic Dramas," in *Journal of English and Germanic Philology,* Vol. 37, October, 1938, pp. 513-23.

[*In the following essay, Dunham analyzes the structure and motivation of the dramatic monologues in three of Grillparzer's dramas:* Sappho, Das goldene Vließ, *and* Des Meeres und der Liebe Wellen.]

Hans Sittenberger in his essay "Der Monolog"[1] distinguishes three types of monologue: (1) the expository monologue; (2) the lyric monologue; (3) the dramatic monologue. The dramatic monologue, according to his definition, is the one which not only fits into the dramatic structure of the play, but which "in seinen einzelnen Gliedern deutlich erkennbar dramatischen Bau aufweist."[2] He continues: "Das trifft bei allen jenen Monologen zu, die aus widerstreitenden Empfindungen zu einem Entschlusse führen, der eine Aenderung der Lage und damit neue Verwicklungen oder Entwicklungen bewirkt."[2]

A monologue of this third type is sometimes built up as though it were a miniature drama. It is possible to identify rising and descending action and a central dramatic conflict. Out of the conflict one or the other of the contending forces becomes dominant and carries the character along in a course of unhindered action, thought, or emotion. When a monologue has this independent unity in addition to its function as an organic part of the drama as a whole it is a true monodrama, i.e. a drama acted by a single character.

Grillparzer's dramas contain interesting examples of all three types of monologue, but the present study is concerned only with the dramatic monologue insofar as it may be called monodrama. The treatment will be limited to the Hellenic (or classical) dramas: ***Sappho, Das goldene Vliess,*** and ***Des Meeres und der Liebe Wellen.*** By analyzing the monologues as to structure and motivation we shall try to show the nature of the dramatic conflict and offer justification for applying the term monodrama.

In ***Sappho*** there are three monologues which merit consideration here.[3] All three are spoken by Sappho. In her monologue at the opening of Act III dramatic interest is centered around the conflict between dream and reality, between the wish to believe and the doubts created by objective evidence. At the beginning of the monologue Sappho is tortured by the memory of Melitta in Phaon's arms. Though she sees her fears of losing her lover already confirmed by the scene she has just witnessed, she struggles to free herself from the thoughts of hateful reality. The dramatic climax is reached when, after recalling the kiss Phaon gave Melitta, Sappho breaks off with the words:

> . . . —fort! ich will's nicht denken! Schon der
> Gedanke tötet tausendfach!—
>
> (801 f.)[4]

The will to believe in Phaon's innocence is stronger than her fear, and she argues with herself that what she has seen is only the expression of a trifling whim and without further significance. Some conflict still continues beyond the climax, but fear has been almost completely suppressed and no further open clash of the opposing forces occurs. During a long flight of rationalizing (803-841) Sappho regains outward composure, and her last doubts are silenced when forced optimism is strengthened by emotional certainty. She finds Phaon sleeping, and his innocent expression and her own love convince her that her fears were groundless. She succumbs to her dream of perfect love and finds it impossible to believe ill of her lover. Disarmed by his smile and eager to hear him speak her name she wakens him and thus paves the way for the disillusionment which follows.

As a monodrama this monologue has very evident shortcomings. The relatively short duration of the active conflict weakens the dramatic force, and the long rationalizing lyric passage detracts from the unity and disturbs the structural balance.

In Sappho's next monologue (Act III, scene ii, 927-975), which comes after she has been convinced of Phaon's faithlessness, a new conflict arises between pride and thwarted love. This time there is no single climax. Feelings of disappointed love alternate with the consciousness of personal pride in such a way that there is a continual course of rising and falling action, a rapid succession of emotional ups and downs. As soon as Sappho recovers from the first shock of her discovery that Phaon is in love with Melitta she feels the acute pain of loss. She asks herself whether it is possible that Sappho is scorned for a slave girl. When she mentions the word "verschmäht" (933) she is stung by its meaning, and her mood immediately changes from pain to violent anger. In a burst of pride she reminds herself of her superiority over Phaon and Melitta, of her poetic genius and her fame. Glorifying herself and her achievements she works herself up to a peak of exultation (939 f.). Then the emotional reaction comes and she bitterly regrets that she ever left her high station (941 ff.). She rationalizes that she has been mistaken in trying to unite art and life. But even when she is expressing forced acceptance of her fate she realizes that she can no longer be content with art alone. There is distinct longing in the words which begin,

> Mag auch das Leben noch so lieblich blinken,
> Mit holden Schmeichellauten zu dir tönen . . .

> (958 f.)

In a moment a third and final shift in mood takes place. Still longing for love, she becomes jealous of Melitta. At the same time pride makes her half-incredulous of the slave girl's charms. Jealousy and curiosity lead her to send for Melitta. The monologue thus ends with a mood which combines elements of both conflicting forces. In this example of monodrama there is a series of climaxes instead of just one, and there is no clear-cut settlement of the conflict. Dramatic life, however, continues through the whole course of the monologue.

In the monologue at the beginning of Act IV (1189-1243) Sappho carries on a dramatic struggle against emotions which threaten to engulf her. Twice emotion rises to a climax. The first time resistance is partially effective, but the force of anger persists and when the second climax is reached Sappho is swept on to action.

The initial portion of the monologue is a lyric passage in which Sappho expresses her great suffering and the longing for the peace and forgetfulness of death (1189-1205). The thought of waking reminds her of the tortures to which she will have to awake. The memory of Phaon's ingratitude arouses her to full awareness of what has happened (1206). Dull pain now gives way to anger. As she describes the crime of ingratitude her anger rises in a crescendo until she becomes almost hysterical. The height of emotion and the first climax of the monologue are reached when she says of ingratitude:

> Er lügt, er raubt, betrügt, schwört falsche Eide,
> Verrät und tötet! Undank! Undank! Undank!

> (1217 f.)

This extreme of emotion frightens Sappho so that she appeals to the gods to protect her from the demons within (1219 ff.). In the relative calm which follows her prayer she recalls to herself the glorious life she had planned for Phaon. Constantly enlarging the list of favors which she wished to bestow on him, she gradually works herself up to a new crest of emotion. The new climax comes with the impassioned outcry:

> Und er—lebt ihr denn noch, gerechte Götter?

> (1232)

This time there is no resistance against passion, and immediately after this line Sappho hits upon her plan for revenge. She now sees the way clear for the gratification of her anger and no longer feels any inhibiting force. The conflict is decided, and the last ten lines of the monologue are filled with the mood of exhilaration.

Of the three monologues so far discussed this last is clearly the strongest and most closely-wrought monodrama. It portrays in highly dramatic form the fluctuations of mood from deepest despair and resignation to resentment and anger, then from fear through regret to rage and finally to exultation.

In the trilogy **Das goldene Vliess** there are three monologues which could be called monodramas. One occurs in **Die Argonauien,** two in **Medea.** The two in **Medea,** as will be pointed out later, may be regarded as parts of one longer monodrama.

The dramatic power of Medea's monologue in Act I of **Die Argonauien** (379-420) lies in the conflict between fear and anxiety on the one hand and duty on the other. Medea enters the gloomy tower room to call upon the gods to help her people against the invading Greeks. At first the mere sense impressions which she receives from the dismal room—sultriness, dampness, darkness—induce a vague feeling of uneasiness. Then a sound startles her and raises anxiety to irrational fear (382 f.). She is able, however, to calm her emotion by reminding herself of the importance of her task. She succeeds in concentrating on the conjuration ritual, but when she completes the wild prayer and receives no response her fear returns, stronger than before. In a moment it displaces all other feelings, and her final impassioned plea to the gods springs from terror rather than from any wish to help her country. The monodrama is thus made up of a brief development to a crest of fear, then descending relative calm, followed by a long passage of intense concentration, and finally an abrupt upward swerve of irresistible terror.

In Act IV of **Medea** occur two monologues (2065-2117; 2125-2152) which are highly important in leading up to Medea's final act, the murder of the children. From the standpoint of dramatic structure these two monologues are in fact two divisions of one long monodrama. The interruption (2118-2124) just at the climax, which breaks the monodrama into two parts, is very brief and serves to heighten the tense dramatic effect of the whole.

The monologue begins with a lyric passage devoted to a description of the night and to a comparison of the uniformity of nature with the instability of man and his fate. Medea then imagines herself listening to the story of her life told by another. She sees herself interrupting the narrative, incredulous that the same person who led the carefree life in Colchis could be capable of her later horrible deeds. Visualizing her youth and describing it as through the eyes of an objective observer, she is carried emotionally upward to a climax of joy. The passage takes on some appearance of dialogue, first by the interjection of questions such as: "Wo geht sie hin?" (2081) and "Was sucht sie Waldespfade?" (2084), and later by the direct address of Medea to her brother and father (2092 ff.).

As she becomes more and more moved by the picture she is painting, Medea drops the rôle of narrator and greets the figures which appear so vividly in her imagination. But just as she reaches the height of pleasure in contemplating her family, a single word shatters the whole illusion. The moment she hears herself say, "gute Tochter!" she sees the irony of the adjective and adds, "Gut? Ha gut!" (2098).

And now after the calm which came with enjoyment of the idyllic scene she has pictured, Medea gives way to a burst of fury. A new train of thought is introduced by her violent exclamation,

> 's ist Lüge! Sie wird dich verraten, Greis!
>
> (2099)

She is then whirled along to a new climax, this time a climax of wild fear and desperation (2117). There is a striking contrast between this passage (2099-2117) and the one preceding (2073-2098). The idyllic passage is in fairly regular blank verse, the form of speech used by the Medea who has tried to adapt herself to civilized Greek ways. But in the later passage, in the heat of violent emotion, she reverts to the wild irregularity of Colchean speech, so that form and content are in agreement. In the first passage mounting calm and peace blot out all thoughts of present despair, and the development is all toward a mood of happy contemplation. The second passage begins with a wild outcry and heaps up horror upon horror of her terrifying life. When she repeats her father's curse and describes its fulfillment her tortured imagination conjures up the figure of Aietes, her father. He seems to be advancing toward her. She can stand no more and in a frenzy of fear flees to the children. This is the climax of emotion and of the monodrama.

After a brief dialogue between Medea and the boy the monologue continues, and this latter half (or second monologue) forms the descending action of the monodrama. As soon as the children leave, Medea returns to thoughts of her predicament and the barren future ahead of her. Bitter hatred of Jason and the Greeks urges her on to the murder of the children and completion of revenge (2127 ff.). Gentler feelings still persist (2141 ff.) and struggle against the "Mordgedanken," thus injecting an element of suspense. Medea hesitates before the deed, but she is driven on by force of circumstances. When she hears the outcry and sees flames rising from the palace she knows it is too late to turn back and so hurries to finish her murderous work.

This monologue not only occupies a key position in the play but is itself a real monodrama containing lyric, epic, and dramatic elements. Almost the whole action of the trilogy passes in review in the brief space of the monodrama. Moreover, Medea's character is here portrayed in practically all its phases. We see her as the thoughtful observer of nature and life, as the carefree young girl, as loving sister and devoted daughter. We see her in the wild fury which is the other side of her nature. We see her tenderness, her suffering, her love, her jealousy, and her hatred. We see her energetic activity and feel her inner conflict.

Here, as in the monologues in *Sappho,* the motivation is dependent upon rapid shifts of mood and feeling.

Of the several examples of monodrama in *Des Meeres und der Leibe Wellen* Hero's monologue in Act III (1003-1060) is the finest and most interesting. The conflict around which this monologue centers is neither as intense nor as stubborn as that experienced by Medea just before she kills her children. The most important function of Hero's monologue is the portrayal of the development of a mood. It is full of fine nuances of feeling and the subtle responses of a sensitive nature to rapidly shifting external and internal stimuli.

In the first ten lines we see the conflict between the asceticism to which Hero has pledged herself and her awakening love. The contradiction, however, causes no emotional upheaval. In the calm self-assurance which is one of her basic traits she thinks to lay aside love as she does her cloak (1020). Nevertheless passion, although it is below the level of consciousness, continues as the motivating force behind all that she says, does, and feels. It is responsible for her restlessness and loneliness. It expresses itself in the maternal tenderness with which she compares the waves with softly whispering children (1027 f.) and in the imagined dialogue between mother and child (1041 f.). Scarcely any disguise of real motive remains when she places the lamp in the window to cheer the wanderer and to gleam across to the opposite shore (1031 ff.). Indeed, the direction of her feeling is so clear at this point that immediately after the reference to the opposite shore Hero becomes aware of what she has been saying. She tries again to extinguish the flame within her (1039 f.), but it only burns more brightly. She does for the moment banish concrete thought of Leander, but the dominant emotion is unchanged. When she finds herself softly singing the voluptuous song about Leda and the swan, she wonders why it so often comes to mind (1045). Her very words, however, about gods no longer climbing to desolate towers and about her own loneliness (1046 ff.) point to the undercurrent of passionate longing. As her restlessness increases Hero wishes that she could play the lyre which she finds in the room, for in music she might find relief from her confused thoughts and feelings (1049 ff.). A moment later comes conscious recognition that she cannot subdue thoughts of Leander, and she finally surrenders to her feelings (1054 ff.).

Through successive shifts of feeling in the monologue there is a progressive development of the central emotion. The partial suppression at the beginning makes love seek other than conscious outlets. Discursiveness and confusion are the result, with passion moving in first one direction, then another. When it threatens to reach consciousness Hero once more tries to suppress it. But when all the pent-up force of emotion at last breaks through the thin veneer of habitual morality, it brings with it clarification and a new integration of thought (1055 ff.).

The dramatic unity of the monodrama is due to the steady persistence of the one emotion from beginning to end.

Animation is achieved not only by the volatility of feeling expressed in words, but by physical activity as well: the laying aside of the cloak, the frequent significant maneuvering of the lamp, the removal of the ornament from her hair, and various changes of position. At several points the illusion of dialogue is created by questions which Hero asks herself and then answers. It is even more dramatically effective when she personifies inanimate objects and talks to them as to intimate friends, as she does with the cloak and the lamp. This is all motivated by her loneliness and longing for human companionship, which reaches its peak in the imagined conversation between mother and child.

In Act IV at another critical point in the drama a monologue by Hero has all the characteristics of monodrama (1772-1815). This is spoken just after she has lighted the lamp which is to guide Leander across the Hellespont. The conflict at the heart of the monologue is the struggle which Hero's will to stay awake wages against fatigue and drowsiness. Even in the opening lines she shows that she is mentally as well as physically weary, for she has already forgotten why the priest wanted her to bring the letter (1772 f.). Her mood of tender, amorous longing finds expression in the lyric passage in which she addresses her lamp (1774 ff.). In her weariness and anticipation of Leander's visit she is still aware, but not intensely aware, of the dangers which lie ahead. She speaks of her intention of watching over the light so that the wind may not extinguish it. She refers also to the oppressive air in the tower, which threatens to put her to sleep, and adds:

> Das aber soll nicht sein, es gilt zu wachen.
>
> (1784)

Fatigue and drowsiness, however, have so dulled Hero's powers of reasoning that she can see no connection between Leander's expected visit and the fact that her uncle has driven her to the point of exhaustion (1785 ff.). Even in her attempt to understand her uncle's motives her speech becomes incoherent and she all but falls asleep (1788 f.). When a moment later she is startled into wakefulness by the sound of the wind, her first thought is not that the lamp may be blown out but that Leander will perhaps come earlier because of the rising wind (1791 f.). Then she scolds herself and once more resumes her vigil.

When definite fear takes shape in her mind that the priest and his servants are suspicious and lying in wait for her lover, Hero is shocked momentarily by the thought of the possible consequences (1797 f.). This is the climax of the monologue. Almost at once, however, the blind optimism of the lover calms her fears. She expresses confidence in her ability to protect Leander from danger (1801 ff.), but even as she speaks fatigue is overpowering her. The unequal conflict is already decided.

In the final section of the monologue (1807-1815) there has ceased to be even a faint struggle against hostile forces. Hero no longer regards the wind as a dangerous threat to her happiness. Instead she welcomes it (1807 f.). The

pleasurable anticipation of the expectant lover merges with physical and mental languor. In this transition between waking and sleeping Hero is susceptible to sensation but incapable of active thought. In a feeling of voluptuous exhilaration she gives herself up to the sensuous enjoyment of the cool breeze and finally falls asleep.

Here, as in the monologue in Act III, purposive forces lack vigor and clarity. They can offer but slight resistance to the power of fatigue, just as in Act III they were ineffective against the surge of emotion. But although the conflict is only the unequal battle against sleep, dramatic suspense is not lacking in the monologue. The alternation of drowsiness and vigilance keeps the outcome in doubt for a time. This suspense reaches its crest with the exclamation, "Mitleidsvolle Götter!" (1797). At this point it still seems possible that fear will dispel all threat of sleep and rouse Hero to aggressive action. But instead there follow only false optimism and gradual forgetfulness of danger.

This monologue, as well as that of Act III, is enlivened by actions and gestures which express changing sensations. Hero sits down when she notices her fatigue, rests her head in her hand when she tries to organize her confused thoughts. She springs to her feet when startled by the sound of the wind. As she gives in to sleep she pulls first one, then the other foot onto the bench. Here, as in the earlier monologue, personifications, this time of the lamp and the wind, add animation and again show Hero's longing for affection.

The priest, Hero's uncle, has three monologues in the drama, but although two of them contain dramatic elements (that beginning with 1352 and that beginning with 1751) the only one which could be called a monodrama is spoken in Act IV (1751 ff.), just after Hero has been sent to the tower to get the letter. Here the dramatic conflict experienced by the priest is between rational thought and emotional inclination, between the conviction that Hero is guilty and affection which would declare her innocent. As he watches her walk away his fondness for the girl who has been as a daughter to him crowds out thoughts of duty. He feels that he must warn her of the misfortune which is ahead (1753 f.). Quickly, however, it occurs to him that Hero's self-assurance and composure are evidence of her guilt (1755). He suppresses his impulse to treat her gently and tells himself that hesitation on his part will lead to the girl's complete ruin (1756 ff.).

But again doubts arise and the priest attempts to excuse Hero by suggesting to himself that she is not necessarily guilty, even if Leander has made bold advances (1761 ff.). At the climax of this apology, however, just as he is doubting that she will go so far as to aid the intruder, the lighted lamp appears in Hero's tower window. Immediately the tension snaps; the dramatic conflict is resolved. The priest cannot resist this final evidence of Hero's complete connivance, and duty and reason now gain undisputed control of his conduct. The last two lines of the monologue, which constitute a brief descending action, show the priest as the relentless judge about to inflict punishment.

We have seen that the various monologues dealt with above vary widely as to length and structure, but that all of them have the characteristics of true monodrama. Monologues of this type appear in some other dramas of Grillparzer,[5] but except in *Die Ahnfrau,* which contains a number of excellent examples, they are of rare occurrence and, as monodramas, not on a par with those in the Hellenic dramas.

We have noted that each of the monologues studied centers around a conflict of emotions or a conflict induced by emotion, and in each case the termination of the conflict either leads directly to or prepares the way for a major event in the larger drama. These peculiarly compact and unified miniature dramas demonstrate nicely the type of motivation which is fundamental with Grillparzer. His characters invariably act in response to feeling and impulse rather than on the basis of reasoned thought. Fluctuations of mood and shifts of feeling are the determining forces in the monologues as in the dramas as a whole. Kleist, as well as Grillparzer, had this highly developed skill in portraying the finest shadings of sensations and states of mind.[6] And in the work of both dramatists this romantic motivation is a basic characteristic.

Notes

1. In *Das literorische Echo,* II, 15, p. 1034 ff.

2. *Ibid.,* p. 1038.

3. A fourth, by Phaon, at the beginning of Act II (456-513), although it contains dramatic elements, is essentially expository and therefore will not be included here.

4. Line references are to the *Historisch-kritische Gesamtausgabe,* Wien: Schroll, 1909 f.

5. *Die Ahnfrau,* II, 753 ff., 1504 ff., IV, 2598 ff., V, 2914 ff., 3184 ff.; *Ein treuer Diener seines Herrn,* II, 772 ff.; *Weh dem, der lügt!* III, 1111 ff., V, 1564 ff. (Stefan Hock edition); *Libussa,* III, 1006 ff.; *Ein Bruderzwist im Hause Habsburg,* V, 2597 ff.

6. For a detailed treatment of this and related problems see Martin Schütze: "Studies in the Mind of Romanticism," *Modern Philology,* XVI, No. 6, XVI, No. 10, XVII, No. 2.

T. C. Dunham (essay date March 1960)

SOURCE: "Symbolism in Grillparzer's *Das goldene Vliess,* in *PMLA,* Vol. 75, March, 1960, pp. 75-82.

[*In the following essay, Dunham offers a symbolic study of* Das goldene Vließ, *maintaining that the many symbols give the trilogy "its rich texture and poetic power."*]

In an age when symbols are being discovered in literary works where critics of an earlier period would never have dreamed of looking for them there is probably little need to defend a study of symbolism in Grillparzer's work.[1] Indeed Grillparzer himself recognized that there is a symbolic element in all art and reproached his own time for its refusal to acknowledge the symbolic aspect of poetic truth.[2] *Das goldene Vließ,* moreover, is not the only drama in which Grillparzer uses symbols. In *Sappho,* for instance, the lyre, the laurel wreath, the rose, the statue of Aphrodite, and the dagger all have symbolic significance. Even the title of *Des Meeres und der Liebe Wellen* reflects symbolic motifs. In that drama subtle variations on the water imagery predominate but are reinforced by symbols such as the dove, the tower, the Leda song, and the lamp. In *Libussa,* to cite one more example, there is a highly developed circle symbolism as well as symbolism involving flowers, vegetation, and metals.

Grillparzer has much to say about the symbolism in *Das goldene Vließ.* While still engaged in the writing he shows his concern with the symbolic force of the trilogy. He feared, among other things, that it might be called a fate-tragedy and was eager to persuade himself that it was not. In October 1819, before completing *Die Argonauten,* he writes: "Halte dir immer gegenwärtig, daß das Stück eigentlich nichts ist als eine Ausführung des Satzes: Das eben ist der Fluch der bösen That, daß sie, fortzeugend, böses muß gebähren. Dieser Satz ist so wichtig als irgend einer in der Welt. Das Vließ ist nur ein *sinnliches Zeichen* dieses Satzes. Es ist da nicht von *Schicksal* die Rede. Ein Unrecht hat ohne Nöthigung von außen das andre zur Folge, und das Vließ *begleitet* sinnbildlich die Begebenheiten, ohne sie zu *bewirken.*"[3] And a few lines farther on he adds: "Phryxus' Fluch ist nicht um ein Haar wirksamer als der Margarethens in *Richard III.*"

Later comments show that Grillparzer was not satisfied with this Aeschylean chain-of-evil idea as the sole meaning of the fleece. One of the most interesting attempts at reinterpretation is a journal entry from the year 1822. Here he writes:

> Das, worauf es bei dem goldenen Vließ ankömmt, ist wohl dieses: Kann das Vließ selbst als ein sinnliches Zeichen des Wünschenswerthen, des mit Begierde Gesuchten, mit Unrecht Erworbenen gelten? Oder vielmehr: ist es als ein solches entsprechend dargestellt? Wenn es das ist, so wird dieses dramatische Gedicht mit der Zeit wohl unter das Beste gezählt werden, was Deutschland in diesem Fache hervorgebracht hat. Ist aber die Darstellung dieses geistigen Mittelpunktes *nicht* gelungen (und so scheint es mir) so kann das Gedicht als Ganzes freilich nicht bestehen, aber die Theile wenigstens werden noch lange dessen harren, der's besser macht. Ich weiß wohl, daß meine Gemüthsstimmung jetzt getrübt ist, aber ich glaube doch, das Werk ist mißlungen.[4]

This passage leaves no doubt that Grillparzer attached great importance to the fleece as symbol. My purpose here is not only to attempt an answer to the question he so morosely poses but also to examine the larger symbolic framework of the trilogy. For the golden fleece is not the only symbol that appears but rather one of many which are woven into the pattern of meaning. Together these symbols give *Das goldene Vließ* much of its rich texture and poetic power.

For purposes of analysis the symbols in the trilogy may be divided into two groups. One set is made up of tangible objects closely associated with the central figures of the drama: the fleece, the statue of the god Peronto, the cave of the dragon, Medea's chest of magic paraphernalia, her veil, her Grecian robe, Kreusa's lyre, and the flaming jar. Another group includes symbols drawn from nature: light, dark, water, and fire.

Since Grillparzer himself brooded over the rôle of the fleece, it is not surprising that critics[5] have called attention to the problematic nature of this central symbol and been bothered by its shifting meanings. And there are such shifts. In the case of Aietes, Pelias, and Kreon the fleece operates not only as the inciter and object of greed in varying intensities but also as the symbol of ill-gotten gains and of the retribution which follows inevitably upon the deeds committed in response to this greed.

With Jason the matter is more complex. For him the glittering fleece is the symbol of a bright new world of adventure and glorious achievement. "Ehregeiz" rather than "Begierde" plunges him into the succession of violent acts from the consequences of which there is no escape. Possession of the once passionately sought treasure brings no lasting satisfaction, for with the passage of time Jason's point of view changes. The fleece thus takes on a new significance. It comes to stand for the intolerable burden of past accomplishments which are at variance with new goals and desires. For the no longer youthful and adventuresome Jason the fleece is a constant reminder of a past which blocks his way into a secure and peaceful future. As Grillparzer puts it, "Das Ganze ist die große Tragödie des Lebens. Daß der Mensch in seiner Jugend sucht, was er im Alter nicht brauchen kann."[6] But of this, more later.

The relation of the fleece to Phryxus presents still another problem, for the "sinnliches Zeichen des ungerechten Gutes" does not seem applicable in his case. But no matter whether Phryxus steals the fleece or merely carries out divine instructions, the fleece symbolizes for him ambition and achievement. To a certain extent, then, the fleece initially has much the same meaning for both Phryxus and Jason. But there is a difference. Rightly or wrongly, Phryxus sees the fleece as the sign of a god's favor, a token of a future where he can gain dignity, respect, and stature. And although, like Jason, a victim of injustice, he has no thought of returning to his homeland and asserting his rights. Unlike Jason, he would be content to stay in Colchis and rule his little bridgehead colony there.[7]

Only Medea among the central characters of the first two parts of the trilogy is free of any desire to possess the fleece. Almost from the beginning she knows, rationally as well as intuitively, that the fleece is a threat to both inner and outer peace. For her it is associated with a male world of violence and cruel passion. But her attempt to save Phryxus from her father's murderous greed and her stubborn, last-ditch struggle to prevent Jason from stealing the fleece both fail. Then she too is sucked into the insidious whirlpool of guilt and revenge.

This brief summary indicates the difficulty of arriving at a single inclusive formula to fit the fleece. But the absence of an unambiguous meaning is not necessarily a weakness. On the contrary, the symbol may gain rather than lose by having multiple levels of meaning. Grillparzer, in other words, may have wrought better than he knew. He was certainly justified in emphasizing the "evil breeds evil" idea, for this is a powerful theme in the drama and is intimately bound up with the fleece. At the same time, however, the fleece is connected with a broader realm of action, is in fact the symbol of what men strive for in the world, whether from good motives or bad. As an object it is useless, nothing but a seductively beautiful and exotic bauble. Just so, in the whole thrust of the drama and in Grillparzer's view in general, the things most men strive for are worthless, illusory, empty. The attempt to achieve the golden fleeces of life will have, according to this interpretation, one of two consequences, or both of them: violence, injustice, destruction on the one hand, or—embroiling the passions as it does—loss of equilibrium and forfeiture of inner harmony.

As a symbol, however, the golden fleece does not exist in isolation. It is a part, a decisive part, to be sure, in a whole network of symbols. And none of these symbols can be understood fully except in relation to the others. It will be well, therefore, to start at the beginning and see how the fleece fits into the larger symbolic pattern of the trilogy. The actual fleece is seen only six times: throughout the second half of the one-act *Der Gastfreund,* twice briefly in Act IV of *Die Argonauten*—in the cavern and at the embarkation from Colchis—and three times in *Medea*—at the beginning as Medea buries it outside the gates of Corinth, in Act IV when she reopens the chest, and in the last scene of Act V as she takes final leave of Jason.

Phryxus first sees the fleece in a dream. This gives an early clue to the origins of the symbol, and a closer look at the content of the dream will support the case for identifying the fleece with irrational forces in man. In the dream a strange god suddenly flashes before Phryxus' eyes with the golden fleece over his shoulders. He is powerful, naked, has long hair and beard, and holds a club in his right hand. The one incongruous element in the otherwise unrelieved impression of primitive violence is the gracious smile. But this incongruity is paralleled by the ambivalence of the cryptic words, "Nimm Sieg und Rache hin." Both the appearance of the god and his words convey the idea of danger as well as triumph. Like primitive passions, the dream both repels and attracts. Although Phryxus compares the apparition to Hercules, his description recalls also Dionysus, as do Jason's comments later on. Jason says that the statue of this god was erected in the dim past by the ancient peoples who came from distant lands and settled Hellas. Since the god apparently has no name in civilized Greece but does in Colchis, one can conclude that, like Dionysus, he comes from the East.

The fact that Phryxus has his dream in the temple of Apollo at Delphi and immediately afterward sees the statue of the unknown god in this same temple might seem to invalidate the interpretation suggested above. On the contrary, this circumstance adds further weight to the theory. The strange god, known to the Colchians as Peronto, has his place in the Greek pantheon but is neutralized there by Apollo. The fleece, which is connected with Peronto and primitive, subterranean drives, exerts its dreadful power only when snatched from the precincts of Apollo. In other words, the Dionysian element ravages human life when removed from Apollonian controls. Seen in this light, Medea's resolve at the end of the trilogy to return the fleece to Delphi does more than unify the parts and bring the tragedy full circle: it gives the final symbolic meaning to the whole. In taking the fleece to Delphi she is doing more than appease the "dunklen Gott" Peronto and hear the verdict of the priests of the temple. She is returning the fleece to the only place where it cannot threaten man: the shelter of Apollo's temple. Thus her explicit renunciation of fame and happiness is accompanied by a symbolic renunciation of those illusory goals and of the passions which drive men toward them. The return of the fleece to the temple of Apollo symbolizes the acceptance of the control of reason and the recognition of "ein einfach Herz und einen stillen Sinn" as the only means of avoiding tragedy.

There is one more point to be made about Phryxus and his dream. If Phryxus is relatively guiltless, then the dream is crucial in his conduct. It arouses in him new and powerful urges that change the course of his life. In effect, the dream vision of Peronto entices him to Colchis and his doom. Phryxus' dream is then comparable to Gustav Aschenbach's vision in front of the mortuary chapel in *Der Tod in Venedig*. Both Peronto and the exotic traveler are emissaries from the realm of the irrational. And as Mann's stranger is related to the symbol of the bamboo jungle with its crouching tiger, so Grillparzer's naked god is connected with dark, forbidding Colchis and its deadly dragon.

After the murder of Phryxus it is no longer the god Peronto who beckons men to disaster but the craving for the fleece which had come originally from Peronto's shoulders. If the case for Peronto as a symbol of the irrational is sound, then there is no essential break in the symbolic continuity when in *Die Argonauten* the god fades from sight and his place is taken by the cave of the dragon. The cave, more clearly than Peronto, mirrors the horrifying depths of the irrational, and the cave has become the new resting-place of the golden fleece.

The fleece, moreover, both as object and as symbol, is connected with aggression, ambition, greed, conquest, with the sword and the spear, in short, with the male principle. It is thus intimately associated with Jason and his fate. The cave, on the other hand, is linked with Medea, both as literal cave and as symbol. Along with the chest and the flame-filled jar it is a female symbol. For Medea, up to the incursions of the Greeks into her world, the passions are as closely guarded and as tightly sealed within her as is the fleece inside the cave. She is, as a matter of fact, a strangely contradictory sorceress. Her command of occult powers seems for the most part a mere surface skill unaccompanied by any deep devotion to the powers of darkness. She reveals an impatience with, perhaps even aversion to, ritual. In *Der Gastfreund* the prayer to the goddess Darimba is something to be disposed of as swiftly as possible. Here she says:

> . . . laßt uns eilen denn! Geh eine hin und spreche das Gebet . . . Und somit genug. Das Opfer ist gebracht, Vollendet das zögernde Geschäft.
>
> (*Der Gastfreund,* 2, 3; 35, 36)

The erotic impulses stirred by the meeting with Phryxus are apparently Medea's first encounter with passion. Her severe castigation of Peritta proves that she has no firsthand knowledge of love and wants none. Her stubborn, tortured resistance to Jason's headlong wooing shows how frightened she is of passion and to what lengths she will go to avoid giving in to it. And it is in the struggle between Jason and Medea and the parallel struggle of Medea with herself that the cave becomes the center of both the external and internal action. On the literal level *Die Argonauten* moves relentlessly toward the cave and the fleece. Symbolically, the movement for Medea is from the edge of tender feeling, which she has fearfully skirted, down into the abyss of passion. In denying Jason entrance to the cave she is barring his way also into the privacy of her being. And just as he cannot enter the actual cave unless she in effect throws open the doors for him, so also he can make no real contact with her until she unlocks the inner recesses of her nature. On another level the symbol is clearly sexual. From this point of view Medea's resistance is a defense of chastity. The penetration of the cave symbolizes Jason's male conquest.

Die Argonauten operates with two symbols at once: the fleece and the cave. For Jason the symbolic movement is primarily toward the fleece and only secondarily toward the cave. For him adventure and fame take precedence over love. He has not only no fear of passion but also no great capacity for deep feeling. This shallowness is underscored rather than contradicted by the fact that, once inside the cave, he is frightened, whereas Medea is outwardly calm. The unspeakable experience with the dragon effects no lasting change in him. Similarly, the union with Medea leaves him relatively untouched. In retrospect he can say that his interest was piqued by her resistance and that "Auf Kampf gestellt rang ich mit ihr, und wie / Ein Abenteuer trieb ich meine Liebe" (*Medea,* 466, 467).

Whereas Jason is aggressive, single-minded, and egoistic, Medea is torn by conflict. For him the battle is positive, for her negative. Jason knows what he wants, Medea knows, rationally, what she does *not* want. He fights for the fleece, she fights against the cave. The climax comes with Medea's frantic final attempt to hold Jason back from the irrevocable last step. Of the fleece and the horrors that lie beyond the last door she says:

> In der Höhle liegt's verwahrt,
> Verteidigt von allen Greueln
> Der List und der Gewalt.
> Labyrinthische Gänge,
> Sinnverwirrend,
> Abgründe, trügerisch bedeckt,
> Dolche unterm Fußtritt,
> Tod im Einhauch,
> Mord in tausendfacher Gestalt,
> Und das Vließ, am Baum hängt's,
> Giftbestrichen,
> Von der Schlange gehütet,
> Die nicht schläft,
> Die nicht schont,
> Unnahbar.

> *(Die Argonauten, 1439-53)*

Here Medea gives not only a breathlessly lurid picture of the literal cave but at the same time a symbolic description of her own subconscious. The psyche is as honeycombed with labyrinthine passages as is the dragon's cave, and its passages too are bewildering to sense. It too is full of treacherously concealed chasms. Insidious attacks from below the surface of consciousness imperil life and sanity. Confinement in the fetid air of unreason means strangulation of the personality. And in the very depths is the nameless monster, the id, the dragon which never sleeps, which is pitiless and unfeeling and beyond the reach and control of reason.

The symbolic effect of this passage, however, is more than that of merely holding the mirror up to human nature. In its focal position just at the climax of *Die Argonauten* it unites past, present, and future. The words tremble with the terror of immediate danger. At the same time they echo the crime of Aietes—"von allen Greueln / Der List und der Gewalt." And finally the "Dolche" point forward to the murder of the children and the "Mord in tausendfacher Gestalt": to the deaths of Absyrtus, Pelias, and Kreusa.

Descent into the cave marks the complete surrender of Medea to Jason as well as to the erotic drives she has heretofore resisted. In a sense she becomes a prisoner of the cave as she loses her own autonomy as a human being and forfeits whatever tranquillity and detachment she had salvaged from the Phryxus catastrophe. At the same time the storming of the cave sets loose the forces that alienate Medea from herself and from her heritage. The dragon now stands between her and her family. The final clash between Greek and barbarian, the violent death of Absyrtus, and the flight from Colchis follow immediately upon the capture of the fleece. The rhythm of *Die Argonauten* is thus a steady, irresistible movement toward the cave and then a brief, headlong catapulting away from it.

The rhythm of the *Medea,* on the other hand, is associated with a new symbol, that of the black chest of magic which Medea carries with her from Colchis to Greece. In this final play of the trilogy the movement is first away from the chest and then gradually back to it again. Just as the entrance into the cave enormously accelerates the pace of *Die Argonauten,* so the opening of the chest in the *Medea* explodes the action into the final catastrophe.

Before inquiring more particularly into the nature of the magic chest as symbol it may be well to see how it relates to the symbols of the first two members of the trilogy. The golden fleece accompanies and, in a certain sense, provokes the external events with which the plot is concerned; it also provides the connection between the other major symbols in the three parts. The gap between Peronto in *Der Gastfreund* and the cave in *Die Argonauten* and the gap between the cave and the magic chest of the *Medea* are both bridged by the fleece. In each instance the object in question is the temporary resting-place of the fleece: the shoulders of Peronto, the cave, the chest. As a symbol, the chest carries a multiple weight of meaning. It is one more embodiment of the irrational, the hidden volcanic urges, but it also represents the Colchian past which Medea cannot avoid carrying with her wherever she goes. At the opening of the play when she buries the chest she is attempting several things at once: to abjure witchcraft, to abandon barbarian customs, and to blot out the past:

> Was mich geknüpft an meiner Väter Heimat
> Ich hab' es in die Erde hier versenkt;
> Die Macht, die meine Mutter mir vererbte,
> Die Wissenschaft geheimnisvoller Kräfte,
> Der Nacht, die sie gebar, gab ich sie wieder . . .

> *(Medea, 128-132)*

The burial of the chest is thus a burial of a part of Medea. She attempts to live with what remains after her Colchian self has been interred, but in so doing she loses one identity and succeeds only partially in establishing a new one. When banishment and Jason's renunciation shatter all her efforts to become a Hellene, this new identity too is lost. She asks Jason, "Allein wer gibt Medeen mir, wer mich?" (*Medea,* 1056). And after her children too have rejected her, she thinks of reclaiming the chest and thus becoming again the Medea she once was: "Zwei Handvoll Erde weg—und es ist mein!" (*Medea,* 1881). But she shrinks back in terror from the thought of thus exhuming herself, for the identity she would gain would be neither the one she had buried nor the new one she had tried to create. To raise the chest from the "finstern Schoß der mütterlichen Erde" would be another unsealing of the dragon's cave, and what would emerge out of the depths this time would be monstrous. Looking toward both the past and this possible future she says:

> Man hat mich bös genannt, ich war es nicht:
> Allein ich fühle, daß man's werden kann.
> Entsetzliches gestaltet sich in mir,
> Ich schaudre . . .

> *(Medea, 1849-52)*

Although terror and a feeling of impotence thus prevent her from regaining the chest, its contents exert attraction as well as repulsion not only for her but for others. The horrors of Medea's past and the dark arts which have enabled Jason to obtain the fleece repel the Hellenic world, but at the same time the fleece, the prize of success and power, entices men. The fact that Kreon, driven by ambition, has the chest dug up and brought back to Medea is one more indication of Medea's entanglement with the past and with the consequences of her earlier acts. As soon as the black, coffin-like chest which had held Medea's Colchian self is again in her possession, the fearful passions of the dragon's cave are once more released. The frenzy which seizes her as she opens the chest repeats the mood at the storming of the cave doors. And in both episodes the fleece occupies a central position. Jason's snatching of the fleece had set in motion destructive forces beyond his control. And now the fleece, which Medea carefully places over the deadly gift to Kreusa, cannot be picked up without dislodging the cover of the insidious vessel and thus spreading fire through the palace.

The theme of shifting identity referred to above is expressed also by three minor symbols in the *Medea*: the veil, the lyre, and the robe. There is some fairly obvious business about removing the dark red veil of sorcery as proof to Jason that Medea has in fact given up her dubious ways. The lyre then comes to stand for the harmonious Hellenic personality, for the "einfaches Herz" Medea would like to acquire. The poignant scene in which she tries unsuccessfully to win Jason back by playing and singing his favorite song ends in frustration and violence. When she smashes the lyre she is not only preventing Kreusa from proving her superiority but is also renouncing the attempt at assimilation, is destroying the new self which she has so earnestly and laboriously cultivated. That the thought of death accompanies her action is clear from her convulsive reaction to Kreusa's exclamation, "Tot!" Medea looks around quickly and says, "Wer?—*Ich* lebe! *lebe!*" (*Medea*, 925). The breathless abruptness of her outcry reveals perhaps the panic fear that she may now have forfeited both selves and thus stand stripped of significant life.

She goes a step farther a few moments later after hearing the edict of the Amphiktyons. Here the shedding of the Greek robe marks the reversion to the barbarism of the veil. And as she herself says, the tearing of the robe symbolizes the severing of her bond with Jason and the destruction of her love. For Medea these are the symbolic meanings, but she learns to her agony that she has neither destroyed her love so easily as the robe nor has she regained the identity which vanished with the veil and the chest.

The major symbols treated above—fleece, Peronto, cave, chest—are constantly reinforced, highlighted, or modified by the nature symbols. Of these latter the most pervasive is light and dark. The simplest meaning of the light-dark opposition is that of the clash of two cultures: civilized

Greece versus barbarian Colchis. Here the contrast is literal as well as figurative, for Colchis is represented as dark, gloomy, forbidding, while Greece is seen as sunny and hospitable. Looked at again from the literal point of view, the whole action of the trilogy develops against a background of shifting light and dark. This alternation between day and night is more than a means of creating a theatrical effect or appropriate atmosphere; it is an important element in the structure of the drama and has meaning in itself.

Each of the three plays of the trilogy begins in darkness or partial darkness. It is daybreak when the curtain rises on *Der Gastfreund. Die Argonauten* opens in "finstere Nacht." *Medea* begins with the darkness before dawn. It becomes lighter during the course of the one-act first play but there is no scene change or any interruption in the flow of time. In the other two plays, however, the sequence is from night to day, to night to day. In *Die Argonauten,* to be sure, the second night-component is darkness—the interior of the cave—rather than actual night, but the effect is much the same as if it were really night. Blended with the real darkness of Act I of *Die Argonauten* is the theme of Medea's magic and the heavy forebodings which have persisted ever since the murder of Phryxus. Acts II and III, concerned with the open conflict between Greek and Colchian and the first stages of the Jason-Medea love conflict, are played in daylight, or what passes for daylight in Colchis. Act IV is divided into two scenes: one in the blackness of the cave, the other on the shore in daylight.

In the *Medea,* Act I, in which Medea begins her attempt at transformation from barbarian to Greek, opens before dawn, but by the end of the act there is bright sunlight— the first in the trilogy. Act II, which contains the fiasco of the lyre-playing and the edict of banishment, takes place in daylight, as does Act III, which is climaxed by the children's rejection of their mother. Act IV, in which Medea regains her chest of magic and carries out her revenge, begins at dusk and proceeds into total darkness. The end of the act is wildly lighted up by the flaming palace. The short last act, which shows Jason in despair and Medea in resignation, takes place at sunrise.

One recurrent pattern in the light-dark, Hellas-Colchis opposition is the fact that only Colchians appear in the darkness with which each member play begins. It is light by the time the Greek Phryxus enters, as it is in *Medea* when Kreon and Kreusa appear. Of the Greeks only Jason and his friend Milo pierce the thickest Colchian gloom, but their entrance in *Die Argonauten* is delayed until the midpoint of Act I. The barbarization of Jason has already begun when he plunges into the water and swims across to Medea's tower and is lost in the darkness.

On quite another level this rhythmic pattern of night and day contributes powerfully to the meaning of the drama. The repeated rising and setting of the sun heightens the awareness of the passage of time and thus reinforces one of the central themes: the tragedy of time and change.

For Medea the light-dark motif is much less the reflection of change than it is of the warring elements in her nature. Her roots are in barbarian soil but, as already pointed out above, she does not belong completely to Colchis even at the beginning. Nor is the ambivalence all below the surface. Both Phryxus and Jason see her immediately as a bright spot in the forbidding gloom of her surroundings. Phryxus' description of her outward appearance catches also the polarity of her nature. To him she is like "der goldne Saum der Wetterwolke" (*Der Gastfreund*, 242). He sees her as "halb Charis" and "halb Mänade" (*Der Gastfreund*, 249). For Jason, as for Phryxus, Medea gleams brightly against the dark background of Colchis. Later on, after he has come to learn something about the relativity of beauty and morality as well as of fame and fortune, he uses images of light and dark to describe to Kreon the impression Medea had first made on him (*Medea*, 451-457).

As pointed out in connection with the symbol of the cave, Medea is not a dedicated sorceress but a sorceress with a bad conscience. To her, magic is indeed a black art. Her gods are "dunkle Götter," "furchtbare Fürsten der Tiefe," the spirits she summons "düstere Geister der schaurigen Nacht" (*Die Argonauten*, 258). Her powers come from the "Unterwelt," the "Schoß der Nacht." These are all images which bear a close relationship to the dragon's cave. But as with the cave symbol, darkness represents not only supernatural forces and death but also primitive, demonic passions. It is significant that the two contiguous realms of death and passion are united in Medea's first response to Jason's sudden intrusion into her tower. She takes him to be Heimdar, the god of death, but she is at the same time inflamed with passion. She thinks that the kiss of the supposed god has marked her as his "dunkles Opfer" (*Die Argonauten*, 572). Here the erotic element expresses itself in a compelling death-wish.

Once she has recognized that the intruder was no god, she pleads with her father to let her escape far into the interior, "Tief, wo nur Wälder und dunkles Geklüft" (*Die Argonauten*, 987). There in the physical darkness she hopes to overcome or at least outlast emotional darkness. For her the emotions are "dunkel" and "trüb" and completely outside the control of the will.

On the other hand, that part of human experience which is outside the dark cave of passion she calls "des Wollens sonniges Reich." The greater the danger of slipping into the "Abgrund," the more tortured is her cry for light. She sees that passion destroys inner equilibrium as darkness blots out light:

> Aber laß uns klar sein, Vater, klar!
> In schwarzen Wirbeln dreht sich's um mich
> Aber ich will hindurch, empor aus Dunkel und Nacht.
>
> (*Die Argonauten*, 1344-46)

The use of the light-dark symbolism in the *Medea* follows closely the pattern already referred to in connection with

the black chest of magic. The first act is concerned initially with burying the chest. In her first speech Medea says:

> Die Zeit der Nacht, der Zauber ist vorbei
> Und was geschieht, ob Schlimmes oder Gutes,
> Es muß geschehn am offnen Strahl des Lichts.
>
> (*Medea*, 4-6)

Then, with the chest returned to the "Schoß der Nacht," her references to darkness and night decrease in frequency. The appearance of Kreusa inspires a brief flurry of light images. Medea responds to the apparent purity and clarity of Kreusa with the words: "Das Herz wie deine Kleider hell und rein. / Gleich einer weißen Taube . . ." (*Medea*, 675-676). She longs for purification through contact with Kreusa: "Senk' einen Strahl von deiner Himmelsklarheit / In diese wunde, schmerzzerrißne Brust" (*Medea*, 680-681).

As Medea proceeds to carry out her resolve to assume Greek ways, and as Jason finds himself less out of joint with his times and his homeland, references to darkness and night disappear. The key words occur only three times in Act II. After this almost complete hiatus the eruption of the night and darkness symbolism in Acts III and IV is all the more startling. The interlude of bright hope has suddenly given way to the darkly ominous mood of the last half of the play. Again the passions of the cave dominate, but this time it is not erotic violence but murderous rage that overcomes Medea. As she had done when Jason sought her love and aid, so now she tries to check and suppress passion. It is no longer a matter of clarity versus obscurity; the shape of passion is now too monstrous even to be looked at. When Gora asks her what she is planning she says:

> Ich gebe mir Müh', nichts zu wollen, zu denken.
> Ob dem schweigenden Abgrund
> Brüte die Nacht.
>
> (*Medea*, 1189-91)

Here both the abyss, which is a link to the cave, and night, as the shroud of darkness and concealment, suggest the intensity of Medea's dread. Emotion rises to the level of panic when specific possibilities of revenge break through into consciousness, and she shrinks back with a breathless

> Still! Still!
> Hinab, wo du herkamst, Gedanke,
> Hinab in Schweigen, hinunter in Nacht!
>
> (*Medea*, 1239-41)

Before the final surrender to the demonic side of her nature Medea tries once more to draw Jason to her, and this effort is accompanied by a reappearance of the light-dark opposition. In their last meeting before the murder of Kreusa and the children both Jason and Medea use images of light, warmth, and vegetation in describing the past. But the darkness of the present creates the nostalgia which sees light where none had actually existed. This self-deception is particularly notable when Medea makes her last appeal for faithfulness. Here in speaking of their early meetings she refers to "das goldne Jugendalter" and to "die schönen Blüten von dem Jugendbaum" (*Medea,* 1473 ff.). Even the sexual image which she uses to recall the beginnings of their love is soft and light:

> Doch du drangst durch mit deinem milden Licht
> Und hell erglänzte meiner Sinne Dunkel.
>
> (*Medea,* 1481-82)

In moments when she faces undistorted reality Medea describes this same event not with such gentleness but with the violent image of the burning brand. Of this, more later.

After she takes her fearful revenge there is no more naïveté or self-deception. Nothing remains but the black pessimism in which she mourns not the death of her children but the fact that they had ever lived at all. Night now stands for the long monotony of dull pain, loneliness, and desolation:

> Was ist der Erde Glück?—Ein Schatten!
> Was ist der Erde Ruhm?—Ein Traum!
> Du Armer! der von Schatten du geträumt!
> Der Traum ist aus, allein die Nacht noch nicht.
>
> (*Medea,* 2366-69)

The tragedy of time and change is frequently represented in the course of the trilogy by the symbol of water. One didactic speech of Medea's pictures man in general and her father in particular as foolish creatures driven along on the waves of time:

> Ein töricht Wesen dünkt mich der Mensch;
> Treibt dahin auf den Wogen der Zeit
> Endlos geschleudert auf und nieder,
> Und wie er ein Fleckchen Grün erspäht
> Gebildet von Schlamm und stockendem Moor
> Und der Verwesung grünlichem Moder,
> Ruft er: *Land*! und rudert drauf hin
> Und besteigt's—und sinkt—und sinkt—
> Und wird nicht mehr gesehn!
>
> (*Die Argonauten,* 230-238)

This extended figure of speech is hardly one of the more inspired passages of the drama but it is nevertheless effective in its unwitting (from the point of view of Medea) applicability to Jason. It is followed almost immediately by Jason's first entrance and his daring swim across to Medea's tower. The image of swimming, landing, and sinking thus foreshadows this particular adventure of Jason as well as his ultimate disaster.

In her first meeting with Kreusa, Medea uses the water symbol to warn the girl of the influences which imperil happiness, security, and harmony. She pictures Kreusa's skiff gliding gently down the stream. But the stream, like time, is always moving and its "Silberwellen" carry all craft finally into the dangerous gray expanse of the sea. Only by clinging to the shelter of the shore, i.e., never

venturing out into the world of action and passion, is there hope of avoiding shipwreck (*Medea,* 389 ff.)

Of the nature symbols there remains only that of fire yet to be discussed. The first references to fire come at the end of *Der Gastfreund* when Medea has a vision of the terrifying consequences of the murder of Phryxus. She sees the Furies with torches in hand and with flaming eyes (*Der Gastfreund,* 500 ff.). The fire motif reappears early in *Die Argonauten* when Medea balefully describes the holocaust to come. The murder of the guest-friend is a spark and the fire it causes can never be quenched until it has burned itself out. She tells her father:

> Da trugst du einen Funken in dein Haus,
> Der glimmt und glimmt und nicht verlöschen wird
> . . .
> Feuer geht aus von dir
> Und ergreift die Stützen deines Hauses
> Das krachend einbricht
> Und uns begräbt.
>
> (*Die Argonauten,* 100, 101, 114-117)

The flames of passion, moreover, are just as uncontrollable as the fires of violence and revenge. But the sensation Medea experiences in her first encounter with Jason is more than the smouldering spark that will later burst into flame; it is sudden, violent conflagration.

> Aus seinem Aug, seiner Hand, seinen Lippen
> Gingen sprühende Funken über mich aus
> Und flammend loderte auf mein Innres.
>
> (*Die Argonauten,* 1030-32)

The explosiveness and intensity of this experience heighten her feeling of impending disaster and lead to even more bizarre imagery in speaking of the fleece:

> Rache strahlet das schimmernde Vließ.
> So oft ich's versuch' in die Zukunft zu schauen
> Flammt's vor mir wie ein blut'ger Komet,
> Droht mir Unheil, findet's mich dort!
>
> (*Die Argonauten,* 1057-60)

Although there are many references to blood on the fleece, there is only one other place where blood and fire are conjoined as in the "blut'ger Komet." When Jason staggers out of the inner cave of the dragon, holding the fleece away from himself, he says: "Berühr's nicht! Feuer! Feuer! Sieh hier die Hand—wie ich's berührt—verbrannt!" (*Die Argonauten,* 1581-82). But Medea, taking his hand, says, "Das ist ja Blut!" Real blood, the sensation of burning, and the accompanying frenzy of fear all point backward to Medea's vision at the end of *Der Gastfreund* and forward to the literal and figurative blood and flames of the final catastrophe.

From the very beginning Jason is associated in Medea's mind with fire. She sees him first as with lightning in his hand, eyes flaming. Later she refers to the burning brand he had hurled into her breast Comet, lightning, and brand are all male symbols, and all cause destruction. The flames ignited in Medea by Jason's brand mount up until "Ruh und Glück und Frieden prasselnd sanker / Von Rauchesqualm und Feuersglut umhüllt" (*Medea,* 622 f.). When not only harmony and tranquillity are lost but also the love of Jason and her children, the flames of fury blaze up in towering, demoniacal revenge. The burned-out palace in the dawn following is the outward image of Medea's state: all passion spent but with no peace of mind.

On the basis of this analysis it seems that Grillparzer's misgivings about the effectiveness of his use of symbol were not well founded. The tragic sense of life is so strong in him that it permeates every aspect of his art. Thus the emotional impact of *Das goldene Vlieβ* derives not only from the tragic events of the drama but in a much more subtle and pervasive way from the symbolic structure of the whole. Herein Grillparzer shows himself as a consummate artist and at the same time as a seer with startling insight into the human psyche.

Notes

1. K. J. Schaum in an unpublished dissertation, "Die Bildund Symbolgestaltung in den Dramen Franz Grillparzers," Princeton, 1955, gives a fairly extensive treatment of the subject. I have found his work helpful and suggestive.

2. *Grillparzers Werke,* Im Auftrage der Reichshaupt- und Residenzstadt Wien, hrsg. v. August Sauer, 2. Abteilung, x, 148. (All quotations are from this edition.)

3. *Werke,* 1. Abteilung, XVII, 301.

4. *Werke,* 2. Abteilung, VIII, 97.

5. Volkelt, Kleinberg, Backmann, et al.

6. *Werke,* 1. Abteilung, XVII, 308.

7. *Der Gastfreund,* pp. 329 ff.

Walter Silz (essay date 1964)

SOURCE: "Grillparzer's Ottokar," in *Germanic Review,* Vol. 39, 1964, pp. 243-61.

[*In the following essay, Silz provides a character study of the protagonist in* König Ottokars Glück und Ende, *King Ottokar, challenging the critical interpretation of the character as a brutal, swaggering tyrant.*]

King Ottokar of Bohemia, the hero of Grillparzer's tragedy *König Ottokars Glück und Ende,* is a person of many aspects and qualities, more perhaps than Grillparzer himself realized; more, certainly, then interpreters of the play have recognized. In the extensive Grillparzer literature, Ottokar is regularly typed as the brutal, blustering tyrant whose many misdeeds culminate in his divorce from his wife Margareta, in consequence of which he comes deservedly to a bad end. This view of him persists,

with minor modifications, from Grillparzer's time to ours. Wilhelm Scherer (whom it is somewhat surprising to think of as a *Niederösterreicher* and acquaintance of Grillparzer's) nearly a century ago condemned Ottokar roundly: "ein übermütiger Prahlhans, kindisch in seinem Hochmut, töricht in seiner eitlen Verblendung, ein Despot von rohen Formen ohne alle Größe"—not to be compared with Napoleon or Richard III, having no claim to our sympathy, for "das bißchen Gewissensbisse im fünften Akte zählt kaum."[1]

Friedrich Gundolf, in another long essay that echoes Scherer's in some degree, could see no redeeming virtue in Grillparzer's hero: "Ottokar ist nichts als ein roher und anmaßender Machtnarr, der gelegentlich sentimentale Anwandlungen hat, als es ihm schlecht geht"; a ruler with none of the grandeur of Macbeth or Richard III: "ohne Zug der Größe so dummstolz, unbillig brutal und widersinnig anmaßend, . . . ein plumper Tor, . . . ein öd hochmütiger Wüterich" who rattles and fumes his hour upon the stage.[2] Most recently, Benno von Wiese has found Ottokar, in his "besinnungslose Hybris," inferior to Wallenstein, merely "ein polternder, ungezügelter, ruhmsüchtiger Barbar" with grotesque traits, intended at best as a critical portrait; hence there is nothing tragic in his fall, however much Grillparzer tried to give him humanly appealing features.[3] Gerhard Fricke is even sharper in his condemnation of Ottokar's mock heroism, rating him as "ein Durchschnittsmensch, dem . . . jedes Moment der Größe geflissentlich genommen ist," and his career as a psychopathological study in the "Großmannssucht eines Kleinen."[4]

That this bombastic tyrant comes to grief as a result of his wrongful abandonment of his wife, Margareta von Österreich, was a view that Grillparzer found already in his chief source, the fourteenth-century *Reimchronik* of Ottokar von Steiermark. This chronicle, written from the Austrian point of view, condemns the divorce and attributes all Ottokar's subsequent troubles to it. Grillparzer indicated his acceptance of this verdict when he compared Ottokar's career to Napoleon's and noted as the final count "zuletzt der Umstand, daß den Wendepunkt von beider Schicksal die Trennung ihrer ersten Ehe und eine zweite Heirat gebildet hatte."[5] In his play, consequently, Grillparzer brings in the divorce as an insistent refrain and makes it the mainspring of events.

And the interpreters have carried on this emphasis. For Fritz Strich, Ottokar's wrong against Margareta is his "erste tragische Verschuldung, welche all sein späteres Unglück auf ihn bringt."[6] For Ilse Münch, this is what makes *Ottokar* a "Schuld-und Sühnedrama"; the hero perishes "weil er aus egoistischer Leidenschaft gefrevelt hat an einem allgemein-verbindlichen ethischen Gesetz."[7] Rudolf Franz ascribes Ottokar's downfall above all to this act: "vorab in seiner selbstsüchtigen Gewalttat gegen die Königin Margarete liegt . . . der Keim zu seinem Sturze."[8] And Walter Naumann sees in the divorce "das unausweichliche Schicksal" that hangs over Ottokar's head like the inexorable curse of the fate-tragedies.[9]

If such is the manifest argument of the play in the eyes of its author and of subsequent interpreters, one must say that there are things in it which are not as simple as they seem, things that Grillparzer himself did not consciously know were there. For *Ottokar,* like other great achievements, was a product of conscious and unconscious work; as Schiller said, "das Bewußtlose mit dem Besonnenen vereinigt macht den poetischen Künstler aus."[10] There were respects in which Grillparzer could dislike and despise his hero, justifying Scherer's opinion that Ottokar "ist mit einer gewissen Antipathie gezeichnet."[11] There were other respects in which he could sympathize with and even identify himself with him. The result is a complex and contradictory character, not wholly satisfactory as a hero, but intensely interesting psychologically and as a self-revelation of his author.

Ottokar could be considered a highly conscious and calculated undertaking. Its production was relatively slow, systematic, and directed by reason. Grillparzer declared, in 1826: "Ottokar ist ein berechnetes Werk (ja berechnet, ins kleinste berechnet . . . !)."[12] In one of his earliest comments on this material, a diary entry of 1819 listing dramatic subjects illustrative of human vices and faults, he ended with "Uibermuth und sein Fall. König Ottokar."[13] At one stage in its evolution, his play bore the title "Eines Gewaltigen Glück und Ende," which shows the intention to present a typical case of a general moral problem.[14] The contemporary figure of Napoleon, to be sure, embodied both "Gewalt" and "Übermut," but "indem ich . . . meine sonstigen historischen Erinnerungen durchmusterte," Grillparzer concluded that Ottokar was a more suitable vehicle for his idea.[15] This procedure strikes us as a perfect illustration of Gottschedian prescriptions "wie eine gute tragische Fabel gemacht werden muß,"[16] and reminds us how close Grillparzer still stood to the *Aufklärung.*

With his conscious mind and from personal conviction, he clearly wished to expose in Ottokar the sins he most condemned in man: egotism, arrogance, aggression, violence. His works early and late prove his deep-seated aversion to the *Machtmensch,* the conqueror and the ruthless adventurer who exploit their fellow-men yet never attain satisfaction or peace within themselves. Consciously, too, he wanted to glorify his native land and the dynasty, established in this very war, that had led it to greatness. This aspect of his historical material, we know, he esteemed a priceless boon for an Austrian writer. On the other hand the creative artist in Grillparzer, the great shaper of dramatic character, could not be content with making Ottokar merely a deterrent example, a bogy. Both deliberately and instinctively, he produced a many-sided hero-villain, appealing and exasperating by turns.

On the negative side, a cardinal difficulty about Ottokar is that he is *shown* to us in his weakness rather than his greatness. His military triumphs are won before the action opens; we have to take them on trust. We do not *see* him achieve anything, but rather throw away the fruits of seemingly undeserved good luck. He appears to do and say all

the wrong things, Rudolf the right ones. Of his intelligent if high-handed *Kulturpolitik,* of his positive relation to his people, we are shown too little, of his faults and blunders too much. This wrong-headed ruler, as Scherer says, hurts those he should cherish, trusts flatterers, is dominated by persons who humiliate him, is audacious and defiant for no reason, and has not even faith in his own stars; why then should all these crowns fall to his lot?[17]

Why, unless on grounds of deep dislike, did Grillparzer make the Ottokar of the opening so brutal and stupid and blind? Why need he ostentatiously disclaim any mourning for his uncle: "Betrauern mag ihn, wer sein Land nicht erbt!" (673), or crudely refer to Margareta in public as "alt und unfruchtbar" (524)? How can he fail to understand what the emissaries of the Empire have plainly said: that this is not an election, but an inquiry (694ff.)? How can he expect them to bring the imperial crown and lay it at his feet, on the chance that he will stoop for it (1185ff.)? He contemptuously spurns election (1245f.) yet confidently expects it (1206-08). Can we believe this man a successful ruler? And how quickly Grillparzer deflates him when adverse news comes! He winces at the mention of Habsburg; he stands for a moment with trembling hands and knees, stammering voice, staring eyes; then he beats a retreat (1220 +). A moment later he reappears, brutally throws his glove into the face of his chancellor and most faithful friend, then takes him by the hand and leads him downstage for a parley (1235 +). This is irrational behavior at its most unpredictable.

It seems incredible that Ottokar should be so willfully blind to the situation at the beginning of Act III (1428ff.); that later, at the meeting on the island, he should persist in his cocksure assertions when he must see that Rudolf holds the trump time after time (1830ff.); that he should boastfully reveal his strategy, now plainly futile (1857-62). Ottokar here looks too much like a straw man, set up to be knocked down again and again, until finally Rudolf "has the floor" for an overlong sermon of sixty-odd lines (1880ff.) during which Ottokar stands by, an actor with nothing to do!

The Climax of the play, in the latter part of Act III, has already too much of Catastrophe in it. Ottokar has been too seriously weakened to last out two more acts as hero. The fourth act, always a problem for a dramatist, is impaired by the fact that the King, who should dominate it, is incapacitated, all but insane. If the theme of this act, as Norbert Fuerst has said, is *Demütigung,*[18] we feel that Grillparzer has heaped too much humiliation on his hero. He exhibits him like a tethered bear at the "side door" of his castle, baited and vilified in turn by persons from his past: the Bürgermeister, Benesch, Berta, and, most cruelly, by his wife Kunigunde. The motif of his disgraceful *Knien* falls like a lash on him all through Act IV.[19] During all this, he is completely passive, broken.

That Kunigunde "gets away with" her savage tongue-whipping, in the presence and with the open cooperation of an impudent vassal, is the measure of the depth to which Grillparzer lets his hero sink. There is no one left in the world who need tremble before him (2190f.). His court is reduced to a single follower. Reviled and spurned by his wife, driven from his home and marriage bed, stricken from the list of princes, vassal to an upstart monarch whom he despised, he is a mere hunted beast of the wilderness. This is more than a man can bear: "Ich kann's nicht tragen, kann nicht leben so!" (2261ff.). He has tried in vain to blot from his mind the memory of his shame; he is ready to kill the last witness to it, even himself if he cannot forget (2280ff.).

From this collapse Grillparzer never raises his hero again to full force. Merely negative factors—wounded pride, self-delusion, inferiority-feeling, resentment—rouse Ottokar to a hollow sort of heroism characterized by the desperate bravado of his tearing up the imperial letter in the Queen's presence. This wins him back a wife whom he immediately rejects (2412ff.). That it was her contempt that goaded him into his ill-fated rebellion he confirms in his final confession:

> Mit Hohn und Spott hat sie mich aufgestachelt,
> Daß blind ich rannte in das Todesnetz,
> Das nun zusammenschlägt ob meinem Scheitel.
>
> (2676-78)

In the last analysis, Ottokar's death is that of a maddened husband more than a king. His domestic troubles, rather than affairs of state, prove his undoing.

At the end of Act IV, this man, formerly *rasch* and impetuous,[20] to his chancellor's consternation denies his very nature by turning to caution and considerateness (2491ff.). We seem to see his established personality breaking up: "Der König hat sein Wesen ausgezogen" (2537). From this point on he becomes refined spiritually but ceases to dominate the action. Act IV ends with Ottokar asleep; Act V begins with Ottokar inactive. Act IV was devoted to his humiliation; Act V shows his remorse,[21] which is an even less dramatic condition. The Queen's outright desertion has finally broken his spirit (2539). He is no longer *im Bilde* topographically or strategically as he faces a final, "unavoidable" battle (2572) which he hopes will bring him peace in death if not in victory (2599).

Grillparzer grants Ottokar personal heroism at the last: he falls as a brave soldier fighting against hopeless odds. But he dies also as a fugitive criminal at the hands of a victim's avenging son. He dies destitute, a beggar who only by the grace of Rudolf's *als ob* investiture still figures as a sovereign.[22]

The man who dies thus ignobly has nevertheless been endowed by the author with attractive and admirable qualities. It is noteworthy that Grillparzer "improved" his hero in comparison with his sources. The *Reimchronik* had Ottokar not only cast off Margareta but let her live in privation and finally, impatient at her survival, order her poisoned:

> und dô si niht wolt ligen tôt,
> wand in dûht ze lanc ir leben,
> dô hiez er ir vergeben.
> sûs nam diu frou ein ende.[23]

The Chronicle records as further grounds for the non-election of Ottokar his burning of Otto von Maissau and his savage killing of Merenberg.[24] Grillparzer omits mention of the first atrocity altogether and postpones the second until after the election, mitigating it then to virtually accidental manslaughter. The fiendish murder of Benesch is not mentioned. Grillparzer conceived his Ottokar as "ohne eigentliche Bösartigkeit, durch die Umstände zur Härte, wohl gar Tyrannei fortgetrieben."[25] He nowhere shows him coldly cruel. Ottokar condemns Merenberg in hot blood, believing him the leading traitor and identifying him with his son who in turn is identified with the King's supreme humiliation. Ottokar acts under great emotional stress and in fact soon relents and shows compassion with his prisoner (2511ff.)—a mollifying touch added by the poet.

When he first appears, flushed with success and self-confidence, Ottokar's bearing is indeed conceited and tactless. Yet we feel that he is often right in the matter, if offensive in manner. His criticism of the Tatars' accouterment (390ff.) is gratuitous but apparently justified. His policy of improving the arts and crafts and raising the cultural level of Bohemia (456ff.)—another motif invented by Grillparzer—can only be applauded, though he pursues it in a way that alienates many of his own people.[26] Even his divorce proceedings, which put him so grievously into the wrong, have a great deal of justification. His *hubris* and bravado in Act I are in large part compensation for a deep feeling of insecurity, of uneasiness about his marital situation. He is in the process of dissolving an unsatisfactory marriage arranged for political reasons, and about to enter into a new union, again in the interests of state and dynasty, not from free personal choice. His initial resentment at Merenberg, who twice puts himself forward in Margaret's behalf, is doubtless due to his own bad conscience about unhappy actions which he does not feel entirely responsible for.

There is a certain nobility in Ottokar's nature and an openness that makes him ready to trust others and slow to suspect them. Even after he has in effect divorced Margareta he continues to confide in her (601ff.) and feels assured of her good will (615). When his Austrian vassals begin to desert him, it is evident that suspicion is new and repugnant to his mind: "Pfui, Argwohn, Spürhund von des Teufels Meute! / Lockst du auch Könige zu deiner Jagd?" (1021f.). If we hear a proud Shakespearean ring in this, there is a like regal dignity in his reproof to Zawisch and Kunigunde (1113-1122); and it does him honor that he leaves these two behind unwatched (end of Act II). Zawisch "trades on" this pride in Ottokar which holds his natural jealously in check; as Grillparzer observed: "Er soll eifersüchtig seyn, sich aber schämen, es auch nur sich selbst zu gestehen."[27]

The King is pictured as an energetic, progressive ruler, a sort of *Vorstudie* to Primislaus in **Libussa.** His ambitions are more patriotic than personal. He has a right to boast of having increased Bohemia's territory and fame; he has not chosen for himself his fathers' easier life of sloth and obscurity; he means to force betterment upon his refractory subjects (489-500). His *Zwangskolonisierung,* unlike Faust's, is not in his own interest but in his country's. There is no indication that he loves the Germans whom he imports; they are for him a temporary means to a national end; indeed, their function is the uncomplimentary one of fleas set in the Bohemian pelt (478ff.).[28] The King's firm faith in "die Seinen" (635) and his sincere devotion to their welfare are apparent all through the play. He will not hear of accusations against his nobles; he insists "Kein Böhme hat noch seinen Herrn verraten" (2436, 2440). As he faces death at the end, he prays God to spare his people: "So triff mich, aber schone meines Volks!" (2863).

The Kanzler testifies (1562ff.) to Ottokar's devotion of all his resources to the task of bettering the economic status of his country, and pictures very briefly the success of this endeavor in terms that remind us of a not uncomparable ruler, Karl August in Goethe's *Ilmenau:* "Es geht der Pflug, der Weber sitzt am Werk, / Der Spinner dreht, der Berg gibt seinen Schatz." Even his adversary Rudolf acknowledges Ottokar's pursuit of the best interests of his people: "Ihr habt der Euren Vorteil stets gewollt" (1928).[29] Ottokar declares that he yielded to Rudolf earlier for the sake of avoiding bloodshed (2391), and—in contrast to the heartless Queen—he feels compunctions now about unleashing "den Teufel Krieg" for new devastation and death (2398ff.). These compunctions are expressed even more poignantly in his final soliloquy (2835ff.). As he launches his last campaign for the power and glory of his country (2443), he renews the solemn oath that binds him to his land and people unto death (2450ff.). For the sake of national solidarity he (unwisely) offers to return to the great nobles the territories, wrongfully appropriated, that he had once wrested from them, and he even courts the support of the traitorous Zawisch in the common cause (2470ff.).

Ottokar, who is so often thought of as a sexual adventurer, is not a "ladies' man" and not particularly clever with women. His flirtation with Berta is of little account. There was never any passion in his marriage with Margareta. He did not marry Kunigunde for love, and he neglects to "cultivate" her, leaving the field open to Zawisch's far superior finesse. Ottokar is essentially a men's man, a soldier, a man of state. His heart is in his work. How naïve and clumsy is his attempt at *Zärtlichkeit* with Kunigunde: "Nu Kunthe, nu, wie geht's?"—with a miscarried chuck under the chin (1006)! This pathetically futile approach is the only blandishment we see him employ toward the woman he is alleged to have married out of sensual passion. Rebuffed, he readily turns away from her to Milota and military affairs.

Again later, when Kunigunde defies him, he does not force the issue, but with a masculine "Mit Weiberlaunen hat

man billig Nachsicht!" (1155) turns quickly to the "real business" of the state. In an ironic reversal of the situation of years ago, when he, the black-haired "Jüngling," faced Margareta, "die Alternde" (329ff.), he appears to Kunigunde an aging, graying man, fit for the woman he left: "die Alternde, / Die Königin des Jammers stand ihm wohl!" (2123f.). That his careworn aspect is due to burdens of war and government makes no difference to Kunigunde ("gleichviel!" 979ff.), but it does in our estimate of the King. He was no darling of success, it seems, even in his years with Margareta, but frequently needed consolation in his troubles: "Du hast mich oft getröstet," he remembers at her coffin (2679).

Grillparzer raises his hero in our eyes, as Schiller did Wallenstein, by contrast with the disloyalty and ingratitude of men he trusted. "Undank," a vice of dark hue in Grillparzer as in Shakespeare, is first in the tale of wrongs that Ottokar pours into the dead Margareta's unhearing ears. On the other hand, a warm light is thrown on him by the love and loyalty he inspires in his chancellor, Braun von Olmütz, who is with him almost constantly from his first entrance to his last exit. One of Grillparzer's most moving closes is that of Act IV: the utterly exhausted King asleep, his head pillowed in the lap of his faithful Kanzler—as it will be again in death at the very end.

If Grillparzer did not sympathize with the triumphant, domineering conqueror of the opening scenes, he could put himself into the place of a victim of marital maladjustments such as he apprehended in his own life. And he could feel with the defeated, despondent ruler wandering incognito like an exile through his realm. The line "Und irrt seitdem im Land herum von Mähren" (1981) led Scherer to surmise that the poet had misunderstood the *Reimchronik* passage which tells that Ottokar, "der ellenhaft" (= der Mannhafte, Mutige), was away in Moravia for a year, mistaking *ellenhaft* to mean "elend, unglücklich."[30] It seems to me not unlikely that there was this misunderstanding, conditioned by a personal memory of misery experienced years before in Moravia, and that it suggested the mournful picture at the opening of Act IV: the fugitive King sitting by the lonely little spring at Kostelez, prophesying gloomily from twigs cast on the water, is the young Grillparzer in this very spot, dangerously ill, abandoned, and facing a blighted future.[31]

The scene of the King's death, too, was shaped by the dramatic poet with perhaps involuntary admiration and sympathy: Ottokar at bay, fearlessly engaging a superior and ungenerous foeman, reminds us of Kleist's Varus and his gallant end, in contradiction to the "propaganda line" of *Die Hermannsschlacht.* Young Merenberg, the Austrian, cuts a sorry figure by comparison, as do the Germans who compete for the ignominious slaughter of the Roman general.

The varying attitudes of the author toward his principal character result in a complex and disunified dramatic personage, an inadequate hero for a historical tragedy.

Sometimes there is a strange lapse in manner between passages in close proximity: immediately after the dignified but astute reproof of lines 1113-22 we hear in lines 1131-36 again the blind braggart of the early scenes. There is too great a gap between the arrogant triumphator of Act I and the crushed and contrite individual of Act V. The new gentleness and insight Ottokar evinces in his encounter with Elisabeth and in his long speech of remorse and self-accusation at Margaret's coffin (2654-83) make for pathos rather than true tragedy.[32] Ottokar, like Napoleon, breaks under misfortune. He lacks the strength to reassert himself. He increases in human value but diminishes in heroic stature. He does not resolutely dominate the action, even in defeat, as Shakespeare's kings do.

Ironically, it is his good qualities, those that make him humanly appealing, that cause his downfall. He fails where a more consistent and ruthless tyrant would have triumphed. No successful hero could afford to be as sensitive to injury and ingratitude and infidelity as he is (2667ff.). If we agree with Volkelt as to the Ottokar of the beginning: "diese Züge der Roheit stimmen zu dem Bilde eines Gewaltherrschers jener Zeit,"[33] surely his scruples about sacrificing the lives of his subjects in battle (2835ff.) are not typical of a warring ruler of the thirteenth century—this is the voice of a nineteenth-century humanitarian.[34]

All through this long, abject, and painful soliloquy, in fact (2826-75), Grillparzer is preaching his creed of humility and humanity, admirable in itself but a clog on his action and a detriment to the dramatic effectiveness of his hero. He started out with a swaggering *Gewaltmensch;* he ends with a humbled penitent.[35] We are invited to join in the simple-minded pathos of Elisabeth's summary: "Ach Gott! / So starb er! Grade da er sanft geworden! / Du armer Herr!" (2949ff.) and in Berta's childlike prayer (2970f.).

Then, having disposed of a sinner rather than a king, Grillparzer the Austrian turns to the concerns of the dynasty that he has fondly shown growing out of this ruin and death. What follows is an appendage, a patriotic *Nachspiel,* no longer a part of the plot, which ended with Ottokar's death. Through the lips of the new emperor, the author underlines like a *fabula docet* his lesson of the perils of *Übermut* and *Gewalt* (2980ff.). But his play has demonstrated much more than this, and the patriotic cheer at the close, like that in Kleist's *Prinz Friedrich von Homburg,* while it begs all other questions for the moment, leaves some weighty ones unanswered.

One of the most insistent of these, a problem that for Grillparzer extended far beyond the limits of this play, is that of marriage and the relation of the sexes in it. Grillparzer was, like Hebbel, preoccupied with what Hebbel called "den zwischen den Geschlechtern anhängigen großen Prozeß," both as a personal problem and as a literary theme. He treated its phenomena less philosophically and more psychologically than Hebbel, and clothed them in more natural, less intentional dramatic figures, but the

problem was with him quite as constantly, from his earliest to his latest works, and the solutions he presents are anything but positive and hopeful.

In *Ottokar,* the matter is centered on the question of divorce. Invariably, interpreters have seen the King's tragic guilt and the cause of his decline in the annulment of his marriage to Queen Margareta; but none of them, so far as I can see, has questioned the nature and validity of the marriage itself.[36] Yet if we look at the evidence of the text, we find a most questionable situation. As Margareta tells Rudolf in Act I, she was a widow, no longer young, no longer fair, worn down with grief, withdrawn from life after the loss of her husband, her children, and her brother, an "unsel'ge Königin der Tränen, / Zum Grab gebeugt durch all der Ihren Tod" (244f.). She had vowed lifelong widowhood and fidelity to her husband's memory: no man should ever so much as touch the hem of her dress, or even a woman kiss her lips.[37]—This virtually monastic vow of celibacy, any modern psychologist would say, must be a formidable hindrance in remarriage and a source of guilt-feelings. She herself, in fact, recognizes that, like Ottokar, she has been guilty of infidelity to marriage vows (364f.); but the recognition is ethical and without psychological depth.

Margareta is a somewhat frail and ascetic figure. From the very opening line, where her physician is urgently sent for, she gives the impression of a suffering woman in a precarious state of health, so that we are prepared for her death within the play. There is something *wehleidig* about her. She tends to make a cult of her grief. Why should she, in replying to Ottokar's request for the deed to her estates, parade the relics of her past misfortunes (659-662)? And why should such a document be deposited with these gruesome mementoes? This throws an odd light on her.

She married Ottokar without even a thought of love, for her country's sake. Distressed by the sight of the devastated land and suffering people, she was willing to promise anything: "Da wollt' ich alles und versprach es ihnen" (326). And so they brought Ottokar and told her this was the man she was to marry. She still remembers him, the black-eyed, black-browed youth standing at a shy distance, contemplating his matrimonial fate. Both these ill-matched persons (in history, he was 23, she 47, and probably Grillparzer so conceived them) are pawns of national exigency and arrangement, victims of royal duty.

Margareta protests that she did not deceive Ottokar in the marriage bargain (239ff.)—but what a bargain! She says she never loved him, never even considered the possibility: "Ich hab' ihn nie geliebt; / Ich dachte nie, ob ich ihn lieben könnte" (334f.); but in looking after him she developed a sort of sisterly or motherly affection, and he in turn something like a son's or younger brother's attachment. At her coffin he speaks to her like a hurt child that can no longer take its troubles to its mother and be comforted: "Und niemand tröstet mich, und niemand hört mich! / Sie haben schlimm an mir getan, Margrete!" (2666f.).

Margareta made it clear at the beginning that she would not, if she could, have any children or, one may conclude, any sexual relations (259). She concedes the naturalness of Ottokar's wish (and that of the State) for a son to succeed him on the throne, but he could not get a legitimate heir if her views prevailed, for she is firmly opposed to divorce. That, she maintains, would be an "Unrecht" (214, 265ff.) and would make their years together "zum Greuel . . . und zum Ärgernis" (290f.)—terms that one would rather apply to this unnatural wedlock itself than to its termination.[38] Yet many persons in the play, from the simple Seyfried to the Emperor, regard the divorce as an unqualified crime and error on Ottokar's part. "Mit ihr habt Ihr das Glück von Euch verbannt," says Rudolf, though at the same time he characterizes Margareta as a "Friedensengel," conciliatory and soothing, a faithfully ministering "liebe Schwester" (1936-40)—hardly the complete description of a wife! And again at the end, Rudolf declares Margareta, not Kunigunde, Ottokar's true wife: "Denn daß sie's blieb, hat sie im Tod erprobt" (2955); but this too simply equates compassionate loyalty with wifehood. Margareta unquestionably had more heart for Ottokar than Kunigunde did, but he was cheated of real marriage in both cases, in different ways.

The King's dalliance with Berta, like that of Alfons with Rahel in *Die Jüdin von Toledo,* is a form of compensation for a loveless marriage, but Ottokar's adventure is of far less emotional depth. To take it as proof of his "sittliche Unverläßlichkeit als Quelle der Unverläßlichkeit seiner besten Vasallen"[39] is to attach too much importance to it. There is nothing to indicate a serious intent, or even a physical liaison, in a flirtation which the simple-minded Berta and some of her kinsmen (*not* the intelligent Zawisch) promoted for their own selfish ends. The Queen, a wise woman, early foresaw its fiasco. She tells us too that the martial bonds uniting her and Ottokar were already very weak before the Rosenbergs, "die bösen Engel des Königs," started their stealthy and persistent work of attrition (206-209),[40] the failure of which they bitterly resent. Here again Ottokar's private life, if indeed he can be said to have one, is at the mercy of alien political interests.

It is so in the case of his remarriage, which has often been grossly misunderstood. The long-standard Ehrhard-Necker biography, for example, declared that not dynastic concern for an heir but simply sensual passion ("Sinnenglut") motivated Ottokar in this step.[41] Ilse Münch ascribed it to his "egoistische Leidenschaft."[42] Fritz Strich saw him succumbing to "dem Ansturm einer gewaltigen Leidenschaft" which like a wild mountain torrent swept away the barriers of his morality and nobility.[43] Of such a passionate attraction of Ottokar to Kunigunde, or of a passionate relationship between them, there is not the slightest trace in Grillparzer's text. Instead, there is abundant evidence that this marriage, entered into for political and dynastic reasons, is a bitter disappointment to both partners. Ottokar is justified in saying that in his personal life as in his administration he has taken the harder course for his country's sake; that it is not youthful desire but national

policy that bids him forsake Margareta and "submit himself" to new marriage bonds: "Es ist ja nicht der Jugend wilder Kitzel, / . . . es ist mein Land, / Das in mir Ehen schließt und Ehen scheidet" (499-515, 592ff.).

When she first intrudes, disguised as a soldier, Kunigunde characterizes herself as forward, unwomanly, and unfeeling; and though Ottokar does not meet her with the misgiving with which he faced his first bride, he soon realizes that he has made an even worse bargain. Ironically, Kunigunde's lot is not unlike that of the woman she supplants: she too has not married for love but under political pressure, and she too cannot forget an earlier man in her life, a more fitting mate, of whom fate deprived her. But where Margareta rises to saintliness, Kunigunde falls to vulgarity. She becomes the very type of the frustrated, embittered wife. Her castigation of Ottokar (2096ff.) voices a deep sexual resentment. She grows harder as he grows softer. The usual roles of man and wife are reversed when he says to her "Gott gönn' Euch was von dem, was hier erwacht [auf seine Brust zeigend] / Und gebe mir die Kraft, die Ihr bewiesen!" (2410f.), and, a moment later, when he shrinks from her touch, appalled by her hardness and cruelty (2415ff.). Her infidelity is the final blow that breaks him down: "Die Flucht der Königin gab ihm den Rest" (2539). He had married Kunigunde in the hope of gaining a wife and heir; there is nothing to show that he ever had the one or the expectation of the other.[44]

Despite this sympathetic portrayal of Ottokar's personal tragedy, it is clear that the author's heart was not with the Bohemian king but with Austria and the first of its Habsburgs. Already at the start, Grillparzer's special interest in Austria is betrayed in Margareta's overlong, dramatically retarding account of her past and the sufferings of her native land. Act III opens with old Merenberg's thanksgiving for the Habsburgs, which contains some of the poet's most beautiful verse. A longer lyrical passage is Ottokar von Horneck's fervid eulogy of Austria and the Austrian character (1672-1704), a warm confession of faith and love but, like the whole Horneck episode, dramatically dispensable. Less often noticed is a similar *con amore* passage in the last act, as the Austrians prepare for battle and the illustrious flags are assigned (2717-49). Throughout the play, the Austrians and their fortunes are kept in view: the effect of their secession on Ottokar's fate, their decisive part in his victory at Marchegg and his defeat at Dürnkrut. The Hungarians and Bohemians, on the other hand, play far less agreeable roles, and there is ground for the charge of national prejudice, though it was probably an unconscious one.[45]

The coincidence of the fall of the Přemyslides and the rise of the Habsburgs seemed to Grillparzer a windfall for an Austrian dramatist: "Wenn nun zugleich aus dem Untergange Ottokars die Gründung der Habsburgischen Dynastie in Österreich hervorging, so war das für einen österreichischen Dichter eine unbezahlbare Gottesgabe und setzte dem Ganzen die Krone auf."[46] There could be no doubt of this benefaction had *Ottokar* been intended as a national

Festspiel—as indeed the poet's brief *Epilog nach der Aufführung* (1825) strongly suggests.[47] The benefaction becomes questionable, however, when we judge the play as genuine tragedy of supra-national stature. From the outset, the Austrian bias tended to elevate Rudolf to the position of a tragic hero, which he could not be, and debase Ottokar to the function of a villain, which he must not become. In a spirit of patriotic moralism Grillparzer could heap on Ottokar all the vices he most condemned in man: selfishness, immoderateness, violence, brutality; and on Rudolf all the virtues he most prized, especially in his fellow-countrymen: simplicity, modesty, measure, common-sense, dutifulness, peaceableness. This threatens to make his play an allegory of the Good and Bad Ruler, a sort of didactic *Fürstenspiegel*. As Ronald Peacock observes, the right and wrong that generate the conflicts within one tragic character are here distributed over two persons.[48]

Many of the earlier interpreters accepted this white/black antithesis. Ehrhard-Necker, for example, saw Rudolf in the island scene as Justice incarnate, the viceregent of God, enthroned in quiet majesty opposite Ottokar in his humbled pride and mundane passion.[49] But even Emil Staiger, much later, accepts the idealization of Rudolf, from the young warrior, "ein Jüngling, wie ihn Gott in seinem Schöpfungsplan erdacht hat," to the triumphant emperor: "Kaiser Rudolf vollendet das Werk."[50] On the other hand, Scherer had charged Grillparzer with partiality for painting Ottokar with too much shadow, Rudolf with too much light, and giving his play two heroes: "hieran krankt die Tragödie."[51] Gundolf, too, found an exaggerated distribution of light and shade that vitiates the tragic effect.[52] And Benno von Wiese recognizes that Rudolf is "eine vaterländisch verherrlichte Gestalt."[53]

From first to last, Rudolf is given every opportunity to distinguish himself *im Guten*. He has a superior, judicial status throughout, the function of an "ideal spectator." He is made a leading figure at Ottokar's court. He first appears as the King's emissary and mediator between him and the Queen. He speaks for the interests of the empire even before he is emperor (375ff.). He is given—unhistorically—a share in Ottokar's victorious campaign and praised by him as a brave man and redoubtable leader (437ff.); his personal valor and leadership are brought to the fore again in the final battle. He is as it were pushed forward by the somewhat contrived error of the imperial delegate who picks up his shield (701 +), and is thus called to the attention of the other envoys. As Grillparzer's chosen mouthpiece he condemns Kunigunde's tactless intrusion (727) as, at the end of the play, he speaks the author's final verdict on her, on Zawisch, on Seyfried, and on Ottokar himself. He defies the King's anger and champions the distressed Queen. For good measure, the anecdote treated in Schiller's ballad is retold—while action and angry Ottokar wait—to prove Rudolf's exemplary piety and humility (747ff.). To this is added a further anecdote which shows that even then the Archbishop of Mainz had an eye on this promising young man (756f.)—

whatever chance Ottokar had against such competition he is allowed to spoil by his haughty behavior! The imperial envoy designates Rudolf as the unhappy queen's escort, thereby associating him with the Holy Roman Empire in an act of mercy: "Wir wollen sie zur sichern Ruhstatt führen"; and we can feel Grillparzer's pride in the ringing line on which they exit: "Gebt Raum der Herzogin von Österreich!" (762, 764).

From line 1330 on, there is open hostility between Ottokar and Rudolf. But our interest and sympathy, contrary to the playwright's intent and to the detriment of his play, go with Rudolf. The universal admiration for him speaks even from Ottokar's stanchest supporter: the Kanzler quite falls out of his role in his praise of the new emperor and detailed knowledge of his doings (1480ff.); Grillparzer seems to sense this when he has Ottokar demur—much too weakly—"Sprichst du so warm für ihn?" (1501).

Magnified by the author's enthusiasm, Rudolf takes interest and force away from the hero without himself being qualified to be a tragic hero. For Rudolf is a completely untragic figure. He does not arouse pity and fear in us, but respect and admiration, which are much colder emotions. He is not truly an opponent of Ottokar, for they move on different levels. They are not, strictly speaking, even rivals for the imperial crown, for Ottokar disdains to contend, and Rudolf is angelically unaware that he is a candidate. Rudolf, himself infallible, is the measure and corrector of the all too fallible Ottokar. He preaches a long sermon to him (1880-1942) which Ottokar interrupts with but a single word, and he moralizes at the end over the slain adversary (2958ff.). The final glorification of victorious Austria in the presence of Ottokar's still warm body may well seem inhuman to anyone who does not share Grillparzer's sympathies.

Rudolf is the ideal male character in the play, as Margareta is the ideal female character. Both are admirable, neither is tragic. Neither has to meet, in the action we see on the stage, a supreme crisis; they are in effect above the battle, clothed in perfection, virtual saintliness. Rudolf to be sure once accuses himself of youthful excesses (1894ff.), but these, unlike Ottokar's, are not shown and do not become dramatically real; we take them as a conversational exaggeration meant to put Ottokar more at his ease.

Rudolf's ideal character has been generally appreciated,[54] but the damage it does to the balance of the play has been little regarded.[55] Rudolf not only detracts from the hero's effect all through, but he diminishes the tragic impact of the ending. Ottokar's disaster is no longer central, but subservient, his death a necessary condition for a better future under Habsburg. We cannot but applaud Rudolf's victory—much as we applaud the fairytale prince who has slain the monster—but this very satisfaction we feel in his triumph clouds our preception of Ottokar's tragedy, our recognition of the incomprehensible vicissitude of human fortunes. The voice of success and exultant patriotism is heard above the still, sad music of humanity.

If Rudolf is no true opponent to Ottokar as hero, neither is Zawisch as villain. Ottokar never actually clashes with Zawisch, the real *Bösewicht* of the play. He comes closest to it in Act IV, and we expect to see him cut down his wife's lover at line 2200: "zum Stoß ausholend." What saves Zawisch in the nick of time is Kunigunde's calling to him from within and a revulsion of Ottokar's pride and chivalry. But this is hardly sufficient psychologically, and it is disappointing dramatically. Or are we to suppose that the Rosenbergs are so powerful and indispensable to Ottokar that he dare not antagonize them? Later on in the act, Zawisch deigns to reappear very briefly and consents to follow his king into battle—for his clan's and country's sake—and Ottokar accepts him with a strangely mild and vague suspicion (2485f.). They never meet again. At the end, Zawisch turns up in the Austrian camp simply as Kunigunde's escort, to be reprimanded by the honorable Rudolf and to stand with hangdog mien beside Ottokar's corpse. Grillparzer created in Zawisch an audacious and fascinating villain, but he failed to make him an adequate opponent for his hero.

His most crucial act of villainy is his intervention in the scene of Ottokar's *Belehnung,* when he cuts the tent-cords and exposes his kneeling king to public view. This action by Zawisch is Grillparzer's invention; it is not in his source. The amazing thing is that no one in the play challenges this overt interference and betrayal, and not one of the many commentators has questioned its plausibility. Yet it is by this act, performed with complete impunity, that the further plot hangs. It is the particular disgrace of having to kneel *in public* that in the last analysis motivates Ottokar's fatal revolt. This makes Zawisch, not Rudolf, the author of Ottokar's downfall—a dubious development!

Ottokar was ready to accept defeat at Rudolf's hands; he was ready, as later passages show, to fulfill the terms of the treaty, including the surrender of his Austrian fiefs. What rankles in him is not even the kneeling per se—for the ever-considerate Rudolf had arranged that this unavoidable formality should be kept private and impersonal (1950-53)—what goads Ottokar into desperate and disastrous rebellion is the humiliation of "Knien im Angesicht des Heers" (2087) which various persons, most bitterly his wife, rub into his raw wounds as a festering venom.

Zawisch's loud words and open movements (1960f. +) must have been witnessed by many people. It is astounding that the conscientious and correct Rudolf takes no notice whatever of an intrusion that vitiates his special arrangements, nor shows any regard for Ottokar's visible and audible consternation: "Ha, Schmach! [Er springt auf und eilt in den Vorgrund]" (1962 +); instead, the Emperor undignifiedly runs after him, banner in hand, and concludes his business impromptu on another spot, as though nothing were amiss. This done, he leaves promptly, calling for cheers to hail what is anything but the "victory of sweet concord" he declares it (1976). All this is quite out of keeping with Rudolf's character as hitherto portrayed and his sense for the dignity of his office and the occasion. The episode leaves a disturbing gap in his armor of perfection.

There was a tradition to the effect that Rudolf himself had instigated the rope-cutting. We may safely assume that Grillparzer knew of this tradition. Though the *Reimchronik* says nothing about it, several other chroniclers do, notably Aeneas Sylvius,[56] and Grillparzer would surely have met it in the course of his "ungeheure Leserei" on the subject. But he would even more surely have suppressed it in his mind. Years later, when he found the motif used in one of Lope's plays, he was quick to condemn it as spoiling Rudolf's portrait.[57]

If it seems incredible for Rudolf to overlook this incident, it is equally incredible that Ottokar makes no attempt to find out and punish the man who exposed him to this egregious humiliation. Seyfried is put forward (1976 +) as a momentary *Blitzableiter,* but, one would think, only a momentary one, a rod too frail to take the tremendous charge of pent-up emotion that makes this one of Grillparzer's most powerful act-closes.

Ottokar's reaction, when it does come (2271ff.), is made ignoble and mean: instead of proceeding against Zawisch, the double author of his disgrace and his wife's unfaithfulness, he defies a minor official and takes reprisal on a defenseless old man, transferring to the man's son the sardonic sneer that must have been on the face of Zawisch (2335f.).

Was Grillparzer insensible of the damage done by the tent episode to the characterization of important persons and to the cogency of his plot? Can we explain this by his latent dislike of his hero and favoritism for his Habsburg opponent? Even so keen a mind as Grillparzer's is apt to be unaware of its prejudices in this area. In later years, he declared **Ottokar** to be his best play,[58] and in a theatrical sense it undoubtedly is. The opening act is a magnificent achievement which he never surpassed and which has been duly praised from Hebbel onward. The whole play abounds with dramatic life and opportunities for fine acting. Character and motive are presented in visible stage action, in contrast and confrontation. The expressive, flexible language, supplemented by eloquent objects and gestures; the skillful stage arrangements, colorful settings and costumes; the management of suspense; the *Stimmungskunst* of crescendo and diminuendo in act-endings—all show the master of theater who completely visualized his work.[59] In the judgment of a recent authority, **Ottokar,** in its consummate synthesis of dramatic form and historical matter, still towers as "ein Gipfelpunkt des deutschen Geschichtsdramas."[60] And its imperfections, one must admit, appear only on repeated critical reading. In the theater, the author's brilliant stage art suffices to cover them, and we are carried along to the triumphant conclusion as the *Bühnendichter* Grillparzer meant us to be.

Notes

1. Wilhelm Scherer, "Franz Grillparzer" (1872), in *Vorträge und Aufsätze* (Berlin, 1874), p. 246.

2. Friedrich Gundolf, "Franz Grillparzer," in *Jahrbuch des Freien Deutschen Hochstifts,* 1931, pp. 54-56.

3. Benno von Wiese, *Die deutsche Tragödie von Lessing bis Hebbel,* 2. Aufl. (Hamburg, 1952), p. 411. B. v. Wiese considers that Ottokar becomes tragic only through the later change and break in his character; but this seems to me to make him pathetic rather than tragic.

4. Gerhard Fricke, *Studien und Interpretationen* (Frankfurt a. M., 1956), p. 275.

5. *Selbstbiographie.* Grillparzer's *Sämtliche Werke,* Stadt Wien edition, Abt. 1, Bd. 16, p. 166. All references for Grillparzer will henceforth be made to section, volume, and page of this edition.

6. Fritz Strich, *Franz Grillparzers Ästhetik* (Berlin, 1905), p. 213.

7. Ilse Münch, *Die Tragik in Drama und Persönlichkeit Franz Grillparzers* (Berlin, 1931), p. 53.

8. Rudolf Franz, *Grillparzers Werke* (Bibliogr. Inst.), III, p. 260.

9. See Walter Naumann's interpretation of the play in *Das deutsche Drama,* ed. B. v. Wiese (Düsseldorf, 1958), I, 406.

10. See Schiller's letter of March 27, 1801, to Goethe, for an interesting brief discussion of this subject.

11. Scherer, op. cit., p. 246.

12. *Tagebuch,* 19. März 1826; Abt. 2, Bd. 8, p. 194.

13. Abt. 2, Bd. 7, p. 241.

14. These terms still linger in the closing lines (2982, 2984).

15. *Selbstbiog.;* Abt. 1, Bd. 16, p. 166.

16. See Gottsched's *Critische Dichtkunst,* 3. Aufl. (Leipzig, 1742), pp. 710f. (2. T., 10. Kap., 11. Abschn.): "Der Poet wählet sich einen moralischen Lehrsatz. . . . Hiernächst sucht er in der Historie solche berühmte Leute, denen etwas ähnliches begegnet ist," etc.

17. Scherer, op. cit., p. 246.

18. Norbert Fuerst, *Grillparzer auf der Bühne* (Wien, 1958), p. 98.

19. It is brought in once more at the very end, 2985 (also 2990+).

20. His very first entry is characteristic: "tritt, ganz gerüstet, . . . rasch auf" (384+); cf. also "(all)zu rasch" (1863, 2431).

21. Fuerst, op. cit., pp. 98f.

22. The simple *action* of Rudolf's taking off his cloak and laying it over Ottokar, without the somewhat self-righteous words, would have sufficed, and the play might well have ended with it. The master of dramatic gesture is superseded by the gratified patriot.

23. *Österreichische Reimchronik,* ed. Jos. Seemüller, in *Monumenta Germaniae Historica,* 5. Bandes 1. Teil (Hannover, 1890), p. 124, lines 9375-78.

24. Ibid., p. 176, lines 13341ff. and 13334ff.

25. *Selbstbiog.;* Abt. 1, Bd. 16, p. 166.

26. Oswald Redlich, the eminent historian, in a lecture on *Grillparzers Verhältnis zur Geschichte* (Wien, 1901), pp. 19f., recognized the admirable traits in Grillparzer's hero and his wish to be "ein schöpferischer Reformator" of his country. This conception, Redlich assures us, the poet could not have found in any publication around 1820; "Er hat geschaut, was die Historiker erst nach ihm erforscht haben."

27. Abt. 1, Bd. 3, p. 339.

28. It is perhaps significant of Ottokar's patriotism that the figure then shifts, identifying his Bohemians with a nobler animal, the horse: 480f.

29. Rudolf adds, echoing Goethe's closing counsel in *Ilmenau:* "Gönnt ihnen Ruh, Ihr könnt nichts Beßres geben!" (1929).

30. Scherer, op. cit., p. 243.

31. *Selbstbiog.;* Abt. 1, Bd. 16, pp. 110f. In the *Tagebücher* too there are passages that show Grillparzer one in spirit with the despondent Ottokar.

32. In a conversation of March 1860, Grillparzer confessed that he had been moved to tears as he wrote Ottokar's speech at Margareta's coffin, and censured himself for this loss of *Abstand.* See *Grillparzers Gespräche,* ed. August Sauer (Wien, 1904ff.), 2. Abt., p. 201.

33. Johannes Volkelt, *Franz Grillparzer als Dichter des Tragischen,* 2. Aufl. (München, 1909), p. 198.

34. Kunigunde is equally out of character in her humanitarian reproaches, 2106-2111.

35. The broken Ottokar, aptly enough, not the successful Rudolf, has something in common with the second Rudolf of the *Bruderzwist:* when Ottokar laughs in wordless self-derision or when the stamps on the ground impatiently (2027+, 2028+), he seems to anticipate the later Rudolf; and his frantic fourfold "fort!" (2420-22) is like Rudolf's sevenfold "allein."

36. Frederic E. Coenen, however, in *Grillparzer's Portraiture of Men* (Chapel Hill, 1951), p. 24, recognized some merit in Ottokar and pointed to line 259 as proof that "Margaret had never been his wife in the real sense."

37. Later, Ottokar displays toward his second wife the same aversion to *Berührung* by the other sex that Margareta must have felt toward him: "Ich sag': berühr' mich nicht!" he cries in frantic revulsion (2414). Sensuous touch plays an important part in Grillparzer's works, doubtless reflecting personal experience.

38. Margareta here anticipates Queen Eleonore, for whom marriage is a sanctification of the "Greuel" of sexual relations (*Die Jüdin von Toledo,* 1202-05).

39. Fuerst, op. cit., p. 93.

40. This is additional exculpation for Ottokar (see also 133f.) The protracted negotiations for the divorce began, in history, less than a year after the marriage, as Grillparzer could read in his sources.

41. Auguste Ehrhard, *Franz Grillparzer,* deutsche Ausgabe von Moritz Necker (München, 1902), pp. 319f.

42. Münch, op. cit., p. 53.

43. Strich, op. cit., p. 213.

44. Kunigunde's "punishment," one might fancy, will come in her union with Zawisch, indicated at the end of the play; for he never loved her but merely used her for his revenge, and he would still be second-best to her "Kumanenführer." Another *Mißheirat* is adumbrated.

45. See Joachim Müller, *Franz Grillparzer* (Stuttgart, 1963), p. 42.

46. *Selbstbiog.;* Abt. 1, Bd. 16, p. 166.

47. Friedrich Sengle, *Das deutsche Geschichtsdrama* (Stuttgart, 1952), p. 102, suggests that *Ottokar* could be taken as a "geschichtlich verkleidetes Festspiel" on the victorious ending of the Wars of Liberation.

48. Ronald Peacock, *The Poet in the Theatre* (New York, 1946), p. 61.

49. Ehrhard-Necker, op. cit., pp. 323f.

50. Emil Staiger, *Meisterwerke deutscher Sprache,* 2. Aufl. (Zürich, 1948), pp. 181, 185.

51. Scherer, op. cit., p. 247.

52. Gundolf, op. cit., p. 55.

53. B. v. Wiese, *Die deut. Tragödie,* 2. Aufl., p. 415.

54. E.g., by Staiger, v. Wiese, and Naumann in the works previously cited. Joachim Müller, *Grillparzers Menschenauffassung* (Weimar, 1934), pp. 58ff., sees him from a religious point of view as "der gerettete und begnadete Mensch," made the bearer of a divine mission and thereby saved from the danger of *hubris.*

55. Gundolf, op. cit., p. 54, concludes that the play is wrongly called a tragedy, for the real hero is not the falling Ottokar but the victorious Rudolf, characterized (p. 56) as an "endlicher, ungefährdeter, sturm-und glutloser Walter."

56. See Abt. 1, Bd. 3, p. 346.

57. See Grillparzer's *Spanische Studien,* around 1850; Abt. 1, Bd. 15, p. 179. Grillparzer's reading of Lope de Vega did not begin until after the writing of *Ottokar.*

58. Summer 1859, *Gespräche,* ed. Sauer, 2. Abt., p. 114.

59. "Der wahre dramatische Dichter *sieht* sein Werk darstellen, indem er es *schreibt.*" Abt. 1, Bd. 14, p. 93 (1837).

60. Sengle, op. cit., p. 104.

Egbert Krispyn (essay date March 1964)

SOURCE: "Grillparzer and the Chorus," in *MLQ,,* Vol. 25, No. 1, March, 1964, pp. 46-56.

[*In the following essay, Krispyn traces Grillparzer's views on the function of the chorus in drama as evinced in his critical and dramatic work.*]

Grillparzer's remarks in "Über die Bedeutung des Chors in der alten Tragödie" have received scant attention in critical literature. Symptomatic of the literary historian's attitude toward this essay is Hartel's study on Grillparzer and antiquity, which mentions it only once in passing.[1] The most extensive treatment of "Über die Bedeutung des Chors" is to be found in the dissertation of Fritz Strich, whose comments on the subject were used by August Sauer as the basis for his note in the critical edition of Grillparzer's works.[2]

Strich stresses the lack of originality in Grillparzer's critical views, which closely adhered to those expressed by Joseph Schreyvogel in *Sonntagsblatt.*[3] Strich furthermore establishes a direct connection between the Grillparzer essay, the fifth Viennese lecture of August Wilhelm von Schlegel, and Schiller's "Über den Gebrauch des Chors in der Tragödie" (which forms the preface to *Die Braut von Messina*). All the points made in "Über die Bedeutung des Chors" have their counterparts in one or both of the other treatises. Strich, moreover, accuses Grillparzer of distorting Schiller's views by overlooking the fact that the latter deals with conditions for reintroducing the chorus in modern tragedy.

The dependence of "Über die Bedeutung des Chors" on other treatments of the topic, its none-too-flawless argumentation, and its fragmentary state—the second half exists only in a rough telegram-style draft—explain in part the lack of interest in it. The only commentator who praises it is the classical scholar Otto Crusius, who sees in it evidence of an unusually highly developed insight into the nature of the theater of antiquity.[4] Yet it would appear that Grillparzer's views on the function of the chorus are of some interest from a Germanistic viewpoint as well, if we take into consideration the time at which he formulated them.

August Sauer dates "Über die Bedeutung des Chors" about September, 1817; in other words, he believes that this essay was written approximately eight months after the première of **Die Ahnfrau** (in the Theater an der Wien on January 31, 1817) and about two months after the completion of his next play, **Sappho.** The immediate reason for the choice of subject of this latter tragedy was Dr. Felix Joel's casual suggestion that Grillparzer write a libretto on the Greek poetess for the composer Weigl. Dr. Joel made his suggestion on June 29, 1817; the play was completed on July 25 of that year. Joel's words could have had such an immediately potent effect only because they fell upon the fertile soil of Grillparzer's long standing interest in the subject matter, which he called "ein Stoff, dessen hervorragende Punkte mich schon in der frühesten Zeit angezogen hatten."[5]

The temporal coincidence of Grillparzer's occupation with *Sappho* and his thoughts on the significance of the chorus is no accident. This, his most classical play, and the essay dealing with the first of the "beiden grossen Hebeln der alten Tragödie: dem *Chor* und dem *Fatum*" (p. 12) are, as is to be expected, intimately related. In fact, his ideas on the meaning of the chorus in the ancient tragedy are determined less by a direct study of the dramaturgical issues involved than by his attitude toward his own play. Basing his argument on the material provided by Schreyvogel, Schiller, and Schlegel in their treatises on the subject, Grillparzer interpreted the significance of the chorus in such a manner as to turn the essay into a commentary on the tragedy *Sappho.*

The general character of this play was determined by Grillparzer's rather horrified reaction to the unsophisticated nature of *Die Ahnfrau*'s success and especially to the critics' insistence that it was an exponent of the fashionable genre of the *Schicksalsdrama.*[6] The dramatist himself referred to this in the draft of a letter to Adolf Müllner in 1818 (the première of *Sappho* was on April 21, 1818):

> Ich konnte mir nicht verhehlen, dass dasjenige, was der *Ahnfrau* den meisten Effekt verschaffte, rohe, rein subjektive Ausbrüche, dass es immer mehr die Empfindungen des Dichters als die der handelnden Personen gewesen waren, was die Zuschauer mit in den wirbelnden Tanz gezogen hatte, in dem zuletzt alles sich herumdrehte, und der Ballettmeister, nach weggeworfenem Taktmesser, auch.—Ich schämte mich.—Ich nahm mir vor, mein nächstes Produkt ein Gegenstück dieses tollen Treibens werden zu lassen, und suchte daher, mit absichtlicher Vermeidung Effekt-reicherer [*sic*], seit lange vorbereiteter Stoffe, nach einem solchen, der es mir möglich machte, mich von den handelnden Personen zu trennen und in der Behandlung eine Ruhe walten zu lassen, die mir des Strebens um so würdiger schien, je fremder sie meiner Individualität ist und je mehr ich daher verzweifelte sie zu erreichen.[7]

This passage makes it clear that Grillparzer regretted above all the subjectivity of *Die Ahnfrau,* the fact that this play in many respects embodied his own experiences and emotions. The most notable cases in point are the character of Jaromir, his attempt to improve his situation by marrying Bertha, and the allusions to an incestuous feeling toward his "Mutter," the ancestress. The poet's feeling of exposure as he watched the first performance of *Die Ahnfrau* undoubtedly resulted from this probably unintentional self-revelation and certainly stimulated his retrospective

aesthetic and dramaturgical objections to the subjective character of this play.[8]

Thus during the gestation period of *Sappho,* a play primarily intended to correct his own "shameful" egocentricity in *Die Ahnfrau,* Grillparzer was preoccupied with the idea that the dramatist should disappear behind his creation and that the dramatis personae should lead an autonomous life, entirely divorced from the author's private circumstances.

From Grillparzer's viewpoint, Schlegel's opinion that the chorus represented "die verkörperte und mit in die Darstellung aufgenommene Theilnahme des Dichters" could therefore appear only as an indictment of the chorus and of the commentator who obviously regarded this aspect as a point in its favor.[9] On the other hand, the draft of a letter to Adolf Müllner does indicate that in at least one respect Schiller's concept of the function of the chorus was quite reconcilable with Grillparzer's objectives concerning *Sappho.* His striving to introduce into the treatment of his subject matter a *Ruhe* which was admittedly foreign to his personality must have made him responsive to these words from the preface to the *Braut von Messina:* "So wie der Chor in die Sprache *Leben* bringt, so bringt er *Ruhe* in die Handlung—aber die schöne und hohe Ruhe, die der Charakter eines edeln Kunstwerkes seyn muss."[10]

Another aspect of the chorus which Schiller presented as an advantage was, however, entirely irreconcilable with Grillparzer's general aesthetic outlook. Schiller stressed the reflexive role of the chorus, saying: "Der Chor *reinigt* also das tragische Gedicht, indem er die Reflexion von der Handlung absondert. . . ." And he expanded this point: "Der Chor verlässt den engen Kreis der Handlung, um sich über Vergangenes und Künftiges, über ferne Zeiten und Völker, über das Menschliche überhaupt zu verbreiten, um die grossen Resultate des Lebens zu ziehen und die Lehren der Weisheit auszusprechen" (p. 10). Schlegel, too, subscribed to this view of the chorus, as is evident from his contention that it must be regarded as the "personificierten Gedanken über die dargestellte Handlung" (p. 76).

The very idea of reflexive literature was inimical to Grillparzer, as he demonstrated with unmistakable clarity by his passion for the Spanish dramatist Lope de Vega, who became his favorite author and was an inexhaustible source of inspiration for him. But long before his discovery of this kindred spirit (during the early 1820's), the Austrian had formulated his own views on this subject. As Farinelli points out:

> Das halbhundertjährige Studium Lope's de Vega von Seite Grillparzers war der glänzendste Protest, der je einem Dichter gegen die Reflektionspoesie gelungen ist. Schon 1818 erklärt Grillparzer ausdrücklich: das Theater solle "ein Zufluchtsort von der Erbärmlichkeit des Alltagslebens und nicht ein reflektierender Spiegel desselben sein." Aus der Betrachtung der Natur und aus der Wiedergabe derselben fliesst wahre, gesunde Poesie.[11]

The difference between Grillparzer's point of view and those of Schiller and Schlegel manifests itself in their claim that the chorus serves the purpose of reflection and extends to the related notion that an ideal abstract quality is inherent in the chorus. According to Schiller, "der Chor ist selbst kein Individuum, sondern ein allgemeiner Begriff" (p. 10), "eine ideale Person" (p. 12). In the tragedy, then, the chorus would have to supply the ideal elements, which must alternate with the sensual ones represented by the action, if the latter were not to destroy the poetic essence of the work (p. 9 f.).

At least in principle, Schlegel agreed with this generalization and idealization of the chorus. He believed that the chorus speaks on behalf of the "gesammten Menschheit" (p. 76), and he commented further about it: "Was er auch in dem einzelnen Stücke Besondres sein und thun mochte, so stellte er überhaupt und zuvörderst den nationalen Gemeingeist, dann die allgemeine menschliche Theilnahme vor. Der Chor ist mit einem Worte der idealisierte Zuschauer" (p. 77).

Grillparzer's general inclination toward naturalness in his art implies the rejection of such theories; as Farinelli expresses it: "Das Begriffliche in der Poesie, wir wissen es, war Grillparzer von Herzen zuwider. Das Begriffsmässige ist ein geschworener Feind des Natürlichen" (p. 225). Grillparzer himself expressly excluded the ideal, the unnatural, when he remarked in 1822, "Ein Kunstwerk muss sein wie die Natur, deren verklärtes Abbild es ist."[12]

Grillparzer was faced with a dilemma. Both Schiller and Schlegel believed that the ideal character of the chorus was its principal feature, the one which really established its *raison d'être* in the tragedy of antiquity and, at least according to the author of the *Malteser* fragment and the *Braut von Messina,* justified its reintroduction into modern drama. If Grillparzer accepted the opinion of these authorities, he would be accepting concepts which from his point of view amounted to an absolute condemnation of the chorus as being entirely incompatible with his idea of the drama. He was not prepared to accept this consequence partly, no doubt, out of respect for ancient tragedy, but principally because his own critical appraisal of *Sappho* had convinced him that the chorus did perform a highly useful function in classical drama.

Grillparzer thus had to refute the central argument in the treatises of Schiller and Schlegel, and to this end he composed his essay "Über die Bedeutung des Chors," leaning heavily on Schreyvogel for his arguments. Taking up Schlegel's terminology, he wrote about the chorus:

> Ob er der idealisierte Zuschauer war? Was heisst das? Er war *der* idealisierte Zuschauer, oder er war *ein* idealisierter Zuschauer? Beides ist falsch. Ersteres, denn der Chor betrachtete nie die Handlung mit den Augen des unbefangenen Zuschauers im Theater, er hatte ferner neben seinem allgemeinen noch immer einen besondern Charakter, je nachdem er aus Greisen, aus Weibern, aus Gefangenen bestand! Aber er war über-

> haupt gar kein Zuschauer durch seine Mitverflochtenheit in der Handlung.
>
> (p. 14)

He continued by quoting examples from classical drama to support his view, repeating the arguments he had already marshaled against Schlegel's conception of the chorus as an idealized observer in a diary note made sometime between April 30, 1816, and April 22, 1817.[13]

His preoccupation with this particular issue is also noticeable in his rejoinder to the argument that the chorus reduced the excessive emotional impact of tragedy on the audience to bearable proportions by "predigesting" the action. Schiller declared:

> das Gemüth des Zuschauers soll auch in der heftigsten Passion seine Freiheit behalten, es soll kein Raub der Eindrücke seyn, sondern sich immer klar und heiter von den Rührungen scheiden, die es erleidet. Was das gemeine Urtheil an dem Chor zu tadeln pflegt, dass er die Täuschung aufhebe, dass er die Gewalt der Affekte breche, das gereicht ihm zu seiner höchsten Empfehlung, denn eben diese blinde Gewalt der Affekte ist es, die der wahre Künstler vermeidet, diese Täuschung ist es, die er zu erregen verschmäht.
>
> (p. 11)

Basically, this aspect of the chorus agrees with Grillparzer's objectives in *Sappho,* which, in contrast to his purpose in *Die Ahnfrau,* were to dispense with crass effects and to avoid drawing the audience into a "wirbelnden Tanz." On the other hand, he detected in this approach a trend toward idealization of the chorus—as well he might, considering Schlegel's comment on this matter, which linked it directly with the conception of the chorus as the idealized observer:

> Der Chor ist mit einem Worte der idealisierte Zuschauer. Er lindert den Eindruck einer tief erschütternden oder tief rührenden Darstellung, indem er dem wirklichen Zuschauer seine eignen Regungen schon lyrisch, also musikalisch ausgedrückt entgegenbringt, und ihn in die Region der Betrachtung hinaufführt.
>
> (p. 77)

Moreover, Grillparzer obviously connected this idea with a remark which Schiller made in a somewhat different context, namely, that the chorus should be "eine lebendige Mauer," which "die Tragödie um sich herumzieht, um sich von der wirklichen Welt rein abzuschliessen, und sich ihren idealen Boden, ihre poetische Freiheit zu bewahren" (p. 7). Paraphrasing this metaphor, Grillparzer asserted his basic premise concerning the chorus in the following observation: "Ob er eine Scheidemauer gegen die Wirklichkeit war? Ich sehe keinen Grund warum der Begriff des Chores auch den Begriff des Ideales involvieren soll. Denn das will man doch sagen, wenn man von einer Scheidemauer gegen die Wirklichkeit redet" (p. 14).

Fritz Strich does Grillparzer an injustice when he singles out this section of "Über die Bedeutung des Chors" for criticism (p. 224). It is true that the remark by Schiller on which Grillparzer based the wording of his comment did refer specifically to the use of the chorus in modern literature, but this does not invalidate Grillparzer's objection. Not only did both Schiller and Schlegel apply the basic notion that the chorus "die Gewalt der Affekte breche" to its use in ancient tragedy as well as to its introduction in contemporary drama, but Grillparzer himself was fundamentally concerned with the role of the lyric element in modern tragedy, namely, in his own *Sappho*! Seen in its proper context, Grillparzer's denial of any direct relationship between chorus and ideality is quite relevant.

Apart from the alleged ideality of the chorus and its related function as a "shock-absorber," Grillparzer was also concerned with another point raised by the earlier commentators. Schiller and Schlegel had made conflicting statements on the public element which the chorus introduces into the proceedings on the stage. Schiller stated that this aspect of the chorus forced the poet to adapt his subject matter to the naïve pattern of life of primitive times, when community affairs were dealt with publicly: "Die Handlungen und Schicksale der Helden und Könige sind schon an sich selbst öffentlich, und waren es in der einfachen Urzeit noch mehr" (p. 8). Schlegel revealed a different historical view, claiming that the monarchic era, from which the heroic themes of ancient tragedy are derived, was marked by an absence of "Öffentlichkeit." In his opinion, the public element inherent in the chorus was inappropriate to the heroic content of the work on which it was superimposed as an act of poetic license by the dramatists who lived in a later republican period, characterized by a public way of life (p. 76 f.).

It is indicative of Grillparzer's general lack of interest in such academic questions and, even more, of his predominantly personal motives for occupying himself with the chorus at this particular time that he did not enter into a discussion of the opposing views advanced by his predecessors. Instead, he noted their common opinion that the chorus does tend to introduce a "Charakter der Öffentlichkeit" into the "Dramen der Alten" and limited himself to expressing his completely personal dramaturgic dislike of this effect: "Ich meines Teiles würde eine Anstalt nicht lieben, die mich zwänge alle Empfindungen und Situazionen die nicht den Charakter der Öffentlichkeit vertragen, aufzugeben" (p. 14).

Grillparzer's indifference to, or even distaste for, abstract theorizing (which is indirectly expressed in his attitude toward the public aspect of the chorus) manifests itself directly and forcefully in the introductory paragraphs of "Über die Bedeutung des Chors," where, with obvious irritation at a certain type of research, he says:

> Wenn wir in unseren Tagen so häufig den Zufall das Ruder führen, beabsichtigte Zwecke vereitelt, und absichtslos angefangenes zum glücklichsten Ende kommen sehen, wenn die Besten unter uns so häufig das Gewohnte tun eben nur weil es gewohnt ist: so soll

> dafür bei den Alten alles Zweck, alles Absicht, alles Plan gewesen sein, ohne dass sie den Zoll der Menschlichkeit auch nur ein einziges Mal entrichtet hätten.

> (p. 11)

These words also reveal the fact that Grillparzer's essay was to a large extent directed against Schlegel, whose equivocation he attacked in similar terms in a diary note of a slightly earlier date: "Überhaupt ist mir Schlegels Sucht, überall tiefen Grund und strenge Zweckmässigkeit zu sehen, wo doch nichts als Zufall waltet, unausstehlich."[14]

If Grillparzer directed his criticism of Schiller's and Schlegel's interpretations of the chorus predominantly against the latter, this was probably due to his deep respect for the creative artist Schiller. Moreover, Schiller's theories (in contrast to those of Schlegel) were at least in some points compatible with his own ideas. This does not alter the fact, however, that he was always fundamentally skeptical of the value of all theoretical speculation on the subject of art, as the following epigram of September, 1869, confirms:

> Die Ästhetik vor allem verpön ich
> Sie spielt ein gefährliches Spiel:
> Die gute nützt sehr wenig,
> Die schlechte schadet sehr viel.[15]

Considering this basic attitude, it is obvious that Grillparzer must have had a specific and personal reason for formulating his own ideas on the chorus. A desire to contradict Schlegel and, to a lesser extent, Schiller, in itself certainly is not sufficient to explain his departure from his antitheoretical principles in writing the essay "Über die Bedeutung des Chors."

But the negative, polemical elements of this treatise serve only as a means of arriving at the one positive characteristic which Grillparzer was prepared to concede to the chorus. The most significant conclusion to be drawn in this matter he offered in almost grudging tones in the final sentence: "Ein wahrer Vorteil des Chors ist aber vielleicht die strenge Scheidung des dramatischen und lyrischen Elements der tragischen Poesie, welche leider bei den Neuern verwischt sind, bei den Alten aber eben durch den Chor sich gesondert zeigen" (p. 14 f.).

Again, Fritz Strich seems to underestimate Grillparzer's intellectual independence when he claims that this idea is obviously taken from Schiller's exposition.[16] The allusion is apparently to the latter's statement that in the tragic poem the chorus "die Reflexion von der Handlung absondert, und eben durch diese Absonderung sie selbst mit poetischer Kraft ausrüstet" (p. 10). That Grillparzer could not have had in mind the same idea as Schiller becomes clear when one considers how vehemently he rejected all reflexive elements in the drama.

Schiller's wording is somewhat ambiguous; grammatically, it could be either the "Reflexion" or the "Handlung" which derives poetic force from the chorus. Both possibilities are consistent with his views: on the one hand, the reflexive chorus is described as a "lyrisches Prachtgewebe" (p. 9); on the other hand, "legt die lyrische Sprache des Chors dem Dichter auf, verhältnissmässig die ganze Sprache des Gedichts zu erheben" (p. 10). In either case, however, Schiller was primarily concerned with the formal aspects of the language in which tragedy is couched. In "Über den Gebrauch des Chors in der Tragödie," the meaning which he attached to the terms concerned is revealed in the following passage from the treatise in which he relates poetic and lyrical qualities to metric speech: "Durch Einführung einer *metrischen Sprache* ist man indess der *poetischen* Tragödie schon um einen grossen Schritt näher gekommen. Es sind einige *lyrische* Versuche auf der Schaubühne glücklich durchgegangen" (p. 7; my italics).

Grillparzer's terminology refers to entirely different aspects of the drama, as may be concluded from his remark concerning *Sappho* that the dramatic element "im Gegensatz der Lyra darin besteht, dass die Gesinnung nur als Substrat der Handlung erscheinen darf."[17] Since, in the letter-draft referred to earlier, he had condemned the intrusion of the dramatist's own feelings into a play, it is clear that the "Gesinnung," which, according to him, should merely provide the substratum of dramatic action and could be expressed directly only in lyrical form, was the "Gesinnung" of the autonomous dramatis personae.

In light of these considerations, it can be concluded that Grillparzer saw in the chorus the means by which the ancient dramatists enabled their characters to speak their own inner thoughts without impeding the action of the tragedy. He was too much a realist and a practical man of the theater, however, to consider reviving the ancient chorus, and he regretfully resigned himself to the fact that the modern playwright lacks such a means of separating the two elements, which consequently merge—generally to the detriment of the drama.

Grillparzer's customary highly self-critical attitude manifests itself in this perception since the modern author he had in mind as exemplifying this regrettable fusion of the incompatible lyrical and dramatic components was himself, the author of *Sappho*. "Über die Bedeutung des Chors" is, in effect, an analysis of certain flaws in the first act of that play which, as the dramatist had to admit, had "nur wenig eigentlich dramatisches Leben."[18] He realized that this shortcoming was due to the inclusion of lyrical scenes which violated the rule that the "Gesinnung" of the characters may manifest itself only through the action:

> Die vorletzte Szene des 1ten Akts ist villeicht die müssigste von allen. Ich wollte jedoch hier, nachdem sich Phaon in der vorigen Szene ausgesprochen, auch Sappho's Erwartungen und Besorgnisse über ihr Verhältniss laut werden lassen, und durch die Art, auf welche Sappho, obgleich poetisirend, ihre Stellung gegen Phaon mit Bangigkeit betrachtet, auf den folgenden Ausbruch vorbereiten. . . . Der Schlussmonolog des ersten Aktes könnte leicht mehr dramatisches Leben

haben, aber ich konnte der Versuchung nicht widerstehen, die zweite der beiden übriggebliebenen Oden Sapphos, die mir zu passen schienen, in dem Stücke, das ihren Namen führt aufzunehmen, damit man mir doch nicht sagen könnte, es sey *gar nichts* von ihrem Geiste darin.[19]

Having written *Sappho* with the express intention of avoiding the error of subjectivism which had marred ***Die Ahnfrau,*** he had been unable to resist the temptation to violate the essence of drama by introducing some lyrical passages. Surely his susceptibility to the lure of such undramatic lyricisms may be ascribed to "heredity"; no genuine Viennese theater-man has ever been able to withstand Erato's seductive charms. That Grillparzer succumbed to them in what was to be his most classical play only confirms that blood is thicker than water, and Parnassus not far from Leopoldstadt.

But having fallen, his artistic conscience troubled him and led him to a preoccupation with the issues later reflected in his essay "Über die Bedeutung des Chors." He arrived at the conclusion that modern tragedy's lack of a chorus, which could have represented the lyric aspects apart from the dramatic substance, was ultimately responsible for the merging of the two elements in *Sappho.*

Grillparzer's finding seems to be valid, but his concern over the matter is somewhat exaggerated. The fusion of the lyric and the dramatic in *Sappho* is not as serious a flaw as Grillparzer, with characteristic self-reproach, assumed. On the contrary, this very feature lends the tragedy its unique character and peculiar appeal. In this issue, one can only side against Grillparzer with Norbert Fürst, who ascribes "theatralische Vollkommenheit" to the play and declares: "Das Wirkungsvollste . . . war die Musik *zwischen* den Zeilen, wie sie treffend ein populärer Musiker der Zeit, Konradin Kreutzer, nach der ersten Aufführung in München andeutete: 'Ich fand das Ganze äusserst harmonisch und musikalisch . . . manchmal glaubte ich, ich müsste Musik-Begleitung—ja selbst Chöre hören!'"[20]

Notes

1. W. Hartel, "Grillparzer und die Antike," *Jahrbuch der Grillparzer-Gesellschaft,* XVII, (1907), 165-89.

2. Fritz Strich, *Franz Grillparzers Ästhetik* (Berlin, 1905), pp. 222 ff. For Grillparzer's works I have used *Sämtliche Werke,* ed. August Sauer, continued by Reinhold Backmann (Vienna, 1909 ff.); "Über die Bedeutung des Chors" appears in Abteilung I, Band 14, pp. 11 ff., and the notes on pp. 232 ff. of the same volume. Subsequent references to "Über die Bedeutung des Chors" will be cited by page number only.

3. Thomas and Karl August West (pseud. J. Schreyvogel), *Gesammelte Schriften* (Braunschweig, 1829), Abt. II, Bd. 2, p. 144.

4. O. Crusius, "Grillparzer und die antike Bühne," *Philologus,* LXIX (1910), 160.

5. Grillparzer, *Sämtliche Werke,* Abt. III, Bd. 1, p. 102.

6. For a discussion and survey of the problems concerning *Die Ahnfrau,* see my article, "Grillparzer and His *Ahnfrau,*" *Germanic Review,* XXXVIII (1963), 209 ff.

7. Grillparzer, *Sämtliche Werke,* Abt. III, Bd. 1, p. 102.

8. See "Grillparzer and His *Ahnfrau.*"

9. August Wilhelm von Schlegel, *Vorlesungen über dramatische Kunst und Litteratur,* ed. Eduard Böcking, 3rd ed. (Leipzig, 1846), Part I, 5th lecture, p. 76. Subsequent references to this volume will be cited by page number only.

10. *Schillers sämmtliche Schriften,* ed. Karl Goedeke *et al.* (Stuttgart, 1872), Bd. 14, p. 11. Subsequent references to this volume will be cited by page number only.

11. Arturo Farinelli, *Grillparzer und Lope de Vega* (Berlin, 1894), p. 222.

12. Quoted by Strich, p. 77.

13. Grillparzer, *Sämtliche Werke,* Abt. II, Bd. 7, p. 88.

14. Grillparzer, *Sämtliche Werke,* Abt. II, Bd. 7, p. 88, diary entry 199.

15. *Ibid.,* Abt. I, Bd. 12, Pt. 1, p. 351.

16. Strich, p. 224. This particular instance demonstrates the validity of what Emil Reich, who does not deal with Grillparzer's chorus-essay, writes about the general relation between the aesthetic theories of the poet and those of Schreyvogel: "Wir werden noch öfter Gelegenheit haben . . . Ähnlichkeiten festzustellen, andererseits aber auch auf Meinungsverschiedenheiten hinzuweisen, die allein schon vor dem Irrthum bewahren können, Grillparzers Kunstansichten von denen Schreyvogels allzu abhängig zu glauben, was gänzlich unrichtig wäre." *Grillparzers Kunstphilosophie* (Vienna, 1890), p. 8 n.

17. Grillparzer, *Sämtliche Werke,* Abt. III, Bd. 1, p. 98.

18. *Ibid.,* p. 98.

19. *Ibid.,* p. 100 f.

20. Norbert Fürst, *Grillparzer auf der Bühne* (Vienna, Munich, 1958), p. 39.

Gerard M. Sweeney (essay date March 1970)

SOURCE: "The *Medea* Howells Saw," in *American Literature,* Vol. 42, No. 1, March, 1970, pp. 83-9.

[*In the following essay, Sweeney differentiates Grillparzer's* Medea *from Euripedes' version and contends that Grillparzer's play was the one that influenced W. D. Howells'* A Modern Instance.]

The connection between *A Modern Instance* and *Medea* has long been an accepted fact. Regarding the genesis of the novel, we are told by William M. Gibson that when Howells "witnessed Francesca Janauschek's fiery recreation on the stage of Medea's love for the self-centered Jason as it turned into hatred and engendered terrible acts of revenge, he said to himself, as he told an interviewer many years later, 'This is an Indiana divorce case . . . and the novel was born.'"[1] We know, furthermore, that Howells first referred to the novel as "that *New Medea.*"[2]

The issue at hand is the authorship of the *Medea* Howells saw. Critics who refer to *Medea* in connection with *A Modern Instance* invariably assume that the play was Euripides' classical drama.[3] But the *Medea* in which Francesca Janauschek starred throughout her career was not the classical Greek tragedy; rather she starred in a romantic German melodrama—part of a trilogy entitled **The Golden Fleece**—written by the Austrian playwright Franz Grillparzer and first staged in Vienna in 1822. In his study of *Franz Grillparzer in England and America,* Arthur Burkhard writes that Grillparzer's *Medea* "was most frequently presented by Mlle. Fanny Janauschek in almost all the major American cities after her debut in this role at the Academy of Music in New York, 9 October 1867."[4] Writing further about Mlle. Janauschek, Burkhard states that she was "distinguished as an actress, colorful as a character, and foremost in most frequently presenting Grillparzer's *Medea* in America."[5] Thus the *Medea* Howells saw Mlle. Janauschek perform in Boston in 1875 was Franz Grillparzer's. And an examination of Grillparzer's alterations of Euripides will reveal that the German play is much closer, in both character delineation and theme, to *A Modern Instance* and that it is easier to envision the novel's springing from the melodrama than from the Euripidean tragedy.

The differences between the two *Medeas* reflect to some extent the differences between romanticism and Greek classicism. Grillparzer adheres to no unity of action or place. The double action of his drama—the divorce and the revenge are separate actions—takes place before the walls of Corinth and then in an apartment and a courtyard of Creon's palace in Corinth. Grillparzer also makes use of several melodramatic theatrical effects: a casket that opens magically, a chalice that bursts forth in flames, and a simulated fire on stage as Creon's palace burns. In the cast of his play, Grillparzer quite naturally displays a technical modernity not present in Euripides. He removes from the plot Aegeus, King of Athens, who in Euripides' drama promises Medea a safe refuge in Athens and whose presence in the play was criticized by Aristotle and other critics as being abrupt and unmotivated. And he removes both the chorus of Corinthian women and the tutor, who serves the earlier drama by foreshadowing the destruction of the children. Grillparzer keeps the other characters, and he adds Creon's daughter, Creusa, who is only spoken of in Euripides.

The differences in incident between the two plays center on the fact that, whereas Euripides' drama opens with the divorce of Jason and Medea, Grillparzer's play is half finished before the divorce is an accomplished fact. Grillparzer's first two acts, therefore, are largely his own invention of the events leading up to the divorce.

As the German *Medea* opens, Medea is seen on the beach, before the walls of Corinth, burying a casket containing sorcerer's devices and the golden fleece. She thus symbolically buries or puts aside her barbaric past before entering Corinth and civilization. She and Jason are still married: they are both outsiders, suppliants begging entrance to the city. And although there is some evidence of friction and malcontent—this largely on Jason's part—the events of Act I do not make an actual separation appear inevitable. As the act closes, Jason, a former resident of Corinth, begs Creon to admit both himself and Medea to the city:

> You must receive us both or neither, my lord!
> My life would be renewed were she away,
> But I must protect what confides itself to me—
>
> (I,vi)[6]

Creon reluctantly agrees to admit them both.

Act II opens inside Creon's palace. Medea, dressed in Grecian garb, is attempting to learn to play the lyre under the tutelage of Creusa, the daughter of Creon and the childhood sweetheart of Jason. But Medea's efforts to learn the arts of civilization as symbolized by the lyre are naturally doomed to failure. Thus in frustration she exclaims to Creusa:

> My hand is only used to handling the
> Javelin, and to doing rough work.
> I fear I shall never learn those
> Things the women of your country do.
>
> (II, i)

Shortly afterward Jason enters and completely ignores Medea as he discusses childhood memories with Creusa. Medea jealously tries to attract his attention by offering to sing a song while accompanying herself on the lyre. She fails completely and smashes the instrument in her anger. Hereupon a herald from Delphi enters and orders both Jason and Medea to leave the city. Creon arrives and countermands half the order: Medea must depart as directed, but Jason will be permitted to remain in Corinth and marry Creusa. Jason offers no opposition to this plan.

From this point Grillparzer's drama approximately parallels Euripides': it deals with the revenge of Medea. However, there are two exceptions. The first of these is a melodramatic scene in Act III wherein Medea unsuccessfully pleads and rages with her children, begging one of them—either one—to accompany her in exile. Both children refuse, however, having become attached to the kindly and civilized Creusa. The second exception lies in the conclusion of the drama. Medea sends to Creusa not a poison cloak, but rather a flaming chalice which kills the princess and ignites the palace. Creon, however, does not die as he does in Euripides' drama. Rather he survives to lament his daughter's death.

The effect of Grillparzer's alterations in general lowers the intensity of both Jason and Medea. His Jason is not so evil or even so foolish as is Euripides'. He does not choose to leave Medea, but he permits the workings of fate to ordain the same result. He at first refuses to leave his wife, even at the price of banishment from civilization; but once established in society, he permits her to be expelled. Jason properly urges the king to permit Medea to retain one of the children; but once the children shun Medea, he steps out of the situation. Thus at whatever point the action of Grillparzer's Jason parallels that of Euripides', it is not because Jason effects the action—as is largely the case in Euripides—but rather because he permits it to happen.

The character of Grillparzer's Medea is similarly pitched at a lower key. She does make an attempt to practice the ways of civilization. And the crimes of her past are reported as less monstrous than they are in Euripides. Unlike her Euripidean counterpart, Grillparzer's Medea did not dismember her brother and throw the pieces from the Argo in order to delay her pursuing father. And although she probably did cause the death of Pelias—she claims he burst a blood vessel when she stole the golden fleece from him—she did not persuade his daughters to boil him in an allegedly youth-giving concoction. Even in her jealousy and hatred Grillparzer's title character does not appear as a dynamic natural force as does Euripides' Medea, the grandfather of whom was the sun god. In fact the quarrels of Jason and Medea seem at times quite petty. One can see this in the strife that arises from Medea's feelings of being ignored by Jason during his reminiscences with Creusa in the palace.

The result of Grillparzer's alterations is that his drama is less universal and more domestic. In Euripides, Jason stupidly fails to comprehend the power that is embodied in his wife. He unleashes this energy or force, and as a result of his mistake a king and a princess are destroyed and an entire civilization disrupted. In Grillparzer, a husband infuriates his wife—who happens to be a sorceress—and the result is that the man's children and fiancée are murdered. His world is destroyed, but the entire civilization is not.

The significance of the foregoing lies in the use Howells made of his source. Like Grillparzer, Howells exercised much freedom in transforming his *New Medea* from the older version. And he employed other sources as well: Bret Harte, to cite one example. Nevertheless, **Medea** is the foundation of the novel, and of the two *Medeas* it is far easier to envision Grillparzer's version as the source of inspiration. On a level of categories, *A Modern Instance* is, like the German **Medea,** melodramatic and not tragic. Its action is realistic and social; it does not pretend to be heroic or universally significant. And what might be called the devices of the plot—those important incidents which are caused by fate and not by the characters—are similarly melodramatic. Bartley's losing the money and the notice of the divorce reaching Ben Halleck are both more akin to the sensationalism of melodrama than to the purity of classical tragedy.

More specifically, Grillparzer's drama shows greater resemblance in both plot and character to *A Modern Instance*. In Euripides' drama, the divorce is an accomplished fact. The plot deals with the title character and the revenge which has been foreshadowed from the beginning. In Grillparzer's play, as in Howells's novel, we see the married hatred and the divorce in progress, as well as the revenge.[7] And this points to another parallel between the two works: the sense of inevitability is the same in both. In Euripides' drama, what is inevitable is that Medea will avenge herself and that the vengeance will take the form of infanticide.[8] In Grillparzer and Howells, however, what is inevitable is that the couples will live in hatred or they will separate. The separations or divorces are not inevitable. Nor are they, strictly speaking, willed by the characters. Rather the divorces are, in both the novel and the play, the effects of fate, operating as some external influence or event. In this light both Bartley Hubbard and the German Jason—in contrast to Euripides' Jason—are more passively than actively evil. Grillparzer's Jason will not desert his wife. But once he is granted citizenship and she is expelled, he will allow her to be banished without him. So too, as Bartley heads westward after his final quarrel with Marcia, he plans to "return after so many months, weeks, days."[9] But his money is stolen, and he finds that he must yield to the fate that is dictated by such a chance event.

Regarding the Medea-Marcia Hubbard parallel, it is precisely because Grillparzer's Medea is set at a lower key that she more precisely resembles Howells's character. While Euripides' Medea is largely an abstraction of the energy of passion and jealousy, Grillparzer's heroine, like Marcia, is more human and in fact commonplace. She is seen trying to repair the marriage that is breaking up. In her attempt to learn the ways of civilization and to keep her husband, she places herself under the tutelage of Creusa, thus resembling Marcia, who comes to Mrs. Halleck for advice. And much akin to Marcia, Grillparzer's Medea is guilt-ridden about having run off with Jason against her father's wishes. We are told that instead of a blessing on her marriage Medea's father pronounced a curse. And late in the play, as she meditates on her past mistakes, Medea feels that she has betrayed her father and that she will be justly punished for this by being "forsaken, avoided / Like a beast of prey, forsaken / By those for whom I forsook . . . [my father]" (IV,v).

A final point of comparison between *A Modern Instance* and Grillparzer's *Medea* is in the theme of civilization and the lack of it. In Euripides' drama, Medea's barbarity is a keystone of the plot—it gives Creon a reason to banish her—but it is not a central thematic issue. Medea is a foreigner in Corinth, but she is also a princess in her own right. And at the end of the play, although she is forced to leave the city, she is not excluded from civilization: she is on her way to accept sanctuary in Athens. In *A Modern Instance,* the issue of civilization is central to Atherton's—and apparently Howells's—comments on Bartley, Marcia, and Ben Halleck. And in Grillparzer's *Medea,* social mores

are similarly central to Medea's attempts to save her marriage by donning the garb and learning the arts of civilization. So too, civilization is crucial for Grillparzer's Jason. It is significant that Medea's murder of his fiancée frustrates Jason's primary goal, his self-centered desire to become a secure citizen of Corinth. Thus the exile that implicitly awaits him stands equated with Medea's murder of Creusa and the children as the poetically just punishments of Jason. Both are equally important. In a similar way, Bartley Hubbard's cleverness and selfishness cause both his "banishment" from the civilized publishing world of Boston and the retaliation of Marcia.[10]

Notes

1. "Introduction," *A Modern Instance* (Boston, 1957), p. v.

2. See letter from Howells to Charles Eliot Norton (Sept. 24, 1876) in *Life in Letters,* ed. Mildred Howells (Garden City, N. Y., 1928), I, 227.

3. E. H. Cady, *The Road to Realism* (Syracuse, N.Y., 1956), p. 207; Kermit Vanderbilt, "Marcia Gaylord's Electra Complex: A Footnote to Sex in Howells," *American Literature,* XXXIV (Nov., 1962), 374, n. 12; Henry Nash Smith and William M. Gibson, eds., *Mark Twain-Howells Letters* (Cambridge, Mass., 1960), I, 362 n. 2.

4. Vienna, 1961, p. 22.

5. Burkhard, p. 22.

6. All quotations from Grillparzer's *Medea* are from the translation made especially for Mlle. Janauschek's performances and printed in a bilingual booklet, the title of which is: *Medea, A Tragedy in Four Acts by Grillparzer, as performed by Mlle. Fanny Janauschek and her company of German artists* . . . (New York, n.d., no name of translator). According to Arthur Burkhard, this version "has every fault a translation can have. The language is commonplace and prosaic; on occasion, vulgar and even illiterate. The German text has numerous misprints; the English rendering is inaccurate and, not infrequently, incorrect" (*Franz Grillparzer,* p. 46).

7. In fact, love and marriage are the topic of a conversation between Grillparzer's Jason and Creusa. What the young and innocent girl has witnessed in the relationship of Jason and Medea causes her to ask in disillusionment, "Who says that the married love each other?" (II,iii).

8. See Eilhard Schlesinger, "On Euripides' *Medea,*" in *Euripides: A Collection of Critical Essays,* ed. Erich Segal (Englewood Cliffs, N.J., 1968), pp. 70-74.

9. *A Modern Instance* (Boston, 1957), p. 277.

10. For his advice and assistance in the preparation of this essay, I wish to thank Mr. Herbert F. Smith of the University of Wisconsin.

R. K. Angress (essay date April 1971)

SOURCE: "*Weh dem, der lügt*: Grillparzer and the Avoidance of Tragedy," in *Modern Language Review,* Vol. 66, No. 2, April, 1971, pp. 355-64.

[*In the following essay, Angress compares* Weh dem, der lügt *to* Ein treuer Diener seines Herrn *and* Das goldene Vließ *in order to "shed new light on the theme, structure and aesthetic intention of* Weh dem, der lügt.*"*]

Grillparzer's comedy has gone through a variety of vicissitudes since its disastrous first performance in 1838, which notoriously caused its author never to write for the stage again. Perhaps no less notoriously, it was later labelled one of 'the three great German comedies', and as such became subject to largely unfavourable comparisons with *Minna von Barnhelm* and *Der zerbrochene Krug.* Because of its clear and graceful structure and the apparent harmlessness of its content, it became a favourite text in German high schools, even more so in Austrian high schools, a fact that did not improve its standing with an adult public. Recent criticism, notably Fritz Martini's valuable article,[1] has shown some of the subtleties in the handling of the truth-falsehood theme, as expressed in the differentiated use of language. Nevertheless, many sensitive readers, including admirers of Grillparzer's other works, find in his comedy an unsettling quality of make-believe, as if the author were patronizing the audience. The moral seems too didactically stated—whether it be the moral of absolute truth or the moral of the need for compromise—and the characters drawn in too heavy-handed a way. It is felt that the subject is childish yet attempts to be classical, that the situation belongs to a nursery tale, not to high comedy.

Yet within the German tradition, the subject matter of *Weh dem, der lügt* is classical enough. It is the subject matter of *Iphigenie auf Tauris.* A post-Goethean play that deals with reconciliation through truthfulness and compromise, achieved by trusting the gods or God and acted out among a group of civilized and a group of primitive men, is clearly a play written in the wake of Goethe's *Iphigenie.*[2] And *Iphigenie* has fallen on evil days in recent times, because it seems too blatantly optimistic.[3] The same cause may underlie the distaste of many readers for Grillparzer's comedy.

An optimistic outlook in a Grillparzer play of the 1830s is indeed something to give pause to anyone familiar with the poet's work. In his tragedies he had amply demonstrated his insight into the power and the intricacies of the destructive instincts in man. And at least two of these tragedies show certain marked parallels to the comedy. The following pages are an attempt to shed new light on the theme, structure and aesthetic intention of *Weh dem, der lügt,* largely through a comparison of this play with *Ein treuer Diener seines Herrn* on the one hand and the Medea trilogy, *Das goldene Vließ,* on the other.

The first comparison, involving *Ein treuer Diener seines Herrn,* should serve to bring into focus the crucial importance of the theme of service in *Weh dem, der lügt.*

In both plays a subject (Bancban and Leon) recognizes the rightful authority vested in his master (King Andreas and Bishop Gregor) and consequently serves him with a loyalty that transcends mere duty, involves his whole being and operates quite independently of the master's ability to enforce his power. In both instances the servant is put to the test by being required to perform a task in the master's absence. In *Ein treuer Diener* it is the master who absents himself, in *Weh dem, der lügt* the servant has to leave, but in either case the service is performed while the master is not present to enforce obedience. In both plays the master's power of attraction lies in the fact that he embodies—or radiates—divine peace:

> Bancban.   Hier wohnt der Frieden; ich bin nur sein Mietsmann, Sein Lehensmann, sein Gast.
>
>   (20f.)
>
> Leon.   In diesem Haus dacht ich, wär Gottesfrieden, Sonst alle Welt im Krieg.
>
>   (55f.)

Both passages occur quite early in the two plays, and even the metaphor, that of the house of peace, is identical.

Both plays are *Bewährungsstücke.*[4] The task which King Andreas sets for Bancban is to preserve the peace, the task which Bishop Gregor sets for Leon is to preserve the truth while engaged in action. Both involve absolutes, and in both instances the servant is asked to do more than he can, given his personal limitations and the wretched condition of the world in which he is to carry out the task. In both cases the servant does his best, with a maximum of good will. In the last act of both plays, servant and master confront one another again, the former to give an account of the completed mission. Here are the words that are exchanged; first, the master's reproach in both instances:

> König.   Bancban, Bancban! du ungetreuer Knecht! Wie hast du deines Herren Haus verwaltet?
>
>   (1976f.)
>
> Bischof.   Nu, hübsch gelogen? Brav dich was vermessen? Mit Lug und Trug verkehrt? Ei ja, ich weiß.
>
>   (1718f.)

Now the servant's reply:

> Bancban.   Herr, gut und schlimm, wies eben möglich war!
>
>   (1978)
>
> Leon.   Nu, gar so rein gings freilich denn nicht ab. Wir haben uns gehütet wie wir konnten.
>
>   (1720f.)

The meaning of these words is essentially the same, only the tone differs to fit a tragic and a comic context respectively. The master is dissatisfied but has to accept the servant's defence, which in both cases runs to the effect that the work was done as well as circumstances permitted. The bishop's humourous recognition of human imperfection is, of course, of a different quality from King Andreas' sorrowful resignation in facing a catastrophe, but the basic attitude is nevertheless the same: the absolute ideal is relinquished when those who represent it are confronted by conditions that are chaotic in one case, confused and confusing in the other. Moreover, in *Ein treuer Diener* the failure is not complete, for, although the peace has been broken and the queen is dead, the heir has been saved and there is hope for the future of the kingdom; while in *Weh dem, der lügt* the success is not complete, for though the curtain drops on a happy couple, the principle of truthfulness has been violated and Edrita's father Kattwald turns back disgruntled and deceived.

The point of these comparisons is that *Weh dem, der lügt* deals not merely with the school problem of how one may lie and yet tell the truth, nor even with the larger problem of how one may need to compromise with half-truths. In the comedy, as in his tragedy *Ein treuer Diener,* Grillparzer shows the forces of violence and irrationality pitted against those of peace and reason. And he concerns himself, as he does in the tragedy, with the nature of freedom and service.[5] Unlike Bancban, who is an old and tested retainer of the king at the beginning of the play in which he appears, Leon seems to be hardly more than a rebellious child at the beginning of his. In course of time, or rather in the course of five acts, he becomes a man, but his development proceeds in such a way that it can always be measured in terms of his relationship to his superiors, i.e. his position as a servant to the bishop and as a slave to Kattwald. He has two masters, one spiritual, one physical. Yet his bondage illuminates his freedom: more than any other character Leon gives the impression of undaunted courage, as he asserts his physical liberty through a sort of footloose independence and his mental freedom through the constant exercise of his critical faculties. Paradoxically, Leon's progress throughout the play consists in his gradual abandoning of these external attributes of freedom and the gradual and voluntary acceptance of bonds, so that ultimately his ability to choose his service and his master constitute both the limit and the triumph of his freedom.

Self-reliance, so often extolled in Protestant literature of the nineteenth century as a virtue, appears here in the comedy of an Austrian Catholic as a thing of dubious value and closely linked to self-delusion. It is no accident that in Act I, when the bishop composes his sermon on truthfulness, he places self-delusion at the core of the problem:

> Gäbs einen Bösewicht? Müßt er sich sagen,
> So oft er nur allein: du bist ein Schurk!
> Wer hielt' sie aus, die eigene Verachtung?
> Allein die Lügen in verschiednem Kleid:
> Als Eitelkeit, als Stolz, als falsche Scham,
> Und wiederum als Großmut und als Stärke,
> Als innre Neigung und als hoher Sinn,
> Als guter Zweck bei etwa schlimmen Mitteln,
> Die hüllen unsrer Schlechtheit Antlitz ein
> Und stellen sich geschäftig vor, wenn sich
> Der Mensch beschaut in des Gewissens Spiegel.
>
> (126-36)

In other words, all deceit can be traced back to self-deceit and has its root in self-love. One is reminded of a recurrent image in Renaissance and Baroque Catholic literature, that of a man staring into a mirror that reflects not his true self but his delusions about himself, an image that is central to Erasmus' *Praise of Folly*. Bidermann's Cenodoxus is undone largely through the machinations of Philautia, self-love, who suggests to him that he is saved and will go to Heaven, when all the while he is damned through believing her. The more worldly Leon is in the habit of thinking that he is right rather than saved, but the choice he has to make is the choice of Cenodoxus: when Leon practises his cunning, he relies on himself, when he decides to speak the truth (end of Act IV) he puts his trust in God.

Leon appears without any family background, his social origin and class are left vague, he has no ties and is as free to choose his future as the medieval context of his story permits. He has made the first step in the right direction before the curtain rises, for he has become part of the bishop's household, having recognized its head as a man of God. The bishop, when Leon first saw him, seemed to see images 'aus einem andern, unbekannten Land' (5). The sight of this man altered Leon's entire career. Instead of enlisting in the army, as had been his intention, he now wanted a humble place in the house of peace:

> Da riefs in mir: dem mußt du dienen, dem,
> Und wärs als Stallbub.
>
> (53f.)

Not the worldly status of the job matters but the master for whom it is done, a lesson which, as we shall shortly see, is conspicuously lost on Atalus. But although Leon has chosen to serve the man of God, he has not yet fully put his trust into him, and accordingly we find him in a state of rebellion at the opening of Act I. By relying on his limited judgement, he mistakes the bishop's motive in saving money for common greed. Defiantly he throws off his apron and cook's knife, the insignia of his calling, thereby removing himself from the orderly hierarchy of the bishop's household. At this point Gregor teaches him his first lesson in humility: the bishop himself bends down to pick up the discarded objects and says:

> Ich mag am Menschen gern ein Zeichen seines Tuns.
> Wie du vor mir standst vorher, blank und bar,
> Du konntest auch so gut ein Tagdieb sein,
> Hinausgehn in den Wald, aufs Feld, auf Böses.
> Die Schürze da sagt mir, du seist mein Koch,
> Und sagt dirs auch.
>
> (196-200)

Both the words and the gestures indicate that Gregor is concerned with bringing the adventurer back from his independence into the enclosure of the communal fold. Notable is the implication that such independence has the potential of wickedness. Leon learns his first lesson sufficiently well to give up his physical freedom by deciding to allow himself to be sold as a slave.

From this point on, his service becomes spiritual: no longer the bishop's cook, his loyalty deepens with absence and distance, and while outwardly a slave he continually asserts his inner freedom. In fact, most of the comic effects of Act II are achieved through a play on this freedom-in-slavery theme: the slave sells himself, the slave asks the buyer to pay a higher sum for him, the slave wants his master to prove himself worthy of the slave's services:

> Ihr müßt erst essen lernen,
> Erst nach und nach den Gaum, die Zunge bilden,
> Bis ihr des Bessern wert seid meiner Kunst.
>
> (602ff.)

Leon over and over refers to the bishop as the master whom both he and Atalus must obey, in spite of and beyond the brute force they appear to be subject to:

> Mir hats eur Ohm vertraut, ich steh ihm ein.
>
> (979)

> Eur Oheim harret eurer—hört ihr wohl?
> Leis mit den Abendwinden, deucht mich, dringt
> Zu uns her sein Gebet, das schützt, das sichert,
> Und Engel mit den breiten Schwingen werden
> Um uns sich lagern wo wir wandelnd gehn.
>
> (986-90)

These lines make it abundantly clear that the human authority of the bishop shades into divine authority, whereas, by contrast, the authority of Kattwald is physical, animal only.

Atalus is in some obvious respects the opposite of Leon, in that he is high-born, snobbish and unrealistic, where Leon is relatively low-born and eminently practical. Moreover, where Leon retains his inner freedom and his self-respect through a complete awareness of his surroundings, as evidenced in his manipulations of his owners, Atalus is intent only on his dignity, i.e. his inner world, his phantasies, and as a direct result has neither freedom nor dignity but merely succeeds in making himself look ridiculous. He is so absorbed in himself that he cannot recognize his own self-interest. He refuses to help Leon in the kitchen, because it seems nobler to him to take care of horses, even though co-operation with Leon might lead to his liberation. At this point Leon reminds him of their true and common master:

> Gält es nur euch, so wär ich nun am Ende;
> Doch euer Oheim wills, und, junger Herr,
> Da werdet ihr wohl müssen.
>
> (805ff.)

Similarly, Bancban overcomes his dislike for Otto von Meran, also a member of the master's family, because he needs him to save the master's child. In the comedy Atalus doubles as both the despicable relative and the child who must be saved.

Yet Atalus' introspective concern with himself makes him at various points not so much the opposite as the distorted reflection of the self-reliant Leon. For example, Atalus complains:

> Wär ich erst wieder heim bei meinem Ohm!
> Der denkt nicht mein und läßt sichs wohl ergehn,
> Indes ich hier bei diesen Heiden schmachte.
>
> (766ff.)

This misjudgement of Gregor's character is in itself no worse than Leon's own in Act I and arises from the same lack of faith. Atalus seems crasser only because he speaks from self-pity whereas Leon's rebellion involved a concern for the bishop's physical welfare, his poor diet. The similarity here is at least as significant as the more obvious difference. Both Leon and Atalus have to learn humility, to set a higher will above their own and to substitute a true hierarchy of values for the artificial one of their imagination. They dislike each other because each recognizes in the other a stubbornness of selfhood that is his own, too. An analysis of the escape may serve to illustrate this point.

At the beginning of Act III, just as Leon explains that the key to the gate is of crucial importance to his plans, a servant comes and takes it. Atalus rejoices:

> Atalus (lachend).   Ha, ha! Damit gings schief!
> Leon.   Freut ihr euch drüber?
> Atalus.   's ist nur, weil du für gar so klug dich hältst.
>
> (928ff.)

This blatant piece of *Schadenfreude* is characteristic of Atalus who cannot put rational self-interest before his petty resentments, but at the same time Atalus has put his finger on Leon's central failing, 'sich für klug halten.' Leon promptly rises to the bait and proceeds to meet Atalus' conceit with an equally strong dose of his own. Having sized up his companion as a contemptible being who does not deserve the freedom he does not even wish for, Leon feels at liberty to provoke him. Atalus is asked to cut down the bridge, a task which he considers, predictably, to be beneath him. Leon agrees and makes a special point of the fact that Atalus must do undignified work and that Leon's own work is on a higher level. 'Ich schleich ins Haus', he says, 'Ihr mögt indes nach Lust im Boden wühlen' (968 f.). And again: 'So recht, mein Maulwurf, wühl dich in den Grund!' (1037). Both remarks clearly indicate his contempt for the man as well as the job.

We must consider this exchange in the light of the context of Act III. It is the act that is most completely dominated by deceit and by Leon's elaborate machinations and plans for the escape. These plans are entirely dependent on his personal ingenuity and they are doomed to failure—unlike his act of faith at the end of Act IV. At the point at which Leon mocks Atalus he has reached the peak of his mood of self-reliance. At the end of the play Leon will say, 'Wahr stets und ganz war nur der Helfer: Gott!' (1722). But in the middle of the play, in Act III, it is not God's help but self-help that he builds on. Accordingly he fails to obtain the all-important key from Kattwald and, stepping out of the house, he faces the digging Atalus again and at the same time is forced to face himself:

> Er gräbt!—O, daß ich ihn gering geachtet,
> Und er genügt dem Wengen was ihm oblag
> Indeß ich scheitre wo ich mich vermaß.
>
> (1117ff.)

Atalus has unwittingly taught Leon a lesson in self-recognition and humility. Having learned this lesson, he is now ready to receive the key, but not through his own efforts, rather through the help of Edrita, and this involves a further humiliation.

Edrita is another person whom Leon has treated with contempt, although with affectionate contempt. Their first encounter in Act II is full of such remarks as:

> Leon.   Je, trifft man ein Geschöpf
> Von einer neuen, niegesehnen Gattung,
> So forscht man wohl, ob es nicht kneipt, nicht sticht,
> Nicht kratzt, nicht beißt; zum mindsten wills die
> Klugheit.
> Edrita.   So hältst du uns für Tiere?
> Leon.   Ei bewahre!
> Ihr seid ein wackres Völkchen. Doch verzeih!
> Vom Tier zum *Menschen* sind der Stufen viele.
>
> (662-8)

Granted that there is humorous undercurrent and a good deal of erotic teasing in these lines; still the joke reveals Leon's penchant to revel in his superiority. We have seen that Atalus, too, is called an animal, a mole. Edrita understands this failing of Leon's for what it is, and she wraps her consternation and pity with so deplorable an attitude into a single word: 'Armseliger!' (669).

The same Edrita whom Leon had put so roundly into her place is needed for the escape. When Leon first finds the key in the gate, he thinks that Heaven has helped him but is reprimanded by the girl, who tells him that he is not good enough to receive help from God and should be glad for what human assistance comes his way:

> Du irrst, kein Engel hilft, da wo der Mensch
> Mit Trug und Falsch an seine Werke geht.
>
> (1132f.)

> Drum hoffe nicht auf Gott bei deinem Tun,
> Ich selber wars, die dir den Schlüssel brachte.
>
> (1139f.)

To be reprimanded by Edrita after he has been shamed by Atalus is a further humiliation for Leon, who quite properly connects what Edrita has said with the bishop's parting words:

>   denk ich seiner Abschiedsworte
> Mit dem was erst nur sprach dein Kindermund
> Ich in Beschämung meine Augen senke.
>
> (1145f.)

'Beschämung' and 'Kindermund' are key words: Leon continues to be humbled by those whom he considers inferior to himself.

In Act IV Leon still learns humility through humiliation. Atalus is for once right when he insists that they should take Edrita along, while Leon wants her to return to her father, where she would remain a heathen and be exposed to the brutality of her people. Leon has to watch Edrita and Atalus side against him, which is a considerable blow to his pride. Atalus for his part now learns to become more aware of others and reaches maturity in Act V, when he recognizes that Leon and Edrita are suited for each other and that he himself is meant to take orders.

The hitherto self-reliant Leon reaches the final stage of his development at the end of Act IV, when he rises from prayer and for the first time speaks the truth without any thought of profiting from it. Where tricks would have failed, faith prevails. Because of factors that they could not have known in advance, the ferryman saves them when he hears who they are, while he would have killed them had they told a lie. In crossing the river all three turn to a new and more deeply Christian stage of their existence, and by the same token they pass from the land of savagery to the land of peace. The contrast between the two sides is very marked towards the end of the play: Kattwald says, before the curtain drops on Act IV, 'Die Hand, den Arm in ihrem Blute baden' (1566), whereas Gregor dismisses his prisoners shortly afterwards with the words, 'Zieht hin in Frieden' (1731) and pointedly insists that there should be no forced conversions.

'Peace and savagery' does not exhaust the qualities of the two countries which the river divides. Again, it will be useful to bring to mind a Grillparzer tragedy that deals with the same theme under a darker aspect, *Das Goldene Vließ,* especially the first two parts of the trilogy. Reduced to its essentials, this play deals with a young man from a highly civilized country who goes forth into the wilderness on a specific errand or quest. He returns from the wilderness bringing with him not only the prize he set out to conquer but also a girl who has fallen in love with him, helped him escape, happens to be the daughter of the barbarous country's ruler and chooses to go with her lover against her father's injunction.—Evidently, this is an accurate account of the plot of *Weh dem, der lügt* as well as of *Das Goldene Vließ.* The story of both Leon and Jason is one of a descent and a return. Jason's pursuit is as ruthless as Leon's might be, if it were not tempered by the bishop's commandment; and where Jason's mission consists in rescuing a stolen object, the fleece, Leon has to free a human being, Atalus. Thus, in the later comedy we find a Christian transformation, with a dash of humanism, of the 'dark' quest of the earlier tragedy. Much can be gained by seeing Leon as a comic Jason, Kattwald as a comic Aietes, Edrita as a Medea without magic powers, and the Rheingau as a Colchis stripped of its demonism. Frankish culture will then be seen as analogous to Greek culture but with an added, and essential, ingredient: Christianity.

That the distinction between the two sides is not one of black and white becomes clear very early in the play, when the bishop, speaking of the Rheingau, says, 'Wo noch die Rohheit, die hier Schein umkleidet / In erster Blöße Mensch und Tier vermengt' (290 f.). Gregor, whose most obvious characteristic is his abhorrence of lies, can naturally have no good opinion of 'Schein'. Naked nature, as it is to be found in the Rheingau, is in some ways superior to deceitful civilization. The land of Christianity is also the land of superficiality and artificiality, of 'Schein'. Leon takes with him to the other side the whole range of his background, from its trivia—good cooking, which he presents as a form of art—to its highest attribute, its religion. In this he demonstrates that the bishop's cook may be one of his lowest servants but is still a servant of Christ. On the other hand, he is also planning to take with him a pack of lies. And thus he comes with an ambiguous mixture of positive and negative values, his art and his artfulness, his cooking and his tricks, the Christianity and the corruption of the Franks.

The Rheingau complements the faults and virtues of Franken with great precision. It is the land of barbarians and of violence, but also the land of uncorrupted nature. Its positive qualities are exemplified in Edrita, whose straightforward simplicity is exactly what the sophisticated and supercilious Frank Leon needs for his salvation. Like Medea's, her relationship to her father is based on mutual suspicion and fear,[6] lacking that respect which is a vital element in the quasi-filial relationship between Leon and the bishop. Like Medea, she warns and helps the stranger with whom she has fallen in love, like Medea she has to contend with the pride of the strangers, but unlike Medea she is a child of nature without nature's demonic powers. It is quite possible that there is an intentional joke on the poet's part in having her gather kitchen herbs in place of the magic herbs that play a role in *Der Gastfreund*. And while Medea must remain an outsider, ultimately an outcast in Greece, Edrita has access to her new country through her conversion.

If the virtues of their respective civilizations can be seen in Edrita and Leon when they are at their best, the faults of the two sides are sketched in Atalus and Galomir. These two characters gain considerably in interest when seen in conjunction. As Galomir represents barbarity due to lack of civilization, so Atalus represents degeneracy due to civilization having removed itself from nature. Atalus' rejection of dirty work and his unhealthy introspection are all due to the aristocratic ideas of high society that have been bred into him. He only sheds them in the course of his escape when he learns to live in open nature and with other human beings.

Galomir, of course, is not even capable of grasping an idea, and his reactions are purely instinctual. He is often pointed to as one of the major flaws of the play, and it would indeed be futile to defend his characterization. However, to understand what went wrong it is essential to understand what was attempted. If the play shows the redeemed and the unredeemed side of human nature on the two banks of the Rhine, in various stages of development and decay, then what was needed in the character of Galomir was an epitome of the dark side of untamed animal forces in man. Galomir had to be a kind of Caliban. It will be recalled that Caliban's relation to a woman he desires takes the form of an attempt at rape, coupled with childishly hurt feelings when he is rebuffed. Grillparzer, too, put his animal-man into a situation where his limitations would appear with regard to a woman, into what should have been an erotic situation: Galomir on stage is Galomir on his wedding day. But here Grillparzer fell victim to the taste of his time. Viennese nineteenth-century comedy would have no attempts at rape or anything approaching a show of brutish sensuality. Yet this is all that Galomir—almost by definition—is capable of. To omit the sensual aspect of his animal nature and still present him as Edrita's suitor results in an absurdity: he becomes an ox when he should be a bull. This is demonstrated in the glaring silliness of the scene in Act IV where he attempts a show of affection for Edrita. To be sure, we must see Galomir as a failure, but as a historically conditioned failure of a particular kind: the Biedermeier attempt and failure to present within a comic framework the unregenerated forces of bestiality in man.

'Vom Tier zum Menschen sind der Stufen viele' (668), Leon says. It is a line that could serve as a motto for the play. The concern with levels of development informs the balance of characters and relationships on the two sides of the Rhine. In each camp there is a ruler who has close personal ties with the younger and more active characters: Kattwald, the man of violence, is flanked by his daughter Edrita and his prospective son-in-law Galomir, while the corresponding couple for Gregor, the man of peace, are his nephew and the servant who is really a spiritual and adopted son. In terms of characters, then, the two sides are evenly matched, which gives the tug-of-war between them an element of fairness. Seen in terms of the play's structure, it becomes altogether appropriate that the crossing of the river should constitute a turning point in the lives of the main characters. It is at the river bank that the girl from the unregenerated country advocates lies and Leon the Frank abandons his wiles and reveals his true, his Christian self. The reversal is significant, since in Act III, when the theft of the key was in question, Edrita rebuked Leon for lying. There she spoke as the forthright child of nature to the crafty man of civilization. That is, the virtues of her side were played out against the faults of his. At the end of Act IV, on the other hand, the truth of Leon's side, which is the truth of God, has the last word.

In *Das Goldene Vließ* the attempt to bring about a union between the wilderness of Colchis and Jason's daylight world ends in catastrophe. The civilization of Greece cannot redeem. Medea is no longer Medea when she abandons the chase and her magic and tries to learn femininity from the blonde Kreusa. There is no humility to be found here, only humiliation. But in *Weh dem, der lügt,* the gap that separates Franken and the Rheingau, symbolically presented by the river and the crossing of the river, can be overcome through trust in God and charitable compromise among men, summed up in the last half-line, with its gentle irony and understatement: 'Sie mögen sich vertragen', essentially an optative variant of Iphigenie's 'Leb wohl' in her last speech.

We return to the question posed at the beginning, concerning the quality of Grillparzer's optimism in this play. It has been shown that the comedy of reconciliation has close ties with two tragedies that deal with the desperate and largely unsuccessful struggle of chaos and order as disparate forces in man. The creator of Otto von Meran and the re-creator of Medea seems to have set himself the task of writing a happy ending where he had hitherto written a bloody one. He did this by reducing the problem and diminishing the characters to doll's size. Kattwald and Galomir *are* make-believe barbarians, and the command that Leon has to follow, always to speak the truth, *is* a sort of game, compared to Bancban's deadly serious instructions to keep the peace. In **Weh dem, der lügt** the final rescue of the fugitives in Act V has a legendary quality: the gates suddenly open after Leon's exclamation: 'Und so begehr ich denn, ich fordre Wunder!' (1687). The solution thus reveals itself as taking place in a day-dream world of wishful (or prayerful) thinking, not in a world which we can readily identify as our own. This sort of distancing effect—one hesitates to speak of alienation—was not at all uncommon on the Viennese stage with its Baroque roots and its gusto for stage tricks and operatic effects. The aesthetic intention of **Weh dem, der lügt** is to a large measure that of an Austrian puppet show on Goethean themes. It is a comedy written by a poet for whom Weimar was long ago and far away and yet ever present, and who was himself firmly rooted in a city where knowledge was increasing and power decaying, a bitter man who did not think much of men's ability 'sich zu vertragen'. He used the ingredients of the witches' cauldron he knew, the stuff of which he previously and subsequently made tragedies and cooked up for once a dish fit for family fare, a comedy. The result has much charm and considerable depth, both enhanced by a quality of stylization that leads to disbelief but also to the willing suspension of disbelief, to borrow Colderidge's useful phrase. A comic fairy tale on man's potential for redeeming himself, **Weh dem, der lügt** is Grillparzer's somewhat sceptical variant of a classic subject, his 'Iphigenie in Vienna'.

Notes

1. '*Weh dem, der lügt* oder von der Sprache im Drama', *Die Wissenschaft von deutscher Sprache und Dichtung. Festschrift für Friedrich Maurer* (Stuttgart, 1963), pp. 438-57. Two other significant contributions to the subject are E. Hock, 'Grillparzers Lustspiel', *Wirkendes Wort*, 4 (1953), 12-23 and Herbert Seidler, 'Grillparzers Lustspiel *Weh dem, der lügt!*', *Jahrbuch der Grillparzergesellschaft*, 3. Folge, 4 (1965), 7-29.

2. For a detailed discussion of this point, see Hock, pp. 17 ff. But already August Sauer, in his notes to the historical-critical edition, points to the similarity between Gregor's crucial line, 'Wer deutet mir die buntverworrne Welt' (1800) and Iphigenie's, 'Daß keiner in sich selbst noch mit den andern/Sich rein und unverworren halten kann' (1658). Franz Grillparzer, *Sämtliche Werke*, ed. August Sauer and Reinhold Backmann (Vienna, 1909-1948), Part I, vol. V, p. 387. Citations from Grillparzer in my text are to this edition, hereafter cited as *Werke*.

3. The most persuasive and best known exponent of this argument is, of course, Erich Heller in his 'Goethe and the Avoidance of Tragedy', *The Disinherited Mind* (New York, 1957), pp. 35-63.

4. Seidler, p. 12, also makes this point in a cursory reference to *Ein treuer Diener*.

5. For a penetrating analysis of the play, see Heinz Politzer, 'Verwirrung des Gefühls. Franz Grillparzer's *Ein treuer Diener seines Herrn*', *Deutsche Vierteljahrsschrift*, 39 (1965), 58-86.

6. See the details noted by Backmann, *Werke*, Part I, vol V, p. 376. Hock, p. 16, calls Edrita 'ein glücklichere Schwester der Medea'.

Penrith Goff (essay date 1974)

SOURCE: "The Play within the Play in Grillparzer's *Des Meeres und der Liebe Wellen*," in *Studies in Nineteenth-Century and Early Twentieth-Century Literature: Essays in Honor of Paul K. Whitaker,* edited by Norman H. Binger and A. Wayne Wonderley, APRAPress, 1974, pp. 22-8.

[*In the following essay, Goff offers a structural analysis of* Des Meeres und der Liebe Wellen, *particularly the "play-within-a-play" technique.*]

Grillparzer's mastery of dramatic effect, gesture, imagery, and symbol in **Des Meeres und der Liebe Wellen** has been abundantly and justly praised; he himself attached great importance to the visual aspects of theater.[1] The structure which holds these various elements together was also of paramount importance to him: "Die Poesie ist eine bildende Kunst wie die Malerei."[2] Scholarship has been reluctant to take note of one of the basic structural features in **Des Meeres und der Liebe Wellen**: the play within the play. An examination of the drama with particular attention to its symmetry and to the role played by the Priest reveals that the love affair between Hero and Leander is staged as a brief drama within the confines of the larger play. It shows further that by virtue of the inner drama and the relationship of the inner drama to the frame, **Des Meeres und der Liebe Wellen** is structurally more closely related to Grillparzer's other plays than has heretofore been acknowledged.

In his discussion of the structure of **Des Meeres und der Liebe Wellen** E.E. Papst points out that the action of the play falls into two halves.[3] In the first half an inner conflict between religious duty and the need to love develops in Hero and reaches its highest pitch midpoint in the play: as she stands at her chamber window, she confesses to herself that she is attracted to Leander and even sends him an imaginary greeting through the night (l. 1060).[4] The conflict becomes externalized when she is startled by a return greeting—one of the most effectively dramatic moments in theater—and Leander appears at the window. The second half of the play brings Hero's dilemma as an external conflict. The symmetry of this two-part structure, Papst observes, "has an affinity with the circular form which characterizes many of Grillparzer's other plays."[5]

Another, more obvious kind of symmetry impresses itself upon even the casual reader (the spectator doubtless to a lesser extent) in many details of the drama's construction: phrases and motifs which foreshadow later developments, symbols embracing the play, phrases repeated or varied showing similarity and contrast between the two halves of the play. A few examples will make this technique clear. The play opens with a striking symbol of Hero's service as a priestess: she weaves a wreath of flowers which denote for her the days she will devote to her goddess, Aphrodite (l. 5-11), and places it on the statue of Amor. The very last action of the play is the removal of the wreath upon Hero's death. In parallel fashion Leander, too, chooses a symbol which denotes his constancy: the trees on the beach (l. 801-02). It is one of these which, broken by the storm that killed him, conceals his body. Leander's complaint in Act II that he is sick with love, "Es schmerzt die Brust" (l. 657), is balanced in Act IV as Hero, waiting for evening, greets the wind blowing from Abydos: "Ich öffne dir die Brust" (l. 1814). Near the end of the first half of the drama Hero is just admitting her interest in Leander but scarcely regrets that she will not see him again: "Im ganzen Leben seh' ich kaum ihn wieder" (l. 1015). Near the end of the second half, a slight variation of the line expresses all the anguish which events in the meanwhile have caused Hero: "Nie wieder dich zu sehen, im Leben nie!" (l. 2059). Perhaps the most pathetic example is the simple variation of verb tense in Hero's description of Leander: "Er ist so schön, so jugendlich, so gut" (l. 799) when she pours out her lament to the Priest after Leander's death: "Er war so jugendlich, so schön" (l. 2026).

The symmetry evident in symbol, motif, and speech extends also to the characters and their interrelationships. As the play begins, both Leander and Hero have rejected a normal mode of life and natural associations with other people. Leander is still grieving over his mother's death; Hero is deeply dissatisfied with her family life: a domineering father, a thoroughly subjugated mother, an abusive older brother. She had welcomed the temple as a refuge from her brother and men like him (l. 305-319). Yet after a brief meeting with Leander she finds herself completely preoccupied with thoughts of him. Although the focus of the play is on Hero, the transformation wrought by love in Leander is just as far-reaching. Leander, who stoutly resisted Naukleros' efforts to interest him in girls, is suddenly consumed by such a passion that he braves the Helle-

spont without regard for his own life. In both cases Grillparzer has pointed up this reversal in the protagonist by showing a reversal in his relationship to a companion. In Act I Naukleros makes a valiant but apparently vain effort to arouse in his friend some interest in the girls they see at the ceremony. In Act IV Leander's eagerness to visit Hero is so great that Naukleros, the stronger of the two men, is unable to restrain him even by force. Hero, whose aloofness had separated her from the other girls at the temple, is suddenly drawn by her love into an intimate friendship with Janthe.

These elements of symmetry set one half of the drama against the other and thus heighten the contrast between the two phases of Hero's psychological development. Many of them also go beyond mere contrast in their function. They embrace segments of the drama, producing not only balance and contrast but a circularity of form. Hero's wreath, for example, encloses nearly the entire play; the tree symbol associated with Leander encloses his life from the point where he declares his love for Hero to the point where the storm kills him and breaks the tree.

A tendency towards circularity is also noticeable in the time settings. The first act begins in the early morning as does the last act. Act III begins at nightfall and Act IV ends just as night is ending. The time settings do not seem forced, yet their symmetry goes beyond what the action would require and what is usual in a Grillparzer play. This circularity does not center around the pivotal line, l. 1060, as it would if it functioned only to contrast the two halves of the play. These elements of symmetry effect a frame enclosing Acts III and IV. This is underscored by the close similarity between the opening lines spoken by the Priest in Act III:

> Des Dienstes heil'ge Pflichten sind vollbracht,
> Der Abend sinkt;
>
>   (l. 891-92)

and the lines with which he closes Act IV:

> —Komm mit, es sinkt die Nacht,
> Und brütet über ungeschehnen Dingen.
> Nun, Himmlische, nun waltet eures Amts!
> Die Schuldigen hält Meer und Schlaf gebunden,
> Und so ist eures Priesters Werk vollbracht:
>
>   (l. 1828-32)

The frame structure of *Des Meeres und der Liebe Wellen* invites comparison to other Grillparzer dramas of similar form. Herbert Seidler has shown that a frame embracing an inner drama is the basic form of *Sappho, König Ottokars Glück und Ende, Ein treuer Diener seines Herrn, Der Traum ein Leben, Weh dem, der lügt, Die Jüdin von Toledo, Libussa,* and *Ein Bruderzwist in Habsburg.*[6] The frame is quite clearly set off from the inner drama in such plays as *Der Traum ein Leben* and *Weh dem, der lügt,* less so in others such as *Sappho* and *Bruderzwist.* At the beginning of each play—the opening of the frame—a task or mission is delegated. This is carried out in the course of the inner drama. The closing of the frame seems to be a return to the beginning of the drama, but the development is actually spiral rather than circular: the protagonist's insight has been greatly deepened by the experiences during the inner drama. The protagonist's performance is judged by the assigner of the mission, in some cases by the protagonist as well, particularly where he also set himself the task. The inner drama contrasts sharply with the frame. The concerns of the characters in the frame are usually directed toward heaven or at any rate the higher powers which govern men's fates. The frame usually represents the reflective life, the vita contemplativa, whereas the inner drama portrays the characters engaged in active life and incurring guilt through their actions.

These features are all present in *Des Meeres und der Liebe Wellen,* as the following analysis will show. The parallel with the Baroque world theater idea, inherent in Grillparzer's use of the frame structure,[7] is more readily apparent in this play than in the others, for the Priest is reminiscent of God, the distributor of roles. He is of course only a human representative for the gods and when he, unlike the God of the Baroque world theater, participates in the inner drama for very human reasons, he places his own authority into question. Thus he as well as the performer of the role is susceptible of judgment.

For the Priest, as for Hero, the consecration culminates long years of hope and planning. It forges another link in the chain of tradition for which he has such high regard. Despite his appearance of cold authoritarianism, the Priest shows genuine affection for Hero. He is confident of her determination (l. 408) but aware of her immaturity. In his attempt to persuade her to seek spiritual fulfillment, to regain the oracular gift which had been in the family tradition, he appeals to her ego. His warning that exclusive preoccupation with religious duties might be taken for self-centeredness (l. 165) seems to stem from a characteristic concern for appearances. Thus, there may be some doubt as to the purity of his motives where Hero is concerned. Nonetheless, whether or not it is truly Hero's fulfillment he desires, he is clearly determined that, having made her choice, she will carry it through. He sees the initiation as marking the beginning of a new task for her, her sacred mission (l. 974). His role is that of spiritual mentor and second father (l. 997), who will provide counsel in the performance of her mission.

Like the Priest, Hero's mother also desires Hero's self-fulfillment and like him she recognizes the selfish nature of Hero's present way of life (l. 329). She has even come to the temple with the hope of persuading Hero to return home: "Das Weib ist glücklich nur an Gattenhand" (l. 320). But Hero is unwilling to accept completely either way of life. To the Priest's urgings that she listen to the oracular voices in the sanctuary at night, she answers that the night is for rest, the day for activity (l. 186). To her mother she praises the joys of "quiet self-possession" (l. 392) she has found at the temple, and the tranquil, unvarying routine of her future as priestess.

In a sense, then, both the Priest and Hero's mother are engaged in competition for Hero. The Priest, apologist for the vita contemplativa, is a forceful, strong-willed man, so uncompromisingly devoted to divine law that he would draw the blood from his own veins "wüsst' er nur einen Tropfen in der Mischung, / Der Unrecht birgt und Unerlaubtes hegt" (l. 1001-02). Hero's mother is a pathetic advocate for the vita activa, the way of life as wife and mother. She is so subjugated she hardly dares to say what weighs so heavily on her heart. For Hero she is a symbol of all that Hero wishes to escape: domestic strife, oppression, disharmony. There could, of course, never be any possibility that Hero would return. Hero knows that her mother is wiser than her father (l. 325), but is not mature enough to understand that her mother wisely accepts the unpleasantness of life as a necessary aspect of the fulfilled active life. On the other hand, Hero also has no conception of what she is renouncing when she takes her vows.

The competition between the Priest and Hero's mother gives rise to a minor skirmish which is actually the first external dramatic conflict in the play. It is precipitated when the Priest orders a dove removed from the grounds. Though the Priest is carrying out temple law—mating animals are forbidden on the premises—Hero's mother is greatly disturbed by the incident, experiencing it as a dramatization of her own fate:

> So reissen sie
> Das Kind auch von der Mutter, Herz vom Herzen,
> Und haben des ihr Spiel.
>
> (l. 339-41)

The word "Spiel" is unfair; the Priest is not, of course, merely amusing himself. A moment later, though, when the Priest in answer to the mother's protests, challenges Hero to return to her mother, he is indeed playing a game. He knows very well that Hero will not surrender the peace and prestige of temple life to go back to the tensions of the outside world. With all the odds in his favor, the Priest is easily victorious in this encounter.

The contest between the Priest and Hero's mother is so unequal and so brief—it spans a mere 50 verses (l. 350-400)—one can easily overlook its significance for the total play. Like many other elements in the first act—imagery, which can be seen later to be symbolic, speeches, which turn out to be prophetic—this incident anticipates later events. It is a prelude to the major conflict of the play, the contest between the two forces which battle for Hero's soul: the attraction of the vita contemplativa and the demands of the vita activa. That contest is much more a challenge to the Priest; his opponent is no cowed woman who appeals to Hero's reason with unconvincing aphorisms, who seems herself adrift in the "desolate, dizzying sea" of everyday life (l. 160) which Hero has fled. It is Leander, vibrant with life, who emerges literally from the sea and speaks directly to Hero's heart.

The first two acts of the play establish the elements which bring the contest about: the Priest's determination that

Hero will be successful in her mission, Hero's irresoluteness to submit herself completely to either way of life, Leander's desperate lovesickness. The contest itself comprises Acts III and IV, the inner drama. It begins with the Priest showing Hero the tower chamber where she is to live and reiterating his wish that she will hear "Götterstimmen halb aus eigner Brust / Und halb aus Höhn, die noch kein Blick ermass—" (l. 967-8). Again she demurs, setting herself a more modest goal: she will attain composure (Sammlung). Having assigned the role and the arena in which it is to be played out, the Priest withdraws, to let the inner play unfold. The tower in and around which the inner play (except for the Naukleros-Leander scene) takes place is a symbol of isolation, as the Priest points out to Hero (l. 894-906). But more than that, it is an objectification of Hero's inner self, the "quiet realm of ordered thought" which she feared would be invaded by men if she returned to the outside world (l. 307-17). Leander's "invasion" of the tower is a dramatic reenactment of what had already happened figuratively in Acts I and II. At first dutifully protesting her obligations as priestess, Hero gradually yields to her now conscious wishes. As she allows the intoxication of love to distract her from her priestly commitment, she passes from the vita meditiva to the vita activa, from the timeless mode of existence to an existence whose most important dimension is time. The transition is dramatized in the interchange during which Leander asks when he may visit again. Hero tells him to come to the next festival (as she had in Act II), when temple law permits outsiders to visit. Then, at his persistence, she gives way, at first in a compromise, and finally surprising him with more than he had dared hope for: "Komm morgen denn!" (l. 1229). When the Priest suspects Hero is not carrying out her mission, he steps into the inner play again, attempting to manipulate events so as to aid her. Thus the inner drama becomes more tightly structured: its immediate goal is the termination of the illicit friendship which will prevent Hero from gaining spiritual fulfillment. To bring this about, the Priest sends Hero on a long futile search for the messenger from her parents, so that by evening she is too exhausted to keep her nightly vigil. After she has fallen asleep, the Priest extinguishes her lamp, having already given orders that the fishermen, who might save Leander's life, are to remain at home that night. Having thus set the stage for the catastrophe of the inner drama, he steps aside again, leaving the conclusion of the episode to the gods:

> Das Holz geschichtet und das Beil gezückt,
> Wend' ich mich ab. Trefft Götter selbst das Opfer.
>
> (l. 1833-34)

With these words the fourth act, and the inner drama, end.

At the end of the inner play in Grillparzer's frame dramas, the characters typically assemble for the closing of the frame. The gathering of characters in *Des Meeres und der Liebe Wellen* (only Hero's parents are absent) is occasioned by the discovery of Leander's body at the beginning of Act V. Since Hero is dazed and reluctant to admit

the episode ended, the Priest attempts to end it for her by rushing Leander's body back to Abydos: "Genug ward nun geklagt ob jenem Fremden" (l. 2023). By keeping the events of the past two days (Acts III and IV) silent, he hopes to restore the former order, even to the extent of having Hero return to her priestly commitment fully unscathed: "So wieder du mein Kind!" (l. 2033).

But a return to the situation at the beginning of the play is not possible. The events of the inner drama have matured Hero. She cannot take up the quest for Sammlung and spiritual fulfillment anew. She has acquired insight into the mystery of human life (l. 2025) and has learned submission to the higher powers: "Nun denn ich hab' gelernt, Gewaltigem mich fügen!/ Die Götter wolltens nicht, da rächten sies" (l. 2047). Finally, Hero, who still refused to commit herself at the beginning of Act III, has by the end of Act IV attained a depth of commitment to love which may be gauged by her use of the same extreme turn of phrase with which the Priest (l. 1000) had expressed his devotion to divine justice:

> O ich will weinen, weinen, mir die Adern öffnen,
> Bis Tränen mich und Blut, ein Meer, umgeben;
>
> (l. 1970-71)

Hero's performance in carrying out her mission is judged with less severity than was to be expected. The Priest is aware of the gravity of her failure but believes she can begin anew:

> Die Götter laut das blut'ge Zeugnis gaben,
> Wie sehr sie zürnen, und wie gross dein Fehl;
> So lass in Demut uns die Strafe nehmen;
>
> (l. 1927-29)

Hero recognizes that she has sinned against the gods but, being firmly committed to her love for Leander, she blames his death on her failure to stay awake and on the Priest's trickery, not on any transgression of law. The Priest, whose course of action seemed to bear the sanction of the gods, is also judged. Janthe's anguished outcry: "Vorsicht'ger Tor, sieh deiner Klugheit Werke!" (l. 2107) and her decision to quit the temple spring from horror at what she regards as momentous human wrong perpetrated in the name of divine law. This plea for humane leniency weighs heavily in its final position in the drama.

Thus, the structure of *Des Meeres und der Liebe Wellen* is much more complex than the outer form would indicate. For the classic story of Hero and Leander, Grillparzer appropriately chose, and adhered in every aspect to, the five-act classic form perfected by Goethe and Schiller. The crux of the play—Hero's psychological development—he portrayed in a two-part structure which harmonizes perfectly with the classic form. To convey his view of the world as the focal point of the tragic antithesis between the human and the divine order, his view of life as a frustrating role for the all-too-fallible humans who play it, he turned once more to the frame structure which he had first used in **Sappho** and which in some variation he used in every major play afterward with the single exception of **Das goldene Vliess.**

Notes

1. See Margaret E. Atkinson, "Grillparzer's Use of Symbol and Image in 'Des Meeres und der Lieben Wellen'," *German Life and Letters* IV (1950/51), 261-77; Joachim Kaiser, *Grillparzers dramatischer Still* (München: Carl Hanser Verlag, 1961); Herbert Seidler, "Zur Sprachkunst in Grillparzers Hero-Tragödie," *Studien zu Grillparzer und Stifter* (Wien, Köln, Graz: Hermann Böhlaus Nachfolger, 1970), pp. 47-65.

2. From the diaries, No. 3188 (1836), in *Franz Grillparzer. Sämtliche Werke* ed. Peter Frank and Karl Pörnbacher (München: Carl Hanser Verlag, 1964), vol. III, p. 238.

3. E.E. Papst, *Grillparzer: Des Meeres und der Liebe Wellen* (London: Edward Arnold Ltd., 1967), pp. 29-52.

4. Line citations refer to the text in *Sämtliche Werke. Historisch-kritische Gesamtausgabe* ed. August Sauer (Wien: Schroll u. Co., 1909-48), section I, vol. 4 ed. Reinhold Backmann (Wien, 1925), pp. 77-211. Quotations, identified by line number only, are also from this edition.

5. Papst, p. 47-48.

6. Herbert Seidler, "Die Kunst der Rahmung in Grillparzers Dramen" in H. Seidler, *Studien zu Grillparzer und Stifter* (Wien, Köln, Graz: Hermann Böhlers Nachfolger, 1970), pp. 118-34. I have summarized only the main points in this excellent essay. In many details, too, Seidler's findings apply to *Des Meeres und der Liebe Wellen,* which he does not include in his study. Kaiser uses the term *Bogenform* for this structure, applying it however more narrowly than Seidler; see Kaiser, *Grillparzers dramatischer Stil,* 109-112.

7. Walter Naumann, *Franz Grillparzer. Das dichterische Werk* (Stuttgart, Berlin, Köln, Mainz: Kohlhammer, [2]1967), pp. 68-69, points out that the Baroque drama (Calderon's *Great World Theater*) and the Viennese folk comedy both employ the scheme assignment—performance—judgment. Cf. also Seidler, *Studien,* p. 134.

Hugo Schmidt (essay date 1974)

SOURCE: "Realms of Action in Grillparzer's *Ein Bruderzwist in Habsburg,*" in *Studies in the German Drama: A Festschrift in Honor of Walter Silz,* edited by Donald H. Crosby and George C. Schoolfield, The University of North Carolina Press, 1974, pp. 149-61.

[*In the following essay, Schmidt places Grillparzer's drama* Ein Bruderzwist in Habsburg *in its historical and intellectual context, asserting that this lends layers of meaning to the play.*]

In trying to come to terms with Grillparzer's **Ein Bruderzwist in Habsburg,** the reader will experience the frustrating sensation that T. S. Eliot formulated so well in his line "That is not what I meant at all." He ponders, tries to see through the veils that obscure the essence of the play. An insight may be about to take shape, but in formulating it, he sees that he is missing his mark. He conveys something, finally, that may be true, vaguely, but not entirely germane. What he was trying to get at remains behind the veil. The play is elusive, and its impact is in its atmosphere, in an area that defies penetration by our interpretative tools.

The action, as a whole, is not difficult to follow. It takes place on a realistic level, and the plot can be paraphrased with ease. True, a paraphrase can never convey the *Gehalt* of a literary work; but here it seems to do less than nothing. For example, would it not impart a more essential aspect of the play to mention that Lukrezia always appears as if out of a dream and almost inexplicably, than to give a precise summary of the peace talks in the second act? Or would a description of Rudolf's gestures not come closer to the *Gehalt* of the play than a limning of his views on unrest and revolution?

Critics have claimed that Grillparzer's play is not stageworthy, that it is a "Gedankendrama,"[1] and that it begins to make sense only after it is comprehended in terms of history and philosophy.[2] The historical and philosophical content is easy to perceive; it is one of the outermost layers of Grillparzer's artistic fabric. Like other historical playwrights, he has taken certain liberties with the actual events, has telescoped time, and has created characters that may have little in common with their historical models. On the philosophical and sociological level, Grillparzer has given voice, through Rudolf, to his conservative views to a degree that is surprising for one who fought frustrating battles against the censorship of an absolutistic era and complained bitterly about the stultifying effect the monarchic system had on the arts. A good comprehension of the intellectual background of the play and its historical content, important though it is, will barely scratch the surface.

The character of Rudolf leads more deeply into the complexities. Obviously, he is not the historical Rudolf. But most critics are willing to forgive Grillparzer his transgressions against history. What is considered a more serious matter is the inconsistency of the character as drawn by the playwright himself. In some scenes, Rudolf's paranoia shows pathological dimensions, in others, he is kind and reveals a sense of humor. He appears to be an apostle of peace and yet is eager to continue the war in Hungary. He is patient and humane in some instances—for example, when he expresses his horror at Ferdinand's ruthless expulsion of the Protestants—and unreasonable in others, for instance, when refusing to listen to a defense of

Field Marshall Rußworm. His threat against Don Cäsar to have him executed if he continues to speak out for Rußworm is inconceivable. On the one hand, he has a deep understanding for matters of the heart—he is horrified by Ferdinand's decision to break with the woman he loves and marry an unloved one for political reasons—on the other, he chastizes Don Cäsar for wooing Lukrezia. Most striking of all, he refuses to permit that medical aid be given to his son, whom he loves deeply, thus causing his death.[3]

Such instances are part of a larger, more general tendency in the play. Grillparzer did not seem overly concerned with a tight, logical structure, a close nexus between the events, or even a careful delineation of cause and effect. Criticizing him on these counts merely reveals a wrong premise on the part of the critic: that Grillparzer, since his creative period followed that of German Classicism, should be measured against Goethe and Schiller and their dramatic technique, which was usually flawless indeed with regard to the details mentioned above. But we know that Grillparzer's art was not indebted primarily to Weimar Classicism; he was not a poor, but at best an unwilling pupil, and probably no pupil at all, of Schiller and Goethe. Commenting, in his diaries, on the historical tragedy—a favorite quotation in recent Grillparzer scholarship—the playwright concedes that there can be no question of the dramatist's need to show cause and effect, but he continues: "Aber wie in der Natur sich höchst selten Ursache und Wirkung wechselseitig ganz decken, so ist, in der Behandlung eine gewisse Inkongruenz beider durchblicken zu lassen, vielleicht die höchste Aufgabe, die ein Dichter sich stellen kann."[4]

"Eine gewisse Inkongruenz": Perhaps a heritage from Baroque drama, passed on to Grillparzer via the Viennese popular theater, it can be traced in the theater tradition in which Grillparzer has his place. Hofmannsthal shows it, for example in *Der Schwierige,* with its somewhat inconsistent portrayal of Hans Karl's character, and the very inconsistent one of Count Hechingen, whose role fluctuates between the comic and the serious. It can be seen in plays that are rooted more directly in the tradition of the Viennese popular theater, above all in Raimund's works, and to a lesser degree in Nestroy's. There the dramatic possibilities of the individual scene, its theatricality, are as important as the progress of the action as a whole. If the playwright wants to make a specific point, or a joke, he will do it, through one of his characters, even though this may cause the character to abandon his role for a moment. Brecht, always eager to acknowledge his indebtedness to Nestroy, has further emphasized these traits and placed them prominently in the development of modern drama.

In the passage quoted above, Grillparzer singled out historical plays as vehicles to show a "certain incongruence." In his own historical plays, as has often been observed, Grillparzer tends to treat the motifs of power and worldly splendor in a negative fashion. For example,

Ottokar's rise is shown in one act, in sequences that have an unreal, dreamlike quality and depict the hero as proud and callous, while his defeat is treated at great length and with a detailed presentation of his growing humanity. The affairs of the world, its power struggles and intrigues, were motifs that Grillparzer used in order to show lack of human substance. In the quoted passage, he did not clarify, either abstractly or through examples, what exactly he had in mind when speaking of incongruence, but it is possible to see in it also the mutual exclusion of external success and human substance, as it prevails in his plays. In *König Ottokars Glück und Ende,* the development of Ottokar as a human being runs contrary to his political fate, to the rise and fall of his power. In *Ein Bruderzwist in Habsburg,* there is no such obvious juxtaposition. And yet, there is a distinct polarity in the play: The action fluctuates between scenes depicting power struggles and court intrigues on the one hand, and scenes presenting the most intimate manifestations of the individual psyche and of human interaction on the other. At least one critic has spoken of the "inner action" of the play.[5] The external and the internal levels of action are not as clearly discernible as in *Ottokar*; they are interwoven in a more subtle fashion, and the difficulty in coming to terms with the play may well be explained by the high degree of subtlety in which the close, private sphere is contraposed to the grandiose, political.

Grillparzer's Rudolf epitomizes the private, intimate sphere. To be sure, he knows the public sphere and is aware of what he owes it. After he bestows his own private order of the Knights of Peace upon Duke Julius, he is obliged to face the Bohemian estates. Preparing to receive them, he asks for his sword and when Julius—no servant is nearby—brings him the sword as well as the imperial robe, Rudolf is uncertain at first: "Ihr bringt den Mantel auch?" but continues, "Habt Ihr doch recht / Die Welt verlangt den Schein. Wir Beide nur / Wir tragen innerhalb des Kleids den Orden."[6] What is essential and important to him is the private, secretly worn order. It is worn inside, close to the heart. Robe and sword are insignia of a realm from which he has withdrawn spiritually. He exhibits them unwillingly. In the last moment, he decides against wearing the sword and asks Julius to put it down somewhere.

Scenes from which Rudolf is absent, scenes of force, political ambition, and intrigue, are fraught with confusion and futility. The peace negotiations in the second act may be cited as the foremost example. The very fact that there are four archdukes present introduces an element of confusion. It may be true that Grillparzer complained about the oversupply of archdukes in the plot[7]; but he could have made use of the historical playwright's most basic prerogative: to eliminate characters from the plot, for the sake of clarity and expediency. He chose not to. The nature of their debate during the conference further confuses the issue and may be taken as an indication that Grillparzer in effect strove for a measure of entanglement in this scene. The actions of the various participants in the debate are motivated in a distorted way. Klesel speaks out for peace;

this may be considered a proper goal for a man of the cloth to pursue, until it becomes evident that he plans to use the conclusion of the peace as an act of revolt against the emperor, and as a crucial step in enhancing Mathias' power. Mathias, Klesel's tool, ought to echo his mentor's views. However, Mathias has lost a battle, once again, and is eager to continue the war in order to have an opportunity for making up the defeat and regaining his personal honor. He is blind to the fact that he will hardly manage a victory with the number of his men cut in half after he had previously been defeated with the forces still intact. Klesel, first upset by Mathias' refusal to speak out for peace, quickly discerns the advantageous side of the situation: If Mathias does not agree with Klesel, for once, the other archdukes will not suspect any foul play on their part and will be less reluctant to go along with Klesel's plans. "Bleibt, Herr, bei eurer Weigrung," he encourages Mathias before Max, Ferdinand, and Leopold enter, "Vielleicht reift unsern Anschlag grade dies" (212). The conference, conducted according to parliamentary procedures, begins in a fashion familiar to all veterans of township, council or faculty meetings: A few words about the table are exchanged— Max is glad that the table cloth is green and not red or blue—one participant is asked to take minutes, another states that he would rather stand than sit because he likes to stand and because he won't sit until he knows what the meeting is all about. Then there is a brief, jocular exchange about Leopold's recent love adventure, and Klesel is asked not to put this into the minutes.

The actual conference, from Max's admonition "zur Sache" to the adjournment, is long by the standards of stage technique: two hundred and forty lines. It is a tour-de-force in the art of conniving and brainwashing. At the beginning of the meeting, none of the archdukes is in favor of concluding the peace; at the end, only Leopold refuses to agree to the treaty. Klesel, the non-voting member of the assembly, masterminds their change of hearts without their noticing it. Some details in the dialog border on the comic. Max chides Mathias for wanting to save face as a commander by continuing the war with his decimated troops. Therefore, Max is against continuing the war. Klesel inquires eagerly, "So seid ihr für den Frieden?" Max: "Ich? Bewahr!" Klesel: "Doch spracht entgegen ihr dem Krieg." Max: "Ei, laßt mich!" (219). The last phrase, which would have to be rendered as "Leave me alone (with your silly logic)," bespeaks the hopeless muddle of the situation. Soon Max and Ferdinand commit themselves to a vote for peace. Mathias states that he might as well join them since he is being outvoted. Leopold reminds him that there would be two of them since he, Leopold, will vote against the treaty. Mathias' remarkable reply is: "Gerade deshalb Frieden auch" (223). Whereas Max's "Laßt mich" at least acknowledged his inability to respond logically, Mathias' answer openly mocks the principle of meaningful discussion.

This bit of parliamentary confusion is set between two scenes that provide a fitting frame. The conference is preceded by a scene in the imperial camp that introduces the motif of confusion on a physical level: A standard bearer relates how the imperial army, caught between two Turkish columns, found itself in such a state of chaos that imperial soldiers pursued and killed other imperial soldiers.[8] There was no leadership during the battle. The troops are close to rebelling. The scene is further complicated by the appearance of a Protestant delegation. A captain comments that he would send them packing if he were the archduke (Mathias); a colonel replies that it was the archduke who had invited them. When the same captain accuses Protestant soldiers of having committed treason by starting the rout during the battle, one soldier contradicts him, saying that it makes no differences, in combat, which religion a soldier favors: "Im Lager hier sind alle Tapfern Brüder" (200).

The motif of fraternal relationships, oddly twisted, is followed through at some length. In the conference scene, two sets of brothers conspire against another brother, the emperor. In the scene just discussed, soldiers are reported to have killed their brothers inadvertently, while members of conflicting religions consider themselves brothers. In the scene following the peace conference, an attempt by Don Cäsar to abduct Lukrezia is thwarted by the appearance of two of the archdukes and their entourages. As in the scene preceding the conference, there occurs the motif of enemy action within one war party. The soldiers hired to perform the abduction flee, and Archduke Leopold comments: "Nicht Türken sinds, des eignen Lagers Auswurf, / Zu Brudermord gezückt das feige Schwert" (235). The only member of the band captured turns out to be the emperor's son.

These scenes comprise the second act, one of the two acts from which Rudolf is absent altogether. The act encompasses a series of incidents that pertain to the world of intrigue, power, and warfare. Nothing is accomplished throughout the act, except that a dubious peace treaty has been concluded, against the emperor's wishes, and that Mathias has been appointed to act in place of the emperor should the latter refuse to ratify the treaty. Both steps leave everyone uneasy, except Klesel, the arbitrator. Leopold comments, "Ihr werdet sehen was ihr angerichtet" (224); and "Wir haben keinen guten Kampf gekämpft" (231). Uncertainty and confusion determine the act, combined with demagoguery and collusion. It illustrates both the dramatic principles that have been outlined above as characteristic of Grillparzer's art: a certain incongruence of cause and effect, and the futility and inscrutability of the affairs of the world. The act does not have the qualities of a *Lesedrama*. It is extremely stageworthy, and the fact that the action is indecisive and confusing is not a weakness but its most salient feature.

One scene in the third act presents a confrontation between the external world with its strifes, and the internal realm, exemplified in the figure of the emperor. The Bohemian estates, newly encouraged by the unrest in the capitol and by the rumor that Archduke Mathias is approaching with armed forces, demand that the emperor sign an agreement granting religious freedom, the "Letter of Majesty." Their arguments are transparent and their demands have the sound of blackmail. Rudolf, fully aware of the nature of their maneuver, responds by speaking to them of love, respect, and belief, and by admonishing them not to question God's wisdom. His words are genuine, simple, direct, and they are poetic. Nevertheless, it is apparent that Rudolf is not reaching them. There is no communication between him and the delegation. He is aware of the falseness of their arguments, but refrains from challenging them. They in turn do not hear what he has to say to them. Their reply, after the close of Rudolf's exhortations, is a renewed request for his approval of their demands. They have talked past each other, each within his own frame of reference. Rudolf signs their document, in disdain, impatient with them, and discouraged. They honor him with an exclamation, "Mit Gut und Blut für unsern Herrn und Kaiser!" (266). Minutes later, they will cheer Mathias as their new champion.

The end of the third act brings to a climax the juxtaposition of the occurences in the physical and the spiritual world. Mathias, in a splendid procession, enters Prague. Bells ring, music is played, and banners are waved. Mathias is shown riding past on a horse, towering over the crowd. The people rush toward him and cheer "Vivat Mathias! Hoch des Landes Recht!" (277). This takes place upstage. Downstage, Duke Julius has tried in vain to persuade Archduke Leopold not to take up arms against Mathias proceeds, Julius turns aside with a gesture of grief. The realms of action are aligned in a striking tableau that concludes the act: Mathias in his glory, the image of a quickly passing worldly triumph; and Julius in his grief, knowing and understanding, the image of introspection, awareness, and integrity.

The play ends with a variation of this scene. Rudolf is dead and Mathias is emperor. Now that he has reached his goal, he is guilt-ridden at his brother's death and wishes he were dead and Rudolf alive. Yet he cannot take his eyes off the imperial insignia that have been brought to him: "Wie ein Magnet ziehts mir die Augen hin / Und täuscht mit Formen, die nicht sind, ich weiß" (337). The people cheer and want to see their new emperor. Reluctantly, Mathias shows himself on the balcony. Again, the shout "Vivat Mathias!" is heard. Back on stage, Mathias kneels and speaks the liturgical formula "Mea culpa, mea culpa, / Mea maxima culpa" (337). The play ends with the shouts of "Vivat Mathias" continuing from the street, and Mathias, on his knees, covering his face with both hands. Like the third act, the fifth closes on a tableau that signifies the deceitfulness and duplicity of power.

Little has been made in criticism of the scene of Lukrezia's death at the hands of Don Cäsar in the fourth act. It does not seem to have any function, in the structure of the play, other than to add to the crimes of the perpetrator and precipitate his downfall. Lukrezia remains a pale, undefined figure to her end. One could view her death as one of Grillparzer's self-contained scenes that are not closely

integrated into the action. However, if the deceitfulness and illusoriness of worldly things is indeed one theme of the play, the scene assumes a subtle significance. Don Cäsar, up to this point nothing more than a rash good-for-nothing, is shown in a new light. He approaches Lukrezia for one more time, but only in search for truth. In a concrete sense, he wants to know who and what Lukrezia really is. "Laßt mich erkennen euch, nur deshalb kam ich; / Zu wissen was ihr seid, nicht was ihr scheint" (282). Lukrezia, vague and shadowy throughout the play, is an embodiment of the evasive element that prevails in the action. Don Cäsar's wish to discover her true self seems plausible to the reader; moreover, the motif of the quest for recognition is pertinent in a play that presents an action veiled in the dusk of futility and doubt. Don Cäsar gains stature in this scene. He reveals himself as a person with substantial thoughts and feelings by asking questions that are only asked by minds that have pondered problems concerning the very nature of existence. But his wish to know Lukrezia remains unfulfilled, as does his larger quest for truth. He fails in trying to penetrate the veil that covers the essence of things:

> Und Recht und Unrecht, Wesen, Wirklichkeit,
> Das ganze Spiel der buntbewegten Welt,
> Liegt eingehüllt in des Gehirnes Räumen,
> Das sie erzeugt und aufhebt wie es will.
> Ich plagte mich mit wirren Glaubenszweifeln,
> Ich pochte forschend an des Fremden Tür,
> Gelesen hab' ich und gehört, verglichen,
> Und fand sie Beide haltlos, Beide leer.
> Vertilgt die Bilder solchen Schattenspiels,
> Blieb nur das Licht zurück, des Gauklers Lampe,
> Das sie als Wesen an die Wände malt,
> Als einz'ge Leidenschaft der Wunsch: zu wissen.

(282)

The truth that Cäsar seeks is present in the play, although he would not recognize it as an answer to his questions. Rudolf embodies truth. He is the still center around which the fleeting matter of the action revolves. This is shown, in part, through his language. Herbert Seidler has demonstrated that Grillparzer's use of *Prunkreden* lends a certain rhythm to his plays. Scenes of action alternate with reflective pauses in which the essence of the action is crystallized in extended speeches resembling monologues. Such passages show a markedly elevated language and poetic refinement.[9] *Ein Bruderzwist* contains several of these *Prunkreden,* all of them spoken by Rudolf. In fact, a good portion of Rudolf's role consists of *Prunkreden.* According to Seidler's count, two are in the first act (ll. 320-346; 391-439), three in the third act (ll. 1233-1276; 1460-1471; 1533-1669), and two in the fourth (ll. 2239-2269; 2286-2428). Altogether, 436 of Rudolf's lines are are spoken in *Prunkreden.* This leaves 427 lines of his role for dialog other than *Prunkreden,*—slightly less than half. In the fourth act, the last in which Rudolf appears, the proportion is 172 lines of *Prunkreden* versus 18 lines of dialog.

These numbers alone testify to the pivotal significance of Rudolf's role. To some extent, these speeches serve to define Rudolf's philosophical outlook. The contraposition of the *vita activa* and the *vita contemplativa,* shown through the action surrounding Rudolf and his own meditative inaction, has been widely discussed in criticism. However, a concentration on the emperor's philosophical and political views neglects the unique features of this character and reduces the play to a contest of intellectual dispositions. In examining the *Prunkreden,* attention must be paid both to their philosophical significance and to their poetic impact. Rudolf's last speech exemplifies Grillparzer's intent to remove his hero to a realm beyond that of the political intrigues he was supposed to cope with and chose to ignore. It is a realm that comes alive in poetry only. In his meditations, Rudolf's thoughts involuntarily converge on religious subjects. The recollection of Christmas takes him back to his childhood, and forward to the threshold of the hereafter. He asks: "Ist hier Musik?" and Julius replies, "Wir hören nichts, o Herr" (305). Only Rudolf hears the music of a realm he is about to enter, and his departure from one world into another is realized convincingly by the poet:

> Mein Geist verirrt sich in die Jugendzeit.
> Als ich aus Spanien kam, wo ich erzogen,
> Und man nun meldete, daß Deutschlands Küste
> Sich nebelgleich am Horizonte zeige,
> Da lief ich aufs Verdeck und offner Arme
> Rief ich: mein Vaterland! Mein teures Vaterland!
> —So dünkt mich nun ein Land in dem ein Vater—
> Am Rand der Ewigkeit emporzutauchen.
> —Ist es denn dunkel hier?—Dort seh' ich Licht
> Und flügelgleich umgibt es meinen Leib.
> —Aus Spanien komm' ich, aus gar harter Zucht,
> Und eile dir entgegen,—nicht mehr deutsches,
> Nein himmlisch Vaterland.—Willst du?—Ich will!
>
> (308)

Here Grillparzer employs the symbol of the voyage, a traditional literary topos, but his poetic power elevates the scene into the realm of the religious and sublime.

Despite Rudolf's saintly death, it is wrong to see in him nothing but a martyr to his age; a man who could not and would not cope with reality; who triumphed, in the end, through his wisdom, kindness, and religious bearing. There are the harsh realities of his occasional ruthlessness and injustice, his whims and pathological capriciousness. Grillparzer did not attempt to pit an unblemished hero against the wicked world. The inner conflict he depicted, as a playwright and poet, is one of atmosphere: the duality between an external action running its futile course in a vague, unfathomable way, and a personage drawn closely and intimately. This duality is at the root of our difficulties in coming to terms with the play, but it is also the source of its strong poetic impact.

Warmth and closeness are created partially through Grillparzer's language. The nature and the characteristics of the playwright's language have long occupied critics. It is unlike Goethe's and Schiller's, unlike Kleist's, unlike Hebbel's. In *Ein Bruderzwist* there is no willful pose in Grill-

parzer's diction; it runs smoothly, softly, and apparently without effort. A good actor would never choose to recite Grillparzer's lines bombastically and at the top of his voice. They require a gentle approach, and they are most effective when spoken with great understanding and feeling. Even the *Prunkreden* are not meant to be declaimed; they simply require greater insight and penetration. The directness of Grillparzer's language is its most prominent characteristic. Some of Rudolph's questions ring with a sense of closeness and familiarity that immediately establishes a link not only between him and the person addressed, but also between him and the reader or spectator. His last words, "Willst du?—Ich will!" (308), are a foremost example of this stylistic quality. The same is true of the inquiry "Ist hier Musik?" (305), and of Rudolf's reply to Ferdinand's proud statement that he has expelled from his territory all Protestants: "Mit Weib und Kind? Die Nächte sind schon kühl" (190). When Don Cäsar states aggressively that only the Lord is judge in matters of religious belief, Rudolf replies: "Ja Gott und du. Ihr Beide, nicht wahr?" (179). The simplicity and candor of these lines is matched by their poetic impact. Occasionally, Grillparzer uses phrases that are almost quaint. Upon realizing that the man he had not recognized was Ferdinand, Rudolf says "All gut!" (182). Rudolf's chamberlain, Rumpf, carries the quaintness of the language a step further. His is a mixture of officialese and a nearly comic, stenographic, private idiom that imitates the emperor's predilection for elliptic remarks. Rumpf's position in the play is never made quite clear. He is a high-ranking official and chargéd'affaires at court, but he also seems to serve as a private secretary and, in a scene where the emperor cannot find his robe and calls for Rumpf, as a valet. Rumpf shows traces of the comic person of the Viennese popular theater, traces that are subtly evident in his language. He uses phrases such as "Huldreichst guten Morgen" (168), "hochgnädige Geduld" (168), "Geht nicht" (167), "Guter Gott!" (177, 178), "Du liebe Zeit!" (170), and the comic Austrian interjection "Je" (167, twice).[10] Rumpf is Rudolf's semicomic foil and counterpart.[11]

Grillparzer's language may have the ring of quaintness even in scenes that do not deal with Rudolf's sequestered world. For example, in the conference scene in the second act, Max invites the other archdukes to sit down at the table with the phrases "Geht sitzen" (214) and "Komm sitzen" (215). In the same scene, Mathias, at a loss for a reply, urges Klesel to answer, formulating his request in a strikingly direct phrase: "Sagt etwas, Klesel!" (216). Shakespeare was a master at such subtle nuances in the dialog, but no author of tragedy in the German language before Grillparzer conveyed such a degree of immediacy with the use of such simple words.

It has been shown that Grillparzer at times chose to forego the use of words altogether in favor of the gesture.[12] In *Ein Bruderzwist,* one of the *Prunkreden* fades away in mumbled sentence fragments and eventually in silence:

> ([Rudolf] Immer leiser sprechend)
> Wenn nun der Herr die Uhr rückt seiner Zeit,

Die Ewigkeit in jedem Glockenschlag
Für die das Oben und das Unten gleich
Ins Brautgemach—des Weltbaus Kräfte eilen
—Gebunden—in der Strahlen Konjunktur—
Und der Malefikus—das böse Trachten—
    (Er verstummt allmählich. Sein Haupt sinkt auf
die
    Brust. Pause.)

(187)

Originally, Grillparzer had planned to complete the passage with its syntax intact and without an indication of Rudolf's voice dying away.[13] The abandonment of the spoken word in favor of the gesture is significant. The gesture, when subtly used, can convey delicate nuances of meaning. In the present play, Grillparzer used gestures to a great extent. Especially those assigned to Rudolf are capable of creating an atmosphere of poignancy. Rudolf is both awesome as a ruler and engaging as a person—a unique combination in a tragic character. On the one hand, he is infirm and helpless; when in a rage against Don Cäsar, he becomes feeble and has to be helped by his guards. He walks on a cane, or supported by Rumpf. On the other hand, Grillparzer gave him the curious agility that is at times peculiar to very old people.

Rudolf shows a certain lack of inhibitions in his gestures. For example, he reacts with an odd, almost childish gesture when reminded of Leopold's unsuccessful attempt to occupy the city: "Der Kaiser droht heftig mit dem Finger in die Ferne" (295). There are several scenes in the play where Rudolf contributes his share to the dialog with gestures only. There is, above all, his entrance in the first act, and the scene at the well in the fourth. On stage, these passages invariably fall flat and give rise to unwanted laughter, unless they are played with great taste and discernment. His gestures not only lend a fascination to the emperor, but also bring him close to the reader and spectator on a human, emotional level. They express more than mere reactions to what he sees and hears; Rudolf communicates through gestures, and at times he gets across fairly complex messages. For example, he criticizes the poor workmanship in one part of a painting without even stepping up to it, and rejects the painting (172). The people about him have learned to understand his silent language. When he looks at two persons engaged in conversation, Rumpf informs them that the emperor wishes to know what is being discussed (296). Rudolf wags his finger threateningly, and Julius knows that he means Leopold (295). When the emperor shows an interest in the key to Don Cäsar's prison, Julius seems to suspect what his intentions are (297).[14] He can be insistent in his sign language: When he extends his hand to great Duke Julius and Julius wants to kiss it, Rudolf withdraws his hand, then extends it again, whereupon Julius takes hold of Rudolf's hand with both of his (293). Grillparzer is able to convey much of his characters' inner qualities through their gestures. They are direct and truthful emanations of their innermost feelings. When giving Leopold permission to bring troops to his aid, Rudolf transmits this instruction through a gesture while off-stage—the ultimate in subtlety: The door

of his private chamber opens to admit Leopold. In the first act, Rudolf hears of the arrival of young Leopold and, overjoyed, demands to see him. Leopold is summoned; he enters when the emperor and his court have lined up, about to proceed to the chapel, and he is taken aback at the sight of the formal arrangement. The Spanish court ceremonial which rules in the imperial castle in Prague is a new experience to the straightforward young man from the Austrian provinces. Rudolf, somewhat curtly, asks him to take his place in the procession, and Ferdinand beckons him to his side. Leopold's spirits must be dampened—he had reason to expect a warmer welcome from the emperor. Rudolf senses this and corrects the situation:

> (Der Zug setzt sich in Bewegung, die beiden Erzherzoge unmittelbar vor dem Kaiser. Nach einigen Schritten tippt Letzterer Erzherzog Leopold auf die Schulter. Dieser wendet sich um und küßt ihm lebhaft die Hand. Der Kaiser winkt ihm liebreich drohend Stillschweigen zu und sie gehen weiter. Die übrigen folgen paarweise.) Der Vorhang fällt.

(193)

The emperor himself takes a quick and secret liberty against the court ceremonial in order to transmit a personal message.

A delicately conveyed, emotional gesture such as this is part of the innermost realm of action in Grillparzer's play. The contrast between this and the realm of the futile, circuitous external action is not primarily one of humanity versus callousness. Rather, it is a contrast between the close and the distant, the inward and the outward, between matter pertaining to the privacy of the heart and matter pertaining to the wordly ambitions of the will and the intellect. Even when Rudolf performs the gesture of dropping the key into the well and in effect executes his son, Grillparzer shows that the dominant emotion prevailing within him during that moment is not cruelty but consuming pain. It is an awesome deed, yet not one performed callously.[15]

The play is open-ended and grants a view into the chaotic times that lie ahead. The external realm is beginning to reign supreme. This prospect is essential to the tragic qualities of the play, as much so as the death of Rudolf and the moral defeat of Mathias. The appearance of young Colonel Wallenstein at the end of the play and his prophecy concerning the duration of the imminent war are often branded by critics as poor in taste. Certainly Wallenstein cuts an offensive figure. Even ruthless Ferdinand is repelled by his overefficiency. Significantly, it is Wallenstein who reports the approach of the emissaries who have come to announce Rudolf's death, and he is the only one to remain untouched by this news. Wallenstein appears as the epitome of the futile ambition that the world has fallen victim to. His figure is odious in the sense that he incorporates all the negative elements of the play. The introduction of a new character in the last scene is not a weakness in the structure of the play comparable to the appearance of Count Bruchsal in Lessing's *Minna von*

Barnhelm. Grillparzer's dramatic art is a match fo such a challenge: Wallenstein, who will not outlive the war that he is so eage to engage in, unwittingly points to the absurdity of his own ambition.

It is in the figure of Wallenstein, in fact, that the theme of the "vanity of the world," apparent throughout the play, is given its last and strongest embodiment. Led on by Wallenstein, almost everyone on stage cheers the outbreak of the war, and the people in the street cheer the new emperor. But the memory of Rudolf permeates the scene: The imperial insignia are on stage, and Mathias performs his final gesture of repentance.

Notes

1. Urs Helmensdorfer, "Ein Bruderzwist in Habsburg," *Grillparzers Bühnenkunst* (Bern: Francke, 1960), p. 99.

2. *Ibid.,* p. 72.

3. Heinz Politzer, in "Grillparzers 'Bruderzwist'—ein Vater-Sohn-Konflikt in Habsburg." *Festschrift für Bernhard Blume* (Göttingen: Vandenhoeck, 1967), pp. 173-194, has thrown a sharp light on the father-son relationship in the play.

4. Franz Grillparzer, *Sämtliche Werke, Historisch-kritische Gesamtausgabe,* ed. A. Sauer. II/8 (Vienna: Gerlach, 1916), 176-177.

5. Kare Langvik-Johannessen, "'Ein Bruderzwist in Habsburg.' Versuch einer Offenlegung der inneren Handlung." *Grillparzer-Forum Forchtenstein* (Heidelberg: Lothar Stiehm), III (1967), 34-42; IV (1968), 43-57. Langvik-Johannessen's foremost concern is the investigation of a psychological basis underlying the action.

6. *Historisch-kritische Gesamtausgabe,* I/6 (Vienna: Scholl, 1927), 259. Future references to this volume will appear by page numbers in the text.

7. Franz Grillparzer, *Gespräche und Charakteristiken seiner Persönlichkeit durch die Zeitgenossen,* ed. A. Sauer 6 vols. (Vienna: Literarischer Verein, 1904-1916), III, 340.

8. The scene is repeated during the retreat of Leopold's forces from Prague. Cf. 289-290.

9. Herbert Seidler, "Prunkreden in Grillparzers Dramen." *Studien zu Grillparzer und Stifter* (Vienna etc.: Böhlau, 1970), pp. 85-117. [First published in 1964 in *Sitzungsberichte der Österreichischen Akademie der Wissenschaften, philosophisch-historische Klasse,* 244/4].

10. Significantly, "je" occurs many times in Grillparzer's comedy, *Weh dem der lügt.*

11. Rumpf is related to a number of servant figures in the Austrian theater tradition, notably to Anton in Hofmannsthal's *Der Turm,* a play that shares a number of themes and motifs with *Ein Bruderzwist,* such as the prophecy of danger to the ruler through

a member of his family, the father-son conflict, the contraposition of corruptness versus purity, and certain inconsistencies in the characterization.

12. E.g., Peter von Matt, *Der Grundriß von Grillparzers Bühnenkunst* (Zürich: Atlantis, 1965), pp. 136 ff.

13. Matt, p. 138.

14. Cf. Politzer, "Bruderzwist," p. 179.

15. One possible interpretation of the scene at the well that—to my knowledge—has not been suggested before would be to see in Rudolf's dropping the key an act of mercy. Since the thwarted abduction of Lukrezia, Don Cäsar has been trying desperately to end his life, first in battle, without succeeding, and now by directly attempting suicide. Could it be that by dropping the key the emperor goes along with his son's intentions and wants to spare him the ignominy of a trial and certain public execution? It is possible to see in Rudolf's words: "Er ist gerichtet, / Von mir, von seinem Kaiser, seinem—/ Herrn!" (297), an assertion that only he, as Don Cäsar's father, should judge him, and a final act of fatherly protection. Seen in this light, the scene is considerably less horrid than, e.g., the killing of Emilia Galotti at her father's hands.

William A. Little (essay date Fall 1975)

SOURCE: "Grillparzer's *Esther*: A Fragment for Good Reason," in *Michigan Germanic Studies,* Vol. 1, No. Fall, 1975, pp. 165-79.

[*In the following essay, Little speculates on the ending of Grillparzer's fragment,* Esther, *and on the reasons why the playwright abandoned the work.*]

With no perceptible voice of dissent critics have perennially acclaimed **Esther** as one of Grillparzer's finest, most mature works, although the poet left it a torso. In 1874 Wilhelm Scherer called it "seine genialste Dichtung,"[1] and nearly a century later Heinz Politzer described it as "ein Produkt aus des Dichters bester Zeit."[2] In the intervening years other critics have expressed much the same opinion, and the "Liebesszene" between Esther and the King was regarded by Emil Reich as "eine der glänzendsten der Weltliteratur,"[3] a view shared by Georg Witkowski: "die grosse Liebesszene . . . zählt zu dem Schönsten in aller Poesie."[4] Although **Esther** is no longer performed so frequently as it once was, Norbert Fuerst asserts, "das Esther-Fragment hat eine Bühnengeschichte, um die andere, vollständige Dramen Grillparzers es beneiden können."[5]

Given the high esteem in which **Esther** has been held and its popularity on the stage, there is an extraordinary lack of secondary literature on the work: one monograph, no dissertations, and only three or four articles, the latest of which appeared nearly fifty years ago.[6] On the other hand,

Esther has been treated in some depth in the biographies by August Ehrhard,[7] Politzer,[8] and Douglas Yates,[9] and in the more specialized studies of Grillparzer's dramas, such as those by Reich, Otto E. Lessing,[10] and Francis Wolf-Cirian.[11] Of particular value also are the introductions to the work by Stefan Hock[12] and Leopold Hradek.[13] The small body of *Esther* criticism, however, has been largely speculative and has generally delat with two major problems: how did Grillparzer intend to end the work, and why did he abandon it? To each of these questions the poet himself provided answers, but he did so late in life, when the frailty of old age may have clouded his memory. Rather than clarifying matters, his comments, at least partially self-contradictory or inaccurate, have tended to confuse them.

In January 1866 in a conversation with Professor Robert Zimmermann Grillparzer outlined the general direction he had intended *Esther* to take: that only Haman was to die and, "zuletzt sollte sich Alles ganz gut lösen, mehr wie im Schauspiel."[14] Two years later, in a lengthy conversation with Frau von Littrow-Bischoff, Grillparzer gave a much more detailed description of his plans, but now both Haman and Zares were to die, and Esther, after having become a "Kanaille," was either to die or live out her life in misery.[15] In several other conversations (with Frankl[16] and Laube[17]) Grillparzer spoke briefly about *Esther,* but on the whole, criticism very early became polarized, depending on whether one accepted the account of Zimmermann or of Frau von Littrow-Bischoff. Alfred von Berger, the strongest advocate of Frau von Littrow-Bischoff's account, maintained that, however one regarded the work, "jedenfalls wäre der Schluss ein herber und diabolischer geworden."[18] (It might be noted that the three early attempts to complete Grillparzer's fragment—by Karl von Heigel in 1888, Rudolf Labres in 1891, and Rudolf Krauss, ca. 1901—all tend to follow Frau von Littrow-Bischoff's version rather than Zimmermann's.) Emil Reich was the first and strongest critic to favor Zimmermann's report over Frau von Littrow-Bischoff's, and with varying degrees of loyalty subsequent critics have fallen generally into one or the other camp.[19]

Speculation on why Grillparzer abandoned the drama has not been marked by such disparate positions, but here again Grillparzer gave a variety of reasons. To Frankl he explained, ". . . ich verlor die Stimmung. Wohl auch, weil die Handlung mir politisch auszuarten drohte,"[20] and to Frau von Littrow-Bischoff he acknowledged that the completed drama could not possibly have been performed in Vienna because of the censorship, and probably could not even have been printed.[21] Wolf-Cirian believed the reason lay in Esther's character as Grillparzer had drawn it in the first two acts: "Allein in den ausgeführten beiden Aufzügen ist Esthers Wesen auf einer so breiten edlen Basis aufgebaut, dass es der Dichter niemals hätte bis zur Canaille erschüttern können, ohne sich selbst zu widersprechen."[22] Similarly, Sigismund Friedmann felt that "die erwähnten guten Eigenschaften [Esthers] verloren gehen müssen, und so mag Grillparzer wohl aus diesem Grunde

die Vollendung dieser Dichtung unterlassen haben."[23] Douglas Yates agrees that Esther's character has been so firmly established that for her "to end as a scoundrel would entail a change in her character of a kind that is insufficiently foreshadowed in the opening acts. . . . But even had he revised the published fragment and developed the motivation of Esther's personality, Grillparzer would have faced a thankless task; for while it may be artistically rewarding to show that in the worst of us there is good which can prevail, it is less so (certainly according to nineteenth-century standards) to show the evil in the best of us."[24] Walter Naumann, in his perceptive study, *Grillparzer: Das dichterische Werk* speculates from a point of view not entirely unrelated to Yates: "In *Esther* ist die Hofwelt mit grimmigem Hohn in mehreren Gestalten dargestellt. Das Unfruchtbare einer solchen negativen Zeichnung mag ein Grund gewesen sein, dass jenes Drama nicht vollendet wurde. Alle Ansätze reiner Karikatur ... sind Fragment geblieben."[25] Nadler, on the other hand, believed that *Esther* had so much in common with *Die Jüdin von Toledo, Libussa,* and *Ein Bruderzwist in Habsburg,* ". . . dass der Dichter nichts Besseres hätte tun können, als *Esther* aus dem Wettbewerb auszuschneiden und seine ganze Kraft auf die drei anderen Stücke zusammenzufassen,"[26] and that ultimately, despite whatever reasons Grillparzer may have given publicly for stopping work on *Esther,* ". . . was ihn dabei wirklich geführt hatte, das waren seine künstlerische Witterung und der natürliche Haushalt seiner Kräfte."[27] Doubtless in all these reasons, in both those given by Grillparzer and those advanced by various critics, there are valid elements, but internal problems in the fragment itself suggest that the poet faced serious problems in character motivation and structure, had he chosen to carry the work to completion.

In the pleasant occupation of speculating whether Zimmermann or Frau von Littrow-Bischoff more accurately reported the poet's real intentions, the work itself has frequently been lost sight of. Ultimately we must deal with what we have, what the poet has left us, the text itself. It is a fragment; in one sense a fragment of a fragment. Of the 979 lines that Grillparzer completed, he released only the first 731 during his lifetime; both in the *Dichterbuch aus Oestreich* (1863) and in the stage performance (1868) the fragment concludes with the love scene between Esther and King Ahasverus. Even after Grillparzer's death, the full text of *Esther* was still not made available in the early "complete" editions (1872 ff.), and it was not until the fifth edition (1887) that the entire fragment was first published. Yet as it stands, this fragmentary work reveals much about Grillparzer's creative process, about his concept of structure and character, and about the reasons why, in this case, he chose to leave the work incomplete.

Esther is Grillparzer's only serious attempt at a biblical drama,[28] and he relied for his material either on the Book of Esther or on Josephus Flavius' *Antiquities of the Jews,*[29] which accords, in a more lengthy fashion, with the Old Testament account. Grillparzer was also well acquainted with Lope de Vega's *La hermosa Ester,* but Lope's influence here has been exaggerated.[30] Grillparzer was also familiar with Racine's *Esther,* but the latter exerted even less influence than Lope.

The genesis of **Esther** can be traced to an early point in the poet's career, and his thoughts for a dramatization of the tale antedated his first acquaintance with either Lope's or Racine's work on the same theme. In 1821 he first mentioned **Esther** in his notes, and although he did not include it in his "Stoffverzeichnis" of 1826, there is no compelling reason to believe that he did not still intend to develop it. In 1829 he returned to the theme and sketched the opening scene between Bigthan and Theres.

As he set about his task, and as he always maintained in later life, Grillparzer intended to follow the Bible, "ganz nach der Bibel,"[31] and in a broad way he did adhere to the biblical account, although by no means "mit ausserordentlicher Treue."[32] The text as it stands in two acts and the beginning of a third is essentially an expansion of parts of Chapter II and the beginning of III of the Book of Esther, and refers back to the banishment of Vasthi, which occurred in Chapter I. From the very beginning Grillparzer allowed himself numerous liberties and made seemingly minor changes. Both had far-reaching implications.

The actual composition of the work was undertaken in three separate stages, and the first section was begun in the summer of 1830:

Stage 1. Summer 1830   lines 1-226
Stage 2. Early 1839 & 1840 lines 226-[717-760]-939
Stage 3. 1848   lines 940-979

By examining these three stages individually it becomes possible to trace Grillparzer's changes in thought and shifts in plan. Simultaneously, it becomes apparent what difficulties the poet would have faced had he continued the drama.

I. Stage 1: 1830 (lines 1-226)

Grillparzer left no indication as to precisely when he began composition of the drama, but on the basis of the paper used, the editors of the *Historischkritische Ausgabe (HKA)* believe the first stage was begun sometime in the summer of 1830.[33] A year earlier Grillparzer had sketched briefly both Bigthan's opening speech and the exchange with Theres (whom he originally called Zares). In the sketch Haman's wife is absent. In the final version there is some question whether or not Bigthan has been in Susa before: the "sonst" in line 2 would seem to indicate that he had, as would the fact that he recognizes Zares as well as Theres (whom he knows well). If he has been in Susa before and he does know Zares, then it is curious that Haman, whom he meets shortly thereafter, is a stranger to him. More important, however, is the question of Bigthan's motivation, of Grillparzer's eventually working him into the plot against Esther. In the Bible Bigthan and Theres (both eunuchs) are the King's chamberlains, and it is they alone who eventually plot against him, although no

reason for their animosity is given. Grillparzer, however, needed to establish a bond with Vasthi, and he did so by making Vasthi send for him and by having Zares remind Bigthan that it was the Queen, "die dich . . . beschützt" (34). On the other hand, in his preliminary sketch Grillparzer included the lines (subsequently deleted): "Doch naht nicht Zares [Theres] dort, mein Freund und Landsmann / Und nun auch Dienstgenoss, seitdem *der König* / Des Schenken Amt, gleich ihm mir anvertraut" (my italics).[34] The changes from the Bible may appear slight, but they were vitally necessary, since Grillparzer intended to build his work around Vasthi's conspiracy; as he noted to himself in the spring of 1830, "Als Hintergrund aller Intrigen am Hofe die verstossene Königin Vasthi, die aber selbst nie erscheint."[35]

The portrait of Bigthan in Act I is hardly that of a potential assassin. Throughout the scene it is Theres who is so enraged by recent events that he ". . . sprudelt Grimm statt klug gemessner Worte" (51). Bigthan, on the other hand, expresses only what appears to be genuine concern at the unfortunate state of affairs. Grillparzer may have realized that Bigthan's role as a conspirator had been only thinly established, since he allows Bigthan to remain silently in the background when he and Theres again appear together later in Act II.

Of all the characters in the **Esther** fragment, none is more fraught with problems than Haman, and especially as he appears in the first section of the work. Indeed, Haman is the key to many of the other problems which would have beset the author in the later acts of the drama. Here Grillparzer's changes from the Bible are particularly significant, insofar as they would have affected the course of the play.

In the 1830 stage in the composition of the work, the poet's attention is focused overwhelmingly on the figure of Haman. Even before he first appears on stage Zares has outlined his character, although her position as lady-in-waiting to the banished Queen hardly allows her remarks to be considered impartial. One point, however, is especially noteworthy since it involves an important departure from the Bible: it was, she asserts, primarily on Haman's advice that the King had decided to ban his Queen:

> Seht Ihr, dort kommet er [Haman]
> Nach dessen Rat der König meist gehandelt
> Als er so schwer tat unsrer hohen Freundin.

> (111-113)

In the biblical account the King had acted on the advice of one Memuchan, but Grillparzer placed the responsibility squarely on Haman's shoulders. Thus to be logical and consistent Haman ought to have done all in his power to prevent the return of Vasthi, since he could certainly expect her to seek revenge, if she succeeded in returning to the throne ("Denn sie ist . . . / . . . rachsüchtig" [664]). Nevertheless, Grillparzer was adamant on constructing a conspiracy by Vasthi in which Haman would eventually take part. As the dramatist sketched it in the spring of 1830, Haman was to be wooed to the side of the Queen, but would not be won over until Act V: "Dem Aman [Haman] werden gleich von vornherein Anträge von ihrer Seite gemacht, die er aber halb mürrisch zurückweist, wie Einer der nicht hören will, gleichsam weil er seiner nicht sicher ist, wenn er einmal gehört hat. Erst im 5. Akt, nach seiner äussersten Demüthigung durch Mardochäus, lässt er die Anträge gleichsam über sich ergehen."[36] Some thirty-five years later, in his conversation with Zimmermann in 1866, Grillparzer still insisted, "Der Haman sollte durch seine Frau verleitet werden, auf die Partei der Königin Vasthi zu treten."[37] In the account Grillparzer gave to Frau von Littrow-Bischoff Haman was to die because of his intended plot to annihilate the Jews. The full development of a Vasthi conspiracy involving Haman, however, could only distract from the main action.

The liberties Grillparzer took with the biblical Haman were both major (as above) and minor. One of the minor changes is illuminating as it suggests that the poet did not keep the Bible or Josephus before him as he planned and wrote. At one place in his notes he refers with blithe innocence to Haman, the husband of Zares and the father of ten sons as "der Verschnittene."

Haman's character as described by Zares and as it derives from his own words in the 1830 section is generally consistent. Zares calls him "klein und ängstlich" (119), but immediately she concedes that he is shrewd in devising "das Nützliche" (122), and as he approaches she speaks of him as "jämmerlich" (125). And to all appearances Haman is genuinely miserable and wretched. We ask ourselves, are his sense of anxiety, his tears (165), his distraught behavior vis-à-vis Bigthan, his eager search for advice from any quarter—are all these hypocritically feigned, and if so why? Or could they not be genuine? Could he not, in fact, be earnestly attempting to devise "das Nützliche"? From what emerges later in the drama, it is clear that these are not his true sentiments or interests, but up to the point to which Grillparzer took the work in 1830 the question certainly remains moot. To be sure, Haman's final speech in the 1830 section (212-226) reveals a willingness to disregard scruples (216), but his insistent call for "Klugheit" (220) does not suggest that his every previous word and gesture has been false and treacherous, as we would have to construe them in the light of Grillparzer's further development of Haman in 1839 and 1840.

Haman's character and role during this part of the exposition (1830) remain ambiguous, and that ambiguity is heightened by the awkwardness of the Haman-Bigthan dialogue. How did Grillparzer expect his audience to receive this exchange? What purpose did he intend to achieve with it? Both Ehrhard and Politzer see in it a reflection of a similar exchange in Grillparzer's early satire, "Das Prius oder die Bekehrung, ein rührendes Drama für Beamte" (1821). Ehrhard maintains that the poet makes of Haman "eine Karikatur auf jene Minister, Präsidenten und Hofräte, die er [Grillparzer] in seiner Beamtenlaufbahn aus der Nähe studieren konnte"; Politzer agrees that "dieser Auftritt gibt sich als eine reine Beamtensatire. . . ." All very well and good, but occurring as it does so early in the dramatic action and so abruptly, it invites at least a second look. Even if one accepts Politzer's interpretation, "der Hochmut, der in diesem Vergessen Hamans liegt, die gleichsam nasale Arroganz seiner Herablassung—sie tragen das Zeichen der unmittelbaren Erfahrung, die Grillparzer in seinem Amtsleben zuteil geworden ist," the nagging problem remains: if Grillparzer was at pains to delineate the character of his villain, a man who would later participate in a plot to assassinate the Queen, and who was capable of genocide, then this aspect of his personality makes him petty and laughable rather than treacherous. What Grillparzer has given us in this vignette of Haman as the *Kleinbeamter* seems both gratuitous and *possenhaft;* it is hardly commensurate with the enormity of the crimes he is later supposed to commit. Otherwise, Haman's character, as it is drawn in the 1830 section, corresponds precisely to his wife's description of him: "klein, ängstlich, jämmerlich," but withal shrewd and resourceful. Haman is the garrulous courtier, the "recht versatile Staatsmann, so eine Art Polonius," as Grillparzer described him to Zimmermann in 1866.

Having advised the King to banish Vasthi, Haman has drawn upon his head the wrath of Zares, his wife, who was also the former Queen's chief lady-in-waiting. Zares may not always have held her husband in high esteem, but Grillparzer does not suggest that prior to the fateful incident Zares has scorned him: "Kein freundlich Wort ward ihm seit jenem Tage" (116). By depicting Zares as hostile to her husband Grillparzer has made two more changes from the Bible. In the Book of Esther Zares does not appear until after Esther had already become Queen, and after both Theres and Bigthan had been hanged for having plotted against the King (Esther 5:10). Moreover, Zares stands firmly aligned with her husband and fully supports him. It is she, in fact, who advises Haman to construct the gallows upon which to hang Mardochai.

II. STAGE 2: 1839-1840 (LINES 227-939)

After an interval of nearly a decade Grillparzer resumed work on *Esther* sometime in the summer of 1839, and working intermittently into 1840, he finished the first act and wrote the second. The poet's first task was to complete the exposition, and he moved directly into the King's monologue, which he had prepared for at the point where he had broken off in 1830 (lines 221-226).

The initial impression given by King Ahasverus is of a man deeply distraught and disappointed. Clearly he is overcome by feelings of anguish, frustration, and rage. "Launenhaft" he may be, but there is no sign of the "asiatischer Despot," as Grillparzer called him in his conversation with Frau von Littrow-Bischoff. Nor does he speak and act like one of those "weichen Männer" (40), of whom Zares had named him an obvious example. Quite the contrary, Ahasverus appears as a monarch who would wish harmony and contentment in his land, who would want to be recognized as benign, not tyrannical. But he has been badly (evilly?) advised and so distrusts and shuns his advisers. At the same time, however, he recognizes the limitation of his power and realizes the extent to which he is dependent upon his own advisers, since his image is largely and simultaneously a reflection of their character: "Seid ihr schlimm, bin ich's auch" (256). Aridai, the brother of Zares, sums up succinctly the King's character in his response to Bigthan's astonished question, "War das der König?"

> Frag' ich doch mich selbst,
> Ob das derselbe Fürst, des sanfter Mut
> Die Liebe war des menschlichen Geschlechts;
> Des Wort Verzeihung hiess, sein Anschaun Gnade.
> Und jetzt zerstört, im Innersten verwandelt.
>
> (272-276)

If the King finds himself in a mood of disappointment and sadness, it is of course a situation for which he is more than partially responsible. Not only had he been ill-advised in demanding that the Queen appear at the feast, but he had then followed equally bad advice by setting her aside. He may have shown himself "weich" in accepting that advice, but he had been uncommonly bull-headed in sticking to his decision. Politzer sees in the Ahasverus-Vasthi confrontation a situation of unyielding stubbornness where "Schlag folgt Gegenschlag." Herein, albeit obscurely, lies the germ for another problem Grillparzer would eventually have had to cope with, had he completed the drama. The King grieves because he has banned the one he loves, yet he is too obstinate to recall her. But love her he does, as Esther points out during her initial conversation with him, when she urges him to bring back "die unersetzte, schwervermisste Freundin!" (656). Vasthi, on the other hand, is evidently more consumed by rage than grief, and the King will soon learn that he had given his love to one whose love would be corrupted (i.e. in the final lines of the fragment, when he reads that "Die Kön'gin Vasthi spinnt geheimen Anschlag . . ." [977]). More extenuating, however, and for the poet more problematic, would be the indelible impression that the King's judgment of people had been faulty—and one had to live with the possibility that it might be faulty on more than one occasion where his heart was concerned—that Esther's character too might degenerate at court, to the point that she might indeed become a "Canaille."

The King's relationship with Vasthi is not only clouded by the question of bad judgment; it also remains one of the unresolved problems of the play. Grillparzer never mentioned Vasthi's later role in his conversation with Zimmermann, and to Frau von Littrow-Bischoff he only noted that the poisoned beaker to be presented by Bigthan was intended for Esther: ". . . der König soll nicht sterben, im Gegenteil, er soll leben für Vasthi." Theres and Bigthan are to be executed for their part in the conspiracy, but Vasthi's fate is ignored. If Grillparzer was determined that she should remain at the center of the court intrigues, then

in one way or in another her presence would have to make itself felt down into the final act of the drama, and it was, in fact, at this point that Grillparzer evidently planned to move Haman to her side in the conflict. If the poet persisted in following that plan, he faced the problem of juggling two distinct major plots, both of which would have competed with each other for pre-eminence: the Vasthi-Haman versus Ahasverus-Esther plot and the Haman versus Mardochai-Jews plot. Haman would naturally have constituted the link between the two, but he would also have had to assume a disproportionately important role in the drama, a role that could easily have overshadowed both Esther and the King.

The brief conclusion of the scene, after the King departs, centers again on Haman, but in the interval of nine years Grillparzer's image of Haman seems to have altered considerably. No longer simply a rather unattractive, but "recht versatiler Staatsmann," Haman has now evolved into an active villain. Moreover, the Haman of 1839 quite effectively obliterates the Haman of 1830 by revealing that he has set his plan of action into motion even before the beginning of the play. He thus vitiates every word and sentiment he had expressed earlier. It is no longer Haman devising "das Nützliche," but Haman scheming "Verrat" (315).

If Haman is at present engaged in a treasonous plan, then it is only logical that he should do so for personal gain, whether for power or prestige, or both. There is no assurance, however, that he will gain either; quite the contrary, his actions now threaten him with double jeopardy.

In the Book of Esther the King is advised by his councillors to inaugurate the search for a new Queen, and it is he who endorses the plan and orders it implemented. In Grillparzer's *Esther* the situation is reversed: the plan to search for a new Queen is conceived by Haman alone and is undertaken on his initiative alone—indeed, Haman conceals the whole affair from the King. The departure from the Bible seems unnecessary, since Haman could have operated with equal cunning and treachery, even were he acting on the King's orders. Acting on his own initiative he invites his own ruin, and at least for a moment at the beginning of Act II, it appears as if his downfall were imminent (490 ff.). Of course, the courtiers believe that Haman intends to set a Queen of his own choice upon the throne, but that achievement is denied him. Haman has no control whatever over the King's choice; he will have to accommodate himself to her and hope that she will be well disposed to him—as he so well recognizes, "Wer nicht gefällt, missfällt und wer missfällt, / Hat ausgelebt, schon lang vor seinem Tode" (541-542). Moreover, one might also argue that Grillparzer has created another problem by making Haman responsible for the search: if it was ordered by Haman, then he should have automatically excluded all Jews, since he was one of the Agagites (Amarkelites), the hereditary enemies of the Jews. Certainly Haman could not have afforded to allow a Jew to become a potential choice for Queen. Finally, Zares' threat, to thwart the plan outlined by Haman, suggests the possibility of yet another, a two-headed conspiracy of her own: to frustrate her husband's intrigue and to initiate her own to restore Vasthi.

The final lines of Act I and all of Act II also belong to the second stage in the composition of the drama and present relatively few instances where Grillparzer had to fashion new material to old, to develop consistently characters whom he had introduced in the first stage of writing. Zares disappears entirely, and although Theres and Bigthan appear briefly in Act II, neither character is developed further. The one figure from the 1830 section with whom Grillparzer still had to contend was Haman, and the poet had already altered his character when he resumed work on the drama. Although Haman's portrait took on sharper definition as the work progressed, the ambiguities in his character remained. As Berthold Auerbach, one of the earliest commentators on *Esther,* noted, "Über den Minister Haman war der Dichter offenbar noch nicht einig mit sich." Clearly, Grillparzer's intentions for Haman were still unsettled, and it may well have been with Haman in mind that the poet later conceded to Emil Kuh that "der erste Akt gefällt mir nicht."

At almost every juncture, whenever Haman appears on stage, Grillparzer's problems increase. In his monologue early in the second act, Haman still gives the impression that he believes what he has done has been for the good of the country: "Ein treuer Diener lohnt sich endlich selbst / Mit dem Bewusstsein, dass er Gutes wollte" (503-504). If the courtiers' comments are to be believed, then either Haman's "Gutes" must be synonymous with "Verrat," or Haman is insensitive to the fact that he has vastly overextended his powers. Certainly, Haman's position is gravely threatened: in the first place the King is furious at the plan itself, and when he discovers—apparently he has not yet done so—that Haman was its instigator, then Haman's influence will indeed be "vernichtet" (490). Secondly, any hope for a successful outcome to Haman's plan is diminishing by the hour, and the selection of a new Queen appears highly unlikely.

When the King enters it is clear from his glance at Haman (post 568) that he has learned Haman's role. Nonetheless, one might note that although "der König zürnt, ob des Versuchs, / Ihn zu beweiben" (492-493), he has inspected, however perfunctorily, the "bunte Reihe" (494) and has laid in readiness the "goldnen Reif, bestimmt für die Gewählte" (718), in the eventuality that he might find someone attractive to him. When he does, Haman's return to grace is assured, and his power restored.

Haman appears only once again in the fragment, near the close of Act II, and here the problems abound. When he enters, his opening lines suggest that he has come directly from the scene with the King in which he was allowed to kiss the King's hand. At the same time, however, it appears that there has been a second interview with the King, in which "der König steckte selber / Sein Siegel mir an

diese meine Hand" (863-864). In any case, with Haman now in possession of the King's seal ring, he has arrived, in his own words, at the pinnacle of his power: "Und all der Glanz ist Macht. / Wer ist noch, der vor mir nicht sinkt in Staub?" (865-866). What further height remains to be scaled—or is Haman simply addicted to intrigue for intrigue's sake? Grillparzer provides no answer, nor does he hint at one in the conversation between Haman and Hiram: "*Haman (leise und schnell):* Habt etwas ihr Geheimes mir zu künden, / Sagt's meiner Frau, lasst's meine Gattin wissen" (904-905).

What possible motivation can the now powerful Haman have for becoming involved with Hiram, Vasthi's loyal Chamberlain? For the "versatile Staatsmann" to involve himself at this point in his career in a conspiracy with Vasthi would be senseless, for there could be no possible gain, only danger. Hiram is what Haman calls him, ". . . der Schatten meines Glücks" (886). At the same time, it is inconceivable that Hiram, who already knows that Haman's plan to place a new Queen on the throne has been successful ("Und Euer Ohr auf neue Töne lauscht" [887]), should confide any of his intentions to Haman. As his parting remark indicates, he sees through Haman's falseness.

When Hiram departs Mardochai attempts to warn Haman of the developing conspiracy. Again, to have acted consistently, Haman should have lent a willing ear to Mardochai's account. To have reported it to the King would have served only to strengthen his position still further. By covering his ears and refusing to listen, Haman abets the plot and automatically becomes an accessory to the act.

In 1840, when Grillparzer broke off work on the drama at the end of Act II, it is certainly possible that he foresaw the problems he would face in the subsequent development of Haman's character and the extent to which retention of the Vasthi conspiracy might complicate the outcome of the play.

III. Stage 3: 1848 (lines 940-979)

When Grillparzer again resumed work on *Esther* early in 1848, he added only the first forty lines of Act III and then abandoned the piece altogether. The eight-year interruption in the composition of the work makes itself felt in an atmosphere of hesitancy and uncertainty. Mardochai's warning, which has been delivered prior to the opening of the scene, is itself ambiguous, and King Ahasverus is uncertain whether to take the message seriously or to regard it as the mischief of "jener Ohrenbläser einer / . . . / Vielleicht ein solch verworfenes Insekt" (963, 969). For her part, Esther equivocates and hesitates unnecessarily before producing the document. The tentative quality in these forty lines suggests that the poet himself was struggling to recapture the threads of his earlier plans.

Little of significance was added in 1848: the King remains, as he had been portrayed in 1839-40, essentially benign, and Esther, though present, speaks a total of less than ten lines. Her denial of Mardochai accords with the biblical tradition, and in this point Grillparzer had no choice; to allow Esther to do otherwise would have contradicted one of the crucial parts of the Bible story. Mardochai's warning, on the other hand, is a blending of the biblical tale with Grillparzer's own invention. As in the Bible the warning reaches the King through Esther, but Grillparzer alters the message in two ways: he places Vasthi at the center of the conspiracy, and he does not specify against whom it is aimed. (Ahasverus, of course, realizes that Esther, not himself, is the intended victim.) With the reading of Mardochai's message the fragment abruptly breaks off, but as it does, it furnishes us with Grillparzer's final word on his intentions. Clearly, he still tenaciously held to his plan to develop Vasthi as the chief conspirator. In the course of eighteen years that basic thought had never changed; indeed, could now no longer be changed. Grillparzer had laid the groundwork too well to alter his plan in 1848.

The steady accumulation of seemingly minor liberties that Grillparzer had taken with the biblical story of Esther could not be reversed, and he faced the problem of having to make yet further, more drastic changes. If, however, he still intended, as he so stoutly maintained, that everything was to be "ganz nach der Bibel," then in 1848 he had two alternatives: to rewrite the first two acts (a task he would not conceivably undertake), or to put the work aside and leave it a fragment. Otherwise he might continue, but along a road that would inexorably draw him further and further away from the Bible. Ultimately, his decision to abandon *Esther* was a tacit acknowledgment that he could not carry the work forward to conclusion as a biblical drama, and that the dramatic and structural problems which had evolved over the long gestational period of composition offered little promise of successful resolution.

Notes

1. Wilhelm Scherer, *Vorträge und Aufsätze zur Geschichte des geistigen Lebens in Deutschland und Österreich* (Berlin: Weidmann, 1874), 268.

2. Heinz Politzer, *Franz Grillparzer oder das abgründige Biedermeier* (Vienna, Munich, Zürich: Verlag Fritz Molden, 1972), 270.

3. Emil Reich, *Grillparzers dramatisches Werk* (Vienna: Saturn, [4]1937), 242.

4. Georg Witkowski, *Das deutsche Drama des neunzehnten Jahrhunderts* (Leipzig: Teubner, 1906), 24.

5. Norbert Fürst, *Grillparzer auf der Bühne* (Vienna, Munich: Manutius, 1958), 226.

6. Leopold Hradek, *Studien zu Grillparzers Altersstil und die Datierung des Estherfragmentes* (Prague-Smichow: Koppe-Bellemann, 1915); S. Lublinski, *Jüdische Charaktere bei Grillparzer, Hebbel und Otto Ludwig* (Literarische Studien; Berlin, 1899); W. Duschinsky, "Über die Quellen und die Zeit der Abfassung von Grillparzers 'Esther'," *Zeitschrift für*

die österreichischen Gymnasien 50 (1899): 961-973; M. Milrath, "Bilder und Vergleiche in Grillparzers *Esther*," *Programm des k. k. deutschen Staatsgymnasiums Prag-Neustadt* (1906); W. Küchler, "Esther bei Calderon, Racine und Grillparzer," *Jahrbuch für Philologie* 1 (1925): 333-354; "Zur Geschichte von Grillparzers Esther-Fragment," *Jahrbuch der Grillparzer-Gesellschaft* 31 (1932): 151-154.

7. August Ehrhard, *Franz Grillparzer: Sein Leben und seine Werke*, tr. Moritz Necker (Munich: Beck, 1910).

8. Politzer, op. cit.

9. Douglas Yates, *Franz Grillparzer* (Cambridge: Cambridge University Press, 1972).

10. Otto E. Lessing, *Grillparzer und das neue Drama* (Munich, Leipzig: Piper, 1905).

11. Francis Wolf-Cirian, *Grillparzers Frauengestalten* (Stuttgart: J. G. Cotta Nachfolger, 1908).

12. *Grillparzers Werke in fünfzehn Teilen,* ed. Stefan Hock (Berlin, Leipzig, Vienna, Stuttgart: Bong, n.d. [1911]), VIII, 9-29.

13. Franz Grillparzer, *Sämtliche Werke, Historisch-kritische Ausgabe im Auftrage der Bundeshauptstadt Wien,* ed. August Sauer, Reinhold Backmann, et al., 42 vols. (Vienna: Scholl, 1909 ff.), I, 7, ed. Leopold Hradek. Hereafter cited as *HKA.* Line numbers in *Esther* are indicated parenthetically after each quotation from the drama.

14. *Grillparzers Gespräche und die Charakteristiken seiner Persönlichkeit durch die Zeitgenossen,* ed. August Sauer. Schriften des literarischen Vereins in Wien, 6 vols., 1904 ff. Part Two (5), (1863-1871), no. 1176 (104). Hereafter cited as *Gespräche.*

15. Ibid., no. 1212 (248).

16. Ibid., no. 1209 (234-236).

17. *HKA,* I, 21, 436.

18. Ibid., 442.

19. Several critics have tried to find a middle road between the conflicting accounts of Zimmermann and Frau von Littrow-Bischoff, most notably Stefan Hock in his introduction to the work; cf. note 12 above.

20. *Gespräche,* 5, no. 1209 (236).

21. Ibid., no. 1212 (245).

22. Wolf-Cirian, 227-228.

23. Sigismund Friedmann, *Das deutsche Drama des neunzehnten Jahrhunderts in seinen Hauptvertretern,* tr. Ludwig Weber (Leipzig: Hermann Seemann Nachfolger, 1902), 1:391n.

24. Yates, 193.

25. Walter Naumann, *Grillparzer: Das dichterische Werk* (Urban Bücher 17; Stuttgart: Kohlhammer, n.d. [1956]), 50.

26. Josef Nadler, *Franz Grillparzer* (Vaduz: Liechtenstein Verlag, 1948), 428.

27. Ibid., 429.

28. Early in his career Grillparzer contemplated two or three other biblical dramas ("Die Nazaräer," "Die letzten Könige von Juda," and "Samson"), but none was carried beyond the stage of preliminary notes and sketches. The poet attended a performance of Handel's oratorio *Samson* on 27 February 1829, and made a few notes afterwards regarding possible dramatization of the theme. At about the same time he was also actively working out his plans for *Esther.*

29. Josephus Flavius, *Antiquities of the Jews,* Book 11, chapter 6.

30. A. Farinelli, *Grillparzer und Lope de Vega* (Berlin: Felber, 1894). See, however, *HKA,* I, 21, 409, and Hock's Introduction (VIII, 27).

31. *Gespräche:* 5, no. 1176 (104) (to Zimmerman).

32. Politzer, 270.

33. *HKA,* I, 21, 447.

34. Ibid., 449.

35. Ibid., 450.

36. Loc. cit.

37. *Gespräche:* 5, no. 1176 (104) (to Zimmermann).

Bruce Thompson (essay date April 1976)

SOURCE: "An Off-Stage Decision: An Examination of an Incident in Grillparzer's *Ein Bruderzwist in Habsburg,*" in *Forum for Modern Language Studies,* Vol. 12, No. 2, April, 1976, pp. 137-48.

[*In the following essay, Thompson considers the lack of dramatic action in* Ein Bruderzwist in Habsburg, *contending that there is a significant dramatic moment in Act IV.*]

The title of Grillparzer's **Ein Bruderzwist in Habsburg** suggests a political conflict on a grand scale, involving, as had been the case in his previous Habsburg drama **König Ottokars Glück und Ende,** possible battle scenes or at least dramatic confrontations of the two principal adversaries, culminating in the triumph of one over the other. In the **Bruderzwist,** however, the conflict between the two brothers is not exploited dramatically, for they meet only once, and then only briefly, during which time Rudolf hardly speaks. Thereafter Rudolf learns of Mathias' movements only by report and not even their armies clash, for at the first sound of shots fired from the ramparts of Prague onto Mathias' advancing army Rudolf orders resistance to cease. Subsequently there is no final scene of triumph, for Mathias closes the play with words of remorse. Moreover, our attention is concentrated primarily on the apparently passive figure of Rudolf, who remains so much

apart from the main forum of events that it has been claimed that the dramatic action could almost survive without him.[1] Thus Grillparzer has been criticised for sacrificing dramatic action for long scenes of reflection and the **Bruderzwist** has been regarded as theatrically his least effective play.[2]

It should not be assumed, however, that the play is entirely lacking in dramatic effect. The opening scene of Act II has been described as "remarkable for its wealth of direct and uninterrupted action".[3] Nor at other times is the stage devoid of theatrical interest, for Grillparzer's attention to visual effect and gesture is as considerable in this play as in any other.[4] Moreover, even while the Emperor himself reflects we are aware that significant political events are taking place in the background. Consequently the contrast between Rudolf's delaying and the threat of future disasters has been seen as "the chief source of dramatic tension in the play".[5] Even so, it is also by no means true that Rudolf does nothing himself to affect the course of events for he takes several decisions which have important consequences. For example in Act I the main action is set going by Rudolf's decision to entrust Mathias with the command of the imperial army in Hungary; in Act III Rudolf yields to the demands of the Bohemian Protestants when he signs the "Majestätsbrief", which may be held to be a direct cause of the Thirty Years' War; he also refuses to allow the Bohemians to resist Mathias' invading troops to which Mathias owes his successful occupation of Prague. These decisions suggest that Rudolf is more involved in the dramatic action of the play than would at first seem apparent. But the most crucial of his decisions is yet to come, namely that taken at the end of Act III to allow Archduke Leopold to bring an army from Passau to relieve Prague. As a result Rudolf loses altogether the loyalty of the Bohemians who unite with Mathias' troops against the invading Passau army. Thus in Act IV Rudolf is isolated in the Hradschin and the way is cleared for the ensuing fatal quarrel between the Mathias-Klesel regime and Archduke Ferdinand. The brief military engagement at the beginning of Act IV is thus but a prelude to the destruction of the Thirty Years' War.

The importance of Rudolf's authorisation of Leopold's attack has not gone unnoticed by critics.[6] For some the significance of the episode lies in the fact that the decision comes too late to rescue Rudolf's authority,[7] which lends the episode a poignant and tragic quality.[8] Grillparzer was himself concerned about the timing of the event, but in connection with the motivation of the decision rather than with its dramatic effect. There were two possibilities which he considered worth noting: either to place the decision after Prokop's audience with Rudolf and the latter's punishment of Cäsar, when his morale would be high and a high-handed action more credible,[9] or after the arrival of Mathias' army, which would provide an appropriate provocation.[10] In the event Grillparzer followed the latter plan, and as Mathias' army approaches, Rudolf speaks of "Zorn" and "Rachsucht" smouldering within him (1705).[11] These feelings come to a head as Klesel enters, arrogantly demanding an audience. The motivation of the decision is thus perfectly clear and psychologically convincing.[12] Rudolf does not simply yield to pressure from Leopold,[13] for his own emotions are positively engaged. Grillparzer's problem was not so much with details of motivation as with the question as to whether Rudolf should be responsible for the decision at all. As two of his main sources suggested that the historical Rudolf may have had no knowledge of the Passau invasion,[14] he originally considered the possibility of having Ferdinand give the authority, and later of having Leopold act on his own initiative. Thus Rudolf's downfall would be brought about ironically through the activities of those who most wished to help him.[15] After all, if Rudolf were shown to permit the attack himself, this decision would involve a violation of his principles.[16] Nevertheless Grillparzer also appreciated at an early stage in his work on the material for this play the dramatic potential of an episode in which Rudolf would eventually by his own action contribute to his own misfortune:

> Am Schluss des III Aktes soll der Kaiser endlich handeln und dadurch noch tiefer ins Unglück stürzen.[17]

Even so, Grillparzer still sought ways of reducing the effect of Rudolf's guilt. For example he considered having Rudolf send a messenger with the order, then a second one to reverse it.[18] Once it had been established, however, that Leopold should appear as a character in the play, it obviously seemed appropriate that Rudolf should give him the order personally. Thus in spite of the uncertainty of the sources concerning this matter, Grillparzer's Rudolf is unambiguously guilty. Yet this brings us to the most striking aspect of the episode—the order is given off-stage. When Leopold arrives, Rudolf, anticipating the nature of his request, flees into an adjoining chamber; Leopold follows, and it is there that the decision is taken, while the stage is occupied by the arrogant Klesel. Instead of witnessing the decision itself, the audience are provided with an alarmed commentary on the situation by Duke Julius.

To place such a critical decision off-stage was clearly a bold and original step, possibly without parallel in European, least of all German, drama.[19] Certainly other dramatists might have made more of the episode. The careful planning, involving political and military calculations, the tortuous deliberations, such as Schiller presented on the part of his Wallenstein and Queen Elizabeth, finally the sheer drama of the moment of decision itself, all could have been presented here to good effect. However, Grillparzer deliberately avoids this kind of approach. The whole episode is given only just over 100 lines of text (1718-1830), the decision itself is a hasty one, and Rudolf is hidden from view at the most important moment.[20] This latter feature is also something which one would not have expected from Grillparzer, who was normally keen to exploit visual theatrical effects and to depict his characters at psychologically interesting moments in full view of the audience. This is particularly the case with Sappho, Medea, Ottokar and Hero. Even in *Die Jüdin von Toledo* where

the King's affair with Rahel takes place between Acts II and III we are made fully aware of his growing feelings for her; in the same play the decision of the nobles to kill Rahel is taken swiftly, obviously after some discussion off-stage (between lines 1528 and 1541), but we have witnessed a long debate on the matter earlier in Act IV and the critical moment is presented on-stage when Manrique appears briefly and notes the Queen's gestures of despair at her husband's attitude (following line 1527). Consequently it is arguable that in the case of Rudolf's decision Grillparzer is departing from his normal practice and is thereby sacrificing an opportunity for presenting onstage a most striking scene, thus lending even further weight to the charge that the *Bruderzwist* is lacking in dramatic action. Furthermore, his treatment of the incident is in the same vein as that of the whole sequence of scenes which involve Leopold and which relate to the raising of the Passau army. Throughout the play Leopold is restricted to brief appearances, first appearing in the final moments of Act I when Rudolf's affection for him is almost furtively indicated in a short sequence of mime action. Thereafter there are occasional references to the Passau army, a short guarded report by Ramee (589 ff.), a furtive discussion to the side of the stage between Ramee and Leopold (669 ff.) and finally a vague suggestion of its purpose by Leopold to Ferdinand (1130 ff.). The topic is alluded to in an atmosphere of conspiracy, and the army's purpose is left obscure. In Act IV the battle scenes are passed over with the minimum of detail, and the episode is closed as it began, in silence, with Rudolf's gesture of reproach in the direction of the now absent Leopold (following line 2143). Thus when Rudolf's decision is taken it seems appropriate that it should be given the discreetest possible coverage. Leopold is not granted an immediate audience, but is momentarily brushed aside (1586): deep in negotiation with the Bohemians, Rudolf wishes the matter to be hushed up for the time being. That the decision itself takes place behind closed doors is consistent with the treatment which Grillparzer gives to the sequence as a whole, whereby it appears that something of considerable significance is being deliberately played down.

In that the decision is also a hasty one, it may be compared with other decisions taken by Rudolf, notably those to place Mathias in command of the army in Hungary, and to sign the "Majestätsbrief".[21] The first is taken reluctantly and rapidly, with little argument or consideration of possible consequences; it is communicated almost in passing to Ferdinand, rather than to Mathias himself, so that we never witness the latter's presumed exaltation. The second is simply indicated in the text as "rasch unterschreibend" (1652) and occurs unexpectedly after a period of delay. Again it seems that Grillparzer is playing down the dramatic potential of his material. A reason for his apparent reluctance to capitalise dramatically on these episodes may be found in the nature of the decisions themselves, which are taken against Rudolf's better judgement and when he is under pressure. In the first case common sense ("Klugheit"—452) would suggest that he should not yield to Mathias' request, but his relatives wish him to. Either he goes against his judgement or loses the good will of his relatives. In the event Rudolf compromises the former in favour of the latter. The circumstances of the second decision are more complex, involving not only Rudolf's political judgement but also his religious and ethical principles. These are embodied in a reverence for the religious, political and social institutions of his day, namely the Catholic Church, the Holy Roman Empire and the feudal hierarchy, all of which he regards as permanent, and with which he would not wish himself nor any other party to tamper. For Rudolf, any social or political change will destroy institutions on which civilisation has been based (1271); what already exists does so in its own right and neither he nor any other man can be certain that a particular change is the correct one; thus his policy is to preserve the status quo by maintaining peace within the confines of the Empire and holding the various hostile parties in a state of balance. Thus he has neither officially recognised the Protestants nor persecuted them, preferring to tolerate their existence unofficially (1560), knowing that any positive action is likely to lead to future bloodshed (1446-9). Rudolf also bases his policy on ethical principles, on a condemnation of selfishness and vanity which he sees embodied in, for example, the empty heroics of Mathias (2309-15) and the presumptuousness of the Protestants 336 f.), and on a hatred of all war. These two principles are united in his plans to found a new order called "Friedensritter" who will preserve peace and whose motto "Nicht ich, nur Gott" expresses more positively Rudolf's detestation of selfishness in a doctrine of self-denial.

Even before Act III commences, political circumstances have forced Rudolf to compromise and to make a choice between conflicting principles. In spite of his hatred for war in general he refuses to end the war with the Turks, deeming it wiser to unite the disparate forces of the Empire against the common foe. The general principle is sacrificed for a political one, for he feels that civil war is the greater of two evils (1193 f.). During the course of Act III the necessity for compromise becomes more pressing and Rudolf's behaviour becomes increasingly contradictory. By now Mathias is marching on Prague and Rudolf's security depends on the loyalty of the Bohemian Protestants who can demand his signature on the "Majestätsbrief" as a condition for their support. Rudolf has again been forced into a dilemma. If he refuses to conciliate the Protestants' demands, Mathias may enter Prague unopposed (see 1526-9). Rudolf will lose all authority, his custodianship of peace and balance in the Empire will cease. If Rudolf signs, however, he will be contradicting his policy of non-alignment, yielding more ground to the Protestants than he would wish. Moreover, as he tells the Bohemians, the concessions made according to the terms of the "Majestäts-brief" would produce an avalanche of demands right down the social and political hierarchy, with ensuing lawlessness and anarchy (1587-1650). Either way, therefore, he must compromise on an aspect of his policy, but he eventually decides, albeit impulsively, in favour of signing, as a result of a chance remark that the Bohemians base their principles on the Holy Scriptures (1651). This, together

with the need to defend "des Reiches Ehre" (1663), at least enables him to half-justify the decision. The decision taken, Grillparzer adds a highly ironic postscript. In meeting the demands of the Bohemians Rudolf has secured their military support, but when shots are fired, he orders resistance to cease (1671), for he perceives that he has touched off the dreaded civil war (1675-9). Thus he immediately cancels out any advantage he may have gained. Clearly he is attempting to return to his pacific principles, but his behaviour seems contradictory, irrational, self-destructive. Now he has sacrificed both principle and military advantage and he finds himself in a worse situation than before! Because Rudolf's decisions are so questionable in that they contradict his better judgement or principles and eventually gain him no obvious advantage, it seems appropriate that Grillparzer should not afford them full dramatic treatment, but should pass over them as quickly as possible.

This then is the background to Rudolf's final decision to permit Leopold to bring the army from Passau. Again it is a decision which contradicts his principles, but in this case there is no contrary principle or policy which could be invoked to half-justify his action. Here he is in no dilemma, but is motivated solely by feelings of anger and a desire for revenge. Previously he had surrendered momentarily and against his will to external pressure of some kind. Here he surrenders not only to Leopold's entreaties, but also wilfully to an inner impulse, his heart being in agreement with Leopold's plan (1720).[22] Thus, fleetingly, Rudolf willingly forsakes his principles altogether and behaves in a selfish and aggressive manner. Consequently it seems appropriate that Grillparzer should choose to depict this unfortunate moment even more discreetly than previous actions which were not so entirely blameworthy. It is difficult, however, to determine whether Grillparzer's decision to place the episode off-stage represents an attempt to detract from Rudolf's guilt or is a tacit admission that it amounts to a major blemish on his hero's career. It is arguable on the one hand that he is suggesting that this is a momentary and unique moment of weakness, insignificant if taken within the context of his career as a whole, so slight in fact as not to be worth staging; on the other that he is banishing the decision from the stage precisely because it constitutes a major crime! Again, on the one hand he has clearly avoided full dramatic treatment of the incident, yet on the other it could be claimed this his refusal to capitalise on its dramatic potential in what could be regarded as the traditional way produces a moment of high drama: Rudolf's flight from the stage paradoxically makes the decision appear more significant than those previous decisions which we have examined. It is as though Rudolf were in this case running away from himself. The dramatic effect is heightened by the consternation of Julius at Klesel's untimely arrival and the latter's loud and brutal behaviour, and reaches its climax when the bell sounds from Rudolf's chamber. The episode is concluded as Julius sounds a note of doom following Leopold's hasty departure (1832 f.). The episode also culminates in a moment of supreme irony. By his action

Rudolf brings about the very thing which he had wished to avoid, himself initiating the civil war which he had prevented when he refused to allow the Bohemians to fire on Mathias' troops. He who has hitherto been presented as the victim of the imperfections of others here provokes his own downfall and joins the ranks of those whom he had condemned for selfish behaviour. At this juncture we may recall Grillparzer's oft-quoted words concerning the contrast between Rudolf and other characters:

> Das Tragische wäre denn doch, dass er das Hereinbre-
> chen der neuen Weltepoche bemerkt, die Anderen aber
> nicht, und dass er fühlt, wie alles Handeln den Herein-
> bruch nur beschleunight.[23]

for it is clear that the tragic effectiveness of the play is heightened by the fact that the all-seeing Rudolf is himself forced by actions of his own to contribute to the "Herein-bruch". Whereas the historical Rudolf was not necessarily guilty in this matter, Grillparzer deliberately chooses that his hero shall be.

Grillparzer's presentation of Rudolf has generally been regarded as a sympathetic one: Rudolf's characteristics and ideas have been identified with Grillparzer's own,[24] he has been praised for his insight into the political situation[25] and for remaining apart from the selfish intrigues of the play,[26] the deterioration in the political situation may be ascribed primarily to the activities of others.[27] Neverthe-less, it is clear that Rudolf is not entirely free from responsibility for the prevailing political confusion. Even his passivity and withdrawal from political affairs have had disastrous results, as Julius points out to him (1329 f.). Clearly one's attitude to Rudolf depends on whether the focus is primarily on his ideas or his achievements, between which there exists an obvious discrepancy.[28] Recently Eve Mason has expressed doubts concerning the validity of his political and religious views, challenging critics who have seen him as the representative of an ideal or interpreted his ideas as the expression of the author's vision of truth.[29] That these more positive interpretations of the character, to which Mason refers, are at best questionable is also sufficiently clear, however, from the evidence of Rudolf's own actions. It is not that we should doubt the purity of Rudolf's intentions. In contrast to the fanatical Ferdinand, the ambitious Mathias, the cunning Klesel and the reckless Leopold, Rudolf's prime aim is to maintain the balance between the hostile parties and so prevent the eruption of the holocaust. This policy is based sincerely on apparently unselfish principles. Unfortunately the very nature of the developing situation forces him at various times to act of his own accord and to make unwelcome choices between his own principles. Conse-quently these are themselves seen to be incompatible with the situation and with the actions which are required of him. Moreover, his attempts to act in accordance with one principle or another produce a pattern of behaviour which is contradictory. That he should eventually abandon his principles altogether and succumb to personal emotions provides the final ironic twist in the series of decisions which he takes in Act III. By his action he makes mockery

of his ideals and policies and of his noble efforts to adhere to these during the difficult circumstances which he has thus far encountered. Though he may stand out at times as a man of principle in a world of compromise, at others he is exposed as one whose principles are sorely compromised by the requirements of his office, until finally he becomes identified by his own action with those whom he has previ-ously outshone.

It is because Grillparzer would not wish to present his hero in a wholly unfavourable light, however, that he has deliberately avoided over-stressing the compromising ac-tions which Rudolf is forced to undertake. Had he built up each unfortunate decision by including long passages of deliberation and calculation, our picture of this highly principled and reluctant politician would have been differ-ent. What we have instead is a series of decisions which are taken rapidly because they are forced upon him by circumstances, and which, instead of wholly condemning him as a villain or a fool, simply cast an ironic light upon his enunciation of his religious and political views. Finally, although we have seen that the dramatic treatment of his last crucial decision by no means suppresses his guilt, but rather draws attention to it with what is arguably a mo-ment of high drama, it is undeniable that more could have been made of the incident, and the absence of Rudolf from the stage in particular diminishes the visual dramatic impact of his guilt. The decision is afforded the significance which it is due, yet it is not stressed out of all proportion to the presentation of the character as a whole. Rudolf is guilty, but he is not seen to be so, and unlike Schiller's Wallenstein who is remembered as the Field-marshal who betrayed his master, Grillparzer's Rudolf will not be saddled only with the reputation of the Emperor who sum-moned an army to attack his own adopted city of Prague.

The depiction of Rudolf's action is thus appropriate to the presentation of a somewhat less than perfect hero who is nevertheles not an outright villain. Grillparzer has deliberately attributed to his hero a crime of which the historical original was not necessarily guilty, but having done so, has not then given it undue emphasis. His treat-ment of this incident is also not inappropriate in a play in which the activities of various characters are presented in a questionable light and are seen to contribute at least indirectly to the ultimate disaster of the Thirty Years' War. The reactions shown by Mathias to his various achieve-ments are suggestive of a lack of enthusiasm for what he has done. Having secured a position of power through the efforts of Klesel, he shows no exaltation, but simply looks at the latter greatly puzzled, contemplating the future in some confusion (1081). Later he desires merely to be left in peace from the political troubles in which he finds himself, and finally he even desires to exchange places with his dead brother, a supreme piece of irony with which to end the play. A similar effect is produced when the Archdukes determine to make peace with the Turks and recognise the ultimate authority of Mathias. It is achieved most strikingly when Ferdinand expresses his misgivings even as he signs the fatal document (1047 f.). The common factor in these cases is the element of contradiction existing between the feelings of the character and the action which he has performed. Just as Rudolf's decisions were taken against his own better judgement, so too do these characters "disagree" with their own decisions or achievements. The effect is to devalue the action which they take. These are no heroic deeds, but shameful actions which will undoubtedly lead to disaster. The element of contradiction existing between characters' attitudes and their actions is suggestive of a lack of control over the situation on their part. Though they do not intend that the ultimate disaster should occur, they are nevertheless directly or indirectly responsible for bringing it about. The sense of helplessness experienced when one is unable to control the course of events initiated by a particular action of one's own is represented in a poetic image by Thurn, to the effect that one's intentions, once translated into action, frequently run away with one like an excited steed, which becomes impossible to halt (2213-22). This comment crystallises in a single image the impression which is created during the play of the nature of different actions on the part of various characters. Yet not all characters consistently believe that action is a bad thing in itself. Ferdinand refers to "Tat" as "den besten Rat" (482); for Leopold "die Klugheit gibt nur Rat, die Tat entscheidet" (1137); Mathias is also bent on decisive action, criticising the Habsburgs for piecemeal politics (922-5). Only Rudolf is consistently determined to avoid taking action. These contrasting attitudes serve both to illustrate character and to signify that there is no clear way out of this particular situation. Both Mathias and Ferdinand come to regret their actions, yet Rudolf learns that it is impossible to remain totally inactive. Twice Julius urges that firm action would have been the better course (1329 f. and 2193 f.). Because the situation is presented in such a way as to suggest that neither a policy of decisive action nor one of laissez-faire is necessarily the right one, it is appropriate that the character who by choice would remain passive should voice his apprehension of activity in general, and it is only to be expected that wilful characters such as Ferdinand and Leopold should at some time hold action in high regard. Our sympathies lie both with Rudolf in his struggle not to compromise his conscience, and with Leopold, who, when condemned for his forthcoming campaign by Julius' harsh "Es ist zu spät", can only say helplessly:

> und früher wars zu früh.
> Wann ist die rechte Zeit?

> (1825 f)

to which no satisfactory answer can be found.

Grillparzer has thus depicted a situation in which neither action nor passivity can provide the answer. The activities which we witness are seen to be questionable and ultimately disastrous. Yet they are also understandable, and, given the situation and the characters involved, inevitable. This impression is conveyed not merely by the conflicting statements made by different characters with differing points of view, but also by the actual presentation

of various actions, i.e. by Grillparzer's skillful use of his dramatic medium. This is particularly the case with regard to decisions taken by Rudolf. By not capitalising on their dramatic potential, by presenting them as taken hastily, with reluctance and regret, Grillparzer suggests their inadvisability. At the same time, by depicting Rudolf as acting under pressure he indicates the unfortunate necessity for action in this particular situation. The most striking of these decisions is that to authorise Leopold's attack. Here Rudolf acts from an inner psychological necessity, but his attempt to run away from the decision, the haste with which it is taken, his immediate and long-lasting regrets following it, and particularly the fact that he is hidden from public view at the crucial moment, are all factors which, whilst suggesting the significance of the decision, ensure that its dramatic impact is diminished. The decision itself is thus not emphasised out of all proportion to the presentation of the character as a whole. Given Rudolf's feelings and situation at the time, the decision is inevitable, but it is appropriate that the decision itself should be taken in obscurity. Grillparzer does not shun the presentation of the imperfections and mistakes of his characters—indeed these represent an essential ingredient in their make-up— but he does not give them undue emphasis. Nor does he avoid actions or decisions which involve violence. For example, during Act IV Rudolf's natural son, Don Cäsar, becomes so enraged at the behaviour of Lukrezia that he shoots her. But the shot is fired into the wings, Lukrezia falls off-stage, and whether she dies or not is left uncertain. Though Cäsar's deed is witnessed by the audience, Grillparzer stops short of a full dramatic treatment of the incident and the result is pushed into obscurity. Similarly when Rudolf drops the key into the well later in the same Act, supposedly thereby condemning Cäsar to death, the result is passed over and we do not witness Cäsar's awful death. In both these incidents Grillparzer is banishing from the stage the disastrous results of a character's behaviour, again refusing to give dramatic events their full due.

If one considers the opportunities for high drama which Grillparzer appears to have deliberately rejected, criticism of the play on the grounds that it is lacking in dramatic action is clearly justified, for though the play is not lacking in incident, the dramatic potential of individual episodes is certainly not fully exploited. However, Grillparzer obviously has good reasons for playing down the drama of these incidents, being concerned not to overstress the guilt of his characters either by depicting the disastrous results of their actions or by over-dramatising their unfortunate decisions. None of the characters in this play are perfect and none inspire our unqualified admiration. On the other hand they cannot be condemned as villains. They are ordinary mortals who either succumb to human weaknesses, find themselves in situations requiring action with which they cannot cope, or take decisions which have unfortunate consequences. In Grillparzer's own words the best of mortals are prone to error and often succumb to external pressures and difficulties, a view of the human situation which is at the heart of tragedy:

> Das Tragische . . . liegt darin, dass der Mensch das

Nichtige des Irdischen erkennt; die Gefahren sieht, welchen der Beste ausgesetzt ist und oft unterliegt; dass er . . . den strauchelnden Mitmenschen bedaure, den fallenden nicht aufhöre zu lieben, wenn er ihn gleich straft.[30]

He goes on to say that the emotions aroused by tragedy include "Menschenliebe" and "Duldsamkeit", emotions which are stimulated in *Ein Bruderzwist in Habsburg* by Grillparzer's discreet and consequently sympathetic treatment of human error.

Notes

1. G. Fricke, "Wesen und Wandel des Tragischen bei Grillparzer", *Studien und Interpretationen*, Frankfurt, 1956, p. 282.

2. Fricke describes the *Bruderzwist* as Grillparzer's "bühnenfremdestes Stück", op. cit. p. 284; Friedrich Gundolf claims that it is "erzählerisch" rather than "dramatisch", "Franz Grillparzer", *Jahrbuch des Freien Deutschen Hochstifts,* Frankfurt, 1931, p. 72; Joachim Müller, reflecting the general import of *Bruderzwist* criticism, concludes that it does not rank with the "theaterwirksamsten Stücken Grillparzers", *Franz Grillparzer*, Sammlung Metzler, Stuttgart, 1963, p. 74.

3. G. A. Wells, *The Plays of Grillparzer,* Oxford, 1969, p. 115.

4. This is especially true of scenes presenting Rudolf himself, e.g. in Act I when his impatient banging on the floor with his stick and the retirement behind the pages of books provide a visual illustration of his lack of interest in politics, and in Act III when stage properties such as the paraphernalia of his chemical laboratory are shown.

5. W. E. Yates, *Grillparzer: a critical introduction,* Cambridge, 1972, p. 243.

6. For Ulrich Fülleborn it is "die Herzpause des Stücks", *Das dramatische Geschehen im Werke Franz Grillparzers,* München, 1966, p. 65; recently H. F. Schafroth has given the episode attention in *Die Entscheidung bei Grillparzer,* Bern, 1971, pp. 76-7.

7. E. Lange, *Franz Grillparzer. Sein Leben und Denken,* Gütersloh, 1894, p. 118; I. Münch, *Die Tragik in Drama und Persönlichkeit Franz Grillparzers,* Bern, 1931, p. 103; B. von Wiese, *Die deutsche Tragödie von Lessing bis Hebbel,* Hamburg, 1948, pp. 443 f. That this is not a universally held interpretation is indicated by R. Schneider, who comments that Rudolf loses his authority because he acts *before* it is too late, *Im Anfang liegt das Ende: Grillparzers Epilog auf die Geschichte,* Baden-Baden, 1946, p. 40.

8. von Wiese, op. cit., p. 450.

9. Sauer edition I, 21, p. 146. References to Grillparzer's own comments on the *Bruderzwist* are taken from *Grillparzer: Sämtliche Werke, Historisch-kritische Gesamtausgabe,* ed. A. Sauer and R. Backmann, Wien, 1909 etc., division I, volume 21 (*Apparent* to the *Bruderzwist,* providing Grillparzer's own notes and comments).

10. Sauer edition, I, 21, p. 145.

11. Line references to the play are taken from the same edition, division I, volume 6.

12. Gerhard Baumann calls it a "psychologischer Meistergriff" in "Ein Bruderzwist in Habsburg", *Das deutsche Drama vom Barock bis zur Gegenwart. Interpretationen,* ed. von Wiese, Düsseldorf, 1958, vol. I, p. 146; one cannot agree with Politzer and Fülleborn who claim that the reasons for the decision are obscure: H. Politzer, *Franz Grillparzer oder das abgründige Biedermeier,* Wien, 1972, p. 359; Fülleborn, op. cit., p. 65.

13. As suggested by Yates, op. cit., p. 246 and Schafroth, op. cit., p. 76. See note 22 below.

14. Franz Christoph Khevenhüller, *Annales Ferdinandei (—1637),* Leipzig, 1721, vol. VII, p. 352, referred to in Sauer edition, I, 21, p. 127; P.Ph. Wolf, *Geschichte Maximilians I und seine Zeit,* München, 1807, vol. II, p. 581, referred to in Sauer edition, I, 21, p. 140.

15. Sauer edition, I, 21, pp. 145-6. Otto Lessing thought the significance of the episode still lay in this aspect of it, *Grillparzer und das neue Drama,* München, 1905, p. 87, but Grillparzer's addition of the vital ingredient, namely Rudolf's personal decision, would appear to invalidate this interpretation.

16. Sauer edition, I, 21, p. 144.

17. Ibid., p. 141.

18. Ibid., p. 145.

19. A celebrated piece of "off-stage drama" occurs in Schiller's *Don Carlos,* Act IV, scene 23, when the King is reported to have wept in his chamber, but this of course does not constitute a major decision.

20. This aspect of the presentation of the decision has rarely been commented on. For example, Wells discusses the incident as though we actually witness the decision itself (op. cit. p. 120). Of critics who do comment on this feature, Baumann assumes that it is a matter of tact: Grillparzer does not wish to depict his hero at such an unbecoming moment (op. cit., p. 446); Schafroth concludes that the episode is a "Warnung vor Entscheidungen, die nicht seiner inneren Überzeugung entspringen" (op. cit., p. 77), but this has nothing to do of course with the staging, or rather non-staging, of the incident.

21. Cf. Schafroth, op. cit., p. 76.

22. Schafroth (loc. cit.) distinguishes between this and the two previous decisions on the grounds that this decision is taken "unter dem Einfluss eines anderen Menschen". In that Leopold puts the request to

Rudolf it could be claimed that Rudolf again here yields to pressure, but in this case the essential and unique ingredient is Rudolf's own emotional sympathy.

23. Sauer edition, I, 21, p. 148.

24. For example, F. Sengle speaks of "Identität von Dichter und Geschichtsfigur", *Das deutsche Geschichtsdrama,* Stuttgart, 1952, p. 108.

25. Baumann, op. cit., p. 428.

26. Fricke, op. cit., p. 282.

27. As claimed by W. Naumann in *Grillparzer: Das dichterische Werk,* Stuttgart, 1956, pp. 40-1.

28. As recognised as early as 1888 by Johannes Volkelt in *Franz Grillparzer als Dichter des Tragischen,* Nördlingen, p. 53.

29. "A new look at Grillparzer's *Bruderzwist*", *German Life and Letters,* XXV, 1972, pp. 102-15. Mason challenges in particular the views of J. P. Stern, J. Nadler, W. Naumann, G. Baumann, G. A. Wells, F. Sengle, and E. E. Papst.

30. Sauer edition, I, 14, pp. 31-2.

Bruce Thompson (essay date 1981)

SOURCE: "The Early Tragedies (1816-23)," in *Franz Grillparzer,* Twayne Publishers, 1981, pp. 27-54.

[*In the following essay, Thompson offers a thematic and stylistic overview of Grillparzer's early dramas.*]

THE EARLY TRAGEDIES (1816-23)

I *DIE AHNFRAU*

For several reasons **Die Ahnfrau** [**The Ancestress**] represents, both in subject-matter and style, an unusual choice for Grillparzer to have made to mark his debut on the Viennese stage. For example, it bears little resemblance to **Blanka von Kastilien,** the tragedy of his youth which had been rejected by the Burgtheater, and which most commentators and editors have relegated to his juvenilia. **Blanka** was written in imitation of Schiller's early verse tragedy *Don Carlos,* the influence of which can be readily perceived in its elevated and occasionally verbose style, in its historical courtly setting, and in its universal theme of the conflict between duty and love. During the six years that passed after the rejection of **Blanka** Grillparzer read widely, particularly Goethe and Shakespeare, and he began his fruitful studies of Spanish drama. He also produced a vast number of notes for possible plays, and from the projects that got under way it is clear that he was still mainly interested in historical material. Yet in his discussion with Schreyvogel in 1816 he mentioned none of these projects, but instead a topic drawn from the world of the horror novel and the *Geisterstücke* ("ghost plays") of the

Viennese popular theater. One reason for Grillparzer's radical change of direction may have been his realization that to be successful on the stage a play must have popular appeal.

In vogue at the time was a genre known as the fate-tragedy, which had been popularized by Zacharias Werner, Christian von Houwald, and Adolf Müllner. Their plays reflect the interest of the Romantics in the irrational and the supernatural, and their characters often appear doomed by some unseen power to commit crimes against those of their own blood. In that it presents the extinction of a family line in horrifyingly dramatic circumstances, involving the murder of the father by the son, an incestuous relationship between brother and sister, and a family ghost, Grillparzer's **Die Ahnfrau** appears to offer a typical example of this genre. The ghost is that of the ancestress of the Borotin family, who was killed by her husband for infidelity, and who, as legend has it, has been doomed to haunt the family until all her descendants are dead. When the play begins, it seems that only Count Borotin and his daughter Bertha are left, for his only son disappeared as a child and is believed to have drowned. Bertha has recently fallen in love with a stranger, Jaromir, who rescued her from robbers in the forest. Now Jaromir seeks sanctuary with them, having apparently himself been attacked by robbers. But his arrival is followed by that of soldiers, who have traced the robbers to the vicinity of Borotin's house. A battle, in which Borotin takes part, is fought between the robbers and the soldiers, and it is revealed that Jaromir is the leader of the robber-band. Worse still, Borotin is fatally wounded by Jaromir, and a captured robber discloses that Jaromir is none other than Borotin's long-lost son. Bertha subsequently dies of a broken heart, and Jaromir perishes in the embrace of the ghost of the ancestress.

In his efforts to achieve theatrical success Grillparzer resorts to the melodramatic devices typical of the fate-tragedy. For example, there is the fatal weapon, the dagger, with which the ancestress was murdered, which hangs ominously on the wall, and which Jaromir also uses to murder his father. The eerie atmosphere of the isolated Gothic hall and of the dark windy night outside also generates feelings of foreboding and terror. At times, too, the playwright descends to the level of popular comedy. For example, Jaromir places a handkerchief over his face so as to avoid being recognized by the soldiers, and the appearances of the ghostly figure spread confusion among the characters to the ghoulish delight of the audience. A significant influence on the play was Calderón, the seventeenth-century Spanish dramatist, whose *La vido es sueño* [*Life is a Dream*] Grillparzer had translated, and whose trochaic verse form he adopted. In places he does achieve the musicality of Calderón's language, often through the use of the kind of syntactical repetitions that the trochaic meter seems to inspire. A characteristic example is afforded by Borotin's envious description of the man fortunate enough to depart this life in the bosom of his family:

Solches Scheiden heißt nicht Sterben;

Denn er lebt im Angedenken,
Lebt in seines Wirkens Früchten,
Lebt in seiner Kinder Taten,
Lebt in seiner Enkel Mund.

(65-9)

(Such a departure is not really a death, for he lives on
in the memory, lives on in the fruits of his labors, lives
on in the deeds of his children, in the stories of his
grandchildren.)

Similar examples abound, with the result that many
speeches have an effusive and declamatory quality. It was
perhaps because of, rather than in spite of, these shortcomings that *Die Ahnfrau* was a sensational success, and the
spectacle of the doomed family is reported to have sent a
shudder of horror through Vienna. Nevertheless, the suggested presence of some supernatural power exercising a
deterministic influence on the lives of the characters, causing them to sin as well as dooming them to destruction,
was a concept that ran contrary to the prevailing intellectual currents of the time, and the critics who attacked
the play as a fate-tragedy do appear to have had a good
case.

Over the years, however, there have been many attempts
to rescue the play from its stigma. It has been pointed out,
for example, that there is no absolute proof that a fatal
force is at work, but only a legend existing in the minds of
the characters. Secondly, the ancestress herself can hardly
be regarded as an emissary of fate, for her main function
is to warn characters of approaching catastrophes. Her appearances represent an attempt to avert them, rather than
to bring them about. Thirdly, the fatal force, if it exists at
all, is given moral implications. It originates in a human
sin, in the adultery of the ancestress, and her guilt seems
to have been passed on to succeeding generations, an
impression which is strengthened by her similarity in appearance to Bertha. Indeed the two are invariably played
by the same actress. Thus *Die Ahnfrau* may be regarded
as a tragedy of inherited guilt, and fate may be interpreted
as an instrument of divine punishment.

But the aspect of the play that has received most attention
is the character treatment. Later in life Grillparzer himself
argued that the action would be entirely convincing even
without the fatalistic elements (G IV, 1088), and it is true
that events seem to result as much from the characters of
those involved as from supernatural activity. Borotin's
own fatalistic and negative attitude may be held responsible
for his failure to dredge the pond after his son's disappearance, and for his pursuit of a lonely existence with his
daughter, apparently cut off from all human society. This
itself may help to explain Bertha's rapid and complete surrender to Jaromir's charms, and in her unquestioning love
for him she exhibits something of the naiveté of the
heroines of the Storm and Stress movement. The main
motivating factor is the character of Jaromir. Brought up
as a robber in ignorance of his noble lineage, he is totally
unscrupulous in his attempts to gain a position in respectable society. He has clearly staged his "rescue" of Bertha

in order to impress her; he deceives her and her father
concerning his identity, and in particular tells Bertha a
succession of lies over his role in the battle between the
robbers and the forces of law and order. In several ways
he is a forerunner of those reckless and egoistic adventur-
ers whom Grillparzer was to treat in later plays.

These features of the play are certainly suggestive of a
character-tragedy, of a tragedy of guilt with strong moral
overtones. We are given the impression that fate is working itself out in the form of human passions, internal
demonic forces which rob the characters of their reason
and freedom of action.[1] In other words, Grillparzer, like
Schiller before him in *Die Braut von Messina* [The Bride
of Messina], has given us a more "modern," and psychologically acceptable, interpretation of fate than that offered
in the fate-tragedies of many of his contemporaries.

But no interpretation of *Die Ahnfrau* can ignore the
supernatural context within which the characters and
events are portrayed. Although events are not predicted in
detail, the legend in which the characters believe is
substantiated by the dramatic outcome and visually by the
appearances of the ghost. Whatever the moral justification
for the downfall of the family, we are left with the impression that this has been contrived by a superior power of
supernatural origin. The death of Jaromir in the ghost's
embrace provides the final conclusive evidence. In *Die
Ahnfrau* Grillparzer attempts to combine psychological
motivation with fatalistic activity, presenting, for the
benefit of the more sophisticated elements of his audience,
the ingredients of character-tragedy within the context of
an irrational and highly popular genre.

Regarding the question as to why Grillparzer should have
chosen to dramatize a fatalistic theme in the first place, we
return to our original assumption that his main purpose
was to achieve theatrical success.[2] It is indeed the dramatic
function of fate that Grillparzer stresses when he attempts
to account for its presence in *Die Ahnfrau* (III, 310-11).
In this connection the influence of Schreyvogel on the
play is of considerable relevance.[3] Much has been made of
Schreyvogel's alterations, but it is apparent that the bulk
of his suggestions were concerned with making the play
more effective dramatically. For example, he attempted to
heighten dramatic tension by having the soldiers converse
on the stage with Jaromir himself, without recognizing
him. He also heightened the atmospheric power of the
play with a speech full of fears and forebodings by Bertha
at the conclusion of the second act. But his most striking
innovations concerned the exploitation of Grillparzer's
fatalistic material for dramatic purposes—in particular,
Grillparzer's use of the ghost as a recurrent visual indication of the presence of fatalistic influence.[4] Its appearances
on stage are used to produce immediately recognizable
ironic effects. For example, its warnings of approaching
disaster contrast markedly with the hopes expressed by
Bertha for her marriage, and again with those of Jaromir,
who assumes he will be purged of all guilt by marrying
into this household. Throughout the play, the characters

are confused by the similarity in appearance between the ghost and Bertha, often misinterpreting the warnings altogether, and we have Schreyvogel to thank for the appearance of the ghost at the moment when Jaromir takes the fatal dagger from the wall. This provides a vivid indication that the use of the dagger may be fatal to the family, but Jaromir actually welcomes the dagger as something which he recalls from the days of his childhood and, with words which have far more sinister implications than he realizes, he senses that fate is inviting him to take it. The young author who chose a fatalistic theme because he felt it would go down well in the theater did indeed profit greatly from his collaboration with Schreyvogel, and thereafter he was to attempt almost always to write with the theater audience in mind.

Grillparzer's dramatic exploitation of his fatalistic material combines with the various pessimistic utterances and gloomy predictions on the part of the characters, as well as with a considerable body of fatalistic imagery, to create a doom-ridden atmosphere[5] to which many critics have understandably been tempted to attribute some more generally symbolic significance. In particular, it has been regarded as an expression of Grillparzer's own fundamentally pessimistic outlook and as a reflection of his own unhappy circumstances at the time.[6] More generally, it has been interpreted as an expression of Romantic *Weltangst,*[7] as a representation of man's dependence on external powers and of his inability to shape his own destiny.[8] If viewed as an exercise in determinism, *Die Ahnfrau* may indeed be regarded as an anticipation of a far more realistic and rationally based view of the human situation which was to be popularized in the dramas of Naturalism later in the nineteenth century. However, Grillparzer himself adamantly denied any intention of representing a universal abstract idea (IV, 270). Apart from some fatalistic outpourings from Borotin and Jaromir, the tragedy contains few statements of philosophical import, which would also suggest that in *Die Ahnfrau* Grillparzer was more concerned with dramatic effects than with thematic content.

II *SAPPHO*

While the controversy over *Die Ahnfrau* was still raging in the summer of 1817, Grillparzer was already at work on his next play, which was to be a tragedy of a very different type. Deliberately avoiding the sensational material of the fate-tragedy, he chose a topic from the life of the Greek poetess Sappho, and in a conscious attempt to recreate the atmosphere of Greek tragedy he achieved at times an elegance and restraint scarcely to be expected from the author of *Die Ahnfrau.*

Because of its formal and stylistic qualities *Sappho* appears to have been written very much in the tradition of German Classicism as exemplified in the verse dramas that Goethe and Schiller wrote during their Weimar period. It is written in iambic blank verse, its diction is stylized, and its tone elevated and dignified, so as to create a more refined or heightened version of reality. There is an absence

of uncontrolled rhetoric, which characterized the longer speeches of *Die Ahnfrau,* and structurally it possesses the kind of simplicity associated with French Classical drama and found in Goethe's own *Iphigenie auf Tauris* and *Torquato Tasso,* with a minimal number of characters, a simple plot, and a strict observation of the unities of time, place, and action.

The heroine is introduced as a successful poetess who returns in triumph from Olympia to an enthusiastic welcome from her people. Act I presents the announcement of her plan to seek domestic happiness through her union in love with the handsome Phaon, a young man whom she has brought home with her from Olympia. But Phaon is bewildered by her offer of love, regarding her more as an exalted goddess than as a woman of flesh and blood. In Act II Sappho's failure is already envisaged, when the preparations for the rose feast, which she has planned in anticipation of her union with Phaon, serve only to bring together Phaon and Melitta, one of her servant girls. By Act III Sappho realizes that her hopes are dashed, and her jealousy is unleashed, to the extent that she threatens Melitta with a dagger. Then in Act IV her jealousy turns to outrage, she attempts to banish Melitta, and when Melitta and Phaon escape together by boat, angrily seeks revenge. In Act V, when the two lovers are brought back by force, Sappho's anger turns to shame, and she eventually throws herself down from a rock into the sea, to return to her true place with the gods. Thus the tragedy is given a symmetrical aspect by Sappho's attempt to regain the exalted image that she possessed at the beginning.

The language of *Sappho,* while restrained and occasionally refined, especially during Sappho's own long, reflective speeches, is scarcely lifeless. It is given expressive power by Grillparzer's frequent use of imagery, much of it drawn from the natural world of hills and valleys, woods and meadows, and the idyllic life of country people. Imagery is used to provide vivid illustration of particular situations. For example, when Sappho describes the poverty of a life devoted to art, she does so in terms of art "begging" from life, turning to Phaon with outstretched arms to provide a visual illustration of the point. Grillparzer's attention to visual detail is also seen in the rose which Melitta wears as visible evidence of Phaon's love for her. Joachim Kaiser, in his analysis of Grillparzer's dramatic style, stresses Grillparzer's symbolic use of objects, mentioning in particular his use in this play of the laurel wreath worn by the poetess, the lyre which she plays, the roses which she intends to use for her love feast, and the noble purple robes which she dons before her suicide.[9]

An element of realism is observable in the language spoken by the servant characters, and in this respect Grillparzer diverges significantly from the techniques of the German Classical drama. In particular, there are half-colloquialisms and short exclamations characteristic of real-life dialogue. "Why are you so angry with us, here we are, you see!" are

Melitta's first words, while Rhamnes comments sarcastically on her naiveté with: "The girl does ask some silly questions!"

Grillparzer also departs from the regularity of the verse form by splitting lines between different speakers, particularly at moments of high drama. For example, as Melitta reaches up to pick a rose from a bush, she falls into Phaon's arms, and he kisses her. The dialogue is arranged as follows:

> MELITTA. Ich falle!
> PHAON.   Nein, ich halte dich!
>
> *der Zweig ist ihren Händen emporschnellend*
> *entschlüpft, sie taumelt und sinkt in Phaons Arme, die*
> *er ihr geöffnet entgegenhält*
>
> MELITTA.   O laß mich!
> PHAON *sie an sich haltend.*
>   Melitta!
> MELITTA.   Weh mir, laß mich! Ach!
> PHAON.   Melitta!
> *er drückt rasch einen Kuß auf ihre Lippen*
>
>   (710f.)

(M: I'm falling! P: No, I'll hold you! *the branch has sprung up and slipped out of her hand, she tumbles and falls into Phaon's arms, which he holds out to catch her.* M: Oh, let me go! P: *holding her to himself.* Melitta! M: Oh dear, let me go! Oh! P: Melitta! *he quickly presses a kiss on to her lips.*)

Here the spectator will be unaware of the existence of verse form, as he concentrates on watching a sequence of dramatic action, whose effectiveness is enhanced when Sappho herself enters fortuitously at this moment.

Grillparzer was first attracted to his material by Sappho's personality. He saw her as a creature of fierce passions, which she had controlled only with great difficulty, until they had broken out at a moment of crisis. It was this psychological crisis that he chose to dramatize, and in his revelation of Sappho's emotions he also shows signs of the Realist's approach. This is not to suggest that he makes no use of traditional Classical devices such as monologues and asides. In Act III Sappho expresses her disappointment over her failure in love in a long monologue, and it is in an aside that she first expresses her misgivings as she looks at Melitta. In this line, "Oh heavens, how beautiful she is!" (1019), she betrays her realization that she has been defeated. But Grillparzer also adds a stage direction to the effect that Sappho covers her face with her hands, thus capturing her emotions both in words and gesture. Sappho's feelings, this time of confusion, are also implied when she gives Melitta conflicting orders, first sending her away to dress, then ordering her to stay and be reprimanded: "Go and change your clothes! Off you go! Stop, where are you going? Stay here! Look at me!" (1088f.). Even a pause in the dialogue is sufficient to suggest her preoccupation after she has seen Phaon and Melitta kiss. Instead of discussing the incident, she pauses and simply says: "Phaon! You left our feast so early. You were

missed!" (719f.). Grillparzer treats such moments of psychological drama very delicately, refusing to overstress them with long speeches of despair or anger. It is from such small beginnings that he eventually moves on to the moment of high drama when Sappho draws the dagger on Melitta. If *Sappho* constituted Grillparzer's first unqualified success in the theater, it is to his credit that he achieved this not through the use of the kind of sensational devices that he employed in *Die Ahnfrau,* but through his subtle and skillful handling of his dramatic medium, in which he pays particular attention to visual elements and to characterization. Nowhere is this more apparent than in his depiction of the development of the love of Phaon and Melitta as something natural and innocent, in contrast to Sappho's conscious selection of Phaon for a specifically selfish purpose. Already Grillparzer was on the way toward the creation of his own characteristic dramatic style.

The main body of critical attention has not, however, been focused on *Sappho*'s dramatic qualities, but on Grillparzer's choice and handling of his main theme. Though he was to concentrate on analyzing Sappho's psychological problems, he also saw the opportunity of presenting them in terms of her position as an artist, and of exploring the general theme of the contrast between art and life. Consequently, *Sappho* has passed into the history of literature as Grillparzer's contribution to the long tradition of works treating the problem of the artist in society, and comparisons have been made particularly with its most obvious predecessor, Goethe's *Torquato Tasso.*

From the early stages of the play, Sappho's problems seem to be caused essentially by her role as artist. For all the fame and glory which she has won, her lofty calling has demanded of her considerable personal sacrifice. Her devotion to her art has meant a life of loneliness, and now with Phaon she hopes to make the crossing from the barren world of art to the golden land of love. But by Act III she has already achieved her insight into the tragic situation of the artist, with her realization that as a poetess she was not entitled to the happiness of an ordinary mortal. Once having chosen her calling she should have remained in the clouds with the gods, and not have ventured into the valleys of life:

> Von beiden Welten eine mußt du wählen,
> *Hast* du gewählt, dann ist kein Rücktritt mehr!
>
>   (952f.)

(Of these two worlds you must choose one, and once the choice is made, there is no return!)

Before her suicide Sappho again recognizes that the practice of her art has involved its necessary deprivations, and that she was not permitted to taste the joys of life to the full. In view of these sentiments it is tempting indeed to regard Sappho as a representative of all great artists, forced to live in splendid poetic isolation, detached from real life.[10]

But Grillparzer's interpretation of the artist's situation is more problematic. Moreover, it would also seem something of an oversimplification to attribute Sappho's suicide solely to the insight that she gains into her situation in Act III. It is at that point that the psychological interest in the play becomes dominant and Grillparzer's exploration of his theme more complex. Here too the serene atmosphere established early in the play by reflective speeches and by the elevated tone of the dialogue erupts into passion, violence, and intrigue with Sappho's outburst of jealous rage. The most crucial moment for an understanding of her suicide occurs at that point in Act V when Phaon expresses deep regret that Sappho in her jealousy and wickedness has destroyed the ideal image of perfection that he once worshipped. Now he begs her to reveal herself again as the goddess she was. And so Sappho takes the lyre and puts on the laurel wreath and purple robe, recapturing her former image, that of the poetess sacred to the gods. This, she feels, is her "true" image. But it is doubtful whether she will be able to sustain it, for her attempt to taste the joys of life has revealed to her her own weaknesses as an ordinary mortal, her jealous passions, even a potentiality for sin and crime. She feels that if she lives on she may well be tempted again to satisfy her human desires. She cannot live on and not "live." And if she suffers a similar reversal, she will again betray the image of perfection that people believe in. At the conclusion, then, Sappho cannot simply return to her art. Only through suicide can she preserve her identity as a divine creature.[11]

Sappho's suicide has been seen as an act of atonement for the betrayal of her art, as though she had offended some universal moral law associated with her calling.[12] She does indeed speak of her death as an atonement for the "final guilt of my life," though she does not specify precisely in what sense she is guilty. It is possible that she may be referring here to her original pursuit of Phaon's love, but her preoccupations in the later stages of the play suggest that she may be concerned about having betrayed her divine image. It is her death that affords her the only means of recapturing and sustaining this image. The play closes, as it began, with an assertion of the gulf between the artist and ordinary mortals, but while the former is still held by others to embody a superior and more perfect mode of existence, Sappho's experience suggests that it is a state that is virtually impossible to attain. It is her tragedy that she possesses ordinary human inclinations which prevent her from living up to the image of the artist which she and others cherish.

Though the image of the artist may be idealized in this play, the nature of the calling is not. Sappho feels that her life as an artist is empty and unfruitful. By contrast, the land of love, with its happy valleys, offers untold delights, and Phaon, endowed with life's most splendid qualities, is "beautiful," "noble," and "worthy." Naturally, after her disappointment, she says precisely the opposite, describing the realm of poetry in terms of flowers, eternal youth, cheerful meadows, and that of life in terms of poverty, treachery, crime, and a barren desert. Ultimately, then, Sappho finds herself faced with a dilemma. Devotion to her calling inevitably involves intolerable personal depriva-

tions; but any attempt to satisfy her more human desires may mean disappointment, a release of sinful passions, and a consequent loss of reputation. Sappho is caught between two equally unattractive alternatives; neither art nor life holds out the prospect of complete happiness.

Grillparzer's view of the artist's dilemma is clearly an extreme and, one suspects, a highly personal one, and differs markedly from those of his predecessors. Goethe's sensitive poet Tasso has his own social problems, and also suffers rejection in love. As a result, he is brought to the brink of madness. But he eventually appears to come to terms with his situation and to be saved by his genius and by the value of his art. This is not the case with Sappho. Devotion to her art offers no such compensation. In the adulation of Sappho by the other characters there is something of the Romantic idealization of the artist as a superior, god-like creature, but we hear little, if anything, of the delights afforded by the adventures of the imagination, or of the ecstasies of the creative act. Sappho finds the demands of her calling too great, gains little happiness from it, is more aware of the disadvantages than the benefits. Grillparzer's artist is an incomplete person, her art is pursued at the expense of her more natural leanings. Viewed in this light, she is not so much a descendant of the Goethean or Romantic artist as a forerunner of the suffering outcasts of the early twentieth century, such as Thomas Mann's Tonio Kröger, who also learns the painful lesson that as an artist he cannot participate in a normal life, and Gustav von Aschenbach, who suffers a degrading and fatal release of passion after a life of discipline and self-control.

III *Das goldene Vließ*

Following the success of **Sappho,** Grillparzer again sought inspiration in Greek legend, and embarked on an adaptation of the story of Medea. Once more it is the figure of a highly strung woman that holds the center of the stage, but in this respect **Das goldene Vließ** [**The Golden Fleece**] marks a considerable advance over **Sappho,** for Grillparzer was here faced with the problem of presenting a heroine who is a genuine criminal, the murderess of her own children. In addition, the relationship between Medea and her husband Jason is analyzed in much greater psychological detail than the Sappho-Phaon relationship, so much so that the **Vließ** has been regarded as one of the first modern tragedies of marriage.[13]

Grillparzer decided at an early stage to present Medea's tragic actions as the culmination of the story of the Golden Fleece, and it was not long before he realized that this vast material would be best embodied in a trilogy rather than in a single tragedy. In the first play, **Der Gastfreund** [**The Host**], the Greek Phrixus has sought hospitality in the barbaric land of Colchis; he is protected, as he thinks, by the fleece of a golden ram, which has been offered to him by the god Peronto. But Peronto is the god of Colchis, and the local king Aietes regards Phrixus' possession of the fleece as theft. To avenge the god, he treacherously murders him.

In this play Grillparzer has deliberately evoked an atmosphere of primitive barbarism in order to illustrate the background of the legend. Just as the servants in *Sappho* were characterized by their occasional colloquialisms, so here the naiveté of the barbarians is reflected in the simplicity of their language. Short lines and phrases, an absence of sophisticated syntax, and a general tone of artlessness, even uncouthness, characterize the following exchange between Medea and her father Aietes:

> AIETES.   Angekommen Männer
>   Aus fernem Land,
>   Bringen Gold, bringen Schätze,
>   Reiche Beute.
> MEDEA.   Wem?
> AIETES.   Uns, wenn wir wollen.
> MEDEA.   Uns?
> AIETES.   's sind Fremde, sind Feinde,
>   Kommen zu verwüsten unser Land.
> MEDEA.   So geh hin und töte sie!
> AIETES.   Zahlreich sind sie und stark bewehrt,
>   Reich an List die fremden Männer,
>   Leicht töten sie *uns*.
> MEDEA.   So laß sie ziehn!
>
>   (97-108)

(A: Men, come from a distant land, bringing gold, bringing treasures, rich booty. M: For whom? A: For us, if we wish. M: For us? A: They're foreigners, enemies, come to lay waste our land. M: Go and kill them, then! A: There are many of them, and well armed, full of cunning, these foreigners, they might easily kill *us*. M: Then let them go.)

Again this is the approach of the Realist, and the episode as a whole, which possesses a distinctly satirical flavor, provides a further illustration of Grillparzer's occasional tendency to deviate from the elevated tone of the dramas of Weimar Classicism. The speech of the Colchians contrasts with the more elegant language of the sophisticated Greek, as also does Aietes's primitive trickery with Phrixus's more civilized approach. The emphasis is on action rather than reflection, whereas when we move on to Greece in the final play the opposite is true.

As Phrixus dies at the end of *Der Gastfreund,* he curses Aietes and calls on the god to avenge him. His call appears to be answered in the second play, *Die Argonauten* [*The Argonauts*], when Jason and his companions come to Colchis in pursuit of the fleece. Jason not only steals the fleece, but also carries off Medea, Aietes's daughter. Moreover, Aietes's son, Absyrtus, commits suicide when Jason attempts to take him hostage. But we are again given some indication that the sequence of catastrophes has not been halted. First Aietes curses Medea for her treachery, and prophesies her unhappiness as Jason's wife, and, then, as he dies, Absyrtus calls for further vengeance on Jason. Their words take us forward into the final play, *Medea,* to the heroine's savage murder of the innocent Kreusa, whom she sees as her rival for Jason's love, and finally to her

destruction of her children. The characters seem inextricably caught up in a chain of revenge and requital which links together the events of the trilogy and generates an atmosphere of doom, which is reinforced by a series of curses, blood-curdling cries, horrific visions, calls for vengeance, and ominous prophecies such as those uttered by Medea to her father after the murder of Phrixus:

> Unglückseliger, was hast du getan?
> Feuer geht aus von dir
> Und ergreift die Stützen deines Hauses,
> Das krachend einbricht
> Und uns begräbt.
>
>   (*Die Argonauten,* 113-7)

(Oh, you wretched man, what have you done? Fire is spreading from you, to devour the very pillars of your house, which will come crashing down and bury us all.)

At such moments we are back in the fatalistic world of *Die Ahnfrau,* and the use of fatalistic imagery, including images of fire, destruction, constriction, entrapment, and bondage, does indeed suggest the influence on events of some higher power.[14]

At times, the impression is given that this power is embodied in the fleece itself, the principal dramatic symbol of the trilogy, and that there is a causal link between the possession of the fleece and the ensuing disasters. Medea herself is convinced that it brings "calamity" and describes it as Phrixus's "fatal gift." The fleece is also given supernatural associations. It is hidden in a remote cave, guarded by a dragon, which threatens all who approach it with fire and poison. Later it is associated with Medea's magic arts, being placed in the chest whose contents bring death to Kreusa. But, significantly, there is no evidence that the fleece itself is an agent of doom, only a belief by individual characters that this is so. It has no death-bringing powers of its own, only by association, and these are in any case triggered by the characters. Grillparzer wanted the fleece to function simply as a symbol of ill-gotten gain (IV, 380), and its real powers are limited to its own dazzling and irresistible qualities. It appeals to Aietes's natural greed and to Jason's youthful ambition, and in this sense does indeed initiate a chain of fatal events. But these events represent the effects, not of some mysterious fateful power, but of ignoble human intentions. It is in their own hearts that the fates of the characters are to be found.

The two characters most fully drawn are Jason and Medea. In *Die Argonauten* Jason comes to Colchis as an adventurer in quest of the fleece, but his pursuit of Medea's love provides the main psychological interest. Jason's wooing of Medea is characterized by his aggression and violence, conveyed vividly by his behavior when he first breaks into her tower. Believing her to be some wild sorceress, he attacks her physically, wounding her in the arm. Then he suddenly seizes her hand and kisses her, rashly disregarding danger in the form of the approaching Colchians. The roughness of Jason's manner and the atmosphere of danger and excitement which is generated here provide striking evidence that in the interests of theatrical effect Grillparzer was prepared to relinquish the principles of dignity and restraint governing the German Classical tragedy.

Equally noteworthy is an absence of tender love scenes. Instead, in a series of brief encounters, Jason fights a running battle for Medea's love. He is attracted to her as to something strange and exotic which he wishes to conquer and possess, persuading her, coaxing her, almost commanding her to surrender to his wishes. Then, having induced her to confess her love for him, he loses no time in enlisting her support in his attempts to capture the fleece, and rides roughshod over her objections, finally carrying her off to Greece, away from her homeland.

But the true shallowness of his feelings is exposed in *Medea*. The omission of the intervening years emphasizes the contrast between the demanding, insistent figure of *Die Argonauten* and the callously indifferent husband. He greets her brusquely and then turns away, preoccupied with more important matters. When she attempts to please him by singing a song from his youth, he is harshly sarcastic. These are the outward symptoms of a marriage gone sour, and some of the longer exchanges between them have a Strindbergian quality in the terseness of the dialogue, the sharpness and bitterness of the tone, in the persistence of Medea's accusations, in Jason's unwillingness to admit error, and in the cruelty of some of his responses. For example, as Medea is about to go into exile, the following exchange takes place:

MEDEA. Jason!
JASON.   umkehrend.
         Was ist?
MEDEA. Es ist das letztemal:
         Das letztemal vielleicht, daß wir uns sprechen!
JASON.   So laß uns scheiden ohne Haß und Groll.
MEDEA. Du hast zu Liebe mich verlockt und fliehst mich?
JASON.   Ich muß.
MEDEA. Du hast den Vater mir geraubt
         Und raubst mir den Gemahl?
JASON.   Gezwungen nur.
MEDEA. Mein Bruder fiel durch dich, du nahmst mir ihn,
         Und fliehst mich?
JASON.   Wie er fiel, gleich unverschuldet.
MEDEA. Mein Vaterland verließ ich, dir zu folgen.
JASON.   Dem eignen Willen folgtest du, nicht mir.
         Hätts dich gereut, gern ließ ich dich zurück!
MEDEA. Die Welt verflucht um deinetwillen mich,
         Ich selber hasse mich um deinetwillen.
         Und du verläßt mich?
JASON.   Ich verlaß dich nicht,
         Ein höhrer Spruch treibt mich von dir hinweg.
                                                    (1556-70)

(M: Jason! J: *turning.* What is it? M: This is the last time, perhaps the very last time that we shall see each

other! J: Then let us part without hatred or bitterness. M: You once seduced me into loving you, and now you shun me? J: I must. M: You robbed me of my father, and now rob me of my husband? J: Only because I am forced to. M: It was because of you that my brother fell, you took him from me, and now you shun me? J: As free from blame as when he fell. M: I left my homeland to follow you. J: You followed your own free will, not me. If you had regretted it, I would gladly have left you behind! M: For your sake the world curses me, for your sake I hate myself, and yet you desert me? J: I am not deserting you. A higher judgment is driving me away from you.)

Admittedly Jason has cause to be dissatisfied. His attempt to introduce the barbarian princess into civilized Greek society has failed. His reception has been hostile, and people recoil in horror from her. She has also been implicated in the murder of his uncle. Initially, then, the tragedy depends on the incompatibility between barbarism and Greek civilization, but ultimately the major factor in the failure of the marriage is the attitude and character of Jason himself. Jason shows no inclination at all to share Medea's fate, but is prepared to get rid of her in order to save his own reputation and future happiness. Bitterly Medea accuses him of seeking her love as an adventurer seeks fame and fortune, of brutally playing with her feelings for his own self-gratification, until casting her aside. Jason is one of Grillparzer's selfish and ambitious heroes, a descendant of Jaromir in *Die Ahnfrau*. Not that he is a truly villainous man, for Kreusa describes a different Jason of the past, a milder and more prepossessing man. But he has been tempted by the lure of adventure, and he learns the bitter lesson of the futility of ambition, ending as a broken man, a singularly unheroic figure, bemoaning the glorious morning which has turned into the blackness of night.

But if Jason bears the major responsibility for the breakdown of the marriage, Medea is by far the more striking figure. She is the first of several female characters in whom Grillparzer has explored the onset of passion, but the bitterness that she displays following Jason's betrayal of her is unique in his tragedies. If Grillparzer was drawing on his personal experiences with Charlotte von Paumgartten, then the Jason-Medea relationship is indeed a revealing piece of *Erlebnisdichtung*.

In *Die Argonauten* Grillparzer depicts Medea essentially as the defenseless victim of Jason's aggression, for she experiences love as an irresistible, bewildering force which takes over her being. Initially she attempts to resist it, regarding Jason as her enemy, suppressing her emotions, refusing to discuss the implications of their initial encounter, enthusiastically cooperating in her father's plans to drive the Greeks from their country. Several spontaneous actions are, however, sufficiently transparent to reveal a growing passion underneath her apparent hostility. At their first encounter she prevents her brother from attacking Jason, at the second she warns Jason that his drink is poisoned. She feels that Jason has kindled a fire within her, with the sparks which emanate from his being. Here the demonic power of love and sexual attraction is represented in a most dangerous form. The image of fire is to recur frequently, in the flames of the venomous dragon which guards the fleece, in the dazzling properties of the fleece itself, and in Medea's own magic arts, which are to consume Kreon's palace in flames. Through the imagery of the trilogy these phenomena become a poetic extension of Medea's passions.[15]

But only in *Medea* do the heroine's passions in themselves become dangerous, when her jealousy is aroused and her love turns to hatred—and this only because of the way the situation has developed and because of Jason's reaction. Grillparzer is clearly intent on presenting Medea as a victim of circumstances rather than as an inherently wicked woman. Her attitude toward the situation is favorably contrasted with Jason's attitude. As *Medea* opens she is seen burying the fleece, attempting to put the past behind her and even to make the marriage work, and on Jason's terms, too, for she is prepared to renounce her barbaric origins and adopt the trappings of Greek civilization. But underneath she is full of resentment, and her hatred begins to show through. Grillparzer captures the nature of her emotions in a striking piece of drama, which occurs when Jason pours scorn on her attempts to play the lyre. As he tries to take the lyre from her, she breaks it into pieces, exulting at this release of her pent-up feelings. With this incident Grillparzer is also beginning his careful delineation of the motivation of her crimes. Medea's bitterness increases when Jason refuses to share her banishment and shows renewed interest in his childhood sweetheart, the Princess Kreusa. But at the end of Act III Medea's feelings come to a head. In response to her appeal that she might take her children with her into exile, Jason agrees that one of them shall accompany her, though on a voluntary basis. But when the choice is put to the children, they both refuse, seeking protection instead with the gentle Kreusa. Medea feels rejected, is filled with a fierce desire for vengeance against one and all. But ultimately the murders are the results of sudden impulses. The decision to kill Kreusa is taken hastily, when Kreon, in his attempt to wrest the fleece from her, suggests that she should send it to Kreusa in its chest. Joyfully she seizes on this opportunity, for she knows the chest conceals her fatal fires. Thereafter, she kills her children, not in a fit of rage, but when she realizes that they may well suffer as a result of her murder of Kreusa. Grillparzer demonstrates that she is pushed to extreme lengths, acting irrationally under pressure rather than with premeditated villainy. It is appropriate that for the murder of Kreusa, Medea should resurrect the fleece and employ her old magic arts. In so doing, she assumes her old identity and returns to her barbaric roots, and the trilogy comes full circle as she indulges in an orgy of primitive vengeance.

Following the savagery of Medea's behavior, it is also fitting that the final scene of *Medea* should have a wild and remote setting, which, with its forests and rocks, is almost identical to the setting used for the opening of the trilogy. Here Jason and Medea encounter each other for the last time, and one might reasonably expect that the chain of vengeance will continue. Jason does indeed reach for his sword to slay Medea, but she stops him with a word. She feels that neither death at the hands of Jason nor indeed suicide would constitute an adequate punishment. While Jason can only bemoan the fate of the children and long for death, Medea conceives of a punishment that is more dire than death, namely, to live on in the knowledge of her crimes. Death would simply amount to an escape from her wretchedness. Instead, Medea, like the Oedipus of Sophocles, will wander the world bearing the pain of her guilt, and will eventually submit herself to the judgment of Apollo. Clearly Grillparzer is bent on giving Medea some stature as a heroine, her strength of character being contrasted to the weakness of the now-broken Jason. She also reminds him of his role in the sequence of tragic events in famous lines denoting the futility of the pursuit of happiness and fame:

> Was ist der Erde Glück?—Ein Schatten!
> Was ist der Erde Ruhm?—Ein Traum!
> Du Armer! der von Schatten du geträumt!
> Der Traum ist aus, allein die Nacht noch nicht.

> (2366-9)

> (What is earthly happiness?—A shadow! What is earthly fame?—A dream! You poor man, who dreamt of shadows! The dream is over, but not yet the night.)

For all his veneer of civilization, Jason must bear his share of the guilt for what has come to pass. Some have seen in Medea's attitude an attempt on Grillparzer's part to endow her with a moral superiority over the unfortunate Jason.[16] But while accusing Jason, she is in no way attempting to detract from her own guilt. Indeed, by deliberately prolonging her agony and suggesting that only a superior being may judge her, she is only underlining her awareness of sin. Though she achieves in her final speech a remarkable calmness, this is not due to any sense of moral superiority or triumph. Here, in the words of T. C. Dunham, it is a matter of "all passion spent, but with no peace of mind."[17] Both the civilized Greek and the barbarian princess are guilty in their different ways, so that the original contrast between barbarism and civilization is both superficial and misleading, and is eventually transcended. The trilogy provides a sorry record of human fallibility, and ends fittingly in an atmosphere of resignation, with an honest appraisal of guilt and a willingness to atone. Nor is the mood alleviated by any act of atonement. The spiritual anguish of Jason and Medea continues beyond the conclusion of this most pessimistic of Grillparzer's early tragedies.

IV *König Ottokars Glück und Ende*

Grillparzer's interest in Greek legend did not diminish after he had completed *Das goldene Vließ,* and while rehearsals were going ahead for the premiere in the winter of 1820-21, he was already planning an adaptation of the story of Hero and Leander. But, following the somewhat modest success of his trilogy, he abandoned his new project and, spurred on by his interest in Napoleon and his discovery of an historical parallel, he returned to a genre that had attracted him in the early years, the historical tragedy. Grillparzer himself felt that **König Ottokars Glück und Ende** [**King Otakar's Rise and Fall**] was his finest play. It encompasses over twenty years of history, is written on the grand scale, in the spirit of Shakespeare's historical pageants, with a large array of characters and spectacular scenes, and has been praised above all for its theatrical qualities; for the opportunities which it affords for fine acting; for its vivid scenes of confrontation and for the visual qualities of the stage action; for its expressive, flexible language, use of eloquent objects and gestures; for its skillful stage arrangements, colorful settings and costumes; all of which for Walter Silz show "the master of theater who completely visualized his work."[18] At last, it seemed, Grillparzer had succeeded in investing a serious tragic subject with popular dramatic appeal. A significant factor was Grillparzer's exploitation of the historical coincidence of Otakar's downfall with the election in 1273 of the first Hapsburg, Rudolph I, as Holy Roman Emperor, and the foundation of the Hapsburg dynasty in Austria. This was a golden opportunity for an Austrian dramatist to introduce a patriotic theme into the play, so Grillparzer idealized Rudolph, bestowing upon him the qualities of the model ruler. Grillparzer's concurrence with the actor Heurteur that the latter should play the role of Rudolf "half like Emperor Francis and half like Saint Florian" (IV, 126) might even indicate that he intended the figure of Rudolf as a tribute to his own emperor. But in view of his experiences following the publication in 1819 of his poem "Campo Vaccino," and his opinions generally of the Metternich regime, it is more likely that he invested Rudolf with qualities that the ruler of his own day did not himself possess, but which he felt had been possessed by Joseph II, who died in the year before Grillparzer was born. In so doing he may have been attempting to put an attractive and misleading gloss over the more serious and potentially dangerous political aspects of the play.

The pivot of the action is the election of Rudolf as emperor instead of Ottokar, and the main issue of conflict is provided by the ensuing dispute between the two over the territories of Austria and Styria, which Ottokar had gained through marriage to Margarethe of Austria. Initially, Ottokar is seen at the height of his power, flushed by recent success in battle, and during the first act he acquires still more lands. When the emissaries arrive from Frankfurt, where the electors have assembled to choose a new emperor, he reaches his zenith, and his people already hail him as emperor. In this first act, however, Ottokar has already made the mistake that will ultimately lead to his downfall. This is his decision to divorce his wife, Margarethe, to marry Kunigunde, niece of the King of Hungary, a decision precipitated in part by Ottokar's desire for an heir, which Margarethe is too old to provide. But Margare-

the herself rejects Ottokar's trumped-up reasons for the divorce, which she regards as an immoral act, as the severance of a sacred bond. Subsequently, complaints are made against him to the electors, who duly turn to Rudolf as someone who is Ottokar's moral superior. By the end of Act II the moral issue has turned into a legal conflict between Ottokar and the new emperor, who has demanded that Ottokar return to the Reich those lands that he had gained when he married Margarethe. The result is a military conflict. There are no actual battle scenes, but two long scenes in their respective camps tell us that Rudolf is in the ascendancy and has already asserted his moral authority over the empire as a whole. When, therefore, Ottokar is persuaded to attend a peace conference near Vienna, he has to surrender the disputed territories and recognize Rudolf's authority. The third act thus ends with Ottokar's submission and the promise of an era of peaceful cooperation. That this is a false climax is revealed in Act IV, when Ottokar returns home from his humiliation. Instead of complying with fresh demands from Rudolf that he surrender hostages which he had taken prior to the conflict, he is goaded into defying Rudolf again, with fatal results in Act V.

The structure of this tragedy encourages a moral interpretation of Ottokar's career, according to which Ottokar is taught a lesson relating both to his defiance of the law and to his conduct generally as a ruler.[19] Tragically, the lesson does not sink home in Act III when reconciliation appears possible, and Ottokar repeats his mistake, only to show signs of genuine moral improvement shortly before his death. Then he regrets his crimes, accusing himself of having had no respect for the human beings whom he has ill-treated and sacrificed for his own cause. These comments amount to Grillparzer's own condemnation of Ottokar's egocentric and tyrannical behavior. The Ottokar who rides roughshod over the interests of others in order to fulfill his own ambitions is another Jason, the private adventurer transferred onto the political stage. Ottokar's reassessment of his career is also strongly suggestive of the Baroque influence on Grillparzer's plays, for at this stage of the tragedy we see the penitent sinner coming to recognize the evil of his ways before submitting himself to the judgment of God.

The touchstone by which Ottokar's behavior may be judged is provided by Rudolf, who describes how as emperor he has lost all interest in himself, and is now unselfishly devoted to the interests of his peoples. The contrast between Ottokar and Rudolf is frequently stressed. In Act I Ottokar is characterized by the set and by his dress. He sits surrounded by the magnificence of his court, dressed in full armor. By contrast Rudolf is shown in a more modest light, in sympathetic conversation with Queen Margarethe. Later as emperor he is seated in his tent, dressed in simple clothes, repairing his helmet with a hammer. He cares nothing for his station or for external magnificence. Ottokar would like to think he has the more commanding and magical personality, but it is Rudolf who is paradoxically the more magnetic figure, and it is a significant feature of the play that characters tend to desert or betray Ottokar, and gravitate toward the more humane and sympathetic Rudolf. It is Ottokar's tragedy that he acquires too late the humility and piety necessary to make him worthy of high office.

But there is more to this tragedy than this conspicuous moral theme. During their confrontation in Act III Rudolf gives a psychological explanation for Ottokar's behavior. He is convinced that in his case power itself has been a corrupting influence, exposing him to temptations and stimulating his desire for more. Rudolf's words bear a striking similarity to Grillparzer's own appraisal of the historical Otakar and of Napoleon, both of whom he felt had been driven more by circumstance than an evil nature to commit acts of tyranny (IV, 117). Margarethe and Seyfried Merenberg, a young Styrian noble at Ottokar's court, are also convinced that Ottokar is not an essentially evil man. For Margarethe he has been misled by others, notably the Rosenbergs, his "bad angels," who have cunningly exploited his desire for an heir, and deliberately flaunted before him their niece Bertha. According to Seyfried, Ottokar has, prior to the divorce, been a model of rectitude. During the play itself, however, we do not see this noble character. Right from the beginning his behavior suggests that of a man drunk with power. He is aggressive, boorish, and arrogant. He treats the friendly Tartars with contempt, brandishing their curved sword and criticizing its design to their faces. When his servants are unable to remove his shin-guard he first asks the Mayor of Prague to perform this menial task, and then rips it off himself and hurls it angrily to the ground. Exultantly he describes the extent of his lands:

Vom Belt bis fern zum adriatschen Golf,
Vom Inn bis zu der Weichsel kaltem Strand
Ist niemand, der nicht Ottokarn gehorcht;
Es hat die Welt seit Karol Magnus Zeiten
Kein Reich noch wie das meinige gesehn.

(605-9)

(From the Baltic to the distant Adriatic, from the Inn to the cold banks of the Vistula, there is no one who does not obey Ottokar. Since the days of Charlemagne the world has seen no empire like mine.)

In Act II his behavior becomes tyrannical, and we witness the possible onset of a reign of terror. Faced with treachery and defection, he can trust no one and plans to make arbitrary arrests. At times it appears that Grillparzer attempts to minimize Ottokar's guilt as far as possible. For example, when he evacuates citizens of Prague from their own homes to make way for skilled German craftsmen, he does so in order to improve the cultural and material circumstances of his peoples. But the impatience that he shows in the face of their objections, his ruthless determination to enforce a policy that he considers best, irrespective of the feelings of those involved, are typical of the despot who, however enlightened his intentions, behaves in a manner that is inhumane and positively Hitlerian. It is a foretaste of the Ottokar whom we are to see in

Act III, when he contemplates the wholesale destruction of areas in which the local population has transferred its loyalty to Rudolf, and when he threatens to reduce Austria to a wasteland. During his moments of remorse before his death he castigates himself precisely on this score, for treating people like garbage with a cynical disregard for their intrinsic value as human beings. The first half of the play is ostensibly a psychological study in tyranny, in which it is Grillparzer's main concern to represent the dangerous extremes to which a man might be pushed by the corrupting influence of power. His fascination with immoral and violent behavior, already seen in Sappho and Medea, is here continued in the political forum.

But Grillparzer's portrait of the tyrant amounts to more than just a succession of wicked deeds. Occasionally, even in the early stages of the play, we glimpse a second Ottokar underneath the mask of confidence which he projects to the outer world, an Ottokar who is weaker, more human, and more vulnerable than even he himself realizes. As the first act progresses, we see that Ottokar's power has been gained more through good fortune—inheritance, marriage, and assistance, ironically from Rudolf in the recent battle—than by his own efforts. A series of dramatic incidents conveys to us the increase in his power, but this is accompanied by a simultaneous series of signals to the audience that tends to undermine his position. As the Austrian and Styrian nobles arrive in succession to offer him their ducal coronets, they first do homage to Margarethe, whom Ottokar is in the process of dismissing, so that their defection is already foreseen by us, if not by Ottokar himself. Then, as the Carinthians bring him yet another crown and Ottokar is hailed prematurely as emperor, old Merenberg, Seyfried's father, is seen sending a message to the electors which will prevent his election. The timing of this incident underlines the fact that the divorce represents a serious piece of political miscalculation.[20] Next, in one of Grillparzer's most celebrated dramatic episodes, we are given vivid evidence of future developments when the emissaries from Frankfurt ask if Ottokar would be prepared to accept the imperial crown should it be offered. Intending to give a broad hint of the electors' intentions, the first emissary raises aloft what he takes to be Ottokar's own shield, but chooses not the white lion of Bohemia, but mistakenly, and prophetically, the red lion of Hapsburg. At this, Ottokar is only momentarily shaken, and he proceeds blindly on his way, still assuming that the crown is his for the taking. This is typical of the attitude that he has displayed throughout, for he has already reacted scornfully to Margarethe's warnings that he is surrounded by traitors, confident that he can sweep aside anything that stands in his way. Ottokar is suffering from delusions of grandeur, and he behaves as though his political greatness were but a reflection of his qualities as a man.

But in the eyes of the audience the image of the all-powerful king is somewhat tarnished, and in the second act Ottokar experiences his first reversal with the news of Rudolf's election. Here the mask of confidence does slip to a remarkable degree. Previous to this, Ottokar had adopted a condescending attitude toward the electors and had even expressed a reluctance to accept the crown. Yet when the news comes, his behavior conveys the full extent of his disappointment. The subtlety of Grillparzer's technique in his revelation of emotions and states of mind is well illustrated here. Instead of having the news conveyed to Ottokar by the formal announcement, he first has the chancellor give the information informally to others. Ottokar is, at the time, boldly announcing his plans for the moment when he becomes emperor, but as he hears the chancellor's words he is visibly shocked. His hand shakes, he stutters, he trembles at the knees, staring for a minute into space. Rapidly he pulls himself together, attempts to continue as though nothing had happened, and greets the public announcement truculently. But for a moment we have been afforded a surprising glimpse of a less confident Ottokar, a man broken by disappointment, who has briefly come face to face with reality. It is an Ottokar whom we shall see again later in the play. But for the time being he resumes his confident front, his delusions return, to the extent that he truly believes he can defy Rudolf on the field of battle. During Act III he is reluctant to admit that Rudolf holds the upper hand, and when he does finally agree to meet him, he assumes he will humiliate him by the sheer force of his personality. Ironically, it is Ottokar who is demoralized by the encounter. The first three acts represent a process whereby Ottokar is reduced in stature, first in the eyes of the audience, and then in his own, when he eventually acknowledges his subservience to the man whom he has hitherto regarded as his inferior.

At this point there occurs a crucial incident which makes it psychologically impossible for Ottokar to accept this situation for long. Rudolf demands that Ottokar should kneel to him to accept the fiefs of Bohemia and Moravia, something which Ottokar is prepared to do, though within the privacy of Rudolf's tent. But when Zawisch von Rosenberg cuts down the entrance to the tent, Ottokar's humiliation becomes a public one. Public shame is something that he cannot bear, and he stands head bowed before rushing from the scene in a great rage. In Act IV we see him broken by the experience. He returns to his native Bohemia in most uncharacteristic fashion, wandering incognito and alone about the countryside. Then, instead of entering Prague with a flourish, he sits dejectedly on the steps outside the city gates, unrecognized by the mayor whom he has insulted in Act I, mocked and humiliated by his second wife Kunigunde. This image of a weaker, downcast Ottokar presents a striking contrast to the earlier one. Here is Ottokar the man, much less impressive, stripped of all pomp and glory. But Ottokar cannot reconcile the manner in which he is now treated with the old Ottokar he once was, and it is his old image that he attempts to resurrect. Unable to bear the memory of his public shame any longer—he shows an almost pathological obsession with his recollection of that moment when he was seen to kneel to Rudolf—he decides to obliterate the memory with a conscious and deliberate reassertion of his old self.[21] Again he is all defiance and bravado, refuses to comply with Rudolf's orders, dismisses Kunigunde,

sends old Merenberg to the tower, and prepares for yet another military adventure. That his performance is inappropriate, both to the circumstances and the man, is subtly suggested when Ottokar proceeds to fall asleep in his chancellor's lap. Our final image of him in this act is that of the weaker mortal, cradled by the older man like a little child.

That Ottokar can never recapture his former glory is confirmed in Act V. On the military front he wavers indecisively, and there is a telling moment before the decisive battle when Ottokar thinks he has Rudolf caught like a mouse in a trap. He laughs, an indication that his delusions have returned, but his laughter is hoarse, and turns into a cough. The physical image mocks his confident words as he is caught off-guard again at a very human moment. Finally he is seen dead, naked as a beggar, his head resting once more in his chancellor's lap, an image which provides another of Grillparzer's eloquent testimonies to the futility of the pursuit of greatness and fame. It also completes Grillparzer's exposure of this self-styled Charlemagne as a king who, underneath his display of self-aggrandizement, is but an ordinary mortal.

Two aspects of the tragedy that contribute to this view of Ottokar are his relationships with his two wives, and the presentation of Zawisch von Rosenbergg. In themselves the two marriages provide interesting and contrasting studies of relationships in which the two parties seem particularly ill-matched. Margarethe is considerably older than Ottokar, and has been more mother to him than wife—there has certainly been no sexual relationship between them. But it is in Act V when, in a highly contrived piece of theater, Ottokar discovers her dead body near the battlefield, that we gain an inkling of the kind of influence she exercised upon him. In a moving scene he appeals to her for her blessing and for comfort, and even begins to acknowledge his errors, as his spiritual communion with her fills him with remorse and softens him. Margarethe was his moral guide, and it was his tragic mistake that he should have repudiated her for the younger woman. His second marriage presents a very different situation. Here the younger Kunigunde is married to the older Ottokar, whom she soon despises as an old man. She succumbs to Zawisch's advances, and then taunts Ottokar mercilessly when his fortunes are low. It is quite understandable that he should respond to these taunts by defying Rudolf once again, and the second fatal rebellion is arguably as much that of the maddened husband as of the humiliated king.[22] Kunigunde's influence is as disastrous as Margarethe's was beneficial, and in the final analysis Ottokar's downfall is brought about as much by events in his domestic life as by affairs of state. The principal function of the presentation of the two marriages is to make Ottokar that much more pathetic a character. Mothered by Margarethe, humiliated by Kunigunde, he is in each case the weaker partner.

The role of Zawisch in relation to Ottokar is similar. Until Act IV, to Ottokar's face at least, he appears to offer loyal support, flattering Ottokar's vanity, even insisting that victory over Rudolf is assured. From the beginning he also appears to be out of sympathy with his relatives' ambitions, mocking them over their failure to marry poor Bertha to Ottokar. Yet, beneath the facade, he is playing a double game. His behavior is at times enigmatic and puzzling, and his motives are never clearly stated, but it soon becomes apparent that his own aspirations are even more presumptuous than those of the other Rosenbergs, his intention being to undermine, and possibly even usurp, Ottokar's position as king. Early in Act II the Rosenbergs capture Seyfried Merenberg with the letter to the Archbishop of Mainz, but Zawisch allows him to escape, presumably because he too wishes to undermine Ottokar's imperial ambitions. He later encourages Ottokar in his defiance of Rudolf to the most foolhardy degree, in order to ensure Ottokar's defeat. Then it is he who cuts down the tent opening, to reveal Ottokar's shame to the world, so destroying all hope of a permanent reconciliation between Ottokar and the emperor. Zawisch is indeed Ottokar's bad angel, playing a Mephistophelian role, driving him to absurd lengths through false praise and encouragement, and thereby engineering his eventual downfall.

Zawisch is one of Grillparzer's most sinister characters, the only true villain in his plays, but an attractive, almost playful villain. Nowhere is his behavior more cynical than in his audacious wooing of Kunigunde, whom he snatches almost from under Ottokar's nose. His protestations of love are delivered in such an exaggerated, ironic, and almost jocular fashion that it is impossible to take them seriously. Much more likely is it that she simply figures in his political plans, which seem well on the way to fruition when we see him blatantly take Ottokar's place beside her in Act IV. Zawisch's success in bringing Ottokar down clearly reflects adversely on Ottokar himself, who seems vulnerable and naive in the face of the machinations of his clever adversary. He is belittled by Zawisch, who exploits and esposes his weaknesses. Ultimately, however, Zawisch is no more successful in achieving his designs than is Ottokar himself. Even before Ottokar's revival, Zawisch flees his presence, eventually to seek sanctuary with Rudolf, who gives him very short shrift indeed. Zawisch fades from the play as a further illustration of the futility of ambition, his career providing a parallel with Ottokar's own. But it is a distorted parallel, and is presented with greater irony. Zawisch pursues his aims through trickery and sexual adventure, with blatant cynicism. Through him Grillparzer makes a mockery of ambition, employing the methods of the satirist to illustrate his moral theme, and introduces the ironical, burlesque atmosphere of the Viennese popular theater.

An atmosphere of a different kind, but which is equally removed from that of the German Classical drama, is created by two brief dramatic sequences in which Grillparzer captures the effect on Bertha von Rosenberg of Ottokar's rejection of her. First, in Act IV, we see her in a deranged state, aimlessly throwing handfuls of soil about her like a child. Then, at the close of the tragedy, she reappears on the field of battle before the dead Ottokar, to knock dementedly on Margarethe's coffin with the words: "Open up, Margarethe, look, your husband is here!" It is at such moments that Grillparzer approaches the episodic style and grotesque realism achieved in the following decade by Georg Büchner, to be developed later by the dramatists of Expressionism.

In several ways *König Ottokar* represents the culmination of the early phase of Grillparzer's development. It provides a more penetrating study of the ambitious self-seeker than either *Die Ahnfrau* or *Das goldene Vlieβ,* and in treating the theme of ambition in a political, as opposed to a private, context, Grillparzer relates the theme to the specific situation of the authoritarian ruler. By representing in the character of Rudolf a standard of behavior by which the attitude and conduct of the hero may be judged, he achieves a fuller and more balanced treatment of the subject. Moreover, Rudolf's triumph enables him to end the tragedy on what is for Grillparzer a uniquely optimistic note. Yet the optimism of the final lines contrasts markedly with the atmosphere surrounding the downfall and death of Ottokar. The exposure of Ottokar's weaknesses and the reduction of this mighty king to the level of unheroic mediocrity provides an even more striking piece of theater than the similar deflation of Jason. In Ottokar, too, we have a further example of a character presented in the grip of an uncontrollable passion, which, though very different from the jealousy and hatred that inspired Sappho and Medea, is even more frightening and far-reaching in its effects. Yet, while noting the overtly moralizing elements of the tragedy, we again discern the approach of the psychologist, bent on affording his audience an insight into the character of his tyrant, providing further illustration of Grillparzer's tendency toward a more realistic dramatic form.

Notes

1. E. R. McDonald, "*Die Ahnfrau:* Franz Grillparzers Metapher des schicksalhaften Lebens," *Maske und Kothurn* 18 (1972): 3-22.

2. As argued by F. Lorenz, "Franz Grillparzers *Ahnfrau:* Eine Schicksalstragödie," *Grillparzer-Forum Forchtenstein 1968* (Hendelberg: Stiehm, 1969), pp. 79-99.

3. Grillparzer's original, unaltered version appears in SB I, 1, 149-256; the final version, which Grillparzer published in 1844, usually called the "stage version," appears in SB I, 1, 9-148 and in Hanser I, 607-708. Critics wishing to demonstrate the effect of Schreyvogel's advice usually compare these two versions.

4. The use of the ghost as a dramatic device has been explored more fully by R. K. Angress, "Das Gespenst in Grillparzers *Ahnfrau,*" *German Quarterly* 45 (1972): 606-19.

5. This is explored especially well by E. R. McDonald.

6. See McDonald, pp. 6-7.

7. Nadler, p. 137.

8. Herbert Kraft, *Das Schicksalsdrama* (Tübingen: Niemeyer, 1974), pp. 68-83); McDonald, p. 14.

9. *Grillparzers dramatischer Stil* (Munich, 1961), pp. 95-100.

10. For example, W. E. Yates (p. 72) interprets her death as symbolic of the acceptance of the artist's need to cut himself off from life.

11. A similar interpretation of her suicide is suggested by Ilse Münch, *Die Tragik in Drama und Persönlichkeit Franz Grillparzers* (Berlin, 1931), p. 33; and G. A. Wells, *The Plays of Grillparzer* (London, 1969), pp. 34-45.

12. For example, W. E. Yates, pp. 65-72.

13. H. Politzer, *Franz Grillparzer* (Vienna, 1972), p. 130.

14. C. S. Baker, "Unifying Imagery Patterns in Grillparzer's *Das goldene Vließ*," *Modern Language Notes* 89 (1974): 392-403.

15. See Baker, pp. 394-98; T. C. Dunham, "Symbolism in Grillparzer's *Das goldene Vließ*," *PMLA* 75 (1960): 75-82.

16. O. E. Lessing, *Grillparzer und das neue Drama* (Munich: Piper, 1905), p. 33; on the other hand W. E. Yates (p. 95) maintains that Medea's crimes are such inhuman atrocities that she can scarcely be regarded as a suitable vehicle for the expression of the moral of the play.

17. "Symbolism in Grillparzer's *Das goldene Vließ*," p. 82.

18. "Grillparzer's Ottokar," *Germanic Review* 39 (1964): 261.

19. W. E. Yates (p. 99) writes: "That Ottokar, like Sappho, is shown as falling short of an absolute ideal, and that this is the *moral* core of his tragedy, is in keeping with a recurrent tendency in Grillparzer's dramatic work."

20. Edward McInnes, "*König Ottokar* and Grillparzer's Conception of Historical Drama," *Essays on Grillparzer,* edited by Thompson and Ward (Hull, 1978), pp. 25-35, discusses Ottokar's political errors.

21. See W. Naumann, "*König Ottokars Glück und Ende,*" *Das deutsche Drama,* edited by von Wiese (Düsseldorf, 1969), I, 413-14.

22. Underlying Silz's interpretation is a strong suggestion that sexual problems lie at the root of Ottokar's behavior.

Roger Nicholls (essay date March 1982)

SOURCE: "The Hero as an Old Man: The Role of Bancbanus in Grillparzer's *Ein Treuer Diener Seines Herrn,*" in *Modern Language Quarterly,* Vol. 43, No. 1, March, 1982, pp. 29-42.

[*In the following essay, Nicholls explores Grillparzer's utilization of Bancbanus as protagonist of* Ein treuer Diener seines Herrn.]

Fundamental to the interpretation of Grillparzer's drama is recognition of the contrast between the expectation aroused by the formal language and structure of his plays and the reality of the inner action. Grillparzer's insistent emphasis on verse as the medium of his drama, his recurrent use of mythological and historical themes, and his vision of himself as the last poet in an age of prose lead us to anticipations that are not realized in practice. There was a time when Grillparzer was regarded as a third classic of German literature beside Goethe and Schiller. Later, more negatively, he was treated as an "Epigone der Klassik."[1] Both associations suggest the atmosphere of *haute tragédie* or at least an attempt to follow Goethe and Schiller in their ambition to re-create in Germany a drama that moves on the heroic scale. In fact, Grillparzer's genius lies in the presentation of man in his limitations; it is his gift to show us the doubts and ambiguities under the surface of our lives, and the conflicts within us out of which human achievements must be built.

Ein treuer Diener seines Herrn needs to be understood in this context. After the intellectualized theater of ***Sappho*** and ***Das goldene Vliess,*** Grillparzer had sought in ***König Ottokars Glück und Ende*** a theme of national celebration to which a diverse audience could respond at different emotional levels. The theater was to become again a focal point of society in which members of the public might unite in a communal experience. In ***Ein treuer Diener,*** likewise, Grillparzer looked for a subject of broad appeal in national history. The original impetus for the play came from plans to celebrate the crowning of the Empress Karoline Auguste as Queen of Hungary. But the plans could not be worked out in time, and Grillparzer's reading of Hungarian histories and chronicles led him away from national pageantry to the choice of an unexpected theme: the story of Bancbanus, an old man with many human weaknesses, who as "loyal servant" to a thirteenth-century Hungarian king is charged with the task of preserving the peace of the realm.

Grillparzer thus openly chooses a protagonist freed from the heroic inheritance of great tragedy. There is evidence enough of human frailty, it is true, in his Sappho and Medea, and much of what we appreciate in these complex and neurotic figures is the author's insight into the conflicts within human consciousness that they reveal. Yet behind the peculiarly modern feeling these heroines evoke we are aware of the significance and grandeur of the traditional themes from which their stories evolve. Again in ***Ottokar,*** although we may see evidence of an unexpected lack of authority and self-assurance in the rapid fall of the protagonist, he remains an imposing figure, a king who in his ambitions visibly incorporates elements of Napoleon. Bancbanus, in contrast, arouses little sense of awe. Under the colorful historical garb of his role as paladin to a medieval king, we see a fussy and pedantic man who at times even borders on the ridiculous and who is described by Grillparzer himself in his *Selbstbiographie* as "ein ziemlich bornierter alter Mann."[2] In terms of Northrop Frye's convenient categorizations, we have not only moved to the stage of "low mimetic" realism, where the hero is superior neither to other men nor to his environment and we respond only in the sense that he is one of us, but we are touching on the "ironic mode," where the protagonist is in some way inferior to us and we look down "on a scene of bondage, frustration, or absurdity."[3]

The character of Bancbanus is one of the main factors to account for the often negative tone in the secondary literature on this play. He is considered too servile and submissive, and the ideal of loyalty which he embodies too much a reflection of the limitations of the Biedermeier. Even critics who appreciate the subtleties and half shades of Grillparzer's work find Bancbanus too stiffly unaffected by feeling and passion to occupy the central role. Heinz Politzer, for instance, calls him a grey figure: "Die Gestalt Bancbanus ist grau wie ihr Haar; . . . Standhaftigkeit macht ihn zum steinernen Gast in einer Welt, die mit ihren Leidenschaften um ihn brandet. . . ."[4] Another sympathetic scholar, Urs Helmensdorfer, says of Bancbanus's central moment of choice: "Seine Loyalität grenzt ans Monströse."[5] Such judgments are understandable, yet behind them we may observe a partial unwillingness to acknowledge the significance of the choice of hero. It is no longer possible in nineteenth-century literature to seek the profound experiences associated with great tragedy. Grillparzer writes in a world deprived of heroes. We cannot anticipate the sense of horror at man's capacity for suffering that tragedy evokes or the curious consolation given us by the significance and dignity inherent in his fate. Yet if our desire for the heroic and the cathartic is not to be fully satisfied, it is still not adequate to say that all tragic force has been replaced by psychological understanding. The inadequacies Bancbanus carries with him are specifically and graphically presented, but at the same time they are also symbolic of all human weaknesses. Despite them he manages to rise to the task imposed on him; he makes of his own limitations virtues by which he can preserve the values he holds most dear. Grillparzer calls his drama a "Trauerspiel," but it is in a deeper sense a morality play. In Act I, King Andreas sets out to defend his rights in a distant land and leaves responsibility at home to his loyal councilor; in Act V, he returns to pronounce judgment on his servant's stewardship of the kingdom. Though Bancbanus is confronted with the deaths of his wife and his queen and the prospect of civil war, he saves the life of the heir to the throne and creates a situation in which peace can be restored. His virtues are not attractive ones, yet they gain from us a grudging recognition of man's determination to respond, to the demands of life and to create some order in the face of chaos.

From the beginning Bancbanus's situation is a delicate one. He shares the regency with Queen Gertrude, but she, hoping to the final moment of the king's departure that he will appoint her brother Otto von Meran as co-regent with her, does not bother to conceal her contempt for the old councilor. The king angrily rebukes her and insists on her cooperation, but the seeds of disorder are clearly present. Otto's pursuit of Erny, Bancbanus's young wife, precipitates the crisis. It is a peculiarity of the drama, often criticized, that the emotional tension of Act III is centered on secondary figures: the complex and unappealing Duke Otto in his attempt to seduce Erny, the nature of Erny's resistance, and the ambivalent reactions of the queen herself. Yet this private and personal conflict leads to the national crisis of Act IV. Erny, trapped by Otto in the queen's quarters and threatened with abduction, commits suicide rather than yield. Her brother, Count Peter, and Bancbanus's brother, Count Simon, seeking revenge and fearing that the queen will succeed in helping Otto escape the country, demand that he be handed over to their authority. Bancbanus is faced with the temptation to join them and revenge himself on the unscrupulous Otto, but does not hesitate in his duty. While they assemble their forces to threaten an attack on the queen in her castle, he attempts to lead her and her son, the crown prince, as well as Otto himself, to safety. As they are escaping, the queen, mistaken for Otto with whom she has exchanged cloaks, is killed. Bancbanus brings the others away and by a dramatic turn of events gives the child into the protection of Otto, while he himself confronts Peter and Simon.

What kind of man is it who is thus able to overcome his misery at his beloved wife's death and rescue her virtual murderer in order to preserve the peace? From the beginning our feelings toward him are uncertain. The opening scene in the drama takes place in the early morning, before dawn. Bancbanus is being dressed to go to court, while outside we hear the shouts and insulting songs of the rowdies, led by Duke Otto, mocking this old man with his young and blooming wife. The servants are nervous and tense, and, though Bancbanus tries to appear calm, his own tension is revealed both by his irritation with their clumsiness and the sententious philosophy with which he tries to sustain himself. It is not necessary to accept totally the description omitted from the final version that he is a "kleine, hagere, etwas gekrümmte Figur" (I, 1318), but he is clearly an unprepossessing man, presented in unfortunate circumstances where he is by no means master of himself or the situation.

The idea of an old man with a young wife pursued by the gallants of the court suggests a comic role. And there are many occasions when Bancbanus comes close to being a comic dupe. At the beginning of Act II, at a meeting of the council after the king's departure, the queen exposes him openly to ridicule. Bored with the legal details with which Bancbanus wrestles, she suddenly brings the meeting to a close. The councilors disappear, leaving Bancbanus, unconscious of their departure, tiresomely searching through his confused papers for the documents he needs. Again, when Otto and Gertrude prepare for festivities, Bancbanus obstinately insists on his duty, setting up his desk outside the queen's rooms to hear the complaints and petitions of the people. He is ridiculed by the courtiers, and his position seems the more ludicrous when we realize that the celebrations are only a pretext for Otto to continue his advances to Erny. But the atmosphere changes. Once the gallery gates have been opened and the people are seen to be thronging outside as they wait for their cases to be heard, matters appear in a different light. Bancbanus is no longer the heavy-footed obstacle to the youthful gaiety of the court. The festivities seem blatantly irresponsible; the courtiers, shallow and absurd. Yet the mood is strangely uncertain, and our feelings find no clear focus. Though Bancbanus's judgments on the cases he hears are vigorous and to the point, they lack the full conviction of authority. His principles of conduct are worthy but are presented so as to seem moralizing and pedantic. Above all, we feel that he is closing his eyes to the realities around him. When Erny pleads to be allowed to leave the dance, he resolutely insists on her doing her duty by remaining in attendance.

It is tempting to treat the scenes here in terms of tragicomedy. A possible parallel might be drawn with *The Wild Duck*.[6] Like Hjalmar Ekdal, Bancbanus seems in part an absurd figure, irritating in his mannerisms, self-engrossed, lacking feeling for reality. Yet both figures are treated with sympathy. In Ibsen at least comic and tragic effects are integrated. Hjalmar is never openly satirized; we cannot mock him or regard him derisively from the outside. We laugh and yet sympathize, recognizing—however unwillingly, for criticism has been slow to accept the implications—that the "life-lie" on which he builds is an essential prop if he is to maintain his existence. Bancbanus's pedantry gives him a similar hold on life. He clings to the letter of the law because it provides a stable source of conduct in the confusions of the world. Recognizing this, we may laugh at him and yet appreciate his dedication to the tasks before him, while still fearing the dangers that are building up. In the end, however, he reveals himself as a far stronger figure than Hjalmar and stronger than the figures around him. Certainly the movement of the act as a whole reverses the usual sequence of comedy. Instead of the victory of youth, traditional to comic action, and the exposure of the pretensions of age, the situation is reversed. The act which begins with the mockery of Bancbanus ends with Erny's contemptuous rejection of Otto and the latter's abysmal collapse. A tender and affectionate scene between Bancbanus and Erny seems to strengthen their relationship. Yet here too Bancbanus's weaknesses impose themselves. As a couple they seem to be more father and daughter than husband and wife. He repeatedly calls her "child," bidding her rest her head on his bosom with closed eyes, like an ostrich burying its head in the sand, as he himself says (line 868). He seems to offer her security and reassurance, but we feel uneasy at their attitudes, sensing on his part an urge to play the father, and on hers a denial of reality, a longing to remain a daughter rather than a woman, a fear perhaps of the desires that Otto may have secretly aroused in her.

The situation at the end of Act II is thus highly ambiguous. We are not sure how to respond or where the action is leading. In Act III, Bancbanus barely appears. His absence is significant for he is able to offer no protection from Otto's attempted abduction of his wife. He arrives only at the end, too late, after Erny has stabbed herself with the dagger which she had seized for protection.

In Act IV, however, we see a different side of Bancbanus. Here is his decisive moment of choice. However uncertain he may have been before in dealing with Otto's mockery, and however much he underestimated the dangers of the situation, he now acts with boldness and decision. Unexpected though the decision is, there is no suggestion of hesitation or doubt. His grief is patent enough. We see a man whose dearest tie to life has been destroyed. Yet he masters his feelings, not by yielding to anger and a natural urge for revenge, but by recognizing the duties still before him. In repudiating the attempts of Simon and Peter to embroil him in actions against the queen, he assumes control of events. It is he who takes decisive action, while Otto is in a helpless state of shock. So great is this growth of stature that Bancbanus readily carries the emotional weight of the final act. Where our attention had earlier moved to Otto, by the last scenes of the drama we are fully prepared to accept that it is Bancbanus's fate in which the moral significance of the drama is invested, and his character and actions which must be weighed in the balance.

The decision to oppose Simon and Peter is of central importance to the interpretation of the drama. It is not sufficient to imply, as do George A. Wells and Herbert W. Reichert,[7] that Grillparzer was faced with the problem of how to motivate Bancbanus's failure to avenge Erny. His refusal to take revenge arises out of his character and becomes the drama's essential theme. In the opening scene Bancbanus shows his control over his feelings. Upset though he is at the abusive behavior of Otto and his companions, he is even more indignant at his servant's wish to open the doors and attack them:

> Bist du so kriegrisch?
> Ich will dir einen Platz im Heere suchen!
> Hier wohnt der Frieden; ich bin nur sein Mietsmann,
> Sein Lehensmann, sein Gast.
> Verhüte Gott, dass er mich lärmend finde
> Und Miet und Wohnung mir auf Umzeit künde!

Bancbanus's eloquence in the preservation of peace sustains him for a while in this scene, both in our eyes and in his own, but in Act II, under the continued provocation of Otto and Gertrude, he must keep his feelings to himself. Here he seems stolid and unimposing; we are ashamed for him in his humiliations. But his refusal to respond is a conscious and deliberate policy; he seeks at all costs to prevent a clash and avoid driving Otto to excess. Perhaps he asks too much of Erny in sending her back to the dance, but he asks it because he is himself under strain and he anticipates in his wife the same determination and control.

Bancbanus's decision after Erny's death is thus well prepared. It seems out of place to talk, as critics have done, of monstrous loyalty or degrading self-abasement in pursuit of the king's demands. Admittedly, Bancbanus's loyalty to the royal family takes some extreme forms. He is unwilling to listen to accusations which challenge or censure their behavior. But while one may understand the liberal sympathies of writers who, from the days when the play was first produced, have objected to the submissive attitude of the hero, their criticisms seem misplaced. Bancbanus's loyalty to the royal family and to his duty is the basis on which he preserves the values of his life. His bitter rejection of Simon's appeal for help in revenge expresses his deepest beliefs.

> Aufrührer! ich mit euch?—Ich bin der Mann des Friedens,
> Der Hüter ich der Ruh—Mich hat mein König
> Geordnet, seinen Frieden hier zu wahren;
> Ich in den Bürgerkrieg mit euch?
> Fluch, Bürgerkrieg! Fluch dir vor allen Flüchen!

The contrast with Simon and Peter is most revealing. Their motives are clear and legitimate enough. They are not villains eager to find an excuse for bloodshed, but men of honor who have seen their family degraded and have reasonable cause to believe that Otto will still escape justice. Simon considers his brother old and feeble, absurdly concerned for the rights of others while unable to protect his own, and thus a source of contempt to all who love honor and courage. But he and Peter take no account of the disastrous consequences of their actions. Sustained by the righteousness of their cause, they shift the blame all too readily onto their enemies for the dangers which result. When Gertrude makes it clear to Peter that she will not hand over Otto and that any attack on him will endanger her own life and that of the heir to the throne, Peter immediately asserts that the responsibility will then be hers (1527-32). Again, after the tragic outcome of the attack, when Peter flings his dagger at what he thinks is the fleeing Otto and kills the queen, Simon refuses to accept the blame. Cursing Otto now as a "double murderer" (1660-61), he forces a fight on Otto's followers and kills one of them in his anger at learning of Otto's escape. Their attitude forces them into open rebellion when the king returns. Obliged to defend themselves, they are prepared to surrender only if the king will offer pardon in advance. Their proud insistence on their own rights and their conviction that they must uphold both their reputation for valor and family honor thus lead to violence and destruction and threaten the breakdown of the state. Only Bancbanus, in the conviction of his mission and confidence gained through the rescue of the crown prince, brings them to submit to the king's mercy.

The incalculable value of peace is a dominant motif in Grillparzer's writings. We may remember Ottokar's moving final speech in which he repents the desperate deeds of his early career. This turn in mood, so different from the Napoleonic egoism of his early life, brings him to recall how many men had been killed in the pursuit of his ambitions:

> Und keiner war von den Gebliebnen allen,

> Den seine Mutter nicht, als sie mit Schmerz geboren,
> Mit Lust gedrückt an ihre Nährerbrust,
> Der Vater nicht als seinen Stolz gesegnet
> Und aufgezogen, jahrelang gehütet.
> Wenn er am Finger sich verletzt die Haut,
> Da liefen sie herbei und bandens ein
> Und sahen zu, bis endlich es geheilt.
> Und 's war ein Finger nur, die Haut am Finger!
> Ich aber hab sie schockweis hingeschleudert
> Und starrem Eisen einen Weg gebahnt
> In ihren warmen Leib.

(2849-60)

Bancbanus is prepared if necessary to sacrifice revenge or justice for the sake of peace. If the death of Otto would restore Erny to him, then perhaps he would act with Peter and Simon. But the danger that Otto will escape his deserts does not move him. Whereas Simon and Peter are motivated by considerations of pride that belong to their rank and caste, Bancbanus's reaction reveals humbleness of heart, an acceptance of the limitations of his claims on the world.

In the way he ignores conventional assumptions of what is required of him and how he should react, Bancbanus reminds us of another Grillparzer peacemaker, Kaiser Rudolf in *Ein Bruderzwist in Habsburg,* whose inner doubts and desperate self-control stand in contrast to the easy self-assurance of the less than adequate men around him. Yet Bancbanus is in some ways a more ambiguous figure than Rudolf. For in acknowledging Bancbanus's achievements, we must also acknowledge his responsibility for the catastrophe. His failures are a product of his character as much as are his successes. If the accomplishment of peace arises from the modesty of his own pretensions, his acceptance of his limitations encouraged the conditions that led to disaster. When the king announces Bancbanus as his choice for regent, the old man responds with fragmentary protests: "Ach, Herr, bedenkt! . . . Ich bin ein schwacher Mann! . . . Bin alt!" (383-86). After the queen has revealed her dislike of the king's choice, Bancbanus says: "Ich sagt euchs, Herr, ich tauge nicht dafür!" (411). He seems unable to formulate the basis of his intuitive reluctance to accept the position. The king easily overrides his protests, yet we feel Bancbanus is right. In accepting the regency, he must accept partial responsibility for the tragedy.

This responsibility may be felt specifically in his relationship to Erny. His failure to aid his wife at the ball helps to bring on the disaster. In part he acts out of delicacy of feeling. Precisely because of the difference in their ages, he hesitates to play the master and exercise authority over her.

> Ich bin wohl alt genug, und du bist jung,
> Ich lebensmüd und ernst, du heiter blühend,
> Was gibt ein Recht mir, also dich zu quälen?
> Weil dus versprachst? Ei, was verspricht der Mensch!
> Weils so die Sitte will? Wer frägt nach Sitte?

(823-27)

He is convinced that he must rely on her feelings and her power of decision, but thereby fails to recognize how much she needs his support. Left to herself, Erny proves too inexperienced and immature to deal with Otto's vigorous advances. Perhaps because of an almost inevitable doubt about her own feelings toward the attractive duke, she overreacts, and by asserting her scorn and contempt, she incites in Otto a violence that might not otherwise have erupted.

It might also be suggested that Bancbanus fails Otto too. By studiously ignoring Otto's insults, he simply increases the duke's sense of humiliation and self-disgust. Otto needs the guidance of someone in authority he can respect. Bancbanus is clearly incapable of providing any help. Evidence of how little he understands the problem is his suggestion of a role for Otto in leading a group of cavalry against some wandering insurgents. He fails totally to realize that, in view of their ambitions, this will seem a gratuitous insult to Otto and Gertrude, a clumsy attempt to ingratiate himself.

But Bancbanus's failure does not lie in specific omissions or decisions; it is rooted in his character. In the early scenes we feel the desperate need for someone to stand up to events and attempt to take control. Bancbanus is an official who has grown old in honorable and faithful service. He deals with his work as it occurs, case by case, trying to do his best, but leaving out of consideration the flow of emotions in the court, the incalculable changes in atmosphere which render the individual cases less important.

At the same time it must be granted that the restrictions of Bancbanus's position make it difficult to see what decisive action he can take. The situation in these early scenes is comparable to that in **Ein Bruderzwist in Habsburg,** although the political and historical setting is far less elaborate. We long for action and yet are gradually oppressed by the recognition that there is no clear path of action available. Bancbanus is an unsatisfactory leader, yet it is impossible to know what satisfactory action can be taken. Grillparzer has put great stress on the ambiguity of the conditions under which he takes over the office. The king spells out the terms in some detail. Bancbanus is invested with legal responsibility but seems to have no corresponding authority and power. The queen is regent and he is her councilor. Although the king insists that nothing can be settled without Bancbanus's agreement and he is answerable for their decisions, this assertion is modified later when the king declares that she is the ruling mind who rules through him. Bancbanus is "Reichsgehilfe," her eyes and ears, her hands and arms (381-82). How then is he to act against her? What can he do if she insists on supporting Otto's excesses?

The significance of this situation is heightened when we remember the particular structure of the drama. Acts I and V serve as a partial frame around the central action. The king's role in setting up the situation and serving as judge

at the end inevitably suggests a symbolic representation of God's world. The favorite baroque theme of the ruler as God's representative standing outside the human action is not carried out here with total consistency any more than it is in other well-known German dramas. We think, for example, of the role of the Elector in *Der Prinz von Homburg* or of the Duke in *Torquato Tasso.* Nevertheless echoes of a higher authority are implicit in the king's role, particularly in the last act when he returns to his divided kingdom. The king's fear that Bancbanus may have been an "ungetreuer Knecht" (1969), together with the final assurance of his real loyalty contained in the title itself, seems a clear allusion to Christ's parable of the talents and the "good and faithful servant" of the Lord. Bancbanus thus comes to stand as a representative for man, his fate an exemplar of the human condition. His weaknesses and inevitable human failings, together with the restrictive conditions of his task, become symbolic of man's fate, "created weak but commanded to be strong." The moral of this situation does not have to be, as F. W. Kaufmann suggests, the acceptance by Bancbanus of a world which "punishes with inner destruction" the transgression of limitations, even when imposed on us against our will.[8] Instead, we may see in Bancbanus's fate an illustration of man burdened by the very nature of life with tasks that go beyond human limits. Although necessarily sharing in responsibility for the tragedy, Bancbanus nevertheless seeks to remain true to the principles of his life and finally manages to bring out of disaster a spirit of reconciliation.

The king's final judgments take fully into account the frailty of the human condition. Indeed, he acknowledges some responsibility for the situation himself, angrily accusing himself of neglect in failing to resist the mood of intransigence and immorality which was to destroy his home and happiness (1917 ff.). Such an attitude, which certainly indicates restrictions on his role as God's representative, is a characteristic turn of Grillparzer's. In **Weh dem, der lügt!** Bishop Gregor, we may recall, similarly sets the conditions of the hero's task and in the end acknowledges the limitations of his own vision. Since the king is himself largely accountable for the disasters that have occurred, he is all the more prepared to act with charity toward others who are involved. Responding to Bancbanus's pleas, he limits punishment of Peter and Simon, in effect the murderers of his wife, to banishment, while Otto too, once he has brought back the crown prince in safety, is permitted to leave the kingdom. For Otto, in fact, a checkered line of Christian grace and mercy may be traced. Bancbanus, seeking to bring the queen and her child across the moat out of the castle, is forced to take them one by one. The queen insists that Otto must be the first to leave, even before the child:

> Dies Kind beschützt
> Schuldlosigkeit mit lilienblankem Schwert;
> Doch diesen suchen sie, und er ist schuldig.

>   (1622-24)

Otto is allowed to escape, not in spite of but because of his guilt, and is thus granted the opportunity for atonement. Bancbanus, by giving the child into Otto's care, grants him, as he says, a last link with life and protection from despair and self-rejection (1985-86). By his rescue of the child Otto sets out on a path toward forgiveness which the king acknowledges in his final words to him: "Zieht hin mit Gott! kein Fluch sei über euch!" (2070).

A further Christian theme may be seen in Bancbanus's conflict with Peter and Simon. We have stressed to what extent his success is a victory of peace over war, of reason over passion, possibly of love over hate, certainly of humility over self-assertion and self-righteousness. The symbolic implications of this victory may be extended if we stress the associations aroused by the names of Bancbanus's opponents. We cannot help seeing here a suggestion of Christ's foremost disciple and the founder of the Church contrasted with Christ himself. In the actions of Simon and Peter after Erny's death we may see a reflection of the church militant ready to fight for its beliefs, opposed to Christ's message of peace. Such an interpretation may find support in the overtones of meaning given to the rescue of the crown prince and in the dream, envisioned in Bancbanus's final speech, of a harmonious new world to be enjoyed during his future reign.

In this context Bancbanus's humility suggests an echo of one of the most mysterious of the Christian beatitudes: "Blessed are the poor in spirit: for theirs is the kingdom of heaven." We may be reminded of the hero of *Der arme Spielmann*. The poor fiddler tells his story of failure and incompetence, even helplessness. He is simple almost to the point of being a fool; but gradually there emerges the realization that there may be another simplicity which is the expression of purity of heart. His stupidity and clumsiness may be nothing compared with his innocence and goodness. We saw Bancbanus first as an almost comic figure, ridiculed by the livelier people around him. Later his character has elements of the Christian fool. And yet the reversal of judgment which takes place in *Der arme Spielmann* never fully occurs here. Bancbanus remains in our mind as a pedantic and limited man, burdened by old age. His victory, won without passion, leaves us little feeling of Christian joy. We are left to wonder whether his achievement is a triumph of Christian humility or whether his humility is not merely an all too easy expression of his own weakness.

It may be that the conclusion of *Der arme Spielmann* is too easy, too sentimental, for us today.[9] **Ein treuer Diener** is more cautious, more subtle, more enigmatic. Yet it is a problem for drama, which traditionally paints in bold and confident colors, to leave us so uncertain in our judgment. If we assert Bancbanus's spiritual victory, insisting on the values of peace and law which he upheld,[10] then we overlook the weakness and tiresome limitations of the old man. Yet if we stress the absence of passion and the cold adherence to rules, then we ignore the elements of moral triumph.

Earlier it was suggested that the play might be considered within the bounds of tragicomedy, but this is not easy to maintain. Elements of the comic have largely disappeared by the end of the action. Moreover, the normal protagonist in tragicomedy is a man we laugh at and yet regard with a certain sympathy and even benevolence. We see in Hjalmar Ekdal's story, as we do, say, in Malvolio's or Alceste's (two often-quoted instances of tragicomic appeal), evidence of an all too human weakness which we can readily acknowledge in ourselves. Bancbanus's faults irritate us. It is difficult to break down the barriers which his weaknesses and even his virtues create. Perhaps the true clue to our sympathy lies in the poignancy of his suffering. In the heat of the action Bancbanus seems to forget his grief at the death of his wife. But when the issues are resolved and the king suggests the possibility of rewards for what he has achieved in the service of his master, we see the terrible emptiness that her loss has caused. Bancbanus's despair finds no relief in outbursts of distress, but lingers within. His life is enveloped in the sorrow and isolation that her death has brought. In the scenes immediately preceding, the drama offers conciliation. The king's son has been saved, Counts Simon and Peter pardoned, even Duke Otto allowed to go in peace. But it is a conciliation based on a shared sense of grief and suffering. Bancbanus's fate confirms this mood. His final decision to reject the king's offers and withdraw from the world of events is influenced by Otto's absolute affirmation that Erny was innocent and had never encouraged his advances. Emphasis is placed once more on the nature of a world in which innocence offers no protection. Bancbanus had sought to avoid the dangers of life through the fulfillment of daily duties, only to be engrossed in larger guilt and responsibility. But his withdrawal does not mean rejection or inner despair. The moral of the play is not like that of **Der Traum ein Leben,** in which a vision of the cruel world outside drives the hero to retreat to his own private corner. Bancbanus has already done what is required of him. Using all his powers in the fulfillment of his given task, he has managed to save the realm from civil war. He has known what it is to live in a threatening world and feels secure of the judgment of posterity. Thus in the midst of sadness there is consolation. In the awareness of grief we recognize the capacity of man to sustain the values by which life may still hold meaning.

Notes

1. A judgment rejected by Emil Staiger, for instance, in his influential discussion, "Grillparzer: *König Ottokars Glück und Ende,*" in *Meisterwerke deutscher Sprache aus dem neunzehnten Jahrhundert,* 2nd ed. (Zürich: Atlantis, 1948), p. 165 f.

2. Franz Grillparzer, *Sämtliche Werke,* ed. Peter Frank and Karl Pörnbacher, 4 vols. (München: Carl Hanser, 1960-65), IV, 153. *Ein treuer Diener* appears in volume 1.

3. *Anatomy of Criticism: Four Essays* (Princeton: Princeton University Press, 1957), p. 34.

4. *Grillparzer oder das abgründige Biedermeier* (Wien: Fritz Molden, 1972), p. 185.

5. *Grillparzers Bühnenkunst* (Bern: Francke, 1960), p. 60.

6. See the discussion of *The Wild Duck* in Karl S. Guthke, *Modern Tragicomedy* (New York: Random House, 1966), pp. 144-65.

7. See Wells, *The Plays of Grillparzer* (London: Pergamon, 1969), p. 23; and Reichert, "The Characterization of Bancbanus in Grillparzer's *Ein treuer Diener seines Herrn*," *SP*, 46 (1949), 70-78, esp. p. 74.

8. *German Dramatists of the Nineteenth Century* (Los Angeles: Lymanhouse, 1940), p. 63.

9. This view has been vigorously represented by the hero of John Irving's bestseller *The World According to Garp* (New York: E. P. Dutton, 1976), p. 88 and *passim*.

10. Cf. Benno von Wiese, *Die deutsche Tragödie von Lessing bis Hebbel* (Hamburg: Hoffmann and Campe, 1948), II, 185: ". . . der Dienst an diesen Werten ist nicht eine Pedanterie, sondern Selbsterfüllung des Ichs, das hier sich verwurzelt weiss."

Marianne Burkhard (essay date 1984)

SOURCE: "Love, Creativity and Female Role: Grillparzer's 'Sappho' and Staël's 'Corinne' Between Art and Cultural Norm," in *Jahrbuch fur Internationale,* Vol. 16, No. 2, 1984, pp. 128-46.

[*In the following essay, Burkhard explores the role of the female poet in* Sappho *and in Madame de Staël's* Corinne.]

Poets and writers are a powerful magnet for the modern imagination. They are considered vivid examples of a complex existence yoked to both the private and the public sphere, the inner laws of creative work and the demands of outside reality. Endowed with nothing but the force of words and images, set against a world of facts and deeds, writers are most exposed to the dichotomy between spirit and reality, between free imagination and actual life in a system of concrete socio-cultural norms.

Yet regarding the poetic mission in tension with social obligations is a relatively recent phenomenon. According to Reinhold Grimm, it arose in the 18th century when writers severed their traditional ties to specific social classes, especially the aristocracy, and assumed a freer, but also more insecure position. In Grimm's words, the poet has henceforth been "more *and* less than the citizen."[1] More apt to infuse life with words, but less capable of actively participating in the world, writers both expose and endure the vicissitudes of social and political processes.

With Goethe's *Torquato Tasso* (1789) and Hölderlin's *Empedokles*-fragments (1797-1800), the 1790's vigorously established the poet as a new literary hero. Yet casting our eyes beyond 1800 and German literature, this period offers even more such figures: Madame de Staël chose a poet as protagonist for her novel *Corinne ou l'Italie,* published in 1807, and Franz Grillparzer earned a theatrical triumph with his drama **Sappho,** written in 1817. Following conventional thinking, Reinhold Grimm summarily mentions **Sappho** as just another *Dichterdrama* which, however, slides into the less tragic, homelier style of the *Biedermeier* because love dominates the dramatic development. Although Grimm points out that Grillparzer created "the first important poet-hero*ine*",[2] he rates Goethe's and Hölderlin's works as more significant commentaries on the poet's position in society. Had Grimm considered Staël's *Corinne,* he could have remarked in a similar way on the dominance of the novel's love story.

In contrast to this approach it is my proposition here to show that **Sappho** and *Corinne* contain an analysis of the woman poet's situation, equally significant to that of the male poets. A careful study of the protagonists' consuming infatuations reveals that the love motif does not detract attention from the poet's existential problem, but rather exacerbates the dilemma of the two women writers. Moreover, by exhibiting the proverbial "power of love" as an absolute and destructive force, Grillparzer and Staël scrutinize cultural norms in a manner comparable to the socio-political analysis in *Tasso* and *Empedokles.* Therefore it is necessary to examine Sappho's and Corinne's calamitous love within the context of role-specific values which inform and suffuse writers and readers at a largely unconscious level. In assessing such culturally sanctioned norms it is actually fortunate that we are able to consider a female poet figure created by a man as well as one created by a woman since the latter's text can adduce direct evidence for the profound effect which cultural values set by male authorities exert on women's thinking and imagination. At the same time, comparisons with Goethe's *Tasso* will provide insights into the way a man devises a male writer's lot.

The three works are not only linked by a common topic and type of protagonist, but also by personal and intellectual connections among the authors. In January 1816, Grillparzer notes the reading of Staël's *Corinne* in his diary,[3] and as an avid reader of Goethe he naturally mentions *Tasso* in the letter explaining **Sappho** to Adolf Müllner.[4] Staël, on her part, had visited Germany in 1803-04 and spent three months in Weimar where she repeatedly met Goethe; in her book *De l'Allemagne* (1810) she discusses *Tasso* at quite some length. In addition, Staël's "dramatic attempts" contain a prose drama *Sapho,* written in 1811, which was, however, neither destined for publication nor even performed in the family circle.[5] Since the idea of this play is, as the editor points out, taken from *Corinne, Sapho* will not be discussed here.

When reading Grillparzer's **Sappho** and Staël's *Corinne* side by side, similarities become easily apparent. Both writers construct their texts along the same line of events leading the poet from triumph and love to the loss of her lover and untimely death. Within this structure there are even more parallels. Both works introduce the protagonist at, or right after, her greatest public triumph. At the beginning of the drama, Sappho returns to Lesbos from Olympia where, in contest with the best poets of Greece, she has won the laurel crown. In Staël's novel, the travelling Englishman Oswald, Lord Nelvil, first sees Rome in the splendor of Corinne's coronation at the Capitol. In the midst of these celebrations the poet's eyes almost magically spot an entranced listener who, despite youth or foreignness, captivates the celebrated woman and soon becomes the object of a novel and passionate love. Yet Corinne as well as Sappho loses this lover to a younger, more conventional woman: Sappho to her naive slave girl Melitta, Corinne to her blond and gentle half-sister Lucile Edgermond, who lives in provincial Northumbria. Neither woman can withstand this loss. In keeping with time-hallowed tradition and the exigencies of drama, Grillparzer has Sappho commit suicide by hurling herself from the Leucadian rock into the sea, while Staël, the novelist, submits Corinne to the slow process of physical decline and emotional death.

At first sight, these facts simply suggest a case of direct influence particularly in view of Grillparzer's remark that his Sappho resembled Corinne who, "perhaps had provided the stimulus" for the play.[6] Further discussion of this direct influence is, however, less interesting than an examination of the possibility that another, larger kind of influence might be at work beneath the surface of the two texts. In other words: The similarities in narrative and psychological sequencing suggest that the very act of imagining the lives of successful women writers is subject to a less visible, yet more pervasive influence of cultural values. In this paper I therefore attempt to demonstrate to what extent general patterns of behavior and thinking determine the creative imagination despite its inherent critical independence.

Staël and Grillparzer show such independence in deciding to relate the life of a woman who was a poet and world-famous.[7] In doing so, they select a subject matter that, for lack of numerous, well-known examples, is not easily accessible to readers' personal experience and historical reflection. To be sure, there were women who had entered the literary arena such as Madame de la Fayette (1634-93) and Mademoiselle de Scudéry (1607-1701) in France or Luise Adelgunde Gottsched (1713-62), Sophie la Roche (1713-1807) and Karoline von Günderrode (1780-1806) in Germany. But even the rather successful French authors were far from being generally renowned, and as authors of novels—considered a female genre—they lacked the distinction of contributing to "high" literature, that is to say, to lyric and epic poetry, or drama.

By choosing a poet-heroine, Staël and Grillparzer had to contend with a two-fold problem. First, they had to find ways of making the protagonist believable both as a famous poet and as a woman, and second, they had to portray her as a character capable of facing a serious, even

tragic dilemma. The latter was no mean feat as women writers were generally considered so unnatural that literary works of the time presented them, if at all, as comic, or even satiric figures.[8] Opposing this common tradition, Grillparzer and Staël had to proceed cautiously, paying heed to the standards used by the public to pass judgment on literary characters and their destinies.

In order to establish the poet's fame in realistic rather than fantastic terms, the protagonist as well as time and place must be selected with care. For Grillparzer, the temporal and geographical setting is, of course, given with the choice of Sappho, yet this choice itself is interesting. Sappho's name has traditionally enjoyed a high artistic reputation despite the fragmentary transmission of her poems. The fact that she lived in an era that has been chronicled very little, i.e. around 600 B.C., removes her at the same time into a more legendary realm. And while Sappho's world-wide renown was a historical fact for Grillparzer's time, nothing is known of an Olympic crown triumph. Also, it is clearly poetic license when Grillparzer has Sappho defeat not only her contemporary Alcaeus but also Anacreon—active a good hundred years later.[9] Combining fact and fiction, the author makes the impression of Sappho's triumph strong, yet also somewhat unreal to the reader. While scholars have long agreed that Grillparzer did not endeavor to create an authentic Greek atmosphere, his play is nevertheless steeped in an atmosphere of remote antiquity just enough to let conventional readers accept Sappho's exceptional accomplishment without questioning its probability.

Staël proceeds in quite a different manner. Setting her story a few years after the French Revolution, she boldly makes Corinne a figure of her own time. Only her name, which is that of a Greek poet in Pindar's time,[10] connects this modern character with a remote past. Presenting Corinne's extraordinary achievements as actual occurrence, Staël clearly took a risk, as a remark in her book *De la littérature* shows. In chapter IV, "Des femmes qui cultivent les lettres" (Of Women Cultivating Literature) she notes:

> . . . il était néanmoins difficile aux femmes de porter noblement la réputation d'auteur, de la concilier avec l'indépendance d'un rang élevé, et de ne perdre rien, par cette réputation, de la dignité, de la grâce, de l'aisance et du naturel qui devaient caractériser leur ton et leurs manières habituelles.
>
> (4, 467)

> (. . . it was nevertheless difficult for women to bear the reputation of author with dignity, to reconcile it [the reputation] with the independence of an elevated rank, without losing anything, through this reputation, of the dignity, the grace, the ease and the natural spontaneity that had to characterize their tone and their customary manners.)

This passage brings Schiller to mind and his statement that the female sex, by nature pliable and inclined toward harmony, in general embodies grace (Anmut), the gentle concord between feelings and thought,[11] or, in Staël's words, the natural ease which must characterize their entire behavior. Such congenial harmony, however, stands in contrast to the noble dignity (Würde) acquired when the spirit overcomes suffering, when the individual proves himself as an autonomous force and, one could say, as a creative spirit striving for, or against, the public's views. Staël and Schiller refer to the cultural principle that associates women first and foremost with immediate beauty, but not with its often arduous creation. In 18th century language we find here equivalents for Nancy Chodorow's modern sociological terms of female being vs. male doing.[12] This fundamental dichotomy confines women to *being* beautiful while men can *create* beauty in art. In the light of all this, it is clear that Corinne must be beautiful and that, moreover, her beauty, grace, sensitivity and natural gifts must be emphasized time and again as the visible and necessary warrants of her authentic feminity.

In addition, Staël carefully predicates the poet's success on specific historical conditions, thus formulating the double message that such accomplishments are possible, but exceptional. Corinne lives in Italy where emotional expression is given value and freedom, and where intuition takes precedence over clear, male rationality. Furthermore, Staël sees Italy's political weakness and fragmentation as favoring a more liberal development in the realm of artistic and spiritual endeavors. Consequently, Italy is more likely than other countries to accept and revere a woman's greatness.[13] England, the country of Corinne's father, where she spends several years, exemplifies the opposite milieu. Living with her father and stepmother in Northumbria, she finds herself in the midst of normal conventions which enjoin women to seek fulfilment only in the role of wife and mother and as their husband's modest, even self-effacing companions.

Unlike Grillparzer Staël was free to assign her poet whatever specific literary pursuit seemed most appropriate. Her decision to make Corinne an improvisor rather than a writer of printed texts carries interesting implications. Exercising an ephemeral art form which cannot create indelible traces in the fabric of a culture, Corinne leaves no "works". She outlives her early death only in the memories of others, especially of Oswald, and in the little art she was able to teach, shortly before dying, to Oswald's young daughter Juliette.

What reasons, we wonder, could have prompted Staël, a rather prolific writer of books herself, to endow Corinne, her alter ego, with such an evanescent mastery? The explanation seems to be twofold. On the one hand, this trait allowed her to stay close to historical reality as she had herself seen several women improvisors during her trip to Italy in 1805. Showing Corinne as one of them lent emphasis to her point that, in the present time, women were able to earn fame as poets. This art form also furnished an historical model for Corinne's general celebrity in the person of Maria Maddalena Morelli, called Corilla Olimpica, who had died in 1800.[14] On the other

hand, Corinne's female art tempers the discrepancy between her sex and her autonomous, successful creativity. It seems obvious that Staël devised this particular situation to insure that conventional readers would accept Corinne as a real woman. In doing so she had, however, to squander an opportunity to present a woman as equal contributor to the lasting cultural monuments created by men.

A glance at Goethe's *Tasso* provides an interesting comparison. The drama captures the moment when Tasso presents his newest and largest work *La Gerusalemme Liberata* to his patron Alphonso d'Este, Duke of Ferrara. This work is an epic poem which, according to the genre, encompasses the world by offering a richly imagined description of how the First Crusade conquered Jerusalem, of how the Western knights regained the East and liberated Christianity's holiest place from the infidels. If Tasso lays claim to this vast universe, he does so not just by virtue of his poetic imagination, but also thanks to the possibility of observing the life at Alphonso's court with all its diplomatic and military action. It is in this highly political environment that the poet, "der tatenlose Jüngling" (the inexperienced youth) comes into contact with the powers that shape reality,[15] and gains the insight necessary for creating works whose poetic vision also illuminates the actual world with its interplay of individual and socio-political forces.

Neither Sappho nor Corinne are in direct touch with a comparable domain of influential action. While generally informed about Italy's political situation, Corinne takes no interest in it; all her thinking revolves around the arts. In addition, her financial independence allows her to devote her life freely to creative pursuits. Unlike Tasso and so many other writers, she lives unencumbered by concerns for a livelihood which might bring economic and political impediments. And unlike her creator, Madame de Staël, she is not harassed by political foes. It is indeed surprising that Staël relegates her protagonist to this non-controversial, contemplative realm of the beaux arts while she herself was embroiled in the world of politics all her life and even enjoyed using her intellectual gifts in the game of power. Yet since politics at that time was considered highly unfeminine, Corinne actually appears as a deliberately stylized image of a woman poet in which Staël's exceptional biography is reduced to the more acceptable spheres of art and beauty. In this respect it is no coincidence that Goethe, experienced in political affairs himself, sees contact with this world as an essential element in Tasso's creative development while Staël eliminates her own experience in this realm as potentially detrimental to Corinne's image both as a poet and a woman. In doing so, she illustrates the reduction which even active women so often impose on themselves for fear of otherwise losing their femininity.

Grillparzer's Sappho displays this self-imposed reduction in a particularly striking way.[16] Upon her triumphant return from Olympia she suddenly announces to friends and neighbors in Lesbos that she has decided to foresake poetry in favor of "ein einfach stilles Hirtenleben" (I,2; 94: [to lead] quietly a simple shepherd's life) and to use her lyre henceforth only for the praise of "häuslich stille Freuden" (96: of tranquil homely joys). This desire for simple domesticity at the side of Phaon is fueled by an acute sense that, for her, art actually is a transgression. Sappho's choice of words demonstrates this when she characterizes writing as "des Vollbringens wahnsinnglühnde Lust" (I,2; 50: my achievement's feverish delight) and when she terms her laurel crown, the symbol of her success in the large world, "ein Verbrechen" and "eine frevle Zier" (11. 57-8: an offense and an impious gaud). Later in the same act, Sappho deplores the artist who, allured by vain renown, ventures out onto the wild sea, into a "graue Unermessli- chkeit" (I,5; 1.403: a boundless gray expanse of open space). Obviously she sees art as an unchartered terra incognita where endless terror accompanies moments of ultimate perfection.

While this experience is not unique among writers, it has particularly problematic implications for Sappho because she is a woman. As portrayed by Grillparzer, she followed her indomitable creative urge and forged ahead, like Faust, into new territories. As a woman, however, she could never avoid feeling guilty for thus neglecting her truly feminine domestic tasks. Because of this fundamental split, the mo- ment of highest success in Olympia is not one of sweet reward, validating all painful risks, but rather one of great- est tension. At this juncture, Sappho therefore suddenly reverts back to Gretchen's world. This turnabout, presented as free decision, is actually marked by a role compulsion whose subliminal power manifests itself in the very abrupt- ness of Sappho's renunciation as well as in her pointedly negative language she uses for her art.

This compulsion takes positive form in Phaon, Sappho's new companion and lover. Though filled with genuine enthusiasm for her poetry and praised for "seiner Gaben Fülle" (I,2; 89: [he is] well endowed with gifts), he ap- pears, first, as an inhibited, immature youth, then, in his relationship with Melitta, as a most average man who is no match for Sappho's strong personality. When falling in love with the simple girl he exhibits conventional male at- titudes that prompt him to seek a woman of unassuming modesty (II,6; 759), distinguished rather for a quiet heart and innocence than "des Ruhmes Lorbeerkronen" (III,6; 1143-45: fame's laurel crowns). Phaon's deepest yearning also reveals itself when his dream, at the beginning of the third act changes Sappho's face "einer Pallas abgestohlen" (III,1, 918: purloined from Pallas' statue) into Melitta's "Kindesangesicht" (919: a child-like face) and replaces the poet's "Götterlieder" (916: [her] sacred songs) with an "irdisch-holdes Lächeln" (917: a winsome smile quite of this earth). Grillparzer's own remark "Phaon and Melitta haben die Partie des Lebens" (Phaon and Melitta play the part of life)[17] clearly implies that the young lovers represent the normal expectations of their respective sex roles.

It is precisely such a normal life that Sappho desires in Olympia more than ever before. With an almost trance- like confidence she selects Phaon trusting that he will pull her gently down "von der Dichtkunst wolkennahen Gipfeln / In dieses Lebens heitre Blütentäler" (I,2; 90-1: from poetry's high summit near the clouds / To life's serene and blossom-covered vales). Thus, his "gifts" do not belong to the spheres of art and spirit, but to that of simple life, and in his very conformity he opens for Sappho a path to a normal female existence. The sudden love of the famous poet for the unknown youth has its causes not only in her sense of aging or her sensitivity heightened by passionate imagination;[18] rather, it is ultimately rooted in the compel- ling female role model that allows for no exceptions. By making Sappho and Phaon so incongruous, Grillparzer displays the insuperable dichotomy which cultural role norms create even in such an independent woman as Sap- pho.

At first, Corinne's case seems to be quite different. For her, Oswald is an equal partner. They both belong to the same social class, and their fathers had even deemed their marriage desirable. More important than this external equality is the fact that his northern proclivity to introspec- tion, and his experience of grief for his dead father have given Oswald the deep and subtle sensitivity which Corinne has not yet found in Italy. And since Oswald's love is kindled in the moment of great triumph at the Capitol he fulfills her fondest hope which, on their first walk through Rome she expresses in the following words:

> Je ne me flattais pas . . . que ce couronnement au Capi- tole me vaudrait un ami; mais cependant, en cherchant la gloire, j'ai toujours espéré qu'elle me ferait aimer. A quoi servirait-elle, du moins aux femmes, sans cet es- poir!
>
> (IV,3; 8, 114)

> (I did not anticipate . . . that the crowning on the Capitol would bring me a friend; yet in seeking renown I have always hoped that it would make me love. What purpose would it [renown] have, at least for women, without this hope!)

Unlike Sappho, Corinne continues to pursue her art. At a ball, she dances her famous tarantella (VI,1), in her own translation of Shakespeare's *Romeo and Juliet* she plays the title role with great success (VII;3) she improvises in Naples (XIII,4), and captivates the public in Venice when impersonating a comic opera part (XVI,2).

A closer examination, however, discovers under this surface the same values that Sappho exhibits more dramati- cally. Corinne's above-quoted opinion that, for women, poetic fame is valuable only when accompanied by love expresses the feeling that drives Sappho in Olympia to her sudden infatuation with Phaon. As women are trained, from childhood on, to center all their thinking and feeling, their entire role conception on love, fame alone cannot grant them true fulfilment. When Sappho describes the importance of a woman's love

> Wie all ihr [der Frau] Sein, ihr Denken und Begehren, Um diesen einz'gen Punkt sich einzig dreht,

. . . . .
[Wie] Das ganze Leben als ein Edelstein
Am Halse hängt der neugebornen Liebe!

(III,1; 827-34)

(How all her being, thinking, her desires / Revolve
about this single point alone. . . . How her complete
existence hangs suspended, / A jewel on the throat of
new-born love!).

she expresses the same sentiment as when Corinne
remarks:

. . . s'il y a quelque chose de religieux dans ce sentiment [amour], c'est parce qu'il fait disparaître tous les
autres intérêts, et se complaît, comme la dévotion, dans
le sacrifice entière de soi-même.

(X,6; 8, 399)

(. . . if there is something religious in this feeling
[love], it is because it makes disappear all the other
interests and takes pleasure, as does devotion, in
sacrificing entirely one's self.)

This juxtaposition demonstrates that Staël as well as her
male colleague, Grillparzer views love as the center, even
the *sine qua non* of a fulfilled life for the woman writer.

To be sure, love is an important companion of fame for
male writers as well. For them requited love is, however,
rather an additional confirmation than the source and basis
for their identity as artists. The love Tasso recognizes in
the words of the princess heightens his self-confidence; in
turn, he measures with assurance his poetry against
Antonio's diplomatic achievements. Indeed, he defends
the value of his creative work against the misconceptions
of the active politician, whereas the dictates of the female
role compel Sappho and Corinne to disparage their artistic
endeavor, their spiritual productivity in comparison with
love.

Although Corinne does not immediately abandon art, her
behavior indicates quite early in the story that her love
jeopardizes her talent. When Oswald introduces an English
acquaintance, Mr. Edgermond, to Corinne, she is for the
first time incapable of improvising: "Le sentiment avait
subjugué tout-à-fait son esprit" (VI,3; 8,221: Feeling had
completely subjugated her spirit.) Only her past reveals
the full import of this passage. Herself a member of the
Edgermond family, she is embarassed to exhibit her talent
before a member of the family whose unmitigated disap-
proval of her creative ambition had forced her to flee back
to Italy. Moreover, this is a moment when her love for Oswald already points to the necessity to present herself to
English traditional society in a favorable light. Finally,
Corinne senses already that despite all his love it will be
difficult for Oswald to marry her, thus fully endorsing her
unusual position. As a matter of fact, upon his return to
England Oswald cannot long resist the appeal of traditional
family life, an appeal so charmingly embodied in the gentle
modesty of Corinne's half-sister Lucile. Just like Sappho,
Corinne sharply collides in her love affair with the prevail-

ing order which, in its pervasive sway, undermines Oswald's love as well as Corinne's confidence.

Besides this external threat from socio-cultural norms
Corinne's art faces an internal one from love itself. In
earlier relations with men she was able to preserve the
independence of her creative work; with Oswald, she is
totally absorbed in her love. Willingly, even eagerly she
now experiences the deeply rooted notions about the
absolute value of love for women and about the bliss total
devotion will bring. In her last improvisation she calls
love "suprême puissance du cœur qui renferme en lui-
même la poésie, l'héroïsme et la religion" (XIII,4; 9, 113:
heart's supreme power encompassing in itself poetry, heroism and religion) while the beloved bestows "divine life"
upon the woman's heart. It is little wonder, that not only
her thoughts and feelings but also her poetic imagination
become ever more dependent on Oswald's presence.

Cette nature, ces beaux-arts que je sens avec vous, et
maintenant, hélas! seulement avec vous, tout deviend-
rait muet pour mon âme . . . ôtez-moi cette terreur [de
partir] . . .

(VII,1; 8, 297)

(This nature, these works of art I experience with you,
and now, unfortunately, only with you, all this would
become mute for my soul . . . deliver me from this
terror [of your departure])

The possibility of Oswald's leaving fills her with terror
because love has deprived her talent of its autonomy and,
thus, the loss of her love would also spell the end of her
art.

What Corinne fears comes true with cruel logic. Once in
England, Oswald marries Lucile without, however, finding
real happiness with her, and in Florence Corinne fades
away, exhausted emotionally as well as creatively. Attempts to express her grief fail:

. . . elle peignait ce qu'elle souffrait; mais ce n'étaient
plus ces idées générales, ces sentiments universels qui
répondent au cœur de tous les hommes; c'était le cri de
la douleur, cri monotone à la longue, . . .

(XVIII,4; 9, 378)

(. . . she depicted what she suffered; but these were
not any more the general ideas, the universal feelings
responding to the hearts of all people; this was the
scream of pain, monotonous in the long run . . .)

Corinne's earlier fear that world and art would become
mute is more than a rhetorical figure; rather, it denotes an
all pervasive paralysis sapping even the foundations of her
creative energy. Sappho, too, describes this experience of
losing the self and the world when, after Phaon openly
declared his love for Melitta, she exclaims:

Bin ich denn noch, und ist denn *etwas* noch?
Dies weite All, es stürzte nicht zusammen
In jenem fürchterlichen Augenblick?

(IV,1; 1189-91)

(Do I still live? Does anything still live? / Did this broad universe not all collapse / in such a fearful moment of despair?)

If George Reinhardt sees in this passage mostly "pathetic fallacy" and "romantic egoism," which all to easily merge the I with the universe,[19] he fails to recognize the fatal nature of this loss of love, a loss that art cannot overcome. Therefore, it is psychologically consistent that Sappho, in her dejection, does not resort to her poetry which she actually considers as an activity past and completed.[20] For the woman writer, the death of her love destroys more than her feelings, it destroys her chance of a normal female existence and, at the same time, her art, her most personal energy.

This deadly effect of unrequited, or lost, love separates Sappho and Corinne from Tasso. However deeply the loss of love affects him, it deprives him neither of his ability to write nor of his will to cling to life. In the midst of his emotional catastrophe he holds on to the one element on which his personality rests: to the power of the word, his poetic talent:

> Nein, alles ist dahin! Nur eines bleibt:
> Die Träne hat uns die Natur verliehen,
> Den Schrei des Schmerzens, wenn der Mann zuletzt
> Es nicht mehr trägt—Und mir noch über alles—
> Sie liess im Schmerz mir Melodie und Rede,
> Die tiefste Fülle meiner Not zu klagen:
> Und wenn der Mensch in seiner Qual verstummt,
> Gab mir ein Gott zu sagen, wie ich leide.
>
> (V,5; 3426-33)

(No: all is gone!—But one thing still remains,—/Tears, balmy tears, kind nature has bestowed. The cry of anguish, when the man at length / Can bear no more— yea, and to me beside, / She leaves in sorrow melody and speech, / To utter forth the fullness of my woe: Though in their mortal anguish men are dumb, / To me a God has given to tell my grief.)

In her grief, the woman writer falls silent, succumbs to mortal weakness while, in the male writer, the talent affirms its divine nature by transcending the catastrophe.

Tasso's tragedy originates in the dichotomy between word and deed, poet and society. However problematic this situation may be, it does not challenge art in itself, but rather questions its place in the world. Through Tasso's love, this always latent conflict fully erupts. For Sappho and Corinne, love itself constitutes the conflict as it threatens art both from without and within. Consequently, a dilemma between love and art develops in which love is equated with what culture designates as the "true nature" of female existence which in its "natural" simplicity cannot be varied. If for male writers, word and deed represent two equal possibilities of existence, love for women writers is not one, but the only approved form of existence compared to which art is alien and therefore cannot outweigh the loss of love.

To what extent art and fame make a woman appear foreign becomes obvious as Phaon decries Sappho now as sinister sorcerer (III,6; V,3), now reveres her as a goddess (I,3; V,3). In both cases he refuses to grant her the very status she so desperately seeks in a life of love and domesticity: the simple status of a female and a human being. In bestowing his love on the homely Melitta rather than on the richly talented Sappho, Phaon affirms the power of the cultural norms which exclude Sappho from the normal status of a woman in bourgeois society. Corinne experiences foreignness and exclusion directly only in England, yet the female role model impinges upon her life even from afar since she has to keep her name and origin secret. Despite external freedom in Italy, she, too, faces an existential dilemma because Oswald cannot fully overcome conventional values and because she herself believes the notion that love represents a woman's highest calling.

A glance at just a few theoretical works reveals the social and philosophical systems that form the background for the two texts. In her books *De la littérature* (1800: On Literature) and *De l'influence des passions sur le bonheur des individus et des nations* (1796: On the Influence of Passions on the Happiness of Individuals and Nations), Staël describes the general position of women quite extensively. In the chapter "Of Women Cultivating Literature" she writes:

> Dès qu'une femme est signalée comme une personne distinguée, le public en général est prévenue contre elle. . . . Tout ce qui sort de ce cours habituel, déplait d'abord à ceux qui considèrent la routine de la vie comme la sauvegarde de la médiocrité.
>
> (*De la littérature* 4, 474)

(As soon as a woman is recognized as a distinguished person, the public in general is prejudiced against her. . . . Whatever departs from this habitual course displeases first those who consider life's routine as the safeguard for mediocrity.)

This attitude is typical for Corinne's stepmother and her father since the concept of mediocrity coincides with their narrow beliefs about women's non-domestic potential. The realm of notable action is reserved for men while "nature" destines women to serve unselfishly men's activities, foregoing any worldly ambitions of their own:

> La gloire même peut être reprochée à une femme, parce qu'il y a contraste entre la gloire et sa destinée naturelle.
>
> (4,475)

(Fame itself can be a reproach to a woman because there is a contrast between fame and her natural destiny.)

This cultural axiom takes an ambivalent form in Oswald since, on the one hand, he loves Corinne with all her fame but, on the other, still succumbs to the traditional system.

Corinne and Sappho also can be seen as examples of the following opinion from the chapter on vanity in *De l'influence des passions:*

En étudiant le petit nombre de femmes qui ont de vrais titres à la gloire, on verra que cet effort de leur nature fut toujours aux dépens de leur bonheur. Après avoir chanté les plus douces leçons de la morale et de la philosophie, Sapho se précipita du haut du rocher de Leucade, . . . Enfin, avant d'entrer dans cette carrière de gloire, . . . les femmes doivent penser que, pour la gloire même, il faut renoncer au bonheur et au repos de la destinée de leur sexe: et qu'il est dans cette carrière bien peu de sorts qui puissent valoir la plus obscure vie d'une femme aimée et d'une mère heureuse.

(3, 107-8)

(When studying the small number of women who have a true claim to fame, one sees that this effort of their nature was always made at the detriment of their happiness. After having sung the loveliest lessons of moral and philosophy, Sapho hurled herself from the top of the Leucadian rock, . . . Finally, before entering a career of fame, . . . women must take into consideration that, for fame itself, they must renounce the happiness and trainquillity of their gender's destiny: and that, in this career, there are very few lots which can counterbalance the most obscure life of a beloved wife and a happy mother.)

Artistic and intellectual talents cost the young Corinne her happiness since Oswald's father feared that, married to Oswald, she would estrange his son from England and traditional lifestyle. While Corinne's flight to Italy is a conscious decision for a career, Sappho in Olympia makes a decision against continuing her career. Yet neither decision, however deliberate each may have been, can resolve the fundamental opposition between art and love.

Whereas Staël focuses on the social background, Friedrich Schiller's essay *Über naive und sentimentalische Dichtung* (1796: On Naive and Sentimental Writing)[21] discusses the nature of poetic writing at great length. On the grounds of Kantian concepts, Schiller defines two fundamental styles of writing. With all his idiosyncratic use of words, such as naive and sentimental, Schiller's definitions are broadly valid and can thus elucidate Staël's and Grillparzer's texts even though these authors had little or no knowledge of them.[22] Werner Vordtriede was the first to apply Schiller's terminology to Grillparzer calling *Sappho* "an exact explication of the sentimental poet".[23] As I have demonstrated in my earlier article, this interpretation must be amended to the effect that Grillparzer portrays a sentimental *woman poet*. Such a designation is, however, a *contradictio in adiecto* since, in Schiller's definition, sentimental poetry is concerned with the absolute and limitless, and is therefore diametrically opposed to that time's conventional notions about women who are seen as absorbed in, and destined for, the limited, immediate present; thus, in Schiller's terminology, they clearly pertain to the naive. Yet Sappho writes in the sentimental manner, she passes beyond the confines of her immediate female realm into the wide open space of the sea and onto "high summits near the clouds" (I,2; 90). As a woman, however, she also clings to the hope for a naive existence, and this prompts her to divert her limitless art to quiet domesticity. Such an attempt to integrate the sentimental into the naive must fail because these two possibilities of existence as well as of writing inhabit separate and contrary positions in the cultural system.

Corinne is, in Schiller's terms, a naive writer. Her graceful beauty, extolled so often, and her art naturally harmonize, forming that undivided unity and autonomous perfect whole that Schiller describes as typical for the naive writer and his art. Corinne falls in with Italian life without ever striving beyond its limits, and she brings Oswald, lost in the dark sorrows for his dead father, back to a bright present and the clarity of classical art. Since a naive existence is commensurate with conventional viewers of female nature, naive writing should not present a basic problem for women. Despite this, Corinne eventually faces a dilemma when her love for Oswald assumes such significance that it consumes her art. Instead of experiencing the world as an immediate whole, as she once did, she now sees it more and more divided into parts as the beauty around her and her feelings cease to complement each other and as her awareness of Oswald's love for English traditions disturbs the simple freedom of her Italian lifestyle. Less and less the world responds to her spirit and emotions until it is muted and Corinne is left with nothing but grief which, in its monotony, fails to evoke response and thus cannot be art. Sooner or later the naive *woman poet* is exposed to the consuming power of love. Corinne, the naive poet, therefore meets as tragic an end as Sappho, the sentimental poet.

The preceding references to Schiller demonstrate that, in elaborating conceptual systems leading male thinkers duplicate and affirm cultural norms that are powerful although they often may seem vague. The theoretical argument sustains Staël's and Grillparzer's poetic vision that a woman poet's life, is ultimately rent by what modern readers would see as a culturally established incompatibility between female nature and spiritual creativity. A woman may be a successful poet as long as the demands and profits of the female role model can be postponed. Yet she necessarily reaches a point where love challenges her creative existence in a much more fundamental manner than this is the case with male poets such as Tasso or Tonio Kröger. For the men, art emerges victorious from the conflict: In the catastrophe Tasso realizes the full potential of creative talent, and for Tonio Kröger art's truly human significance is born in the very conflict that compels the artist to love life from afar. For Sappho and Corinne, lost and impossible love cannot bear poetic fruit because their nature is so bound to immediate presence that the loss of love annihilates their sense of identity. Or, in modern terms: For the women, art succumbs to the cultural norm of a one-dimensional female role.

Of course, this model does not only operate within the poetic cosmos, it also affects poetic imagination by setting limits to what authors, themselves embedded in the cultural system, are able to conceive and willing to depict for a usually conventional public from which they expect applause. Thus, deviations from ingrained patterns need to be presented cautiously if they are to find sympathetic understanding in readers. Viewed in this light, Staël's and Grillparzer's decision to let their protagonists die of lovers' grief appears as traditional counterbalance to their defiantly male careers. Is this, then, a signal of the author's ultimate yielding to conventions, or rather a deliberate strategy to reassure the general public that they do not aim at total revolution?

With regard to Grillparzer, critics have implicitly assumed that male thinking prevailed, contending that his main concern lies more with the woman than the poet. Yet in his surprising juxtaposition of Sappho with the average man Phaon he provides insight into the compulsion of general role norms. This insight, unusual for a man of that time, enables Grillparzer to see in Sappho's relation with Phaon, traditionally construed as comic, the core of a tragedy, which is, however, a tragedy of cultural values rather than of passionate love. His criticism is implied in this choice of the tragic mode that moves public and readers to deplore Sappho's untimely death and to grasp, intuitively at least, the impossibility of reconciling autonomous creativity to the inflexible female role.

In principle, Staël assumes the same attitude. She, too, expresses her criticism indirectly describing the status quo which, even under favorable conditions, precipitates a tragic end. Moving readers to exclaim with Ophelia "O what a noble mind is here o'er thrown!" she suggests that readers take a more critical look at behavior patterns designated as "natural" only by sociocultural convention.

Yet since Staël is a woman, her text raises more expectations which, in turn, could cause modern readers to find great fault with her lack of overt criticism. To be fair we must bring her situation into full relief. By making Corinne an improvisor and by subjecting her art to her love, Staël clearly submits her character to a feminization designed to make her as acceptable a woman as possible. This constitutes a case of self-censure which is surprising only because it comes from an author who, in her own career, had already gone much further, in terms both of writing and of political involvement. Yet this very discrepancy should give us pause, since more than any theoretical pronouncement it underscores the power of prevailing norm that kept even such a self-confident woman as Staël from portraying her own achievement directly, thus advancing it as a realistic possibility or women. Despite this, Staël's own biography provides an indirect counterbalance to Corinne. Though she experienced the loss of love intensely, she overcame these repeated disappointments, continued her writing, and was therefore able to relate Corinne's death and destruction. In doing so, she reached what for women, is the necessary first level of emancipation and implied criticism.[24] At this state the destructive fate, be it death or madness, is not just mutely suffered, but described and named.

Another point to consider is the public. Perhaps Staël's own experiences taught her that a wider readership was not yet willing to take Corinne seriously if she were not dependent on love. The risk was probably too great that such a figure would be seen as unnatural and unwomanly, and would therefore be dismissed as comic or impossible. To avoid this, Corinne's undiminished femininity had to be affirmed in her devotion to, and dependence on, love. The dominance of love alone could reassure skeptics that poetry and fame need not destroy female sensitivity and that women could be creative artists without forfeiting their emotional depth.

If Staël and Grillparzer succeeded in establishing a *woman* as a powerful poet, they did so at the ultimate expense of art; to sustain the poet's credibility as a woman they had to destroy her creative individuality. Sappho's and Corinne's triumph as serious *Dichterheldinnen*, poetheroines, requires the annihilation of their talent. This cruel contradiction is inherent in the prevailing value system that deprived women of the freedom to realize their spiritual, non-domestic potential without being subjected to personal guilt, social disapprobation and cultural prescription.

The portrayal of women as successful writers and impressive characters impels Staël and Grillparzer to explore the tragic implications of the protagonists' position in a patriarchal world. In this process, they are led to demonstrate to what extent social and psychological mechanisms determine role expectations at an unconscious and thus unquestioned level. The result is less a tragedy of art (Kunsttragödie) than a tragedy of culture (Kulturtragödie). And while the dramas focusing on male writers comment on the artist's ambivalent place in the socio-political context, *Sappho* and *Corinne* comment on women's onedimensional place in the cultural value system. Instead of taking issue with political power in the normal sense of the word, Staël and Grillparzer make a statement on the politics of culture, that is to say, on the less visible and far less changeable distribution of power in the general notions regarding men's and women's roles. Therefore, the *Dichterinnendrama* is not a derivative of the *Dichterdrama* with its focus on the male writer's socio-political dilemma, but rather its equal counterpart bringing to light the woman writer's tragic position between art and cultural norm.

Notes

1. Reinhold Grimm, "Dichter-Helden: *Tasso, Empedokles* und die Folgen", *Basis: Jahrbuch für deutsche Gegenwartsliteratur* 7 (1977), p. 9. Cf. also Emil Staiger, "Goethes Zweifel am Wesen des Dichters", *Anzeiger der österreichischen Akademie der Wissenschaften*, Philosophisch-historische Klasse, 113 (1976), Nr. 8, p. 218.

2. Grimm, p. 16; Grimm's emphasis.

3. Cf. August Sauer (ed.), *Grillparzers Werke*, Part 2, vol. 1: *Tagebücher und literarische Skizzenhefte* I 1808-21 (Wien: Gerlach-Wiedling, 1914), p. 78.

4. Letter dated end of February/beginning of March, cited in Karl Pörnbacher (ed.), *Franz Grillparzer:*

Dichter über ihre Dichtungen (München: Heimeran, 1970), p. 105.

5. Cf. "Avertissement de l'éditeur" [Auguste-Louis de Staël] in Madame la Baronne de Staël, *OEuvres complètes* (Paris: Treuttel et Würtz, 1820-1), vol. 16, i-iii. All Staël quotations refer to this edition and are given in the text with the volume number preceding the page number. In order to facilitate locating quotes for *Corinne* in other editions, books and chapters are also indicated. The translations are my own.

6. Quoted in Pörnbacher (cf. 4), p. 108.

7. Cf. also Sigrid Weigel, "Der schielende Blick: Thesen zur Geschichte weiblicher Schreibpraxis" in *Die Verborgene Frau: Sechs Beiträge zu einer feministischen Literaturwissenschaft* (Berlin: Argument, 1983), pp. 93-95.

8. Cf. Dolores Whelan's study *Gesellschaft im Wandel: Der Engel mausert sich. Das Bild der Frau in den Komödien Eduard von Bauernfelds: 1830-1870.* Europäische Hochschulschriften, Series I, vol. 223 (Bern: Peter Lang, 1978), pp. 109-22.

9. Cf. Phaon's description of the Olympian contest Act I, Scene 3, 11.218-20. To facilitate locating quotations in different editions and the translation, quotations are identified by act, scene and line numbers. I am quoting the translation of Arthur Burkhard, *Sappho* (Yarmouth Port/MA: Register Press, 1953).

10. Corinne was a Boeotian poet living around 500 B.C. In a footnote (9,487), Staël mentions that she gave lessons to Pindar; Pauly-Wissowa's *Realencyclopädie der klassischen Altertumswissenschaften* terms this an "invention."

11. Cf. Schiller, *Über Anmut und Würde* [On Grace and Dignity]; for a translation cf. *Schillers Complete Works in 8 volumes* (New York: Collier, 1902), vol. 8.

12. Cf. Nancy Chodorow, "Being and Doing: A Cross-Cultural Examination of the Socialization of Males and Females" in Vivian Gornick/Barbara MOran (eds.), *Woman in Sexist Society* (New York: Basic Books, 1971), 259-91.

13. Cf. Madelyn Gutwirth, *Madame de Staël, Novelist: The Emergence of the Artist as Woman* (Urbana: University of Illinois Press, 1978), pp. 208-15.

14. Cf. Gutwirth, p. 173 and footnote 13.

15. *Torquato Tasso* I,3; 11.426-36. For the translation cf. Anna Swanwick, *Torquato Tasso* in *The Complete Works of Johann Wolfgang von Goethe* (New York: Collier, n.d.), vol. 6, pp. 99-100.

16. For a more thorough discussion of Sappho's motivation cf. my article "Die letzte Schuld des Lebens': Grillparzers *Sappho* als Tragödie der schreibenden Frau" in *Monatshefte* 74 (1982), 122-138.

17. Quoted in Pörnbacher (cf. note 4), p. 105.

18. Critics belabor this last point again and again, cf. Douglas Yates in *Franz Grillparzer: A Critical Biography* (Oxford: Blackwell, 1946), pp. 35-6; G.A. Wells in *The Plays of Grillparzer* (London: Pergamon, 1969); and, most recently, Robert Mühlher in "Das Doppelantlitz des Eros in Grillparzers Sappho" in K. Bartsch / O. Goltschnigg / G. Melzer / W.H. Schober (eds.), *Die andere Welt: Aspekte der österreichischen Literatur des 19. und 20. Jahrhunderts* (Bern: Francke, 1979), pp. 54-5.

19. Cf. "A Reading of Grillparzer's *Sappho*" in Donald H. Crosby / George C. Schoolfield (eds.), *Studies in the German Drama* (Chapel Hill: University of North Carolina Press, 1974), p. 134.

20. In act IV, Sappho considers her poetry as a land lost (IV,2; 1272ff.) and in act V her lyre reminds her "an verflossne Zeit" (V,5; 1926: of the days gone by) while in her last monologue she says that she has "fulfilled" what the gods asked her to do (V,6; 2001).

21. The translation cited in footnote 11 renders the German "naiv" with the English word "simple".

22. According to the diary, Grillparzer had read Schiller's essays, yet being unimpressed, he disposes of them summarily; cf. *Tagebücher I* (see note 3), p. 48 (entry of June 19, 1810). In *De l'Allemagne* Staël does not mention Schiller's essays at all.

23. Cf. "Grillparzers Beitrag zum poetischen Nihilismus" in *Trivium* 9 (1951), 105.

24. Cf. also Weigel, p. 103.

FURTHER READING

Criticism

Baker, Christa Suttner. "Structure and Imagery in Grillparzer's *Sappho*." *Germanic Review* 48 (1973): 44-55.
    Perceives a "dynamic balance between independence and interdependence among the various acts rather than stasis resulting from such autonomy seems to characterize *Sappho*."

Gordon, Philip. "Franz Grillparzer: Critic of Music." *Musical Quarterly* 11, No. 2 (October 1916): 552-61.
    Highlights Grillparzer's role in the Viennese musical circle, tracing its effects upon his work.

Hitchman, Sybil. *The World as Theatre in the Works of Franz Grillparzer.* Berne: Peter Lang, 1979, 246p.
    Full-length critical study of Grillparzer's work.

Kaufmann, Friedrich Wilhelm. "Franz Grillparzer: 1791-1872." In *German Dramatists of the Nineteenth Century.* Freeport, N.Y.: Books for Libraries Press, 1940 (Reprint, 1970), 215p.

Analysis of the philosophical bases of the dramas, illustrating how Grillparzer adapted various theories in forming his unique worldview.

Morris, I. V. "Grillparzer's Individuality as a Dramatist." *Modern Language Quarterly* 18, No. 2 (June 1957): 83-99.

Examines the sources and prevalent influences that shaped the dramas and illustrates how, in combining diverse sources, Grillparzer achieved his philosophy of drama.

Mulholland, Gabrielle. "Some Problems in Translating Grillparzer." *German Life & Letters* XIX, No. 3 (April 1966): 178-89.

Asserts that translators of Grillparzer's plays must "keep in mind the live performance on the stage, whether out of loyalty to an audience today."

Robinson, J. G. "Franz Grillparzer." In *Essays and Addresses on Literature*. Freeport, N.Y.: Books for Libraries Press, 1935 (Reprint, 1968), 314p.

General discussion of Grillparzer's work, noting the changes in his literary reputation.

Roe, Ian F. "Classical Vocabulary in Grillparzer's Early Work." *Modern Language Review* 77, No. 4 (October 1982): 860-75.

Determines the influence of German Classicism on Grillparzer's work.

Root, Winthrop H. "Grillparzer's *Sappho* and Thomas Mann's *Tonio Kröger*." *Monatshefte für Deutsschen Unterrich* XXIX, No. 2 (February 1937): 59-64.

An analysis of the similarities and differences between the two works in subject matter and style.

Stein, Gisela. *The Inspiration Motif in the Works of Franz Grillparzer*. The Hague: Martinus Nijhoff, 1955, 223p.

Study of the myriad sources of Grillparzer's work with special consideration of *Libussa*.

Stenberg, Peter. "Strindberg and Grillparzer: Contrasting Approaches to the War of the Sexes." *Canadian Review of Comparative Literature* I, No. 1 (Winter 1974): 65-75.

Finds common thematic concerns of Strindberg and Grillparzer.

Wells, George A. *The Plays of Grillparzer*. London: Pergamon Press, 1969, 173p.

Examination of the dramatic effectiveness of Grillparzer's plays.

Yates, Douglas. *Franz Grillparzer: A Critical Biography*. Oxford: Basil, Blackwell & Mott, 1946, 188p.

A critical assessment focusing on the biographical aspects of Grillparzer's work.

Yates, W. E. *Grillparzer: A Critical Introduction*. Cambridge: Cambridge University Press, 1972, 276p.

A critical survey of Grillparzer's work.

Additional coverage of Grillparzer's life and career is contained in the following sources published by the Gale Group: *Dictionary of Literary Biography*, Vol. 133 and *Short Story Criticism*, Vol. 37.

Beth Henley
1952-

(Full name Elizabeth Becker Henley) American dramatist.

INTRODUCTION

Beth Henley is a popular contemporary playwright. She is best known for her tragicomedies that depict female protagonists who struggle to define themselves outside of their relationships with their families and their relationships with men. Commentators praise Henley's strong regional voice and her humorous portrayal of small-town Southern life, prompting comparisons with other Southern playwrights, such as Eudora Welty and Tennessee Williams.

BIOGRAPHICAL INFORMATION

The daughter of an attorney and an actress, Henley was born on May 8, 1952, in Jackson, Mississippi. Her childhood in Mississippi provides the background for a number of her works. In 1974 she received her B.F.A. from Southern Methodist University. Initially, Henley wanted to become an actress; discouraged by the lack of quality parts for Southern women, she turned to playwrighting. Henley's first play, *Am I Blue* (1973), was produced while a student. In 1976 Henley moved to Los Angeles and three years later her second play, *Crimes of the Heart,* was produced. In 1981 this play won a Pulitzer Prize for drama and a New York Drama Critics Circle Award for best new American play. Following this nascent success, Henley has continued to write plays as well as screenplays, earning an Academy Award nomination for her adaptation of *Crimes of the Heart* in 1986.

MAJOR WORKS

One of the defining characteristics of Henley's plays is the struggle of women to satisfactorily define their roles in society independent of romantic and familial relationships. Henley's most successful play, *Crimes of the Heart,* has been compared to the works of Eudora Welty for its compassionate portrayal of a bizarre family dealing with the underlying horrors of small-town life. The story centers on the reunion of three sisters: Meg, just back from a failed attempt at a singing career in Hollywood; Lenny, single and desperate; and Babe, the youngest sister, who shot her husband because she "didn't like his looks." Henley achieves the comic-absurdist mood of the play by employing a surface realism typical of more naturalistic works. *The Miss Firecracker Contest* (1980) is an insight-

ful look at a small-town beauty pageant in Mississippi; in the process, it focuses on the obsession with youth and beauty found in American popular culture and its detrimental effects on women. Henley's *Abundance* (1989) chronicles the friendship of two pioneer women as they struggle with unhappy marriages and personal dissatisfaction.

CRITICAL RECEPTION

Henley's plays have received mixed reviews throughout her career. After her early critical and commercial success with *Crimes of the Heart,* Henley's later work has failed to reach that same level of popularity. Critics often praise Henley's ability to blend the sympathetic and the absurd to create unique and eccentric characters. Her recurring small-town, Southern settings have led many commentators to compare her to other prominent Southern writers such as Flannery O'Connor. Yet some reviewers consider her male characters underdeveloped and the maturation of her characters implausible. Moreover, Henley's use of black humor has been derided by some critics, as well as her use of metaphor, which has been deemed confusing and ineffective.

PRINCIPAL WORKS

Plays

Am I Blue? 1973
Crimes of the Heart 1979
The Miss Firecracker Contest 1980
The Wake of Jamey Foster 1982
The Debutante Ball 1985
The Lucky Spot 1987
Abundance 1989
Control Freaks 1992
Beth Henley: Four Plays 1994
Impossible Marriage 1998

Screenplays

The Moon Watcher 1983
Crimes of the Heart 1986
Nobody's Fool 1986
True Stories [with David Byrne and Stephen Tobolowsky] 1986
Miss Firecracker 1989

OVERVIEWS AND GENERAL STUDIES

Karen Jaehne (essay date May-June 1989)

SOURCE: "Beth's Beauties," in *Film Comment*, Vol. 25, No. 3, May-June, 1989, pp. 9-15.

[*In the following essay, Jaehne critiques* Miss Firecracker *as a work that examines "how beauty affects who we are and who we wanna be."*]

In *Miss Firecracker* Mary Steenburgen clears her throat to deliver her keynote speech, "My Life as a Beauty." She explains how she won her title, "Miss Firecracker," (she's beautiful) and why she will always reign supreme (she's unassailably beautiful). The audiences in the theater and onscreen giggle uncomfortably, because we are supposed to have transcended Queen for a Day consciousness (sure, but being a beauty queen hasn't hurt Diane Sawyer). *Miss*

Firecracker asks, among other things, how beauty affects who we are and who we wanna be.

Steenburgen as Elain is passably beautiful, but she radiates her right to rule in life as Astonishingly Beautiful as she once ruled on the parade float. She's mastered Inner Float. And, as her creator, Beth Henley, says in her best Mississippi maiden voice, "Ah think everybuddy wahnts to be byutuhful. Or at least to have someone else think of them that way."

Miss Firecracker is the very epitome of pageantry, but Henley thinks there's more to beauty than a bunch of roses and a tiara. It's not just that beauty is in the eye of the beholder, or that beauty is a cliché that keeps girls busy. Like Chicken Little, when struck by beauty all the politically-correct feminists see the sky falling in and the soul evaporating into thin air. Says our heroine, Holly Hunter as Carnelle, after losing the beauty contest but triumphantly gaining her soul, "I don't know what you can reasonably hope for in life."

What constitutes beauty—in the threatened absence of significance (pace *Slaves of New York,* which failed to satirize the subject)—may be the best parlor/locker-room issue of the 20th century, even if most people don't look to beauty contests for much more than centerfold models, and certainly not for explanations of the relative merits of anti-art or anti-fashion. "You'd think," says Elain's brother Delmount, who loves her to distraction, "after you left me in that lunatic asylum, I'd know better than to trust you." Maybe that's man's lot: to figure out how far to trust beauty.

Beauty is one of the main concerns of that which we call (by virtue of grant applications) art, if nothing else. Henley loves to let Beauty strut its stuff, poking fun at it as it glides by on life's runway. How did beauty become simultaneously enshrined and debased in America, or more specifically in the South—Mecca for America's peachfuzz maidens? The only thing that this particular beauty, Elain, actually knows about it is that it allows her to be admired—not as a sex object but rather as an objet d'art, pedestal included.

If you reverse the perspective, as *Miss Firecracker* does, and look at those who aspire to and admire Elain's beauty, the picture focuses sharp as a stiletto heel on how and why the American beauty came to inspire fear and pity. The beast within is sneaky, savage, scared and comically self-obsessed, making the beauty's beatific image all the more important, all the more impenetrable. Beauty kills, they say; but what's even worse, it maims. And now that that's settled, we can all sleep a little more safely—or just a little more, period.

Miss Firecracker's real heroine, however, is Henley's other creation, Carnelle, who is, as her name implies, a carnal beauty, but to us no less beautiful for being less ethereal than Elain. Carnelle's options are limited to the other side of Yazoo City's tracks and the mockery of her sexual exploits as the local "Miss Hot Tamale." So she worships her ice-queen cousin Elain so desperately that she staggers in her footsteps into the local Miss Firecracker contest—not only to finish dead last but to be royally betrayed. Why are we not surprised?

Since Henley's first play, *Crimes of the Heart* (1979), which she herself adapted for the screen, through *Nobody's Fool* and *True Stories* (both 1986) with David Byrne, she has analyzed the ways women conform to or rebel against standards of femininity, standards more rigid than the Honor Code at Notre Dame. Ultimately, her women are all shades of Scarlet, not of the Letter but of the Wind.

What with beauty queens turning out to be shoplifters and centerfolds, the film that Henley adapted from her 1980 play, *The Miss Firecracker Contest,* did not augur well for the Misses themselves or for the scales of justice found in beauty pageantry. Yet Henley loves her characters too much to leave them stranded in satiric social commentary. "Self-esteem," she says, "is the only thing that can save a woman from the traps of other people's definitions.

"Don't get stuck in this notion," Henley says with an unexpected commanding authority, "that beauty is problematic only in the South. Look at Hollywood." She waves a hand in an extremely graceful gesture for somebody clearly outraged. Henley went to Los Angeles in the Seventies to become an actress but found her niche in the New York theater as a wordsmith.

"The vanity principle here is so out of line—tanning salons, plastic surgery, constant cosmetic everything. I love the people in Mississippi. They don't have time to worry about it or the money to spend on it. Or the places to go to show off what they bought and did to themselves. They have beliefs about beauty that may seem antiquated but they know it's not something you can operate on to make it better." What is it, then? "Oh, I don't know, but it's a bit like beauty as something natural, innate, a blessing and, sometimes, an excuse for not being anything else, you know?"

At the heart of *Miss Firecracker,* one senses awe at the power of beauty such as Elain's. Henley, who keeps herself more *au naturel* than Hollywood or Manhattan allow, admits to a preoccupation with beauty that "varies with a woman's age, her work and even her social stature, don't you think?" One of the first experiences of awe that she recalls is "watching my Mama. She is what I think of as truly beautiful. I would be hanging on the doorknob when I was a little girl, watching Mama get dressed up to go out. The way she put on mascara and powder . . . then she'd step so gracefully into a dress and then the high heels. To me it was a bit of magic that was beyond my reach, maybe beyond my understanding of what it meant at the time."

Hints of a feminist consciousness raise the next question: what is the significance of these trappings of transforma-

tion? "Hahahahaha," she laughs very discreetly, raising her eyes in coy resistance. "I don't claim to make any feminist or ideological statements. We all know what it's like as kids to watch Miss America pageants on television. I didn't write *Miss Firecracker* to criticize beauty contests, to show them as social problems. I just wanted to show how that contest becomes an opportunity for a girl to fulfill a dream of being beautiful and winning some recognition for it.

"What a woman does to herself in the name of beauty is very complicated and private, and what makes her feel good about herself should not be subject to ideology." One might think Scarlet O'Hara was the godmother of post-feminism, which holds that you put on the dress and put out the man—a phenomenon that has succeeded the proposition that to be a woman is to put on the pants and be equal to a man.

The Southern literary tradition is full of women in dust-bowls and gilded cages flapping their wings briefly, then lying down to die. Henley has a line that recalls their misery, when a character bemoans her fate, "I thought I was a victim of broken dreams." But Henley's carny (Scott Glenn), himself a gypsy, loves Carnelle enough not to trap her in Yazoo City. He cites "eternal grace" as something Carnelle can expect and tells her, "You can change your dreams." Henley shows through the tragi-comedy of Carnelle's defeat at the beauty contest the way to change: face those dreams and move on. In the end, Carnelle is victorious and Elain a miserable mess, because Elain is stuck as Miss Firecracker unto the grave. As ambivalent about beauty as Henley's work is, one thing seems certain: she's looking for the transformation of beauty into character—or vice-versa—that raises beauty from the stuff of the in-crowd and cheerleading to a mature and transcendental state of grace.

Henley's victory over the chivalry that patronizes women in order to claim their accomplishments—the South's "Our Women" starts sounding like "Our Blacks"—is also part of their literary tradition in which the writer decamps from the world she writes about. Henley inched out of Mississippi to attend Southern Methodist University, study drama, and go west to Hollywood, only to find herself still defined as a Southern writer.

With that comes the story of how Henley repudiated her Pulitzer. "It was very hard to come back to my hometown after I had won the prize," she told writer Jan Stuart, "and the people were showering me with attention. I felt very false, because in high school, I was a mediocre student, I was terribly shy, I didn't go to homecoming. I wasn't a cheerleader. I thought, why do they like me now? They didn't like me then."

Much the same response came when she realized that the people who had signed her Pulitzer prize were the same folks who'd trashed her play *The Wake of Jamey Foster.* And so, she reasoned, "If I've got to believe these people when they tell me I'm good, then I've got to believe them when they tell me I'm bad. I refused to give them that power over me. I chucked it in the garbage."

Apart from the undercurrent of hypocrisy, some genuinely funny ideas provide the grace notes for a comic vision of Mississippi life, not the least of which is the alliance of underdogs. To provide her with a baton-twirler's costume to show off her talent at the beauty pageant, Carnelle breathlessly hunts down the only seamstress who'll take the work—Alfre Woodard as Popeye—and interrupts her current contract, making costumes for bull-frogs. "My aunt used to make those," says Henley, "when she was a little girl, and my mother told me about it."

"But the gut-sucker machines," she says forthrightly, "well, they have those in the catfish farms in Mississippi. When we were adapting the play, I wanted to show Carnelle working, so I put her in a sock factory. But then Tommy (director Thomas Schlamme) went down there and thought the catfish farm was just unbelievably perfect. It was really something we had sort of left open and let the location determine, I guess. Films allow you to do that in a way theater doesn't."

The location in *Miss Firecracker* runs the risk of over-determining the film. It's the South in a way rarely seen at the bijou. It's the South where lovely young Babe can shoot her husband and make us love her for it, as in *Crimes of the Heart,* or where a gal's sister can try to hang herself from a chandelier and bring down the whole house. It's the South of Beth Henley where Brer Rabbit meets Eugene O'Neill.

"I like to read Chekhov and Shakespeare, and I love Sam Shepard, and the literature that maps out great tragedies," says Henley, "but in my own writing I can't see the situations I look at without laughing. I back into comedy. I can't help it."

Although her work offers eccentric characters full of ornate habits and language, Henley herself is studiously under-stated. Arriving from the first run-through of her new play, *Abundance,* she enters a bar in Century City where guys with guts full of beer are boring themselves through Oscar night in front of the tavern's television. Heads turn but turn back quickly, when her modest figure glides through the door. Nothing flashy, nothing even Californian or remotely theatrical about Beth Henley would lead you to think she is a playwright, a wit.

She declares her hunger and gets right down to ordering. She drinks a ginger ale and some designer water and then orders a glass of wine. Her cheerful drawl is at once pragmatic and lady-like. She eats with gusto, forking in salad ravenously, then slowing down for half a plate of pasta—reminiscent of the scene in *Gone with the Wind* in which the girls eat their biscuits before the party lest they reveal animal appetites inappropriate to the ante-bellum belle. Suddenly, she is the Southern lady whom *Fire-cracker* producer Frank Perry has described as the "iron butterfly."

"I don't like labels," she says, "but Elain could be seen that way. Mary brought a lot to that character, levels of desperation, need and spirit, a lot of spirit. Very complex, really. I think it's dangerous to label somebody like that 'cause you might end up insulting someone. A Southern Belle is also supposed to exemplify a lot of good qualities like graciousness, kindness, a genteelness, you know?

"Sometimes I think it got twisted in people's perceptions, because the facade got more real or stronger than the woman. You had to cover up so many of your true feelings about this facade that enormous anger built up underneath. People can't always be that kind and gracious and thoughtful of others. Elain has this wonderful way of trying to be nice, but it really winds up being about herself. . . ."

The Southern Belle may be an anachronism to the rest of the nation, but in the South, she is alive and well—and suffering, which is as it should be, prone as she is to headaches and histrionics. Her "life as a beauty" is an invisible shield to protect her from the reality of working women whose hands don't deserve to be lily-white, and to guarantee that she will always feel somehow unworthy of the veneration she craves. And she will lay the back of her hand to her forehead and weep to have her gilded cage door opened. Then she will faint at the prospect of an escape. The smelling salts of Security will revive her, and she will stare soulfully at the tiara she once won in a Miss Turnip contest, which is better than a Prime USDA Meat inspection stamp on a side of beef. The Southern Belle (who, like the Jewish Mother, need not be born one to become one) wants to have her turnips and eat 'em, too. Beth Henley gives us this creature in dozens of pastel shades, nuances and neuroses.

"Elain can't really be loved in the purest sense of the word," says Henley, "because she won't let anybody know her. She doesn't have enough self-esteem to let other people control their own perception of her. She's just not what she wished she were."

"I respond more than most people to Beth's humor, because I'm Southern," says Mary Steenburgen. "She writes about what I am. My humor is very Southern, and it's as hard to describe as Jewish humor." In fact, it's the humor of the vanquished, who secretly believe they have won. In the South, the Confederate flag is as prominent as Laura Ashley.

Steenburgen offers an interesting insight into what lay beneath the gentility of Southerners: "You're told from the time you're little that you're not as intelligent as other people, but that you're real nice, probably a lot nicer. Southerners sort of retreat into a sly use of words; we derive pleasure from regional slang."

Henley cultivates her ideas carefully, "seeing how people tolerate each other or even just their own lives," she says "Of course I 'believe' in my characters. To me, they're more than real. More real than people you might get to know."

One actress who knows both Henley and her characters very well is Holly Hunter, whom many consider Henley's alter ego. Hunter has been in almost all of Henley's plays. "When she wasn't, there was always a good reason," says Henley. "Everybody thinks of us in tandem," says Hunter, "but sometimes I just don't fit, y'know?" Sounds like a good fit, in fact, since Henley's best characters don't fit. It was Hunter's newsroom neurotic in *Broadcast News* that goosed that film with the feeling that a Henley creation got loose in James Brooks' broadcast.

"Beth has a really different point of view," says Holly, "really different." Long pause while she considers how they're different. "Beth grew up with such a strong sense of her own culture. Maybe it was more oppressive to her than it seems, 'cause it sort of fits her in some ways. Like how she talks and is so considerate of other people. But in other ways, she's just trying to shuck it. She had an awareness of it that most people don't have, I think, even if they embrace it and they live it. They're probably not as conscious of how it affects their lives as Beth is."

Because Beth and Holly both come from the South, it is tempting to lump them in with the Belles, easier in Henley's case then Hunter's. It's a temptation, however, that deserves resisting, because the only thing these two gals do seem to have in common is that they up and skedaddled outta there, only to get stuck in an elevator together in New York.

Hunter tells the story. "A long, long time ago, a casting director introduced me to Ulu Grosbard, when he was going to direct *The Pope of Greenwich Village*. Ulu told me there was somebody he wanted me to meet. No role, just more introductions, y'know? So, one day I'm set up to meet this woman and I get in an elevator where this is all s'posed to happen, and another woman gets in. And the elevator gets stuck between floors. For about 15 minutes. Finally, after this helpless feelin' . . . just hangin' there, stuck, she turns to me and says in her matter-o'-fact way, 'You must be Holly Hunter?' So I grin, 'cause like I'm not late anymore, all the sudden, and I say, 'Are you Beth Henley?' Boy, was I glad to meet her."

Hunter's relief has resonance beyond the elevator. The two of them have become like Tweedledee and Tweedledum, like the Cheshire Cat and his smile, like Alice and Wonderland. It takes Holly Hunter to rip the propriety out of Henley's work, to rough up the genteel edges and let her raspy throat give voice to Henley's disgruntled cats on their hot tin roofs. Hunter claims it's partly because she's from Georgia and "country," while "Beth is from a really different part of the South, a different kind of world."

Henley is one of four daughters of a Mississippi politician and actress Lydy Henley, while Hunter grew up on a farm with shorthorn cattle and four brothers. "I think family has a lot more to do with how a person develops," says Hunter, "than geography. I always wanted to be like my older brother, Kip, and I kinda modeled my speech patterns after him. I just never had the pressures of Southern life that Beth experienced. I had a pretty regular childhood, all-American with a bit different accent."

Hunter and Henley share an exasperation at the way people try to be cute about their being from the South. It sometimes is almost enough to send them back to beat their feet on the Mississippi mud. "Beth and I are not much alike. I mean, she's so feminine," Hunter concludes. Why, see for yourself: Holly—no makeup, dressed in East Village black with big horsehair buttons on her sweater; Henley—brown jacket, print skirt and a lapel pin of two doves kissing.

Holly Hunter is—no doubt about it—and always was the grit and life of *Miss Firecracker*. "Frankly, I was real worried about doin' the movie after getting it to that pitch of perfection on stage. I was really afraid it wouldn't spring to life like things should for the camera. But there were plenty of changes that allowed me to do things that had just rattled around in my head before.

"You know I couldn't play Carnelle so young anymore. I had to crank into her character the changes I'd gone through myself, so she's quite a bit different in the movie. Older and not quite as likely to fall apart over her crazy need to win a beauty contest."

Is Holly Hunter now or has she ever been a beauty queen?

"Lord, no," she croaks, "I mean . . . well, of course I knew girls in high school who . . . well, sure, some of my best friends participated, but that was their deal. You don't break up a friendship over something like that."

Hunter's hand pulls on her straight brown hair. Her eyes burn as she says, "I always felt somehow insulted by them. It's like taking 20,000 steps back. Major, major backwards action, a beauty contest. All the priorities and values and things that make a woman a worthy human being are reduced to such stupid categories that don't have much to do with most of our lives anyway. Like talent! How many people have a talent that they can go onstage with?"

Well, Holly Hunter, for one. Her greatest accomplishment in *Miss Firecracker* is her reaction shot to another contestant's reading of Scarlet's famous turnip field soliloquy. Taking a sharp thwack at this locus classicus of Hollywood-imposed heritage, Henley writes the moment truthfully in all its complexity: the faux-Scarlet claws the earth of Tara, raging against her fate, hilariously and embarrassingly chomping on a carrot and mewling in wretched excess in quest of the only kind of heroine the South knows—the kind it takes to be Miss Firecracker.

But Carnelle watches from the wings, mesmerized, weeping.

Up until that moment, the movie is entertaining; Hunter is a pip and her wacky family is Southern Gothic. Then suddenly, in Carnelle's response to all this kitsch, her culture reaches out and claims her with Hollywood's most memorable portrait of the Southern Belle. No matter how ludicrous, no matter how mortifying, no matter that its beauty won't grace the cover of *Vogue*. It is the soil of all the sunflowers in the sun.

Beth Henley has updated beauty for us in Carnelle: as vulnerable, lovable and beautiful as a woman can be. "If her cultural memory of a plantation icon or her personal memory of Elain waving graciously from her Miss Firecracker parade float gave her the courage to change her life, to get out of the rut, more power to them all," says Henley, dabbing the pasta from her mouth.

Suddenly a cheer goes up in the next room, and we hear Jodie Foster's voice—as unmistakable in its own way as Holly Hunter's—thanking the Academy. "I'm so glad Jodie won," says Beth, breaking into a scarecrow's grin. "I voted for her." Like Carnelle, Jodie Foster is "someone who could take it on the chin," as *Miss Firecracker* concludes. And that's no Southern Belle. Another one of those moments occurs, when our culture claims us, and we grin at each other, acknowledging what it means to reveal the soul instead of to revel in good looks. "Yeah," says Henley, "I'd really like to create a lot of characters like that. Feisty, Real, And beautiful."

Janet V. Haedicke (essay date March 1993)

SOURCE: "'A Population [and Theater] at Risk': Battered Women in Henley's *Crimes of the Heart* and Shepard's *A Lie of the Mind*," in *Modern Drama*, Vol. 36, No. 1, March, 1993, pp. 83-95.

[*In the following essay, Haedicke compares the depiction of domestic violence in Shepard's* A Lie of the Mind *and Henley's* Crimes of the Heart, *asserting that Shepard's postmodernist drama "ignites a politics beyond Henley's modernist drama, which can kindle only kitchen fires."*]

"The weeping of women who are wives—what is more bitter?"[1]

Oft-castigated for its preponderance of family drama, American theater seems unprotestingly to cede stature to British theater, which has moved from "kitchen-sink" realism to presumably more universal and political plays. Yet the charge of triviality levelled against American "diaper drama"[2] in the theater dissipates in the face of the domestic drama currently being played on the cultural stage: statistics indicate that "An American resident is 'more likely to be physically assaulted, beaten, and killed in the home at the hands of a loved one than any place else, or by anyone else.'"[3] That many such residents are women led former U.S. Surgeon-General C. Everett Koop in 1989 to decry wife-battering as "an overwhelming moral, economic, and public health burden that our society can no longer bear" and to identify battered women as "a population at risk."[4] Current Surgeon-General Antonia No-

vello in 1992 backed a surprising American Medical Association declaration of domestic violence against women as an epidemic requiring intervention by health officials.[5] Should they escape their kitchens for the theater, those four million women assaulted annually would hardly find American family plays trivial or apolitical.

This is not to imply, however, that any such play is by nature politically progressive, even if it directly addresses the issue of family violence. Ironically, Beth Henley's *Crimes of the Heart,* widely lauded as a breakthrough since its 1981 Pulitzer was the first for a woman in twenty-three years, emerges as ultimately regressive compared to Sam Shepard's 1985 *A Lie of the Mind,* vehemently attacked by feminist critics as exemplifying the playwright's macho vision.[6] Prompted by the ever-suspect politics of the Pulitzer, which has since rewarded female escape through suicide and meaning through maternity,[7] this treacherous stance finds theoretical ground in the location of Henley's play within a modernist, albeit feminist, epistemology and Shepard's within a postmodernist, more politically feminist, one. Further outcry from feminists who attack postmodern theory's decentering of the subject as a negation of agency may be deflected by Wendy Brown's cogent response to the current critical (in every sense of the word) debate.

Brown argues that "postmodernity signifies a pervasive condition"[8] as distinguished from postmodern theory, which signifies, like the current modernist position, a response to that condition. Thus it is epoch, not theory, which poses a threat to formulating an effective alternative politics. The cultural-spatial disorientation of postmodernism has produced an identity politics and a strategic fundamentalism "rooted not [conservatively] in a coherent tradition but [reactionarily] in a fetishized, decontextualized fragment or icon of such a narrative—'the American flag,' 'the great books,' 'the traditional family.'"[9] Insisting that even an issue from the Left, such as feminism, can become just such "reactionary foundationalism" when it poses as a necessary good, Brown contends that modernist feminism's rejection of postmodern theory as apolitical actually reflects an antipolitical preference for reason over power, truth over politics, security over freedom, discoveries over decisions, and identities over pluralities. It is such reactionary modernism which renders Henley's *Crimes of the Heart* Pulitzerly palatable and, not coincidentally, precludes encouragement of a feminist alternative politics to counter familial and social violence.

Literalizing both the "kitchen-sink" disparagement of domestic drama and the historical relegation of women to the private sphere, *Crimes of the Heart* takes place entirely in the kitchen of the MaGrath family home in Hazlehurst, Mississippi. Moreover, Henley specifies the time as "In the fall; five years after Hurricane Camille,"[10] thereby associating the turbulence in the lives of the MaGrath sisters with the turbulence of a Nature constructed as feminine. Indeed, these women seem to spawn turbulence, since the central crime of the play and the catalyst for their reunion is the youngest sister's shooting of her husband Zackery, the town's most prominent lawyer. The play opens on the oldest sister, Lenny, a stereotypical Southern spinster, pathetically celebrating her thirtieth birthday alone with a candle on a cookie in Old Grandaddy's kitchen, where she now sleeps. Summoned by Lenny, middle sister Meg returns from California, where she has pursued a singing career but achieved only a mental breakdown. Out on bail, the youngest sister, Babe, with "*an angelic face*" and "*pink pocketbook*" (18), refuses to offer any explanation for the shooting other than "I just didn't like his stinking looks!" (19).

Babe's lawyer, Barnette, whose fondness for his client stems from her selling him a cake at a bazaar, reveals to Meg medical charts which indicate that Zackery has "brutalized and tormented" (27) Babe over the past four years. Confronted by Meg's demand for a reason for Zackery's abuse (as if any could exist), Babe replies: "I don't know! He started hating me, 'cause I couldn't laugh at his jokes" (29). Thus wife-battering is the crime behind the crime here, aligning Babe's attempted homicide with that "nearly three-fourths of the violence perpetrated by women [which] is committed in self-defense."[11] So cursory, however, is Henley's treatment of this motive, to which the play never again even alludes, that its significance is occluded. Indeed, most critics seem oblivious to the fact that Babe is a battered woman, concentrating instead on the self-destructive violence of the sisters' behavior; even those who do acknowledge the abuse treat it as a "detail."[12] Henley further undercuts the impact of the issue by Babe's wackiness. Surely it is not only the undeniably sensitive perspective of a Southern female spectator which finds Henley's humor reductionist, a perpetuation of magnolia mush rather than the Southern Gothic comedy ascribed by admirers. Babe's preparing and drinking lemonade after the shooting to the point of pseudo-pregnancy ("my stomach kind of swoll all up" [35]) and then offering a glass to the prostrate, bleeding Zackery renders trivial rather than grotesque the image of family violence. Attempts at feminist recuperation of this scene lead to such stretches as "Lemonade must quench the thirst for masculine validation that neither her father [who abandoned them] nor Zachary [sic] may be depended upon to satisfy."[13] This critical excess, however, is at least partially absolved by the palpability in the play of that thirst in each of the sisters.

Indeed, the immediate motive for Babe's crime proves to be not self-defense but the defense of her fifteen-year-old black lover, whom Zackery struck and shoved off the porch. Initially planning to shoot herself, Babe remembers her mother's hanging herself with her cat: "Then I realized—that's right I realized how I didn't want to kill myself! And she—she probably didn't want to kill herself. She wanted to kill him, and I wanted to kill him, too. I wanted to kill Zackery, not myself. 'Cause I—I wanted to live!" (31-32). Often cited as exemplifying the rise of female assertiveness in the play, the passage reflects only a reactive subjectivity underscored by Babe's two subsequent

suicide attempts, which Henley renders farcical by a broken rope and a failed Plath-imitation. Likewise, the female desire here smacks of pathetic need, a sexual stereotyping worsened by its racial and regional echoes:

> MEG I'm amazed, Babe. I'm really, completely amazed. I didn't even know you were a liberal.
>
> BABE Well, I'm not! I'm not a liberal! I'm a democratic! I was just lonely! I was so lonely. And he was good. Oh, he was so, so good. I'd never had it that good. We'd always go out into the garage and—
>
> (31)

This Southern-apolitical-middle-class-white-lily-awakened-by-double-named-mindless-lower-class-black-stud scenario offends further when Meg sees the pictures taken by Zackery's sister of Babe and Willie Jay in the garage: "Well, he certainly *has* grown. You were right about that. My, oh, my" (61, emphasis in original). Parodic female assertiveness continues in Babe's admirable but undeniably maternalistic protection of Willie Jay, who is eventually shipped north by Babe's savior Barnette. Even more regressive than Babe's rescue-relationship, founded on pound cake and talk of the "Christmas angel" (36), is Meg's purported regeneration through the realization that "I could want someone" (57) who no longer wants her. Worse still is Lenny's recovery via the telephoned confession of her "shrunken ovary" to her beau from the Lonely Hearts Club of the South, who miraculously wants a non-breeder.

Understandably eliding this overtly schematized self-discovery through male validation, feminist criticism of the play focuses on the rebirth of identity through female and family bonding. Overcome by her real birthday cake, Lenny has a vision of "Just this one moment and we were all laughing," which the play's final image concretizes: "*the lights change and frame [the sisters] in a magical, golden, sparkling glimmer*" (72). Such a vision—Lenny's and Henley's—represents a reaction to rather than an "ultimate rejection of [mediating patriarchal forces]"[14] and thus reflects the reactionary foundationalism of modernist feminism, which posits Truth in individualized subjectivity (consciousness raising) and refuses to deconstruct the subject though insisting on gender as a construct. As Brown insists, "Since women's subordination is partly achieved through the construction and positioning of us as private—sexual, familial, emotional—and is produced and inscribed in the domain of both domestic and psychic interiors, then within modernity, the voicing of women's experience acquires an inherently confessional cast."[15]

Henley inadvertently reproduces this construction and succumbs to Foucault's "internal ruse of confession,"[16] which opposes truth and freedom to silence and power. Clinging to illusory icons of unity in identity and in family, denying the "groundlessness of *discovered* norms or visions,"[17] Henley's women offer, at best, only the power of Nietzsche's "slave morality," a power of reaction and a politics of *ressentiment*. **Crimes of the Heart,** then, dramatizes what Brown terms "feminist hesitations" rather than a feminist politics. So tempting for feminists is this equation of confessional truth with moral good that Joan Cocks also warns against *ressentiment* and resistance politics, which risks becoming a "sanctification of powerlessness, a celebration of weakness, a championing of victim status."[18] The sisters' party seems just this sort of celebration, and Henley's play, just this sort of championing. **Crimes of the Heart** leaves us with saxophone strains in the theater, but, since the music echoes the pathos of Babe's career ambitions on this instrument that she has never played, with no transformative politics to counter violence against women in the family.

Shepard, on the other hand, consistently dramatizes the urgency of a move beyond *ressentiment* in his family plays, which denaturalize rather than revalidate individualism and the traditional family. Although to posit Shepard as feminist is to risk banishment from the ranks, Shepard's dramaturgy increasingly offers that "Democratic political space" essential for feminism.[19] On Shepard's stage, Oedipal politics is foregrounded in the violence of its faltering rather than, as many feminist critics claim, supported in a covert ratification of violence against women through realistic representation. Even *A Lie of the Mind*, the most overtly violent and ostensibly realistic of the family plays, belies Lynda Hart's accusation of a "pornographic vision,"[20] since that very vision (or male gaze) constitutes the lie of the title. Much as Shepard's postmodern theatricalism disrupts the surface illusion of causal, Newtonian realism, Jake's beating of his wife, Beth, splays open the violent illusion of binary vision, its subject-object poles inevitably gendered and hierarchized. Instead of Henley's reactionary foundationalism in iconizing family, Shepard presents an indictment of family structure as not only the site but also the cause of violence against women.

The stage set, which physically separates Jake from Beth until play's end through the "infinite space"[21] of the "*middle neutral territory*" (21), renders concrete the binary construction of gender, which psychically separates them. Both replay their childhoods at the foundation of subjectivity, the family home. Beth has regressed to a childlike state as a result of brain damage from the battering; Jake, as a result of a mental collapse from the belief that he has killed his wife. On each side of the stage and country is enacted an Oedipal scenario, which mimics the theatricalism inherent in the cultural construction of gender roles.[22] Stripped of his pants, the adult Jake is imprisoned in his short boyhood bed by a mother driven to incestuous attachment by her husband's desertion and subsequent death. The presence of the father weighs heavily, not only as "Some disease he left behind" (91) in his wife, Lorraine, but also in the pressure on Jake, who comments on the box of his father's ashes retrieved from under his bed: "He's kinda' heavy" (39). A military man "always cookin' up some weird code" (36), Jake's father personifies the monolithic masculinism which encodes meanings or inscribes "Truths." As the pantless Jake stares at the Second World War model airplanes dangling from the ceiling and dons his father's bomber jacket, Shepard provides

a telescopic image of the originary violence of the Oedipal legacy. Recent research having shifted the psychological determinant in date rape from the rapist's hostility towards the mother to that towards the father, David Lisak maintains that hypermasculinity provoked by paternal distance spawns violence against women.[23] Lisak's warning about this by-product of gender-divided families finds its echo in Shepard's drama. Jake's repeated abuse of Beth ("I saw her face. It was bad this time" [2]) perpetuates, according to his brother, Frankie, a childhood pattern of violence ("Well you kicked the shit out of that [milk] goat you loved so much . . ." [13]). Jake himself implicates his father in the violence of his gaze. When the voyeuristic image of Beth, who is "*simply his vision*" (41), blacks out as he moves towards it, he blows into the box of ashes.

Whereas Henley confines battering wholly to pre-text, Shepard assaults the spectator with its evidence. Beth first appears in a hospital bed, head bandaged, face bruised. The witnessing of her laborious recovery physically elicits shock and horror, which remain even as her precarious steps and fragmented speech metaphorically evoke the construction of subjectivity: "Who fell me? Iza—Iza name? Iza name to come. Itz—Itz—Inza man. Inza name" (6). Permeating the play is this postmodern insistence on subjects constituted linguistically and thus decentered, which refutes modernist notions of unmediated and centered (or gendered) identity. Moreover, Shepard's alternating narrative and persistent doubling of Beth and Jake[24] do not so much posit Jake as an *equal* victim of machismo as emphasize their mutual construction on the Oedipal stage where gender roles are scripted.[25] Beth's first lucid words, "Am I a mummy now?" (4), suggest a pun encouraged by further conflation of marriage and maternity with lifelessness and weakness. Meg, Beth's submissive mother, confuses her history with that of her own mother until her husband, Baylor, disdainfully clarifies who was actually "locked up" (30).

Beth associates history's erasure of women with psychology's inscription of castration, both signifying female absence to verify male presence. To Frankie, mistaken for a deer and shot in the leg by her father, she suggests the possibility of amputation. Showing an incredulous Frankie the "Knife tracks" of her "*nonexistent scar,*" Beth parodies the Freudian biological fiction of a female scar of inferiority and the Lacanian linguistic fiction of female lack:[26]

> BETH . . . No brain. Cut me out. Cut. Brain. Cut.
>
> FRANKIE No, Beth, look—They didn't—they didn't operate did they? Nobody said anything about that.
>
> BETH They don't say. Secret. Like my old Mom. Old. My Grand Mom. Old.
>
> They cut her. Out. Disappeared. They don't say her name now. She's gone.
>
> Vanish. . . . My Father sent her someplace. Had her gone.

(73-74)

This theatricalization of the Oedipal myth of female castration exposes feminine absence or weakness as a masculine binary construct, a lie of the mind to sustain subject/object dominance and foster male subjectivity by subjection. Rebelling against her brother Mike's role of male as hunter-protector to female as domestic-dependent, Beth screams: "You make an enemy. In me. In me! An enemy. You. You. You think me. You think you know. You think. You have a big idea" (45).

The "You" accused in the play is the masculinist, militarist cultural complex, which perpetuates paradigmatic binary logic: psychology's phallus versus lack, language's symbolic versus imaginary, history's fact versus fiction, metaphysics' presence versus absence, all encoded as male versus female. Subjectivity is thus constructed by opposition and exclusion. Here lies the "lie," the source of violence in the world and in the play. Jake's latest beating of Beth erupted ("Why didn't I see it comin'. I been good for so long" [2]) from his own vision of infidelity at a play rehearsal; like Mike, Jake "thinks her": "I knew what she was up to even if she didn't" (11). Jake's violent aversion to acting ("This acting shit is more real than the real world to her" [10]) signals a modernist aversion to shifting subjectivity ("She was unrecognizable" [10]) as a threat to unified identity, which the men guard as dogs guard their territory. Juxtaposed dramatically against the bravado of barking dogs is the vulnerability of silent deer, one of whose hindquarters Mike plops onstage in triumph over his father in their hunting rivalry. At this reminder of Oedipal severing, Beth marvels, "You cut him in half?" (80), echoing verbally Shepard's theatrical undercutting of gender "reality" and dramatic "realism." When Meg uncharacteristically refutes her husband in claiming that hunting is war, not art, she tells him to go ahead and leave, since the women have actually taken care of themselves anyway. Citing her mother's description of males and females as "'Two opposite animals'" (103), Meg exasperates Baylor with her claim that now "Beth's got male in her" (104).

Beth responds to her disorientation, which makes emblematic the cultural/spatial disorientation of a postmodern world, by moving beyond the androgynous reconciliation posited by modernist identity politics to a denaturalization of Oedipal identity. Remaining with "Naked" feet (43) rather than choosing between fuzzy slippers and work boots, Beth mocks the cultural construction of gender as opposition accepted by her foremothers and encoded in clothes. To Frankie's discomfort, she removes her father's plaid shirt, insisting that he "need it" (71) to cover his wound (feminized weakness or castration), and giggles at the burden of fixating gendered identity: "Look how big a man is. So big. He scares himself. His shirt scares him. He puts his scary shirt on so it won't scare himself. He can't see it when it's on him. Now he thinks it's him. . . . Jake was scared of shirts. . . . This is like a custom. . . . For play. Acting" (74-75). The association of tradition, acting, and identity reveals Beth's abdication of foundationalism as she parodies romantic love, though she has claimed to love Jake still. Pushing Frankie down on the sofa and giggling, "You fight but all the time you want . . . me on your face" (76), Beth mimics the progression from romance to rape mentality and the male fantasy of "her mouth says no but her eyes say yes," which disclaims sexual violence.

Rescripting her own marriage, Beth directs Frankie to "Pretend" the Jake role: "But soft. . . . Like a woman-man. . . . Without hate" (76). Over Frankie's protestations that "It's not good for my [penis] leg," Beth proposes *pretending* their way into "a love we never knew" (77). Attacks on Shepard for validating romantic love's pornographic objectification of women ignore the theatricalism foregrounded in this scene as in the rest of the play, a theatricalism which insists on the theatricalism of post-Heisenberg culture itself. Beth subverts through mimicry the simulacrum of scripted love and its inscription of violence. Her final appearance in bizarre clothing *"straight out of the fifties"* (111) mocks the mentality of those like her father who see such a "roadhouse chippie" (111) as fair prey.[27] Further, this presentation of sexuality as a gendered representation, a "custom" wherein Beth "looks equally like a child playing dress-up and like a hooker,"[28] underscores the horror of Jake's gaze, whereby perception equals Truth and shifts in identity must be brutally quashed.

Beth's fragmented yet oracular speech, like Tilden's in *Buried Child,* suggests agency within mediated subjectivity: "I get the thought. Mixed. It dangles. Sometimes the thought just hangs with no words there. . . . It speaks. Speeches. In me. Comes and goes" (72-73). Shepard's postmodern thematics and theatricalism preclude viewing as reactionary foundationalism Beth's assertions to Frankie that "We'll be in a whole new world" (114) and undermine modernist drama's inscription of the present and the past. Unlike Henley's, the female emergence dramatized here moves beyond the confessional voicing of female experience in the private sphere, hence beyond *ressentiment* and subordination. The revelation by Jake's sister that the son plotted the father's death in Mexico by challenging him to a bar-to-bar "First one to America!" (94) footrace prompts Lorraine's recognition that keeping house was "just a dream of theirs . . . to keep me on the hook" (96). She thus urges her daughter, once banished to reinstate the son in his throne-room, towards freedom from Oedipal rule. Setting afire the icons of the past and family tradition-photos and *"paraphernalia from the men"* (115), Lorraine plans for them to "Do a little jig" and then "Just walk" (120) as the house burns.

In jarring juxtaposition, a still pantless Jake emerges in the center space, *"walking on his knees straight toward the audience with the American flag between his teeth and stretched taut on either side of his head"* (120), these *"reins"* held by a rifle-armed Mike. Thus confronted, the audience stands implicated in the violence inherent in modernist fundamentalism's fetishized iconography. Jake is subjugated by the flag with which his country awarded his dead father's military mindset and in the spirit of which he rendered his wife "red and black and blue" (3).[29] Though Mike attempts vengeance in the name of family, his Oedipal territory, too, is eroding as he inadvertently points the rifle at his father, who has demanded the flag wrapped around it. More concerned with fighting for the blanket that has shrouded Frankie *"like a mummy"* (124)[30] and with sanctifying "the flag of our nation" (123) than with Mike's captive, Baylor solicits Meg's help in folding the flag "letter perfect" (130). Her presence recognized by neither parent, Beth hears Jake's confession, which echoes her own former disconnected speech: "Everything in me lies. But you. You Stay. You are true" (128-29). Jake has been driven back to Beth by not a vision but a voice, "a voice I knew once but now it's changed. It doesn't know me either. Now. It used to but not now. I've scared it into something else. Another form" (85).

Though Jake's bequeathing of Beth to his protesting brother obviously raises feminist ire, Frankie exists only as a vocalization of Beth, whose voice, as Jake has recognized, now presages transformation. The feminist possibilities capsulized in Beth's speech find interdisciplinary underscoring in Donna Haraway's call for a postmodernist feminist position for scientists: "Feminism loves another science: the sciences and politics of interpretation, translation, stuttering, and the partly understood. Feminism is about the sciences of the multiple subject."[31] Although Nancy Love faults this notion of "situated knowledges" as still too rooted in objectivity and vision, she perceives in Haraway's vocal metaphors a subtextual emphasis on democratic discourse. Love advocates vocal metaphor as signalling an extra-foundationalist "political epistemology [as opposed to the epistemological politics of visual imagery] and, with it, a political transformation . . . an empowerment/knowledge regime,"[32] which makes democratic discourse possible. Shepard's emphasis on vocal metaphors pushes the play beyond a "championing of victim status" and renders its final vision a created revision rather than the "discovered vision" of Henley's sisters. As Jake exits, shrouded in the patriarchal blanket, and Baylor exits, clinging to its analogue, the flag, Meg refuses to follow her husband, who has rewarded her folding efforts with his first kiss in twenty years. With hand to cheek, Meg descries Lorraine's fire across stage and country: "Looks like a fire in the snow. How could that be?" (131). Only the most myopic perspective is persuaded here of a reawakening of passion in marriage and the reinscription of unity. Nor does Shepard grieve for the failed reconciliation of constructed opposites.[33] As its sheer theatricalism insists, the bucket fire, which burns as the stage lights fade, heralds a Phoenix-rite wherein wives no longer weep in Oedipus's house.

Shepard's postmodernist theater thus ignites a politics beyond Henley's modernist drama, which can kindle only kitchen fires. Rather than recentering the subject in a subjective, moral Truth, which replays the heart's crimes, Shepard decenters the subject in a political, amoral truth, which reveals the mind's lie. No "sanctification of powerlessness" but the voice of power, such truth creates in the cultural theater that discourse in a "democratic political space" which constitutes a feminist politics beyond *ressentiment*. Providing the quintessential forum for vocal metaphors and thus for a political epistemology, theater can become that space where theory scripts praxis. Shepard himself hails "Words as living incantations and not as symbols. Taken in this way, the organization of living, breathing words as they hit the air between the actor and the audience actually possesses the power to change our chemistry."[34] Hardly giving voice to macho nostalgia, this alleged pornographer confronts the dangers of fixated (gendered) vision and fulfills Haraway's edict that "The interrogation for the limits and violence of vision is part of the politics of learning to revision."[35] Thus does Shepard evoke a transformative politics: "What I'm trying to get at here is that the real quest of a writer is to penetrate into another world. A world behind the form. The contradiction is that as soon as that world opens up, I tend to run the other way. It's scary because I can't answer to it from what I know."[36] And run the masculinist in him and in his audience might, since that "world behind the form," that future beyond the present, must embrace feminism, a feminism which must, in turn, embrace postmodernism. As American family drama moves from Henley's theater of causal identity to Shepard's theater of chaotic multiplicity, it calls for the American family to vacate the site of subjectivity by opposition and subjugation by gender for one of subjectivity in difference and connection in contradiction. Then mainstream theater becomes a voice for the margins in the mainstream, a voice of empowerment for those populations at risk.[37] With such voice, in the words of one battered, "Raggedy Ann Takes a Stand"[38] onstage in the theater of American culture.

Notes

1. Nancy Hoffman, "A Journey into Knowing: Agnes Smedley's *Daughter of Earth*" in Florence Howe, ed., *Tradition and the Talents of Women* (Urbana, IL, 1991), 174.

2. Martin Esslin's use of the term reflects his perception of a "deep anti-intellectual, anti-ideological bias" in American drama. "'Dead! And Never Called Me Mother!': The Missing Dimension in American Drama," *Studies in the Literary Imagination,* 21:2 (Fall 1988), 28. Robert Brustein also faults contemporary American theater as family "guilt-mongering" but objects to the limitations of causal as opposed to metaphorical theater more than to domestic drama itself, "The Crack in the Chimney: Reflections on Contemporary American Playwriting," *Theater,* 9:2 (Spring 1978), 29.

3. Sara Munson Deats and Lagretta Tallent Lenker, Introduction, in Deats and Lenker, eds., *The Aching Hearth: Family Violence in Life and Literature* (New York, 1991), 1.

4. Cited in ibid., 3.

5. Jill Smolowe, "What the Doctor Should Do," *Time,* 29 June 1992, 57.

6. Lynda Hart, for example, sees the play as verifying Florence Falk's location of Shepard in the realm of "Male Homo Erectus" (69) and insists that the family plays mitigate male violence by placing it "within the context of romantic ideology." "Sam Shepard's Pornographic Visions," *Studies in the Literary Imagination,* 21:2 (Fall 1988), 73.

7. Marsha Norman's *'night, Mother* garnered the prize in 1983; Wendy Wasserstein's *The Heidi Chronicles,* in 1989.

8. Wendy Brown, "Feminist Hesitations, Postmodern Exposures," *Differences,* 3:1 (Spring 1991), 64.

9. Ibid., 68.

10. Beth Henley, *Crimes of the Heart* (New York, Dramatists Play Service, 1982), 4. Subsequent page references to the play are to this edition and will appear in my text.

11. Deats and Lenker, 4.

12. Karen L. Laughlin, "Criminality, Desire, and Community: A Feminist Approach to Beth Henley's *Crimes of the Heart," Women and Performance,* 3:1 (1986), 44.

13. Laura Morrow, "Orality and Identity in *'night, Mother* and *Crimes of the Heart," Studies in American Drama, 1945-Present,* 3 (1988), 34.

14. Laughlin, 48. Morrow reflects critical consensus in claiming that each sister is "reborn as an individual as a consequence of her redefinition of her identity and rediscovery of her ability to love" (38).

15. Brown, 73.

16. Cited in ibid., 73.

17. Ibid., 77, emphasis in original.

18. Joan Cocks, "Augustine, Nietzsche, and Contemporary Body Politics," *Differences,* 3:1 (Spring 1991), 145. Unlike Brown, Cocks acknowledges the problematics of Nietzsche for feminists but presents an equally convincing argument for his relevance.

19. Brown, 79.

20. Hart, 82. Hart agrees with Sue-Ellen Case that Shepard's family plays evince a "heterosexist ideology linked with its stage partner realism" (80). This prevalent position in feminist drama criticism, though based on feminist film criticism, ignores the evolution therein beyond the anti-narrative postulation of an inescapable "male gaze."

21. Sam Shepard, *A Lie of the Mind* (New York, New American Library, 1986), set description preceding Act One. Subsequent page references to the play are to this edition and will appear in my text.

22. David DeRose finds the play a "surprisingly tame vision of love and subsequent violence American style" devoid of Shepard's trademark theatricality and mythic imagery. "Slouching towards Broadway: Shepard's *A Lie of the Mind," Theater,* 17:2 (1986), 69. If, however, the Oedipal complex is recognized as myth and its cultural inscription as theatrical, then Shepard here demystifies this "American style" conjunction of love and violence.

23. David Lisak, "Sexual Aggression, Masculinity, and Fathers," *Signs,* 16:2 (Winter 1991), 238-62.

24. Rosemarie Bank details the doubling in the play as manifesting a "Self as Other" transformation in the "heterotopic climate of postmodern drama." "Self as Other: Sam Shepard's *Fool for Love* and *A Lie of the Mind*" in June Schlueter, ed., *Feminist Rereadings of Modern American Drama* (Rutherford, NJ, 1989), 239.

25. Shepard does view his father and himself in his father's wake as victims of machismo. Jonathan Cott, "The Rolling Stone Interview: Sam Shepard," *Rolling Stone,* 18 December 1986, 172.

26. Mary Jacobus rejects Freud's female-as-castrated image ("she develops, like a scar, a sense of inferiority"), dismissing penis envy as a "defensive fiction," "An '*idée fixe*' designed to stabilize an original undecidability . . . by projecting the boy's threatened loss or 'cut' onto the girl's scarred psyche." *Reading Women* (New York, 1986), 114.

27. A recent *Time* survey indicates that 53 per cent of American adults over fifty believe that a woman is "partly to blame" for rape if "she dresses provocatively." Nancy Gibbs, "When Is It Rape?" *Time,* 3 June 1991, 51.

28. Sheila Rabillard, "Sam Shepard: Theatrical Power and American Dreams," *Modern Drama,* 30 (1987), 69.

29. This conflation of patriotism, the military, and familial and sexual violence recurs in Shepard's most recent play, *States of Shock,* when the uniformed father beats the war-castrated son, whose identity he denies, as White Man masturbates, both to the rhythm of visual and auditory weapon blasts. The theatricalization of war (so frightening in the Middle East) epitomizes Shepard's view of the violence of fixating gendered identity: "There's some hidden, deeply rooted thing in the Anglo male American that has to do with inferiority, that has to do with not being a man, and always, continually having to *act* out some idea of manhood that invariably is violent." Michiko Kakutani, "Myths, Dreams, and Realities-Sam Shepard's America," *New York Times,* 29 January 1984, sec. 2, 26, emphasis mine.

30. Males fighting over a blanket mantle/shroud also provides a *leitmotif* in *Buried Child,* revealing Shepard's focus on the mummification of the patriarch.

31. Donna Haraway, "Situated Knowledges: The Science Question in Feminism and the Privilege of Partial Perspective," *Feminist Studies,* 14 (Fall 1988), 589.

32. Nancy S. Love, "Politics and Voice(s): An Empowerment/Knowledge Regime," *Differences,* 3:1 (Spring 1991), 86.

33. Having established oppositions between same-sex characters, Gregory Lanier nonetheless insists on the "balanced opposition" between male and female and sees tragedy in the "futility of ever achieving a single, unified resolution." "Two Opposite Animals: Structural Pairing in Sam Shepard's *A Lie of the Mind,*" *Modern Drama,* 34 (1991), 419.

34. Sam Shepard, "Visualization, Language and the Inner Library," *Drama Review,* 21:4 (December 1977), 53.

35. Haraway cited by Love, 93.

36. Shepard, "Visualization," 55.

37. Only burgeoning public awareness can account for the shamefully belated but auspicious changes in the legal system signalled by a recognition in some states of Battered Women's Syndrome as a legal defense and grounds for clemency.

38. Deborah Eve Grayson, "Raggedy Ann Takes a Stand," cited by Nicholas Mazza, "When Victims Become Survivors: Poetry and Battered Women" in *The Aching Hearth,* 40.

Alan Clarke Shepard (essay date March 1993)

SOURCE: "Aborted Rage in Beth Henley's Women," in *Modern Drama,* Vol. 36, No. 1, March, 1993, pp. 96-108.

[*In the following essay, Shepard explores the effects of the feminist movement on the female protagonists of Henley's plays, in particular examining the recurring images of homicide and suicide.*]

Beth Henley's tragicomedies study the effects of the feminist movement upon a few, mostly proletarian women in rural Mississippi, who are more likely to read *Glamour* than Cixous and Clement's *The Newly Born Woman.*[1] We are invited to sympathize with isolated heroines whose fantasies demonstrate the difficulty of conceiving female subjectivity while entrenched in patriarchal epistemes, whose resilience is expressed in their canny, survivalist compromises with the codes of passive southern womanhood.[2] Their compromises may be precisely located in the recurring imagery of homicide and suicide that pervades Henley's scripts. Take Elain in *The Miss Firecracker Contest* (1979),[3] for example, an aging beauty queen in flight from a suffocating marriage and motherhood. When her estranged husband worries that she may kill their children in a fit of fury, Elain answers him by quashing the idea of her repressed rage spiraling murderously out of control: "Oh, for God's sake, Franklin, no one's going to bake them into a pie!"[4] Franklin, borrowing from classical tragedy, baits Elain to circumscribe, even to annul her anger and her flight. One subtext of his inflammatory trope of filicide is that Elain's bid for greater autonomy threatens to incite a domestic "tragedy" (50). Yet the word "tragedy" is Elain's own assessment of impending doom. Though Franklin makes her "ill" (24), without him she is "feeling nothing but terror and fear and loneliness!" (50). And so, after a few minutes of "reckless" infamy under the wisteria bushes with an alcoholic carnival hand, she expects to return to her "dreary, dreary life" (101). No Medea she, Elain occupies the periphery of *Miss Firecracker,* but the arc of her brief rebellion illuminates a paradigm of female surrender running through Henley's plays. The southern heroines populating her tragicomedies frequently erupt in anger toward those (including themselves) who engineer or sustain the emotionally impoverishing circumstances of their private lives; and just as often, they retreat from the schemes of violence bred by that anger. They relish murderous and suicidal fantasies, they repudiate them. The problematics of their rage is my subject.

The shadow of violent death is diffused across Henley's landscapes At times it is treated with the *sprezzatura* of black comedy. Accidents of nature abound, wacky in their studied randomness: Carnelle's father has died chasing "the Tropical Ice Cream truck" (*Firecracker,* 12), her Uncle George fell "to his death trying to pull this bird's nest out from the chimney" (12); Popeye's brother has been fatally bitten "by a water moccasin down by the Pearl River" (12); Lenny's horse Billy Boy has been "struck dead" by lightning;[5] Jamey Foster has been fatally "kicked in the head by a cow";[6] an orphanage has burnt, blood vessels burst, cars and pigs exploded. Katty observes that "life is so full of unknown horror" (*Wake,* 8).

But at other times the half-baked threats of homicide and suicide swerve toward the rant of revenge tragedies. Unlike accidents of nature, these threats have knowable if not justifiable causes, reactions to betrayals and injustices made visible as the plays unfold. Yet the fantasies of murder entertained by these heroines signify no commitment to the principle that drives revenge tragedies, namely that revenge is an heroic prerogative of the wronged party, for traditionally revenge has been a masculine mode, from which these heroines mostly draw back. The fantasies secreted in Henley's texts are indeed not so much retributive as palliative. They are strategies of coping with the residual scars of emotional abandonment, or with a fresh crisis of the same, a recurring motif in Henley's art. Consider those of the widow Marshael in *The Wake of Jamey Foster* (1982). Estranged from her husband Jamey, who eventually dies from being filliped in the head—by a cow—during a pastoral tryst with his mistress Esmerelda, Marshael is abandoned a second time in a thunderstorm by family friend Brocker Slade, to whom she has turned in her grief, as they are travelling home from the hospital bed of her then-critically-ill husband. Slade later surfaces at Marshael's house to launch a half-hearted campaign to cajole her into forgiveness, cooing, "God, M., honey, [. . .] I'm about ready to run jump into the Big Black River." To his self-pity she replies coolly, "Well, don't forget to hang a heavy stone around your scrawny old neck" (47-48). But recommending his suicide is as far as Marshael's rage goes. It rapidly devolves into despair, with Marshael vesting herself in the role of invalid. The particular stresses of earlier days, inscribed in the "purple and swollen" (20) ulcers on her gums, the rash on her knuckles, have now become general and overwhelming: she is, she says, "sick of betrayal! Sick!" (47), echoing Elain's sentiment in *Miss Firecracker* that her husband Franklin makes her "ill." Yet as in *Firecracker,* again it is a man who is both the source and the cure of a heroine's disease. *The Wake of Jamey Foster* ends in a tableau of Slade soothing Marshael to sleep with the lullaby "This Old Man Comes Rolling Home," in whose refrain (of the same words) Marshael takes comfort from its implicit promise of Slade's enduring paternal presence.[7] He is redeemed, no longer a "scrawny old neck," but an "old *man*" (my emphasis). As the cure suggests, then, Marshael's rage against betrayal is not a liberating or even die-breaking action signalling her escape from heterosexist oppression, but a conservative, paradigmatic strategy for recuperating an emotionally dysfunctional man.

The embryo of this pattern of repudiated rage appears in *Am I Blue* (1972), the first of Henley's plays to be staged. *Am I Blue* investigates the pressures of gender relations, specifically of sexual initiation, felt by two adolescents, Ashbe and John Polk (or J.P.). They meet in a seedy New Orleans bar, return to the apartment Ashbe shares with her always absent father, and, compromising, agree to dance until dawn. Against our gendered expectations that men are always the sexual aggressor, it is the younger Ashbe who presses J.P. to have intercourse. When he refuses, fearing that Ashbe would "get neurotic, or pregnant, or some damn thing,"[8] she retaliates—she feigns having poisoned his drink dyed a suspicious blue: impulsively she hypothesizes his murder, only to recant the fiction immediately, then internalizes her anger, which, though tied to J.P.'s refusal, speaks of larger rejections and wounds.

Yet more striking than Ashbe's threat of the mickeyed highball are the fantasies of murder entertained by both teenagers. Enroute to the apartment, Ashbe, scooping up a stray hat from the street, wonders aloud whether it might not have been "a butcher's who slaughtered his wife or a silver pirate with a black bird on his throat"; J.P. fears that she "probably [has] got some gang of muggers waiting to kill me" (12). While he registers the practical risks of picking up a stranger in a bar, she romanticizes murder; the pirate Blackbeard roams the interstices of her imagination. In Ashbe's terms, a pirate's violence both creates and signifies his autarkic self; and Ashbe, virtually alone in the world, vicariously produces one, too, through her well-developed fantasy life, which privileges the swashbuckler mode, where violence is glamorous, sovereign, and artificial. But other fragments of her fantasy life belie her pose of nonchalance toward violence. They show Ashbe

grappling with feelings of inexplicable rage, inexplicable to her because she possesses only an adolescent, even nascent, sense of herself as an autonomous being. For example, she describes visiting a grocery to smash bags of marshmallows (14), an act of rage comically diverted from its true object; she claims to have stolen ashtrays from the Screw Inn (it discriminates against the helpless, she says pointedly), and to have practiced the passive-aggressive art of voodoo against a clique of schoolmates. From all this, J.P. avers that Ashbe is "probably one of those people that live in a fantasy world" (17). In the most bizarre flight of fancy, she holds out hope of having sex with J.P. so that she might conceive, then travel to Tokyo for an abortion, explaining that she is "so sick of school I could smash every marshmallow in sight" (24). Mary Field Belenky and others have observed that oppressed women who are reconstituting themselves as autonomous subjects sometimes use "the imagery of birth, rebirth and childhood to describe their experience of a nascent self."[9] But Ashbe's struggle to develop as a subject results only in the cross-eyed impulses to smash marshmallows and to conceive only to abort. The latter mirrors the pattern of repudiated rage: she imagines internalizing, then expelling not only a fetus, but also the pressures of conventional commitments imposed upon young women to reproduce; to please and serve men, whatever the cost (recall Ashbe's imaginary butcher who slashes his wife's throat); to disavow the aggression typically associated with the masculine sphere. In the end, however, like Marshael, Ashbe abandons her resistance and, encircled by J.P.'s arms, dances to Billie Holiday. Relinquishing the murderous power of a blue mickey for "the blues" as soon as a man's company is even provisionally secured, Ashbe goes passive toward her own pain. Even the play's interrogative title serves notice of her surrender to the external regulation of her own feelings: *Am I Blue?*

Henley's heroines who have passed beyond adolescence do not similarly romanticize the murder and mutilation of women in later texts, where the playwright explores relationships between men's abuse of women and women's surprising, apparent diffidence or even absence of rage in return. Breaking the conspiracy of silence that surrounds domestic abuse, a conspiracy once silently tolerated, then contested, by Babe in *Crimes of the Heart* (1981), for example, whose medical history narrates the injuries inflicted by her husband, Zackery, these texts map out the cycle of emotional and physical battering. The abuse comes first; and though bids for greater subjectivity sometimes follow a sudden escalation of the abuse,[10] enduring, transformative rage seldom does, for that is largely a privilege of "autarkic selfhood,"[11] about which Henley's women, like Ashbe, seldom more than fantasize. If it is true, as George Mariscal has said, "that all forms of subjectivity are conceived in a bitter struggle for power and hegemony,"[12] then the absence of rage or its diffident expression by Henley's abused women invites us to study the strategies by which the men organize, control, even amputate the heroines' "bitter struggle."

Key moments expose the violence against women inscribed in the institutions of marriage and motherhood in Henley's plays. Two marriages near the brink of collapse—one peripheral, one central to a plot—illustrate their strategies. In *The Wake of Jamey Foster* Katty and Wayne Foster arrive to mourn Jamey's sudden death. The wake itself Henley depicts humorously; it is the spectacle of Wayne's treatment of Katty that transforms comedy into tragicomedy. Like Delmount in *Miss Firecracker,* who dreams at night of women's bodies dismembered (100), Katty and Wayne live in a violently phallic universe. Wayne, who calls Katty a "twat" (*Wake,* 36), sexually harrasses his sister-in-law Collard, confident that men are entitled to control women's bodies: calling her "Charlotte," imposing his preference for her "proper name," he lifts her chin, marking her as his sexual property. Collard protests: "Lifting my chin up like that—you're making me feel like some sort of goddamn horse—[. . .] Oh, so you do like your women dirty?" (49). Katty witnesses this exchange, and immediately moves to protect her own claim to Wayne's twisted affections: "Just because I lose those babies is no reason to treat me viciously—no reason at all! You know I can't help it!" (50)—as if it might be possible ever to justify such abuse. Falsely blaming herself, Katty fails to see, as Collard does, how he is titillated by dehumanizing women into chattel. Yet what Katty has seen precipitates a household crisis. She barricades herself in shame in an upstairs bath, emerging much later to announce, in sorrow and frustration,

> I hate the me I have to be with him. If only I could have the baby it would give me someone to love and make someone who'd love me. There'd be a reason for having the fine house and the lovely yard.
>
> (57)

Of course the same impulse that has driven Katty to mold herself to Wayne's desire for a submissive wife keeps her from reconfiguring her life. She remains committed to their marriage, answering Marshael's inquiry into her next move with numb resignation: "Why, nothing. That's all I can do. I don't have children or a career like you do. Anyway I don't like changes" (58). Katty takes refuge behind the "incompetency 'demands' of the conventional feminine role."[13]

What makes Katty interesting as a specimen of rage repudiated is not her response to Wayne's cruelty but a childhood experience she confides during an intimate talk with the other women, who have congregated in Marshael's bedroom to comfort and cheer her as she mourns. The lights go up on them in the midst of their trading stories of the cruelest thing they have ever done. The segue to Katty's story suggests its dramaturgic importance:

> KATTY (*Pulling at her hair with glee.*) Oh, it's so awful! It's too horrible! You won't think I'm sweet anymore!
>
> COLLARD We don't care! We don't care!
>
> PIXROSE No, we don't care! Tell us!
>
> (54-55)

Collard and Pixrose function as a Greek chorus. They deliver the judgment of a community of women—"We don't care! We don't care!"—that sharply contrasts with the conventional commitment to sentimentality imposed upon women by the male characters in these texts. Moreover, it is possible to hear in Pixrose's "Tell us" a resemblance of a similar moment in *Portrait of the Artist* in which Joyce may be punning on the Greek noun *telos.*[14] Like Stephen Dedalus, who is engaged in challenging the authority of the Roman Catholic Church to establish the ultimate purpose of life, Katty challenges with her story of girlhood violence the authority of men to establish the *telos* of women:

> KATTY One Easter Sunday I was walking to church with my maid, Lizzie Pearl. Well, I was all dressed to kill for in my white ruffled dress and my white Easter bonnet and carrying my white parasol. Well, we had to pass by the Dooleys' house, and the Dooleys were always known as white trash, and that bunch really despised me. Well, Harry and Virginia Dooley came up and shoved me down into a huge mudhole. [. . .] [Later that day] [. . .] Lizzie Pearl and I sneaked back over to their back yard and yanked the chirping heads off of every one of their colored Easter chicks-We murdered them *all* with our bare hands!
>
> (55)

It is difficult to reconcile this portrait of Katty with the other that prevails. In Wayne's absence, she paints herself "with glee" as fully capable of retaliating violently against indignities she has suffered. In Wayne's presence, however, she regresses to the role of a child, even using baby-talk to soothe him as he pretends to grieve the loss of his brother: "Why we're all gonna do every little bitty thing we can do to unburden poor, old Papa Sweet Potato" (9).

Katty's regression is intriguingly linked to her apparent inability to carry a fetus to term. Because Wayne reduces Katty to a "twat," he continuously snuffs out her adult interiority, where interiority signifies not simply an emotional and physical readiness to bear children but also a mature knowledge of the terrain of one's own imagination, memory, and will. This link between male sexuality and the death of female interiority is reiterated elsewhere in *The Wake* when Collard abruptly propositions Slade: "Brocker, honey . . . you gonna leave me forever unravished?" (46-47). With his eye on Marshael instead, Brocker Slade refuses, and Collard, affronted, strikes back: "Oh, Marshael. Right, Marshael. Well, that's all right then. 'Course she's nothing like me. She doesn't caress death and danger with open legs" (47). Here Collard represents heterosexual intercourse as an act of heroic bravado, a potentially fatal sacrifice on the woman's part. (The metaphor also evokes the literal risk of death that women face during childbirth.) Later, her observation that sex with men threatens the death of the female subject is explicitly linked to Katty's instinctive regression. As Slade serenades Marshael from outside her window, Collard, protecting her sister as well as herself, throws a nest of bird's eggs at him, then assigns him responsibility: "Look!

Now you've made me murder these baby eggs! I've done murder!" (62). Just as Collard sacrifices the embryonic lives of birds in a feeble attempt to ward off the dangers of Slade's predatory and at this time unwanted sexual advances toward Marshael, so Katty has killed Easter chicks to signify her resistance to the conventions of feminine obsequiousness, perhaps even to the expectation of motherhood. It is no accident of the text that Katty remains childless, her body expelling the embryonic fruits of her sexual relations with Wayne to preserve what little interiority is left her by their marriage. She controls her uterus if nothing else.

Although these narratives of "murder" intuitively link Katty and Collard, Collard is distinguished by openly resisting the imposition of patriarchal conventions. As we have seen, she furiously rejects sexual harassment from her brother-in-law Wayne, and in another memorable scene, as he insists that Marshael attend Jamey's wake, like it or not, Collard mocks him: "Look, just because you'll always have the taste of leather in your mouth, doesn't mean the rest of us have to" (67). Turning upon Wayne the equestrian metaphor previously applied to herself, Collard scorns him for having accepted the patriarchal bridle. Reversing the sign, she emphasizes the double standard by which men profit, and women suffer, from submitting to patriarchy—we know that Wayne has become a powerful small-town banker, Katty his slave. Yet it is also Collard who most articulates the toll of women's resistance against patriarchy. Ambivalent toward Slade, whom she once invited to "ravish" her, Collard is even more ambivalent toward her own reproductive freedom. In a magnetic scene, she recounts for the other women the aftermath of her abortion, which she imagines to be a violent act:

> I went out and ate fried chicken. Got a ten-piece bucket filled with mashed potatoes and gravy, coleslaw, and a roll. First it tasted good and greasy and gooey. Then I felt like I was eating my baby's skin and flesh and veins and all. I got so sick—
>
> (58)

In contrast to Ashbe's flippant scheme to parlay an abortion into a Tokyo vacation in *Am I Blue,* this painful memory illustrates the anguishing material consequences of Collard's resolve not to be bridled. It leaves her not simply "sick," but nightmarishly guilty. Again Henley records the cost of women's liberation in graphic images of animal dismemberment.[15] Associating the fetus and the fried chicken, which is the third appearance in *The Wake of Jamey Foster* of the trope of fowl destroyed (Easter chicks/bird eggs/fried chicken) as a sign of challenge to the conventions of gender, especially of the obligation to nurture, Collard imagines herself feeding off her own interior: "I felt like I was eating my baby's skin and flesh and veins." From another point of view, though, Collard is not a cannibal but a survivor. In this instance, to reject the fetus is to preserve her nascent claim to self-determination. Perhaps it is that claim that produces as much guilt as the abortion itself.

If Henley's plays collectively forecast the high price yet to be paid by virtually everyone for the manifold inequities long borne by women, the most expansive treatment of this idea is in *Crimes of the Heart.* Not the fairy tale of female bonding that Lorimar made it out to be in its 1986 production, *Crimes of the Heart* studies the origins and effects of domestic abuse, tracing the rise and fall of its principal heroine's rage, fingering the female conspirators of culturally sanctioned violence against women, exposing the link between sexism and racism, suggesting the often grave costs of women's coming to know themselves as wholly volitional beings.

Hovering over the MaGrath family in *Crimes of the Heart* is a curse as particular as any in Ibsen, Tennessee Williams, or Sam Shepard, and as general as post-classical Western culture itself: long ago, the matriarch of the Ma-Grath clan, in fury and despair, hanged herself and her cat in the fruit cellar of the family home. Her suicide affirmed for her daughters the ideological link between women's exercise of self-determination and Death, a link dating at least from early Christian constructions of Eve's primal disobedience.[16] *Crimes of the Heart* dramatizes its continuing damage to the next generation, especially through the fallout from Babe and Zackery Botrelle's exploded marriage. Long physically abused by "the richest and most powerful man in all of Hazlehurst" (21), Babe has denied the significance of her own fractures and bruises, breaking free only after watching Zack maul Willie Jay, her fifteen-year-old African-American lover. Although Babe is enraged by Zack's racism and his consequent physical abuse of Willie Jay,[17] Babe's first response is to think of suicide, as her mother had done, then epiphanically to reject suicide as a viable response to explosive anger:

> Why, I was gonna shoot off my own head! [. . .] I thought about Mama . . . how she'd hung herself. Then I realized—that's right, I realized how I didn't want to kill myself! And she—she probably didn't want to kill herself.
>
> (49)

Instead, fittingly, she shoots Zack in the belly, inflicting *quid pro quo* an ironic even if uncalculated revenge on a "bully" who had threatened to cut out Willie's "gizzard" (42, 49). Though Babe is no avenger, her shooting Zackery might seem to presage a heroine's decisive new commitment to self-determination. But near the end of *Crimes of the Heart* Henley dashes that hope, having Babe comically regress toward suicide. Without success she tries to hang, then to asphyxiate herself in a gas oven. Babe suffers the by-now-familiar arc: once vented, her rage boomerangs. In effect she mentally implodes, just as her compatriot Marshael does in *The Wake* Recall that Marshael, though liberated by her husband's sudden death from one cycle of emotional neglect, is still furiously angry at him, confessing that she feels as if "a hole's been shot through me, and all my insides have been blown out somewhere else" (*Wake,* 43).

In earlier plays, heroines abort their rage or, what amounts to the same thing, turn it inward, for obliquely palpable reasons that spectators must infer. In *Crimes,* however, the playwright delivers a direct cause of Babe's reversal, namely Zackery's intention to commit her to the Whitfield psychiatric hospital (114). His plan disorients but also catalyzes Babe, who *"slams the phone down and stares wildly ahead:* He's not. He's not. [. . .] I'll do it. I will. And he won't" (114). The indicative verbs here signify that Babe again turns to suicide as the only gesture of self-determination available in a universe otherwise controlled by those such as her estranged lawyer-husband, who is ominously confident that psychiatric clinics stand ready to isolate, punish, and perhaps reprogram women who, in their rage, repudiate the hegemony of men. Zackery is obviously a "total criminal" (43), as Babe's defense lawyer claims. Yet Henley insists we not dismiss him as an aberrant loner, but see him as an integral member of a community that permits, even expects, men to abuse women, and that expects women to cope with it by clinging to the theorem of female martyrdom. That theorem is best expressed in a colloquial commonplace by Elain, the ex-beauty queen, who counsels Carnelle on her loss of the Miss Firecracker title: "Just try to remember how Mama was enlightened by her affliction" (*Firecracker,* 80). Though none of the women in *Crimes of the Heart* has in so many words similarly advised Babe to tough out Zackery's abuse, Babe has nevertheless learned well not to expect others to validate her supposedly unfeminine rage, neither before nor after she shoots Zackery. Thus when her sister Lenny and cousin Chick question Babe as to motive, she is virtually mute, offering only that she "didn't like [Zackery's] looks" (27). Obviously ridiculous, this red herring intensifies her silence. Elizabeth Stanko observes that abused women's silence "is linked to an understanding of [their] powerlessness; it is a recognition of the contradictory expectations of femaleness and probable judgments others commonly render about any woman's involvement in male violence."[18] Henley sharpens her critique of women who collude with oppressive forces by depicting Babe's attorney Barnette Lloyd as steadfastly supportive of his accused client, suggesting how little one's gender necessarily dictates one's politics.

Indeed, in small ways and large, Lenny and especially Chick reproduce the inequities of gender that have been insinuated into every social discourse. Lenny, for example, anticipates Zack's psychiatric prescription, telling Meg, "I believe Babe is ill. I mean in-her-head ill" (17). Lenny fails to see how her diagnosis reinforces a double standard of provocation, in which men's "retaliatory behavior is acceptable," and women's is not.[19] But it is cousin Chick, who works the system well enough to have been accepted to membership in the Hazlehurst Ladies' Social League, who is Zackery's far more malignant if still unwitting conspirator. Deploying the concept of "shame" to police other women, Chick consistently attacks what she takes to be the MaGraths' lack of obedience to a code of womanhood that emphasizes decorum, not subjectivity; submission, not independence. She is not simply a watchdog, but a burlesque[20] obsessed by "the skeletons in the MaGraths' closet" (6), her anger rising as the sisters' violations mount.

After spying Meg returning from a night with Doc, for example, Chick bashes Meg in order to recruit Lenny into conscious alliance with the model of suffocating female subjectivity endorsed by the Ladies' Social League.[21] Chick pities not Meg but Lenny:

> You must be so ashamed! You must just want to die! Why, I always said that girl was nothing but cheap Christmas trash! [. . .] Meg's a low-class tramp and you need not have one more blessed thing to do with her and her disgusting behavior.
>
> (112)

When Lenny refuses to concede Meg's depravity, Chick explodes, inadvertently revealing the root of her anger:

> I've just about had my fill of you trashy MaGraths and your trashy ways: hanging yourselves in cellars; carrying on with married men; shooting your own husbands! [. . .] *[Turning toward Babe]* And don't you think she's not gonna end up at the state prison farm or in some-mental institution. Why, it's a clear-cut case of manslaughter with intent to kill! [. . .] That's what everyone's saying, deliberate intent to kill! And you'll pay for that! Do you hear me? You'll pay!
>
> (112-13)

"Manslaughter," from the lexicon of law, aptly describes Chick's judgment of the MaGraths' violations, their budding refusals to "pay" into a patriarchal discourse that brands women "cheap Christmas trash," that blames the victim for spouse abuse, that again insinuates death as the inevitable consequence of women's self-determination ("you must just want to die!"). In Chick's eyes, resistance is indeed man/slaughter.

Against Chick's slavish dependence upon pernicious communal values, Henley juxtaposes Meg's apparently fierce independence. Faced with the artifacts of her sister's medical history, for example, which records the consequences of Zack's spousal violence, Meg rants, "This is madness! Did he do this to her? I'll kill him; I will—I'll fry his blood!" (43); in the Senecan image Meg boldly claims the prerogative of revenge abdicated by most of Henley's other heroines. And later, she quells Babe's self-recriminations by erasing the privileged line between sanity and madness, declaring, "Why, you're just as perfectly sane as anyone walking the streets of Hazlehurst, Mississippi" (119); in Meg's circuitous compliment we may hear an indictment of the citizenry for continuing to tolerate domestic violence.

In these moments of bravado Meg seems stronger than Babe for openly resisting the forces under which Babe has long suffered, but elsewhere Henley suggests that Meg likewise suffers from deep ambivalence about the scope and strength of her own freedom. Feigning heroic indifference toward the dangers of smoking, for example, she reiterates the link between women's self-determination and death that led her mother to hang herself in the fruit cellar: "That's what I like about [smoking], Chick—taking a drag off of death. [. . .] Mmm! Gives me a sense of controlling my own destiny. What power! What exhilaration! Want a drag?" (28). Unlike Lenny and Babe, who seem glued to Hazlehurst, Meg has attempted to wrest her destiny away from the Ladies' Social League by exiling herself to Los Angeles, a move that demonstrates autonomy and mobility. In L.A., though, she has met failure. Once an aspiring singer, she has succumbed to clerking for a dog food company (23), and in her words has recently gone "insane," winding up in the psychiatric ward of L.A. County Hospital (85). The cause, as we gradually come to see, is the residual effects of her mother's suicide. Much like Carnelle in **Miss Firecracker,** who laments that "people've been dying practically all my life," and "I guess I should be used to it by now" (12), Meg has stoically attempted to block out the pain of having been the one to discover her mother's body.[22] Yet Babe recalls that during girlhood outings to the public library and the Dixieland Drugstore,

> Meg would spend all her time reading and looking through this old black book called *Diseases of the Skin.* It was full of the most sickening pictures you've ever seen. Things like rotting-away noses and eyeballs drooping off down the sides of people's faces, and scabs and sores and eaten-away places. [At Dixieland Drugs, examining a crippled-children poster, Meg would say] "See, I can stand it. I can stand it. Just look how I'm gonna be able to stand it."
>
> (66-67)

The memory illustrates Meg's resolve to steel herself against loss, an early decision that continues to sabotage her life as an adult. Reversing the usual pattern in Henley's plays, it has been Meg who abandoned her sometime lover Doc, rather than vice versa, during Hurricane Camille: returned from L.A., she confesses to him, "It was my fault to leave you. I was crazy. I thought I was choking. I felt choked!" (84). Meg's fear of "choking"[23] not only recalls her mother's suicide by hanging, but also illuminates what is for her virtually a synaptic link between romantic alliances with men and the potential snuffing out of her own life. But, she tells Doc, "I was crazy." Apologizing, labelling her earlier perceptions of risk as signs of mental illness, Meg now repudiates her own intuition and thus repatriates herself into the Hazlehurst community. À la Elain in **Miss Firecracker,** she too "comes home."

Meg's maneuver is consonant with the pattern of surrender that is woven through Henley's scripts. We may conclude that these heroines engage in quasi-feminist rebellion, if they engage in it at all, for psychological rather than political motives. Babe makes the point best when she refutes what is to her the alarming possibility that she intended her interracial liaison with Willie Jay to be a political statement: "I'm not a liberal! I'm a democratic! I was just lonely! I was so lonely! And he was so good" (48). Babe's verbal slip—an adjective for a noun—reveals an inarticulate command of the political, at least disqualifying her from playing the conscious iconoclast. As in this instance, Henley's heroines seem not to recognize as such the feminist awakenings that bubble to the surfaces of their consciousnesses, as they seek to repair and preserve their lives within the system they have inherited. Yet they come to life inside Henley's crucible of populist tragicomedy, in which regressive comic fantasies and tragic aspirations collide; osmotically the heroines have absorbed some of the energies of the feminist movement, and in their own ways, they grope toward liberty.[24]

Notes

1. On the implications of community for Henley's characters, other commentators have tended to read more optimistically. Hargrove, for example, finds "ultimately cheering and sustaining" the fact "That each play ends with two or more characters joined together in a bond of human solidarity" (Nancy D. Hargrove, "The Tragicomic Vision of Beth Henley's Drama," *Southern Quarterly,* 22: 4 [1984] 69); Harbin emphasizes the "awakened sense of the restorative powers of familial trust and communion" in *Crimes of the Heart,* but concedes that the other plays leave characters suspended in "hopeless resignation" (Billy J. Harbin "Familial Bonds in the Plays of Beth Henley," *Southern Quarterly,* 25: 3 [1987], 88, 93); Laughlin, emphasizing *Crimes of the Heart,* too, claims it "proposes a vision of women bonding with each other and dramatizes a joyful celebration of this bond" (Karen L. Laughlin, "Criminality, Desire and Community: A Feminist Approach to Beth Henley's *Crimes of the Heart,*" *Women and Performance: A Journal of Feminist Theory,* 3: 1 [1986], 48). I argue that Henley dramatizes a far more ambiguous vision of community, of "female bonding" in particular.

2. For discussion of politically radical heroines in the tradition of Southern proletarian fiction, see Sylvia Jenkins Cook, "Poor Whites, Feminists, and Marxists," in *From "Tobacco Road" to Route 66* (Chapel Hill, 1976), 98-124.

3. Years in parentheses refer to the date of first production.

4. Beth Henley, *The Miss Firecracker Contest* (Garden City, NY, 1985), 38. Hereafter cited as *Firecracker.*

5. Beth Henley, *Crimes of the Heart* (New York, 1982), 19. Hereafter cited as *Crimes.*

6. Beth Henley, *The Wake of Jamey Foster* (New York, 1983), 12. Hereafter cited as *Wake.*

7. Harbin mistakenly argues that Marshael's "grim suffering remains unrelieved throughout the play" (93).

8. Beth Henley, *Am I Blue* (New York, 1982), 23.

9. Mary Field Belenky *et al., Women's Ways of Knowing: The Development of Self, Voice, and Mind* (New York, 1986), 82.

10. Belenky points out that many women start a transition to subjectivist autonomy and power only

11. Gordon Braden, *Renaissance Tragedy and the Senecan Tradition: Anger's Privilege* (New Haven, 1985), 2.

12. George Mariscal, "The Other Quixote," in Nancy Armstrong and Leonard Tennenhouse, eds., *The Violence of Representation* (New York, 1989), 113.

13. Belenky, 104. Belenky is citing N. Livson and H. Peskin, "Psychological Health at Age 40: Predictions from Adolescent Personality," in D. Eichorn *et al.*, eds., *Present and Past in Mid-life* (New York, 1981), 191.

14. Edmund L. Epstein, *The Ordeal of Stephen Dedalus: The Conflict of the Generations in James Joyce's "A Portrait of the Artist as a Young Man"* (Carbondale, IL, 1971), 10.

15. Henley uses the technique to comic advantage when Marshael bites the ears off a chocolate Easter rabbit as the play opens.

16. Elaine Pagels cites Tertullian, a second-century Carthaginian theologian, excoriating women: "You are the devil's gateway . . . You are she who persuaded him whom the devil did not dare attack . . . *do you not know that every one of you is an Eve?*" See *Adam, Eve, and the Serpent* (New York, 1988), 63 (her emphasis).

17. Belenky *et al.* observe that abused women often respond by continuing to care for others, but not for themselves (166).

18. Elizabeth Stanko, *Intimate Intrusions: Women's Experience of Male Violence* (London, 1985), 72. Laughlin (43) says that "Elissa Gelfand and others have highlighted the tendency of (predominantly male) criminologists to explain the female criminal's surprising departure from the expected patterns of inactivity and domesticity as 'monstrous'."

19. James Ptacek, "Why Do Men Batter Their Wives?" in Kersti Yllö and Michele Bograd, eds., *Feminist Perspectives on Wife Abuse* (Newbury Park, CA, 1988), 145.

20. Jacobs traces the literary evolution of caricatures of the southern poor white to William Byrd II's *History of the Dividing Line* (1728), not published until 1841, but circulating in manuscript much earlier. Robert D. Jacobs, "*Tobacco Road*: Lowlife and the Comic Tradition," in Louis D. Rubin, Jr., ed., *The American South: Portrait of a Culture* (Baton Rouge, 1980), 206-26. Hargrove notes that Chick's name fits her: she "is nervous, nosy, and bossy, verbally 'pecking' at everyone" (63).

21. Laughlin observes that Chick's "attempts to divide or degrade the Magrath [sic] sisters play directly into the hands of the patriarchal order" (55).

22. Hargrove admires the characters' collective "strength or stoicism," declaring that "perhaps the dominant theme of her drama ultimately is the value of love" (55).

23. See Mac Sam's ironic observation, "I was almost choked to death by my mama's umbilical cord at birth" (*Firecracker*, 63).

24. Thanks to my colleagues Linda K. Hughes, Robert Donahoo, and Rob McDonald for reading earlier drafts of this essay, and especially to Steven Wozniak for his encouragement and counsel.

An earlier version of this paper was presented on 14 February 1992 before a session of the Southern Humanities Conference, meeting at the University of North Carolina, Chapel Hill. Thanks to Professors Annette Cox for inviting me and Roberta Rosenberg for good conversation about *Crimes of the Heart.*

Paul Rosefeldt (essay date 1995)

SOURCE: "Trapped in the Father's Dying World: Beth Henley's *Crimes of the Heart* and Anton Chekhov's *The Three Sisters*," in *The Absent Father in Modern Drama*, Peter Lang, 1995, pp. 75-82.

[*In the following essay, Rosefeldt links Henley's* Crimes of the Heart *to the Chekhovian tradition, in particular to the drama* The Three Sisters.]

Another play that focuses on the daughter's relationship to an absent father is Beth Henley's ***Crimes of the Heart.*** ***Crimes of the Heart*** is not a play about the daughter's withdrawal into the world of the father, but it is a play in which an absent father figure dominates the lives of three women. Both *'night, Mother* and ***Crimes of the Heart*** started at the Actors' Theatre in Louisville, played Off-Broadway, won a Pulitzer Prize, and had successful Broadway runs. Both plays made instant successes out of women playwrights and sparked heated debates among feminist critics. Like *'night, Mother,* ***Crimes of the Heart*** is about relationships among women who have led troubled lives and are seeking desperate solutions to their problems. According to Morrow, the protagonists in both plays have "been influenced by mothers who were literally or figuratively abandoned by their husbands" (23). However, these protagonists are all influenced by men who are absent from the action of the play. More specifically, both feature an absent father or father figure.

Other than the feminist debate, criticism of ***Crimes of the Heart*** has focused on the issue of truths versus gimmicks. For some reason, critics tend to denigrate a comedy for creating a series of joke lines and for setting up contrived events. Walter Kerr sees ***Crimes of the Heart*** as "overloaded with quirky behavior" ("Offbeat" D3). He feels that "the characters tend to lose weight and substance as they reach farther and farther for one more brass ring" (31). Howard Kissel notes that "the story though funny, never seems true" (140). Michael Feingold feels that Henley gossips about her characters "never at any point coming close to the truth in their lives" (106). Frank Rich, however, takes an opposite view. He feels that Henley "refuses to tell jokes at all" and that her "characters always stick to the unvarnished truth and the truth is funnier than any invented wisecracks" ("Unvarnished Laughs" C21). Clive Barnes notes that the play can capture "the basic truth behind the improbabilities" ("'Crimes'" 137). Nancy Hargrove finds Henley's portrayal of the human condition "realistic" and "painfully honest" (89).

Comedy by its very nature treats behavior that is outrageous; yet critics want to validate a "serious comedy" by focusing primarily on its verisimilitude. *Crimes of the Heart* is indeed an entertaining play written to evoke laughter; yet behind the play is a psychological pattern that links the drama to the absent father.

First, much of the plot is structured around a series of absent fathers. The father of the MaGrath sisters left their mother, and his absence leads the MaGraths to move from Vicksburg to Hazlehurst so they can live with their maternal grandfather, Old Granddaddy. Old Granddaddy, a surrogate father to the sisters, is now in the hospital dying. Much of the play's action is surrounded around the absent patriarch. Also, Doc, Meg's old boyfriend whom she abandoned, is back in Hazlehurst because "his father died a couple of months ago," and Doc is "seeing to his property" (24). In other words, a dead father has brought him back to town where he will meet Meg again. Barnette Lloyd, the young lawyer who keeps Babe out of jail, is seeking revenge for the destruction of his father. He is willing to take a case against Zackery Botrelle because Zackery ruined Barnette's father: "He took away his job, his home, his health, and his respectability" (62). Barnette is interjected into the plot to revenge the wounding of an absent father. Even Charlie Hill can become a prospective husband for Lenny because he has renounced the state of fatherhood and doesn't want to raise "little snot-nosed pigs" (116). *Crimes of the Heart* is inscribed within the world of the absent father.

The most obvious absent father is Jimmy MaGrath. Like the Wingfield father, he seems to be noted for his ambiguous smile. Meg despises his "white teeth" (31), and when she sees a picture of him "clowning on the beach" (71), she says, "Turn the page . . . we can't do worse than this" (71). Babe holds him and his absence responsible for the death of her mother and the old yellow cat that the mother hung beside herself. "I bet if Daddy hadn't left, they'd still be alive" (31). The MaGrath father, who has disappeared completely from their lives, is not only held responsible for the mother's death, which has emotionally scarred the sisters, but he is also responsible for leaving them stranded in the house of Old Granddaddy, who has a disastrous effect in shaping their lives.

Critics seem to agree on the role that Old Granddaddy plays in the lives of the MaGrath sisters. E. D. Huntley notes, "The absent Old Granddaddy is in some ways the guiltiest character in the play because his 'crimes' have precipitated the self-destructive sins of the MaGrath sisters" (410). Adler contends that he has "controlled and

limited their lives more decisively than the shadow of their mother's suicide" (44). And Jonnie Guerra points out how "the sister's victimization by Old Granddaddy's misguided plans" demonstrates "the destructive power of a male-dominated society" (125).

Old Granddaddy, the only father figure that the sisters identify with, is a key structural device in the play. His off-stage dying sets a deathwatch atmosphere against which the actions of the drama are played. Lenny has already moved her cot into the kitchen to "be close and hear him at night if he needed something" (19). Early in the play, the audience knows that "Old Granddaddy's gotten worse in the hospital" (12). Even though Meg has been brought home by Babe's legal problems, she and Lenny must inevitably face Old Granddaddy, who has "blood vessels popping in his brain" (20). As the sisters are beset with a series of crises, Act Two ends on the jolting announcement that Old Granddaddy has had a stroke. Act Three begins with an announcement that he is in a coma and that his death is imminent. As an absent father who controls the progress of the play, Old Granddaddy and his dying absorb a considerable portion of the drama.

Reflecting his dying, the world itself is filled with disease and decay. From Lenny's hair "falling out" (18) and Meg's "slicing pains" (20) to Mrs. Porter's tumor in her bladder, illness is pervasive. Meg reads Old Granddaddy's book on diseases of the skin and looks at "rotting away noses and eyeballs drooping off down the sides of people's faces" (66) while Babe keeps a scrapbook about the unpleasant things in her life, like her mother's death. Also, Old Granddaddy, who is turning "white and milky" (69) and has "almost evaporated" (69), is not alone among the wounded men. Shot by Babe, Zackery is in the hospital with a bullet wound in his stomach. Doc, lured by Meg to stay in a hurricane, has a crushed leg and has abandoned a promising medical career. The battered Willy Jay is uprooted and sent North. Lloyd Barnette, though not physically injured, has to give up his personal vendetta. Not to mention the fact that Mama's cat gets hung and Lenny's horse Billy Boy is struck by lightning. The world of death, disease, and loss is a wasteland world that revolves around the dying of Old Granddaddy, the absent father figure.

Although the sisters have not doubled Old Granddaddy, they have tried to live out his dreams for them. He has filled them with illusions that have led them into self-destructive lifestyles. Old Granddaddy designated Babe "the prettiest and most perfect of the three" (21). He was proud to see her married to Zackery Botrelle, "the richest and most powerful man in Hazlehurst" (22). Old Granddaddy felt that Zackery was "the right man for her whether she knew it or not" (22). It was Old Granddaddy's, not Babe's dream, that she would "skyrocket right to the heights of Hazlehurst society" (22). When asked whether she was happy on her wedding day, she can only reply that she "was drunk with champagne" (71). Babe is not suited to be among the social set. Furthermore, Old Granddaddy's dream husband turns out to be a callous and abusive man, so Babe seeks love and understanding in the arms of a fifteen-year-old black boy and shoots her husband when he strikes the boy. Following the path Old Granddaddy has pointed out for her has left Babe alienated, perplexed, and suicidal.

Old Granddaddy has also led Meg astray. He has pumped Meg up with ideas of becoming a Hollywood celebrity. He told her that with her singing talent all she needed was "exposure," and she could make her "own breaks" (23). In the American mythos, the Hollywood dream factory again provides an illusory escape for lost children. Like Tom, Austin, and Pavlo, Meg follows the path of the movies. Old Granddaddy wants her to put her foot "in one of those blocks of cement they have in Hollywood" (23). Ironically, Meg is metaphorically stuck in cement, trapped in the dream she and Old Granddaddy share. Resentfully, she tells Lenny, "I think I've heard that [Hollywood speech] and I'll probably hear it again when I visit him in the hospital" (23). Meg has also been driven to the brink of madness trying to live the role Old Granddaddy has cast her in. Unable to attain success, she winds up working for a dog food company. When Old Granddaddy sends her money to come home for Christmas, she can't because she undergoes a nervous breakdown. She psychologically loses her singing voice partially to get even with Old Granddaddy for whom she has been singing and winds up in the L.A. County Hospital's psychiatric ward.

Interestingly, Meg's trauma is connected with Christmas. Psychologists have discovered that Christmas time brings on depression and emotional crises in troubled people. But Christmas as a "holiday gone wrong" seems to be a focal theme in some of the dramas of the absent father. Nora's tragedy begins on Christmas. Jessie decides she is going to kill herself on Christmas. She even notes that "Jesus was a suicide" (18). Interestingly, Jesus does die at the bidding of the Absent Father and dies to return to the Father. The Christian ethos always points toward a return to the Father. Christmas brings forth the hope of a savior, but Meg, who cannot find a savior, goes crazy at Christmas. Chick even labels her "cheap Christmas trash" (6). At a Christmas bazaar, Babe does find Barnette, a savior figure who keeps her out of jail. However, despite his rescue, Babe attempts suicide. Thus, the Christmas theme of salvation sent from the Father reverses itself into one of despair and hopelessness.

Since Meg's Christmas rewards never come, she is forced to engage in storytelling. Like Willy, Biff, and Pavlo, she creates grandiose fabrications. She lies to Old Granddaddy, telling him she has made a record album and has a role in a movie called *Singing in a Shoe Factory,* a title which contrasts the glamour of being in Hollywood with the mundane job she has at a dog food company. Like Biff, Meg is forced to create a false identity in order to please a father figure. Meg confesses, "I hate myself when I lie for that old man. I do. I feel so weak. Then I have to do at least three or four things that I know he'd despise just to get even with the miserable, old bossy man!" (69).

Whether she tries to fulfill Old Granddaddy's vision of what she should be or whether she acts to spite him, Meg is still controlled by Old Granddaddy.

Like Babe and Meg, Lenny too is acting out Old Granddaddy's image of what she should be. Old Granddaddy has made Lenny feel self-conscious about her "shrunken ovary" (34). Meg accuses Lenny of living out her life "as Old Granddaddy's nursemaid" (79). The one man she has had a relationship with she stopped seeing "because of Old Granddaddy" (79). Old Granddaddy told Lenny that the man would not marry her because she could not have children. Meg tries to convince Lenny she can have a romantic attachment and that "Old Granddaddy's the only one who seems to think otherwise" (80). Lenny feels that Old Granddaddy has always wanted to see them happy. "He went out of his way to make a home for us, to treat us like we were his own children. All he ever wanted was the best for us" (69-70). Thus, the sisters are trapped in an ambivalent relationship with a father figure. Old Granddaddy, the surrogate father, has determined what is best for the sisters, and they feel guilty not following his wishes.

However, Old Granddaddy's attempts to manufacture happy lives for his surrogate daughters have left them miserable and debilitated. The way Old Granddaddy has influenced them can be seen in the way he treated the young girls on the day of their mother's funeral. Old Granddaddy bought them "banana splits for breakfast" (72) and "shoved them down" (72) the girls until they got sick. His attempts to fill them with the rich desserts of life have left them physically and mentally ill. Meg says, "He keeps trying to make us happy and we end up getting stomach aches and turning green and throwing up in the flower arrangements" (73). Babe shoots her husband, then swills down three glasses of her favorite lemonade until she is bloated. Meg tries to harden herself against the tragedies of life by looking at pictures of crippled children, then buying "a double scoop ice cream cone" (67). When Lenny is filled full of Old Granddaddy's advice, she says "I'm gonna vomit" (81).

Although they follow the advice of Old Granddaddy, their feelings toward this absent father figure are ambivalent. Lenny has made a birthday wish that "Old Granddaddy would be put out of his pain" (95) and feels guilty when he goes into a coma. Rebelling against Old Granddaddy, Meg proclaims, "I sang right up into the trees! But not for Old Granddaddy. None of it was to please him" (99). Then, she announces in defiance, "He's just gonna have to take me like I am and if that sends him into a coma, that's just too damn bad" (99). Ironically, he has just been sent into a coma, and Meg's line provokes hysterical laughter.

Critics have commented on the difficulty of accepting this line. Leo Sauvage finds it in poor taste. He notes that nervous laughter may occur when someone falls down, but points out, "I've never heard of a similar physiological outbreak occurring when a family member is told a sick relative is in the hospital near dying" (20). Walter Kerr also comments on the difficulty of playing such a scene, but notes that the director of the Broadway production has "orchestrated the two-way personal collapse perfectly" in order to set up a perfect "alternating of grief and manic glee" ("Offbeat" D31). Brendan Gill notes that the sisters' outburst into laughter "strikes us as the most natural thing in the world to do" (183). The difficulty of playing such a scene which skirts a fine line between comedy and horror is connected to the sisters' ambivalent feeling toward an absent father figure.

This ambivalence brings up another problematic point in the play—its resolution. According to Morrow, "Lenny's birthday cake foreshadows her being surrounded by enduring and increasing circles of love" (37). Yet one is inclined to agree with Guerra's less sanguine conclusion. According to Guerra, Lenny's statement that the laughter of the sisters was just for a moment can only "remind the audience of the uncertain fates of these women and raise doubts that either their new closeness or their new selves can be sustained" (126). The resolution is uncertain because the ending is clearly linked to the sisters' reactions to Old Granddaddy. First, the mysterious, unrevealed birthday wish is closely connected to Lenny's first birthday wish that Old Granddaddy will be put out of his misery and to Babe's conclusion that birthday wishes sometimes "don't even count when you do have a cake" (96). Second, the final scene of the three sisters laughing replicates the previous laughter scene over Old Granddaddy's coma. Their laughter comes more out of hysteria than joy. Third, the scene in which the sisters begin to stuff themselves with an enormous birthday cake for breakfast reenacts Old Granddaddy's stuffing them full of banana splits for breakfast. Even though they have made some discoveries about themselves, their moment of laughter and their gorging of themselves with birthday cake can only offer them what Old Granddaddy has been offering them all along: solace and a life full of empty desserts. Perhaps those trapped in the world of the absent father can do no more than find ways to get through the bad days.

Despite its noticeable and much commented upon affinity to American Southern Gothic, _Crimes of the Heart,_ like _'night, Mother,_ is linked to an earlier dramatic tradition— the Chekhovian tradition. Adler feels that the "three Ma-Grath sisters bear little resemblance to Anton Chekhov's" (47); however, Jean Gagen and Joanne Karpinski have both uncovered remarkable similarities in _Crimes of the Heart_ and Chekhov's _The Three Sisters._ Both critics find likenesses in the lives of the sisters. "Lenny, like Olga, has aged prematurely in a self-defeating effort to carry out a nurturing role and never expects to have a man" (Karpinski 230). Just as Lenny takes care of Old Granddaddy, Olga takes in Anfisa, the old family nurse (Gagen 119). Babe, like Masha, feels stuck in an unhappy marriage and finds a more sympathetic partner outside this bond. And like Meg, "Irina gets sidetracked in a meaningless job despite lofty career expectations and has doubts about making a commitment to a man that truly loves her" (Karpinski 230).

Both plays are also full of the details of daily life (Gagen 120) and display "infiltrations of the comic into depictions of frustration, disenchantment, and failure" (Gagen 121), creating a "tragicomic tone" (Karpinski 234).

A more significant comparison lies in the structure of the two plays. Gagen notes that in both plays "most of the significant action, whether external or internal, takes place offstage and is reported" (120). This focus on offstage action sets up the drama of absent characters, the most noticeable being the absent father. Gagen notes that both plays have "invisible characters who never appear on stage, yet play significant roles in the action" (120). She points out the two absent fathers: the "father of the Prozorov sisters, who was responsible for bringing them to the provincial town which they despise" and "Old Granddaddy, who has been an obvious force in the lives of the MaGrath sisters" (120). Karpinski also notes how "both sets of sisters have inherited a suffocating value system, reinforced by emotional ties to a dominating male figure not present on stage" (230).

Both dramas open on the death or dying of an absent father figure. The first line of _The Three Sisters_ is "It's exactly a year ago since father died" (73). In fact, Olga reenacts the death of the father. As the clock strikes twelve, she relives her father's death and says, "The clock struck twelve then too" (73). Early in the first act of _**Crimes of the Heart,**_ Old Granddaddy's worsening condition is announced. Thus, the dying fathers are very present. Both plays combine death and dying of the father with the distorted celebration of a birthday. The anniversary of the Prozorov father's death and its reenactment in Olga's opening monologue takes place on Irina's name day, just like Lenny's birthday coincides with Old Granddaddy's dying. Both birthdays are filled with unusual celebrations. Chick gives Lenny a box of left-over Christmas candy, which Meg destroys. Irina's brother-in-law gives her a pedantic book which he had already given her as an Easter present. And the old doctor who was in love with Irina's mother (a spurious father figure) inappropriately gives her an anniversary present. In the world of the absent father, a celebration of renewal is tinged with incongruities, thus casting doubt on the efficacy of the celebration.

Both sets of sisters have been given unrealistic expectations by their absent fathers. Just as Old Granddaddy gave the MaGrath sisters unsuitable goals, the Prozorov father has overeducated his children. Andrew, the brother of the Prozorov sisters says "Our father . . . inflicted education on us" and "thanks to Father my sisters and I know French, German, and English, and Irina knows Italian too" (84). But Masha bemoans that in a small town this knowledge is a "useless luxury" like "having a sixth finger" (84). The father has raised them to expect a cultured life and then left them in a small town where they cannot reach their potential (Karpinski 232). Tied to a life of drudgery, Olga, like Lenny, feels "her youth and energy draining" and "would marry the first man who would come along provided he was decent and honest" (119). Masha, like

Babe, married at eighteen. Like Babe, she married a man who would fit the expectations of her absent father. She thought her husband would be "the wisest of men," and he turned out to be a disappointment. Masha, a general's daughter, also remembers the officers that graced her father's parties. She believes that the "most civilized and cultured people are the military" (93). She engages in an affair with Vershinin, an officer who served in the same brigade as her father and knew him personally (another father substitute), and she is disappointed when he is sent away to Poland. Irina is also disappointed in her prospects for the future and in a prospective marriage partner. When most of the town is on fire, and her brother has mortgaged off the paternal estate, she can only say, "I can't remember the Italian word for 'window' or 'ceiling' either" (119). The education that her father gave her is receding into the past, just like his world. She realizes that she "is losing touch with everything fine and genuine in life" (119). Just as in *Ghosts* and *Miss Julie,* the world of her absent father is burning down around her, and the patriarchal estate is being jeopardized.

Both plays end with a final tableau of the three sisters together consoling one another and looking forward to better times. Gagen believes the MaGrath sisters have more "hope in the end" and Karpinski finds the ending of **Crimes of the Heart** to be in "a brighter key" (283) than the finale of *The Three Sisters.* Yet both plays are held bound by the attachment to the absent father. The Ma-Grath sisters are condemned to repeat Old Granddaddy's eating ritual and the Prozorov sisters listen to the "rousing tune" (139) of a military band which can be compared to the "band playing when they took father to the cemetery" (73). Significantly, his funeral was held on a day of "heavy rain and sleet" and just like Willy's funeral "not many people came" (73). Both plays end on a nostalgic longing for a childhood world and vague, uncertain hopes for the future.

The lost daughters in *'night, Mother, Hedda Gabler,* **Crimes of the Heart,** and *The Three Sisters* are all haunted by an absent father. The mysterious fathers have no first names. Daddy Cates, General Gabler, Old Granddaddy, and the Prozorov father are shady patriarchal figures connected with death and dying. They have all trapped their daughters in a world of illusion. As the daughters double or live out the dreams of the father, they find themselves facing death or a childhood world of dreams and fragile hopes. Whether the father represents a dying aristocratic order as he does in *Hedda Gabler* and *The Three Sisters,* the shallow values of materialistic success as in **Crimes of the Heart,** or the private world of withdrawal and renunciation of family as in *'night, Mother,* the trajectory of the daughter is propelled by his absence and what he represents.

CRIMES OF THE HEART

CRITICAL COMMENTARY

Joseph Parisi (essay date July 1983)

SOURCE: A review of *Crimes of the Heart,* in *Booklist,* Vol. 79, No. 21, July, 1983, p. 1383.

[*In the following review of the published play, Parisi offers a laudatory assessment of* Crimes of the Heart.]

No wonder this play [**Crimes of the Heart**] won the Pulitzer—it has just about everything: sex, manslaughter, suicide, cat-slaying (all discreetly offstage), and abundant humor and humanity (front and center). In the grand, grotesque tradition of Southern Gothic, Henley's hilarious examination of hearth and heartstrings suggests parallels with Tennessee Williams and Flannery O'Connor. But such comparisons would be unfair, for Henley's distinct talents—though equally moving as those masters'—are more consistently comic. Her three sisters—would-be-murderer Babe, lounge-singer dropout Meg, and incipient spinster Lenny—are uniquely wacky, sensual, vulnerable, and, despite their incredible behavior, utterly believable. Foiled ambition, long-simmering frustration, and fantastic fumbling are economically combined in a complicated but cleverly managed plot, whose improbable twists are as winning as the demented dialogue. But through the controlled madness, Henley delivers several home truths about family and familial relations. Expect in-house readers to ignore any Silence, Please signs. When word gets out about this book, libraries may need extra copies.

ABUNDANCE

PRODUCTION REVIEWS

Variety (review date 10 May 1989)

SOURCE: A review of *Abundance,* in *Variety,* Vol. 335, No. 4, May 10, 1989, p. 120.

[*In the following negative review, the critic asserts that* Abundance *"is dragged down by its lack of an idea of where it's going or what it intends to accomplish."*]

Story [of **Abundance**] begins in the Wyoming Territory as two women, fresh off the train, wait to meet their future husbands. They become friends, for lack of other acquaintances, and the play follows them through a somewhat stormy 25-year relationship.

The women end up in very different situations. One marries a man who brutalizes her and turns her life into poverty-ridden despair. The other marries a kindly but timid fellow with money.

As the years go by, it's apparent that the most striking qualities about these four are their weaknesses. One man is a lout, his wife trades innocence for cynicism, the other woman has an affair with the brute, and the rich husband simply avoids reality.

In the midst of this is thrown a contrived plot twist as one of the women is captured by Indians, a rather convenient cliffhanger at the end of Act I.

It seems evident that Henley was not sure where she wanted this play to go. The styles in Act I and II vary from an ironic dark comedy to a slower-paced drama that attempts to confront some of the issues raised.

Director Ron Lagomarsino does a good job of keeping some sense of coherence to an uncohesive story, although his actors have trouble with their timing. The strongest one in the crew is Jimmie Ray Weeks as the passive husband.

Abundance is dragged down by its lack of an idea of where it's going or what it intends to accomplish. There are some fine moments and it's an interesting idea, but confusing.

John Simon (review date 12 November 1990)

SOURCE: "Yo, Kay," in *New York,* Vol. 23, No. 44, November 12, 1990, pp. 92-3.

[*In the following review, Simon offers a negative assessment of* Abundance.]

As one watches with trepidation the talented Beth Henley making a fool of herself in *Abundance,* one tries to figure out what could have led the worthy author of *Crimes of the Heart* to this malfeasance of the mind. Such a crime against one's reputation (even lesser plays by Miss Henley used to show a passel of offbeat felicities) invites critical detective work.

Knowing only what I read in the papers about Miss Henley's private life, I can nevertheless speculate that *Abundance* is somehow the playwright's own story projected onto a mythic plane, or, more precisely, the Great Plains of the once wild and fabled West. This, then, would be a final, cathartic reckoning with an ex-husband and a female friend, a story of friendship, marriage, adultery, and reciprocal betrayals, from which only the camaraderie of the two women emerges in the end, bloody, battered, but uncowed.

It is about two mail-order brides who go out West circa 1868 (i.e., swinging 1968), where they are to marry men who turn out to be bitterly disappointing. The waifish, dreamy Bess (note the similarity to "Beth") ends up with the brother of her deceased suitor, the handsome but brutally egocentric Jack, who strays from the path of straight boorishness only as far as utter swinishness. The energetic and enthusiastic pioneer woman, Macon, gets William, an elderly widower with only one peeper and looks that—even after he acquires a glass eye that he calls a present for his wife—could frighten biggish children.

The couples end up as neighbors in the Wyoming Territory, where they proceed to entangle and disentangle over a quarter century in various bizarre ways that I cannot reveal without depriving *Abundance* of its one meager asset. As in *Crimes of the Heart,* sisterhood (though here only figurative) is weird, wild, and beautiful, but instead of an impish warmth we get an overheated feyness. The play has as many reversals and unexpected reunions as Thomas Berger's *Little Big Man,* but the only strong feeling it generates is dismay, even if you are willing to suspend your disbelief six feet high.

Finally, there is the mystery of the fifth character (or wheel) in this basically four-character play, Professor Elmore Crome, a Boswell-cum-Svengali-cum-Barnum. He may perhaps be explained by the play's dedication "with love to Robert Darnell and the spirit of Darnelley Points." This, I surmise, is a professor at SMU who taught Miss Henley playwriting—albeit not spelling, else his system would be memorialized as Darnelly, not Darnelley, Points. But whatever those points were, Miss Henley has turned them against her own breast and wounded herself to the quick.

As if the play didn't have problems in abundance, Bess is enacted by Amanda Plummer, an actress with the most limited repertoire from whose constituents sanity of any kind is conspicuously missing. Miss Plummer mumbles at the flies and natters into her navel, and manages stunningly to avoid any connection with her fellow actors, her audience, her part. Conversely, Tess Harper, as Macon, is able to endow the hackneyed role of an intrepid but finally frustrated frontierswoman (periodically regenerated and refrustrated) with as much humanity as a contraption made of matchsticks and rubber bands can bear. As William, Lanny Flaherty succeeds at the neat trick of being simultaneously comic, odious, and pathetic, but not at the neater one of making it matter. As Jack, Michael Rooker is certainly handsome, arrogant, and repellent, but his inward deadness arrives a couple of hours ahead of schedule. Not having had the pleasure of knowing Mr. Darnell, I can't evaluate Keith Reddin's pipsqueaky performance, but by the time Crome makes his entrance, it's hard to give a darn.

Adrianne Lobel's scenery, a mountain view in front of which two reversible log cabins on twin turntables interact more satisfyingly than the cast, is always winning. Ron

Lagomarsino, aware of the nomadic lure of the West, directs the actors off their butts and onto their nimble feet whenever possible with much skulking, stalking, and flouncing on and off, thus providing us with a month's supply of walking, standing, and sitting bull.

James S. Torrens (review date 8 December 1990)

SOURCE: "Trying Them Out Off Broadway," in *America*, Vol. 163, No. 18, December 8, 1990, p. 453–54.

[*In the following review, Torrens provides a positive assessment of* Abundance.]

Abundance by Beth Henley, author of *Crimes of the Heart,* proves ample to the imagination, intriguing in its Victorian-homespun language ("We're to wed,""I cherish rings,""We'd drink plentiful"), and abundantly theatrical. Produced at the Manhattan Theatre Club and staged inventively by Ron Lagomarsino, its scene is set in an anti-heroic Wild West. *Abundance* beings with taped music of two fiddlers, one slightly dissonant with the other, to prepare us for a prairie saga a bit off-kilter. This fiddling recurs during every scene change—whenever one of the two halves of the stage revolves, allowing glimpses of mountain scenery on the drop at stage rear.

As *Abundance* opens, two mail-order brides await their husbands along the slat wall of a prairie main street. One, Bess Johnson (Amanda Plummer), is a bundle of anxieties; the other, Macon Hill (Tess Harper), starry-eyed and ready for adventure. To put it oddly, as the play does by design, Macon allows as she has "come out West to see the elephant." What will the husbands be like? Jack Flan (played by Murphy Guyer, an understudy) is 100-percent churl—slovenly, wasting no attention or approval on Bess his wife (who bends every effort to please), raising no finger to sustain the two of them. The other, Mister Curtis (Lanny Flaherty), with an inflamed face, a patch, and later a glass eye, revulses Macon, with her romantic fancies, despite the good will and hard work he lavishes.

Macon, living with Curtis, concentrates on making their spread prosper, even beyond what Curtis thinks it will bear. She concentrates, in other words, on abundance. The other two, reduced to penury, have to beg from them and then, when Jack burns his cabin down, take refuge with Macon and Curtis. Jack has been setting his eyes on Macon; Bess, unable to endure this menage, goes wandering out into the wild, where she supposedly perishes. End of Act One.

In Act Two the tables turn. Bess, nine years later, has been found among the Ogalallas as a squaw. An anthropologist lures her back into "civilization" by confabulating a book with her and touring her around on the lecture platform, with Jack now as her subdued lackey. Meanwhile, Macon's mismanagement and tyranny have ruined the ranch and driven Curtis off. She takes up a gypsy existence and at

the play's end, in her dire straits, is visited by Bess, the one true friend (though the play has never really shown it), whose luck too by this time is running down. The elephant, the vast promise of the West, abundance, has proved illusory.

CONTROL FREAKS

PRODUCTION REVIEWS

Tom Jacobs (review date 9 August 1993)

SOURCE: A review of *Control Freaks*, in *Variety*, Vol. 351, No. 13, August 9, 1993, p. 35.

[*In the following mixed review, Jacobs maintains that* Control Freaks *"is often as darkly hilarious as it is startling."*]

Control Freaks is almost surely the first R-rated play to use the services of Flying by Foy. Beth Henley's latest comedy, a mixture of sexual perversity and serial acrobatics, is often as darkly hilarious as it is startling.

Henley falters in the final scenes, when she unwisely attempts to shift the mood radically and explain her characters' bizarre behavior. But the play contains wonderful writing, and the production proves she is an excellent director of her own work.

As the play opens, Carl Willard (Bill Pullman) has just brought home his fourth wife, Betty (Carol Kane). Her presence annoys his sister, known only as Sister (Holly Hunter).

Carl, whose surface attempts to embody coolness hide his increasing desperation to accomplish something—anything—before he gets much older, wants to buy a nearby building and open a furniture store.

To finance the deal, he figures he can convince Sister to give up her inheritance. He assumes he can get the rest from Paul Casper (Wayne Pere), the owner of the building and a man he sees as a potential husband to Sister. Sister doesn't want to part with her money, but she does like the idea of getting married.

This quiet woman is suffering from the mother of all identity crises; she talks to herself in a series of different voices late at night and spends each day in a different wig in an apparent attempt to find her long-repressed personality.

The four-way battle for control over the group's destiny provides dramatic thrust as well as entertainment value as the characters find creative ways to humiliate one another.

These involve sex games, glasses of wine laced with rat poison and—in the play's best scene—an insincere marriage proposal from Paul to Sister. Her transparent—and increasingly traumatic—attempts to appear not too eager are extremely amusing.

Hunter gives a virtuoso—not to mention brave—performance, brilliantly embodying Sister's many moods and, in the less-effective-than-expected finale, strapping on a harness and twisting about above the audience.

Each actor uses body language superbly in this physical play.

Kane brings an appropriate hard edge to her character's ditziness, while Pullman and Pere play two distinct types of slimy men to perfection.

Sets, costumes and lighting are adequate without reaching the inspired level of the acting.

BETH HENLEY: FOUR PLAYS

CRITICAL COMMENTARY

English Studies (review date May 1994)

SOURCE: A review of *Four Plays,* in *English Studies,* Vol. 75, No. 3, May, 1994, p. 259–61.

[*In the following review, the critic offers a laudatory review of the plays collected in* Four Plays.]

Four Plays, by Beth Henley, is a collection of plays written since *Crimes of the Heart* (1981) and demonstrates that she may well be the best dramatist now writing in America. Chekhov has long been the inspiration for American dramatists and actors, but Henley develops his legacy in original directions of her own. In *The Wake of Jamey Foster* (1983) the bizarre decision of his white-trash mother to have an open-coffin wake in the living room of his house focusses the contemplation of a failed marriage and a failed life. 'And now he's really gone' says his wife, 'He's out of the whole deal; and I don't even know what we felt for each other. Stupid. Lord . . .'. The presence of the body in the house unleashes all kinds of fascinating responses in the various members of the family. Henley's humour softens horror and suffering, but never obscures it. She shows the power of love between people and the importance of small moments of fellow-feeling even between enemies. She puts most faith in friendship, its staying power. *The Miss Firecracker Contest* (1985) reveals depths in even the most objectionable characters and the enormous toughness in some of life's apparent losers, particularly women in old-fashioned Southern towns. Brutal conditions cannot destory their

victims as long as emotional support comes from somewhere. Henley is not an advocate for any social cause. Ugly people are simply out there doing destructive things and people manage to survive in spite of them—a miracle she uncovers again and again. It is a pleasure to turn to a writer whose vision is so distinctive. Her dialogue is her own stylization of the way people talk, as every original dramatist's is, but it gets very close to the way people communicate, to the small, symbolic phrases and gestures which define our place in the world or else drive us off it. The last two, most recent, plays, *The Lucky Spot* (1987), and *Abundance* (1990) are stylized historical-psychological reconstructions set in the 1930s and in the 70s and 80s of the last century. The first tells the story of a crazy reunion between a man and the jailed wife who has ruined his life. The second is the story of two women who have answered advertisements for brides in the American West. One of them gets abducted by Indians and she subsequently makes capital out of this by contributing to the genocidal anti-Indian propaganda which accompanied the settlement of the West. . . .

IMPOSSIBLE MARRIAGE

PRODUCTION REVIEWS

John Simon (review date 26 October 1998)

SOURCE: "The Boys in the Sand," in *New York,* Vol. 31, No. 41, October 26, 1998, pp. 82-3.

[*In the following excerpt, Simon deems* Impossible Marriage *ditzy and uninteresting.*]

The program for Beth Henley's *Impossible Marriage* says, "The play is in three parts and is performed without intermission." "Three parts," something you might say about the division of Gaul, is grandiose nonsense: This 90-minute scribble is in three *scenes.* But Henley's playwriting career *is* in three parts. The first was fey and sort of likable; the second flaky and fairly exasperating. Now we are in the third, which is bananas. Totally.

Even the characters' names are ditsy. We are in the garden of a country house near Savannah owned by Kandall (not Kendall) Kingsley. Her daughter Floral (not Flora) looks to be about twelve months pregnant, and is married to the supposed philanderer Jonsey (pronounced Jonesy) Whitman, who keeps announcing how handsome he is and says he has never slept with his wife or anyone else. He tells her, "I thought you knew my attention to others was merely to make *us* appear normal." Floral's younger sister, Pandora, is getting married to a famous, much older foreign writer, Edvard Lunt: The *v* makes him Norwegian, as in Grieg or Munch; the Lunt, Swedish, as in Alfred. His accent, however, is Slavic. His crazy son is named Sidney and looks like a nerdy yeshiva boy. There is also the Reverend Jonathan Larence (not Lawrence).

In word and action, they are all space cadets, nay, space generals or marshals. About the goldfish she starved, Pandora says, "I do not understand why I should throw out a fish just because it's dead." "Forgive me," says the entering Sidney to Kandall. "For what?" "For being in your line of vision." He is sure that his mother will commit suicide if Edvard marries Pandora: "After Mummy kills herself, I will take my own life with an unsharpened hatchet," and his seven siblings will follow suit. "I allowed mosquitoes to suck my blood with impunity," the self-unfrocked Larence declares. "In attempting to follow your amorphous train of thought, I seem to have derailed," Edvard tells Floral, something we can all empathize with.

Insofar as it is about anything, the play is about whether Pandora wants to marry Edvard or not, will marry him or won't. And about who is the father of Floral's unborn child that may never get born, given Floral's propensity for going off to "roll down the hills," which with her ballooning shape must come easy. The former man of God, on the other hand, favors lying in ditches for repentance. If you suspect the two are cut from the same (nonclerical) cloth, you are more right than you realize. But whatever you may think of the rest of the play, you will love Pandora's wedding dress: blue, sheer, with enormous gossamer wings attached to her shoulders and wrists.

Holly Hunter, who has made a career of portraying Henley heroines, perpetrates yet another one here. Like a true alter ego, she has progressed along the same path to loopiness as her author. She attitudinizes, struts, stomps, contorts, collapses, utters weird sounds, and grimaces clownishly, and to make it even more unbearable, reeks of "Aren't I the cutest?" The others, especially the always appealing Lois Smith, do the best they can, although Gretchen Cleevely's ingenue antics weigh heavily on the stomach. She may well be the next Holly Hunter.

This coagulated whimsy has been staged operatically by Stephen Wadsworth, so that countless lines are spoken out at the audience by actors not looking at one another, perhaps to keep themselves from giggling. The production is handsomely designed, but not enough so as to hold the interest for 90 minutes.

FURTHER READING

Criticism

Getz, Ricki R. Review of *Crimes of the Heart. Kliatt* 17, No. 3 (Spring 1983): 20.
    Positive assessment of *Crimes of the Heart.*

Paulk, J. Sara. Review of *The Debutante Ball. Library Journal* 116, No. 17 (15 October 1991): 80.
    Recommends the book version of Henley's play.

Tischler, N. Review of *The Debutante Ball. Choice* 29, No. 8 (April 1992): 1225.
    Mixed assessment of *The Debutante Ball.*

Review of *Abundance. Variety* 341, No. 4 (5 November 1990): 84.
    Mixed review of the play, contending that "the lack of overall pizzazz and a satisfactory dramatic resolution makes it unlikely the play would make the grade with a larger Broadway audience."

Additional coverage of Henley's life and career is contained in the following sources published by the Gale Group: *Contemporary Authors,* **Vol. 107;** *Contemporary Authors New Revision Series,* **Vols. 32, 73;** *Contemporary Authors Bibliographical Series,* **Vol. 3;** *Contemporary Literary Criticism,* **Vol. 23;** *Dictionary of Literary Biography Yearbook,* **Vol. 86;** *DISCovering Authors 3.0; DISCovering Authors Modules: Dramatists, Most-studied Authors; Drama Criticism,* **Vol. 6;** *Drama for Students,* **Vol. 2;** **and** *Major 20th-Century Writers,* **Vols. 1, 2.**

Neil Simon
1927-

(Full name Marvin Neil Simon) American comedy writer, dramatist, and screenwriter

INTRODUCTION

Neil Simon's career as a writer of comedy has been marked by a series of successes which have turned his name into a recognizable theatrical commodity. Simon began his early work during the golden age of television in the 1950s for weekly programs featuring Sid Cesar, Jackie Gleason, Red Buttons, and Phil Silvers. Simon continued his long career as a Broadway playwright with a string of hits season after season, to work in Hollywood writing original screenplays and adapting his stage plays for film. The hallmark of his comedy from the simpler, lighthearted early plays to the later darker ones has been the comic presentation of perplexing and even painful experience.

BIOGRAPHICAL INFORMATION

Neil Simon was born in New York City, in the Bronx, into what would now be called a dysfunctional family. His father, Irving Simon, was a garment salesman who regularly abandoned the family for long stretches. His woe-beset mother, Mamie Simon, worked at Gimbel's department store in order to support the family. Simon graduated from DeWitt Clinton High School at sixteen, entered New York University in the U.S. Army Air Force reserve program, and was sent by the Army to Colorado where he attended the University of Denver. After he returned from the army in 1946, Simon got a job at the New York offices of Warner Brothers, where his older brother Danny worked. When they heard that Goodman Ace, the comedy writer and radio personality was looking for material, the brothers submitted some of their work and were hired to write for him. For the next fifteen years Simon wrote for the foremost radio and television comedians and contributed sketches for Broadway reviews like *New Faces*. In 1961, with the success of *Come Blow Your Horn,* Simon began a career as the most commercially successful playwright in Broadway history. Simon also regularly adapts his plays for film and has written a number of original screenplays.

MAJOR WORKS

Had he never written anything after 1961, Simon would still be remembered as a major contributor to enormously

successful television programs which were watched weekly by millions, and for which he won several Emmy Awards. In 1961, however, his play *Come Blow Your Horn* inaugurated a second immensely successful career as a Broadway writer who has enjoyed a record number of hits. Among them are *The Odd Couple* (1965) about two divorced men who share an apartment and recapitulate with each other the problems that destroyed their marriages, and *The Prisoner of Second Avenue* (1971) which is about the terrors of living in New York City. Additionally, Simon penned the smashes *The Sunshine Boys* (1972) about aging vaudevillians and *The Brighton Beach Trilogy*—*Brighton Beach Memoirs* (1982), *Biloxi Blues* (1984), *Broadway Bound* (1986)—which are all drawn from his family life and passage from home. With *Lost in Yonkers* (1991), Simon won both a Pulitzer Prize and a Drama Desk Award. Simon also won a Tony for *Biloxi Blues* in 1985.

CRITICAL RECEPTION

Although Simon's work at first was neglected by serious critics, and he was often considered a gag writer or a writer of situation comedy for Broadway, most of Simon's plays have been box office smashes. Much of Simon's work earns favorable reviews from daily newspaper reviewers and often draws audiences in record numbers. After his initial success with lighter comedies, Simon began to write plays with a darker edge. Critics and audiences deemed some of these like *The Gingerbread Lady* (1970), *God's Favorite* (1974), and especially *Fools* (1981) as weaker than Simon's regular contribution. Simon himself closed *Jake's Women* (1992) the first time around before it got to Broadway. But he came back even stronger, writing plays which more deeply explored pain and conflict, finding laughter inside adversity, with the autobiographical *Brighton Beach Trilogy,* and the award winning *Lost in Yonkers* (1991).

PRINCIPAL WORKS

Plays

Come Blow Your Horn [with Danny Simon] 1961
Little Me [adaptor; based on the novel by Patrick Dennis] (musical) 1962
Barefoot in the Park 1963
The Odd Couple [revised 1985] 1965
The Star-Spangled Girl 1966
Sweet Charity [adaptor; from the screenplay *The Nights of Cabiria* by Federico Fellini] 1966
Plaza Suite 1968
Promises, Promises [adaptor; from the screenplay *The Apartment* by Billy Wilder and I. A. L. Diamond] 1968
Last of the Red Hot Lovers 1969
The Gingerbread Lady 1970
The Prisoner of Second Avenue 1971
The Sunshine Boys 1972
The Good Doctor 1973
God's Favorite 1974
California Suite 1976
Chapter Two 1977
They're Playing Our Song 1978
I Ought to Be in Pictures 1980
Fools 1981
Brighton Beach Memoirs 1982
Biloxi Blues 1984
Broadway Bound 1986
Rumors 1988
Lost in Yonkers (musical comedy) 1991
Jake's Women 1992
Laughter on the 23rd Floor (comedy) 1993
London Suite 1995

Screenplays

The Out-of-Towners 1970
The Heartbreak Kid [adaptor; from the short story by Bruce Jay Friedman] 1972
Murder by Death 1976
The Goodbye Girl 1977
The Cheap Detective 1978
Seems Like Old Times 1980
Only When I Laugh 1981
Max Dugan Returns 1983
The Lonely Guy [with Ed Weinberger and Stan Daniels] 1984
The Slugger's Wife 1985
The Marrying Man 1991

Memoirs

Rewrites 1996

*Simon also adapted these plays for film.

AUTHOR COMMENTARY

Jackson R. Bryer with Neil Simon (interview date 1991)

"An Interview with Neil Simon," in *Studies in American Drama, 1945-Present*, Vol. 6, No. 2, 1991, pp. 153-76.

[*In the following interview, Simon discusses his plays, his development as a playwright, how he writes, Hollywood, the role of the actor, and his disinclination to be a director.*]

A critic has described Neil Simon as "relentlessly prolific." By virtually any accepted standard, he is the most successful playwright in the history of the American theatre. In thirty years, his 26 Broadway shows (including revivals of **Little Me** and **The Odd Couple**) have played a total of well over 15,000 performances. When **The Star-Spangled Girl** opened in December 1966, Simon had four Broadway productions running simultaneously. Despite this popular success and general critical approval, Simon did not win his first Tony Award for Best Play until 1985 (**Biloxi Blues**), although he had won the Tony for Best Author of a Play for **The Odd Couple** in 1965. His most recent play, **Lost in Yonkers,** won both the Pulitzer Prize for Drama and the Tony Award for Best Play in 1991.

Simon's Broadway productions include the plays **Come Blow Your Horn** (1961), **Barefoot in the Park** (1963), **The Odd Couple** (1965), **The Star-Spangled Girl** (1966), **Plaza Suite** (1968), **Last of the Red-Hot Lovers** (1969), **The Gingerbread Lady** (1970), **The Prisoner of Second Avenue** (1971), **The Sunshine Boys** (1972), **The Good**

Doctor (1973), *God's Favorite* (1974), *California Suite* (1977), *Chapter Two* (1977), *I Ought to Be in Pictures* (1980), *Fools* (1981), *Brighton Beach Memoirs* (1983), *Biloxi Blues* (1985), *Broadway Bound* (1986), *Rumors* (1988), and *Lost in Yonkers* (1991). His 1990 play, *Jake's Women,* closed before reaching New York. He has written the books for the musicals *Little Me* (1962), *Sweet Charity* (1966), *Promises, Promises* (1968), and *They're Playing Our Song* (1979). Besides the adaptations of several of his plays for the movies, his screenplays are *The Out-of-Towners, The Heartbreak Kid, Murder By Death, The Goodbye Girl, The Cheap Detective, Seems Like Old Times, Only When I Laugh, Max Dugan Returns, The Slugger's Wife,* and *The Marrying Man.*

Born, like George M. Cohan, on the Fourth of July, in 1927 in the Bronx, New York, he grew up there and in the Washington Heights section of Manhattan with his only sibling, his brother Danny. He early received the nickname "Doc" for his ability to mimic the family doctor. When their parents, Irving (a garment salesman) and Mamie (who often worked at department stores to support the family during her husband's frequent absences), divorced, the two boys went to live with relatives in Forest Hills, Queens, and Simon attended high school there and at De-Witt Clinton in Manhattan. After brief military service at the end of World War II, he worked for several years with his brother as a comedy writer for radio and television. In 1953, he married Joan Baim, a dancer, who died of cancer in 1973. His second wife was actress Marsha Mason; he is now married to Diane Lander. He has two grown daughters and a step-daughter.

This interview was conducted on January 23, 1991, in Simon's suite at the Willard Hotel in Washington, DC, while he was preparing *Lost in Yonkers* (then playing at Washington's National Theatre) for its Broadway opening. The interview was transcribed by Drew Eisenhauer.

You always say that very early on you knew you wanted to be a playwright.

I wanted to be a writer very early on. It's not quite true about the playwrighting thing. I started writing the first play when I was thirty and got it on when I was thirty-three, so that's fairly old to be starting as a playwright.

Most young people want to write poetry or want to write novels. When you knew you wanted to be a writer, was it always writing plays that you wanted to do?

I started out with different aims and ambitions. I grew up in the world of radio so the first couple of jobs I had were in radio and then television. I think I was setting my sights for film. I'm not quite sure when I decided to do plays. I know when I actually did so which was after years of working on *Your Show of Shows* with Sid Caesar, and *The Bilko Show.* I said I didn't want to spend the rest of my life doing this—writing for someone else—I wanted to do my own work. So I started writing the first play, *Come*

Blow Your Horn, and it took me almost three years to do the twenty-some complete new versions before I got it on. When I did get it on, I said, "My God, three years!" and I was exhausted. I had only taken other little jobs just to make a living, since I had a wife and two children. But once the play hit, *Come Blow Your Horn* subsidized the next one which was a musical, *Little Me,* and that subsidized writing *Barefoot in the Park,* and then I was making enough money so I could do this full-time.

So, in a sense, your playwrighting grew out of writing for TV and radio in that writing for TV and radio was basically working within a dramatic form? That's what really led to the playwrighting.

Right. I started off just writing jokes for newspaper columns and things and then working on *Your Show of Shows* and *Bilko. Your Show of Shows* was writing sketches and *Bilko* was like a half-hour movie; so I was learning the dramatic form. Then I worked for about two years with Max Liebman, who was the producer of *Your Show of Shows,* doing specials. It was a very good education for me because we were updating pretty famous musical books of the past—*Best Foot Forward* and *Knickerbocker Holiday.* We would throw the book out completely and use the score; we would sort of follow the story line but use our own dialogue. So I was able to step in the footprints of previous writers and learn about the construction from them.

What was the purpose of those? Were they for television?

Yes. We did about twenty of them, two shows a month. One show would be a book show. A couple of them were originals; one was *The Adventures of Marco Polo,* and we used the music of Rimsky-Korsakoff. So I was really learning a lot about construction. I had made a few abortive attempts to write plays during that time—one with another writer on the *The Bilko Show*—and it was going nowhere. I always had my summers off because in those days we did 39 shows a year on television in consecutive weeks and you had something like thirteen weeks off in the summer in which I would try to write plays; and I would say, "Wow, this is tough!" Finally, I went to California to do a television special—for Jerry Lewis of all people. I had quit *Your Show of Shows*—it had finally gone off the air—and so I was free-lancing. I went out there for six weeks. In about ten days I wrote the whole show and I said to Jerry Lewis, "What'll I do, I've got all this time?" He said, "I've got other things to do. Just do what you want until we go into rehearsal." And I started to write *Come Blow Your Horn,* which was almost a satirical or a farcical look at my upbringing with my parents. I was on the way but it took three years to do that, as I said.

As a child, and as a young adult, did you read plays and did you go to the theatre?

I went to the theatre. I read quite a good deal. I went to the library; I used to take out about three books a week, but they weren't about the theatre. It wasn't until I was about fourteen or fifteen that I saw my very first play, *Native Son,* the Richard Wright book and play.

A strange thing for a fourteen or fifteen year-old to go see, wasn't it?

There was a local theatre in upper Manhattan, in Washington Heights where I lived. It was called the Audubon Theatre. It used to be a movie house and then they used it for acts—sort of vaudeville acts but I wouldn't really call it vaudeville. They started doing that all over New York at the time when the theatre was truly flourishing. You not only played Broadway, you could go to Brooklyn and Manhattan and the Bronx and there were theatres that did their versions of plays that had closed on Broadway. So I went to this local theatre and saw *Native Son* and was mesmerized by what the theatre could do. I had also acted in plays in public school and in junior high school, so I had a little glimpse of that; but acting is a lot different from writing. I think that slowly, as my parents started to take me to the theatre more, mostly musicals (I remember seeing *Oklahoma!*; it was—for its time—so innovative and so original), in the back of my mind I thought about that. But all during those years I was working with my brother and I thought that the only way to write a play was to do it by yourself, because one needed an individual point of view. Even if we were to write about our own family background, his point of view would be completely different from mine, and so it would get diminished somehow and watered down. When I wrote **Come Blow Your Horn,** I never even told him about it. It meant that I would have to make a break with him after ten years of writing together. The break was pretty traumatic. It was worse than leaving home because one expects that, but this was breaking up a partnership that he started because he was looking for a partner. He doesn't like to work by himself, and he always noticed and encouraged the sense of humor I had. I didn't have a sense of construction; he had that, and I was wonderful with lines and with the comedy concepts. Finally, when I did **Come Blow Your Horn,** I knew I had to step away. Partly I think it had to do with my being married; I began to feel my own oats and wanted the separation.

Can you speak at all about plays or playwrights that impressed you, influenced you, early or late?

Well, it was any good playwright. I didn't have favorites. In terms of comedy, I guess maybe Moss Hart and George S. Kaufman. A play that neither one of them wrote, Garson Kanin's *Born Yesterday,* I thought was a wonderful comedy, and I liked *Mr. Roberts* too; but I was as intrigued by the dramas as I was by the comedies. It wasn't until sometime later that I decided what I wanted to write was drama and tell it as comedy. I was such an avid theatre-goer, especially when I first married Joan. You could go to the theatre then twice a week and not catch the whole season on Broadway and even off-Broadway. *Streetcar Named Desire* probably made the greatest impression on

me, that and *Death of a Salesman.* These are not comedies. Although I knew I was not up to writing a drama as yet, I thought when I wrote something it would be from a comedy point of view.

If you could have written one play that was written by somebody else, what would that play be?

The question has been asked a lot and I generally say *A Streetcar Named Desire.* I have a certain affinity for that play; so does everyone else in America for that matter, I think. *Death of a Salesman* I thought was maybe the best American play I've ever seen—but it lacked humor. The humor that I saw in *Streetcar Named Desire* came out of a new place for humor. It came out of the character of Stanley Kowalski saying, "I have this lawyer acquaintance of mine" and talking about the Napoleonic Code. It was the way he talked that got huge laughs, and I knew that this was not comedy; it was character comedy and that's what I aimed for later on. If I were able to write a play, an American play, I would say it would be *Streetcar.*

The same quality is present in The Glass Menagerie, *too. That play also has some very funny moments in it, but they grow very organically out of Amanda and out of her situation.*

Yes. Even in Eugene O'Neill, who really lacks humor, I found humor in *Long Day's Journey,* in James Tyrone's meanness with money—turning out the light bulbs all the time and being so cheap. That was a play that I said to myself when I saw it, "I could never write that but I would love to write like that," to write my own *Long Day's Journey.* I have an oblique sense of humor; I see comedy—or humor, not comedy (there's a difference)—in almost everything that I've gone through in life, I'd say, with the exception of my wife's illness and death. Humor has become so wide open today that it's almost uncensored on television. It's all part of the game now. As I said, *Long Day's Journey* impressed me very much early on, and the writings of August Wilson impress me very much today. There's great humor in them and great sense of character and story-telling; it's almost old-fashioned playwrighting, in a way. There are not many playwrights who write like he does.

I think some of the humor in O'Neill comes from the Irish quality in those plays, the whole Sean O'Casey tradition of Irish drama where the humor and the seriousness are very closely juxtaposed; and I wonder whether there isn't something similar in the Jewish idiom, with humor coming out of serious situations. Do you feel that is a factor in your own plays?

I'm sure it is, but I find it a very difficult thing to talk about because I'm unaware of anything being particularly Jewish. This present play, **Lost in Yonkers,** is about a Jewish family but rarely is it mentioned or brought up. But the humor comes out of the Jewish culture as I know it. It's fatalistic; everything bad is going to happen. In the opening scene, the father talks about his troubles with his wife dying, being at a loss about what to do with the boys and so worried about how they're going to look well and be presented well to the grandmother. It's all out of fear; there's no sense of confidence, because he knows what he's up against. The mother is, I think, more German than Jew, because she was brought up in Germany, and her culture is German. So one doesn't ever get a picture that she was brought up in a Jewish home in which they paid attention to the services. I would doubt very much if they were Orthodox Jews. But it's there someplace, and it's so deeply embedded in me and so inherent in me that I am unaware of its quality. When I write something I don't think, "Oh, this is Jewish." At one time I thought I did, that I needed Jewish actors, but I found that people like Jack Lemmon or George C. Scott or Maureen Stapleton were equally at home with my material and they gave great performances. I rarely work with Jewish actors now; there are very few of them in *Lost in Yonkers.* However, in making the film of *Brighton Beach Memoirs,* when we did not get Jewish women to play the mother and the sister, it didn't sound right. Blythe Danner and Judith Ivey, as wonderful as they are, did not sound right. To the gentile ear it may not sound wrong, but still the audiences are aware that something is not quite organic. They don't know what it is; they can't name it. The difference came when Linda Lavin played in *Broadway Bound* and was right on the button and had the sense of truth. I think it's true too with O'Neill. He doesn't have to have Irish actors but Jewish actors playing O'Neill would have to have a very wide range to be able to do it well.

You have always said you stopped writing for TV because you wanted control, because you wanted to be on your own, not to have network executives and ad men running your creative life. But didn't the same sort of thing start to happen after a bit when you started to write for the stage, where producers like Saint-Subber wanted you to write a particular kind of play?

Saint used terms that no longer exist; they come from the turn of the century. He talked about "the carriage trade," those people, not necessarily Jewish, maybe New York society or wealthier people, who we wanted to appeal to as well. When I wrote *Barefoot in the Park* I think in an earlier version I made them a Jewish family without saying so. Saint said stay away from that because we're going to miss the carriage trade, so to speak; so maybe I was aware of it. Certainly it was in *The Odd Couple,* with Oscar Madison, only because Walter Matthau played it. I was aware of that in the beginning and then gradually got away from it until I got specifically Jewish when I was writing the autobiographical plays. In *Chapter Two,* something made me lean toward an actor like Judd Hirsch playing the leading character George because I knew the cadences and the attitudes came from me, so I thought that character had to be Jewish but I didn't call him Jewish. In these plays—I'm talking about "The Trilogy" (*Brighton Beach Memoirs, Biloxi Blues,* and *Broadway Bound*) and about *Lost in Yonkers*—they are Jewish families, you can't

get away from it. Some plays are just not; *Barefoot in the Park* was not necessarily at all. *The Odd Couple* has proven not to be because it's the most universal play I've written. They do it in Japan as often as they do it here now. It's done all over the world constantly because it is such a universal situation. Two people living together cannot get along all the time and it made it unique that it was two men. It seemed like such a simple idea that you thought surely someone would have written a play about it, but no one ever did up until that time. It was the idea or concept that made it so popular and then the execution.

Which of your plays gave you the most trouble and which was the easiest?

Rumors gave me the most trouble because of the necessities of farce. One has to get the audience to dispel their sense of truth, and they must believe in the premise even though we know it's about three feet off the ground. It has to be filled with surprises, and it has to move at a breakneck pace. People have to be in jeopardy constantly; the minute the jeopardy stops and they can sit back and relax, it's like a train that runs out of steam. And it has to be funny every minute. It was like constructing a murder mystery, an Agatha Christie mystery in which you are kept in suspense, only it had to go at a much greater pace than any of Agatha Christie's stories. I wanted to do it because I wanted to try the form. In a sense I was buoyed by watching an interview with Peter Shaffer, whom I respect enormously. I think he's a wonderful playwright. *Amadeus* is one of my favorite plays, again a play with a great concept—an original one—about professional jealousy. The interviewer said, "Why did you write *Black Comedy*?" And he said, "Well, it was a farce, and everyone wants to write one farce in their life." I had tried bits and pieces of it; the third act of *Plaza Suite,* with the father and mother trying to get the girl out of the locked bathroom, is a farce. But it only ran for thirty minutes and it wasn't a full-blown piece, so I wanted to try that. That was the most difficult. None of them come easy.

What happened with *Brighton Beach* was interesting. I wrote thirty-five pages and stopped and put it away for nine years; and when I came back to it, somehow the play had been written in my head over those nine years without thinking of it so I wrote it completely from beginning to end without stopping. But that's only the beginning of the process. You can never say any play is written easily because you write it once, and then you write it again, and then you write it again; then you have a reading of it, and then you go into rehearsal in which you write it ten more times. So they all present their difficulties. But I can't think of any one play where it was really easy, where I didn't have a difficult time with it.

Have your writing methods changed over the years? You say you wrote **Come Blow Your Horn** *twenty times. Is that still true, that you write a play over and over again, or do you find that you're getting better at it?*

If I do write it over and over and over again, it means that the play has some serious flaw. I wrote *Jake's Women* seven times, almost from beginning to end, before I put it on the stage; so I never really corrected the serious flaw. With this play, *Lost in Yonkers,* the first version was fairly close to what we have now. I did two more versions before we went into rehearsal but I had less trouble with the construction of the play. It just seemed to lead to the right thing. It has to do with the beginnings of the play, with how each of the characters is introduced and how each of them has his own problem. Manny Azenberg, our producer, has always said that if I reach page thirty-five it is almost always a "go" project. Sometimes I get to page twenty-five or so, and I start to look ahead and say, "What are you going to write about? What else could possibly happen?" I've come up with some wonderful beginnings of situations and don't always know where they're going but sort of know what they're going to be.

Billy Wilder, the director, once said to me (he was talking about a film but I think it applies to a play as well), "If you have four great scenes, you've got a hit." He says if you don't have those great scenes then you're not going to make it. When I wrote *The Sunshine Boys,* the whole play came to me at once in a sense. Since I fashioned it somewhat (even though I didn't know them) after the careers of Smith and Dale, and got the premise that they had not spoken to each other in eleven years and then they were being offered this job to work together and didn't want to speak to each other, I said, well, they've got to get together. That's the first funny interesting conflict, then the rehearsal, then the actual doing of the show on the air. I knew that they could cause great conflict and problems with each other, and then there would be the denouement of finally getting together. I said there's those four scenes. I don't think about that all the time, but that time I knew where it was going—there was a play there—so I sat down with some sense of confidence.

Others just unfold themselves. When I was writing *Lost in Yonkers,* I knew I had these four characters in my mind. I had witnessed somebody who has this dysfunction of not being able to breathe properly and I never thought about using it; but it suddenly came to mind in this dysfunctional family which the mother has created. When you write you're always trying to catch up with your thoughts. They're ahead of you, like the carrot in front of the rabbit or the horse. If it's always there ahead of you then you know that each day that you go to work you will be able to write something. It's awful when you are writing a play and you get to page forty and you come to your office in the morning and say, "Well, what do I write today? Where does it go?" I want to leave it the night before saying to myself, "I know what that next scene is tomorrow" and I look forward to the next day.

How do you get started on a play? Do you usually start with an idea, or with a character?

First it starts with a desire, to write a play, and then the next desire is what kind of play do you want to write. When I finished *Broadway Bound,* I said I do not want to

write another play like this right now. I've done a play that in degrees develops more seriously because I thought that *Broadway Bound* dealt more truthfully with my family and with the kind of writing I wanted to do than anything I had done in the past. I did not have an idea for the next one, and so sometimes you just play around with an idea. I said I wanted to write a farce, and I just sat down and thought of the opening premise. It literally started with how it looked. Most farces are about wealthy people. They're not about people who are poor because their lives are in conflict all the time. They must be satirical; you want to make jabs at them socially. These were all fairly prominent people, and I wanted them all to show up in black tie and their best gowns because I knew whatever it was that I was going to write they would be a mess at the end of the evening—either emotionally or physically—with their clothes tattered and torn. I thought of it as a mystery. I had no idea where it was going. The host had attempted suicide and was not able to tell them what happened, the hostess wasn't there, and there was no food: that's all I knew. I had read (I read a great deal of biographies of writers and artists) that Georges Simenon wrote most of his murder mysteries without knowing who was going to be murdered and who the murderer was. He picked a place, a set of situations, just something that intrigued him. I think almost anyone can sit down and write the first five pages of a murder mystery because you don't have to leave any clues. You just think of some wild situation that sounds interesting. It's only the really great mystery writers who know where to take it. *The Thin Man* is one of the most complicated books I've ever read. I don't think Dashiell Hammett is given enough credit. That's really literature, that book. What was your original question?

How you got the ideas for plays.

I never really can remember the moment, maybe with a few exceptions. *The Odd Couple* came out of watching my brother and the man he was living with at that time. They had both just gotten divorced, had decided to live together to cut down expenses, and they were dating girls. I said what an incredible idea for a play. *Barefoot* came out of my own experiences with my wife. Strangely enough, *Barefoot in the Park* started in Switzerland. The first version of it—this really happened—was when my wife and I went on our honeymoon to St. Moritz, Switzerland, met an elderly couple, and decided to go hiking with them. My wife then—Joan died in '73—was a wonderful athlete and she and the older man were practically jumping up this mountain while his wife and I staggered behind, and I was angry at Joan for being able to jump like a goat up this mountain. Then I realized that it had too exotic an atmosphere and I wanted to locate it in a place where one could relate to it more. I thought about that tiny apartment that we actually lived in that was five flights up and had a shower and no bath; it had a hole in the skylight in which it snowed. So I used all of those things. You don't know that when you're sitting down to write it. It's an adventure; it's really jumping into this big swimming pool and hoping there's going to be water when you hit.

How has the experience of writing musicals and writing films been different and why do you continue to do them when you don't need to? Why have you continued to write in collaborative situations and seemingly against the whole idea of wanting to be independent?

I do it because I think I have to keep writing all the time. Each year I want to be doing something. I wouldn't know how to take a year off and do nothing. I would feel it a wasted year of my life, unless I did something else productive that I love—but I haven't found anything. I think that even at this age I'm still growing and that I want to do as much as I can before I can't do it anymore. Again, I think, what do you want to do following what you have just done? I was about to start another play that I had in mind but I still haven't quite licked where it's going and I'm not ready to do it. It's not that I won't have anything on next year, but I won't have anything to work on. So I'm toying with the idea of doing a musical now which is like a breather, even though the musical is a much more collaborative and a much more debilitating effort than anything else in the theatre could be. The movies have been in the past—some of them—such good experiences that I was usually eager to do one again. The movie industry has changed enormously. I did ten films with Ray Stark. Nine of them were successful and one was terrible. But for all of them, Ray Stark was the producer; he always got me a good director, always got a good cast, and was really the blocking back for me, the runner, with the studio. I almost never had to deal with the studio. This last experience I had, *The Marrying Man,* was enough to make me say I never want to do a film again.

I did have good experiences doing *The Heartbreak Kid* and *The Goodbye Girl,* even *Murder By Death. Murder By Death* is not a great work of art but it's great fun. In my reveries I used to wish that I were older in the Thirties and in the early Forties and could write for Cary Grant and Humphrey Bogart and Jimmy Stewart. One of the great thrills I had in Hollywood was when I met some of these people and they said, "Gee, I wish I could have done a picture with you!" When Cary Grant said that to me, I said, "Wow, what I've missed!" Those actors who were, I think, in some ways (the best of them) superior to some of the actors we have today, carried none of the weight that the actors do today. Now even a small star, a starlet, has something to say about the picture. I will deal with the director always, with the producer seldom but sometimes, the studio hardly ever, and with an actor never. I will listen to an actor's inabilities to find what he needs to accomplish in a part and try to accommodate that, but not because he wants to be portrayed in a certain way. On the stage Manny Azenberg and I must have fired eight to ten actors over the years because we found they were not fulfilling what we wanted. An actor's training is mostly with dead playwrights, so when they do the classics they

don't expect any rewrites. I want them to feel the same thing. I rewrite more than anybody I know; I just do it over and over. I'm still giving pages and new lines on *Lost in Yonkers* and will do it until we open. But they'll always come to you and say, "I'm having trouble with this line. Can you think if there's another way of me saying it that makes it more comfortable?" I'll say, "I'll rewrite it if it makes it more comfortable for the character, not for you." When they understand that then we can find a way to do it.

To give you a really good example of the difference between films and plays for me, a director of a play will come to me and say, "What do you think about this section? I'm not so sure that this is working. Do you think you could find something else?" And I'll either agree with him or disagree with him and write it or rewrite it, but he does nothing about it until I rewrite it. He'll even come to me about a sentence or a couple of words. That play is sold to the films, and he becomes the director. He shoots the film, then invites me to the first cut, and three major scenes are missing. I say, "What happened to those scenes?" He says, "They didn't work for me." It now has become his script; it's not mine anymore. And the only way to control that is to direct your own films which I don't want to do. I'm not a director. I don't want to spend all that time. I love writing. I hate directing. I hate hanging around the rehearsals. I do it when I'm working and I need to do something, but just to stand there and watch—I don't want to do it. So I do the films, but I'm not really very happy with them. Musicals are something else, because when you work with some of the best people (I worked with Bob Fosse a number of times and I thought he was really a genius; I worked with Michael Bennett a few times, even a little bit on *Chorus Line*), that's great fun. That's like being invited to the party, so you just do it.

You talk about rewriting. When you're readying a play like **Lost in Yonkers** *and you're doing the rewriting, to whom are you responding when you do the rewrites? Is it purely your own responses when you're in the theatre? Or do you also respond to critics, or the director, or an actor?*

All of them. Not an actor so much, a director yes, a critic sometimes. If a critic says something that's valid, and especially if it's backed up by another critic who hits on the same point, I say, "I've got to address this." When you're writing it over and over again and then you're in rehearsal and you're out of town and you start to try it, you've lost all objectivity. Now you need the audience to be objective for you (and they are totally) and you listen to them. Sometimes the actor will come to me and say, "This line isn't getting a laugh." And I say, "I never intended it to." They assume that everything they should say when the situation is comic should get a laugh. I say, "No, no, no, this is character; it's pushing the story ahead." That never happens in any of the dramatic scenes in *Lost in Yonkers.* Very few of those lines were ever changed because they don't have the difficulty in expecting a reaction from the audience. I rewrite just watching what it is that I hear wrong. And sometimes I can watch a play and after about eight or nine performances, I say, "I don't like that." There was a producer who once said to me, "Only look at the things that don't work in the play. The good things will take care of themselves, don't worry about that. Don't say, 'I know this stuff doesn't work but look at all the good things I have.'" He said, "The bad things'll do you in every time." So I concentrate on the bad things; and after I get whatever I think is unworthy of the play out, then I start to hear it more objectively. I stay away for two or three performances and come back and say, "We need something much better than that." When you first see that play up on a stage for the first time in front of an audience, all you care about is that the baby is delivered and is well and has all its arms and legs and moves. Then you say, "OK, now starts its education."

I teach a course in Modern American Drama, and many of the playwrights in the course, people like John Guare and Beth Henley, are considered by the "establishment" to be serious playwrights who write plays that contain comic moments. Neil Simon, on the other hand, is considered a writer of funny plays that are occasionally serious. That strikes me as unfair because, especially in the most recent of your plays, like "The Trilogy" and now **Lost in Yonkers,** *the proportion of humor to seriousness is if anything less comedy than in, say,* Crimes of the Heart.

Crimes of the Heart is a comedy.

Yes, but Henley is considered a serious playwright.

I don't consider it necessarily unfair. I just think it's inaccurate. Unfair means that I'm being picked on for not writing serious, which is better than comedy, which I don't hold to be true. For the most part, I think I have written, with the exception of **Rumors** and the musicals (starting even with **The Odd Couple**), a serious play which is told through my own comic point of view. There are no serious moments in **The Odd Couple;** but when I first sat down to write it, naive as this may be, I thought it was sort of a black comedy, because in most comedies up to that point, there were always women in the play and a romantic relationship. Here there were none; the relationship was between these two men. **Plaza Suite,** with a husband and wife getting a divorce after twenty-three years, was basically a serious play that had comedy in it. The audience at that time was so trained to laugh at what I wrote that, in Boston, Mike Nichols and I kept taking out all the funny lines in the first act—and they found other places to laugh.

I write with a sense of irony and even with lines that are not funny, sometimes the audience senses the irony when they are sophisticated enough and they see the humor. That's why I always need really good productions for the plays to work. I once met a woman who said, "You know, I've never been a fan of yours." and I said, "Oh, that's OK." and she said, "Now I'm a big fan!" and I said, "What happened?" She said, "Well, I come from"—it was either

Wyoming or Montana—and she said, "I've only seen dinner theatre productions of your plays in which they would play all the plays on one superficial level. They played it all as comedy, and then I read the plays and I said, this isn't comedy at all." I remember people walking out of **Prisoner of Second Avenue** confused because some would say, "This wasn't funny." I didn't mean it to be funny; I thought it was a very serious subject, especially at that time. It was the beginning of people being so age-conscious with the man of forty-eight years old losing his job and finding it very difficult to start all over again which is true even today. That to me was a serious play that had a great deal of comedy.

I use the comedy in a way to get the audience's attention and then sort of pull the rug from underneath them. That's how I view life: things are wonderful, things are going along just great, and then a telephone call comes and just pulls the rug from under you. Some tragic thing, some tragic event, has happened in your life, and I say if it can happen in life I want to do that in the theatre. It took a long time to convince audiences and critics that one could write a play that way. I remember reading Lillian Hellman saying, "Never mix comedy and drama in the same play; the audiences won't understand it." They say to me, "What are you writing?" and I'll mention something, and they say, "Is it a comedy?" I say, "No it's a play." They say, "Is it a drama?" and I say, "It's a play. It has everything in it."

When you look back over your career to date, how has Neil Simon changed as a playwright? In other interviews you've mentioned the idea of the tapestry play, that you're now writing about more than two people as the focus of the plays. I assume that's one way, but are there other ways that you see your plays changing?

Well, in a glacier-like way. They move slowly; I don't make sudden overnight changes. I think back to **Chapter Two,** which was the story of the guilt a man feels who has lost a spouse and feels too guilty or is made to feel too guilty by his children or other relatives to go ahead in another relationship. There were people who spent the next fifteen or twenty years or the rest of their lives never moving on with it. In my own case, I was encouraged by my daughters to move on when I met somebody else. But still you get that kick of guilt, not a high kick, a kick in the gut, of guilt much like the survivors of the Holocaust when those who lived felt guilty all their lives. So the man in the play was not able to give himself the enjoyment and the latitude of exploring this new relationship without always pulling in the guilt of being alive and his wife being dead. Around that point, it's what I started to look for in almost every play. I think if there's any change it's that way. It's not necessary for me to be conceived of as a serious playwright because the word is so bandied about I think that it gets misinterpreted, serious meaning the intention is lofty. It isn't any loftier than comedy can be, but I don't write a pure comedy anymore, with the exception of **Rumors** where I intentionally did. I try to write plays about human emotions. I don't write plays about society. I find I can't. They become very current plays, and I like plays to be able to last for fifty or a hundred years or so. These are plays that contain serious subject matter. *Lost in Yonkers* is very well disguised, not that I meant it to be, but I couldn't open up the play showing the tragic side of Bella. It only came out when she was confronted with this chance to better her life and she didn't quite know how to do it and didn't get the permission of her mother who was the one who stunted her growth in the first place. That has to be built to, and I see how the audience is taken by surprise as it goes on. If they leave after that first act, they say, "It's nice, it's funny, it's cute." And then the second act just hits them so hard. It's what you leave the theatre with, not what's going on in the beginning of the play, that's important.

Perhaps this analogy will seem far-fetched to you, but one could say that it took O'Neill almost his whole creative life to write a play like Long Day's Journey, *where, as he said, he "faced his dead at last." He had started to do it with* Ah, Wilderness! *in a more light-hearted way.* Ah, Wilderness! *and* Long Day's Journey *are really the same play but one is weighted towards a comedic treatment and the other towards a more tragic approach. It seems to me that you could say the same thing about* **Brighton Beach Memoirs** *and* **Broadway Bound**: **Brighton Beach Memoirs** *is your* Ah, Wilderness!, *and* **Broadway Bound** *is your* Long Day's Journey. *You started to confront your family directly in* **Brighton Beach,** *particularly through Eugene's narration in a comic way, and then in* **Broadway Bound** *you did so much more seriously.*

There was a really valid reason for that. With *Brighton Beach* my mother was still alive, so she could come and enjoy it and *Biloxi Blues* as well. She died after that so she never saw *Broadway Bound.* I would not have written *Broadway Bound* if my parents were alive. I couldn't have put them up on the stage that way. I don't think I put them in an unsympathetic light certainly, but in a truthful one in a way. I was probably harsher on my father than I was on my mother; at that time in our lives, I really think she was the one who caused the anguish in the family. But I have more of an understanding of him now having lived through some of the same things myself.

So you think it was basically the death of your mother that enabled you to write **Broadway Bound** *when you did?*

It freed me to do it. I reveal things about her, her inability to be close and emotional. I don't remember ever being hugged by my mother as far back as being a child. I always knew that she loved me, but she was unable to show emotion. I did talk about something that happened to my mother personally, that she was burned in a fire; the grandfather talks about that. I don't go into it in **Broadway Bound** but it must have affected their marriage very much—how she was scarred. She was actually scarred on the front, not on the back as in the play.

And you never could have done that if she'd still been alive?

No, I couldn't. When O'Neill wrote *Long Day's Journey* he put it in a drawer and said it couldn't be done until twenty-five years after his death, which didn't happen of course; his wife had it done. I sort of felt that way. *Chapter Two* was cathartic for me. It helped me get rid of my own guilt by sharing it with the world. But *Broadway Bound* was not cathartic. It was an attempt to try to understand my family and my own origins. It's a play of forgiveness, and I didn't realize it until somebody associated with the play—the set designer or a costume designer—said after the reading, "It's a love letter to his mother." I had a very up and down relationship with my mother. I used to get angry at her very often, and I loved her too, but there was no way for either one of us to show it—and so there it is on the stage. I remember in real life once I gave a surprise birthday party for my mother—she really was surprised—and we brought out the cake. She couldn't smile or say, "This is wonderful." She just looked at me as she was about to cut the cake and said, "I'm still angry with you from last week when you did such and such." It was the only way she could deal with it. So when I wrote the play, what I had to do after listening to the first reading when I didn't have that scene about George Raft, I said I've got to show the other side of my mother, show her when she was happy. I like that when in the second act of a play, you begin to show what really is information that happened way before that, to give it late in the play.

Do you have a favorite among your own plays? The last one you wrote?

Yes, it's generally that. It suddenly becomes the one that you're working on; but when I think of my favorite, I think about what my experience was when I wrote it and put it on. Was that a good time in my life, in my personal life and in doing the play? With some of the plays I had terrible times doing the play yet the play came out very well; other times it was great fun doing it. I think the greatest kick I got on an opening night—when I knew I was sort of catapulted into another place in my life—was the opening night of *The Odd Couple.* It was accepted on such a high level by everyone. It was what you dream about—Moss Hart in *Act One*—the hottest ticket in town. That night was a terrific night!

What about as a craftsman? Which of the plays are you proudest of as a piece of writing?

Structurally I like *The Sunshine Boys,* and I like this one structurally.

The Sunshine Boys *is my favorite Simon play so far because of the integration of comedy and seriousness and because of the organic nature of that integration. Maybe it's an accident of the subject matter because you're dealing with comedians.*

You're dealing with comedians which gives you license for them to be funny. But the seriousness in the play was inherent too; it wasn't always written about because you knew that they were old, you knew they couldn't deal with things. One was really fighting for his way of life to continue, the other was quite satisfied to be retired and live in another way; so there was something classic about it. It just seems to hark back to another period in time. That play is done by more national theatres in Europe—in England or even Germany—because they relate to it in some part of their own culture, to the old vaudevillians and what's happened to them. They've died out. That's another play that sat in the drawer for six months after I wrote twenty-five pages of it until I had lunch with Mike Nichols and said, "I'm kind of stuck. I have a play." I started to tell him the idea and he said, "That sounds wonderful!" That's sometimes all I need; that's like a great review. "You really like that, Mike?" "Yes." And I went ahead and wrote the whole thing.

Can you think of plays that exceeded your expectations and plays that you had great expectations for that never reached them once you saw them on stage?

That's an interesting question because I think I always know what the reception is going to be. I'm rarely surprised. Sometimes I write a play knowing it's not going to succeed. There's a psychological subconscious will to fail after writing four or five hits—you don't deserve that much. I pick a subject matter that is so far out—something that I would not do right now. Not one that's more dangerous and that's taking more of a chance with an audience, but one that's almost guaranteed not to be commercially successful (not that I always know when it's going to be). *The Odd Couple* and *Barefoot in the Park* fooled me because they were so early in my career. I didn't know what to expect. When they were both such big hits, I was really shocked. But a play that I knew I wanted to write for a reason other than artistic or commercial success was something like *God's Favorite.*

God's Favorite was my way of dealing with my wife's death. It was *Waiting for Godot* for me; I could not understand the absurdity of a thirty-nine-year-old beautiful, energetic woman dying so young. It was railing at God to explain to me why He did this thing, so I used the *Book of Job.* One critic cried on television in his anger: "How dare you do this to the *Book of Job!*" Yet there were critics like Walter Kerr, a devout Catholic, who loved it, just adored it. And so I wasn't too surprised that we weren't a major success, but I learned in hindsight that it was not a Broadway play. It should have been done off-Broadway as *Fools* should have been. *Fools* I did in a way like *Rumors.* Again it was farce in a sense. I just loved the premise. It's almost Hebraic culturally like the towns written about by Sholem Aleichem in which there were stupid people (without ever going into the reasons why) and I had a curse in my town. I thought it was good. Mike Nichols came up and did it; we had a good time. If we had done it in a small theatre, it would have been fine—Playwrights Horizons or something like that—but not with the expectations of a Broadway audience paying whatever it was at the time, expecting a certain kind of play.

I remember when we did *The Good Doctor,* which was another play written during my wife's illness when they discovered that she would not live. I was just sitting up in the country and I wanted to write to keep myself going and I read a short story by Chekhov called "The Sneeze"; and, just to kill time, I dramatized it. And I said, "Gee, this would be fun, to do all Russian writers and do comic pieces—or non-comic pieces—by them." I couldn't find any, so in order to give unity to the evening I decided to do Chekhov because he had written so many newspaper pieces where he got paid by the word and I found as many of them as I could. Then when I tried them out of town some of them didn't work, so I wrote my own Chekhov pieces and some of the critics pointed them out and said, "This one is so Chekhovian." which wasn't his at all! I don't mean that as flattery to me but as not knowing by some of the critics. I remember a woman in New Haven coming up the aisle and she said to me, "This isn't Neil Simon." So I asked, "Do you like it or do you not like it?" She said, "I don't know. It's just not Neil Simon." I have to overcome their expectations of me so that they don't get to see what they want to see. It's like going to see Babe Ruth at a baseball game; if he hits two singles and drives in the winning run, it's not a Babe Ruth game.

How do you feel about the current relationship between the theatre and film and TV? It's a cliché that television is ruining the theatre, that we are a culture of filmgoers not theatregoers. Do you feel those are valid kinds of observations? You once said you thought the biggest obstacle to theatre was the price of theatre tickets. Do you think it's really that?

That's one of them. It's only one of them. No, there's enough money around, I think, for people to go to Broadway theatre. I think we've lost the writers more than anything. David Richards of the *New York Times* recently said to me, "Do you realize you may be the only one left around who repeatedly works for the Broadway theatre?" And I said, "Well, they're all gone." Edward Albee hardly writes at all. Arthur Miller has grown older and writes occasionally for the theatre but rarely for Broadway; it's usually for Lincoln Center or someplace else. David Mamet now would rather direct and write his own films. Sam Shepard was never a Broadway writer. There are no repeat writers—the Tennessee Williamses, the George S. Kaufmans, or even Jean Kerr in terms of comedy. You talk to anybody today, especially in California, and they will use writing as a stepping stone to becoming a director. They want to be directors; it has to be about control. Even a promising young writer like John Patrick Shanley has a big success with *Moonstruck* after he had small success in the theatre. We had said this is an interesting playwright, he does *Moonstruck,* and then he wants to direct—so he does *Joe Versus the Volcano* and I'm sure he just wants to keep on directing. Nora Ephron writes a couple of movies that are nice and now she wants to direct. I have no desire to direct at all. I see the soundness of it, in terms of movies. As I said before, I have no control over what goes on up on the screen or what's cut later. Between the director and the actors you lose all of that.

It's almost a mystery as to what's happened in the theatre. I think it's just changing. It's becoming regional theatre and the plays are in a sense getting smaller, not necessarily in their scope. *Six Degrees of Separation* is a wonderful play; I really like that play. I'm not so sure if it had opened on Broadway at the Plymouth Theatre that it would have gotten the kind of attention, the demands for seats. It's viewed from a different perspective when it's presented in an off-Broadway atmosphere. You see what happens when they transfer plays. One of the few that transferred fairly well was *The Heidi Chronicles,* but even when you're watching *The Heidi Chronicles,* you say this isn't really a Broadway play. That could be a misnomer too because it makes it sound crass and commercial, but *Amadeus* is a Broadway play and I think it's a great play. I think most of Peter Shaffer's plays are wonderful plays: *Five Finger Exercise* and the one about the Incas, *The Royal Hunt of the Sun.* Tennessee Williams didn't write off-Broadway plays except at the end of his career when the plays got smaller in their scope. *Cat on a Hot Tin Roof* is a beautiful play, but it's got size to it, and there is no one around who does that anymore. It's changed, I guess maybe the way painting has changed. I don't know who the great portrait painters are anymore if they exist at all. I think it's economics that changes it. In the theatre now they are catering to an international audience. Who comes to America now but the people who have money—the Japanese or the Germans? They don't all understand English but if they go see a musical like *Cats* they don't have to. Even *Phantom of the Opera*—if you don't understand it you can still enjoy it. If a play runs two years it is amazing. Most musical hits will run ten years now. You can't get *Cats* out of that theatre. *Phantom* will be there forever. It will be interesting to see what happens with *Miss Saigon* because it has this amazing anti-American number. When I saw it in London, you could almost cheer it, but if when it opens in March this war is still going on there may be some repercussions.

One of the things that occurred to me when I was watching **Lost in Yonkers** *the other night is that you're one of the cleanest playwrights I know, even though you write about very intimate things.*

You write to what fits the play. There are all sorts of four-letter words in **Rumors** because these are very contemporary people. In **Lost in Yonkers,** you're dealing with the 1940's and you're not only trying to emulate a play that might have existed in that time, but certainly what life was like at that time. And that kind of language, street language, I at least didn't hear that much. I never heard it at home, except maybe in a violent argument between my mother and father. It's interesting to watch playwrights like Tennessee Williams and Arthur Miller who never resorted to that language but found another language that was more potent. In doing **The Marrying Man** with Kim Basinger and Alec Baldwin, which was just an awful experience, she did this scene in which she was sitting in a box at the opera in Boston. She used to be Bugsy Siegal's girlfriend but is found by this guy who's a multimillionaire

and they get married; they're forced to get married through no intention of their own. Later on, they fall in love and get remarried. She's sitting in Boston and a man in the box is annoying her as she's sort of kissing the ear of Alec Baldwin. He keeps shushing her and she says, "Oh, come on, this opera isn't even in English, you can't understand it"; and it goes on and finally she adlibs, "Oh, go fuck yourself." And I said, "Wait, you can't say that." It had nothing to with my thinking that the language is offensive; it's so wrong for the character and for the tone of the movie. It's a movie that takes place in 1948. It's OK when the Alec Baldwin character and his four cronies are in the car. They use all sorts of language; but for her to use it in that place seemed so wrong for me. So it wasn't being prudish about anything; you've just got to use it where it's got some weight. Sometimes I would use "fuck you" or whatever it is once in a play, and it has much more impact than just using it all the way through. I like it when David Mamet does it sometimes like in *American Buffalo.* It is said so often that it is no longer offensive. It bothers some people I know; they don't want to hear it. But it never bothers me. I think he writes in such wonderful rhythms and cadences that the language is so important, so precise.

Linda Lavin once said à propos of **Last of the Red-Hot Lovers,** *in which she was then appearing: "People come to the theatre to see their lives verified. They haven't been offended. The life they lead hasn't been challenged, it's been reaffirmed." And I think you once said, "recognition" is what you'd like to see your plays be all about. Let me be a devil's advocate and say that one should come out of the theatre upset, as Edward Albee insists. I don't mean necessarily emotionally upset but something should have changed. You shouldn't have been patted on the head, you should have been disturbed.* **Lost in Yonkers** *can be a very disturbing play in that way.*

Oh, absolutely.

Do you think you've changed in that respect?

Yes. I remember that when I did **Plaza Suite** and I wrote the first act about the husband who's having the affair with the secretary, the general manager for the play read it and said, "You can't do this play." I said, "Why not?" He said, "Do you know how many men come from out of town and meet their secretary or somebody and come to this play. They'll be so embarrassed." I said, "Good, that's what I want to do. I want to shake people up." So I don't think I was trying to reaffirm middle-class values. In **Last of the Red-Hot Lovers,** the man was trying to have an affair. I found him sort of a pitiful character not even being able to break through that. I saw him as an Everyman in a way who finally had the courage to try to break out but didn't know how to do it. Sometimes those labels stick with you. But as I said it's a glacier. It moves along and it changes and it pulls along the debris with it. I don't think I write that way. I think why I get bandied about a lot by critics is because of the success ratio. There must be something wrong when it appeals to so many people around the world. They hate it that I've become a wealthy person from the plays.

You can't be any good if you're wealthy!

Yes. I remember at the time reading about Tennessee Williams's wealth, which was relative compared to today's market, but he was a fairly wealthy man because he was so successful. But he also took such chances with plays like *Camino Real.* He was a poet and he made his reputation on plays like *The Glass Menagerie* and *Streetcar Named Desire.* It's because I do write plays that for the most part are so popular. I never mind a bad review from a good critic who has liked some of the work in the past and then says, "No, you didn't do it this time." I say that's valid and I can accept it. I don't expect a rave from Frank Rich. Frank Rich always will find fault. He's tough to figure out because he'll write a very middling review of **Brighton Beach** and talk about its faults and at the end of it say, "One hopes there will be a chapter two to **Brighton Beach.**" He finds fault with the play yet he wants to see a sequel to it! I had no intention of writing a trilogy, I just wrote **Brighton Beach.** When I read his notice I said, well, I'll do another play. You still don't think about a trilogy because if the second play fails, who wants to see the sequel to a failure? So I wrote **Biloxi Blues,** which he loved. It won the Tony Award, and so I did the third one which he again then finds fault with by saying, "I missed it being a great play." He gives it a negative sounding review by saying it almost reaches great heights but doesn't.

You have to steel yourself. You become very thick-skinned after a while because you're out there naked and they are writing about you personally. They don't write about your work as much as who you are in the reviews. In a way I think the theatre has been changed a lot by critics who are now looking to make names for themselves. It bothers me that critics are hailed as personalities. Siskel and Ebert, good critics or bad critics it makes no difference to me, I hate that they are celebrities and have such power. Fortunately, there are so many people who write reviews for films, and people generally make up their mind to go see a film before they read the reviews. Not so with the theatre. The reviews mean everything. If you get a bad review in the *New York Times,* you can still exist but you've got to overcome it.

No, that's not exactly true. You *can still exist. Neil Simon can still exist. A lot of other people can't with a bad review in the* Times.

Well, it depends on the play. There have been a few that have existed without it, but it's very hard. Rich loved **Biloxi Blues** and the first day after **Biloxi Blues** opened we did an enormous amount of business, twice what we did on **Brighton Beach Memoirs.** But **Brighton Beach Memoirs** ran twice as long as **Biloxi Blues.** The audience seeks out what they want and **Brighton Beach,** next to **The Odd Couple,** is played more than any play I've ever

done. There is something about the idealization of the family in that play that we all dream about. They know it's an idealization. It's like looking back on your family album and seeing it better than it was.

But it's not Ah, Wilderness! *It's not that sappy.*

Well, those were sappier days.

There's a lot of what happens in **Broadway Bound** *underneath the surface of* **Brighton Beach.**

Oh, yes—the mother's hurt when she finds out that the father has had this heart attack and that the boy has lost all the money.

What do you think you've done differently in **Lost in Yonkers?** *What would you say has inched the glacier forward with this play?*

I've written about much darker people than I ever have before. I've written about normal people in dark situations before—the death of spouses, the break-up of marriages (tragedies in proportion to their own lives at that time like in **Brighton Beach**), anti-semitism and anti-homosexuality in **Biloxi.** But in this play, I really wrote about dysfunctional people and the results of a woman who was beaten in Germany who in order to teach her children to survive teaches them only to survive and nothing else. That's much further than I've gone in any other play, so it's deeper. It's why I want to do a musical next year because I need really sure footing to go on to the next place. That doesn't mean I need to write about people even more dysfunctional, but as a matter of fact the play that I've been working on and haven't been able to lick quite yet is about two people in a sanitarium who have had breakdowns and find solace in each other almost more than in the doctor. I've written about thirty pages of it and I've had it there for two years and I'm anxious to write it, but each play comes when its time is ripe. Who knows if at some point I lose faith in the musical I'm working on, I'll probably go back and start to write that play. Right now, all I want to do is get out of Washington, go home, rest, come back, do the stuff in New York. Then I forget all about **Lost in Yonkers.** They all become a piece of the past for me. I've learned from them, and then they only come up in interviews like this when you talk about them. I don't think of the plays. I don't try to remember or go back or ever read them and see what I've done to see how I could do that again. I want to go to some other place. I'm just hoping that there'll even be a theatre enough around for people to want to go see these plays.

James Lipton with Neil Simon (interview date Winter 1992)

"Neil Simon: The Art of Theater X," in *The Paris Review,* Vol. 34, No. 125, Winter, 1992, pp. 167-213.

[In the following interview, Simon discusses the development of his plays from light to dark comedies.]

Legend has it that on his deathbed the actor Edmund Gwenn answered director John Ford's "What is dying like?" with a reflective, "Dying is easy. Comedy is hard."

By any measure—quantity, quality, popular success, renown—Neil Simon is the preeminent purveyor of comedy in the last half of the twentieth century. Like the work of most writers of comedy, from Aristophanes to Woody Allen, Simon's humor is written to be spoken. And heard. For Simon the art of humor is both communal (each member of the audience in league with all the other members of the audience) and collegial (playwright and performers in league with the audience—a relationship Simon will describe as a "shared secret"). Fielding, Twain and Thurber can be savored in one's lap, but verbal, visual humor, like misery, loves company. Simon is not only skillful at his craft but prolific as well. He is the author of more than twenty plays, including **Come Blow Your Horn, Barefoot in the Park, The Odd Couple,** *the Brighton Beach trilogy,* **Prisoner of Second Avenue, Plaza Suite** *and* **Lost in Yonkers.**

These pages are the winnowing of sixteen hours of taped conversation in Simon's office on the second floor of a Spanish colonial apartment building in the Beverly Hills flats—several miles, a thousand vertical feet and a dozen social strata below the Bel Air hilltop home Simon shares with his wife Diane and their daughter Bryn.

The writer's no-nonsense work space, impersonal in its laidback Southern Californian setting, is conspicuously empty (no secretary, no phone calls, no distractions) but intensely personal in the memorabilia that have, as Simon explains, "sort of gravitated" there over the years.

Halfway through the tour of the apartment Simon stopped abruptly and remarked, in apparent surprise, on how many of the room's furnishings date from the house on Manhattan's East Sixty-second Street where he lived with his first wife, Joan: chairs, tables, photographs, paintings—some painted by Joan, a framed letter from her, written in cryptic, Joycean prose and signed, "Klarn." The baseball paraphernalia on display reflects another side of Simon's life. His substantial collection of antique caps and autographed balls, with a recent emphasis on Bobby Bonilla, would knock the knee-socks off the playwright's baseball-mad alter ego, Eugene Jerome.

There are the usual theatrical souvenirs and a few unusual ones: a telegram from the president of Columbia University informing Simon of his Pulitzer Prize for **Lost in Yonkers,** *a Neil Simon* Time *magazine cover, a poster from the Moscow production of* **Biloxi Blues,** *signed by the cast, "Dear Neil Simon, We love you and your plays. We had worked on this performance with enjoy."*

"Doc" Simon, so called from his childhood habit of mimicking the family doctor, is tall and fit, despite the chronic back problems that have curtailed his tennis playing in recent years. We sat at a massive, polished tree-stump coffee table covered with the tools of his trade: pens neatly stacked (by the cleaning woman, he hastened to say), scripts, finished and unfinished, books and the long pads on which he writes. We laughed frequently as we discussed his plays, opinions and past. Even when the talk turned as serious as some of his recent scripts, the face that peered over the tree stump like a Bronx leprechaun bore two indelible Simon trademarks: the eyes of an insatiably curious and slightly guarded child, shielded by horn-rimmed glasses, and a faint, constant, enigmatic smile. . . . What is this man smiling at? Perhaps the shared secret.

[Lipton]: *Lillian Hellman once said she always began work on a play with something very small—a scene, or even two vague lines of dialogue whose meaning was utterly unknown to her. What starts you, what makes you think there's a play there?*

[Simon]: As many plays as I've written—twenty-seven, twenty-eight—I can't recollect a moment when I've said "This would make a good play." I never sit down and write bits and pieces of dialogue. What I might do is make a few notes on who's in the play, the characters I want, where it takes place and the general idea of it. I don't make any outlines at all. I just like to plunge in. I'll start right from page one because I want to hear how the people speak. Are they interesting enough for me? Have I captured them? It goes piece by piece, brick by brick. I don't know that I have a play until I've reached thirty, thirty-five pages.

Have you ever started thematically?

I *think* about thematic plays, but I don't believe I write them. Nothing really takes shape until I become specific about the character and the dilemma he's in. *Dilemma* is the key word. It is always a dilemma, not a situation. To tell the truth, I really don't know what the theme of the play is until I've written it and the critics tell me.

Every playwright, every director, every actor, speaks about conflict. We're all supposed to be in the conflict business. When you speak of dilemma, are you talking about conflict?

Yes. In **Broadway Bound** I wanted to show the anatomy of writing comedy—with the older brother teaching Eugene, which was the case with my brother Danny and me. Stan keeps asking Eugene for the essential ingredient in comedy, and when Eugene can't answer, Stan says, "Conflict!" When he asks for the *other* key ingredient, and Eugene can only come up with, "*More* conflict?" Stan says, "The key word is *wants*. In every comedy, even drama, somebody has to want something and want it bad. When somebody tries to stop him—that's conflict." By the time you know the conflicts, the play is already written in your mind. All you have to do is put the words down. You don't have to outline the play, it outlines itself. You go by sequential activity. One thing follows the other. But it all starts with that first seed, conflict. As Stan says, it's got to be a very, very strong conflict, not one that allows the characters to say, "Forget about this! I'm walking out." They've got to stay there and fight it out to the end.

You said that it isn't until you get to page thirty-five that you know whether or not you've got a play. Are there times when you get to page thirty-five and decide the conflict isn't strong enough, and the play disappears to languish forever in a drawer?

I've got infinitely more plays in the drawer than have seen the lights of the stage. Most of them never come out of the drawer, but occasionally one will, and it amazes me how long it has taken to germinate and blossom. The best example would be **Brighton Beach Memoirs.** I wrote the first thirty-five pages of the play and gave it to my children, Nancy and Ellen, and Marsha, my wife at the time. They read it and said, "This is incredible. You've got to go on with it." I showed it to my producer, Manny Azenberg, and to Gordon Davidson, and they said, "This is going to be a great play." I knew the play was a turn in style for me, probing more deeply into myself, but maybe the pressure of the words "great play" scared me, so I put it away. Periodically, I would take it out and read it, and I wouldn't know how to do it. After nine years I took it out one day, read the thirty-five pages, picked up my pen and the pad I write on and finished the play in six weeks. I have the feeling that in the back of your mind there's a little writer who writes while you're doing other things, because I had no trouble at that point. Obviously, what had happened in the ensuing years in my life made clear to me what it should be about. Somewhere in the back of my head I grew up, I matured. I was ready to write that play. Sometimes it *helps* to have some encouragement. Once I was having dinner with Mike Nichols, and he asked, "What are you doing?" I said, "I'm working on a play about two ex-vaudevillians who haven't worked together or seen each other in eleven years, and they get together to do an Ed Sullivan Show." He said, "That sounds wonderful. Go back and finish it." So I did. It was as though a critic had already seen the play and said, "I love it." But there are many, many plays that get to a certain point and no further. For years I've been trying to write the play of what happened to me and the seven writers who wrote Sid Caesar's "Your Show of Shows." But I've never got past page twenty-two because there are seven conflicts rather than one main conflict. I've been writing more subtext and more subplot lately—but in this situation *everybody* was funny. I didn't have somebody to be serious, to anchor it. I always have to find the anchor. I have to find the Greek chorus in the play, the character who either literally talks to the audience or talks to the audience in a sense. For example, Oscar in **The Odd Couple** is the Greek chorus. he watches, he perceives how Felix behaves, and he comments on it. Felix then comments back on what Oscar is, but Oscar is the one who is telling us what the play is about. More recently, in the Brighton Beach trilogy, I've been *literally* talking to the

audience, through the character of Eugene, because it is the only way I can express the writer's viewpoint. The writer has inner thoughts, and they are not always articulated on the stage—and I want the audience to be able to get inside his head. It's what I did in **Jake's Women.** In the first try out in San Diego the audience didn't know enough about Jake because all he did was react to the women in his life, who were badgering him, trying to get him to open up. We didn't know who Jake was. So I introduced the device of him talking to the audience. Then he became the fullest, richest character in the play, because the audience knew things I never thought I would reveal about Jake—and possibly about myself.

Will you return to the "Show of Shows" play?

I do very often think about doing it. What was unique about that experience was that almost every one of the writers has gone on to do really major things: Mel Brooks's whole career . . . Larry Gelbart . . . Woody Allen . . . Joe Stein who wrote *Fiddler on the Roof* . . . Michael Stewart who wrote *Hello, Dolly* . . . it was a group of people only Sid Caesar knew how to put together. Maybe it was trial and error because the ones who didn't work fell out, but once we worked together it was the most excruciatingly hilarious time in my life. It was also one of the most painful because you were fighting for recognition, and there was no recognition. It was very difficult for me because I was quiet and shy, so I sat next to Carl Reiner and whispered my jokes to him. He was my spokesman, he'd jump up and say, "He's got it! He's got it!" Then Carl would say the line, and I would hear it, and I'd laugh because I thought it was funny. But when I watched the show on a Saturday night with my wife, Joan, she'd say, "That was your line, wasn't it?" and I'd say, "I don't remember." What I *do* remember is the screaming and fighting—a cocktail party without the cocktails, everyone yelling lines in and out, people getting very angry at others who were slacking off. Mel Brooks was the main culprit. We all came in to work at ten o'clock in the morning, but he showed up at one o'clock. We'd say, "That's it. We're sick and tired of this. Either Mel comes in at ten o'clock or we go to Sid and do something about it." At about ten to one, Mel would come in with a straw hat, fling it across the room and say "Lindy made it!" and everyone would fall down hysterical. He didn't need the eight hours we put in. He needed four hours. He is, maybe, the most uniquely funny man I've ever met. That inspired me. I wanted to be around those people. I've fooled around with this idea for a play. I even found a title for it, *Laughter on the Twenty-third Floor,* because I think the office was on the twenty-third floor. From that building we looked down on Bendel's and Bergdorf Goodman and Fifth Avenue, watching all the pretty girls go by through binoculars. Sometimes we'd set fire to the desk with lighter fluid. We should have been arrested, all of us.

If you ever get past page twenty-two, how would you deal with Mel and Woody and the others? Would they appear as themselves?

No, no, no! They'd all be fictitious. It would be like the Brighton Beach trilogy, which is semi-autobiographical.

It feels totally autobiographical. I assumed it was.

Everyone does. But I've told interviewers that if I meant it to be autobiographical I would have called the character Neil Simon. He's not Neil. He's Eugene Jerome. That gives you greater latitude for fiction. It's like doing abstract painting. You see your own truth in it, but the abstraction is the art.

When did you realize there was a sequel to **Brighton Beach Memoirs?**

It got a middling review from Frank Rich of *The New York Times,* but he said at the end of it, "One hopes that there is a chapter two to *Brighton Beach.*" I thought, he's asking for a sequel to a play that he doesn't seem to like!

Are you saying Frank Rich persuaded you to write **Biloxi Blues?**

No, but I listened to him saying, "I'm interested enough to want to know more about this family." Then, Steven Spielberg, who had gone to see *Brighton Beach,* got word to me, suggesting the next play should be about my days in the army. I was already thinking about that, and I started to write *Biloxi Blues,* which became a play about Eugene's rites of passage. I discovered something very important in the writing of *Biloxi Blues.* Eugene, who keeps a diary, writes in it his belief that Epstein is homosexual. When the other boys in the barracks read the diary and assume it's true, Eugene feels terrible guilt. He's realized the responsibility of putting something down on paper, because people tend to believe everything they read.

The Counterfeiters ends with the diary André Gide kept while he was writing the book, and in it he says he knows he's writing well when the dialectic of the scene takes over, and the characters seize the scene from him, and he's become not a writer but a reader. Do you sometimes find that your characters have taken the play away from you and are off in their own direction?

I've *always* felt like a middleman, like the typist. Somebody somewhere else is saying, "This is what they say now. This is what they say next." Very often it is the characters themselves, once they become clearly defined. When I was working on my first play, **Come Blow Your Horn,** I was told by fellow writers that you must outline your play, you must know where you're going. I wrote a complete, detailed outline from page one to the end of the play. In the writing of the play, I didn't get past page fifteen when the characters started to move away from the outline. I tried to pull them back in, saying, "Get back in there. This is where you belong. I've already diagrammed your life." They said, "No, no, no. This is where I want to go." So, I started following them. In the second play, **Barefoot in the Park,** I outlined the first two acts. I said,

"I'll leave the third act a free-for-all, so I can go where I want." I never got through that outline either. In *The Odd Couple.* I outlined the first act. After a while I got tired of doing even that. I said, "I want to be as surprised as anyone else." I had also read a book on playwriting by John van Druten, in which he said, "Don't outline your play, because then the rest of it will just be work. It should be joy. You should be discovering things the way the audience discovers them." So, I stopped doing it.

Gide writes about being surprised by the material coming up on the typewriter. He finds himself laughing, shocked, sometimes dismayed . . .

Sometimes I start laughing—and I've had moments in this office when I've burst into tears. Not that I thought the audience might do that. The moment had triggered a memory or a feeling that was deeply hidden. That's catharsis. It's one of the main reasons I write the plays. It's like analysis without going to the analyst. The play becomes your analysis. The writing of the play is the most enjoyable part of it. It's also the most frightening part because you walk into a forest without a knife, without a compass. But if your instincts are good, if you have a sense of geography, you find that you're clearing a path and getting to the right place. If the miracle happens, you come out at the very place you *wanted* to. But very often you have to go back to the beginning of the forest and start walking through it again, saying, "I went that way. It was a dead end." You cross out, cross over. You meet new friends along the way, people you never thought you'd meet. It takes you into a world you hadn't planned on going to when you started the play. The play may have started out to be a comedy, and suddenly you get into a place of such depth that it surprises you. As one critic aptly said, I wrote *Brighton Beach Memoirs* about the family I *wished* I'd had instead of the family I *did* have. It's closer to *Ah, Wilderness* than my reality.

When did you realize that **Brighton Beach Memoirs** *and* **Biloxi Blues** *were part of a trilogy?*

I thought it seemed odd to leave the Eugene saga finished after two plays. Three is a trilogy—I don't even know what two plays are called. So, I decided to write the third one, and the idea came immediately. It was back to the war theme again, only these were domestic wars. The boys were having guilts and doubts about leaving home for a career writing comedy. Against this played the war between the parents. I also brought in the character of the socialist grandfather who was constantly telling the boys, "You can't just write jokes and make people laugh." Against this came Blanche from the first play, **Brighton Beach,** trying to get the grandfather to move to Florida to take care of his aging, ill wife. To me, setting people in conflict with each other is like what those Chinese jugglers do, spinning one plate, then another, then another. I wanted to keep as many plates spinning as I could.

What exactly do you mean when you call The Brighton Beach Trilogy semi-autobiographical?

It means the play may be based on incidents that happened in my life—but they're not written the way they happened. **Broadway Bound** comes closest to being really autobiographical. I didn't pull any punches with that one. My mother and father were gone when I wrote it, so I did tell about the fights, and what it was like for me as a kid hearing them. I didn't realize until someone said after the first reading that the play was really a love letter to my mother! She suffered the most in all of it. She was the one that was left alone. Her waxing that table didn't exist in life, but it exists symbolically for *me*. It's the abstraction I was talking about.

Speaking of abstraction, there's something mystifying to audiences—and other writers—about what the great comedy writers do. From outside, it seems to be as different from what most writers are able to do as baseball is from ballet. I'm not going to ask anything quite as fatuous as "What is humor?" but I am asking—is it genetic, is it a mind-set, a quirk? And, most important, can it be learned—or, for that matter, taught?

The answer is complex. First of all, there are various styles and attitudes towards comedy. When I worked on "Your Show of Shows," Larry Gelbart was the wittiest, cleverest man I'd ever met, Mel Brooks the most outrageous. I never knew what I was. I *still* don't know. Maybe I had the best sense of construction of the group. I only know some aspects of my humor, one of which involves being completely literal. To give you an example, in **Lost in Yonkers,** Uncle Louie is trying to explain the heartless grandmother to Arty. "When she was twelve years old, her old man takes her to a political rally in Berlin. A horse goes down and crushes Ma's foot. Nobody ever fixed it. It hurts every day of her life, but I never once seen her take even an aspirin." Later, Arty says to his older brother, "I'm afraid of her, Jay. A horse fell on her when she was a kid, and she hasn't taken an aspirin yet." It's an almost exact repetition of what Louie told him and this time it gets a huge laugh. That mystifies me. In **Prisoner of Second Avenue,** you knew there were terrible things tormenting Peter Falk. He sat down on a sofa that had stacks of pillows, like every sofa in the world, and he took one pillow after the other and started throwing them angrily saying, "You pay $800 for a sofa, and you can't sit on it because you got ugly little pillows shoved up your back!" There is no joke there. Yet, it was an enormous laugh—because the audience identified. That, more or less, is what is funny to me: saying something that's instantly identifiable to everybody. People come up to you after the show and say, "I've always thought that, but I never knew anyone *else* thought it." It's a shared secret between you and the audience.

You've often said that you've never consciously written a joke in one of your plays.

I try never to think of jokes as jokes. I confess that in the early days, when I came from television, plays like **Come Blow Your Horn** would have lines you could lift out that would be funny in themselves. That to me would be a "joke," which I would try to remove. In **The Odd Couple** Oscar had a line about Felix, "He's so panicky he wears his seatbelt at a drive-in movie." That could be a Bob Hope joke. I left it in because I couldn't find anything to replace it.

Have you ever found that a producer, director or actor objected to losing a huge laugh that you were determined to cut from the play?

An actor, perhaps, yes. They'll say, "But that's my big laugh." I say, "But it hurts the scene." It's very hard to convince them. Walter Matthau was after me constantly on **The Odd Couple,** complaining not about one of his lines, but one of Art Carney's. He'd say, "It's not a good line." A few days later, I received a letter from a doctor in Wilmington. It said, "Dear Mr. Simon, I loved your play, but I find one line really objectionable. I wish you would take it out." So, I took the line out and said, "Walter, I've complied with your wishes. I got a letter from a prominent doctor in Wilmington who didn't like the line . . ." He started to laugh, and then I realized, "You son of a bitch, *you're* the doctor!" And he was. Those quick lines, the one-liners attributed to me for so many years—I think they come purely out of character, rather than out of a joke. Walter Kerr once came to my aid by saying, "to be or not to be" is a one-liner. If it's a dramatic moment no one calls it a one-liner. If it gets a laugh, suddenly it's a one-liner. I think one of the complaints of critics is that the people in my plays are funnier than they would be in life, but have you ever seen *Medea?* The characters are a lot more dramatic in that than they are in life.

You've also said that when you began writing for the theater you decided to try to write comedy the way dramatists write plays—writing from the characters out, internally, psychologically . . .

Yes. What I try to do is make dialogue come purely out of character, so that one character could never say the lines that belong to another character. If it's funny, it's because I'm telling a story about characters in whom I may find a rich vein of humor. When I started writing plays I was warned by people like Lillian Hellman, "You do not mix comedy with drama." But my theory was, if it's mixed in life, why can't you do it in a play? The very first person I showed **Come Blow Your Horn** to was Herman Shumlin, the director of Hellman's *The Little Foxes.* He said, "I like the play, I like the people, but I don't like the older brother." I said, "What's wrong with him?" He said, "Well, it's a comedy. We have to like everybody." I said, "In *life* do we have to like everybody?" In the most painful scene in **Lost in Yonkers,** Bella, who is semiretarded, is trying to tell the family that the boy she wants to marry is also retarded. It's a poignant situation, and yet the information that slowly comes out—and the way the family is third-degreeing her—becomes hilarious, because it's mixed with someone else's pain. I find that what is most poignant is often most funny.

*In the roll-call scene in **Biloxi Blues** you riff for several pages on one word, one syllable: "Ho." It builds and builds in what I've heard you call a "run."*

I learned from watching Chaplin films that what's most funny isn't a single moment of laughter but the moments that come on top of it, and on top of *those.* I learned it from the Laurel and Hardy films too. One of the funniest things I ever saw Laurel and Hardy do was try to undress in the upper berth of a train—together. It took ten minutes, getting the arms in the wrong sleeves and their feet caught in the net, one terrible moment leading to another. I thought, there could be no greater satisfaction for me than to do that to an audience. Maybe "Ho" also came from sitting in the dark as a kid, listening to Jack Benny's running gags on the radio. In **Barefoot in the Park,** when the telephone man comes up five or six flights of stairs, he arrives completely out of breath. When Paul makes *his* entrance, *he's* completely out of breath. When the mother makes her entrance, *she's* completely out of breath. Some critics have written, "You milk that out-of-breath joke too much." My answer is, "You mean because it's happened three times, when they come up the fourth time they shouldn't be out of breath anymore?" It's *not* a joke, it's the natural thing. Like "Ho." Those boys are petrified on their first day in the army, confronted by this maniac sergeant.

Do you pace the lines so the laughs don't cover the dialogue or is that the director's job? Do you try to set up a rhythm in the writing that will allow for the audience's response?

You don't know where the laughs are until you get in front of an audience. Most of the biggest laughs I've ever had I never knew were big laughs. Mike Nichols used to say to me, "Take out all the little laughs because they hurt the big ones." Sometimes the little laughs aren't even *meant* to be laughs. I mean them to further the play, the plot, the character, the story. They're written unwittingly . . . strange word to pick. I cut them, and the laugh pops up somewhere else.

When did you first realize you were funny?

It started very early in my life—eight, nine, ten years old—being funny around the other kids. You single out one kid on your block or in the school who understands what you're saying. He's the only one who laughs. The other kids only laugh when someone tells them a joke: "Two guys got on a truck . . ." I've never done that in my life. I don't like telling jokes. I don't like to hear someone say to me, "Tell him that funny thing you said the other day." It's repeating it. I have no more joy in it. Once it's said, for me it's over. The same is true once it's written—I have no more interest in it. I've expelled whatever it is I needed to exorcise, whether it's humorous or painful. Generally, painful. Maybe the humor is to cover the pain up, or maybe it's a way to share the experience with someone.

Has psychoanalysis influenced your work?

Yes. Generally I've gone into analysis when my life was in turmoil. But I found after a while I was going when it *wasn't* in turmoil. I was going to get a college education in human behavior. I was talking not only about myself; I was trying to understand my wife, my brother, my children, my family, anybody—including the analyst. I can't put everything in the plays down to pure chance. I want them to reveal what makes people tick. I tend to analyze almost everything. I don't think it started because I went through analysis. I'm just naturally that curious. The good mechanic knows how to take a car apart; I love to take the human mind apart and see how it works. Behavior is absolutely the most interesting thing I can write about. You put that behavior in conflict, and you're in business.

Would you describe your writing process? Since you don't use an outline, do you ever know how a play will end?

Sometimes I think I do—but it doesn't mean that's how the play *will* end. Very often you find that you've written past the end, and you say, "Wait a minute, it ended *here.*" When I started to write **Plaza Suite** it was going to be a full three-act play. The first act was about a wife who rents the same suite she and her husband honeymooned in at the Plaza Hotel twenty-three years ago. In the course of the act the wife finds out that the husband is having an affair with his secretary, and at the end of the act the husband walks out the door as champagne and hors d'oeuvres arrive. The waiter asks, "Is he coming back?" and the wife says, "Funny you should ask that." I wrote that and said to myself, "That's the end of the play, I don't want to *know* if he's coming back." That's what made me write three one-act plays for **Plaza Suite.** I don't *like* to know where the play is going to end. I purposely won't think of the ending because I'm afraid, if I know, even subliminally, it'll sneak into the script, and the audience will know where the play is going. As a matter of fact, I never know where the play is going in the *second act.* When **Broadway Bound** was completed, I listened to the first reading and thought, there's not a moment in this entire play where I see the mother happy. She's a miserable woman. I want to know *why* she's miserable. The answer was planted in the beginning of the play: the mother kept talking about how no one believed she once danced with George Raft. I thought, the boy should ask her to talk about George Raft, and as she does, she'll reveal everything in her past.

The scene ends with the now-famous moment of the boy dancing with the mother the way Raft did—if he did.

Yes. People have said, "It's so organic, you had to have known you were writing to that all the time." But I *didn't* know it when I sat down to write the play. I had an interesting problem when I was writing **Rumors.** I started off with just a basic premise: I wanted to do an elegant farce. I wrote it right up to the last two pages of the play, the denouement in which everything has to be explained— and I didn't know what it was! I said to myself, "Today's the day I have to write the explanation. All right, just think it out." I *couldn't* think it out. So I said, "Well then, go sentence by sentence." I couldn't write it sentence by sentence. I said, "Go word by word. The man sits down and tells the police the story. He starts off with, 'It was six o'clock.'" That much I could write. I kept going until everything made sense. That method takes either insanity or egocentricity—or a great deal of confidence. It's like building a bridge over water without knowing if there's land on the other side. But I do have confidence that when I get to the end of the play, I will have gotten so deeply into the characters and the situation I'll find the resolution.

So you never write backwards from a climactic event to the incidents and scenes at the beginning of the play that will take you to it?

Never. The linkages are done by instinct. Sometimes I'll write something and say, "Right now this doesn't mean very much, but I have a hunch that later on in the play it will mean something." The thing I always do is play back on things I set up without any intention in the beginning. The foundation of the play is set in those first fifteen or twenty minutes. Whenever I get in trouble in the second act, I go back to the first act. The answers always lie there. One of the lines people have most often accused me of working backwards from is Felix Ungar's note to Oscar in **The Odd Couple.** In the second act, Oscar has reeled off the laundry list of complaints he has about Felix, including "the little letters you leave me." Now, when Felix is leaving one of those notes, telling Oscar they're all out of cornflakes, I said to myself, "How would he sign it? I know he'd do something that would annoy Oscar." So I signed it "Mr. Ungar." Then I tried "Felix Ungar." Then I tried "F.U." and it was as if a bomb had exploded in the room. When Oscar says, "It took me three hours to figure out that F.U. was Felix Ungar," it always gets this huge laugh.

Felix Unger also appears in **Come Blow Your Horn.** *I wanted to ask why you used the name twice.*

This will give you an indication of how little I thought my career would amount to. I thought **The Odd Couple** would probably be the end of my career, so it wouldn't make any difference that I had used Felix Ungar in **Come Blow Your Horn.** It was a name that seemed to denote the prissiness of Felix, the perfect contrast to the name of Oscar. Oscar may not sound like a strong name, but it did to me— maybe because of the *K* sound in it.

So you subscribe to the K-*theory expressed by the comedians in* **The Sunshine Boys**—K *is funny.*

Oh, I do. Not only that, *K* cuts through the theater. You say a *K*-word, and they can hear it.

Let's talk about the mechanics of writing, starting with where you write.

I have this office. There are four or five rooms in it, and no one is here but me. No secretary, no one, and I've

never once in the many years that I've come here ever felt lonely, or even alone. I come in and the room is filled with—as corny as it might sound—these characters I'm writing, who are waiting each day for me to arrive and give them life. I've also written on airplanes, in dentist's offices, on subways. I think it's true for many writers. You blank out whatever is in front of your eyes. That's why you see writers staring off into space. They're not looking at "nothing," they're visualizing what they're thinking. I never visualize what a play will look like on stage, I visualize what it looks like in *life.* I visualize being in that room where the mother is confronting the father.

What tools do you use? Do you use a 1928 Underwood the way real writers are supposed to? Or a computer? You mentioned using a pad and pencil . . .

I wrote my early plays at the typewriter because it was what writers looked like in *His Girl Friday.*

Lots of crumpled pages being flung across the room?

Yes. But my back started to get so bad from bending over a typewriter eight hours a day, five or six days a week that I couldn't do it anymore, so I started to write in pads. Then a curious thing happened. I was in England and found that they have pads over there with longer pages and thinner spaces between the lines. I liked that because I could get much more on a single page. At a single glance I could see the rhythm of the speeches. If they're on a smaller page with wide spaces you don't get a sense of the rhythm. You have to keep turning. So, I write in these pads. Sometimes I write on both sides of the page, but I always leave myself lots of room to make notes and cross things out. I'll write about three pages, then go to the typewriter and type that out. Then the next day I'll read those three pages again and maybe not like them, and go back to the notebook—write it out, make changes, and then retype it. The typing is boring for me, but I can't use a word processor. It feels inhuman. It seems to me that every script comes out of a computer looking like it was written by the same person. My typewriter has its own characteristics, its own little foibles. Even there, I black out parts and write marginal notes. I'd like it to be neat, but I don't like to send it to a professional typist because they invariably correct my purposely made grammatical errors. I try to write the way people speak, not the way people *should* speak.

When you're writing dialogue, do you write it silently or speak it aloud?

I never *thought* I spoke the lines until my family told me I did. They said they could walk by and tell if it was going well or not by the rhythm of it. I guess I want to see if I'm repeating words, and, because I write primarily for the stage, I want to make sure the words won't be tripping badly over some tongues.

Do you play the parts, I mean, really *play them and get into them?*

Yes. When I wrote the Sergeant Bilko show my father asked me naively, "Do you just write Sergeant Bilko's lines or do you write the other lines too?" When you write a play, maybe even a novel, you become *everybody*. It may seem like I only write the lines spoken by the character who is like Neil Simon, but, in **Lost in Yonkers,** I'm also the grandmother—and Bella. And to do that you have to *become* that person. That's the adventure, the joy, the release that allows you to escape from your own boundaries. To be Grandma every other line for a couple of pages takes you into another being. It's interesting how many people ask, "Was this your grandmother?" I say, "No, I didn't have a grandmother like that," and they say, "Then how do you know her?" I know what she *sounds* like. I know what she *feels* like. The boys describe it when they say, "When you kiss her it's like kissing a cold prune." I describe her in a stage direction as being a very tall, buxom woman. But she doesn't necessarily have to be tall and buxom. She just has to appear that way to the boys. You can't really use that as physical description, but it will convey something to the actress.

And to the actors playing the two boys.

Yes. Those directions are very important.

Family seems to be more than a predilection or interest, it is a near obsession with you. Even if you're writing about a couple, in comes an extended family of friends or the blood-related aunts, uncles, cousins, fathers and mothers with which your plays abound. Is that because family has played such an important role, for good and ill, in your life?

Well, for one thing, it's a universal subject. For example, when **Come Blow Your Horn** was playing, the theater doorman, a black man in his sixties, was standing in the back of the theater, laughing his head off. I went over to him after the play and asked, "Why were you laughing so much?" He said, "That's my family up there." I don't write social and political plays, because I've always thought the family was the microcosm of what goes on in the world. I write about the small wars that eventually become the big wars. It's also what I'm most comfortable with. I am a middle-class person, I grew up in a middle-class neighborhood. I try now and then to get away from the family play, but it amazes me that I've spent the last thirty-one years writing plays primarily about either my family or families very close to it. Maybe the answer is that at some point along the way you discover what it is you do best, and writing about the family unit and its extensions is what I do best.

Your introduction to the first published collection of your work is called "The Writer as Schizophrenic." The word observer *comes up repeatedly in your conversation, your interviews and, especially, in your plays. Have you always seen yourself as an outsider, an observer?*

Yes, that started very early, when my parents would take me to visit family. They'd offer me a cookie or a piece of fruit, but no one *spoke* to me, because they knew I had nothing to contribute. I wasn't offended. I just thought it was the accepted norm. And that led me to believe that I was somehow invisible. On radio shows like "The Shadow," there *were* invisible people. And movies were coming out—"The Invisible Man," with Claude Rains. To me, invisible seemed the greatest thing you could be! If I could have one wish, it was to be invisible. First of all, you could go to any baseball game you wanted to. Free. You could go into any girl's house and watch her get undressed! But it works another way too. It means there's no responsibility. You don't have to integrate, to contribute. This becomes a part of your personality.

Does that detachment apply to your personal relationships as pervasively as to your work?

I'm not quite sure who I am besides the writer. The writer is expressive, the other person can sit in a room and listen and not say anything. It's very hard for me to get those two people together. In the middle of a conversation or a confrontation, I can suddenly step outside it. It's like Jekyll turning into Mr. Hyde without the necessity of taking the potion. It's why the Eugene character speaks to the audience in the trilogy: because, in a sense, he is invisible. The other characters in the play don't see him talking to the audience. They go right about their business. As I wrote it, I thought: I'm now living my perfect dream—to be invisible.

In **Barefoot in the Park,** *Corie says, "Do you know what you are? You're a watcher. There are watchers in the world, and there are doers, and the watchers sit around watching the doers do."*

In all three of my marriages I've been accused of this separation. "You're not listening to me. You're not looking at me." When you asked about where I write, I said anywhere. I just stare into space. That's happened when I was talking to my wife. I could be looking at her and not thinking about what she's saying. It's rude. It's selfish, I guess. But it's what happens; some other thought has taken its place. One of the worst and most frightening examples of that was the first time I was ever on television. I went on the Johnny Carson show. I was standing behind that curtain, hearing them give my credits. Then they said, "And here he is, the prolific playwright, Neil Simon." I walked out and froze. I thought, my God, I'm out here, I've got to deliver something, I've got to be humorous, that's what they expect of me. I sat down opposite Johnny Carson, and he asked his first question, which was fairly lengthy. After the first two words I heard *nothing*. I only saw his lips moving. I said to myself, "I've got all this time not to do anything. In other words, while his lips are moving I'm all right." So, my mind just wandered. I was looking around, saying, "Well, forty million people are watching me, I wonder if my brother's going to watch this, what's he going to think of it?" When Johnny's lips stopped, I was on. But I had no answer because I'd never heard the question. So, I said something like, "That reminds me of something Johnny," and went into something completely irrelevant that fortunately was funny, and we just seemed to move on with the conversation. It happens while I'm speaking to students at a college or university. I'll be talking. I'll look over the room and see one face not interested, and I'm gone, I'm lost. I wish I were out there, sitting among the invisible, but I'm up there having to deliver. The demands of coming up with something every minute are very difficult. In a sense, being in this office, I am invisible because I can stop. When I'm writing, there's no pressure to come up with the next line. I always need that escape hatch, that place to go that's within myself. I've tried coming to terms with it. I feel, as long as it doesn't bother someone else, I'm happy with it. When it *does* bother someone else, then I'm in trouble.

And your characters share this watcher/doer problem?

Felix in *The Odd Couple* isn't a watcher—or a doer. He's stuck. He's reached a certain point in his life and developed no further. *Most* of my characters are people who are stuck and can't move. The grandmother in *Lost in Yonkers* has been stuck for the last seventy years. The mother in *Broadway Bound*—she's *really* stuck.

I remember George in **Chapter Two** *saying, "I'm stuck, Jennie . . . I'm just stuck some place in my mind, and it's driving me crazy." Going back to* **Barefoot in the Park,** *Corie's pretty hard on your surrogate Neil when she tells him he's not a doer. But, come to think of it, what could be more venturesome and brave—or foolhardy—than the real Neil opening a play on Broadway and exposing it to the critics and the audience?*

It *is* the most frightening thing in the world—and it was almost a matter of life and death for Joan and me with *Come Blow Your Horn.* If it had failed I would have been forced to move to California and become a comedy writer in television. But I don't worry about it anymore, and I think not being fearful of what's going to happen has allowed me to write so much. If I *do* worry, I say I won't do the play, because that means I don't think it's that good.

Is the opposite true? Can you anticipate a hit?

I never think of the plays as being hits when I write them. Well, I thought *Rumors,* of all plays, would be a really good commercial comedy if I wrote it well. I thought *The Odd Couple* was a black comedy. I never thought it was going to be popular, ever.

It's your most popular play, isn't it? All over the world.

Yes. And I thought it was a grim, dark play about two lonely men. I thought *The Sunshine Boys* wouldn't be a popular play, but it was very well received. *Chapter Two* was another one I doubted, because when you touch on a character's guilt, you touch on the *audience's* guilt, and that makes them uncomfortable. Yet the play turned out to

be very successful because it was a universal theme. *Lost in Yonkers* is an enormous success, but I thought I was writing the bleakest of plays. What I liked about it was that I thought it was Dickensian: two young boys left in the hands of dreadful people. What I was afraid of was that I would hear words like *melodrama.*

You heard "Pulitzer Prize." There are several plays that don't seem to fit in your canon. In plays like **The Good Doctor, Rumors, Fools** *and* **God's Favorite** *you seem to have a different agenda, there's a different relationship between you and the play than the one you've described. Could that explain their lack of critical and popular success?*

I wrote *The Good Doctor* soon after I learned my wife had a year and a half to live. She didn't know that. On the advice of the doctors, I'd elected not to tell her, and I wanted to keep on working, so it would seem to her that everything was normal. I was reading Chekhov's short stories and decided, just for practice, to translate one of them into my own language, my own humor. I knew it was a diversion. After a performance, a woman grabbed me in the foyer and said, "This is not Neil Simon!" *Fools* was an experiment that didn't work. *God's Favorite* is an absurdist black comedy about Job that was written as an outcry of anger against Joan's death. My belief in God had vanished when this beautiful young girl was dying. I wasn't Archibald MacLeish. I thought it would be pretentious for me to try to write something like a dramatic *JB.* So, I wrote it as a black comedy, and it did help me get through that period. Sometimes you write a play just for the sake of working at it. It's my craft. I'm allowed to go in any direction I want. I hate being pushed into certain places. Walter Kerr once wrote that he thought I was successful because I didn't listen to what was in fashion in the theater and went my own way at my peril, and that sometimes I suffered for it, and at other times I broke through. With *Lost in Yonkers* I suddenly heard from critics who said, "This is a new voice for Neil Simon. We want you to go deeper and deeper into this area." At the same time other critics complained, "I don't like this as much. It's not as funny as the old plays." They wanted *Barefoot in the Park* and *The Odd Couple.* I could have spent my whole life writing the *Barefoot in the Parks* and *Odd Couples,* which I certainly don't denigrate, because I love them—but, where would I have gone with my life? I would have been standing still, grinding out the same story time after time after time. What I've done, I think, is take the best of me and the best of my observations and try to deepen them to reform them and re-flesh them. At some point along the way you discover what it is you do best. Recently I've been reading Samuel Beckett's biography. When he was about forty-four years old, he said he wanted to write monologue. It was his way of expressing himself to the world. *He* was shy, too. In a sense, I think many of my plays are dramatized monologues. It's like sitting around the fire and telling you the story of my life and my father and my mother and my cousins and my aunts. In *Lost in Yonkers* I know I'm one of those two boys, probably the younger one. Who that grandmother is, who Aunt Bella is, with her adolescent mind, I don't know.

You seem to be saying that **Lost in Yonkers** *is even less autobiographical than the Brighton Beach trilogy.*

I'd say **Lost in Yonkers** isn't autobiographical at all. You asked me earlier whether I write thematic plays. I don't, but I have a feeling that in **Lost in Yonkers** there was a theme within me that was crying to get out, a common denominator that got to everybody. In the last fifteen, twenty years, a phrase has come into prominence that didn't exist in my childhood: dysfunctional family. My mother's and father's constant breakups seemed to show little concern for my brother and me. It was like coming from *five* broken families. That pain lingers. Writing plays is a way of working out your life. That's why I can never conceive of stopping, because I would stop the investigation of who I am and what I am.

You have the reputation of being a tireless, even an eager, rewriter. How much of the rewriting is done during the first drafts of the play, and how much do you rewrite after the play has gone into rehearsal?

I would say that I do no fewer than three to four major rewrites on a play before we go into rehearsal. I write the play, put it aside, take it out six months later, read it. By then I've forgotten everything about the play. It's as though someone had sent it to me in the mail and I'm reading it for the first time. I can tell right away what I don't and do like. That becomes a very easy rewrite: you just get rid of the stuff you don't like. Then we start auditions for actors, so I keep hearing the words every day. After a while I can't stand some of them, and I start to rewrite, so, in later auditions, the actors get a better script to read. I finally say it's the last draft before we go into rehearsal, and we have a reading of the play in a room with just the producer, director and a few of the other people who will work on the play, one month before rehearsal. At that reading we have the entire cast, so now I know what it's going to sound like. Based on that reading, I'll do another major rewrite. It's rare that I would ever do what they do in musicals: "Why don't we switch scene four and scene two?" I write in a linear way, so that everything falls apart if you take anything out. Sometimes, if even a few sentences come out of the play, something suffers for it later on. Once the play opens out of town, the most important rewriting begins, based on not only the audience's and the out-of-town critics' reactions, but the reactions of ourselves, the actors, and some people we've invited to see the play and comment. I also listen—if I can, to the audience's comments on the way out of the theater. That becomes harder now that I've lost my invisibility.

How do you remain objective with all those voices in your ear?

Mostly it's my own intuition. I bring in rewrites no one has asked for. I'll suddenly come in with five pages, and

the director and the actors will say, "You didn't like the other stuff?" I'll say, "I think this is better." If you bring in seven pages, maybe three will work. That's a big percentage. You're way ahead of the game. An analogy for it would be if you were in college and took a test, and your grade came back. You got a sixty-three on the test, and they say, "Come back tomorrow. You'll be given exactly the same test. There'll be no new questions." Well, you're going to get an eighty-four on the second test. You'll have had chances to fix it. That's what happens to a play. Day by day, it gets better and better. In the case of **Jake's Women,** in the first production a couple of years ago, there were a lot of things wrong. It was miscast, I had a director I was unfamiliar with who didn't really understand my process. We opened with a play that was about a sixty-two on a possible grade of a hundred. I brought the play up to about a seventy-eight. As we got toward the end of the run, just prior to going to New York, I thought, you can't get by in New York with a seventy-eight. You need at least a ninety-six or ninety-seven. So, I said to everyone, let's just pull it. And we did. I thought it was dead forever, because I'd put so much into it and wasn't able to save it. Two years later I took another crack at it and did a major rewrite in which, as I've told you, I had Jake speak to the audience. The play took a whole new turn. I thought it was finally up in the ninety-percent bracket.

If a play is truly flawed, how much can you do to improve it?

Well, in the case of something like **The Gingerbread Lady,** which *was* a flawed play, the producer was going to put up a closing notice in Boston. Maureen Stapleton, who was starring in the play, came to me and said, "If you close this play I'll never speak to you again." She said, "This is a potentially wonderful play. It needs work but don't walk away from it!" I thought, what a reasonable thing to say, because all it amounted to was more of my time. The producer said he wanted to close, to save me "from the slings and arrows of the critics in New York." I said, "I can take the slings and arrows. I've had enough success up to now. I'll *learn* from this one." What finally made up my mind, after reading three terrible reviews in Boston, was, while waiting at the airport for my plane, I picked up *The Christian Science Monitor,* and the review was a letter addressed to me. It said, "Dear Neil Simon, I know you're probably going to want to close this play, but I beg of you, don't do it. This is potentially the best play you have written. You're going into a whole new genre, a whole new mode of writing. Don't abandon it." So, I called the producer and said, "Please don't close the play. Let's run in Boston and see what happens." Then, I didn't want to get on a plane and arrive in New York an hour later; I wanted a four-hour trip on a train, so I could start the rewrite. By the time I got to New York I had rewritten fifteen pages of the play. I stayed in New York for a week and came back with about thirty-five new pages. And we went to work. The play was never a major success, but we did have a year's run, and sold it to the movies. Maureen Stapleton won the Tony Award, and Marsha Mason, who played the lead in the film version, got an Oscar nomination. So, something good came out of persevering.

Your plays have become darker in the last several years. Is this a sign of maturity or a wish to be taken seriously, since comedy generally isn't as highly regarded as so-called "serious plays?"

Maybe the plays matured because *I* matured. I *do* want to be taken more seriously, yet I want to hear the laughter in the theater. The laughs are very often the same gratification to the audience as letting themselves cry. They're interchangeable emotions.

Most of the darker plays take place in your childhood. Does that mean that your childhood was dark, or that your view of your childhood and perhaps of the world has darkened as you've matured?

My view of my childhood was always dark, but my view of the world has darkened considerably. The darkness in my plays reflects the way the world is *now*. The darkness in the plays, strangely enough, seems more beautiful to me. I think anything that is truthful has beauty in it. Life without the dark times is unrealistic. I don't want to write unrealistically anymore.

What do you consider your strongest suit as a writer? And what in your view is your weakest suit?

I think my blue suit is my weakest.

I knew it would come to this.

I think my greatest weakness is that I can't write outside of my own experience. I'm not like Paddy Chayefsky who could go off and do six months of research and then write something extremely believable. I'd *like* to write about Michelangelo, but I don't *know* Michelangelo. I don't know what his life was like. I wish I could extend myself, but I don't think that's going to happen. I might play around with it from time to time. Those are the ones that wind up in the drawer.

If you ever have a fire sale of the contents of that drawer, call me. What would you say is your particular strength?

I think it's construction. Maybe what I write is out-moded today, the "well-made play"—a play that tells you what the problem is, then shows you how it affects everybody, then resolves it. Resolution doesn't mean a happy ending—which I've been accused of. I don't think I write happy endings. Sometimes I have *hopeful* endings, sometimes optimistic ones. I try never to end the play with two people in each other's arms—unless it's a musical. When I was writing three-act plays, a producer told me the curtain should always come down on the beginning of the fourth act. A play should never really come to an end. The audience should leave saying, "What's going to happen to them now?" As the plays progressed, some people wanted darker endings. Some critics even said the ending

of *Lost in Yonkers* wasn't dark enough. But I can't write a play as dark and bleak and wonderful as *A Streetcar Named Desire*. I fall in some gray area. There is so much comedy within the dramas or so much drama within the comedies.

In her interview for The Paris Review, *Dorothy Parker said she got her character names from the telephone book and obituary columns. Do you have a system for naming your characters?*

There was a time I used to take baseball players' names. The famous ones were too obvious, so you had to take names like Crespi. There was a guy named Creepy Crespi who played for the St. Louis Cardinals. Crespi would be a good name, although I've never used it.

It's got a nice K sound in it.

Yes. I try to name the character the way the character looks to me. I spend more time on the titles of plays than on the names of the characters. What I've tried to do over the years is take an expression from life that has a double entendre in it, for example, the musical *Promises, Promises,* so that every time people speak the words it sounds like they're talking about your play. Or *The Odd Couple*—people sometimes say, "They're sort of an odd couple." If you mention an odd couple now, you think of the play. I've seen the words maybe a thousand times in newspapers since, and it seems as if I originated the term, which, of course, I didn't. *Come Blow Your Horn* comes from the nursery rhyme. *Barefoot in the Park* came from what the play was about. There's a line in the play that comes from my life, when Joan used to say to me, "Stop being a fuddy-duddy. Let's go to Washington Square Park and walk barefoot in the grass." *Chapter Two* was, literally, the second chapter of my life, after my wife Joan died, and I married Marsha. *Prisoner of Second Avenue* was a good title for a play about a man who loses his job and is left to live in that little apartment on Second Avenue while his wife goes to work. He has nothing to do but walk around the room 'til he knows exactly how many feet each side is—so he's literally a prisoner. *The Gingerbread Lady* is a bad title. I liked the title and then had to make up a phrase about the gingerbread lady to make it fit. The film title was better: *Only When I Laugh. The Star-Spangled Girl* was a better title than a play. I liked *Last of the Red Hot Lovers.* It seemed familiar. It comes from Sophie Tucker's slogan, "Last of the Red Hot Mamas." *Lost in Yonkers*—I love the word Yonkers, and I wanted to put the play in a specific place. I said to myself, "*What* in Yonkers?" These boys are lost, Bella is lost, this family is *all* lost . . . in Yonkers. *Jake's Women* is literally about a man named Jake and three women. Again, there's the *K* sound in Jake.

Let's talk about stage directors. How much can a director help a play? Or, conversely, hurt it?

Well, in the early days, I worked principally with Mike Nichols. He was after me day and night. "This scene isn't good enough. Work on this. Fix this." He'd call me at two or three in the morning, to the point where I'd say, "Mike, give me a chance, leave me alone. You're on my back all the time." But, I always knew he was right. I wasn't that experienced a playwright. The way I work now—with Gene Saks—the conversation is generally short. He might say to me, "There's something wrong with this scene." I'll say, "I know what you mean. Let me go home and work on it." I'm much less influenced by the director now than I was before. I depend on the director in terms of *interpretation* of the play. With *The Brighton Beach Trilogy* and *Lost in Yonkers,* I watched with clenched fists and teeth as Gene was directing, thinking, that's wrong, it's all wrong what he's doing. Then, suddenly, I *saw* what he was doing, and said, "Oh God! He has to go step by step to get to this place, trying all his things, the way *I* would try them at the writer's table."

How much do actors influence you? Is it ever the case that the personality of an actor influences you to remold the character to the actor, playing into what you now perceive to be the actor's strength?

I might do that. But what I try to do in terms of rewriting is always to benefit the *character,* not the actor. There's something an actor sometimes says that drives me crazy: "I would never do that." I say you're *not* doing this, the *character* is. The one thing I almost always look for is the best actor, not the funniest actor. I rarely, rarely cast a comedian in a play. The best comedian I ever had in a play was George C. Scott. He was funnier than anybody in the third act of *Plaza Suite* because he was playing King Lear. He knew the essence of comedy is not to play "funny." I remember, at the first reading of *Barefoot in the Park,* the whole cast was laughing at every line in the play. When we finished the reading, Mike Nichols said, "Now forget it's a comedy. From here on we're playing *Hamlet.*"

I notice in the printed plays that you use ellipses, italics and all-caps. I assume the ellipses are meant to tell the actors when you want them to pause, the italics are meant to give emphasis, and that all-caps ask for added emphasis, even volume.

Yes. They are a first indication to the actor and the director. Some of those emphases change enormously in the rehearsal period, but I also have to worry about what's going to be done in stock and amateur and European productions, so I hope it's a guide to what I meant. *The Prisoner of Second Avenue* opens in the dark. All we see is a cigarette, as Mel Edison comes in. The part was played by Peter Falk. He sat down on the sofa, took a puff of the cigarette, and in the dark we heard, "Aaaahhhhhhh." I don't know how you're going to be able to spell that, but it's got a lot of *h*s in it—a *lot* of them. It got a huge laugh because the audience heard two thousand years of suffering in that "Aaaahhhhhh." When Peter left and other actors played the part, they would go, "Ahh." There weren't enough *h*s, and the line wasn't funny. People tell me that

when they study my work in acting class, the teachers have to give them the sounds, the nuances, the way the lines are said. I guess Shakespeare can be said a thousand different ways, but in certain kinds of lines—for example, that run on "Ho" in *Biloxi Blues*—everything depends on the timing of it. I've always considered all of this a form of music. I wish I could write tempo directions, like *allegro* and *adagio.* That's why I put dots between words or underline certain words, to try to convey the sense of music, dynamics and rhythm.

Do the critics ever help you, shedding light on your work, regardless of whether they're praising or damning it?

Walter Kerr gave me one of the best pieces of criticism I've ever had. In the first line of his review of *The Star-Spangled Girl,* he said, "Neil Simon didn't have an idea for a play this year, but he wrote it anyway." That was exactly what had happened. Elliot Norton was very helpful to me in Boston with *The Odd Couple.* His title of the opening night review was, "Oh, for a Third Act." He wasn't going to waste his time telling everyone how good the first two acts were. His job, he felt, was to make me make the third act better. And his suggestion to me was to bring back the Pigeon sisters. I said, "Good idea," brought back the Pigeon sisters, and the play worked. More important than the reviews, it's the audience that tells you whether or not you've succeeded. A week prior to the opening of the play you know if it's going to work or not. If ninety percent of the critics say it doesn't work, well, you already knew that without having to read the reviews. On the other hand, the opening night of *Little Me,* Bob Fosse and I were standing in the back of the theater. The producers had allowed a black-tie audience to come from a dinner to the theater. They'd eaten, they'd had drinks, they all knew each other—that's the worst audience you can get. About three-quarters of the way through the first act, a man got up, so drunk he could hardly walk, and staggered up the aisle looking for the men's room. As he passed Bob and me, he said, "This is the worst piece of crap I've seen since *My Fair Lady!*" Go figure out what *that* means.

Maybe the reason comedies like **Barefoot in the Park,** **The Odd Couple** *and* **The Sunshine Boys** *are sometimes underrated is quite simply that the audience is laughing at them—rather than worrying, weeping, learning—or doing any of the other virtuous things an audience is reputed to be doing at a drama. However, I think most writers would agree that it is relatively easy to make people cry and very, very hard to make them laugh.*

Billy Wilder, whom I respect enormously, once confided in me, "Drama's a lot easier than comedy." He found some of the brilliant dramas he wrote, like *Sunset Boulevard,* much easier to write than the comedies. Comedies are relentless, especially a farce like *Some Like It Hot.* **Rumors** was the most difficult play I ever wrote because not only did every moment of that play have to further the story, complicate it and keep the characters in motion—*literal* motion, swinging in and out of doors—but the audience had to laugh at every *attempt* at humor. You don't have five minutes where two people can sit on a sofa and just say, "What am I doing with my life, Jack? Am I crazy? Why don't I get out of this?" You can do that in a drama. You can't do it in a farce.

Do you make it a point to see the plays of other playwrights?

When I was in my late teens and early twenties, I went to the theater a lot. There was always a Tennessee Williams play to see or a great English play. It was such an education. I learned more from bad plays than from good ones. Good plays are a mystery. You don't know what it is that the playwright did right. More often than not you see where a work fails. One of the things I found interesting was that a lot of comedy came from drunks on the stage. If a character was drunk he was funny. I thought, wouldn't it be great to write characters who are as funny as drunks, but are not drunk. In other words, bring out the *outrageousness* of them, and the only way you can do that is to put them in such a tight corner that they have to say what's really on their minds. That's where the humor comes from.

Are you a good audience for other people's work? Do you laugh in the theater? I know some writers who are just not good audiences. Would you call yourself a good audience?

I'd call myself a *great* audience. I'm appreciative of good work, no matter what its form—comedy, drama, musical. I saw *Amadeus* four times. *A Streetcar Named Desire* I could see over and over. When I'm in England I go to some of the most esoteric English plays, plays that never even come over here, and I'm just amazed at them. I've recently caught up with the works of Joe Orton. I love Tom Stoppard's plays *Jumpers* and *Travesties,* and I admire the work of Peter Schaffer. If it's good theater, yes, I'm the best audience. I'm out there screaming.

Comedy has changed in a very noticeable way in the last thirty years. Subjects and language that were taboo are now almost obligatory. Do you think that indicates progress?

I like the fact that one can touch on subjects one wouldn't have dealt with in years gone by. The things that Lenny Bruce got arrested for you can find on any cable station today. Television situation comedy doesn't seem as funny to me as what Chaplin and Buster Keaton did without words. There are a few good comedians, but by and large I don't think comedy is a lot better today.

You seem to exercise a certain constraint over the language of your plays. Even **Biloxi Blues** *doesn't use the kind of profanity and obscenity I remember from my days at that same airfield.*

I think to say *fuck* once in an entire play is much more shocking than to say it sixty times. Four of the last five plays I've written took place in the thirties and forties, when profanity wasn't used on stage—or in the home. The fifth play, **Rumors,** is contemporary, and it's *filled* with profanity. But I don't need profanity. I love language, and I'd rather find more interesting ways to use it than take the easy way out.

Every playwright has fingerprints. You've mentioned thinking of your plays in musical terms, and one fingerprint of yours seems to be the "aria." At a certain point in almost every one of your plays a character in extremis *launches into an extended list of all the catastrophes that are happening to him. In* **Come Blow Your Horn,** *Alan says, "You're using my barber, my restaurants, my ticket broker, my apartment and my socks. How's it going, kid? Am I having fun?" In* **Plaza Suite** *the father explodes, "You can take all the Eislers, all the hors d'oeuvres and go to Central Park and have an eight thousand dollar picnic! I'm going down to the Oak Room with my broken arm, with my drenched, rented, ripped suit and I'm going to get blind!" Are you aware of doing that?*

Yes, it's a fingerprint. You'll notice that those arias always come near the end of the play. The character has reached the point where he can't contain himself anymore, and everything comes spurting out, like a waterfall, a cascade of irritations. Just mentioning one of them wouldn't be funny, but to mention *all* the irritations wraps up a man's life in one paragraph.

The words you use to describe your comedy are words that are generally associated not with comedy at all, but with tragedy. You've talked about catharsis and your characters exploding when they can't bear the pain anymore.

Yes. That's why I don't find television comedy very funny—because it's hardly ever about anything important. I think the weightier comedy is, the funnier it is. To me, Chaplin's films are masterpieces. Remember him running after a truck with the red warning flag that has fallen off it?

And he doesn't see hundreds of rioting radicals falling enthusiastically in behind him . . .

So he gets busted and goes to jail as their leader.

Maybe when the record is written a hundred years from now it will turn out that all our comedy writers, from Chaplin and Keaton to you and Woody Allen, were writing tragedies. What's the cliché? Comedy is tragedy plus time. How fine is the line between tragedy and comedy?

It's almost invisible. I think Mel Brooks is one of the funniest people in the world, but when he makes a picture like *Spaceballs,* he's telling us, "This is foolishness. No one is in danger," so the audience knows it's too inconsequential to laugh at. But when he does a picture like *High Anxiety* or *Young Frankenstein* there's something at stake. He's taken a frightening idea and twisted it, so we're able to laugh at it.

Here comes a difficult question . . .

As long as it doesn't have to do with math.

I don't know a writer who wouldn't say that—or a musician who isn't good *at math. Because music is mathematical, I guess.*

But so are plays. As surely as two plus two is four, the things you write in the play must add up to some kind of logical figure. In **Broadway Bound,** when Stan is teaching Eugene the craft of comedy, Eugene says, "It's just a comedy sketch. Does it have to be so logical? We're not drawing the plans for the Suez Canal," and Stan says, "Yes we are. It's not funny if it's not believable."

Well, now that we've covered math and logic, here's the difficult question. You write repeatedly about an uptight man and a liberating woman: is that because it's a reflection of your relationship with the women in your life—or because you feel it's a common and important theme?

The answer is quite simple. It's because I'm an uptight man who's been married to three liberated women. Joan was the first liberated woman I ever met and the most unconventional. She introduced me to more ways of looking at life than I'd ever dreamed of. She was more adventuresome than I'd ever been. She would jump from a plane in a parachute, and I'm the uptight man who would say, "You're crazy." Marsha was the same way. She was a feminist and had me marching in parades with a flag, yelling for women's rights. It's not that I didn't believe in women's rights, but I'm not an activist. Diane is an environmentalist, an ecologist and also a fighter for the rights of women. Go over all the plays. With the exception of **The Odd Couple** and **The Sunshine Boys,** you'll find that the women are not only stronger but more interesting characters than the men. Again, the men are usually the Greek chorus. That's me sitting there, little Neil, born Marvin, observing the world—verbally, from a very safe place, which is what the man does in **Barefoot in the Park,** which is what he does in **Chapter Two,** in almost every play.

In the theater, in films, rugged men usually liberate unfulfilled women. From what you say, your plays reverse that convention.

Yes. I never feel threatened by women. I have enormous respect for them. I would also usually rather be with them than with men. I'm not much of a male bonder. I have male friends, obviously. I belong to tennis clubs. But in a social situation, I'd generally rather talk to a woman because it's like a play: you're getting the opposite point of view. You talk to a man, you're getting your own point of view. It becomes redundant. But when you're with a woman, that's when the sparks fly, that's when it's most interesting.

Plays these days are usually in two acts rather than three, and you are using more and shorter scenes. Is that the result of changes in stage technology? Are you being influenced by film?

I think I've been influenced by films, which have been influenced by television and commercials. Today you can see a one-minute commercial with about forty setups in it. There's a need to pace things differently because the audience's attention span has grown shorter. **Biloxi Blues** was the first major example of that because I had fourteen set changes. What also helped speed things along was that I started writing plays with larger casts, so there were many more entrances and exits. Also, having a narrator makes big time-leaps possible. I *am* influenced by new technologies and techniques, but that doesn't mean I'm following the fashions. It just means that I'm moving to another phase in my career—I'm becoming less literal and more abstract.

You've mentioned finding your characters waiting for you every time you walk into your office. Dickens complained that he hated to end his books because he didn't want to say good-bye to the characters he'd been living with.

That's why I don't go back to see my plays again, because they belong to someone else—to the actors and the audience. That process happens in a series of events. First, you finish writing the play, and everyone reads it. Then you go into rehearsal. Day by day, it slowly becomes the director's and the actors'. They're still asking me questions. I'm still participating. I'm still the father of these children. They get onstage, and soon the play is finished. They no longer need me! I feel locked out, I'm not part of them. After the play opens, I'm almost embarrassed to go backstage, because it's the place that belongs to the director and the actors. I'm just the man who introduced the characters to them. It's a very, very sad feeling for me. What happens eventually—it may sound cold—is that I disown them. I have no interest in seeing the plays again. In fact, it's painful, especially when a play has run for a long time and new actors have come in to replace the original cast. When I walk into that theater, it's as if I were picking up my family album, and turning the pages to see my mother and father and aunt and cousins—and I say, "This isn't my family!" So, you give it up and go on to the next play.

And the next. And the next.

Every time I write a play it's the beginning of a new life for me. Today as I listen to you read excerpts from these plays and talk about them, it makes me feel nostalgic about how wonderful those days were—but I'm enjoying *these* days of writing, even though I see that the sun is setting.

OVERVIEWS AND GENERAL STUDIES

Clifford A. Ridley (essay date 20 November 1971)

"Neil Simon, Boffmeister," in *The National Observer,* Vol. 10, No. 46, November 20, 1971, p. 24.

[*In the following essay, Ridley observes that in* The Prisoner of Second Avenue *Simon has moved from the cheerful innocence of his early comedies to a comedy painfully aware of distress and hopelessness.*]

As **The Prisoner of Second Avenue** begins to unfold, it's clear that Mel Edison (Peter Falk) is your prototypical middle-class New Yorker. A 46-year-old account executive who has lived six years in his 14th floor apartment—handsomely realized by Richard Sylbert—at Second Avenue and 88th Street, he is beset by all the existential woes of the urban condition.

It's 89 degrees outside, but it's an airconditioned 12 in his living room. The stewardesses next door play *Raindrops Keep Fallin' on My Head* at 3 in the morning. All his food is artificial, and health food makes him sick. Dogs bay in the streets; garbage piles up in the courtyard. "In three years," he says, "this apartment is going to be on the second floor."

Mel Edison, in brief, is quite literally losing his sanity; and in establishing this condition, Neil Simon has done his best work to date. His new "comedy" opened last week at the Eugene O'Neill Theater in New York (I saw it at the last Washington tryout). If it is not a wholly successful play, it is a wholly admirable one.

PARADE OF CATASTROPHE

In those opening moments, Simon catches the feel of New York existence, the sense of raw nerve ends rubbing crazily against each other, about as well as anyone ever has. If art consists in appropriating the stuff of everyday existence and stripping it down to essentials, he has made a mad, dissonant art form out of ordinary urban clay. His concern is reminiscent of *Little Murders,* but where Jules Feiffer saw the urban world in terms of surreal, unseen, almost Godlike forces at play, Simon sees it as a congeries of tangible, petty irritations. Feiffer's Alfred has been deadened by the city, stripped of all his responses; Simon's Mel still greets each successive indignity with a wisecrack, although he knows it does no good. He has only to turn on his television—a large screen appears on the curtain between scenes—to hear of an endless parade of strikes, muggings, abductions, and other catastrophes that make his circumstances pale by comparison.

Still, those circumstances grow worse. His apartment is robbed—denuded of money, clothing, liquor, and TV set. ("Nothing to drink and nothing to watch!" he wails at the point of total despair, and in its evocation of modern loss the cry is as bone-chilling as anything in Euripides.) And in an economy move, he is fired from his job.

YOU KNOW HIS MIND

At this point Mel's predicament begins to seem a good deal less laughable than it looked at the outset, and Simon wisely cools the play down, forcing your sympathy for a man who is in fact at the brink of mental collapse. Simon has attempted this tragicomic blend before—notably in the first playlet of **Plaza Suite,** the first act of **Last of the Red Hot Lovers,** and almost all of **The Gingerbread Lady**—but he is singularly successful here because he has set you up so well. His evocation of the daily harassments in urban life has been so meticulous, so concrete, that you know the battered condition of Mel Edison's mind as you have known little else in the Simon canon.

And then Simon does an unfortunate thing. As Mel stands on his balcony during a shouting match with an upstairs neighbor, he gets a bucket of water dumped on him. Actually, it's not a bad metaphor—the crowning insult, all that—but in this context, in this play by this playwright, it shatters the mood. It's okay, Mabel; we can start laughing again. Curtain.

The second and last act is a mixed assortment. At the outset, Mel has been out of work seven weeks and his wife (Lee Grant) has gone to work to support the two of them. It is a devastating, funny portrait of a bored and useless man that Simon paints here, shading slowly toward Mel's total mental collapse. Yet the collapse itself is overdrawn and improbable, and again the playwright draws laughs where he needs them least.

Did he perhaps *intend* to create a laughable breakdown? I don't think so, for he follows it with a break-the-ice sort of family conference at which Mel's brother and sisters agree to furnish him X amount of dollars toward his recovery—so long as X is very small. Another devastating scene, this, and matters proceed briskly to the final curtain, at which—you may have guessed it—Mel is doused for a second time. And by this point, Neil Simon is sounding very much like Jules Feiffer, for Mel and Edna—like Alfred—ultimately conclude that if you can't beat urban insanity, you might as well join it. At the final curtain they stare out from their tastefully upholstered sofa, as alone and indomitable as the couple in *American Gothic,* awaiting their revenge.

This is a different Neil Simon than the one who used to laugh just for the hell of it; if you want to know *how* different, I refer you to *The Comedy of Neil Simon,* an anthology of work from **Come Blow Your Horn** to **Last of the Red Hot Lovers.** Yet in another sense he's not so different; in a sense Neil Simon's journey is the journey of many of us over the past several years.

There's a clear connection, after all, between the 6th floor, walk-up love nest of **Barefoot in the Park** and the 14th-floor, express-elevator strait jacket of **The Prisoner of Second Avenue.** Mel and Edna Edison could be the Corie and Paul Bratter of that 1963 comedy grown up, but the timing is wrong: Mel and Edna have children in college. Wait, however: Suppose we assume that Corie and Paul didn't move into their loft in 1963, but in 1953? Then it all works out.

And they did, you know, for the fact is that comedy in 1963 dealt with a world that had stopped existing for almost everyone but newlyweds and comedy writers. Simon and his comperes had their details right, but the mood was wrong, their characters still believed in the perfectibility of man and his works, although many people in real life did not. Today, however, the message reaches us a hundred times a day. And so the toilet that was cute in *Barefoot in the Park,* flushing only if you pulled the handle *up,* has become a gurgling monster in *The Prisoner of Second Avenue,* refusing to *stop* flushing until the handle is jiggled.

EDNA'S LAMENT

This is the key to the change in Neil Simon, along with the change in many of us: In eight years, that damned toilet has been fixed tens of times, and it still doesn't work. Nothing works. Or as Edna Edison puts it: "Is the whole world going out of business?"

Yet there are still people who choose to ignore all this, who visit a Neil Simon play in the expectation of recapturing the world of *Barefoot in the Park,* of guffawing mindlessly at unreal and untroubled people. That is why the twin dousings in *The Prisoner of Second Avenue* are so unfortunate: Coming from Neil Simon, the old boffmeister, they trigger an avalanche of brainless and cruel laughter that I'm convinced Simon did not intend. I must ask you to forgive the cliche here, but at these moments, and during Mel's crackup as well, Simon is asking us to laugh because it hurts too much to cry. But that's not the kind of laughter he's getting.

It's a shame. Directed with *eclat* by Mike Nichols and performed to near perfection by Peter Falk and Lee Grant, *The Prisoner of Second Avenue* is a much better play than it likely will receive credit for being.

Helen McMahon (essay date October 1975)

"A Rhetoric of American Popular Drama: The Comedies of Neil Simon," in *Players Magazine,* Vol. 51, No. 1, October, 1975, pp. 11-15.

[*In the following essay, McMahon argues that Simon introduces serious themes in his plays, which challenge accepted attitudes and practices, only to later trivialize them and reinforce a conservative status quo.*]

Critical opinion of Neil Simon's plays during his fourteen years as a playwright has been, in general, mocking and pejorative; yet his plays just as consistently have been box office hits. Almost all of them have been converted into films, a television series derived from *The Odd Couple* ran for several years, and his plays are the staple of Summer Theatres and Community Theatres. Seven of his plays are listed as "long runs," having achieved more than 500 continuous performances on Broadway. Simon's second play, *Barefoot in the Park* (1963), with a run of 1,530

performances, is fifteenth on that list of some 243 plays, not too far behind *South Pacific, Oklahoma, My Fair Lady, Hello Dolly, Life with Father,* and *Fiddler on the Roof* (the play that now tops the list with 3,242 performances). Twice in his career, Simon was represented on Broadway with three and four plays running simultaneously. Not surprisingly, however, he has never won the New York Drama Critics Circle Award or the Pulitzer Prize for Drama.

Some recent reviews of Simon's latest play may suggest the problems involved. The epigraph for Walter Kerr's favorable review of *God's Favorite* reads: "Neil Simon has been more than clever. Would you go for diabolical?"[1] Kerr begins by defending Simon's takeoff of the Book of Job, suggesting that it is "material for broad farce." He calls it a satyr play, defining the genre for us as "a burlesque of harrowing tragic material." "Because the material is innately funny," Kerr continues, "it needs no profound original message of its own to deliver and (is) allowed an open-door policy on jokes . . ." He admits Simon's inclination for simple-reflex gags, even providing us with an example on one; but he invites us not to be deterred by them because, he says, *God's Favorite* doesn't function that way—from joke to joke.[2]

In describing a particular scene, Kerr uses actor names rather than character names. This association of actor with character is especially apt in discussing Simon's play's because a certain kind of sad-faced comic actor, a Walter Matthau or a Nancy Walker, for instance, does much to sustain the equivocal attitudes implicit in the plays. Kerr tells us that God's emissary, played by Charles Nelson Reilly, "a flutter of a fellow," comes by bicycle from Jackson Heights to deliver God's message to the American Job, Vincent Gardenia. We have learned earlier that the devil looks like Robert Redford.

> But Mr. Gardenia's family, huddled in parkas and stocking caps because the heat's gone off, hasn't [heard the news yet]. It is inclined to be extremely dubious as Mr. Gardenia explains about messengers from Jackson Heights, devils, and all that. "The messenger saw the Devil?" asks son Terry Kiser with a curl of his lip. "What's he look like?" Mr. Gardenia doesn't answer immediately. He simply stands there, mouth open like a stapler that hasn't been punched yet, unable to speak the words that are so patently absurd. In his pause a laugh comes up, starting small and delayed and then expanding in discovery; it turns into a wave that engulfs the house. The audience is exactly as far ahead of Simon as Simon wants it to be; an adopted and rather strabysmic angle of vision is writing its own play, gags and all. Mr. Simon has been more than clever. Would you go for diabolical?

Jack Kroll offers an entirely different perspective of Simon's work:

> Like an annual outbreak of warts, the critic's yearly problem is back—what in God's name to do about Neil Simon? . . . like that battered but unbowed institution [the Presidency], the institution called Neil Simon still

stands, calmly flicking the critical pigeon droppings from his lapels. Nevertheless, here goes one more dive-bombing run right between Simon's spectacles. My megaton dropping this year is as follows: Neil Simon is just what we deserve . . . As with all funny guys, Simon's real subject is the pain of it all. But unlike Chaplin, Keaton, Fields, the Marx Brothers, he does not detonate human experience into grenades of laughter whose shrapnel rips up the pomposity of homo sap. Instead, Simon trivializes experience with a shower of one-liners that tickle, sometimes hit a valuable spot, but never draw blood. Simon is the gagman laureate of the Age of Triviality . . . In *The Odd Couple* Simon trivialized the pangs of divorce into the problem of using the washing machine; in *The Prisoner of Second Avenue* he trivialized urban anxiety into the annoyance of thin walls and faulty air conditioning in high-rise apartment buildings.[3]

Kroll's examples of trivializing are both ridiculing devices and deceptions. For every problem, whether it be growing old or losing a job, getting married or divorced, Simon focuses—not on the problem—but on the physical surroundings of the setting and on the personal idiosyncracies of his stereotype characters. An apt example, in the third one-act of *Plaza Suite,* is the mother's concern, on her daughter's wedding day, for a run in her stocking and the need to keep up appearances. All during the scene the torn stocking gets more emphasis than the conflict between parents and daughter.

In direct contrast with Walter Kerr, Brendan Gill's response to *God's Favorite* is "one of indignation":

> I would have expected to content myself with reporting that, despite its having been written as a comedy, it amounts to a grim and often distressing medley of trumped-up, unfunny jokes, ill told and thoroughly unsuited to the action they purport to embody; instead, I find that I feel more strongly about the play than that. I find that it looms before me as a colossal impertinence—a jeer not at religion, though Mr. Simon in his ignorance manages to affront both Judaism and Christianity, but at literature.[4]

These few critics, whether they like or dislike Simon, do seem to suggest that he is in the service of the stock response and that he mixes his modes. Depending on the critic, Simon writes Boffo comedies or "bastard tragedies" when he should be writing satires.

One last quotation from the weeklies because it links the new Simon play with other Broadway hits and makes an interesting generalization about a certain kind of popular Broadway play. In a review of a Murray Schisgal play (*All Over Town*), which opened a few weeks after *God's Favorite,* Jack Kroll writes that

> Schisgal's play belongs to a kind of New Conservative black comedy that includes Neil Simon's new play, *God's Favorite,* Bruce Jay Friedman's "Scuba Duba," Mel Brooks' "Blazing Saddles" and, at a higher level, Saul Bellow's "The Last Analysis." These comedies operate in that area where, as Bellow says,

"laughter turns into insanity." The insanity these writers see is the breakdown of the old order with its comfortable certainties, now replaced . . . with 'strikes, revolution, anarchy, chaos.'

> The problem with much of this work is that the writers are really lamenting not the breakup of old faiths, but the comfort that has been lost with this breakup. Tragedy is the flea in the pelt of comedy, but in Simon, Friedman and Schisgal the real tragedy is the sheer inconvenience that urban middle-class chaps like themselves have to undergo as the old order changeth.[5]

The old order—if we can construct it from the seeming anxieties of Simon's characters—appears to be made up of washing machines, air-conditioners, stockings, uncollected garbage, cute apartments, etc. They add up to an idolatry of creature comforts, the worship of which is disturbed by the exigencies of life and by the presence of other people—landladies, neighbors, wives, fathers, and children. Simon's plays are actually "tragedies of the middle class" posing as zany escapist entertainment. Perhaps it is the deception that bothers the critic because the plays do seem to contradict themselves.

The problem, I think, is both moral and aesthetic. In comedy the nature of the characters and the conflicts they experience are normally the platforms from which the humor is launched. The conflict, even in farce, ought to be established and apparently resolved. We don't need to be too serious about conflict in farce, of course, except in terms of the ending—the assumption being that one side overcomes the other and the other is reconciled to the new situation.

In Simon's plays, which operate without a clear thematic structure, the conflict is blurred. He begins each play with contrasting character types—one sloppy man vs. one neat man; one swinging bachelor vs. one shy young man; one radical and one patriot; one free spirit and one conservative—each apparently motivated, or defined rather, by slogans and a particular illusion about life. The goal or philosophy, if you will, of any particular character—protagonist or antaganist—has to do with appearances—one conforming, more or less, to the conventions of the old world, of neatness and comfortable financial success, and the other experimenting with all kinds of freedom and the conventions (fads) of the new. The situation in which these disparate characters are located is of a serious and often sentimental nature and relates to problems of middle age, marriage, divorce, identity, and, of course, sex and success; but the characters are not allowed to be serious about them for very long. The contrasting characters, limiting themselves to trivial concerns, only suggest a conflict, which will be resolved in an apparently "happy ending." Not unexpectedly, given this kind of fuzzy conflict, the plays will be resolved by compromise.

Simon manipulates his characters and his materials with certain devices which, in performance with skillful direction and a certain type of actor, disguise the flaws in reasoning. In the text, however, Simon fails to accomplish the transformation from conflict to resolution. He appears to abandon the structural conflict until the end of the plays and to focus on the disparate natures of his characters. These contrasting attitudes, then, are the source of invective and vituperative and the primary tenor of his plays. Between the beginning and end, the plays more or less wander toward their destinations through a series of vaudeville routines.

Whatever the apparent conflict, Simon's plays conclude surreptitiously on the side of conservatism. Each of the comedies ends—after having equivocated the conflict—in a return to the status quo. The characters have only changed hats with each other. The plays really should be satires, but the playwright conspires with his manic joking and diversionary tactics to outlaw reality, because reality would necessitate recognition and change and the dismissal of illusions rather than equivocation, conversion and compromise.

Despite Simon's strategies, it may be that he depends too much on the realistic mode to depict his fantasies; and stage realism, even in comedy, makes certain thematic and technical demands which he ignores. Simon shares some of the problems of Arthur Miller's suffering characters. He continues in the later part of the twentieth century to flirt with the American dream, and his characters seem to want to have it both ways.

In the play where Simon uses two contrasting men, brothers or friends, one of them compromises in some way his initial swinging bachelor position (usually to marriage) and the other quite without motivation takes up the characteristics or role of the one who marries (***Come Blow Your Horn, Star Spangled Girl,*** and ***The Odd Couple***). There is much laughter, and one boy always gets a girl. The happy ending or the new society which is usually formed at the end of comedies is thus in Simon not new, but only made to seem new.

The third one-act of ***Plaza Suite*** is a good example of this kind of switch or ambiguity in Simon. Financially successful parents, hard working urban New Yorkers, have rented rooms at the Plaza for their daughter's wedding. As the act begins, the daughter, Mimsey, is discovered locked in the bathroom and refusing to talk to her parents. This suggested conflict introduces thirty or so minutes of the parents pleading, threatening, feeling sorry for themselves, or, complaining about a torn stocking, a ripped morning coat, the cost of the wedding ($8,000), the ingratitude of "college graduates," and having devoted their lives' effort to giving their daughter the fanciest wedding this side of Hollywood. This serious-cum-farcical situation climaxes in the father's venturing onto the hotel ledge to get to the bathroom window. After the gag situations have reached nadir or zenith, the girl agrees to see her father and tells him that she is afraid her marriage will be like theirs. This motive, viable as it may seem, introduces a serious idea and a sentimental moment. It is not, however, examined or transformed. Instead, the situation is undercut in a deadly

fashion with a kind of joke. The parents send for the fiance. He appears, cool and calm in his cutaway, is told of the situation, walks to the bathroom door and says, "Mimsey? . . . This is Bordon . . . Cool it!" He then leaves the room, "without looking at the parents," and "without showing any more emotion." The girl comes out of the bathroom without a murmur and is glowingly ready for the wedding.

Farce and sentiment are mixed: absurd and pitiable situation-comedy parents do battle with a "spoiled darling" daughter; she introduces a *soupcon* of concern about the meaning of life; and the problem is resolved with a phrase: "Cool it." The expression may be contemporary but the behavior of the characters, including the young man, is finally banal and conservative. There is laughter in this play because Simon has exploited the surface of the familiar frenzy of weddings; but there is an underlying morbidity also because he has injected into a skit about a wedding certain sordid complaints about life. If it is true that laughter arises from feeling of superiority, then these comedies are indeed cruel in their intentions. However, unlike Buster Keaton, these characters are unable to get up and walk away from the fall.

An excerpt from Oliver Goldsmith's essay, "A Comparison between Sentimental and Laughing Comedy" (1772), may be useful as an analogy here:

> Yet notwithstanding . . . the universal practice of former ages, a new species of dramatic composition has been introduced under the name of *sentimental comedy,* in which the virtues of private life are exhibited, rather than the vices exposed; and the distresses rather than the faults of mankind make our interest in the piece. These comedies have had of late great success, perhaps from their novelty, and also from their flattering every man in his favourite foible. In these plays almost all the characters are good, and exceedingly generous; they are lavish enough of their tin money on the stage; and though they want humour, have abundance of sentiment and feeling. If they happen to have faults or foibles, the spectator is taught not only to pardon, but to applaud them, in consideration of the goodness of their hearts; so that folly, instead of being ridiculed, is commended, and the comedy aims at touching our passions, without the power of being pathetic. In this manner we are likely to lose one great source of entertainment on the stage; for while the comic poet is invading the province of the tragic muse, he leaves her lovely sister quite neglected.[6]

The principle of Simon's techniques, then, is to switch from any consistent consideration of an idea to a gag. In addition to this oscillation between the serious and the joke and the equivocal conflict between two opposite types with the same goal, many other devices support Simon's slight of hand. Multiple associations are made with the world outside the play: the characters are familiar types from other popular Broadway plays, television, the film, and the novel; the actors who perform in Simon's plays share the same familiarity; and the setting of each play in apartments in different areas of New York City—uptown, downtown, East and West sides—provides additional associations and instant familiarity with subjects not explored in the plays. And, finally, topical allusions to middle and lower class experience in New York City, to assorted news items, and to the world of fad and fashion of any given period fill the gaps in structure and give an appearance of reality.

An example from an early play may demonstrate Simon's principle of switching back and forth between opposites, which allows his characters, at the end of the action, to have it both ways. In *Barefoot in the Park,* a romantic, well-to-do, free spirited, sexy girl rents a fifth floor apartment (sixth counting the front stoop) which the newly-wed husband has not yet seen. Although climbing the stairs exhaustedly provides much of the comedy and takes up a certan amount of time, the conflict established is between craziness and stuffiness, between freedom and responsibility, between new fashions and old fashions. The adventurous girl has been known to walk barefoot in Central Park, but her new husband is a briefcase carrying young lawyer who gasps when he climbs the stairs and has no inclination or time for the new and adventurous. A neighbor is introduced. He is a 58-year-old bluebeard and lives in the attic above their flat. In order to get to his room, when he is locked out for non-payment of rent, he has to go through their bedroom window and walk along the ridge of the house to his attic. He is a foil for both the girl and her husband. This Victor doesn't puff when he climbs the stairs; in fact, he savors every moment of life. He even surpasses the girl in intensity of living. After an elaborate experience which consists of eating an "exotic" appetizer and traveling to Staten Island to eat an "exotic," if horrible, meal, the differences between the tired and stuffy husband and the fun-loving and apparently never-tiring Victor are made more than clear. Apparent differences in character climax in a quarrel which promises to dissolve the marriage. Suddenly, as if by magic, a happy ending is achieved. The husband gets drunk, walks barefoot in the park (in February), and the girl, responding to her mother's advice and to love, is tamed.

Although this early play uses typical Simon devices and is generated by a conflict between old ways and new, it doesn't worry the critic because it is, perhaps, Simon's only straight romantic farce—the characters are young and goodlooking and the problems are minimal. The experience in Simon's other plays, however, is more serious and, often, tawdry. They are, therefore, more resistant to contrived happy endings: while one faction in the plays stresses bourgeois creature comforts and old world responsibility, the other flirts with bourgeois sins which, more often than not, hint at extra-marital sex. We seem then, to have characters with the instincts of one order adopting temporarily the behavior of the pervailing new order.

Actually, Simon's characters all belong to the old order—both the middle-aged characters and the spoiled children;

but they give lip service to whatever is topical in the new movements. Walking barefoot becomes a part of the conflict in Simon's second play written in 1963 at about the time that students in colleges were taking their shoes off all over the world. Critcizing LBJ, making jokes about LSD and "burning draft cards" are the topical allusion in *Star Spangled Girl* (1966).

The conflict in this particular play is, on the surface, one between two young men and a girl. The young men publish an avant garde magazine which criticizes the President, the Government, the Establishment, etc.; the girl who provides the opposition and the sex is a 150 percent American Patriot. But these arm-chair radicals are at the same time hypocrites and chauvinists. They manipulate and patronize their women. The bulk of the play, a dozen absurd actions which are meant to define sexual desire of one of the young men for the girl, is his pursuit of this sexy girl. The complications derive from her exasperation with him. The play ends with her falling inexplicably in love with the other young man who has not pursued her but who, in fact, has shouted at her and ordered her about. The response of Sophie in *Girl* is thus unlike the response of Mimsey to Bordon in *Plaza Suite.* And the ending that undercuts the apparent conflict between the old order and new order is the impending marriage of a pseudo-radical to the Star Spangled Girl. The curtain comes down on the girl singing the "Battle Hymn of the Republic" as she cleans the boys' apartment.

In *Come Blow Your Horn,* an early play, the hero is a swinging thirty-three-year-old bachelor. The first act defines him: he spends the act manipulating girls in and out of his apartment and resisting, via wisecrack, any suggestion that he follow in the footsteps of his plastic-fruit manufacturing father. At the end of the play, he will marry and "settle down," and his formerly shy brother will take up his bachelor habits and apartment. In *Last of the Red Hot Lovers,* a sad-looking, fat, middle-aged married man tries, unsuccessfully and self-pityingly, to have an affair in his mother's apartment between 3:30 and 5:00 with women he has picked up (one to an act). This man salvages his desire for an affair at the end of the play by telephoning his wife to come to the apartment.

The plays, then, share a certain subject matter and plot structure, have a veneer of topicality and are supported by gags, jokes, and absurd behavior. Variations on the themes of unobtainable vain fantasies are played out, but the plays all end in the marriage bed, however devious and deceitful the way has been. The vagaries of sex and guilt, inadequacy and machismo (the plays are, to say the least, chauvinistic as well) have been circumscribed and made manageable.

Simon's plays are technically unsatisfying because he uses a disjointed tragi-comic story line with an enormous number of realistic and cliche details and verbal and sight gags to distract from the disjointed story. For the same reasons, the plays are thematically unsatisfying. Simon finally doesn't create a myth. Instead he utilizes the details of several myths. This kind of topicality allows for an appearance of reality at the same time that it lessens its virulence. If Simon has a theme in his bag of tricks, it may be that he is trying "to justify the ways of man to God." But his exploitation of the safe and familiar prevents exploration of the serious or the comic

Notes

1. *The New York Times,* December 22, 1975, p. 5.

2. See Gerald M. Berkowitz's article, "Neil Simon and His Amazing Laugh Machine," *Players* 47:3, February, 1972.

3. *Newsweek,* December 23, 1974, p. 56.

4. *The New Yorker,* December 23, 1974, pp. 53-54.

5. *Newsweek,* January 13, 1975, p. 51.

6. Bernard F. Dukore, *Dramatic Theory and Criticism* (New York: Holt, Reinhart and Winston, Inc.), 1974, p. 425.

Robert K. Johnson (essay date 1983)

Neil Simon, Twayne Publishers, 1983, pp. 16-22, 34-42, 43-51.

[*In the following excerpts, Johnson argues that the third act of* The Odd Couple, *is flawed because Simon has created such fully realized characters that he is unable to manipulate them convincingly for the happy ending he has contrived. Johnson also states that in* Plaza Suite *Simon is showing that outward success may not be enough, and that* Last of the Red Hot Lovers *does not meet the challenge it sets for itself to mediate the conflict between self-isolating cynicism and concerned human contact.*]

THE ODD COUPLE

It is significant that Simon originally envisioned **The Odd Couple** as "a black comedy."[1] He wanted to push beyond the simple comedy formats of **Come Blow Your Horn** and **Barefoot in the Park.** The tryout troubles that the new play incurred are also significant. On the first day of rehearsals, Simon realized that he had a weak third act. He began revising it that day and continued altering it throughout the long tryout period.

The play opens with a poker game held at Oscar Madison's apartment, the setting for all the scenes. Felix Ungar is late joining his friends, for earlier in the day his wife and he separated. Oscar, divorced from his wife, Blanche, offers to let Felix move in with him, and Felix accepts the invitation. The two men, however, immediately begin to get on each other's nerves. Oscar is lazy, disorganized, and sloppy. Felix is compulsively neat and a hypochondriac.

During another poker game two weeks later, the friction between the two men intensifies. A few nights later, Oscar

arranges a double-date for Felix and himself with Cecily and Gwen Pigeon. On that evening, Oscar upsets Felix by thoughtlessly causing the meal Felix has cooked to burn up. Felix spoils everyone else's mood by delivering a morose monologue about his separation from his wife and two children. The next evening Oscar, still fuming, tells Felix to move out of the apartment, and Felix does so. But it is clear to Oscar's poker-playing cronies, back for another game, that Oscar feels guilty about throwing Felix out into the night. Then Felix returns with the Pigeon sisters to collect the rest of his things; the two women, taking pity on Felix, have invited him to share their quarters. Oscar is surprised, but relieved, and the two men part amicably.

Simon skillfully makes the weekly poker games an entertaining means of presenting expository information about Oscar and Felix and highlighting the domestic changes in the two men's lives. Simon underscores those changes by contrasting them with the sameness of the poker-game format. During the game in Act One, for instance, the audience quickly learns that Oscar is more than a bit of a slob. He offers his friends "brown sandwiches and green sandwiches." When asked what the green is, he replies, "It's either very new cheese or very old meat." One friend, Roy, commenting on Oscar's housecleaning inabilities, observes, "His refrigerator's been broken for two weeks. I saw milk standing in there that wasn't even in the bottle."[2] Even though Oscar is a highly paid sportswriter, he owes the other players money. Through a phonecall from his ex-wife, the audience discovers he is three or four weeks behind in alimony payments. Because it is unusual for Felix to be late for the game, the other men worry aloud about him. By this means, Simon sketches in much of Felix's basic personality. Particular emphasis is placed on his hypochondria and other fears and on his compulsive desire for neatness.

After the other men leave, Oscar and Felix elaborate on their own personalities, particularly their faults. Felix speaks of coming home after his wife and the hired help had cleaned all the rooms and cleaning the rooms again himself. A good cook, he recooked all the meals. Oscar describes some of his own marital faults. He let his cigars burn holes in the furniture and he drank too much. He insensitively dragged his wife to a hockey game to "celebrate" their tenth wedding anniversary.

Still, the two men reveal more about themselves to the audience than they do to each other. Oscar, for instance, is not wholly the happy-go-lucky guy he appears to be. He humorously admits to his friends that he loves to bluff while playing poker. It becomes evident, however, that he puts up a front in other ways, too. Although he seems unconcerned about living alone, he tells Felix, "When you walk into eight empty rooms every night it hits you in the face like a wet glove" (244). When Felix remains hesitant about moving in, Oscar blurts out that he truly wants Felix to move in, and that he is not just doing Felix a favor. He says, "I can't stand living alone" (248).

Felix, too, gives himself away more than he realizes when he declares himself a better cook and, by implication, a better financial manager and housecleaner than his wife, Frances. He is so intent on listing his faults he fails to perceive that he is, in fact, almost entirely absorbed in himself. Unlike the audience, Felix is startled when told he is full of self-love, an observation Oscar makes when he states he has "never *seen* anyone so in love" (246) with himself as Felix is. This same shoe, however, also fits Oscar's foot. Oscar says he is impossible to live with; but he does not really believe this is so—else he would not invite Felix to come live with him.

In point of fact, for all the self-criticism the two engage in, neither man truly thinks he is such a bad guy. Each is tacitly convinced his good qualities far outweigh his faults. Moreover, each believes that some of the faults confessed to are actually either not faults at all or are faults bred and subsumed by virtues. Deep down in their hearts, both men believe they are by no means entirely to blame for the demise of their marriages. Coming full circle, Oscar asserts, "It takes two to make a rotten marriage" (246). Although not conscious of what they are doing, they think they now, by creating a happy "marriage," are about to prove how decisively their good points eclipse their bad points.

They do not, however, live happily ever after. The first indications of trouble are the direct comments they exchange at the poker game in Act Two. Cleverly, Simon counterpoints the friction between Oscar and Felix by means of the other four participants in the card game. Vinnie and Murray, similar to Felix in temperament, appreciate the changes Felix has rendered in the apartment. They relish especially the striking improvement in the quality of the food offered. Speed and Roy, akin to Oscar in personality, are irritated by the innovations. Roy goes so far as to say he preferred things the way they were before Felix moved in. Felix's self-love prevents him from discerning how annoying his housekeeper's quirks are. Finally sensing Oscar's mounting anger, he says in surprise, "I didn't realize I irritated you that much" (259).

The double-date ignites the final blowup. Before the big evening begins, Felix tells Oscar he will cook the dinner for the foursome; he also promises not to dwell on his unhappy past. Elated, Oscar exclaims, "That's the new Felix I've been waiting for" (266). Oscar's high hopes for the get-together, however, prove unfounded. Almost as soon as he leaves Felix alone with the two women in order to make everyone a drink, Felix breaks his promise. Because he obviously thrives on brooding about his woes, he tells the women how lonely and unhappy he is away from his wife and children. As he verbalizes his feelings for the first extended time since the end of his marriage, the full weight of his sad situation hits him—so much so he breaks down and begins crying. The Pigeon sisters, touched by Felix's sorrow, become teary themselves. Returning to the "party," Oscar finds three very somber people and becomes incensed at Felix. In order to hurt Felix, Oscar informs him that his London broil is ruined.

The whole matter of the food for dinner makes it clear that Felix is not the only one of the two men who continues to display unpleasant, annoying traits. One reason the meat is spoiled is that Oscar promised to be home at seven o'clock and then did not arrive home until eight—without bothering to inform Felix he would be late. Nonetheless, it still would have been possible for Felix to serve a succulent dinner if it had been served right away, as Felix had wanted it to be. But Oscar insists that they all have a drink first. To top it all off, while he is out in the kitchen mixing drinks, Oscar neglects to check on the London broil. In sum, Oscar is as uncaring as Felix is overly fussy.

When Felix's anger prompts him to declare he will not join Oscar and the ladies in the latters' apartment for the rest of the evening, Oscar says, "You mean you're not going to make any effort to change? This is the person you're going to be—until the day you die?" Felix responds with, "We are what we are" (284). In point of fact, neither man wants to change or thinks he should.

Despite the revisions Simon fashioned during the play's tryout run, the third act dips below the high quality of the preceding acts. Simon himself wrote that *The Odd Couple* is basically a sound play, but that the "seams show a bit in the third act. I rewrote it five times out of town. I think I needed one more town."[3] Because Simon is a master of the rewrite, it is entirely possible that, if allowed more time, he would have made his third act as fine a piece of work as the first two acts are. Even in its present form, the third act deserves praise.

The two men's final confrontation is thoroughly gripping. It is also quite funny. Oscar tries to bully Felix by declaring that everything in the apartment is his own; he concludes, "The only thing here that's yours is you" (286). Felix will not be intimidated. He reminds Oscar that he pays half the rent and then rattles Oscar by threatening to walk around in Oscar's bedroom. Oscar counters by commanding Felix to remove the plate of spaghetti from the poker table. When Felix needles Oscar for not recognizing that the food is linguini, not spaghetti, Oscar hurls the plate against the kitchen wall and states, "Now it's garbage!" (287).

Their confrontation peaks as Felix asks Oscar to be less vague regarding what it is about Felix that bothers him. Felix inquires, "What is it, the cooking? The cleaning? The crying?" Oscar answers, "It's the cooking, cleaning and crying" (288). Felix unloads on Oscar, describing him as "one of the biggest slobs in the world" as well as unreliable and irresponsible. Not to be outdone, Oscar states that he was merely a little dejected after living alone in the apartment for six months, but that now, after living with Felix for only three weeks, "I am about to have a nervous breakdown" (290).

Simon, however, did not wish the play to end with the two men angrily going their separate ways. He wanted a happy ending, an ending that left the audience still tickled by and fond of Felix and Oscar. To achieve this, Simon decided to have the two men part amicably, respecting each other as much or more than they did before they roomed together. Like the characters themselves, the audience is to believe that as a result of their living together, Oscar and Felix have had a positive effect on each other.

In an effort to create a change in Felix's character, Simon has Felix come out of his shell a little and release some of his long-suppressed anger and frustration. Oscar is so surprised by Felix's comparatively uninhibited behavior that he remarks, "What's this? A display of temper?" (289). When Felix believes his wife, Frances, has phoned the apartment, he instructs Murray, who answered the phone, to tell Frances that he "is not the same man she kicked out three weeks ago" (300). Simon indicates that Oscar has changed, too. Although Oscar suppressed whatever modicum of guilt he felt for causing his marriage to end in divorce, he now admits to feeling guilty about throwing Felix out of the apartment. A further indication of his change in personality, and an indication of Felix's effect on him, occurs at the very end of the play. Oscar—for the first time ever—reprimands the other poker players for their sloppiness. He protests, "Watch your cigarettes, will you? This is my house, not a pig sty" (301). Furthermore, both men acknowledge that they have helped each other. Oscar says that Felix should thank him for doing two things—taking Felix in and throwing him out. Felix responds, "You're right, Oscar. Thanks a lot" (299).

All the same, Simon's attempt to create a happy ending for a play that started out as "a black comedy" does not work. By the time he wrote this play, Simon had become too skillful at presenting realistic characters for him suddenly to reduce Oscar and Felix in the third act to puppets he could pull any way he wanted to. When he wrote ***Come Blow Your Horn***, he could arrange his happy ending without a great deal of difficulty because, except for Mr. Baker, the characters were little more than slickly depicted, broad types. In ***Barefoot in the Park***, Simon produced much more lifelike characters, particularly in Paul, Corie, and, most of all, Mrs. Banks. Consequently, it was harder for Simon to make the characters do whatever he wanted them to do in order to end the play on a cheery note. Hence the partially flawed resolution of that play.

Oscar and Felix are vivid personalities in the first two acts of ***The Odd Couple***. There was no way that Simon could force these two characters to do whatever he wanted them to do in Act Three. The main point dramatized in Act Two is that Oscar and Felix have learned nothing from the failures of their marriages. They are exactly the way they were while married. Because they doggedly insist on asserting their considerable egos, it is abundantly clear they will never change. The "marriage" between them was bound to end in an angry "divorce."

Although Oscar was largely to blame for the failure of his marriage with Blanche, he felt little remorse. That he would instantly be filled with intense guilt feelings about

his "breakup" with Felix—a "breakup" for which he was at most only fifty percent to blame—is quite implausible. It is even more unlikely that he, the great bluffer, would almost immediately confess to his friends how guilty he felt. Nor would Felix sincerely assume a major portion of the blame. Rather, he would talk—endlessly, if allowed—about his "flaws," but simultaneously make it clear that all his "flaws" were actually the result of his superiority to Oscar.

Walter Kerr brought the point home when he wrote, "Those two men haven't learned anything from their marital quarrels that will help them share an apartment now, and they aren't going to learn anything from their quarrels now that will help them next time around. . . . They aren't going anywhere, except into new failures."[4] Simon himself perceived this truth, although he did not proceed to honor his perception. In Act Three he presents an insightful exchange between Murray and Oscar. Having just banished Felix, Oscar is already worried about his friend, whom Oscar envisions wandering aimlessly through the streets all night. He tells Murray that the primary reason for his concern is that he was the one who sent Felix out into the night in the first place. Murray contradicts him:

> Murray: Frances sent him out in the first place. *You* sent him out in the second place. And whoever he lives with next will send him out in the third place. Don't you understand? It's Felix. He does it to himself.
>
> Oscar: Why?
>
> Murray: I don't know why. *He* doesn't know why.
>
> (296)

Simon shows the audience why. Neither Felix nor Oscar will ever live happily with someone else because they are both incapable of doing what Simon in ***Barefoot in the Park*** wisely suggested people should do. Neither man will compromise. Each is a willful egotist.

Simon, then, has to take "the blame" for creating two main characters who are so vibrantly alive they cannot be mechanically manipulated during the play's closing minutes. Nonetheless, like ***Barefoot in the Park, The Odd Couple*** is, overall, good in so many ways it easily overrides its third-act weaknesses. The play's high quality results not only from its superb delineation of two interesting individuals, but from the incongruous juxtaposition of those two individuals. As Howard Taubman stated, Simon's "instinct for incongruity is faultless."[5] It was, in fact, inevitable that Simon's plays move toward a major emphasis on the incongruous, for Simon sees incongruity as a primary feature of human reality. In his introduction to *The Comedy of Neil Simon*, he describes an argument his wife and he were having in the kitchen. In the middle of the argument, his wife "picked up a frozen veal chop recently left out on the table to defrost, and hurled it at me, striking me just above the right eye. I was so stunned I could barely react; stunned not by the blow nor the intent, but by the absurdity that I, a grown man, had just been hit in the head with a frozen veal chop."[6] So, too, one reason Simon writes comedies instead of tragedies is his acute awareness of how much of a man's life is riddled with comic incongruities.

Oscar and Felix's attempt to share living quarters, it can be argued, is the most captivating dramatization of incongruity Simon has yet created. The two men are wildly incompatible roommates. The humor ries out of their clashing personality traits and domestic habits—and out of how preposterous the very idea of their living together is. They, of course, see nothing incongruous about trying to room together. An awareness of the incongruous depends on a person's ability to remove himself far enough from a situation he is a part of to see that situation from a second, less subjective point of view. Self-love presents Oscar and Felix from obtaining this perspective. Indeed, the core of **The Odd Couple** is Simon's successful presentation of the serious dangers of self-love.

But perhaps the final triumph of Simon's play is that Oscar Madison and Felix Ungar—and Simon's whole concept of "the odd couple"—have become as much a part of our cultural folklore as Babbitt, Superman, Holden Caulfield, and Archie Bunker.

PLAZA SUITE

Both **The Odd Couple** and **Promises, Promises** indicate that Simon was gravitating toward writing comedies consisting of more than a stream of funny lines. **Plaza Suite,** a highly successful blend of humor and character study, completes the transition. Later, discussing his shift to this goal, Simon stated, "I used to ask, 'What is a funny situation?' Now I ask, 'What is a sad situation and how can I tell it humorously?'"[7]

"VISITOR FROM MAMARONECK"

Plaza Suite consists of three one-act plays, all taking place in the same hotel suite. The first play, **"Visitor from Mamaroneck,"** depicts the marital situation of Karen and Sam Nash. Aware that her husband has become increasingly indifferent to her after more than twenty years of marriage, Karen suspects he is having an affair with his secretary, Jean McCormack. So, while their house is repainted, Karen rents what she believes to be the same suite that Sam and she stayed in one their honeymoon. She has bought a sexy negligee and has deliberately not packed any pajamas for Sam. Sam soon joins her, but is totally preoccupied with his looks and with completing a big business deal. When Miss McCormack appears with data containing an error, Sam decides the two of them must meet back at the office to check the problem out. After Miss McCormack leaves, Karen confronts Sam with the fact that their marriage is deteriorating and asks him if he is having an affair with his secretary. Eventually Sam confesses he is. At first Karen tells him she will accept his

need for an affair with a younger woman; later, she asks him to end the affair. Although he loves Karen, Sam will not agree to her request and leaves to meet his secretary.

While **Promises, Promises** dealt with a husband and "the other woman," this one-acter centers on the conflict between the husband and wife. Simon stresses two additional conflicts—the turmoil within the husband and, above all, the turmoil within the wife. Initially, Karen is trying solely to keep the lid on the situation. Her goal is simply to rekindle the love Sam and she felt for each other in the early years of their marriage. She believes that if she can do that, she can defuse any problems bred by the deterioration of the marriage.

That her plan is a calculated one does not mean she has attained a coolly detached view of her predicament. On the contrary, the tension Karen feels is readily apparent. Learning from the bellhop that a famous New York building has been torn down, she immediately applies this fact to her own situation. She says that is how things are these days: if something is old, it is torn down. Other facets of Karen's personality are quickly revealed. She is a scrapper, which prepares the audience for Karen's later confrontation with Sam. Indeed, she fights even when she is sure she will lose. Before Sam arrives, she orders some hors d'oeuvres over the phone, stressing that she does not want any anchovies. Yet she expects (justifiably, as it turns out) that she will be served anchovies all the same. It is equally plausible that Karen would suspect the truth concerning Sam and his secretary, for she is remarkably willing to confront the truth. The stage directions state, "Karen is forty-eight years old, and she makes no bones about it."[8] She looks in the mirror and declares, "You are definitely some old lady" (500). Karen's honesty, however, has done more than lead her to realize her marriage is in trouble; it is one of the basic reasons the marriage *is* in trouble. Her husband will not accept that he is aging, and he resents Karen's acceptance of middle age. He even encourages her to lie about her age.

With Sam's entrance, the plot focuses directly on the marital relationship. It becomes clear that Sam expects Karen to concentrate selflessly on his needs and desires, but that when she does so, he takes her for granted. He recognizes her individual existence only when she fails to aid him competently. Karen's perceptiveness and her desire for a particularly pleasant evening with her husband pull her in two directions. Her suspicions concerning the possibility of Sam's infidelity mount. For one thing, although Sam explains his gruffness with her by stating he has a bad headache, he is all charm while talking with Miss McCormack on the phone. He also sidesteps Karen's comment that she has seen less and less of him at night in the past month. Still, she resolutely resumes cajoling Sam.

The situation intensifies when Sam decides he must meet Miss McCormack back at the office. Watching Sam primp and shave in front of the mirror, Karen intuits that Sam and Miss McCormack have previously arranged to meet this evening. Crushingly disappointed that her plan for a special evening with her husband is collapsing, she asks him if he is having an affair with his secretary. At first Sam denies everything. Then Karen says that "if at this stage" of Sam's life he wants to have "a small, quiet affair with a young, skinny woman," she would understand. Instantly Sam replies, "What do you mean, at this stage of my life?" (527).

Now the play scrutinizes Sam's character—for Karen has hit Sam where he lives. Earlier, Karen had lamented, "I'm not insane about getting older. It happens to everyone. It's happened to you. You're fifty-one years old." Sam retorted, "That's the difference between us. I don't accept it. I don't have to accept being fifty-one" (521). Karen's newest allusion to his age leads Sam for the first time to open up to Karen—and to himself. He takes primary responsibility for their marriage turning sour. Next, he confesses, "When I came home after the war . . . I had my whole life in front of me. And all I dreamed about, all I wanted, was to get married, and to have children . . . and to make a success of my life. . . . Well, I was very lucky. . . . I got it all. . . . Marriage, the children . . . more money than I ever dreamed of making." Puzzled, Karen asks, "Then what is it you want?" Sam blurts, "I just want to do it all over again . . . I would like to start the whole damned thing right from the beginning."

Karen's response to this poignant disclosure may be interpreted as a gag designed to keep the play from becoming too serious. She says, "Well, frankly, Sam, I don't think the Navy will take you again." It *is* a funny comeback. But it is more than that. Her remark reminds Sam that he cannot go back in time. It asks him to accept his present situation. For Karen senses that if Sam will accept the reality of his situation, their marriage has a chance.

Consequently, when Sam replies in turn, "Well, it won't be because I can't pass the physical," Karen is deeply shaken. She realizes that their marriage is in an even more precarious state than she previously surmised it was. She bluntly, unhumorously says aloud exactly what she is thinking: "I think you want to get out and you don't know how to tell me" (529). When Sam starts to leave, Karen for the first time lashes out at him, demanding that he stay and discuss their situation. Rocked again when Sam confesses that he is having an affair with his secretary, Karen reneges on her willingness to go along with such a development.

Karen is caught in a cruel dilemma. She knows that if she does not battle to break up the affair, Sam, in his obsession to "keep young," will become so enamored of Miss McCormack he will seek a divorce. Yet Karen is equally aware that if she pressures Sam to end the affair, she will become in his eyes a nagging, unattractive woman. She tells him she knows her criticism of him "makes everything nice and simple for you. Now you can leave here the martyred, misunderstood husband" (534). At her wit's end, she pleads with Sam to stay in the suite with her. Sam,

however, will not let himself surrender to age. Although his awareness that Karen is a fine woman prevents him from deciding then and there to divorce her, he feels he has to leave—at least for this night.

Neither of them knows if he will come back.

"VISITOR FROM HOLLYWOOD"

In the second sketch, **"Visitor from Hollywood,"** movie producer Jesse Kiplinger arranges a meeting in his suite with his old high-school girlfriend Muriel Tate. Muriel, well aware that Jesse has become famous, is both intrigued and intimidated by his fame. She talks about leaving for home throughout the early stages of the conversation. After Jesse tells her that his private life is as much of a failure as his professional life is a success, Muriel relaxes. They begin kissing. Later, while Jesse starts to remove her dress, Muriel starts asking him gossipy questions about other famous Hollywood personalities.

As in the previous one-acter, Simon uses a familiar situation. The first story features the eternal triangle. The situation in this second one-acter is that of the cosmopolitan male's attempt to seduce the uncosmopolitan female. Simon breathes new life into this situation by focusing not on the act of seduction, but on the motivations of the seducer and the seduced. Simon shows how complicated a simple seduction can be. The seduction is simple because both Jesse and Muriel want it to take place. What complicates matters is that each wants more out of the seduction than a sexual interlude.

Initially, Muriel is so impressed by Jesse's fame she is uncertain she can be a satisfactory sexual partner. After they kiss, she nervously asks Jesse, "Was it good?" Startled, he only after a moment or two has the presence of mind to reply, "It was a superb kiss" (547). Another problem arises when, early in the conversation, Jesse brushes aside Muriel's questions about glamorous Hollywood because he does not want to be reminded of his life out there. He wants to recapture the manly confidence he felt when young. Disillusioned by his personal experiences while in California, he sees Muriel as a symbol of his comparatively more innocent pre-Hollywood life. After their high-school years, however, Muriel's life became dismally mundane; and she is not at all interested in reliving "days gone by." Jesse's appeal for her is precisely that he symbolizes the Hollywood life-style she fantasizes about. When, for instance, he blurts out that his newest picture is "a piece of crap" (546), Muriel will have none of it. She quotes how much money it has made and ponders its chances of winning an Academy Award.

As a result, for a good while, no seduction takes place. Instead, each of them continues to pursue his or her private obsession. Jesse elaborates on his renewed interest in Muriel by telling her she is "the only, solitary, real, honest-to-goodness, unphoney woman" (548) he has been with since he went to Hollywood seventeen years ago. He tells her he remembers exactly what she wore the day he left her to go to Hollywood. He begs her never to change from "the sweet, simple way you are" (550). Muriel does not follow Jesse's lead. When he speaks of the day he left for California, Muriel states, "I remember when your first picture came to Tenafly" (549). All her reflections concerning their high-school years and her life thereafter relate directly to his later success. She informs him that their old high-school friends tease her, telling her, "If I married you instead of Larry, I'd be living in Hollywood now" (549). In response to his pleas that she never change, she says, "Do you know Frank Sinatra?" (550). More than a little drunk on vodka stingers, Muriel blurts out, "I suppose you'll go back to Hollywood and have a big laugh with Otto Preminger over this" (551).

Jesse's preoccupation with himself finally subsides enough for him to become aware of Muriel's fear of inadequacy. Quickly he begins reassuring her that he has only the warmest feelings for her. Then, as a further means of wooing Muriel, but also because he sincerely needs to express the unhappiness churning within him, Jesse tells Muriel the truth about himself. He confesses he has been humiliated both financially and sexually by his three former wives. Staggered by these defeats, he yearns for the unthreatening atmosphere of innocence he is convinced existed back when he dated Muriel. He wants this so much he ignores a blatantly obvious fact—namely, that Muriel is not now (if she ever was) the uncomplicated high-school sweetheart he persists in believing she still is. He also does not confront the pathetic contradiction in, on the one hand, his delight in Muriel's supposed innocence and, on the other hand, his desire to have sexual intercourse with her in order to reassure himself about his sexual prowess.

Jesse's confession provides the pivotal turn in his present relationship with Muriel. His words stoke Muriel's self-confidence. Previously, she had shuttled back and forth concerning how much free time she had. Now she relaxes and declares, "I've got plenty of time" (554). She completes the job of getting drunk. She admits her own marriage is a mess. She literally not once, but twice throws her arms around Jesse. And she insists he tell her some Hollywood gossip.

Sensing "victory," Jesse states what truly does express the sad—vain—hope both Muriel and he have. He says, "The world can change for one hour" (558).

Thus, both Muriel's daydream and Jesse's "come true." She is made love to by a Hollywood Celebrity. He makes love to an Innocent Woman. Muriel does not want to see, beneath the celebrity, a pathetically insecure, egotistical human being interested only in reasserting his masculinity by sleeping with a middle-aged groupie. Jesse ignores the fact Muriel has become a frustrated, calculating, hard-drinking housewife. On this day both Jesse and Muriel fornicate a fantasy. Consequently, they do not change their drab lives one iota.

Thematically, this one-acter ties in with the other two segments of *Plaza Suite* and with other writings by Simon.

As Edythe M. McGovern observed concerning Jesse, Sam Nash, and Roy Hubley, the main male character in the third one-acter, "There is an interesting commonality among the three principal male characters. . . . Each man has achieved the visible trappings of success as our middle-class world views that phenomenon. Each has reached the forty to fifty age bracket and somehow discovered that 'winning the goal' does not necessarily bring the satisfactions associated with that feat."[9] Jesse and Muriel also prove a point Simon dramatizes through the characters in *Last of the Red-Hot Lovers,* through Faye Medwick and Leo Schneider in *Chapter Two,* and through the Fran Kubelik/Jeff Sheldrake relationship in *Promises, Promises*—namely, that a relationship founded on sex without love is an emotionally bankrupt relationship.

"VISITOR FROM FOREST HILLS"

The third one-act play is much lighter fare. In **"Visitor from Forest Hills"** a prospective bride, Mimsey, locks herself in the suite's bathroom minutes before she is to be married. Unable to entice Mimsey out of the bathroom, Norma, her mother, phones her husband, Roy, downstairs. As soon as he arrives on the scene, he, too, attempts to convince Mimsey to unlock the bathroom door. He also attempts to break the door down and to climb in through the bathroom window. Finally, when her parents converse with her more calmly, Mimsey tells them what is bothering her. Still, she does not come out of the bathroom until her fiancé comes to speak to her.

Here Simon presents in semifarcical fashion the problems of communication and of making a serious commitment to another person when one is intensely aware of the dangers involved. The first problem dominates. When Norma phones downstairs, her future son-in-law's father is the first one to speak with her, and she tells him everything is going along beautifully; the instant her husband gets on the phone her suppressed desperation explodes in words. Yet it is only when Roy enters the suite that she tells him exactly what the problem is. For a minute, Roy does not believe what Norma tells him; then he pigheadedly decides that Norma must have caused the problem by saying the wrong thing to Mimsey.

The problem of communicating is even more effectively dramatized when, before Roy arrives, Norma tells Mimsey, "I know what you're going through now, sweetheart, you're just nervous." Failing to gain an immediate response from Mimsey, Norma shouts, "Mimsey, if you don't care about your life, think about mine. Your father'll kill me" (561). What becomes increasingly clear is that, in large part, Mimsey refuses to come out of the bathroom because her parents fail to use the right approach with her. Norma should have continued concentrating on what Mimsey was thinking and feeling on her wedding day. Instead, Norma selfishly switched her concern to herself—to her fear about what Roy would say to her when he discovered what Mimsey had done.

Norma's selfishness is more than matched by her husband's. As soon as he enters the suite he says, "Why are you standing here? There are sixty-eight people down there drinking my liquor" (562). Roy's first words to Mimsey are, "This is your father. I want you and your four-hundred-dollar wedding dress out of there in five seconds!" (564). He asks Mimsey nothing; nor does he offer to discuss the situation. He simply issues a command stressing what preoccupies him most—the amount of money that the wedding is costing him.

Both Norma and Roy proceed to pay dearly for their almost continuous self-absorption. Norma rips her stockings while trying to peek through the bathroom-door keyhole. Later, pounding on the door, she breaks her diamond ring. Roy almost breaks his arm when he rams his shoulder into the door. His coat is ripped as he attempts to climb into the bathroom via the window.

Only when Norma begins to concentrate on how Mimsey feels do the parents make any progress. At one point, she exclaims to Roy, "Is that all you care about? What it's costing you? Aren't you concerned about your daughter's happiness?" (565). Later, in a moment of exhaustion, Norma says to Roy, "I'll tell you who can get into that bathroom. Someone with love and understanding. Someone who cares about that poor kid who's going through some terrible decision now and needs help. Help that only *you* can give her and that *I* can give her" (577). Momentarily humbled by this insight, Roy for the first time tries seriously to communicate with his daughter. Soon Mimsey talks quietly with him in the bathroom, after which Roy phones the bridegroom, Borden, and asks him to come up. Roy then explains to Norma that their daughter is afraid that Borden and she will become exactly like her parents, whose marriage, filled with incessant bickering, the audience has just seen on display.

When Borden arrives, Roy says, "It seems you're the only one who can communicate with her." Borden strides to the bathroom door and says, "Mimsey? . . . This is Borden. . . . Cool it!" (581). With these few comically cryptic words—and the strength and reassurance offered in his tone and manner—Borden has communicated with Mimsey. Mimsey comes out of the bathroom. Her parents, who have exchanged thousands of words with each other, but who have rarely communicated love for one another, are left bewildered. So, they once again do what they have always done: they turn on each other. Roy says, "What kind of a person is that to let your daughter marry?" Norma snaps back, "Roy, don't aggravate me. I'm warning you" (582).

Despite the faint scent of sadness that permeates the atmosphere of all three segments of *Plaza Suite,* especially the first two, many critics regarded Simon's latest comedy as no different from all his previous work. Or they considered it retrogressive. Walter Kerr was more perceptive. He wrote that "a shadow of substance has become the base for the joke" in Simon's comedies. Kerr went on to point out that Americans tend to disbelieve that a comedy can contain any serious point. He stated, "One of

the crazy mistakes we make in the contemporary theater is that in supposing that if something is serious at all it must be thoroughly, thumpingly serious." Kerr concluded: "There *are* small truths . . . truths of a size that can be accommodated in—and almost cheerfully covered over by—a quip."[10] Amid the laughter it evokes, *Plaza Suite* offers incisive character delineations that dramatize several insights into human experience. To perceive these insights, however, and to perceive the high quality of Simon's finest creative achievements, one must accept the possibility that a writer can simultaneously make people laugh and offer them valuable insights.

LAST OF THE RED-HOT LOVERS

Although *Last of the Red-Hot Lovers,* like *Plaza Suite,* is a mixture of character delineation, humor, and observations about contemporary life, there are important differences in the two plays. While all three segments of *Plaza Suite* are soundly constructed, the second act of *Last of the Red-Hot Lovers* is flawed. On the other hand, in the later play Simon scrutinizes various attitudes toward the human experience more intently and directly than he ever ventured to do before.

Plaza Suite featured three couples occupying the same rooms over a period of approximately six months. *Last of the Red-Hot Lovers* spotlights one man, Barney Cashman, and the three women he directs, in turn, to his mother's apartment during the course of ten months' time. The first woman to join Barney in the apartment is Elaine Navazio, who frequented the restaurant he owns. Barney, aware of the sexual revolution going on throughout the country, wants one romantic extramarital experience before he moves toward old age. Elaine simply wants sex. In his attempt to make the encounter more than a merely sexual one, Barney keeps talking and talking until Elaine becomes irritated and walks out.

Although Barney vows never again to try to set up an extramarital sexual tryst, he forsakes his vow nine months later. Accidentally meeting Bobbi Michele in the park one afternoon, he lends her money so she can hire an accompanist for her theater audition. The next day, she comes to his mother's apartment, supposedly in order to pay him back. She sees, though, that Barney will not pressure her either for the money or for sexual favors in lieu of the money. She also perceives that her descriptions of her "far out" life fascinate him; so she makes herself comfortable, talks at great length, and finally badgers Barney into smoking some marijuana with her before she leaves.

Within a month, Barney arranges a rendezvous with Jeanette Fisher. Jeanette and her husband, Mel, are good friends of Barney and his wife, Thelma. Barney is much more aggressive than he was on the two previous occasions. Jeanette, however, brooding about Mel's having an affair with another woman, is too depressed to follow through on her previous impulse to have sex with Barney. Instead, she leads Barney into a debate about whether there are any decent people in the world. Barney ultimately convinces her there are. Feeling less melancholy, Jeanette leaves. Barney phones his wife, Thelma, and tries to coax her into coming to the apartment for sex.

Barney, like the three husbands in *Plaza Suite,* is undergoing a middle-age crisis. Barney's crisis, however, is not caused by a desire to be young again, or by the need to prove his sexual prowess and rebuild his self-confidence, or by a daughter who bewilders him. Barney has become intensely aware of his own mortality. Realizing that he has settled into a bland life-style, and that other people's lives are freer and more exciting, Barney wants more out of his life.

When Elaine Navazio responds to his overtures while in his restaurant, Barney gives her the address of his mother's apartment and hurries there to wait for her. The setting symbolizes part of Barney's inner conflict. The building is new, but the furniture is old, "from another generation."[11] Barney and his values are from another, more conservative generation; but now, like the younger generation, he wants to "swing"—at least a little. His conflicting desires are underscored very quickly in the opening scene. Barney tells Elaine that she looks like someone who should be named Irene. She looks in the mirror and remarks, "No, I look like an Elaine Navazio" (587). Barney wants to see Elaine as an "Irene"—see her within a romantic context. Elaine sticks to reality. Thus, long before Barney articulates the point aloud, it is evident that he wants sex, but that he wants it to be part of a romantic interlude. Elaine wants a brief, intense sexual coupling.

Elaine relishes living on a sensuous level. She wants cigarettes, which she forgot to bring, and many refills of her liquor glass. She speaks straightforwardly and specifically of Barney's physically attractive features. She tells Barney that she gets intense cravings to "eat, to touch, to smell, to see, to do," and that for her a "sensual, physical pleasure" can only "be satisfied at *that* particular moment" (594—95). By no coincidence, then, she is the one who keeps bringing the conversation back to the question of when are they going to have sex.

Barney is shocked and dismayed by her directness and her starkly limited desires. While insisting he is not a prude, he repeatedly stresses that he does not want "just" a sexual encounter. He describes his intentions as "of a romantic nature" (598). In defense of choosing his mother's unexotic apartment for their meeting, he says, "I thought a motel was a little sordid" (599). When Elaine complains about Barney's incessant talking, he explains, "I just thought you might be interested in knowing a little bit more about me" (599). Goaded by her jibes, he says, "I find it disturbing, and a little sad, that your attitude towards people is so detached" (601). In sum, he cannot, after all, be like the young swingers he has heard about who have sex, plain and straight, with total strangers.

Nervous and upset, he ultimately succeeds in "humanizing" his encounter with Elaine even more than he wanted

to. As Jesse Kiplinger did with Muriel Tate, Barney reveals more about himself and his problems than he originally intended to do. He tells Elaine that other than with his wife, he has had only one sexual experience in his whole life: one night when he was young his brother took him to a middle-aged whore in New Jersey. He goes on to say that although he is for all practical purposes a success in life, he feels he has missed out on many things. What aroused this feeling in him was his increasing awareness of death—that "for the first time in my life I think about dying" (611). He became unhappy that he could be aptly described in one word: "nice." He asked himself, "Shouldn't there be something else besides opening the restaurant eleven o'clock every morning?" (611). So, he started daydreaming about having one extramarital experience, "an experience so rewarding and fulfilling that it would last me the rest of my life" (612).

Seeking to make his daydream come true, Barney gets far more than he bargained for, just as Chuck did when he pursued his dream girl, Fran, in *Promises, Promises.* For one thing, Elaine tells him, "If you want undying love and romance, take a guitar and go to Spain" (608). She also informs him that the whore he slept with might well have been her mother. When he preaches to her and inquires about her marriage, she lashes out, "I didn't come up here to get reformed," and tells him to "leave my sex life alone" (600).

Elaine does not want to analyze her situation, for she does not have any hope of improving her lot in life. She simply wants a moment of unthinking sensuous pleasure. She states, "I happen to like the pure physical act of making love. It warms me, it stimulates me and it makes me feel like a woman" (609). In other words, while Jesse Kiplinger and Muriel Tate kid themselves into believing that "the world can change for one hour," Elaine entertains no such illusion. She believes nothing will change the basically bleak human condition.

By the time the third-act curtain falls, the play reveals that in Simon's opinion Elaine's outlook is excessively grim. Thus, when, at his most sentimental, Barney describes Elaine as "sad and pitiful" (608), his description is not without validity. Yet Elaine, stung by this description, touches on the truth, too. She retorts that Barney is the pitiful one—and so much of a hypocrite that he should be in no hurry to pass judgment on others. She points out to him that as much as he is presently concerned about "poor" Elaine, once their afternoon together ends he will pray fervently that she never enters his restaurant again. She declares, "I don't know your problems and I don't care. . . . No one really cares about anything or anyone in this world except himself." She concludes that the only sensible guideline is: "If you can't taste it, touch it or smell it, forget it!" (609).

Timidly exploring the world at large, Barney has met someone living in a state of resigned, yet intense desperation that minimizes—at least temporarily—his middle-aged awareness that he will eventually die. In fact, Elaine is in far worse physical shape than Barney is. She repeatedly is racked by coughing fits so severe she is forced to hold onto furniture in order to keep from collapsing. Near the end of their rendezvous, Elaine tells Barney that "no one gives a good crap about you dying because a lot of people discovered it ahead of you. We're all dying, Mr. Cashman" (612).

Elaine's attack on Barney's musings about the human condition articulates a view of reality unmatched in fierceness by any other character's philosophy of life in any Simon play to date. It is a far tougher point of view, for instance, than either Fran's or Sheldrake's in *Promises, Promises*. It is so powerful that Barney will only begin to try fumblingly to undercut Elaine's beliefs ten months later—in Act Three—when he arranges to meet Jeanette in the apartment. A major flaw in Act Two is that it barely touches on the challenge Elaine's philosophy of life presented to Barney.

Nine months after his talk with Elaine, Barney again ventures beyond the world he knows best. Having helped Bobbi Michele out financially, he hopes his rendezvous with her will culminate in sex. But Bobbi comes at Barney from too many directions for him to steer her where he wants to go. It is not really even a matter of Bobbi defeating him in a battle of wills, for no conflict takes place. Barney almost immediately bogs down in merely trying to figure Bobbi out. Eventually, he gives up the effort. He is reduced to being a fascinated listener whom she pressures into operating on her terms. What dilutes dramatic interest still further is that, like Barney, the audience has no way of figuring Bobbi out. Various interpretations of Bobbi's character are suggested via her chatter early on. Unfortunately the rest of the scene merely keeps circling back to those same possible interpretations. It is no wonder that during the tryout period Simon worked more on this middle act than on the other two.

One of the few things that can be said about Bobbi with confidence is that she does not have a firm grip on reality. Not long after she arrives at the apartment, she says, "I love this neighborhood. . . . I once had a girl friend who lived on this block. Forty-seventh between First and York." Barney has to correct her: "This is Thirty-seventh" (615). She also tells Barney he is shorter than he looked the day before, and that she remembered him as having a moustache.

At times she appears to be one of life's helpless victims. Barney, for instance, feels sorry for Bobbi while she tells him a man in the airplane seat next to hers pawed her during a recent flight. Barney is startled to learn soon afterward that she gave her "assailant" her phone number. She complains about receiving obscene phone calls; but then it turns out that, instead of hanging up, she listens to the obscenities for fifteen minutes at a clip. She is sometimes equally misleading when describing less bizarre episodes in her life. Speaking about her audition the day

before, she tells Barney that David Merrick thought she was fabulous. Pressed by Barney about this reference to Merrick, she backs off, claiming only that *someone* with a moustache sitting out front praised her. She adds that she would have gotten the part, but the producers wanted a black girl. Yet when Barney later mentions she was turned down at the audition, she snaps, "I didn't say they turned me down. I said they took the black girl" (631).

Bobbi's angry outburst points to another facet of her personality. She undergoes sudden shifts of mood. When a roommate is slow to answer Bobbi's phonecall, Bobbi stops her blithe chatter and remarks coldly, "She hears the phone. She's just a lazy bitch" (620). Nor is she always as naive as she would like Barney to believe. More than a little paranoiac, she laments how cruel people have been to her, including the men with whom she has supposedly had affairs. Then she shrewdly comments, "Married men are rarely vicious. They're too guilty" (624). Although she appears not to listen to what Barney says, he mumbles something about smoking marijuana with her sometime, and later she reminds him of his promise and forces him to light up.

The only mild suspense in this scene resides in the question: what will Bobbi say next? But the audience's curiosity concerning the degree of truth in Bobbi's stories is stymied by there being no objective means of comparing her statements with the reality of her situation. All one can safely say is that while such characters as the "lovers" Jesse and Muriel tried to live an illusion, Bobbi's problem is much worse. She has no more than a tenuous hold on reality.

Still, some of the dialogue near the end of Act Two is important thematically to the play as a whole. Bobbi reassures Barney—and herself—that it is only a matter of time before others recognize her genuine talent as a performer. Then, in another shift of mood, she paranoiacally insists, "People don't want to see you make good . . . they're all jealous . . . they're all rotten . . . they're all vicious" (635). This declaration, as Edythe M. McGovern has pointed out, somewhat parallels Elaine Navazio's outlook on life.[12] Thus, Bobbi's statement reminds the audience that the challenge to refute this outlook has still not been met.

Bitter because she was turned down at the audition, Bobbi speaks of gaining revenge on the world by writing a book telling of all her encounters with men. Barney is instantly nervous. He says, "I'm sure once in a while you must have met some *nice* men" (629). She calms him down by reassuring him that she will not mention someone as sensitive as him in her book. Significantly, Barney no longer sees his being a "nice" person in a totally negative light.

In Act Two, while high on marijuana, Barney muses, "So many things I wanted to do . . . but I'll never do 'em," and adds, "Trapped . . . we're all trapped" (635). Yet, less than a month later, he makes one last attempt to wriggle out of the "trap" he is in and find an extramarital sexual moment of bliss. Responding to remarks his friend Jeanette makes at a social gathering, Barney arranges a rendezvous with her. Like Elaine and Bobbi, Jeanette has a grim view of life. Jeanette, however, is markedly different from the other two women. She does not try to suppress or evade her darker moods. On the contrary, she wallows in depression. While Elaine escapes into sensual pleasure and Bobbi into fantasy and paranoia, Jeanette broods about the human condition.

Typically, Simon wastes little time setting things into motion. Moments after she enters the apartment, Jeanette begins to sob. As soon as she stops sobbing, she says, "Why am I here, Barney?" (637). The range of Jeanette's probing will not prove very wide. She will make no serious references to religious creeds, politics, or philosophical tenets. Nonetheless, she will, in her tense, fretful way, ask fundamental questions.

Employing a realistic and comic framework, Simon shows Jeanette and Barney stumbling toward these questions. Jeanette does say early on that she thinks Barney is "basically a good person" (638)—an important point they will return to; but the comment is made amid a series of remarks that deflate Barney, for Jeanette is busy stressing how physically unattractive she finds Barney. Barney at this time is totally uninterested in fundamental questions. The defeats he suffered in his previous extramarital encounters have honed his sexual frustrations to a keen edge. He is now in almost the exact frame of mind that Elaine was in ten months earlier. He does not want chitchat. He wants sex.

Ironically, Barney has waited too long and has picked the wrong partner for his current mood. Jeanette is as unsensuous a person as Elaine was sensuous. Elaine craved certain foods; Jeanette states, "I can *not* taste food" (643). Jeanette also tells Barney, "I don't particularly enjoy sex" (639). Embodying a somber moral awareness and a strong sense of guilt, she is appalled by the same contemporary promiscuity that so intrigues Barney. Barney tries to ply Jeanette with drinks, but she doggedly states, "You're not going to have a good time with me" (642).

Barney wanted to humanize his relationship with Elaine by finding out something about her. With Jeanette, Barney keeps trying to dodge her attempts to instigate a meaningful conversation. Jeanette asks him if her husband, Mel, has talked to Barney about her. Barney brushes aside the very possibility. He does the same thing when Jeanette inquires whether Mel ever spoke to him about Mel's affair with another woman. She asks him if he feels guilty about meeting her in the apartment. Exasperated, Barney finally says to Jeanette, "Why probe deeply into everything?" (641).

Barney's success at avoiding Jeanette's attempts to draw him into a serious conversation ends when Jeanette asks him if he thinks death is terrible. This question snags him.

For it was his intensified awareness of death that nurtured his desire for an affair. He replies that he does think death is terrible. Jeanette immediately follows up with another question, "You mean you enjoy your life?" Barney, all seriousness now, responds, "I *love* living. I have some problems with my *life,* but living is the best thing they've come up with so far" (644).

Because Jeanette sincerely wants to learn some affirmative reasons why she should go on living, she asks Barney how much of life he actually enjoys. Pressed for a precise answer, he says, "Fifty-one, fifty-two percent" (645). Jeanette then asks him if he thinks there are many decent people in the world, and Barney resumes trying to sidestep Jeanette's series of questions. When she challenges him to name three decent people, however, he—hoping to wrap the whole matter up and get on with the sex—allows himself to accept the challenge. Barney cites his wife, Thelma, as one of the three.

Jeanette is reluctant to put Thelma on her list of three immediately, and now, thoroughly exasperated, Barney begins to shuttle back and forth in mood. He, on the one hand, again wants to blot out the whole conversation by focusing strictly on sex. He becomes increasingly sexually aggressive—almost threatening. On the other hand, he is gnawed at by the still unresolved question of what should be the final judgment of human beings. At one point, he claims, "We're not indecent, we're not unloving. We're human" (650). Later, sexually impatient, he tells Jeanette, "All right, we're all no good" (652).

The climax of the play, the climax that Simon has been moving toward—albeit not all that steadily—since Act One occurs when Jeanette, genuinely frightened by Barney's sexual advances, begs him to stop. She blurts out, "I know you're not like this," and goes on to say, "You're quiet. You're intelligent." Then she exclaims, "You're decent! You *are,* Barney!" (654-55). These statements stop Barney in his tracks. In Act One, a comment by Elaine made Barney realize he unconsciously and fruitlessly kept trying to rid his hands of the smell of the fish he prepared for the customers in his restaurant. Jeanette's comments make him equally aware that—as he said to Bobbi—"We're all trapped." Just as he can never rid his hands of the smell of fish, he can never escape from the trap of his basic nature. Barney gains the same humbling but helpful self-knowledge that all four characters in *Barefoot in the Park* and Fran in *Promises, Promises* gained—and that Oscar and Felix in *The Odd Couple* never gained. Barney finally accepts that he will never be a part of the new sexual revolution, for he is precisely the type of man he told Elaine he was—a nice guy.

Abandoning his sexual scheme, Barney gets Jeanette to admit that Thelma is gentle, loving, and decent. He makes Jeanette see that, however many other kinds of people there are in the world, a significant number of people are decent, even though these people—because they are human—are imperfect. Paradoxically, thanks to Barney and to her own insistence on confronting her problems, although Jeanette originally wallowed in melancholy, she leaves the apartment much less imprisoned by depression than Elaine and Bobbi.

Despite all the plays and movie scripts he wrote after ***Last of the Red-Hot Lovers,*** Simon thus far in his career has never come any closer to stating directly his fundamental opinion of the human experience than he does in this play. This opinion cannot be considered wildly optimistic. He makes no mention of a loving God. He does not posit a heaven; rather, death is inevitable and final. He does not deny that much of our daily world is cold and indifferent to us, and is permeated by evil and insanity. Weighing the good and the bad in life, Simon sees the scale tipping ever so slightly toward the good. What tips the scale is that some people, such as Barney, but not Elaine, try to comfort others as well as to find comfort for themselves.

Notes

1. Linderman, "Playboy Interview," p. 74.

2. All page references are to *The Odd Couple* in *The Comedy of Neil Simon,* pp. 220-21.

3. Simon, "Notes from the Playwright," pp. 3-4.

4. Walter Kerr, "What Simon Says," *New York Times Magazine,* 22 March 1970, p. 14.

5. Howard Taubman, review of *The Odd Couple, New York Times,* 11 March 1965, p. 36.

6. Simon, "Notes from the Playwright," p. 3.

7. Zimmerman, "Neil Simon," pp. 52, 55.

8. All page references are to *Plaza Suite* in *The Comedy of Neil Simon,* p. 497.

9. McGovern, *Neil Simon,* p. 58.

10. Walter Kerr, "Simon's Funny—Don't Laugh," *New York Times,* 25 February 1968, Section 2, p. 5.

11. All page references are to *Last of the Red-Hot Lovers* in *The Comedy of Neil Simon,* p. 585.

12. McGovern, *Neil Simon,* p. 77.

FURTHER READING

Criticism

Bryer, Jackson R. "Neil Simon." In *The Playwright's Art: Conversations with Contemporary American Dramatists,* pp.221-40. New Jersey: Rutgers University Press, 1995, 316p.

An interview touching on Simon's life, times, and works.

Gilman, Richard. "A Hit and A Success." In *Common and Uncommon Masks: Writings on Theatre 1961-1970,* pp. 198-200. New York: Random House, 1971, 319p.

An appreciative review of *Barefoot In the Park* as being better than other Broadway hits.

Kerr, Walter. "Money and Uglier Matters." In *God on the Gymnasium Floor, and Other Theatrical Adventures,* pp. 214-39. New York: Simon and Schuster, 1977, 320p.

Presents a discussion of the economics of the Broadway theatre.

———. *Thirty Plays Hath November: Pain and Pleasure in the Contemporary Theatre,* pp. 297-301. New York: Simon and Schuster, 1969, 343p.

An appreciative review of *Plaza Suite.*

McGovern, Edythe M. *Neil Simon: A Critical Study,* New York: Frederick Ungar Publishing Co., 1979, 196p.

The first book length study of Simon's plays attempts to evaluate them as literature rather than merely as hits.

Richards, David. "The Last of the Red Hot Playwrights." *The New York Times* Sec. 6, Col. 1 (17 February 1991): 30.

Profiles Simon as the last successful playwright writing regularly for Broadway.

Rhinehart, Brian and Norman N. Holland. "Jake's Women: A Dialogue." In *Neil Simon: A Casebook,* edited by Gary Konas, pp.173-188. New York: Garland Publishing, 1997, 242p.

A discussion of *Jake's Women* considering the play from a postmodern psychoanalytic point of view.

Additional coverage of Simon's life and career is contained in the following sources published by the Gale Group: *Authors and Artists for Young Adults,* **Vol. 32;** *Authors in the News,* **Vol. 1;** *Contemporary Authors,* **Vols. 21-24R;** *Contemporary Authors New Revision Series,* **Vols. 26, 54, 87;** *Contemporary Literary Criticism,* **Vols. 6, 11, 31, 39, 70;** *Dictionary of Literary Biography,* **Vol. 7;** *DISCovering Authors 3.0; DISCovering Authors Modules: Dramatists; Drama for Students,* **Vols. 2, 6; and** *Major 20th-Century Writers,* **Eds. 1, 2.**

How to Use This Index

The main references

> **Calvino, Italo**
>   1923-1985 .... **CLC 5, 8, 11, 22, 33, 39,
>   73; SSC 3**

list all author entries in the following Gale Literary Criticism series:

BLC = *Black Literature Criticism*
CLC = *Contemporary Literary Criticism*
CLR = *Children's Literature Review*
CMLC = *Classical and Medieval Literature Criticism*
DA = *DISCovering Authors*
DAB = *DISCovering Authors: British*
DAC = *DISCovering Authors: Canadian*
DAM = *DISCovering Authors: Modules*
         DRAM: Dramatists Module; MST: Most-Studied Authors Module;
         MULT: Multicultural Authors Module; NOV: Novelists Module;
         POET: Poets Module; POP: Popular Fiction and Genre Authors Module
DC = *Drama Criticism*
HLC = *Hispanic Literature Criticism*
LC = *Literature Criticism from 1400 to 1800*
NNAL = *Native North American Literature*
NCLC = *Nineteenth-Century Literature Criticism*
PC = *Poetry Criticism*
SSC = *Short Story Criticism*
TCLC = *Twentieth-Century Literary Criticism*
WLC = *World Literature Criticism, 1500 to the Present*

The cross-references

> See also CANR 23; CA 85-88;
> obituary CA116

list all author entries in the following Gale biographical and literary sources:

AAYA = *Authors & Artists for Young Adults*
AITN = *Authors in the News*
BEST = *Bestsellers*
BW = *Black Writers*
CA = *Contemporary Authors*
CAAS = *Contemporary Authors Autobiography Series*
CABS = *Contemporary Authors Bibliographical Series*
CANR = *Contemporary Authors New Revision Series*
CAP = *Contemporary Authors Permanent Series*
CDALB = *Concise Dictionary of American Literary Biography*
CDBLB = *Concise Dictionary of British Literary Biography*
DLB = *Dictionary of Literary Biography*
DLBD = *Dictionary of Literary Biography Documentary Series*
DLBY = *Dictionary of Literary Biography Yearbook*
HW = *Hispanic Writers*
JRDA = *Junior DISCovering Authors*
MAICYA = *Major Authors and Illustrators for Children and Young Adults*
MTCW = *Major 20th-Century Writers*
SAAS = *Something about the Author Autobiography Series*
SATA = *Something about the Author*
YABC = *Yesterday's Authors of Books for Children*

Literary Criticism Series
Cumulative Author Index

A/C Cross
See Lawrence, T(homas) E(dward)

Abasiyanik, Sait Faik 1906-1954
See Sait Faik
See also CA 123

Abbey, Edward 1927-1989 .... **CLC 36, 59**
See also CA 45-48; 128; CANR 2, 41; DA3;
MTCW 2

Abbott, Lee K(ittredge) 1947- .... **CLC 48**
See also CA 124; CANR 51; DLB 130

Abe, Kobo 1924-1993 ..... **CLC 8, 22, 53, 81;
DAM NOV**
See also CA 65-68; 140; CANR 24, 60;
DLB 182; MTCW 1, 2

Abelard, Peter c. 1079-c. 1142 ..... **CMLC 11**
See also DLB 115, 208

Abell, Kjeld 1901-1961 .... **CLC 15**
See also CA 111

Abish, Walter 1931- .... **CLC 22**
See also CA 101; CANR 37; DLB 130, 227

Abrahams, Peter (Henry) 1919- .... **CLC 4**
See also BW 1; CA 57-60; CANR 26; DLB
117, 225; MTCW 1, 2

Abrams, M(eyer) H(oward) 1912- .. **CLC 24**
See also CA 57-60; CANR 13, 33; DLB 67

Abse, Dannie 1923- . **CLC 7, 29; DAB; DAM
POET**
See also CA 53-56; CAAS 1; CANR 4, 46,
74; DLB 27; MTCW 1

Achebe, (Albert) Chinua(lumogu) 1930-
.... **CLC 1, 3, 5, 7, 11, 26, 51, 75, 127;
BLC 1; DA; DAB; DAC; DAM MST,
MULT, NOV; WLC**
See also AAYA 15; BW 2, 3; CA 1-4R;
CANR 6, 26, 47; CLR 20; DA3; DLB
117; MAICYA; MTCW 1, 2; SATA 38,
40; SATA-Brief 38

Acker, Kathy 1948-1997 .... **CLC 45, 111**
See also CA 117; 122; 162; CANR 55

Ackroyd, Peter 1949- .... **CLC 34, 52**
See also CA 123; 127; CANR 51, 74; DLB
155, 231; INT 127; MTCW 1

Acorn, Milton 1923- .... **CLC 15; DAC**
See also CA 103; DLB 53; INT 103

Adamov, Arthur 1908-1970 .... **CLC 4, 25;
DAM DRAM**
See also CA 17-18; 25-28R; CAP 2; MTCW
1

Adams, Alice (Boyd) 1926-1999 . **CLC 6, 13,
46; SSC 24**
See also CA 81-84; 179; CANR 26, 53, 75,
88; DLB 234; DLBY 86; INT CANR-26;
MTCW 1, 2

Adams, Andy 1859-1935 .... **TCLC 56**
See also YABC 1

Adams, Brooks 1848-1927 .... **TCLC 80**
See also CA 123; DLB 47

Adams, Douglas (Noel) 1952- .. **CLC 27, 60;
DAM POP**
See also AAYA 4, 33; BEST 89:3; CA 106;
CANR 34, 64; DA3; DLBY 83; JRDA;
MTCW 1; SATA 116

Adams, Francis 1862-1893 .... **NCLC 33**

Adams, Henry (Brooks) 1838-1918
... **TCLC 4, 52; DA; DAB; DAC; DAM
MST**
See also CA 104; 133; CANR 77; DLB 12,
47, 189; MTCW 1

Adams, Richard (George) 1920- .. **CLC 4, 5,
18; DAM NOV**
See also AAYA 16; AITN 1, 2; CA 49-52;
CANR 3, 35; CLR 20; JRDA; MAICYA;
MTCW 1, 2; SATA 7, 69

Adamson, Joy(-Friederike Victoria)
1910-1980 .... **CLC 17**
See also CA 69-72; 93-96; CANR 22;
MTCW 1; SATA 11; SATA-Obit 22

Adcock, Fleur 1934- .... **CLC 41**
See also CA 25-28R, 182; CAAE 182;
CAAS 23; CANR 11, 34, 69; DLB 40

Addams, Charles (Samuel) 1912-1988
.... **CLC 30**
See also CA 61-64; 126; CANR 12, 79

Addams, Jane 1860-1945 .... **TCLC 76**

Addison, Joseph 1672-1719 .... **LC 18**
See also CDBLB 1660-1789; DLB 101

Adler, Alfred (F.) 1870-1937 .... **TCLC 61**
See also CA 119; 159

Adler, C(arole) S(chwerdtfeger) 1932-
.... **CLC 35**
See also AAYA 4; CA 89-92; CANR 19,
40; JRDA; MAICYA; SAAS 15; SATA
26, 63, 102

Adler, Renata 1938- .... **CLC 8, 31**
See also CA 49-52; CANR 5, 22, 52;
MTCW 1

Ady, Endre 1877-1919 .... **TCLC 11**
See also CA 107

A.E. 1867-1935 .... **TCLC 3, 10**
See also Russell, George William

Aeschylus 525B.C.-456B.C. . **CMLC 11; DA;
DAB; DAC; DAM DRAM, MST; DC 8;
WLCS**
See also DLB 176

Aesop 620(?)B.C.-(?)B.C. .... **CMLC 24**
See also CLR 14; MAICYA; SATA 64

Affable Hawk
See MacCarthy, Sir(Charles Otto) Desmond

Africa, Ben
See Bosman, Herman Charles

Afton, Effie
See Harper, Frances Ellen Watkins

Agapida, Fray Antonio
See Irving, Washington

Agee, James (Rufus) 1909-1955 .... **TCLC 1,
19; DAM NOV**

See also AITN 1; CA 108; 148; CDALB
1941-1968; DLB 2, 26, 152; MTCW 1

Aghill, Gordon
See Silverberg, Robert

Agnon, S(hmuel) Y(osef Halevi) 1888-1970
.... **CLC 4, 8, 14; SSC 30**
See also CA 17-18; 25-28R; CANR 60;
CAP 2; MTCW 1, 2

Agrippa von Nettesheim, Henry Cornelius
1486-1535 .... **LC 27**

Aguilera Malta, Demetrio 1909-1981
See also CA 111; 124; CANR 87; DAM
MULT, NOV; DLB 145; HLCS 1; HW 1

Agustini, Delmira 1886-1914
See also CA 166; HLCS 1; HW 1, 2

Aherne, Owen
See Cassill, R(onald) V(erlin)

Ai 1947- .... **CLC 4, 14, 69**
See also CA 85-88; CAAS 13; CANR 70;
DLB 120

Aickman, Robert (Fordyce) 1914-1981
.... **CLC 57**
See also CA 5-8R; CANR 3, 72

Aiken, Conrad (Potter) 1889-1973 .. **CLC 1,
3, 5, 10, 52; DAM NOV, POET; PC 26;
SSC 9**
See also CA 5-8R; 45-48; CANR 4, 60;
CDALB 1929-1941; DLB 9, 45, 102;
MTCW 1, 2; SATA 3, 30

Aiken, Joan (Delano) 1924- .... **CLC 35**
See also AAYA 1, 25; CA 9-12R, 182;
CAAE 182; CANR 4, 23, 34, 64; CLR 1,
19; DLB 161; JRDA; MAICYA; MTCW
1; SAAS 1; SATA 2, 30, 73; SATA-Essay
109

Ainsworth, William Harrison 1805-1882
.... **NCLC 13**
See also DLB 21; SATA 24

Aitmatov, Chingiz (Torekulovich) 1928-
.... **CLC 71**
See also CA 103; CANR 38; MTCW 1;
SATA 56

Akers, Floyd
See Baum, L(yman) Frank

Akhmadulina, Bella Akhatovna 1937-
.... **CLC 53; DAM POET**
See also CA 65-68

Akhmatova, Anna 1888-1966 ... **CLC 11, 25,
64, 126; DAM POET; PC 2**
See also CA 19-20; 25-28R; CANR 35;
CAP 1; DA3; MTCW 1, 2

Aksakov, Sergei Timofeyvich 1791-1859
.... **NCLC 2**
See also DLB 198

Aksenov, Vassily
See Aksyonov, Vassily (Pavlovich)

Akst, Daniel 1956- .... **CLC 109**
See also CA 161

Anderson, C. Farley
　　See Mencken, H(enry) L(ouis); Nathan, George Jean
Anderson, Jessica (Margaret) Queale 1916-
　　.. **CLC 37**
　　See also CA 9-12R; CANR 4, 62
Anderson, Jon (Victor) 1940- . **CLC 9; DAM POET**
　　See also CA 25-28R; CANR 20
Anderson, Lindsay (Gordon) 1923-1994
　　.. **CLC 20**
　　See also CA 125; 128; 146; CANR 77
Anderson, Maxwell 1888-1959 ...... **TCLC 2; DAM DRAM**
　　See also CA 105; 152; DLB 7, 228; MTCW 2
Anderson, Poul (William) 1926- ..... **CLC 15**
　　See also AAYA 5, 34; CA 1-4R, 181; CAAE 181; CAAS 2; CANR 2, 15, 34, 64; CLR 58; DLB 8; INT CANR-15; MTCW 1, 2; SATA 90; SATA-Brief 39; SATA-Essay 106
Anderson, Robert (Woodruff) 1917-
　　............................ **CLC 23; DAM DRAM**
　　See also AITN 1; CA 21-24R; CANR 32; DLB 7
Anderson, Sherwood 1876-1941 .... **TCLC 1, 10, 24; DA; DAB; DAC; DAM MST, NOV; SSC 1; WLC**
　　See also AAYA 30; CA 104; 121; CANR 61; CDALB 1917-1929; DA3; DLB 4, 9, 86; DLBD 1; MTCW 1, 2
Andier, Pierre
　　See Desnos, Robert
Andouard
　　See Giraudoux, (Hippolyte) Jean
Andrade, Carlos Drummond de ..... **CLC 18**
　　See also Drummond de Andrade, Carlos
Andrade, Mario de 1893-1945 .... **TCLC 43**
Andreae, Johann V(alentin) 1586-1654
　　.. **LC 32**
　　See also DLB 164
Andreas-Salome, Lou 1861-1937 .. **TCLC 56**
　　See also CA 178; DLB 66
Andress, Lesley
　　See Sanders, Lawrence
Andrewes, Lancelot 1555-1626 .... **LC 5**
　　See also DLB 151, 172
Andrews, Cicily Fairfield
　　See West, Rebecca
Andrews, Elton V.
　　See Pohl, Frederik
Andreyev, Leonid (Nikolaevich) 1871-1919
　　.. **TCLC 3**
　　See also CA 104; 185
Andric, Ivo 1892-1975 .... **CLC 8; SSC 36**
　　See also CA 81-84; 57-60; CANR 43, 60; DLB 147; MTCW 1
Androvar
　　See Prado (Calvo), Pedro
Angelique, Pierre
　　See Bataille, Georges
Angell, Roger 1920- .... **CLC 26**
　　See also CA 57-60; CANR 13, 44, 70; DLB 171, 185
Angelou, Maya 1928- ... **CLC 12, 35, 64, 77; BLC 1; DA; DAB; DAC; DAM MST, MULT, POET, POP; PC 32; WLCS**
　　See also AAYA 7, 20; BW 2, 3; CA 65-68; CANR 19, 42, 65; CDALBS; CLR 53; DA3; DLB 38; MTCW 1, 2; SATA 49
Anna Comnena 1083-1153 .... **CMLC 25**
Annensky, Innokenty (Fyodorovich) 1856-1909 .... **TCLC 14**
　　See also CA 110; 155
Annunzio, Gabriele d'
　　See D'Annunzio, Gabriele
Anodos
　　See Coleridge, Mary E(lizabeth)

Anon, Charles Robert
　　See Pessoa, Fernando (Antonio Nogueira)
Anouilh, Jean (Marie Lucien Pierre) 1910-1987 .... **CLC 1, 3, 8, 13, 40, 50; DAM DRAM; DC 8**
　　See also CA 17-20R; 123; CANR 32; MTCW 1, 2
Anthony, Florence
　　See Ai
Anthony, John
　　See Ciardi, John (Anthony)
Anthony, Peter
　　See Shaffer, Anthony (Joshua); Shaffer, Peter (Levin)
Anthony, Piers 1934- ... **CLC 35; DAM POP**
　　See also AAYA 11; CA 21-24R; CANR 28, 56, 73; DLB 8; MTCW 1, 2; SAAS 22; SATA 84
Anthony, Susan B(rownell) 1916-1991
　　.. **TCLC 84**
　　See also CA 89-92; 134
Antoine, Marc
　　See Proust, (Valentin-Louis-George-Eugene-) Marcel
Antoninus, Brother
　　See Everson, William (Oliver)
Antonioni, Michelangelo 1912- .... **CLC 20**
　　See also CA 73-76; CANR 45, 77
Antschel, Paul 1920-1970
　　See Celan, Paul
　　See also CA 85-88; CANR 33, 61; MTCW 1
Anwar, Chairil 1922-1949 .... **TCLC 22**
　　See also CA 121
Anzaldua, Gloria (Evanjelina) 1942-
　　See also CA 175; DLB 122; HLCS 1
Apess, William 1798-1839(?) .... **NCLC 73; DAM MULT**
　　See also DLB 175; NNAL
Apollinaire, Guillaume 1880-1918 . **TCLC 3, 8, 51; DAM POET; PC 7**
　　See also CA 152; MTCW 1
Appelfeld, Aharon 1932- .. **CLC 23, 47; SSC 42**
　　See also CA 112; 133; CANR 86
Apple, Max (Isaac) 1941- .... **CLC 9, 33**
　　See also CA 81-84; CANR 19, 54; DLB 130
Appleman, Philip (Dean) 1926- .... **CLC 51**
　　See also CA 13-16R; CAAS 18; CANR 6, 29, 56
Appleton, Lawrence
　　See Lovecraft, H(oward) P(hillips)
Apteryx
　　See Eliot, T(homas) S(tearns)
Apuleius, (Lucius Madaurensis) 125(?)-175(?) .... **CMLC 1**
　　See also DLB 211
Aquin, Hubert 1929-1977 .... **CLC 15**
　　See also CA 105; DLB 53
Aquinas, Thomas 1224(?)-1274 ... **CMLC 33**
　　See also DLB 115
Aragon, Louis 1897-1982 . **CLC 3, 22; DAM NOV, POET**
　　See also CA 69-72; 108; CANR 28, 71; DLB 72; MTCW 1, 2
Arany, Janos 1817-1882 .... **NCLC 34**
Aranyos, Kakay
　　See Mikszath, Kalman
Arbuthnot, John 1667-1735 .... **LC 1**
　　See also DLB 101
Archer, Herbert Winslow
　　See Mencken, H(enry) L(ouis)
Archer, Jeffrey (Howard) 1940- ..... **CLC 28; DAM POP**
　　See also AAYA 16; BEST 89:3; CA 77-80; CANR 22, 52; DA3; INT CANR-22
Archer, Jules 1915- .... **CLC 12**

　　See also CA 9-12R; CANR 6, 69; SAAS 5; SATA 4, 85
Archer, Lee
　　See Ellison, Harlan (Jay)
Arden, John 1930- ..... **CLC 6, 13, 15; DAM DRAM**
　　See also CA 13-16R; CAAS 4; CANR 31, 65, 67; DLB 13; MTCW 1
Arenas, Reinaldo 1943-1990 . **CLC 41; DAM MULT; HLC 1**
　　See also CA 124; 128; 133; CANR 73; DLB 145; HW 1; MTCW 1
Arendt, Hannah 1906-1975 .... **CLC 66, 98**
　　See also CA 17-20R; 61-64; CANR 26, 60; MTCW 1, 2
Aretino, Pietro 1492-1556 .... **LC 12**
Arghezi, Tudor 1880-1967 .... **CLC 80**
　　See also Theodorescu, Ion N.
　　See also CA 167; DLB 220
Arguedas, Jose Maria 1911-1969 ... **CLC 10, 18; HLCS 1**
　　See also CA 89-92; CANR 73; DLB 113; HW 1
Argueta, Manlio 1936- .... **CLC 31**
　　See also CA 131; CANR 73; DLB 145; HW 1
Arias, Ron(ald Francis) 1941-
　　See also CA 131; CANR 81; DAM MULT; DLB 82; HLC 1; HW 1, 2; MTCW 2
Ariosto, Ludovico 1474-1533 .... **LC 6**
Aristides
　　See Epstein, Joseph
Aristophanes 450B.C.-385B.C. ...... **CMLC 4; DA; DAB; DAC; DAM DRAM, MST; DC 2; WLCS**
　　See also DA3; DLB 176
Aristotle 384B.C.-322B.C. ... **CMLC 31; DA; DAB; DAC; DAM MST; WLCS**
　　See also DA3; DLB 176
Arlt, Roberto (Godofredo Christophersen) 1900-1942 ..... **TCLC 29; DAM MULT; HLC 1**
　　See also CA 123; 131; CANR 67; HW 1, 2
Armah, Ayi Kwei 1939- ..... **CLC 5, 33, 136; BLC 1; DAM MULT, POET**
　　See also BW 1; CA 61-64; CANR 21, 64; DLB 117; MTCW 1
Armatrading, Joan 1950- .... **CLC 17**
　　See also CA 114; 186
Arnette, Robert
　　See Silverberg, Robert
Arnim, Achim von (Ludwig Joachim von Arnim) 1781-1831 .... **NCLC 5; SSC 29**
　　See also DLB 90
Arnim, Bettina von 1785-1859 ..... **NCLC 38**
　　See also DLB 90
Arnold, Matthew 1822-1888 .... **NCLC 6, 29, 89; DA; DAB; DAC; DAM MST, POET; PC 5; WLC**
　　See also CDBLB 1832-1890; DLB 32, 57
Arnold, Thomas 1795-1842 .... **NCLC 18**
　　See also DLB 55
Arnow, Harriette (Louisa) Simpson 1908-1986 .... **CLC 2, 7, 18**
　　See also CA 9-12R; 118; CANR 14; DLB 6; MTCW 1, 2; SATA 42; SATA-Obit 47
Arouet, Francois-Marie
　　See Voltaire
Arp, Hans
　　See Arp, Jean
Arp, Jean 1887-1966 .... **CLC 5**
　　See also CA 81-84; 25-28R; CANR 42, 77
Arrabal
　　See Arrabal, Fernando
Arrabal, Fernando 1932- .. **CLC 2, 9, 18, 58**
　　See also CA 9-12R; CANR 15
Arreola, Juan Jose 1918- ...... **SSC 38; DAM MULT; HLC 1**

See also CA 113; 131; CANR 81; DLB 113;
HW 1, 2

Arrian c. 89(?)-c. 155(?) .... **CMLC 43**
See also DLB 176

Arrick, Fran .... **CLC 30**
See also Gaberman, Judie Angell

Artaud, Antonin (Marie Joseph) 1896-1948
...... **TCLC 3, 36; DAM DRAM; DC 14**
See also CA 104; 149; DA3; MTCW 1

Arthur, Ruth M(abel) 1905-1979 .... **CLC 12**
See also CA 9-12R; 85-88; CANR 4; SATA
7, 26

Artsybashev, Mikhail (Petrovich) 1878-1927
.... **TCLC 31**
See also CA 170

Arundel, Honor (Morfydd) 1919-1973
.... **CLC 17**
See also CA 21-22; 41-44R; CAP 2; CLR
35; SATA 4; SATA-Obit 24

Arzner, Dorothy 1897-1979 .... **CLC 98**

Asch, Sholem 1880-1957 .... **TCLC 3**
See also CA 105

Ash, Shalom
See Asch, Sholem

Ashbery, John (Lawrence) 1927- . **CLC 2, 3,
4, 6, 9, 13, 15, 25, 41, 77, 125; DAM
POET; PC 26**
See also CA 5-8R; CANR 9, 37, 66; DA3;
DLB 5, 165; DLBY 81; INT CANR-9;
MTCW 1, 2

Ashdown, Clifford
See Freeman, R(ichard) Austin

Ashe, Gordon
See Creasey, John

Ashton-Warner, Sylvia (Constance)
1908-1984 .... **CLC 19**
See also CA 69-72; 112; CANR 29; MTCW
1, 2

Asimov, Isaac 1920-1992 .... **CLC 1, 3, 9, 19,
26, 76, 92; DAM POP**
See also AAYA 13; BEST 90:2; CA 1-4R;
137; CANR 2, 19, 36, 60; CLR 12; DA3;
DLB 8; DLBY 92; INT CANR-19; JRDA;
MAICYA; MTCW 1, 2; SATA 1, 26, 74

Assis, Joaquim Maria Machado de
See Machado de Assis, Joaquim Maria

Astley, Thea (Beatrice May) 1925- . **CLC 41**
See also CA 65-68; CANR 11, 43, 78

Aston, James
See White, T(erence) H(anbury)

Asturias, Miguel Angel 1899-1974 ... **CLC 3,
8, 13; DAM MULT, NOV; HLC 1**
See also CA 25-28; 49-52; CANR 32; CAP
2; DA3; DLB 113; HW 1; MTCW 1, 2

Atares, Carlos Saura
See Saura (Atares), Carlos

Atheling, William
See Pound, Ezra (Weston Loomis)

Atheling, William, Jr.
See Blish, James (Benjamin)

Atherton, Gertrude (Franklin Horn)
1857-1948 .... **TCLC 2**
See also CA 104; 155; DLB 9, 78, 186

Atherton, Lucius
See Masters, Edgar Lee

Atkins, Jack
See Harris, Mark

Atkinson, Kate .... **CLC 99**
See also CA 166

Attaway, William (Alexander) 1911-1986
.... **CLC 92; BLC 1; DAM MULT**
See also BW 2, 3; CA 143; CANR 82; DLB
76

Atticus
See Fleming, Ian (Lancaster); Wilson,
(Thomas) Woodrow

Atwood, Margaret (Eleanor) 1939- . **CLC 2,
3, 4, 8, 13, 15, 25, 44, 84, 135; DA; DAB;**

**DAC; DAM MST, NOV, POET; PC 8;
SSC 2; WLC**
See also AAYA 12; BEST 89:2; CA 49-52;
CANR 3, 24, 33, 59; DA3; DLB 53; INT
CANR-24; MTCW 1, 2; SATA 50

Aubigny, Pierre d'
See Mencken, H(enry) L(ouis)

Aubin, Penelope 1685-1731(?) .... **LC 9**
See also DLB 39

Auchincloss, Louis (Stanton) 1917- . **CLC 4,
6, 9, 18, 45; DAM NOV; SSC 22**
See also CA 1-4R; CANR 6, 29, 55, 87;
DLB 2; DLBY 80; INT CANR-29;
MTCW 1

Auden, W(ystan) H(ugh) 1907-1973 . **CLC 1,
2, 3, 4, 6, 9, 11, 14, 43, 123; DA; DAB;
DAC; DAM DRAM, MST, POET; PC
1; WLC**
See also AAYA 18; CA 9-12R; 45-48;
CANR 5, 61; CDBLB 1914-1945; DA3;
DLB 10, 20; MTCW 1, 2

Audiberti, Jacques 1900-1965 .... **CLC 38;
DAM DRAM**
See also CA 25-28R

Audubon, John James 1785-1851 . **NCLC 47**

Auel, Jean M(arie) 1936- .... **CLC 31, 107;
DAM POP**
See also AAYA 7; BEST 90:4; CA 103;
CANR 21, 64; DA3; INT CANR-21;
SATA 91

Auerbach, Erich 1892-1957 .... **TCLC 43**
See also CA 118; 155

Augier, Emile 1820-1889 .... **NCLC 31**
See also DLB 192

August, John
See De Voto, Bernard (Augustine)

Augustine 354-430 ...... **CMLC 6; DA; DAB;
DAC; DAM MST; WLCS**
See also DA3; DLB 115

Aurelius
See Bourne, Randolph S(illiman)

Aurobindo, Sri
See Ghose, Aurabinda

Austen, Jane 1775-1817 ..... **NCLC 1, 13, 19,
33, 51, 81; DA; DAB; DAC; DAM MST,
NOV; WLC**
See also AAYA 19; CDBLB 1789-1832;
DA3; DLB 116

Auster, Paul 1947- .... **CLC 47, 131**
See also CA 69-72; CANR 23, 52, 75; DA3;
DLB 227; MTCW 1

Austin, Frank
See Faust, Frederick (Schiller)

Austin, Mary (Hunter) 1868-1934 . **TCLC 25**
See also CA 109; 178; DLB 9, 78, 206, 221

Averroes 1126-1198 .... **CMLC 7**
See also DLB 115

Avicenna 980-1037 .... **CMLC 16**
See also DLB 115

Avison, Margaret 1918- .... **CLC 2, 4, 97;
DAC; DAM POET**
See also CA 17-20R; DLB 53; MTCW 1

Axton, David
See Koontz, Dean R(ay)

Ayckbourn, Alan 1939- .... **CLC 5, 8, 18, 33,
74; DAB; DAM DRAM; DC 13**
See also CA 21-24R; CANR 31, 59; DLB
13; MTCW 1, 2

Aydy, Catherine
See Tennant, Emma (Christina)

Ayme, Marcel (Andre) 1902-1967 .. **CLC 11;
SSC 41**
See also CA 89-92; CANR 67; CLR 25;
DLB 72; SATA 91

Ayrton, Michael 1921-1975 .... **CLC 7**
See also CA 5-8R; 61-64; CANR 9, 21

Azorin .... **CLC 11**
See also Martinez Ruiz, Jose

Azuela, Mariano 1873-1952 . **TCLC 3; DAM
MULT; HLC 1**
See also CA 104; 131; CANR 81; HW 1, 2;
MTCW 1, 2

Baastad, Babbis Friis
See Friis-Baastad, Babbis Ellinor

Bab
See Gilbert, W(illiam) S(chwenck)

Babbis, Eleanor
See Friis-Baastad, Babbis Ellinor

Babel, Isaac
See Babel, Isaak (Emmanuilovich)

Babel, Isaak (Emmanuilovich) 1894-1941(?)
.... **TCLC 2, 13; SSC 16**
See also Babel, Isaac
See also CA 104; 155; MTCW 1

Babits, Mihaly 1883-1941 .... **TCLC 14**
See also CA 114

Babur 1483-1530 .... **LC 18**

Baca, Jimmy Santiago 1952-
See also CA 131; CANR 81, 90; DAM
MULT; DLB 122; HLC 1; HW 1, 2

Bacchelli, Riccardo 1891-1985 .... **CLC 19**
See also CA 29-32R; 117

Bach, Richard (David) 1936- .... **CLC 14;
DAM NOV, POP**
See also AITN 1; BEST 89:2; CA 9-12R;
CANR 18, 93; MTCW 1; SATA 13

Bachman, Richard
See King, Stephen (Edwin)

Bachmann, Ingeborg 1926-1973 ..... **CLC 69**
See also CA 93-96; 45-48; CANR 69; DLB
85

Bacon, Francis 1561-1626 .... **LC 18, 32**
See also CDBLB Before 1660; DLB 151,
236

Bacon, Roger 1214(?)-1292 .... **CMLC 14**
See also DLB 115

Bacovia, George .... **TCLC 24**
See also Bacovia, G.; Vasiliu, Gheorghe
See also DLB 220

Badanes, Jerome 1937- .... **CLC 59**

Bagehot, Walter 1826-1877 .... **NCLC 10**
See also DLB 55

Bagnold, Enid 1889-1981 ..... **CLC 25; DAM
DRAM**
See also CA 5-8R; 103; CANR 5, 40; DLB
13, 160, 191; MAICYA; SATA 1, 25

Bagritsky, Eduard 1895-1934 .... **TCLC 60**

Bagrjana, Elisaveta
See Belcheva, Elisaveta

Bagryana, Elisaveta 1893-1991 .... **CLC 10**
See also Belcheva, Elisaveta
See also CA 178; DLB 147

Bailey, Paul 1937- .... **CLC 45**
See also CA 21-24R; CANR 16, 62; DLB
14

Baillie, Joanna 1762-1851 .... **NCLC 71**
See also DLB 93

Bainbridge, Beryl (Margaret) 1934- . **CLC 4,
5, 8, 10, 14, 18, 22, 62, 130; DAM NOV**
See also CA 21-24R; CANR 24, 55, 75, 88;
DLB 14, 231; MTCW 1, 2

Baker, Elliott 1922- .... **CLC 8**
See also CA 45-48; CANR 2, 63

Baker, Jean H. .... **TCLC 3, 10**
See also Russell, George William

Baker, Nicholson 1957- . **CLC 61; DAM POP**
See also CA 135; CANR 63; DA3; DLB
227

Baker, Ray Stannard 1870-1946 .. **TCLC 47**
See also CA 118

Baker, Russell (Wayne) 1925- .... **CLC 31**
See also BEST 89:4; CA 57-60; CANR 11,
41, 59; MTCW 1, 2

Bakhtin, M.
See Bakhtin, Mikhail Mikhailovich

Bakhtin, M. M.
　See Bakhtin, Mikhail Mikhailovich
Bakhtin, Mikhail
　See Bakhtin, Mikhail Mikhailovich
Bakhtin, Mikhail Mikhailovich 1895-1975
　..................................... **CLC 83**
　See also CA 128; 113
Bakshi, Ralph 1938(?)- .... **CLC 26**
　See also CA 112; 138
Bakunin, Mikhail (Alexandrovich)
　1814-1876 .... **NCLC 25, 58**
Baldwin, James (Arthur) 1924-1987 . **CLC 1,
　2, 3, 4, 5, 8, 13, 15, 17, 42, 50, 67, 90,
　127; BLC 1; DA; DAB; DAC; DAM
　MST, MULT, NOV, POP; DC 1; SSC
　10, 33; WLC**
　See also AAYA 4, 34; BW 1; CA 1-4R; 124;
　CABS 1; CANR 3, 24; CDALB 1941-
　1968; DA3; DLB 2, 7, 33; DLBY 87;
　MTCW 1, 2; SATA 9; SATA-Obit 54
Bale, John 1495-1563 .... **LC 62**
　See also DLB 132
Ballard, J(ames) G(raham) 1930- .... **CLC 3,
　6, 14, 36, 137; DAM NOV, POP; SSC 1**
　See also AAYA 3; CA 5-8R; CANR 15, 39,
　65; DA3; DLB 14, 207; MTCW 1, 2;
　SATA 93
Balmont, Konstantin (Dmitriyevich)
　1867-1943 .... **TCLC 11**
　See also CA 109; 155
Baltausis, Vincas
　See Mikszath, Kalman
Balzac, Honore de 1799-1850 .. **NCLC 5, 35,
　53; DA; DAB; DAC; DAM MST, NOV;
　SSC 5; WLC**
　See also DA3; DLB 119
Bambara, Toni Cade 1939-1995 ..... **CLC 19,
　88; BLC 1; DA; DAC; DAM MST,
　MULT; SSC 35; WLCS**
　See also AAYA 5; BW 2, 3; CA 29-32R;
　150; CANR 24, 49, 81; CDALBS; DA3;
　DLB 38; MTCW 1, 2; SATA 112
Bamdad, A.
　See Shamlu, Ahmad
Banat, D. R.
　See Bradbury, Ray (Douglas)
Bancroft, Laura
　See Baum, L(yman) Frank
Banim, John 1798-1842 .... **NCLC 13**
　See also DLB 116, 158, 159
Banim, Michael 1796-1874 .... **NCLC 13**
　See also DLB 158, 159
Banjo, The
　See Paterson, A(ndrew) B(arton)
Banks, Iain
　See Banks, Iain M(enzies)
Banks, Iain M(enzies) 1954- .... **CLC 34**
　See also CA 123; 128; CANR 61; DLB 194;
　INT 128
Banks, Lynne Reid .... **CLC 23**
　See also Reid Banks, Lynne
　See also AAYA 6
Banks, Russell 1940- ... **CLC 37, 72; SSC 42**
　See also CA 65-68; CAAS 15; CANR 19,
　52, 73; DLB 130
Banville, John 1945- .... **CLC 46, 118**
　See also CA 117; 128; DLB 14; INT 128
Banville, Theodore (Faullain) de 1832-1891
　....................................... **NCLC 9**
Baraka, Amiri 1934- . **CLC 1, 2, 3, 5, 10, 14,
　33, 115; BLC 1; DA; DAC; DAM MST,
　MULT, POET, POP; DC 6; PC 4;
　WLCS**
　See also Jones, LeRoi
　See also BW 2, 3; CA 21-24R; CABS 3;
　CANR 27, 38, 61; CDALB 1941-1968;
　DA3; DLB 5, 7, 16, 38; DLBD 8; MTCW
　1, 2

Barbauld, Anna Laetitia 1743-1825
　....................................... **NCLC 50**
　See also DLB 107, 109, 142, 158
Barbellion, W. N. P. .... **TCLC 24**
　See also Cummings, Bruce F(rederick)
Barbera, Jack (Vincent) 1945- .... **CLC 44**
　See also CA 110; CANR 45
Barbey d'Aurevilly, Jules Amedee 1808-1889
　....................................... **NCLC 1; SSC 17**
　See also DLB 119
Barbour, John c. 1316-1395 .... **CMLC 33**
　See also DLB 146
Barbusse, Henri 1873-1935 .... **TCLC 5**
　See also CA 105; 154; DLB 65
Barclay, Bill
　See Moorcock, Michael (John)
Barclay, William Ewert
　See Moorcock, Michael (John)
Barea, Arturo 1897-1957 .... **TCLC 14**
　See also CA 111
Barfoot, Joan 1946- .... **CLC 18**
　See also CA 105
Barham, Richard Harris 1788-1845
　....................................... **NCLC 77**
　See also DLB 159
Baring, Maurice 1874-1945 .... **TCLC 8**
　See also CA 105; 168; DLB 34
Baring-Gould, Sabine 1834-1924 . **TCLC 88**
　See also DLB 156, 190
Barker, Clive 1952- ..... **CLC 52; DAM POP**
　See also AAYA 10; BEST 90:3; CA 121;
　129; CANR 71; DA3; INT 129; MTCW
　1, 2
Barker, George Granville 1913-1991
　....................... **CLC 8, 48; DAM POET**
　See also CA 9-12R; 135; CANR 7, 38; DLB
　20; MTCW 1
Barker, Harley Granville
　See Granville-Barker, Harley
　See also DLB 10
Barker, Howard 1946- .... **CLC 37**
　See also CA 102; DLB 13, 233
Barker, Jane 1652-1732 .... **LC 42**
Barker, Pat(ricia) 1943- .... **CLC 32, 94**
　See also CA 117; 122; CANR 50; INT 122
Barlach, Ernst (Heinrich) 1870-1938
　....................................... **TCLC 84**
　See also CA 178; DLB 56, 118
Barlow, Joel 1754-1812 .... **NCLC 23**
　See also DLB 37
Barnard, Mary (Ethel) 1909- .... **CLC 48**
　See also CA 21-22; CAP 2
Barnes, Djuna 1892-1982 ... **CLC 3, 4, 8, 11,
　29, 127; SSC 3**
　See also CA 9-12R; 107; CANR 16, 55;
　DLB 4, 9, 45; MTCW 1, 2
Barnes, Julian (Patrick) 1946- .... **CLC 42;
　DAB**
　See also CA 102; CANR 19, 54; DLB 194;
　DLBY 93; MTCW 1
Barnes, Peter 1931- .... **CLC 5, 56**
　See also CA 65-68; CAAS 12; CANR 33,
　34, 64; DLB 13, 233; MTCW 1
Barnes, William 1801-1886 .... **NCLC 75**
　See also DLB 32
Baroja (y Nessi), Pio 1872-1956 .... **TCLC 8;
　HLC 1**
　See also CA 104
Baron, David
　See Pinter, Harold
Baron Corvo
　See Rolfe, Frederick (William Serafino
　Austin Lewis Mary)
Barondess, Sue K(aufman) 1926-1977
　....................................... **CLC 8**
　See also Kaufman, Sue
　See also CA 1-4R; 69-72; CANR 1

Baron de Teive
　See Pessoa, Fernando (Antonio Nogueira)
Baroness Von S.
　See Zangwill, Israel
Barres, (Auguste-) Maurice 1862-1923
　....................................... **TCLC 47**
　See also CA 164; DLB 123
Barreto, Afonso Henrique de Lima
　See Lima Barreto, Afonso Henrique de
Barrett, (Roger) Syd 1946- .... **CLC 35**
Barrett, William (Christopher) 1913-1992
　....................................... **CLC 27**
　See also CA 13-16R; 139; CANR 11, 67;
　INT CANR-11
Barrie, J(ames) M(atthew) 1860-1937
　............. **TCLC 2; DAB; DAM DRAM**
　See also CA 104; 136; CANR 77; CDBLB
　1890-1914; CLR 16; DA3; DLB 10, 141,
　156; MAICYA; MTCW 1; SATA 100;
　YABC 1
Barrington, Michael
　See Moorcock, Michael (John)
Barrol, Grady
　See Bograd, Larry
Barry, Mike
　See Malzberg, Barry N(athaniel)
Barry, Philip 1896-1949 .... **TCLC 11**
　See also CA 109; DLB 7, 228
Bart, Andre Schwarz
　See Schwarz-Bart, Andre
Barth, John (Simmons) 1930- .. **CLC 1, 2, 3,
　5, 7, 9, 10, 14, 27, 51, 89; DAM NOV;
　SSC 10**
　See also AITN 1, 2; CA 1-4R; CABS 1;
　CANR 5, 23, 49, 64; DLB 2, 227; MTCW
　1
Barthelme, Donald 1931-1989 . **CLC 1, 2, 3,
　5, 6, 8, 13, 23, 46, 59, 115; DAM NOV;
　SSC 2**
　See also CA 21-24R; 129; CANR 20, 58;
　DA3; DLB 2, 234; DLBY 80, 89; MTCW
　1, 2; SATA 7; SATA-Obit 62
Barthelme, Frederick 1943- .... **CLC 36, 117**
　See also CA 114; 122; CANR 77; DLBY
　85; INT 122
Barthes, Roland (Gerard) 1915-1980
　....................................... **CLC 24, 83**
　See also CA 130; 97-100; CANR 66;
　MTCW 1, 2
Barzun, Jacques (Martin) 1907- ..... **CLC 51**
　See also CA 61-64; CANR 22
Bashevis, Isaac
　See Singer, Isaac Bashevis
Bashkirtseff, Marie 1859-1884 ..... **NCLC 27**
Basho
　See Matsuo Basho
Basil of Caesaria c. 330-379 .... **CMLC 35**
Bass, Kingsley B., Jr.
　See Bullins, Ed
Bass, Rick 1958- .... **CLC 79**
　See also CA 126; CANR 53, 93; DLB 212
Bassani, Giorgio 1916- .... **CLC 9**
　See also CA 65-68; CANR 33; DLB 128,
　177; MTCW 1
Bastos, Augusto (Antonio) Roa
　See Roa Bastos, Augusto (Antonio)
Bataille, Georges 1897-1962 .... **CLC 29**
　See also CA 101; 89-92
Bates, H(erbert) E(rnest) 1905-1974
　..... **CLC 46; DAB; DAM POP; SSC 10**
　See also CA 93-96; 45-48; CANR 34; DA3;
　DLB 162, 191; MTCW 1, 2
Bauchart
　See Camus, Albert
Baudelaire, Charles 1821-1867 ...... **NCLC 6,
　29, 55; DA; DAB; DAC; DAM MST,
　POET; PC 1; SSC 18; WLC**
　See also DA3

Bourget, Paul (Charles Joseph) 1852-1935
.... **TCLC 12**
See also CA 107; DLB 123

Bourjaily, Vance (Nye) 1922- ...... **CLC 8, 62**
See also CA 1-4R; CAAS 1; CANR 2, 72;
DLB 2, 143

Bourne, Randolph S(illiman) 1886-1918
.... **TCLC 16**
See also CA 117; 155; DLB 63

Bova, Ben(jamin William) 1932- .... **CLC 45**
See also AAYA 16; CA 5-8R; CAAS 18;
CANR 11, 56; CLR 3; DLBY 81; INT
CANR-11; MAICYA; MTCW 1; SATA 6,
68

Bowen, Elizabeth (Dorothea Cole) 1899-1973
...... **CLC 1, 3, 6, 11, 15, 22, 118; DAM
NOV; SSC 3, 28**
See also CA 17-18; 41-44R; CANR 35;
CAP 2; CDBLB 1945-1960; DA3; DLB
15, 162; MTCW 1, 2

Bowering, George 1935- .... **CLC 15, 47**
See also CA 21-24R; CAAS 16; CANR 10;
DLB 53

Bowering, Marilyn R(uthe) 1949- ... **CLC 32**
See also CA 101; CANR 49

Bowers, Edgar 1924-2000 .... **CLC 9**
See also CA 5-8R; CANR 24; DLB 5

Bowie, David .... **CLC 17**
See also Jones, David Robert

Bowles, Jane (Sydney) 1917-1973 .... **CLC 3,
68**
See also CA 19-20; 41-44R; CAP 2

Bowles, Paul (Frederick) 1910-1999 . **CLC 1,
2, 19, 53; SSC 3**
See also CA 1-4R; 186; CAAS 1; CANR 1,
19, 50, 75; DA3; DLB 5, 6; MTCW 1, 2

Box, Edgar
See Vidal, Gore

Boyd, Nancy
See Millay, Edna St. Vincent

Boyd, William 1952- .... **CLC 28, 53, 70**
See also CA 114; 120; CANR 51, 71; DLB
231

Boyle, Kay 1902-1992 .... **CLC 1, 5, 19, 58,
121; SSC 5**
See also CA 13-16R; 140; CAAS 1; CANR
29, 61; DLB 4, 9, 48, 86; DLBY 93;
MTCW 1, 2

Boyle, Mark
See Kienzle, William X(avier)

Boyle, Patrick 1905-1982 .... **CLC 19**
See also CA 127

Boyle, T. C. 1948-
See Boyle, T(homas) Coraghessan

Boyle, T(homas) Coraghessan 1948-
... **CLC 36, 55, 90; DAM POP; SSC 16**
See also BEST 90:4; CA 120; CANR 44,
76, 89; DA3; DLBY 86; MTCW 2

Boz
See Dickens, Charles (John Huffam)

Brackenridge, Hugh Henry 1748-1816
.... **NCLC 7**
See also DLB 11, 37

Bradbury, Edward P.
See Moorcock, Michael (John)
See also MTCW 2

Bradbury, Malcolm (Stanley) 1932-
.... **CLC 32, 61; DAM NOV**
See also CA 1-4R; CANR 1, 33, 91; DA3;
DLB 14, 207; MTCW 1, 2

Bradbury, Ray (Douglas) 1920- ... **CLC 1, 3,
10, 15, 42, 98; DA; DAB; DAC; DAM
MST, NOV, POP; SSC 29; WLC**
See also AAYA 15; AITN 1, 2; CA 1-4R;
CANR 2, 30, 75; CDALB 1968-1988;
DA3; DLB 2, 8; MTCW 1, 2; SATA 11,
64

Bradford, Gamaliel 1863-1932 ..... **TCLC 36**
See also CA 160; DLB 17

Bradley, David (Henry), Jr. 1950- . **CLC 23,
118; BLC 1; DAM MULT**
See also BW 1, 3; CA 104; CANR 26, 81;
DLB 33

Bradley, John Ed(mund, Jr.) 1958- . **CLC 55**
See also CA 139

Bradley, Marion Zimmer 1930-1999
.... **CLC 30; DAM POP**
See also AAYA 9; CA 57-60; 185; CAAS
10; CANR 7, 31, 51, 75; DA3; DLB 8;
MTCW 1, 2; SATA 90; SATA-Obit 116

Bradstreet, Anne 1612(?)-1672 ..... **LC 4, 30;
DA; DAC; DAM MST, POET; PC 10**
See also CDALB 1640-1865; DA3; DLB
24

Brady, Joan 1939- .... **CLC 86**
See also CA 141

Bragg, Melvyn 1939- .... **CLC 10**
See also BEST 89:3; CA 57-60; CANR 10,
48, 89; DLB 14

Brahe, Tycho 1546-1601 .... **LC 45**

Braine, John (Gerard) 1922-1986 .... **CLC 1,
3, 41**
See also CA 1-4R; 120; CANR 1, 33; CD-
BLB 1945-1960; DLB 15; DLBY 86;
MTCW 1

Bramah, Ernest 1868-1942 .... **TCLC 72**
See also CA 156; DLB 70

Brammer, William 1930(?)-1978 ..... **CLC 31**
See also CA 77-80

Brancati, Vitaliano 1907-1954 ...... **TCLC 12**
See also CA 109

Brancato, Robin F(idler) 1936- .... **CLC 35**
See also AAYA 9; CA 69-72; CANR 11,
45; CLR 32; JRDA; SAAS 9; SATA 97

Brand, Max
See Faust, Frederick (Schiller)

Brand, Millen 1906-1980 .... **CLC 7**
See also CA 21-24R; 97-100; CANR 72

Branden, Barbara .... **CLC 44**
See also CA 148

Brandes, Georg (Morris Cohen) 1842-1927
.... **TCLC 10**
See also CA 105

Brandys, Kazimierz 1916- .... **CLC 62**

Branley, Franklyn M(ansfield) 1915-
.... **CLC 21**
See also CA 33-36R; CANR 14, 39; CLR
13; MAICYA; SAAS 16; SATA 4, 68

Brathwaite, Edward (Kamau) 1930-
.... **CLC 11; BLCS; DAM POET**
See also BW 2, 3; CA 25-28R; CANR 11,
26, 47; DLB 125

Brautigan, Richard (Gary) 1935-1984
. **CLC 1, 3, 5, 9, 12, 34, 42; DAM NOV**
See also CA 53-56; 113; CANR 34; DA3;
DLB 2, 5, 206; DLBY 80, 84; MTCW 1;
SATA 56

Brave Bird, Mary 1953-
See Crow Dog, Mary (Ellen)
See also NNAL

Braverman, Kate 1950- .... **CLC 67**
See also CA 89-92

Brecht, (Eugen) Bertolt (Friedrich)
1898-1956 .... **TCLC 1, 6, 13, 35; DA;
DAB; DAC; DAM DRAM, MST; DC 3;
WLC**
See also CA 104; 133; CANR 62; DA3;
DLB 56, 124; MTCW 1, 2

Brecht, Eugen Berthold Friedrich
See Brecht, (Eugen) Bertolt (Friedrich)

Bremer, Fredrika 1801-1865 .... **NCLC 11**

Brennan, Christopher (John) 1870-1932
.... **TCLC 17**
See also CA 117; DLB 230

Brennan, Maeve 1917-1993 .... **CLC 5**
See also CA 81-84; CANR 72

Brent, Linda
See Jacobs, Harriet A(nn)

Brentano, Clemens (Maria) 1778-1842
.... **NCLC 1**
See also DLB 90

Brent of Bin Bin
See Franklin, (Stella Maria Sarah) Miles
(Lampe)

Brenton, Howard 1942- .... **CLC 31**
See also CA 69-72; CANR 33, 67; DLB 13;
MTCW 1

Breslin, James 1930-
See Breslin, Jimmy
See also CA 73-76; CANR 31, 75; DAM
NOV; MTCW 1, 2

Breslin, Jimmy .... **CLC 4, 43**
See also Breslin, James
See also AITN 1; DLB 185; MTCW 2

Bresson, Robert 1901(?)-1999 .... **CLC 16**
See also CA 110; 187; CANR 49

Breton, Andre 1896-1966 . **CLC 2, 9, 15, 54;
PC 15**
See also CA 19-20; 25-28R; CANR 40, 60;
CAP 2; DLB 65; MTCW 1, 2

Breytenbach, Breyten 1939(?)- . **CLC 23, 37,
126; DAM POET**
See also CA 113; 129; CANR 61; DLB 225

Bridgers, Sue Ellen 1942- .... **CLC 26**
See also AAYA 8; CA 65-68; CANR 11,
36; CLR 18; DLB 52; JRDA; MAICYA;
SAAS 1; SATA 22, 90; SATA-Essay 109

Bridges, Robert (Seymour) 1844-1930
.... **TCLC 1; DAM POET; PC 28**
See also CA 104; 152; CDBLB 1890-1914;
DLB 19, 98

Bridie, James .... **TCLC 3**
See also Mavor, Osborne Henry
See also DLB 10

Brin, David 1950- .... **CLC 34**
See also AAYA 21; CA 102; CANR 24, 70;
INT CANR-24; SATA 65

Brink, Andre (Philippus) 1935- ...... **CLC 18,
36, 106**
See also CA 104; CANR 39, 62; DLB 225;
INT 103; MTCW 1, 2

Brinsmead, H(esba) F(ay) 1922- ..... **CLC 21**
See also CA 21-24R; CANR 10; CLR 47;
MAICYA; SAAS 5; SATA 18, 78

Brittain, Vera (Mary) 1893(?)-1970 . **CLC 23**
See also CA 13-16; 25-28R; CANR 58;
CAP 1; DLB 191; MTCW 1, 2

Broch, Hermann 1886-1951 .... **TCLC 20**
See also CA 117; DLB 85, 124

Brock, Rose
See Hansen, Joseph

Brodkey, Harold (Roy) 1930-1996 .. **CLC 56**
See also CA 111; 151; CANR 71; DLB 130

Brodsky, Iosif Alexandrovich 1940-1996
See Brodsky, Joseph
See also AITN 1; CA 41-44R; 151; CANR
37; DAM POET; DA3; MTCW 1, 2

Brodsky, Joseph 1940-1996 .... **CLC 4, 6, 13,
36, 100; PC 9**
See also Brodsky, Iosif Alexandrovich
See also MTCW 1

Brodsky, Michael (Mark) 1948- ...... **CLC 19**
See also CA 102; CANR 18, 41, 58

Brome, Richard 1590(?)-1652 .... **LC 61**
See also DLB 58

Bromell, Henry 1947- .... **CLC 5**
See also CA 53-56; CANR 9

Bromfield, Louis (Brucker) 1896-1956
.... **TCLC 11**
See also CA 107; 155; DLB 4, 9, 86

Broner, E(sther) M(asserman) 1930-
.... **CLC 19**
See also CA 17-20R; CANR 8, 25, 72; DLB
28

Bronk, William (M.) 1918-1999 ...... **CLC 10**
See also CA 89-92; 177; CANR 23; DLB
165

See also AAYA 23; CDBLB 1832-1890;
DA3; DLB 21, 55, 70, 159, 166; JRDA;
MAICYA; SATA 15

Dickey, James (Lafayette) 1923-1997
.. **CLC 1, 2, 4, 7, 10, 15, 47, 109; DAM
NOV, POET, POP**
See also AITN 1, 2; CA 9-12R; 156; CABS
2; CANR 10, 48, 61; CDALB 1968-1988;
DA3; DLB 5, 193; DLBD 7; DLBY 82,
93, 96, 97, 98; INT CANR-10; MTCW 1,
2

Dickey, William 1928-1994 .... **CLC 3, 28**
See also CA 9-12R; 145; CANR 24, 79;
DLB 5

Dickinson, Charles 1951- .... **CLC 49**
See also CA 128

Dickinson, Emily (Elizabeth) 1830-1886
. **NCLC 21, 77; DA; DAB; DAC; DAM
MST, POET; PC 1; WLC**
See also AAYA 22; CDALB 1865-1917;
DA3; DLB 1; SATA 29

Dickinson, Peter (Malcolm) 1927- . **CLC 12,
35**
See also AAYA 9; CA 41-44R; CANR 31,
58, 88; CLR 29; DLB 87, 161; JRDA;
MAICYA; SATA 5, 62, 95

Dickson, Carr
See Carr, John Dickson

Dickson, Carter
See Carr, John Dickson

Diderot, Denis 1713-1784 .... **LC 26**

Didion, Joan 1934- . **CLC 1, 3, 8, 14, 32, 129;
DAM NOV**
See also AITN 1; CA 5-8R; CANR 14, 52,
76; CDALB 1968-1988; DA3; DLB 2,
173, 185; DLBY 81, 86; MTCW 1, 2

Dietrich, Robert
See Hunt, E(verette) Howard, (Jr.)

Difusa, Pati
See Almodovar, Pedro

Dillard, Annie 1945- . **CLC 9, 60, 115; DAM
NOV**
See also AAYA 6; CA 49-52; CANR 3, 43,
62, 90; DA3; DLBY 80; MTCW 1, 2;
SATA 10

Dillard, R(ichard) H(enry) W(ilde) 1937-
.... **CLC 5**
See also CA 21-24R; CAAS 7; CANR 10;
DLB 5

Dillon, Eilis 1920-1994 .... **CLC 17**
See also CA 9-12R, 182; 147; CAAE 182;
CAAS 3; CANR 4, 38, 78; CLR 26; MAI-
CYA; SATA 2, 74; SATA-Essay 105;
SATA-Obit 83

Dimont, Penelope
See Mortimer, Penelope (Ruth)

Dinesen, Isak -1962 . **CLC 10, 29, 95; SSC 7**
See also Blixen, Karen (Christentze
Dinesen)
See also MTCW 1

Ding Ling .... **CLC 68**
See also Chiang, Pin-chin

Diphusa, Patty
See Almodovar, Pedro

Disch, Thomas M(ichael) 1940- .. **CLC 7, 36**
See also AAYA 17; CA 21-24R; CAAS 4;
CANR 17, 36, 54, 89; CLR 18; DA3;
DLB 8; MAICYA; MTCW 1, 2; SAAS
15; SATA 92

Disch, Tom
See Disch, Thomas M(ichael)

d'Isly, Georges
See Simenon, Georges (Jacques Christian)

Disraeli, Benjamin 1804-1881 . **NCLC 2, 39,
79**
See also DLB 21, 55

Ditcum, Steve
See Crumb, R(obert)

Dixon, Paige
See Corcoran, Barbara

Dixon, Stephen 1936- .... **CLC 52; SSC 16**
See also CA 89-92; CANR 17, 40, 54, 91;
DLB 130

Doak, Annie
See Dillard, Annie

Dobell, Sydney Thompson 1824-1874
.... **NCLC 43**
See also DLB 32

Doblin, Alfred .... **TCLC 13**
See also Doeblin, Alfred

**Dobrolyubov, Nikolai Alexandrovich
1836-1861** .... **NCLC 5**

Dobson, Austin 1840-1921 .... **TCLC 79**
See also DLB 35; 144

Dobyns, Stephen 1941- .... **CLC 37**
See also CA 45-48; CANR 2, 18

Doctorow, E(dgar) L(aurence) 1931-
.... **CLC 6, 11, 15, 18, 37, 44, 65, 113;
DAM NOV, POP**
See also AAYA 22; AITN 2; BEST 89:3;
CA 45-48; CANR 2, 33, 51, 76; CDALB
1968-1988; DA3; DLB 2, 28, 173; DLBY
80; MTCW 1, 2

Dodgson, Charles Lutwidge 1832-1898
See Carroll, Lewis
See also CLR 2; DA; DAB; DAC; DAM
MST, NOV, POET; DA3; MAICYA;
SATA 100; YABC 2

Dodson, Owen (Vincent) 1914-1983
.... **CLC 79; BLC 1; DAM MULT**
See also BW 1; CA 65-68; 110; CANR 24;
DLB 76

Doeblin, Alfred 1878-1957 .... **TCLC 13**
See also Doblin, Alfred
See also CA 110; 141; DLB 66

Doerr, Harriet 1910- .... **CLC 34**
See also CA 117; 122; CANR 47; INT 122

Domecq, H(onorio Bustos)
See Bioy Casares, Adolfo

Domecq, H(onorio) Bustos
See Bioy Casares, Adolfo; Borges, Jorge
Luis

Domini, Rey
See Lorde, Audre (Geraldine)

Dominique
See Proust, (Valentin-Louis-George-
Eugene-) Marcel

Don, A
See Stephen, SirLeslie

Donaldson, Stephen R. 1947- . **CLC 46, 138;
DAM POP**
See also CA 89-92; CANR 13, 55; INT
CANR-13

Donleavy, J(ames) P(atrick) 1926- ... **CLC 1,
4, 6, 10, 45**
See also AITN 2; CA 9-12R; CANR 24, 49,
62, 80; DLB 6, 173; INT CANR-24;
MTCW 1, 2

Donne, John 1572-1631 .... **LC 10, 24; DA;
DAB; DAC; DAM MST, POET; PC 1;
WLC**
See also CDBLB Before 1660; DLB 121,
151

Donnell, David 1939(?)- .... **CLC 34**

Donoghue, P. S.
See Hunt, E(verette) Howard, (Jr.)

Donoso (Yanez), Jose 1924-1996 ... **CLC 4, 8,
11, 32, 99; DAM MULT; HLC 1; SSC
34**
See also CA 81-84; 155; CANR 32, 73;
DLB 113; HW 1, 2; MTCW 1, 2

Donovan, John 1928-1992 .... **CLC 35**
See also AAYA 20; CA 97-100; 137; CLR
3; MAICYA; SATA 72; SATA-Brief 29

Don Roberto
See Cunninghame Graham, Robert
(Gallnigad) Bontine

Doolittle, Hilda 1886-1961 ...... **CLC 3, 8, 14,
31, 34, 73; DA; DAC; DAM MST,
POET; PC 5; WLC**
See also H. D.
See also CA 97-100; CANR 35; DLB 4, 45;
MTCW 1, 2

Dorfman, Ariel 1942- ..... **CLC 48, 77; DAM
MULT; HLC 1**
See also CA 124; 130; CANR 67, 70; HW
1, 2; INT 130

Dorn, Edward (Merton) 1929-1999 . **CLC 10,
18**
See also CA 93-96; 187; CANR 42, 79;
DLB 5; INT 93-96

Dorris, Michael (Anthony) 1945-1997
.... **CLC 109; DAM MULT, NOV**
See also AAYA 20; BEST 90:1; CA 102;
157; CANR 19, 46, 75; CLR 58; DA3;
DLB 175; MTCW 2; NNAL; SATA 75;
SATA-Obit 94

Dorris, Michael A.
See Dorris, Michael (Anthony)

Dorsan, Luc
See Simenon, Georges (Jacques Christian)

Dorsange, Jean
See Simenon, Georges (Jacques Christian)

Dos Passos, John (Roderigo) 1896-1970
..... **CLC 1, 4, 8, 11, 15, 25, 34, 82; DA;
DAB; DAC; DAM MST, NOV; WLC**
See also CA 1-4R; 29-32R; CANR 3;
CDALB 1929-1941; DA3; DLB 4, 9;
DLBD 1, 15; DLBY 96; MTCW 1, 2

Dossage, Jean
See Simenon, Georges (Jacques Christian)

Dostoevsky, Fedor Mikhailovich 1821-1881
.... **NCLC 2, 7, 21, 33, 43; DA; DAB;
DAC; DAM MST, NOV; SSC 2, 33;
WLC**
See also DA3

Doughty, Charles M(ontagu) 1843-1926
.... **TCLC 27**
See also CA 115; 178; DLB 19, 57, 174

Douglas, Ellen .... **CLC 73**
See also Haxton, Josephine Ayres; William-
son, Ellen Douglas

Douglas, Gavin 1475(?)-1522 .... **LC 20**
See also DLB 132

Douglas, George
See Brown, George Douglas

Douglas, Keith (Castellain) 1920-1944
.... **TCLC 40**
See also CA 160; DLB 27

Douglas, Leonard
See Bradbury, Ray (Douglas)

Douglas, Michael
See Crichton, (John) Michael

Douglas, (George) Norman 1868-1952
.... **TCLC 68**
See also CA 119; 157; DLB 34, 195

Douglas, William
See Brown, George Douglas

Douglass, Frederick 1817(?)-1895 . **NCLC 7,
55; BLC 1; DA; DAC; DAM MST,
MULT; WLC**
See also CDALB 1640-1865; DA3; DLB 1,
43, 50, 79; SATA 29

Dourado, (Waldomiro Freitas) Autran 1926-
.... **CLC 23, 60**
See also CA 25-28R; 179; CANR 34, 81;
DLB 145; HW 2

Dourado, Waldomiro Autran 1926-
See Dourado, (Waldomiro Freitas) Autran
See also CA 179

Dove, Rita (Frances) 1952- ...... **CLC 50, 81;
BLCS; DAM MULT, POET; PC 6**
See also BW 2; CA 109; CAAS 19; CANR
27, 42, 68, 76; CDALBS; DA3; DLB 120;
MTCW 1

Flecker, (Herman) James Elroy 1884-1915
.... **TCLC 43**
See also CA 109; 150; DLB 10, 19
Fleming, Ian (Lancaster) 1908-1964 . **CLC 3,
30; DAM POP**
See also AAYA 26; CA 5-8R; CANR 59;
CDBLB 1945-1960; DA3; DLB 87, 201;
MTCW 1, 2; SATA 9
Fleming, Thomas (James) 1927- ..... **CLC 37**
See also CA 5-8R; CANR 10; INT CANR-
10; SATA 8
Fletcher, John 1579-1625 .... **LC 33; DC 6**
See also CDBLB Before 1660; DLB 58
Fletcher, John Gould 1886-1950 .. **TCLC 35**
See also CA 107; 167; DLB 4, 45
Fleur, Paul
See Pohl, Frederik
Flooglebuckle, Al
See Spiegelman, Art
Flora, Fletcher 1914-1969
See Queen, Ellery
See also CA 1-4R; CANR 3, 85
Flying Officer X
See Bates, H(erbert) E(rnest)
Fo, Dario 1926- .... **CLC 32, 109; DAM
DRAM; DC 10**
See also CA 116; 128; CANR 68; DA3;
DLBY 97; MTCW 1, 2
Fogarty, Jonathan Titulescu Esq.
See Farrell, James T(homas)
Follett, Ken(neth Martin) 1949- .... **CLC 18;
DAM NOV, POP**
See also AAYA 6; BEST 89:4; CA 81-84;
CANR 13, 33, 54; DA3; DLB 87; DLBY
81; INT CANR-33; MTCW 1
Fontane, Theodor 1819-1898 .... **NCLC 26**
See also DLB 129
Foote, Horton 1916- .... **CLC 51, 91; DAM
DRAM**
See also CA 73-76; CANR 34, 51; DA3;
DLB 26; INT CANR-34
Foote, Shelby 1916- ... **CLC 75; DAM NOV,
POP**
See also CA 5-8R; CANR 3, 45, 74; DA3;
DLB 2, 17; MTCW 2
Forbes, Esther 1891-1967 .... **CLC 12**
See also AAYA 17; CA 13-14; 25-28R; CAP
1; CLR 27; DLB 22; JRDA; MAICYA;
SATA 2, 100
Forche, Carolyn (Louise) 1950- ..... **CLC 25,
83, 86; DAM POET; PC 10**
See also CA 109; 117; CANR 50, 74; DA3;
DLB 5, 193; INT 117; MTCW 1
Ford, Elbur
See Hibbert, Eleanor Alice Burford
Ford, Ford Madox 1873-1939 . **TCLC 1, 15,
39, 57; DAM NOV**
See Chaucer, Daniel
See also CA 104; 132; CANR 74; CDBLB
1914-1945; DA3; DLB 162; MTCW 1, 2
Ford, Henry 1863-1947 .... **TCLC 73**
See also CA 115; 148
Ford, John 1586-(?) .... **DC 8**
See also CDBLB Before 1660; DAM
DRAM; DA3; DLB 58
Ford, John 1895-1973 .... **CLC 16**
See also CA 187; 45-48
Ford, Richard 1944- .... **CLC 46, 99**
See also CA 69-72; CANR 11, 47, 86; DLB
227; MTCW 1
Ford, Webster
See Masters, Edgar Lee
Foreman, Richard 1937- .... **CLC 50**
See also CA 65-68; CANR 32, 63
Forester, C(ecil) S(cott) 1899-1966 . **CLC 35**
See also CA 73-76; 25-28R; CANR 83;
DLB 191; SATA 13

Forez
See Mauriac, Francois (Charles)
Forman, James Douglas 1932- .... **CLC 21**
See also AAYA 17; CA 9-12R; CANR 4,
19, 42; JRDA; MAICYA; SATA 8, 70
Fornes, Maria Irene 1930- . **CLC 39, 61; DC
10; HLCS 1**
See also CA 25-28R; CANR 28, 81; DLB
7; HW 1, 2; INT CANR-28; MTCW 1
Forrest, Leon (Richard) 1937-1997 . **CLC 4;
BLCS**
See also BW 2; CA 89-92; 162; CAAS 7;
CANR 25, 52, 87; DLB 33
Forster, E(dward) M(organ) 1879-1970
..... **CLC 1, 2, 3, 4, 9, 10, 13, 15, 22, 45,
77; DA; DAB; DAC; DAM MST, NOV;
SSC 27; WLC**
See also AAYA 2; CA 13-14; 25-28R;
CANR 45; CAP 1; CDBLB 1914-1945;
DA3; DLB 34, 98, 162, 178, 195; DLBD
10; MTCW 1, 2; SATA 57
Forster, John 1812-1876 .... **NCLC 11**
See also DLB 144, 184
Forsyth, Frederick 1938- .... **CLC 2, 5, 36;
DAM NOV, POP**
See also BEST 89:4; CA 85-88; CANR 38,
62; DLB 87; MTCW 1, 2
Forten, Charlotte L. .... **TCLC 16; BLC 2**
See Grimke, Charlotte L(ottie) Forten
See also DLB 50
Foscolo, Ugo 1778-1827 .... **NCLC 8**
Fosse, Bob .... **CLC 20**
See also Fosse, Robert Louis
Fosse, Robert Louis 1927-1987
See Fosse, Bob
See also CA 110; 123
Foster, Stephen Collins 1826-1864 . **NCLC 26**
Foucault, Michel 1926-1984 . **CLC 31, 34, 69**
See also CA 105; 113; CANR 34; MTCW
1, 2
Fouque, Friedrich (Heinrich Karl) de la
Motte 1777-1843 .... **NCLC 2**
See also DLB 90
Fourier, Charles 1772-1837 .... **NCLC 51**
Fournier, Pierre 1916- .... **CLC 11**
See also Gascar, Pierre
See also CA 89-92; CANR 16, 40
Fowles, John (Philip) 1926- . **CLC 1, 2, 3, 4,
6, 9, 10, 15, 33, 87; DAB; DAC; DAM
MST; SSC 33**
See also CA 5-8R; CANR 25, 71; CDBLB
1960 to Present; DA3; DLB 14, 139, 207;
MTCW 1, 2; SATA 22
Fox, Paula 1923- .... **CLC 2, 8, 121**
See also AAYA 3; CA 73-76; CANR 20,
36, 62; CLR 1, 44; DLB 52; JRDA; MAI-
CYA; MTCW 1; SATA 17, 60
Fox, William Price (Jr.) 1926- .... **CLC 22**
See also CA 17-20R; CAAS 19; CANR 11;
DLB 2; DLBY 81
Foxe, John 1516(?)-1587 .... **LC 14**
See also DLB 132
Frame, Janet 1924- . **CLC 2, 3, 6, 22, 66, 96;
SSC 29**
See also Clutha, Janet Paterson Frame
France, Anatole .... **TCLC 9**
See also Thibault, Jacques Anatole Francois
See also DLB 123; MTCW 1
Francis, Claude 19(?)- .... **CLC 50**
Francis, Dick 1920- ...... **CLC 2, 22, 42, 102;
DAM POP**
See also AAYA 5, 21; BEST 89:3; CA 5-8R;
CANR 9, 42, 68; CDBLB 1960 to Present;
DA3; DLB 87; INT CANR-9; MTCW 1,
2
Francis, Robert (Churchill) 1901-1987
.... **CLC 15**
See also CA 1-4R; 123; CANR 1

Frank, Anne(lies Marie) 1929-1945
...... **TCLC 17; DA; DAB; DAC; DAM
MST; WLC**
See also AAYA 12; CA 113; 133; CANR
68; DA3; MTCW 1, 2; SATA 87; SATA-
Brief 42
Frank, Bruno 1887-1945 .... **TCLC 81**
See also DLB 118
Frank, Elizabeth 1945- .... **CLC 39**
See also CA 121; 126; CANR 78; INT 126
Frankl, Viktor E(mil) 1905-1997 .... **CLC 93**
See also CA 65-68; 161
Franklin, Benjamin
See Hasek, Jaroslav (Matej Frantisek)
Franklin, Benjamin 1706-1790 . **LC 25; DA;
DAB; DAC; DAM MST; WLCS**
See also CDALB 1640-1865; DA3; DLB
24, 43, 73
Franklin, (Stella Maria Sarah) Miles
(Lampe) 1879-1954 .... **TCLC 7**
See also CA 104; 164
Fraser, (Lady) Antonia (Pakenham) 1932-
.... **CLC 32, 107**
See also CA 85-88; CANR 44, 65; MTCW
1, 2; SATA-Brief 32
Fraser, George MacDonald 1925- ..... **CLC 7**
See also CA 45-48, 180; CAAE 180; CANR
2, 48, 74; MTCW 1
Fraser, Sylvia 1935- .... **CLC 64**
See also CA 45-48; CANR 1, 16, 60
Frayn, Michael 1933- .... **CLC 3, 7, 31, 47;
DAM DRAM, NOV**
See also CA 5-8R; CANR 30, 69; DLB 13,
14, 194; MTCW 1, 2
Fraze, Candida (Merrill) 1945- .... **CLC 50**
See also CA 126
Frazer, J(ames) G(eorge) 1854-1941
.... **TCLC 32**
See also CA 118
Frazer, Robert Caine
See Creasey, John
Frazer, Sir James George
See Frazer, J(ames) G(eorge)
Frazier, Charles 1950- .... **CLC 109**
See also AAYA 34; CA 161
Frazier, Ian 1951- .... **CLC 46**
See also CA 130; CANR 54, 93
Frederic, Harold 1856-1898 .... **NCLC 10**
See also DLB 12, 23; DLBD 13
Frederick, John
See Faust, Frederick (Schiller)
Frederick the Great 1712-1786 .... **LC 14**
Fredro, Aleksander 1793-1876 .... **NCLC 8**
Freeling, Nicolas 1927- .... **CLC 38**
See also CA 49-52; CAAS 12; CANR 1,
17, 50, 84; DLB 87
Freeman, Douglas Southall 1886-1953
.... **TCLC 11**
See also CA 109; DLB 17; DLBD 17
Freeman, Judith 1946- .... **CLC 55**
See also CA 148
Freeman, Mary E(leanor) Wilkins 1852-1930
.... **TCLC 9; SSC 1**
See also CA 106; 177; DLB 12, 78, 221
Freeman, R(ichard) Austin 1862-1943
.... **TCLC 21**
See also CA 113; CANR 84; DLB 70
French, Albert 1943- .... **CLC 86**
See also BW 3; CA 167
French, Marilyn 1929- .... **CLC 10, 18, 60;
DAM DRAM, NOV, POP**
See also CA 69-72; CANR 3, 31; INT
CANR-31; MTCW 1, 2
French, Paul
See Asimov, Isaac
Freneau, Philip Morin 1752-1832 .. **NCLC 1**
See also DLB 37, 43
Freud, Sigmund 1856-1939 .... **TCLC 52**

See also CA 115; 133; CANR 69; MTCW 1, 2

Friedan, Betty (Naomi) 1921- .... **CLC 74**
See also CA 65-68; CANR 18, 45, 74; MTCW 1, 2

Friedlander, Saul 1932- .... **CLC 90**
See also CA 117; 130; CANR 72

Friedman, B(ernard) H(arper) 1926-
.... **CLC 7**
See also CA 1-4R; CANR 3, 48

Friedman, Bruce Jay 1930- ... **CLC 3, 5, 56**
See also CA 9-12R; CANR 25, 52; DLB 2, 28; INT CANR-25

Friel, Brian 1929- .. **CLC 5, 42, 59, 115; DC 8**
See also CA 21-24R; CANR 33, 69; DLB 13; MTCW 1

Friis-Baastad, Babbis Ellinor 1921-1970
.... **CLC 12**
See also CA 17-20R; 134; SATA 7

Frisch, Max (Rudolf) 1911-1991 .. **CLC 3, 9, 14, 18, 32, 44; DAM DRAM, NOV**
See also CA 85-88; 134; CANR 32, 74; DLB 69, 124; MTCW 1, 2

Fromentin, Eugene (Samuel Auguste) 1820-1876 .... **NCLC 10**
See also DLB 123

Frost, Frederick
See Faust, Frederick (Schiller)

Frost, Robert (Lee) 1874-1963 . **CLC 1, 3, 4, 9, 10, 13, 15, 26, 34, 44; DA; DAB; DAC; DAM MST, POET; PC 1; WLC**
See also AAYA 21; CA 89-92; CANR 33; CDALB 1917-1929; CLR 67; DA3; DLB 54; DLBD 7; MTCW 1, 2; SATA 14

Froude, James Anthony 1818-1894
.... **NCLC 43**
See also DLB 18, 57, 144

Froy, Herald
See Waterhouse, Keith (Spencer)

Fry, Christopher 1907- .... **CLC 2, 10, 14; DAM DRAM**
See also CA 17-20R; CAAS 23; CANR 9, 30, 74; DLB 13; MTCW 1, 2; SATA 66

Frye, (Herman) Northrop 1912-1991
.... **CLC 24, 70**
See also CA 5-8R; 133; CANR 8, 37; DLB 67, 68; MTCW 1, 2

Fuchs, Daniel 1909-1993 .... **CLC 8, 22**
See also CA 81-84; 142; CAAS 5; CANR 40; DLB 9, 26, 28; DLBY 93

Fuchs, Daniel 1934- .... **CLC 34**
See also CA 37-40R; CANR 14, 48

Fuentes, Carlos 1928- . **CLC 3, 8, 10, 13, 22, 41, 60, 113; DA; DAB; DAC; DAM MST, MULT, NOV; HLC 1; SSC 24; WLC**
See also AAYA 4; AITN 2; CA 69-72; CANR 10, 32, 68; DA3; DLB 113; HW 1, 2; MTCW 1, 2

Fuentes, Gregorio Lopez y
See Lopez y Fuentes, Gregorio

Fuertes, Gloria 1918- .... **PC 27**
See also CA 178, 180; DLB 108; HW 2; SATA 115

Fugard, (Harold) Athol 1932- . **CLC 5, 9, 14, 25, 40, 80; DAM DRAM; DC 3**
See also AAYA 17; CA 85-88; CANR 32, 54; DLB 225; MTCW 1

Fugard, Sheila 1932- .... **CLC 48**
See also CA 125

Fukuyama, Francis 1952- .... **CLC 131**
See also CA 140; CANR 72

Fuller, Charles (H., Jr.) 1939- .... **CLC 25; BLC 2; DAM DRAM, MULT; DC 1**
See also BW 2; CA 108; 112; CANR 87; DLB 38; INT 112; MTCW 1

Fuller, Henry Blake 1857-1929 ... **TCLC 103**
See also CA 108; 177; DLB 12

Fuller, John (Leopold) 1937- .... **CLC 62**
See also CA 21-24R; CANR 9, 44; DLB 40

Fuller, Margaret
See Ossoli, Sarah Margaret (Fuller marchesa d')

Fuller, Roy (Broadbent) 1912-1991 . **CLC 4, 28**
See also CA 5-8R; 135; CAAS 10; CANR 53, 83; DLB 15, 20; SATA 87

Fuller, Sarah Margaret 1810-1850
See Ossoli, Sarah Margaret (Fuller marchesa d')

Fulton, Alice 1952- .... **CLC 52**
See also CA 116; CANR 57, 88; DLB 193

Furphy, Joseph 1843-1912 .... **TCLC 25**
See also CA 163; DLB 230

Fussell, Paul 1924- .... **CLC 74**
See also BEST 90:1; CA 17-20R; CANR 8, 21, 35, 69; INT CANR-21; MTCW 1, 2

Futabatei, Shimei 1864-1909 .... **TCLC 44**
See also CA 162; DLB 180

Futrelle, Jacques 1875-1912 .... **TCLC 19**
See also CA 113; 155

Gaboriau, Emile 1835-1873 .... **NCLC 14**

Gadda, Carlo Emilio 1893-1973 ...... **CLC 11**
See also CA 89-92; DLB 177

Gaddis, William 1922-1998 .. **CLC 1, 3, 6, 8, 10, 19, 43, 86**
See also CA 17-20R; 172; CANR 21, 48; DLB 2; MTCW 1, 2

Gage, Walter
See Inge, William (Motter)

Gaines, Ernest J(ames) 1933- ..... **CLC 3, 11, 18, 86; BLC 2; DAM MULT**
See also AAYA 18; AITN 1; BW 2, 3; CA 9-12R; CANR 6, 24, 42, 75; CDALB 1968-1988; CLR 62; DA3; DLB 2, 33, 152; DLBY 80; MTCW 1, 2; SATA 86

Gaitskill, Mary 1954- .... **CLC 69**
See also CA 128; CANR 61

Galdos, Benito Perez
See Perez Galdos, Benito

Gale, Zona 1874-1938 .... **TCLC 7; DAM DRAM**
See also CA 105; 153; CANR 84; DLB 9, 78, 228

Galeano, Eduardo (Hughes) 1940- . **CLC 72; HLCS 1**
See also CA 29-32R; CANR 13, 32; HW 1

Galiano, Juan Valera y Alcala
See Valera y Alcala-Galiano, Juan

Galilei, Galileo 1546-1642 .... **LC 45**

Gallagher, Tess 1943- ..... **CLC 18, 63; DAM POET; PC 9**
See also CA 106; DLB 212

Gallant, Mavis 1922- . **CLC 7, 18, 38; DAC; DAM MST; SSC 5**
See also CA 69-72; CANR 29, 69; DLB 53; MTCW 1, 2

Gallant, Roy A(rthur) 1924- .... **CLC 17**
See also CA 5-8R; CANR 4, 29, 54; CLR 30; MAICYA; SATA 4, 68, 110

Gallico, Paul (William) 1897-1976 .... **CLC 2**
See also AITN 1; CA 5-8R; 69-72; CANR 23; DLB 9, 171; MAICYA; SATA 13

Gallo, Max Louis 1932- .... **CLC 95**
See also CA 85-88

Gallois, Lucien
See Desnos, Robert

Gallup, Ralph
See Whitemore, Hugh (John)

Galsworthy, John 1867-1933 ... **TCLC 1, 45; DA; DAB; DAC; DAM DRAM, MST, NOV; SSC 22; WLC**
See also CA 104; 141; CANR 75; CDBLB 1890-1914; DA3; DLB 10, 34, 98, 162; DLBD 16; MTCW 1

Galt, John 1779-1839 .... **NCLC 1**
See also DLB 99, 116, 159

Galvin, James 1951- .... **CLC 38**
See also CA 108; CANR 26

Gamboa, Federico 1864-1939 .... **TCLC 36**
See also CA 167; HW 2

Gandhi, M. K.
See Gandhi, Mohandas Karamchand

Gandhi, Mahatma
See Gandhi, Mohandas Karamchand

Gandhi, Mohandas Karamchand 1869-1948
.... **TCLC 59; DAM MULT**
See also CA 121; 132; DA3; MTCW 1, 2

Gann, Ernest Kellogg 1910-1991 .... **CLC 23**
See also AITN 1; CA 1-4R; 136; CANR 1, 83

Garber, Eric 1943(?)-
See Holleran, Andrew
See also CANR 89

Garcia, Cristina 1958- .... **CLC 76**
See also CA 141; CANR 73; HW 2

Garcia Lorca, Federico 1898-1936 . **TCLC 1, 7, 49; DA; DAB; DAC; DAM DRAM, MST, MULT, POET; DC 2; HLC 2; PC 3; WLC**
See also CA 104; 131; CANR 81; DA3; DLB 108; HW 1, 2; MTCW 1, 2

Garcia Marquez, Gabriel (Jose) 1928-
.... **CLC 2, 3, 8, 10, 15, 27, 47, 55, 68; DA; DAB; DAC; DAM MST, MULT, NOV, POP; HLC 1; SSC 8; WLC**
See also AAYA 3, 33; BEST 89:1, 90:4; CA 33-36R; CANR 10, 28, 50, 75, 82; DA3; DLB 113; HW 1, 2; MTCW 1, 2

Garcilaso de la Vega, El Inca 1503-1536
See also HLCS 1

Gard, Janice
See Latham, Jean Lee

Gard, Roger Martin du
See Martin du Gard, Roger

Gardam, Jane 1928- .... **CLC 43**
See also CA 49-52; CANR 2, 18, 33, 54; CLR 12; DLB 14, 161, 231; MAICYA; MTCW 1; SAAS 9; SATA 39, 76; SATA-Brief 28

Gardner, Herb(ert) 1934- .... **CLC 44**
See also CA 149

Gardner, John (Champlin), Jr. 1933-1982
. **CLC 2, 3, 5, 7, 8, 10, 18, 28, 34; DAM NOV, POP; SSC 7**
See also AITN 1; CA 65-68; 107; CANR 33, 73; CDALBS; DA3; DLB 2; DLBY 82; MTCW 1; SATA 40; SATA-Obit 31

Gardner, John (Edmund) 1926- .... **CLC 30; DAM POP**
See also CA 103; CANR 15, 69; MTCW 1

Gardner, Miriam
See Bradley, Marion Zimmer

Gardner, Noel
See Kuttner, Henry

Gardons, S. S.
See Snodgrass, W(illiam) D(e Witt)

Garfield, Leon 1921-1996 .... **CLC 12**
See also AAYA 8; CA 17-20R; 152; CANR 38, 41, 78; CLR 21; DLB 161; JRDA; MAICYA; SATA 1, 32, 76; SATA-Obit 90

Garland, (Hannibal) Hamlin 1860-1940
.... **TCLC 3; SSC 18**
See also CA 104; DLB 12, 71, 78, 186

Garneau, (Hector de) Saint-Denys 1912-1943
.... **TCLC 13**
See also CA 111; DLB 88

Garner, Alan 1934- .... **CLC 17; DAB; DAM POP**
See also AAYA 18; CA 73-76, 178; CAAE 178; CANR 15, 64; CLR 20; DLB 161; MAICYA; MTCW 1, 2; SATA 18, 69; SATA-Essay 108

Garner, Hugh 1913-1979 .... **CLC 13**
See also CA 69-72; CANR 31; DLB 68

Glasgow, Ellen (Anderson Gholson) 1873-1945 .... **TCLC 2, 7; SSC 34**
See also CA 104; 164; DLB 9, 12; MTCW 2

Glaspell, Susan 1882(?)-1948 . **TCLC 55; DC 10; SSC 41**
See also CA 110; 154; DLB 7, 9, 78, 228; YABC 2

Glassco, John 1909-1981 .... **CLC 9**
See also CA 13-16R; 102; CANR 15; DLB 68

Glasscock, Amnesia
See Steinbeck, John (Ernst)

Glasser, Ronald J. 1940(?)- .... **CLC 37**

Glassman, Joyce
See Johnson, Joyce

Glendinning, Victoria 1937- .... **CLC 50**
See also CA 120; 127; CANR 59, 89; DLB 155

Glissant, Edouard 1928- . **CLC 10, 68; DAM MULT**
See also CA 153

Gloag, Julian 1930- .... **CLC 40**
See also AITN 1; CA 65-68; CANR 10, 70

Glowacki, Aleksander
See Prus, Boleslaw

Gluck, Louise (Elisabeth) 1943- . **CLC 7, 22, 44, 81; DAM POET; PC 16**
See also CA 33-36R; CANR 40, 69; DA3; DLB 5; MTCW 2

Glyn, Elinor 1864-1943 .... **TCLC 72**
See also DLB 153

Gobineau, Joseph Arthur (Comte) de 1816-1882 .... **NCLC 17**
See also DLB 123

Godard, Jean-Luc 1930- .... **CLC 20**
See also CA 93-96

Godden, (Margaret) Rumer 1907-1998
.... **CLC 53**
See also AAYA 6; CA 5-8R; 172; CANR 4, 27, 36, 55, 80; CLR 20; DLB 161; MAI-CYA; SAAS 12; SATA 3, 36; SATA-Obit 109

Godoy Alcayaga, Lucila 1889-1957
..... **TCLC 2; DAM MULT; HLC 2; PC 32**
See also BW 2; CA 104; 131; CANR 81; HW 1, 2; MTCW 1, 2

Godwin, Gail (Kathleen) 1937- .... **CLC 5, 8, 22, 31, 69, 125; DAM POP**
See also CA 29-32R; CANR 15, 43, 69; DA3; DLB 6, 234; INT CANR-15; MTCW 1, 2

Godwin, William 1756-1836 .... **NCLC 14**
See also CDBLB 1789-1832; DLB 39, 104, 142, 158, 163

Goebbels, Josef
See Goebbels, (Paul) Joseph

Goebbels, (Paul) Joseph 1897-1945
.... **TCLC 68**
See also CA 115; 148

Goebbels, Joseph Paul
See Goebbels, (Paul) Joseph

Goethe, Johann Wolfgang von 1749-1832
. **NCLC 4, 22, 34, 90; DA; DAB; DAC; DAM DRAM, MST, POET; PC 5; SSC 38; WLC**
See also DA3; DLB 94

Gogarty, Oliver St. John 1878-1957
.... **TCLC 15**
See also CA 109; 150; DLB 15, 19

Gogol, Nikolai (Vasilyevich) 1809-1852
.... **NCLC 5, 15, 31; DA; DAB; DAC; DAM DRAM, MST; DC 1; SSC 4, 29; WLC**
See also DLB 198

Goines, Donald 1937(?)-1974 . **CLC 80; BLC 2; DAM MULT, POP**

See also AITN 1; BW 1, 3; CA 124; 114; CANR 82; DA3; DLB 33

Gold, Herbert 1924- .... **CLC 4, 7, 14, 42**
See also CA 9-12R; CANR 17, 45; DLB 2; DLBY 81

Goldbarth, Albert 1948- .... **CLC 5, 38**
See also CA 53-56; CANR 6, 40; DLB 120

Goldberg, Anatol 1910-1982 .... **CLC 34**
See also CA 131; 117

Goldemberg, Isaac 1945- .... **CLC 52**
See also CA 69-72; CAAS 12; CANR 11, 32; HW 1

Golding, William (Gerald) 1911-1993
. **CLC 1, 2, 3, 8, 10, 17, 27, 58, 81; DA; DAB; DAC; DAM MST, NOV; WLC**
See also AAYA 5; CA 5-8R; 141; CANR 13, 33, 54; CDBLB 1945-1960; DA3; DLB 15, 100; MTCW 1, 2

Goldman, Emma 1869-1940 .... **TCLC 13**
See also CA 110; 150; DLB 221

Goldman, Francisco 1954- .... **CLC 76**
See also CA 162

Goldman, William (W.) 1931- ..... **CLC 1, 48**
See also CA 9-12R; CANR 29, 69; DLB 44

Goldmann, Lucien 1913-1970 .... **CLC 24**
See also CA 25-28; CAP 2

Goldoni, Carlo 1707-1793 .... **LC 4; DAM DRAM**

Goldsberry, Steven 1949- .... **CLC 34**
See also CA 131

Goldsmith, Oliver 1728-1774 . **LC 2, 48; DA; DAB; DAC; DAM DRAM, MST, NOV, POET; DC 8; WLC**
See also CDBLB 1660-1789; DLB 39, 89, 104, 109, 142; SATA 26

Goldsmith, Peter
See Priestley, J(ohn) B(oynton)

Gombrowicz, Witold 1904-1969 ... **CLC 4, 7, 11, 49; DAM DRAM**
See also CA 19-20; 25-28R; CAP 2

Gomez de la Serna, Ramon 1888-1963
.... **CLC 9**
See also CA 153; 116; CANR 79; HW 1, 2

Goncharov, Ivan Alexandrovich 1812-1891
.... **NCLC 1, 63**

Goncourt, Edmond (Louis Antoine Huot) de 1822-1896 .... **NCLC 7**
See also DLB 123

Goncourt, Jules (Alfred Huot) de 1830-1870
.... **NCLC 7**
See also DLB 123

Gontier, Fernande 19(?)- .... **CLC 50**

Gonzalez Martinez, Enrique 1871-1952
.... **TCLC 72**
See also CA 166; CANR 81; HW 1, 2

Goodman, Paul 1911-1972 .... **CLC 1, 2, 4, 7**
See also CA 19-20; 37-40R; CANR 34; CAP 2; DLB 130; MTCW 1

Gordimer, Nadine 1923- .... **CLC 3, 5, 7, 10, 18, 33, 51, 70, 123; DA; DAB; DAC; DAM MST, NOV; SSC 17; WLCS**
See also CA 5-8R; CANR 3, 28, 56, 88; DA3; DLB 225; INT CANR-28; MTCW 1, 2

Gordon, Adam Lindsay 1833-1870
.... **NCLC 21**
See also DLB 230

Gordon, Caroline 1895-1981 ...... **CLC 6, 13, 29, 83; SSC 15**
See also CA 11-12; 103; CANR 36; CAP 1; DLB 4, 9, 102; DLBD 17; DLBY 81; MTCW 1, 2

Gordon, Charles William 1860-1937
See Connor, Ralph
See also CA 109

Gordon, Mary (Catherine) 1949- .. **CLC 13, 22, 128**
See also CA 102; CANR 44, 92; DLB 6; DLBY 81; INT 102; MTCW 1

Gordon, N. J.
See Bosman, Herman Charles

Gordon, Sol 1923- .... **CLC 26**
See also CA 53-56; CANR 4; SATA 11

Gordone, Charles 1925-1995 .... **CLC 1, 4; DAM DRAM; DC 8**
See also BW 1, 3; CA 93-96; 180; 150; CAAE 180; CANR 55; DLB 7; INT 93-96; MTCW 1

Gore, Catherine 1800-1861 .... **NCLC 65**
See also DLB 116

Gorenko, Anna Andreevna
See Akhmatova, Anna

Gorky, Maxim 1868-1936 ... **TCLC 8; DAB; SSC 28; WLC**
See also Peshkov, Alexei Maximovich
See also MTCW 2

Goryan, Sirak
See Saroyan, William

Gosse, Sir Edmund (William) 1849-1928
.... **TCLC 28**
See also CA 117; DLB 57, 144, 184

Gotlieb, Phyllis Fay (Bloom) 1926- . **CLC 18**
See also CA 13-16R; CANR 7; DLB 88

Gottesman, S. D.
See Kornbluth, C(yril) M.; Pohl, Frederik

Gottfried von Strassburg fl. c. 1210-
.... **CMLC 10**
See also DLB 138

Gould, Lois .... **CLC 4, 10**
See also CA 77-80; CANR 29; MTCW 1

Gourmont, Remy (-Marie-Charles) de 1858-1915 .... **TCLC 17**
See also CA 109; 150; MTCW 2

Govier, Katherine 1948- .... **CLC 51**
See also CA 101; CANR 18, 40

Goyen, (Charles) William 1915-1983
.... **CLC 5, 8, 14, 40**
See also AITN 2; CA 5-8R; 110; CANR 6, 71; DLB 2; DLBY 83; INT CANR-6

Goytisolo, Juan 1931- .. **CLC 5, 10, 23, 133; DAM MULT; HLC 1**
See also CA 85-88; CANR 32, 61; HW 1, 2; MTCW 1, 2

Gozzano, Guido 1883-1916 .... **PC 10**
See also CA 154; DLB 114

Gozzi, (Conte) Carlo 1720-1806 ... **NCLC 23**

Grabbe, Christian Dietrich 1801-1836
.... **NCLC 2**
See also DLB 133

Grace, Patricia Frances 1937- .... **CLC 56**
See also CA 176

Gracian y Morales, Baltasar 1601-1658
.... **LC 15**

Gracq, Julien .... **CLC 11, 48**
See also Poirier, Louis
See also DLB 83

Grade, Chaim 1910-1982 .... **CLC 10**
See also CA 93-96; 107

Graduate of Oxford, A
See Ruskin, John

Grafton, Garth
See Duncan, Sara Jeannette

Graham, John
See Phillips, David Graham

Graham, Jorie 1951- .... **CLC 48, 118**
See also CA 111; CANR 63; DLB 120

Graham, R(obert) B(ontine) Cunninghame
See Cunninghame Graham, Robert (Gallnigad) Bontine
See also DLB 98, 135, 174

Graham, Robert
See Haldeman, Joe (William)

Graham, Tom
See Lewis, (Harry) Sinclair

Graham, W(illiam) S(idney) 1918-1986
.... **CLC 29**
See also CA 73-76; 118; DLB 20

See also CA 25-28R; CANR 11, 44, 84;
DLB 5, 193

Guest, Edgar A(lbert) 1881-1959 . **TCLC 95**
See also CA 112; 168

Guest, Judith (Ann) 1936- .... **CLC 8, 30;
DAM NOV, POP**
See also AAYA 7; CA 77-80; CANR 15,
75; DA3; INT CANR-15; MTCW 1, 2

Guevara, Che .... **CLC 87; HLC 1**
See also Guevara (Serna), Ernesto

Guevara (Serna), Ernesto 1928-1967
.... **CLC 87; DAM MULT; HLC 1**
See also Guevara, Che
See also CA 127; 111; CANR 56; HW 1

Guicciardini, Francesco 1483-1540 ... **LC 49**

Guild, Nicholas M. 1944- .... **CLC 33**
See also CA 93-96

Guillemin, Jacques
See Sartre, Jean-Paul

Guillen, Jorge 1893-1984 ..... **CLC 11; DAM
MULT, POET; HLCS 1**
See also CA 89-92; 112; DLB 108; HW 1

Guillen, Nicolas (Cristobal) 1902-1989
.... **CLC 48, 79; BLC 2; DAM MST,
MULT, POET; HLC 1; PC 23**
See also BW 2; CA 116; 125; 129; CANR
84; HW 1

Guillevic, (Eugene) 1907- .... **CLC 33**
See also CA 93-96

Guillois
See Desnos, Robert

Guillois, Valentin
See Desnos, Robert

Guimaraes Rosa, Joao 1908-1967
See also CA 175; HLCS 2

Guiney, Louise Imogen 1861-1920 . **TCLC 41**
See also CA 160; DLB 54

Guiraldes, Ricardo (Guillermo) 1886-1927
.... **TCLC 39**
See also CA 131; HW 1; MTCW 1

Gumilev, Nikolai (Stepanovich) 1886-1921
.... **TCLC 60**
See also CA 165

Gunesekera, Romesh 1954- .... **CLC 91**
See also CA 159

Gunn, Bill .... **CLC 5**
See also Gunn, William Harrison
See also DLB 38

Gunn, Thom(son William) 1929- . **CLC 3, 6,
18, 32, 81; DAM POET; PC 26**
See also CA 17-20R; CANR 9, 33; CDBLB
1960 to Present; DLB 27; INT CANR-33;
MTCW 1

Gunn, William Harrison 1934(?)-1989
See Gunn, Bill
See also AITN 1; BW 1, 3; CA 13-16R;
128; CANR 12, 25, 76

Gunnars, Kristjana 1948- .... **CLC 69**
See also CA 113; DLB 60

Gurdjieff, G(eorgei) I(vanovich)
1877(?)-1949 .... **TCLC 71**
See also CA 157

Gurganus, Allan 1947- . **CLC 70; DAM POP**
See also BEST 90:1; CA 135

Gurney, A(lbert) R(amsdell), Jr. 1930-
.... **CLC 32, 50, 54; DAM DRAM**
See also CA 77-80; CANR 32, 64

Gurney, Ivor (Bertie) 1890-1937 .. **TCLC 33**
See also CA 167

Gurney, Peter
See Gurney, A(lbert) R(amsdell), Jr.

Guro, Elena 1877-1913 .... **TCLC 56**

Gustafson, James M(oody) 1925- . **CLC 100**
See also CA 25-28R; CANR 37

Gustafson, Ralph (Barker) 1909- ... **CLC 36**
See also CA 21-24R; CANR 8, 45, 84; DLB
88

Gut, Gom
See Simenon, Georges (Jacques Christian)

Guterson, David 1956- .... **CLC 91**
See also CA 132; CANR 73; MTCW 2

Guthrie, A(lfred) B(ertram), Jr. 1901-1991
.... **CLC 23**
See also CA 57-60; 134; CANR 24; DLB
212; SATA 62; SATA-Obit 67

Guthrie, Isobel
See Grieve, C(hristopher) M(urray)

Guthrie, Woodrow Wilson 1912-1967
See Guthrie, Woody
See also CA 113; 93-96

Guthrie, Woody .... **CLC 35**
See also Guthrie, Woodrow Wilson

Gutierrez Najera, Manuel 1859-1895
See also HLCS 2

Guy, Rosa (Cuthbert) 1928- .... **CLC 26**
See also AAYA 4; BW 2; CA 17-20R;
CANR 14, 34, 83; CLR 13; DLB 33;
JRDA; MAICYA; SATA 14, 62

Gwendolyn
See Bennett, (Enoch) Arnold

H. D. .... **CLC 3, 8, 14, 31, 34, 73; PC 5**
See also Doolittle, Hilda

H. de V.
See Buchan, John

Haavikko, Paavo Juhani 1931- . **CLC 18, 34**
See also CA 106

Habbema, Koos
See Heijermans, Herman

Habermas, Juergen 1929- .... **CLC 104**
See also CA 109; CANR 85

Habermas, Jurgen
See Habermas, Juergen

Hacker, Marilyn 1942- ..... **CLC 5, 9, 23, 72,
91; DAM POET**
See also CA 77-80; CANR 68; DLB 120

Haeckel, Ernst Heinrich (Philipp August)
1834-1919 .... **TCLC 83**
See also CA 157

Hafiz c. 1326-1389(?) .... **CMLC 34**

Hafiz c. 1326-1389 .... **CMLC 34**

Haggard, H(enry) Rider 1856-1925
.... **TCLC 11**
See also CA 108; 148; DLB 70, 156, 174,
178; MTCW 2; SATA 16

Hagiosy, L.
See Larbaud, Valery (Nicolas)

Hagiwara Sakutaro 1886-1942 .... **TCLC 60;
PC 18**

Haig, Fenil
See Ford, Ford Madox

Haig-Brown, Roderick (Langmere)
1908-1976 .... **CLC 21**
See also CA 5-8R; 69-72; CANR 4, 38, 83;
CLR 31; DLB 88; MAICYA; SATA 12

Hailey, Arthur 1920- .... **CLC 5; DAM NOV,
POP**
See also AITN 2; BEST 90:3; CA 1-4R;
CANR 2, 36, 75; DLB 88; DLBY 82;
MTCW 1, 2

Hailey, Elizabeth Forsythe 1938- .... **CLC 40**
See also CA 93-96; CAAS 1; CANR 15,
48; INT CANR-15

Haines, John (Meade) 1924- .... **CLC 58**
See also CA 17-20R; CANR 13, 34; DLB
212

Hakluyt, Richard 1552-1616 .... **LC 31**

Haldeman, Joe (William) 1943- ...... **CLC 61**
See also Graham, Robert
See also CA 53-56, 179; CAAE 179; CAAS
25; CANR 6, 70, 72; DLB 8; INT
CANR-6

Hale, Sarah Josepha (Buell) 1788-1879
.... **NCLC 75**
See also DLB 1, 42, 73

Haley, Alex(ander Murray Palmer)
1921-1992 . **CLC 8, 12, 76; BLC 2; DA;
DAB; DAC; DAM MST, MULT, POP**
See also AAYA 26; BW 2, 3; CA 77-80;
136; CANR 61; CDALBS; DA3; DLB 38;
MTCW 1, 2

Haliburton, Thomas Chandler 1796-1865
.... **NCLC 15**
See also DLB 11, 99

Hall, Donald (Andrew, Jr.) 1928- .... **CLC 1,
13, 37, 59; DAM POET**
See also CA 5-8R; CAAS 7; CANR 2, 44,
64; DLB 5; MTCW 1; SATA 23, 97

Hall, Frederic Sauser
See Sauser-Hall, Frederic

Hall, James
See Kuttner, Henry

Hall, James Norman 1887-1951 ... **TCLC 23**
See also CA 123; 173; SATA 21

Hall, Radclyffe -1943
See Hall, (Marguerite) Radclyffe
See also MTCW 2

Hall, (Marguerite) Radclyffe 1886-1943
.... **TCLC 12**
See also CA 110; 150; CANR 83; DLB 191

Hall, Rodney 1935- .... **CLC 51**
See also CA 109; CANR 69

Halleck, Fitz-Greene 1790-1867 ... **NCLC 47**
See also DLB 3

Halliday, Michael
See Creasey, John

Halpern, Daniel 1945- .... **CLC 14**
See also CA 33-36R; CANR 93

Hamburger, Michael (Peter Leopold) 1924-
.... **CLC 5, 14**
See also CA 5-8R; CAAS 4; CANR 2, 47;
DLB 27

Hamill, Pete 1935- .... **CLC 10**
See also CA 25-28R; CANR 18, 71

Hamilton, Alexander 1755(?)-1804
.... **NCLC 49**
See also DLB 37

Hamilton, Clive
See Lewis, C(live) S(taples)

Hamilton, Edmond 1904-1977 .... **CLC 1**
See also CA 1-4R; CANR 3, 84; DLB 8;
SATA 118

Hamilton, Eugene (Jacob) Lee
See Lee-Hamilton, Eugene (Jacob)

Hamilton, Franklin
See Silverberg, Robert

Hamilton, Gail
See Corcoran, Barbara

Hamilton, Mollie
See Kaye, M(ary) M(argaret)

Hamilton, (Anthony Walter) Patrick
1904-1962 .... **CLC 51**
See also CA 176; 113; DLB 191

Hamilton, Virginia 1936- ..... **CLC 26; DAM
MULT**
See also AAYA 2, 21; BW 2, 3; CA 25-28R;
CANR 20, 37, 73; CLR 1, 11, 40; DLB
33, 52; INT CANR-20; JRDA; MAICYA;
MTCW 1, 2; SATA 4, 56, 79

Hammett, (Samuel) Dashiell 1894-1961
.... **CLC 3, 5, 10, 19, 47; SSC 17**
See also AITN 1; CA 81-84; CANR 42;
CDALB 1929-1941; DA3; DLB 226;
DLBD 6; DLBY 96; MTCW 1, 2

Hammon, Jupiter 1711(?)-1800(?) . **NCLC 5;
BLC 2; DAM MULT, POET; PC 16**
See also DLB 31, 50

Hammond, Keith
See Kuttner, Henry

Hamner, Earl (Henry), Jr. 1923- .... **CLC 12**
See also AITN 2; CA 73-76; DLB 6

Hampton, Christopher (James) 1946-
.... **CLC 4**
See also CA 25-28R; DLB 13; MTCW 1

Head, Bessie 1937-1986 ... **CLC 25, 67; BLC 2; DAM MULT**
See also BW 2, 3; CA 29-32R; 119; CANR 25, 82; DA3; DLB 117, 225; MTCW 1, 2

Headon, (Nicky) Topper 1956(?)- ... **CLC 30**

Heaney, Seamus (Justin) 1939- .... **CLC 5, 7, 14, 25, 37, 74, 91; DAB; DAM POET; PC 18; WLCS**
See also CA 85-88; CANR 25, 48, 75, 91; CDBLB 1960 to Present; DA3; DLB 40; DLBY 95; MTCW 1, 2

Hearn, (Patricio) Lafcadio (Tessima Carlos) 1850-1904 .... **TCLC 9**
See also CA 105; 166; DLB 12, 78, 189

Hearne, Vicki 1946- .... **CLC 56**
See also CA 139

Hearon, Shelby 1931- .... **CLC 63**
See also AITN 2; CA 25-28R; CANR 18, 48

Heat-Moon, William Least .... **CLC 29**
See also Trogdon, William (Lewis)
See also AAYA 9

Hebbel, Friedrich 1813-1863 .... **NCLC 43; DAM DRAM**
See also DLB 129

Hebert, Anne 1916-2000 ...... **CLC 4, 13, 29; DAC; DAM MST, POET**
See also CA 85-88; 187; CANR 69; DA3; DLB 68; MTCW 1, 2

Hecht, Anthony (Evan) 1923- .... **CLC 8, 13, 19; DAM POET**
See also CA 9-12R; CANR 6; DLB 5, 169

Hecht, Ben 1894-1964 .... **CLC 8**
See also CA 85-88; DLB 7, 9, 25, 26, 28, 86; TCLC 101

Hedayat, Sadeq 1903-1951 .... **TCLC 21**
See also CA 120

Hegel, Georg Wilhelm Friedrich 1770-1831
.... **NCLC 46**
See also DLB 90

Heidegger, Martin 1889-1976 .... **CLC 24**
See also CA 81-84; 65-68; CANR 34; MTCW 1, 2

Heidenstam, (Carl Gustaf) Verner von 1859-1940 .... **TCLC 5**
See also CA 104

Heifner, Jack 1946- .... **CLC 11**
See also CA 105; CANR 47

Heijermans, Herman 1864-1924 ... **TCLC 24**
See also CA 123

Heilbrun, Carolyn G(old) 1926- ..... **CLC 25**
See also CA 45-48; CANR 1, 28, 58

Heine, Heinrich 1797-1856 ...... **NCLC 4, 54; PC 25**
See also DLB 90

Heinemann, Larry (Curtiss) 1944- . **CLC 50**
See also CA 110; CAAS 21; CANR 31, 81; DLBD 9; INT CANR-31

Heiney, Donald (William) 1921-1993
See Harris, MacDonald
See also CA 1-4R; 142; CANR 3, 58

Heinlein, Robert A(nson) 1907-1988 . **CLC 1, 3, 8, 14, 26, 55; DAM POP**
See also AAYA 17; CA 1-4R; 125; CANR 1, 20, 53; DA3; DLB 8; JRDA; MAICYA; MTCW 1, 2; SATA 9, 69; SATA-Obit 56

Helforth, John
See Doolittle, Hilda

Hellenhofferu, Vojtech Kapristian z
See Hasek, Jaroslav (Matej Frantisek)

Heller, Joseph 1923-1999 ..... **CLC 1, 3, 5, 8, 11, 36, 63; DA; DAB; DAC; DAM MST, NOV, POP; WLC**
See also AAYA 24; AITN 1; CA 5-8R; 187; CABS 1; CANR 8, 42, 66; DA3; DLB 2, 28, 227; DLBY 80; INT CANR-8; MTCW 1, 2

Hellman, Lillian (Florence) 1906-1984
.. **CLC 2, 4, 8, 14, 18, 34, 44, 52; DAM DRAM; DC 1**
See also AITN 1, 2; CA 13-16R; 112; CANR 33; DA3; DLB 7, 228; DLBY 84; MTCW 1, 2

Helprin, Mark 1947- ...... **CLC 7, 10, 22, 32; DAM NOV, POP**
See also CA 81-84; CANR 47, 64; CDALBS; DA3; DLBY 85; MTCW 1, 2

Helvetius, Claude-Adrien 1715-1771 . **LC 26**

Helyar, Jane Penelope Josephine 1933-
See Poole, Josephine
See also CA 21-24R; CANR 10, 26; SATA 82

Hemans, Felicia 1793-1835 .... **NCLC 71**
See also DLB 96

Hemingway, Ernest (Miller) 1899-1961
... **CLC 1, 3, 6, 8, 10, 13, 19, 30, 34, 39, 41, 44, 50, 61, 80; DA; DAB; DAC; DAM MST, NOV; SSC 1, 25, 36, 40; WLC**
See also AAYA 19; CA 77-80; CANR 34; CDALB 1917-1929; DA3; DLB 4, 9, 102, 210; DLBD 1, 15, 16; DLBY 81, 87, 96, 98; MTCW 1, 2

Hempel, Amy 1951- .... **CLC 39**
See also CA 118; 137; CANR 70; DA3; MTCW 2

Henderson, F. C.
See Mencken, H(enry) L(ouis)

Henderson, Sylvia
See Ashton-Warner, Sylvia (Constance)

Henderson, Zenna (Chlarson) 1917-1983
.... **SSC 29**
See also CA 1-4R; 133; CANR 1, 84; DLB 8; SATA 5

Henkin, Joshua .... **CLC 119**
See also CA 161

Henley, Beth .... **CLC 23; DC 6, 14**
See also Henley, Elizabeth Becker
See also CABS 3; DLBY 86

Henley, Elizabeth Becker 1952-
See Henley, Beth
See also CA 107; CANR 32, 73; DAM DRAM, MST; DA3; MTCW 1, 2

Henley, William Ernest 1849-1903 . **TCLC 8**
See also CA 105; DLB 19

Hennissart, Martha
See Lathen, Emma
See also CA 85-88; CANR 64

Henry, O. .... **TCLC 1, 19; SSC 5; WLC**
See also Porter, William Sydney

Henry, Patrick 1736-1799 .... **LC 25**

Henryson, Robert 1430(?)-1506(?) ..... **LC 20**
See also DLB 146

Henry VIII 1491-1547 .... **LC 10**
See also DLB 132

Henschke, Alfred
See Klabund

Hentoff, Nat(han Irving) 1925- .... **CLC 26**
See also AAYA 4; CA 1-4R; CAAS 6; CANR 5, 25, 77; CLR 1, 52; INT CANR-25; JRDA; MAICYA; SATA 42, 69; SATA-Brief 27

Heppenstall, (John) Rayner 1911-1981
.... **CLC 10**
See also CA 1-4R; 103; CANR 29

Heraclitus c. 540B.C.-c. 450B.C. . **CMLC 22**
See also DLB 176

Herbert, Frank (Patrick) 1920-1986
...... **CLC 12, 23, 35, 44, 85; DAM POP**
See also AAYA 21; CA 53-56; 118; CANR 5, 43; CDALBS; DLB 8; INT CANR-5; MTCW 1, 2; SATA 9, 37; SATA-Obit 47

Herbert, George 1593-1633 .... **LC 24; DAB; DAM POET; PC 4**
See also CDBLB Before 1660; DLB 126

Herbert, Zbigniew 1924-1998 .... **CLC 9, 43; DAM POET**
See also CA 89-92; 169; CANR 36, 74; DLB 232; MTCW 1

Herbst, Josephine (Frey) 1897-1969
.... **CLC 34**
See also CA 5-8R; 25-28R; DLB 9

Heredia, Jose Maria 1803-1839
See also HLCS 2

Hergesheimer, Joseph 1880-1954 .. **TCLC 11**
See also CA 109; DLB 102, 9

Herlihy, James Leo 1927-1993 .... **CLC 6**
See also CA 1-4R; 143; CANR 2

Hermogenes fl. c. 175- .... **CMLC 6**

Hernandez, Jose 1834-1886 .... **NCLC 17**

Herodotus c. 484B.C.-429B.C. ..... **CMLC 17**
See also DLB 176

Herrick, Robert 1591-1674 .... **LC 13; DA; DAB; DAC; DAM MST, POP; PC 9**
See also DLB 126

Herring, Guilles
See Somerville, Edith

Herriot, James 1916-1995 .... **CLC 12; DAM POP**
See also Wight, James Alfred
See also AAYA 1; CA 148; CANR 40; MTCW 2; SATA 86

Herris, Violet
See Hunt, Violet

Herrmann, Dorothy 1941- .... **CLC 44**
See also CA 107

Herrmann, Taffy
See Herrmann, Dorothy

Hersey, John (Richard) 1914-1993 .. **CLC 1, 2, 7, 9, 40, 81, 97; DAM POP**
See also AAYA 29; CA 17-20R; 140; CANR 33; CDALBS; DLB 6, 185; MTCW 1, 2; SATA 25; SATA-Obit 76

Herzen, Aleksandr Ivanovich 1812-1870
.... **NCLC 10, 61**

Herzl, Theodor 1860-1904 .... **TCLC 36**
See also CA 168

Herzog, Werner 1942- .... **CLC 16**
See also CA 89-92

Hesiod c. 8th cent. B.C.- .... **CMLC 5**
See also DLB 176

Hesse, Hermann 1877-1962 . **CLC 1, 2, 3, 6, 11, 17, 25, 69; DA; DAB; DAC; DAM MST, NOV; SSC 9; WLC**
See also CA 17-18; CAP 2; DA3; DLB 66; MTCW 1, 2; SATA 50

Hewes, Cady
See De Voto, Bernard (Augustine)

Heyen, William 1940- .... **CLC 13, 18**
See also CA 33-36R; CAAS 9; DLB 5

Heyerdahl, Thor 1914- .... **CLC 26**
See also CA 5-8R; CANR 5, 22, 66, 73; MTCW 1, 2; SATA 2, 52

Heym, Georg (Theodor Franz Arthur) 1887-1912 .... **TCLC 9**
See also CA 106; 181

Heym, Stefan 1913- .... **CLC 41**
See also CA 9-12R; CANR 4; DLB 69

Heyse, Paul (Johann Ludwig von) 1830-1914
.... **TCLC 8**
See also CA 104; DLB 129

Heyward, (Edwin) DuBose 1885-1940
.... **TCLC 59**
See also CA 108; 157; DLB 7, 9, 45; SATA 21

Hibbert, Eleanor Alice Burford 1906-1993
.... **CLC 7; DAM POP**
See also BEST 90:4; CA 17-20R; 140; CANR 9, 28, 59; MTCW 2; SATA 2; SATA-Obit 74

Hichens, Robert (Smythe) 1864-1950
.... **TCLC 64**
See also CA 162; DLB 153

See also CA 49-52; CAAS 17; CANR 1, 33, 87; DLB 53

Hood, Thomas 1799-1845 .... **NCLC 16**
See also DLB 96

Hooker, (Peter) Jeremy 1941- .... **CLC 43**
See also CA 77-80; CANR 22; DLB 40

hooks, bell .... **CLC 94; BLCS**
See also Watkins, Gloria Jean
See also MTCW 2

Hope, A(lec) D(erwent) 1907- ..... **CLC 3, 51**
See also CA 21-24R; CANR 33, 74; MTCW 1, 2

Hope, Anthony 1863-1933 .... **TCLC 83**
See also CA 157; DLB 153, 156

Hope, Brian
See Creasey, John

Hope, Christopher (David Tully) 1944-
.... **CLC 52**
See also CA 106; CANR 47; DLB 225; SATA 62

Hopkins, Gerard Manley 1844-1889
.... **NCLC 17; DA; DAB; DAC; DAM MST, POET; PC 15; WLC**
See also CDBLB 1890-1914; DA3; DLB 35, 57

Hopkins, John (Richard) 1931-1998 . **CLC 4**
See also CA 85-88; 169

Hopkins, Pauline Elizabeth 1859-1930
.... **TCLC 28; BLC 2; DAM MULT**
See also BW 2, 3; CA 141; CANR 82; DLB 50

Hopkinson, Francis 1737-1791 .... **LC 25**
See also DLB 31

Hopley-Woolrich, Cornell George 1903-1968
See Woolrich, Cornell
See also CA 13-14; CANR 58; CAP 1; DLB 226; MTCW 2

Horace 65B.C.-8B.C. .... **CMLC 39**
See also DLB 211

Horatio
See Proust, (Valentin-Louis-George-Eugene-) Marcel

Horgan, Paul (George Vincent O'Shaughnessy) 1903-1995 ...... **CLC 9, 53; DAM NOV**
See also CA 13-16R; 147; CANR 9, 35; DLB 212; DLBY 85; INT CANR-9; MTCW 1, 2; SATA 13; SATA-Obit 84

Horn, Peter
See Kuttner, Henry

Hornem, Horace Esq.
See Byron, George Gordon (Noel)

Horney, Karen (Clementine Theodore Danielsen) 1885-1952 .... **TCLC 71**
See also CA 114; 165

Hornung, E(rnest) W(illiam) 1866-1921
.... **TCLC 59**
See also CA 108; 160; DLB 70

Horovitz, Israel (Arthur) 1939- ..... **CLC 56; DAM DRAM**
See also CA 33-36R; CANR 46, 59; DLB 7

Horton, George Moses 1797(?)-1883(?)
.... **NCLC 87**
See also DLB 50

Horvath, Odon von
See Horvath, Oedoen von
See also DLB 85, 124

Horvath, Oedoen von 1901-1938 .. **TCLC 45**
See also Horvath, Odon von; von Horvath, Oedoen
See also CA 118

Horwitz, Julius 1920-1986 .... **CLC 14**
See also CA 9-12R; 119; CANR 12

Hospital, Janette Turner 1942- .... **CLC 42**
See also CA 108; CANR 48

Hostos, E. M. de
See Hostos (y Bonilla), Eugenio Maria de

Hostos, Eugenio M. de
See Hostos (y Bonilla), Eugenio Maria de

Hostos, Eugenio Maria
See Hostos (y Bonilla), Eugenio Maria de

Hostos (y Bonilla), Eugenio Maria de
1839-1903 .... **TCLC 24**
See also CA 123; 131; HW 1

Houdini
See Lovecraft, H(oward) P(hillips)

Hougan, Carolyn 1943- .... **CLC 34**
See also CA 139

Household, Geoffrey (Edward West)
1900-1988 .... **CLC 11**
See also CA 77-80; 126; CANR 58; DLB 87; SATA 14; SATA-Obit 59

Housman, A(lfred) E(dward) 1859-1936
... **TCLC 1, 10; DA; DAB; DAC; DAM MST, POET; PC 2; WLCS**
See also CA 104; 125; DA3; DLB 19; MTCW 1, 2

Housman, Laurence 1865-1959 ...... **TCLC 7**
See also CA 106; 155; DLB 10; SATA 25

Howard, Elizabeth Jane 1923- .... **CLC 7, 29**
See also CA 5-8R; CANR 8, 62

Howard, Maureen 1930- ...... **CLC 5, 14, 46**
See also CA 53-56; CANR 31, 75; DLBY 83; INT CANR-31; MTCW 1, 2

Howard, Richard 1929- .... **CLC 7, 10, 47**
See also AITN 1; CA 85-88; CANR 25, 80; DLB 5; INT CANR-25

Howard, Robert E(rvin) 1906-1936 . **TCLC 8**
See also CA 105; 157

Howard, Warren F.
See Pohl, Frederik

Howe, Fanny (Quincy) 1940- .... **CLC 47**
See also CA 117; CAAE 187; CAAS 27; CANR 70; SATA-Brief 52

Howe, Irving 1920-1993 .... **CLC 85**
See also CA 9-12R; 141; CANR 21, 50; DLB 67; MTCW 1, 2

Howe, Julia Ward 1819-1910 .... **TCLC 21**
See also CA 117; DLB 1, 189, 235

Howe, Susan 1937- .... **CLC 72**
See also CA 160; DLB 120

Howe, Tina 1937- .... **CLC 48**
See also CA 109

Howell, James 1594(?)-1666 .... **LC 13**
See also DLB 151

Howells, W. D.
See Howells, William Dean

Howells, William D.
See Howells, William Dean

Howells, William Dean 1837-1920 . **TCLC 7, 17, 41; SSC 36**
See also CA 104; 134; CDALB 1865-1917; DLB 12, 64, 74, 79, 189; MTCW 2

Howes, Barbara 1914-1996 .... **CLC 15**
See also CA 9-12R; 151; CAAS 3; CANR 53; SATA 5

Hrabal, Bohumil 1914-1997 ...... **CLC 13, 67**
See also CA 106; 156; CAAS 12; CANR 57; DLB 232

Hroswitha of Gandersheim c. 935-c. 1002
.... **CMLC 29**
See also DLB 148

Hsi, Chu 1130-1200 .... **CMLC 42**

Hsun, Lu
See Lu Hsun

Hubbard, L(afayette) Ron(ald) 1911-1986
.... **CLC 43; DAM POP**
See also CA 77-80; 118; CANR 52; DA3; MTCW 2

Huch, Ricarda (Octavia) 1864-1947
.... **TCLC 13**
See also CA 111; DLB 66

Huddle, David 1942- .... **CLC 49**
See also CA 57-60; CAAS 20; CANR 89; DLB 130

Hudson, Jeffrey
See Crichton, (John) Michael

Hudson, W(illiam) H(enry) 1841-1922
.... **TCLC 29**
See also CA 115; DLB 98, 153, 174; SATA 35

Hueffer, Ford Madox
See Ford, Ford Madox

Hughart, Barry 1934- .... **CLC 39**
See also CA 137

Hughes, Colin
See Creasey, John

Hughes, David (John) 1930- .... **CLC 48**
See also CA 116; 129; DLB 14

Hughes, Edward James
See Hughes, Ted
See also DAM MST, POET; DA3

Hughes, (James) Langston 1902-1967
. **CLC 1, 5, 10, 15, 35, 44, 108; BLC 2; DA; DAB; DAC; DAM DRAM, MST, MULT, POET; DC 3; PC 1; SSC 6; WLC**
See also AAYA 12; BW 1, 3; CA 1-4R; 25-28R; CANR 1, 34, 82; CDALB 1929-1941; CLR 17; DA3; DLB 4, 7, 48, 51, 86, 228; JRDA; MAICYA; MTCW 1, 2; SATA 4, 33

Hughes, Richard (Arthur Warren)
1900-1976 .... **CLC 1, 11; DAM NOV**
See also CA 5-8R; 65-68; CANR 4; DLB 15, 161; MTCW 1; SATA 8; SATA-Obit 25

Hughes, Ted 1930-1998 . **CLC 2, 4, 9, 14, 37, 119; DAB; DAC; PC 7**
See also Hughes, Edward James
See also CA 1-4R; 171; CANR 1, 33, 66; CLR 3; DLB 40, 161; MAICYA; MTCW 1, 2; SATA 49; SATA-Brief 27; SATA-Obit 107

Hugo, Richard F(ranklin) 1923-1982
.... **CLC 6, 18, 32; DAM POET**
See also CA 49-52; 108; CANR 3; DLB 5, 206

Hugo, Victor (Marie) 1802-1885 ... **NCLC 3, 10, 21; DA; DAB; DAC; DAM DRAM, MST, NOV, POET; PC 17; WLC**
See also AAYA 28; DA3; DLB 119, 192; SATA 47

Huidobro, Vicente
See Huidobro Fernandez, Vicente Garcia

Huidobro Fernandez, Vicente Garcia
1893-1948 .... **TCLC 31**
See also CA 131; HW 1

Hulme, Keri 1947- .... **CLC 39, 130**
See also CA 125; CANR 69; INT 125

Hulme, T(homas) E(rnest) 1883-1917
.... **TCLC 21**
See also CA 117; DLB 19

Hume, David 1711-1776 .... **LC 7, 56**
See also DLB 104

Humphrey, William 1924-1997 .... **CLC 45**
See also CA 77-80; 160; CANR 68; DLB 212

Humphreys, Emyr Owen 1919- ...... **CLC 47**
See also CA 5-8R; CANR 3, 24; DLB 15

Humphreys, Josephine 1945- .... **CLC 34, 57**
See also CA 121; 127; INT 127

Huneker, James Gibbons 1857-1921
.... **TCLC 65**
See also DLB 71

Hungerford, Pixie
See Brinsmead, H(esba) F(ay)

Hunt, E(verette) Howard, (Jr.) 1918- . **CLC 3**
See also AITN 1; CA 45-48; CANR 2, 47

Hunt, Francesca
See Holland, Isabelle

Hunt, Kyle
See Creasey, John

Hunt, (James Henry) Leigh 1784-1859
.... **NCLC 1, 70; DAM POET**
See also DLB 96, 110, 144

Keates, Jonathan 1946(?)- .... **CLC 34**
See also CA 163

Keaton, Buster 1895-1966 .... **CLC 20**

Keats, John 1795-1821 .... **NCLC 8, 73; DA; DAB; DAC; DAM MST, POET; PC 1; WLC**
See also CDBLB 1789-1832; DA3; DLB 96, 110

Keble, John 1792-1866 .... **NCLC 87**
See also DLB 32, 55

Keene, Donald 1922- .... **CLC 34**
See also CA 1-4R; CANR 5

Keillor, Garrison .... **CLC 40, 115**
See also Keillor, Gary (Edward)
See also AAYA 2; BEST 89:3; DLBY 87; SATA 58

Keillor, Gary (Edward) 1942-
See Keillor, Garrison
See also CA 111; 117; CANR 36, 59; DAM POP; DA3; MTCW 1, 2

Keith, Michael
See Hubbard, L(afayette) Ron(ald)

Keller, Gottfried 1819-1890 .. **NCLC 2; SSC 26**
See also DLB 129

Keller, Nora Okja 1965- .... **CLC 109**
See also CA 187

Kellerman, Jonathan 1949- . **CLC 44; DAM POP**
See also BEST 90:1; CA 106; CANR 29, 51; DA3; INT CANR-29

Kelley, William Melvin 1937- .... **CLC 22**
See also BW 1; CA 77-80; CANR 27, 83; DLB 33

Kellogg, Marjorie 1922- .... **CLC 2**
See also CA 81-84

Kellow, Kathleen
See Hibbert, Eleanor Alice Burford

Kelly, M(ilton) T(errence) 1947- ..... **CLC 55**
See also CA 97-100; CAAS 22; CANR 19, 43, 84

Kelman, James 1946- .... **CLC 58, 86**
See also CA 148; CANR 85; DLB 194

Kemal, Yashar 1923- .... **CLC 14, 29**
See also CA 89-92; CANR 44

Kemble, Fanny 1809-1893 .... **NCLC 18**
See also DLB 32

Kemelman, Harry 1908-1996 .... **CLC 2**
See also AITN 1; CA 9-12R; 155; CANR 6, 71; DLB 28

Kempe, Margery 1373(?)-1440(?) .. **LC 6, 56**
See also DLB 146

Kempis, Thomas a 1380-1471 .... **LC 11**

Kendall, Henry 1839-1882 .... **NCLC 12**
See also DLB 230

Keneally, Thomas (Michael) 1935- .. **CLC 5, 8, 10, 14, 19, 27, 43, 117; DAM NOV**
See also CA 85-88; CANR 10, 50, 74; DA3; MTCW 1, 2

Kennedy, Adrienne (Lita) 1931- .... **CLC 66; BLC 2; DAM MULT; DC 5**
See also BW 2, 3; CA 103; CAAS 20; CABS 3; CANR 26, 53, 82; DLB 38

Kennedy, John Pendleton 1795-1870
.... **NCLC 2**
See also DLB 3

Kennedy, Joseph Charles 1929-
See Kennedy, X. J.
See also CA 1-4R; CANR 4, 30, 40; SATA 14, 86

Kennedy, William 1928- . **CLC 6, 28, 34, 53; DAM NOV**
See also AAYA 1; CA 85-88; CANR 14, 31, 76; DA3; DLB 143; DLBY 85; INT CANR-31; MTCW 1, 2; SATA 57

Kennedy, X. J. .... **CLC 8, 42**
See also Kennedy, Joseph Charles
See also CAAS 9; CLR 27; DLB 5; SAAS 22

Kenny, Maurice (Francis) 1929- .... **CLC 87; DAM MULT**
See also CA 144; CAAS 22; DLB 175; NNAL

Kent, Kelvin
See Kuttner, Henry

Kenton, Maxwell
See Southern, Terry

Kenyon, Robert O.
See Kuttner, Henry

Kepler, Johannes 1571-1630 .... **LC 45**

Kerouac, Jack ..... **CLC 1, 2, 3, 5, 14, 29, 61**
See also Kerouac, Jean-Louis Lebris de
See also AAYA 25; CDALB 1941-1968; DLB 2, 16; DLBD 3; DLBY 95; MTCW 2

Kerouac, Jean-Louis Lebris de 1922-1969
See Kerouac, Jack
See also AITN 1; CA 5-8R; 25-28R; CANR 26, 54; DA; DAB; DAC; DAM MST, NOV, POET, POP; DA3; MTCW 1, 2; WLC

Kerr, Jean 1923- .... **CLC 22**
See also CA 5-8R; CANR 7; INT CANR-7

Kerr, M. E. .... **CLC 12, 35**
See also Meaker, Marijane (Agnes)
See also AAYA 2, 23; CLR 29; SAAS 1

Kerr, Robert .... **CLC 55**

Kerrigan, (Thomas) Anthony 1918- . **CLC 4, 6**
See also CA 49-52; CAAS 11; CANR 4

Kerry, Lois
See Duncan, Lois

Kesey, Ken (Elton) 1935- ... **CLC 1, 3, 6, 11, 46, 64; DA; DAB; DAC; DAM MST, NOV, POP; WLC**
See also AAYA 25; CA 1-4R; CANR 22, 38, 66; CDALB 1968-1988; DA3; DLB 2, 16, 206; MTCW 1, 2; SATA 66

Kesselring, Joseph (Otto) 1902-1967
.... **CLC 45; DAM DRAM, MST**
See also CA 150

Kessler, Jascha (Frederick) 1929- ..... **CLC 4**
See also CA 17-20R; CANR 8, 48

Kettelkamp, Larry (Dale) 1933- ...... **CLC 12**
See also CA 29-32R; CANR 16; SAAS 3; SATA 2

Key, Ellen (Karolina Sofia) 1849-1926
.... **TCLC 65**

Keyber, Conny
See Fielding, Henry

Keyes, Daniel 1927- ..... **CLC 80; DA; DAC; DAM MST, NOV**
See also AAYA 23; CA 17-20R, 181; CAAE 181; CANR 10, 26, 54, 74; DA3; MTCW 2; SATA 37

Keynes, John Maynard 1883-1946
.... **TCLC 64**
See also CA 114; 162, 163; DLBD 10; MTCW 2

Khanshendel, Chiron
See Rose, Wendy

Khayyam, Omar 1048-1131 .... **CMLC 11; DAM POET; PC 8**
See also DA3

Kherdian, David 1931- .... **CLC 6, 9**
See also CA 21-24R; CAAS 2; CANR 39, 78; CLR 24; JRDA; MAICYA; SATA 16, 74

Khlebnikov, Velimir .... **TCLC 20**
See also Khlebnikov, Viktor Vladimirovich

Khlebnikov, Viktor Vladimirovich 1885-1922
See Khlebnikov, Velimir
See also CA 117

Khodasevich, Vladislav (Felitsianovich) 1886-1939 .... **TCLC 15**
See also CA 115

Kielland, Alexander Lange 1849-1906
.... **TCLC 5**

See also CA 104

Kiely, Benedict 1919- .... **CLC 23, 43**
See also CA 1-4R; CANR 2, 84; DLB 15

Kienzle, William X(avier) 1928- .... **CLC 25; DAM POP**
See also CA 93-96; CAAS 1; CANR 9, 31, 59; DA3; INT CANR-31; MTCW 1, 2

Kierkegaard, Soren 1813-1855 .... **NCLC 34, 78**

Kieslowski, Krzysztof 1941-1996 .. **CLC 120**
See also CA 147; 151

Killens, John Oliver 1916-1987 .... **CLC 10**
See also BW 2; CA 77-80; 123; CAAS 2; CANR 26; DLB 33

Killigrew, Anne 1660-1685 .... **LC 4**
See also DLB 131

Killigrew, Thomas 1612-1683 .... **LC 57**
See also DLB 58

Kim
See Simenon, Georges (Jacques Christian)

Kincaid, Jamaica 1949- .... **CLC 43, 68, 137; BLC 2; DAM MULT, NOV**
See also AAYA 13; BW 2, 3; CA 125; CANR 47, 59; CDALBS; CLR 63; DA3; DLB 157, 227; MTCW 2

King, Francis (Henry) 1923- ...... **CLC 8, 53; DAM NOV**
See also CA 1-4R; CANR 1, 33, 86; DLB 15, 139; MTCW 1

King, Kennedy
See Brown, George Douglas

King, Martin Luther, Jr. 1929-1968
.... **CLC 83; BLC 2; DA; DAB; DAC; DAM MST, MULT; WLCS**
See also BW 2, 3; CA 25-28R; CANR 27, 44; CAP 2; DA3; MTCW 1, 2; SATA 14

King, Stephen (Edwin) 1947- ... **CLC 12, 26, 37, 61, 113; DAM NOV, POP; SSC 17**
See also AAYA 1, 17; BEST 90:1; CA 61-64; CANR 1, 30, 52, 76; DA3; DLB 143; DLBY 80; JRDA; MTCW 1, 2; SATA 9, 55

King, Steve
See King, Stephen (Edwin)

King, Thomas 1943- .. **CLC 89; DAC; DAM MULT**
See also CA 144; DLB 175; NNAL; SATA 96

Kingman, Lee .... **CLC 17**
See also Natti, (Mary) Lee
See also SAAS 3; SATA 1, 67

Kingsley, Charles 1819-1875 .... **NCLC 35**
See also DLB 21, 32, 163, 190; YABC 2

Kingsley, Sidney 1906-1995 .... **CLC 44**
See also CA 85-88; 147; DLB 7

Kingsolver, Barbara 1955- .... **CLC 55, 81, 130; DAM POP**
See also AAYA 15; CA 129; 134; CANR 60; CDALBS; DA3; DLB 206; INT 134; MTCW 2

Kingston, Maxine (Ting Ting) Hong 1940-
.... **CLC 12, 19, 58, 121; DAM MULT, NOV; WLCS**
See also AAYA 8; CA 69-72; CANR 13, 38, 74, 87; CDALBS; DA3; DLB 173, 212; DLBY 80; INT CANR-13; MTCW 1, 2; SATA 53

Kinnell, Galway 1927- ... **CLC 1, 2, 3, 5, 13, 29, 129; PC 26**
See also CA 9-12R; CANR 10, 34, 66; DLB 5; DLBY 87; INT CANR-34; MTCW 1, 2

Kinsella, Thomas 1928- .... **CLC 4, 19, 138**
See also CA 17-20R; CANR 15; DLB 27; MTCW 1, 2

Kinsella, W(illiam) P(atrick) 1935- . **CLC 27, 43; DAC; DAM NOV, POP**
See also AAYA 7; CA 97-100; CAAS 7; CANR 21, 35, 66, 75; INT CANR-21; MTCW 1, 2

Kinsey, Alfred C(harles) 1894-1956
.... **TCLC 91**
See also CA 115; 170; MTCW 2
Kipling, (Joseph) Rudyard 1865-1936
... **TCLC 8, 17; DA; DAB; DAC; DAM MST, POET; PC 3; SSC 5; WLC**
See also AAYA 32; CA 105; 120; CANR 33; CDBLB 1890-1914; CLR 39, 65; DA3; DLB 19, 34, 141, 156; MAICYA; MTCW 1, 2; SATA 100; YABC 2
Kirkland, Caroline M. 1801-1864 . **NCLC 85**
See also DLB 3, 73, 74; DLBD 13
Kirkup, James 1918- .... **CLC 1**
See also CA 1-4R; CAAS 4; CANR 2; DLB 27; SATA 12
Kirkwood, James 1930(?)-1989 .... **CLC 9**
See also AITN 2; CA 1-4R; 128; CANR 6, 40
Kirshner, Sidney
See Kingsley, Sidney
Kis, Danilo 1935-1989 .... **CLC 57**
See also CA 109; 118; 129; CANR 61; DLB 181; MTCW 1
Kissinger, Henry A(lfred) 1923- .... **CLC 137**
See also CA 1-4R; CANR 2, 33, 66; MTCW 1
Kivi, Aleksis 1834-1872 .... **NCLC 30**
Kizer, Carolyn (Ashley) 1925- . **CLC 15, 39, 80; DAM POET**
See also CA 65-68; CAAS 5; CANR 24, 70; DLB 5, 169; MTCW 2
Klabund 1890-1928 .... **TCLC 44**
See also CA 162; DLB 66
Klappert, Peter 1942- .... **CLC 57**
See also CA 33-36R; DLB 5
Klein, A(braham) M(oses) 1909-1972
.... **CLC 19; DAB; DAC; DAM MST**
See also CA 101; 37-40R; DLB 68
Klein, Norma 1938-1989 .... **CLC 30**
See also AAYA 2; CA 41-44R; 128; CANR 15, 37; CLR 2, 19; INT CANR-15; JRDA; MAICYA; SAAS 1; SATA 7, 57
Klein, T(heodore) E(ibon) D(onald) 1947-
.... **CLC 34**
See also CA 119; CANR 44, 75
Kleist, Heinrich von 1777-1811 ..... **NCLC 2, 37; DAM DRAM; SSC 22**
See also DLB 90
Klima, Ivan 1931- .... **CLC 56; DAM NOV**
See also CA 25-28R; CANR 17, 50, 91; DLB 232
Klimentov, Andrei Platonovich 1899-1951
.... **TCLC 14; SSC 42**
See also CA 108
Klinger, Friedrich Maximilian von 1752-1831 .... **NCLC 1**
See also DLB 94
Klingsor the Magician
See Hartmann, Sadakichi
Klopstock, Friedrich Gottlieb 1724-1803
.... **NCLC 11**
See also DLB 97
Knapp, Caroline 1959- .... **CLC 99**
See also CA 154
Knebel, Fletcher 1911-1993 .... **CLC 14**
See also AITN 1; CA 1-4R; 140; CAAS 3; CANR 1, 36; SATA 36; SATA-Obit 75
Knickerbocker, Diedrich
See Irving, Washington
Knight, Etheridge 1931-1991 . **CLC 40; BLC 2; DAM POET; PC 14**
See also BW 1, 3; CA 21-24R; 133; CANR 23, 82; DLB 41; MTCW 2
Knight, Sarah Kemble 1666-1727 .... **LC 7**
See also DLB 24, 200
Knister, Raymond 1899-1932 .... **TCLC 56**
See also CA 186; DLB 68
Knowles, John 1926- . **CLC 1, 4, 10, 26; DA; DAC; DAM MST, NOV**

See also AAYA 10; CA 17-20R; CANR 40, 74, 76; CDALB 1968-1988; DLB 6; MTCW 1, 2; SATA 8, 89
Knox, Calvin M.
See Silverberg, Robert
Knox, John c. 1505-1572 .... **LC 37**
See also DLB 132
Knye, Cassandra
See Disch, Thomas M(ichael)
Koch, C(hristopher) J(ohn) 1932- .. **CLC 42**
See also CA 127; CANR 84
Koch, Christopher
See Koch, C(hristopher) J(ohn)
Koch, Kenneth 1925- ... **CLC 5, 8, 44; DAM POET**
See also CA 1-4R; CANR 6, 36, 57; DLB 5; INT CANR-36; MTCW 2; SATA 65
Kochanowski, Jan 1530-1584 .... **LC 10**
Kock, Charles Paul de 1794-1871 . **NCLC 16**
Koda Rohan 1867-
See Koda Shigeyuki
Koda Shigeyuki 1867-1947 .... **TCLC 22**
See also CA 121; 183; DLB 180
Koestler, Arthur 1905-1983 . **CLC 1, 3, 6, 8, 15, 33**
See also CA 1-4R; 109; CANR 1, 33; CD-BLB 1945-1960; DLBY 83; MTCW 1, 2
Kogawa, Joy Nozomi 1935- ... **CLC 78, 129; DAC; DAM MST, MULT**
See also CA 101; CANR 19, 62; MTCW 2; SATA 99
Kohout, Pavel 1928- .... **CLC 13**
See also CA 45-48; CANR 3
Koizumi, Yakumo
See Hearn, (Patricio) Lafcadio (Tessima Carlos)
Kolmar, Gertrud 1894-1943 .... **TCLC 40**
See also CA 167
Komunyakaa, Yusef 1947- .... **CLC 86, 94; BLCS**
See also CA 147; CANR 83; DLB 120
Konrad, George
See Konrad, Gyorgy
Konrad, Gyorgy 1933- .... **CLC 4, 10, 73**
See also CA 85-88; DLB 232
Konwicki, Tadeusz 1926- ...... **CLC 8, 28, 54, 117**
See also CA 101; CAAS 9; CANR 39, 59; DLB 232; MTCW 1
Koontz, Dean R(ay) 1945- ... **CLC 78; DAM NOV, POP**
See also AAYA 9, 31; BEST 89:3, 90:2; CA 108; CANR 19, 36, 52; DA3; MTCW 1; SATA 92
Kopernik, Mikolaj
See Copernicus, Nicolaus
Kopit, Arthur (Lee) 1937- ... **CLC 1, 18, 33; DAM DRAM**
See also AITN 1; CA 81-84; CABS 3; DLB 7; MTCW 1
Kops, Bernard 1926- .... **CLC 4**
See also CA 5-8R; CANR 84; DLB 13
Kornbluth, C(yril) M. 1923-1958 ... **TCLC 8**
See also CA 105; 160; DLB 8
Korolenko, V. G.
See Korolenko, Vladimir Galaktionovich
Korolenko, Vladimir
See Korolenko, Vladimir Galaktionovich
Korolenko, Vladimir G.
See Korolenko, Vladimir Galaktionovich
Korolenko, Vladimir Galaktionovich 1853-1921 .... **TCLC 22**
See also CA 121
Korzybski, Alfred (Habdank Skarbek) 1879-1950 .... **TCLC 61**
See also CA 123; 160

Kosinski, Jerzy (Nikodem) 1933-1991
.... **CLC 1, 2, 3, 6, 10, 15, 53, 70; DAM NOV**
See also CA 17-20R; 134; CANR 9, 46; DA3; DLB 2; DLBY 82; MTCW 1, 2
Kostelanetz, Richard (Cory) 1940- . **CLC 28**
See also CA 13-16R; CAAS 8; CANR 38, 77
Kotlowitz, Robert 1924- .... **CLC 4**
See also CA 33-36R; CANR 36
Kotzebue, August (Friedrich Ferdinand) von 1761-1819 .... **NCLC 25**
See also DLB 94
Kotzwinkle, William 1938- ... **CLC 5, 14, 35**
See also CA 45-48; CANR 3, 44, 84; CLR 6; DLB 173; MAICYA; SATA 24, 70
Kowna, Stancy
See Szymborska, Wislawa
Kozol, Jonathan 1936- .... **CLC 17**
See also CA 61-64; CANR 16, 45
Kozoll, Michael 1940(?)- .... **CLC 35**
Kramer, Kathryn 19(?)- .... **CLC 34**
Kramer, Larry 1935- . **CLC 42; DAM POP; DC 8**
See also CA 124; 126; CANR 60
Krasicki, Ignacy 1735-1801 .... **NCLC 8**
Krasinski, Zygmunt 1812-1859 ...... **NCLC 4**
Kraus, Karl 1874-1936 .... **TCLC 5**
See also CA 104; DLB 118
Kreve (Mickevicius), Vincas 1882-1954
.... **TCLC 27**
See also CA 170; DLB 220
Kristeva, Julia 1941- .... **CLC 77**
See also CA 154
Kristofferson, Kris 1936- .... **CLC 26**
See also CA 104
Krizanc, John 1956- .... **CLC 57**
See also CA 187
Krleza, Miroslav 1893-1981 ...... **CLC 8, 114**
See also CA 97-100; 105; CANR 50; DLB 147
Kroetsch, Robert 1927- . **CLC 5, 23, 57, 132; DAC; DAM POET**
See also CA 17-20R; CANR 8, 38; DLB 53; MTCW 1
Kroetz, Franz
See Kroetz, Franz Xaver
Kroetz, Franz Xaver 1946- .... **CLC 41**
See also CA 130
Kroker, Arthur (W.) 1945- .... **CLC 77**
See also CA 161
Kropotkin, Peter (Aleksieevich) 1842-1921
.... **TCLC 36**
See also CA 119
Krotkov, Yuri 1917- .... **CLC 19**
See also CA 102
Krumb
See Crumb, R(obert)
Krumgold, Joseph (Quincy) 1908-1980
.... **CLC 12**
See also CA 9-12R; 101; CANR 7; MAI-CYA; SATA 1, 48; SATA-Obit 23
Krumwitz
See Crumb, R(obert)
Krutch, Joseph Wood 1893-1970 .... **CLC 24**
See also CA 1-4R; 25-28R; CANR 4; DLB 63, 206
Krutzch, Gus
See Eliot, T(homas) S(tearns)
Krylov, Ivan Andreevich 1768(?)-1844
.... **NCLC 1**
See also DLB 150
Kubin, Alfred (Leopold Isidor) 1877-1959
.... **TCLC 23**
See also CA 112; 149; DLB 81
Kubrick, Stanley 1928-1999 .... **CLC 16**
See also AAYA 30; CA 81-84; 177; CANR 33; DLB 26

See also CA 5-8R; 121; CANR 33; DLB
53; MTCW 1, 2; SATA-Obit 50
Laurent, Antoine 1952- .... **CLC 50**
Lauscher, Hermann
See Hesse, Hermann
Lautreamont, Comte de 1846-1870
.... **NCLC 12; SSC 14**
Laverty, Donald
See Blish, James (Benjamin)
Lavin, Mary 1912-1996 . **CLC 4, 18, 99; SSC
4**
See also CA 9-12R; 151; CANR 33; DLB
15; MTCW 1
Lavond, Paul Dennis
See Kornbluth, C(yril) M.; Pohl, Frederik
Lawler, Raymond Evenor 1922- ..... **CLC 58**
See also CA 103
Lawrence, D(avid) H(erbert Richards)
1885-1930 ... **TCLC 2, 9, 16, 33, 48, 61,
93; DA; DAB; DAC; DAM MST, NOV,
POET; SSC 4, 19; WLC**
See also CA 104; 121; CDBLB 1914-1945;
DA3; DLB 10, 19, 36, 98, 162, 195;
MTCW 1, 2
Lawrence, T(homas) E(dward) 1888-1935
.... **TCLC 18**
See also Dale, Colin
See also CA 115; 167; DLB 195
Lawrence of Arabia
See Lawrence, T(homas) E(dward)
Lawson, Henry (Archibald Hertzberg)
1867-1922 .... **TCLC 27; SSC 18**
See also CA 120; 181; DLB 230
Lawton, Dennis
See Faust, Frederick (Schiller)
Laxness, Halldor .... **CLC 25**
See also Gudjonsson, Halldor Kiljan
Layamon fl. c. 1200- .... **CMLC 10**
See also DLB 146
Laye, Camara 1928-1980 .. **CLC 4, 38; BLC
2; DAM MULT**
See also BW 1; CA 85-88; 97-100; CANR
25; MTCW 1, 2
Layton, Irving (Peter) 1912- ...... **CLC 2, 15;
DAC; DAM MST, POET**
See also CA 1-4R; CANR 2, 33, 43, 66;
DLB 88; MTCW 1, 2
Lazarus, Emma 1849-1887 .... **NCLC 8**
Lazarus, Felix
See Cable, George Washington
Lazarus, Henry
See Slavitt, David R(ytman)
Lea, Joan
See Neufeld, John (Arthur)
Leacock, Stephen (Butler) 1869-1944
.... **TCLC 2; DAC; DAM MST; SSC 39**
See also CA 104; 141; CANR 80; DLB 92;
MTCW 2
Lear, Edward 1812-1888 .... **NCLC 3**
See also CLR 1; DLB 32, 163, 166; MAI-
CYA; SATA 18, 100
Lear, Norman (Milton) 1922- .... **CLC 12**
See also CA 73-76
Leautaud, Paul 1872-1956 .... **TCLC 83**
See also DLB 65
Leavis, F(rank) R(aymond) 1895-1978
.... **CLC 24**
See also CA 21-24R; 77-80; CANR 44;
MTCW 1, 2
Leavitt, David 1961- ... **CLC 34; DAM POP**
See also CA 116; 122; CANR 50, 62; DA3;
DLB 130; INT 122; MTCW 2
Leblanc, Maurice (Marie Emile) 1864-1941
.... **TCLC 49**
See also CA 110
Lebowitz, Fran(ces Ann) 1951(?)- .. **CLC 11,
36**
See also CA 81-84; CANR 14, 60, 70; INT
CANR-14; MTCW 1

Lebrecht, Peter
See Tieck, (Johann) Ludwig
le Carre, John .... **CLC 3, 5, 9, 15, 28**
See also Cornwell, David (John Moore)
See also BEST 89:4; CDBLB 1960 to
Present; DLB 87; MTCW 2
Le Clezio, J(ean) M(arie) G(ustave) 1940-
.... **CLC 31**
See also CA 116; 128; DLB 83
Leconte de Lisle, Charles-Marie-Rene
1818-1894 .... **NCLC 29**
Le Coq, Monsieur
See Simenon, Georges (Jacques Christian)
Leduc, Violette 1907-1972 .... **CLC 22**
See also CA 13-14; 33-36R; CANR 69;
CAP 1
Ledwidge, Francis 1887(?)-1917 ... **TCLC 23**
See also CA 123; DLB 20
Lee, Andrea 1953- .. **CLC 36; BLC 2; DAM
MULT**
See also BW 1, 3; CA 125; CANR 82
Lee, Andrew
See Auchincloss, Louis (Stanton)
Lee, Chang-rae 1965- .... **CLC 91**
See also CA 148; CANR 89
Lee, Don L. .... **CLC 2**
See also Madhubuti, Haki R.
Lee, George W(ashington) 1894-1976
.... **CLC 52; BLC 2; DAM MULT**
See also BW 1; CA 125; CANR 83; DLB
51
Lee, (Nelle) Harper 1926- . **CLC 12, 60; DA;
DAB; DAC; DAM MST, NOV; WLC**
See also AAYA 13; CA 13-16R; CANR 51;
CDALB 1941-1968; DA3; DLB 6;
MTCW 1, 2; SATA 11
Lee, Helen Elaine 1959(?)- .... **CLC 86**
See also CA 148
Lee, Julian
See Latham, Jean Lee
Lee, Larry
See Lee, Lawrence
Lee, Laurie 1914-1997 .... **CLC 90; DAB;
DAM POP**
See also CA 77-80; 158; CANR 33, 73;
DLB 27; MTCW 1
Lee, Lawrence 1941-1990 .... **CLC 34**
See also CA 131; CANR 43
Lee, Li-Young 1957- .... **PC 24**
See also CA 153; DLB 165
Lee, Manfred B(ennington) 1905-1971
.... **CLC 11**
See also Queen, Ellery
See also CA 1-4R; 29-32R; CANR 2; DLB
137
Lee, Shelton Jackson 1957(?)- ..... **CLC 105;
BLCS; DAM MULT**
See also Lee, Spike
See also BW 2, 3; CA 125; CANR 42
Lee, Spike
See Lee, Shelton Jackson
See also AAYA 4, 29
Lee, Stan 1922- .... **CLC 17**
See also AAYA 5; CA 108; 111; INT 111
Lee, Tanith 1947- .... **CLC 46**
See also AAYA 15; CA 37-40R; CANR 53;
SATA 8, 88
Lee, Vernon .... **TCLC 5; SSC 33**
See also Paget, Violet
See also DLB 57, 153, 156, 174, 178
Lee, William
See Burroughs, William S(eward)
Lee, Willy
See Burroughs, William S(eward)
Lee-Hamilton, Eugene (Jacob) 1845-1907
.... **TCLC 22**
See also CA 117
Leet, Judith 1935- .... **CLC 11**
See also CA 187

Le Fanu, Joseph Sheridan 1814-1873
.... **NCLC 9, 58; DAM POP; SSC 14**
See also DA3; DLB 21, 70, 159, 178
Leffland, Ella 1931- .... **CLC 19**
See also CA 29-32R; CANR 35, 78, 82;
DLBY 84; INT CANR-35; SATA 65
Leger, Alexis
See Leger, (Marie-Rene Auguste) Alexis
Saint-Leger
**Leger, (Marie-Rene Auguste) Alexis
Saint-Leger** 1887-1975 . **CLC 4, 11, 46;
DAM POET; PC 23**
See also CA 13-16R; 61-64; CANR 43;
MTCW 1
Leger, Saintleger
See Leger, (Marie-Rene Auguste) Alexis
Saint-Leger
Le Guin, Ursula K(roeber) 1929- .... **CLC 8,
13, 22, 45, 71, 136; DAB; DAC; DAM
MST, POP; SSC 12**
See also AAYA 9, 27; AITN 1; CA 21-24R;
CANR 9, 32, 52, 74; CDALB 1968-1988;
CLR 3, 28; DA3; DLB 8, 52; INT CANR-
32; JRDA; MAICYA; MTCW 1, 2; SATA
4, 52, 99
Lehmann, Rosamond (Nina) 1901-1990
.... **CLC 5**
See also CA 77-80; 131; CANR 8, 73; DLB
15; MTCW 2
Leiber, Fritz (Reuter, Jr.) 1910-1992
.... **CLC 25**
See also CA 45-48; 139; CANR 2, 40, 86;
DLB 8; MTCW 1, 2; SATA 45; SATA-
Obit 73
Leibniz, Gottfried Wilhelm von 1646-1716
.... **LC 35**
See also DLB 168
Leimbach, Martha 1963-
See Leimbach, Marti
See also CA 130
Leimbach, Marti .... **CLC 65**
See also Leimbach, Martha
Leino, Eino .... **TCLC 24**
See also Loennbohm, Armas Eino Leopold
Leiris, Michel (Julien) 1901-1990 ... **CLC 61**
See also CA 119; 128; 132
Leithauser, Brad 1953- .... **CLC 27**
See also CA 107; CANR 27, 81; DLB 120
Lelchuk, Alan 1938- .... **CLC 5**
See also CA 45-48; CAAS 20; CANR 1, 70
Lem, Stanislaw 1921- .... **CLC 8, 15, 40**
See also CA 105; CAAS 1; CANR 32;
MTCW 1
Lemann, Nancy 1956- .... **CLC 39**
See also CA 118; 136
Lemonnier, (Antoine Louis) Camille
1844-1913 .... **TCLC 22**
See also CA 121
Lenau, Nikolaus 1802-1850 .... **NCLC 16**
L'Engle, Madeleine (Camp Franklin) 1918-
.... **CLC 12; DAM POP**
See also AAYA 28; AITN 2; CA 1-4R;
CANR 3, 21, 39, 66; CLR 1, 14, 57; DA3;
DLB 52; JRDA; MAICYA; MTCW 1, 2;
SAAS 15; SATA 1, 27, 75
Lengyel, Jozsef 1896-1975 .... **CLC 7**
See also CA 85-88; 57-60; CANR 71
Lenin 1870-1924
See Lenin, V. I.
See also CA 121; 168
Lenin, V. I. .... **TCLC 67**
See also Lenin
Lennon, John (Ono) 1940-1980 . **CLC 12, 35**
See also CA 102; SATA 114
Lennox, Charlotte Ramsay 1729(?)-1804
.... **NCLC 23**
See also DLB 39
Lentricchia, Frank (Jr.) 1940- .... **CLC 34**
See also CA 25-28R; CANR 19

Lenz, Siegfried 1926- .... **CLC 27; SSC 33**
See also CA 89-92; CANR 80; DLB 75

Leonard, Elmore (John, Jr.) 1925- . **CLC 28, 34, 71, 120; DAM POP**
See also AAYA 22; AITN 1; BEST 89:1, 90:4; CA 81-84; CANR 12, 28, 53, 76; DA3; DLB 173, 226; INT CANR-28; MTCW 1, 2

Leonard, Hugh .... **CLC 19**
See also Byrne, John Keyes
See also DLB 13

Leonov, Leonid (Maximovich) 1899-1994
.... **CLC 92; DAM NOV**
See also CA 129; CANR 74, 76; MTCW 1, 2

Leopardi, (Conte) Giacomo 1798-1837
.... **NCLC 22**

Le Reveler
See Artaud, Antonin (Marie Joseph)

Lerman, Eleanor 1952- .... **CLC 9**
See also CA 85-88; CANR 69

Lerman, Rhoda 1936- .... **CLC 56**
See also CA 49-52; CANR 70

Lermontov, Mikhail Yuryevich 1814-1841
.... **NCLC 47; PC 18**
See also DLB 205

Leroux, Gaston 1868-1927 .... **TCLC 25**
See also CA 108; 136; CANR 69; SATA 65

Lesage, Alain-Rene 1668-1747 .... **LC 2, 28**

Leskov, Nikolai (Semyonovich) 1831-1895
.... **NCLC 25; SSC 34**

Lessing, Doris (May) 1919- . **CLC 1, 2, 3, 6, 10, 15, 22, 40, 94; DA; DAB; DAC; DAM MST, NOV; SSC 6; WLCS**
See also CA 9-12R; CAAS 14; CANR 33, 54, 76; CDBLB 1960 to Present; DA3; DLB 15, 139; DLBY 85; MTCW 1, 2

Lessing, Gotthold Ephraim 1729-1781 . **LC 8**
See also DLB 97

Lester, Richard 1932- .... **CLC 20**

Lever, Charles (James) 1806-1872 . **NCLC 23**
See also DLB 21

Leverson, Ada 1865(?)-1936(?) ..... **TCLC 18**
See also Elaine
See also CA 117; DLB 153

Levertov, Denise 1923-1997 . **CLC 1, 2, 3, 5, 8, 15, 28, 66; DAM POET; PC 11**
See also CA 1-4R, 178; 163; CAAE 178; CAAS 19; CANR 3, 29, 50; CDALBS; DLB 5, 165; INT CANR-29; MTCW 1, 2

Levi, Jonathan .... **CLC 76**

Levi, Peter (Chad Tigar) 1931-2000 . **CLC 41**
See also CA 5-8R; 187; CANR 34, 80; DLB 40

Levi, Primo 1919-1987 ..... **CLC 37, 50; SSC 12**
See also CA 13-16R; 122; CANR 12, 33, 61, 70; DLB 177; MTCW 1, 2

Levin, Ira 1929- .... **CLC 3, 6; DAM POP**
See also CA 21-24R; CANR 17, 44, 74; DA3; MTCW 1, 2; SATA 66

Levin, Meyer 1905-1981 .... **CLC 7; DAM POP**
See also AITN 1; CA 9-12R; 104; CANR 15; DLB 9, 28; DLBY 81; SATA 21; SATA-Obit 27

Levine, Norman 1924- .... **CLC 54**
See also CA 73-76; CAAS 23; CANR 14, 70; DLB 88

Levine, Philip 1928- . **CLC 2, 4, 5, 9, 14, 33, 118; DAM POET; PC 22**
See also CA 9-12R; CANR 9, 37, 52; DLB 5

Levinson, Deirdre 1931- .... **CLC 49**
See also CA 73-76; CANR 70

Levi-Strauss, Claude 1908- .... **CLC 38**
See also CA 1-4R; CANR 6, 32, 57; MTCW 1, 2

Levitin, Sonia (Wolff) 1934- .... **CLC 17**

See also AAYA 13; CA 29-32R; CANR 14, 32, 79; CLR 53; JRDA; MAICYA; SAAS 2; SATA 4, 68, 119

Levon, O. U.
See Kesey, Ken (Elton)

Levy, Amy 1861-1889 .... **NCLC 59**
See also DLB 156

Lewes, George Henry 1817-1878 . **NCLC 25**
See also DLB 55, 144

Lewis, Alun 1915-1944 ..... **TCLC 3; SSC 40**
See also CA 104; DLB 20, 162

Lewis, C. Day
See Day Lewis, C(ecil)

Lewis, C(live) S(taples) 1898-1963 ... **CLC 1, 3, 6, 14, 27, 124; DA; DAB; DAC; DAM MST, NOV, POP; WLC**
See also AAYA 3; CA 81-84; CANR 33, 71; CDBLB 1945-1960; CLR 3, 27; DA3; DLB 15, 100, 160; JRDA; MAICYA; MTCW 1, 2; SATA 13, 100

Lewis, Janet 1899-1998 .... **CLC 41**
See also Winters, Janet Lewis
See also CA 9-12R; 172; CANR 29, 63; CAP 1; DLBY 87

Lewis, Matthew Gregory 1775-1818
.... **NCLC 11, 62**
See also DLB 39, 158, 178

Lewis, (Harry) Sinclair 1885-1951 . **TCLC 4, 13, 23, 39; DA; DAB; DAC; DAM MST, NOV; WLC**
See also CA 104; 133; CDALB 1917-1929; DA3; DLB 9, 102; DLBD 1; MTCW 1, 2

Lewis, (Percy) Wyndham 1882(?)-1957
.... **TCLC 2, 9; SSC 34**
See also CA 104; 157; DLB 15; MTCW 2

Lewisohn, Ludwig 1883-1955 .... **TCLC 19**
See also CA 107; DLB 4, 9, 28, 102

Lewton, Val 1904-1951 .... **TCLC 76**

Leyner, Mark 1956- .... **CLC 92**
See also CA 110; CANR 28, 53; DA3; MTCW 2

Lezama Lima, Jose 1910-1976 ... **CLC 4, 10, 101; DAM MULT; HLCS 2**
See also CA 77-80; CANR 71; DLB 113; HW 1, 2

L'Heureux, John (Clarke) 1934- .... **CLC 52**
See also CA 13-16R; CANR 23, 45, 88

Liddell, C. H.
See Kuttner, Henry

Lie, Jonas (Lauritz Idemil) 1833-1908(?)
.... **TCLC 5**
See also CA 115

Lieber, Joel 1937-1971 .... **CLC 6**
See also CA 73-76; 29-32R

Lieber, Stanley Martin
See Lee, Stan

Lieberman, Laurence (James) 1935-
.... **CLC 4, 36**
See also CA 17-20R; CANR 8, 36, 89

Lieh Tzu fl. 7th cent. B.C.-5th cent. B.C.
.... **CMLC 27**

Lieksman, Anders
See Haavikko, Paavo Juhani

Li Fei-kan 1904-
See Pa Chin
See also CA 105

Lifton, Robert Jay 1926- .... **CLC 67**
See also CA 17-20R; CANR 27, 78; INT CANR-27; SATA 66

Lightfoot, Gordon 1938- .... **CLC 26**
See also CA 109

Lightman, Alan P(aige) 1948- .... **CLC 81**
See also CA 141; CANR 63

Ligotti, Thomas (Robert) 1953- ..... **CLC 44; SSC 16**
See also CA 123; CANR 49

Li Ho 791-817 .... **PC 13**

Liliencron, (Friedrich Adolf Axel) Detlev von 1844-1909 .... **TCLC 18**
See also CA 117

Lilly, William 1602-1681 .... **LC 27**

Lima, Jose Lezama
See Lezama Lima, Jose

Lima Barreto, Afonso Henrique de 1881-1922 .... **TCLC 23**
See also CA 117; 181

Limonov, Edward 1944- .... **CLC 67**
See also CA 137

Lin, Frank
See Atherton, Gertrude (Franklin Horn)

Lincoln, Abraham 1809-1865 .... **NCLC 18**

Lind, Jakov .... **CLC 1, 2, 4, 27, 82**
See also Landwirth, Heinz
See also CAAS 4

Lindbergh, Anne (Spencer) Morrow 1906-
.... **CLC 82; DAM NOV**
See also CA 17-20R; CANR 16, 73; MTCW 1, 2; SATA 33

Lindsay, David 1876(?)-1945 .... **TCLC 15**
See also CA 113; 187

Lindsay, (Nicholas) Vachel 1879-1931
.... **TCLC 17; DA; DAC; DAM MST, POET; PC 23; WLC**
See also CA 114; 135; CANR 79; CDALB 1865-1917; DA3; DLB 54; SATA 40

Linke-Poot
See Doeblin, Alfred

Linney, Romulus 1930- .... **CLC 51**
See also CA 1-4R; CANR 40, 44, 79

Linton, Eliza Lynn 1822-1898 .... **NCLC 41**
See also DLB 18

Li Po 701-763 .... **CMLC 2; PC 29**

Lipsius, Justus 1547-1606 .... **LC 16**

Lipsyte, Robert (Michael) 1938- .... **CLC 21; DA; DAC; DAM MST, NOV**
See also AAYA 7; CA 17-20R; CANR 8, 57; CLR 23; JRDA; MAICYA; SATA 5, 68, 113

Lish, Gordon (Jay) 1934- . **CLC 45; SSC 18**
See also CA 113; 117; CANR 79; DLB 130; INT 117

Lispector, Clarice 1925(?)-1977 ..... **CLC 43; HLCS 2; SSC 34**
See also CA 139; 116; CANR 71; DLB 113; HW 2

Littell, Robert 1935(?)- .... **CLC 42**
See also CA 109; 112; CANR 64

Little, Malcolm 1925-1965
See Malcolm X
See also BW 1, 3; CA 125; 111; CANR 82; DA; DAB; DAC; DAM MST, MULT; DA3; MTCW 1, 2

Littlewit, Humphrey Gent.
See Lovecraft, H(oward) P(hillips)

Litwos
See Sienkiewicz, Henryk (Adam Alexander Pius)

Liu, E 1857-1909 .... **TCLC 15**
See also CA 115

Lively, Penelope (Margaret) 1933- . **CLC 32, 50; DAM NOV**
See also CA 41-44R; CANR 29, 67, 79; CLR 7; DLB 14, 161, 207; JRDA; MAICYA; MTCW 1, 2; SATA 7, 60, 101

Livesay, Dorothy (Kathleen) 1909- .. **CLC 4, 15, 79; DAC; DAM MST, POET**
See also AITN 2; CA 25-28R; CAAS 8; CANR 36, 67; DLB 68; MTCW 1

Livy c. 59B.C.-c. 17 .... **CMLC 11**
See also DLB 211

Lizardi, Jose Joaquin Fernandez de 1776-1827 .... **NCLC 30**

Llewellyn, Richard
See Llewellyn Lloyd, Richard Dafydd Vivian
See also DLB 15

Llewellyn Lloyd, Richard Dafydd Vivian
1906-1983 .... **CLC 7, 80**
See also Llewellyn, Richard
See also CA 53-56; 111; CANR 7, 71;
SATA 11; SATA-Obit 37

Llosa, (Jorge) Mario (Pedro) Vargas
See Vargas Llosa, (Jorge) Mario (Pedro)

Lloyd, Manda
See Mander, (Mary) Jane

Lloyd Webber, Andrew 1948-
See Webber, Andrew Lloyd
See also AAYA 1; CA 116; 149; DAM
DRAM; SATA 56

Llull, Ramon c. 1235-c. 1316 .... **CMLC 12**

Lobb, Ebenezer
See Upward, Allen

Locke, Alain (Le Roy) 1886-1954 . **TCLC 43;
BLCS**
See also BW 1, 3; CA 106; 124; CANR 79;
DLB 51

Locke, John 1632-1704 .... **LC 7, 35**
See also DLB 101

Locke-Elliott, Sumner
See Elliott, Sumner Locke

Lockhart, John Gibson 1794-1854 . **NCLC 6**
See also DLB 110, 116, 144

Lodge, David (John) 1935- .. **CLC 36; DAM
POP**
See also BEST 90:1; CA 17-20R; CANR
19, 53, 92; DLB 14, 194; INT CANR-19;
MTCW 1, 2

Lodge, Thomas 1558-1625 .... **LC 41**

Lodge, Thomas 1558-1625 .... **LC 41**
See also DLB 172

Loennbohm, Armas Eino Leopold 1878-1926
See Leino, Eino
See also CA 123

Loewinsohn, Ron(ald William) 1937-
.... **CLC 52**
See also CA 25-28R; CANR 71

Logan, Jake
See Smith, Martin Cruz

Logan, John (Burton) 1923-1987 ...... **CLC 5**
See also CA 77-80; 124; CANR 45; DLB 5

Lo Kuan-chung 1330(?)-1400(?) .... **LC 12**

Lombard, Nap
See Johnson, Pamela Hansford

London, Jack .... **TCLC 9, 15, 39; SSC 4;
WLC**
See also London, John Griffith
See also AAYA 13; AITN 2; CDALB 1865-
1917; DLB 8, 12, 78, 212; SATA 18

London, John Griffith 1876-1916
See London, Jack
See also CA 110; 119; CANR 73; DA;
DAB; DAC; DAM MST, NOV; DA3;
JRDA; MAICYA; MTCW 1, 2

Long, Emmett
See Leonard, Elmore (John, Jr.)

Longbaugh, Harry
See Goldman, William (W.)

Longfellow, Henry Wadsworth 1807-1882
.. **NCLC 2, 45; DA; DAB; DAC; DAM
MST, POET; PC 30; WLCS**
See also CDALB 1640-1865; DA3; DLB 1,
59, 235; SATA 19

Longinus c. 1st cent. - .... **CMLC 27**
See also DLB 176

Longley, Michael 1939- .... **CLC 29**
See also CA 102; DLB 40

Longus fl. c. 2nd cent. - .... **CMLC 7**

Longway, A. Hugh
See Lang, Andrew

Lonnrot, Elias 1802-1884 .... **NCLC 53**

Lopate, Phillip 1943- .... **CLC 29**
See also CA 97-100; CANR 88; DLBY 80;
INT 97-100

Lopez Portillo (y Pacheco), Jose 1920-
.... **CLC 46**
See also CA 129; HW 1

Lopez y Fuentes, Gregorio 1897(?)-1966
.... **CLC 32**
See also CA 131; HW 1

Lorca, Federico Garcia
See Garcia Lorca, Federico

Lord, Bette Bao 1938- .... **CLC 23**
See also BEST 90:3; CA 107; CANR 41,
79; INT 107; SATA 58

Lord Auch
See Bataille, Georges

Lord Byron
See Byron, George Gordon (Noel)

Lorde, Audre (Geraldine) 1934-1992
...... **CLC 18, 71; BLC 2; DAM MULT,
POET; PC 12**
See also BW 1, 3; CA 25-28R; 142; CANR
16, 26, 46, 82; DA3; DLB 41; MTCW 1,
2

Lord Houghton
See Milnes, Richard Monckton

Lord Jeffrey
See Jeffrey, Francis

Lorenzini, Carlo 1826-1890
See Collodi, Carlo
See also MAICYA; SATA 29, 100

Lorenzo, Heberto Padilla
See Padilla (Lorenzo), Heberto

Loris
See Hofmannsthal, Hugo von

Loti, Pierre .... **TCLC 11**
See also Viaud, (Louis Marie) Julien
See also DLB 123

Lou, Henri
See Andreas-Salome, Lou

Louie, David Wong 1954- .... **CLC 70**
See also CA 139

Louis, Father M.
See Merton, Thomas

Lovecraft, H(oward) P(hillips) 1890-1937
.... **TCLC 4, 22; DAM POP; SSC 3**
See also AAYA 14; CA 104; 133; DA3;
MTCW 1, 2

Lovelace, Earl 1935- .... **CLC 51**
See also BW 2; CA 77-80; CANR 41, 72;
DLB 125; MTCW 1

Lovelace, Richard 1618-1657 .... **LC 24**
See also DLB 131

Lowell, Amy 1874-1925 ... **TCLC 1, 8; DAM
POET; PC 13**
See also CA 104; 151; DLB 54, 140;
MTCW 2

Lowell, James Russell 1819-1891 .. **NCLC 2,
90**
See also CDALB 1640-1865; DLB 1, 11,
64, 79, 189, 235

Lowell, Robert (Traill Spence, Jr.)
1917-1977 ... **CLC 1, 2, 3, 4, 5, 8, 9, 11,
15, 37, 124; DA; DAB; DAC; DAM
MST, NOV; PC 3; WLC**
See also CA 9-12R; 73-76; CABS 2; CANR
26, 60; CDALBS; DA3; DLB 5, 169;
MTCW 1, 2

Lowenthal, Michael (Francis) 1969-
.... **CLC 119**
See also CA 150

Lowndes, Marie Adelaide (Belloc) 1868-1947
.... **TCLC 12**
See also CA 107; DLB 70

Lowry, (Clarence) Malcolm 1909-1957
.... **TCLC 6, 40; SSC 31**
See also CA 105; 131; CANR 62; CDBLB
1945-1960; DLB 15; MTCW 1, 2

Lowry, Mina Gertrude 1882-1966
See Loy, Mina
See also CA 113

Loxsmith, John
See Brunner, John (Kilian Houston)

Loy, Mina ..... **CLC 28; DAM POET; PC 16**
See also Lowry, Mina Gertrude
See also DLB 4, 54

Loyson-Bridet
See Schwob, Marcel (Mayer Andre)

Lucan 39-65 .... **CMLC 33**
See also DLB 211

Lucas, Craig 1951- .... **CLC 64**
See also CA 137; CANR 71

Lucas, E(dward) V(errall) 1868-1938
.... **TCLC 73**
See also CA 176; DLB 98, 149, 153; SATA
20

Lucas, George 1944- .... **CLC 16**
See also AAYA 1, 23; CA 77-80; CANR
30; SATA 56

Lucas, Hans
See Godard, Jean-Luc

Lucas, Victoria
See Plath, Sylvia

Lucian c. 120-c. 180 .... **CMLC 32**
See also DLB 176

Ludlam, Charles 1943-1987 ...... **CLC 46, 50**
See also CA 85-88; 122; CANR 72, 86

Ludlum, Robert 1927- ... **CLC 22, 43; DAM
NOV, POP**
See also AAYA 10; BEST 89:1, 90:3; CA
33-36R; CANR 25, 41, 68; DA3; DLBY
82; MTCW 1, 2

Ludwig, Ken .... **CLC 60**

Ludwig, Otto 1813-1865 .... **NCLC 4**
See also DLB 129

Lugones, Leopoldo 1874-1938 ..... **TCLC 15;
HLCS 2**
See also CA 116; 131; HW 1

Lu Hsun 1881-1936 .... **TCLC 3; SSC 20**
See also Shu-Jen, Chou

Lukacs, George .... **CLC 24**
See also Lukacs, Gyorgy (Szegeny von)

Lukacs, Gyorgy (Szegeny von) 1885-1971
See Lukacs, George
See also CA 101; 29-32R; CANR 62;
MTCW 2

Luke, Peter (Ambrose Cyprian) 1919-1995
.... **CLC 38**
See also CA 81-84; 147; CANR 72; DLB
13

Lunar, Dennis
See Mungo, Raymond

Lurie, Alison 1926- .... **CLC 4, 5, 18, 39**
See also CA 1-4R; CANR 2, 17, 50, 88;
DLB 2; MTCW 1; SATA 46, 112

Lustig, Arnost 1926- .... **CLC 56**
See also AAYA 3; CA 69-72; CANR 47;
DLB 232; SATA 56

Luther, Martin 1483-1546 .... **LC 9, 37**
See also DLB 179

Luxemburg, Rosa 1870(?)-1919 .... **TCLC 63**
See also CA 118

Luzi, Mario 1914- .... **CLC 13**
See also CA 61-64; CANR 9, 70; DLB 128

Lyly, John 1554(?)-1606 .... **LC 41; DAM
DRAM; DC 7**
See also DLB 62, 167

L'Ymagier
See Gourmont, Remy (-Marie-Charles) de

Lynch, B. Suarez
See Bioy Casares, Adolfo; Borges, Jorge
Luis

Lynch, B. Suarez
See Bioy Casares, Adolfo

Lynch, David (K.) 1946- .... **CLC 66**
See also CA 124; 129

Lynch, James
See Andreyev, Leonid (Nikolaevich)

See also CA 45-48; CANR 2, 32, 63; DA3; DLB 113; HW 1, 2; MTCW 1, 2

Pulitzer, Joseph 1847-1911 .... **TCLC 76**
See also CA 114; DLB 23

Purdy, A(lfred) W(ellington) 1918- .. **CLC 3, 6, 14, 50; DAC; DAM MST, POET**
See also CA 81-84; CAAS 17; CANR 42, 66; DLB 88

Purdy, James (Amos) 1923- ... **CLC 2, 4, 10, 28, 52**
See also CA 33-36R; CAAS 1; CANR 19, 51; DLB 2; INT CANR-19; MTCW 1

Pure, Simon
See Swinnerton, Frank Arthur

Pushkin, Alexander (Sergeyevich) 1799-1837
.... **NCLC 3, 27, 83; DA; DAB; DAC; DAM DRAM, MST, POET; PC 10; SSC 27; WLC**
See also DA3; DLB 205; SATA 61

P'u Sung-ling 1640-1715 ...... **LC 49; SSC 31**

Putnam, Arthur Lee
See Alger, Horatio Jr., Jr.

Puzo, Mario 1920-1999 ...... **CLC 1, 2, 6, 36, 107; DAM NOV, POP**
See also CA 65-68; 185; CANR 4, 42, 65; DA3; DLB 6; MTCW 1, 2

Pygge, Edward
See Barnes, Julian (Patrick)

Pyle, Ernest Taylor 1900-1945
See Pyle, Ernie
See also CA 115; 160

Pyle, Ernie 1900-1945 .... **TCLC 75**
See also Pyle, Ernest Taylor
See also DLB 29; MTCW 2

Pyle, Howard 1853-1911 .... **TCLC 81**
See also CA 109; 137; CLR 22; DLB 42, 188; DLBD 13; MAICYA; SATA 16, 100

Pym, Barbara (Mary Crampton) 1913-1980
.... **CLC 13, 19, 37, 111**
See also CA 13-14; 97-100; CANR 13, 34; CAP 1; DLB 14, 207; DLBY 87; MTCW 1, 2

Pynchon, Thomas (Ruggles, Jr.) 1937-
. **CLC 2, 3, 6, 9, 11, 18, 33, 62, 72, 123; DA; DAB; DAC; DAM MST, NOV, POP; SSC 14; WLC**
See also BEST 90:2; CA 17-20R; CANR 22, 46, 73; DA3; DLB 2, 173; MTCW 1, 2

Pythagoras c. 570B.C.-c. 500B.C. . **CMLC 22**
See also DLB 176

Q
See Quiller-Couch, SirArthur (Thomas)

Qian Zhongshu
See Ch'ien Chung-shu

Qroll
See Dagerman, Stig (Halvard)

Quarrington, Paul (Lewis) 1953- .... **CLC 65**
See also CA 129; CANR 62

Quasimodo, Salvatore 1901-1968 .... **CLC 10**
See also CA 13-16; 25-28R; CAP 1; DLB 114; MTCW 1

Quay, Stephen 1947- .... **CLC 95**

Quay, Timothy 1947- .... **CLC 95**

Queen, Ellery .... **CLC 3, 11**
See also Dannay, Frederic; Davidson, Avram (James); Deming, Richard; Fairman, Paul W.; Flora, Fletcher; Hoch, Edward D(entinger); Kane, Henry; Lee, Manfred B(ennington); Marlowe, Stephen; Powell, Talmage; Sheldon, Walter J.; Sturgeon, Theodore (Hamilton); Tracy, Don(ald Fiske); Vance, John Holbrook

Queen, Ellery, Jr.
See Dannay, Frederic; Lee, Manfred B(ennington)

Queneau, Raymond 1903-1976 .... **CLC 2, 5, 10, 42**

See also CA 77-80; 69-72; CANR 32; DLB 72; MTCW 1, 2

Quevedo, Francisco de 1580-1645 ..... **LC 23**

Quiller-Couch, SirArthur (Thomas)
1863-1944 .... **TCLC 53**
See also CA 118; 166; DLB 135, 153, 190

Quin, Ann (Marie) 1936-1973 .... **CLC 6**
See also CA 9-12R; 45-48; DLB 14, 231

Quinn, Martin
See Smith, Martin Cruz

Quinn, Peter 1947- .... **CLC 91**

Quinn, Simon
See Smith, Martin Cruz

Quintana, Leroy V. 1944-
See also CA 131; CANR 65; DAM MULT; DLB 82; HLC 2; HW 1, 2

Quiroga, Horacio (Sylvestre) 1878-1937
.... **TCLC 20; DAM MULT; HLC 2**
See also CA 117; 131; HW 1; MTCW 1

Quoirez, Francoise 1935- .... **CLC 9**
See also Sagan, Francoise
See also CA 49-52; CANR 6, 39, 73; MTCW 1, 2

Raabe, Wilhelm (Karl) 1831-1910 . **TCLC 45**
See also CA 167; DLB 129

Rabe, David (William) 1940- . **CLC 4, 8, 33; DAM DRAM**
See also CA 85-88; CABS 3; CANR 59; DLB 7, 228

Rabelais, Francois 1483-1553 .... **LC 5, 60; DA; DAB; DAC; DAM MST; WLC**

Rabinovitch, Sholem 1859-1916
See Aleichem, Sholom
See also CA 104

Rabinyan, Dorit 1972- .... **CLC 119**
See also CA 170

Rachilde
See Vallette, Marguerite Eymery

Racine, Jean 1639-1699 . **LC 28; DAB; DAM MST**
See also DA3

Radcliffe, Ann (Ward) 1764-1823 . **NCLC 6, 55**
See also DLB 39, 178

Radiguet, Raymond 1903-1923 .... **TCLC 29**
See also CA 162; DLB 65

Radnoti, Miklos 1909-1944 .... **TCLC 16**
See also CA 118

Rado, James 1939- .... **CLC 17**
See also CA 105

Radvanyi, Netty 1900-1983
See Seghers, Anna
See also CA 85-88; 110; CANR 82

Rae, Ben
See Griffiths, Trevor

Raeburn, John (Hay) 1941- .... **CLC 34**
See also CA 57-60

Ragni, Gerome 1942-1991 .... **CLC 17**
See also CA 105; 134

Rahv, Philip 1908-1973 .... **CLC 24**
See also Greenberg, Ivan
See also DLB 137

Raimund, Ferdinand Jakob 1790-1836
.... **NCLC 69**
See also DLB 90

Raine, Craig 1944- .... **CLC 32, 103**
See also CA 108; CANR 29, 51; DLB 40

Raine, Kathleen (Jessie) 1908- .... **CLC 7, 45**
See also CA 85-88; CANR 46; DLB 20; MTCW 1

Rainis, Janis 1865-1929 .... **TCLC 29**
See also Plieksans, Janis
See also CA 170; DLB 220

Rakosi, Carl 1903- .... **CLC 47**
See also Rawley, Callman
See also CAAS 5; DLB 193

Raleigh, Richard
See Lovecraft, H(oward) P(hillips)

Raleigh, Sir Walter 1554(?)-1618 ...... **LC 31, 39; PC 31**
See also CDBLB Before 1660; DLB 172

Rallentando, H. P.
See Sayers, Dorothy L(eigh)

Ramal, Walter
See de la Mare, Walter (John)

Ramana Maharshi 1879-1950 .... **TCLC 84**

Ramoacn y Cajal, Santiago 1852-1934
.... **TCLC 93**

Ramon, Juan
See Jimenez (Mantecon), Juan Ramon

Ramos, Graciliano 1892-1953 .... **TCLC 32**
See also CA 167; HW 2

Rampersad, Arnold 1941- .... **CLC 44**
See also BW 2, 3; CA 127; 133; CANR 81; DLB 111; INT 133

Rampling, Anne
See Rice, Anne

Ramsay, Allan 1684(?)-1758 .... **LC 29**
See also DLB 95

Ramuz, Charles-Ferdinand 1878-1947
.... **TCLC 33**
See also CA 165

Rand, Ayn 1905-1982 ..... **CLC 3, 30, 44, 79; DA; DAC; DAM MST, NOV, POP; WLC**
See also AAYA 10; CA 13-16R; 105; CANR 27, 73; CDALBS; DA3; DLB 227; MTCW 1, 2

Randall, Dudley (Felker) 1914-2000 . **CLC 1, 135; BLC 3; DAM MULT**
See also BW 1, 3; CA 25-28R; CANR 23, 82; DLB 41

Randall, Robert
See Silverberg, Robert

Ranger, Ken
See Creasey, John

Ransom, John Crowe 1888-1974 . **CLC 2, 4, 5, 11, 24; DAM POET**
See also CA 5-8R; 49-52; CANR 6, 34; CDALBS; DA3; DLB 45, 63; MTCW 1, 2

Rao, Raja 1909- .... **CLC 25, 56; DAM NOV**
See also CA 73-76; CANR 51; MTCW 1, 2

Raphael, Frederic (Michael) 1931- .. **CLC 2, 14**
See also CA 1-4R; CANR 1, 86; DLB 14

Ratcliffe, James P.
See Mencken, H(enry) L(ouis)

Rathbone, Julian 1935- .... **CLC 41**
See also CA 101; CANR 34, 73

Rattigan, Terence (Mervyn) 1911-1977
.... **CLC 7; DAM DRAM**
See also CA 85-88; 73-76; CDBLB 1945-1960; DLB 13; MTCW 1, 2

Ratushinskaya, Irina 1954- .... **CLC 54**
See also CA 129; CANR 68

Raven, Simon (Arthur Noel) 1927- . **CLC 14**
See also CA 81-84; CANR 86

Ravenna, Michael
See Welty, Eudora

Rawley, Callman 1903-
See Rakosi, Carl
See also CA 21-24R; CANR 12, 32, 91

Rawlings, Marjorie Kinnan 1896-1953
.... **TCLC 4**
See also AAYA 20; CA 104; 137; CANR 74; CLR 63; DLB 9, 22, 102; DLBD 17; JRDA; MAICYA; MTCW 2; SATA 100; YABC 1

Ray, Satyajit 1921-1992 . **CLC 16, 76; DAM MULT**
See also CA 114; 137

Read, Herbert Edward 1893-1968 .... **CLC 4**
See also CA 85-88; 25-28R; DLB 20, 149

Rossetti, Christina (Georgina) 1830-1894
.... NCLC 2, 50, 66; DA; DAB; DAC;
DAM MST, POET; PC 7; WLC
See also DA3; DLB 35, 163; MAICYA;
SATA 20

Rossetti, Dante Gabriel 1828-1882 . NCLC 4,
77; DA; DAB; DAC; DAM MST,
POET; WLC
See also CDBLB 1832-1890; DLB 35

Rossner, Judith (Perelman) 1935- .... CLC 6,
9, 29
See also AITN 2; BEST 90:3; CA 17-20R;
CANR 18, 51, 73; DLB 6; INT CANR-
18; MTCW 1, 2

Rostand, Edmond (Eugene Alexis)
1868-1918 ...... TCLC 6, 37; DA; DAB;
DAC; DAM DRAM, MST; DC 10
See also CA 104; 126; DA3; DLB 192;
MTCW 1

Roth, Henry 1906-1995 ... CLC 2, 6, 11, 104
See also CA 11-12; 149; CANR 38, 63;
CAP 1; DA3; DLB 28; MTCW 1, 2

Roth, Philip (Milton) 1933- . CLC 1, 2, 3, 4,
6, 9, 15, 22, 31, 47, 66, 86, 119; DA;
DAB; DAC; DAM MST, NOV, POP;
SSC 26; WLC
See also BEST 90:3; CA 1-4R; CANR 1,
22, 36, 55, 89; CDALB 1968-1988; DA3;
DLB 2, 28, 173; DLBY 82; MTCW 1, 2

Rothenberg, Jerome 1931- .... CLC 6, 57
See also CA 45-48; CANR 1; DLB 5, 193

Roumain, Jacques (Jean Baptiste) 1907-1944
.... TCLC 19; BLC 3; DAM MULT
See also BW 1; CA 117; 125

Rourke, Constance (Mayfield) 1885-1941
.... TCLC 12
See also CA 107; YABC 1

Rousseau, Jean-Baptiste 1671-1741 ..... LC 9

Rousseau, Jean-Jacques 1712-1778 .. LC 14,
36; DA; DAB; DAC; DAM MST; WLC
See also DA3

Roussel, Raymond 1877-1933 .... TCLC 20
See also CA 117

Rovit, Earl (Herbert) 1927- .... CLC 7
See also CA 5-8R; CANR 12

Rowe, Elizabeth Singer 1674-1737 .... LC 44
See also DLB 39, 95

Rowe, Nicholas 1674-1718 .... LC 8
See also DLB 84

Rowley, Ames Dorrance
See Lovecraft, H(oward) P(hillips)

Rowling, J(oanne) K. 1966(?)- ...... CLC 137
See also AAYA 34; CA 173; CLR 66; SATA
109

Rowson, Susanna Haswell 1762(?)-1824
.... NCLC 5, 69
See also DLB 37, 200

Roy, Arundhati 1960(?)- .... CLC 109
See also CA 163; CANR 90; DLBY 97

Roy, Gabrielle 1909-1983 .... CLC 10, 14;
DAB; DAC; DAM MST
See also CA 53-56; 110; CANR 5, 61; DLB
68; MTCW 1; SATA 104

Royko, Mike 1932-1997 .... CLC 109
See also CA 89-92; 157; CANR 26

Rozewicz, Tadeusz 1921- . CLC 9, 23; DAM
POET
See also CA 108; CANR 36, 66; DA3; DLB
232; MTCW 1, 2

Ruark, Gibbons 1941- .... CLC 3
See also CA 33-36R; CAAS 23; CANR 14,
31, 57; DLB 120

Rubens, Bernice (Ruth) 1923- .. CLC 19, 31
See also CA 25-28R; CANR 33, 65; DLB
14, 207; MTCW 1

Rubin, Harold
See Robbins, Harold

Rudkin, (James) David 1936- .... CLC 14
See also CA 89-92; DLB 13

Rudnik, Raphael 1933- .... CLC 7
See also CA 29-32R

Ruffian, M.
See Hasek, Jaroslav (Matej Frantisek)

Ruiz, Jose Martinez .... CLC 11
See also Martinez Ruiz, Jose

Rukeyser, Muriel 1913-1980 . CLC 6, 10, 15,
27; DAM POET; PC 12
See also CA 5-8R; 93-96; CANR 26, 60;
DA3; DLB 48; MTCW 1, 2; SATA-Obit
22

Rule, Jane (Vance) 1931- .... CLC 27
See also CA 25-28R; CAAS 18; CANR 12,
87; DLB 60

Rulfo, Juan 1918-1986 ..... CLC 8, 80; DAM
MULT; HLC 2; SSC 25
See also CA 85-88; 118; CANR 26; DLB
113; HW 1, 2; MTCW 1, 2

Rumi, Jalal al-Din 1297-1373 ...... CMLC 20

Runeberg, Johan 1804-1877 .... NCLC 41

Runyon, (Alfred) Damon 1884(?)-1946
.... TCLC 10
See also CA 107; 165; DLB 11, 86, 171;
MTCW 2

Rush, Norman 1933- .... CLC 44
See also CA 121; 126; INT 126

Rushdie, (Ahmed) Salman 1947- ... CLC 23,
31, 55, 100; DAB; DAC; DAM MST,
NOV, POP; WLCS
See also BEST 89:3; CA 108; 111; CANR
33, 56; DA3; DLB 194; INT 111; MTCW
1, 2

Rushforth, Peter (Scott) 1945- .... CLC 19
See also CA 101

Ruskin, John 1819-1900 .... TCLC 63
See also CA 114; 129; CDBLB 1832-1890;
DLB 55, 163, 190; SATA 24

Russ, Joanna 1937- .... CLC 15
See also CA 5-28R; CANR 11, 31, 65; DLB
8; MTCW 1

Russell, George William 1867-1935
See Baker, Jean H.
See also CA 104; 153; CDBLB 1890-1914;
DAM POET

Russell, (Henry) Ken(neth Alfred) 1927-
.... CLC 16
See also CA 105

Russell, William Martin 1947- .... CLC 60
See also CA 164; DLB 233

Rutherford, Mark .... TCLC 25
See also White, William Hale
See also DLB 18

Ruyslinck, Ward 1929- .... CLC 14
See also Belser, Reimond Karel Maria de

Ryan, Cornelius (John) 1920-1974 ... CLC 7
See also CA 69-72; 53-56; CANR 38

Ryan, Michael 1946- .... CLC 65
See also CA 49-52; DLBY 82

Ryan, Tim
See Dent, Lester

Rybakov, Anatoli (Naumovich) 1911-1998
.... CLC 23, 53
See also CA 126; 135; 172; SATA 79;
SATA-Obit 108

Ryder, Jonathan
See Ludlum, Robert

Ryga, George 1932-1987 ...... CLC 14; DAC;
DAM MST
See also CA 101; 124; CANR 43, 90; DLB
60

S. H.
See Hartmann, Sadakichi

S. S.
See Sassoon, Siegfried (Lorraine)

Saba, Umberto 1883-1957 .... TCLC 33
See also CA 144; CANR 79; DLB 114

Sabatini, Rafael 1875-1950 .... TCLC 47
See also CA 162

Sabato, Ernesto (R.) 1911- .... CLC 10, 23;
DAM MULT; HLC 2
See also CA 97-100; CANR 32, 65; DLB
145; HW 1, 2; MTCW 1, 2

Sa-Carniero, Mario de 1890-1916 . TCLC 83

Sacastru, Martin
See Bioy Casares, Adolfo

Sacastru, Martin
See Bioy Casares, Adolfo

Sacher-Masoch, Leopold von 1836(?)-1895
.... NCLC 31

Sachs, Marilyn (Stickle) 1927- .... CLC 35
See also AAYA 2; CA 17-20R; CANR 13,
47; CLR 2; JRDA; MAICYA; SAAS 2;
SATA 3, 68; SATA-Essay 110

Sachs, Nelly 1891-1970 .... CLC 14, 98
See also CA 17-18; 25-28R; CANR 87;
CAP 2; MTCW 2

Sackler, Howard (Oliver) 1929-1982
.... CLC 14
See also CA 61-64; 108; CANR 30; DLB 7

Sacks, Oliver (Wolf) 1933- .... CLC 67
See also CA 53-56; CANR 28, 50, 76; DA3;
INT CANR-28; MTCW 1, 2

Sadakichi
See Hartmann, Sadakichi

Sade, Donatien Alphonse Francois, Comte
de 1740-1814 .... NCLC 47

Sadoff, Ira 1945- .... CLC 9
See also CA 53-56; CANR 5, 21; DLB 120

Saetone
See Camus, Albert

Safire, William 1929- .... CLC 10
See also CA 17-20R; CANR 31, 54, 91

Sagan, Carl (Edward) 1934-1996 .. CLC 30,
112
See also AAYA 2; CA 25-28R; 155; CANR
11, 36, 74; DA3; MTCW 1, 2; SATA 58;
SATA-Obit 94

Sagan, Francoise .... CLC 3, 6, 9, 17, 36
See also Quoirez, Francoise
See also DLB 83; MTCW 2

Sahgal, Nayantara (Pandit) 1927- .. CLC 41
See also CA 9-12R; CANR 11, 88

Said, Edward W. 1935- .... CLC 123
See also CA 21-24R; CANR 45, 74; DLB
67; MTCW 2

Saint, H(arry) F. 1941- .... CLC 50
See also CA 127

St. Aubin de Teran, Lisa 1953-
See Teran, Lisa St. Aubin de
See also CA 118; 126; INT 126

Saint Birgitta of Sweden c. 1303-1373
.... CMLC 24

Sainte-Beuve, Charles Augustin 1804-1869
.... NCLC 5

Saint-Exupery, Antoine (Jean Baptiste
Marie Roger) de 1900-1944 .. TCLC 2,
56; DAM NOV; WLC
See also CA 108; 132; CLR 10; DA3; DLB
72; MAICYA; MTCW 1, 2; SATA 20

St. John, David
See Hunt, E(verette) Howard, (Jr.)

Saint-John Perse
See Leger, (Marie-Rene Auguste) Alexis
Saint-Leger

Saintsbury, George (Edward Bateman)
1845-1933 .... TCLC 31
See also CA 160; DLB 57, 149

Sait Faik .... TCLC 23
See also Abasiyanik, Sait Faik

Saki .... TCLC 3; SSC 12
See also Munro, H(ector) H(ugh)
See also MTCW 2

Sala, George Augustus .... NCLC 46

Saladin 1138-1193 .... CMLC 38

Salama, Hannu 1936- .... CLC 18

Salamanca, J(ack) R(ichard) 1922- . **CLC 4, 15**
   See also CA 25-28R

Salas, Floyd Francis 1931-
   See also CA 119; CAAS 27; CANR 44, 75, 93; DAM MULT; DLB 82; HLC 2; HW 1, 2; MTCW 2

Sale, J. Kirkpatrick
   See Sale, Kirkpatrick

Sale, Kirkpatrick 1937- .... **CLC 68**
   See also CA 13-16R; CANR 10

Salinas, Luis Omar 1937- .... **CLC 90; DAM MULT; HLC 2**
   See also CA 131; CANR 81; DLB 82; HW 1, 2

Salinas (y Serrano), Pedro 1891(?)-1951
   .... **TCLC 17**
   See also CA 117; DLB 134

Salinger, J(erome) D(avid) 1919- . **CLC 1, 3, 8, 12, 55, 56, 138; DA; DAB; DAC; DAM MST, NOV, POP; SSC 2, 28; WLC**
   See also AAYA 2; CA 5-8R; CANR 39; CDALB 1941-1968; CLR 18; DA3; DLB 2, 102, 173; MAICYA; MTCW 1, 2; SATA 67

Salisbury, John
   See Caute, (John) David

Salter, James 1925- .... **CLC 7, 52, 59**
   See also CA 73-76; DLB 130

Saltus, Edgar (Everton) 1855-1921 . **TCLC 8**
   See also CA 105; DLB 202

Saltykov, Mikhail Evgrafovich 1826-1889
   .... **NCLC 16**

Samarakis, Antonis 1919- .... **CLC 5**
   See also CA 25-28R; CAAS 16; CANR 36

Sanchez, Florencio 1875-1910 .... **TCLC 37**
   See also CA 153; HW 1

Sanchez, Luis Rafael 1936- .... **CLC 23**
   See also CA 128; DLB 145; HW 1

Sanchez, Sonia 1934- .. **CLC 5, 116; BLC 3; DAM MULT; PC 9**
   See also BW 2, 3; CA 33-36R; CANR 24, 49, 74; CLR 18; DA3; DLB 41; DLBD 8; MAICYA; MTCW 1, 2; SATA 22

Sand, George 1804-1876 ... **NCLC 2, 42, 57; DA; DAB; DAC; DAM MST, NOV; WLC**
   See also DA3; DLB 119, 192

Sandburg, Carl (August) 1878-1967 . **CLC 1, 4, 10, 15, 35; DA; DAB; DAC; DAM MST, POET; PC 2; WLC**
   See also AAYA 24; CA 5-8R; 25-28R; CANR 35; CDALB 1865-1917; CLR 67; DA3; DLB 17, 54; MAICYA; MTCW 1, 2; SATA 8

Sandburg, Charles
   See Sandburg, Carl (August)

Sandburg, Charles A.
   See Sandburg, Carl (August)

Sanders, (James) Ed(ward) 1939- . **CLC 53; DAM POET**
   See also CA 13-16R; CAAS 21; CANR 13, 44, 78; DLB 16

Sanders, Lawrence 1920-1998 .... **CLC 41; DAM POP**
   See also BEST 89:4; CA 81-84; 165; CANR 33, 62; DA3; MTCW 1

Sanders, Noah
   See Blount, Roy (Alton), Jr.

Sanders, Winston P.
   See Anderson, Poul (William)

Sandoz, Mari(e Susette) 1896-1966 . **CLC 28**
   See also CA 1-4R; 25-28R; CANR 17, 64; DLB 9, 212; MTCW 1, 2; SATA 5

Saner, Reg(inald Anthony) 1931- ...... **CLC 9**
   See also CA 65-68

Sankara 788-820 .... **CMLC 32**

Sannazaro, Jacopo 1456(?)-1530 .... **LC 8**

Sansom, William 1912-1976 .... **CLC 2, 6; DAM NOV; SSC 21**
   See also CA 5-8R; 65-68; CANR 42; DLB 139; MTCW 1

Santayana, George 1863-1952 ...... **TCLC 40**
   See also CA 115; DLB 54, 71; DLBD 13

Santiago, Danny .... **CLC 33**
   See also James, Daniel (Lewis)
   See also DLB 122

Santmyer, Helen Hoover 1895-1986 . **CLC 33**
   See also CA 1-4R; 118; CANR 15, 33; DLBY 84; MTCW 1

Santoka, Taneda 1882-1940 .... **TCLC 72**

Santos, Bienvenido N(uqui) 1911-1996
   .... **CLC 22; DAM MULT**
   See also CA 101; 151; CANR 19, 46

Sapper .... **TCLC 44**
   See also McNeile, Herman Cyril

Sapphire
   See Sapphire, Brenda

Sapphire, Brenda 1950- .... **CLC 99**

Sappho fl. 6th cent. B.C.- .. **CMLC 3; DAM POET; PC 5**
   See also DA3; DLB 176

Saramago, Jose 1922- .... **CLC 119; HLCS 1**
   See also CA 153

Sarduy, Severo 1937-1993 .... **CLC 6, 97; HLCS 1**
   See also CA 89-92; 142; CANR 58, 81; DLB 113; HW 1, 2

Sargeson, Frank 1903-1982 .... **CLC 31**
   See also CA 25-28R; 106; CANR 38, 79

Sarmiento, Domingo Faustino 1811-1888
   See also HLCS 2

Sarmiento, Felix Ruben Garcia
   See Dario, Ruben

Saro-Wiwa, Ken(ule Beeson) 1941-1995
   .... **CLC 114**
   See also BW 2; CA 142; 150; CANR 60; DLB 157

Saroyan, William 1908-1981 .. **CLC 1, 8, 10, 29, 34, 56; DA; DAB; DAC; DAM DRAM, MST, NOV; SSC 21; WLC**
   See also CA 5-8R; 103; CANR 30; CDALBS; DA3; DLB 7, 9, 86; DLBY 81; MTCW 1, 2; SATA 23; SATA-Obit 24

Sarraute, Nathalie 1900-1999 .. **CLC 1, 2, 4, 8, 10, 31, 80**
   See also CA 9-12R; 187; CANR 23, 66; DLB 83; MTCW 1, 2

Sarton, (Eleanor) May 1912-1995 .... **CLC 4, 14, 49, 91; DAM POET**
   See also CA 1-4R; 149; CANR 1, 34, 55; DLB 48; DLBY 81; INT CANR-34; MTCW 1, 2; SATA 36; SATA-Obit 86

Sartre, Jean-Paul 1905-1980 ... **CLC 1, 4, 7, 9, 13, 18, 24, 44, 50, 52; DA; DAB; DAC; DAM DRAM, MST, NOV; DC 3; SSC 32; WLC**
   See also CA 9-12R; 97-100; CANR 21; DA3; DLB 72; MTCW 1, 2

Sassoon, Siegfried (Lorraine) 1886-1967
   . **CLC 36, 130; DAB; DAM MST, NOV, POET; PC 12**
   See also CA 104; 25-28R; CANR 36; DLB 20, 191; DLBD 18; MTCW 1, 2

Satterfield, Charles
   See Pohl, Frederik

Satyremont
   See Peret, Benjamin

Saul, John (W. III) 1942- ..... **CLC 46; DAM NOV, POP**
   See also AAYA 10; BEST 90:4; CA 81-84; CANR 16, 40, 81; SATA 98

Saunders, Caleb
   See Heinlein, Robert A(nson)

Saura (Atares), Carlos 1932- .... **CLC 20**
   See also CA 114; 131; CANR 79; HW 1

Sauser-Hall, Frederic 1887-1961 ..... **CLC 18**

See also Cendrars, Blaise
   See also CA 102; 93-96; CANR 36, 62; MTCW 1

Saussure, Ferdinand de 1857-1913
   .... **TCLC 49**

Savage, Catharine
   See Brosman, Catharine Savage

Savage, Thomas 1915- .... **CLC 40**
   See also CA 126; 132; CAAS 15; INT 132

Savan, Glenn 19(?)- .... **CLC 50**

Sayers, Dorothy L(eigh) 1893-1957
   .... **TCLC 2, 15; DAM POP**
   See also CA 104; 119; CANR 60; CDBLB 1914-1945; DLB 10, 36, 77, 100; MTCW 1, 2

Sayers, Valerie 1952- .... **CLC 50, 122**
   See also CA 134; CANR 61

Sayles, John (Thomas) 1950- . **CLC 7, 10, 14**
   See also CA 57-60; CANR 41, 84; DLB 44

Scammell, Michael 1935- .... **CLC 34**
   See also CA 156

Scannell, Vernon 1922- .... **CLC 49**
   See also CA 5-8R; CANR 8, 24, 57; DLB 27; SATA 59

Scarlett, Susan
   See Streatfeild, (Mary) Noel

Scarron
   See Mikszath, Kalman

Schaeffer, Susan Fromberg 1941- .... **CLC 6, 11, 22**
   See also CA 49-52; CANR 18, 65; DLB 28; MTCW 1, 2; SATA 22

Schary, Jill
   See Robinson, Jill

Schell, Jonathan 1943- .... **CLC 35**
   See also CA 73-76; CANR 12

Schelling, Friedrich Wilhelm Joseph von 1775-1854 .... **NCLC 30**
   See also DLB 90

Schendel, Arthur van 1874-1946 .. **TCLC 56**

Scherer, Jean-Marie Maurice 1920-
   See Rohmer, Eric
   See also CA 110

Schevill, James (Erwin) 1920- .... **CLC 7**
   See also CA 5-8R; CAAS 12

Schiller, Friedrich 1759-1805 . **NCLC 39, 69; DAM DRAM; DC 12**
   See also DLB 94

Schisgal, Murray (Joseph) 1926- ...... **CLC 6**
   See also CA 21-24R; CANR 48, 86

Schlee, Ann 1934- .... **CLC 35**
   See also CA 101; CANR 29, 88; SATA 44; SATA-Brief 36

Schlegel, August Wilhelm von 1767-1845
   .... **NCLC 15**
   See also DLB 94

Schlegel, Friedrich 1772-1829 ...... **NCLC 45**
   See also DLB 90

Schlegel, Johann Elias (von) 1719(?)-1749
   .... **LC 5**

Schlesinger, Arthur M(eier), Jr. 1917-
   .... **CLC 84**
   See also AITN 1; CA 1-4R; CANR 1, 28, 58; DLB 17; INT CANR-28; MTCW 1, 2; SATA 61

Schmidt, Arno (Otto) 1914-1979 ..... **CLC 56**
   See also CA 128; 109; DLB 69

Schmitz, Aron Hector 1861-1928
   See Svevo, Italo
   See also CA 104; 122; MTCW 1

Schnackenberg, Gjertrud 1953- ...... **CLC 40**
   See also CA 116; DLB 120

Schneider, Leonard Alfred 1925-1966
   See Bruce, Lenny
   See also CA 89-92

Schnitzler, Arthur 1862-1931 . **TCLC 4; SSC 15**
   See also CA 104; DLB 81, 118

37, 60; DAB; DAM DRAM, MST; DC 7
See also CA 25-28R; CANR 25, 47, 74; CDBLB 1960 to Present; DA3; DLB 13, 233; MTCW 1, 2

Shakey, Bernard
See Young, Neil

Shalamov, Varlam (Tikhonovich) 1907(?)-1982 .... **CLC 18**
See also CA 129; 105

Shamlu, Ahmad 1925- .... **CLC 10**

Shammas, Anton 1951- .... **CLC 55**

Shandling, Arline
See Berriault, Gina

Shange, Ntozake 1948- ... **CLC 8, 25, 38, 74, 126; BLC 3; DAM DRAM, MULT; DC 3**
See also AAYA 9; BW 2; CA 85-88; CABS 3; CANR 27, 48, 74; DA3; DLB 38; MTCW 1, 2

Shanley, John Patrick 1950- .... **CLC 75**
See also CA 128; 133; CANR 83

Shapcott, Thomas W(illiam) 1935- . **CLC 38**
See also CA 69-72; CANR 49, 83

Shapiro, Jane .... **CLC 76**

Shapiro, Karl (Jay) 1913- . **CLC 4, 8, 15, 53; PC 25**
See also CA 1-4R; CAAS 6; CANR 1, 36, 66; DLB 48; MTCW 1, 2

Sharp, William 1855-1905 .... **TCLC 39**
See also CA 160; DLB 156

Sharpe, Thomas Ridley 1928-
See Sharpe, Tom
See also CA 114; 122; CANR 85; DLB 231; INT 122

Sharpe, Tom .... **CLC 36**
See also Sharpe, Thomas Ridley
See also DLB 14

Shaw, Bernard
See Shaw, George Bernard
See also BW 1; MTCW 2

Shaw, G. Bernard
See Shaw, George Bernard

Shaw, George Bernard 1856-1950 . **TCLC 3, 9, 21, 45; DA; DAB; DAC; DAM DRAM, MST; WLC**
See also Shaw, Bernard
See also CA 104; 128; CDBLB 1914-1945; DA3; DLB 10, 57, 190; MTCW 1, 2

Shaw, Henry Wheeler 1818-1885 . **NCLC 15**
See also DLB 11

Shaw, Irwin 1913-1984 .... **CLC 7, 23, 34; DAM DRAM, POP**
See also AITN 1; CA 13-16R; 112; CANR 21; CDALB 1941-1968; DLB 6, 102; DLBY 84; MTCW 1, 21

Shaw, Robert 1927-1978 .... **CLC 5**
See also AITN 1; CA 1-4R; 81-84; CANR 4; DLB 13, 14

Shaw, T. E.
See Lawrence, T(homas) E(dward)

Shawn, Wallace 1943- .... **CLC 41**
See also CA 112

Shea, Lisa 1953- .... **CLC 86**
See also CA 147

Sheed, Wilfrid (John Joseph) 1930- . **CLC 2, 4, 10, 53**
See also CA 65-68; CANR 30, 66; DLB 6; MTCW 1, 2

Sheldon, Alice Hastings Bradley 1915(?)-1987
See Tiptree, James, Jr.
See also CA 108; 122; CANR 34; INT 108; MTCW 1

Sheldon, John
See Bloch, Robert (Albert)

Sheldon, Walter J. 1917-
See Queen, Ellery
See also AITN 1; CA 25-28R; CANR 10

Shelley, Mary Wollstonecraft (Godwin) 1797-1851 .... **NCLC 14, 59; DA; DAB; DAC; DAM MST, NOV; WLC**
See also AAYA 20; CDBLB 1789-1832; DA3; DLB 110, 116, 159, 178; SATA 29

Shelley, Percy Bysshe 1792-1822 . **NCLC 18, 93; DA; DAB; DAC; DAM MST, POET; PC 14; WLC**
See also CDBLB 1789-1832; DA3; DLB 96, 110, 158

Shepard, Jim 1956- .... **CLC 36**
See also CA 137; CANR 59; SATA 90

Shepard, Lucius 1947- .... **CLC 34**
See also CA 128; 141; CANR 81

Shepard, Sam 1943- ... **CLC 4, 6, 17, 34, 41, 44; DAM DRAM; DC 5**
See also AAYA 1; CA 69-72; CABS 3; CANR 22; DA3; DLB 7, 212; MTCW 1, 2

Shepherd, Michael
See Ludlum, Robert

Sherburne, Zoa (Lillian Morin) 1912-1995 .... **CLC 30**
See also AAYA 13; CA 1-4R; 176; CANR 3, 37; MAICYA; SAAS 18; SATA 3

Sheridan, Frances 1724-1766 .... **LC 7**
See also DLB 39, 84

Sheridan, Richard Brinsley 1751-1816 .. **NCLC 5, 91; DA; DAB; DAC; DAM DRAM, MST; DC 1; WLC**
See also CDBLB 1660-1789; DLB 89

Sherman, Jonathan Marc .... **CLC 55**

Sherman, Martin 1941(?)- .... **CLC 19**
See also CA 116; 123; CANR 86

Sherwin, Judith Johnson 1936-
See Johnson, Judith (Emlyn)
See also CANR 85

Sherwood, Frances 1940- .... **CLC 81**
See also CA 146

Sherwood, Robert E(mmet) 1896-1955 .... **TCLC 3; DAM DRAM**
See also CA 104; 153; CANR 86; DLB 7, 26

Shestov, Lev 1866-1938 .... **TCLC 56**

Shevchenko, Taras 1814-1861 .... **NCLC 54**

Shiel, M(atthew) P(hipps) 1865-1947 .... **TCLC 8**
See also Holmes, Gordon
See also CA 106; 160; DLB 153; MTCW 2

Shields, Carol 1935- ...... **CLC 91, 113; DAC**
See also CA 81-84; CANR 51, 74; DA3; MTCW 2

Shields, David 1956- .... **CLC 97**
See also CA 124; CANR 48

Shiga, Naoya 1883-1971 .... **CLC 33; SSC 23**
See also CA 101; 33-36R; DLB 180

Shikibu, Murasaki c. 978-c. 1014 . **CMLC 1**

Shilts, Randy 1951-1994 .... **CLC 85**
See also AAYA 19; CA 115; 127; 144; CANR 45; DA3; INT 127; MTCW 2

Shimazaki, Haruki 1872-1943
See Shimazaki Toson
See also CA 105; 134; CANR 84

Shimazaki Toson 1872-1943 .... **TCLC 5**
See also Shimazaki, Haruki
See also DLB 180

Sholokhov, Mikhail (Aleksandrovich) 1905-1984 .... **CLC 7, 15**
See also CA 101; 112; MTCW 1, 2; SATA-Obit 36

Shone, Patric
See Hanley, James

Shreve, Susan Richards 1939- .... **CLC 23**
See also CA 49-52; CAAS 5; CANR 5, 38, 69; MAICYA; SATA 46, 95; SATA-Brief 41

Shue, Larry 1946-1985 .... **CLC 52; DAM DRAM**
See also CA 145; 117

Shu-Jen, Chou 1881-1936
See Lu Hsun
See also CA 104

Shulman, Alix Kates 1932- .... **CLC 2, 10**
See also CA 29-32R; CANR 43; SATA 7

Shuster, Joe 1914- .... **CLC 21**

Shute, Nevil .... **CLC 30**
See also Norway, Nevil Shute
See also MTCW 2

Shuttle, Penelope (Diane) 1947- .... **CLC 7**
See also CA 93-96; CANR 39, 84, 92; DLB 14, 40

Sidney, Mary 1561-1621 .... **LC 19, 39**

Sidney, Sir Philip 1554-1586 . **LC 19, 39; DA; DAB; DAC; DAM MST, POET; PC 32**
See also CDBLB Before 1660; DA3; DLB 167

Siegel, Jerome 1914-1996 .... **CLC 21**
See also CA 116; 169; 151

Siegel, Jerry
See Siegel, Jerome

Sienkiewicz, Henryk (Adam Alexander Pius) 1846-1916 .... **TCLC 3**
See also CA 104; 134; CANR 84

Sierra, Gregorio Martinez
See Martinez Sierra, Gregorio

Sierra, Maria (de la O'LeJarraga) Martinez
See Martinez Sierra, Maria (de la O'LeJarraga)

Sigal, Clancy 1926- .... **CLC 7**
See also CA 1-4R; CANR 85

Sigourney, Lydia Howard (Huntley) 1791-1865 .... **NCLC 21, 87**
See also DLB 1, 42, 73

Siguenza y Gongora, Carlos de 1645-1700 .... **LC 8; HLCS 2**

Sigurjonsson, Johann 1880-1919 .. **TCLC 27**
See also CA 170

Sikelianos, Angelos 1884-1951 ..... **TCLC 39; PC 29**

Silkin, Jon 1930- .... **CLC 2, 6, 43**
See also CA 5-8R; CAAS 5; CANR 89; DLB 27

Silko, Leslie (Marmon) 1948- .. **CLC 23, 74, 114; DA; DAC; DAM MST, MULT, POP; SSC 37; WLCS**
See also AAYA 14; CA 115; 122; CANR 45, 65; DA3; DLB 143, 175; MTCW 2; NNAL

Sillanpaa, Frans Eemil 1888-1964 .. **CLC 19**
See also CA 129; 93-96; MTCW 1

Sillitoe, Alan 1928- .. **CLC 1, 3, 6, 10, 19, 57**
See also AITN 1; CA 9-12R; CAAS 2; CANR 8, 26, 55; CDBLB 1960 to Present; DLB 14, 139; MTCW 1, 2; SATA 61

Silone, Ignazio 1900-1978 .... **CLC 4**
See also CA 25-28; 81-84; CANR 34; CAP 2; MTCW 1

Silver, Joan Micklin 1935- .... **CLC 20**
See also CA 114; 121; INT 121

Silver, Nicholas
See Faust, Frederick (Schiller)

Silverberg, Robert 1935- .... **CLC 7; DAM POP**
See also AAYA 24; CA 1-4R; 186; CAAE 186; CAAS 3; CANR 1, 20, 36, 85; CLR 59; DLB 8; INT CANR-20; MAICYA; MTCW 1, 2; SATA 13, 91; SATA-Essay 104

Silverstein, Alvin 1933- .... **CLC 17**
See also CA 49-52; CANR 2; CLR 25; JRDA; MAICYA; SATA 8, 69

Silverstein, Virginia B(arbara Opshelor) 1937- .... **CLC 17**
See also CA 49-52; CANR 2; CLR 25; JRDA; MAICYA; SATA 8, 69

See also BW 1, 3; CA 124; 89-92; CANR 80; DLB 48, 76
Tolstoi, Aleksei Nikolaevich
    See Tolstoy, Alexey Nikolaevich
Tolstoy, Alexey Nikolaevich 1882-1945
    .... **TCLC 18**
    See also CA 107; 158
Tolstoy, Count Leo
    See Tolstoy, Leo (Nikolaevich)
Tolstoy, Leo (Nikolaevich) 1828-1910
    . **TCLC 4, 11, 17, 28, 44, 79; DA; DAB; DAC; DAM MST, NOV; SSC 9, 30; WLC**
    See also CA 104; 123; DA3; SATA 26
Tomasi di Lampedusa, Giuseppe 1896-1957
    See Lampedusa, Giuseppe (Tomasi) di
    See also CA 111
Tomlin, Lily .... **CLC 17**
    See also Tomlin, Mary Jean
Tomlin, Mary Jean 1939(?)-
    See Tomlin, Lily
    See also CA 117
Tomlinson, (Alfred) Charles 1927- .. **CLC 2, 4, 6, 13, 45; DAM POET; PC 17**
    See also CA 5-8R; CANR 33; DLB 40
Tomlinson, H(enry) M(ajor) 1873-1958
    .... **TCLC 71**
    See also CA 118; 161; DLB 36, 100, 195
Tonson, Jacob
    See Bennett, (Enoch) Arnold
Toole, John Kennedy 1937-1969 .... **CLC 19, 64**
    See also CA 104; DLBY 81; MTCW 2
Toomer, Jean 1894-1967 .. **CLC 1, 4, 13, 22; BLC 3; DAM MULT; PC 7; SSC 1; WLCS**
    See also Pinchback, Eugene; Toomer, Eugene; Toomer, Eugene Pinchback; Toomer, Nathan Jean; Toomer, Nathan Pinchback
    See also BW 1; CA 85-88; CDALB 1917-1929; DA3; DLB 45, 51; MTCW 1, 2
Torley, Luke
    See Blish, James (Benjamin)
Tornimparte, Alessandra
    See Ginzburg, Natalia
Torre, Raoul della
    See Mencken, H(enry) L(ouis)
Torrence, Ridgely 1874-1950 .... **TCLC 97**
    See also DLB 54
Torrey, E(dwin) Fuller 1937- .... **CLC 34**
    See also CA 119; CANR 71
Torsvan, Ben Traven
    See Traven, B.
Torsvan, Benno Traven
    See Traven, B.
Torsvan, Berick Traven
    See Traven, B.
Torsvan, Berwick Traven
    See Traven, B.
Torsvan, Bruno Traven
    See Traven, B.
Torsvan, Traven
    See Traven, B.
Tournier, Michel (Edouard) 1924- ... **CLC 6, 23, 36, 95**
    See also CA 49-52; CANR 3, 36, 74; DLB 83; MTCW 1, 2; SATA 23
Tournimparte, Alessandra
    See Ginzburg, Natalia
Towers, Ivar
    See Kornbluth, C(yril) M.
Towne, Robert (Burton) 1936(?)- .... **CLC 87**
    See also CA 108; DLB 44
Townsend, Sue .... **CLC 61**
    See also Townsend, Susan Elaine
    See also AAYA 28; SATA 55, 93; SATA-Brief 48

Townsend, Susan Elaine 1946-
    See Townsend, Sue
    See also CA 119; 127; CANR 65; DAB; DAC; DAM MST; INT 127
Townshend, Peter (Dennis Blandford) 1945- .... **CLC 17, 42**
    See also CA 107
Tozzi, Federigo 1883-1920 .... **TCLC 31**
    See also CA 160
Tracy, Don(ald Fiske) 1905-1976(?)
    See Queen, Ellery
    See also CA 1-4R; 176; CANR 2
Traill, Catharine Parr 1802-1899 . **NCLC 31**
    See also DLB 99
Trakl, Georg 1887-1914 ..... **TCLC 5; PC 20**
    See also CA 104; 165; MTCW 2
Transtroemer, Tomas (Goesta) 1931-
    .... **CLC 52, 65; DAM POET**
    See also CA 117; 129; CAAS 17
Transtromer, Tomas Gosta
    See Transtroemer, Tomas (Goesta)
Traven, B. (?)-1969 .... **CLC 8, 11**
    See also CA 19-20; 25-28R; CAP 2; DLB 9, 56; MTCW 1
Treitel, Jonathan 1959- .... **CLC 70**
Trelawny, Edward John 1792-1881
    .... **NCLC 85**
    See also DLB 110, 116, 144
Tremain, Rose 1943- .... **CLC 42**
    See also CA 97-100; CANR 44; DLB 14
Tremblay, Michel 1942- .... **CLC 29, 102; DAC; DAM MST**
    See also CA 116; 128; DLB 60; MTCW 1, 2
Trevanian .... **CLC 29**
    See also Whitaker, Rod(ney)
Trevor, Glen
    See Hilton, James
Trevor, William 1928- . **CLC 7, 9, 14, 25, 71, 116; SSC 21**
    See also Cox, William Trevor
    See also DLB 14, 139; MTCW 2
Trifonov, Yuri (Valentinovich) 1925-1981
    .... **CLC 45**
    See also CA 126; 103; MTCW 1
Trilling, Diana (Rubin) 1905-1996 . **CLC 129**
    See also CA 5-8R; 154; CANR 10, 46; INT CANR-10; MTCW 1, 2
Trilling, Lionel 1905-1975 ..... **CLC 9, 11, 24**
    See also CA 9-12R; 61-64; CANR 10; DLB 28, 63; INT CANR-10; MTCW 1, 2
Trimball, W. H.
    See Mencken, H(enry) L(ouis)
Tristan
    See Gomez de la Serna, Ramon
Tristram
    See Housman, A(lfred) E(dward)
Trogdon, William (Lewis) 1939-
    See Heat-Moon, William Least
    See also CA 115; 119; CANR 47, 89; INT 119
Trollope, Anthony 1815-1882 .. **NCLC 6, 33; DA; DAB; DAC; DAM MST, NOV; SSC 28; WLC**
    See also CDBLB 1832-1890; DA3; DLB 21, 57, 159; SATA 22
Trollope, Frances 1779-1863 .... **NCLC 30**
    See also DLB 21, 166
Trotsky, Leon 1879-1940 .... **TCLC 22**
    See also CA 118; 167
Trotter (Cockburn), Catharine 1679-1749
    .... **LC 8**
    See also DLB 84
Trotter, Wilfred 1872-1939 .... **TCLC 97**
Trout, Kilgore
    See Farmer, Philip Jose
Trow, George W. S. 1943- .... **CLC 52**
    See also CA 126; CANR 91

Troyat, Henri 1911- .... **CLC 23**
    See also CA 45-48; CANR 2, 33, 67; MTCW 1
Trudeau, G(arretson) B(eekman) 1948-
    See Trudeau, Garry B.
    See also CA 81-84; CANR 31; SATA 35
Trudeau, Garry B. .... **CLC 12**
    See also Trudeau, G(arretson) B(eekman)
    See also AAYA 10; AITN 2
Truffaut, Francois 1932-1984 .. **CLC 20, 101**
    See also CA 81-84; 113; CANR 34
Trumbo, Dalton 1905-1976 .... **CLC 19**
    See also CA 21-24R; 69-72; CANR 10; DLB 26
Trumbull, John 1750-1831 .... **NCLC 30**
    See also DLB 31
Trundlett, Helen B.
    See Eliot, T(homas) S(tearns)
Truth, Sojourner 1797(?)-1883 ..... **NCLC 94**
Tryon, Thomas 1926-1991 . **CLC 3, 11; DAM POP**
    See also AITN 1; CA 29-32R; 135; CANR 32, 77; DA3; MTCW 1
Tryon, Tom
    See Tryon, Thomas
Ts'ao Hsueh-ch'in 1715(?)-1763 .... **LC 1**
Tsushima, Shuji 1909-1948
    See Dazai Osamu
    See also CA 107
Tsvetaeva (Efron), Marina (Ivanovna) 1892-1941 .... **TCLC 7, 35; PC 14**
    See also CA 104; 128; CANR 73; MTCW 1, 2
Tuck, Lily 1938- .... **CLC 70**
    See also CA 139; CANR 90
Tu Fu 712-770 .... **PC 9**
    See also DAM MULT
Tunis, John R(oberts) 1889-1975 .... **CLC 12**
    See also CA 61-64; CANR 62; DLB 22, 171; JRDA; MAICYA; SATA 37; SATA-Brief 30
Tuohy, Frank .... **CLC 37**
    See also Tuohy, John Francis
    See also DLB 14, 139
Tuohy, John Francis 1925-
    See Tuohy, Frank
    See also CA 5-8R; 178; CANR 3, 47
Turco, Lewis (Putnam) 1934- .... **CLC 11, 63**
    See also CA 13-16R; CAAS 22; CANR 24, 51; DLBY 84
Turgenev, Ivan 1818-1883 ..... **NCLC 21, 37; DA; DAB; DAC; DAM MST, NOV; DC 7; SSC 7; WLC**
Turgot, Anne-Robert-Jacques 1727-1781
    .... **LC 26**
Turner, Frederick 1943- .... **CLC 48**
    See also CA 73-76; CAAS 10; CANR 12, 30, 56; DLB 40
Tutu, Desmond M(pilo) 1931- .... **CLC 80; BLC 3; DAM MULT**
    See also BW 1, 3; CA 125; CANR 67, 81
Tutuola, Amos 1920-1997 ..... **CLC 5, 14, 29; BLC 3; DAM MULT**
    See also BW 2, 3; CA 9-12R; 159; CANR 27, 66; DA3; DLB 125; MTCW 1, 2
Twain, Mark 1835-1910 ..... **TCLC 6, 12, 19, 36, 48, 59; SSC 34; WLC**
    See also Clemens, Samuel Langhorne
    See also AAYA 20; CLR 58, 60, 66; DLB 11, 12, 23, 64, 74
20/1631
    See Upward, Allen
Tyler, Anne 1941- . **CLC 7, 11, 18, 28, 44, 59, 103; DAM NOV, POP**
    See also AAYA 18; BEST 89:1; CA 9-12R; CANR 11, 33, 53; CDALBS; DLB 6, 143; DLBY 82; MTCW 1, 2; SATA 7, 90
Tyler, Royall 1757-1826 .... **NCLC 3**
    See also DLB 37

See also DLB 1

Vesaas, Tarjei 1897-1970 .... **CLC 48**
See also CA 29-32R

Vialis, Gaston
See Simenon, Georges (Jacques Christian)

Vian, Boris 1920-1959 .... **TCLC 9**
See also CA 106; 164; DLB 72; MTCW 2

Viaud, (Louis Marie) Julien 1850-1923
See Loti, Pierre
See also CA 107

Vicar, Henry
See Felsen, Henry Gregor

Vicker, Angus
See Felsen, Henry Gregor

Vidal, Gore 1925- ..... **CLC 2, 4, 6, 8, 10, 22, 33, 72; DAM NOV, POP**
See also AITN 1; BEST 90:2; CA 5-8R; CANR 13, 45, 65; CDALBS; DA3; DLB 6, 152; INT CANR-13; MTCW 1, 2

Viereck, Peter (Robert Edwin) 1916-
.... **CLC 4; PC 27**
See also CA 1-4R; CANR 1, 47; DLB 5

Vigny, Alfred (Victor) de 1797-1863
.... **NCLC 7; DAM POET; PC 26**
See also DLB 119, 192

Vilakazi, Benedict Wallet 1906-1947
.... **TCLC 37**
See also CA 168

Villa, Jose Garcia 1904-1997 .... **PC 22**
See also CA 25-28R; CANR 12

Villarreal, Jose Antonio 1924-
See also CA 133; CANR 93; DAM MULT; DLB 82; HLC 2; HW 1

Villaurrutia, Xavier 1903-1950 ..... **TCLC 80**
See also HW 1

Villehardouin 1150(?)-1218(?) ...... **CMLC 38**

Villiers de l'Isle Adam, Jean Marie Mathias Philippe Auguste, Comte de 1838-1889
.... **NCLC 3; SSC 14**
See also DLB 123

Villon, Francois 1431-1463(?) ..... **LC 62; PC 13**
See also DLB 208

Vine, Barbara .... **CLC 50**
See also Rendell, Ruth (Barbara)
See also BEST 90:4

Vinge, Joan (Carol) D(ennison) 1948-
.... **CLC 30; SSC 24**
See also AAYA 32; CA 93-96; CANR 72; SATA 36, 113

Violis, G.
See Simenon, Georges (Jacques Christian)

Viramontes, Helena Maria 1954-
See also CA 159; DLB 122; HLCS 2; HW 2

Virgil 70B.C.-19B.C.
See Vergil

Visconti, Luchino 1906-1976 .... **CLC 16**
See also CA 81-84; 65-68; CANR 39

Vittorini, Elio 1908-1966 .... **CLC 6, 9, 14**
See also CA 133; 25-28R

Vivekananda, Swami 1863-1902 ... **TCLC 88**

Vizenor, Gerald Robert 1934- ...... **CLC 103; DAM MULT**
See also CA 13-16R; CAAS 22; CANR 5, 21, 44, 67; DLB 175, 227; MTCW 2; NNAL

Vizinczey, Stephen 1933- .... **CLC 40**
See also CA 128; INT 128

Vliet, R(ussell) G(ordon) 1929-1984 . **CLC 22**
See also CA 37-40R; 112; CANR 18

Vogau, Boris Andreyevich 1894-1937(?)
See Pilnyak, Boris
See also CA 123

Vogel, Paula A(nne) 1951- .... **CLC 76**
See also CA 108

Voigt, Cynthia 1942- .... **CLC 30**
See also AAYA 3, 30; CA 106; CANR 18, 37, 40; CLR 13, 48; INT CANR-18; JRDA; MAICYA; SATA 48, 79, 116; SATA-Brief 33

Voigt, Ellen Bryant 1943- .... **CLC 54**
See also CA 69-72; CANR 11, 29, 55; DLB 120

Voinovich, Vladimir (Nikolaevich) 1932-
.... **CLC 10, 49**
See also CA 81-84; CAAS 12; CANR 33, 67; MTCW 1

Vollmann, William T. 1959- . **CLC 89; DAM NOV, POP**
See also CA 134; CANR 67; DA3; MTCW 2

Voloshinov, V. N.
See Bakhtin, Mikhail Mikhailovich

Voltaire 1694-1778 .... **LC 14; DA; DAB; DAC; DAM DRAM, MST; SSC 12; WLC**
See also DA3

von Aschendrof, BaronIgnatz
See Ford, Ford Madox

von Daeniken, Erich 1935- .... **CLC 30**
See also AITN 1; CA 37-40R; CANR 17, 44

von Daniken, Erich
See von Daeniken, Erich

von Hartmann, Eduard 1842-1906
.... **TCLC 96**

von Heidenstam, (Carl Gustaf) Verner
See Heidenstam, (Carl Gustaf) Verner von

von Heyse, Paul (Johann Ludwig)
See Heyse, Paul (Johann Ludwig von)

von Hofmannsthal, Hugo
See Hofmannsthal, Hugo von

von Horvath, Odon
See Horvath, Oedoen von

von Horvath, Oedoen -1938
See Horvath, Oedoen von
See also CA 184

von Liliencron, (Friedrich Adolf Axel) Detlev
See Liliencron, (Friedrich Adolf Axel) Detlev von

Vonnegut, Kurt, Jr. 1922- . **CLC 1, 2, 3, 4, 5, 8, 12, 22, 40, 60, 111; DA; DAB; DAC; DAM MST, NOV, POP; SSC 8; WLC**
See also AAYA 6; AITN 1; BEST 90:4; CA 1-4R; CANR 1, 25, 49, 75, 92; CDALB 1968-1988; DA3; DLB 2, 8, 152; DLBD 3; DLBY 80; MTCW 1, 2

Von Rachen, Kurt
See Hubbard, L(afayette) Ron(ald)

von Rezzori (d'Arezzo), Gregor
See Rezzori (d'Arezzo), Gregor von

von Sternberg, Josef
See Sternberg, Josef von

Vorster, Gordon 1924- .... **CLC 34**
See also CA 133

Vosce, Trudie
See Ozick, Cynthia

Voznesensky, Andrei (Andreievich) 1933-
.... **CLC 1, 15, 57; DAM POET**
See also CA 89-92; CANR 37; MTCW 1

Waddington, Miriam 1917- .... **CLC 28**
See also CA 21-24R; CANR 12, 30; DLB 68

Wagman, Fredrica 1937- .... **CLC 7**
See also CA 97-100; INT 97-100

Wagner, Linda W.
See Wagner-Martin, Linda (C.)

Wagner, Linda Welshimer
See Wagner-Martin, Linda (C.)

Wagner, Richard 1813-1883 .... **NCLC 9**
See also DLB 129

Wagner-Martin, Linda (C.) 1936- .. **CLC 50**
See also CA 159

Wagoner, David (Russell) 1926- .. **CLC 3, 5, 15**
See also CA 1-4R; CAAS 3; CANR 2, 71; DLB 5; SATA 14

Wah, Fred(erick James) 1939- .... **CLC 44**
See also CA 107; 141; DLB 60

Wahloo, Per 1926- .... **CLC 7**
See also CA 61-64; CANR 73

Wahloo, Peter
See Wahloo, Per

Wain, John (Barrington) 1925-1994 . **CLC 2, 11, 15, 46**
See also CA 5-8R; 145; CAAS 4; CANR 23, 54; CDBLB 1960 to Present; DLB 15, 27, 139, 155; MTCW 1, 2

Wajda, Andrzej 1926- .... **CLC 16**
See also CA 102

Wakefield, Dan 1932- .... **CLC 7**
See also CA 21-24R; CAAS 7

Wakoski, Diane 1937- .... **CLC 2, 4, 7, 9, 11, 40; DAM POET; PC 15**
See also CA 13-16R; CAAS 1; CANR 9, 60; DLB 5; INT CANR-9; MTCW 2

Wakoski-Sherbell, Diane
See Wakoski, Diane

Walcott, Derek (Alton) 1930- ... **CLC 2, 4, 9, 14, 25, 42, 67, 76; BLC 3; DAB; DAC; DAM MST, MULT, POET; DC 7**
See also BW 2; CA 89-92; CANR 26, 47, 75, 80; DA3; DLB 117; DLBY 81; MTCW 1, 2

Waldman, Anne (Lesley) 1945- .... **CLC 7**
See also CA 37-40R; CAAS 17; CANR 34, 69; DLB 16

Waldo, E. Hunter
See Sturgeon, Theodore (Hamilton)

Waldo, Edward Hamilton
See Sturgeon, Theodore (Hamilton)

Walker, Alice (Malsenior) 1944- .. **CLC 5, 6, 9, 19, 27, 46, 58, 103; BLC 3; DA; DAB; DAC; DAM MST, MULT, NOV, POET, POP; PC 30; SSC 5; WLCS**
See also AAYA 3, 33; BEST 89:4; BW 2, 3; CA 37-40R; CANR 9, 27, 49, 66, 82; CDALB 1968-1988; DA3; DLB 6, 33, 143; INT CANR-27; MTCW 1, 2; SATA 31

Walker, David Harry 1911-1992 ..... **CLC 14**
See also CA 1-4R; 137; CANR 1; SATA 8; SATA-Obit 71

Walker, Edward Joseph 1934-
See Walker, Ted
See also CA 21-24R; CANR 12, 28, 53

Walker, George F. 1947- . **CLC 44, 61; DAB; DAC; DAM MST**
See also CA 103; CANR 21, 43, 59; DLB 60

Walker, Joseph A. 1935- ...... **CLC 19; DAM DRAM, MST**
See also BW 1, 3; CA 89-92; CANR 26; DLB 38

Walker, Margaret (Abigail) 1915-1998
. **CLC 1, 6; BLC; DAM MULT; PC 20**
See also BW 2, 3; CA 73-76; 172; CANR 26, 54, 76; DLB 76, 152; MTCW 1, 2

Walker, Ted .... **CLC 13**
See also Walker, Edward Joseph
See also DLB 40

Wallace, David Foster 1962- ... **CLC 50, 114**
See also CA 132; CANR 59; DA3; MTCW 2

Wallace, Dexter
See Masters, Edgar Lee

Wallace, (Richard Horatio) Edgar 1875-1932
.... **TCLC 57**
See also CA 115; DLB 70

Wallace, Irving 1916-1990 .... **CLC 7, 13; DAM NOV, POP**

Wells, H(erbert) G(eorge) 1866-1946 .... **TCLC 6, 12, 19; DA; DAB; DAC; DAM MST, NOV; SSC 6; WLC**
See also AAYA 18; CA 110; 121; CDBLB 1914-1945; CLR 64; DLB 34, 70, 156, 178; MTCW 1, 2; SATA 20

Wells, Rosemary 1943- .... **CLC 12**
See also AAYA 13; CA 85-88; CANR 48; CLR 16; MAICYA; SAAS 1; SATA 18, 69, 114

Welty, Eudora 1909- .... **CLC 1, 2, 5, 14, 22, 33, 105; DA; DAB; DAC; DAM MST, NOV; SSC 1, 27; WLC**
See also CA 9-12R; CABS 1; CANR 32, 65; CDALB 1941-1968; DA3; DLB 2, 102, 143; DLBD 12; DLBY 87; MTCW 1, 2

Wen I-to 1899-1946 .... **TCLC 28**

Wentworth, Robert
See Hamilton, Edmond

Werfel, Franz (Viktor) 1890-1945 .. **TCLC 8**
See also CA 104; 161; DLB 81, 124

Wergeland, Henrik Arnold 1808-1845 .... **NCLC 5**

Wersba, Barbara 1932- .... **CLC 30**
See also AAYA 2, 30; CA 29-32R, 182; CAAE 182; CANR 16, 38; CLR 3; DLB 52; JRDA; MAICYA; SAAS 2; SATA 1, 58; SATA-Essay 103

Wertmueller, Lina 1928- .... **CLC 16**
See also CA 97-100; CANR 39, 78

Wescott, Glenway 1901-1987 . **CLC 13; SSC 35**
See also CA 13-16R; 121; CANR 23, 70; DLB 4, 9, 102

Wesker, Arnold 1932- .. **CLC 3, 5, 42; DAB; DAM DRAM**
See also CA 1-4R; CAAS 7; CANR 1, 33; CDBLB 1960 to Present; DLB 13; MTCW 1

Wesley, Richard (Errol) 1945- .... **CLC 7**
See also BW 1; CA 57-60; CANR 27; DLB 38

Wessel, Johan Herman 1742-1785 .... **LC 7**

West, Anthony (Panther) 1914-1987
.... **CLC 50**
See also CA 45-48; 124; CANR 3, 19; DLB 15

West, C. P.
See Wodehouse, P(elham) G(renville)

West, Cornel (Ronald) 1953- .... **CLC 134; BLCS**
See also CA 144; CANR 91

West, (Mary) Jessamyn 1902-1984 .. **CLC 7, 17**
See also CA 9-12R; 112; CANR 27; DLB 6; DLBY 84; MTCW 1, 2; SATA-Obit 37

West, Morris L(anglo) 1916-1999 .... **CLC 6, 33**
See also CA 5-8R; 187; CANR 24, 49, 64; MTCW 1, 2

West, Nathanael 1903-1940 ..... **TCLC 1, 14, 44; SSC 16**
See also CA 104; 125; CDALB 1929-1941; DA3; DLB 4, 9, 28; MTCW 1, 2

West, Owen
See Koontz, Dean R(ay)

West, Paul 1930- .... **CLC 7, 14, 96**
See also CA 13-16R; CAAS 7; CANR 22, 53, 76, 89; DLB 14; INT CANR-22; MTCW 2

West, Rebecca 1892-1983 .. **CLC 7, 9, 31, 50**
See also CA 5-8R; 109; CANR 19; DLB 36; DLBY 83; MTCW 1, 2

Westall, Robert (Atkinson) 1929-1993
.... **CLC 17**
See also AAYA 12; CA 69-72; 141; CANR 18, 68; CLR 13; JRDA; MAICYA; SAAS 2; SATA 23, 69; SATA-Obit 75

Westermarck, Edward 1862-1939 . **TCLC 87**

Westlake, Donald E(dwin) 1933- ..... **CLC 7, 33; DAM POP**
See also CA 17-20R; CAAS 13; CANR 16, 44, 65; INT CANR-16; MTCW 2

Westmacott, Mary
See Christie, Agatha (Mary Clarissa)

Weston, Allen
See Norton, Andre

Wetcheek, J. L.
See Feuchtwanger, Lion

Wetering, Janwillem van de
See van de Wetering, Janwillem

Wetherald, Agnes Ethelwyn 1857-1940
.... **TCLC 81**
See also DLB 99

Wetherell, Elizabeth
See Warner, Susan (Bogert)

Whale, James 1889-1957 .... **TCLC 63**

Whalen, Philip 1923- .... **CLC 6, 29**
See also CA 9-12R; CANR 5, 39; DLB 16

Wharton, Edith (Newbold Jones) 1862-1937
... **TCLC 3, 9, 27, 53; DA; DAB; DAC; DAM MST, NOV; SSC 6; WLC**
See also AAYA 25; CA 104; 132; CDALB 1865-1917; DA3; DLB 4, 9, 12, 78, 189; DLBD 13; MTCW 1, 2

Wharton, James
See Mencken, H(enry) L(ouis)

Wharton, William (a pseudonym) . **CLC 18, 37**
See also CA 93-96; DLBY 80; INT 93-96

Wheatley (Peters), Phillis 1754(?)-1784
..... **LC 3, 50; BLC 3; DA; DAC; DAM MST, MULT, POET; PC 3; WLC**
See also CDALB 1640-1865; DA3; DLB 31, 50

Wheelock, John Hall 1886-1978 ..... **CLC 14**
See also CA 13-16R; 77-80; CANR 14; DLB 45

White, E(lwyn) B(rooks) 1899-1985
.... **CLC 10, 34, 39; DAM POP**
See also AITN 2; CA 13-16R; 116; CANR 16, 37; CDALBS; CLR 1, 21; DA3; DLB 11, 22; MAICYA; MTCW 1, 2; SATA 2, 29, 100; SATA-Obit 44

White, Edmund (Valentine III) 1940-
.... **CLC 27, 110; DAM POP**
See also AAYA 7; CA 45-48; CANR 3, 19, 36, 62; DA3; DLB 227; MTCW 1, 2

White, Patrick (Victor Martindale) 1912-1990 ..... **CLC 3, 4, 5, 7, 9, 18, 65, 69; SSC 39**
See also CA 81-84; 132; CANR 43; MTCW 1

White, Phyllis Dorothy James 1920-
See James, P. D.
See also CA 21-24R; CANR 17, 43, 65; DAM POP; DA3; MTCW 1, 2

White, T(erence) H(anbury) 1906-1964
.... **CLC 30**
See also AAYA 22; CA 73-76; CANR 37; DLB 160; JRDA; MAICYA; SATA 12

White, Terence de Vere 1912-1994 . **CLC 49**
See also CA 49-52; 145; CANR 3

White, Walter
See White, Walter F(rancis)
See also BLC; DAM MULT

White, Walter F(rancis) 1893-1955
.... **TCLC 15**
See also White, Walter
See also BW 1; CA 115; 124; DLB 51

White, William Hale 1831-1913
See Rutherford, Mark
See also CA 121

Whitehead, Alfred North 1861-1947
.... **TCLC 97**
See also CA 117; 165; DLB 100

Whitehead, E(dward) A(nthony) 1933-
.... **CLC 5**
See also CA 65-68; CANR 58

Whitemore, Hugh (John) 1936- ...... **CLC 37**
See also CA 132; CANR 77; INT 132

Whitman, Sarah Helen (Power) 1803-1878
.... **NCLC 19**
See also DLB 1

Whitman, Walt(er) 1819-1892 . **NCLC 4, 31, 81; DA; DAB; DAC; DAM MST, POET; PC 3; WLC**
See also CDALB 1640-1865; DA3; DLB 3, 64, 224; SATA 20

Whitney, Phyllis A(yame) 1903- .... **CLC 42; DAM POP**
See also AITN 2; BEST 90:3; CA 1-4R; CANR 3, 25, 38, 60; CLR 59; DA3; JRDA; MAICYA; MTCW 2; SATA 1, 30

Whittemore, (Edward) Reed (Jr.) 1919-
.... **CLC 4**
See also CA 9-12R; CAAS 8; CANR 4; DLB 5

Whittier, John Greenleaf 1807-1892
.... **NCLC 8, 59**
See also DLB 1

Whittlebot, Hernia
See Coward, Noel (Peirce)

Wicker, Thomas Grey 1926-
See Wicker, Tom
See also CA 65-68; CANR 21, 46

Wicker, Tom .... **CLC 7**
See also Wicker, Thomas Grey

Wideman, John Edgar 1941- ..... **CLC 5, 34, 36, 67, 122; BLC 3; DAM MULT**
See also BW 2, 3; CA 85-88; CANR 14, 42, 67; DLB 33, 143; MTCW 2

Wiebe, Rudy (Henry) 1934- . **CLC 6, 11, 14, 138; DAC; DAM MST**
See also CA 37-40R; CANR 42, 67; DLB 60

Wieland, Christoph Martin 1733-1813
.... **NCLC 17**
See also DLB 97

Wiene, Robert 1881-1938 .... **TCLC 56**

Wieners, John 1934- .... **CLC 7**
See also CA 13-16R; DLB 16

Wiesel, Elie(zer) 1928- ..... **CLC 3, 5, 11, 37; DA; DAB; DAC; DAM MST, NOV; WLCS**
See also AAYA 7; AITN 1; CA 5-8R; CAAS 4; CANR 8, 40, 65; CDALBS; DA3; DLB 83; DLBY 87; INT CANR-8; MTCW 1, 2; SATA 56

Wiggins, Marianne 1947- .... **CLC 57**
See also BEST 89:3; CA 130; CANR 60

Wight, James Alfred 1916-1995
See Herriot, James
See also CA 77-80; SATA 55; SATA-Brief 44

Wilbur, Richard (Purdy) 1921- ... **CLC 3, 6, 9, 14, 53, 110; DA; DAB; DAC; DAM MST, POET**
See also CA 1-4R; CABS 2; CANR 2, 29, 76, 93; CDALBS; DLB 5, 169; INT CANR-29; MTCW 1, 2; SATA 9, 108

Wild, Peter 1940- .... **CLC 14**
See also CA 37-40R; DLB 5

Wilde, Oscar (Fingal O'Flahertie Wills) 1854(?)-1900 .. **TCLC 1, 8, 23, 41; DA; DAB; DAC; DAM DRAM, MST, NOV; SSC 11; WLC**
See also CA 104; 119; CDBLB 1890-1914; DA3; DLB 10, 19, 34, 57, 141, 156, 190; SATA 24

Wilder, Billy .... **CLC 20**
See also Wilder, Samuel
See also DLB 26

Author Index

DC Cumulative Nationality Index

ALGERIAN

Camus, Albert **2**

AMERICAN

Albee, Edward (Franklin III) **11**
Baldwin, James (Arthur) **1**
Baraka, Amiri **6**
Brown, William Wells **1**
Bullins, Ed **6**
Chase, Mary (Coyle) **1**
Childress, Alice **4**
Chin, Frank (Chew Jr.) **7**
Elder, Lonne III **8**
Fornes, Maria Irene **10**
Fuller, Charles (H. Jr.) **1**
Glaspell, Susan **10**
Gordone, Charles **8**
Gray, Spalding **7**
Hansberry, Lorraine (Vivian) **2**
Hellman, Lillian (Florence) **1**
Henley, Beth **6, 14**
Hughes, (James) Langston **3**
Hurston, Zora Neale **12**
Hwang, David Henry **4**
Kennedy, Adrienne (Lita) **5**
Kramer, Larry **8**
Kushner, Tony **10**
Mamet, David (Alan) **4**
Mann, Emily **7**
Miller, Arthur **1**
Norman, Marsha **8**
Odets, Clifford **6**
Shange, Ntozake **3**
Shepard, Sam **5**
Sheridan, Richard Brinsley **1**
Simon, (Marvin) Neil **14**
Terry, Megan **13**
Valdez, Luis (Miguel) **10**
Wasserstein, Wendy **4**
Wilder, Thornton (Niven) **1**
Williams, Tennessee **4**
Wilson, August **2**
Zindel, Paul **5**

AUSTRIAN

Bernhard, Thomas **14**
Grillparzer, Franz **14**
Hofmannsthal, Hugo von **4**

BARBADIAN

Kennedy, Adrienne (Lita) **5**

CUBAN

Fornes, Maria Irene **10**

CZECH

Capek, Karel **1**
Havel, Vaclav **6**

ENGLISH

Ayckbourn, Alan **13**
Beaumont, Francis **6**
Behn, Aphra **4**
Churchill, Caryl **5**
Congreve, William **2**
Dekker, Thomas **12**
Dryden, John **3**
Fletcher, John **6**
Jonson, Ben(jamin) **4**
Kyd, Thomas **3**
Lyly, John **7**
Marlowe, Christopher **1**
Middleton, Thomas **5**
Orton, Joe **3**
Shaffer, Peter (Levin) **7**
Stoppard, Tom **6**
Webster, John **2**

FRENCH

Anouilh, Jean (Marie Lucien Pierre) **8**
Artaud, Antonin (Marie Joseph) **14**
Beaumarchais, Pierre-Augustin Caron de **4**
Camus, Albert **2**
Dumas, Alexandre (fils) **1**
Ionesco, Eugene **12**
Marivaux, Pierre Carlet de Chamblain de **7**
Moliere **13**
Perrault, Charles **12**
Rostand, Edmond (Eugene Alexis) **10**
Sartre, Jean-Paul **3**
Scribe, (Augustin) Eugene **5**

GERMAN

Brecht, (Eugen) Bertolt (Friedrich) **3**
Schiller, Friedrich **12**

GREEK

Aeschylus **8**
Aristophanes **2**
Euripides **4**
Menander **3**
Sophocles **1**

IRISH

Friel, Brian **8**
Goldsmith, Oliver **8**
O'Casey, Sean **12**
Sheridan, Richard Brinsley **1**
Synge, (Edmund) J(ohn) M(illington) **2**

ITALIAN

Fo, Dario **10**
Pirandello, Luigi **5**

JAPANESE

Mishima, Yukio **1**
Zeami **7**

NIGERIAN

Clark Bekedermo, J(ohnson) P(epper) **5**
Soyinka, Wole **2**

NORWEGIAN

Ibsen, Henrik (Johan) **2**

ROMAN

Seneca, Lucius Annaeus **5**
Terence **7**

ROMANIAN

Ionesco, Eugene **12**

RUSSIAN

Chekhov, Anton (Pavlovich) **9**
Gogol, Nikolai (Vasilyevich) **1**
Turgenev, Ivan **7**

SOUTH AFRICAN

Fugard, (Harold) Athol **3**

SPANISH

Calderon de la Barca, Pedro **3**
de Molina, Tirso **13**
Garcia Lorca, Federico **2**

ST. LUCIAN

Walcott, Derek (Alton) **7**

DC Cumulative Title Index

451

Andria (Terence) **7**:214, 216, 218, 220-26, 234, 251
Andromache (Euripides) **4**:101-03, 121
Andromeda (Euripides) **4**:96
Angel City (Shepard) **5**:359-61, 368, 372, 375-76, 393
The Angel That Troubled the Waters (Wilder) **1**:481
Angels in America: A Gay Fantasia on National Themes (Kushner) **10**:213-18, 220, 229-40, 242-83
Anger (Ionesco)
    See *La Colère*
Anger (Menander)
    See *Org(em)*
Anna-Anna (Brecht)
    See *Die sieben Todsünden der Kleinburger*
The Anniversary (Chekhov)
    See *Zhubilei*
Annulla Allen: The Autobiography of a Survivor (Mann) **7**:101, 103-04, 1115
"Annus Mirabilis: The Year of Wonders, 1666" (Dryden) **3**:158, 199-01, 204, 212-14
Another Life (Walcott) **7**:329
Another Moon Called Earth (Stoppard) **6**:347, 352
Another Part of the Forest (Hellman) **1**:185, 188-90, 207, 209
Antigone (Anouilh) **8**:70, 72, 78, 80, 82, 84, 88-104, 109
Antigon(em) (Sophocles) **1**:414-15, 417, 422-26, 431, 433, 435-42, 460
Antiope (Euripides) **4**:104, 121
The Ants (Churchill) **5**:7
Anything for a Quiet Life (Middleton) **5**:165
Anything for a Quiet Life (Webster) **2**:436
Aoi no ue (Mishima) **1**:354, 361
Apocolocyntosis Divi Claudii (Seneca) **5**:323
The Apparition (Menander) **3**:346
Appearances Are Deceiving (Bernhard)
    See *Der Schein trügt*
Appius and Virginia (Webster) **2**:437
Apprendre à marcher (Ionesco) **12**:238
Approaching Simone (Terry) **13**:281, 283, 296, 302, 306, 308, 315-16, 333
El Aquiles (de Molina) **13**:203-04, 206, 249
Arabella (Hofmannsthal) **4**:193-4, 196
The Aran Islands (Synge) **2**:400-01, 415
The Arbitrants (Menander)
    See *Epitrepontes*
The Arbitration (Menander)
    See *Epitrepontes*
El árbol del mejor fruto (de Molina) **13**:204, 206
Gli arcangeli non giocano al flipper (Fo) **10**:9, 11, 30-32
Archangels Do Not Play Pinball (Fo)
    See *Gli arcangeli non giocano al flipper*
Ardele; or, The Daisy (Anouilh)
    See *Ardèle; ou, La marguerite*
Ardèle; ou, La marguerite (Anouilh) **8**:76, 78, 81, 85-7
L'Argent du diable (Sejour) **10**:334, 340
Die Argonauten (Grillparzer) **14**:224, 227-33, 284-85
The Argonauts (Grillparzer)
    See *Die Argonauten*
Ariadne (Hofmannsthal)
    See *Ariadne auf Naxos*
Ariadne auf Naxos (Hofmannsthal) **4**:167, 173, 194
Arlequin poli par l'amour (Marivaux) **7**:124, 126, 129-30, 132, 147, 149-50, 155, 163-65
Arm Yourself or Harm Yourself: A One-Act Play: A Message of Self-Defense to Black Men (Baraka) **6**:8, 15
Artist Descending a Staircase (Stoppard) **6**:294, 308-09, 312, 314-15, 347
As Well as Before, Better than Before (Pirandello)
    See *Come prima, meglio di prima*

As You Desire Me (Pirandello)
    See *Come tu mi vuoi*
Ashikari (Zeami) **7**:348, 350
Así que pasen cinco años (Garcia Lorca) **2**:199-200, 202, 204, 206, 213
Asinaria (Plautus) **6**:242, 275-78, 286, 290
Aspis (Menander) **3**:362, 364, 366, 368-70
The Assassins (Camus)
    See *Les justes*
Assembly of Women (Aristophanes)
    See *Ekklesiazousai*
The Assignation (Dryden) **3**:167-68, 188
"At a Spiritualist Seance" (Chekhov) **9**:33
"At Christmas-Time" (Chekhov) **9**:36
At One's Goal (Bernhard)
    See *Am Ziel*
"At Sea" (Chekhov) **9**:32-4
At the Exit (Pirandello)
    See *All'uscita*
At the Gate (Pirandello)
    See *All'uscita*
"An Attack of Nerves" (Chekhov) **9**:122
Attempted Rescue on Avenue B (Terry) **13**:288
The Audience (Garcia Lorca)
    See *El público*
Audience (Havel) **6**:150-51, 156-57, 163, 166, 170-73, 175
Aufstieg und Fall der Stadt Mahagonny (Brecht) **3**:19-20, 27
"The Augsburg Chalk Circle" (Brecht)
    See "Der Augsburger Kreidekreis"
"Der Augsburger Kreidekreis" (Brecht) **3**:81
Aulularia (Plautus) **6**:241-42, 244-46, 249, 278-79, 281-83
"Aunt Maggie, the Strong One" (Friel) **8**:213
Aureng-Zebe (Dryden) **3**:154, 158, 160-62, 168-69, 177, 179, 184, 188, 190-91, 193-96, 198, 212, 216-17
Aurora (Fornes) **10**:82, 87, 90, 125
l'autre Tartuffe; ou La mère coupable (Beaumarchais) **4**:2-6, 10-12, 14, 18, 20, 25
The Autumn Garden (Hellman) **1**:188, 190-91, 208
L'avare (Moliere) **13**:38, 49, 61-62, 64, 74, 86-87, 90, 98, 153, 158-74
L'Avenir est dans les oeufs (Ionesco) **12**:199-200, 205, 208, 212, 226, 239, 254
Les Aventuriers (Sejour) **10**:342
Averígüelo Vargas (de Molina) **13**:202
Aveva due pisotle con gli occhi bianchi e neri (Fo) **10**:9, 11
Awake and Sing! (Odets) **6**:205-07, 209, 211, 214-16, 223-32, 234
Aya no tsuzumi (Mishima) **1**:361-62, 363-66, 368-70, 372
L'azione parlata (Pirandello) **5**:215, 217, 233
Baal (Brecht) **3**:15-16, 25-6, 34, 78
Babes in the Bighouse (Terry) **13**:281, 289, 302, 316-20, 330, 332
Baby Doll (Williams) **4**:371-72
The Babylonians (Aristophanes) **2**:9, 18, 35-6, 41
Bacchae (Aeschylus) **8**:16
Bacchae (Euripides) **4**:96, 98-9, 101-5, 107-9, 121-2, 142-4, 152-3, 156-7
The Bacchae (Ionesco) **12**:223
The Bacchae of Euripides: A Communion Rite (Soyinka) **2**:366, 368
Bacchanals (Euripides)
    See *Bacchae*
The Bacchants (Euripides)
    See *Bacchae*
Bacchides (Plautus) **6**:242, 246, 250-51, 255, 262-64, 290
The Bacchis Sisters (Plautus)
    See *Bacchides*
The Bachelor (Turgenev)
    See *Kholostiak*
Bachelor Girls (Wasserstein) **4**:366
Back Bog Beast Bait (Shepard) **5**:359-60

Bad Temper (Menander)
    See *Org(em)*
Le bal des voleurs (Anouilh) **8**:71, 75
Balance of Terror (Shaffer) **7**:183
The Bald Prima Donna (Ionesco)
    See *La cantatrice chauve*
The Bald Soprano (Ionesco)
    See *La cantatrice chauve*
The Ballad of the Sad Café (Albee) **11**:20, 27, 37, 40-1, 47, 53, 56, 61, 76, 133, 175, 362
Bam Bam! It's the Police (Fo)
    See *Pum pum chi è? La polizia!*
La Bamba (Valdez) **10**:355-56, 383
La banda y la flor (Calderon de la Barca) **3**:104
Bandido! (Valdez) **10**:380, 383-86
Bang Bang Who's There? Police! (Fo)
    See *Pum pum chi è? La polizia!*
The Banqueters (Aristophanes) **2**:8, 18, 42
"The Baptism" (Baraka) **6**:10-12, 15-17, 25, 30, 32
Ba-Ra-Ka (Baraka) **6**:15
The Barber of Seville, or, The Pointless Precaution (Beaumarchais)
    See *Le barbier de Séville; ou, La précaution inutile*
Le barbier de Séville; ou, La précaution inutile (Beaumarchais) **4**:2-9, 11-2, 14-18, 21-5, 30-1
Barefoot in the Park (Simon) **14**:334-35, 337-38, 342, 347, 349, 351-52, 354-55, 357-59, 362-63, 365, 372
Bartholomew Fair (Jonson) **4**:227, 229, 232, 235, 240, 242, 248, 256-59, 263, 276
Bartleby (Albee) **11**:53
Basic Handbook for the Actor (Fo)
    See *Manuale minimo dell'Attore*
Bataille de dames; ou, Un duel en amour (Scribe) **5**:247-49, 253
Batrakhoi (Aristophanes) **2**:4, 6, 13-14, 16-17, 40, 45, 47-51, 68
The Battle at Yashima (Zeami)
    See *Yashima*
Battle of Angels (Williams) **4**:371, 383, 391
The Battle of Shrivings (Shaffer) **7**:183-84, 189-90, 197, 202, 205
The Bear (Chekhov)
    See *Medved*
A Beast Story (Kennedy) **5**:76, 89, 91-2
Beautie (Jonson)
    See *Masque of Beauty*
"The Beauties" (Chekhov) **9**:153
"Because of the King of France" (Kennedy) **5**:90
Becket; or, The Honor of God (Anouilh)
    See *Becket; ou, L'honneur de Dieu*
Becket; ou, L'honneur de Dieu (Anouilh) **8**:85, 88, 91, 95, 104-10
Bedroom Farce (Ayckbourn) **13**:11-12, 17, 19-20, 22
The Bee (Goldsmith) **8**:281
Beef, No Chicken (Walcott) **7**:320, 323-25
Before Retirement (Bernhard)
    See *Vor dem Ruhestand*
Before the Marriage (Menander) **3**:346
Beggar's Bush (Beaumont) **6**:84
Beggar's Bush (Fletcher) **6**:84
The Beggar's Opera (Havel) **6**:151, 163
The Begging Priest (Menander) **3**:346
A Begonia for Miss Applebaum (Zindel) **5**:425
Behind the Green Curtains (O'Casey) **12**:274, 279-80
Die beiden Götter (Hofmannsthal) **4**:169
Being and Nothingness: An Essay on Phenomenological Ontology (Sartre)
    See *L'être et le néant: Essai d'ontologie phénoménologique*
Bellerophon (Euripides) **4**:104
The Bellman of London, or Roque's Horn-Book (Dekker) **12**:4
Ben Jonson: Selected Works (Jonson) **4**:277
Bernabé (Valdez) **10**:352-53, 355, 366, 377-79, 381, 393

Title Index

Title Index

Title Index

Title Index

ISBN 0-7876-3142-6

9 780787 631420

90000